P9-DFC-877

UNIVERSITY CASEBOOK SERIES

EDITORIAL BOARD

ROBERT C. CLARK
DIRECTING EDITOR
Former Dean & Distinguished Service Professor
Harvard University

DANIEL A. FARBER
Sho Sato Professor of Law
University of California at Berkeley

OWEN M. FISS
Sterling Professor of Law
Yale University

HERMA HILL KAY
Dean & Barbara Nachtrieb Armstrong Professor of Law
University of California, Berkeley

HAROLD HONGJU KOH
Dean & Gerard C. & Bernice Latrobe Smith Professor of International Law
Yale Law School

SAUL LEVMORE
Dean & William B. Graham Professor of Law
University of Chicago

THOMAS W. MERRILL
Charles Keller Beekman Professor of Law
Columbia Law School

ROBERT L. RABIN
A. Calder Mackay Professor of Law
Stanford University

CAROL M. ROSE
Gordon Bradford Tweedy Professor of Law & Organization
Yale University

DAVID L. SHAPIRO
William Nelson Cromwell Professor of Law
Harvard University

KATHLEEN M. SULLIVAN
Stanley Morrison Professor of Law and
Former Dean of the School of Law
Stanford University

CASES AND MATERIALS

FUNDAMENTALS OF CORPORATE TAXATION

SIXTH EDITION

by

STEPHEN A. LIND
Albert R. Abramson Distinguished Professor of Law,
University of California, Hastings College of the Law

STEPHEN SCHWARZ
Professor of Law Emeritus,
University of California, Hastings College of the Law

DANIEL J. LATHROPE
Professor of Law,
University of California, Hastings College of the Law

JOSHUA D. ROSENBERG
Professor of Law,
University of San Francisco School of Law

FOUNDATION PRESS
NEW YORK, NEW YORK
2005

THOMSON

WEST

Foundation Press, of Thomson/West, has created this publication to provide you with accurate and authoritative information concerning the subject matter covered. However, this publication was not necessarily prepared by persons licensed to practice law in a particular jurisdiction. Foundation Press is not engaged in rendering legal or other professional advice, and this publication is not a substitute for the advice of an attorney. If you require legal or other expert advice, you should seek the services of a competent attorney or other professional.

© 1985, 1987, 1991, 1997, 2002 FOUNDATION PRESS
© 2005 By FOUNDATION PRESS
       395 Hudson Street
       New York, NY 10014
       Phone Toll Free 1–877–888–1330
       Fax (212) 367–6799
       fdpress.com

Printed in the United States of America

ISBN 1–58778–831–4

TEXT IS PRINTED ON 10% POST CONSUMER RECYCLED PAPER

To our families

*

PREFACE

Since the Fifth Edition of *Fundamentals of Corporate Taxation* was published in 2002, the federal tax environment continued in its now familiar state of disequilibrium, reinforcing the status of tax textbooks as one of the world's most perishable commodities. Before the ink was dry, rates on ordinary income and capital gains were reduced again, albeit not permanently. And in 2003, for the first time in modern tax history, Congress provided significant relief from the double tax to investors in C corporations by reducing the tax rate on most dividends. A year later, Congress passed the American Jobs Creation Act of 2004, a bloated tax bill that adds many new targeted tax breaks for C corporations, widens the eligibility gates for S corporation status, adds to the patchwork quilt of anti-abuse rules, and steps up the attack on corporate tax shelters. These developments, along with the usual flow of regulations and a trickle of interesting new published rulings, more than justified a new edition and offered yet another opportunity to cure some minor viruses that may have infected our earlier efforts.

The relentless barrage of tax legislation and regulations presents an ongoing challenge to instructors who seek to provide manageable coverage of an overwhelming body of material. Although some level of detail is unavoidable in a corporate tax course, we pause at the outset to remind ourselves and others of the importance of teaching the "fundamentals." As we said in the Preface to the First Edition:

> * * * [I]n our collective experience, we have been troubled by a common denominator in the many fine corporate tax casebooks and texts: their sheer bulk. In this book and a previously published companion volume, Fundamentals of Partnership Taxation, we attempt to chart a different course by bringing the "fundamentals" philosophy to the teaching of taxation of the business enterprise. * * * [T]he fundamentals approach involves selectivity of subject matter, emphasis on basic concepts, avoidance of esoteric detail and realistic depth of coverage. To those ends, this volume is the product of self restraint—although perhaps not enough. At times, we opted for over inclusion to accommodate the varied teaching biases and favorite cases and topics of experienced instructors (including ourselves). We have continued, however, to select and edit cases with care. Lengthy citations, obscure questions and meanderings into minutia have been avoided. Throughout the book, we have made an effort to remember what it was like when we studied cor-

porate tax; this volume is designed as a teaching book, not the definitive treatise. And so, of course, we expect students to do the reading!

We also believe that the most effective way to teach and learn tax fundamentals is by the problem method. This book thus contains a comprehensive yet manageable set of problems to accompany every major topic. The problems are designed to help students decipher the statute and apply it in a wide variety of alternative fact situations. Some are "building block" problems with specific answers. We are mindful, however, of the tendency to become preoccupied with technical trivia and have also included some more sophisticated (and realistic) problems with a planning orientation.

The primary sources in any tax course are the Code and Regulations. But the statute frequently is unintelligible when read out of context. To provide a foundation of understanding, this book includes extensive explanatory text to accompany the problems and a selection of cases, rulings, legislative history and other materials. The goal of the text is not merely to paraphrase the Code. In addition to describing the workings of the statute, we have attempted to explain why it works the way it does. If presented as a purely mechanical exercise, the problem method can degenerate into a mindless series of computations, leaving one without insights into the function of the statute, the relationship between sections and the broad principles governing the taxation of corporations and shareholders. By first explaining the "why" as well as the "how," we hope that even the computational problems will serve as launching pads for the discussion of more important policy and planning issues.

Turning to organization and emphasis, the Sixth Edition retains the pedagogically proven "cradle to grave" organization of its predecessors. Chapter 1 provides an introduction to business enterprise taxation, offering perspective on the influential policies that have shaped Subchapter C and analyzing the profound changes that have occurred over the past two decades. Chapter 1 also surveys the corporate regular and alternative minimum taxes and highlights contemporary policy issues, including proposals to "integrate" the corporate and individual income taxes and efforts to curb abusive tax shelters. Chapters 2 and 3, which examine corporate formations and capital structure, set the stage for a study of Subchapter C's double tax regime and the bias in favor of debt that has helped taxpayers avoid its full impact.

Chapters 4 through 6 cover operating distributions, stock redemptions, and stock dividends (including Section 306 stock). For a brief time after passage of the Tax Reform Act of 1986, these chapters lost much of their vitality because ordinary income and capital gains were taxed at the same rate. Then, as many predicted, a meaningful capital gains rate preference was restored, breathing new life into these operational chapters and validating our decision to retain textual discussion and problems even when the

stakes were low. Now, with the decision—not yet permanent—to tax qualified dividends and long-term capital gains at the same reduced rate, it is
deja vu all over again. Where the historical agenda was to avoid dividend
treatment and "bail out" corporate earnings at capital gains rates, now the
major advantage of a capital gains bailout is recovery of basis. As we await
the outcome, if any, of the long-promised "fundamental tax reform," this
"transitional" edition does its best to discuss the planning implications of
the current landscape. But mindful that nothing is certain, many of the traditional materials have been retained, except for a few cases that no longer
seemed to be worth the time and effort. It will be up to instructors to decide
how much emphasis to give to characterization issues in view of these (temporarily?) altered stakes.

Complete liquidations and taxable acquisitions are addressed in Chapters 7 and 8. The discussion of taxable stock acquisitions offers selective
coverage of Section 338 without, we hope, getting too bogged down in
arcane minutia. Chapters 9 through 12 cover the still vibrant topics of tax-
free reorganizations and divisions, including the rules and limitations
affecting carryovers of corporate tax attributes. Chapter 9, on acquisitive
reorganizations, selectively incorporates many new final regulations on a
variety of topics (most notably, continuity of proprietary interest), and several recent published rulings have been included to enliven this chapter's
emphasis on transactional as well as doctrinal analysis.

Chapter 13, covering affiliated corporations, was extensively updated
and revised in an earlier edition. Depending on time and interest, many
instructors may choose not to cover this material. For those who wish students to achieve literacy, not mastery, this chapter offers what we hope is a
coherent primer on the intricacies of multiple tax benefits, Section 482 allocations, and consolidated groups.

Chapter 14, which examines the accumulated earnings and personal
holding company penalty taxes, remains at the end of Part II. The significance of these taxes has declined almost to the vanishing point now that dividends and long-term capital gains are taxed at the same rate. Although
this chapter remains virtually intact, it has become a historical relic, and we
encourage instructors to think through their coverage decisions carefully.

Part Three (Chapter 15) is devoted to S corporations, which remain a
popular alternative for businesses whose structure can accommodate to a
simpler pass-through taxing regime. Similar surveys of Subchapter S are
included in our companion volume, Fundamentals of Partnership Taxation,
and in Fundamentals of Business Enterprise Taxation, an alternative text
for a combined course on corporate and partnership tax. Tax professors
continue to debate whether S corporations are best covered in corporate tax,
a course on pass-through entities, or a combined business enterprise taxation course offering. Our books accommodate any of these approaches.

Turning to matters of style, we assume that the text will be assigned
with the most recent edition of the Code and Regulations. Suggested
assignments to these sources are provided for each topic. Instructors should

review these assignments carefully, editing when necessary to ensure that they are consistent with the desired coverage. Deletions from cases and other authorities have been made freely, with asterisks used to denote substantive omissions, but citations and internal cross references in excerpted materials have been deleted without so indicating. Editorial additions are in brackets. Footnotes to the original text are numbered consecutively within each section, and many footnotes have been deleted from cases without renumbering those that remain. The text is current as of April 1, 2005.

The authors extend special thanks to Professor Bruce McGovern for his many constructive suggestions and invaluable assistance in updating several chapters on an earlier edition when he was an LL.M student at the University of Florida College of Law. We remain indebted to many former students who assisted on prior editions, particularly: Ted Brooks, Mitch Salamon, Ray Kawasaki, Terri Murray, Jim Potratz, Jeff Anthony, Garo Kalfayan, Steve Vogelsang, Julie Divola, Joe Bartlett, Marilyn Cleveland, Chris Detzel, and Jeffrey Essner.

We also express our gratitude to Steve Lind and Josh Rosenberg, who have ended their active participation as co-authors, for their thoughtful contributions to the development of this text and to its many previous editions. And, as always, we are indebted to the administration of Hastings College of the Law for its research, logistical and moral support.

STEPHEN SCHWARZ

DANIEL J. LATHROPE

San Francisco, California
May, 2005

SUMMARY OF CONTENTS

TABLE OF CONTENTS

TABLE OF INTERNAL REVENUE CODE SECTIONS

TABLE OF TREASURY REGULATIONS

*

TABLE OF REVENUE RULINGS

TABLE OF MISCELLANEOUS RULINGS

*

TABLE OF CASES

Principal cases are in bold type. Non-principal cases are in roman type. References are to Pages.

TABLE OF AUTHORITIES

*

FUNDAMENTALS OF CORPORATE TAXATION

*

PART ONE

INTRODUCTION

CHAPTER 1

AN OVERVIEW OF THE TAXATION OF CORPORATIONS AND SHAREHOLDERS

A. INTRODUCTION

1. TAXATION OF BUSINESS ENTITIES

Since the time when the British Crown begrudgingly recognized collective profit-seeking enterprises,[1] the artificial legal entity known as the "corporation" has served as a principal vehicle for conducting business in a capitalist economic system. Legal advisors to the earliest American corporations spent much of their time defining the relationship between the corporation and the state and developing hoary doctrines to regulate corporate governance and control. It was not until late in the 19th century that the genteel world of corporate law was jolted by the emergence of the income tax as a principal government revenue raising device. The life of the corporate lawyer would never be the same again. From the ill-fated Income Tax of 1894, which at the time was viewed as a Socialist plot because it imposed a two percent tax on individual and corporate net income,[2] to the Payne–Aldrich Tariff Act of 1909, which imposed a modest one percent tax on corporate net income over $5,000,[3] to the Sixteenth Amendment and beyond, the income tax gradually came to influence how corporations conducted their affairs. It is now well acknowledged, though often lamented, that the federal tax law has invaded virtually every aspect of American business life. It shapes and often twists management decisions and generally is an unpleasant distraction to those who would prefer to devote their full resources to the pursuit of profit.

The decision to superimpose an income tax on a system that recognized artificial entities as separate from their owners raised a fundamental structural question. Simply put, the dilemma confronting the architects of the federal income tax was whether to treat corporations, partnerships, trusts and other vehicles for conducting business as separate taxable entities or as an aggregate of the underlying owners.

---

1. See generally Eisenberg, Cases and Materials on Corporations 1 (unabridged 8th ed. 2000).

2. See Bittker & Lokken, Federal Income Taxation of Income, Estates and Gifts ¶ 1.1.2 (3d ed.1999); see also Pollock v. Farm-ers' Loan & Trust Co., 157 U.S. 429, 15 S.Ct. 673 (1895).

3. See Bittker & Eustice, Federal Income Taxation of Corporations and Shareholders ¶ 1.01 (7th ed. 2000).

Since the earliest income tax acts, a corporation has been treated as a distinct taxable entity, separate and apart from its shareholders. Once that policy decision was made, a host of additional questions followed. What rates should be applied to corporate income? Should they resemble the graduated rates applicable to individuals or is a flat rate more appropriate? How should the tax system treat transactions between a corporation and its shareholders? If a corporation already has been taxed on its earnings, should those earnings be taxed again when they are distributed to the shareholders? If so, is it appropriate to give the corporation a deduction for the amount of the distribution? In short, must corporate income be taxed twice—once when earned by the corporation and again, after distribution to the shareholders?[4]

The answers to these and many other questions will unfold throughout this text. But it serves no purpose to hide the ball on the most fundamental question. Congress, having decided to treat the corporation as a separate taxpaying entity, went on to adopt a double tax regime. A tax is imposed annually, at the rates set forth in Section 11, on the taxable income of a corporation. That income is effectively taxed again when distributed to the shareholders in the form of dividends, which are not deductible by the distributing corporation but are taxed to noncorporate shareholders at the same preferential rate as long-term capital gains.[5] Because the corporation is treated as a separate taxable entity, transactions between corporations and their shareholders are taxable events. The tax consequences of these transactions and other major changes and adjustments in a corporation are governed by Subchapter C (Sections 301 to 385) of the Internal Revenue Code of 1986, a challenging and fascinating body of law that is the principal subject of this book. Corporations subject to the double tax regime also draw their identity (and monogram) from Subchapter C. Collectively, the Code refers to them as "C corporations."[6]

Congress made a markedly different policy decision in the case of partnerships, which are treated by Subchapter K of the Code as pass-through entities that do not pay federal income tax. Instead, partners include their respective shares of partnership income, deductions, losses and other items when determining their tax liability.[7] Ongoing adjustments to the basis of a partner's interest in the partnership ensure that income and losses are not taxed (or deducted) twice.[8] Partnerships are treated as entities, however, for purposes of selecting a taxable year, computing and characterizing partnership income, filing information returns, making elections, undergoing an audit by the Internal Revenue Service and in several substantive contexts, such as formation and termination, transactions

---

4. See, e.g., McLure, Must Corporate Income Be Taxed Twice? (1979).

5. I.R.C. § 1(h)(11). For corporate shareholders, some relief from a potential triple tax is provided by a 70, 80 or 100 percent dividends received deduction under Section 243. See Section B1 of this chapter, infra.

6. I.R.C. § 1361(a)(2).

7. I.R.C. § 701.

8. I.R.C. § 705.

between partners and partnerships, and sales of partnership interests.[9] The principal features of a pass-through tax regime are: (1) income generated by the business is taxed only once to the beneficial owners of the enterprise, whether or not they receive current distributions, and (2) losses pass through to the owners and, subject to various timing limitations,[10] may be deducted against income from other sources. More recently, the tax benefits of the partnership pass-through system have been extended to limited liability companies, an increasingly popular form of legal entity.[11]

The double tax regime generally applicable to corporations and the pass-through system governing partnerships and limited liability companies represent the Code's two fundamental alternatives for taxing business enterprises. To level the playing field and respond to the special problems of unique industries, Congress occasionally has deviated from these two basic models. Thus, to minimize the role of taxes on the choice of form for smaller businesses, certain closely held corporations may elect under Subchapter S to be treated as conduits.[12] Conversely, to preclude widely held businesses from disincorporating to escape the double tax regime of Subchapter C, most "publicly traded" partnerships are treated as corporations for tax purposes.[13] Other types of hybrid entities qualify for pass-through treatment if they satisfy requirements designed to limit the nature of their business operations,[14] and corporations in certain discrete industries are governed by specialized taxing regimes.[15] Despite these departures from the norm, the central question remains—shall business profits be subjected to one or two levels of tax? The debate on this question is ongoing and will arise repeatedly throughout the text.

2. INFLUENTIAL POLICIES

Four broad tax policy decisions have shaped the development of Subchapter C and contributed to its corpulent physique. The interrelationship of these policies influences taxpayer behavior regarding the type of entity in which to conduct a business enterprise, capital structure and financing of corporate activities, dividend and compensation policy, estate planning and a myriad of other tax and business planning decisions. During the recent past, the policies underlying Subchapter C have been in a state of disequilibrium as Congress has tinkered with the tax rates as part of the

---

9. I.R.C. §§ 721; 707; 741. See generally, Lind, Schwarz, Lathrope & Rosenberg, Cases and Materials on Fundamentals of Partnership Taxation (7th ed. 2005).

10. See I.R.C. §§ 704(d); 465; 469.

11. See Section C2b of this chapter, infra.

12. These are known as "S corporations." I.R.C. § 1361(a)(1). The Code imposes no limit on the value of an S corporation, but eligibility for Subchapter S status is restricted to corporations having not more than 100 shareholders or more than one class of stock.

See Section 1B4 of this chapter and Chapter 15, infra.

13. See I.R.C. § 7704 and Section C2b of this chapter, infra.

14. See e.g., Subchapter M, governing regulated investment companies (mutual funds) and real estate investment trusts.

15. See, e.g., Subchapter L (Insurance Companies), Subchapter H (banks and trust companies), and Subchapter F (tax-exempt organizations and cooperatives).

budget-driven tax legislative process.[1] An overview of the past and current synergy of these influential policies is appropriate before moving on.

The Double Tax. The concept at the heart of Subchapter C is the double taxation of corporate income. Earnings are taxed once at the corporate level when earned and again when distributed as dividends to shareholders.[2] This decision to treat corporations as separate taxable entities, distinct from their shareholders, has been controversial.[3] Some of the debate is over the incidence of the corporate tax—whether it is borne by shareholders, employees, corporate managers, consumers of the company's goods or services, or investors in general.[4] Critics also point to the adverse impact of the tax on the allocation of economic resources; its complexity; and many other evils, including three distinct biases: (1) against corporate as opposed to noncorporate investment (because only corporate capital is subject to a second tax); (2) in favor of excessive debt financing for businesses organized as C corporations; and (3) in favor of retention of earnings at the corporate level as opposed to distribution of dividends.[5]

If a double tax is accepted as the appropriate corporate taxing model, the discussion then turns to the "integrity" of the corporate-level tax. For example, should the corporate income tax apply not only to operating profits but also to distributions of appreciated property and sales in connection with corporate liquidations? The outcome of this controversy will unfold as these and other transactions are studied later in this text. For now, it is sufficient to observe that in the Tax Reform Act of 1986 the defenders of the corporate income tax largely prevailed on these theoretical questions. The results were a strengthened double tax regime, an increase in the tax costs of operating a profitable business as a C corporation, and greater pressure on techniques to reduce these costs. More recently, the pendulum has shifted in the other direction, most notably with the reduction in the tax rate on dividends. Beginning in 2003 and continuing at least

---

1. See generally Zolt, "Corporate Taxation After the Tax Reform Act of 1986: A State of Disequilibrium," 66 N.C.L.Rev. 839 (1988).

2. Of course, corporations have been adept at minimizing their taxable income, and many shareholders, such as pension funds and nonprofit organizations, generally do not pay taxes on the dividends they receive.

3. See generally Goode, The Corporate Income Tax (1951); McLure, "Integration of the Personal and Corporate Income Taxes: The Missing Element in Recent Tax Reform Proposals," 88 Harv.L.Rev. 532 (1975).

4. See e.g., Harberger, "The Incidence of the Corporation Income Tax," 70 J.Pol.Econ. 215 (1962); Klein, "The Incidence of the Corporation Income Tax: A Lawyer's View of a Problem in Economics," 65 Wisc. L.Rev. 576 (1965). Lest there be any suspense, economists have concluded that they are unable to ascertain who bears the burden of the corporate tax. See generally Break, "The Incidence and Economic Effects of Taxation," in The Economics of Public Finance (Brookings 1974).

5. See generally American Law Institute, Federal Income Tax Project—Subchapter C 341–355 (1982). Commentators also point to the "compensating biases" in the individual income tax, such as the rate structure, the capital gains preference and the ability of individuals to obtain a stepped-up basis in property held at death. See Zolt, supra note 1, at 845–846, and text accompanying notes 6–11, infra.

until 2009, most dividends received by noncorporate shareholders are taxed at the same 15 percent maximum rate as long-term capital gains.[6]

The desire to avoid the double tax on corporate profits while obtaining limited liability for all the owners of a business has fueled the emergence of new legal forms, such as the limited liability company. Entities similar to the LLC have long been used in other countries. Examples include the Latin American *limitada* and the German *Gesellschaft mit besechrankter Haftung* ("GmbH").[7] The origins of the LLC in the United States can be traced to the search by foreign investors in the oil and gas industry for a U.S. business entity that would combine limited liability protection for all owners with one level of taxation. Because nonresident aliens may not own stock in an S corporation, the investors' objectives could not be met using the corporate form. So they began lobbying state legislatures, and by the late 1970's Wyoming had enacted the first domestic limited liability company statute.[8] LLCs were not practically viable, however, until the Internal Revenue Service ruled, first privately and then in a 1989 published ruling, that a Wyoming LLC would be treated as a partnership rather than a corporation for tax purposes.[9]

The explosive growth of the LLC as a "best of all worlds" legal form breathed new life into the business enterprise tax policy debate. Consider the following questions. Why does the Internal Revenue Code have two separate pass-through tax regimes for closely held business enterprises, one (Subchapter K) for partnerships and LLCs and the other (Subchapter S) for certain corporations, each with different qualification standards and operative provisions?[10] If a single pass-through regime were adopted, would Subchapter K be preferable to Subchapter S, or would some combination of the two be the best approach?[11] Why are C corporations singled out for a double tax regime? Is it because they enjoy limited liability under state law? Presumably not, because LLCs are not subject to Subchapter C. Does the rise of the LLC undermine the policy underlying the double tax and threaten to destroy the corporate tax base? Would it make more sense to limit Subchapter C to large corporations (based on revenues) or publicly traded entities? Or should there be a single one-tier tax regime for all

---

6. I.R.C. § 1(h)(11)(A). See Chapter 4A2, infra.

7. See Carney, "Limited Liability Companies: Origins and Antecedents," 66 U.Colo. L.Rev. 855 (1995).

8. See Hamill, "The Limited Liability Company: A Catalyst Exposing The Corporate Integration Question," 95 Mich. L. Rev. 393, 399 (1996), for a history of LLC's rise from obscurity to its current position as a mainstream form of business entity.

9. Rev. Rul. 88–76, 1988–2 C.B. 361. See Section C1 of this chapter, infra.

10. See Lokken, "Taxation of Private Business Firms: Imagining a Future Without

Subchapter K," 4 Fla. Tax Rev. 249 (1999); Schwidetzky, "Is it Time to Give the S Corporation a Proper Burial?", 15 Va. Tax Rev. 591 (1996); Rands, "Pass through Entities and Their Unprincipled Differences Under Federal Tax Law," 49 SMU L. Rev. 15 (1995).

11. See Eustice, "Subchapter S Corporations and Partnerships: A Search for the Passthrough Paradigm," 39 Tax L. Rev. 345 (1989); August, "Benefits and Burdens of Subchapter S in a Check-the-Box World," 4 Fla. Tax Rev. 287 (1999).

business income without regard to the organizational form?[12] The remaining chapters provide an opportunity to reconsider these issues as you study the Code's two corporate tax regimes in greater depth.

Rates on Ordinary Income. For C corporations with significant taxable income, the corporate income tax is essentially a 34 or 35 percent flat rate tax with no preferential rate for long-term capital gains.[13] Corporations with smaller amounts of income, however, can take advantage of lower rates (15 and 25 percent) on their first $75,000 of taxable income.[14] Individuals pay tax at graduated rates beginning at 10 percent of taxable income and peaking at a nominal rate of 35 percent.[15] And profits of C corporations are potentially taxed both at the corporate and shareholder levels when they are distributed as dividends or when the shareholders sell their stock.

At first glance, the highest individual and corporate rates appear to be the same, but a true comparison is a bit more complex. The effective marginal rate for some individuals may be higher than 35 percent on some income because of the disallowance of itemized deductions and the phase-out of personal exemptions for high-income taxpayers.[16] Beginning in 2003 and continuing until 2009, dividends received by noncorporate shareholders are taxed at the same preferential 15 percent maximum rate as long-term capital gains.[17] Other variables that may affect the overall tax burden include the corporate and individual alternative minimum taxes; a long list of corporate tax benefits, ranging from accelerated depreciation to targeted subsidies for particular industries, that lower the effective corporate tax rate; and employment taxes imposed on owners who also perform services for the business.

At one time, when the maximum individual tax rate on ordinary income peaked at 70 percent or higher and the top corporate rate was 46 percent, C corporations served as a refuge from the steeper individual rates. This rate differential prompted privately held firms to conduct their business and investment activities as C corporations rather than pass-through entities because their income was taxed at lower rates and could remain in corporate solution to compound at the these tax-preferred rates until the business was sold or liquidated. In the meantime, shareholders who wished to withdraw earnings utilized tax efficient strategies to avoid the sting of the double tax. For example, owner-employees of a C corporation typically have distributed profits in the form of salary and fringe

---

12. See, e.g., Yin, "The Future Taxation of Private Business Firms," 4 Fla. Tax Rev. 141 (1999); Klein & Zolt, "Business Form, Limited Liability, and Tax Regimes: Lurching Toward a Coherent Outcome," 66 Colo.L.Rev. 1001 (1995).

13. I.R.C. §§ 11; 1201(a).

14. I.R.C. 11(b). Certain corporations with major shareholders who render personal services, such as professional corporations of lawyers, accountants, architects, and the like,

are not entitled to the lower marginal corporate rates. I.R.C. §§ 11(b)(2); 448(d)(2).

15. I.R.C. § 1.

16. See I.R.C. §§ 68; 151(d)(3). The phase-outs are themselves being phased out, however, and are scheduled for repeal by 2010, but just for one year unless Congress makes the repeal permanent.

17. I.R.C. § 1(h)(11).

benefits that are tax-deductible by the corporation and, in the case of many fringe benefits, excludable by the owner-employee. Shareholders also can loan funds or lease property to a C corporation and withdraw earnings in the form of tax-deductible interest or rent.

To be sure, the Service had weapons to combat these self-help strategies. Payments of salary or interest could be attacked as unreasonable compensation or disguised dividends but usually these arguments were reserved for the most egregious cases. Congress also enacted penalty taxes to patrol against excessive accumulations or avoidance of the individual progressive rates.[18] With foresight and good planning, however, an active business that paid reasonable compensation and justified any accumulations of earnings on the basis of reasonable business judgment could avoid constructive dividends and the corporate penalty taxes with relative ease.

For many C corporations, these tax saving strategies have withstood the test of time. A study by the Joint Committee on Taxation revealed that in 1993, 61 percent of all C corporations reported no taxable income and another 37 percent reported taxable income of less than $355,000.[19] More recent data indicates that in 2001, 49 percent of all C corporations reported no taxable income, and only 35 percent of C corporations had any corporate tax liability after tax credits were taken into account.[20]

But some of the key variables have changed along with the tax rates. Today, with individuals and C corporations subject to the same top rate and with dividends and long-term capital gains taxed at a maximum rate of 15 percent, the C corporation earnings accumulation strategy is much less compelling than when corporations enjoyed a significant tax rate advantage over individuals. This rate parity, together with the prospect of two levels of tax when a C corporation is sold, provides a greater incentive to use a pass-through entity instead of a C corporation, particularly if the business intends to distribute its earnings currently, does not have owners who work for the firm, or holds assets that are likely to appreciate in value over a relatively short time horizon. It would be rare, for example, for a venture investing in real estate or financial assets for current income or capital appreciation (or both) to operate as a C corporation because the costs of doing so would be prohibitive in light of the double tax. In some cases, however, C corporations still offer tax savings, especially for businesses that are able to pay out most of their earnings as compensation to their high-income owners.

Preferential Capital Gains Rates. The decision to tax long-term capital gains at substantially lower rates than ordinary income is another feature of the tax system that historically eased the tax burden of conducting a business as a C corporation. Rather than paying dividends, tax advisors

---

18. See I.R.C. § 531 et seq. (accumulated earnings tax); § 541 (personal holding company tax).

19. Joint Committee on Taxation, Impact of Small Business of Replacing the Federal Income Tax 5 (J.C.S., 3–96, April 23, 1996).

20. Statistics of Income—2001, Corporation Income Tax Returns, Table 22 (2004).

devised techniques to "bail out" earnings at capital gains rates. A "bailout" is a distribution of earnings in a transaction, such as a redemption of stock, that qualifies as a "sale or exchange," enabling the shareholder to recover all or part of her stock basis and to benefit from preferential capital gain treatment on any realized gain.[21] In some cases, such as where the shareholder has died and the basis of her stock has been stepped up to its date-of-death value, the bailout may be accomplished tax-free.[22] Over the years, Congress responded with complex anti-bailout provisions to ensure that distributions resembling dividends would be taxed as ordinary income.[23]

Now that dividends and capital gains are taxed at the same preferential rates, the traditional incentive for a bailout has just about disappeared. Under the new rate regime, the tax goal of a bailout will not be to convert dividend income to capital gain but rather to enable shareholders to recover all or part of the basis in their stock. It is unlikely that this will tip the scales in favor of using a C corporation but this new type of bailout continues to raise challenging tax issues for the many closely held businesses that currently operate as C corporations.

Nonrecognition. Under the realization principle, gains and losses are not taxable until they are realized in a sale, exchange or other event that makes the gain or loss "real" and more easily measurable. The nonrecognition concept assumes that certain realization events should not be impeded by the imposition of a tax. Transactions that qualify for nonrecognition treatment may go forward on a tax-free basis on the theory that they are mere changes in form which result in a continuity of investment. To ensure that any realized gain or loss is merely deferred rather than eliminated, the typical nonrecognition provision includes corollary rules providing for transferred and exchanged bases and tacked holding periods.[24] The nonrecognition principle pervades Subchapter C, affecting transactions ranging from the simple corporate formation to complex mergers and acquisitions.

The opportunity to qualify a corporate transaction for nonrecognition has assumed even greater importance with the strengthening of the corporate tax. A corporation must pay tax on the appreciation in its assets on a sale or distribution in connection with a complete liquidation.[25] Standing in sharp contrast are acquisitions known as tax-free reorganizations, which ordinarily are free of tax to all the parties, albeit with the trade-off of transferred bases and a carryover of other tax attributes. Taxpayers are

---

21. Subchapter C includes many provisions to patrol against bailout transactions that are essentially equivalent to dividend distributions. See, e.g., I.R.C. §§ 302; 304; 306.

22. The date-of-death basis rule in Section 1014 is scheduled to be replaced by a carryover basis regime (with some exceptions) in 2010 (but for one year only) when the estate tax is repealed. See I.R.C. § 1022.

23. See, e.g., I.R.C. §§ 302; 304; 306.

24. See, e.g., I.R.C. § 1031, which provides for nonrecognition on certain like-kind exchanges.

25. See Chapter 7B2, infra. Certain taxable acquisitions of stock will continue to trigger only shareholder-level gain but the bases of the acquired corporation's assets will transfer to the purchaser.

thus encouraged to structure sales of a corporate business to come within an applicable nonrecognition provision in order to avoid (or at least defer) tax at the corporate and shareholder levels.

Perspective. In the first edition of this book, published in 1985, we observed that "[t]he corporate tax system previewed here is not engraved in stone," and predicted that "change is in the air, and tax lawyers and students must be prepared, often at a moment's notice, to discard old concepts and master new ones."[26] Before the ink was dry, Congress enacted the historic Tax Reform Act of 1986. Subsequent developments, most recently the significant rate reduction for qualified dividends, have contributed to an unstable tax environment—and frequent revisions of tax textbooks.

And so once again, as in each prior edition, we ask—what of that future? Although the spirited debate over Subchapter C appears to have subsided, tax policy issues continue to dominate the contemporary political debate. As always, tax lawyers (and students) must be prepared, often with little notice, to discard old concepts and master new ones. To assist in that process, policy readings have been interspersed throughout the text. Later in this chapter, for example, students are invited to examine how aggressive tax shelter activity is contributing to an erosion of the corporate income tax, and to consider the pros and cons of "integration" of the corporate and individual income taxes.[27] Other proposals emanating from Congress, the Treasury Department, the American Law Institute, and commentators are considered in connection with the specific trouble spots to which they relate.

3.   THE COMMON LAW OF CORPORATE TAXATION

Although the study of corporate taxation principally involves the application of complex statutes to particular transactions, the Code is not the only analytical tool. In scrutinizing taxpayer behavior, the courts at an early date went beyond the literal statutory language and began to formulate a set of doctrines that have become the "common law" of federal taxation. Some of these principles, such as the assignment of income doctrine, were encountered in the basic income tax course. Unlike the Code, which often provides bright-line rules for solving problems, the judicial doctrines are imprecise. The very vagueness of these pronouncements, however, has contributed to their influence. When the system is working, they loom large in the tax advisor's conscience and serve to thwart aggressive schemes that literally comply with the statute but are incompatible with its intended purpose.[1] This introductory survey is in-

26. Lind, Schwarz, Lathrope & Rosenberg, Cases and Materials on Fundamentals of Corporate Taxation 3–4 (1st ed. 1985).

27. See generally "Colloquium on Corporate Integration," 47 Tax L.Rev. 427 (1992); Warren, "The Relation and Integration of Individual and Corporate Income Taxes," 94 Harv.L.Rev. 719 (1981); McNulty,

"Reform of the Individual Income Tax By Integration of the Corporate Income Tax," 46 Tax Notes 1445 (Mar. 19, 1990)

1. See generally Bittker & Lokken, Federal Taxation of Income, Estates and Gifts ¶ 4.3.1 (3d ed. 1999).

tended to preview some of the reasoning that lies at the heart of this tax jurisprudence.

Viewed most broadly, the judicial doctrines ask a simple question that is central to almost every transaction studied in this text. Have the taxpayers actually done what they, and their documents, represent, or are the economic realities of the transaction—and the attendant tax consequences—other than what the taxpayers purport them to be? The tests used to resolve this question bear many labels which are often used interchangeably. What follows is a summary of the terminology that will soon become familiar.

Sham Transaction and Economic Substance Doctrines. If a transaction is a "sham," it will not be respected for tax purposes. A "sham" sometimes is defined as a transaction that never actually occurred but is represented by the taxpayer to have transpired—with favorable tax consequences of course.[2] One court has colorfully described a sham as an "attempt by a taxpayer to ward off tax blows with paper armor,"[3] in a purported transaction that "gives off an unmistakably hollow sound when it is tapped."[4]

Because a "sham" often connotes near fraudulent behavior, the courts tend to reserve this doctrine for the more egregious cases. But the pejorative term also has been used to describe kinds of transactions that are challenged under the closely related economic substance doctrine. In one typically overlapping formulation, the Fourth Circuit offered the following two-part test to define a sham:[5]

> To treat a transaction as a sham, the court must find that the taxpayer was motivated by no business purpose other than obtaining tax benefits in entering the transaction, and that the transaction has no economic substance because no reasonable possibility of a profit exists.

The courts also are not consistent in their application of the economic substance doctrine. Some apply a two-part test requiring a taxpayer first to establish the presence of economic substance (an objective inquiry) and then a business purpose (a subjective test).[6] Others will respect a transaction if it has either a business purpose or economic substance.[7] Still others reject a rigid two-step analysis and consider economic substance and

---

2. See, e.g., Knetsch v. United States, 364 U.S. 361, 81 S.Ct. 132 (1960).

3. Waterman Steamship Corp. v. Commissioner, 430 F.2d 1185 (5th Cir.1970), cert. denied, 401 U.S. 939, 91 S.Ct. 936 (1971).

4. Id. at 1196, quoting United States v. General Geophysical Co., 296 F.2d 86, 89 (5th Cir.1961), cert. denied, 369 U.S. 849, 82 S.Ct. 932 (1962).

5. Rice's Toyota World, Inc. v. Commissioner, 752 F.2d 89, 91 (4th Cir.1985); Winn–Dixie Stores, Inc. v. Commissioner, 254 F.3d 1313 (11th Cir.2001). See also Kirchman v. Commissioner, 862 F.2d 1486 (11th Cir. 1989). For cases where courts have declined to characterize a questionable transaction as a sham, see Compaq v. Commissioner, 277 F.3d 778 (5th Cir.2001); IES Industries, Inc. v. United States, 253 F.3d 350 (8th Cir.2001).

6. See, e.g., Pasternak v. Commissioner, 990 F.2d 893, 898 (6th Cir. 1993).

7. Rice's Toyota World v. Commissioner, supra note 5; see also IES Industries v. Commissioner, 253 F.3d 350, 358 (8th Cir. 2001).

business purpose merely as "precise factors" to help determine whether a transaction has any practical economic effects apart from securing tax benefits.[8]

Substance Over Form. The form of a transaction frequently is determinative of its tax consequences. Since the early days of the income tax, however, the courts have been willing to go beyond the formal papers and evaluate the "substance" of a transaction. A familiar example is the proper classification of a business arrangement as a sale or a lease.[9] The documents used by the taxpayer may use one label, but the courts are not inhibited from examining the arrangement and restructuring it for tax purposes to comport with the economic realities.

The tension between form and substance will be evident throughout the chapters that follow. Is a corporate instrument "debt," as the taxpayer contends, or "equity," as the Service usually will assert? Is a payment to a shareholder-employee really "compensation" or is it a disguised dividend? Who, in substance, made a sale of corporate assets—the corporation or its shareholders? It is impossible to generalize as to when and how this doctrine will be applied. Individual cases turn on unique fact pressures and the court's attitude toward tax avoidance.[10]

Despite the influence of this doctrine over time, the courts have shown some reluctance to accept recent attempts by the Service to restructure legitimate transactions to reach a result that will produce more revenue. The Tax Court, for example, is wary of extending the judicial doctrines where Congress has mandated that particular results shall flow from a given form and the taxpayers have carefully structured an otherwise legitimate transaction to comply with the statutory requirements.[11]

Business Purpose. The business purpose doctrine is conceptually linked to the sham, economic substance, and substance-versus-form tests. A transaction motivated by a business purpose usually is compared to one that has no substance, purpose or utility apart from tax avoidance. As originally formulated by Judge Learned Hand,[12] the business purpose doctrine was applied to deny tax-free status to a transaction that would not have been consummated but for the tax savings that would result if its form were respected. The doctrine took hold and has become an independent requirement for tax recognition of many transactions.[13]

---

8. See, e.g., ACM Partnership v. Commissioner, 157 F.3d 231 (3d Cir. 1998), cert. denied, 526 U.S. 1017, 119 S.Ct. 1251 (1999).

9. See, e.g., Frank Lyon Co. v. United States, 435 U.S. 561, 98 S.Ct. 1291 (1978).

10. See, e.g., Grove v. Commissioner, infra p. 274, where the majority and dissenting opinion evidence a sharply conflicting philosophy about the use of the substance-versus-form doctrine in tax cases.

11. See, e.g., Esmark, Inc. v. Commissioner, 90 T.C. 171 (1988), affirmed 886 F.2d

1318 (7th Cir.1989). See also United Parcel Service of America, Inc. v. Commissioner, infra p. 26; Compaq Computer Corp. v. Commissioner, 277 F.3d 778 (5th Cir.2001); Black & Decker Corp. v. United States, 340 F.Supp. 2d 621 (D. Md. 2004).

12. See Helvering v. Gregory, 69 F.2d 809 (2d Cir.1934).

13. See, e.g., Reg. § 1.355–2(b), requiring a corporate business purpose to qualify as a tax-free corporate division under Section 355.

Step Transaction Doctrine. When courts apply the step transaction doctrine, they combine (or "step") formally distinct transactions to determine the tax treatment of the single integrated series of events. The doctrine frequently is applied in conjunction with the other judicial tests.

The courts disagree on the standard to be employed in applying the step transaction doctrine. Some require a binding legal commitment to complete all the steps from the outset before combining them, while others require only a "mutual interdependence" of steps or a preconceived intent to reach a particular end result.[14]

The meaning and scope of all this overlapping common law tax jurisprudence has befuddled (and yet challenged) tax advisors for decades. Our goal here is to identify the principal terminology and give fair warning that literal compliance with the Code may not be enough for a transaction to pass muster. Students should not expect to master a precise or consistent explanation of the judicial doctrines. It will be enough simply to develop a sense of smell for the kinds of cases in which the doctrines might be invoked.[15]

B.   THE CORPORATION AS A SEPARATE TAXABLE ENTITY

1.   THE CORPORATE INCOME TAX

Code: §§ 11(a), (b)(1) & (2); 63(a). Skim §§ 199(a), (b), (c); 243(a); 1201(a); 1211(a); 1212(a)(1).

Students are often surprised to learn that a study of corporate taxation devotes very little time to the determination of a corporation's tax liability. The reason is that the concepts used in making that determination already should have been mastered in the basic federal income tax course. Those same broad principles—gross income, deductions, assignment of income, timing and characterization—apply in computing the taxable income of a C corporation, and we only need to pause briefly to discuss the rate structure and a few other special rules applicable to C corporations.

Rates. A C corporation, like an individual, is a separate taxable entity for federal income tax purposes. The corporation selects its own taxable year and method of accounting, computes its taxable income under applicable principles of the tax law and otherwise is generally treated like any other taxable person. The corporate rates are found in Section 11, which provides a limited number of brackets for lower income corporations but

---

14. This doctrine is analyzed in some detail in connection with corporate liquidations and corporate reorganizations. See, e.g., Commissioner v. Court Holding Co., infra p. 333.

15. For an analysis of the state of the judicial doctrines, see McMahon, "Random Thoughts on Applying Judicial Doctrines to Interpret the Internal Revenue Code," 54 SMU L. Rev. 195 (2001); Canellos, "A Tax Practitioner's Perspective on Substance, Form and Business Purpose in Structuring Business Transactions and in Tax Shelters," 54 SMU L. Rev. 47 (2001). For application of the judicial doctrines in connection with the Service's war against corporate tax shelters, see Section B5 of this chapter, infra.

becomes an essentially flat rate tax for more profitable companies. The maximum corporate rate is 35 percent on a corporation's taxable income in excess of $10,000,000.[1] For corporate income under $10,000,000 the rates are as follows:[2]

Taxable Income	Rate
$0 to $50,000	15%
$50,001 to $75,000	25%
$75,001 to $10,000,000	34%

The simple schedule above is modified, however, to prevent the most profitable corporations from enjoying the benefits of the lower graduated rates. Section 11(b) imposes an additional five percent tax on taxable income in excess of $100,000 up to a maximum increase of $11,750, which is the amount of tax savings from the lower rates on the first $75,000 of taxable income. This rate "bubble" in effect creates a 39 percent marginal bracket on taxable income between $100,000 and $335,000. In addition, corporations with taxable income in excess of $15,000,000 must increase their tax by the lesser of three percent of the excess, or $100,000. As a result of this second (double?) bubble, corporations with taxable income over $18,333,333 are taxed at a flat 35 percent rate on all their income.

To prevent doctors, lawyers, entertainers and other incorporated service providers from taking advantage of the lower marginal corporate rates, Section 11(b)(2) denies the benefit of those rates to any "qualified personal service corporation" as defined in Section 448(d)(2). Incorporated service businesses are thus subject to a 35 percent flat rate tax on all their taxable income. In general, a "qualified personal service corporation" is a corporation substantially engaged in the performance of services in the fields of health, law, engineering, architecture, accounting, actuarial science, performing arts, or consulting, if substantially all of the corporation's stock is held (directly or indirectly) by employees performing services for the corporation, retired employees, or the estates of employees or retirees.[3]

Determination of Taxable Income. Section 63(a) defines taxable income as "gross income minus the deductions allowed by this chapter." In the case of a corporation, this amount generally is determined by applying the same principles and Code sections applicable to individuals. A few differences, primarily attributable to the distinct status of the corporation as an artificial business entity, are worth mentioning.

First, because a corporation has no "personal" expenses, it is not entitled to any personal or dependency exemptions and, unlike an individual, it receives no standard deduction. Corporations thus are not concerned with distinguishing between "above-the-line" deductions allowable in reaching adjusted gross income and "below-the-line" itemized deductions or in applying the Section 67 two percent of adjusted gross income floor to

1. I.R.C. § 11(b).   **3.** I.R.C. § 448(d)(2).

2. Id.

"miscellaneous itemized deductions" or the Section 68 overall limitation on itemized deductions.

In addition, most of the personal deductions allowed to individuals are not available to corporations. For example, a corporation is not entitled to a medical expense deduction under Section 213 or a spousal support deduction under Section 215. Moreover, Section 212, which allows a deduction for certain expenses incurred for the production of income or maintenance of income-producing property or for tax advice, is expressly applicable only to individuals. Corporations need not worry however, because virtually all of their ordinary expenses in the pursuit of profit are deductible under Section 162.

On the other hand, certain *limitations* on the deductibility of personal expenses of individuals do not apply to corporations. For example, Section 165(c), which limits the deductibility of nonbusiness losses; Section 166(d), which characterizes nonbusiness bad debts as short-term capital losses; and Section 183(a), which limits deductions for activities not motivated by profit, are among a number of restrictive sections that do not apply to C corporations. This is because it is generally assumed that all of a corporation's activities are motivated by the pursuit of profit.[4]

By virtue of their unique status, corporations are entitled to one important deduction not available to individuals. To prevent multiple taxation as earnings wend their way through a chain of corporations, corporate shareholders generally are entitled to deduct 70 percent (or, in some cases, 80 or 100 percent) of the dividends they receive from other corporations. The effect of the 70 percent dividends received deduction is that corporations are subject to tax at a maximum rate of 10.5 percent on dividends—an amount derived by applying the top 35 percent corporate rate to the 30 percent includable portion of the dividends.

The remaining differences in the treatment of corporations and individuals are the result of a conscious legislative choice to treat them differently. For example, the percentage limitation on corporate charitable deductions is 10 percent of taxable income as compared to an overall 50 percent limit on individual charitable contributions.[5] The at-risk limitations in Section 465 and the passive loss limitations in Section 469, which are aimed at tax shelter activities of individual taxpayers, generally do not apply to C corporations.[6] And publicly traded corporations may not deduct more than $1 million per year for otherwise reasonable compensation paid to certain high-level corporate executives.[7]

---

4. Certain payments made by a corporation to or on behalf of its shareholders may be nondeductible because they are in fact dividends, but their disallowance is the result of the classification of the payments as constructive dividends rather than the "personal" nature of the payments. See Chapter 4E, infra.

5. I.R.C. § 170(b)(2).

6. I.R.C. §§ 465(a)(1); 469(a)(2)(B), (j)(1). See Chapter 3C, supra.

7. I.R.C. § 162(m). This limitation only applies to the chief executive officer and the four other most highly compensated executives. I.R.C. § 162(m)(3). Various types of commissions and performance-based compensation are exempt. I.R.C. § 162(m)(4). Tax advisors have been adept at designing com-

Another significant difference relates to the treatment of corporate capital losses. Corporations may deduct capital losses only to the extent of capital gains during the taxable year. Although the excess may not be applied against ordinary income, it may be carried back for three years and carried forward for five years. By contrast, individuals are permitted to deduct capital losses to the extent of capital gains, and up to $3,000 of excess losses may be deducted against ordinary income. Unused capital losses may be carried forward indefinitely by an individual taxpayer.[8]

Deduction for Domestic Production Activities. The stated maximum corporate income tax rate of 35 percent will be reduced by approximately 3 percent when the Section 199 deduction for domestic production activities is fully phased in.[9] This generous new tax benefit was the centerpiece of the American Jobs Creation Act of 2004, which repealed a longstanding export subsidy ruled illegal by the World Trade Organization.[10] To compensate for the lost tax break, Congress added the deduction, which permits U.S. taxpayers engaged in certain domestic production activities to deduct a specified percentage (3 percent in 2005–2006, 6 percent in 2007–2009, and 9 percent in 2010 and thereafter) of the lesser of their taxable income or "qualified production activities income."[11] The deduction is allowed for purposes of both the regular and alternative minimum taxes.[12]

Section 199 is a typically complex provision littered with definitions and special rules. In keeping with the "fundamentals" philosophy of the text, the following discussion is limited to a few highlights. "Qualified production activities income," the base on which the deduction is determined, equals a taxpayer's "domestic production gross receipts" reduced by the sum of: (1) the cost of goods sold allocable to those receipts, (2) other allocable expenses, and (3) a ratable portion of other not directly allocable deductions and losses.[13] The key term that unlocks the gate to the deduction is "domestic production gross receipts," which are gross receipts derived from various "production" activities within the United States. "Production" is much broader than just "manufacturing." It includes farming, equipment leasing, licensing of software and films (but not if the film is "pornographic"), construction, production of electricity, natural gas and drinking water, and even some service businesses such as engineering or architecture.[14] As a result, many companies that did not benefit from the repealed export subsidy will qualify for the new deduction.

pensation plans to avoid the impact of this provision.

8. I.R.C. §§ 1211, 1212.

9. I.R.C. § 199. The deduction is effective for taxable years beginning after December 31, 2004.

10. Another generous provision added by the 2004 legislation creates a one-year amnesty for companies to repatriate profits earned outside the United States at a reduced tax rate of 5.25 percent. I.R.C. § 965(a). Technology and pharmaceutical companies with large amount of overseas cash especially will benefit from this "tax holiday."

11. I.R.C. § 199(a). The deduction cannot exceed 50 percent of "W–2 wages" (defined as wages and certain elective deferrals, such as contributions to Section 401(k) plans) paid by the taxpayer as an employer during the taxable year. I.R.C. § 199(b).

12. I.R.C. § 199(d)(6).

13. I.R.C. § 199(c)(1).

14. I.R.C. § 199(c)(4).

The statute draws some fine lines in determining what activities qualify for the deduction. Profits from the sale of food and beverages prepared by the taxpayer at a retail establishment, such as restaurants and facilities selling take-out food items, do not qualify,[15] but profits from processing food (e.g., from an in-store bakery in a supermarket) are eligible for the tax break.[16] As explained in the legislative history, "the gross receipts of a meat packing establishment" qualify but "the activities of a master chef who creates a venison sausage for his or her restaurant menu" do not.[17] U.S. companies that roast coffee beans and use them to brew coffee for sale qualify for the deduction on the roasting but not the brewing activity.[18] The Service has been delegated the authority to provide additional guidance through regulations.[19]

The Section 199 deduction was part of a massive tax bill intended by Congress to stimulate the creation of new jobs within the United States. It is already clear that deciphering the intricacies of this new deduction will boost the gross receipts of law and accounting firms, but the definition of "domestic production" does not yet extend to the services provided by tax advisers.

Taxable Year and Accounting Method. Most C corporations have the flexibility to adopt either a calendar year or a fiscal year as their annual accounting period.[20] Certain "personal service corporations" must use a calendar year, however, unless they can show a business purpose for using a fiscal year.[21] For this purpose, a "personal service corporation" is one whose principal activity is the performance of personal services that are substantially performed by "employee-owners" who collectively own more than 10 percent (by value) of the corporation's stock.[22] This generally forces most personal service corporations to use a calendar year, subject to an exception in Section 444 which permits them to elect to adopt or change to a fiscal year with a "deferral period" of not more than three months.[23] As a result, a personal service corporation that otherwise would be required to use a calendar year may elect a taxable year ending September 30, October 31 or November 30. To prevent any tax savings that might result from the use of a fiscal year, personal service corporations making a Section 444

---

15. I.R.C. § 199(c)(4)(B).

16. H.R. Rep. No. 108–755, 108th Cong., 2d Sess. 13 (2004).

17. Id. at 12.

18. Id. at 13.

19. I.R.C. § 199(d)(7). The Service issued detailed guidance in I.R.S. Notice 2005–14, 2005–7 I.R.B. 1.

20. See generally I.R.C. § 441. A fiscal year is any period of 12 months ending on the last day of any month other than December. I.R.C. § 441(e).

21. I.R.C. § 441(i)(1). Deferral of income to shareholders is not treated as a business purpose. Id.

22. I.R.C. §§ 269A(b)(1); 441(i)(2). An employee-owner is defined as any employee who owns, on any day during the taxable year, any of the outstanding stock of the corporation after applying certain attribution rules. I.R.C. § 269A(b)(2), as modified by I.R.C. § 441(i)(2).

23. I.R.C. § 444(b)(2). The "deferral period" of a taxable year is the number of months between the beginning of the taxable year elected and the close of the required taxable year that ends within the taxable year elected.

election must make certain minimum distributions (e.g., primarily of compensation) to employee-owners during the portion of the employee's fiscal year that ends on December 31.[24] If these minimum distribution requirements are not met, the electing corporation must defer certain otherwise currently deductible payments (e.g., compensation) to employee-owners.[25] A personal service corporation that establishes a business purpose for a fiscal year is not required to make a Section 444 election and is not subject to these distribution requirements and deduction limitations.[26]

In general, C corporations are required to use the accrual method of accounting.[27] Exemptions are provided for corporations engaged in the farming business, "qualified personal service corporations"[28] and any other corporation whose average annual gross receipts for a three-year measuring period preceding the taxable year do not exceed $5 million.[29]

In addition to these general accounting rules, Section 267 regulates certain transactions between corporations and their shareholders to prevent the acceleration of losses on related party transactions and to preclude timing advantages when the corporation and its owner-employees use different methods of accounting. For example, Section 267(a)(1) provides that losses from sales or exchanges of property between an individual shareholder and a more-than–50 percent-owned corporation may not be deducted.[30] The forced matching rules in Section 267(a)(2) prevent an accrual method corporation from accruing and deducting compensation paid to a cash method owner-employee in the year when the services are performed but deferring payment until the following taxable year to provide the employee with a timing advantage. When an owner-employee owns, directly or indirectly, more than 50 percent of the payor corporation, the corporation's deduction is deferred until such time as the owner-employee includes the amount in income.[31]

Credits. Like any taxpayer engaged in business or investment activities, a corporation is entitled to several valuable tax credits. The most significant is the foreign tax credit, which is available to corporations with

24. See generally I.R.C. § 280H.

25. I.R.C. § 280H(a), (b), (c).

26. I.R.S. Notice 88–10, 1988–1 C.B. 478.

27. I.R.C. § 448(a).

28. This is the same category of corporations that is deprived of the lower graduated rates in Section 11. Substantially all of the activities of the corporation must involve the performance of services in the fields of health, law, engineering, accounting, architecture, actuarial science, performing arts, or consulting, and substantially all of the stock must be held by employees, their estates or their heirs. I.R.C. § 448(d)(2).

29. I.R.C. § 448(b).

30. The loss disallowance applies to transactions between related parties as defined in Section 267(b). A corporation and its more-than–50 percent (measured by value) shareholders are considered related. I.R.C. § 267(b)(2). Percentage ownership is determined after application of attribution rules in Section 267(c).

31. I.R.C. § 267(a)(2). This section also may apply to payments of interest and other deductible expenses. In the case of personal service corporations, the corporation and *any* owner-employee (regardless of the percentage ownership) are treated as related parties for purposes of the forced matching rules in Section 267. Id.

income from foreign sources.[32] Others include the rehabilitation and energy credits,[33] the work opportunity credit,[34] and the credit for research expenditures.[35]

2. THE CORPORATE ALTERNATIVE MINIMUM TAX

Code: §§ 55(a), (b)(1)(B) & (2), (c)(1), (d)(2) & (3)(A), (e)(1); 56(a)(1)(A), (c)(1), (g)(1), (2), (3), (4)(A)–(C)(ii), (6); 57(a)(5)(A), (6). Skim § 53.

C Corporations also are potentially subject to the alternative minimum tax ("AMT"), which is designed "to ensure that no taxpayer with substantial economic income can avoid significant tax liability by using exclusions, deductions and credits."[1] The AMT generally can be described as a flat rate tax which is imposed on a broader income base than the taxable income yardstick used for the regular corporate tax. But that deceptively simple description only begins to explain a complex statutory scheme that takes many twists and turns before reaching "alternative minimum taxable income," the base that Congress believed was a truer measure of a corporation's economic results.

The corporate AMT is payable only to the extent that it exceeds a corporation's regular tax liability.[2] The AMT generally is 20 percent of the amount by which a corporation's alternative minimum taxable income, as defined in Section 55(b)(2), exceeds a $40,000 exemption amount.[3] "Alternative minimum taxable income" ("AMTI") is the corporation's taxable income, increased by various tax preference items and adjusted to eliminate certain timing benefits (e.g., accelerated cost recovery) that are available under the regular tax.[4] Certain "small" corporations are exempt from the corporate AMT. To qualify for this exemption for a taxable year, a corporation's average annual gross receipts must be $7.5 million or less for all preceding three-taxable-year periods (taking into account only taxable years beginning after 1993).[5] In its first year of existence, a corporation is exempt from the AMT regardless of its gross receipts.[6]

Section 56 lists the principal adjustments made in arriving at a corporation's alternative minimum taxable income.[7] Many are narrow and beyond the scope of this text, but a few adjustments will be familiar to

---

32. I.R.C. § 27.

33. I.R.C. §§ 46–48.

34. I.R.C. § 51.

35. I.R.C. § 41.

1. S. Rep. No. 99–313, 99th Cong., 2d Sess. 518 (1986). See generally Lathrope, The Alternative Minimum Tax—Compliance and Planning with Analysis (1994).

2. I.R.C. § 55(a).

3. I.R.C. § 55(b), (d)(2). The $40,000 exemption amount is phased out at the rate of 25 cents for each dollar that a corporation's alternative minimum taxable income exceeds $150,000. I.R.C. § 55(d)(3)(A). The

exemption is thus fully phased out when a corporation's alternative minimum taxable income reaches $310,000.

4. I.R.C. § 55(b)(2).

5. I.R.C. § 55(e)(1)(A). The $7.5 million limit is reduced to $5 million for the first three-taxable-year period taken into account. I.R.C. § 55(e)(1)(B).

6. I.R.C. § 55(e)(1)(C).

7. Certain specialized adjustments in Section 58 also must be made. I.R.C. § 55(b)(2)(A).

students who have completed the basic income tax course. For example, depreciation on tangible personal property eligible for the 200 percent declining balance method under the regular tax is limited to the 150 percent declining balance method for AMT purposes.[8] A special net operating loss, known as the "alternative minimum tax net operating loss," also must be used in computing alternative minimum taxable income.[9]

In extending the AMT concept to corporations, Congress was responding to several highly publicized cases of corporations that reported significant operating profits in their financial statements to shareholders but paid minimal amounts of corporate income tax.[10] In an effort to improve perceptions, Section 56(g) requires an upward AMTI adjustment equal to 75 percent of the amount by which "adjusted current earnings" ("ACE") exceed AMTI determined without regard to this adjustment or AMT net operating losses ("pre–ACE AMTI").[11] The purpose of the ACE adjustment is to reach an even more accurate measure of a corporation's economic performance. ACE is determined by starting with pre–ACE AMTI and making several additional adjustments.[12]

Understanding the final round of ACE adjustments requires a brief introduction to the concept of "earnings and profits." The principal function of earnings and profits is to determine whether distributions paid by C corporations to their shareholders are dividends or a return of capital.[13] The computation of earnings and profits begins with taxable income and requires a number of adjustments which are designed to provide a truer measure of the corporation's economic performance. Consequently, certain amounts that were excluded from gross income for purposes of computing pre–ACE AMTI but that are taken into account in determining a corporation's "earnings and profits" must be included in determining ACE. An example is tax-exempt municipal bond interest, which increases a corporation's wealth but (except for interest on certain private activity bonds) is not included in the AMT base. Similarly, items that are disallowed as deductions in computing earnings and profits are added back for ACE purposes. An example is the 70 percent dividends received deduction for corporate shareholders.[14]

8. I.R.C. § 56(a)(1)(A)(ii). For property placed in service after 1986 but before 1999, AMT depreciation also must be computed using the longer class lives prescribed by the alternative depreciation system of Section 168(g). I.R.C. § 56(a)(1)(A)(i).

9. In general, the AMT net operating loss must be computed in a manner consistent with the adjustments and preferences in the alternative minimum tax scheme. The special net operating loss may not offset more than 90 percent of a corporation's alternative minimum taxable income, determined without the net operating loss deduction. I.R.C. § 56(a)(4), (d). Net operating losses carried back from taxable years ending in 2001 or 2002 and carryforwards of net operating loss-

es to those years are not subject to the 90 percent limitation. I.R.C. § 56(d)(1)(A)(ii).

10. See, e.g., Citizens for Tax Justice, "Corporate Taxpayers and Corporate Free-loaders," 29 Tax Notes 947 (Dec. 2, 1985).

11. A negative adjustment also is allowed—i.e., pre–ACE AMTI may be reduced by 75 percent of the excess of pre–ACE AMTI over ACE. I.R.C. § 56(g)(2).

12. I.R.C. § 56(g)(3).

13. See I.R.C. §§ 301; 316; and Chapter 4, infra.

14. See I.R.C. § 243(a). An exception is provided for deductions that qualify for a 100 or 80 percent dividends received deduction,

Once ACE is determined, the final step is to increase pre–ACE AMTI by 75 percent of the excess of ACE over pre–ACE AMTI.[15] After this orgy of adjustments, one wonders why Congress did not simply adopt ACE (or earnings and profits, for that matter) as the base for the corporate AMT. The answer presumably is political compromise, a force that has complicated the tax system in general and the alternative minimum tax in particular.

The determination of AMTI requires one more step. Once the required Section 56 adjustments are made, a corporation must increase taxable income by the amount of certain tax preference items, most of which are very specialized. Some of the more familiar preferences included in Section 57(a) are: (1) the excess of percentage depletion over cost depletion; (2) excess intangible drilling costs; and (3) tax-exempt interest on certain private activity bonds issued after August 7, 1986.

A limited number of credits may be applied against a corporation's alternative minimum tax liability.[16] In addition, a minimum tax credit is allowed against a corporation's *regular* tax liability. The minimum credit was enacted in recognition of the fact that many of the alternative minimum tax adjustments and items of tax preference reflect deferral of tax liability rather than permanent tax avoidance. An adjustment thus is required so that taxpayers do not lose these benefits altogether.[17] In general, Section 53(a) allows a corporation's alternative minimum tax to be credited against regular tax liability (reduced by certain other credits) in later years.[18] The minimum tax credit may be carried over until it is fully used, but it cannot be used as a credit against the alternative minimum tax.[19]

Not surprisingly, the corporate AMT is unpopular in the business community, which has placed complete repeal of this tax high on its wish list of proposed legislation. Advocates of tax simplification also have recommended a phase-out and eventual repeal of both the individual and corporate AMT.[20] Although these proposals have broad support in Congress, the revenue loss from AMT repeal would be substantial, and the best guess is that the AMT will remain part of the corporate tax landscape unless and until it can be given a proper burial as part of a comprehensive overall of the federal tax system.

3.   MULTIPLE CORPORATIONS

Code: Skim §§ 1501; 1502; 1503; 1504(a), (b); 1551; 1561; 1563.

Because corporations are easier to create than individuals, multiple corporations might be used to save taxes. For example, if Sole Shareholder

provided that the dividends are paid from earnings that were taxable to the payor. I.R.C. § 56(g)(4)(C)(ii).

15. As noted earlier, if pre–ACE AMTI exceeds ACE, then pre–ACE AMTI is decreased by the difference. See note 11, supra.

16. See I.R.C. § 38(c)(regular investment tax credit); § 59(a) (alternative minimum tax foreign tax credit).

17. S. Rep. No. 99–313, supra note 1, at 521.

18. I.R.C. § 53(a), (b), (d)(1)(B).

19. I.R.C. § 53(c).

20. See, e.g., Staff of the Joint Committee on Taxation, Study of the Overall State of the Federal Tax System and Recommendations for Simplification, vol. II, pp. 2–23 (JCS–3–01, April 2001).

owns a corporation that generates $1,000,000 of net income annually, he might be tempted to divide the enterprise into 20 separate companies, each with an annual income of $50,000 and each therefore taxed at a maximum rate of only 15 percent. This income-splitting ploy is precluded by Section 1561, which denies certain multiple tax benefits to a "controlled group of corporations."[1] Generally speaking, corporations are a controlled group if they constitute either a "parent-subsidiary controlled group" or a "brother-sister controlled group" under ownership tests in Section 1563.

The Code also contains provisions which permit an "affiliated group of corporations" to elect to consolidate its results for purposes of tax reporting.[2] In broad outline, the effect of a consolidated return election is to treat the affiliated group as a single corporate entity for tax purposes. The consolidated return rules are covered in more detail in Chapter 13, and selected issues involving consolidated returns are raised in the context of various transactions discussed later in this book. The ownership test applied to determine whether corporations are affiliated, however, is used in several provisions of Subchapter C[3] and is worth a brief glance at this early juncture. Section 1504(a)(2) employs an 80 percent of voting power and value standard to test corporate ownership of another corporation. That standard is met if a corporation possesses at least 80 percent of the total voting power of the stock in another corporation and has at least 80 percent of the total value of the stock of such corporation. For purposes of this test, certain nonconvertible, nonvoting preferred stock is disregarded.[4]

4. THE S CORPORATION ALTERNATIVE

As previewed earlier, Subchapter C's strengthened double tax regime has created an incentive for closely held businesses to select a legal form that qualifies for pass-through tax treatment. For businesses that require the corporate form for nontax reasons,[1] Subchapter S of the Code provides a relatively simple but not always accessible means to achieve this goal. Enacted to reduce the tax influences on the choice of entity decision, Subchapter S permits the shareholders of a "small business corporation" to elect to be taxed under a conduit approach similar to the taxation of partnerships. Subchapter S's role as an alternative to the two-tier system applicable to C corporations merits a brief introduction to its provisions.[2]

---

1. Section 1551 limits controlled groups to one use of the lower rates in Section 11(b). The entire group's income must be combined for purposes of applying Section 11. See Chapter 13, infra.

2. I.R.C. §§ 1501–1504.

3. See, e.g., I.R.C. §§ 332(b)(1); 336(e)(1); 338(d)(3).

4. I.R.C. § 1504(a)(4).

1. For businesses that do not require the corporate form but desire limited liability for all their owners, the limited liability company is emerging as an entity of choice. See Section C2b of this chapter, infra.

2. For detailed coverage of S corporations, see Chapter 15, infra.

The principal obstacle to making an S election are the eligibility requirements found in the Code's definition of "small business corporation" in Section 1361. In general, a corporation may make an S election only if it has not more than 100 shareholders who must be individuals other than nonresident aliens, estates or certain trusts,[3] and an S corporation may not have more than one class of stock.[4]

The income of an S corporation generally is subject to a single, shareholder-level tax.[5] The income, losses, deductions and credits of an S corporation pass through to its shareholders, but the character of those items is determined at the corporate level.[6] Basis and distribution rules are designed to assure that the shareholders may receive previously taxed income without paying additional tax.[7]

Even though S corporations and their shareholders are taxed under a special regime, S corporations remain "corporations" for purposes of Subchapter C.[8] Thus, the two corporate subchapters often operate in tandem when an S corporation engages in transactions, such as distributions of appreciated property, stock redemptions and liquidations, that are subject to Subchapter C.[9]

PROBLEM

Boots, Inc. is a "C" corporation engaged in the shoe manufacturing business. It also holds a small portfolio of securities and is engaged in a passive equipment leasing activity. Boots is a calendar year, accrual method taxpayer with two equal shareholders, Emil and Betty, who are unrelated cash method taxpayers. Use the rates in § 11 to determine Boots, Inc.'s tax liability, and assume for convenience that Emil and Betty each are taxable at a combined federal and state flat tax rate of 40% on ordinary income and a combined flat rate of 20% on qualified dividends and long-term capital gains. During the current year, Boots has the following income and expense items and makes no distributions to its shareholders:

Income:	
Gross profit—sale of inventory	$2,500,000
Dividends received	100,000
Capital gains	200,000
Municipal bond interest (not private activity bond)	10,000
Expenses and Losses:	
Operating Expenses	600,000

3. I.R.C. § 1361(b)(1)(A), (B), (C). Members of a "family," broadly defined, may elect to be treated as one shareholder for purposes of this requirement. I.R.C. § 1361(c)(1).

4. I.R.C. § 1361(b)(1)(D).

5. But see I.R.C. §§ 1374 and 1375, which impose a corporate-level tax on certain S corporations that previously were C corporations.

6. I.R.C. § 1366(a), (b).

7. I.R.C. §§ 1367(a); 1368(a), (b).

8. I.R.C. § 1371(a)(1).

9. See Chapter 15G, infra.

ACRS depreciation (5–year property; $4,000,000 cost;
  all placed in service in current year; no § 168(k)
  depreciation elected)   800,000
Net loss from passive leasing activity   130,000
Capital losses   220,000

(a) Determine Boots, Inc.'s taxable income and its regular tax liability for the current year.

(b) What result in (a), above, if Boots distributes $330,000 each to Emil and Betty as qualified dividends?

(c) What result in (a), above, if instead of paying dividends Boots pays Emil and Betty salaries of $500,000 each? What other strategies could Emil and Betty employ to reduce the impact of the corporate "double tax"? In general, what are the risks of these strategies. See, e.g., §§ 79; 105(a), (b); 106; 119; 162(a)(2); 163; 267; 1363(a); 1366(a)(1), (c).

5. CORPORATE TAX SHELTERS

The corporate income tax base has been eroding as a result of the proliferation of transactions being marketed for the specific purpose of substantially reducing the tax liability of profitable corporations and their high-income executives.[1] Loosely defined as "corporate tax shelters," the characteristics of these transactions generally are: (1) realization of tax losses without corresponding economic loss through transactions having questionable economic substance apart from the desire to reduce United States income taxes; (2) realization of income by "tax-indifferent" facilitators, such as foreign affiliates, domestic corporations with soon-to-expire loss carryovers, and tax-exempt organizations; (3) reliance on the literal language or ambiguities in the Internal Revenue Code to support a result that may be technically defensible but is inconsistent with the spirit of the law and well-accepted tax principles; (4) marketing of transactions under a veil of secrecy by entrepreneurial accounting firms and investment banks in exchange for enormous fees; (5) inconsistent treatment for financial accounting and tax purposes of items resulting from the same transaction; and (6) the willingness of corporate managers and their advisors, emboldened by "reasoned" opinions of tax counsel[2] and the knowledge that IRS audits have been reduced, to play "audit roulette" by taking questionable tax return reporting positions with the hope (and expectation?) that they will never be scrutinized. A crisper and perhaps more informative defini-

---

1. See, e.g., Joint Committee on Taxation, Background and Present Law Relating to Tax Shelters (JCX–19–02), March 19, 2002; Symposium, "Business Purpose, Economic Substance, and Corporate Tax Shelters," 54 SMU L. Rev. 3 (2001); Symposium on Corporate Tax Shelters, Part I, 55 Tax L. Rev. No. 2 (Winter 2002); Part II, 55 Tax L. Rev. No. 3 (Spring 2002).

2. An opinion of counsel assuring a taxpayer that a transaction is "more likely than not" to achieve its intended purpose, ordinarily insulates the taxpayers from various civil penalties. See, e.g., I.R.C. § 6662(a), (d); Reg. § 1.6662–4.

tion has been proposed by Professor Michael Graetz, who has characterized a tax shelter as "a deal done by very smart people that, absent tax considerations, would be very stupid."[3]

An attack on corporate tax shelters has been proceeding for a number of years on multiple fronts. Developments are ongoing and include legislation, regulations, changes to the rules governing tax practice before the Internal Revenue Service, and a sprinkling of test cases involving high profile taxpayers. Key components of the campaign include: (1) disallowance of tax benefits derived in certain types of "listed" tax avoidance transactions;[4] (2) a heightened disclosure regime, requiring taxpayers to put the Service on notice if they have engaged in "reportable" transactions and requiring promoters and tax advisors to "register" corporate tax shelters before the transaction occurs;[5] (3) an enhanced substantial understatement penalty regime for items attributable to corporate tax shelters;[6] (4) stiff no-fault penalties for failure to comply with the tax shelter disclosure requirements;[7] and (5) heightened regulation of the conduct of professional advisors who provide opinion letters and participate in the marketing of corporate tax shelters.[8] To bolster this assault, some commentators have gone so far as to propose that public companies be required to compute their taxable income by reference to the income reported for financial accounting purposes, with only limited deviations permitted for valid tax policy reasons.[9]

As demonstrated by the *United Parcel Service* case, which follows in the text, the Service's success in the test cases has been mixed as it has unleashed its familiar arsenal of "common law" doctrines[10] in an attempt to disallow the intended tax benefits from tax-motivated transactions. Not surprisingly, the Tax Court has been somewhat more inclined to apply the venerable judicial doctrines than the generalist judges of the courts of appeals.[11]

3. See, e.g., Tom Herman, "Tax Report," Wall St. J. at A-1 (Feb. 10, 1999).

4. A "listed" transaction is one that the Service formally determines to have a potential for tax avoidance or evasion. The "list" continues to grow, mostly through published notices and other guidance. See, e.g., Notice 2001-17, 2001-9 I.R.B. 730, identifying a contingent liability shelter as a listed transaction.

5. See, e.g., I.R.C. §§ 6011 (taxpayer must disclose reportable transaction); 6111 (organizers and promoters must register potentially illegal shelters with the IRS); 6112 (promoters must maintain lists of clients who purchase potentially illegal tax shelters and, on request, must disclose these client lists to the IRS); and Reg. §§ 1.6011-4; 301.6711-1.

6. I.R.C. §§ 6662(d)(1)(B); 6662A.

7. I.R.C. §§ 6707; 6707A; 6708.

8. See, e.g., 31 U.S. § 330(b), (d) and various implementing changes to Circular 230, which regulates professionals who practice before the Treasury Department (including the IRS).

9. See, e.g., Yin, "Getting Serious About Corporate Tax Shelters: Taking a Lesson from History," 54 SMU L. Rev. 209 (2001).

10. See Section A3 of this chapter, supra.

11. See, e.g., Coltec Industries, Inc. v. United States, 62 Fed. Cl. 716 (Ct. Fed. Cl. 2004); Black & Decker v. United States, 340 F. Supp. 2d 621 (D. Md. 2004); Compaq v. Commissioner, 277 F.3d 778 (5th Cir.2001), rev'g, 113 T.C. 214 (1999); United Parcel Service of America, Inc. v. Commissioner, 254 F.3d 1014 (11th Cir.2001), rev'g 78 T.C.M. 262 (1999). The Service's greatest success to

United Parcel Service of America, Inc. v. Commissioner

United States Court of Appeals, Eleventh Circuit, 2001.
254 F.3d 1014.

■ Cox, CIRCUIT JUDGE:

The tax court held United Parcel Service of America, Inc. (UPS) liable for additional taxes and penalties for the tax year 1984. UPS appeals, and we reverse and remand.

I. Background

UPS, whose main business is shipping packages, had a practice in the early 1980s of reimbursing customers for lost or damaged parcels up to $100 in declared value.[1] Above that level, UPS would assume liability up to the parcel's declared value if the customer paid 25per additional $100 in declared value, the "excess-value charge." If a parcel were lost or damaged, UPS would process and pay the resulting claim. UPS turned a large profit on excess-value charges because it never came close to paying as much in claims as it collected in charges, in part because of efforts it made to safeguard and track excess-value shipments. This profit was taxed; UPS declared its revenue from excess-value charges as income on its 1983 return, and it deducted as expenses the claims paid on damaged or lost excess-value parcels.

UPS's insurance broker suggested that UPS could avoid paying taxes on the lucrative excess-value business if it restructured the program as insurance provided by an overseas affiliate. UPS implemented this plan in 1983 by first forming and capitalizing a Bermuda subsidiary, Overseas Partners, Ltd. (OPL), almost all of whose shares were distributed as a taxable dividend to UPS shareholders (most of whom were employees; UPS stock was not publicly traded). UPS then purchased an insurance policy, for the benefit of UPS customers, from National Union Fire Insurance Company. By this policy, National Union assumed the risk of damage to or loss of excess-value shipments. The premiums for the policy were the excess-value charges that UPS collected. UPS, not National Union, was responsible for administering claims brought under the policy. National Union in turn entered a reinsurance treaty with OPL. Under the treaty, OPL assumed risk commensurate with National Union's, in exchange for premiums that equal the excess-value payments National Union got from UPS, less commissions, fees, and excise taxes.

Under this plan, UPS thus continued to collect 25per $100 of excess value from its customers, process and pay claims, and take special measures to safeguard valuable packages. But UPS now remitted monthly the excess-value payments, less claims paid, to National Union as premiums on the policy. National Union then collected its commission, excise taxes, and

date, however, has been in a federal district court. See Long–Term Capital Holdings v. United States, 330 F.Supp. 3d 122 (D. Conn. 2004).

1. These facts synopsize the high points of the tax court's long opinion, which is published at 78 T.C.M. (CCH) 262, 1999 WL 592696.

fees from the charges before sending the rest on to OPL as payments under the reinsurance contract. UPS reported neither revenue from excess-value charges nor claim expenses on its 1984 return, although it did deduct the fees and commissions that National Union charged.

The IRS determined a deficiency in the amount of the excess-value charges collected in 1984, concluding that the excess-value payment remitted ultimately to OPL had to be treated as gross income to UPS. UPS petitioned for a redetermination. Following a hearing, the tax court agreed with the IRS.

It is not perfectly clear on what judicial doctrine the holding rests. The court started its analysis by expounding on the assignment-of-income doctrine, a source rule that ensures that income is attributed to the person who earned it regardless of efforts to deflect it elsewhere. See United States v. Basye, 410 U.S. 441, 450, 93 S.Ct. 1080, 1086, 35 L.Ed.2d 412 (1973). The court did not, however, discuss at all the touchstone of an ineffective assignment of income, which would be UPS's control over the excess-value charges once UPS had turned them over as premiums to National Union. See Comm'r v. Sunnen, 333 U.S. 591, 604, 68 S.Ct. 715, 722, 92 L.Ed. 898 (1948). The court's analysis proceeded rather under the substantive-sham or economic-substance doctrines, the assignment-of-income doctrine's kissing cousins. See United States v. Krall, 835 F.2d 711, 714 (8th Cir.1987) (treating the assignment-of-income doctrine as a subtheory of the sham-transaction doctrine). The conclusion was that UPS's redesign of its excess-value business warranted no respect. Three core reasons support this result, according to the court: the plan had no defensible business purpose, as the business realities were identical before and after; the premiums paid for the National Union policy were well above industry norms; and contemporary memoranda and documents show that UPS's sole motivation was tax avoidance. The revenue from the excess-value program was thus properly deemed to be income to UPS rather than to OPL or National Union. The court also imposed penalties.

UPS now appeals, attacking the tax court's economic-substance analysis and its imposition of penalties. The refrain of UPS's lead argument is that the excess-value plan had economic substance, and thus was not a sham, because it comprised genuine exchanges of reciprocal obligations among real, independent entities. The IRS answers with a before-and-after analysis, pointing out that whatever the reality and enforceability of the contracts that composed the excess-value plan, UPS's postplan practice equated to its preplan, in that it collected excess-value charges, administered claims, and generated substantial profits. The issue presented to this court, therefore, is whether the excess-value plan had the kind of economic substance that removes it from "shamhood," even if the business continued as it had before. The question of the effect of a transaction on tax liability, to the extent it does not concern the accuracy of the tax court's fact-finding, is subject to de novo review. * * * We agree with UPS that this was not a sham transaction, and we therefore do not reach UPS's challenges to the tax penalties.

II. Discussion

I.R.C. §§ 11, 61, and 63 together provide the Code's foundation by identifying income as the basis of taxation. Even apart from the narrower assignment-of-income doctrine—which we do not address here—these sections come with the gloss, analogous to that on other Code sections, that economic substance determines what is income to a taxpayer and what is not. See Caruth Corp. v. United States, 865 F.2d 644, 650 (5th Cir.1989) (addressing, but rejecting on the case's facts, the argument that the donation of an income source to charity was a sham, and that the income should be reattributed to the donor); United States v. Buttorff, 761 F.2d 1056, 1061 (5th Cir.1985) (conveying income to a trust controlled by the income's earner has no tax consequence because the assignment is insubstantial); Zmuda v. Comm'r, 731 F.2d 1417, 1421 (9th Cir.1984) (similar). This economic-substance doctrine, also called the sham-transaction doctrine, provides that a transaction ceases to merit tax respect when it has no "economic effects other than the creation of tax benefits." Kirchman, 862 F.2d at 1492.[2] Even if the transaction has economic effects, it must be disregarded if it has no business purpose and its motive is tax avoidance. See Karr, 924 F.2d at 1023 (noting that subjective intent is not irrelevant, despite *Kirchman*'s statement of the doctrine); Neely v. United States, 775 F.2d 1092, 1094 (9th Cir.1985); see also Frank Lyon Co. v. United States, 435 U.S. 561, 583–84, 98 S.Ct. 1291, 1303, 55 L.Ed.2d 550 (1978) (one reason requiring treatment of transaction as genuine was that it was "compelled or encouraged by business or regulatory realities"); Gregory v. Helvering, 293 U.S. 465, 469, 55 S.Ct. 266, 267, 79 L.Ed. 596 (1935) (reorganization disregarded in part because it had "no business or corporate purpose").

The kind of "economic effects" required to entitle a transaction to respect in taxation include the creation of genuine obligations enforceable by an unrelated party. *See Frank Lyon Co.,* 435 U.S. at 582–83, 98 S.Ct. at 1303 (refusing to deem a sale-leaseback a sham in part because the lessor had accepted a real, enforceable debt to an unrelated bank as part of the deal). The restructuring of UPS's excess-value business generated just such obligations. There was a real insurance policy between UPS and National Union that gave National Union the right to receive the excess-value charges that UPS collected. And even if the odds of losing money on the policy were slim, National Union had assumed liability for the losses of UPS's excess-value shippers, again a genuine obligation. A history of not losing money on a policy is no guarantee of such a future. Insurance companies indeed do not make a habit of issuing policies whose premiums do not exceed the claims anticipated, but that fact does not imply that insurance companies do not bear risk. Nor did the reinsurance treaty with

---

2. *Kirchman,* which is binding in this circuit, differs in this respect from the oft-used statement of the doctrine derived from Rice's Toyota World, Inc. v. Comm'r, 752 F.2d 89, 91–92 (4th Cir.1985). *Rice's Toyota World,* unlike *Kirchman,* requires a tax-avoidance purpose as well as a lack of substance; *Kirchman* explicitly refuses to examine subjective intent if the transaction lacks economic effects.

OPL, while certainly reducing the odds of loss, completely foreclose the risk of loss because reinsurance treaties, like all agreements, are susceptible to default.

The tax court dismissed these obligations because National Union, given the reinsurance treaty, was no more than a "front" in what was a transfer of revenue from UPS to OPL. As we have said, that conclusion ignores the real risk that National Union assumed. But even if we overlook the reality of the risk and treat National Union as a conduit for transmission of the excess-value payments from UPS to OPL, there remains the fact that OPL is an independently taxable entity that is not under UPS's control. UPS really did lose the stream of income it had earlier reaped from excess-value charges. UPS genuinely could not apply that money to any use other than paying a premium to National Union; the money could not be used for other purposes, such as capital improvement, salaries, dividends, or investment. These circumstances distinguish UPS's case from the paradigmatic sham transfers of income, in which the taxpayer retains the benefits of the income it has ostensibly forgone. See, e.g., Zmuda v. Comm'r, 731 F.2d at 1417 (income "laundered" through a series of trusts into notes that were delivered to the taxpayer as "gifts"). Here that benefit ended up with OPL. There were, therefore, real economic effects from this transaction on all of its parties.

The conclusion that UPS's excess-value plan had real economic effects means, under this circuit's rule in *Kirchman,* that it is not per se a sham. But it could still be one if tax avoidance displaced any business purpose. The tax court saw no business purpose here because the excess-value business continued to operate after its reconfiguration much as before. This lack of change in how the business operated at the retail level, according to the court, betrayed the restructuring as pointless.

It may be true that there was little change over time in how the excess-value program appeared to customers. But the tax court's narrow notion of "business purpose"—which is admittedly implied by the phrase's plain language—stretches the economic-substance doctrine farther than it has been stretched. A "business purpose" does not mean a reason for a transaction that is free of tax considerations. Rather, a transaction has a "business purpose," when we are talking about a going concern like UPS, as long as it figures in a bona fide, profit-seeking business. See ACM P'ship v. Comm'r, 157 F.3d 231, 251 (3d Cir.1998). This concept of "business purpose" is a necessary corollary to the venerable axiom that tax-planning is permissible. See Gregory v. Helvering, 293 U.S. 465, 469, 55 S.Ct. 266, 267, 79 L.Ed. 596 (1935) ("The legal right of a taxpayer to decrease the amount of what otherwise would be his taxes, or altogether avoid them, by means which the law permits, cannot be doubted."). The Code treats lots of categories of economically similar behavior differently. For instance, two ways to infuse capital into a corporation, borrowing and sale of equity, have different tax consequences; interest is usually deductible and distributions to equityholders are not. There may be no tax-independent reason for a taxpayer to choose between these different ways of financing the business, but it does not mean that the taxpayer lacks a "business purpose." To conclude otherwise would prohibit tax-planning.

The caselaw, too, bears out this broader notion of "business purpose." Many of the cases where no business purpose appears are about individual income tax returns, when the individual meant to evade taxes on income probably destined for personal consumption; obviously, it is difficult in such a case to articulate any *business* purpose to the transaction. See, e.g., Gregory, 293 U.S. at 469, 55 S.Ct. at 267 (purported corporate reorganization was disguised dividend distribution to shareholder); Knetsch v. United States, 364 U.S. 361, 362–65, 81 S.Ct. 132, 133–35, 5 L.Ed.2d 128 (1960) (faux personal loans intended to generate interest deductions); Neely v. United States, 775 F.2d 1092, 1094 (9th Cir.1985) (one of many cases in which the taxpayers formed a trust, controlled by them, and diverted personal earnings to it). Other no-business-purpose cases concern tax-shelter transactions or investments by a business or investor that would not have occurred, *in any form,* but for tax-avoidance reasons. See, e.g., ACM P'ship, 157 F.3d at 233–43 (sophisticated investment partnership formed and manipulated solely to generate a capital loss to shelter some of Colgate–Palmolive's capital gains); Kirchman, 862 F.2d at 1488–89 (option straddles entered to produce deductions with little risk of real loss); Karr, 924 F.2d at 1021 (facade of energy enterprise developed solely to produce deductible losses for investors); Rice's Toyota World, Inc. v. Comm'r, 752 F.2d 89, 91 (4th Cir.1985) (sale-leaseback of a computer by a car dealership, solely to generate depreciation deductions). By contrast, the few cases that accept a transaction as genuine involve a bona fide business that—perhaps even by design—generates tax benefits. See, e.g., Frank Lyon, 435 U.S. at 582–84, 98 S.Ct. at 1302–04 (sale-leaseback was part of genuine financing transaction, heavily influenced by banking regulation, to permit debtor bank to outdo its competitor in impressive office space); Jacobson v. Comm'r, 915 F.2d 832, 837–39 (2d Cir.1990) (one of many cases finding that a bona fide profit motive provided a business purpose for a losing investment because the investment was not an obvious loser ex ante).

The transaction under challenge here simply altered the form of an existing, bona fide business, and this case therefore falls in with those that find an adequate business purpose to neutralize any tax-avoidance motive. True, UPS's restructuring was more sophisticated and complex than the usual tax-influenced form-of-business election or a choice of debt over equity financing. But its sophistication does not change the fact that there was a real business that served the genuine need for customers to enjoy loss coverage and for UPS to lower its liability exposure.

We therefore conclude that UPS's restructuring of its excess-value business had both real economic effects and a business purpose, and it therefore under our precedent had sufficient economic substance to merit respect in taxation. It follows that the tax court improperly imposed penalties and enhanced interest on UPS for engaging in a sham transaction. The tax court did not, however, reach the IRS's alternative arguments in support of its determination of deficiency, the reallocation provisions of

I.R.C. §§ 482 and 845(a). The holding here does not dispose of those arguments, and we therefore must remand for the tax court to address them in the first instance.

III. Conclusion

For the foregoing reasons, we reverse the judgment against UPS and remand the action to the tax court for it to address in the first instance the IRS's contentions under §§ 482 and 845(a).

REVERSED AND REMANDED.

■ RYSKAMP, DISTRICT JUDGE, dissenting:

I respectfully dissent. Although I agree with the majority's recitation of the facts as well as its interpretation of the applicable legal standard, I find that its reversal of the tax court is contrary to the great weight of the evidence that was before the lower court. The majority, as well as the tax court below, correctly finds that the question before the Court is whether UPS's insurance arrangements with NUF and OPL are valid under the sham-transaction doctrine. Under the sham-transaction doctrine, UPS's transaction ceases to merit tax respect when it has no "economic effects other than the creation of tax benefits," Kirchman v. Comm'r, 862 F.2d 1486, 1492 (11th Cir.1989), or has no business purpose and its sole motive is tax avoidance. See Karr v. Comm'r, 924 F.2d 1018, 1023 (11th Cir.1991). Thus the question before the Court is not strictly whether UPS had a tax avoidance motive when it formulated the scheme in question, but rather whether there was some legitimate, substantive business reason for the transaction as well. There clearly was not.

As the tax court articulated in great detail in its well-reasoned 114–page opinion, the evidence in this case overwhelmingly demonstrates that UPS's reinsurance arrangement with NUF and OPL had no economic significance or business purpose outside of UPS's desire to avoid federal income tax, and was therefore a sham transaction. First, the tax court based its decision upon evidence that the scheme in question was subjectively motivated by tax avoidance. For example, the evidence showed that tax avoidance was the initial and sole reason for the scheme in question, that UPS held off on the plan for some time to analyze tax legislation on the floor of the United States House of Representatives, and that a letter sent to AIG Insurance from UPS detailing the scheme claimed that AIG would serve in merely a "fronting" capacity and would bear little or no actual risk. The evidence thus showed that this scheme was hatched with only tax avoidance in mind.

Second, the tax court based its decision on overwhelming evidence that UPS's scheme had no real economic or business purpose outside of tax avoidance. For example, the evidence showed that NUF's exposure to loss under the plan (except in the very unlikely event of *extreme* catastrophe) was infinitesimal, and that UPS nevertheless continued to fully bear the administrative costs of the EVC program. NUF was only liable for losses not covered by another insurance policy held by UPS, yet UPS still collected the EVC's and deposited the money into UPS bank accounts, still processed EVC claims, and continued to pay all EVC claims out of UPS bank accounts (while collecting the accrued interest for itself). All NUF really did in the scheme was collect over $1 million in fees and expenses before passing the EVC income on to OPL, which was of course wholly owned by UPS shareholders. In essence, NUF received an enormous fee from UPS in exchange for nothing.

Moreover, the tax court systematically rejected every explanation of the scheme put forth by UPS. UPS claimed that the scheme was meant to avoid violation of state insurance laws, yet the evidence showed no real concern for such laws and that in fact UPS was well aware that federal preemption of these state laws likely made its old EVC plan legal. UPS claimed that it intended OPL to become a full-line insurer someday, yet the evidence showed that it was nevertheless unnecessary to specifically use *EVC income* for such a capital investment. UPS claimed that elimination of the EVC income allowed it to increase its rates, yet one of its own board members testified that this explanation was untrue. I also note that UPS's claim that OPL was a legitimate insurance company fails in light of the fact that OPL was charging a substantially inflated rate for EVCs. Evidence in the tax court showed that in an arms-length transaction with a legitimate insurance company, EVC rates would have been approximately half those charged by UPS (and in turn passed on to OPL), providing further evidence that the transaction was a sham. In sum, UPS failed to show any legitimate business reason for giving up nearly $100 million in EVC income in 1984.

For these reasons, I would affirm the holding of the tax court and find that UPS's arrangement with NUF and OPL was a sham transaction subject to federal tax liability.

NOTE

Legislation has been proposed to "codify" the economic substance doctrine. In 2004, the Senate approved a provision under which a transaction under scrutiny would pass muster for tax purposes only if the taxpayer established that (1) the transaction changes in a meaningful way (apart from federal income taxes) the taxpayer's economic position, and (2) there is a substantial non-tax purpose for the taxpayer to enter into the transaction and the transaction is a reasonable means of accomplishing such purpose.[3] This proposal would have made it clear that the economic substance doctrine requires both an objective inquiry regarding the economic effects of the transaction on the taxpayer and a subjective inquiry regarding the taxpayer's motives.

The codification approach was met with substantial opposition from lobbyists and practitioners, who viewed it as impractical and overbroad. To date, the proposal has come close (having been included by the Senate in several tax bills) but it has not yet survived a House–Senate conference.

3. H.Conf. Rep. No. 108–755, 108th Cong., 2d Sess. 445 (2004).

Corporate tax shelters continue to stimulate spirited discussion, and they have become a favorite topic of journalists[4] and tax academics. The new disclosure and penalty rules appear to be sending a clearer message to promoters and taxpayers alike that overly aggressive behavior may result in serious economic consequences beyond disallowance of the claimed tax benefits. As always in this area, interested observers should stay tuned for future developments.

6.   The Integration Alternative

The double tax on corporate profits has always been controversial. Economists and corporate finance theorists contend that it creates economic distortions and is inequitable, especially when compared to the pass-through treatment available to businesses that operate as partnerships, limited liability companies, or S corporations. Calls frequently have been made for "integration" of the individual and corporate income taxes into a single comprehensive system,[1] and the federal income tax began to move in that direction by reducing the burden of the double tax with the introduction in 2003 of a preferential 15 percent rate on qualified dividends received by noncorporate shareholders.[2]

Although many developed countries have adopted an integration model to tax business income,[3] the conventional wisdom is that a fully integrated system in the United States is not realistic in the near term. A separate tax on corporations is a politically popular way to raise revenue. Proponents of the classic double tax system have argued that the concentration of economic power represented by the earnings of at least public companies is an appropriate object of a tax system that purports to be built on principles of fairness and ability to pay. Many closely held businesses are able to avoid the double tax by operating as partnerships or S corporations. Even if they do not qualify for pass-through treatment, virtually all well-advised closely held C corporations have engaged in many "self-help" integration techniques (such as payments of deductible compensation or interest) to avoid the sting of the corporate tax. Moreover, a large of amount of the taxable income of publicly traded corporation is only taxed once because of the significant concentration of stock held by tax-exempt pension funds and charitable endowments.

4. See, e.g., Johnston, Perfectly Legal (2004), for an investigative reporter's perspective on the phenomenon.

1. See, e.g., McLure, "Integration of the Personal and Corporate Income Taxes: The Missing Element in Recent Tax Reform Proposals," 88 Harv.L.Rev. 532 (1975); Canellos, "Corporate Tax Integration: By Design or By Default?" in Corporate Tax Reform: A Report of the Invitational Conference on Subchapter C 129 (Am. Bar Ass'n Section on Taxation; N.Y. State Bar Ass'n Tax Section, 1988); Graetz & Warren, "Integration of Corporate and Individual Income Taxes: An Introduction," 84 Tax Notes 1767 (Sept. 27, 1999).

2. See Chapter 4A2, infra.

3. Among the countries with fully or partially integrated business taxation regimes are Canada, Germany, France, Australia, Italy, and the United Kingdom.

Despite these practical and political realities, proponents of integration continue to argue that the corporate income tax increases the cost of capital for U.S. corporations. It is said to be an indirect tax on shareholders rather than a cost of doing business that is passed on to consumers. So viewed, the tax violates notions of vertical equity (by uniformly taxing income earned indirectly by dissimilarly situated shareholders) and horizontal equity (because income earned through a C corporation is taxed more heavily than the same item of income earned through a proprietorship, S corporation or partnership).[4] Free-market economists contend that integration would encourage corporate earnings to be more freely distributed to shareholders, who then could decide whether to reinvest in the business instead of leaving that reinvestment decision to corporate managers.

With the ongoing theoretical interest in integration, it is worth pausing to consider how such a system might be implemented. The potential integration models fall into two broad categories. The first, referred to as "full" or "complete" integration, would eliminate the corporate income tax and apply a pass-through taxing system to C corporations and their shareholders. A leading alternative is "partial" integration, which typically contemplates different types of tax relief for dividends paid by a corporation. Variations include giving shareholders a tax credit equal to a percentage of dividends paid or allowing shareholders to exclude from gross income a portion of dividends received during the year. Alternatively, the corporation could be permitted to deduct some or all of the dividends it pays its shareholders. The excerpts below survey the major integration prototypes.

Excerpt From Canellos, "Tax Integration by Design or by Default?"

Reprinted in Corporate Tax Reform: A Report of the Invitational Conference on Subchapter C 132–35 (American Bar Association, Section of Taxation; New York State Bar Association, Tax Section, 1988.)*

Formal Means for Achieving Integration

If it is determined that there should be some formal integration of corporate and shareholder taxation, the next issue is to choose among the range of techniques for achieving such integration. These techniques differ in terms of whether (1) double taxation is mitigated with respect to both retained and distributed assets; and (2) the actual taxpayer on corporate earnings is the corporation or the shareholder.

The purest form of integration is referred to as full or complete integration, and in effect represents the system of tax applicable to partnerships and S corporations. Under full integration, corporate earnings are

---

4. See Canellos, supra note 1, at 130–131.

* Reprinted by permission of Peter C. Canellos; American Bar Association; and New York State Bar Association. Copyright © American Bar Association, 1988. All Rights Reserved.

attributed on some basis to shareholders who pay tax on them whether or not distributed. In turn, corporate losses flow through to shareholders for deduction by them subject to applicable restrictions on such flow through (such as basis rules, at risk rules, and the new passive loss limitations). The mechanics of existing full integration schemes differ. Thus, in the case of S corporations, the "entity" nature of the corporation predominates more than in the case of partnerships, which under Subchapter K are more often viewed as aggregates. As an example, the basis of corporate assets is generally not affected by sales of the S corporation's stock, whereas Section 754 allows for such an adjustment in the case of sales of partnership interests.

A scheme of complete integration was recommended in the 1977 Treasury Department study entitled "Blueprints for Basic Tax Reform." Under that system, the holder of corporate shares on the first day of the corporation's taxable year would be attributed all the earnings of the corporation for the taxable year. His basis would be increased by any allocated earnings, and would be decreased by distributions and losses. Where shares were sold during the taxable year, the seller would not be taxed on the current year's income, nor would he have any basis increase in respect of such income. Given the premise of "Blueprints" that capital gain and ordinary income would be taxed alike, the exclusion of current year's income was fully offset by the failure to increase basis for current year's income.

"Blueprints" dealt at length with the administrative difficulties of a fully integrated scheme. Thus, the problem of taxing shareholders on amounts not received was to be ameliorated through a system of corporate remittance of a "withholding" tax. This tax was to be considered paid on behalf of shareholders. The audit adjustment problem was to be solved by having the adjustment treated as an income or deduction item attributed to those persons holding shares on the first day of the year in which the adjustment was made. Despite these efforts to grapple with the problems of full integration, "Blueprints" never got off the drawing board. In this respect, it shares the fate of all other schemes for applying a full integration system to corporations in general. In this connection, full integration systems were considered and rejected by Canada and Germany for reasons of theory as well as practicality.

A second system of integration provides for a deemed paid credit for shareholders receiving distributions. The corporation is the initial taxpayer. In essence, tax paid by the corporation on distributed earnings would be attributed to shareholders. Distributions would be "grossed up" and the shareholder would apply the attributed tax as a credit against his tax on the "grossed up" dividend. In effect, this system taxes the shareholder in much the same way in which United States domestic corporations are taxed on distributions from foreign subsidiaries. The credit system has been adopted in many foreign countries and represents the generally prevailing corporate integration system.

The credit system raises a number of serious issues. First, there is the issue whether credit should be allowed only for corporate taxes actually paid. If so, integration has the effect of cutting back on corporate tax preferences such as investment tax credits, as well as possibly eliminating the benefit of foreign tax credits. Second, there is the issue whether tax should be paid by the corporation in connection with distributions (the advance corporation tax in the United Kingdom being an example). Such a tax payment assures that the Treasury will receive tax equal to the credit claimed by shareholders and represents in effect a corporate minimum tax applicable even if preferences would otherwise reduce the effective rate of corporate "mainstream" tax below the rate of attributed credit. A third significant issue is whether the credit should be made available to foreign shareholders in domestic corporations. Such credit has generally not been provided to foreign shareholders in the absence of tax treaties. Indeed, a major advantage of the credit system is the leverage which it provides to the taxing jurisdiction in negotiating favorable treaties with other countries.

A third system of integration reduces the corporate tax on distributed profits. This can be achieved by either a dividends-paid deduction or a split-rate system which taxes distributed earnings at a lower rate than retained earnings. The split-rate system had been used in Germany prior to Germany's adoption of the credit system. A dividends-paid deduction had been recommended in the 1984 Treasury Department Tax Reform Proposals, as well as the House version of the 1986 Act. This system of integration relieves corporate tax on distributed earnings at the corporate level rather than offsetting the second tax otherwise payable by shareholders. It raises some of the same issues discussed above in the case of the credit system. In addition, it raises other serious concerns. First, unless measures are taken to alter this result, a dividends-paid deduction or split-rate system has the effect of allowing corporate earnings to pass untaxed to shareholders who are not taxpayers (e.g., tax-exempt organizations and foreign shareholders). The Treasury Department's tax reform proposals would have sought to recapture some of the tax lost as the result of distributions to foreign shareholders by imposing a special withholding tax on dividends qualifying for the dividends-paid deduction. It acknowledged, however, that such a withholding tax would violate most existing tax treaties.

A final system for achieving integration with respect to distributed earnings is to exclude such distributions from the recipient's income.* This system would permit a shareholder to exclude from income dividends paid from a "previously taxed income" account. Issues raised by this system of integration include whether a selling shareholder should receive a basis increase for undistributed, previously-taxed income allocated to his account; and the allocation of distributions among the categories of previously-taxed income, pre-integration earnings, and earnings accumulated after

---

* An analysis of this approach is contained in Peel, A Proposal for Eliminating Double Taxation of Corporate Dividends, 39 Tax Lawyer 1 (1985).

integration which had not been previously taxed (for example, because of corporate tax preferences).

As this short summary demonstrates, difficult issues must be considered and dealt with in determining which, if any, path to express integration should be taken. Typically, the integration scheme which is adopted is tailored to meet the needs of the particular taxing jurisdiction—its historic tax system, the nature of its capital markets, the role of inward and outward international investment, and other factors. Where integration was adopted, it followed a long period of scholarly analysis and political input. Much of that work has already been undertaken in the United States. Despite these efforts, however, we are no closer to formal integration than we were in the sixties. Indeed, the 1986 Act has gone in the opposite direction by increasing the relative burden of corporate as compared with individual income taxes.

Integration of Individual and Corporate Tax Systems

Report of the Department of the Treasury.
January, 1992.

EXECUTIVE SUMMARY

WHAT IS INTEGRATION AND WHY SHOULD IT BE BENEFICIAL?

Currently, our tax system taxes corporate profits distributed to shareholders at least twice—once at the shareholder level and once at the corporate level. If the distribution is made through multiple unrelated corporations, profits may be taxed more than twice. If, on the other hand, the corporation succeeds in distributing profits in the form of interest on bonds to a tax-exempt or foreign lender, no U.S. tax at all is paid.

The two-tier system (i.e., imposing tax on distributed profits in the hands of shareholders after taxation at the corporate level) is often referred to as a classical tax system. Over the past two decades, most of our trading partners have modified their corporate tax systems to "integrate" the corporate and shareholder taxes to mitigate the impact of imposing two levels of tax on distributed corporate profits. Most typically, this has been accomplished by providing the shareholder with a full or partial credit for taxes paid at the corporate level.

Integration would reduce three distortions inherent in the classical system:

(a) *The incentive to invest in noncorporate rather than corporate businesses.* Current law's double tax on corporations creates a higher effective tax rate on corporate equity than on non-corporate equity. The additional tax burden encourages "self-help" integration through disincorporation.

(b) *The incentive to finance corporate investments with debt rather than new equity.* Particularly in the 1980's, corporations issued substantial amounts of debt. By 1990, net interest expense reached a postwar high of 19 percent of corporate cash flow.

(c) *The incentive to retain earnings or to structure distributions of corporate profits in a manner to avoid the double tax.* Between 1970 and 1990, corporations' repurchases of their own shares grew from $1.2 billion (or 5.4 percent of dividends) to $47.9 billion (or 34 percent of dividends). By 1990, over one-quarter of corporate interest payments were attributable to the substitution of debt for equity through share repurchases.

These distortions raise the cost of capital for corporate investments; integration could be expected to reduce it. To the extent that an integrated system reduces incentives for highly-leveraged corporate capital structures, it would provide important non-tax benefits by encouraging the adoption of capital structures less vulnerable to instability in times of economic downturn. The Report contains estimates of substantial potential economic gains from integration. Depending on its form, the Report estimates that integration could increase the capital stock in the corporate sector by $125 billion to $500 billion, could decrease the debt-asset ratio in the corporate sector by 1 to 7 percentage points and could produce an annual gain to the U.S. economy as a whole from $2.5 billion to $25 billion.

PROTOTYPES

This Report defines four integration prototypes and provides specifications for how each would work. [The prototypes described are: (1) a dividend exclusion; (2) a shareholder allocation under which all corporate income is allocated to shareholders and taxed in a manner similar to partnership income under current law; (3) a comprehensive business income tax (CBIT); and (4) an imputation credit.] For administrative reasons that the Report details, we have not recommended the shareholder allocation prototype * * *. Simplification concerns led us to prefer the dividend exclusion to any form of the imputation credit prototype.

In the dividend exclusion prototype, shareholders exclude dividends from income because they have already been taxed at the corporate level. Dividend exclusion provides significant integration benefits and requires little structural change in the Internal Revenue Code. When fully phased in, dividend exclusion would cost approximately $13.1 billion per year.

CBIT is, as its name implies, a much more comprehensive and larger scale prototype and will require significant statutory revision. CBIT represents a long-term, comprehensive option for equalizing the tax treatment of debt and equity. It is not expected that implementation of CBIT would begin in the short term, and full implementation would likely be phased in over a period of about 10 years. In CBIT, shareholders and bondholders exclude dividends and interest received from corporations from income, but neither type of payment is deductible by the corporation. Because debt and equity receive identical treatment in CBIT, CBIT better achieves tax neutrality goals than does the dividend exclusion prototype. CBIT is self-financing and would permit lowering the corporate rate to the maximum individual rate of 31 percent on a revenue neutral basis, even if capital gains on corporate stock were fully exempt from tax to shareholders.

POLICY RECOMMENDATIONS

In addition to describing prototypes, the Report makes several basic policy recommendations which we believe should apply to any integration proposal ultimately adopted:

(a) *Integration should not result in the extension of corporate tax preferences to shareholders.* This structure is grounded in both policy and revenue concerns and has been adopted by every country with an integrated system. The mechanism for preventing pass-through of preferences varies; some countries utilize a compensatory tax mechanism and others simply tax preference-sheltered income when distributed (as we recommend in the dividend exclusion prototype). Both of these mechanisms are discussed in the Report.

(b) *Integration should not reduce the total tax collected on corporate income allocable to tax-exempt investors.* Absent this restriction, business profits paid to tax-exempt entities could escape all taxation in an integrated system. This revenue loss would prove difficult to finance and would exacerbate distortions between taxable and tax-exempt investors.

(c) *Integration should be extended to foreign shareholders only through treaty negotiations, not by statute.* This is required to assure that U.S. shareholders receive reciprocal concessions from foreign tax jurisdictions.

(d) *Foreign taxes paid by U.S. corporations should not be treated, by statute, identically to taxes paid to the U.S. Government.* Absent this limitation, integration could eliminate all U.S. taxes on foreign source profits in many cases.

* * *

OBJECTIVES OF THE REPORT

This Report is not a legislative proposal but rather a source document to begin the debate on the desirability of integration. This Report concludes that integration is desirable and presents a variety of integration mechanisms. A major reform such as integration should be undertaken only after appropriate deliberation and consideration of public comments. In light of the increasing isolation of the United States as one of the few remaining countries with a classical tax system, serious consideration of integration is now appropriate.

* * *

NOTE

In December, 1992, the Treasury Department followed up on its report by publishing a specific proposal for integration based on a dividend exclusion.[1] In March, 1993, the American Law Institute released its "Reporter's Study" of corporate tax integration.[2] Much like the Treasury report, the ALI study criticizes the classical double-tax regime. The ALI's recommended cure is a shareholder imputation credit system generally along the lines discussed in the earlier Canellos excerpt. As summarized in the Reporter's Study:[3]

> The proposed approach would convert the separate corporate income tax into a withholding tax with respect to dividends. Because some dividends will not have borne a corporate tax prior to distribution, an auxiliary dividend withholding tax is necessary to assure that shareholders do not receive tax credits for taxes that have never been paid at the corporate level. No double tax would result, because payments of regular corporate tax would be considered prepayments of the auxiliary tax. On the other hand, certain dividends may be free of corporate tax as a result of deliberately enacted corporate tax preferences that should be passed through to shareholders. Finally, in order to minimize differential treatment of debt and equity, a withholding tax on corporate interest payments would be desirable. Four proposals implement this basic system of integration:

> 1.   A withholding tax will be levied on dividend distributions; payments of corporate tax will be fully creditable against the withholding tax.

> 2.   Shareholders will receive a refundable tax credit for the dividend withholding tax.

> 3.   Certain corporate tax preferences can be passed through to shareholders.

> 4.   A withholding tax will be levied on payments of corporate interest; that tax will be fully creditable by and refundable to the recipients of such interest payments.

After this flurry of activity in the early and mid–1990's, the integration debate went back into hibernation. Historically, the business community has not embraced the concept of integration, preferring instead to work within the existing system with its many opportunities to reduce or eliminate the corporate income tax. Corporate lobbyists continue to focus their attention on expanding corporate tax preferences (such as accelerated depreciation, research and development incentives, and targeted tax credits) and repealing the corporate alternative minimum tax. Some commentators have suggested that corporate managers view integration as a threat to their power base because it would force them to act more as stewards of

---

1. See U.S. Treasury Dept., A Recommendation for Integration of the Individual and Corporate Income Tax Systems (1992).

2. See Warren, "Integration of the Individual and Corporate Income Taxes," Reporter's Study of Corporate Tax Integration (American Law Institute, 1993)(hereinafter "Reporter's Study").

3. Reporter's Study, supra note 2, at 4–5.

shareholders interests.[4] it seemed more and more likely that integration would remain a topic for occasional academic discourse rather than a viable political reality.

And then, surprising the skeptics, President George W. Bush revived the integration debate in early 2003 with a bold proposal that became the controversial centerpiece of his economic stimulus package. The original proposal was reminiscent of the Treasury Department's dividend exclusion prototype. It provided for a 100 percent exclusion for all dividends paid out of income previously taxed at the corporate level. The excerpt below is from a Treasury Department press release explaining the proposal and providing an overview of some of the details. Keep in mind that the description of "current law" is as it was prior to individual taxpayer rate reductions enacted in 2003.

Description of President's Dividend Exclusion Proposal

U.S. Dept. of the Treasury, Jan. 21, 2003.

Eliminate the Double Taxation of Corporate Earnings

Current Law

Income earned by a corporation is taxed at the corporate level, generally at the rate of 35 percent. If the corporation distributes earnings to shareholders in the form of dividends, the income generally is taxed a second time at the shareholder level (at rates as high as 38.6 percent). If a corporation instead retains its earnings, the value of corporate stock will reflect the retained earnings. When shareholders sell their stock, that additional value will be taxed as capital gains (generally at a maximum rate of 20 percent for long-term capital gains). The combined rate of tax on corporate income can be as high as 60 percent, far in excess of rates of tax imposed on other types of income.

Reasons for Change

The double taxation of corporate profits creates significant economic distortions.

- First, double taxation creates a bias in favor of debt as compared to equity, because payments of interest by the corporation are deductible while returns on equity in the form of dividends and retained earnings are not. Excessive debt increases the risks of bankruptcy during economic downturns.

- Second, double taxation of corporate profits creates a bias in favor of unincorporated entities (such as partnerships and limited liability companies), which are not subject to the double tax.

- Third, because dividends are taxed at a higher rate than are capital gains, double taxation of corporate profits encourages a corporation

4. See, e.g., Arlen & Weiss, "A Political Theory of Corporate Taxation," 105 Yale L. J. 325 (1995).

to retain its earnings rather than distribute them in the form of dividends. This lessens the pressure on corporate managers to undertake only the most productive investments because corporate investments funded by retained earnings may receive less scrutiny than investments funded by outside equity or debt financing.

- Fourth, double taxation encourages corporations to engage in transactions such as share repurchases rather than to pay dividends because share repurchase permit the corporation to distribute earnings at reduced capital gains tax rates.

- Fifth, double taxation increases incentives for corporations to engage in transactions for the sole purpose of minimizing their tax liability.

By eliminating double taxation, the proposal will reduce tax-induced distortions that, in the current tax system, encourage firms to use debt rather than equity finance and to adopt noncorporate rather than corporate structures. Because shareholders will be exempt from tax only on distributions of previously taxed corporate income, the proposal will reduce incentives for certain types of corporate tax planning. In addition, the proposal will enhance corporate governance by eliminating the current bias against the payment of dividends. Dividends can provide evidence of a corporation's underlying financial health and enable investors to evaluate more readily a corporation's financial condition. This, in turn, increases the accountability of corporate management to its investors.

Proposal

Overview

The proposal would integrate the corporate and individual income taxes so that corporate earnings generally will be taxed once and only once. Under the proposal, public and private corporations would be permitted to distribute nontaxable dividends to their shareholders to the extent that those dividends are paid out of income previously taxed at the corporate level. The proposal generally would be effective for distributions made on or after January 1, 2003, with respect to corporate earnings after 2000.

To calculate the amount that can be distributed to its shareholders without further tax, a corporation will compute an excludable dividend amount (EDA) for each year. The EDA reflects income of the corporation that has been fully taxed. Thus, for example, a corporation with $100 of income that pays $35 of U.S. income taxes will have an EDA of $65 that can be distributed as excludable dividends.

If an amount would be a dividend under current law, it will be treated as an excludable dividend to the extent of EDA. Excludable dividends will not be taxed to shareholders. If a corporation's distributions during a calendar year exceed its EDA, only a proportionate amount of each distribution will be treated as an excludable dividend. Ordering rules are provided below for distributions that exceed EDA.

The capital gains tax on the sale of stock will be retained. Without further change, this would create an incentive for corporations to distribute previously taxed income as excludable dividends rather than retaining earnings for future investment. This is because excludable dividends would not be taxed to the shareholders but capital gains that represent retained earnings would be taxed to the shareholders when they sell their shares.

To ensure that distributions and retentions of previously taxed earnings are treated similarly, shareholders will be permitted to increase their basis in their shares to reflect that the retained earnings have already been taxed at the corporate level. As an alternative to distributing excludable dividends, corporations generally may allocate throughout the year all or a portion of the EDA to provide these basis increases. The basis increases will not be taxable. The effect of the basis increases will be to reduce the capital gains realized when shareholders sell their stock to the extent that the sales price reflects the corporation's retained, previously taxed earnings.

NOTE

The Bush Administration's proposal received a mixed response from Congress and the business community. Opponents argued that it was too complex, favored the wealthy without providing any immediate economic stimulus, and contributed to the federal budget deficit. Tax-privileged sectors, such as issuers of municipal bonds, banks, insurance companies, and real estate investment trusts, were concerned that their existing tax preferences would be undermined. Tax-exempt shareholders, such as pension funds and charitable foundations, as well as companies that were losing money or able to shelter their income from the corporate income tax, had little to gain from the proposal.

Supporters argued that eliminating the double tax on corporate earnings was a long overdue correction to a flawed system that encouraged excessive corporate debt, discouraged the payment of dividends and, in so doing, contributed to a misallocation of capital by favoring retained earnings over cash payouts. Some proponents predicted that a full dividend exclusion would make corporate managers more accountable to shareholders and increase shareholder confidence in the credibility of corporate earnings reports.

It became clear as the debate raged that the Bush dividend exclusion proposal would not be enacted because of its complexity and revenue effect. The ultimate compromise—a 15 percent maximum rate on both qualified dividends and most long-term capital gains—took a small step toward integrating the corporate and individual income taxes. Notably, dividends qualify for the reduced rate whether or not they are paid out of income previously taxed at the corporate level. Some of the details are discussed in Chapter 4.

C. CORPORATE CLASSIFICATION

1. IN GENERAL

Code: § 7701(a)(3).

The classification of a business relationship may have profound tax consequences. Entities classified as C corporations are subject to the double tax regime of Subchapter C, while the tax treatment of partnerships is governed by the single tax pass-through regime of Subchapter K. The classification area has a rich and textured history, as the stakes have changed in response to shifting tax incentives to utilize one form of business entity over another. After decades of strife, much confusion, and reams of boilerplate classification opinion letters issued by high-priced counsel, there is good news. Beginning in 1997, the Internal Revenue Service simplified this topic considerably (and shortened your reading assignment) by adopting a classification system that as a practical matter permits a closely held unincorporated business to elect its taxing regime.

For tax purposes, Section 7701 defines a corporation to include "associations, joint-stock companies, and insurance companies." Thus, if an entity is an unincorporated "association," it will be classified as a corporation. The longstanding, pre–1997 classification regulations did not define the term "association." Instead, they listed six characteristics ordinarily found in a "pure" corporation: (1) associates (i.e., two or more persons joining together in shared control and ownership of the venture); (2) an objective to carry on business and divide the gains therefrom; (3) continuity of life (a corporation continues in existence despite the death or withdrawal of one or more shareholders); (4) centralization of management (i.e., management responsibility is vested in directors and is not exercised directly by the shareholders); (5) limited liability (shareholders are not personally liable for corporate debts); and (6) free transferability of interests (i.e., shareholders may dispose of their shares).[1] The regulations then explained that "an organization will be treated as an association if the corporate characteristics are such that the organization more nearly resembles a corporation than a partnership or trust."[2] Under those regulations, characteristics common to corporations and partnerships (associates and a business objective) were disregarded in classifying an entity as an association or a partnership. The remaining characteristics (continuity of life, centralized management, limited liability, and free transferability of interests) were then weighted equally and an organization was classified as an association only if it had three of the remaining corporate characteristics.[3]

The pre–1997 regulations were issued at a time when professional service providers (e.g., doctors and lawyers), forbidden from incorporating under state law, attempted to form entities that qualified as "associations" taxable as corporations. Their tax planning agenda was to qualify for tax advantages, such as qualified retirement plans and tax-free fringe benefits, that were then available to corporations and their employees but not to partnerships and partners.[4] The Treasury's mission was to make it more

---

1. Reg. § 301.7701–2(a)(1) (pre–1997).

2. Id.

3. Reg. § 1.7701–2(a) (pre–1997).

4. United States v. Kintner, 216 F.2d 418 (9th Cir.1954). Cf. Morrissey v. Commissioner, 296 U.S. 344, 56 S.Ct. 289 (1935). Virtually all of the advantages of corporate

difficult for unincorporated entities to qualify as corporations for federal tax purposes, but its efforts were undercut by the subsequent willingness of state legislators to permit the formation of professional corporations.[5]

One result of this early fray was that the old regulations reflected an anti-association, pro-partnership bias. This redounded to the benefit of high-income taxpayers seeking to shelter their compensation, dividends, or interest income with losses from strategically structured investment activities in real estate and other tax-favored industries. Limited partnerships became the vehicle of choice for these "tax shelters" because they permitted losses to pass through to investors, allowed the partners to maximize those losses by including their share of partnership debt in the basis of their partnership interests, and provided protection for the limited partners against personal liability for debts of the enterprise. These goals could not be achieved in a C or S corporation. The Service's effort to convince the courts that limited partnerships should be classified as "associations" was unsuccessful.[6] Even after tax shelters were derailed by the Tax Reform Act of 1986, the Service continued to issue stringent guidelines for limited partnerships seeking a favorable classification ruling.[7] Most tax advisors bypassed the ruling process, and the well informed easily were able to structure a limited partnership that would avoid "association" classification.

In the 1980's, limited liability companies (LLCs) emerged on the scene and quickly became touted as the "best of all worlds" alternative for conducting a closely held business. An LLC is an unincorporated entity in which the owners, called "members," have limited liability for the enterprise's debts and claims even if they participate in management. Members of an LLC have great flexibility in structuring the governance of their venture through the LLC's "operating agreement." LLCs are now authorized in every state, but some states still prohibit a single-member LLC.[8] The Internal Revenue Service gave a major boost to the LLC movement in 1988 by classifying a Wyoming LLC as a partnership for federal tax purposes.[9] That ruling was followed by others making it clear that an LLC could be structured as either an association or a partnership depending on the flexibility provided by state law and the desires of the members.[10]

---

classification in the retirement plan context have been eliminated.

5. See, e.g., West's Ann. Cal. Corp. Code §§ 13400–13410; Maryland Code, Corporations and Associations, Title 5, Subtitle 1 (1999); West's Florida Statutes Annotated, ch. 621.

6. See Larson v. Commissioner, 66 T.C. 159 (1976).

7. See, e.g., Rev. Proc. 89–12, 1989–1 C.B. 798; Rev. Proc. 91–13, 1991–1 C.B. 477.

8. See generally Gazur, "The Limited Liability Experiment: Unlimited Flexibility, Uncertain Role," 58 L. & Contemp. Prob. 135 (1995); "F. Hodge O'Neal Corporate and Securities Law Symposium: Limited Liability Companies," 73 Wash U.L.Q. 369 (1995).

9. Rev. Rul. 88–76, 1988–2 C.B. 360.

10. See Rev. Rul. 93–38, 1993–1 C.B. 233, where LLCs formed under the Delaware statute were classified as an association or a partnership depending on the terms of the LLC agreement.

2.   CORPORATIONS VS. PARTNERSHIPS

a.   "CHECK–THE–BOX" REGULATIONS

Code: § 7701(a)(3).

Regulations: §§ 301.7701–1(a)(1) & (2);–2(a), (b)(1)–(3), (c)(1) & (2);–3(a), (b)(1).

The pre–1997 classification regulations were based on the traditional state-law differences between a pure corporation and other types of organizations, such as partnerships.[1] State law developments, however, largely blurred the classic distinctions between corporations and the unincorporated forms for doing business. For example, the increasingly popular LLC offers all its investors (including those involved in management) limited liability for obligations of the venture—a characteristic traditionally available only in a corporation—along with classification as a partnership for federal tax purposes.

The Service eventually concluded that the state law differences between corporations and partnerships had narrowed to such a degree that the venerable corporate resemblance test for classifying unincorporated entities should be abandoned in favor of a simpler classification regime that is generally elective.[2] To that end, the regulations have discarded the four-factor classification system, which was de facto elective for individuals with skilled tax advisors, and replaced it with a "check-the-box" system in which most new unincorporated entities automatically will be classified as partnerships for federal tax purposes unless the entity elects to be an association taxable as a C corporation.

General Classification Rules. The regulations only apply to entities that are treated for federal tax purposes as being separate from their owners.[3] If an organization recognized as a separate entity for federal tax purposes is not a trust, it is a "business entity" under the regulations.[4] Certain business entities are automatically classified as corporations.[5] Most importantly, a business entity organized under a federal or state statute that refers to the entity as "incorporated" or as a "corporation," "body corporate," or "body politic," is treated as a corporation for federal tax purposes,[6] as are other business entities taxable as corporations under other Code provisions, such as publicly traded partnerships which are treated as corporations under Section 7704.[7]

Under the regulations, a noncorporate business entity (an "eligible entity") with at least two members is classified as a partnership unless an election is made for the entity to be classified as an association. Thus,

---

1. Reg. § 301.7701–2(a)(1) (pre–1997).

2. Preamble to Final Regulations on Simplification of Entity Classification Rules, 61 Fed. Reg. 66584 (Dec. 18, 1986). The elective regime became effective as of January 1, 1997. Reg. § 301.7701–1(f).

3. See Reg. § 301.7701–1(a).

4. Reg. § 301.7701–2(a).

5. Reg. § 301.7701–2(b)(1) through (8).

6. Reg. § 301.7701–2(b)(1).

7. Reg. § 301.7701–2(b)(7). See Section C2b of this chapter, infra, for a discussion of publicly traded partnerships.

partnership status is the default classification for unincorporated entities with two or more members.[8]

Single-Owner Organizations. The regulations treat a noncorporate business entity that has a single owner as a "tax nothing." A single-owner entity is disregarded for tax purposes and treated as an extension of its owner unless the entity elects to be classified as an association and thus taxed as a C corporation.[9] Consequently, if no such election is made, the entity is treated for federal tax purposes as if it were a sole proprietorship (if owned by an individual), or a branch or division (if owned by another business entity, such as a C corporation)[10] This rule is particularly useful in the vast majority of states which permit single-member LLCs.

An entity that is solely owned by a husband and wife as community property may be treated by its owners as either a disregarded entity or a partnership unless the entity elects to be taxed as a C corporation.[11]

Foreign Organizations. The regulations list certain business entities formed in specific jurisdictions (e.g., a public limited company formed in Hong Kong) that will be automatically classified as a corporation.[12] In the absence of a contrary election, other foreign entities are classified as: (1) a partnership if the entity has two or more members and at least one member does not have limited liability, (2) an association if all members have limited liability, or (3) disregarded as an entity separate from its owner if the entity has a single owner that does not have limited liability.[13]

Existing Entities. Under the "check-the-box" system, an existing business entity generally retains the same classification that it claimed under the prior regulations unless it elects otherwise. An exception is provided for an entity with a single owner that claimed to be a partnership under the earlier regulations but which is disregarded as an entity separate from its owner under the current version.[14]

Election. A classification election under the regulations may be designated as effective up to 75 days before or twelve months after the election is filed.[15] The election generally must be signed either by (1) each member of the electing entity, including prior members affected by a retroactive election, or (2) by an officer, manager, or member authorized to make the election.[16] If an entity makes a classification election, a new classification election generally cannot be made for 60 months, unless the Service allows

---

8. Reg. §§ 301.7701–2(c)(1), 301.7701–3(a), 301.7701–3(b)(1)(i).

9. Reg. §§ 301.7701–2(c)(2), 301.7701–3(a), 301.7701–3(b)(1)(ii).

10. Reg. § 1.301.7701–2(a). See Miller, "The Strange Materialization of the Tax Nothing," 87 Tax Notes 685 (May 5, 2000).

11. Rev. Proc. 2002–69, §§ 3.02, 4.01–4.02, 2002–2 C.B. 831. If such an entity changes its classification for tax purposes, the change is treated as a conversion of the entity. Id. at § 4.03.

12. Reg. § 301.7701–2(b)(8).

13. Reg. § 301.7701–3(b)(2)(i). Limited liability generally exists if the member has no personal liability for the debts of or claims against the entity by reason of being a member. Reg. § 301.7701–3(b)(2)(ii).

14. Reg. § 301.7701–3(b)(3).

15. Reg. § 301.7701–3(c)(1)(iii).

16. Reg. § 301.7701–3(c)(2).

such an election and more than 50 percent of the ownership interests in the entity are owned by persons that did not own any interests when the first election was made.[17]

Change in Number of Members of an Entity. The regulations provide that the classification of an eligible entity as an association generally is not affected by any change in the numbers of members of the entity.[18] But if an eligible entity (such as a limited liability company) is classified as a partnership and its membership is reduced to one member, it becomes a disregarded entity.[19] A single-member disregarded entity also is classified as a partnership if it gains more than one member.[20]

Elective Changes in Classification. The regulations also prescribe the tax consequences when an entity makes a valid election to change its tax classification. If a partnership elects to be reclassified as an association, it is deemed to contribute all of its assets and liabilities to the association for stock and then to liquidate by distributing the stock to its partners.[21] If an association elects to be classified as a partnership, it is deemed to liquidate by distributing all of its assets and liabilities to its shareholders who then contribute the assets and liabilities to a newly formed partnership.[22] If an association with one owner elects to be classified as a disregarded entity, it is deemed to liquidate by distributing all of its assets and liabilities to the single owner.[23] Finally, if a disregarded entity elects to be classified as an association, the owner is deemed to contribute all of the assets and liabilities of the entity to the association for stock in the association.[24]

The tax treatment of a change in classification is determined under all relevant provisions of the Internal Revenue Code and general principles of tax law, including the step transaction doctrine.[25] An election to change the classification of an eligible entity is treated as occurring at the start of the day for which the election is effective.[26]

b. PUBLICLY TRADED PARTNERSHIPS

Code: § 7704.

For a brief time after enactment of the Tax Reform Act of 1986, the publicly traded partnership ("PTP") surfaced as a refuge from the costly double tax regime of Subchapter C. Unlike an S corporation, a PTP could have an unlimited number of shareholders. It could register its limited partnership interests, known as "units," with the Securities and Exchange

---

17. Reg. 301.7701–3(c)(1)(iv).

18. Reg. § 301.7701–3(f)(1).

19. Reg. § 301.7701–3(f)(2).

20. Id.

21. Reg. § 301.7701–3(g)(1)(i).

22. Reg. § 301.7701–3(g)(1)(ii).

23. Reg. § 301.7701–3(g)(1)(iii). If an association is deemed to liquidate under Section 332 (relating to complete liquidations of certain corporate subsidiaries), the election to change classification is considered to be the adoption of a plan of liquidation. Reg. § 301.7701–3(g)(2)(ii).

24. Reg. § 301.7701–3(g)(1)(iv).

25. Reg. § 301.7701–3(g)(2).

26. Reg. § 301.7701–3(g)(3)(i). Transactions deemed to occur as a result of the election are treated as occurring immediately before the close of the day before the election is effective. Id.

Commission, and the units were freely tradable on a securities exchange or in the over-the-counter market. A profitable PTP thus avoided the corporate income tax and passed through its income to noncorporate limited partners at the lower individual rates.

Alarmed at the proliferation of PTPs and the potential erosion of the corporate tax base, Congress responded by enacting Section 7704, which classifies certain PTPs as corporations for tax purposes. As defined, a "publicly traded partnership" is any partnership whose interests are: (1) traded on an established securities market, or (2) readily tradable on a secondary market (or its substantial equivalent).[27] An important exception from reclassification is provided for partnerships if 90 percent or more of their gross income consists of certain passive-type income items (e.g., interest, dividends, real property rents, gains from the sale of real property and income and gains from certain natural resources activities).[28]

The regulations generally provide that an interest is "readily tradable" if "taking into account all of the facts and circumstances, the partners are readily able to buy, sell, or exchange their partnership interests in a manner that is comparable, economically, to trading on an established securities market."[29]

3. CORPORATIONS VS. TRUSTS

Regulations: § 301.7701–4(a), (b).

Trusts, like corporations, may be taxpaying entities, but the income taxation of trusts differs from the taxation of corporations in several important respects. First, a corporation is taxed on its profits as they are earned under the relatively flat rates in Section 11. If it later distributes the remaining after-tax earnings as dividends, the shareholders are subject to a second tax. But there is no double tax on trust income. Under the complex rules of Subchapter J, trust income currently distributed to beneficiaries is generally not taxed to the trust. Rather, the income is taxed to the recipient beneficiaries to the extent of the trust's "distributable net income." If, however, trust income is accumulated, it is taxed to the trust when earned under the rates in Section 1(e) but normally not taxed again when distributed to the beneficiaries. Also, corporate shareholders who receive dividends are taxable at ordinary income rates, regardless of the character of the corporation's earnings. By contrast, trust income retains its tax character in the hands of the beneficiaries.

The regulations distinguish between "ordinary trusts" created to take title to property for the purpose of protecting and conserving it for the beneficiaries, and "business" or "commercial" trusts which are created to carry on a business for profit. An ordinary trust is classified as a "trust" and taxed under Subchapter J.[1] A business trust, on the other hand, is a

---

27. I.R.C. § 7704(b).

28. I.R.C. § 7704(c).

29. Reg. § 1.7704–1(c)(1).

1. Reg. § 301.7701–4(a).

business entity that is classified under the check-the-box regulations.[2] Because a business trust is an unincorporated entity, it will be classified as a partnership for federal tax purposes if it has two or more members and does not make an election to be classified as a corporation.[3]

D. RECOGNITION OF THE CORPORATE ENTITY

The premise underlying Subchapter C is that a corporation is an entity separate and apart from its shareholders. In addition to questions of classification, issues have arisen over the years as to whether an entity organized as a corporation under state law should be respected as such for tax purposes. These cases often involve corporations that are formed to avoid state usury laws or to act as nontaxable agents of a related partnership. The case below is the Supreme Court's most recent pronouncement on this issue.

Commissioner v. Bollinger

Supreme Court of the United States, 1988.
485 U.S. 340, 108 S.Ct. 1173.

■ JUSTICE SCALIA delivered the opinion of the Court.

Petitioner the Commissioner of Internal Revenue challenges a decision by the United States Court of Appeals for the Sixth Circuit holding that a corporation which held record title to real property as agent for the corporation's shareholders was not the owner of the property for purposes of federal income taxation. 807 F.2d 65 (1986). We granted certiorari, 482 U.S. 913, 107 S.Ct. 3183, 96 L.Ed.2d 672 (1987), to resolve a conflict in the courts of appeals over the tax treatment of corporations purporting to be agents for their shareholders. * * *

I.

Respondent Jesse C. Bollinger, Jr., developed, either individually or in partnership with some or all of the other respondents, eight apartment complexes in Lexington, Kentucky. (For convenience we will refer to all the ventures as "partnerships.") Bollinger initiated development of the first apartment complex, Creekside North Apartments, in 1968. The Massachusetts Mutual Life Insurance Company agreed to provide permanent financing by lending $1,075,000 to "the corporate nominee of Jesse C. Bollinger, Jr." at an annual interest rate of eight percent, secured by a mortgage on the property and a personal guaranty from Bollinger. The loan commitment was structured in this fashion because Kentucky's usury law at the time limited the annual interest rate for noncorporate borrowers to seven percent. Ky.Rev.Stat. §§ 360.010, 360.025 (1972). Lenders willing to pro-

---

2. Reg. § 301.7701–4(b).

3. Reg. § 301.7701–2(c)(1);–3(a), (b)(1)(i).

vide money only at higher rates required the nominal debtor and record title holder of mortgaged property to be a corporate nominee of the true owner and borrower. On October 14, 1968, Bollinger incorporated Creekside, Inc., under the laws of Kentucky; he was the only stockholder. The next day, Bollinger and Creekside, Inc., entered into a written agreement which provided that the corporation would hold title to the apartment complex as Bollinger's agent for the sole purpose of securing financing, and would convey, assign, or encumber the property and disburse the proceeds thereof only as directed by Bollinger; that Creekside, Inc., had no obligation to maintain the property or assume any liability by reason of the execution of promissory notes or otherwise; and that Bollinger would indemnify and hold the corporation harmless from any liability it might sustain as his agent and nominee.

Having secured the commitment for permanent financing, Bollinger, acting through Creekside, Inc., borrowed the construction funds for the apartment complex from Citizens Fidelity Bank and Trust Company. Creekside, Inc., executed all necessary loan documents including the promissory note and mortgage, and transferred all loan proceeds to Bollinger's individual construction account. Bollinger acted as general contractor for the construction, hired the necessary employees, and paid the expenses out of the construction account. When construction was completed, Bollinger obtained, again through Creekside, Inc., permanent financing from Massachusetts Mutual Life in accordance with the earlier loan commitment. These loan proceeds were used to pay off the Citizens Fidelity construction loan. Bollinger hired a resident manager to rent the apartments, execute leases with tenants, collect and deposit the rents, and maintain operating records. The manager deposited all rental receipts into, and paid all operating expenses from, an operating account, which was first opened in the name of Creekside, Inc., but was later changed to "Creekside Apartments, a partnership." The operation of Creekside North Apartments generated losses for the taxable years 1969, 1971, 1972, 1973, and 1974, and ordinary income for the years 1970, 1975, 1976, and 1977. Throughout, the income and losses were reported by Bollinger on his individual income tax returns.

Following a substantially identical pattern, seven other apartment complexes were developed by respondents through seven separate partnerships. For each venture, a partnership executed a nominee agreement with Creekside, Inc., to obtain financing. (For one of the ventures, a different Kentucky corporation, Cloisters, Inc., in which Bollinger had a 50 percent interest, acted as the borrower and titleholder. For convenience, we will refer to both Creekside and Cloisters as "the corporation.") The corporation transferred the construction loan proceeds to the partnership's construction account, and the partnership hired a construction supervisor who oversaw construction. Upon completion of construction, each partnership actively managed its apartment complex, depositing all rental receipts into, and paying all expenses from, a separate partnership account for each apartment complex. The corporation had no assets, liabilities, employees, or bank accounts. In every case, the lenders regarded the partnership as the owner of the apartments and were aware that the corporation was acting as agent of the partnership in holding record title. The partnerships reported the income and losses generated by the apartment complexes on their partnership tax returns, and respondents reported their distributive share of the partnership income and losses on their individual tax returns.

The Commissioner of Internal Revenue disallowed the losses reported by respondents, on the ground that the standards set out in National Carbide Corp. v. Commissioner, 336 U.S. 422, 69 S.Ct. 726, 93 L.Ed. 779 (1949), were not met. The Commissioner contended that *National Carbide* required a corporation to have an arm's-length relationship with its shareholders before it could be recognized as their agent. Although not all respondents were shareholders of the corporation, the Commissioner took the position that the funds the partnerships disbursed to pay expenses should be deemed contributions to the corporation's capital, thereby making all respondents constructive stockholders. Since, in the Commissioner's view, the corporation rather than its shareholders owned the real estate, any losses sustained by the ventures were attributable to the corporation and not respondents. Respondents sought a redetermination in the United States Tax Court. The Tax Court held that the corporations were the agents of the partnerships and should be disregarded for tax purposes. On appeal, the United States Court of Appeals for the Sixth Circuit affirmed. 807 F.2d 65 (1986). We granted the Commissioner's petition for certiorari.

II.

For federal income tax purposes, gain or loss from the sale or use of property is attributable to the owner of the property. * * * The problem we face here is that two different taxpayers can plausibly be regarded as the owner. Neither the Internal Revenue Code nor the regulations promulgated by the Secretary of the Treasury provide significant guidance as to which should be selected. It is common ground between the parties, however, that if a corporation holds title to property as agent for a partnership, then for tax purposes the partnership and not the corporation is the owner. Given agreement on that premise, one would suppose that there would be agreement upon the conclusion as well. For each of respondents' apartment complexes, an agency agreement expressly provided that the corporation would "hold such property as nominee and agent for" the partnership, and that the partnership would have sole control of and responsibility for the apartment complex. The partnership in each instance was identified as the principal and owner of the property during financing, construction, and operation. The lenders, contractors, managers, employees, and tenants—all who had contact with the development—knew that the corporation was merely the agent of the partnership, if they knew of the existence of the corporation at all. In each instance the relationship between the corporation and the partnership was, in both form and substance, an agency with the partnership as principal.

The Commissioner contends, however, that the normal indicia of agency cannot suffice for tax purposes when, as here, the alleged principals

are the controlling shareholders of the alleged agent corporation. That, it
asserts, would undermine the principle of Moline Properties v. Commissioner, 319 U.S. 436, 63 S.Ct. 1132, 87 L.Ed. 1499 (1943), which held that a
corporation is a separate taxable entity even if it has only one shareholder
who exercises total control over its affairs. Obviously, *Moline's* separate-
entity principle would be significantly compromised if shareholders of
closely held corporations could, by clothing the corporation with some
attributes of agency with respect to particular assets, leave themselves free
at the end of the tax year to make a claim—perhaps even a good-faith
claim—of either agent or owner status, depending upon which choice turns
out to minimize their tax liability. The Commissioner does not have the
resources to audit and litigate the many cases in which agency status could
be thought debatable. Hence, the Commissioner argues, in this shareholder
context he can reasonably demand that the taxpayer meet a prophylactical-
ly clear test of agency.

We agree with that principle, but the question remains whether the
test the Commissioner proposes is appropriate. The parties have debated at
length the significance of our opinion in National Carbide Corp. v. Commissioner, supra. In that case, three corporations that were wholly owned
subsidiaries of another corporation agreed to operate their production
plants as "agents" for the parent, transferring to it all profits except for a
nominal sum. The subsidiaries reported as gross income only this sum, but
the Commissioner concluded that they should be taxed on the entirety of
the profits because they were not really agents. We agreed, reasoning first,
that the mere fact of the parent's control over the subsidiaries did not
establish the existence of an agency, since such control is typical of all
shareholder-corporation relationships, id., 336 U.S. at 429–434, 69 S.Ct., at
730–732; and second, that the agreements to pay the parent all profits
above a nominal amount were not determinative since income must be
taxed to those who actually earn it without regard to anticipatory assignment, id., at 435–436, 69 S.Ct., at 733–734. We acknowledged, however,
that there was such a thing as "a true corporate agent . . . of [an] owner-
principal," id., at 437, 69 S.Ct., at 734, and proceeded to set forth four
indicia and two requirements of such status, the sum of which has become
known in the lore of federal income tax law as the "six *National Carbide*
factors":

> "[1] Whether the corporation operates in the name and for the
> account of the principal, [2] binds the principal by its actions, [3]
> transmits money received to the principal, and [4] whether receipt
> of income is attributable to the services of employees of the
> principal and to assets belonging to the principal are some of the
> relevant considerations in determining whether a true agency
> exists. [5] If the corporation is a true agent, its relations with its
> principal must not be dependent upon the fact that it is owned by
> the principal, if such is the case. [6] Its business purpose must be
> the carrying on of the normal duties of an agent." Id., at 437, 69
> S.Ct., at 734 (footnotes omitted).

We readily discerned that these factors led to a conclusion of nonagency in *National Carbide* itself. There each subsidiary had represented to its customers that it (not the parent) was the company manufacturing and selling its products; each had sought to shield the parent from service of legal process; and the operations had used thousands of the subsidiaries' employees and nearly $20 million worth of property and equipment listed as assets on the subsidiaries' books. Id., at 425, 434, 438, and n. 21, 69 S.Ct., at 728, 732–733, 734, and n. 21.

The Commissioner contends that the last two *National Carbide* factors are not satisfied in the present case. To take the last first: The Commissioner argues that here the corporation's business purpose with respect to the property at issue was not "the carrying on of the normal duties of an agent," since it was acting not as the agent but rather as the owner of the property for purposes of Kentucky's usury laws. We do not agree. It assuredly was not acting as the owner in fact, since respondents represented themselves as the principals to all parties concerned with the loans. Indeed, it was the lenders themselves who required the use of a corporate nominee. Nor does it make any sense to adopt a contrary-to-fact legal presumption that the corporation was the principal, imposing a federal tax sanction for the apparent evasion of Kentucky's usury law. To begin with, the Commissioner has not established that these transactions were an evasion. Respondents assert without contradiction that use of agency arrangements in order to permit higher interest was common practice, and it is by no means clear that the practice violated the spirit of the Kentucky law, much less its letter. It might well be thought that the borrower does not generally require usury protection in a transaction sophisticated enough to employ a corporate agent—assuredly not the normal *modus operandi* of the loan shark. That the statute positively envisioned corporate nominees is suggested by a provision which forbids charging the higher corporate interest rates "to a corporation, the principal asset of which shall be the ownership of a one (1) or two (2) family dwelling." Ky.Rev.Stat. § 360.025(2) (1987)—which would seem to prevent use of the nominee device for ordinary home-mortgage loans. In any event, even if the transaction did run afoul of the usury law, Kentucky, like most States, regards only the lender as the usurer, and the borrower as the victim. See Ky.Rev.Stat. § 360.020 (1987) (lender liable to borrower for civil penalty), § 360.990 (lender guilty of misdemeanor). Since the Kentucky statute imposed no penalties upon the borrower for allowing himself to be victimized, nor treated him as *in pari delictu,* but to the contrary enabled him to pay back the principal without any interest, and to sue for double the amount of interest already paid (plus attorney's fees), see Ky.Rev.Stat. § 360.020 (1972), the United States would hardly be vindicating Kentucky law by depriving the usury victim of tax advantages he would otherwise enjoy. In sum, we see no basis in either fact or policy for holding that the corporation was the principal because of the nature of its participation in the loans.

Of more general importance is the Commissioner's contention that the arrangements here violate the fifth *National Carbide* factor—that the corporate agent's "relations with its principal must not be dependent upon the fact that it is owned by the principal." The Commissioner asserts that this cannot be satisfied unless the corporate agent and its shareholder principal have an "arm's-length relationship" that includes the payment of a fee for agency services. The meaning of *National Carbide*'s fifth factor is, at the risk of understatement, not entirely clear. Ultimately, the relations between a corporate agent and its owner-principal are *always* dependent upon the fact of ownership, in that the owner can cause the relations to be altered or terminated at any time. Plainly that is not what was meant, since on that interpretation all subsidiary-parent agencies would be invalid for tax purposes, a position which the *National Carbide* opinion specifically disavowed. We think the fifth *National Carbide* factor—so much more abstract than the others—was no more and no less than a generalized statement of the concern, expressed earlier in our own discussion, that the separate-entity doctrine of *Moline* not be subverted.

In any case, we decline to parse the text of *National Carbide* as though that were itself the governing statute. As noted earlier, it is uncontested that the law attributes tax consequences of property held by a genuine agent to the principal; and we agree that it is reasonable for the Commissioner to demand unequivocal evidence of genuineness in the corporation-shareholder context, in order to prevent evasion of *Moline*. We see no basis, however, for holding that unequivocal evidence can only consist of the rigid requirements (arm's-length dealing plus agency fee) that the Commissioner suggests. Neither of those is demanded by the law of agency, which permits agents to be unpaid family members, friends, or associates. See Restatement (Second) of Agency §§ 16, 21, 22 (1958). It seems to us that the genuineness of the agency relationship is adequately assured, and tax-avoiding manipulation adequately avoided, when the fact that the corporation is acting as agent for its shareholders with respect to a particular asset is set forth in a written agreement at the time the asset is acquired, the corporation functions as agent and not principal with respect to the asset for all purposes, and the corporation is held out as the agent and not principal in all dealings with third parties relating to the asset. Since these requirements were met here, the judgment of the Court of Appeals is

Affirmed.

■ Justice Kennedy took no part in the consideration or decision of this case.

*

PART TWO

TAXATION OF C CORPORATIONS

CHAPTER 2

FORMATION OF A CORPORATION

A. INTRODUCTION TO SECTION 351

Code: §§ 351(a), (c), (d)(1)–(2); 358(a), (b)(1); 362(a), (e); 368(c); 1032(a); 1223(1), (2); 1245(b)(3).

Regulations: §§ 1.351–1(a), (b); 1.358–1(a), –2(b)(2); 1.362–1(a); 1.1032–1(a), (d).

Policy of Section 351. In order to commence business operations, a corporation needs assets. It normally acquires these assets—known as the initial "capital" of a corporation—by issuing shares of stock in exchange for cash or other property, or by borrowing. When a corporation raises its equity capital by issuing stock solely for cash, the tax consequences are routine: the shareholder simply has made a cash purchase and takes a cost basis in the shares acquired.[1] If the corporation issues stock for property other than cash, the exchange would be a taxable event without a special provision of the Code. The shareholder would recognize gain or loss equal to the difference between the fair market value of the stock received and the adjusted basis of the property transferred to the corporation.[2] The exchange also might be taxable to the corporation. Its gain—more theoretical than real—would be the excess of the fair market value of the cash and property received over the corporation's zero basis in the newly issued shares.

A simple example illustrates the possibilities. Assume that A decides to form Venture, Inc. by transferring appreciated property with a value of $100 and a basis of $10 in exchange for Venture stock with a value of $100. A would realize $90 of gain and, in theory, Venture might be said to realize $100 of gain by issuing its stock. If both parties were taxed on this simple transaction, however, corporate formations would be severely impeded. To remove these tax obstacles, Congress long ago decided that routine incorporations should be tax free to the shareholders and the corporation. At the shareholder level, Section 351(a) provides that no gain or loss shall be recognized if property is transferred to a corporation by one or more persons solely in exchange for its stock if the transferor or transferors of property are in "control" of the corporation "immediately after the exchange." Section 351 applies both to transfers to newly formed and preexisting corporations provided that the transferors of property have "control" immediately after the exchange. At the corporate level, Section 1032(a) provides that a corporation shall not recognize gain or loss on the

---

1. I.R.C. § 1012.

2. I.R.C. § 1001(a).

receipt of money or other property in exchange for its stock (including treasury stock).[3] These general rules are accompanied by special basis provisions and are subject to several exceptions, all of which will be discussed as this chapter unfolds.

The policy of Section 351 is one familiar to nonrecognition provisions. The transfer of appreciated or depreciated property to a corporation controlled by the transferor is viewed as a mere change in the form of a shareholder's investment. Consider, for example, the sole proprietor who decides to incorporate an ongoing business. The proprietor clearly *realizes* gain in a theoretical sense when the assets of the business are exchanged for all of the new corporation's stock. But he has neither "cashed out" nor appreciably changed the nature of his investment. He owns and operates the same business with the same assets, only now in corporate solution. Incorporation does not seem to be the appropriate occasion to impose a tax if the transferred assets have appreciated or to allow a deductible loss if the assets have decreased in value.

This policy is more difficult to defend in the case of a minority shareholder. Consider a taxpayer who exchanges appreciated land with a basis of $40 and a fair market value of $100 for a ten percent stock interest in a newly formed corporation with a total net worth of $1,000. As a result of the exchange, the taxpayer's continuing interest in the land has been significantly reduced, and he now owns a ten percent interest in a variety of other assets. Presumably, the exchange should be taxable and he should recognize $60 of gain. Similarly, if two or more unrelated taxpayers join together and transfer various assets to a new corporation in exchange for its stock, they arguably have changed the form of their investment; each now owns a part of several assets in corporate solution rather than all of the assets previously owned directly. Despite these arguments, Congress chose not to make such fine distinctions, perhaps because its primary goal in enacting Section 351 was to facilitate a wide variety of corporate formations. Section 351 thus is broad enough to embrace transfers of property by a group of previously unrelated persons—provided, of course, that the specific statutory requirements set forth below have been met.[4]

Basic Requirements. The three major requirements to qualify for nonrecognition of gain or loss under Section 351 are as follows:

(1) One or more persons (including individuals, corporations, partnerships and other entities) must transfer "property" to the corporation;

(2) The transfer must be solely in exchange for stock of the corporation; and

---

3. See Reg. § 1.1032–1(a).

4. But see I.R.C. § 351(e)(1), which disallows nonrecognition in the case of a "transfer of property to an investment company." This provision is intended to preclude a group of taxpayers from achieving a tax-free diversification of their investment portfolio through an exchange with a newly formed investment company. See Reg. § 1.351–1(c) for the details.

(3) The transferor or transferors, as a group, must be in "control" of the corporation "immediately after the exchange."

"Control" for this purpose is defined by Section 368(c) as "the ownership of stock possessing at least 80 percent of the total combined voting power of all classes of stock entitled to vote and at least 80 percent of the total number of shares of all other classes of stock of the corporation." These requirements are not as simple as they may first appear. Section 351 contains several statutory terms of art, each of which has raised issues over the years. Before studying the requirements in detail, however, it is necessary to complete the basic statutory scheme by turning to the corollary rules on basis and holding period.

Shareholder Basis and Holding Period. If Section 351 applies to a transfer, any gain or loss realized by the shareholder is not currently recognized. The policy of nonrecognition requires the preservation of these tax attributes to prevent total forgiveness of the unrecognized gain or forfeiture of any unrecognized loss. This goal is achieved by Section 358(a)(1), which provides that the basis of the stock ("nonrecognition property") received in a Section 351 exchange shall be the same as the basis of the property transferred by the shareholder to the corporation. Returning to the introductory example, if A transfers property to Venture, Inc. with a basis of $10 and a fair market value of $100 for stock with a value of $100 in a transaction governed by Section 351, A's basis in the stock will be $10. Assuming no decrease in the value of the stock, the $90 of gain that went unrecognized on the exchange will be recognized if and when A sells the stock.[5]

In keeping with this policy, Section 1223(1) provides that where a transferor receives property with an "exchanged basis,"[6] such as stock in a Section 351 exchange, the holding period of that property is determined by including the period during which he held the transferred property if the transferred property is a capital asset or a Section 1231 asset; if it is not, the transferor's holding period begins on the date of the exchange.

Tax Consequences to Transferee Corporation. On the corporate side, Section 1032 provides that a corporation does not recognize gain or loss when it issues stock in exchange for money or property. Moreover, a corporation that receives property in exchange for its stock in a Section 351 exchange steps into the shoes of the transferor. Section 362(a) generally prescribes a transferred basis—i.e., the corporation's basis in any property

---

5. If a shareholder dies without selling the stock, however, his basis will be stepped up (or down) to its fair market value on the date of his death (or six months thereafter, if the alternate valuation date is elected for federal estate tax purposes). I.R.C. § 1014(a). This would be the case, of course, if the shareholder had simply continued to hold the transferred assets out of corporate solution and thus is not inconsistent with the policy of Section 358.

6. See I.R.C. § 7701(a)(44), which defines "exchanged basis property" as property having a basis determined in whole or in part by reference to other property held at any time by the person for whom the basis is to be determined. "Exchanged basis property" is a subspecies of "substituted basis property," which also includes "transferred" (formerly "carryover") basis property. See I.R.C. § 7701(a)(42)–(44).

received in a Section 351 exchange is the same as the transferor's basis, thus preserving the gain or loss inherent in the asset for later recognition by the corporation. And Section 1223(2) provides that if property has a transferred (i.e., carryover) basis to the corporation, the transferor's holding period likewise will carry over.

Limitations on Transfer of Built-in Losses. When controlling shareholders transfer noncash assets to a corporation in a Section 351 exchange, the economic gain or loss inherent in those assets is reflected in both the transferor's stock basis and the transferee corporation's basis in the assets. This potential for duplication of the same economic gain or loss has been a longstanding feature of the Section 351 nonrecognition scheme. When Congress discovered that some U.S. corporations were exploiting these rules by deducting the same losses twice, it did what came naturally and enacted yet another statutory watchdog to limit the recognition of losses. In so doing, it not only curtailed a potentially abusive tax shelter but also adversely affected many other transactions that may not be motivated by tax avoidance.

If property with a net built-in loss is transferred to a corporation in a Section 351 transaction or as a contribution to capital, the transferee corporation's aggregate adjusted basis of such property is limited to the fair market value of the transferred property immediately after the transfer.[7] Transferred property has a "net built-in loss" when the aggregate adjusted basis of the property exceeds its fair market value. If multiple properties are transferred in the same transaction, some with built-in gains and others with built-in losses, the basis limitation only applies when there is a net built-in loss.[8] If more than one property with a built-in loss is transferred, the aggregate reduction in basis is allocated among the properties in proportion to their respective built-in losses immediately before the transaction.[9] Alternatively, the shareholder and the corporation may jointly elect to reduce the shareholder's basis in the stock that it receives to its fair market value.[10] If the election is made, the assets continue to have a built-in loss in the hands of the transferee corporation, but the loss will not be duplicated on the disposition of the shareholder's stock.

§362(e)

More to Come. All these basis rules are subject to modifications to be discussed later in this chapter,[11] and both Sections 358 and 362 apply to a variety of corporate transactions other than Section 351. For the moment, however, it is best to ignore these distractions and focus on the policy of

---

7. I.R.C. § 362(e)(2).

8. I.R.C. § 362(e)(2)(A)(ii). Similar basis limitation rules apply to transactions where there is an "importation of a net built-in loss," such as a transfer of loss property to a domestic corporation by a person not subject to U.S. tax. See I.R.C. § 362(e)(1). The non-importation rule is designed to prevent the shifting of losses from transferors who are not subject to U.S. tax, such as a foreign person or a domestic tax-exempt entity, to transferees who are taxable and can use the loss.

9. I.R.C. § 362(e)(2)(B).

10. I.R.C. § 362(e)(2)(C).

11. See Section C1 of this chapter, infra.

continuity of tax characteristics that is an essential corollary to the nonrecognition principle of Section 351.

PROBLEM

A, B, C, D and E, all individuals, form X Corporation to engage in a manufacturing business. X issues 100 shares of common stock. A transfers $25,000 cash for 25 shares; B transfers inventory with a value of $10,000 and a basis of $5,000 for 10 shares; C transfers unimproved land with a value of $20,000 and a basis of $25,000 for 20 shares; D transfers equipment with a basis of $5,000 and a value of $25,000 (prior depreciation taken was $20,000) for 25 shares; and E transfers a $20,000 (face amount and value) installment note for 20 shares. E received the note in exchange for land with a $2,000 basis that he sold last year. The note is payable over a five-year period, beginning in two years, at $4,000 per year plus market rate interest.

(a) What are the tax consequences (gain or loss recognized, basis and holding period in the stock received) to each of the transferors? As to E, see I.R.C. § 453B(a); Reg. § 1.453–9(c)(2). *None, they are nonrecognition. Subject to nonrecognition w/ carry-over basis*

(b) What are the tax consequences (gain recognized, basis and holding period in each of the assets received) to X Corporation? *Same.*

(c) Assume all the same facts except that C transfers two parcels of unimproved land (Parcel #1 and Parcel #2), each with a value of $10,000. C's basis in Parcel #1 is $15,000 and C's basis in Parcel #2 is $8,000. What result to C and X Corporation?

(d) There was $5,000 of gain inherent in the inventory transferred by B. If X Corporation later sells the inventory for $10,000, and B sells his stock for $10,000, how many times will that $5,000 of gain be taxed? Is there any justification for this result?

B. REQUIREMENTS FOR NONRECOGNITION OF GAIN OR LOSS UNDER SECTION 351

The introductory problem illustrates that a tax-free exchange is easily accomplished if a group of individuals forms a corporation by transferring property solely in exchange for common stock. But variations abound in the world of corporate formations, and the desires of the parties for a more complex transaction may conflict with the policy of nonrecognition. This section explores the requirements of Section 351 in more depth and shows that it often is possible, through careful planning, to reconcile these competing objectives.

1. "CONTROL" IMMEDIATELY AFTER THE EXCHANGE

Code: §§ 351(a); 368(c).

Regulations: § 1.351–1(a)(1).

Section 351 applies only if the transferors of property, as a group, "control" the corporation immediately after the exchange. For this purpose, "control" is defined by Section 368(c) as: (1) the ownership of at least 80 percent of the total combined voting power of all classes of stock entitled to vote, and (2) at least 80 percent of the total number of shares of all other classes of stock. The dual standard apparently was designed to ensure that the requisite control would not exist unless the transferors owned more than 80 percent of both the voting power and the total value of the corporation. Both prongs of the "control" test raise potentially thorny definitional questions—e.g., what is "stock entitled to vote?"; how is "voting power" determined? But these questions seldom arise in practice either because the routine corporate formation involves only one class of voting common stock or the transferors of property collectively emerge from the exchange owning 100 percent of all classes of stock.

The requisite control must be obtained by one or more transferors of "property" who act in concert under a single integrated plan. There is no limit on the number of transferors, and some may receive voting stock while others receive nonvoting stock. If the corporation issues more than one class of nonvoting stock, the Service requires that the transferor group must own at least 80 percent of *each* class.[1]

To be part of an integrated plan, the transfers need not be simultaneous. It is sufficient if the rights of the parties are "previously defined" and the agreement proceeds with an "expedition consistent with orderly procedure."[2] More important than timing is whether the transfers are mutually interdependent steps in the formation and carrying on of the business. Thus, it is possible for transfers separated by less than an hour to be considered separately for purposes of the control requirement or for transfers several years apart to be treated as part of an integrated plan.[3]

Finally, the transferors of property must be in control "immediately after the exchange." Momentary control will not suffice if the holdings of the transferor group fall below the required 80 percent as a result of dispositions of stock in a taxable transaction pursuant to a binding agreement or a prearranged plan.[4] But a voluntary disposition of stock, particularly in a donative setting, should not break control even if the original transferor of property parts with the shares moments after the incorporation exchange.[5]

As illustrated by the case below, the courts have taken a practical approach to this much-litigated issue, focusing less on timing and more on the previously defined rights and obligations of the parties.

1. Rev.Rul. 59–259, 1959–2 C.B. 115.

2. Reg. § 1.351–1(a)(1).

3. Compare Henricksen v. Braicks, 137 F.2d 632 (9th Cir.1943), with Commissioner v. Ashland Oil & Refining Co., 99 F.2d 588 (6th Cir.1938).

4. See American Bantam Car Co. v. Commissioner, 11 T.C. 397 (1948), affirmed per curiam, 177 F.2d 513 (3d Cir.1949), cert. denied, 339 U.S. 920, 70 S.Ct. 622 (1950).

5. See D'Angelo Associates, Inc. v. Commissioner, 70 T.C. 121 (1978); Stanton v. United States, 512 F.2d 13 (3d Cir.1975).

Intermountain Lumber Co. v. Commissioner

United States Tax Court, 1976.
65 T.C. 1025.

Always Petitioner

Always Respondent

■ WILES, JUDGE: * * *

[From 1948 until March, 1964, Dee Shook owned a sawmill in Montana, where Milo Wilson had logs processed into rough lumber for a fee. The rough lumber was processed into finished lumber at a separate plant jointly owned by Shook and Wilson. In March, 1964, the sawmill was damaged by fire. Shook and Wilson wanted to replace it with a larger facility, but Shook was financially unable to do so. Shook convinced Wilson to personally coguarantee a $200,000 loan to provide financing and, in return, Wilson insisted on becoming an equal shareholder with Shook in the rebuilt sawmill enterprise.

On May 28, 1964, Shook, Wilson and two other individuals incorporated S & W Sawmill, Inc. ("S & W"). Minutes of the first meeting of shareholders on July 7, 1964, recited in part that "Mr. Shook informed the meeting that a separate agreement was being prepared between he and Mr. Wilson providing for the sale of one-half of his stock to Mr. Wilson." Several days later, Shook transferred his sawmill site to S & W in exchange for 364 shares of S & W common stock. The company also issued one share to each of its four incorporators. No other stock was issued. On the same day, Shook and Wilson entered into "An Agreement for Sale and Purchase of Stock" under which Wilson was to purchase 182 shares of Shook's stock for $500 per share, plus annual interest, to be paid in installments. As each principal payment on the purchase price was made, a proportionate number of shares of stock were to be transferred on the corporate records and delivered to Wilson. A certificate for the 182 shares was placed in escrow. Shook also executed an irrevocable proxy granting Wilson voting rights in the 182 shares.

On August 19, 1964, S & W borrowed $200,000 from an outside lender, in part upon the personal guarantees of Shook and Wilson. On July 1, 1967, the taxpayer in this case, Intermountain Lumber Co. (referred to in the opinion as "petitioner"), acquired all the outstanding S & W stock from Shook and Wilson. S & W became a wholly owned subsidiary of Intermountain, and the companies filed consolidated tax returns for the years involved in this controversy.

Question:

The specific question before the Tax Court related to the tax basis of S & W's assets for purposes of depreciation claimed on the Intermountain Lumber group's consolidated return. In a role reversal, the Service contended that the transfer of assets to S & W was tax-free under Section 351, requiring S & W to take a transferred basis in the assets under Section 362. In support of a higher cost basis, the taxpayer argued that the incorporation did not qualify under Section 351 because Mr. Shook did not have control immediately after the exchange. Ed.]

OPINION

Section 351 provides, in part, that no gain shall be recognized if property is transferred to a corporation by one or more persons solely in exchange for stock or securities ["or securities" was deleted from the statute in 1989. Ed.] in such corporation and immediately after the exchange such person or persons are in control of the corporation. "Control" is defined for this purpose in section 368(c) as ownership of stock possessing at least 80 percent of the total combined voting power of all classes of stock entitled to vote and at least 80 percent of the total number of shares of all other classes of stock of the corporation.

In this case, respondent is in the unusual posture of arguing that a transfer to a corporation in return for stock was nontaxable under section 351, and Intermountain is in the equally unusual posture of arguing that the transfer was taxable because section 351 was inapplicable. The explanation is simply that Intermountain purchased all stock of the corporation, S & W, from its incorporators, and that Intermountain and S & W have filed consolidated income tax returns for years in issue. Accordingly, if section 351 was applicable to the incorporators when S & W was formed, S & W and Intermountain must depreciate the assets of S & W on their consolidated returns on the incorporators' basis. Sec. 362(a). If section 351 was inapplicable, and the transfer of assets to S & W was accordingly to be treated as a sale, S & W and Intermountain could base depreciation on those returns on the fair market value of those assets at the time of incorporation, which was higher than the incorporators' cost and which would accordingly provide larger depreciation deductions. Secs. 167(g), 1011, and 1012.

Petitioner thus maintains that the transfer to S & W of all of S & W's property at the time of incorporation by the primary incorporator, one Dee Shook, was a taxable sale. It asserts that section 351 was inapplicable because an agreement for sale required Shook, as part of the incorporation transaction, to sell almost half of the S & W shares outstanding to one Milo Wilson over a period of time, thereby depriving Shook of the requisite percentage of stock necessary for "control" of S & W immediately after the exchange.

Respondent, on the other hand, maintains that the agreement between Shook and Wilson did not deprive Shook of ownership of the shares immediately after the exchange, as the stock purchase agreement merely gave Wilson an option to purchase the shares. Shook accordingly was in "control" of the corporation and the exchange was thus nontaxable under section 351.

Respondent has abandoned on brief his contention that Wilson was a transferor of property and therefore a person to also be counted for purposes of control under section 351. Respondent is correct in doing so, since Wilson did not transfer any property to S & W upon its initial formation in July of 1964. Wilson's agreement to transfer cash for corporate stock in March of 1965 cannot be considered part of the same transaction.

Since Wilson was not a transferor of property and therefore cannot be counted for control under section 351, William A. James, 53 T.C. 63, 69 (1969), we must determine if Shook alone owned the requisite percentage of shares for control. This determination depends upon whether, under all facts and circumstances surrounding the agreement for sale of 182 shares between Shook and Wilson, ownership of those shares was in Shook or Wilson.

A determination of "ownership," as that term is used in section 368(c) and for purposes of control under section 351, depends upon the obligations and freedom of action of the transferee with respect to the stock when he acquired it from the corporation. Such traditional ownership attributes as legal title, voting rights, and possession of stock certificates are not conclusive. If the transferee, as part of the transaction by which the shares were acquired, has irrevocably foregone or relinquished at that time the legal right to determine whether to keep the shares, ownership in such shares is lacking for purposes of section 351. By contrast, if there are no restrictions upon freedom of action at the time he acquired the shares, it is immaterial how soon thereafter the transferee elects to dispose of his stock or whether such disposition is in accord with a preconceived plan not amounting to a binding obligation. * * *

After considering the entire record, we have concluded that Shook and Wilson intended to consummate a sale of the S & W stock, that they never doubted that the sale would be completed, that the sale was an integral part of the incorporation transaction, and that they considered themselves to be coowners of S & W upon execution of the stock purchase agreement in 1964. These conclusions are supported by minutes of the first stockholders meeting on July 7, 1964, at which Shook characterized the agreement for sale as a "sale"; minutes of a special meeting on July 15, 1964, at which Shook stated Wilson was to "purchase" half of Shook's stock; the "Agreement for Sale and Purchase of Stock" itself, dated July 15, 1964, which is drawn as an installment sale and which provides for payment of interest on unpaid principal; Wilson's deduction of interest expenses in connection with the agreement for sale, which would be inconsistent with an option; the S & W loan agreement, in which Shook and Wilson held themselves out as the "principal stockholders" of S & W and in which S & W covenanted to equally insure Shook and Wilson for $100,000; the March 1965 stock purchase agreement with S & W, which indicated that Shook and Wilson "*are* to remain *equal* "(emphasis added) shareholders in S & W; the letter of May 1967 from Shook and Wilson to Intermountain, which indicated that Wilson owed Shook the principal balance due on the shares as an unpaid obligation; and all surrounding facts and circumstances leading to corporate formation and execution of the above documents. Inconsistent and self-serving testimony of Shook and Wilson regarding their intent and understanding of the documents in evidence is unpersuasive in view of the record as a whole to alter interpretation of the transaction as a sale of stock by Shook to Wilson.

We accordingly cannot accept respondent's contention that the substance varied from the form of this transaction, which was, of course, labeled a "sale." The parties executed an "option" agreement on the same day that the "agreement for sale" was executed, and we have no doubt that they could and indeed did correctly distinguish between a sale and an option.

The agreement for sale's forfeiture clause, which provided that Wilson forfeited the right to purchase a proportionate number of shares for which timely principal payments were not made, did not convert it into an option agreement. Furthermore, the agreement for sale made no provision for forgiving interest payments on the remaining principal due should principal payments not be made on earlier dates; indeed, it specifically provided that "Interest payment must always be kept current before any delivery of stock is to be made resulting from a payment of principal."

We thus believe that Shook, as part of the same transaction by which the shares were acquired (indeed, the agreement for sale was executed before the sawmill was deeded to S & W), had relinquished when he acquired those shares the legal right to determine whether to keep them. Shook was under an obligation, upon receipt of the shares, to transfer the stock as he received Wilson's principal payments. * * * We note also that the agreement for sale gave Wilson the right to prepay principal and receive all 182 shares at any time in advance. Shook therefore did not own, within the meaning of section 368(c), the requisite percentage of stock immediately after the exchange to control the corporation as required for nontaxable treatment under section 351.

We note also that the basic premise of section 351 is to avoid recognition of gain or loss resulting from transfer of property to a corporation which works a change of form only. See Bittker & Eustice, Federal Income Taxation of Corporations and Shareholders, par. 3.01, p. 3–4 (3d ed. 1971). Accordingly, if the transferor sells his stock as part of the same transaction, the transaction is taxable because there has been more than a mere change in form. * * * In this case, the transferor agreed to sell and did sell 50 percent of the stock to be received, placed the certificates in the possession of an escrow agent, and granted a binding proxy to the purchaser to vote the stock being sold. Far more than a mere change in form was effected.

We accordingly hold for petitioner.

NOTE

The Service has taken a pragmatic (some might say "nuanced") view of the issue in *Intermountain Lumber* when the subsequent disposition of stock, even though planned, is not taxable. Revenue Ruling 2003–51[1] involved a plan by two corporations, referred to here as X Co. and Y Co., to consolidate certain businesses in a holding company structure. To accomplish that goal, X Co. transferred $40 of business assets to a wholly owned

---

1.   2003–1 C.B. 938.

subsidiary, X Sub Co., for X Sub Co. stock (the first transfer). Then, pursuant to a preexisting agreement, X Co. transferred its X Sub Co. stock to Y Sub Co., a subsidiary of Y Co., for stock of Y Sub Co. (the second transfer). At the same time as the second transfer, Y Co. also contributed $30 of cash to Y Sub Co. for additional stock (the third transfer). Finally, Y Sub Co. transferred its own business assets, the assets it received from X Co., and the $30 it got from Y Co. to X Sub Co. (the fourth transfer). When the dust settled, X Co. and Y Co. owned 40 percent and 60 percent, respectively, of Y Sub Co. and Y Sub Co. owned 100 percent of X Sub Co. The issue in the ruling was the tax results of the first transfer. X Co. clearly would have qualified for nonrecognition of gain under Section 351 on the first transfer but for its preexisting obligation to also make the second transfer. In holding that the first transfer satisfied the "control immediately after the exchange requirement," Revenue Ruling 2003–51 distinguishes between prearranged dispositions of stock that are taxable and those that are nontaxable:

> Treating a transfer of property that is followed by ... *a prearranged sale of the stock* received as a transfer described in § 351 is not consistent with Congress' intent in enacting § 351 to facilitate rearrangement of the transferor's interest in its property. Treating a transfer of property that is followed by *a nontaxable disposition of the stock* received as a transfer described in § 351 is not necessarily inconsistent with the purposes of § 351. Accordingly, the control requirement may be satisfied in such a case, even if the stock received is transferred pursuant to a binding commitment in place upon the transfer of the property in exchange for the stock. (Emphasis added.)

Revenue Ruling 2003–51 also notes that its result is supported by the fact that the transaction could have been rearranged to more directly qualify for nonrecognition under Section 351. For example, X Co. could have contributed the business assets directly to Y Sub Co. for Y Sub Co. stock at the same time as Y Co. contributed the $30 of cash to the subsidiary. Those transfers would have been protected by Section 351. Y Sub Co. could have then transferred its assets to a newly formed X Sub Co. in a second tax-free Section 351 exchange. Thus, Revenue Ruling 2003–51 concludes that treating X Co.'s first transfer as within Section 351 is not inconsistent with the purposes of that section.

2. TRANSFERS OF "PROPERTY" AND SERVICES

Regulations: § 1.351–1(a)(1), (2).

If the transferors of "property" must have control immediately after the exchange, the question then becomes: what is "property?" Although the term is not specifically defined for purposes of Section 351, it has been broadly construed to include cash, capital assets, inventory, accounts receivable, patents, and, in certain circumstances, other intangible assets such as nonexclusive licenses and industrial know-how.[1]

Section 351(d)(1) specifically provides, however, that stock issued for services shall not be considered as issued in return for property.[2] This rule makes good sense in the case of a promoter of the enterprise or even the company lawyer, each of whom contributes no capital but still receives stock in exchange for services rendered to the corporation. Inasmuch as the stock is compensation for those services, the tax consequences are properly determined under Sections 61 and 83.

Apart from realizing ordinary income, a person who receives stock solely in exchange for services may cause the other parties to the incorporation to recognize gain or loss. The pure service provider is not considered a transferor of property and may not be counted as part of the control group for purposes of qualifying the exchange under Section 351. But if a person receives stock in exchange for both property and services, *all* of his stock is counted toward the 80 percent control requirement.[3]

These rules offer some tempting opportunities for the tax planner. Assume, for example, that Promoter and Investor join forces to form a new corporation. In exchange for his services, Promoter receives 25 percent of the corporation's common stock. In exchange for $500,000 of highly appreciated property, Investor receives the other 75 percent. Investor, as the only transferor of property, does not have control and thus must recognize gain on the transaction unless Promoter somehow can qualify as a transferor of property—a status easily achieved, perhaps, by the mere transfer of $100 in cash.

Life is not so simple in the world of Subchapter C. To prevent such facile maneuvering around the control requirement, the regulations provide that the stock will not be treated as having been issued for property if the primary purpose of the transfer is to qualify the exchanges of the other property transferors for nonrecognition and if the stock issued to the nominal transferor is "of relatively small value" in comparison to the value of the stock already owned or to be received for services by the transferor.[4] In other words, the accommodation transfer gambit fails if the value of the property transferred is *de minimis* relative to the stock received for services. This regulation has been interpreted generously by the Service in Revenue Procedure 77–37,[5] which provides that property transferred "will not be considered to be of relatively small value * * * if the fair market value of the property transferred is equal to, or in excess of, 10 percent of the fair market value of the stock already owned (or to be received for services) by * * * [the transferor]."

1. See, e.g., E.I. Du Pont de Nemours & Co. v. United States, 471 F.2d 1211 (Ct.Cl. 1973); Rev.Rul. 64–56, 1964–1 C.B. 133 (industrial know-how); Rev.Rul. 69–357, 1969–1 C.B. 101 (money is "property").

2. See also Reg. § 1.351–1(a)(1)(i).

3. Reg. § 1.351–1(a)(1)(ii), –1(a)(2) Example (3).

4. Reg. § 1.351–1(a)(1)(ii). See also Estate of Kamborian v. Commissioner, 469 F.2d 219 (1st Cir.1972).

5. 1977–2 C.B. 568, § 3.07.

3. SOLELY FOR "STOCK"

Code: Skim § 351(g).

The final requirement for nonrecognition is that the transfers of property be made "solely" in exchange for "stock" of the controlled corporation. "Stock" generally means an equity investment in the company, and in this context the term has presented relatively few definitional problems. It does not include stock rights or warrants.[1] At one time, Section 351(a) applied to transfers of property solely in exchange for both stock and corporate debt securities, but the term "securities" eventually was deleted. A "security" was construed by the courts as a relatively long-term debt obligation (e.g., a bond or debenture) which provided the holder with a continuing degree of participation in corporate affairs, albeit as a creditor.[2] After the amendment, debt securities received in a Section 351 transaction, along with all forms of nonsecurity debt (e.g., a short-term note), are treated as boot, leaving only stock to qualify as nonrecognition property.

Certain preferred stock with debt-like characteristics, labelled by Section 351(g)(2) as "nonqualified preferred stock," is treated as "other property" (i.e., boot) rather than stock for purposes of Sections 351 and 356 (relating to recognition of gain or loss on certain otherwise tax-free corporate acquisitions). "Nonqualified preferred stock" is generally defined as preferred stock[3] with any of the following characteristics: (1) the stockholder has the right to require the issuing corporation or a "related person"[4] to redeem or purchase the stock, (2) the issuer or a related person is required to redeem or purchase the stock, (3) the issuer or a related person has the right to redeem or purchase the stock and, as of the issue date, it is more likely than not that such right will be exercised, or (4) the dividend rate on such stock varies in whole or in part with reference to interest rates, commodity prices, or similar indices.[5] The first three of these categories apply only if the right or obligation with respect to the redemption or purchase of the stock may be exercised within the 20–year period beginning on the issue date of the stock, and such right or obligation is not subject to a contingency which, as of the issue date, makes remote the likelihood of the redemption or purchase.[6]

---

1. Reg. § 1.351–1(a)(1), last sentence.

2. Camp Wolters Enterprises, Inc. v. Commissioner, 22 T.C. 737 (1954), affirmed, 230 F.2d 555 (5th Cir.1956), cert. denied, 352 U.S. 826, 77 S.Ct. 39 (1956).

3. For this purpose, "preferred stock" is stock which is limited and preferred as to dividends and does not participate in corporate growth to any significant extent. I.R.C. § 351(g)(3)(A). Stock is not treated as participating in corporate growth to any significant extent unless there is a real and meaningful likelihood of the shareholder actually participating in the corporation's earnings and growth. Id.

4. Persons are "related" if they bear any of the relationships described in Sections 267(b) or 707(b), such as family members, controlling shareholders or partners, a corporate affiliate, etc. I.R.C. § 351(g)(3)(B).

5. I.R.C. § 351(g)(2)(A).

6. I.R.C. § 351(g)(2)(B).

The effect of Section 351(g) is to treat debt-like preferred stock as boot, resulting in potential recognition of gain (but generally not loss) to the recipient under Section 351(b). A taxpayer is allowed to recognize a loss, however, if only nonqualified preferred stock is received in an exchange.[7] The legislative history indicates that nonqualified preferred stock still will be treated as "stock" for all other purposes until the Treasury provides otherwise in prospective regulations issued under the authority of Section 351(g)(4).[8] This hybrid status as boot for gain recognition purposes but stock for other purposes is more significant in connection with tax-free acquisitive reorganizations, which are covered later in the text.[9]

PROBLEMS

1. Consider whether the following transactions qualify under Section 351:

   (a) A and B are unrelated individuals. A forms Newco, Inc. on January 2 of the current year by transferring property with a basis of $10,000 and a value of $50,000 for all 50 shares of Newco common stock. On March 2, in an unrelated transaction, B transfers property with a basis of $1,000 and a value of $10,000 for 10 shares of Newco nonvoting preferred stock (that is not nonqualified preferred stock).

   (b) Same as (a), above, except the transfers by A and B were part of a single integrated plan.

   (c) Same as (b), above, except A transferred 25 of her 50 shares to her daughter, D, as a gift on March 5 (three days after B's transfer). What if A's gift to D were on January 5?

   (d) Same as (b), above, except that two months after B's transfer, A sold 15 shares to E pursuant to a preexisting oral understanding, without which Newco would not have been formed.

2. Mr. Java ("Java") has operated a chain of coffee houses as a sole proprietorship over the past three years and is now interested in expanding his horizons and limiting his liability. To do so, he wishes to incorporate, raise $150,000 of additional capital and hire an experienced person to manage the business. He has located Venturer, who is willing to invest $150,000 cash and Manager, who has agreed to serve as chief operating officer if the terms are right.

   The parties have decided to join forces and form Java Jyve, Inc. ("Jyve") to expand the coffee house business and offer access to the Internet at every location. Java will transfer assets with an aggregate basis of $50,000 and a fair market value of $200,000 (do not be concerned with the character of the individual assets for this problem); Venturer will contribute $150,000 cash; and Manager will enter into a five-year employ-

---

7. I.R.C. § 351(g)(1)(B).

8. Staff of Joint Committee on Taxation, General Explanation of Tax Legislation

Enacted in 1997, 105th Cong., 1st Sess. 210 (1997).

9. See Chapter 17, infra.

ment contract. Java would like effective control of the business; Venturer is interested in a guaranteed preferred return on his investment but also wants to share in the growth of the company; and Manager wants to be fairly compensated (she believes her services are worth approximately $80,000 per year) and receive stock in the company, but she can not afford to make a substantial cash investment. All the parties wish to avoid adverse tax consequences.

Consider the following alternative proposals and evaluate whether they meet the tax and non-tax objectives of the parties:

(a) In exchange for their respective contributions, Java will receive 200 shares and Venturer will receive 150 shares of Jyve stock. Manager will agree to a salary of $40,000 per year for five years and will receive 150 shares of Jyve common stock upon the incorporation. (Assume that the value of the stock is $1,000 per share.)

(b) Same as (a), above, except Manager will receive compensation of $80,000 per year and will pay $150,000 for her Jyve stock. Any difference if Manager, unable to raise the cash, gave Jyve her unsecured $150,000 promissory note, at market rate interest, payable in five equal installments, in exchange for her 150 shares?

(c) Same as (a), above, except Manager will pay $1,000 for her 150 shares and the incorporation documents specify that she is receiving those shares in exchange for her cash contribution rather than for future services.

(d) Same as (c), above, except Manager will pay $20,000 cash rather than $1,000.

(e) Same as (d), above, except Manager will receive only 20 shares of stock without restrictions; the other 130 shares may not be sold by Manager for five years and will revert back to the corporation if Manager should cease to be an employee of the company during the five-year period. See I.R.C. § 83. Would you advise Manager to make a § 83(b) election in this situation? What other information would you need?

(f) In general, is there another approach to structuring the formation of Jyve that would harmonize the goals of the founders?

C. TREATMENT OF BOOT

1. IN GENERAL

Code: §§ 351(b); 358(a), (b)(1); 362(a). Skim § 351(g).

Regulations: §§ 1.351–2(a); 1.358–1, –2; 1.362–1.

In the introductory section of this chapter, a simple example illustrated the need for Section 351. Recall that A decided to form Venture, Inc. by transferring appreciated property with a value of $100 and a basis of $10 in exchange for Venture stock with a value of $100. Without a special provision of the Code, A would have recognized a $90 gain on the exchange. But since A received solely stock and owned 100 percent of Venture, the transaction qualified for nonrecognition under Section 351. To preserve the gain that went unrecognized, A took a $10 exchanged basis in the Venture stock under Section 358, and Venture took a $10 transferred basis in the contributed assets under Section 362. If A had received more than one class of stock, the transaction still would have qualified under Section 351, and A would have been required to allocate his aggregate exchanged basis of $10 among the various classes of stock received in proportion to their relative fair market values.[1]

But suppose that A, perhaps motivated by the tax advantages of corporate debt,[2] capitalizes Venture, Inc. with the same $100 asset by taking back common stock with a value of $80 and a corporate note with a value of $20. The transaction fails to qualify under Section 351(a) because A, although clearly in "control" of Venture, has not exchanged his $100 asset "solely" in exchange for stock. A's position is not unlike the real estate investor who, desiring a tax-free like-kind exchange, trades his highly appreciated $500,000 building in exchange for other real estate with a value of $450,000 and $50,000 of cash to even out the deal. The question for both A and the real estate investor becomes: should the presence of this "other property," known in tax parlance as "boot," require full recognition of their realized gain, or should there be a statutory middle ground?

The question is answered by Section 351(b). It provides that if an exchange otherwise would have qualified under Section 351(a) but for the fact that the transferor received "other property or money" in addition to stock, then the transferor's realized gain (if any) must be recognized to the extent of the cash plus the fair market value of the other property received. Translated more concisely, Section 351(b) provides that any gain realized by a transferor on an otherwise qualified Section 351(a) exchange must be recognized only to the extent of the boot received. The gain is characterized by reference to the character of the assets transferred, taking into account the impact of the recapture of depreciation provisions.[3] Despite the presence of boot, however, no *loss* may be recognized under Section 351(b).[4]

In the example where A receives $80 of stock and a $20 corporate note in exchange for his $100 asset with a $10 basis, Section 351(b) will require A to recognize $20 of his $90 realized gain.[5] This makes sense, of course, because to the extent that A has transferred his asset in exchange for

---

1. Reg. § 1.358–2(b)(2).

2. See Chapter 3A, infra.

3. See I.R.C. §§ 1245(b)(3); 1250(d)(3). Also relevant is I.R.C. § 1239, which characterizes the recognized gain on the transfer of depreciable property to a corporation as ordinary income if the transferor and certain related parties own more than 50 percent of the value of the transferee corporation's stock.

4. See also I.R.C. § 267(a)(1), disallowing losses on sales or exchanges between related taxpayers, including an individual and a corporation more than 50 percent in value of which is owned by the individual (actually or through attribution rules).

5. This example only addresses the *amount* of A's gain. The *timing* of gain triggered by the receipt of installment boot is considered in Section C2 of the chapter, infra.

property other than stock, he has changed not merely the form of his investment but the substance as well. To that extent, nonrecognition treatment is inappropriate.

As noted earlier, if a shareholder transfers property in a tax-free Section 351(a) transaction, the unrecognized gain on the transfer will be preserved through an exchanged basis in the transferor's stock and again through a transferred basis in the corporation's assets. But if a shareholder recognizes some gain as a result of the receipt of boot, not all of his realized gain must be accounted for at a later time. To avoid this potential double recognition of gain, the shareholder may increase his basis in the stock, securities and other property received by an amount equal to the gain recognized on the transfer.[6] This higher basis will result in less gain (or more loss) if and when the shareholder later sells the property received from the corporation.

The shareholder's combined basis in the stock, securities and other property received from the corporation thus equals the basis in the property transferred to the corporation increased by the gain recognized on the transfer. This total basis then must be allocated between the nonrecognition property (i.e., the stock) and the boot. Since any gain recognized by the shareholder is attributable to the boot, and since his continuing investment is represented by the nonrecognition property, the unrecognized gain inherent in the property transferred to the corporation should now lurk in the nonrecognition property. These goals are achieved by assigning the boot a fair market value basis and allocating the remaining basis to the nonrecognition property. The basis of the nonrecognition property is thus an exchanged basis, increased by the gain recognized on the transfer, and, finally, decreased by the fair market value of the boot (including cash) received.[7]

Applying these rules to our previous example, if A received $80 of Venture, Inc. stock and a $20 note in exchange for his $100 asset with a basis of $10, his recognized gain would be $20—the fair market value of the boot. A's basis in the note would be $20, its fair market value. A's basis in the stock would be determined as follows:

Basis of Asset Transferred	$ 10
Less: Fair Market Value of Note Received	(20)
Plus: Gain Recognized	20
Basis of Stock	$ 10

The arithmetic makes sense. Remember that the value of the Venture stock was $80. By assigning the stock a $10 basis, Section 358 preserves the $70 of realized gain that went unrecognized on the partially tax-free exchange. There is no more gain to be preserved, so it is logical to give the boot a fair market value basis.[8]

6. I.R.C. § 358(a)(1)(B)(ii).

7. I.R.C. § 358(a)(2).

8. As before, this example only address-es the amount of gain recognized under Sec-

At the corporate level, Section 362(a) provides that the corporation's basis in the property received on a Section 351 exchange is the same as the transferor's basis, increased by any gain recognized on the exchange. This rule ensures that any gain or loss not recognized by the shareholder will be reflected in the corporation's basis in the transferred assets. Returning one last time to the example, since A recognized $20 of gain on the exchange, Venture's basis in the transferred asset would be $30 (a $10 transferred basis in A's hands plus $20 gain recognized).

If a transferor exchanges several assets in exchange for stock and boot, the transaction becomes more complex. For purposes of determining the gain recognized (and, if relevant, the character of that gain), it becomes necessary to allocate the boot among the transferred assets. Similar allocations are required to determine the basis of the assets in the hands of the corporation. Although these questions rarely arise in the routine corporate formation, they have titillated tax commentators and caused unnecessary anguish to students of corporate tax.[9] The ruling below is the Service's attempt at an orderly resolution of this problem.

Revenue Ruling 68–55

1968–1 Cum.Bull. 140.

Advice has been requested as to the correct method of determining the amount and character of the gain to be recognized by Corporation X under section 351(b) of the Internal Revenue Code of 1954 under the circumstances described below.

Corporation Y was organized by X and A, an individual who owned no stock in X. A transferred $20x$ dollars to Y in exchange for stock of Y having a fair market value of $20x$ dollars and X transferred to Y three separate assets and received in exchange stock of Y having a fair market value of $100x$ dollars plus cash of $10x$ dollars.

In accordance with the facts set forth in the table below if X had sold at fair market value each of the three assets it transferred to Y, the result would have been as follows:

	Asset I	**Asset II**	**Asset III**
Character of asset	Capital asset held more than 6 months.	Capital asset held not more than 6 months.	Section 1245 property.
Fair market value	$22x$	$33x$	$55x$
Adjusted basis	40x	20x	25x
Gain (loss)	($18x$)	$13x$	$30x$
Character of gain or loss	Long-term capital loss.	Short-term capital gain.	Ordinary income.

tion 351(b) and the resulting basis consequences.

9. For the seminal article on boot allocation, see Rabinovitz, "Allocating Boot in Section 351 Exchanges," 24 Tax L.Rev. 337 (1969). For an exhaustive (and exhausting) update, see Cohen & Whitney, "Revisiting the Allocation of Boot in Section 351 Exchanges," 48 Tax Lawyer 959 (1995).

The facts in the instant case disclose that with respect to the section 1245 property the depreciation subject to recapture exceeds the amount of gain that would be recognized on a sale at fair market value. Therefore, all of such gain would be treated as ordinary income under section 1245(a)(1) of the Code.

Under section 351(a) of the Code, no gain or loss is recognized if property is transferred to a corporation solely in exchange for its stock and immediately after the exchange the transferor is in control of the corporation. If section 351(a) of the Code would apply to an exchange but for the fact that there is received, in addition to the property permitted to be received without recognition of gain, other property or money, then under section 351(b) of the Code gain (if any) to the recipient will be recognized, but in an amount not in excess of the sum of such money and the fair market value of such other property received, and no loss to the recipient will be recognized.

The first question presented is how to determine the amount of gain to be recognized under section 351(b) of the Code. The general rule is that each asset transferred must be considered to have been separately exchanged. See the authorities cited in Revenue Ruling 67–192, C.B. 1967–2, 140, and in Revenue Ruling 68–23, page 144, this Bulletin, which hold that there is no netting of gains and losses for purposes of applying sections 367 and 356(c) of the Code. Thus, for purposes of making computations under section 351(b) of the Code, it is not proper to total the bases of the various assets transferred and to subtract this total from the fair market value of the total consideration received in the exchange. Moreover, any treatment other than an asset-by-asset approach would have the effect of allowing losses that are specifically disallowed by section 351(b)(2) of the Code.

The second question presented is how, for purposes of making computations under section 351(b) of the Code, to allocate the cash and stock received to the amount realized as to each asset transferred in the exchange. The asset-by-asset approach for computing the amount of gain realized in the exchange requires that for this purpose the fair market value of each category of consideration received must be separately allocated to the transferred assets in proportion to the relative fair market values of the transferred assets. See section 1.1245–4(c)(1) of the Income Tax Regulations which, for the same reasons, requires that for purposes of computing the amount of gain to which section 1245 of the Code applies each category of consideration received must be allocated to the properties transferred in proportion to their relative fair market values.

Accordingly, the amount and character of the gain recognized in the exchange should be computed as follows:

	Total	Asset I	Asset II	Asset III
Fair market value of asset transferred	$110x	$22x	$33x	$55x
Percent of total fair market value		20%	30%	50%
Fair market value of Y stock received in exchange	$100x	$20x	$30x	$50x
Cash received in exchange	10x	2x	3x	5x
Amount realized	$110x	$22x	$33x	$55x
Adjusted basis		40x	20x	25x
Gain (loss) realized		($18x)	$13x	$30x

Under section 351(b)(2) of the Code the loss of 18x dollars realized on the exchange of Asset Number I is not recognized. Such loss may not be used to offset the gains realized on the exchanges of the other assets. Under section 351(b)(1) of the Code, the gain of 13x dollars realized on the exchange of Asset Number II will be recognized as short-term capital gain in the amount of 3x dollars, the amount of cash received. Under sections 351(b)(1) and 1245(b)(3) of the Code, the gain of 30x dollars realized on the exchange of Asset Number III will be recognized as ordinary income in the amount of 5x dollars, the amount of cash received.

NOTE

Overall understanding of Section 351 may be enhanced by an analysis of the additional results to the shareholder ("X") and the corporation ("Y") in the transaction described in Revenue Ruling 68–55. X's basis in the Y stock received will be an exchanged basis ($40 from Asset I, plus $20 from Asset II, plus $25 from Asset III = $85), increased by its total gain recognized on the transfer ($3 on Asset II, plus $5 on Asset III = $8) and decreased by the fair market value of the boot (including cash) received ($10) for a total basis of $83 ($85 + $8 − 10).

The next question is X's holding period for the stock. X received stock worth $100 together with $10 cash for assets with a value of $110 (Asset I $22, Asset II $33, Asset III $55). Thus, it could be said that $^{22}\!/_{110}$ of the stock was received in exchange for Asset I, $^{33}\!/_{110}$ was received in exchange for Asset II, and $^{55}\!/_{110}$ was received in exchange for Asset III. In that event, each share could be considered to have a split holding period allocated in proportion to the fair market value of the transferred assets.[1]

The next step is a determination of Y's basis in the assets received. In the ruling, Y's basis in those assets will be their adjusted bases in X's hands ($40 for Asset I, plus $20 for Asset II, plus $25 for Asset III) increased by the gain recognized to X (zero on Asset I, plus $3 on Asset II, plus $5 on Asset III) for a total of $93 ($40 + $20 + $25 + $3 + $5). Nothing in the Code, regulations or rulings explains how this basis is allocated among the assets. The underlying premise of Section 362, however, is that any gain or

---

1. This approach was adopted by the Service in Rev.Rul. 85–164, 1985–2 C.B. 117. In so ruling, the Service rejected an alternative approach, under which some shares would take a tacked holding period and other shares a holding period commencing as of the date of the exchange. The latter approach would permit a shareholder selling a portion of his holdings to designate shares with the longer holding period.

loss which is realized but not recognized by the transferor on the Section 351 transfer will be recognized by the corporation on a later sale. This concept is carried out by giving each separate asset its original transferred basis and then increasing the basis by the amount of gain recognized by the transferor on that asset.[2] On the facts in Revenue Ruling 68–55, Y's basis in Asset I would be $40 (transferred basis) since no gain or loss was recognized on that asset. If Y sells Asset I for its $22 fair market value, it then will recognize the $18 loss realized but not recognized by the transferor. Y's basis in Asset II would be $23 (transferred basis of $20 increased by the $3 of gain recognized on Asset II). Of the $13 of realized gain on Asset II, $3 already has been recognized, and Y will recognize the $10 additional gain if it sells that asset for its fair market value of $33. Finally, Asset III will take a basis of $30 (transferred basis of $25, increased by $5 gain recognized) so that if Y sold the asset for its fair market value of $55, it will recognize the $25 additional realized gain that was not recognized by X.

2. TIMING OF SECTION 351(b) GAIN

Proposed Regulations: § 1.453–1(f)(1)(iii), –(f)(3)(i), (ii), (iii) Example (1).

The preceding discussion concerned the amount of gain recognized by a transferor who receives boot in a Section 351 transaction. What about the timing of that gain? If the boot is cash or other corporate property, the transferor recognizes any Section 351(b) gain immediately upon receipt of the boot. But gain is more typically recognized when a shareholder transfers appreciated property in exchange for a mixture of stock and corporate debt instruments.[1] In that event, the question becomes—*when* must that gain be recognized? And if the gain may be deferred, what is the resulting impact on the shareholder's basis in her stock under Section 358 and the corporation's basis in its assets under Section 362? The answers lie in the relationship between Section 351 and the installment sale rules in Section 453.

For many years, it was not clear whether a shareholder could defer the reporting of Section 351 gain triggered by the receipt of corporate debt obligations. The Code resolves this question in an analogous context by permitting deferral of gain for installment boot received in a Section 1031 like-kind exchange and certain other corporate nonrecognition transactions.[2] In proposed regulations, the Treasury extended this rule to allow a transferor who receives installment boot in a Section 351(b) transaction to defer gain until payments are received on the corporate debt.[3] The regula-

2. See, e.g., P.A. Birren & Son v. Commissioner, 116 F.2d 718 (7th Cir.1940).

1. For the tax incentives to capitalize a corporation with debt, see Section F of this chapter, infra.

2. I.R.C. § 453(f)(6).

3. Prop.Reg. § 1.453–1(f)(3)(ii). Any gain attributable to recapture of depreciation

or dispositions of dealer property cannot be deferred. I.R.C. § 453(i), (*l*). See generally Cain, "Taxation of Boot Notes in a 351/453 Transaction," 27 S. Texas L.Rev. 61 (1985); Dentino & Walker, "Impact of the Installment Sales Revision Act of 1980 on Evidences of Indebtedness in a Section 351 Transaction," 9 J.Corp. Tax'n 330 (1983).

tions also permit a transferor to immediately increase the basis in any nonrecognition property received (e.g., stock) by the transferor's total potential recognized gain, but they delay the corporation's corresponding Section 362(a) basis increase in its assets until the transferor actually recognizes gain on the installment method.[4]

The operation of the proposed regulations is best illustrated by an example. In a conventional installment sale (i.e., a deferred payment sale not made in conjunction with a nonrecognition provision), Section 453 directs the seller to construct a fraction by dividing the realized gain (known in Section 453 parlance as the "gross profit") by the total principal payments to be received on the sale ("total contract price").[5] The seller then applies the fraction to each payment received to determine the gain recognized in the year of sale and as installment payments are later received. Adopting the facts of our continuing example, assume A sells his appreciated asset ("Gainacre"), which has an adjusted basis of $10 and a fair market value of $100, for $80 cash and a $20 note with market rate interest and principal payable in equal installments over the next five years. A's realized gain is $90. A's total payments received will be $100: $80 in the year of sale and $20 in subsequent years. Under the installment method, $90/100$, or 90 percent, of each payment received must be reported as taxable gain.

Now assume that A transfers Gainacre to Venture, Inc., in exchange for 80 shares of Venture stock (worth $80), and a $20 Venture five-year note. A again realizes $90 of gain but recognizes that gain only to the extent of the $20 boot received. For timing purposes, the regulations divide the exchange into two separate transactions: a Section 351(a) nonrecognition exchange to the extent of the stock received by the transferor and an installment sale to the extent of the boot received. The basis of the transferred property is first allocated to the nonrecognition transaction. The regulations implement this bifurcation approach as follows:[6]

1. A's basis in Gainacre ($10) is first allocated to the Venture stock ("nonrecognition property")[7] received in the exchange in an amount up to the fair market value of that property. The entire $10 of basis is thus allocated to the $80 of Venture stock received by A.

2. If the transferor's basis in the transferred property exceeds the fair market value of the nonrecognition property received, that "excess basis" is then allocated to the installment portion of the transaction. There is no excess basis to allocate in this example because the Gainacre basis ($10) does not exceed the value of the nonrecognition property (stock worth $80).

---

4. Prop. Reg. § 1.453–1(f)(3)(ii).

5. I.R.C. § 453(c). For purposes of this and subsequent examples, assume that the property sold is unencumbered and is otherwise eligible for installment sale treatment.

6. Prop.Reg. § 1.453–1(f)(1)(iii);–1(f)(3)(ii).

7. The proposed regulations refer to nonrecognition property as "permitted property." Prop.Reg. § 1.453–1(f)(1)(i).

3. Section 453 is then applied to the installment portion of the transaction. For this purpose, the "selling price" is the sum of the face value of the installment obligation ($20 here) and the fair market value of any other boot (none here). Where, as here, there are no liabilities, the total contract price is the same as the selling price ($20). The gross profit is the selling price less any "excess basis" allocated to the installment obligation ($20–0 = $20). A's gross profit ratio is thus $^{20}\!/_{20}$, or 100%. To determine his recognized gain, A applies that percentage to any boot received in the year of sale and to payments as they are received on the installment note. A thus recognizes no gain in the year of the exchange; his entire $20 "boot" gain is recognized as the note is paid off over the next five years. Note that the gross profit ratio is normally 100% if the boot received is less than the realized gain.[8]

For purposes of determining a shareholder's basis in the nonrecognition property received in a Section 351/453 transaction, the regulations treat the shareholder as electing out of the installment method.[9] Returning to the example, A's basis in his Venture stock under Section 358 is $10, determined as follows: $10 (A's basis in Gainacre) decreased by $20 (total boot received by A) and increased by $20 (the entire gain A would have recognized if he reported all his gain in the year of sale).

Determining the corporation's basis in the transferred property is more complicated. Adopting what one commentator has called a "roller-coaster basis" approach,[10] the regulations provide that the corporation's basis in the transferred property is the same as the transferor's basis increased by the gain recognized only if, as and when that gain is actually recognized. In the example, Venture initially takes a transferred basis of $10 in Gainacre, and that basis gradually is increased by $20 as Venture pays off the note and A recognizes his deferred gain on the installment method.[11] Query whether this rollercoaster basis approach is appropriate, considering that Venture in effect has incurred a liability in connection with its acquisition of Gainacre. If the teachings of the *Crane* case are followed, it would seem that Venture should be permitted to increase its basis by the full $20 liability notwithstanding that A may defer his boot

---

8. If the boot exceeds the transferor's realized gain, then some of the basis of the transferred property must be allocated to the installment portion of the transaction. For example, assume the same transaction, except A's basis in Gainacre is $90 and his realized gain is thus only $10. Although A receives $20 of boot, his recognized gain is limited to $10 under Section 351(b). The proposed regulations again direct A to allocate his basis in Gainacre ($90) to the Venture stock received but only up to the fair market value of that "nonrecognition property" ($80 here). The $10 "excess basis" is allocated to the installment sale, resulting in a gross prof-

it of $10 ($20 selling price less $10 excess basis) and a gross profit ratio of ½. A thus must report ½ of each payment received on the note as taxable gain.

9. Prop.Reg. § 1.453–1(f)(3)(ii).

10. See Bogdanski, "Closely Held Corporations: Section 351 and Installment 'Boot,' "11 J.Corp.Tax'n 268 (1984).

11. Id. Suppose Venture sells Gainacre prior to the due date of the note. Should Venture recognize a loss when the note is eventually paid off? See Prop. Reg. § 1.453–1(f)(3)(iii) Example (1).

gain over five years. An immediate step-up in basis of the transferred property would be particularly appealing to the corporation when the property is depreciable real estate with no lurking recapture gain.

PROBLEM

A, B and C form X Corporation by transferring the following assets, each of which has been held long-term:

Transferor	Asset	Adj. Basis	F.M.V.
A	Equipment (all § 1245 gain)	$15,000	$22,000
B	Inventory	7,000	20,000
	Land	25,000	10,000
C	Land	20,000	50,000

In exchange, A receives 15 shares of X common stock (value—$15,000), $2,000 cash and 100 shares of X preferred stock (value—$5,000), B receives 15 shares of X common stock (value—$15,000) and $15,000 cash, and C receives 10 shares of X common stock (value—$10,000), $5,000 cash and X's note for $35,000, payable in two years. None of the transferors is a "dealer" in real estate. Assume that the preferred stock issued to A is not "nonqualified preferred stock."

 (a) What are the tax consequences (gain or loss realized and recognized, basis and holding period) of the transfers described above to each shareholder and to X Corporation?

 (b) What result to C in (a), above, if instead of land, C transferred depreciable equipment with the same adjusted basis and fair market value as the land and an original cost to C of $50,000? See § 453(i).

D.   ASSUMPTION OF LIABILITIES

Code: §§ 357(a)–(c); 358(d). Skim § 357(d).

Regulations: §§ 1.357–1, –2; 1.358–3.

Many corporate formations involve the transfer of encumbered property or the assumption of liabilities by the transferee corporation. In most circumstances, a taxpayer who is relieved of a debt in connection with the disposition of property must include the debt relief in the amount realized even if the debt is nonrecourse. This is the teaching of the celebrated *Crane* case,[1] and the Supreme Court took a similar approach nine years earlier in United States v. Hendler.[2] Interpreting the corporate reorganization provisions, the Court held in *Hendler* that the assumption and subsequent payment of the transferor's liabilities by a transferee corporation constitut-

---

1. Crane v. Commissioner, 331 U.S. 1, 67 S.Ct. 1047 (1947).

2. 303 U.S. 564, 58 S.Ct. 655 (1938).

ed boot to the transferor. If that rule applied to a corporate formation, however, many incorporations of a going business would become taxable events to the extent of the liabilities assumed, and the policy of Section 351 would be seriously frustrated.

To prevent this result, Congress promptly responded to *Hendler* by enacting the statutory predecessor of Section 357. Section 357(a) now provides that the assumption of a liability[3] by a transferee corporation in a Section 351 exchange (and several other transactions to be studied later) will neither constitute boot nor prevent the exchange from qualifying under Section 351. Rather than treating the debt relief as boot, the Code postpones the recognition of any gain attributable to the transferred liabilities. This deferral is accomplished by Section 358(d), which reduces the basis in the stock received in the exchange by treating the relieved liabilities as "money received" by the transferor for purposes of determining the shareholder's basis.

Section 357 is subject to two exceptions. The first (Section 357(b)) prevents abuse and the second (Section 357(c)) avoids the tax taboo of a negative basis. Under the Section 357(b) "tax avoidance" exception, the assumption of a liability is treated as boot if the taxpayer's "principal purpose" in transferring the liability was the avoidance of federal income taxes or was not a bona fide business purpose. This essentially factual determination is made after "taking into consideration the nature of the liability and the circumstances in the light of which the arrangement for the assumption or acquisition was made."[4] If an improper purpose exists, all the relieved liabilities, not merely the evil debts, are treated as boot.[5] Section 357(b) was designed to prevent taxpayers from transferring personal obligations to a newly formed corporation or from achieving a "bail out without boot" by borrowing against property on the eve of incorporation and then transferring the encumbered asset to the corporation. Perhaps because the rule is more draconian than necessary, it has been sparingly applied.[6]

The purpose of the second exception is more technical. Section 357(c) provides that if the sum of the liabilities assumed by the corporation exceed

---

3. A recourse liability is treated as "assumed" if, based on all the facts and circumstances, the transferee has agreed to, and is expected to, satisfy the liability, whether or not the transferor has been relieved of the liability. A nonrecourse liability is generally treated as having been assumed by any transferee who takes an asset subject to the liability. I.R.C. § 357(d)(1).

4. I.R.C. § 357(b)(1). In evaluating whether the business purpose is bona fide, the regulations require both the transferor and the corporation to demonstrate a *"corporate* business reason" (emphasis added) for the assumption of the liabilities when they report a Section 351 transaction on their income tax returns. Reg. § 1.351–3(a)(6), –3(b)(7).

5. Reg. § 1.357–1(c).

6. Section 357(b) is accompanied by an odd burden of proof rule providing that in "any suit" where the taxpayer has the burden of proving the absence of an improper purpose, that burden shall not be met unless the taxpayer "sustains such burden by the clear preponderance of the evidence." I.R.C. § 357(b)(2). This standard adds little to the normal burden of proof imposed in tax litigation and has largely been ignored by the courts.

the aggregate adjusted bases of the properties transferred by a particular transferor,[7] the excess shall be considered as gain from the sale or exchange of the property.[8] A simple illustration explains the need for this exception. Assume our friend, A, forms Venture, Inc. by transferring a building with an adjusted basis of $30, a fair market value of $100 and an outstanding mortgage of $55. In exchange, Venture issues common stock with a value of $45 and takes the building subject to the $55 mortgage. If Section 357(a) applied, without more, A would recognize no gain on the exchange, but pause to consider his basis in the stock under Section 358. It would be $30 (the basis of the building), less $55 (the liability, treated as boot for basis purposes under Section 358(d)), or a *minus* $25. Although tax scholars have debated the issue, the Code abhors a negative basis.[9] Section 357(c) conveniently avoids that taboo by requiring A to recognize $25 gain (the excess of the $55 liability over his $30 adjusted basis). A's basis then becomes zero, and the Code is not further complicated by the mysteries of algebra.

Section 357(c) is itself subject to an exception. Under general tax principles, a taxpayer who is relieved of a liability that would be deductible if paid directly by the taxpayer does not recognize gain if the debt is discharged because any potential income would be offset by a corresponding deduction upon payment.[10] For example, a lender's discharge of a borrower's $1,000 interest expense on a home mortgage is economically equivalent to the lender's transfer of $1,000 cash to the borrower (gross income) and a retransfer of $1,000 cash as interest by the borrower to the lender (offsetting deduction). Taken together, these transactions should not result in any net income to the borrower.[11] In keeping with this approach, Section 357(c)(3) excludes from the term "liabilities," for purposes of determining the excess of liabilities over basis, any obligation that would give rise to a deduction if it had been paid by the transferor[12] or which would be

---

7. Section 357(c) is applied on a transferor-by-transferor basis. Rev.Rul. 66–142, 1966–2 C.B. 66.

8. According to the regulations, the character of the Section 357(c) gain is determined by allocating the gain among the transferred assets in proportion to their respective fair market values. Reg. § 1.357–2(a). As the problems illustrate, this approach is anomalous insofar as it may require an allocation of gain to an asset with no realized gain.

9. For a contrary view on the viability of a negative basis, see Cooper, "Negative Basis," 75 Harv.L.Rev. 1352 (1962).

10. See I.R.C. § 108(e)(2), which provides that no income shall be realized from the discharge of indebtedness to the extent the payment of the liability would have given rise to a deduction.

11. Cf. I.R.C. § 7872. The example assumes that the interest is deductible "qualified residence interest" under Section 163(h).

12. Excepted from this exception are obligations which, when incurred, resulted in the creation of, or an increase in, the basis of any property—e.g., obligations to pay for small tools purchased on credit. I.R.C. § 357(c)(3)(B). To illustrate, assume cash method Proprietor ("P") buys $100 of small tools on credit, promising to pay the seller in two months. Pending payment of the obligation, P has a $100 basis in the tools (P's cost). One month later, P transfers the tools and the related obligation to a new corporation in a Section 351 transaction. The obligation is appropriately treated as a "liability" for purposes of Section 357(c)—but not to worry because the amount of that liability is offset by P's basis in the transferred tools. In comparison, contingent liabilities that have

described in Section 736(a).[13] These same types of obligations also are not treated as "liabilities" for purposes of determining the basis of the stock received by the transferor under Section 358.[14]

The origin of this exception is best understood by looking back to the difficulties encountered by cash basis proprietors who incorporated a going business prior to the enactment of Section 357(c)(3). Consider the plight of Accountant ("A"), a cash basis taxpayer whose sole proprietorship consisted of the following assets and liabilities:

Assets	Adj. Basis	F.M.V.
Cash	$100	$100
Accounts Receivable	0	200
Equipment	50	250
	$150	$550
Liabilities		
Accounts payable		$400

Assume A incorporates his business by transferring all the assets to Newco in exchange for $150 of Newco stock and Newco's assumption of the $400 accounts payable. If the payables are "liabilities" for purposes of Section 357(c)(1), A recognizes $250 gain—the excess of the $400 liabilities assumed by Newco over the $150 aggregate adjusted basis of the assets transferred to the corporation. A's adjusted basis in the Newco stock would be zero.[15]

The harshness of this result becomes apparent when it is compared to an economically equivalent transaction. Suppose, for example, that A had retained the payables, transferred the $550 in assets to Newco in exchange for $150 of Newco stock and $400 cash and then used the cash to pay his creditors. Although A would recognize $400 gain under Section 351(b), that gain would be offset by the $400 deduction that A would receive on payment of the payables. Alternatively, A could have avoided any gain simply by retaining sufficient assets to pay the deductible accounts payable.

not yet given rise to a capital expenditure (and thus have not created or increased basis) are not included in determining the amount of liabilities assumed by the transferee. See Rev. Rul. 95–74, infra, p. 104.

13. Section 736(a) applies to payments made to a retiring partner or to a deceased partner's successor in interest in liquidation of that partner's interest in the partnership. See Chapter 8, supra. Section 736(a) payments, like accounts payable of a cash basis taxpayer, have the effect of reducing gross income when paid and thus are appropriately excluded from "liabilities" for purposes of Section 357(c) and 358(d).

14. I.R.C. § 358(d)(2). But see I.R.C. § 358(h), a specialized anti-abuse rule, which

generally provides that if the basis of stock received in a Section 351 transaction exceeds its fair market value, that basis must be stepped down (but not below fair market value) by the amount of any liabilities not taken into account under Section 358(d) (e.g., "deductible" or contingent liabilities that do not result in a basis reduction) and assumed by the corporation.

15. A's basis is derived as follows: $150 (basis in assets transferred by A) minus $400 (liabilities assumed by Newco, treated as "money received" for basis purposes) plus $250 (gain recognized by A). I.R.C. § 358(a)(1), (d)(1).

As these examples illustrate, the inclusion of accounts payable as "liabilities" for purposes of Section 357(c) often caused cash basis taxpayers to recognize more gain by having their obligations assumed than they would have recognized if they received equivalent cash boot or withheld sufficient assets to pay the liabilities. Several courts attempted to cure this anomaly by excluding certain deductible liabilities from the scope of Section 357(c), but the cases lacked a uniform rationale.[16] To resolve these ambiguities and halt the litigation, Congress amended Sections 357(c) and 358(d) to provide that deductible obligations no longer would be considered "liabilities" for these limited purposes. Congress also indicated that this exception was not intended to affect either the transferee corporation's tax treatment of the excluded liabilities or the definition of liabilities for any other provision of the Code, including Sections 357(a) and 357(b).[17]

If all else fails, a transferor can avoid recognizing Section 357(c) gain simply by contributing additional cash to the corporation in an amount equal to the excess of assumed liabilities over the aggregate adjusted basis of the other contributed assets. A more intriguing question is whether a cash poor transferor can eliminate the gain by remaining personally liable on the assumed debts or by transferring a personal note to the corporation for the Section 357(c) excess. The courts are confused by these questions, as evidenced by the *Peracchi* case and the Note following.

Peracchi v. Commissioner

United States Court of Appeals, Ninth Circuit, 1998.
143 F.3d 487.

■ KOZINSKI, CIRCUIT JUDGE:

We must unscramble a Rubik's Cube of corporate tax law to determine the basis of a note contributed by a taxpayer to his wholly-owned corporation.

The Transaction

The taxpayer, Donald Peracchi, needed to contribute additional capital to his closely-held corporation (NAC) to comply with Nevada's minimum premium-to-asset ratio for insurance companies. Peracchi contributed two parcels of real estate. The parcels were encumbered with liabilities which together exceeded Peracchi's total basis in the properties by more than half a million dollars. As we discuss in detail below, under section 357(c),

---

16. See Focht v. Commissioner, 68 T.C. 223 (1977)("liability" under Sections 357(c) and 358(d) limited to obligations which, if transferred, cause gain recognition under *Crane* case); Thatcher v. Commissioner, 61 T.C. 28 (1973), reversed in part and affirmed in part 533 F.2d 1114 (9th Cir.1976)(analyze transaction as "ordinary exchange" and give transferor constructive deduction for accounts payable discharged by corporation in same year as transfer to the extent of the lesser of accounts receivable or Section 357(c) gain); Bongiovanni v. Commissioner, 470 F.2d 921 (2d Cir.1972)(Section 357(c) only applies to "tax liabilities"—i.e., liens, mortgages, etc.).

17. Staff of Joint Committee on Taxation, General Explanation of the Revenue Act of 1978, 96th Cong., 1st Sess. 219–220 (1979).

contributing property with liabilities in excess of basis can trigger immediate recognition of gain in the amount of the excess. In an effort to avoid this, Peracchi also executed a promissory note, promising to pay NAC $1,060,000 over a term of ten years at 11% interest. Peracchi maintains that the note has a basis equal to its face amount, thereby making his total basis in the property contributed greater than the total liabilities. If this is so, he will have extracted himself from the quicksand of section 357(c) and owe no immediate tax on the transfer of property to NAC. The IRS, though, maintains that (1) the note is not genuine indebtedness and should be treated as an unenforceable gift; and (2) even if the note is genuine, it does not increase Peracchi's basis in the property contributed.

The parties are not splitting hairs: Peracchi claims the basis of the note is $1,060,000, its face value, while the IRS argues that the note has a basis of zero. If Peracchi is right, he pays no immediate tax on the half a million dollars by which the debts on the land he contributed exceed his basis in the land; if the IRS is right, the note becomes irrelevant for tax purposes and Peracchi must recognize an immediate gain on the half million. The fact that the IRS and Peracchi are so far apart suggests they are looking at the transaction through different colored lenses. To figure out whether Peracchi's lens is rose-tinted or clear, it is useful to take a guided tour of sections 351 and 357 and the tax law principles undergirding them.

Into the Lobster Pot: Section 351[2]

The Code tries to make organizing a corporation pain-free from a tax point of view. A capital contribution is, in tax lingo, a "nonrecognition" event: A shareholder can generally contribute capital without recognizing gain on the exchange.[3] It's merely a change in the form of ownership, like moving a billfold from one pocket to another. See I.R.C. § 351. So long as the shareholders contributing the property remain in control of the corporation after the exchange, section 351 applies: It doesn't matter if the capital contribution occurs at the creation of the corporation or if-as here-

---

2. "Decisions to embrace the corporate form of organization should be carefully considered, since a corporation is like a lobster pot: easy to enter, difficult to live in, and painful to get out of." Boris I. Bittker & James S. Eustice, Federal Income Taxation of Corporations and Shareholders ¶ 2.01[3] (6th ed.1997) (footnotes omitted) (hereinafter Bittker & Eustice).

3. The income tax often operates as a tax on transactions. Regardless of when a taxpayer realizes accretions to his economic wealth, income is usually recognized when a measuring event occurs, such as receipt of a paycheck or the "sale or exchange" of property. But the Code exempts certain sales and

exchanges from recognition, such as when a sale is involuntary, or merely a change in the form of ownership, or otherwise warrants nonrecognition. See generally Boris I. Bittker & Lawrence Lokken, Federal Taxation of Income, Estates and Gifts ¶ 44.1.1 (2d ed. 1990) ("The Code contains numerous nonrecognition provisions covering a wide range of transactions that have little in common except that they have elicited a legislative judgment that the taxpayer's realized gain or loss should not be taxed or deducted when the exchange or other event occurs.") Congress has not deemed the organization of a corporation an appropriate event for recognition of income.

the company is already up and running. The baseline is that Peracchi may contribute property to NAC without recognizing gain on the exchange.

Gain Deferral: Section 358(a)

Peracchi contributed capital to NAC in the form of real property and a promissory note. Corporations may be funded with any kind of asset, such as equipment, real estate, intellectual property, contracts, leaseholds, securities or letters of credit. The tax consequences can get a little complicated because a shareholder's basis in the property contributed often differs from its fair market value. The general rule is that an asset's basis is equal to its "cost." See I.R.C. § 1012. But when a shareholder like Peracchi contributes property to a corporation in a nonrecognition transaction, a cost basis does not preserve the unrecognized gain. Rather than take a basis equal to the fair market value of the property exchanged, the shareholder must substitute the basis of that property for what would otherwise be the cost basis of the stock. This preserves the gain for recognition at a later day: The gain is built into the shareholder's new basis in the stock, and he will recognize income when he disposes of the stock.

The fact that gain is deferred rather than extinguished doesn't diminish the importance of questions relating to basis and the timing of recognition. In tax, as in comedy, timing matters. Most taxpayers would much prefer to pay tax on contributed property years later—when they sell their stock—rather than when they contribute the property. Thus what Peracchi is seeking here is gain deferral: He wants the gain to be recognized only when he disposes of some or all of his stock.

Continuity of Investment: Boot and Section 351(b)

Continuity of investment is the cornerstone of nonrecognition under section 351. Nonrecognition assumes that a capital contribution amounts to nothing more than a nominal change in the form of ownership; in substance the shareholder's investment in the property continues. But a capital contribution can sometimes allow a shareholder to partially terminate his investment in an asset or group of assets. For example, when a shareholder receives cash or other property in addition to stock, receipt of that property reflects a partial termination of investment in the business. The shareholder may invest that money in a wholly unrelated business, or spend it just like any other form of personal income. To the extent a section 351 transaction resembles an ordinary sale, the nonrecognition rationale falls apart.

Thus the central exception to nonrecognition for section 351 transactions comes into play when the taxpayer receives "boot"—money or property other than stock in the corporation-in exchange for the property contributed. See I.R.C. § 351(b). Boot is recognized as taxable income because it represents a partial cashing out. It's as if the taxpayer contributed part of the property to the corporation in exchange for stock, and sold part of the property for cash. Only the part exchanged for stock represents a continuation of investment; the part sold for cash is properly recognized as yielding income, just as if the taxpayer had sold the property to a third party.

Peracchi did not receive boot in return for the property he contributed. But that doesn't end the inquiry: We must consider whether Peracchi has cashed out in some other way which would warrant treating part of the transaction as taxable boot.

Assumption of Liabilities: Section 357(a)

The property Peracchi contributed to NAC was encumbered by liabilities. Contribution of leveraged property makes things trickier from a tax perspective. When a shareholder contributes property encumbered by debt, the corporation usually assumes the debt. And the Code normally treats discharging a liability the same as receiving money: The taxpayer improves his economic position by the same amount either way. See I.R.C. § 61(a)(12). NAC's assumption of the liabilities attached to Peracchi's property therefore could theoretically be viewed as the receipt of money, which would be taxable boot. See United States v. Hendler, 303 U.S. 564, 58 S.Ct. 655, 82 L.Ed. 1018 (1938).

The Code takes a different tack. Requiring shareholders like Peracchi to recognize gain any time a corporation assumes a liability in connection with a capital contribution would greatly diminish the nonrecognition benefit section 351 is meant to confer. Section 357(a) thus takes a lenient view of the assumption of liability: A shareholder engaging in a section 351 transaction does not have to treat the assumption of liability as boot, even if the corporation assumes his obligation to pay. See I.R.C. § 357(a).

This nonrecognition does not mean that the potential gain disappears. Once again, the basis provisions kick in to reflect the transfer of gain from the shareholder to the corporation: The shareholder's substitute basis in the stock received is decreased by the amount of the liability assumed by the corporation. See I.R.C. § 358(d), (a). The adjustment preserves the gain for recognition when the shareholder sells his stock in the company, since his taxable gain will be the difference between the (new lower) basis and the sale price of the stock.

Sasquatch and The Negative Basis Problem: Section 357(c)

Highly leveraged property presents a peculiar problem in the section 351 context. Suppose a shareholder organizes a corporation and contributes as its only asset a building with a basis of $50, a fair market value of $100, and mortgage debt of $90. Section 351 says that the shareholder does not recognize any gain on the transaction. Under section 358, the shareholder takes a substitute basis of $50 in the stock, then adjusts it downward under section 357 by $90 to reflect the assumption of liability. This leaves him with a basis of minus $40. A negative basis properly preserves the gain built into the property: If the shareholder turns around and sells the stock the next day for $10 (the difference between the fair market value and the debt), he would face $50 in gain, the same amount as if he sold the property without first encasing it in a corporate shell.[8]

---

8. If the taxpayer sells the property outright, his amount realized includes the full amount of the mortgage debt, see Crane v. Commissioner, 331 U.S. 1, 14, 67 S.Ct.

But skeptics say that negative basis, like Bigfoot, doesn't exist. Compare Easson v. Commissioner, 33 T.C. 963, 970, 1960 WL 1347 (1960) (there's no such thing as a negative basis) with Easson v. Commissioner, 294 F.2d 653, 657–58 (9th Cir.1961) (yes, Virginia, there is a negative basis). Basis normally operates as a cost recovery system: Depreciation deductions reduce basis, and when basis hits zero, the property cannot be depreciated farther. At a more basic level, it seems incongruous to attribute a negative value to a figure that normally represents one's investment in an asset. Some commentators nevertheless argue that when basis operates merely to measure potential gain (as it does here), allowing negative basis may be perfectly appropriate and consistent with the tax policy underlying nonrecognition transactions. See, e.g., J. Clifton Fleming, Jr., The Highly Avoidable Section 357(c): A Case Study in Traps for the Unwary and Some Positive Thoughts About Negative Basis, 16 J. Corp. L. 1, 27–30 (1990). Whatever the merits of this debate, it seems that section 357(c) was enacted to eliminate the possibility of negative basis. See George Cooper, Negative Basis, 75 Harv. L.Rev. 1352, 1360 (1962).

Section 357(c) prevents negative basis by forcing a shareholder to recognize gain to the extent liabilities exceed basis. Thus, if a shareholder contributes a building with a basis of $50 and liabilities of $90, he does not receive stock with a basis of minus $40. Instead, he takes a basis of zero and must recognize a $40 gain.

Peracchi sought to contribute two parcels of real property to NAC in a section 351 transaction. Standing alone the contribution would have run afoul of section 357(c): The property he wanted to contribute had liabilities in excess of basis, and Peracchi would have had to recognize gain to the extent of the excess, or $566,807 * * *.[10]

The Grift: Boosting Basis with a Promissory Note

Peracchi tried to dig himself out of this tax hole by contributing a personal note with a face amount of $1,060,000 along with the real property. Peracchi maintains that the note has a basis in his hands equal to its face value. If he's right, we must add the basis of the note to the basis of the real property. Taken together, the aggregate basis in the property contributed would exceed the aggregate liabilities [including the note at face value, the aggregate basis of the contributed properties would be $2,041,406 and would exceed the $1,548,213 of aggregate liabilities, Eds.].

Under Peracchi's theory, then, the aggregate liabilities no longer exceed the aggregate basis, and section 357(c) no longer triggers any gain. The government argues, however, that the note has a zero basis. If so, the

1047, 91 L.Ed. 1301 (1947), and the result is as follows: Amount realized ($10 cash + $90 debt)—$50 Basis = $50 gain.

10. Peracchi remained personally liable on the debts encumbering the property transferred to NAC. NAC took the property subject to the debts, however, which is enough to trigger gain under the plain language of section 357(c). See Owen v. Commissioner, 881 F.2d 832, 835–36 (9th Cir.1989).

note would not affect the tax consequences of the transaction, and Peracchi's $566,807 in gain would be taxable immediately.[11]

Are Promises Truly Free?

Which brings us (phew!) to the issue before us: Does Peracchi's note have a basis in Peracchi's hands for purposes of section 357(c)?[12] The language of the Code gives us little to work with. The logical place to start is with the definition of basis. Section 1012 provides that "[t]he basis of property shall be the cost of such property...." But "cost" is nowhere defined. What does it cost Peracchi to write the note and contribute it to his corporation? The IRS argues tersely that the "taxpayers in the instant case incurred no cost in issuing their own note to NAC, so their basis in the note was zero." * * * See Alderman v. Commissioner, 55 T.C. 662, 665, 1971 WL 2488 (1971); Rev. Rul. 68–629, 1968–2 C.B. 154, 155.[13] Building on this premise, the IRS makes Peracchi out to be a grifter: He holds an unenforceable promise to pay himself money, since the corporation will not collect on it unless he says so.

It's true that all Peracchi did was make out a promise to pay on a piece of paper, mark it in the corporate minutes and enter it on the corporate books. It is also true that nothing will cause the corporation to enforce the note against Peracchi so long as Peracchi remains in control. But the IRS ignores the possibility that NAC may go bankrupt, an event that would suddenly make the note highly significant. Peracchi and NAC are separated by the corporate form, and this gossamer curtain makes a difference in the shell game of C Corp organization and reorganization. Contributing the note puts a million dollar nut within the corporate shell, exposing Peracchi to the cruel nutcracker of corporate creditors in the event NAC goes bankrupt. And it does so to the tune of $1,060,000, the full face amount of the note. Without the note, no matter how deeply the corporation went into debt, creditors could not reach Peracchi's personal assets. With the note on the books, however, creditors can reach into Peracchi's pocket by enforcing the note as an unliquidated asset of the corporation.

---

11. The government does not dispute that the note and the two parcels of real estate were contributed as part of the same transaction for purposes of section 351. Their bases must therefore be aggregated for purposes of section 357(c).

12. Peracchi owned all the voting stock of NAC both before and after the exchange, so the control requirement of section 351 is satisfied. Peracchi received no boot (such as cash or securities) which would qualify as "money or other property" and trigger recognition under 351(b) alone. Peracchi did not receive any stock in return for the property contributed, so it could be argued that the exchange was not "solely in exchange for stock" as required by section 351. Courts have consistently recognized, however, that issuing stock in this situation would be a

meaningless gesture: Because Peracchi is the sole shareholder of NAC, issuing additional stock would not affect his economic position relative to other shareholders. See, e.g., Jackson v. Commissioner, 708 F.2d 1402, 1405 (9th Cir.1983).

13. We would face a different case had the Treasury promulgated a regulation interpreting section 357(c). A revenue ruling is entitled to some deference as the stated litigating position of the agency which enforces the tax code, but not nearly as much as a regulation. Ruling 68–629 offers no rationale, let alone a reasonable one, for its holding that it costs a taxpayer nothing to write a promissory note, and thus deserves little weight.

The key to solving this puzzle, then, is to ask whether bankruptcy is significant enough a contingency to confer substantial economic effect on this transaction. If the risk of bankruptcy is important enough to be recognized, Peracchi should get basis in the note: He will have increased his exposure to the risks of the business-and thus his economic investment in NAC-by $1,060,000. If bankruptcy is so remote that there is no realistic possibility it will ever occur, we can ignore the potential economic effect of the note as speculative and treat it as merely an unenforceable promise to contribute capital in the future.

When the question is posed this way, the answer is clear. Peracchi's obligation on the note was not conditioned on NAC's remaining solvent. It represents a new and substantial increase in Peracchi's investment in the corporation.[14] The Code seems to recognize that economic exposure of the shareholder is the ultimate measuring rod of a shareholder's investment. Cf. I.R.C. § 465 (at-risk rules for partnership investments). Peracchi therefore is entitled to a step-up in basis to the extent he will be subjected to economic loss if the underlying investment turns unprofitable. Cf. HGA Cinema Trust v. Commissioner, 950 F.2d 1357, 1363 (7th Cir.1991) (examining effect of bankruptcy to determine whether long-term note contributed by partner could be included in basis). See also Treas. Reg. § 1.704–1(b)(2)(ii)(c)(1) (recognizing economic effect of promissory note contributed by partner for purposes of partner's obligation to restore deficit capital account).

The economics of the transaction also support Peracchi's view of the matter. The transaction here does not differ substantively from others that would certainly give Peracchi a boost in basis. For example, Peracchi could have borrowed $1 million from a bank and contributed the cash to NAC along with the properties. Because cash has a basis equal to face value, Peracchi would not have faced any section 357(c) gain. NAC could then have purchased the note from the bank for $1 million which, assuming the bank's original assessment of Peracchi's creditworthiness was accurate, would be the fair market value of the note. In the end the corporation would hold a million dollar note from Peracchi-just like it does now-and Peracchi would face no section 357(c) gain.[15] The only economic difference

14. We confine our holding to a case such as this where the note is contributed to an operating business which is subject to a non-trivial risk of bankruptcy or receivership. NAC is not, for example, a shell corporation or a passive investment company; Peracchi got into this mess in the first place because NAC was in financial trouble and needed more assets to meet Nevada's minimum premium-to-asset ratio for insurance companies.

15. In a similar vein, Peracchi could have first swapped promissory notes with a third party. Assuming the bona fides of each note, Peracchi would take a cost basis in the third party note equal to the face value of the note he gave up. Peracchi could then contribute the third party note to NAC, and (thanks to the added basis) avoid any section 357(c) gain. NAC could then close the circle by giving the third party note back to the third party in exchange for Peracchi's note, leaving Peracchi and NAC in exactly the same position they occupy now. The IRS might attack these maneuvers as step transactions, but that would beg the question: Does the contribution of a shareholder's note to his wholly-owned corporation have any real economic effect, or is it just so much window dressing? If the debt has real economic effect, it

between the transaction just described and the transaction Peracchi actual-ly engaged in is the additional costs that would accompany getting a loan from the bank. Peracchi incurs a "cost" of $1 million when he promises to pay the note to the bank; the cost is not diminished here by the fact that the transferor controls the initial transferee. The experts seem to agree: "Section 357(c) can be avoided by a transfer of enough cash to eliminate any excess of liabilities over basis; and since a note given by a solvent obligor in purchasing property is routinely treated as the equivalent of cash in determining the basis of the property, it seems reasonable to give it the same treatment in determining the basis of the property transferred in a s 351 exchange." Bittker & Eustice ¶ 3.06[4][b].

We are aware of the mischief that can result when taxpayers are permitted to calculate basis in excess of their true economic investment. See Commissioner v. Tufts, 461 U.S. 300, 103 S.Ct. 1826, 75 L.Ed.2d 863 (1983). For two reasons, however, we do not believe our holding will have such pernicious effects. First, and most significantly, by increasing the taxpayer's personal exposure, the contribution of a valid, unconditional promissory note has substantial economic effects which reflect his true economic investment in the enterprise. The main problem with attributing basis to nonrecourse debt financing is that the tax benefits enjoyed as a result of increased basis do not reflect the true economic risk. Here Peracchi will have to pay the full amount of the note with after-tax dollars if NAC's economic situation heads south. Second, the tax treatment of nonrecourse debt primarily creates problems in the partnership context, where the entity's loss deductions (resulting from depreciation based on basis inflated above and beyond the taxpayer's true economic investment) can be passed through to the taxpayer. It is the pass-through of losses that makes artificial increases in equity interests of particular concern. See, e.g., Levy v. Commissioner, 732 F.2d 1435, 1437 (9th Cir.1984). We don't have to tread quite so lightly in the C Corp context, since a C Corp doesn't funnel losses to the shareholder.[16]

We find further support for Peracchi's view by looking at the alterna-tive: What would happen if the note had a zero basis? The IRS points out that the basis of the note in the hands of the corporation is the same as it was in the hands of the taxpayer. Accordingly, if the note has a zero basis for Peracchi, so too for NAC. See I.R.C. § 362(a).[17] But what happens if

shouldn't matter how the shareholder struc-tures the transaction. The only substantive difference between the avoidance techniques just discussed-swapping notes or borrowing from a third party-and the case here is the valuation role implicitly performed by the third party. A bank would not give Peracchi the face value of the note unless his credit warranted it, while we have no assurance that NAC wouldn't do so. We readily ac-knowledge that our assumptions fall apart if the shareholder isn't creditworthy. Here, the government has stipulated that Peracchi's net worth far exceeds the value of the note, so creditworthiness is not at issue. But we limit our holding to cases where the note is in fact worth approximately its face value.

16. Our holding therefore does not ex-tend to the partnership or S Corp context.

17. But see Lessinger v. Commissioner, 872 F.2d 519 (2d Cir.1989). In Lessinger, the Second Circuit analyzed a similar transac-tion. It agreed with the IRS's (faulty) premise that the note had a zero basis in the taxpay-

NAC—perhaps facing the threat of an involuntary petition for bankruptcy—turns around and sells Peracchi's note to a third party for its fair market value? According to the IRS's theory, NAC would take a carryover basis of zero in the note and would have to recognize $1,060,000 in phantom gain on the subsequent exchange, even though the note did not appreciate in value one bit. That can't be the right result.

Accordingly, we hold that Peracchi has a basis of $1,060,000 in the note he wrote to NAC. The aggregate basis exceeds the liabilities of the properties transferred to NAC under section 351, and Peracchi need not recognize any section 357(c) gain.

Genuine Indebtedness or Sham?

The Tax Court never reached the issue of Peracchi's basis in the note. Instead, it ruled for the Commissioner on the ground that the note is not genuine indebtedness. The court emphasized two facts which it believed supported the view that the note is a sham: (1) NAC's decision whether to collect on the note is wholly controlled by Peracchi and (2) Peracchi missed the first two years of payments, yet NAC did not accelerate the debt. These facts certainly do suggest that Peracchi paid imperfect attention to his obligations under the note, as frequently happens when debtor and creditor are under common control. But we believe the proper way to approach the genuine indebtedness question is to look at the face of the note and consider whether Peracchi's legal obligation is illusory. And it is not. First, the note's bona fides are adequate: The IRS has stipulated that Peracchi is creditworthy and likely to have the funds to pay the note; the note bears a market rate of interest commensurate with his creditworthiness; the note has a fixed term. Second, the IRS does not argue that the value of the note is anything other than its face value; nothing in the record suggests NAC couldn't borrow against the note to raise cash. Lastly, the note is fully transferable and enforceable by third parties, such as hostile creditors. On the basis of these facts we hold that the note is an ordinary, negotiable, recourse obligation which must be treated as genuine debt for tax purposes. See Sacks v. Commissioner, 69 F.3d 982, 989 (9th Cir.1995).

The IRS argues that the note is nevertheless a sham because it was executed simply to avoid tax. Tax avoidance is a valid concern in this context; section 357(a) does provide the opportunity for a bailout transaction of sorts. For example, a taxpayer with an unencumbered building he wants to sell could take out a nonrecourse mortgage, pocket the proceeds,

er's hands. But then, brushing aside the language of section 362(a), the court concluded that the note had a basis in the corporation's hands equal to its face value. The court held that this was enough to dispel any section 357(c) gain to the taxpayer, proving that two wrongs sometimes do add up to a right. We agree with the IRS that Lessinger's approach is untenable. Section 357(c) contemplates measuring basis of the property contributed in the hands of the taxpayer, not the corpora- tion. Section 357 appears in the midst of the Code sections dealing with the effect of capital contributions on the shareholder; sections 361 et seq., on the other hand, deal with the effect on a corporation, and section 362 defines the basis of property contributed in the hands of the corporation. Because we hold that the note has a face value basis to the shareholder for purposes of section 357(c), however, we reach the same result as Lessinger.

and contribute the property to a newly organized corporation. Although the gain would be preserved for later recognition, the taxpayer would have partially cashed out his economic investment in the property: By taking out a nonrecourse mortgage, the economic risk of loss would be transferred to the lender. Section 357(b) addresses this sort of bailout by requiring the recognition of gain if the transaction lacks a business purpose.

Peracchi's capital contribution is not a bailout. Peracchi contributed the buildings to NAC because the company needed additional capital, and the contribution of the note was part of that transaction. The IRS, in fact, stipulated that the contribution had a business purpose. Bailout potential exists regardless of whether the taxpayer contributes a note along with the property; section 357(b), not 357(c), is the sword the Service must use to attack bailout transactions.

Is the note a gift?

The IRS also offers a more refined version of the sham transaction argument: The note was really a gift to NAC because Peracchi did not receive any consideration from the exchange. The IRS admits that the tax deferral resulting from avoiding section 357(c) gain is a benefit to Peracchi. It argues, nonetheless, that this is not enough to make the bargain enforceable because it works no detriment to NAC. This argument would classify all contributions of capital as gifts. A corporation never gives up anything explicitly when it accepts a capital contribution. Instead, the corporation implicitly promises to put the money to good use, and its directors and officers undertake the fiduciary duty to generate the highest possible return on the investment. The contribution of the note was no more a gift than the contribution of $1 million in cash to the corporation would have been; it does not reflect the "detached and disinterested generosity" which characterizes a gift for purposes of federal income taxation. See Commissioner v. Duberstein, 363 U.S. 278, 285, 80 S.Ct. 1190, 4 L.Ed.2d 1218 (1960).

The Aftermath

We take a final look at the result to make sure we have not placed our stamp of approval on some sort of exotic tax shelter. We hold that Peracchi is entitled to a step up in basis for the face value of the note, just as if he contributed cash to the corporation. See I.R.C. § 358. If Peracchi does in fact keep his promise and pay off the note with after tax dollars, the tax result is perfectly appropriate: NAC receives cash, and the increase in basis Peracchi took for the original contribution is justified. Peracchi has less potential gain, but he paid for it in real dollars.

But what if, as the IRS fears, NAC never does enforce the note? If NAC goes bankrupt, the note will be an asset of the estate enforceable for the benefit of creditors, and Peracchi will eventually be forced to pay in after tax dollars. Peracchi will undoubtedly have worked the deferral mechanism of section 351 to his advantage, but this is not inappropriate where the taxpayer is on the hook in both form and substance for enough cash to offset the excess of liabilities over basis. By increasing his personal exposure to the creditors of NAC, Peracchi has increased his economic investment in the corporation, and a corresponding increase in basis is wholly justified.[20]

Conclusion

We hold that Peracchi has a basis of $1,060,000 in the note, its face value. As such, the aggregate liabilities of the property contributed to NAC do not exceed its basis, and Peracchi does not recognize any § 357(c) gain. The decision of the Tax Court is REVERSED. The case is remanded for entry of judgment in favor of Peracchi.

■ FERNANDEZ, CIRCUIT JUDGE, DISSENTING:

Is there something that a taxpayer, who has borrowed hundreds of thousands of dollars more than his basis in his property, can do to avoid taxation when he transfers the property? Yes, says Peracchi, because by using a very clever argument he can avoid the strictures of 26 U.S.C. § 357(c). He need only make a promise to pay by giving a "good," though unsecured, promissory note to his corporation when he transfers the property to it. That is true even though the property remains subject to the encumbrances. How can that be? Well, by preparing a promissory note the taxpayer simply creates basis without cost to himself. * * * Thus he can extract a large part of the value of the property, pocket the funds, use them, divest himself of the property, and pay the tax another day, if ever at all.

But as with all magical solutions, the taxpayer must know the proper incantations and make the correct movements. He cannot just transfer the property to the corporation and promise, or be obligated, to pay off the encumbrances. That would not change the fact that the property was still subject to those encumbrances. According to Peracchi, the thaumaturgy that will save him from taxes proceeds in two simple steps. He must first prepare a ritualistic writing—an unsecured promissory note in an amount equal to or more than the excess of the encumbrances over the basis. He must then give that writing to his corporation. That is all.[1] But is not that just a "promise to pay," which "does not represent the paying out or reduction of assets?" Don E. Williams Co. v. Commissioner, 429 U.S. 569, 583, 97 S.Ct. 850, 858, 51 L.Ed.2d 48 (1977). Never mind, he says. He has nonetheless increased the total basis of the property transferred and avoided the tax. I understand the temptation to embrace that argument, but I see no real support for it in the law.

20. What happens if NAC does not go bankrupt, but merely writes off the note instead? Peracchi would then face discharge of indebtedness income to the tune of $1,060,000. This would put Peracchi in a worse position than when he started, since discharge of indebtedness is normally treated as ordinary income. Peracchi, having increased his basis in the stock of the corporation by $1,060,000 would receive a capital loss (or less capital gain) to that extent. But the shift in character of the income will normally work to the disadvantage of a taxpayer in Peracchi's situation.

1. What is even better, he need not even make payments on the note until after the IRS catches up with him. I, by the way, am dubious about the proposition that the Tax Court clearly erred when it held that the note was not even a genuine indebtedness.

Peracchi says a lot about economic realities. I see nothing real about that maneuver. I see, rather, a bit of sortilege that would have made Merlin envious. The taxpayer has created something—basis—out of nothing.

Thus, I respectfully dissent.

NOTE

An Alternative Rationale. As noted in Judge Kozinski's opinion in *Peracchi*, the Second Circuit reached a similar result in Lessinger v. Commissioner,[1] but its rationale was different. The Second Circuit concluded that a shareholder's basis in his own note equals its face amount because, necessarily, the note's basis to the corporation was face value. While it may lead to an equitable result, this backwards reasoning is not supported by the Code. The following excerpt from a commentary on *Lessinger* illustrates the court's faulty logic:[2]

> Before turning to the court's application of Section 357(c) to the note—a genuinely intriguing question—one should clear the air about the general question of the basis on which Section 357(c) must be focusing. To say that this is the corporation's basis in the transferred assets is preposterous. If nothing else, such a reading will in many cases be circular. Section 362(a) gives the corporation a carryover basis in the assets received from the shareholder, increased by any gain recognized by the shareholder on the exchange. The classic instance of recognized gain on a Section 351 exchange is under Section 357(c); thus, one cannot determine a corporation's basis in its assets without first determining the shareholder's gain under Section 357(c). To declare, as the Second Circuit did, that the amount of the gain generally turns on the corporation's basis in its assets leads to an endless circle.

> To illustrate, assume a shareholder transfers to a corporation, Blackacre, in which the shareholder has a basis of $30,000, subject to a mortgage of $40,000. To determine the gain under Section 357(c) under the appellate decision in *Lessinger,* one would have to first determine the corporation's basis under Section 362(a). Under the latter section, however, the corporation's basis must reflect the gain under Section 357(c), and thus, one must compute the shareholder's gain in order to determine the corporation's basis. Perhaps the court meant that one should determine the corporation's basis without regard to the debt, or that Section 357(c) looks at different bases depending on whether a shareholder note or

1.   872 F.2d 519 (2d Cir.1989).

2.   Bogdanski, "Shareholder Debt, Corporate Debt: Lessons from *Leavitt* and *Lessinger,*" 16 J.Corp.Tax'n 348, 352–53 (1990). For a competing view, see Quiring, "Section 357(c) and the Elusive Basis of the Issuer's Note," 57 Tax Law. 97 (2003), and for the rebuttal, see Bogdanski, "Section 358 and *Crane*—A Reply to My Critics," 57 Tax Law. 905 (2004). See also Lazar, "*Lessinger, Peracchi*, and the Emperor's New Clothes; Covering a Section 357(c) Deficit with Invisible (or Nonexistent) Property," 58 Tax Law. 41 (2004).

hard assets are being transferred, but these are even more thoroughly incredible stretches of the Code language.

Perhaps the Second Circuit was trying to say that Mr. Lessinger should receive "basis credit" for his own note because of his future obligation to transfer cash to the corporation or its creditors. In other contexts, a taxpayer's acceptance of even a nonrecourse liability on the acquisition of property gives rise to a cost basis that includes the amount of the future obligation.[3] If Mr. Lessinger's liability were genuine and enforceable by the corporation's creditors, as the court concluded, he arguably is as much entitled to basis credit as is the purchaser of property financed with nonrecourse debt.

Effect of Shareholder's Continuing Personal Liability. The courts have been less sympathetic on a closely related question: whether a shareholder's continuing personal liability on debts transferred to a corporation in a Section 351 transaction causes those debts to be excluded for purposes of Section 357(c). The Tax Court has consistently rejected the notion that transferred liabilities are excluded from the Section 357(c) arithmetic if the transferring shareholder remains personally liable for the debt.[4] The Ninth Circuit once appeared to disagree but later had a change of heart. In *Jackson v. Commissioner*,[5] that court held that Section 357(c) did not apply on an incorporation of a partnership where the taxpayer's share of the partnership's liabilities exceeded his adjusted basis in the transferred partnership interest but the taxpayer remained personally liable on the debts. On these facts, the court reasoned that the corporation had not assumed any liabilities and thus the taxpayer did not have any Section 357(c) gain. This result was criticized by courts and commentators,[6] but it is consistent with the Second Circuit's reasoning in *Lessinger* that taxpayers enjoy no economic benefit (and thus no taxable gain) for the excess of transferred liabilities over basis when they retain genuine personal liability on the debts. In a later case, the Ninth Circuit upheld the Tax Court's finding of Section 357(c) gain on a transfer of encumbered equipment to a controlled corporation where the liabilities exceeded the taxpayer's basis even though the transferor had guaranteed the liabilities and remained personally liable following the transfer.[7] Although the court purported to distinguish its earlier *Jackson* holding as not involving property subject to debt, the two decisions are difficult to reconcile.

In a more recent case,[8] the taxpayers, in connection with the incorporation of their family farming business, contributed assets subject to

3. Parker v. Delaney, 186 F.2d 455 (1st Cir.1950). Cf. Crane v. Commissioner, 331 U.S. 1, 67 S.Ct. 1047 (1947); Commissioner v. Tufts, 461 U.S. 300, 103 S.Ct. 1826 (1983).

4. See, e.g., Smith v. Commissioner, 84 T.C. 889 (1985), affirmed, 805 F.2d 1073 (D.C.Cir.1986); Rosen v. Commissioner, 62 T.C. 11 (1974), affirmed in unpublished opinion, 515 F.2d 507 (3d Cir.1975).

5. 708 F.2d 1402 (9th Cir.1983).

6. See, e.g., Estate of Juden v. Commissioner, 865 F.2d 960, 962 (8th Cir.1989); Bogdanski, "Of Debt, Discharge, and Discord": Jackson v. Commissioner, 10 J.Corp.Tax'n 357 (1984).

7. Owen v. Commissioner, 881 F.2d 832 (9th Cir.1989), cert. denied, 493 U.S. 1070, 110 S.Ct. 1113 (1990).

8. Seggerman Farms, Inc. v. Commissioner, 308 F.3d 803 (7th Cir. 2002).

liabilities that exceeded the aggregate adjusted basis of the transferred assets. The taxpayers remained liable as guarantors on the debts. The Seventh Circuit, affirming the Tax Court, held that the taxpayers recognized Section 357(c) gain on the incorporation and, in so holding, followed the line of cases strictly interpreting the statute. Citing *Peracchi* and *Lessinger*, the taxpayers contended that a strict reading of Section 357(c) was based on "outdated precedent" and urged the court to exercise its equitable power to craft a judicial exception to the plain language of the statute. Both the Tax Court and Seventh Circuit declined the invitation to do so and distinguished the pro-taxpayer cases on the ground that personal guaranties of corporate debt are not the same as incurring debt to the corporation. The court reasoned that a guaranty is not an economic outlay but merely a promise to pay in the future if certain events should occur.

The uneasy relationship between owner debt, entity debt and basis is raised in many settings. Similar conceptual questions will resurface with varying results in other contexts involving C and S corporations.[9]

Determination of Amount of Liability Assumed. Section 357(d) attempts to clarify the amount and effect of liability assumptions under Section 357 and several other provisions covered later in the text. A recourse liability is treated as having been "assumed" if, based on all the facts and circumstances, the transferee has agreed to and is expected to satisfy the liability, whether or not the transferor has been relieved of it.[10] Nonrecourse liabilities generally are treated as having been assumed by a transferee who takes an asset subject to the liability, except the amount is reduced by the lesser of: (1) the amount of such liability which an owner of other assets not transferred to the transferee and also subject to such liability has agreed with the transferee to, and is expected to, satisfy, or (2) the fair market value of those other assets.[11] The purpose of this convoluted exception is to prevent double counting the same liability for basis adjustment purposes.

Section 357(d) was enacted to eliminate an arcane corporate tax shelter that exploited ambiguities in the interpretation of the phrase "transferred subject to a liability" in an earlier version of Section 357.[12] Most of the abusive transactions were used by domestic corporations to overstate the basis of encumbered assets received in transfers from foreign affiliates that were not subject to U.S. tax and thus were indifferent to any potential

---

9. See, e.g., Chapter 3B, infra (treatment of shareholder guaranteed debt for purposes of characterizing debt and equity in C corporation's capital structure); Chapter 15D, infra (treatment of shareholder debt and S corporation debt guaranteed by shareholders in determining basis of S corporation stock under Section 1366); I.R.C. § 752 (allocation of liabilities in determining partner's basis in partnership interest and for other purposes).

10. I.R.C. § 357(d)(1)(A). Where more than one person agrees to satisfy a liability,

only one of them would be "expected" to satisfy it.

11. I.R.C. § 357(d)(2). See also I.R.C. § 362(d), which limits the basis of property in the hands of the transferee to effectuate a similar policy against double counting.

12. See Staff of Joint Committee on Taxation, Description of Revenue Provisions Contained in the President's Fiscal Year 2000 Budget Proposal 197, JCS–1–99, 106th Cong., 1st Sess. (1999).

Section 357(c) gain triggered by the transfer. If the plan succeeded, the domestic corporation would benefit from excessive depreciation deductions, tax losses, or reduced gain on a future sale of the asset.[13]

Fortunately, the confusing language in Section 357(d) rarely affects most simple incorporations. But it raises some questions (and offers planning opportunities) that could arise in a purely domestic, non-abusive setting. For example, recourse debt is treated as assumed only if the transferee has agreed and is expected to satisfy it. As one commentator has asked, "expected by whom"—the transferee, the transferor, or both?[14] Without such an agreement and expectation, a liability would not be treated as "assumed," perhaps eliminating a Section 357(c) problem that otherwise might have existed. A similar factual inquiry may be required with nonrecourse debt, which generally is treated as "assumed" unless a third party has pledged other assets as collateral and "has agreed to, and is expected to, satisfy" the obligation.[15]

As for planning, it has been suggested that Section 357(c) problems could be avoided, at least with respect to recourse debt, if a shareholder who transfers encumbered property to a controlled corporation enters into an agreement with the corporation providing that the shareholder will satisfy the debt. In that event, the debt would not be treated as "assumed" under Section 357(d), and neither Section 357(a) nor Section 357(c) would apply to the transfer.[16] This strategy would be an alternative to contributing a note to the corporation in the amount of the potential Section 357(c) gain.

PROBLEMS

1. A organized X Corporation by transferring the following: inventory with a basis of $20,000 and a fair market value of $10,000 and unimproved land held for several years with a basis of $20,000, a fair market value of $40,000 and subject to a recourse debt of $30,000. In return, A received 20 shares of X stock (fair market value, $20,000) and X took the land subject to the debt.

 (a) Assuming no application of Section 357(b), how much gain, if any, does A recognize and what is A's basis and holding period in the stock?

 (b) What result in (a), above, if the basis of the land were only $5,000?

13. See Department of Treasury, White Paper, "The Problem of Corporate Tax Shelters: Discussion, Analysis and Legislative Proposals," App. A (July 1, 1999).

14. Bogdanski, "Section 357(d)—Old Can, New Worms," 27 J. Corp. Tax'n 17, 22–23 (2000). See also Banks–Golub, "Recent Amendments to Code Sec. 357: Congress Responds to 'Artificial Basis Creation,' "78 Taxes 19 (2000).

15. The Service has announced that it is studying these and other complex issues and considering whether to issue regulations specifying the "requirements of an agreement between the transferor and transferee regarding which party will satisfy a liability and how such an agreement must be evidenced." Ann. 2003–37, 2003–1 C.B. 1025.

16. See Bodgdanski, supra note 15, at 26–28.

(c) In (b), above, what is the character of A's recognized gain under Reg. § 1.357–2(b)? Does this result make sense? How else might the character of A's gain be determined?

(d) In (b), above, what is X Corporation's basis in the properties received from A?

(e) What might A have done to avoid the recognition of gain in (b), above?

2. B organized Y Corporation and transferred a building with a basis of $100,000 and a fair market value of $400,000. The building was subject to a first mortgage of $80,000 which was incurred two years ago for valid business reasons. Two weeks before the incorporation of Y, B borrowed $10,000 for personal purposes and secured the loan with a second mortgage on the building. In exchange for the building, Y Corporation will issue $310,000 of Y common stock to B and will take the building subject to the mortgages.

(a) What are the tax consequences to B on the transfer of the building to Y Corporation?

(b) What result if B did not borrow the additional $10,000 and, instead, Y Corporation borrowed $10,000 from a bank and gave B $310,000 of Y common stock, $10,000 cash and will take the building subject to the $80,000 first mortgage?

(c) Is the difference in results between (a) and (b), above, justified?

(d) When might there be legitimate business reasons for a corporation assuming a transferor's debt or taking property subject to debt?

E. SPECIAL PROBLEMS

1. INCORPORATION OF A GOING BUSINESS

The preceding sections were designed to illustrate the basic requirements and exceptions for qualifying as a tax-free incorporation. For pedagogical reasons, the problems have involved relatively isolated fact patterns, and it has been assumed that the Code and regulations will provide an answer to virtually every question. When a going business is incorporated, however, matters may become more complex. The mix of assets transferred by a sole proprietorship or partnership may include "ordinary income" property, such as accounts receivable and inventory, and the corporation may assume accounts payable, contingent liabilities, and supplies the cost of which was deducted by the transferor prior to the incorporation. Questions arise as to the proper taxpayer to report the receivables and to deduct the payables. In addition, these items potentially raise a broad issue that will recur throughout our study of Subchapter C: to what extent must a nonrecognition provision yield to judicially created "common law" principles of taxation or to more general provisions of the Code?

This section examines the special problems raised by midstream transfers and, in so doing, provides an opportunity to review concepts introduced earlier in the chapter.

Hempt Brothers, Inc. v. United States

United States Court of Appeals, Third Circuit, 1974.
490 F.2d 1172, cert. denied 419 U.S. 826, 95 S.Ct. 44 (1974).

■ ALDISERT, CIRCUIT JUDGE.

[A cash method partnership transferred all its assets, including $662,820 in zero basis accounts receivable, to a newly formed corporation in exchange for all the corporation's stock. Because the exchange qualified under Section 351, the Service contended that the partnership's zero basis in the receivables carried over to the corporation under Section 362, causing the corporation to realize income upon their collection. In an odd reversal of roles, because the statute of limitations had run on earlier years, the corporation contended that the receivables were not "property" within the meaning of Section 351 and that their transfer to the corporation was an assignment of income by the partnership, subjecting the partners to tax when the receivables were transferred or collected and providing the corporation with a cost (i.e., fair market value) basis and no income upon collection. The Court thus was required to address the relationship between Section 351 and the assignment of income doctrine.]

I.

Taxpayer argues here, as it did in the district court, that because the term "property" as used in Section 351 does not embrace accounts receivable, the Commissioner lacked statutory authority to apply principles associated with Section 351. The district court properly rejected the legal interpretation urged by the taxpayer.

The definition of Section 351 "property" has been extensively treated by the Court of Claims in E.I. Du Pont de Nemours and Co. v. United States, 471 F.2d 1211, 1218–1219 (Ct.Cl.1973), describing the transfer of a non-exclusive license to make, use and sell area herbicides under French patents:

> Unless there is some special reason intrinsic to * * * [Section 351] * * * the general word "property" has a broad reach in tax law. * * * For section 351, in particular, courts have advocated a generous definition of "property," * * * and it has been suggested in one capital gains case that nonexclusive licenses can be viewed as property though not as capital assets. * * *

> We see no adequate reason for refusing to follow these leads.

We fail to perceive any special reason why a restrictive meaning should be applied to accounts receivables so as to exclude them from the general meaning of "property." Receivables possess the usual capabilities and attributes associated with jurisprudential concepts of property law. They may be identified, valued, and transferred. Moreover, their role in an ongoing business must be viewed in the context of Section 351 application. The presence of accounts receivable is a normal, rather than an exceptional accoutrement of the type of business included by Congress in the transfer to a corporate form. They are "commonly thought of in the commercial world as a positive business asset." As aptly put by the district court: "There is a compelling reason to construe 'property' to include * * * [accounts receivable]: a new corporation needs working capital, and accounts receivable can be an important source of liquidity." Hempt Bros., Inc. v. United States, supra, at 1176. In any event, this court had no difficulty in characterizing a sale of receivables as "property" within the purview of the "no gain or loss" provision of Section 337 as a "qualified sale of property within a 12–month period." Citizens' Acceptance Corp. v. United States, 462 F.2d 751, 756 (3d Cir.1972).

The taxpayer next makes a strenuous argument that "[t]he government is seeking to tax the wrong person."[4] It contends that the assignment of income doctrine as developed by the Supreme Court applies to a Section 351 transfer of accounts receivable so that the transferor, not the transferee-corporation, bears the corresponding tax liability. It argues that the assignment of income doctrine dictates that where the right to receive income is transferred to another person in a transaction not giving rise to tax at the time of transfer, the transferor is taxed on the income when it is collected by the transferee; that the only requirement for its application is a transfer of a right to receive ordinary income; and that since the transferred accounts receivable are a present right to future income, the sole requirement for the application of the doctrine is squarely met. In essence, this is a contention that the nonrecognition provision of Section 351 is in conflict with the assignment of income doctrine and that Section 351 should be subordinated thereto. Taxpayer relies on the seminal case of Lucas v. Earl, 280 U.S. 538, 50 S.Ct. 16, 74 L.Ed. 600 (1930), and its progeny for support of its proposition that the application of the doctrine is mandated whenever one transfers a right to receive ordinary income.

On its part, the government concedes that a taxpayer may sell for value a claim to income otherwise his own and he will be taxable upon the proceeds of the sale. Such was the case in Commissioner v. P.G. Lake, Inc., 356 U.S. 260, 78 S.Ct. 691, 2 L.Ed.2d 743 (1958), in which the taxpayer-corporation assigned its oil payment right to its president in consideration for his cancellation of a $600,000 loan. Viewing the oil payment right as a right to receive future income, the Court applied the reasoning of the assignment of income doctrine, normally applicable to a gratuitous assignment, and held that the consideration received by the taxpayer-corporation was taxable as ordinary income since it essentially was a substitute for that which would otherwise be received at a future time as ordinary income.

---

4. We put aside the pragmatic consideration that the transferee-corporate taxpayer raises the argument that the partnership should be taxed at a time when the statute of limitations has presumably run against the transferor partners, who ostensibly are the stockholders of the new corporation.

Turning to the facts of this case, we note that here there was the transfer of accounts receivable from the partnership to the corporation pursuant to Section 351. We view these accounts receivable as a present right to receive future income. In consideration of the transfer of this right, the members of the partnership received stock—a valid consideration. The consideration, therefore, was essentially a substitute for that which would otherwise be received at a future time as ordinary income to the cash basis partnership. Consequently, the holding in *Lake* would normally apply, and income would ordinarily be realized, and thereby taxable, by the cash basis partnership-transferor at the time of receipt of the stock.

But the terms and purpose of Section 351 have to be reckoned with. By its explicit terms Section 351 expresses the Congressional intent that transfers of property for stock or securities will not result in recognition. It therefore becomes apparent that this case vividly illustrates how Section 351 sometimes comes into conflict with another provision of the Internal Revenue Code or a judicial doctrine, and requires a determination of which of two conflicting doctrines will control.

As we must, when we try to reconcile conflicting doctrines in the revenue law, we endeavor to ascertain a controlling Congressional mandate. Section 351 has been described as a deliberate attempt by Congress to facilitate the incorporation of ongoing businesses and to eliminate any technical constructions which are economically unsound.

Appellant-taxpayer seems to recognize this and argues that application of the *Lake* rationale when accounts receivable are transferred would not create any undue hardship to an incorporating taxpayer. "All a taxpayer [transferor] need do is withhold the earned income items and collect them, transferring the net proceeds to the Corporation. Indeed * * * the transferor should retain both accounts receivable and accounts payable to avoid income recognition at the time of transfer and to have sufficient funds with which to pay accounts payable. Where the taxpayer [transferor] is on the cash method of accounting [as here], the deduction of the accounts payable would be applied against the income generated by the accounts receivable."

While we cannot fault the general principle "that income be taxed to him who earns it," to adopt taxpayer's argument would be to hamper the incorporation of ongoing businesses; additionally it would impose technical constructions which are economically and practically unsound. None of the cases cited by taxpayer, including *Lake* itself, persuades us otherwise. In *Lake* the Court was required to decide whether the proceeds from the assignment of the oil payment right were taxable as ordinary income or as long term capital gains. Observing that the provision for long term capital gains treatment "has always been narrowly construed so as to protect the revenue against artful devices," 356 U.S. at 265, 78 S.Ct. at 694, the Court predicated its holding upon an emphatic distinction between a conversion of a capital investment—"income-producing property"—and an assignment of income *per se*. "The substance of what was assigned was the right to receive future income. The substance of what was received was the present value of income which the recipient would otherwise obtain in the future."

Ibid., at 266, 78 S.Ct. at 695. A Section 351 issue was not presented in *Lake*. Therefore the case does not control in weighing the conflict between the general rule of assignment of income and the Congressional purpose of nonrecognition upon the incorporation of an ongoing business.

We are persuaded that, on balance, the teachings of *Lake* must give way in this case to the broad Congressional interest in facilitating the incorporation of ongoing businesses. As desirable as it is to afford symmetry in revenue law, we do not intend to promulgate a hard and fast rule. We believe that the problems posed by the clash of conflicting internal revenue doctrines are more properly determined by the circumstances of each case. Here we are influenced by the fact that the subject of the assignment was accounts receivable for partnership's goods and services sold in the regular course of business, that the change of business form from partnership to corporation had a basic business purpose and was not designed for the purpose of deliberate tax avoidance, and by the conviction that the totality of circumstances here presented fit the mold of the Congressional intent to give nonrecognition to a transfer of a total business from a non-corporate to a corporate form.

But this too must be said. Even though Section 351(a) immunizes the transferor from immediate tax consequences, Section 358 retains for the transferors a potential income tax liability to be realized and recognized upon a subsequent sale or exchange of the stock certificates received. As to the transferee-corporation, the tax basis of the receivables will be governed by Section 362.

* * *

Revenue Ruling 95–74

1995–2 Cum.Bull. 36.

ISSUES

(1) Are the liabilities assumed by S in the § 351 exchange described below liabilities for purposes of §§ 357(c)(1) and 358(d)?

(2) Once assumed by S, how will the liabilities in the § 351 exchange described below be treated?

FACTS

Corporation P is an accrual basis, calendar-year corporation engaged in various ongoing businesses, one of which includes the operation of a manufacturing plant (the Manufacturing Business). The plant is located on land purchased by P many years before. The land was not contaminated by any hazardous waste when P purchased it. However, as a result of plant operations, certain environmental liabilities, such as potential soil and groundwater remediation, are now associated with the land.

In Year 1, for bona fide business purposes, P engages in an exchange to which § 351 of the Internal Revenue Code applies by transferring substantially all of the assets associated with the Manufacturing Business, including the manufacturing plant and the land on which the plant is located, to a newly formed corporation, S, in exchange for all of the stock of S and for S's assumption of the liabilities associated with the Manufacturing Business, including the environmental liabilities associated with the land. P has no plan or intention to dispose of (or have S issue) any S stock. S is an accrual basis, calendar-year taxpayer.

P did not undertake any environmental remediation efforts in connection with the land transferred to S before the transfer and did not deduct or capitalize any amount with respect to the contingent environmental liabilities associated with the transferred land.

In Year 3, S undertakes soil and groundwater remediation efforts relating to the land transferred in the § 351 exchange and incurs costs (within the meaning of the economic performance rules of § 461(h)) as a result of those remediation efforts. Of the total amount of costs incurred, a portion would have constituted ordinary and necessary business expenses that are deductible under § 162 and the remaining portion would have constituted capital expenditures under § 263 if there had not been a § 351 exchange and the costs for remediation efforts had been incurred by P.
* * *

LAW AND ANALYSIS

Issue 1: * * * The legislative history of § 351 indicates that Congress viewed an incorporation as a mere change in the form of the underlying business and enacted § 351 to facilitate such business adjustments generally by allowing taxpayers to incorporate businesses without recognizing gain. * * * Section 357(c)(1), however, provides that the transferor recognizes gain to the extent that the amount of liabilities transferred exceeds the aggregate basis of the assets transferred.

A number of cases concerning cash basis taxpayers were litigated in the 1970s with respect to the definition of "liabilities" for purposes of § 357(c)(1), with sometimes conflicting analyses and results. * * * In response to this litigation, Congress enacted § 357(c)(3) to address the concern that the inclusion in the § 357(c)(1) determination of certain deductible liabilities resulted in "unforeseen and unintended tax difficulties for certain cash basis taxpayers who incorporate a going business." S.Rep. No. 1263, 95th Cong., 2d Sess. 184–85 (1978), 1978–3 C.B. 482–83.

Congress concluded that including in the § 357(c)(1) determination liabilities that have not yet been taken into account by the transferor results in an overstatement of liabilities of, and potential inappropriate gain recognition to, the transferor because the transferor has not received the corresponding deduction or other corresponding tax benefit. Id. To prevent this result, Congress enacted § 357(c)(3)(A) to exclude certain deductible liabilities from the scope of § 357(c), as long as the liabilities had not resulted in the creation of, or an increase in, the basis of any property (as provided in s 357(c)(3)(B)). * * *

While § 357(c)(3) explicitly addresses liabilities that give rise to deductible items, the same principle applies to liabilities that give rise to capital expenditures as well. Including in the § 357(c)(1) determination those liabilities that have not yet given rise to capital expenditures (and thus have not yet created or increased basis) with respect to the property of the transferor prior to the transfer also would result in an overstatement of liabilities. Thus, such liabilities also appropriately are excluded in determining liabilities for purposes of § 357(c)(1). * * *

In this case, the contingent environmental liabilities assumed by S had not yet been taken into account by P prior to the transfer (and therefore had neither given rise to deductions for P nor resulted in the creation of, or increase in, basis in any property of P). As a result, the contingent environmental liabilities are not included in determining whether the amount of the liabilities assumed by S exceeds the adjusted basis of the property transferred by P pursuant to § 357(c)(1).

Due to the parallel constructions and interrelated function and mechanics of §§ 357 and 358, liabilities that are not included in the determination under § 357(c)(1) also are not included in the § 358 determination of the transferor's basis in the stock received in the § 351 exchange. * * * Therefore, the contingent environmental liabilities assumed by S are not treated as money received by P under § 358 for purposes of determining P's basis in the stock of S received in the exchange.

Issue 2: In Holdcroft Transp. Co. v. Commissioner, 153 F.2d 323 (8th Cir.1946), the Court of Appeals for the Eighth Circuit held that, after a transfer pursuant to the predecessor to § 351, the payments by a transferee corporation were not deductible even though the transferor partnership would have been entitled to deductions for the payments had the partnership actually made the payments. The court stated generally that the expense of settling claims or liabilities of a predecessor entity did not arise as an operating expense or loss of the business of the transferee but was a part of the cost of acquiring the predecessor's property, and the fact that the claims were contingent and unliquidated at the time of the acquisition was not of controlling consequence.

In Rev. Rul. 80–198, 1980–2 C.B. 113, an individual transferred all of the assets and liabilities of a sole proprietorship, which included accounts payable and accounts receivable, to a new corporation in exchange for all of its stock. The revenue ruling holds, subject to certain limitations, that the transfer qualifies as an exchange within the meaning of § 351(a) and that the transferee corporation will report in its income the accounts receivable as collected and will be allowed deductions under § 162 for the payments it makes to satisfy the accounts payable. In reaching these holdings, the revenue ruling makes reference to the specific congressional intent of § 351(a) to facilitate the incorporation of an ongoing business by making the incorporation tax free. The ruling states that this intent would be equally frustrated if either the transferor were taxed on the transfer of the accounts receivable or the transferee were not allowed a deduction for payment of the accounts payable. * * *

The present case is analogous to the situation in Rev. Rul. 80–198. For business reasons, P transferred in a § 351 exchange substantially all of the assets and liabilities associated with the Manufacturing Business to S, in exchange for all of its stock, and P intends to remain in control of S. The costs S incurs to remediate the land would have been deductible in part and capitalized in part had P continued the Manufacturing Business and incurred those costs to remediate the land. The congressional intent to facilitate necessary business readjustments would be frustrated by not according to S the ability to deduct or capitalize the expenses of the ongoing business.

Therefore, on these facts, the Internal Revenue Service will not follow the decision in Holdcroft Transp. Co. v. Commissioner, 153 F.2d 323 (8th Cir.1946). Accordingly, the contingent environmental liabilities assumed from P are deductible as business expenses under § 162 or are capitalized under § 263, as appropriate, by S under S's method of accounting (determined as if S has owned the land for the period and in the same manner as it was owned by P).

HOLDINGS

(1) The liabilities assumed by S in the § 351 exchange described above are not liabilities for purposes of § 357(c)(1) and § 358(d) because the liabilities had not yet been taken into account by P prior to the transfer (and therefore had neither given rise to deductions for P nor resulted in the creation of, or increase in, basis in any property of P).

(2) The liabilities assumed by S in the § 351 exchange described above are deductible by S as business expenses under § 162 or are capital expenditures under § 263, as appropriate, under S's method of accounting (determined as if S has owned the land for the period and in the same manner as it was owned by P).

LIMITATIONS

The holdings described above are subject to § 482 and other applicable sections of the Code and principles of law, including the limitations discussed in Rev. Rul. 80–198, 1980–2 C.B. 113 (limiting the scope of the revenue ruling to transactions that do not have a tax avoidance purpose).
* * *

NOTE

Receivables and Payables. When there is a valid business purpose for the transfer of receivables and payables on the incorporation of a going business, the Service will issue a ruling that the transferee corporation (and not the transferor) must report the receivables in income as they are collected and deduct the payables when they are paid.[1] This position is consistent with the Government's position in *Hempt Brothers* that the

1. Rev.Rul. 80–198, 1980–2 C.B. 113.
See also Rev.Rul. 95–74, p. 104 supra.

assignment of income doctrine normally will not override Section 351. But to prevent abuse in situations where receivables are accumulated or payables prepaid in anticipation of the incorporation, the Service has noted the following limitations:[2]

> Section 351 of the Code does not apply to a transfer of accounts receivable which constitute an assignment of an income right in a case such as Brown v. Commissioner, 40 B.T.A. 565 (1939), aff'd 115 F.2d 337 (2d Cir.1940). In *Brown,* an attorney transferred to a corporation, in which he was the sole owner, a one-half interest in a claim for legal services performed by the attorney and his law partner. In exchange, the attorney received additional stock of the corporation. The claim represented the corporation's only asset. Subsequent to the receipt by the corporation of the proceeds of the claim, the attorney gave all of the stock of the corporation to his wife. The United States Court of Appeals for the Second Circuit found that the transfer of the claim for the fee to the corporation had no purpose other than to avoid taxes and held that in such a case the intervention of the corporation would not prevent the attorney from being liable for the tax on the income which resulted from services under the assignment of income rule of Lucas v. Earl, 281 U.S. 111, 50 S.Ct. 241 (1930). Accordingly, in a case of a transfer to a controlled corporation of an account receivable in respect of services rendered where there is a tax avoidance purpose for the transaction (which might be evidenced by the corporation not conducting an ongoing business), the Internal Revenue Service will continue to apply assignment of income principles and require that the transferor of such a receivable include it in income when received by the transferee corporation.

> Likewise, it may be appropriate in certain situations to allocate income, deductions, credits, or allowances to the transferor or transferee under section 482 of the Code when the timing of the incorporation improperly separates income from related expenses. See Rooney v. United States, 305 F.2d 681 (9th Cir.1962), where a farming operation was incorporated in a transaction described in section 351(a) after the expenses of the crop had been incurred but before the crop had been sold and income realized. The transferor's tax return contained all of the expenses but none of the farming income to which the expenses related. The United States Court of Appeals for the Ninth Circuit held that the expenses could be allocated under section 482 to the corporation, to be matched with the income to which the expenses related. Similar adjustments may be appropriate where some assets, liabilities, or both, are retained by the transferor and such retention results in the income of the transferor, transferee, or both, not being clearly reflected.

2.   Id.

Tax Benefit Rule. Even when a transferor clearly contributes "property" to a newly formed corporation, a problem may arise if the transferor deducted the cost of that property prior to the incorporation. Under the tax benefit rule, if an amount has been deducted and a later event occurs that is fundamentally inconsistent with the premise on which the deduction was initially based, the earlier deduction must be effectively "cancelled out" by the recognition of income equal to the amount previously deducted.[3] For example, a taxpayer who pays $1,000 for minor office supplies to be used in his business would deduct that amount when paid on the assumption that those supplies soon would be exhausted. If that taxpayer later incorporates before the supplies are used and receives $1,000 of stock in the exchange, an event has occurred that is inconsistent with the presumption upon which the earlier deduction was based. But recognition of $1,000 of current income on the transfer of the supplies to a controlled corporation in exchange for its stock is also inconsistent with Section 351.

Whether or not the tax benefit rule overrides Section 351 is unsettled. In Nash v. United States,[4] an accrual method taxpayer transferred accounts receivable to a newly formed corporation in exchange for stock. The taxpayer already had included the receivables in income and also had deducted a reserve for bad debts. Applying the tax benefit rule, the Service argued that the taxpayer should be taxed on an amount equal to the previously deducted bad debt reserve because the taxpayer's presumption that some of those debts would turn bad while held in his business had proved erroneous. Although the debts still might become worthless, that event would occur only when they were held by the new corporation—a separate business. The Supreme Court held that the net amount the taxpayer had included in his income as a result of the receivables (i.e., the excess of all accrued receivables over the deducted reserve for bad debts) equalled the value of the stock received for the receivables, so that the earlier deduction for the reserve for bad debts was not inappropriate and did not generate income under the tax benefit rule.

The specific fact pattern addressed in *Nash* is no longer important because accrual method taxpayers are now generally precluded from deducting a reserve for bad debts. Moreover, in a subsequent case, the Supreme Court held that the tax benefit rule applies whenever a later unforeseen event is "fundamentally inconsistent" with the premise underlying a taxpayer's earlier deduction.[5] This broader holding suggests that the Court might uphold application of the tax benefit rule in another factual setting involving a transfer to a newly formed corporation. On the other hand, the Code specifically provides that the depreciation recapture provi-

3. See Bittker & Lokken, Federal Taxation of Income, Estates and Gifts ¶ 5.7.1 (3d ed. 1999).

4. 398 U.S. 1, 90 S.Ct. 1550 (1970). See also Rev.Rul. 78–280, 1978–2 C.B. 139.

5. Hillsboro Nat'l Bank v. Commissioner, 460 U.S. 370, 103 S.Ct. 1134 (1983).

sions, which are grounded on tax benefit rule principles, do not override Section 351.[6]

PROBLEM

Architect, a cash basis taxpayer, has been conducting a business as a sole proprietorship for several years. Architect decides to incorporate, and on July 1 of the current year he forms Design, Inc., to which he transfers the following assets:

Asset	A.B.	F.M.V.
Accounts Receivable	$ 0	$ 60,000
Supplies	0	20,000
Unimproved Land	60,000	120,000
Total	$ 60,000	$200,000

The land was subject to contingent environmental liabilities that Architect had not taken into account (i.e., had not deducted or capitalized) for tax purposes at the time of the incorporation. The supplies were acquired nine months ago and their cost was immediately deducted by Architect as an ordinary and necessary business expense.

In exchange, Architect receives 100 shares of Design common stock with a fair market value of $100,000. In addition, Design assumes $70,000 of accounts payable to trade creditors of Architect's sole proprietorship and a $30,000 bank loan incurred by Architect two years ago for valid business reasons, and it assumed the environmental liabilities associated with the land.

Design elects to become a cash method, calendar year taxpayer. During the remainder of the current year, it pays $30,000 of the accounts payable and collects $40,000 of the accounts receivable transferred by Architect. In the following taxable year, Design paid $20,000 in environmental remediation expenses that qualified for a current deduction when paid or accrued under Section 162.

(a) What are the tax consequences (gain or loss recognized, basis and holding period) of the incorporation to Architect and Design, Inc.?

(b) Who will be taxable upon collection of the accounts receivable: Architect, Design or both?

(c) When Design pays the accounts payable assumed from Architect and incurs the environmental remediation costs, may it properly deduct these expenses?

(d) Assume that Architect is in the highest marginal individual tax bracket and Design, Inc. anticipates no significant taxable income for the current year. What result if Architect decides to pay (and

---

6. See, e.g., I.R.C. § 1245(b)(3).

deduct) personally all the accounts payable and transfers the accounts receivable to the corporation?

(e) Would your answers be any different if Architect had been an accrual method taxpayer?

(f) Is Design, Inc. limited in its choice of accounting method (i.e., cash or accrual) or taxable year? See §§ 441; 448.

2. CONTINGENT LIABILITY TAX SHELTERS

Black & Decker Corp. v. United States

United States District Court, Maryland, 2004.
2004 WL 2051215.

■ QUARLES, DISTRICT JUDGE.

Black & Decker Corporation ("B & D") has sued the United States of America for a refund of federal taxes in the amount of $57,358,030, plus interest, which it contends were erroneously assessed and collected for the years 1995 through 2000. Pending is the United States' motion for summary judgment. For the reasons discussed below, the motion for summary judgment will be denied.

BACKGROUND

[In 1998, Black & Decker Corporation ("B & D") sold three businesses, generating significant capital gains. Later that same year, B & D engaged in a transaction known as a "contingent liability tax shelter," with the objective of generating a capital loss to offset the significant gain. To that end, B & D and several other entities created a new corporation, Black & Decker Health Management, Inc. ("BDHMI"). B & D transferred $561 million in cash in exchange for a class of preferred stock with a value of $1 million and BDHMI's assumption of contingent employee and retiree healthcare benefit claims with an actuarially determined present value of $560 million. B & D obtained the cash from bank loans. Shortly thereafter, BDHMI loaned the funds back to B & D in exchange for promissory notes, and B & D repaid the bank loans. B & D's stated business purpose for this transaction, which was based on advice from an accounting firm that charged $2 million for its services, was a desire to outsource employee and retiree medical claims in order to control costs.

One month after BDHMI was formed, B & D sold its preferred stock to a third party (a trust controlled by a former B & D employee who was serving as a facilitator) for $1 million. B & D, taking the position that its basis in the BDHMI stock was $561 million, claimed a $560 million capital loss on the sale. It applied a portion of the loss to offset its gain on the same of the three businesses and carried back and forward the remaining capital loss to offset gains in prior and future years.

The key issue in the case was whether B & D's basis in the preferred stock was $561 million or $1 million. In claiming that its basis was $561 million, B & D relied on Revenue Ruling 95–74, supra p. 104. It contended that it was not required to reduce its stock basis by the "contingent" liabilities assumed by BDHMI because they were not "liabilities" for purposes of Sections 357(c)(1) and 358(d). The Service argued that B & D's stock basis equalled the $561 million cash transferred less the $560 million liabilities assumed, or $1 million, so that there was no loss on the sale of the stock.

These facts have been derived from the court's memorandum opinion rendered in August, 2004, and a summary of other documents filed in the case in Burke, "Black & Decker's Contingent Liability Shelter: 'A Thing of Grace and Beauty'?" 106 Tax Notes 577 (Jan. 31, 2005). Ed.]

ANALYSIS

For the purposes of its motion for summary judgment, the United States has assumed that B & D's transaction with BDHMI qualifies as a transfer to corporation controlled by transferor under 26 U.S.C. § 351. Section 351 provides that no gain or loss shall be recognized if property is transferred to a corporation solely in exchange for stock in such corporation and immediately after the exchange the transferor is in control of the corporation. Applying § 351 to the transaction between B & D and BDHMI, the value of the new shares that BDHMI issued to B & D would be $561 million dollars, the value of the property that B & D contributed to BDHMI in the exchange.

Section 358(d) provides, however, that when, in a § 351 exchange, the transferee assumes a liability of the transferor, such assumption shall be treated as money received by the transferor on the exchange. Applying § 358(d) to the B & D transaction, the value of the $560 million dollars worth of contingent healthcare claims assumed by BDHMI for B & D would be deducted from the original value of the stock that B & D received in the exchange (i.e., $561 million dollars—$560 million dollars = $1 million dollars).

Section 357(c)(3)(A) provides that if the contingent liabilities transferred would give rise to a deduction, then the amount of such liabilities shall be excluded in determining the amount of liabilities assumed. Because the contingent liabilities that B & D transferred to BDHMI would have been deductible as ordinary business expenses for B & D, B & D asserts that by virtue of § 357(c)(3)(A), it need not recognize the transfer of contingent liabilities to BDHMI. Accordingly, B & D argues that the value of the stock it received in the exchange is $561 million dollars, thus when it sold the stock to an investor for $1 million dollars, it incurred a substantial capital loss.

The United States contends that the contingent liabilities transferred to BDHMI are not deductible to BDHMI, but to B & D, because the healthcare expenses of B & D employees are B & D's ordinary business expenses; whereas BDHMI merely *pays* B & D employees' healthcare claims. In that case, B & D could double-deduct the contingent liabilities by (1) not recognizing their transfer on the 1998 exchange, and (2) deducting the amount of the contingent employee healthcare claims as they become payable.

The tax code should not be interpreted to allow taxpayers the practical equivalent of a double-deduction absent a clear declaration of intent by Congress. United States v. Skelly Oil Co., 394 U.S. 678, 684, 89 S.Ct. 1379, 22 L.Ed.2d 642 (1969) (citing Charles Ilfeld Co. v. Hernandez, 292 U.S. 62, 68, 54 S.Ct. 596, 78 L.Ed. 1127 (1934); United States v. Ludey, 274 U.S. 295, 47 S.Ct. 608, 71 L.Ed. 1054 (1927)). The United States argues, therefore, that § 357(c)(3)(A) must mean that contingent liabilities assumed by a transferee in a § 351 exchange need not be recognized if the liabilities assumed would have given rise to a deduction for the *transferee*.

Section 357(c)(3)(A) does not explicitly state whether contingent liabilities must be deductible by the transferor or the transferee in a § 351 exchange to fall within the exception. When a statute's language is ambiguous, the court must refer to its legislative history for guidance. Holland v. Big River Minerals Corp., 181 F.3d 597, 603 (4th Cir.1999).

The legislative history to § 357(c) lends no support to the United States' suggested interpretation. Section 357(c) was enacted as part of the Revenue Act of 1978. The Senate Report accompanying the bill explains that "for purposes of section 357(c) . . . the amount of liabilities assumed or to which the property transferred is subject, the amount of a liability would be excluded . . . to the extent payment thereof by the *transferor* would have given rise to a deduction." S. Rep. No. 95–1263, at 185 (1978) (emphasis added). The Senate Report also notes that "the provision is not intended to affect the corporate-transferees' tax accounting for the excluded liabilities." Id.; see also Joint Comm. on Taxation, 95th Cong., General Explanation of Revenue Act of 1978, at 219 (Comm. Print 1979). Section 357(c) was subsequently amended by the Technical Corrections Act of 1979 ("the 1979 Act"). The legislative history to the 1979 Act explains that "liabilities may be excluded under this provision only to the extent payment thereof by the *transferor* would have given rise to a deduction. A liability would not be excluded under this provision to the extent the liability has already been deducted by the transferor." S. REP. NO. 96–498, at 62 (1980) (emphasis added).

Moreover, the Internal Revenue Service has focused on the transferor's deductibility when applying § 357(c)(3)(A). See, e.g., Rev. Rul. 95–74, 1995–2 C.B. 36 (1995) (contingent liabilities assumed by transferee had not been taken into account by transferor prior to transfer, thus they had not yet given rise to a deduction for the transferor and should not have been included in determining the transferor's basis in the transferred property).

Because the Court is unable to find support for the United States' interpretation of § 357(c)(3)(A), the United States' motion for summary judgment must be denied.

[At a later stage of this proceeding, the Service argued that the transaction was a tax avoidance vehicle that must be disregarded. For purposes of this summary judgment motion, B & D conceded that tax avoidance was its sole motivation for the transaction but nonetheless claimed that it had "economic substance" aside from tax benefits. The court agreed with B & D, concluding that "[t]he BDHMI transaction . . . had very real economic implications for every beneficiary of B & D's employee benefits program, as well as for the parties to the transaction." Black & Decker Corp. v. United States, 340 F.Supp.2d 621 (D. Md. 2004). Ed.]

NOTE

Black & Decker is a good illustration of the corporate tax shelter phenomenon that was previewed in Chapter 1. If successful, the transaction under scrutiny accelerated a tax loss to offset an already realized gain and, in some cases, the same loss was duplicated.

Contingent liability shelters are now largely blocked by Section 358(h), which was not applicable for the taxable year at issue in *Black & Decker*. It provides that if, after application of the general Section 358 stock basis rules, a transferor's basis exceeds the fair market value of the stock received in a Section 351 transaction, the transferor must reduce that basis by the amount of any "liability"[1] assumed by another person as part of the exchange if a basis reduction was not otherwise required under Section 358(d). This would be the case where the assumed liability was contingent or excluded under Section 357(c)(3). The basis step-down rule does not apply where the trade or business with which the liability is associated or substantially all of the assets with which the liability is associated are transferred to the person assuming the liability as part of the exchange.[2]

3. INTENTIONAL AVOIDANCE OF SECTION 351

Section 351 is not an elective provision. It applies whenever its requirements are met. Historically, some taxpayers attempted to avoid Section 351 in order to recognize a loss[1] or to step-up the basis of an asset after recognizing a gain to increase the transferee corporation's cost recovery deductions.[2] When long-term capital gains enjoy a significant tax rate preference, taxpayers have also found it advantageous to freeze appreciation as capital gain on an asset that was about to be converted into "ordinary income" property—e.g., land held for investment that the taxpayer intended to subdivide. In these cases, the tax savings achieved by converting ordinary income into capital gain outweighed the disadvantage of accelerating recognition of part of the gain.

---

1. For this purpose, a "liability" includes any fixed or contingent obligation to make payment without regard to whether the obligation is otherwise taken into account for tax purposes. I.R.C. § 358(h)(3).

2. I.R.C. § 358(h)(2).

1. Recognition of losses in this manner on a sale between a controlling (more than 50 percent) shareholder and a corporation would be limited by Section 267.

2. But see I.R.C. § 1239, which characterizes gain on sales of property between related taxpayers (e.g., a corporation and a more–than–50–percent shareholder) as ordinary income if the property is depreciable in the hands of the transferee.

Planning to avoid Section 351 may present as great a challenge as satisfying its requirements. As illustrated by the *Intermountain Lumber* case earlier in the chapter,[3] one potentially successful avoidance strategy is to break control after the exchange by a prearranged disposition of more than 20 percent of the stock. Another possibility is to structure an incorporation transfer as a taxable "sale" rather than a tax-free Section 351 exchange.[4]

To illustrate the sale technique, assume Investor owns undeveloped land with an adjusted basis of $50,000 and a fair market value of $300,000. Investor intends to subdivide the land and sell home sites at an aggregate sales price of $500,000. If he developed the land as an individual, Investor would recognize $450,000 of ordinary income.[5] But with long-term capital gains taxed at a significantly lower rate than ordinary income, Investor may benefit by selling the land to a controlled corporation for $300,000 of corporate installment obligations. He would recognize $250,000 of predevelopment capital gain on the sale, the corporation would take a $300,000 stepped-up basis in the land, and the future ordinary income would be limited to $200,000.

The sale strategy was successful in Bradshaw v. United States,[6] where the taxpayer transferred 40 acres of Georgia land in which he had a basis of $8,500 to a new corporation in exchange for $250,000 of unsecured corporate installment notes. The corporation's only other capital was a $4,500 automobile transferred on the same day in exchange for common stock. The court treated the transfer of land as a sale and permitted the taxpayer to report his gain on the installment method.[7] In so doing, the court rejected the Service's claim that the notes were really stock even though it conceded that the corporation was thinly capitalized. A contrary result was reached in Burr Oaks Corp. v. Commissioner,[8] where three taxpayers transferred land to a corporation in exchange for two-year notes with a face amount of $330,000. The corporation's only equity capital was $4,500. The court held that the transfer was a nontaxable Section 351 exchange rather than a sale because the notes, payment of which was dependent on the profitability of an undercapitalized corporation, were really preferred stock.

In the last analysis, resolution of the "Section 351 vs. sale" issue turns on the facts in each case and the court's inclination to reclassify what the taxpayer labels "debt" into what the Service believes to be "equity."[9]

---

3. See p. 64, supra.

4. See generally Bittker & Eustice, Federal Income Taxation of Corporations and Shareholders ¶ 3.14 (7th ed. 2000).

5. For convenience, assume no upward adjustments to basis during the subdivision phase.

6. 683 F.2d 365 (Ct.Cl.1982).

7. The deferral achieved by the taxpayer in *Bradshaw* is foreclosed under current law. Because a shareholder and his wholly owned corporation are "related parties," a later sale of the land by the corporation will accelerate recognition of any gain that otherwise would be deferred on the shareholder's installment sale to the corporation. I.R.C. § 453(e), (f)(1).

8. 365 F.2d 24 (7th Cir.1966), cert. denied, 385 U.S. 1007, 87 S.Ct. 713 (1967). See also Aqualane Shores, Inc. v. Commissioner, 269 F.2d 116 (5th Cir.1959).

9. See Section F of this chapter, supra.

F.   Collateral Issues

1.   Contributions to Capital

Code: §§ 118(a); 362(a)(2), (c).

Regulations: § 1.118–1.

When a shareholder transfers property to a corporation and does not receive stock or other consideration in exchange, the transaction is a contribution to capital. Although Section 351 does not apply to capital contributions, the contributing shareholder does not recognize gain or loss on a contribution of property other than cash to a corporation. Instead, the shareholder may increase the basis in her stock by the amount of cash and the adjusted basis of any contributed property.[1] Contributions to capital by shareholders also are excludable from the gross income of the transferee corporation.[2] The corporation's basis in property received as a nontaxable shareholder contribution to capital is the same as the transferor's basis.[3]

If a sole shareholder transfers property to a corporation, or if all shareholders transfer property in the same proportion as their holdings, the issuance of new stock has no economic significance. After some waffling on the issue,[4] the courts now agree that issuance of stock in these circumstances would be "a meaningless gesture" and consequently have held that such transfers are constructive Section 351 exchanges.[5]

Majority shareholders of a financially distressed corporation may surrender some of their stock back to the company in order to improve its credit rating. The proper tax treatment of a voluntary non-pro rata contribution of stock perplexed the courts for many years, as taxpayers sought to immediately deduct their basis in the surrendered shares as an ordinary loss while the Service contended that the surrender was akin to a contribution to capital. The *Fink* case, below, is the Supreme Court's resolution of this question.

---

1. Reg. § 1.118–1.

2. I.R.C. § 118(a). Contributions to capital by a nonshareholder (e.g., a transfer of property by a municipality to encourage the corporation to build a facility within the city limits) also are excludable. Reg. § 1.118–1.

3. I.R.C. § 362(a)(2). This rule parallels Section 362(a)(1), which provides that the corporation takes a transferred basis in property received in a Section 351 exchange. For the corporation's basis in property contributed by a nonshareholder, see I.R.C. § 362(c).

4. See, e.g., Abegg v. Commissioner, 429 F.2d 1209 (2d Cir.1970), cert. denied, 400 U.S. 1008, 91 S.Ct. 566 (1971).

5. See, e.g., Peracchi v. Commissioner, supra p. 85. As *Peracchi* illustrates, applying Section 351 to contributions to capital by a sole shareholder may be significant insofar as it triggers the application of other Code sections, such as Section 357, to the transaction.

Commissioner v. Fink

Supreme Court of the United States, 1987.
483 U.S. 89, 107 S.Ct. 2729.

■ JUSTICE POWELL delivered the opinion of the Court.

The question in this case is whether a dominant shareholder who voluntarily surrenders a portion of his shares to the corporation, but retains control, may immediately deduct from taxable income his basis in the surrendered shares.

I

Respondents Peter and Karla Fink were the principal shareholders of Travco Corporation, a Michigan manufacturer of motor homes. Travco had one class of common stock outstanding and no preferred stock. Mr. Fink owned 52.2 percent, and Mrs. Fink 20.3 percent, of the outstanding shares.[87] Travco urgently needed new capital as a result of financial difficulties it encountered in the mid–1970s. The Finks voluntarily surrendered some of their shares to Travco in an effort to "increase the attractiveness of the corporation to outside investors." * * * Mr. Fink surrendered 116,146 shares in December 1976; Mrs. Fink surrendered 80,000 shares in January 1977. As a result, the Finks' combined percentage ownership of Travco was reduced from 72.5 percent to 68.5 percent. The Finks received no consideration for the surrendered shares, and no other shareholder surrendered any stock. The effort to attract new investors was unsuccessful, and the corporation eventually was liquidated.

On their 1976 and 1977 joint federal income tax returns, the Finks claimed ordinary loss deductions totaling $389,040, the full amount of their adjusted basis in the surrendered shares.[2] The Commissioner of Internal Revenue disallowed the deductions. He concluded that the stock surrendered was a contribution to the corporation's capital. Accordingly, the Commissioner determined that the surrender resulted in no immediate tax consequences, and that the Finks' basis in the surrendered shares should be added to the basis of their remaining shares of Travco stock.

In an unpublished opinion, the Tax Court sustained the Commissioner's determination for the reasons stated in Frantz v. Commissioner, * * *. In *Frantz* the Tax Court held that a stockholder's non pro rata surrender of shares to the corporation does not produce an immediate loss. The court reasoned that "[t]his conclusion * * * necessarily follows from a recognition of the purpose of the transfer, that is, to bolster the financial position of [the corporation] and, hence, to protect and make more valuable [the stockholder's] retained shares." Because the purpose of the shareholder's surrender is "to decrease or avoid a loss on his overall investment," the Tax Court in Frantz was "unable to conclude that [he] sustained a loss at the time of the transaction." "Whether [the shareholder] would sustain a

---

2. The unadjusted basis of shares is their cost. 26 U.S.C. § 1012. Adjustments to basis are made for, among other things, "ex-penditures, receipts, losses, or other items, properly chargeable to capital account." § 1016(a)(1).

loss, and if so, the amount thereof, could only be determined when he subsequently disposed of the stock that the surrender was intended to protect and make more valuable." The Tax Court recognized that it had sustained the taxpayer's position in a series of prior cases. But it concluded that these decisions were incorrect, in part because they "encourage[d] a conversion of eventual capital losses into immediate ordinary losses." Id., at 182.

In this case, a divided panel of the Court of Appeals for the Sixth Circuit reversed the Tax Court. 789 F.2d 427 (1986). The court concluded that the proper tax treatment of this type of stock surrender turns on the choice between "unitary" and "fragmented" views of stock ownership. Under the " 'fragmented view,' ""each share of stock is considered a separate investment," and gain or loss is computed separately on the sale or other disposition of each share. According to the " 'unitary view,' ""the 'stockholder's entire investment is viewed as a single indivisible property unit,' "ibid. (citation omitted), and a sale or disposition of some of the stockholder's shares only produces "as ascertainable gain or loss when the stockholder has disposed of his remaining shares." The court observed that both it and the Tax Court generally had adhered to the fragmented view, and concluded that "the facts of the instant case [do not] present sufficient justification for abandoning" it. It therefore held that the Finks were entitled to deduct their basis in the surrendered shares immediately as an ordinary loss, except to the extent that the surrender had increased the value of their remaining shares. The Court of Appeals remanded the case to the Tax Court for a determination of the increase, if any, in the value of the Finks' remaining shares that was attributable to the surrender.

Judge Joiner dissented. Because the taxpayers' "sole motivation in disposing of certain shares is to benefit the other shares they hold[,] * * * [v]iewing the surrender of each share as the termination of an individual investment ignores the very reason for the surrender." He concluded: "Particularly in cases such as this, where the diminution in the shareholder's corporate control and equity interest is so minute as to be illusory, the stock surrender should be regarded as a contribution to capital."

We granted certiorari to resolve a conflict among the circuits, 479 U.S. 960, 107 S.Ct. 454, 93 L.Ed.2d 401 (1986), and now reverse.

II

A

It is settled that a shareholder's voluntary contribution to the capital of the corporation has no immediate tax consequences. 26 U.S.C. § 263; 26 CFR § 1.263(a)–2(f) (1986). Instead, the shareholder is entitled to increase the basis of his shares by the amount of his basis in the property transferred to the corporation. See 26 U.S.C. § 1016(a)(1). When the shareholder later disposes of his shares, his contribution is reflected as a smaller taxable gain or a larger deductible loss. This rule applies not only to transfers of cash or tangible property, but also to a shareholder's forgiveness of a debt owed to him by the corporation. 26 CFR § 1.61–12(a)

(1986). Such transfers are treated as contributions to capital even if the other shareholders make proportionately smaller contributions, or no contribution at all. The rules governing contributions to capital reflect the general principle that a shareholder may not claim an immediate loss for outlays made to benefit the corporation. We must decide whether this principle also applies to a controlling shareholder's non pro rata surrender of a portion of his shares.

B

The Finks contend that they sustained an immediate loss upon surrendering some of their shares to the corporation. By parting with the shares, they gave up an ownership interest entitling them to future dividends, future capital appreciation, assets in the event of liquidation, and voting rights.[7] Therefore, the Finks contend, they are entitled to an immediate deduction. See 26 U.S.C. §§ 165(a) and (c)(2). In addition, the Finks argue that any non pro rata stock transaction "give[s] rise to immediate tax results." For example, a non pro rata stock dividend produces income because it increases the recipient's proportionate ownership of the corporation.[8] By analogy, the Finks argue that a non pro rata surrender of shares should be recognized as an immediate loss because it reduces the surrendering shareholder's proportionate ownership.

Finally, the Finks contend that their stock surrenders were not contributions to the corporation's capital. They note that a typical contribution to capital, unlike a non pro rata stock surrender, has no effect on the contributing shareholder's proportionate interest in the corporation. Moreover, the Finks argue, a contribution of cash or other property increases the net worth of the corporation. For example, a shareholder's forgiveness of a debt owed to him by the corporation decreases the corporation's liabilities. In contrast, when a shareholder surrenders shares of the corporation's own stock, the corporation's net worth is unchanged. This is because the corporation cannot itself exercise the right to vote, receive dividends, or receive a share of assets in the event of liquidation. G. Johnson & J. Gentry, Finney and Miller's Principles of Accounting 538 (7th ed. 1974).[9]

III

A shareholder who surrenders a portion of his shares to the corporation has parted with an asset, but that alone does not entitle him to an

---

7. As a practical matter, however, the Finks did not give up a great deal. Their percentage interest in the corporation declined by only four percent. Because the Finks retained a majority interest, this reduction in their voting power was inconsequential. Moreover, Travco, like many corporations in financial difficulties, was not paying dividends.

8. In most cases, however, stock dividends are not recognized as income until the shares are sold. See 26 U.S.C. § 305.

9. Treasury stock—that is, stock that has been issued, reacquired by the corporation, and not canceled—generally is shown as an offset to shareholder's equity on the liability side of the balance sheet. G. Johnson & J. Gentry, Finney & Miller's Principles of Accounting 538 (7th ed. 1974).

immediate deduction. Indeed, if the shareholder owns less than 100 percent of the corporation's shares, any non pro rata contribution to the corporation's capital will reduce the net worth of the contributing shareholder.[10] A shareholder who surrenders stock thus is similar to one who forgives or surrenders a debt owed to him by the corporation; the latter gives up interest, principal, and also potential voting power in the event of insolvency or bankruptcy. But, as stated above, such forgiveness of corporate debt is treated as a contribution to capital rather than a current deduction. The Finks' voluntary surrender of shares, like a shareholder's voluntary forgiveness of debt owed by the corporation, closely resembles an investment or contribution to capital. See B. Bittker & J. Eustice, Federal Income Taxation of Corporations and Shareholders ¶ 3.14, p. 3–59 (4th ed. 1979) ("If the contribution is voluntary, it does not produce gain or loss to the shareholder"). We find the similarity convincing in this case.

The fact that a stock surrender is not recorded as a contribution to capital on the corporation's balance sheet does not compel a different result. Shareholders who forgive a debt owed by the corporation or pay a corporate expense also are denied an immediate deduction, even though neither of these transactions is a contribution to capital in the accounting sense.[11] Nor are we persuaded by the fact that a stock surrender, unlike a typical contribution to capital, reduces the shareholder's proportionate interest in the corporation. This Court has never held that every change in a shareholder's percentage ownership has immediate tax consequences. Of course, a shareholder's receipt of property from the corporation generally is a taxable event. See 26 U.S.C. §§ 301, 316. In contrast, a shareholder's transfer of property to the corporation usually has no immediate tax consequences. § 263.

The Finks concede that the purpose of their stock surrender was to protect or increase the value of their investment in the corporation.[12] They hoped to encourage new investors to provide needed capital and in the long run recover the value of the surrendered shares through increased dividends or appreciation in the value of their remaining shares. If the surrender had achieved its purpose, the Finks would not have suffered an

---

10. For example, assume that a shareholder holding an 80 percent interest in a corporation with a total liquidation value of $100,000 makes a non pro rata contribution to the corporation's capital of $20,000 in cash. Assume further that the shareholder has no other assets. Prior to the contribution, the shareholder's net worth was $100,000 ($20,000 plus 80 percent of $100,000). If the corporation were immediately liquidated following the contribution, the shareholder would receive only $96,000 (80 percent of $120,000). Of course such a non pro rata contribution is rare in practice. Typically a shareholder will simply purchase additional shares.

11. It is true that a corporation's stock is not considered an asset of the corporation. A corporation's own shares nevertheless may be as valuable to the corporation as other property contributed by shareholders, as treasury shares may be resold. This is evidenced by the fact that corporations often purchase their own shares on the open market.

12. Indeed, if the Finks did not make this concession their surrender probably would be treated as a non-deductible gift. See 26 CFR § 25.2511–1(h)(1) (1986).

economic loss. See Johnson, Tax Models for Nonprorata Shareholder Contributions, 3 Va.Tax.Rev. 81, 104–108 (1983). In this case, as in many cases involving closely-held corporations whose shares are not traded on an open market, there is no reliable method of determining whether the surrender will result in a loss until the shareholder disposes of his remaining shares. Thus, the Finks' stock surrender does not meet the requirement that an immediately deductible loss must be "actually sustained during the taxable year." 26 CFR § 1.165–1(b) (1986).

reasoning

Finally, treating stock surrenders as ordinary losses might encourage shareholders in failing corporations to convert potential capital losses to ordinary losses by voluntarily surrendering their shares before the corporation fails. In this way shareholders might avoid the consequences of 26 U.S.C. § 165(g)(1), that provides for capital loss treatment of stock that becomes worthless. Similarly, shareholders may be encouraged to transfer corporate stock rather than other property to the corporation in order to realize a current loss.[14]

We therefore hold that a dominant shareholder who voluntarily surrenders a portion of his shares to the corporation, but retains control, does not sustain an immediate loss deductible from taxable income. Rather, the surrendering shareholder must reallocate his basis in the surrendered shares to the shares he retains.[15] The shareholder's loss, if any, will be recognized when he disposes of his remaining shares. A reallocation of basis is consistent with the general principle that "[p]ayments made by a stockholder of a corporation for the purpose of protecting his interest therein must be regarded as [an] additional cost of his stock," and so

14. Our holding today also draws support from two other sections of the Code. First, § 83 provides that, if a shareholder makes a "bargain sale" of stock to a corporate officer or employee as compensation, the "bargain" element of the sale must be treated as a contribution to the corporation's capital. * * * To be sure, Congress was concerned in § 83 with transfers of restricted stock to employees as compensation rather than surrenders of stock to improve the corporation's financial condition. In both cases, however, the shareholder's underlying purpose is to increase the value of his investment.

Second, if a shareholder's stock is redeemed—that is, surrendered to the corporation in return for cash or other property—the shareholder is not entitled to an immediate deduction unless the redemption results in a substantial reduction in the shareholder's ownership percentage. §§ 302(a), (b), (d); 26 CFR § 1.302–2(c) (1986). Because the Finks' surrenders resulted in only a slight reduction in their ownership percentage, they would

not have been entitled to an immediate loss if they had received consideration for the surrendered shares. 26 U.S.C. § 302(b). Although the Finks did not receive a direct payment of cash or other property, they hoped to be compensated by an increase in the value of their remaining shares.

15. The Finks remained the controlling shareholders after their surrender. We therefore have no occasion to decide in this case whether a surrender that causes the shareholder to lose control of the corporation is immediately deductible. In related contexts, the Code distinguishes between minimal reductions in a shareholder's ownership percentage and loss of corporate control. See § 302(b)(2) (providing "exchange" rather than dividend treatment for a "substantially disproportionate redemption of stock" that brings the shareholder's ownership percentage below 50 percent); § 302(b)(3) (providing similar treatment when the redemption terminates the shareholder's interest in the corporation).

cannot be deducted immediately. Our holding today is not inconsistent with the settled rule that the gain or loss on the sale or disposition of shares of stock equals the difference between the amount realized in the sale or disposition and the shareholder's basis in the particular shares sold or exchanged. See 26 U.S.C. § 1001(a); 26 CFR § 1.1012–1(c)(1) (1986). We conclude only that a controlling shareholder's voluntary surrender of shares, like contributions of other forms of property to the corporation, is not an appropriate occasion for the recognition of gain or loss.

In this case we use the term "control" to mean ownership of more than half of a corporation's voting shares. We recognize, of course, that in larger corporations—especially those whose shares are listed on a national exchange—a person or entity may exercise control in fact while owning less than a majority of the voting shares. See Securities Exchange Act of 1934, § 13(d), 48 Stat. 894, 15 U.S.C. § 78m(d) (requiring persons to report acquisition of more than 5 percent of a registered equity security).

IV

For the reasons we have stated, the judgment of the Court of Appeals for the Sixth Circuit is reversed.

It is so ordered.

■ JUSTICE BLACKMUN concurs in the result.

■ JUSTICE WHITE, concurring.

Although I join the Court's opinion, I suggest that there is little substance in the reservation in footnote 15 of the question whether a surrender of stock that causes the stockholder to lose control of the corporation is immediately deductible as an ordinary loss. Of course, this case does not involve a loss of control; but as I understand the rationale of the Court's opinion, it would also apply to a surrender that results in loss of control. At least I do not find in the opinion any principled ground for distinguishing a loss-of-control case from this one.

■ JUSTICE SCALIA, concurring in the judgment.

I do not believe that the Finks' surrender of their shares was, or even closely resembles, a shareholder contribution to corporate capital. Since, however, its purpose was to make the corporation a more valuable investment by giving it a more attractive capital structure, I think that it was, no less than a contribution to capital, an "amount paid out * * * for * * * betterments made to increase the value of * * * property," 26 U.S.C. § 263(a)(1), and thus not entitled to treatment as a current deduction.

[The dissenting opinion of Mr. Justice Stevens has been omitted. Ed.]

2.   ORGANIZATIONAL AND START-UP EXPENSES

Code: §§ 195; 212(3); 248.

Regulations: § 1.248–1(b).

A corporation incurs a variety of expenses in connection with its incorporation. Section 248 permits a corporation to elect to deduct currently up to $5,000 of its "organizational expenditures" in the taxable year in which it begins business, but this $5,000 maximum current deduction is reduced by the amount by which total organizational expenditures exceed $50,000.[1] Organizational expenditures that are not currently deductible must be amortized over the 180–month period beginning with the month in which the corporation begins business.[2] A similar rule is provided for "start-up expenditures,"[3] which generally are amounts the corporation incurs after formation but before beginning business operations.

"Organizational expenditures" are defined as expenditures which are: (1) incident to the creation of the corporation, (2) chargeable to capital account, and (3) of a character which, if expended to create a corporation having a limited life, would be amortizable over that life.[4] Examples include legal fees for drafting the corporate charter and bylaws, fees paid to the state of incorporation, and necessary accounting services.[5] Specifically excluded are the costs of issuing or selling stock and expenditures connected with the transfer of assets to the corporation, presumably because such expenses do not create an asset that is exhausted over the life of the corporation.[6] "Start-up expenditures" are amounts that the corporation could have deducted currently as trade or business expenses if they had been incurred in an ongoing business. Pure capital expenditures, such as costs of acquiring a particular asset, are neither organizational nor start-up expenditures and must be capitalized and added to the basis of the asset.

Whether or not they are borne by the corporation, certain items are considered as expenses of the shareholders and, as such, they may neither be deducted nor amortized by the corporation. For example, expenses connected with the acquisition of stock (e.g., appraisal fees) must be capitalized and added to the shareholder's basis in the stock.[7]

PROBLEM

A currently conducts a computer software manufacturing business as a sole proprietorship. With the assistance of B, a wealthy investor, A plans to incorporate and then expand the business. A will contribute the assets and liabilities of her proprietorship and B will invest enough cash to give him a 49 percent interest in the corporation. After numerous appraisals, lengthy negotiations and considerable expense, A and B have agreed that the net

---

1. I.R.C. § 248(a)(1). Prior to October 22, 2004, Section 248 permitted a corporation to elect to amortize all of its organizational expenditures over a period of sixty months or more beginning with the month in which the corporation commenced business.

2. I.R.C. § 248(a)(2).

3. I.R.C. § 195(b).

4. I.R.C. § 248(b).

5. Reg. § 1.248–1(b)(2).

6. Reg. § 1.248–1(b)(3)(i). See S.Rep. No. 1622, 83d Cong.2d Sess. 224.

7. See Woodward v. Commissioner, 397 U.S. 572, 90 S.Ct. 1302 (1970); United States v. Hilton Hotels Corp., 397 U.S. 580, 90 S.Ct. 1307 (1970).

worth of A's proprietorship is $510,000. B thus will contribute $490,000 cash for his 49 percent interest.

To what extent do the following expenses incurred in connection with the incorporation constitute organizational expenditures that are either currently deductible or amortizable under Section 248:

(a) $3,000 in fees paid by A for appraisals of her proprietorship for purposes of the negotiations with B.

(b) Is there any difference in (a), above, if the appraisal fees are paid by the corporation?

(c) Legal fees paid by the corporation for the following services:

   (i) drafting the articles of incorporation, by laws and minutes of the first meeting of directors and shareholders;

   (ii) preparation of deeds and bills of sale transferring A's assets to the corporation;

   (iii) application for a permit from the state commissioner of corporations to issue the stock and other legal research relating to exempting the stock from registration under federal securities laws;

   (iv) preparation of a request for a Section 351 ruling from the Internal Revenue Service;

   (v) drafting a buy-sell agreement providing for the repurchase of shares by the corporation in the event A or B dies or becomes incapacitated.

(d) Same as (c), above, except the legal fees were all paid by A.

CHAPTER 3

THE CAPITAL STRUCTURE OF A CORPORATION

A. INTRODUCTION

The organizers of a business venture face a major decision in planning the capital structure of their company. The simplest method of raising corporate capital is by issuing stock in exchange for contributions of money, property or services. Stock—known as "equity" in corporate finance parlance—may be common or preferred, and either type may be issued in various classes with different rights and priorities as to voting, dividends, liquidations, convertibility, and the like. A corporation also may raise capital by borrowing, either from the same insider group that owns the company's stock or from banks and other outside lenders. Corporate debt typically is evidenced by a variety of instruments including bonds, notes and more exotic hybrid securities such as convertible debentures. Although both shareholders and creditors contribute capital, their relationship to the corporation is markedly different. As one early case put it, a shareholder is "an adventurer in the corporate business," taking risk and profit from success, while a creditor, "in compensation for not sharing the profits, is to be paid independently of the risk of success, and gets a right to dip into capital when the payment date arrives."[1]

To some extent, decisions concerning the proper mix of debt and equity are made without regard to tax considerations. Most businesses rely on both short and long-term debt to finance their operations. Quite apart from taxes, traditional corporate finance theorists believed that debt financing contributed to a higher rate of investment return. This conventional wisdom did not go unchallenged. In their well known writings on corporate finance, Professors Modigliani and Miller took the view that, assuming away taxes and other factors, the value of a corporation is unrelated to the amount of debt used in its capital structure.[2] On the other hand, excessive debt has its pitfalls, and CFO's of conservatively managed public companies may be reluctant to risk insolvency or a shaky credit rating by loading the corporate balance sheet with liabilities.[3] In short, innumerable factors other than taxes affect corporate financing decisions.

1. Commissioner v. O.P.P. Holding Corp., 76 F.2d 11, 12 (2d Cir.1935).

2. For a general discussion of the debate, see Klein & Coffee, Business Organiza-tion and Finance, Legal and Economic Principles 347–380 (9th ed. 2004).

3. The statement in the text is belied by the surge of debt financing that accompanied the corporate mergers and restructur-

Although the tax system may not always drive financing behavior, it profoundly influences the capital structure of both publicly traded and closely held C corporations. Consider the decision facing A and B, who each plan to invest $100,000 on the formation of closely held Newco, Inc. At first glance, it might seem that issuing any Newco debt to A and B would be a needless exercise. If the investors agree on their respective contributions and the allocation of ownership and voting power, what difference does it make whether they hold stock, bonds or notes? The answer is often found in the Internal Revenue Code, which distinguishes between debt and equity for tax purposes, tipping the scales in favor of issuing a healthy dose of debt. This tax bias toward debt financing is influential both at the time of formation and on later occasions in a corporation's life cycle.

The principal advantage of issuing debt as opposed to equity is avoidance of the "double tax." Even though most dividends now qualify for a preferential tax rate, they still are includible in a shareholder's income and are not deductible by the corporation. The earnings represented by these dividends are thus taxed at both the corporate and shareholder levels.[4] But interest paid on corporate debt, while also includible in the recipient's income, is deductible by the corporation.[5] Assuming the owners of the business desire some ongoing return on their investment, there is an incentive to distribute earnings with tax-deductible dollars.[6]

Several other features of the tax law reflect a bias in favor of debt over equity. The repayment of principal on a corporate debt is a tax-free return of capital to the lender. If the amount repaid exceeds the lender's basis in the debt, the difference generally is treated as a capital gain under Section 1271. In contrast, when a corporation redeems (i.e., buys back) stock from a shareholder—a transaction quite similar to the repayment of a debt—the entire amount received may be taxed as a dividend if the shareholder or related persons continue to own stock in the corporation.[7]

The issuance of debt at the time of incorporation also may provide a defense against subsequent imposition of the accumulated earnings tax.[8]

---

ings of the 1980's and the significant increases in corporate debt in 2000 and 2001. See, e.g., Zuckerman, "Climb of Corporate Debt Trips Analysts' Alarm," Wall St. Journal, Dec. 31, 2001, at C1 (reporting that U.S. corporations were incurring debt at record levels as of the end of 2001). The nontax risks of excessive debt were well documented by the collapse of the junk bond market in the early 1990's and the bankruptcy boom of 2001–2002 (e.g., Enron), but the tax system continues to provide incentives for C corporations to engage in debt-financed acquisitions and stock repurchases.

4. The dividends received deduction provides some additional tax relief for corporate shareholders. See I.R.C. § 243 and Chapter 4A, infra.

5. I.R.C. § 163(a).

6. But see Andrews, "Tax Neutrality Between Equity Capital and Debt," 30 Wayne L.Rev. 1057 (1984), suggesting that this traditional "simple view" is inadequate because it fails to recognize the opportunity for corporations to raise equity capital by accumulating earnings—a process that redounds to the benefit of shareholders without subjecting them to tax until the earnings are distributed or the shares are sold.

7. I.R.C. § 302. See Chapter 5C, infra.

8. I.R.C. § 531 et seq. See Chapter 14B, supra.

The obligation to repay a debt at maturity may qualify as a "reasonable business need," justifying an accumulation of corporate earnings,[9] while the same type of accumulation for a redemption of stock normally is not regarded as reasonable for purposes of the accumulated earnings tax.[10]

The choice between debt and equity has significant tax ramifications in many other contexts. For example, the classification of a corporate investment may have an impact on whether transfers of property to a corporation qualify for nonrecognition under Section 351. Complete nonrecognition of gain or loss is available only when the contributing taxpayer receives solely stock. Conversely, taxpayers who wish to recognize gain on the transfer of property to a controlled corporation may attempt to accomplish their objective by taking back boot in the form of installment debt obligations.[11] That goal will be thwarted if the notes are reclassified as stock. Classification of an interest in a corporation also may control the character of a loss if the investment becomes worthless.[12]

The tax distinctions between debt and equity have fueled an ongoing policy debate. The relationship between the favorable tax treatment of debt and the explosive growth in debt-financed corporate acquisitions have captured the public's attention for several decades. But Congress to date has declined to embrace a comprehensive legislative solution to the problems of excessive debt. Instead, it has been content to enact narrowly targeted provisions aimed at isolated abuses that are seen as threats to the integrity of the corporate income tax. The excerpt below from a Congressional study on the income tax aspects of corporate financial structures, which predates the reduced tax rate on qualified dividends, offers some general insights into the debt vs. equity policy debate.

Excerpt From Joint Committee on Taxation, Federal Income Tax Aspects of Corporate Financial Structures

101st Cong., 1st Sess. pp. 53–58 (Jan. 18, 1989).

A. Tax Advantage of Debt Versus Equity

The total effect of the tax system on the incentives for corporations to use debt or equity depends on the interaction between the tax treatment at the shareholder and corporate levels.

The case of no income taxes.—In a simple world without taxes or additional costs in times of financial distress, economic theory suggests that the value of a corporation, as measured by the total value of the outstanding debt and equity, would be unchanged by the degree of leverage of the

---

9. Reg. § 1.537–2(b)(3). Repayment of debt owed to shareholders, however, may be subjected to greater scrutiny. See Smoot Sand & Gravel Corp. v. Commissioner, 241 F.2d 197 (4th Cir.1957), cert. denied 354 U.S. 922, 77 S.Ct. 1383 (1957).

10. See, e.g., Bittker & Eustice, Federal Income Taxation of Corporations and Shareholders ¶ 7.07 (7th ed. 2000).

11. See Section 2F2 of this chapter, infra.

12. See Section D of this chapter, infra.

firm. This conclusion explicitly recognizes that debt issued by the corporation represents an ownership right to future income of the corporation in a fashion similar to that of equity. In this simple world there would be no advantage to debt or to equity and the debt-equity ratio of the firm would not affect the cost of financing investment.

Effect of corporate income tax

Tax advantages

Taxes greatly complicate this analysis. Since the interest expense on debt is deductible for computing the corporate income tax while the return to equity is not, the tax at the corporate level provides a strong incentive for debt rather than equity finance.

Table IV-A.—Effect of Debt Financing on Returns to Equity Investment

Item	All-equity corporation	50–percent debt-financed corporation
Beginning Balance Sheet:		
Total assets	$1,000	$1,000
Debt..............................	0	500
Shareholders' equity	1,000	500
Income Statement:		
Operating income.................	150	150
Interest expense	0	50
Taxable income...................	150	100
Income tax	51	34
Income after corporate tax	99	66
Return on Equity [1] (percent)..........	9.9	13.2

The advantages of debt financing can be illustrated by comparing two corporations with $1,000 of assets that are identical except for financial structure: the first is entirely equity financed; while the second is 50–percent debt financed. Both corporations earn $150 of operating income. The all-equity corporation pays $51 in corporate tax [this and later examples assume a 34 percent corporate income tax rate, Ed.] and retains or distributes $99 of after-tax income ($150 less $51). Thus, as shown in Table IV–A, the return on equity is 9.9 percent ($99 divided by $1,000).

The leveraged corporation is financed by $500 of debt and $500 of stock. If the interest rate is 10 percent, then interest expense is $50 (10 percent times $500). Taxable income is $100 after deducting interest expense. The leveraged corporation is liable for $34 in corporate tax (34 percent times $100) and distributes or retains $66 of after-tax income ($100 less $34). Consequently, the return on equity is 13.2 percent ($66 divided by $500). Thus, as shown in Table IV–A, increasing the debt ratio from

---

1. Return on equity is computed as income after corporate tax divided by beginning shareholders' equity.

zero to 50 percent increases the rate of return on equity from 9.9 to 13.2 percent.

This arithmetic demonstrates that a leveraged corporation can generate a higher return on equity (net of corporate income tax) than an unleveraged company or, equivalently, that an unleveraged company needs to earn a higher profit before corporate tax to provide investors the same return net of corporate tax as could be obtained with an unleveraged company. More generally, the return on equity rises with increasing debt capitalization so long as the interest rate is less than the pre-tax rate of return on corporate assets. This suggests that the Code creates an incentive to raise the debt-equity ratio to the point where the corporate income tax (or outstanding equity) is eliminated.

Costs of financial distress

With higher levels of debt the possibility of financial distress increases, as do the expected costs to the firm which occur with such distress. These additional costs include such items as the increase in the costs of debt funds; constraints on credit, expenditure or operating decisions; and the direct costs of being in bankruptcy. These expected costs of financial distress may, at sufficiently high debt-equity ratios, offset the corporate tax advantage to additional debt finance.

Effect of shareholder income tax

The above analysis focuses solely on the effect of interest deductibility at the corporate level. Shareholder-level income taxation may offset to some degree the corporate tax incentive for corporate debt relative to equity.

Shareholder treatment of debt and equity

The conclusion that debt is tax favored relative to equity remains unchanged if interest on corporate debt and returns on equity are taxed at the same effective rate to investors. In this case, the returns to investors on both debt and equity are reduced proportionately by the income tax; the advantage to debt presented by corporate tax deductibility remains. One noteworthy exception exists if the marginal investments on both debt and equity are effectively tax-exempt. Given the previously documented importance of tax-exempt pension funds in the bond and equity markets, this case may be of some importance.

Shareholder level tax treatment of equity

In general, returns to shareholders and debtholders are not taxed the same. Although dividends, like interest income, are taxed currently, equity income in other forms may reduce the effective investor-level tax on equity below that on debt. First, the firm may retain earnings and not pay dividends currently. In general, the accumulation of earnings by the firm will cause the value of the firm's shares to rise. Rather than being taxed currently on corporate earnings, a shareholder will be able to defer the taxation on the value of the retained earnings reflected in the price of the stock until the shareholder sells the stock. Thus, even though the tax rates on interest, dividends, and capital gains are the same [the tax rates were the same for a few years after the Tax Reform Act of 1986; under current law, <u>interest is taxable as ordinary income while long-term capital gains and qualified dividends are taxed at preferential rates,</u> Ed.], the ability to defer the tax on returns from equity reduces the effective rate of individual tax on equity investment below that on income from interest on corporate debt.

Other aspects of capital gain taxation serve to reduce further the individual income tax on equity. Since tax on capital gain is normally triggered after a voluntary recognition event (e.g., the sale of stock), the taxpayer can time the realization of capital gain income when the effective rate of tax is low. The rate of tax could be low if the taxpayer is in a low or zero tax bracket because other income is abnormally low, if other capital losses shelter the capital gain, or if changes in the tax law cause the statutory rate on capital gains to be low. Perhaps most important, the step up in the adjusted tax basis of the stock upon the death of the shareholder may permit the shareholder's heirs to avoid tax completely on capital gains. For all these reasons, the effective rate of tax on undistributed earnings may be already quite low.

Corporations can distribute their earnings to owners of equity in forms that generally result in less tax to shareholders than do dividend distributions. Share repurchases have become an important method of distributing corporate earnings to equity holders. When employed by large publicly traded firms, repurchases of the corporation's own shares permit the shareholders to treat the distribution as a sale of stock (i.e., to obtain capital gain treatment, and recover the basis in the stock without tax). The remaining shareholders may benefit because they have rights to a larger fraction of the firm and may see a corresponding increase in the value of their shares. Thus, less individual tax will generally be imposed on a $100 repurchase of stock than on $100 of dividends. In addition, share repurchases allow shareholders to choose whether to receive corporate distributions by choosing whether to sell or retain shares, so as to minimize tax liability.

Acquisitions of the stock of one corporation for cash or property of another corporation provides a similar method for distributing corporate earnings out of corporate solution with less shareholder tax than through a dividend. The target shareholders generally treat the acquisition as a sale and recover their basis free of tax. For purposes of analyzing the individual tax effect of corporate earnings disbursements, this transaction can be thought of as equivalent to a stock merger of the target with the acquiror followed by the repurchase of the target shareholders' shares by the resulting merged firm. The result is similar to the case of a share repurchase in that cash is distributed to shareholders with less than the full dividend tax, except that two firms are involved instead of one.

Since dividends typically are subject to more tax than other methods for providing returns to shareholders, the puzzle of why firms pay dividends remains. Because dividends are paid at the discretion of the firm, it appears that firms cause their shareholders to pay more tax on equity income than is strictly necessary. Until a better understanding of corporate distribution policy exists, the role of dividend taxation on equity financing decisions remain uncertain.

To summarize, although the current taxation of dividends to investors is clearly significant, there are numerous reasons why the overall individual tax on equity investments may be less than that on interest income from debt. Since the effective shareholder tax on returns from equity may be less than that on debt holdings, the shareholder tax may offset some or all of the advantage to debt at the corporate level.

Interaction of corporate and shareholder taxation

With shareholders in different income tax brackets, high tax rate taxpayers will tend to concentrate their wealth in the form of equity and low tax rate taxpayers will tend to concentrate their wealth in the form of debt. The distribution of wealth among investors with different marginal tax rates affects the demand for investments in the form of debt or equity. The interaction between the demand of investors, and the supply provided by corporations, determines the aggregate amount of corporate debt and equity in the economy.

At some aggregate mix between debt and equity, the difference in the investor-level tax on income from equity and debt may be sufficient to offset completely, at the margin, the apparent advantage of debt at the corporate level. Even if the difference in investor tax treatment of debt and equity is not sufficient to offset completely the corporate tax advantage, the advantage to debt may be less than the corporate-level tax treatment alone would provide.

* * *

Implications for policy

The analysis above suggests that any policy change designed to reduce the tax incentive for debt must consider the interaction of both corporate and shareholder taxes. For example, proposals to change the income tax rates for individuals or corporations will change the incentive for corporate debt. Likewise, proposals to change the tax treatment of tax-exempt entities may alter the aggregate mix and distribution of debt and equity.

In addition, proposals to reduce the bias toward debt over equity, for example, by reducing the total tax on dividends, must confront the somewhat voluntary nature of the dividend tax. Since the payment of dividends by corporations generally is discretionary and other means exist for providing value to shareholders with less tax, corporations can affect the level of shareholder level tax incurred. Until a better understanding of the determinants of corporate distribution behavior exists, the total impact of policies designed to reduce the bias between debt and equity are uncertain.

* * *

NOTE

The traditional tax bias for debt over equity has been weakened now that qualified dividends are taxed at the same preferential rate as long-term capital gains. The Bush Administration's original proposal to allow a 100 percent shareholder-level exclusion for dividends paid from previously taxed corporate earnings would have largely eliminated the bias and profoundly altered the stakes for future capital structure decisions.

The 15 percent rate on qualified dividends, assuming it becomes permanent,[1] is a major step toward neutralizing the debt vs. equity distinction. As long as dividends are taxed at preferential rates, equity investments will be more attractive to taxable investors. Not all shareholders pay taxes, however—e.g., tax-exempt pension funds and charities—and corporations still benefit from the ability to deduct interest paid on corporate debt. It thus seems premature to relegate the discussion of capital structure in this chapter to the recycling bin.

B.   DEBT VS. EQUITY

Taxpayers have considerable flexibility to structure corporate instruments as debt or equity. In view of the sharply disparate tax treatment of debt and equity, it is hardly surprising that the Service may be unwilling to accept the taxpayer's label as controlling.[1] Form would be elevated over substance if every piece of paper embossed with a corporate seal and bearing the label "debt" were treated as such for tax purposes. To prevent tax avoidance through the use of excessive debt, the Service may recast a purported debt obligation as equity. The tax consequences of a recharacterization can be extremely unpleasant. An interest payment becomes a dividend and the corporation loses its deduction. If and when the note is repaid, the "creditor" finds himself in the role of shareholder, and the "loan repayment" may turn into a taxable dividend instead of a tax-free return of capital.

It is one thing to list the advantages of debt and identify the unfortunate ramifications of reclassification. It is quite another to describe with any precision the process employed by the courts and the Service to determine whether a particular instrument is debt or equity. The case law first approaches the issue by describing a spectrum. At one end is equity, a risk investment with the potential to share in corporate profits. At the other end is debt, evidenced by the corporation's unconditional promise to pay back the contributed funds, with market rate interest, at a fixed maturity date. A pure equity investor—the shareholder—has voting rights and upside potential. A pure debt holder—the creditor—is an outsider with

---

1. Unless extended, the preferential rate will expire at the end of 2008.

1. The characterization of an instrument at its issuance is binding on the issuer, but not the Service. I.R.C. § 385(c)(1). A holder of an instrument generally is bound by the issuer's characterization unless the holder discloses an inconsistent position on a tax return. I.R.C. § 385(c)(2).

no prospect of sharing in the growth of the enterprise. Many classification controversies involve "hybrid securities" having features common to both debt and equity, and the courts must decide whether these instruments falling in the middle of the spectrum are closer to one end or the other.

Any process that looks at something decidedly gray and tries to determine whether it more closely resembles black or white is bound to be frustrating. And so it is here. The litigated cases are legion and the court decisions have been aptly vilified as a "jungle"[2] and a "viper's tangle."[3] The issue is murky because classification of an obligation as debt or equity traditionally is treated as a question of fact to be resolved by applying vague standards that require the weighing of many factors.[4] In a manner reminiscent of the approach to determining whether an asset is "held primarily for sale to customers," the courts have spewed forth laundry lists of "factors," but it is difficult to discern which are controlling in a given case. Exhaustive research leaves one with the firm conviction that the courts are applying an amorphous and highly unsatisfactory "smell test."

Synthesizing the decisional morass is a perilous enterprise, but the principal factors enunciated by the courts over the years may be summarized as follows:[5]

Form of the Obligation. Labels are hardly controlling, but the decisions provide some guidance for a corporation that wishes to avoid reclassification of debt as equity. At a minimum, debt instruments should bear the usual indicia of debt—an unconditional promise to pay; a specific term; remedies for a default; and a stated, reasonable rate of interest, payable in all events.[6] Equity characteristics should be avoided. For example, the likelihood of reclassification is far greater with a hybrid instrument that makes payment of interest contingent on earnings or provides the holder with voting rights.[7]

The Debt/Equity Ratio. The debt/equity ratio of a corporation is the ratio of the company's liabilities to the shareholders' equity. The ratio has long been used as a tool to determine whether a corporation is thinly capitalized. Thin capitalization, in turn, creates a substantial risk that what purports to be debt will be reclassified as equity on the theory that no

---

2. Commissioner v. Union Mutual Insurance Co. of Providence, 386 F.2d 974, 978 (1st Cir.1967).

3. Bittker & Eustice, Federal Income Taxation of Corporations and Shareholders ¶ 4.04 (4th ed. 1979).

4. For this reason, the Service ordinarily declines to issue advance rulings on the classification on an instrument as debt or equity. Rev. Proc. 2005–3, § 4.02(1), 2005–1 C.B. 118, 125.

5. See generally Plumb, "The Federal Income Tax Significance of Corporate Debt: A Critical Analysis and a Proposal," 26 Tax L.Rev. 369 (1971); Stone, "Debt–Equity Distinctions in the Tax Treatment of the Corporation and Its Shareholders," 42 Tulane L.Rev. 251 (1968). For a more contemporary summary, see Hariton, "Essay: Distinguishing Between Equity and Debt in the New Financial Environment," 49 Tax L. Rev. 499 (1994).

6. See Wood Preserving Corp. v. United States, 347 F.2d 117, 119 (4th Cir.1965).

7. See Fellinger v. United States, 363 F.2d 826 (6th Cir.1966).

rational creditor would lend money to a corporation with such nominal equity.

The trouble with this attempt at quantification is that the cases are inconsistent as to what constitutes an excessive debt/equity ratio. For example, depending on all the other factors, a debt/equity ratio of 3–to–1, which most would regard as conservative, has been held to be excessive,[8] while ratios of 50–to–1 and higher have been held to be acceptable.[9] Some cases apply different norms for different industries,[10] others ignore the ratio entirely,[11] and some evaluate the ratio in the context of the overall growth prospects of the business.[12]

And how is the debt/equity ratio to be computed? Consider some of the basic questions on which there is disagreement. Is debt limited to shareholder debt or does it include debts to outsiders?[13] Does outside debt include accounts payable to trade creditors or only long-term liabilities? What about shareholder guaranteed debt?[14] In determining "equity," are assets taken into account at their book value (i.e., adjusted basis) or fair market value?[15] The differences in approach can be considerable.

Intent Some cases have turned on the "intent" of the parties to create a debtor-creditor relationship.[16] "Intent" presumably is not gleaned by a subjective inquiry; it would be meaningless to place the corporate insiders on the witness stand and ask whether they "intended" to be shareholders

---

8. See Schnitzer v. Commissioner, 13 T.C. 43 (1949).

9. See Bradshaw v. United States, 231 Ct.Cl. 144, 683 F.2d 365, 367–68 (1982)(50–to–1 ratio not fatal because corporation was likely to and did in fact pay off debts when due); Baker Commodities, Inc. v. Commissioner, 48 T.C. 374 (1967), affirmed, 415 F.2d 519 (9th Cir.1969), cert. denied, 397 U.S. 988, 90 S.Ct. 1117 (1970)(692–to–1 ratio is acceptable because cash flow and earning power of business could cover payments).

10. Compare Tomlinson v. 1661 Corp., 377 F.2d 291 (5th Cir.1967)(improved real estate; debt traditionally high) with John Lizak, Inc. v. Commissioner, 28 T.C.M. 804 (1969)(construction business less able to carry heavy debt burden).

11. See Gooding Amusement Co. v. Commissioner, 23 T.C. 408, 419 (1954), affirmed, 236 F.2d 159 (6th Cir.1956), cert. denied, 352 U.S. 1031, 77 S.Ct. 595 (1957).

12. See, e.g., Delta Plastics, Inc. v. Commissioner, 85 T.C.M. 940 (2003) (26–to–1 ratio was acceptable because likely success of business would reduce ratio to 4–to–1 within three years).

13. Compare Ambassador Apartments, Inc. v. Commissioner, 50 T.C. 236, 245 (1968), affirmed, 406 F.2d 288 (2d Cir. 1969)(consider outside debt) with P.M. Finance Corp. v. Commissioner, 302 F.2d 786, 788 (3d Cir.1962) (consider only shareholder debt).

14. Compare Murphy Logging Co. v. United States, 378 F.2d 222 (9th Cir. 1967)(disregard shareholder guaranteed debt) with Plantation Patterns, Inc. v. Commissioner, 462 F.2d 712 (5th Cir.1972), cert. denied, 409 U.S. 1076, 93 S.Ct. 683 (1972)(shareholder guaranteed debt recharacterized as equity contribution by guarantor.)

15. See Nye v. Commissioner, 50 T.C. 203, 216 (1968). In Bauer v. Commissioner, 748 F.2d 1365 (9th Cir.1984), the court computed stockholders' equity by adding together paid-in capital and retained earnings and arrived at outside debt/equity ratios for different years ranging from approximately 2 to 1 to 8 to 1. The Tax Court had determined a ratio for one year of approximately 92 to 1 by limiting shareholders' equity to initial paid-in capital.

16. See Gooding Amusement Co. v. Commissioner, 236 F.2d 159 (6th Cir.1956), cert. denied, 352 U.S. 1031, 77 S.Ct. 595 (1957).

or creditors. The more reasoned decisions measure "intent" by objective criteria such as the lender's reasonable expectation of repayment, evaluated in light of the financial condition of the company, and the corporation's ability to pay principal and interest.[17] Hindsight also plays a role. For example, if the corporation consistently fails to pay interest or repay debts when they are due, its claim to debtor status may be highly questionable.[18]

Proportionality In a closely held setting, debt held by the shareholders in the same proportion as their stock holdings normally raises the eyebrows of the Service.[19] The rationale is that if debt is held in roughly the same proportion as stock, the "creditors" have no economic incentive to act like creditors by setting or enforcing the terms of the so-called liability. The unanswered question is whether proportionality, without other negative factors, is sufficient in itself to convert the obligation into stock.[20]

Subordination. If a corporation has borrowed from both shareholders and outside sources, the independent creditors frequently will require that the shareholder debt be subordinated to the claims of general creditors. Although subordination of inside debt would appear to be inevitable if significant unsecured outside financing is desired, some courts have regarded it as the smoking pistol.[21] Once again, however, it is difficult to advise a client with any certainty that subordination is fatal per se. The economic realities of closely held corporate life would suggest that it should not be determinative, but it grows in importance when combined with other negative factors such as thin capitalization and proportionality.[22]

This distillation of factors barely scratches the surface. The *Fin Hay Realty* case, which follows, provides an illustration of one court's approach to the problem.[23]

Fin Hay Realty Co. v. United States

United States Court of Appeals, Third Circuit, 1968.
398 F.2d 694.

OPINION OF THE COURT

■ FREEDMAN, CIRCUIT JUDGE.

We are presented in this case with the recurrent problem whether funds paid to a close corporation by its shareholders were additional

---

17. Fin Hay Realty Co. v. United States, 398 F.2d 694 (3d Cir.1968); Gilbert v. Commissioner, 248 F.2d 399 (2d Cir.1957).

18. See Slappey Drive Industrial Park v. United States, 561 F.2d 572, 582 (5th Cir.1977); Estate of Mixon v. United States, 464 F.2d 394, 409 (5th Cir.1972).

19. See Charter Wire, Inc. v. United States, 309 F.2d 878, 880 (7th Cir.1962), cert. denied, 372 U.S. 965, 83 S.Ct. 1090 (1963).

20. For a negative view, see Harlan v. United States, 409 F.2d 904, 909 (5th Cir. 1969)(proportionality may be considered but has no significant importance).

21. See P.M. Finance Corp. v. Commissioner, 302 F.2d 786, 789–90 (3d Cir.1962); R.C. Owen Co. v. Commissioner, 23 T.C.M. 673, 676 (1964), affirmed, 351 F.2d 410 (6th Cir.1965), cert. denied, 382 U.S. 967, 86 S.Ct. 1272 (1966).

22. See Tyler v. Tomlinson, 414 F.2d 844 (5th Cir.1969).

23. For a more thorough examination, see Plumb, supra note 5, a classic article that somehow manages to survey this vexing subject with only 1,591 footnotes.

contributions to capital or loans on which the corporation's payment of interest was deductible under § 163 of the Internal Revenue Code of 1954.

The problem necessarily calls for an evaluation of the facts, which we therefore detail.

Fin Hay Realty Co., the taxpayer was organized on February 14, 1934, by Frank L. Finlaw and J. Louis Hay. Each of them contributed $10,000 for which he received one-half of the corporation's stock and at the same time each advanced an additional $15,000 for which the corporation issued to him its unsecured promissory note payable on demand and bearing interest at the rate of six per cent per annum. The corporation immediately purchased an apartment house in Newark, New Jersey, for $39,000 in cash. About a month later the two shareholders each advanced an additional $35,000 to the corporation in return for six per cent demand promissory notes and next day the corporation purchased two apartment buildings in East Orange, New Jersey, for which it paid $75,000 in cash and gave the seller a six per cent, five year purchase money mortgage for the balance of $100,000.

Three years later, in October, 1937, the corporation created a new mortgage on all three properties and from the proceeds paid off the old mortgage on the East Orange property, which had been partially amortized. The new mortgage was for a five year term in the amount of $82,000 with interest at four and one-half per cent. In the following three years each of the shareholders advanced an additional $3,000 to the corporation, bringing the total advanced by each shareholder to $53,000, in addition to their acknowledged stock subscriptions of $10,000 each.

Finlaw died in 1941 and his stock and notes passed to his two daughters in equal shares. A year later the mortgage, which was about to fall due, was extended for a further period of five years with interest at four per cent. From the record it appears that it was subsequently extended until 1951.[3] In 1949 Hay died and in 1951 his executor requested the retirement of his stock and the payment of his notes. The corporation thereupon refinanced its real estate for $125,000 and sold one of the buildings. With the net proceeds it paid Hay's estate $24,000 in redemption of his stock and $53,000 in retirement of his notes. Finlaw's daughters then became and still remain the sole shareholders of the corporation.

Thereafter the corporation continued to pay and deduct interest on Finlaw's notes, now held by his two daughters. In 1962 the Internal Revenue Service for the first time declared the payments on the notes not allowable as interest deductions and disallowed them for the tax years 1959 and 1960. The corporation thereupon repaid a total of $6,000 on account of the outstanding notes and in the following year after refinancing the

---

3. The corporation's tax returns show a continuing decline in the principal of the debt until that year.

mortgage on its real estate repaid the balance of $47,000. A short time later the Internal Revenue Service disallowed the interest deductions for the years 1961 and 1962. When the corporation failed to obtain refunds it brought this refund action in the district court. After a nonjury trial the court denied the claims and entered judgment for the United States. 261 F.Supp. 823 (D.N.J.1966). From this judgment the corporation appeals.

This case arose in a factual setting where it is the corporation which is the party concerned that its obligations be deemed to represent a debt and not a stock interest. In the long run in cases of this kind it is also important to the shareholder that his advance be deemed a loan rather than a capital contribution, for in such a case his receipt of repayment may be treated as the retirement of a loan rather than a taxable dividend.[6] There are other instances in which it is in the shareholder's interest that his advance to the corporation be considered a debt rather than an increase in his equity. A loss resulting from the worthlessness of stock is a capital loss under § 165(g), whereas a bad debt may be treated as an ordinary loss if it qualifies as a business bad debt under § 166. Similarly, it is only if a taxpayer receives debt obligations of a controlled corporation that he can avoid the provision for nonrecognition of gains or losses on transfers of property to such a corporation under § 351.[8] These advantages in having the funds entrusted to a corporation treated as corporate obligations instead of contributions to capital have required the courts to look beyond the literal terms in which the parties have cast the transaction in order to determine its substantive nature.

In attempting to deal with this problem courts and commentators have isolated a number of criteria by which to judge the true nature of an investment which is in form a debt: (1) the intent of the parties; (2) the identity between creditors and shareholders; (3) the extent of participation in management by the holder of the instrument; (4) the ability of the corporation to obtain funds from outside sources; (5) the "thinness" of the capital structure in relation to debt; (6) the risk involved; (7) the formal indicia of the arrangement; (8) the relative position of the obligees as to other creditors regarding the payment of interest and principal; (9) the voting power of the holder of the instrument; (10) the provision of a fixed rate of interest; (11) a contingency on the obligation to repay; (12) the source of the interest payments; (13) the presence or absence of a fixed maturity date; (14) a provision for redemption by the corporation; (15) a provision for redemption at the option of the holder; and (16) the timing of the advance with reference to the organization of the corporation.

---

6. The partial retirement of an equity interest may be considered as essentially equivalent to a dividend under § 302, while the repayment of even a debt whose principal has appreciated is taxed only as a capital gain under [§ 1271(a)(1). Ed.]

8. A taxpayer might wish to avoid § 351 when he transfers depreciated property to the corporation and seeks to recognize the loss immediately and also when the transferred property is to be resold by the corporation but will not qualify for capital gains treatment in the hands of the corporation.

While the Internal Revenue Code of 1954 was under consideration, and after its adoption, Congress sought to identify the criteria which would determine whether an investment represents a debt or equity, but these and similar efforts have not found acceptance.[10] It still remains true that neither any single criterion nor any series of criteria can provide a conclusive answer in the kaleidoscopic circumstances which individual cases present. See John Kelley Co. v. Commissioner of Internal Revenue, 326 U.S. 521, 530, 66 S.Ct. 299, 90 L.Ed. 278 (1946).

The various factors which have been identified in the cases are only aids in answering the ultimate question whether the investment, analyzed in terms of its economic reality, constitutes risk capital entirely subject to the fortunes of the corporate venture or represents a strict debtor-creditor relationship. Since there is often an element of risk in a loan, just as there is an element of risk in an equity interest, the conflicting elements do not end at a clear line in all cases.

In a corporation which has numerous shareholders with varying interests, the arm's-length relationship between the corporation and a shareholder who supplies funds to it inevitably results in a transaction whose form mirrors its substance. Where the corporation is closely held, however, and the same persons occupy both sides of the bargaining table, form does not necessarily correspond to the intrinsic economic nature of the transaction, for the parties may mold it at their will with no countervailing pull. This is particularly so where a shareholder can have the funds he advances to a corporation treated as corporate obligations instead of contributions to capital without affecting his proportionate equity interest. Labels, which are perhaps the best expression of the subjective intention of parties to a transaction, thus lose their meaningfulness.

To seek economic reality in objective terms of course disregards the personal interest which a shareholder may have in the welfare of the corporation in which he is a dominant force. But an objective standard is one imposed by the very fact of his dominant position and is much fairer than one which would presumptively construe all such transactions against the shareholder's interest. Under an objective test of economic reality it is useful to compare the form which a similar transaction would have taken had it been between the corporation and an outside lender, and if the

---

10. The original House version of the 1954 Code, H.R. 8300, 83d Cong., 2d Sess., contained a provision, § 312, which distinguished between "securities", "participating stock", and "nonparticipating stock". Only payments with regard to "securities" were deductible by the corporation as interest. See proposed § 275. "Securities" were defined as unconditional obligations to pay a sum certain with an unconditional interest requirement not dependent on corporate earnings. The Senate rejected the proposed classification on the ground that it was inflexible. See S.Rep. No. 1622, 83d Cong., 2d Sess., 1954 U.S.C.Cong. & Admin.News, pp. 4621, 4673.

A similar list of determinants was proposed in 1957 by an advisory group to a subcommittee of the House Committee on Ways and Means, but was not acted upon.

In 1954 the American Law Institute embodied such a test in § x500 of its draft income tax statute. See ALI Federal Tax Project, Income Tax Problems of Corporations and Shareholders 396 (1958).

shareholder's advance is far more speculative than what an outsider would make, it is obviously a loan in name only.

In the present case all the formal indicia of an obligation were meticulously made to appear. The corporation, however, was the complete creature of the two shareholders who had the power to create whatever appearance would be of tax benefit to them despite the economic reality of the transaction. Each shareholder owned an equal proportion of stock and was making an equal additional contribution, so that whether Finlaw and Hay designated any part of their additional contributions as debt or as stock would not dilute their proportionate equity interests. There was no restriction because of the possible excessive debt structure, for the corporation had been created to acquire real estate and had no outside creditors except mortgagees who, of course, would have no concern for general creditors because they had priority in the security of the real estate. The position of the mortgagees also rendered of no significance the possible subordination of the notes to other debts of the corporation, a matter which in some cases this Court has deemed significant.

The shareholders here, moreover, lacked one of the principal advantages of creditors. Although the corporation issued demand notes for the advances, nevertheless, as the court below found, it could not have repaid them for a number of years. The economic reality was that the corporation used the proceeds of the notes to purchase its original assets, and the advances represented a long term commitment dependent on the future value of the real estate and the ability of the corporation to sell or refinance it. Only because such an entwining of interest existed between the two shareholders and the corporation, so different from the arm's-length relationship between a corporation and an outside creditor, were they willing to invest in the notes and allow them to go unpaid for so many years while the corporation continued to enjoy the advantages of uninterrupted ownership of its real estate.

It is true that real estate values rose steadily with a consequent improvement in the mortgage market, so that looking back the investment now appears to have been a good one. As events unfolded, the corporation reached a point at which it could have repaid the notes through refinancing, but this does not obliterate the uncontradicted testimony that in 1934 it was impossible to obtain any outside mortgage financing for real estate of this kind except through the device of a purchase money mortgage taken back by the seller.

It is argued that the rate of interest at six per cent per annum was far more than the shareholders could have obtained from other investments. This argument, however, is self-defeating, for it implies that the shareholders would damage their own corporation by an overcharge for interest. There was, moreover, enough objective evidence to neutralize this contention. The outside mortgage obtained at the time the corporation purchased the East Orange property bore interest at the rate of six per cent even though the mortgagee was protected by an equity in excess of forty per cent of the value of the property. In any event, to compare the six per cent interest rate of the notes with other 1934 rates ignores the most salient feature of the notes—their risk. It is difficult to escape the inference that a prudent outside businessman would not have risked his capital in six per cent unsecured demand notes in Fin Hay Realty Co. in 1934. The evidence therefore amply justifies the conclusion of the district court that the form which the parties gave to their transaction did not match its economic reality.

It is argued that even if the advances may be deemed to have been contributions to capital when they were originally made in 1934, a decisive change occurred when the original shareholder, Finlaw, died and his heirs continued to hold the notes without demanding payment. This, it is said could be construed as a decision to reinvest, and if by 1941 the notes were sufficiently secure to be considered bona fide debt, they should now be so treated for tax purposes. Such a conclusion, however, does not inevitably follow. Indeed, the weight of the circumstances leads to the opposite conclusion.

First, there is nothing in the record to indicate that the corporation could have readily raised the cash with which to pay off Finlaw's notes on his death in 1941. When Hay, the other shareholder, died in 1949 and his executor two years later requested the retirement of his interest, the corporation in order to carry this out sold one of its properties and refinanced the others. Again, when in 1963 the corporation paid off the notes held by Finlaw's daughters after the Internal Revenue Service had disallowed the interest deductions for 1961 and 1962 it again refinanced its real estate. There is nothing in the record which would sustain a finding that the corporation could have readily undertaken a similar financing in 1941, when Finlaw died even if we assume that the corporation was able to undertake the appropriate refinancing ten years later to liquidate Hay's interest. Moreover, there was no objective evidence to indicate that in 1941 Finlaw's daughters viewed the notes as changed in character or in security, or indeed that they viewed the stock and notes as separate and distinct investments. To indulge in a theoretical conversion of equity contributions into a debt obligation in 1941 when Finlaw died would be to ignore what such a conversion might have entailed. For Finlaw's estate might then have been chargeable with the receipt of dividends at the time the equity was redeemed and converted into a debt. To recognize retrospectively such a change in the character of the obligation would be to assume a conclusion with consequences unfavorable to the parties, which they themselves never acknowledged.

The burden was on the taxpayer to prove that the determination by the Internal Revenue Service that the advances represented capital contributions was incorrect. The district court was justified in holding that the taxpayer had not met this burden.

The judgment of the district court will be affirmed.

[The dissenting opinion of Judge VAN DUSEN has been omitted. Ed.]

NOTE

The types of financial instruments available to investors have proliferated. As one commentator has described the reality of today's world of corporate finance, "[i]n exchange for capital, corporations can offer investors any set of rights that can be described by words, subject to any conceivable set of qualifications, and in consideration of any conceivable set of offsetting obligations."[1]

The flexibility afforded corporate issuers has contributed to an array of exotic products that seek "best of both worlds" treatment—i.e., debt for tax purposes and equity for regulatory, financial rating, and accounting purposes. These hybrid instruments have been created and marketed by large financial institutions and Wall Street law firms who have advised corporate issuers that they may deduct the "interest" paid on the purported debt while treating the instruments as equity for financial statement or regulatory purposes.

In the mid–1990's, Wall Street and the Service skirmished over the tax treatment of so-called monthly income preferred securities ("MIPs"), a creation of the large investment bank, Goldman Sachs. A MIP commonly has significant equity features. Typically, the obligation term was 50 to 100 years, the "debt" was subordinated to other corporate indebtedness, and the issuer had the right to defer interest payments for up to five years. On the debt side, the lender was entitled to the repayment of the full amount of his investment and had the rights typically enjoyed by a creditor to enforce the terms of the obligation on a default.[2]

In its reaction to MIPs and similar financing vehicles, the Service noted that characterization of an instrument for federal tax purposes depends on all the facts and circumstances, with no particular factor being conclusive in deciding whether an instrument is debt or equity.[3] It announced "particular interest" in instruments that contained a variety of equity features, including an unreasonably long maturity or the ability to repay the instrument's principal with corporate stock. The pronouncement went on to address both of those factors and included a distinct warning to practitioners about relying on the precedential value of specific cases and rulings. Concerning length of maturity, the Service noted the case law supporting debt characterization for instruments with a 50–year term,[4] but

---

1. Hariton, "Distinguishing Between Equity and Debt in the New Financial Environment," 49 Tax L.Rev. 499, 501 (1994).

2. MIPs transactions are described in more detail in Hariton, supra note 1; Sheppard, "News Analysis: Treasury Stands Up to Wall Street," 63 Tax Notes 386 (1994); and Sheppard, "News Analysis: Toward Straightforward Section 385 Guidance," 65 Tax Notes 664 (1994).

3. Notice 94–47, 1994–1 C.B. 357. Notice 94–48, 1994–1 C.B. 357 addresses a variation of the MIPs strategy in which a corpo-

ration forms a partnership which issues notes to third-party investors and then purchases newly issued preferred stock of the corporation. Notice 94–48 states that the Service believes the overall substance of the arrangement is simply an issuance of preferred stock by the corporation and suggests different theories for denying the corporation an interest deduction.

4. See Monon Railroad v. Commissioner, 55 T.C. 345 (1970), *acq.* 1973–2 C.B. 3.

it cautioned that even in the case of terms of less than 50 years, debt characterization may not be appropriate for an instrument with significant equity characteristics. The Service also noted that the reasonableness of an instrument's term has to include consideration of factors such as an obligation to relend funds and the issuer's ability to satisfy the instrument.[5] But the Treasury Department's efforts to eliminate MIPs ultimately were beaten back by a lobbying blitz on behalf of a coalition of investment banks, law firms and corporate borrowers.[6]

As for the form of payment, the Service has ruled that an instrument may be classified as debt where a holder has the right to be repaid in cash or stock.[7] Thus, if a holder is required to accept payment of principal solely in stock, the instrument does not qualify as debt. Similarly, if an instrument provides a holder with a choice between repayment in cash or stock but is structured to ensure a selection of the stock, the instrument will not qualify as debt.[8]

Section 163(l) may limit a corporation's interest deduction in the case of debt payable in equity by disallowing a deduction for interest (including accrued original issue discount) paid or accrued on a "disqualified debt instrument," which is generally defined as any corporate debt payable in equity of the issuer or a related party.[9] Debt is treated as payable in stock if a substantial amount of the principal or interest is required either: (1) to be paid or converted into stock of the issuer or a related party, or (2) to be determined by reference to stock of the issuer or related party.[10] Debt also is treated as payable in stock if the issuer has the option to pay, convert, or determine the amount of principal or interest by reference to its stock or stock of a related party.[11]

Despite all the cautionary notes from the Service and occasional legislation, the financial services industry continues to market a dizzying array of hybrid security "products" that allow public companies to claim interest deductions on their tax returns while avoiding debt classification on their books.[12] Known generically as "trust preferred securities" and labelled with various trademarked acronyms, the standard terms are fairly similar and include maturities of from 20 to 30 years, a fixed interest rate,

5. Notice 94–47, 1994–1 C.B. 357.

6. See, e.g., McKinnon and Hitt, "How Treasury Lost in Battle to Quash a Dubious Security: Instrument Issued by Enron and Others Can be Used as Both Debt and Equity," Wall St. Journal, Feb. 4, 2002, at A1.

7. Rev. Rul. 85–119, 1985–2 C.B. 60.

8. Notice 94–47, supra note 3.

9. I.R.C. § 163(l)(2). "Related party" is defined by reference to Sections 267(b) and 707. I.R.C. § 163(l)(4).

10. I.R.C. § 163(l)(3)(A) & (B).

11. An instrument also is treated as payable in stock if it is part of an arrange-

ment reasonably expected to result in such payment with or by reference to the stock. I.R.C. § 163(l)(3)(C). Examples include nonrecourse debt secured principally by the issuer's stock or debt convertible at the holder's option when it is substantially certain the conversion right will be exercised.

12. See Sheppard, "The Nine Lives of Equity–Linked Securities," 92 Tax Notes 597 (Aug. 6, 2001); McKinnon, "Congressional Probe to Examine Enron's Tax–Avoidance Strategies," Wall St. Journal, Feb. 19, 2002, at A6.

and a right on the part of the issuer to defer interest payments for up to five years at a time.

C.   THE SECTION 385 SAGA

Code: § 385.

Background. In the course of its deliberations on the Tax Reform Act of 1969, Congress concluded that determined effort was needed to alleviate the uncertainties flowing from the debt/equity case law, especially in light of "the increasing use of debt for corporate acquisition purposes."[1] Frustrated in its attempt to draft precise definitions, Congress delegated the chore to the executive branch by enacting Section 385, which authorizes the Treasury to promulgate such regulations "as may be necessary or appropriate" to determine for all tax purposes whether an interest in a corporation is to be treated as stock or debt. Section 385(b) requires the regulations to set forth "factors" to be taken into account in determining whether a debtor-creditor relationship exists and specifies the following factors which may (but need not) be included in the regulations:

1. Form—i.e., whether the instrument is evidenced by a written, unconditional promise to pay a sum certain on demand or on a specific date in return for an adequate consideration and bears a fixed interest rate.   *Debt*

2. Subordination to any indebtedness of the corporation. *Equity*

3. The debt/equity ratio.

4. Convertibility into stock. *Equity*

5. Proportionality—i.e., the relationship between holdings of stock in the corporation and holdings of the purported debt interest being scrutinized.

The Regulations Project. Section 385 was hailed by leading commentators as "perhaps the most important and potentially far-reaching corporate provision added by the Tax Reform Act of 1969,"[2] and the literature was replete with predictions as to the content of the regulations.[3] In March, 1980, 11 years after Section 385 was enacted, the Treasury issued a lengthy, detailed and controversial set of proposed regulations.[4] "Final" regulations were promulgated in December, 1980,[5] followed by amendments

1. S.Rep. No. 91–552, 91st Cong., 1st Sess. 511 (1969), reprinted in 1969–3 C.B. 423, 511. See also H.R.Rep. No. 91–413, 91st Cong., 1st Sess. 265 (1969), reprinted in 1969–3 C.B. 200, 265.

2. Bittker & Eustice, Federal Income Taxation of Corporations and Shareholders, ¶ 4.05 (3rd ed. 1971).

3. Id. at 4–16 to 4–19. See also Recommendations as to Federal Tax Distinction be-

tween Corporate Stock and Indebtedness, N.Y. State Bar Association Tax Section Committee on Reorganization Problems, 25 Tax Lawyer 57 (1971).

4. 45 Fed.Reg. 18957 (1980).

5. T.D. 7747 (filed Dec. 29, 1980), 45 Fed.Reg. 86438 (Dec. 31, 1980), known as the "December 29" regulations.

and effective date extensions, but all versions of the regulations were withdrawn in 1983[6] and the project has since been abandoned.

Although detailed examination of the now long defunct regulations would not be productive, some features are noteworthy if only because they represented a concentrated attempt to bring order out of the chaos. For example, the regulations[7] distinguished straight debt from hybrid instruments, appropriately relegating hybrid securities to second class status. A "hybrid" was defined as an instrument convertible into stock or providing for any contingent payment to the holder.[8] In virtually all cases, hybrids would have been treated as preferred stock for tax purposes, at least if they were not held by independent creditors.[9] Straight debt—defined as anything other than a hybrid instrument[10]—still had a fighting chance of avoiding reclassification if certain other requirements were met.

The concept of proportionality played a central role in the regulatory scheme because "it generally makes little economic difference (aside from tax consequences) whether proportionate shareholder advances are made as debt or equity * * *."[11] Elaborate definitions of proportionality were provided, and special scrutiny was required for instruments held in substantial proportion to equity investments.[12]

Another contribution of the regulations was their precise definition of two debt/equity ratios—"outside" (which took into account *all* liabilities, including those to independent creditors) and "inside" (considering only shareholder debt).[13] Corollary rules provided that assets were to be reflected at adjusted basis rather than fair market value and trade liabilities were to be disregarded.[14] The debt/equity ratio was used to determine whether a corporation's debt was "excessive". A debt was excessive if the instrument's terms and conditions, viewed in combination with the corporation's financial structure, would not have been satisfactory to a bank or other financial institution making ordinary commercial loans.[15] It was not excessive, however, if the outside debt/equity ratio did not exceed 10–to–1 and the inside debt/equity ratio did not exceed 3–to–1.[16] Thus, even proportionate straight debt issued for cash would not be reclassified if it fell within this safe harbor from "excessive debt" and bore a "reasonable"

6. T.D. 7920, 48 Fed.Reg. 31054 (July 6, 1983).

7. Unless otherwise indicated, citations which follow are to the December 30, 1981 version of the regulations.

8. Prop.Reg. § 1.385–3(d).

9. Prop.Reg. § 1.385–0(c)(2).

10. Prop.Reg. § 1.385–3(e).

11. T.D. 7747, 45 Fed.Reg. 86438, 86440 (Explanation of Changes), reprinted in 1981–1 C.B. 143.

12. Prop.Reg. § 1.385–6. In general, proportional straight debt instruments were

treated as debt only if issued to "independent creditors" or if they were marketable instruments issued by a public company; otherwise they generally were reclassified as equity unless they were: (a) issued for cash or, if issued for property, the stated annual interest rate was "reasonable," and (b) the corporation did not have "excessive debt" at the time the instrument was issued. Prop.Reg. § 1.385–6(a)(3), (e), (g).

13. Prop.Reg. § 1.385–6(g)(4).

14. Prop.Reg. § 1.385–6(h).

15. Prop.Reg. § 1.385–6(f)(2).

16. Prop.Reg. § 1.385–6(g)(3).

(within specified ranges) interest rate. Variations on these themes abounded.

The regulations were withdrawn because lobbyists convinced the Treasury that they would have a negative impact on particular industries and on small businesses generally.[17] Although some of the regulatory themes ultimately may be adopted by the courts, the Treasury is unlikely to initiate the mobilization that would be required to resurrect this project.

Bifurcation of Instruments. Despite the Treasury's lack of success in implementing the goals of Section 385, Congress has not given up hope. Section 385 was amended to allow (but not require) the Treasury to classify an interest having significant debt and equity characteristics as "in part stock and in part indebtedness."[18] According to the legislative history, bifurcation may be appropriate where a debt instrument provides for payments that are dependent to a significant extent on corporate performance, such as through "equity kickers" (i.e., provisions in a debt instrument that provide the holder with an equity interest in certain circumstances), contingent interests (which are dependent on corporate performance), significant deferral of payment, subordination, or an interest rate high enough to suggest a significant risk of default.[19]

If the Treasury accepts this Congressional challenge, several options might be considered. One approach would disallow interest deductions in excess of a specified rate of return to investors on the theory that a higher than normal risk is tantamount to an equity investment. For example, the regulations might specify a reference rate (such as the rate on comparable-term Treasury obligations) that is relatively risk-free and permit interest paid up to that rate to be deductible but deny a deduction for the additional "risk" element because it is more akin to a dividend. Under this type of broad disallowance approach, a corporation that issued a 20–year $100,000 unsecured debt instrument paying 14 percent interest (14,000 per year) at a time when comparable Treasury bonds were yielding 10 percent would be permitted to deduct only $10,000 per year as interest and the remaining $4,000 per year would be a nondeductible dividend.[20]

Another option is to limit bifurcation to instruments that provide for a combination of a fixed return and an additional return based on earnings. The regulations might treat the fixed return as interest while classifying the performance-based component as a nondeductible dividend. A closely related alternative, which finds isolated support in the case law, would be

17. See, e.g., Levin & Bowen, "The Section 385 Regulations Regarding Debt Versus Equity: Is the Cure Worse than the Malady?" 35 Tax Lawyer 1 (1981).

18. I.R.C. § 385(a). This regulatory authority may be exercised on a prospective basis only.

19. H.Rep. No. 101–247, 101st Cong., 1st Sess. 1236 (1989).

20. In narrowly targeted situations, Congress began moving in this direction with the legislation enacted in 1989. See, e.g., I.R.C. §§ 163(e)(5), (i). Query whether any broader approach would discriminate against start-up companies or firms engaged in high-risk businesses?

to divide one instrument into separate components—i.e., one part as debt and another as equity.[21]

Obligation of Consistency. Section 385(c) provides that a corporate issuer's characterization of an instrument as debt or equity at the time of issuance shall be binding on the issuer and all holders of the interest—but not binding, of course, on the Service. This rule of consistency does not apply, however, to holders who disclose on their tax return that they are treating the interest in a manner inconsistent with the issuer's characterization.

The Future. Perhaps in the 22d century, when the Section 385 regulations are reissued, we will know the Treasury's thinking on these questions.

PROBLEMS

1. Aristocrat, Baker and Chef have formed Chez Guevara, Inc. ("Chez") to operate a gourmet restaurant and bakery previously operated by Chef as a sole proprietorship. Aristocrat will contribute $80,000 cash, Baker will contribute a building with a fair market value of $80,000 and an adjusted basis of $20,000, and Chef will contribute $40,000 cash and the goodwill from his proprietorship which the parties agree is worth $40,000 and has a zero basis. In return, each of the parties will receive 100 shares of Chez common stock, the only class outstanding.

Chez requires at least $1,800,000 of additional capital in order to renovate the building, acquire new equipment and provide working capital. It has negotiated a $900,000 loan from Friendly National Bank on the following terms: interest will be payable at two points above the prime rate, determined semi-annually, with principal due in ten years and the loan will be secured by a mortgage on the renovated restaurant building.

Evaluate the following alternative proposals for raising the additional $900,000 needed to commence business, focusing on the possibility that the Service will reclassify corporate debt instruments as equity:

(a) Aristocrat, Baker and Chef each will loan Chez $300,000, and each will take back a $300,000 five-year corporate note with variable interest payable at one point below the prime rate, determined annually.

(b) Same as (a), above except that each of the parties will take back $300,000 of 10% 20–year subordinated income debentures; interest will be payable only out of the net profits of the business.

(c) Same as (a), above, except that the $900,000 loan from Friendly National Bank will be unsecured but personally guaranteed by Aristocrat, Baker and Chef, who will be jointly and severally liable.

---

21. Two courts have used this approach with respect to so-called hybrid instruments. See Richmond, Fredericksburg and Potomac R.R. v. Commissioner, 528 F.2d 917 (4th Cir. 1975); Farley Realty Corp. v. Commissioner, 279 F.2d 701 (2d Cir.1960). In most other cases, the courts have applied an all-or-nothing approach.

(d) Aristocrat will loan the entire $900,000, taking back a $900,000 corporate note with terms identical to those described in (a), above.

(e) Same as (d), above, except that commencing two years after the incorporation, Chez ceases to pay interest on the notes because of a severe cash flow problem.

2. In view of the confused state of the law, how can a tax advisor plan the capital structure of a corporation to avoid the risk of reclassification of debt as equity. From the standpoint of the tax advisor, is the vagueness of the law in this area preferable to more detailed "bright line" rules in the Code or regulations? Which approach is preferable as a matter of policy?

D.   CHARACTER OF GAIN OR LOSS ON CORPORATE INVESTMENT

Code: §§ 165(g)(1), (2); 166(a), (d), (e); 1244(a)–(c). Skim §§ 1045; 1202.

Regulations: §§ 1.165–5(a)–(c); 1.166–5; 1.1244(a)–1(a), (b).

Since equity and debt securities held by investors are capital assets, gain or loss on the sale of stock, bonds and other debt instruments generally is a capital gain or loss.[1] As discussed below, the Code also includes a few special characterization rules, some to stimulate investment and others to clarify the tax treatment of transactions that technically do not constitute a "sale or exchange."

Gain on Sale of Qualified Small Business Stock. To encourage long-term investment in small start-up companies, Section 1202 permits noncorporate shareholders to exclude from gross income 50 percent of the gain from a sale or exchange of "qualified small business stock" held for more than five years.[2] To qualify its stock for this tax benefit, the issuer must be a C corporation with aggregate gross assets of $50 million or less at the time the stock is issued.[3] That's the good news. The bad news is that long-term capital gain from the sale of qualified small business stock—known as "Section 1202 gain"—is taxed at a maximum rate of 28 percent.[4] As a result, the maximum effective rate on a sale of qualified small business stock, after taking into account the 50 percent exclusion, is 14 percent, which is not much better than the generally applicable 15 percent maximum rate.[5]

---

1. In some cases, where the original issue discount and market discount rules apply, all or part of the gain on the sale or maturity of a debt instrument may be ordinary income. See generally I.R.C. §§ 1271–1275.

2. I.R.C. § 1202(a)(1). To qualify, the shareholder must be an original issuee of the stock. The exclusion is generally available for up to $10 million of recognized gain per qualifying corporation. § 1202(b)(1). In some cases involving larger investors, higher limits may apply.

3. I.R.C. § 1202(c)(1), (d).

4. I.R.C. § 1(h)(4), (7).

5. When Section 1202 was first enacted, the rate differential was six percent. For more bad news, see I.R.C. § 57(a)(7), which requires seven percent of the excluded portion of Section 1202 gain to be treated as a

A more meaningful tax benefit is provided by Section 1045, which allows noncorporate shareholders to elect to defer otherwise taxable gain from a sale of qualified small business stock held for more than six months by rolling over the proceeds into new qualified small business stock within 60 days of the sale.

Worthless Securities. Even the most optimistic taxpayers who embark on a business venture are well advised to anticipate the tax consequences if their endeavor should result in a loss. Sole proprietors, partners (including members of limited liability companies) and shareholders in an S corporation usually may deduct the losses from their business operations as they are incurred if they materially participate in the activity.[1] But shareholders or creditors of a C corporation normally must be content to recognize a capital loss at the time their investment is sold or becomes worthless. If a loss results from the worthlessness of stock or debt evidenced by a "security" which is a capital asset, the calamity is treated as a hypothetical sale or exchange on the last day of the taxable year in which the loss is incurred.[2]

Debts Not Evidenced by a Security. The tax consequences of losses sustained on a debt not evidenced by a security are governed by the bad debt deduction rules in Section 166. Business bad debts are ordinary losses, while nonbusiness bad debts are artificially treated as short-term capital losses.[3] When a shareholder who is also an employee loans money to a closely held corporation and later is not repaid, an issue arises over whether the loan was made as an investment or in a trade or business carried on by the taxpayer. In the *Generes* case, below, the Supreme Court resolved a conflict on the appropriate standard to be applied in making that determination.

United States v. Generes

Supreme Court of the United States, 1972.
405 U.S. 93, 92 S.Ct. 827.

■ MR. JUSTICE BLACKMUN delivered the opinion of the Court.

A debt a closely held corporation owed to an indemnifying shareholder-employee became worthless in 1962. The issue in this federal income tax refund suit is whether, for the shareholder-employee, that worthless obligation was a business or a nonbusiness bad debt within the meaning and reach of §§ 166(a) and (d) of the Internal Revenue Code of 1954, as amended, 26 U.S.C. §§ 166(a) and (d), and of the implementing Regulations § 1.166–5.

The issue's resolution is important for the taxpayer. If the obligation was a business debt, he may use it to offset ordinary income and for

---

tax preference item under the alternative minimum tax.

1. See generally I.R.C. § 469 for limitations on the timing of losses incurred in a passive activity.

2. See I.R.C. §§ 165(g)(1), (g)(2).

3. I.R.C. § 166(a), (d).

carryback purposes under § 172 of the Code, 26 U.S.C. § 172. On the other hand, if the obligation is a nonbusiness debt, it is to be treated as a short-term capital loss subject to the restrictions imposed on such losses by § 166(d)(1)(B) and §§ 1211 and 1212, and its use for carryback purposes is restricted by § 172(d)(4). The debt is one or the other in its entirety, for the Code does not provide for its allocation in part to business and in part to nonbusiness.

In determining whether a bad debt is a business or a nonbusiness obligation, the Regulations focus on the relation the loss bears to the taxpayer's business. If, at the time of worthlessness, that relation is a "proximate" one, the debt qualifies as a business bad debt and the aforementioned desirable tax consequences then ensue.

The present case turns on the proper measure of the required proximate relation. Does this necessitate a "dominant" business motivation on the part of the taxpayer or is a "significant" motivation sufficient?

Tax in an amount somewhat in excess of $40,000 is involved. The taxpayer, Allen H. Generes, prevailed in a jury trial in the District Court. See 67–2 U.S.T.C. ¶ 9754 (E.D.La.). On the Government's appeal, the Fifth Circuit affirmed by a divided vote. 427 F.2d 279 (C.A.5 1970). Certiorari was granted, 401 U.S. 972, 91 S.Ct. 1189, 28 L.Ed.2d 321 (1971), to resolve a conflict among the circuits.

I

The taxpayer as a young man in 1909 began work in the construction business. His son-in-law, William F. Kelly, later engaged independently in similar work. During World War II the two men formed a partnership in which their participation was equal. The enterprise proved successful. In 1954 Kelly–Generes Construction Co., Inc., was organized as the corporate successor to the partnership. It engaged in the heavy-construction business, primarily on public works projects.

The taxpayer and Kelly each owned 44% of the corporation's outstanding capital stock. The taxpayer's original investment in his shares was $38,900. The remaining 12% of the stock was owned by a son of the taxpayer and by another son-in-law. Mr. Generes was president of the corporation and received from it an annual salary of $12,000. Mr. Kelly was executive vice-president and received an annual salary of $15,000.

The taxpayer and Mr. Kelly performed different services for the corporation. Kelly worked full time in the field and was in charge of the day-to-day construction operations. Generes, on the other hand, devoted no more than six to eight hours a week to the enterprise. He reviewed bids and jobs, made cost estimates, sought and obtained bank financing, and assisted in securing the bid and performance bonds that are an essential part of the public-project construction business. Mr. Generes, in addition to being president of the corporation, held a full-time position as president of a savings and loan association he had founded in 1937. He received from the association an annual salary of $19,000. The taxpayer also had other sources of income. His gross income averaged about $40,000 a year during 1959–1962.

Taxpayer Generes from time to time advanced personal funds to the corporation to enable it to complete construction jobs. He also guaranteed loans made to the corporation by banks for the purchase of construction machinery and other equipment. In addition, his presence with respect to the bid and performance bonds is of particular significance. Most of these were obtained from Maryland Casualty Co. That underwriter required the taxpayer and Kelly to sign an indemnity agreement for each bond it issued for the corporation. In 1958, however, in order to eliminate the need for individual indemnity contracts, taxpayer and Kelly signed a blanket agreement with Maryland whereby they agreed to indemnify it, up to a designated amount, for any loss it suffered as surety for the corporation. Maryland then increased its line of surety credit to $2,000,000. The corporation had over $14,000,000 gross business for the period 1954 through 1962.

In 1962 the corporation seriously underbid two projects and defaulted in its performance of the project contracts. It proved necessary for Maryland to complete the work. Maryland then sought indemnity from Generes and Kelly. The taxpayer indemnified Maryland to the extent of $162,104.57. In the same year he also loaned $158,814.49 to the corporation to assist it in its financial difficulties. The corporation subsequently went into receivership and the taxpayer was unable to obtain reimbursement from it.

In his federal income tax return for 1962 the taxpayer took his loss on his direct loans to the corporation as a nonbusiness bad debt. He claimed the indemnification loss as a business bad debt and deducted it against ordinary income. Later he filed claims for refund for 1959–1961, asserting net operating loss carrybacks under § 172 to those years for the portion, unused in 1962, of the claimed business bad debt deduction.

In due course the claims were made the subject of the jury trial refund suit in the United States District Court for the Eastern District of Louisiana. At the trial Mr. Generes testified that his sole motive in signing the indemnity agreement was to protect his $12,000–a-year employment with the corporation. The jury, by special interrogatory, was asked to determine whether taxpayer's signing of the indemnity agreement with Maryland "was proximately related to his trade or business of being an employee" of the corporation. The District Court charged the jury, over the Government's objection, that significant motivation satisfies the Regulations' requirement of proximate relationship.[6] The court refused the Government's request for an instruction that the applicable standard was that of dominant rather than significant motivation.[7]

6. "A debt is proximately related to the taxpayer's trade or business when its creation was significantly motivated by the taxpayer's trade or business, and it is not rendered a non-business debt merely because there was a non-qualifying motivation as well, even though the non-qualifying motivation was the primary one."

7. "You must, in short, determine whether Mr. Generes" dominant motivation

After twice returning to the court for clarification of the instruction given, the jury found that the taxpayer's signing of the indemnity agreement was proximately related to his trade or business of being an employee of the corporation. Judgment on this verdict was then entered for the taxpayer.

The Fifth Circuit majority approved the significant-motivation standard so specified and agreed with a Second Circuit majority in Weddle v. Commissioner, 325 F.2d 849, 851 (1963), in finding comfort for so doing in the tort law's concept of proximate cause. Judge Simpson dissented. 427 F.2d, at 284. He agreed with the holding of the Seventh Circuit in Niblock v. Commissioner, 417 F.2d 1185 (1969), and with Chief Judge Lumbard, separately concurring in Weddle, 325 F.2d, at 852, that dominant and primary motivation is the standard to be applied.

II

A.   The fact responsible for the litigation is the taxpayer's dual status relative to the corporation. Generes was both a shareholder and an employee. These interests are not the same, and their differences occasion different tax consequences. In tax jargon, Generes' status as a shareholder was a nonbusiness interest. It was capital in nature and it was composed initially of tax-paid dollars. Its rewards were expectative and would flow, not from personal effort, but from investment earnings and appreciation. On the other hand, Generes' status as an employee was a business interest. Its nature centered in personal effort and labor, and salary for that endeavor would be received. The salary would consist of pre-tax dollars.

Thus, for tax purposes it becomes important and, indeed, necessary to determine the character of the debt that went bad and became uncollectible. Did the debt center on the taxpayer's business interest in the corporation or on his nonbusiness interest? If it was the former, the taxpayer deserves to prevail here. * * *

B.   Although arising in somewhat different contexts, two tax cases decided by the Court in recent years merit initial mention. In each of these cases a major shareholder paid out money to or on behalf of his corporation and then was unable to obtain reimbursement from it. In each he claimed a deduction assertable against ordinary income. In each he was unsuccessful in this quest:

1.   In Putnam v. Commissioner, 352 U.S. 82 (1956), the taxpayer was a practicing lawyer who had guaranteed obligations of a labor newspaper corporation in which he owned stock. He claimed his loss as fully deductible

in signing the indemnity agreement was to protect his salary and status as an employee or was to protect his investment in the Kelly–Generes Construction Co.

"Mr. Generes is entitled to prevail in this case only if he convinces you that the dominant motivating factor for his signing the indemnity agreement was to insure the receiving of his salary from the company. It is insufficient if the protection or insurance of his salary was only a significant secondary motivation for his signing the indemnity agreement. It must have been his dominant or most important reason for signing the indemnity agreement."

in 1948 under § 23(e)(2) of the 1939 Code. The standard prescribed by that statute was incurrence of the loss "in any transaction entered into for profit, though not connected with the trade or business." The Court rejected this approach and held that the loss was a nonbusiness bad debt subject to short-term capital loss treatment under § 23(k)(4). The loss was deductible as a bad debt or not at all. See Rev.Rul. 60–48, 1960–1 Cum.Bull. 112.

2.   In Whipple v. Commissioner, 373 U.S. 193 (1963), the taxpayer had provided organizational, promotional, and managerial services to a corporation in which he owned approximately an 80% stock interest. He claimed that this constituted a trade or business and, hence, that debts owing him by the corporation were business bad debts when they became worthless in 1953. The Court also rejected that contention and held that Whipple's investing was not a trade or business, that is, that "[d]evoting one's time and energies to the affairs of a corporation is not of itself, and without more, a trade or business of the person so engaged." 373 U.S., at 202. The rationale was that a contrary conclusion would be inconsistent with the principle that a corporation has a personality separate from its shareholders and that its business is not necessarily their business. The Court indicated its approval of the Regulations' proximate-relation test:

> "Moreover, there is no proof (which might be difficult to furnish where the taxpayer is the sole or dominant stockholder) that the loan was necessary to keep his job or was otherwise proximately related to maintaining his trade or business as an employee. Compare Trent v. Commissioner, [291 F.2d 669 (C.A.2 1961)]." 373 U.S., at 204.

The Court also carefully noted the distinction between the business and the nonbusiness bad debt for one who is both an employee and a shareholder.[8]

These two cases approach, but do not govern, the present one. They indicate, however, a cautious and not a free-wheeling approach to the business bad debt. Obviously, taxpayer Generes endeavored to frame his case to bring it within the area indicated in the above quotation from Whipple v. Commissioner.

III

We conclude that in determining whether a bad debt has a "proximate" relation to the taxpayer's trade or business, as the Regulations specify, and thus qualifies as a business bad debt, the proper measure is that of dominant motivation, and that only significant motivation is not sufficient. We reach this conclusion for a number of reasons:

A.   The Code itself carefully distinguishes between business and nonbusiness items. It does so, for example, in § 165 with respect to losses, in

---

8. "Even if the taxpayer demonstrates an independent trade or business of his own, care must be taken to distinguish bad debt losses arising from his own business and those actually arising from activities peculiar to an investor concerned with, and participating in, the conduct of the corporate business." 373 U.S., at 202.

§ 166 with respect to bad debts, and in § 162 with respect to expenses. It gives particular tax benefits to business losses, business bad debts, and business expenses, and gives lesser benefits, or none at all, to nonbusiness losses, nonbusiness bad debts, and nonbusiness expenses. It does this despite the fact that the latter are just as adverse in financial consequence to the taxpayer as are the former. But this distinction has been a policy of the income tax structure ever since the Revenue Act of 1916, § 5(a), 39 Stat. 759, provided differently for trade or business losses than it did for losses sustained in another transaction entered into for profit. And it has been the specific policy with respect to bad debts since the Revenue Act of 1942 incorporated into § 23(k) of the 1939 Code the distinction between business and nonbusiness bad debts. 56 Stat. 820.

The point, however, is that the tax statutes have made the distinction, that the Congress therefore intended it to be a meaningful one, and that the distinction is not to be obliterated or blunted by an interpretation that tends to equate the business bad debt with the nonbusiness bad debt. We think that emphasis upon the significant rather than upon the dominant would have a tendency to do just that.

B. Application of the significant-motivation standard would also tend to undermine and circumscribe the Court's holding in Whipple and the emphasis there that a shareholder's mere activity in a corporation's affairs is not a trade or business. As Chief Judge Lumbard pointed out in his separate and disagreeing concurrence in Weddle, supra, 325 F.2d, at 852–853, both motives—that of protecting the investment and that of protecting the salary—are inevitably involved, and an inquiry whether employee status provides a significant motivation will always produce an affirmative answer and result in a judgment for the taxpayer.

C. The dominant-motivation standard has the attribute of workability. It provides a guideline of certainty for the trier of fact. The trier then may compare the risk against the potential reward and give proper emphasis to the objective rather than to the subjective. As has just been noted, an employee-shareholder, in making or guaranteeing a loan to his corporation, usually acts with two motivations, the one to protect his investment and the other to protect his employment. By making the dominant motivation the measure, the logical tax consequence ensues and prevents the mere presence of a business motive, however small and however insignificant, from controlling the tax result at the taxpayer's convenience. This is of particular importance in a tax system that is so largely dependent on voluntary compliance.

D. The dominant-motivation test strengthens and is consistent with the mandate of § 262 of the Code, 26 U.S.C. § 262, that "no deduction shall be allowed for personal, living, or family expenses" except as otherwise provided. It prevents personal considerations from circumventing this provision.

E. The dominant-motivation approach to § 166(d) is consistent with that given the loss provisions in § 165(c)(1), see, for example, Imbesi v. Commissioner, 361 F.2d 640, 644 (C.A.3 1966), and in § 165(c)(2), see

Austin v. Commissioner, 298 F.2d 583, 584 (C.A.2 1962). In these related areas, consistency is desirable. See also, Commissioner v. Duberstein, 363 U.S. 278, 286 (1960).

F.   We see no inconsistency, such as the taxpayer suggests, between the Government's urging dominant motivation here and its having urged only significant motivation as the appropriate standard for the incurrence of liability for the accumulated-earnings tax under § 531 of the 1954 Code, 26 U.S.C. § 531, and for includability in the gross estate, for federal estate tax purposes, of a transfer made in contemplation of death under § 2035, 26 U.S.C. § 2035. Sections 531 and 2035 are Congress' answer to tax avoidance activity. * * *

G.   The Regulations' use of the word "proximate" perhaps is not the most fortunate, for it naturally tempts one to think in tort terms. The temptation, however, is best rejected, and we reject it here. In tort law factors of duty, of foreseeability, of secondary cause, and of plural liability are under consideration, and the concept of proximate cause has been developed as an appropriate application and measure of these factors. It has little place in tax law where plural aspects are not usual, where an item either is or is not a deduction, or either is or is not a business bad debt, and where certainty is desirable.

IV

The conclusion we have reached means that the District Court's instructions, based on a standard of significant rather than dominant motivation, are erroneous and that, at least, a new trial is required. We have examined the record, however, and find nothing that would support a jury verdict in this taxpayer's favor had the dominant-motivation standard been embodied in the instructions. Judgment n.o.v. for the United States, therefore, must be ordered. * * *

As Judge Simpson pointed out in his dissent, 427 F.2d, at 284–285, the only real evidence offered by the taxpayer bearing upon motivation was his own testimony that he signed the indemnity agreement "to protect my job," that "I figured in three years' time I would get my money out," and that "I never once gave it [his investment in the corporation] a thought."

The statements obviously are self-serving. In addition, standing alone, they do not bear the light of analysis. What the taxpayer was purporting to say was that his $12,000 annual salary was his sole motivation, and that his $38,900 original investment, the actual value of which prior to the misfortunes of 1962 we do not know, plus his loans to the corporation, plus his personal interest in the integrity of the corporation as a source of living for his son-in-law and as an investment for his son and his other son-in-law, were of no consequence whatever in his thinking. The comparison is strained all the more by the fact that the salary is pre-tax and the investment is taxpaid. With his total annual income about $40,000, Mr. Generes may well have reached a federal income tax bracket of 40% or more for a joint return in 1958–1962. §§ 1 and 2 of the 1954 Code, 68A Stat. 5 and 8. The $12,000 salary thus would produce for him only about

$7,000 net after federal tax and before any state income tax. This is the figure, and not $12,000, that has any possible significance for motivation purposes, and it is less than ⅕ of the original stock investment.

We conclude on these facts that the taxpayer's explanation falls of its own weight, and that reasonable minds could not ascribe, on this record, a dominant motivation directed to the preservation of the taxpayer's salary as president of Kelly–Generes Construction Co., Inc.

The judgment is reversed and the case is remanded with direction that judgment be entered for the United States.

It is so ordered.

■ Mr. Justice Powell and Mr. Justice Rehnquist took no part in the consideration or decision of this case.

[The concurring opinion of Mr. Justice Marshall and the dissenting opinion of Mr. Justice Douglas have been omitted. Ed.]

NOTE

After *Generes*, it became almost impossible for shareholders to avoid nonbusiness bad debt treatment if they sustain a loss in their creditor capacity. Whatever their roles, corporate insiders generally are regarded as investors.[1]

These rules place corporate investors who suffer losses at a tax disadvantage relative to those who conduct their affairs through other business vehicles. In the case of a small business, this dichotomy makes little sense and may prove to be particularly unfair to those who are forced into the C corporation form for nontax reasons. In the same legislation that produced the earliest version of Subchapter S, Congress provided some limited relief by enacting Section 1244 in order to "encourage the flow of new funds into small business" by placing small business shareholders on more of a par with proprietors and partners.[2] If certain detailed statutory requirements are met, an individual shareholder may (within limits) treat a loss from the sale, exchange or worthlessness of "Section 1244 stock" as an ordinary loss even if it might otherwise have been treated as a capital loss.

Because Section 1244 was designed to stimulate investment in small businesses, only individual taxpayers and partnerships (but not trusts and estates) who were original issuees of the stock are eligible for ordinary loss treatment.[3] Donees, heirs and other transferees of the original investor will continue to be limited to capital loss treatment under Section 165.

---

1. See, e.g., Benak v. Commissioner, 77 T.C. 1213 (1981); but see Bowers v. Commissioner, 716 F.2d 1047 (4th Cir.1983).

2. H.R.Rep. No. 2198, 85th Cong., 1st Sess. (1958), reprinted in 1959–2 C.B. 709, 711.

3. I.R.C. § 1244(a). A partner qualifies for a Section 1244 ordinary loss only if he was a partner when the partnership acquired the stock. Reg. § 1.1244(a)–1(b)(2). The regulations also provide that ordinary loss treatment is not available to a partner who has received the stock in a distribution from the partnership. Reg. § 1.1244(a)–1(b). Unlike a

Section 1244 stock may be either common or preferred stock that has been issued for money or property.[4] Stock issued for services thus does not qualify.[5] To prevent the benefits of Section 1244 from extending beyond the small business community, its reach is limited to stock of a "small business corporation," a status achieved if the aggregate amount of money and other property received by the corporation for stock, as a contribution to capital and as paid-in surplus does not exceed $1,000,000.[6] This determination is made at the time the stock is issued, but the $1,000,000 cap includes both amounts received for the newly issued stock and any stock previously issued by the corporation.[7]

Qualification under Section 1244 when the stock is issued does not automatically guarantee that an ordinary loss will be allowed when a loss is realized. Section 1244(c)(1)(C) also requires that, for the five taxable years ending before the year in which the loss was sustained, the corporation must have derived more than 50 percent of its aggregate gross receipts from sources other than passive investment income items (royalties, rents, dividends, interest, annuities and sales or exchanges of stock or securities). The requirement is designed to preclude ordinary loss treatment to shareholders of corporations engaged primarily in investment rather than active business activities. If these investment losses had been incurred directly, the taxpayer would have been limited to capital loss treatment and the corporate form should not facilitate an end run around this limitation. If the loss is sustained before the corporation has a five-year measuring period, then the gross receipts test is applied by substituting the taxable years ending before the date of the loss in which the corporation was in existence.[8]

The aggregate amount that may be treated by the taxpayer as an ordinary loss for any one taxable year may not exceed $50,000 or, in the case of married couple filing a joint return, $100,000.[9] In the case of partnerships, the limit is determined separately as to each partner.[10]

Section 1244 is a "no lose" provision in the sense that nothing is lost by passing a corporate resolution declaring that an equity interest is being issued as Section 1244 stock even if the stock ultimately fails to qualify. Although there is no longer a requirement for a formal plan, it generally is regarded as good practice to include a reference to Section 1244 in the corporate resolution approving the issuance of stock in a qualifying corpo-

---

partnership, an S corporation is not eligible for ordinary loss treatment under Section 1244. Rath v. Commissioner, 101 T.C. 196 (1993).

4.   I.R.C. § 1244(c)(1)(B).

5.   Reg. § 1.1244(c)–1(d).

6.   I.R.C. § 1244(c)(3).

7.   Id. See also Reg. § 1.1244(c)–2(b). If the capital receipts exceed $1,000,000, the corporation may designate certain shares as

Section 1244 stock provided that the amounts received for such designated stock do not exceed $1,000,000 less amounts received for stock or as capital contributions in prior years.

8.   I.R.C. § 1244(c)(2)(A).

9.   I.R.C. § 1244(b).

10.   Reg. § 1.1244(b)–1(a).

ration, if only to remind the shareholders that ordinary loss treatment is available if that unhappy event should later occur.

PROBLEM

High Technologies, Inc. ("Hi–Tech") is a small semiconductor company owned and operated by Thelma High and Allen Woody. Thelma and Allen formed Hi–Tech three years ago by each contributing $400,000 in exchange for 50% of the corporation's common stock. Hi–Tech has been planning a major expansion of its manufacturing facility and has decided to seek outside financing. It recently approached Jennifer Leech about the possibility of her investing $200,000 in Hi–Tech.

After investigating the corporation's financial position, Jennifer has decided to make the investment. Her objectives are to obtain maximum security while at the same time participating in Hi–Tech's potential growth. Jennifer also is concerned about the rapid change in computer technology and would like to plan for the most favorable tax consequences in the unfortunate event that her investment in Hi–Tech becomes worthless. Consider to what extent Jennifer will realize her goals if, in the alternative, her investment takes the following forms:

(a) A $200,000 unregistered five-year Hi–Tech note bearing market rate interest.   §166

(b) A $200,000 Hi–Tech registered bond bearing market rate interest.   §165

(c) A $190,000 Hi–Tech registered bond bearing market rate interest and warrants to purchase Hi–Tech common stock at a favorable price.   §165(g)(1)

(d) $200,000 of Hi–Tech common stock.   §1244

(e) $200,000 of Hi–Tech convertible preferred stock.   §1244

(f) Same as (d), above, except that Thelma and Allen originally capitalized Hi–Tech by each contributing $500,000.   §165

(g) Same as (d), above, except that Jennifer plans to give the Hi–Tech common stock to her son, Peter, as a wedding gift.   §165

(h) Same as (d), above, except that Jennifer and her son, Peter, will purchase the Hi–Tech common stock through Leech Associates, a venture capital partnership.   §165 §1244

CHAPTER 4

NONLIQUIDATING DISTRIBUTIONS

A. INTRODUCTION

1. DIVIDENDS: IN GENERAL

Code: §§ 243(a), (b)(1); 301(a), (c); 316(a); 317(a).

Regulations: §§ 1.301–1(c); 1.316–1(a)(1)–(2).

It was once said that a corporation derives no greater pleasure than through making distributions to its shareholders. As one court observed, "like the 'life-rendering pelican,' [a corporation] feeds its shareholders upon dividends."[1] In the case of a close corporation, however, this colorful marine analogy fails to capture reality. Closely held companies, influenced by the federal tax law, typically resist paying dividends and expend considerable energy to avoid the sting of the double tax. Many public companies retain profits for internal expansion, to finance acquisitions, or to repurchase their own stock.[2] But if an enterprise is successful, the pressure may mount to distribute earnings to the shareholders, and distributions often occur in connection with major changes in a corporation's capital structure, such as liquidations, mergers and recapitalizations. At that point, it becomes necessary to classify the distribution as a taxable dividend, a nontaxable return of capital, or as gain from a sale of the shareholder's stock. Simple as the task may seem, drawing these lines has been a central issue in the taxation of corporations and shareholders. Not surprisingly, the statutory scheme is complex and sometimes even illogical.

Distributions come in many forms. A corporation may distribute its own stock or debt obligations; redeem (i.e., repurchase) stock from its shareholders by distributing cash or property; or distribute its net assets in liquidation of the entire business. The tax consequences of these and other more complex transactions are considered in later chapters.[3] This chapter lays a foundation by examining the corporate and shareholder level tax treatment of nonliquidating (or "operating") distributions of cash or property—distributions loosely referred to as "dividends" by those unfamiliar with Subchapter C. We are about to learn, however, that not all distributions classified as dividends under state law or designated as such in the corporate minutes are dividends for federal tax purposes.

1. Commissioner v. First State Bank of Stratford, 168 F.2d 1004, 1009 (5th Cir.1948), cert. denied, 335 U.S. 867, 69 S.Ct. 137 (1948).

2. For an expanded discussion of the influence of federal tax law on corporate dividend policy, see Section A3 of this chapter, infra.

3. See Chapters 5–7, infra.

Determining the tax consequences of a nonliquidating distribution requires an excursion through several sections of the Code. Section 301 governs the amount and classification to corporate and noncorporate shareholders of distributions of "property" made by a C corporation with respect to its stock.[4] Under Section 301(c)(1), distributions that are "dividends" within the meaning of Section 316 must be included in gross income.[5] In order to prevent multiple taxation, corporate shareholders may deduct 70 percent (or sometimes 80 or 100 percent) of the dividends they receive.[6] Dividends received by noncorporate shareholders are usually taxed at preferential long-term capital gains rates.[7] Distributions that are not dividends are first treated as a recovery of the shareholder's basis in his stock, and any excess over basis is treated as gain from the sale or exchange of the stock.[8]

Section 316(a) defines a "dividend" as any distribution of property made by a corporation to its shareholders out of (1) earnings and profits accumulated after February 28, 1913 ("accumulated earnings and profits") or (2) earnings and profits of the current taxable year ("current earnings and profits"). "Earnings and profits," a term of art to be examined in more detail below, is a concept that attempts to distinguish distributions of corporate profits from returns of capital. Section 316(a) also includes two irrebuttable presumptions: every distribution is deemed to be made out of earnings and profits to the extent that they exist and is deemed to be made from the most recently accumulated earnings and profits.

In testing for dividend status, the regulations look first to current earnings and profits, determined as of the close of the taxable year in which the distribution is made.[9] A distribution out of current earnings and profits is thus a taxable dividend even if the corporation has an historical deficit. This seemingly harsh rule was enacted many years ago as a relief measure to permit corporations with deficits to pay dividends and thus avoid an undistributed profits tax then in effect. Although the tax was later repealed, the "nimble dividend" rule survived without any Congressional

4. Distributions to shareholders in their other capacities (e.g., employee, creditor, lessor) are thus not embraced by Section 301. "Property" is deemed to include money and other corporate assets but not stock in the distributing corporation or rights to acquire stock. I.R.C. § 317(a).

5. See also I.R.C. § 61(a)(7).

6. I.R.C. § 243(a), (b)(1), (c). See Chapter 1B1 supra. Potential abuses of the dividends received deduction are policed by an assortment of Code provisions. See Section F of this chapter, infra.

7. I.R.C. § 1(h)(11). See Section A2 of this chapter, infra.

8. I.R.C. § 301(c)(2), (3). The rules in the text apply to distributions by C corpora-

tions that do not file a consolidated return. Distributions received by one member of a consolidated group from another member generally are tax-free, but the distributee must reduce its basis in the stock of the payor by the amount of the distribution. See Reg. § 1.1502–13(f)(2)(ii) and Chapter 13B, supra. Distributions by S corporations also are tax-free to the extent of the shareholder's basis, and any excess is treated as gain from a sale of the S corporation stock. § 1368(b). The rules are more complex if an S corporation has accumulated earnings and profits from a time when it was a C corporation. § 1368(c). See Chapter 15E, infra.

9. Reg. § 1.316–1(a)(1).

explanation of why it was still necessary.[10] The rule at least simplifies the inquiry because it is rare for a company to make distributions during a period when it is operating at a loss. Only when distributions exceed current earnings and profits must reference be made to the historical track record of the corporation.

The dual focus in Section 316 on current and accumulated earnings and profits may produce anomalous results because dividend status is determined by reference to the corporation's overall financial success rather than the gain or loss realized by a particular shareholder. To be sure, most dividends represent an increase in the shareholder's wealth rather than a return of capital, but this is not inevitable under the current scheme. For example, the existence of accumulated earnings and profits will cause a distribution to be classified as a dividend even if those profits were earned before the shareholder acquired his stock.

To illustrate, assume that Shareholder forms Corporation with initial paid-in capital of $110. During its first year of operation, Corporation earns $20 and distributes $30 to Shareholder. The distribution consists of a $20 dividend (out of current earnings and profits) and a $10 return of capital, and Shareholder reduces his stock basis by $10 to $100. In year two, assume Corporation earns $50 and makes no distributions, ending the year with $50 of accumulated earnings and profits. At the beginning of year three, Buyer (an individual) acquires all the stock of Corporation for $150, and Shareholder realizes a $50 long-term capital gain. Assume further that Corporation, now wholly owned by Buyer, suffers a $10 loss in year three, causing its accumulated earnings and profits account to decrease to $40. If Corporation breaks even in year four but distributes $30, Buyer is taxed on the entire distribution because it is made from accumulated earnings and profits. But in substance Buyer has received merely a return of capital. After all, he paid $150 for the stock, and the company has since lost $10 while distributing $30 to Buyer, who is understandably surprised to realize $30 of ordinary income even though the value of his investment has declined.

In an academically tidy world, the curious result illustrated above should not occur. Instead, the tax treatment of distributions should depend on the gain or loss realized by the shareholder rather than the corporation's financial track record over time. Ideally, Shareholder should be taxed at ordinary income rates to the extent that the gain on a sale of his stock is attributable to undistributed corporate earnings while he was a shareholder. It then would be unnecessary to tax those earnings again when they are distributed to Buyer, who logically should be treated as receiving a return of capital rather than a $30 dividend.

In the early days of the income tax, taxpayers in Buyer's position argued that distributions out of preacquisition earnings should not be

---

10. See Bittker & Eustice, Federal Income Taxation of Corporations and Share- holders ¶ 8.02[3] (7th ed. 2000).

taxable since they did not represent any real gain to the shareholder. The Supreme Court put this argument to rest, reasoning:[11]

> Dividends are the appropriate fruit of stock ownership, are commonly reckoned as income, and are expended as such by the stockholder without regard to whether they are declared from the most recent earnings, or from a surplus accumulated from the earnings of the past, or are based upon the increased value of the property of the corporation. The stockholder is, in the ordinary case, a different entity from the corporation, and Congress was at liberty to treat the dividends as coming to him *ab extra,* and as constituting a part of his income when they came to hand.

Despite its conceptual flaws, the present approach is defensible on practical grounds. Since shares in publicly held corporations are traded daily, it would be difficult to determine precisely the corporation's earnings during the period that any particular shareholder held his stock. The current scheme at least ensures that earnings will be taxed to some shareholder, even if that shareholder may not be the theoretically correct one. Moreover, the presumption that distributions are made out of a corporation's earnings and profits to the extent they exist often eliminates the chore of tracing the source of a distribution and considerably simplifies the system.[12]

2. QUALIFIED DIVIDENDS

Code: § 1(h)(11).

For most of our tax history, dividends have been taxed as ordinary income. Relief from multiple taxation has been provided to corporate shareholders by the Section 243 dividends received deduction. From time to time, individual shareholders also have received very modest relief from double taxation, most often in the form of a limited dividend exclusion that ranged from $50 to $400 before it was repealed in 1986.

As previewed in Chapter 1,[1] President George W. Bush made eliminating double taxation of corporate earnings a centerpiece of economic stimulus legislation introduced in early 2003. The eventual compromise was a

---

11. Lynch v. Hornby, 247 U.S. 339, 343, 38 S.Ct. 543, 545 (1918).

12. In a 1983 report on Subchapter C reform, the Senate Finance Committee Staff recommended repeal of the earnings and profits limitation and proposed to tax all ordinary distributions as dividends, with limited relief for distributions made to the original contributing shareholder within three years of the contribution. See Staff of the Senate Finance Committee, Preliminary Report on the Reform and Simplification of the Income Taxation of Corporations, 98th Cong., 1st Sess. 77–78 (Comm.Print 98–85, 1983). The proposal was deleted from the staff's final report. See Staff of the Senate Finance Committee, Subchapter C Revision Act of 1985: A Final Report Prepared by the Staff, 99th Cong., 1st Sess. (S.Prt. 99–47, 1985). For some other alternatives to the present scheme, see Andrews, " 'Out of Its Earnings and Profits': Some Reflections on the Taxation of Dividends," 69 Harv.L.Rev. 1403 (1956); Blum, "The Earnings and Profits Limitation on Dividend Income: A Reappraisal," 53 Taxes 68 (1975).

1. See pp. 41–43, supra.

rate reduction on certain "qualified dividend income" received by non-corporate shareholders. Effective for eligible dividends received from January 1, 2003 through December 31, 2008, the maximum rate on qualified dividend income is reduced to 15 percent for taxpayers whose ordinary income otherwise would be taxed at higher rates, and to 5 percent for lower-income taxpayers whose ordinary income would be taxed in the 10 or 15 percent marginal brackets. Technically, these rate reductions have been implemented by including "qualified dividend income" within the definition of "net capital gain" in Section 1(h), which provides for the maximum rate on long-term capital gains for noncorporate taxpayers.[2] The dividend rate reduction applies for both the regular tax and the individual alternative minimum tax.

To be eligible for the reduced rates, a dividend must be received from a domestic corporation or a foreign corporation that meets certain criteria.[3] Unlike President Bush's original proposal, a qualified dividend need not be derived from earnings that were taxed at the corporate level. But some income items that are labelled "dividends" do not qualify for the rate reduction. Familiar examples are credit union and money market fund dividends, "dividends" paid on hybrid corporate instruments (e.g., certain types of preferred stock that are treated as debt by the issuing corporation), and payments in lieu of dividends on stock that has loaned as part of a short sale transaction.[4] Corporate payors must identify which dividends are "qualified" on the Form 1099's that they send at the end of the year, but shareholders are responsible for determining if they comply with the holding period requirements discussed below.

To prevent arbitrage opportunities on short-term trades, the common stock with respect to which the dividend was paid must have been held by the taxpayer for more than 60 days in the 121–day period beginning 60 days before the stock's ex-dividend date.[5] The ex-dividend date is the first date on which a share with respect to which a dividend has been declared is sold without the buyer being entitled to the dividend.[6] Without this rule, a taxpayer could acquire stock shortly before becoming entitled to a dividend, sell the stock at a loss after holding it at least 30 days (to avoid the wash sale loss disallowance rules under Section 1091), use the loss to offset short-term capital gain or up to $3,000 of ordinary income if the taxpayer has no capital gains, but still pay tax on the dividend at the preferential

---

2. I.R.C. § 1(h)(11)(A). Although qualified dividends are treated as net capital gain for rate reduction purposes, they are still ordinary income and may not be offset by capital losses without being subject to the $3,000 limitation in Section 1211(b).

3. I.R.C. § 1(h)(11)(B)(ii).

4. I.R.C. § 1(h)(11)(B)(ii).

5. I.R.C. § 1(h)(11)(B)(iii), which imports, with some modifications, similar holding period limitations on the corporate dividends received deduction and requires a longer holding period (91 days during the 181–day period beginning 90 days before the ex-dividend date) for dividends paid with respect to preferred stock. See I.R.C § 246 and Section F2 of this chapter, infra.

6. Under stock exchange rules, the ex-dividend date is typically three days before the date on which shareholders of record are entitled to receive a declared dividend.

rate. Several other rules have been included to prevent opportunistic exploitation of the rate reduction.[7]

3. IMPACT OF TAXES ON CORPORATE DIVIDEND POLICY

The distribution policies of closely held C corporations are largely motivated by the goal of getting corporate profits to the shareholders at the lowest tax cost. For that reason, closely held companies typically have resisted paying dividends, preferring instead to distribute earnings in the form of tax-deductible salary, interest or rent, or to engage in transactions (such as redemptions) where shareholders can bailout earnings at capital gains rates.[1]

The dividend policies of publicly traded corporations vary widely. Many "old economy" companies adhere to the tradition of paying quarterly dividends, increasing them at regular intervals and rarely reducing their payouts unless the company is in serious financial difficulty. Most "new economy" companies, such as those in the technology sector, have generally opted not to pay dividends, hoping instead to reward investors with increased share prices.

What is it that motivates public companies to pay dividends and to what extent do the tax laws influence corporate dividend policy? These questions have stimulated a lively theoretical debate.[2] Leaving aside taxes, one view is that dividends serve as a signal to the financial markets of a company's profitability and future expectations[3], enhancing shareholder value through their positive impact on the price of the stock. Other theorists contend that, apart from taxes and transaction costs, shareholders should be indifferent to a corporation's dividend policy because they reap the same benefit when the stock price increases to reflect undistributed earnings and they are free to generate "homemade dividends" by strategically timed sales of stock.[4] Throughout this debate, there also is much discussion of the different interests of corporate managers and shareholders, and the potential "agency costs" when managers use retained earnings

---

7. See, e.g., I.R.C. § 1(h)(11)(D)(ii), which provides that if an individual taxpayer receives qualified dividend income for one or more dividends that are "extraordinary dividends" as defined in Section 1059, any loss on a later disposition of the stock on which the dividends were paid shall be treated as long-term capital loss to the extent of the dividend even if the stock was held for one year or less, and I.R.C. §§ 1(h)(11)(D)(i) and 163(d)(4)(A), providing that qualified dividend income is excluded from "net investment income" for purposes of the limitations on deduction of investment interest unless the taxpayer elects to have the dividend taxed at ordinary income rates.

1. See, e.g., Chapters 1A2 & 3A, supra, & 5A, infra.

2. See generally Hamilton, Business Basics for Law Students § 12.11 (3d ed. 2002); Klein & Coffee, Business Organization and Finance 395 (9th ed. 2004). For a historical perspective, see Bank "Rethinking Double Taxation's Role in Dividend Policy: A Historical Approach," 56 Tax L. Rev. 463 (2003).

3. Hamilton, supra note 2, at § 12.12.

4. See, e.g., Modigliani & Miller, "Dividend Policy, Growth, and the Valuation of Shares," 34 J. of Bus. 411 (1961), for an early articulation of the "dividend irrelevance" theory.

to make suboptimal investments or simply hoard cash.[5] Encouraging dividends is said to counteract this form of managerial empire building and imposes a measure of discipline. Returning the money to investors in the form of dividends, so the argument goes, allows capital to be redirected more efficiently and promotes economic growth.[6]

As for the impact of taxes on corporate dividend policy, the traditional view is that the "double tax" on corporate profits lowers a shareholder's return on investment. It follows from this thesis that lower tax rates will lead to higher dividends and new investments by the shareholders who receive them. Others contend that dividend tax cuts do not cause corporations to increase their payouts because institutional shareholders, such as pension funds and large charities, don't pay taxes. These contrarians also argue that since most new investments are made by corporations from retained earnings, dividend tax rate reductions are not an effective investment stimulus.

Beginning in the 1980's and continuing until 2003, dividends became less fashionable. In explaining this decline, corporate finance theorists argued that shareholders benefit more when a corporation deploys its available cash for business expansion, acquisition of other companies, or the selective repurchase of its own stock, all with the goal of raising the stock price. Retention of earnings also was seen as tax efficient because shareholders desiring liquidity could sell their stock and realize tax-favored capital gains at their own pace.[7]

Proponents of tax relief for dividends focused primarily on the harsh effects of the double tax on corporate earnings. They argued that taxing dividends at the highest ordinary income rates encouraged corporations to hoard cash, locking in huge stockpiles of capital that could be reinvested more efficiently if it were distributed and redeployed by the shareholders. Accounting scandals and sub-optimal investments also increased the pressure on corporate managers to legitimize their reported profits by providing a source of regular cash flow to shareholders.

The early evidence is mixed, but it suggests that the 2003 dividend tax cuts have influenced corporate behavior and contributed to a resurgence of dividends. A dramatic example was Microsoft Corporation's decision to distribute $32 billion as an extraordinary dividend at the end of 2004, use another $30 billion to repurchase stock over the next four years, and raise its modest quarterly dividend.[8] More generally, aggregate dividends rose nine percent in the quarter after the new rate went into effect. One early study nonetheless downplayed the effects of the tax cuts, noting that dividend increases for the first few calendar quarters were concentrated in

---

5. See, e.g., Easterbrook, "Two Agency-Cost Explanations of Dividends," 74 Am. Econ. Rev. 650 (1984).

6. See Moore & Kerpen, "Show Me the Money! Dividend Payouts after the Bush Tax Cut (Cato Institute, Oct. 11, 2004).

7. See Engler, "A Missing Piece to the Dividend Agency Costs of Mutual Funds," 25 Cardozo L. Rev. 215, 217–220 (2003).

8. Guth & Thurm, Microsoft to Dole Out its Cash Hoard, Wall St. Journal, July 21, 2004, at A1.

a handful of outlier companies dominated by insiders making special one-time distributions.[9]

Another study, using data over a longer time period, concluded that dividends had risen sharply along several dimensions.[10] First, the fraction of public companies paying dividends began to increase in 2003 for the first time in more than two decades; second, many firms that had been paying regular dividends raised their payouts significantly after the tax cut; and third, a few companies such as Microsoft paid special one-time dividends.[11] A report issued by Standard and Poors at the end of 2004 supports the view that the combination of tax cuts and shareholder pressure has contributed to a surge in dividend payments.[12] In the 19 months since the dividend tax cut was enacted, companies in the S & P 500 announced 421 dividend increases, with 24 companies paying dividends for the first time.[13] But the average yield on the S & P 500 stocks is still only 1.6 percent, much lower than over most of its history (from 1945 through the early 1980's, dividend yields on the S & P 500 ranged between three and six percent) and lower than the yields in most foreign markets.[14]

Despite the stock market gains that followed the 2003 economic stimulus legislation, the initial reaction of the financial markets to the dividend tax cut does not suggest that investors are favoring dividend-paying stocks over growth investments with little or no dividend yield. According to one study, from October 2002 through January, 2005, nondividend-paying stocks produced significantly stronger returns than dividend-paying stocks (63 percent vs. 52 percent).[15] Investors, it appears, continue to look for the highest possible total return, which they think is more likely to come from stock appreciation than dividends. Moreover, capital gains rates were reduced at the same time the dividend tax cut went into effect, and long-term investors enjoy the additional advantage of deferring tax on their capital gains.

B. EARNINGS AND PROFITS

Code: § 312(a), (c), (f)(1), (k)(1)–(3); 316(a). Skim § 312(n).

Regulations: § 1.312–6(a), (b), (d) (first sentence), 1.312–7(b)(1) (first sentence).

The Code makes it clear that distributions are dividends only to the extent that they come from the corporation's earnings and profits, but it

---

9. Blouin, Raedy & Shackelford, "Did Dividends Increase Immediately After the 2003 Reduction in Tax Rates?" (NBER Working Paper 10301, Feb. 2004), available at www.nber.org/papers/w10301.

10. Chetty & Saez, "Do Dividend Payments Respond to Taxes? Preliminary Evidence from the 2003 Tax Cut," (NBER Working Paper 10572), available at www.nber.org/papers/w10572.

11. Id.

12. Opdyke, "Tax Cut, Shareholder Pressure Stoke Surge in Stock Dividends," Wall St. Journal, Jan. 18, 2005, at A1.

13. Id.

14. Id. In 2004, S & P companies distributed approximately 34 percent of their profits as dividends, as compared to the historical average of 54 percent. Id.

15. See, e.g., Browning, "Dividend Stocks Haven't Caught Investors' Fancy," Wall St. Journal, Jan. 31, 2005, at C1.

curiously does not take the extra step and actually define earnings and profits. Section 312 describes the effects of certain transactions on earnings and profits, and the accompanying regulations provide ample elaboration, but a precise definition of the term is nowhere to be found in the Code or regulations.[1] The function of the earnings and profits concept, however, is clear: it is a measuring device used to determine the extent to which a distribution is made from a corporation's economic income as opposed to its taxable income or paid-in capital.

The meaning of earnings and profits, which is a phrase peculiar to the tax law, has evolved over the years. It is roughly analogous (but not identical) to the accounting concept of retained earnings (sometimes called "earned surplus") in that neither amount includes initial paid-in capital or subsequent contributions to capital. The primary difference is that retained earnings are decreased by stock distributions and contingency reserves. If earnings and profits were similarly reduced, a company could avoid ever making a taxable distribution simply by ensuring that its distributions were preceded by nontaxable stock dividends or the establishment of reserves for contingencies. Earnings and profits also are not identical to taxable income. The earnings and profits account is intended to measure the economic performance of the corporation. In contrast, taxable income does not provide a true financial picture because that concept is cluttered with a host of policy incentives and relief provisions that bear little or no relationship to the corporation's capacity to pay dividends.

Although earnings and profits can be determined by making adjustments to either retained earnings or taxable income, the traditional approach is to start with a corporation's taxable income and to make adjustments that fall into the four broad categories discussed below. In general, the same accounting method used by the corporation to determine its taxable income is employed in determining earnings and profits.[2]

1. *Certain items excluded from taxable income must be added back.* Items that represent true financial gain but are exempt from tax, such as municipal bond interest, life insurance proceeds and federal tax refunds and otherwise excludable discharge of indebtedness income (unless coupled with a basis reduction under Section 1017) are included in earnings and profits.[3] Contributions to capital and gains that are realized but not recognized for tax purposes (e.g., like-kind exchanges, Section 351 trans-

---

1. For a history of the earnings and profits concept, see Rudick, " 'Dividends' and 'Earnings or Profits' Under the Income Tax Law: Corporate Non–Liquidating Distributions," 89 U.Pa.L.Rev. 865 (1941).

2. Reg. § 1.312–6(a).

3. Reg. § 1.312–6(b). In the case of life insurance, the Service has ruled that earnings and profits are increased by the proceeds collected less the aggregate premiums paid by the corporation. Rev.Rul. 54–230, 1954–1 C.B. 114. For discharge of indebtedness income, see I.R.C. § 312(*l*)(1).

fers, involuntary conversions under Section 1033) are not added back in computing earnings and profits.[4]

2. *Certain items deductible in determining taxable income must be added back.* Certain deductions and benefits allowed in computing taxable income which do not reflect a real decrease in corporate wealth are not permitted or are restricted in determining earnings and profits. For example, a deductible item that involves no actual expenditure, such as the Section 243 dividends received deduction, must be added back to taxable income in determining earnings and profits. Similarly, the depletion allowance must be based on the corporation's cost of a depletable asset even if the corporation deducts percentage depletion in computing taxable income.[5]

3. *Certain nondeductible items must be subtracted.* Some items not allowed as deductions in computing taxable income in fact represent actual expenditures that diminish a corporation's capacity to pay dividends. These items reduce earnings and profits. For example, federal income taxes paid during the year by a cash method corporation will reduce earnings and profits,[6] as will losses and expenses disallowed under provisions such as Sections 265 (expenses allocable to tax-exempt income), 267 (losses between related taxpayers) and 274 (travel and entertainment expenses) and charitable contributions in excess of the ten percent corporate limitation. In addition, net operating losses and capital losses in excess of capital gains reduce earnings and profits in the year they are incurred. In order to avoid a double tax benefit, they may not be carried back or forward in determining earnings and profits.

4. *Certain timing adjustments must be made.* Finally, a variety of adjustments are required to override timing rules that allow corporations to artificially defer income or accelerate deductions in computing taxable income.[7] For example, a corporation may not use the generally applicable accelerated cost recovery system (ACRS) of Section 168 in determining earnings and profits. Instead, the cost of depreciable property must be recovered in computing earnings and profits under the alternative depreciation system, which employs the straight line method using specially prescribed and generally longer recovery periods than ACRS.[8] The corporation thus must increase its taxable income by the excess accelerated depreciation allowed for tax purposes.[9] Similarly, if the corporation has elected to

---

4. I.R.C. § 312(f)(1).

5. Reg. § 1.312–6(c).

6. Rev.Rul. 70–609, 1970–2 C.B. 78; Webb v. Commissioner, 572 F.2d 135 (5th Cir.1978). A few courts, however, have permitted a cash method corporation to reduce its earnings and profits in the year to which the federal taxes relate even though the taxes have not yet been paid. See e.g., Drybrough v. Commissioner, 238 F.2d 735 (6th Cir.1956).

7. See generally I.R.C. § 312(n). To prevent abuse of the dividends received de-duction, the Section 312(n) adjustments do not apply to distributions to any 20 percent or more corporate shareholders. I.R.C. § 301(e). The effect of this rule is to reduce earnings and profits only in determining the amount of any dividend to major corporate shareholders. See Section F5 of this chapter, infra.

8. I.R.C. §§ 312(k)(3)(A); 168(g)(2).

9. The adjusted basis of the property determined under this special provision also is used in determining the impact of a sale or other disposition of property on earnings and

expense the cost of eligible property under Section 179, it must amortize that expense ratably over five years in determining earnings and profits.[10] Additional earnings and profits timing rules require a corporation to capitalize otherwise amortizable construction period interest and taxes and to amortize normally deductible mineral exploration costs and intangible drilling expenses over extended time periods.[11]

On the income side, realized gains that are deferred for taxable income purposes under the installment sale method of Section 453 or by the completed contract method of accounting must be currently included in earnings and profits.[12] Moreover, for earnings and profits purposes, gains on the sale of inventory must be reported under the standard first-in-first-out (FIFO) method rather than the last-in-first-out (LIFO) method.[13]

It should be apparent by now that earnings and profits is simply a tax accounting concept designed to better measure a corporation's true financial results. It is an artificial "account" created by the Code—not an actual bank account or liquid fund set aside by the corporation for the payment of dividends. There is no statute of limitations on earnings and profits issues, and a corporation sometimes will face the onerous task of reconstructing many years of financial history in order to determine the tax consequences of a current distribution.[14]

PROBLEM

X Corporation is a cash method, calendar year taxpayer. During the current year, X has the following income and expenses:

Gross profits from sales	$20,000
Salaries paid to employees	10,250
Tax-exempt interest received	3,000
Dividends received from IBM	5,000
Depreciation (X purchased 5–year property in the current year for $14,000; assume the property has a 7–year class life; no § 179 election was made and X elected not to take the special depreciation allowance in § 168(k))	2,800
LTCG on a sale of stock	2,500
LTCL on a sale of stock	5,000
LTCL carryover from prior years	1,000
Estimated federal income taxes paid	800

Determine X's taxable income for the current year and its current earnings and profits.

---

profits. I.R.C. § 312(f)(1). In virtually all cases, this rule will cause corporations to have different bases in property for purposes of determining taxable income and earnings and profits.

10.   I.R.C. § 312(k)(3)(B).

11.   I.R.C. § 312(n)(1), (2).

12.   I.R.C. § 312(n)(5), (6).

13.   I.R.C. § 312(n)(4).

14.   Because it usually is an inherently factual question, the Service will not issue a ruling on the amount of a corporation's earnings and profits. Rev.Proc. 2005–3, § 3.01(29), 2005–1 C.B. 118, 120.

C. DISTRIBUTIONS OF CASH

Code: §§ 301(a), (b), (c); 312(a); 316(a).

Regulations: §§ 1.301–1(a), (b); 1.316–2(a)–(c).

The taxation of cash distributions by a corporation with respect to its stock is relatively straightforward. The amount of the distribution is simply the amount of money received by the shareholder.[1] That amount is taxable as a dividend to the extent of the distributing corporation's current or accumulated earnings and profits.[2] Amounts distributed in excess of available earnings and profits are first applied against and reduce the basis of the shareholder's stock and, to the extent that they exceed the shareholder's basis, they are treated as gain from the sale or exchange of the stock.[3] The distributing corporation generally is permitted to reduce its earnings and profits by the amount of money distributed, except that earnings and profits may be reduced as a result of a distribution only to the extent they exist.[4] Thus, while a deficit in earnings and profits may result from corporate operations, a deficit may not be created or increased by a distribution.[5]

When there are insufficient current earnings and profits available to cover all cash distributions made during the year, earnings and profits must be allocated to the distributions in order to determine dividend status under the following rules:[6]

(1) First, current earnings and profits, determined as of the end of the year, are prorated among the distributions by using the following formula:[7]

$$\frac{\text{Current E \& P}}{\text{allocated to distribution}} = \frac{\text{Amount of}}{\text{distribution}} \times \frac{\text{Total current E \& P}}{\text{Total distributions}}$$

(2) Next, accumulated earnings and profits are allocated chronologically to distributions (i.e., on a first-come, first-served basis).[8]

(3) If the corporation has a current loss but has accumulated earnings and profits from prior years, it will be necessary to determine the amount of accumulated earnings and profits available on the date of distribution. Unless the loss can be earmarked to a particular period, the current deficit is prorated to the date of the distribu-

---

1. The same rule applies to corporate and noncorporate distributees. I.R.C. § 301(b).

2. I.R.C. §§ 301(c)(1); 316(a).

3. I.R.C. § 301(c)(2), (3).

4. I.R.C. § 312(a).

5. Id.

6. This allocation method is significant only if there is a change in shareholder interests during the year or on a non pro rata distribution.

7. Reg. § 1.316–2(b), (c) Example.

8. Id.

tion.[9]

Revenue Ruling 74–164, below, and the problem which follows test your ability to understand and apply these principles.

Revenue Ruling 74–164

1974–1 Cum.Bull. 74.

Advice has been requested concerning the taxable status of corporate distributions under the circumstances described below.

X corporation and *Y* corporation each using the calendar year for Federal income tax purposes made distributions of $15,000 to their respective shareholders on July 1, 1971, and made no other distributions to their shareholders during the taxable year. The distributions were taxable as provided by section 301(c) of the Internal Revenue Code of 1954.

Situation 1.

At the beginning of its taxable year 1971, *X* corporation had earnings and profits accumulated after February 28, 1913, of $40,000. It had an operating loss for the period January 1, 1971 through June 30, 1971, of $50,000 but had earnings and profits for the entire year 1971 of $5,000.

Situation 2.

At the beginning of its taxable year 1971, *Y* corporation had a deficit in earnings and profits accumulated after February 28, 1913, of $60,000. Its net profits for the period January 1, 1971 through June 30, 1971, were $75,000 but its earnings and profits for the entire taxable year 1971 were only $5,000.

Situation 3.

Assume the same facts as in *Situation* 1 except that *X* had a deficit in earnings and profits of $5,000 for the entire taxable year 1971.

Situation 4.

Assume the same facts as in *Situation* 1 except that *X* had a deficit in earnings and profits of $55,000 for the entire taxable year 1971.

Section 301(a) and 301(c) of the Code provides, in part, that: (1) the portion of a distribution of property made by a corporation to a shareholder with respect to its stock which is a dividend (as defined in section 316), shall be included in the shareholder's gross income; (2) the portion of the distribution which is not a dividend shall be applied against and reduce the adjusted basis of the stock; and (3) the portion which is not a dividend to the extent that it exceeds the adjusted basis of the stock and is not out of increase in value accrued before March 1, 1913, shall be treated as gain from the sale or exchange of property.

9.   Reg. § 1.316–2(b).

Section 316(a) of the Code provides that the term "dividend" means any distribution of property made by a corporation to its shareholders out of its earnings and profits accumulated after February 28, 1913, or out of its earnings and profits of the taxable year computed as of the close of the taxable year without diminution by reason of any distribution made during the year, and *without regard to the amount of earnings and profits at the time the distribution was made.*

Section 1.316–2(a) of the Income Tax Regulations provides, in part, that in determining the source of a distribution, consideration should be given first, to the earnings and profits of the taxable year; and second, to the earnings and profits accumulated since February 28, 1913, only in the case where, and to the extent that, the distributions made during the taxable year are not regarded as out of the earnings and profits of that year.

Applying the foregoing principles, in *Situation* 1, the earnings and profits of *X* corporation for the taxable year 1971 of $5,000 and the earnings and profits accumulated since February 28, 1913, and prior to the taxable year 1971, of $40,000 were applicable to the distribution paid by it on July 1, 1971. Thus, $5,000 of the distribution of $15,000 was paid from the earnings and profits of the taxable year 1971 and the balance of $10,000 was paid from the earnings and profits accumulated since February 28, 1913. Therefore, the entire distribution of $15,000 was a dividend within the meaning of section 316 of the Code.

In *Situation* 2 the earnings and profits of *Y* corporation for the taxable year 1971 of $5,000 were applicable to the distribution paid by *Y* corporation on July 1, 1971. *Y* corporation had no earnings and profits accumulated after February 28, 1913, available at the time of the distribution. Thus, only $5,000 of the distribution by *Y* corporation of $15,000 was a dividend within the meaning of section 316 of the Code. The balance of such distribution, $10,000 which was not a dividend, applied against and reduced the adjusted basis of the stock in the hands of the shareholders, and to the extent that it exceeded the adjusted basis of the stock was gain from the sale or exchange of property.

In the case of a deficit in earnings and profits for the taxable year in which distributions are made, the taxable status of distributions is dependent upon the amount of earnings and profits accumulated since February 28, 1913, and available at the dates of distribution. In determining the amount of such earnings and profits, section 1.316–2(b) of the regulations provides, in effect, that the deficit in earnings and profits of the taxable year will be prorated to the dates of distribution.

Applying the foregoing to Situations 3 and 4 the distribution paid by *X* corporation on July 1, 1971, in each situation was a dividend within the meaning of section 316 of the Code to the extent indicated as follows:

Situation #3

Accumulated Earnings and Profits (E & P) 1/1	$ 40,000
E & P deficit for entire taxable year ($5,000) Prorate to date of distribution 7/1 (½ of $5,000)	(2,500)
E & P available 7/1	$ 37,500
Distribution 7/1 ($15,000)	(15,000) taxable as a dividend
E & P deficit from 7/1–12/31	(2,500)
Accumulated E & P balance 12/31	$ 20,000

Situation #4

Accumulated E & P 1/1	$ 40,000
E & P deficit for entire taxable year ($55,000) Prorate to date of distribution 7/1 (½ of $55,000)	(27,500)
E & P available 7/1	$ 12,500
Distribution 7/1 ($15,000)	(12,500) taxable as a dividend
E & P deficit from 7/1–12/31	(27,500)
Accumulated E & P balance 12/31	$(27,500)

NOTE

Situations 3 and 4 of Revenue Ruling 74–164 do not consider the possibility of earmarking the 1971 deficit to the first half of the year. Under the regulations,[1] if the deficit were sustained in the first half of 1971, the full deficit (not just one-half) would reduce the accumulated earnings and profits available to characterize the July 1 distribution as a dividend. This would not affect the result in Situation 3 but it would change the result in Situation 4, where there would be no dividend.

PROBLEM

Ann owns all of the common stock (the only class outstanding) of Pelican Corporation. Prior to the transactions below and as a result of a § 351 transfer, Ann has a $10,000 basis in her Pelican stock. What results to Ann and Pelican in each of the following alternative situations?

(a) In year one Pelican has $5,000 of current and no accumulated earnings and profits and it distributes $17,500 to Ann?

(b) Pelican has a $15,000 accumulated deficit in its earnings and profits at the beginning of year two. In year two Pelican has $10,000 of current earnings and profits and it distributes $10,000 to Ann.

(c) Pelican has $10,000 of accumulated earnings and profits at the beginning of year two and $4,000 of current earnings and profits in year two. On July 1 of year two, Ann sells half of her Pelican stock to Baker Corporation for $15,000. On April 1 of year two, Pelican distributes $10,000 to Ann, and on October 1 of year 2, Pelican distributes $5,000 to Ann and $5,000 to Baker.

---

1. Reg. § 1.316–2(b).

(d) Same as (c), above, except that Pelican has a $10,000 deficit in earnings and profits in year 2 as a result of its business operations.

D.   DISTRIBUTIONS OF PROPERTY

1.   CONSEQUENCES TO THE DISTRIBUTING CORPORATION

a.   BACKGROUND: THE *GENERAL UTILITIES* DOCTRINE

Under the double tax regime of Subchapter C, profits from the sale of appreciated corporate property are taxed twice—first to the corporation when it sells the property and again to the shareholders when the sales proceeds are distributed as dividends. What if a corporation *distributes* appreciated property to its shareholders? The shareholders, of course, receive a taxable dividend to the extent the distribution is out of current or accumulated earnings and profits. Should the distributing corporation also recognize gain—just as if it had sold the property for its fair market value? Or is the corporation entitled to nonrecognition of gain because the property was distributed rather than sold? Does the answer depend on the shareholder's basis in the distributed property? If tax relief is appropriate, should nonliquidating distributions be treated less favorably than liquidating distributions? And what about distributions of loss property? Simple as they may seem, these are among the most controversial questions ever spawned by Subchapter C. The answers will come gradually. The coverage in this chapter is limited to nonliquidating distributions. To set the stage, we begin with a brief history of the rise and fall of what has become known as the *General Utilities* doctrine.

In General Utilities & Operating Co. v. Helvering,[1] the Supreme Court first considered the corporate-level tax consequences of a nonliquidating distribution of appreciated property by a corporation to its shareholders. The facts were straightforward. General Utilities Corporation had located a buyer for corporate property with a value of $1,000,000 and an adjusted basis of $2,000. Hoping to escape the large corporate-level tax that would be imposed on a sale by the corporation, General Utilities distributed the property to its shareholders with an "understanding" (but not a legal commitment) that they would sell the targeted property to the prospective buyer. Four days later, the shareholders sold the property to the buyer on the same terms negotiated by the corporation. The Service contended that the distribution was a taxable event at the corporate level.

By the time the controversy reached the Supreme Court, the government's principal argument was based on the premise that General Utilities had created an indebtedness to its shareholders by declaring a dividend. It went on to contend that using appreciated property to discharge that indebtedness was a taxable event. Apparently confining its decision to these narrow grounds, the Court held that the corporation recognized no gain because the distribution was not a "sale" and the corporation did not

---

1.   296 U.S. 200, 56 S.Ct. 185 (1935).

discharge indebtedness with appreciated assets.[2] Despite this limited holding, it long was assumed that *General Utilities* stood for the broader proposition that a distributing corporation does not recognize gain or loss when it makes a distribution in kind with respect to its stock.[3]

The result in *General Utilities* raised fundamental policy questions that went to the heart of the double tax regime. The decision created a significant and arguably unwarranted tax distinction between a distribution in kind of appreciated property and a sale of that same property by the corporation followed by a distribution of the proceeds to the shareholders. In the case of a sale at the corporate level, the corporation recognizes gain and correspondingly must increase its earnings and profits. On distribution of the sale proceeds, the shareholders also are taxed to the extent of the corporation's earnings and profits. Under *General Utilities,* however, the corporation could distribute the same asset to the shareholders without recognizing gain. To be sure, the shareholders were taxable on the distribution, but the asset appreciation escaped tax at the corporate level, and a noncorporate shareholder took the asset with a fair market value basis.[4] This simple comparison demonstrates that the tax treatment of distributions in kind is critical to the integrity of the double tax regime. Because the *General Utilities* doctrine was incompatible with the double tax, it was criticized by commentators.[5]

Despite these deficiencies, Congress codified *General Utilities* in the 1954 Code by enacting Section 311(a)(2), which provides that a corporation generally does not recognize gain or loss on a nonliquidating distribution of property.[6] This nonrecognition rule was never absolute. Over the years, the courts applied "common law" doctrines, such as assignment of income[7] and the tax benefit rule,[8] and substance over form,[9] to override Section 311(a)

---

2. The government also argued that the subsequent sale by the shareholders of the assets could be attributed to the corporation, but the Court declined to consider that question since it had not been raised below. Ten years later, in Commissioner v. Court Holding Co., 324 U.S. 331, 65 S.Ct. 707 (1945), the government successfully advanced the attribution argument in the context of a liquidating distribution. See Chapter 16B2, infra. In *General Utilities,* the government alternatively contended that a distribution of appreciated property by a corporation in and of itself constitutes a realization event, but the Court did not address this argument. See Bittker & Eustice, Federal Income Taxation of Corporations and Shareholders ¶ 8.20[2] n. 313 (7th ed. 2000).

3. See, e.g., Commissioner v. Godley's Estate, 213 F.2d 529, 531 (3d Cir.1954), cert. denied 348 U.S. 862, 75 S.Ct. 86 (1954). Even before the 1954 Code, however, the *General Utilities* nonrecognition rule was subject to judicially-created exceptions, such as the assignment of income doctrine. See S.Rep. No. 1622, 83rd Cong., 2d Sess. 247 (1954).

4. I.R.C. § 301(d).

5. See, e.g., Block, "Liquidations Before and After Repeal of *General Utilities*," 21 Harv.J.Legis. 307 (1984); Blum, "Taxing Transfers of Incorporated Business: A Proposal for Improvement," 52 Taxes 516 (1974); Raum, "Dividends in Kind: Their Tax Aspects," 63 Harv.L.Rev. 593 (1950).

6. Prior to 1987, Section 336 provided a similar nonrecognition rule for liquidating distributions. See Chapter 7B2, infra.

7. See, e.g., Commissioner v. First State Bank of Stratford, 168 F.2d 1004 (5th Cir. 1948), cert. denied, 335 U.S. 867, 69 S.Ct. 137 (1948).

8. Cf. Hillsboro National Bank v. Commissioner, 460 U.S. 370, 103 S.Ct. 1134 (1983).

and attribute income back to the corporation. Congress also chipped away at the doctrine with various specialized statutory exceptions until 1986, when it repealed *General Utilities* in the context of both nonliquidating and liquidating distributions of appreciated property.[10]

b. CORPORATE GAIN OR LOSS

Code: § 311.

Although the nonrecognition rule in Section 311(a)(2) remains in the Code, Section 311(b) stands that rule on its head for nonliquidating distributions of appreciated property. If a corporation distributes appreciated property (other than its own obligations) in a nonliquidating distribution, it must recognize gain in an amount equal to the excess of the fair market value of the property over its adjusted basis. If the distributed property is subject to a liability or if the distributee shareholder assumes a liability in connection with the distribution, the fair market value of the distributed property is treated as not less than the amount of the liability.[11] The deceptive "general" rule of Section 311(a)(2) still applies, however, to disallow recognition of loss on a distribution of property that has declined in value. The objective of this statutory regime is to strengthen the corporate income tax by ensuring that appreciated property may not leave corporate solution and take a stepped-up basis in the hands of the distributee shareholder without the imposition of a corporate-level tax on the appreciation.[12]

The *General Utilities* doctrine thus no longer applies to nonliquidating distributions of appreciated property. A later chapter examines the repeal of the doctrine in the area of complete liquidations.[13] Despite what appears to be parallel treatment, some differences between the treatment of liquidating and nonliquidating distributions persist, raising lingering policy issues. For example, a distributing corporation generally may recognize a loss on a liquidating distribution of property with a built-in loss.[14] Should nonliquidating distributions be treated similarly? Is the "general" loss disallowance rule in Section 311(a)(2) an indefensible trap for the uninformed? In considering these questions, one should keep in mind that the double tax regime has not been universally accepted, and some have argued that relief through limited *General Utilities* type exceptions would be appropriate.[15]

---

9. Bush Brothers & Co. v. Commissioner, 668 F.2d 252 (6th Cir.1982); Waltham Netoco Theatres, Inc. v. Commissioner, 401 F.2d 333 (1st Cir.1968). But see Anderson v. Commissioner, 92 T.C. 138 (1989).

10. See also Chapter 7B2, infra.

11. I.R.C. § 311(b)(2), incorporating the rule for liquidating distributions in I.R.C. § 336(b).

12. Cf. S.Rep.No. 98–169, 98th Cong., 2d Sess. 177 (1984); H.R.Rep.No. 99–426, 99th Cong., 1st Sess. 282 (1985).

13. See Chapter 7B2, infra.

14. I.R.C. § 336(a), (d).

15. Compare Thompson, "An Analysis of the Proposal to Repeal General Utilities with an Escape Hatch," 31 Tax Notes 1121 (June 16, 1986) with Yin, "General Utilities Repeal: Is Tax Reform Really Going to Pass it By?" 31 Tax Notes 1111 (June 16, 1986).

c. EFFECT ON THE DISTRIBUTING CORPORATION'S EARNINGS AND PROFITS

Code: § 312(a)(3), (b), (c), (f)(1).

Regulations: § 1.312–3.

Nonliquidating distributions of property have several effects upon the earnings and profits of the distributing corporation. Gain recognized by the corporation on the distribution naturally increases current earnings and profits.[16] Following a property distribution, the distributing corporation may reduce accumulated earnings and profits (to the extent thereof) under Section 312(a)(3) by the adjusted basis of the distributed property. On a distribution of appreciated property (other than a corporation's own debt obligations), this rule is modified by Section 312(b)(2), which provides that the earnings and profits reduction rule in Section 312(a)(3) is applied by substituting the fair market value of the property for its adjusted basis. This special rule logically allows a corporation distributing appreciated property to make a downward adjustment to accumulated earnings and profits in an amount equal to the full fair market value of the property. The net result of these earnings and profits adjustments—the first relating to the gain recognized on the distribution and the second relating to the effect of the distribution itself—is the same as if the corporation had sold the property (increasing current earnings and profits by the gain recognized) and then distributed cash equal to the fair market value of the property (decreasing accumulated earnings and profits by that amount).

Section 312(c) cryptically adds that "proper adjustment" shall be made for liabilities either assumed by the shareholder or to which the property is subject. Section 1.312–3 of the regulations provides that the "proper adjustment" is a reduction in the Section 312(a)(3) charge to earnings and profits for liabilities assumed or to which the property is subject. This adjustment thus *decreases* the charge to earnings and profits and properly reflects the fact that relief from the liability is an economic benefit to the distributing corporation.

2. CONSEQUENCES TO THE SHAREHOLDERS

Code: §§ 301(a), (b), (c), (d).

The rules governing the shareholder level tax consequences of property distributions are essentially the same as those for cash distributions. The amount of the distribution is the fair market value of the distributed property, reduced by any liabilities assumed by the shareholder or to which the property is subject;[1] that amount is taxed under the now familiar

---

16. I.R.C. § 312(b)(1), (f)(1). For this purpose and for purposes of determining gain recognized, the adjusted basis of any property is its adjusted basis for purposes of computing earnings and profits. I.R.C. § 312(b), flush language. For example, tangible property depreciated for tax purposes under the accelerated cost recovery system must be depreciated for "E & P" purposes under the § 168(g)(2) alternative depreciation system and thus may have a different "E & P" adjusted basis.

1. I.R.C. § 301(b). The fair market value of the distributed property is determined

principles in Section 301(c). The shareholder's basis in the distributed property is its fair market value as of the date of the distribution.[2]

PROBLEM

Zane, an individual, owns all of the outstanding common stock in Sturdley Utilities Corporation. Zane purchased his Sturdley stock seven years ago and his basis is $8,000. At the beginning of the current year, Sturdley had $25,000 of accumulated earnings and profits and no current earnings and profits. Determine the tax consequences to Zane and Sturdley in each of the following alternative situations:

(a) Sturdley distributes inventory ($20,000 fair market value; $11,000 basis) to Zane.

(b) Same as (a), above, except that, before the distribution, Sturdley has no current or accumulated earnings and profits.

(c) Sturdley distributes land ($20,000 fair market value; $11,000 basis) which it has used in its business. Zane takes the land subject to a $16,000 mortgage.

(d) Assume Sturdley has $15,000 of current earnings and profits (in addition to $25,000 of accumulated earnings and profits) and it distributes to Zane land ($20,000 fair market value; $30,000 basis) which it held as an investment. Compare the result if Sturdley first sold the land and then distributed the proceeds.

(e) Assume again that Sturdley has $25,000 of accumulated earnings and profits at the beginning of the current year. Sturdley distributes machinery used in its business ($10,000 fair market value, zero adjusted basis for taxable income purposes, and $2,000 adjusted basis for earnings and profits purposes). The machinery is five-year property and has a seven-year class life, was purchased by Sturdley for $14,000 on July 1 of year one (no § 179 election was made), and the distribution is made on January 1 of year seven. See I.R.C. §§ 168(g)(2), 312(k)(3); Reg. § 1.312–15(d).

3.   DISTRIBUTIONS OF A CORPORATION'S OWN OBLIGATIONS

Code: §§ 311(a), (b)(1); 312(a)(2). Skim §§ 312(o); 1272(a)(1); 1273(a)(1).

Regulations: § 1.301–1(d)(1)(ii).

By virtue of the parenthetical in Section 311(b)(1)(A), "(other than an obligation of such corporation)", the general gain recognition rule does not apply to distributions by a corporation of its own debt obligations. Consequently, the eroded Section 311(a) continues to govern this situation. At the shareholder level, both the amount of the distribution and the distribu-

as of the date of distribution. I.R.C.   **2.** I.R.C. § 301(d).
§ 301(b)(3).

tee shareholder's basis are equal to the fair market value of the obligation.[1] The distributing corporation's earnings and profits are reduced by the principal amount of the obligation or, in the case of an obligation having original issue discount, by its issue price.[2]

The legislative history that follows describes two Congressional concerns involving distributions of a corporation's own obligations and the statutory solutions.

Excerpt From the Senate Finance Committee Explanation of the Tax Reform Act of 1984
S.Rep. No. 98–169, 98th Cong., 2d Sess. 188–89 (1984).

Distributions By a Corporation of Debt Obligations Having a Fair Market Value Less Than Par (sec. 47 of the bill and sec. 312 of the Code)

Present Law

A distribution by a corporation constitutes a dividend only if out of current or accumulated earnings and profits. The fair market value of property distributed as a dividend is includible in the gross income of an individual shareholder.

A corporation can distribute as a dividend its own debt obligations. Those obligations may have a fair market value less than their face amount. That is, they may carry a stated interest rate which is below the prevailing market rate. In such a case, an individual shareholder would have dividend income in an amount equal to the value of the obligations distributed to him. But the corporation may contend that, under present law, it can reduce its earnings and profits by the principal amount of such obligations (sec. 312(a)). The result could be to eliminate earnings and profits at the cost of a relatively small dividend tax. Distributions made by a corporation with no earnings and profits are not dividends but a return of capital.

Furthermore, taxpayers may argue that, under present law, such an obligation is not subject to the original issue discount rules. If that is correct, a shareholder on the cash basis may report no income with respect to the discount until it is paid, and the income may qualify as capital gain. Similarly, an accrual basis obligor may claim interest deductions currently on a straight-line or ratable rather than a constant rate basis, thereby accelerating deduction of the discount.

Reasons for Change

The committee does not believe that a dividend distribution should reduce earnings and profits by more than the amount includible as a dividend in the gross income of an individual recipient of such a distribu-

---

1. Reg. §§ 1.301–1(d)(1)(ii), –1(h)(2)(i).   2. I.R.C. § 312(a)(2).

tion. Furthermore, the committee believes that obligations distributed by a corporation that bear economic discount should be subject to the general original issue discount rules.

Explanation of Provisions

In the case of a dividend distribution by a corporation of its own debt securities at a discount, the corporation's earnings and profits are to be reduced by the issue price of the securities at the time of the distribution (determined under the original issue discount rules). Furthermore, any such securities are to be subject to the original issue discount rules. These provisions apply, however, only if the instruments distributed in fact represent indebtedness of the distributing corporation rather than equity. The provisions are not intended to create any inference that purported debt obligations distributed by a corporation should be treated as debt. The characterization of such instruments is governed by generally applicable provisions of present law. Furthermore, no inference is intended as to the proper treatment with respect to discount instruments distributed as dividends under present law.

PROBLEM

Andy owns all of the outstanding stock of Debt Corporation. Andy's stock basis is $100,000. Debt has $100,000 of accumulated earnings and profits and no current earnings and profits. On January 1 of this year, Debt distributed a $100,000 note, payable in 30 years, to Andy. The note bears no interest and because of that fact, the length of the obligation, and the relatively small size of Debt Co., the note currently has a fair market value of $5,000. Assume $5,000 is also the "issue price" of the note for purposes of original issue discount computations. On February 1 of this year, Debt Co. distributed $100,000 cash to Andy. How are the results of these distributions affected by the statutory changes discussed above?

E.   CONSTRUCTIVE DISTRIBUTIONS

Code: Skim § 7872(a), (c)(1)(C).

Regulations: § 1.301–1(j).

Historically, dividend distributions often combined the worst of all possible worlds from a tax standpoint: they were fully taxable to noncorporate shareholders at the highest ordinary income rates but were not deductible by the distributing corporation. To avoid the double tax, closely held C corporations have attempted to distribute earnings in a form that may be deductible at the corporate level. Notable examples include a corporation's payment of: (1) excessive compensation to shareholders or their relatives;[1] (2) expenses paid for the personal benefit of shareholders

---

1. For the legal standards used in making this determination, see, e.g., Exacto

Spring Corp. v. Commissioner, 196 F.3d 833 (7th Cir.1999), and compare Charles

(e.g., travel or entertainment, legal expenses);[2] (3) excessive rent for corporate use of shareholder property;[3] and (4) interest on shareholder debt that in substance represents equity.[4] If these payments are not what they purport to be—i.e., if they are not *really* salary, rent or interest, etc., or if they are primarily for the personal benefit of shareholders—they risk being reclassified by the Service as a constructive dividend. In that event, the corporate level deduction will be disallowed. Other disguised dividend strategies include labeling what in reality is a distribution as a loan to the shareholder,[5] bargain sales or rentals of corporate property to shareholders[6] and interest free loans.[7]

The constructive dividend area has produced many entertaining controversies involving blatant attempts by taxpayers to milk their corporations while avoiding the double tax. The prototype transaction involves a direct payment or receipt of an economic benefit by the shareholder, and resolution of the issue requires an evaluation of all the facts and circumstances, applying broad standards such as "reasonable compensation;" "shareholder benefit vs. corporate benefit" and "intent."[8] The case and ruling below illustrate some typical fact patterns and issues in this area. They are followed by a Note discussing the changing stakes now that most dividends are taxed at a preferential rate.

Nicholls, North, Buse Co. v. Commissioner

Tax Court of the United States, 1971.
56 T.C. 1225.

[Nicholls, North, Buse Co. ("Nicholls") was a Wisconsin corporation in the food-brokerage and food-packing businesses. All of the Nicholls voting common stock was owned by Herbert and Charlotte Resenhoeft, who were married. Herbert served as president and a director of the corporation. Nicholls nonvoting common stock was owned by Herbert, Charlotte and their two sons, Robert and James. James was also an employee of Nicholls.

Herbert Resenhoeft previously had personally owned two boats: *Pea Picker I* and *Pea Picker II*. In 1964, Nicholls acquired a new 52–foot yacht—*Pea Picker III*—at a total cost of $68,290. Nicholls' Board of Directors unanimously approved the purchase of *Pea Picker III* and provid-

---

McCandless Tile Service v. United States, 191 Ct.Cl. 108, 422 F.2d 1336 (1970) with Elliotts, Inc. v. Commissioner, 716 F.2d 1241 (9th Cir.1983).

2. See, e.g., Ashby v. Commissioner, 50 T.C. 409 (1968); Hood v. Commissioner, 115 T.C. 172 (2000).

3. See, e.g., International Artists, Ltd. v. Commissioner, 55 T.C. 94 (1970).

4. See Chapter 3, supra.

5. See, e.g., Williams v. Commissioner, 627 F.2d 1032 (10th Cir.1980).

6. See, e.g., Honigman v. Commissioner, 466 F.2d 69 (6th Cir.1972).

7. Compare Zager v. Commissioner, 72 T.C. 1009 (1979) with I.R.C. § 7872. See also Rountree Cotton Co. v. Commissioner, 113 T.C. 422 (1999), aff'd by order, 12 Fed.Appx. 641 (10th Cir.2001).

8. See generally, Bittker & Eustice, Federal Income Taxation of Corporations and Shareholders ¶ 8.05 (7th ed. 2000).

ed in a corporate resolution that "any expenses incurred in the personal use of the boat are to be borne by H.A. Resenhoeft and an accurate log is to be kept of all business use." During 1964, $1,144.72 was charged to Herbert for personal use of *Pea Picker III*.

Both Robert and James were free to operate *Pea Picker III*, without special permission. Herbert was unable to operate the yacht and had little technical knowledge about yachting. James was the principal operator of *Pea Picker III* and was the family boating enthusiast. In fact, James negotiated Nicholls' purchase of the yacht. During 1964, the use of *Pea Picker III* included personal use by James.

In its original notice of deficiency to Herbert, the Service took the position that he was taxable on $68,878.72, the purchase price for the yacht plus yacht expenses for the year. Later, the Service alternatively argued that Herbert was taxable on a dividend equal to the fair rental value of *Pea Picker III*. Ed.]

The issues with regard to individual petitioner Resenhoeft resolve themselves down to the following: (a) Was there a constructive dividend; (b) may the use of the yacht by James, a stockholder in his own right, be imputed to his father who was in control of the corporation to make the father the recipient of the constructive dividend; and (c) is the measure of the dividend the purchase price of the craft plus actual operating expenses or is the fair rental value of the use of the yacht during the period in question the appropriate measure?

(a) It is well established that any expenditure made by a corporation for the personal benefit of its stockholders, or the making available of corporate-owned facilities to stockholders for their personal benefit, may result in the receipt by the stockholders of a constructive dividend. * * * Upon consideration of all the evidence, including the possible instances of unrecorded personal use, we conclude that *Pea Picker III* was used for business purposes 25 percent and for personal purposes 75 percent of the time in 1964.

(b) Since we have found that there was personal use constituting under some circumstances a dividend, the next question is, to whom was the benefit directed? Resenhoeft has established by convincing evidence that he was not interested in the yacht for his own personal pleasure as a boating enthusiast. He had little knowledge of the workings of such craft, could not operate them himself, and played no direct part in the purchase of *Pea Picker III* or the sale of her predecessor. However, to the extent that he was present on an occasion of personal use, he received a benefit and an argument that others benefited as well is of no avail here. * * * He shared in the friendships and joined in the social activity on board on those occasions.

The question remains, however, whether James' personal use of *Pea Picker III* on occasions when Resenhoeft was not present may nevertheless be attributed to Resenhoeft. The essential elements underlying the taxation of assigned income to the assignor were set down in Helvering v. Horst, 311

U.S. 112 (1940). The Court stated in that case that: "The power to dispose of income is the equivalent of 'ownership' of it and the exercise of that power to procure the payment of income to another is the 'enjoyment' and hence the 'realization' of the income by him who exercises it." In this case Resenhoeft personally owned well over 50 percent of all voting stock and together with his wife owned all of it, and in addition was the president of the company and on the board of directors. It is manifestly clear that it was Resenhoeft's decision that the corporation acquire *Pea Picker III*. Resenhoeft's decision to allow the use of the boat by his sons as they desired and without direct control over either the circumstances of use or the maintenance of appropriate supportive documentation must be given particular emphasis. There is no indication here that information regarding the actual use of the boat, or the type of records maintained, was being kept from Resenhoeft or that he had no way of learning the truth. * * *

The principle of assignment was applied to constructive dividends in Byers v. Commissioner, 199 F.2d 273 (C.A.8, 1952), certiorari denied 345 U.S. 907 (1953). See also Commissioner v. Makransky, 321 F.2d 598 (C.A.3, 1963). We remain unpersuaded that Resenhoeft's purpose in agreeing to the acquisition of a large pleasure craft was only to benefit the corporation. This is particularly so in light of his prior personal ownership of *Pea Picker I* and *II* which were available for the use and benefit of his sons. Once it is understood that Resenhoeft was in complete control of the events, the fact that James, the principle user of the boat for noncorporate purposes, was a mature adult and a shareholder in his own right becomes irrelevant.

(c) Although we have determined that there was a dividend, and that the dividend must be attributed to Resenhoeft, we have yet to ascertain the amount of the dividend. Two standards have been used on different occasions, the first being the initial cost of the facility and the second, the approximate rental value for the period at issue. The standard to be chosen rests on the facts and circumstances of the event rather than on which year (the initial year of purchase or a subsequent year) happens to be before the Court, as was argued by respondent in his briefs. In *Louis Greenspon, supra*, the Court held that continued corporate ownership of farm equipment used by the petitioner shareholder prevented the assessment of a constructive dividend based on the purchase price of the equipment. No determination of a dividend was made based on the rental value since respondent failed to raise that issue. Our holding in *Greenspon* that ownership of the asset is a principal factor has not been altered by subsequent cases involving the year an asset was acquired. Although in some cases subsequent to *Greenspon* we have determined the amount of the dividend to be the acquisition cost, in those cases the evidence clearly pointed to shareholder ownership, * * * or the location of title could not be determined and therefore was presumptively in the shareholder. * * * These cases have not been followed when the title was clearly with the corporation. * * *

In this case, ownership continued to rest with Nicholls. The bill of sale was made in Nicholls' name, Nicholls' principal creditor was informed of the purchase and the yacht's intended devotion to corporate purposes, a license to operate short-wave radio equipment installed on *Pea Picker III* was acquired in the corporate name, registration by U.S. Customs was attempted in the corporate name, registration and licensing was received from the State of Wisconsin in the corporate name, and sales tax was paid by the corporation although a significant savings would have resulted by treating this as a purchase by Resenhoeft. Although a listing in the Lake Michigan Yachting Association catalogue showed James as the owner of the *Pea Picker III*, the association provided no means for noting corporate ownership, and registration in whatever name offered values significant to the corporation as well as to James. Therefore we hold that petitioner has not received a constructive dividend equivalent to the cost of acquisition of *Pea Picker III*.

The issue yet remaining is whether there is another more appropriate measure of the constructive dividend, a dividend which we have already decided Resenhoeft received.

Respondent's alternative theory is that the fair rental value of *Pea Picker III* for the period of use in 1964 is the measure of the dividend received; furthermore, respondent argues that the testimony of the captain in charge of delivering *Pea Picker III* from Florida corroborates the minimum rental value alleged in respondent's amended answer. The amended answer alleged that the fair value was not less than Nicholls' combined depreciation and operating expenses, $4,578.86, of which $1,144.72 concededly was included as income by Resenhoeft at the time he filed his 1964 return. Since we have already determined that Resenhoeft should be charged with 75 percent of the total value of the use of the yacht rather than 100 percent as argued by respondent, the remaining amount actually in dispute is $2,289.42. * * *

Ordinarily, respondent's alternative allegation would be determinative since petitioner has offered no evidence showing that determination to be in error. However, since the theory of a dividend based on rental value comprises a separate issue, involving distinct factual questions, and was raised by the Commissioner for the first time in his amended answer, the rental value suggested by the Commissioner may not be given the presumption it would otherwise be due * * *. Upon Considering all evidence, including the rental value of similar craft used in dissimilar water, we hold that the full rental value of *Pea Picker III* for the period following the shakedown cruise and ending with the final storage of the boat was $4,000. Resenhoeft gained personal benefit and therefore received a constructive dividend from his own use and the use of the craft by his sons equaling 75 percent of the above rental value; of that amount he has voluntarily recognized income to the extent of $1,144.72. We have no reason to believe Nicholls' earnings and profits were insufficient for the payment of a taxable dividend of the amount determined above.

Revenue Ruling 69–630

1969–2 Cum. Bull. 112.

Advice has been requested as to the treatment of a "bargain sale" between two corporate entities controlled by the same shareholder(s).

A, an individual, owns all of the stock of X corporation and all of the stock of Y corporation. In 1967, A caused X to sell certain of its property to Y for less than an arm's length price. It has been determined that such sale had as one of its principal purposes the avoidance of Federal income tax and resulted in a significant understatement of X's taxable income.

Section 482 of the Internal Revenue Code * * * provides authority to distribute, apportion, or allocate gross income, deductions, and credits among related organizations, trades, or businesses if it is necessary in order to clearly reflect the income of such entities or to prevent the evasion of taxes.

Section 482 of the Code applies to bargain sale transactions between brother-sister corporations that result in significant shifting of income. Where an allocation is made under section 482 of the Code as a result of a bargain sale between brother-sister corporations, the amount of the allocation will be treated as a distribution to the controlling shareholder(s) with respect to the stock of the entity whose income is increased and as a capital contribution by the controlling shareholder(s) to the other entity involved in the transaction giving rise to the section 482 allocation.

Accordingly, in the instant case, the income of X for 1967 will be increased under section 482 of the Code to reflect the arm's length price of the property sold to Y. The basis of the property in the hands of Y will also be increased to reflect the arm's length price. * * * Furthermore, the amount of such increase will be treated as a distribution to A, the controlling shareholder, with respect to his stock of X and as a capital contribution by A to Y.

* * *

NOTE

The reduced rate on qualified dividends has changed the stakes and planning agenda in some traditional scenarios. The distinction between compensation and a constructive dividend provides a good illustration. Compensation continues to be taxable at the highest ordinary income rates and is subject to employment taxes equal to 12.4 percent of the social security wage base of $90,000 (in 2005) and a 2.9 percent medicare tax on all wages while dividends are taxed at a maximum rate of 15 percent and are not subject to employment taxes. But compensation and the employer's share of employment taxes are deductible while dividends are not.

Under the "old arithmetic," with wages and dividends taxed at the same ordinary income rate, it almost always was advantageous to classify distributions to shareholder-employees as compensation rather than a dividend so that the corporation could deduct the payment. Under current law, however, as long as dividends are taxable at only 15 percent, there now are situations where the aggregate amount of federal taxes is lower if payments are classified as dividends rather than compensation. Important variables are the corporate and individual tax rates and the impact of employment taxes.[1]

To illustrate, consider first the following simple example in a world where wages are not subject to employment taxes, and all income of C corporations and individuals is taxed at a 35 percent rate except for dividends, which are taxed at 15 percent. Assume that X Corporation has $100,000 of earnings to distribute to A, its only employee and shareholder, and is evaluating whether to classify the distribution as a dividend or compensation. The overall tax results are as follows:

	Compensation	Dividend
X's Taxable Income Before Payment to A	$100,000	$100,000
Corporate Income Tax	0	35,000
Payment to A	100,000	65,000
A's Income Tax	35,000	9,750
Net Amount to A	65,000	55,250

The traditional incentive to classify the distribution as compensation remains in this example, despite the lower tax rate on dividends, because of the continuing negative effect of the double tax when a C corporation taxable at the highest marginal rate (35 percent) pays dividends.

Now assume the same facts, except reflect the reality that A is subject to employment taxes of 12.4 percent on the first $90,000[2] of wages and 2.9 percent on all wages, with half of these taxes paid by X Corp. (which can deduct them) and half by A. Assuming that X Corp. has $100,000 available to pay to A before any corporate-level income or employment taxes, the tax results are as follows:

	Compensation[3]	Dividend
X's Taxable Income Before Payment to A	$100,000	$100,000
Employment Taxes (X's share)	6,930	0
Corporate Income Tax	0	35,000
Payment to A	93,070	65,000
Employment Taxes (A's share)	6,930	0
A's Income Tax	32,575	9,750
Net Amount to A	53,565	55,250

1. For more extended analysis of these issues and other variables, see Feld, "Dividends Reconsidered," 101 Tax Notes 1117 (Dec. 1, 2003); Jewett, "Characterization of Income: Compensation vs. Dividends," 103 Tax Notes 1501 (June 21, 2004).

2. This is the wage base in effect for 2005.

3. These computations assume that X has $100,000 available for payment of wages to A before X pays the employer's share of employment taxes (6.2 percent of the first $90,000 of wages plus 1.45% of all wages). A's wages were determined using the following formula: wages ("W") = $100,000 − .062 (90,000) − .0145W.

When employment taxes are taken into account, there is a slight overall advantage to dividend classification. As A's compensation rises, however, the benefit of dividend classification will diminish because the 12.4 percent social security tax is only imposed on the first $90,000 of wages. With larger distributions, the traditional bias toward compensation persists because of the negative impact of the double tax.

The incentives also change if the corporation or the shareholder pays tax at lower marginal rates. If the corporation's taxable income falls within the lower rate brackets in Section 11, that reduces the amount of double tax paid and favors a dividend. Alternatively, if the shareholder pays tax on ordinary income at lower rates, that will favor compensation because the relative tax advantage for dividends will not be as great.

F. ANTI-AVOIDANCE LIMITATIONS ON THE DIVIDENDS RECEIVED DEDUCTION

1. IN GENERAL

Code: §§ 243(a)(1), (3), (c); 246(a)(1), (b)(1), (c); 246A; 1059(a), (b), (c), (d), (e)(1). Skim §§ 243(b)(1); 1059(e)(2), (3), (f).

Dividends received by corporate shareholders are treated more generously for tax purposes than dividends received by individuals. If corporate shareholders were taxed in full on the dividends they receive, corporate profits would be subjected to a minimum of three levels of taxation—once when earned, a second time when received as dividends by the corporate shareholder, and again when distributed to the ultimate noncorporate shareholder. To alleviate this multiple taxation, Section 243 generally permits corporate shareholders to deduct 70 percent of dividends received from other corporations. The deduction is increased to 80 percent if the corporate shareholder owns 20 percent or more (by vote or value) of the distributing corporation[1] and to 100 percent for certain "qualifying" dividends if the payor and recipient corporations are members of the same affiliated group.[2] As a result, a maximum of only 30 percent of dividends received by corporate shareholders are subject to tax, for a maximum effective rate of 10.5 percent.[3] The availability of this deduction has inspired tax advisors to devise techniques to take advantage of the lower effective rate on dividends received by corporate shareholders. This section examines ongoing Congressional efforts to curtail some of these abuses.

1. I.R.C. § 243(c).

2. I.R.C. § 243(a)(3). The term "affiliated group" is generally defined by reference to the rules governing affiliated corporations that file consolidated tax returns. I.R.C. § 243(b)(2). A simple example would be a corporate parent and an 80 percent or more subsidiary. See I.R.C. § 1504(a). A "qualifying dividend" must be paid from earnings and profits accumulated with the payor and recipient corporations are members of the same affiliated group. I.R.C. § 243(b)(1).

3. The 10.5 percent effective rate is derived by multiplying the 30 percent includible portion of the dividends by the 35 percent maximum corporate rate.

2. SPECIAL HOLDING PERIOD REQUIREMENTS

The dividends received deduction may motivate corporate shareholders to convert capital gain (taxable at the 35 percent maximum corporate rate) to tax sheltered dividend income (taxable at a maximum rate of 10.5 percent). Assume, for example, that Converter Corporation acquires 100 shares of Distributor, Inc. for $5,250 shortly before the stock goes "ex-dividend."[4] Converter holds the stock, collects a $250 dividend, includes only 30% ($75) in income, and then sells the stock for its post-dividend value of $5,000, claiming a short-term capital loss of $250 which is available to offset other capital gains normally taxable at 35 percent. Without any patrolling mechanism, this maneuver enables a corporate shareholder to convert short-term gain into 70 percent sheltered income.

An earlier version of Section 246(c) attempted to close this loophole by denying any dividends received deduction unless the stock was held for more than 15 days (90 days for certain preferred stock), but corporations concocted methods to diminish the risk of loss during this brief 15–day holding period. Congress responded by increasing the holding period in Section 246(c) to more than 45 days during the 91–day period[5] beginning on the date which is 45 days before the stock goes ex-dividend.[6] In the case of certain preferred stock, the required holding period is 90 days during the 181–day period beginning on the date which is 90 days before the ex-dividend date.[7] The 45 or 90–day period is tolled whenever the corporate shareholder diminishes its risk of loss with respect to the stock in any one of several specified manners.[8] As a result, a corporation is not entitled to the dividends received deduction unless it is willing to hold the stock and incur a genuine market risk for the requisite period of time.

3. EXTRAORDINARY DIVIDENDS: BASIS REDUCTION

If the dividend to be received is extraordinarily large in relation to the price of the stock, a corporate shareholder may incur a minimal risk of loss even if it holds the stock for more than 45 days. This opportunity was illustrated by a dramatic example of a tax-motivated "dividend stripping" transaction described in a Congressional committee report:[9]

> Chrysler's cumulative preferred stock sells at $36 per share shortly before Chrysler is scheduled to distribute $11.69 per share of back dividends. Corporation X has a short-term capital gain of $1 million, on which it will owe tax of $460,000 [the example uses the

---

4. The "ex-dividend" date is the first date that a buyer of the stock with respect to which a dividend has been declared is not entitled to receive the dividend.

5. The former 90–day period was increased to 91 days by § 406(f)(1) of the Working Families Tax Relief Act of 2004.

6. I.R.C. § 246(c)(1)(A). For purposes of counting the number of days, the date of

disposition but not the date of acquisition is included. I.R.C. § 246(c)(3).

7. I.R.C. § 246(c)(2).

8. I.R.C. § 246(c)(4). See Reg. § 1.246–5.

9. Joint Committee on Taxation, Tax Shelter Proposals and Other Tax–Motivated Transactions, 98th Cong., 2d Sess. 39–40 (1984).

pre–1987 46 percent corporate rate.] It buys 85,000 shares of Chrysler preferred for $3,060,000 and holds it for 91 days. When the stock goes ex-dividend, the price drops to $24.31 per share. Assume corporation X eventually sells the stock for $24.31. Corporation X has a capital loss of $11.69 per share, or $993,650, which reduces the tax on its capital gain to $2,921, or by $457,079. It receives a dividend of $993,650, of which 85 percent [now 70 percent.], or $844,603 is excluded. The tax on the rest of the dividend is $68,562. Thus, the transaction saves $457,079 of capital gain tax at a price of $68,562 of dividend tax, a net gain of $388,517. This gain is likely to exceed, by far, whatever economic consequences result from fluctuations in the market value of Chrysler preferred during the 91–day mandatory holding period.

To deter this opportunity for tax arbitrage, Congress enacted Section 1059, which provides that a corporate shareholder receiving an "extraordinary dividend" must reduce its basis in the underlying stock (but not below zero) by the amount of the nontaxed (i.e., deductible) portion of the dividend if the corporation has not held the stock for more than two years before the "dividend announcement date"—i.e., the earliest date when the distributing corporation declares, announces or agrees to the amount or payment of the dividend.[10]

To fully understand the workings of Section 1059, some definitions are in order. An "extraordinary dividend" is defined in terms of the size of the dividend in relation to the shareholder's adjusted basis in the underlying stock. A dividend is extraordinary if it exceeds certain threshold percentages—five percent of the shareholder's adjusted basis in the case of most preferred stock and ten percent of the adjusted basis in the case of any other stock.[11] To prevent easy avoidance of these percentage tests, all dividends received by a shareholder with respect to any shares of stock which have ex-dividend dates within the same period of 85 consecutive days are combined and treated as one dividend.[12] Under an alternate test, a taxpayer may elect to determine the status of a dividend as extraordinary by reference to the fair market value (rather than the adjusted basis) of the stock as of the day before the ex-dividend date.[13] This election could be beneficial if the stock had appreciated substantially from the time when it was acquired by the shareholder.

---

10. I.R.C. § 1059(a)(1), (d)(5). A distribution that otherwise would constitute an extraordinary dividend will not be considered as such if the shareholder has held the stock during the entire existence of the corporation or any predecessor corporation. I.R.C. § 1059(d)(6).

11. I.R.C. § 1059(c)(1), (2).

12. I.R.C. § 1059(c)(3)(A). In addition, all dividends received with respect to a share of stock which have ex-dividend dates during the same period of 365 consecutive days are treated as extraordinary if the aggregate of such dividends exceeds 20 percent of the basis in such stock. I.R.C. § 1059(c)(3)(B). These rules are extended to include dividends received with respect to shares of stock having a substituted basis. I.R.C. § 1059(c)(3)(C).

13. I.R.C. § 1059(c)(4). This option is available only if the taxpayer establishes the fair market value of the stock to the satisfaction of the Commissioner.

The basis reduction required by Section 1059 is only for the "nontaxed portion" of an extraordinary dividend. The "nontaxed portion" is the total amount of the dividend reduced by the taxable portion—i.e., the portion of the dividend includible in gross income after application of the dividends received deduction.[14] The basis reduction generally occurs immediately before any sale or disposition of the stock.[15] If the nontaxed portion of an extraordinary dividend exceeds the shareholder's adjusted basis in the stock, any excess is treated as gain from the sale or exchange of property in the taxable year in which the extraordinary dividend is received.[16]

The general definition of "extraordinary dividend" is broadened in two special situations. Section 1059(e)(1) provides that any amount treated as a Section 301 distribution to a corporate shareholder shall be an extraordinary dividend, irrespective of the shareholder's holding period in the stock or the size of the distribution, if it is a distribution in redemption of stock which is: (1) part of a partial liquidation of the redeeming corporation[17], or (2) is non pro rata as to all shareholders.[18] In addition, a corporate shareholder will recognize immediate gain with respect to any redemption treated as a dividend (in whole or in part) when the nontaxed portion of the dividend exceeds the basis of the shares surrendered if the redemption is treated as a dividend because of the holding of options that are treated as constructively owned by the shareholder under Section 318.[19] This rather obscure provision was enacted in response to a few highly publicized transactions where corporate taxpayers sought to structure sales of stock as "dividend" redemptions in order to shelter their gain through the dividends received deduction.

Two other special rules carve out liberalizing exceptions. First, certain distributions between an affiliated group of corporations that qualify for the 100 percent dividends received deduction under Section 243(b)(1) are not treated as extraordinary dividends.[20] Second, special relief is provided for "qualified preferred dividends," which are defined as dividends payable with respect to any share of stock which provides for fixed preferred dividends payable not less than annually and was not acquired with dividends in arrears.[21] A "qualified preferred dividend" is not treated as an extraordinary dividend if the dividends received by the shareholder during the period it owned the stock do not exceed an annualized rate of 15 percent of the lower of (a) the shareholder's adjusted basis or (b) the liquidation preference of the stock, and the stock is held by the shareholder

---

14. I.R.C. § 1059(b).

15. I.R.C. § 1059(d)(1)(A). Section 1059(d)(1)(B) provides that in testing for an extraordinary dividend under Section 1059(c)(1), any reduction in basis required by reason of a prior distribution is treated as occurring at the beginning of the ex-dividend date for such distribution.

16. I.R.C. § 1059(a)(2). This treatment avoids the tax taboo of a negative basis. Cf. I.R.C. § 357(c) and Chapter 2D, supra.

17. "Partial liquidation" is defined for this purpose under the tests in Section 302(e). See Chapter 5D, infra.

18. The tax consequences of stock redemptions are covered in Chapter 5, infra.

19. I.R.C. § 1059(e)(1)(A)(iii).

20. I.R.C. § 1059(e)(2).

21. I.R.C. § 1059(e)(3)(C)(i).

for over five years.[22] The theory for this complex exception is that, unlike the typical extraordinary dividend, a qualified preferred dividend offers no potential for effectively purchasing a dividend that accrued prior to the date on which the stock was acquired.

4. DEBT-FINANCED PORTFOLIO STOCK

Corporate shareholders also exploited the dividends received deduction by borrowing funds to acquire dividend paying stock. For example, assume Leverage Corporation borrows $10,000 at 10 percent interest to purchase $10,000 of stock that will pay dividends at an 8 percent annual return ($800 per year). Leverage fully deducts the $1,000 interest expense against ordinary income but only $240 of the $800 dividend received would be taxable if the 70 percent dividends received deduction is available. The deduction thus turns this otherwise uneconomic transaction into a profitable low risk arbitrage maneuver. The interest deduction results in an annual tax savings of $350 ($1,000 × 35%) while the tax owed on the dividends would be $84 if the corporation were in the maximum 35 percent bracket. For an annual outlay of $1,000 in interest and $84 in tax, Leverage receives $800 in income and a tax savings of $350, for a $66 after-tax benefit.

Section 246A precludes this strategy by reducing Leverage's dividends received deduction to the extent the dividends are attributable to "debt-financed portfolio stock." A similar policy is reflected in Section 265(a)(2), which denies a deduction for interest incurred to purchase or carry tax-exempt municipal bonds. Thus, if the "portfolio stock" is entirely debt-financed, Section 246A denies any dividends received deduction. If it is debt-financed in some lesser percentage, then that same percentage of the dividends received deduction is denied.[23] In all events, however, the reduction in the dividends received deduction may not exceed the amount of any interest deduction allocable to the dividend (i.e., to the borrowed funds directly attributable to the stock).[24]

Stock is "debt-financed" if it is "portfolio stock" that is encumbered by "portfolio indebtedness" during a "base period" prescribed in the statute.[25] "Portfolio stock" is defined as any stock of a corporation unless the corporate shareholder owns either: (1) 50 percent of the total voting power and value of the corporation or (2) at least 20 percent of the total voting power and value and five or fewer corporate shareholders own at least 50 percent of the voting power and value, excluding preferred stock.[26] "Portfolio indebtedness" means any indebtedness directly attributable to the investment in the portfolio stock.[27] This means that the stock must have been purchased with borrowed funds or that the borrowing must be

---

22. I.R.C. § 1059(e)(3)(A), (B). If all these requirements are met except for the five year holding period, the exclusion from extraordinary dividend treatment is more limited. I.R.C. § 1059(e)(3)(A)(ii).

23. I.R.C. § 246A(a), (d).

24. I.R.C. § 246A(e).

25. I.R.C. § 246A(c)(1), (d)(4).

26. I.R.C. § 246A(c)(2), (4).

27. I.R.C. § 246A(d)(3)(A).

directly traceable to the acquisition, such as where the stock was pledged as security for a subsequently incurred debt in a case where the corporation reasonably could have been expected to sell the stock rather than incur the indebtedness.[28]

To illustrate, assume that Leverage Corporation acquires 100 shares of publicly traded X Corp. stock for $10,000, paying $6,000 cash from corporate funds and borrowing the $4,000 balance. X Corp. pays Leverage an annual dividend of $1,000. The stock is debt-financed to the extent of $4,000. The percentage of debt-financing is thus 40 percent (the "average portfolio indebtedness," as defined by Section 246A(d)). Under the convoluted formula in Section 246A(a), Leverage subtracts 40 percent from 100 percent and then multiplies the result (60 percent here) by the usual 70 percent dividends received deduction percentage, to reach 42 percent. That lower figure is substituted for 70 percent in determining Leverage's Section 243 deduction. When Leverage receives its $1,000 dividend, it may deduct only $420 (rather than the usual $700).

5.   SECTION 301(e)

The adjustments to earnings and profits required by Sections 312(k) and 312(n) for depreciation and other timing items frequently result in an increase to a corporation's earnings and profits[29] and may cause earnings and profits to exceed the corporation's taxable income. For example, a corporation that reports a gain on the installment method may not defer the gain for purposes of determining its earnings and profits.[30] The increase in earnings and profits resulting from these adjustments often ensures that a distribution will be fully taxable as a dividend to noncorporate shareholders. Because of the dividends received deduction, this may prove to be a bonanza to a corporate shareholder. The following example from the legislative history illustrates one type of abuse that concerned Congress:[31]

> For example, assume that P Corporation owns 100 percent of the stock of X Corporation, that P's basis in such stock is $200, that P and X file separate income tax returns, and that X has no current or accumulated earnings and profits. Assume further that X sells an asset for a $1,000 installment note, realizing an $800 gain. Finally, assume that X borrows $500 secured by the installment note and distributes the $500 to P. Under [Section 312(n)], absent a special rule, X Corporation's earnings and profits would be increased by the amount of gain on the installment sale, and P would treat the $500 distribution as a dividend. Thus P would

---

28. H.R.Rep. No. 98–432, 98th Cong., 2d Sess. 1181 (1984).

29. The purpose of these adjustments is to ensure that a corporation's earnings and profits more accurately reflect its true economic performance. See Section B of this chapter, supra.

30. I.R.C. § 312(n)(5).

31. Staff of the Joint Committee on Taxation, General Explanation of the Revenue Provisions of the Deficit Reduction Act of 1984 (hereinafter "1984 Act General Explanation"), 98th Cong., 2d Sess. 183 (1984).

include the $500 in income but would likely qualify for a 100–percent dividends received deduction. If P later sold its X stock for $200 (the value of that stock if it is assumed that X will ultimately have a $300 tax liability, in present value terms, on account of the installment sale), it would not recognize gain or loss on the sale. As a result, P would have realized an overall profit of $500.

Section 301(e) prevents the result illustrated above by providing that the adjustments required by Sections 312(k) and 312(n) shall not be made for purposes of determining the taxable income of (and the adjusted basis of stock held by) any "20 percent corporate shareholder."[32] A 20 percent corporate shareholder is any corporation entitled to a dividends received deduction with respect to a distribution that owns, directly or through the Section 318 attribution rules, either (1) stock in the distributing corporation possessing at least 20 percent of the total combined voting power, or (2) at least 20 percent of the total value of all of the distributing corporation's stock, except nonvoting preferred stock.[33]

The general effect of Section 301(e) is to reduce the distributing corporation's earnings and profits in determining the tax consequences of distributions to 20 percent corporate shareholders. This reduction, in turn, may cause a distribution to be treated as a return of capital coupled with a reduction in the basis of the distributing corporation's stock. Without Section 301(e), the same distribution likely would have been a tax-free dividend with no basis reduction. Thus, applying Section 301(e) to the earlier example, X Corporation will have no earnings and profits for purposes of determining the tax consequences of a distribution to P Corporation. In the absence of earnings and profits, $200 of the distribution by X to P will be a return of capital under Section 301(c)(2), and $300 will be taxed to P as gain from the sale or exchange of its X stock under Section 301(c)(3). P's basis in its X stock will be reduced to zero and it will recognize a $200 gain on the later sale of the stock.[34]

PROBLEM

On June 1, Publicly Held Corporation's common stock is selling for $15 per share. On that date, Publicly Held declares a dividend of $1 per share, payable on June 12 to shareholders of record as of June 8. Investor Corporation purchases 1,000 shares of Publicly Held common stock for $15,000 on June 3 (two days before the June 5 ex-dividend date), collects a $1,000 dividend on June 12 and sells the stock for $14,000 on June 15.

(a) What are the tax consequences to Investor Corporation?

(b) What result in (a), above, if Investor sold the stock on December 1, instead of June 15?

---

32. I.R.C. § 301(e)(1).

33. I.R.C. § 301(e)(2).

34. 1984 Act General Explanation, supra note 29, at 183.

(c) What result in (b), above, if Publicly Held had paid a second $1 per share dividend on August 15, and the ex-dividend date was August 5?

(d) What result in (c), above, if the August dividend is $2 per share but Investor holds the Publicly Held stock for 25 months before selling it?

(e) What result if Investor purchased the Publicly Held stock by borrowing $15,000, secured by the stock, and Investor paid $1,200 interest during the year and received $1,000 of dividends?

(f) What result in (e), above, if Investor had borrowed only $7,500 of the $15,000 used to buy the stock?

G.   Use of Dividends in Bootstrap Sales

TSN Liquidating Corp. v. United States

United States Court of Appeals, Fifth Circuit, 1980.
624 F.2d 1328.

■ Randall, Circuit Judge:

This case presents the question whether assets distributed to a corporation by its subsidiary, immediately prior to the sale by such corporation of all the capital stock of such subsidiary, should be treated, for federal income tax purposes, as a dividend or, as the district court held, as part of the consideration received from the sale of such capital stock. We hold that on the facts of this case, the assets so distributed constituted a dividend and we reverse the judgment of the district court.

In 1969, TSN Liquidating Corporation, Inc. ("TSN"), which was then named "Texas State Network, Inc.," owned over 90% of the capital stock of Community Life Insurance Company ("CLIC"), an insurance company chartered under the laws of the State of Maine. In early 1969, negotiations began for the purchase of CLIC by Union Mutual Life Insurance Company ("Union Mutual"). On May 5, 1969, TSN and the other CLIC stockholders entered into an Agreement of Stock Purchase (the "Stock Purchase Agreement") with Union Mutual for the sale of the capital stock of CLIC to Union Mutual. The Stock Purchase Agreement provided that there would be no material adverse change in the business or assets of CLIC prior to the closing "except that as of closing certain shares and capital notes as provided in Section '4.(i).' above will not be a part of the assets of [CLIC]." Since the purchase price of the capital stock of CLIC under the Stock Purchase Agreement was based primarily on the book value (or, in some instances, market value) of those assets owned by CLIC on the closing date, the purchase price would be automatically reduced by the elimination of such shares and notes from the assets of CLIC. On May 14, 1969, as contemplated by the Stock Purchase Agreement, the Board of Directors of CLIC declared a dividend in kind, payable to stockholders of record as of

May 19, 1969, consisting primarily of capital stock in small, public companies traded infrequently and in small quantities in the over-the-counter market. On May 20, 1969, the closing was held and Union Mutual purchased substantially all the outstanding capital stock of CLIC, including the shares held by TSN. The final purchase price paid by Union Mutual to the selling stockholders of CLIC was $823,822, of which TSN's share was $747,436. Union Mutual thereupon contributed to the capital of CLIC $1,120,000 in municipal bonds and purchased from CLIC additional capital stock of CLIC for $824,598 in cash paid to CLIC.

In its income tax return for the fiscal year ended July 31, 1969, TSN reported its receipt of assets from CLIC as a dividend and claimed the 85% dividends received deduction available to corporate stockholders pursuant to § 243(a)(1) of the Internal Revenue Code of 1954. TSN also reported its gain on the sale of the capital stock of CLIC on the installment method pursuant to § 453 of the Code. [Under current law, installment sale treatment would not be allowed if the CLIC stock were publicly traded. I.R.C. § 453(k)(2). Ed.] On audit, the Internal Revenue Service treated the distribution of the assets from CLIC to TSN as having been an integral part of the sale by TSN of capital stock of CLIC to Union Mutual, added its estimate ($1,677,082) of the fair market value of the assets received by TSN to the cash ($747,436) received by TSN on the sale, and disallowed the use by TSN of the installment method for reporting the gain on the sale of the capital stock of CLIC since aggregating the fair market value of the distributed assets and the cash resulted in more than 30% of the proceeds from the sale being received in the year of sale. TSN paid the additional tax due as a result of such treatment by the Internal Revenue Service, filed a claim for a refund and subsequently instituted this action against the Internal Revenue Service.

The district court made the following findings of fact in part II of its opinion:

> With regard to the negotiations between CLIC and Union Mutual in early 1969, the Court finds that Union Mutual was interested in purchasing CLIC and proposed a formula for valuing the assets, liabilities, and insurance in force, which, together with an additional amount, would be the price paid for the CLIC stock.

> The investment portfolio of CLIC was heavily oriented toward equity investments in closely held over-the-counter securities. At least in the mind of CLIC's officers, the makeup of CLIC's investment portfolio was affecting its ability to obtain licenses in various states. As early as the Spring of 1968, the management and principal stockholders of CLIC had begun to seek a solution to the investment portfolio problem. The Court finds, however, that CLIC had never formulated a definite plan on how to solve its investment portfolio problem.

> Union Mutual did not like CLIC's investment portfolio but considered bonds to be more in keeping with insurance industry responsibilities. The management of CLIC regarded the Union

Mutual offer as a good one, and tried without success to get Union Mutual to take the entire investment portfolio.

Accordingly, the [Stock Purchase Agreement] required CLIC to dispose some of the investment portfolio assets. Thus, the price that would be paid for the CLIC stock was based upon a formula which valued the assets after excluding certain stocks.

* * *

Plaintiff's disposition of the undesirable over-the-counter stock was necessitated by its sale arrangements with Union Mutual. Plaintiff had no definite plans prior to its negotiations with Union Mutual as to how to get rid of the undesirable stock, when it was to get rid of the undesirable stock, or even that it would definitely get rid of the undesirable stock. Accordingly, the Court finds that the dividend in kind of 14 May 1969 was part and parcel of the purchase agreement with Union Mutual.

TSN Liquidating Corp. v. United States, 77–2 U.S.Tax Cas. ¶ 9741 at 88,523 (N.D.Tex.1977). In part III of its opinion, the district court made the following additional findings:

Union Mutual was interested in purchasing the stock of an approximately $2 million corporation in order that that corporation might be licensed to do business in other states. As of 30 April 1969, CLIC had assets of $2,115,138. On 14 May 1969, CLIC declared a dividend valued at approximately $1.8 million. As a result of this dividend, CLIC was left with assets totaling approximately $300,000. The final purchase price paid by Union Mutual to the selling shareholders of CLIC was $823,822. In addition, Union Mutual contributed $1,120,000 of municipal bonds to the capital of CLIC and purchased additional shares of stock of CLIC for $824,598. Thus, subsequent to closing on 20 May 1969, CLIC was worth $2,400,000. Thus, CLIC was worth $2 million when the [Stock Purchase Agreement] was signed on 5 May 1969 and worth over $2 million immediately after closing.

There was no business purpose served in this case by the dividend declared by CLIC prior to the sale of all its stock to Union Mutual. It is evident that the dividend benefitted the shareholders of CLIC and not CLIC itself. There was no benefit or business purpose in CLIC's declaration of the dividend separate and apart from the sale. The Court finds that the dividend would not, and could not, have been made without the sale.

* * *

What actually happened in the period 5 through 20 May 1969 was that the stockholders received $1.8 million in virtually tax-free stocks, as well as over $800,000 in cash, for a total of approximately $2.6 million. This was certainly a fair price for a corporation valued at the time of sale at $2,115,138, and reflects a premium paid for good will and policies in force, as well as the fact that CLIC was an existing business with licenses in eight or nine states. Hence, a $2 million corporation was sold for $2.6 million including the dividend and the cash.

After noting the time-honored principle that the incidence of taxation is to be determined by the substance of the transaction rather than by its form and the related principle that the transaction is generally to be viewed as a whole and not to be separated into its component parts, the district court held:

> The distribution of assets to [TSN] from its subsidiary, CLIC, immediately prior to [TSN's] disposition of its entire stock interest in CLIC should be treated as a part of the gain from the sale of the stock. Thus, the Court concludes that the in-kind distribution of 14 May 1969 to the stockholders of CLIC is taxable to [TSN] as gain from the sale of its stock. The alleged dividend was merely intented [sic] to be part of the purchase price paid by Union Mutual to CLIC for its stock.

The district court relied for its holding primarily on the cases of Waterman Steamship Corp. v. Commissioner, 430 F.2d 1185 (5th Cir.1970), cert. denied, 401 U.S. 939, 91 S.Ct. 936, 28 L.Ed.2d 219 (1971), and Basic, Inc. v. United States, 549 F.2d 740 (Ct.Cl.1977), all discussed infra.

On appeal, TSN argues that the cases relied upon by the district court are exceptions to what TSN characterizes as the established rule, namely, that assets removed from a corporation by a dividend made in contemplation of a sale of the stock of that corporation, when those assets are in good faith to be retained by the selling stockholders and not thereafter transferred to the buyer, are taxable as a dividend and not as a part of the price paid for the stock for the reason that, in economic reality and in substance, the selling stockholders did not sell and the buyer did not purchase or pay for the excluded assets. The principal cases cited by TSN for its position are Gilmore v. Commissioner, 25 T.C. 1321 (1956), Coffey v. Commissioner, 14 T.C. 1410 (1950), and Rosenbloom Finance Corp. v. Commissioner, 24 B.T.A. 763 (1931). According to TSN, the controlling distinction between the *Coffey* line of cases relied upon by TSN and the *Waterman* line of cases relied upon by the district court is whether the buyer negotiated to acquire and pay for the stock, exclusive of the assets distributed out as a dividend, on the one hand, or whether the buyer negotiated to acquire and pay for the stock, including the assets which were then the subject of a sham distribution designed to evade taxes, on the other hand. In the former case, according to TSN, there is a taxable dividend; in the latter case there is not.

We begin by noting that the district court was certainly correct in its position that the substance of the transaction controls over the form and that the transaction should be viewed as a whole, rather than being separated into its parts. Further, having reviewed the record, we are of the view that the operative facts found so carefully by the district court are entirely accurate (except for the valuation of the distributed assets, as to which we express no opinion). We differ with the district court only in the legal characterization of those facts and in the conclusion to be drawn therefrom. We agree with TSN that this case is controlled by the *Coffey, Gilmore* and *Rosenbloom* cases rather than by the *Waterman* and *Basic* cases relied upon by the district court.

In *Coffey,* the principal case relied upon by TSN, the taxpayers owned the stock of Smith Brothers Refinery Co., Inc. and were negotiating for the sale of such stock. Representatives of the purchasers and representatives of the sellers examined and discussed the various assets owned by Smith Brothers Refinery Co., Inc., and the liabilities of the company, with a view to reaching an agreement upon the fair market value of the stock. During these negotiations, the representatives of the purchasers and of the sellers could not agree upon the value of certain assets (including a contingent receivable referred to as the Cabot payment). The representatives of the purchasers informed the representatives of the sellers that the sellers could withdraw those assets from the assets of the company and that they would buy the stock without those assets being a part of the sale, thereby eliminating the necessity for arriving at a valuation of those assets in determining the value of the stock on a net worth basis. The contract of sale provided that the unwanted assets would be distributed by the corporation as a dividend prior to the sale of the stock. The selling stockholders contended before the tax court, as the Internal Revenue Service does in the case before this court, that the Cabot payment distributed to them as a dividend in kind was "part of the consideration for stock sold and that any profit resulting from its receipt by them is taxable as a capital gain." The tax court rejected that contention because it was contrary to the substance of the transaction:

> We do not agree with petitioners that they received the Cabot payment as part of the consideration for the sale of their stock. The purchasers did not agree to buy their stock and then turn over to them $190,000 and the Cabot payment in consideration therefor. From the testimony above set forth it is apparent that they were not interested in the Cabot payment, did not want it included in the assets of the corporation at the time they acquired its stock, and negotiated with petitioners to acquire stock of a corporation whose assets did not include the unwanted Cabot payment. * * * They received $190,000 for their stock. Under the contract of sale, they did not sell or part with their interest in the Cabot contract. It was expressly reserved by them and was a distribution they received as stockholders by virtue of the reservation.

Coffey, 14 T.C. at 1417, 1418. The tax court held the distribution to be a dividend.

In *Gilmore,* the purchasers of corporate stock did not wish to pay for quick assets owned by the corporation, namely cash on hand and United States bonds, and the parties provided for a presale dividend to exclude them from the assets to be transferred to the purchaser by means of the sale of the corporate stock. The tax court held that the assets distributed to the stockholders by means of a dividend were taxable as a dividend and not as a part of the sales proceeds for the corporate stock:

> It may be true the parties could have reached much the same result and have avoided some tax consequences to the stockholders by casting the transaction in the form of a higher purchase offer that would have included all of the quick assets. But this just was not done. * * * The [purchasers] chose to make this offer, one that "waived" the quick assets after payment of indebtedness. * * * The [purchasers] did not agree to pay the stockholders $6.50 or any other sum from the surplus. They "waived any claim" to the surplus and consented that it "may be paid to the present stockholders." * * *
>
> In *T.J. Coffey, Jr.,* 14 T.C. 1410, a situation similar to the one here was before the Court and we held that the corporate distributions there involved were not a part of the consideration for the sale of stock.

Gilmore, 25 T.C. at 1323, 1324.

In *Rosenbloom,* the sole stockholder of Joseph S. Finch Company was Rosenbloom Finance Corporation. Rosenbloom entered into a contract for the sale of all the capital stock of Joseph S. Finch Company to Shenley Products Company. With respect to the unwanted assets, the contract provided:

> "All other assets of every character whatsoever owned by the Finch Company at the time of the transfer of said shares of stock, as herein provided, shall be transferred to the party of the first part (petitioner) by dividend distribution, prior to the consummation of the sale of said shares of stock herein provided for."

Rosenbloom, 24 B.T.A. at 769. The board of tax appeals held that the assets distributed to Rosenbloom Finance Corporation by Joseph S. Finch Company should be treated as an ordinary dividend and not as an amount distributed in partial liquidation.

The Internal Revenue Service states that it does not disagree with the holdings in *Coffey, Gilmore* and *Rosenbloom,* but it takes the position that they do not apply in the circumstances of this case. The Internal Revenue Service focuses on the receipt by the selling stockholders of CLIC of investment assets, followed immediately by an infusion by Union Mutual of a like amount of investment assets into CLIC, and says that the reinfusion of assets brings the case before the court within the "conduit rationale" of *Waterman.* In *Waterman,* Waterman Steamship Corporation ("Waterman") was the owner of all the outstanding capital stock of Pan–Atlantic Steamship Corporation ("Pan–Atlantic") and Gulf Florida Terminal Company, Incorporated ("Gulf Florida"). Malcolm P. McLean made an offer to Waterman to purchase all the outstanding capital stock of Pan–Atlantic and Gulf Florida for $3,500,000. Since Waterman's tax basis for the stock of the subsidiaries totaled $700,000, a sale of the capital stock of the subsidiaries for $3,500,000 would have produced a taxable gain of approximately $2,800,000. Because the treasury regulations on consolidated returns provided that the dividends received from an affiliated corporation are exempt from tax, a sale of capital stock of the subsidiaries for $700,000, after a dividend payment to Waterman by the subsidiaries of $2,800,000, would, at least in theory, have produced no taxable gain. The Board of Directors of Waterman rejected McLean's offer, but authorized Waterman's president to submit a counter proposal providing for the sale of all the capital stock in the subsidiaries for $700,000, but only after the subsidiaries paid dividends to Waterman in the aggregate amount of $2,800,000. As finally consummated, the dividends and the sale of the capital stock of the subsidiaries took the following form:

(1) Pan–Atlantic gave a promissory note to Waterman for $2,800,000 payable in 30 days as a "dividend."

(2) One hour later, Waterman agreed to sell all of the capital stock of Pan–Atlantic and Gulf Florida for $700,000.

(3) Thirty minutes later, after the closing of the sale of the capital stock of the subsidiaries had occurred, Pan–Atlantic held a special meeting of its new Board of Directors, and the Board authorized Pan–Atlantic to borrow $2,800,000 from McLean and a corporation controlled by McLean. Those funds were used by Pan–Atlantic promptly to pay off the $2,800,000 note to Waterman (which was not yet due).

In its tax return for the fiscal year involved, Waterman eliminated from income the $2,800,000 received as a dividend from Pan–Atlantic and reported $700,000 as the sales price of the capital stock of the two subsidiaries. Since Waterman's tax basis for the stock was the same as the sales price therefor, no taxable gain was realized on the sale. On audit, the Internal Revenue Service took the position that Waterman had realized a long-term capital gain of $2,800,000 on the sale of the capital stock of the subsidiaries and increased its taxable income accordingly. On appeal from a judgment by the tax court in favor of the taxpayer, the Internal Revenue Service contended that the rules applicable to situations where a regular dividend has been declared are not applicable when the parties contemplate that a purported dividend is to be inextricably tied to the purchase price and where, as was the case before the court, the amount of the dividend is not a true distribution of corporate profits. The Internal Revenue Service argued that the funds were supplied by the buyer of the stock, with the corporation acting as a mere conduit for passing the payment through to the seller. This court agreed with the Internal Revenue Service:

The so-called dividend and sale were one transaction. The note was but one transitory step in a total, pre-arranged plan to sell the stock. We hold that in substance Pan–Atlantic neither declared nor paid a dividend to Waterman, but rather acted as a mere conduit for the payment of the purchase price to Waterman.

Waterman, 430 F.2d at 1192. The opinion of this court began with this sentence:

> This case involves another attempt by a taxpayer to ward off tax blows with paper armor.

Id. at 1185. The opinion stressed the sham, tax motivated aspects of the transaction:

> Here, McLean originally offered Waterman $3,500,000 for the stock of Pan–Atlantic and Gulf Florida. Waterman recognized that since its basis for tax purposes in the stock was $700,180, a taxable gain of approximately $2,800,000 would result from the sale. It declined the original offer and proposed to cast the sale of the stock in a two step transaction. Waterman proposed to McLean that it would sell the stock of the two subsidiaries for $700,180 after it had extracted $2,800,000 of the subsidiaries' earnings and profits. It is undisputed that Waterman intended to sell the two subsidiaries for the original offering price—with $2,800,000 of the amount disguised as a dividend which would be eliminated from income under Section 1502. Waterman also intended that none of the assets owned by the subsidiaries would be removed prior to the sale. Although the distribution was cast in the form of a dividend, the distribution was to be financed by McLean with payment being made to Waterman through Pan–Atlantic. To inject substance into the form of the transaction, Pan–Atlantic issued its note to Waterman before the closing agreement was signed. The creation of a valid indebtedness however, cannot change the true nature of the transaction. * * *

> * * *

> The form of the transaction used by the parties is relatively unimportant, for the true substance and effect of their agreement was that McLean would pay $3,500,000 for all of the assets, rights and liabilities represented by the stock of Pan–Atlantic and Gulf Florida.

Id. at 1194–95. This court concluded its opinion in *Waterman* by cautioning against "giving force to 'a purported [dividend] which gives off an unmistakably hollow sound when it is tapped.'" Id. at 1196 (quoting United States v. General Geophysical Co., 296 F.2d 86, 89 (5th Cir.1961), cert. denied, 369 U.S. 849, 82 S.Ct. 932, 8 L.Ed.2d 8 (1962)). A final footnote to the opinion stated that the decision should not be interpreted as standing for the proposition that a corporation which is contemplating a sale of its subsidiary's stock could not under any circumstances distribute its subsidiaries' profits prior to the sale without having such distribution deemed part of the purchase price. Id. at 1196 n. 21.

In summary, in *Waterman,* the substance of the transaction, and the way in which it was originally negotiated, was that the purchaser would pay $3,500,000 of its money to the seller in exchange for all the stock of the two subsidiaries and none of the assets of those subsidiaries was to be removed and retained by the sellers. In the case before the court, the district court found that Union Mutual did not want and would not pay for the assets of CLIC which were distributed to TSN and the other stockholders of CLIC. Those assets were retained by the selling stockholders. The fact that bonds and cash were reinfused into CLIC after the closing, in lieu of the unwanted capital stock of small, publicly held corporations, does not convert this case from a *Coffey* situation, in which admittedly unwanted assets were distributed by the corporation to its stockholders and retained by them, into a *Waterman* situation, in which the distribution of assets was clearly a sham, designed solely to achieve a tax free distribution of assets ultimately funded by the purchaser. Indeed, the Internal Revenue Service does not argue, in the case before the court, that the transaction was in any respect a sham. Instead, the Service would have us hold that the mere infusion of assets into the acquired company after the closing, assets which are markedly different in kind from the assets that were distributed prior to the closing, should result in the disallowance of dividend treatment for the distribution of the unwanted assets, and the Service cites *Waterman* as authority for that proposition. We view the sham aspect—the hollow sound—of the transaction described in *Waterman* as one of the critical aspects of that decision, and we decline to extend the *Waterman* rule to a case which admittedly does not involve a sham and which, in other important respects, is factually different from *Waterman*.

The Internal Revenue Service also cites *Basic* as authority for the disallowance of dividend treatment for the distribution of the unwanted assets in this case. Basic Incorporated ("Basic") owned all the capital stock of Falls Industries Incorporated ("Falls"), which in turn owned all the stock of Basic Carbon Corporation ("Carbon"). Carborundum Company ("Carborundum") made an initial offer to acquire all the assets of Falls and Carbon. This offer failed to gel when Basic demanded that Carborundum agree to indemnify Basic for any tax assessments that might become payable on the transaction in excess of those which Basic could anticipate and compute in advance, a proposal that was unacceptable to Carborundum. Carborundum then made a second proposal to acquire directly from Basic the capital stock of Falls and the capital stock of Carbon and requested that Basic transfer the ownership of the capital stock of Carbon from Falls to Basic prior to the transaction. In order to achieve that, Falls distributed the capital stock of Carbon to Basic as a dividend, which put Basic in the position of owning the capital stock of both Falls and Carbon. The sale of such capital stock to Carborundum was then consummated. In its federal income tax return for the year involved, Basic reported dividend income from Falls in the amount of $500,000 as a result of its receipt of the capital stock of Carbon. It thereupon claimed a dividends received deduction in the amount of 85% of the dividend pursuant to § 243(a)(1) of the Code. Finally, it reported a long-term capital gain of $2,300,000 from the sale to Carborundum of the shares of Falls and Carbon. On audit, the Internal Revenue Service determined that the gain from the sale of the shares of capital stock of Falls and Carbon should be increased by the amount of the purported dividend. On those facts, the court of claims held that the distribution of the capital stock of Carbon by Falls to Basic was not a true dividend but was part of the total transaction by which Basic, in substance, sold the capital stock of Falls and Carbon to Carborundum:

> Under the facts and circumstances presented here, plaintiff has not shown that there was a reason for the transfer of the Carbon stock from Falls to Basic aside from the tax consequences attributable to that move. Accordingly, for purposes of taxation, the transfer was not a dividend within the meaning of Section 316(a)(1). Instead, it should be regarded as a transfer that avoided part of the gain to be expected from the sale of the business to Carborundum, and should, therefore, be now taxed accordingly.

Basic, 549 F.2d at 749. Basic was a conduit through which an asset, the capital stock of Carbon, was passed to the buyer. The substance of the transaction was a brief removal of the "dividend" asset (the Carbon stock) on the way to the hands of the waiting buyer. In the case before the court, unlike the situation that obtained in *Basic,* the distributed assets were retained by the stockholders to whom they were distributed, rather than being immediately transferred to the purchaser.

As additional support for its position, the court in *Basic* focused on the absence of a business purpose, viewed from the standpoint of Falls, for the payment of a dividend of a valuable corporate asset, i.e., the capital stock of Carbon, by Falls to Basic. The district court, in the case before this court, applied the same test to the payment of the dividend of the unwanted assets by CLIC to TSN, the controlling stockholder of CLIC, and found that, strictly from the standpoint of CLIC, the dividend was lacking in business purpose and, indeed, could not have taken place apart from the sale and the subsequent infusion of investment assets into CLIC by Union Mutual. However, it seems to us to be inconsistent to take the position that substance must control over form and that a transaction must be viewed as a whole, rather than in parts, and at the same time to state that the business purpose of one participant in a multi-party transaction (particularly where the participant is a corporation controlled by the taxpayer and is not itself a party to the sale transaction) is to be viewed in isolation from the over-all business purpose for the entire transaction. We agree that the transaction must be viewed as a whole and we accept the district court's finding of fact that the dividend of the unwanted assets was "part and parcel of the purchase arrangement with Union Mutual," motivated specifically by Union Mutual's unwillingness to take and pay for such assets. That being the case, we decline to focus on the business purpose of one participant in the transaction—a corporation controlled by the taxpayer— and instead find that the business purpose for the transaction as a whole, viewed from the standpoint of the taxpayer, controls. The facts found by the district court clearly demonstrate a business purpose for the presale dividend of the unwanted assets which fully explains that dividend. We note that there is no suggestion in the district court's opinion of any tax avoidance motivation on the part of the taxpayer TSN. The fact that the dividend may have had incidental tax benefit to the taxpayer, without more, does not necessitate the disallowance of dividend treatment.

Having concluded that the pre-sale distribution by CLIC to its stockholders (including TSN) of assets which Union Mutual did not want, would not pay for and did not ultimately receive is a dividend for tax purposes, and not part of the purchase price of the capital stock of CLIC, we reverse the judgment of the district court and remand for proceedings consistent with this opinion.

Reversed and remanded.

NOTE

Life is not as simple today as it was when the successful tax plan in *TSN Liquidating* was concocted. Several additional provisions of the Code now must be considered in evaluating the continuing viability of a pre-sale distribution of unwanted assets by a corporate shareholder.

As noted earlier,[1] Section 301(e) requires, solely for purposes of computing the amount of any taxable dividend income to a 20 percent or more corporate shareholder and the shareholder's basis in the stock of the distributing corporation, that the distributing corporation's earnings and profits must be determined without regard to the special adjustments in Sections 312(k) and 312(n). Section 301(e), however, will not necessarily impair the technique used in *TSN Liquidating;* it merely limits the utility of pre-acquisition dividend strips to situations where the distributing corporation has substantial earnings and profits before the required earnings and profits timing adjustments.

A more serious impediment is the possibility of a downward adjustment in the basis of the corporate shareholder's stock as a result of the pre-sale dividend. If TSN had been required to reduce the basis in its CLIC stock by the amount of the dividends received deduction that it was allowed on the distribution, the transaction would have lost its allure. A basis reduction would have placed TSN in the position of trading a dollar of dividend income for a dollar of gain on the subsequent sale of its CLIC stock. Since corporations do not enjoy a capital gains preference, they usually are indifferent to the distinction between ordinary income and capital gain.[2] Does current law cause TSN to suffer a basis reduction as a result of the pre-sale dividend? The answer is no unless the distribution is subject to Section 1059. That section requires a basis reduction for the amount of any "extraordinary dividend" which was not taxed to a corporate shareholder because of the dividends received deduction where the stock has not been held for more than two years before the announcement of the dividend.[3] Because of its size (roughly $1.67 million, according to the facts of the case), the dividend to TSN appears to be "extraordinary" under the tests in Section 1059(c). But TSN nonetheless could have avoided any

---

1. See Section F5 of this chapter, supra.

2. Other tax attributes, however, might cause TSN to prefer one or the other type of income. For example, if TSN had unused capital losses, it might prefer capital gains on the sale to fully taxable dividend income.

3. I.R.C. § 1059(a). See Section F3 of this chapter, supra.

basis reduction if it had held its CLIC stock for more than two years before the dividend was announced.

One final obstacle must be mentioned in the interests of full disclosure. If TSN and CLIC were affiliated corporations and elected to file a consolidated tax return,[4] TSN would have been required to reduce its basis in the CLIC stock as a result of the dividend. The consolidated return regulations, which treat an "affiliated group" as a single taxpaying entity, logically eliminate intracorporate dividends from the consolidated group's joint gross income.[5] The dividend is considered a mere reshuffling of profits within a single taxpayer which should not generate additional income. The regulations also provide that a parent's basis in the stock of a subsidiary is generally reduced by the full amount of any excluded intercompany dividend.[6] It follows that the strategy employed in *TSN Liquidating* has no appeal in the context of a consolidated group.

Despite these technical hurdles, a pre-sale dividend is still viable if the selling parent corporation has held the stock of a subsidiary for more than two years and the corporations do not file a consolidated return. The Tax Court's decision in Litton Industries, Inc. v. Commissioner[7] illustrates the importance of form and timing to the success of this technique. The issue in *Litton* was whether a $30 million dividend, paid to Litton by a wholly owned subsidiary in the form of a negotiable promissory note five months prior to Litton's sale of the subsidiary's stock to Nestle Corporation, was truly a dividend rather than part of the proceeds received by Litton on the sale of the stock. The promissory note was later satisfied by Nestle at the same time that it purchased the stock. Dividend treatment was preferable to Litton because of the shelter provided by what was then an 85 percent dividends received deduction.

Distinguishing Waterman Steamship Corp. v. Commissioner[8] (discussed in *TSN Liquidating* at pages 198–201 of the text, supra), the Tax Court held that the payment was a dividend. Favorable (and distinguishing) factors were: (1) unlike *Waterman Steamship,* the dividend and subsequent sale in *Litton* were substantially separated in time (over five months in *Litton* was better than the few hours in *Waterman*); (2) at the time the dividend was declared, no formal action had been taken by the parent to initiate a sale to Nestle and "[t]here was no definite purchaser waiting in the wings with the terms and conditions of sale already agreed upon;"[9] and (3) as in *TSN Liquidating,* the overall transaction was not a sham because a business purpose was served by the dividend. In rejecting the Service's contention that the dividend and subsequent sale of the subsidiary should be treated as one transaction for tax purposes, the court reasoned:[10]

The term "dividend" is defined in section 316(a) as a distribution by a corporation to its shareholders out of earnings and

4. See Chapter 13, supra.
5. Reg. § 1.1502–13(f)(2)(ii).
6. Reg. § 1.1502–32(b)(2), (3)(v).
7. 89 T.C. 1086 (1987).
8. 430 F.2d 1185 (5th Cir.1970).
9. 89 T.C. at 1099.
10. Id. at 1099–1100.

profits. The parties have stipulated that Stouffer had earnings and profits exceeding $30 million at the time the dividend was declared. This Court has recognized that a dividend may be paid by a note. T.R. Miller Mill Co. v. Commissioner, 37 B.T.A. 43, 49 (1938), affd. 102 F.2d 599 (5th Cir.1939). Based on these criteria, the $30 million distribution by Stouffer would clearly constitute a dividend if the sale of Stouffer had not occurred. We are not persuaded that the subsequent sale of Stouffer to Nestle changes that result merely because it was more advantageous to Litton from a tax perspective.

It is well established that a taxpayer is entitled to structure his affairs and transactions in order to minimize his taxes. This proposition does not give a taxpayer carte blanche to set up a transaction in any form which will avoid tax consequences, regardless of whether the transaction has substance. Gregory v. Helvering, 293 U.S. 465 (1935). A variety of factors present here preclude a finding of sham or subterfuge. Although the record in this case clearly shows that Litton intended at the time the dividend was declared to sell Stouffer, no formal action had been taken and no announcement had been made. There was no definite purchaser waiting in the wings with the terms and conditions of sale already agreed upon. At that time, Litton had not even decided upon the form of sale of Stouffer. Nothing in the record here suggests that there was any prearranged sale agreement, formal or informal, at the time the dividend was declared.

Petitioner further supports its argument that the transaction was not a sham by pointing out Litton's legitimate business purposes in declaring the dividend. Although the code and case law do not require a dividend to have a business purpose, it is a factor to be considered in determining whether the overall transaction was a sham. T.S.N. Liquidating Corp. v. United States, 624 F.2d 1328 (5th Cir.1980). Petitioner argues that the distribution allowed Litton to maximize the gross after-tax amount it could receive from its investment in Stouffer. From the viewpoint of a private purchaser of Stouffer, it is difficult to see how the declaration of a dividend would improve the value of the stock since creating a liability in the form of a promissory note for $30 million would reduce the value of Stouffer by approximately that amount. However, since Litton was considering disposing of all or part of Stouffer through a public or private offering, the payment of a dividend by a promissory note prior to any sale had two advantages. First, Litton hoped to avoid materially diminishing the market value of the Stouffer stock. At that time, one of the factors considered in valuing a stock, and in determining the market value of a stock was the "multiple of earnings" criterion. Payment of the dividend by issuance of a promissory note would not substantially alter Stouffer's earnings. Since many investors were relatively unsophisticated, Litton may have been quite right that it could increase its investment in Stouffer by at least some portion of the $30 million dividend. Second, by declaring a dividend and paying it by a promissory note prior to an anticipated public offering, Litton could avoid sharing the earnings with future additional shareholders while not diminishing to the full extent of the pro rata dividend, the amount received for the stock. Whether Litton could have come out ahead after Stouffer paid the promissory note is at this point merely speculation about a public offering which never occurred. The point, however, is that Litton hoped to achieve some business purpose, and not just tax benefits, in structuring the transaction as it did.

Under these facts, where the dividend was declared 6 months prior to the sale of Stouffer, where the sale was not prearranged, and since Stouffer had earnings and profits exceeding $30 million at the time the dividend was declared, we cannot conclude that the distribution was merely a device designed to give the appearance of a dividend to a part of the sales proceeds. In this case, the form and substance of the transaction coincide; it was not a transaction entered into solely for tax reasons, and it should be recognized as structured by petitioner.

PROBLEM

Strap Corporation is the sole shareholder of X, Inc. Strap and X do not file a consolidated return, and Strap has held its X stock for more than two years. Strap has a $150,000 basis in its X stock. Boot is a prospective buyer and is willing to purchase all of the X stock, but he is unable to pay the $500,000 price demanded by Strap even though he believes it to be fair. X has $100,000 cash on hand and an ample supply of earnings and profits. To solve these problems, the parties have agreed on the following plan: Strap Corporation will cause X, Inc. to distribute $100,000 to it as a dividend. Promptly thereafter, Strap will sell its X stock to Boot for $400,000. What are the tax consequences of this plan? What if Strap were an individual rather than a corporation?

CHAPTER 5

REDEMPTIONS AND PARTIAL LIQUIDATIONS

A. INTRODUCTION

Code: §§ 302; 317(b).

Proposed Regulations: § 1.302–5(a), (b), (c).

The Logic of Section 302. Shareholders generally recognize a capital gain or loss on the sale of some or all of their stock. Assume, for example, that A purchased 100 shares of X Corporation stock two years ago for $1,000. If A sells 50 of those shares to B, an unrelated outsider, for $750, he will recognize a $250 long-term capital gain. But what if A made the same sale to the corporation? Should that transaction, known as a redemption, also generate a $250 long-term capital gain? We need more facts to answer the question. If A is one of several X shareholders and owns a small percentage of the corporation's stock, a sale of stock to the corporation may be similar (for tax purposes) to a sale to B. But if X has few shareholders and ample earnings and profits and A is a major shareholder, the transaction begins to resemble a dividend.

To illustrate, assume that A's 100 shares constitute all of X Corporation's outstanding stock. In that event, A's "sale" of 50 shares to the corporation in exchange for $750 cash is indistinguishable from a nonliquidating distribution of $750. Although A has surrendered a stock certificate for 50 shares, his proportionate interest in the corporation remains unchanged. When the smoke clears, A continues to control all corporate decisions and he remains the sole shareholder, entitled to 100 percent of X's net assets upon a liquidation. Yet without altering his interest in the business, A has extracted $750 from the corporate coffers. This is the essence of a dividend! But if the "sale" to X were respected, A would be permitted to use a proportionate amount of his stock basis ($500) to offset an equivalent amount of income, and any resulting gain will be taxed at preferential capital gains rates. If A were permitted to avoid dividend characterization with such ease, proportionate redemption programs by shareholders of closely held corporations quickly would become a national sport whenever the shareholders have a substantial basis in their stock.

These simple examples identify the fundamental problem in determining the shareholder level tax consequences of a redemption. A line must be drawn between redemptions having the effect of a dividend—that is, transactions that enable shareholders to withdraw cash or other property while leaving their proportionate interest intact—and redemptions that resemble sales because they result in a meaningful reduction in the shareholder's proportionate interest. Under prior law, there was only one vague standard to resolve this question. A redemption was treated as an operating distribution and taxed as a dividend to the extent of the corporation's current and accumulated earnings and profits unless it was not "essentially equivalent to a taxable dividend."[1] Cases were resolved by looking to all the facts and circumstances, including the corporation's "business purpose" and the "net effect" of the transaction.[2]

The enactment of Section 302 introduced a commendable degree of certainty in an area where predictions had been precarious. Section 302(a) provides that a redemption will be treated as an "exchange" if it satisfies one of four statutory tests in Section 302(b). "Exchange" status means that the shareholder generally will recognize capital gain or loss to the extent of the difference between the amount of the distribution and the shareholder's basis in the redeemed stock. A redemption falling outside of Section 302(b) is treated under Section 302(d) as a "distribution to which Section 301 applies." Under the rules studied in the preceding chapter, the distribution will be a dividend to the extent of the corporation's current and accumulated earnings and profits, then a return of capital to the extent of the shareholder's basis in the redeemed stock, and finally gain from the sale or exchange of the stock to the extent of any balance.

Section 302(b) is thus the nerve center for determining the shareholder-level tax consequences of a redemption and the principal focus of this chapter. Three of the four statutory tests (Sections 302(b)(1)–(3)) examine whether there has been a sufficient reduction in the shareholder's ownership interest in the corporation to justify treating the redemption as an exchange. To obtain a more accurate measure, the shareholder's interest before and after the redemption is determined after application of the constructive ownership rules in Section 318.[3] Section 302(b)(4) shifts the focus to the corporate level and provides exchange treatment for any distribution that qualifies as a "partial liquidation" under Section 302(e) because it involves a genuine contraction of the distributing corporation's business.

Basis Consequences. If a redemption is treated as a sale, the basis of the redeemed stock is taken into account in determining the shareholder's gain or loss. If a redemption is treated as a dividend, the regulations historically have provided that the shareholder's basis in the redeemed stock does not disappear but may be added to the basis of the shareholder's retained stock. If the shareholder no longer owns any stock after the

---

1. Internal Revenue Code of 1939, § 115(g).

2. See Bittker & Eustice, Federal Income Taxation of Corporations and Shareholders ¶ 9.01 (7th ed. 2000). Another line of authority treated a redemption as not "essentially equivalent to a taxable dividend" if it involved a contraction in the corporation's business activities. This test focused on events at the corporate rather than the shareholder level and gave birth to the tax concept known as a "partial liquidation." The remnants of this concept are considered in Section F of this chapter, infra.

3. I.R.C. § 302(c)(1).

redemption, the basis of the redeemed stock may be added to the basis of stock held by family members or entities whose stock was attributed to the redeemed shareholder under Section 318. The regulations have never been specific about how this basis shift should be allocated when there is more than one related shareholder.[4]

The Service has issued proposed regulations that would change these longstanding rules, as applied to simple redemptions and a number of other transactions (well beyond appropriate "fundamentals" coverage) where the rules of Section 302 are implicated.[5] If and when they become final, the proposed regulations will apply (among other places) to redemptions taxable as dividends where the redeemed shareholder owns no stock of the redeeming corporation (a complete redemption) or still owns some stock (a partial redemption).[6] They generally would treat "dividend redemptions" as triggering a loss, in the amount of the shareholder's basis in the redeemed stock, that is recognized and characterized at the time of the redemption but not "taken into account" (i.e., deducted) until a later date specified by the regulations.[7] Under the general rule, a redeemed shareholder may take the loss into account on a "final inclusion date," which is defined as the first date when events occur that, if they occurred at the time of the redemption, would have caused the redemption to be treated as an exchange under Section 302 or, alternatively, on the last day that the shareholder could take the loss into account, such as immediately before the shareholder's death or upon the liquidation of a corporate shareholder.[8] Under a special rule, all or part of the deferred loss may be taken into account earlier, on an "accelerated loss inclusion date," such as when the redeemed shareholder recognizes a gain from the sale of his shares, or must take into account gain recognized on a distribution under Section 301(c)(3), but only to the extent of that gain.[9]

To illustrate the operation of these rules, assume A, an individual shareholder, acquired all 100 shares of X Corporation for $100,000. Several years later, X redeems 60 shares for $150,000, all of which is treated as a dividend. The current regulations would treat A as having a $100,000 basis in his remaining 40 shares. Under the proposed regulations, A would recognize a $60,000 deferred loss (equal to A's basis in the redeemed stock) at the time of the redemption. The character and source of that loss (e.g., short or long-term) would be determined at that time, and the basis of A's remaining shares would be $40,000. The $60,000 deferred capital loss could be "taken into account" (i.e., deducted, subject to the limitations on deductions of capital losses) on the "final inclusion date," such as when A sells his remaining stock to an unrelated party, or if A never makes another sale, on the date of A's death.[10]

---

4. Reg. § 1.302–2(c), providing for "proper adjustment of the remaining stock."

5. REG–150313–01, 67 Fed. Reg. 64331–64345 (Oct. 18, 2002).

6. Prop. Reg. § 1.302–5(a).

7. Id.

8. Prop. Reg. §§ 1.302–5(b)(3).

9. Prop. Reg. §§ 1.302–5(b)(4); 1.302–5(f) Examples 3 & 4.

10. See, e.g., Prop. Reg. § 1.302–5(f) Examples 1–2.

Alternatively, assume that several years after the redemption A sells 15 of his remaining 40 shares to an unrelated person and realizes a $20,000 capital gain on the sale. The proposed regulations would treat the sale as an "accelerated loss inclusion date" and permit A to utilize his deferred loss to the extent of the $20,000 gain recognized. A would continue to hold the remaining $40,000 deferred loss in abeyance until the next accelerated loss inclusion date (to the extent of gain recognized) or, if later, the final inclusion date.[11]

These complex rules were designed to combat abusive corporate tax shelter transactions (well beyond the scope of our coverage) that exploited the current regulatory rule, usually by shifting basis from a foreign shareholder not subject to U.S. tax to a related U.S. taxpayer who then utilized the additional basis to increase loss or reduce taxable gain.[12]

Tax Consequences to Distributing Corporation. Whether a redemption is treated as an exchange or a Section 301 distribution at the shareholder level, the tax consequences to the distributing corporation of a distribution of property in a redemption are governed by Section 311. The distributing corporation recognizes gain on a distribution of appreciated property, but it may not recognize loss on a distribution of property that has declined in value.[13]

Changing Stakes. The tax stakes on a redemption have changed considerably over the years. They are influenced by several variables, such as the type of shareholder (individual or corporate), the shareholder's basis in the redeemed stock, and the applicable tax rates for dividends and capital gains. For most of our tax history, noncorporate shareholders preferred a redemption to be treated as a sale of stock resulting in recovery of the shareholder's basis and recognition of more lightly taxed capital gain. Corporate shareholders prefer dividend treatment because they can shelter most of the distribution if they qualify for the dividends received deduction or completely exclude dividends received from other members of an affiliated group of corporations that file a consolidated tax return.

The 15 percent maximum rate on qualified dividends has altered the stakes for individual shareholders. With the dividend and long-term capital gains rates now the same, the major advantage to treating a redemption as an exchange is the shareholder's ability to recover the basis of the redeemed stock in determining gain or loss. In some cases, this still provides an incentive to qualify a redemption as an exchange, but not as much as when exchange treatment offered both recovery of basis and a significant capital gains rate preference and hardly at all where a noncorporate shareholder's stock basis is nominal. In special situations, such as where a shareholder has excess capital losses that will offset capital gains but not qualified dividends, or on a deferred payment redemption where install-

---

11. See, e.g., Prop. Reg. § 1.302–5(f) Examples 3–7.

12. See Notice 2001–45, 2001–33 I.R.B. 129.

13. I.R.C. § 311(a), (b). For the details and the effect of a redemption on the distributing corporation's earnings and profits, see Section E of this chapter, infra.

ment sale reporting under Section 453 would benefit the shareholder, exchange treatment also will be preferable.

The Nontax Context. Redemptions are used to accomplish a variety of corporate and shareholder planning objectives. In the case of closely held corporations, a redemption may be the vehicle for a shift of corporate control or for the buyout of a dissatisfied or deceased shareholder. Stock redemptions by publicly traded companies also have become increasingly common transactions.[14] Keep these contexts in mind in studying the somewhat mechanical aspects of Section 302 at the beginning of this chapter. Later sections explore some of the planning opportunities provided by Section 302.

B.   CONSTRUCTIVE OWNERSHIP OF STOCK

Code: §§ 302(c)(1); 318.

Regulations: § 1.318–1(a), (b), –2, –3(a), (b), –4.

Any system that purports to measure the change in a shareholder's proportionate interest in a corporation would be ineffective if it failed to consider the holdings of closely related shareholders. Returning to our introductory example, assume that A and his daughter, D, each own 50 of the 100 outstanding shares of X Corporation and A sells 30 of his shares to the corporation for $450. A's actual percentage ownership drops from 50 percent (50 out of 100 shares) to 29 percent (20 out of 70 shares). Has he substantially reduced his proportionate interest? Looking only to A's *actual* ownership, the reduction is substantial, but the remaining shares are owned by a close relative. With appropriate skepticism, the drafters of the Code concluded that in determining stock ownership for purposes of the Section 302(b) tests for exchange treatment, an individual taxpayer or entity should be considered as owning stock owned by certain family members and related entities under elaborate attribution rules set forth in Section 318.[1]

Section 318 is one of several sets of constructive ownership rules in the Internal Revenue Code[2] and applies only when it is expressly made applicable by another provision of the Code.[3] Its principal role is in the redemption area, where it treats a taxpayer as "owning" stock that is actually owned by various related parties. The attribution rules in Section 318 fall into the following four categories.

1.   *Family Attribution.* An individual is considered as owning stock owned by his spouse, children, grandchildren and parents. Siblings and in-

---

14.   See Chapter 8F2, infra, which discusses the tax and nontax motivations for stock repurchases by public companies.

1.   I.R.C. § 302(c)(1).

2.   Other constructive ownership provisions include Sections 267(c), 341(e)(8), and 544.

3.   Section 318(b) contains a partial list of cross references to sections applying Section 318.

laws are not part of the "family" for this purpose, and there is no attribution from a grandparent to a grandchild.[4]

2. *Entity to Beneficiary Attribution.* Stock owned by or for a partnership or estate is considered as owned by the partners or beneficiaries in proportion to their beneficial interests.[5] A person ceases to be a "beneficiary" of an estate for this purpose when she receives all property to which she is entitled (e.g., a specific bequest) and the possibility that she must return the property to satisfy claims is remote.[6] Stock owned by a trust (other than a qualified employees' trust) is considered as owned by the beneficiaries in proportion to their actuarial interests in the trust. In the case of grantor trusts, stock is considered owned by the grantor or other person who is taxable on the trust income.[7] Stock owned by a corporation is considered owned proportionately (comparing the value of the shareholder's stock to the value of all stock) by a shareholder who owns, directly or through the attribution rules, 50 percent or more in value of that corporation's stock.[8]

3. *Beneficiary to Entity Attribution.* Stock owned by partners or beneficiaries of an estate is considered as owned by the partnership or estate.[9] All stock owned by a trust beneficiary is attributed to the trust except where the beneficiary's interest is "remote" and "contingent." Grantor trusts are considered to own stock owned by the grantor or other person taxable on the income of the trust.[10] All the stock owned by a 50 percent or more shareholder of a corporation is attributed to the corporation.[11]

4. *Option Attribution.* A person holding an option to acquire stock is considered as owning that stock.[12]

These general rules are supplemented by a set of "operating rules" in Section 318(a)(5), which generally authorize chain attribution (e.g., parent to child to child's trust) except that there can be no double family attribution (e.g., no attribution from parent to child to child's spouse) or "sidewise" attribution (e.g., stock attributed to an entity from a partner, beneficiary or shareholder may not be reattributed from that entity to another partner, beneficiary or shareholder).[13] In addition, option attribution takes precedence over family attribution where both apply.[14] For

---

4. I.R.C.   § 318(a)(1).   Cf.   I.R.C. § 318(a)(5)(B).

5. I.R.C. § 318(a)(2)(A).

6. Reg. § 1.318–3(a).

7. I.R.C. § 318(a)(2)(B).

8. I.R.C. § 318(a)(2)(C).

9. I.R.C. § 318(a)(3)(A).

10. I.R.C.   § 318(a)(3)(B).   Contingent interests are considered remote if the actuarial value of the interest is 5 percent or less of the value of the trust property, assuming the trustee exercises maximum discretion in favor of the beneficiary.

11. I.R.C. § 318(a)(3)(C).

12. I.R.C. § 318(a)(4). "Options" have been interpreted to include warrants and convertible debentures. Rev.Rul. 68–601, 1968–2 C.B. 124. Even options that are exercisable after the lapse of a fixed period of time are considered as options from the time they are granted. Rev.Rul. 89–64, 1989–1 C.B. 91.

13. I.R.C. § 318(a)(5)(A), (B), (C).

14. I.R.C. § 318(a)(5)(D).

Section 318 purposes, an S corporation is treated as a partnership, and S corporation shareholders are treated like partners.[15]

The problems below test your ability to apply the attribution rules in some typical factual contexts.

PROBLEMS

1. Wham Corporation has 100 shares of common stock outstanding. Twenty-five shares are owned by Grandfather, 20 shares are owned by Mother (Grandfather's Daughter), 15 shares are owned by Mother's Daughter, 10 shares are owned by Mother's adopted Son, and the remaining 30 shares are owned by Grandmother's estate, of which Mother is a 50% beneficiary. One of Mother's cousins is the other beneficiary of the estate. Mother also has an option to purchase 5 of Son's shares. How much Wham stock do Grandfather, Mother's Daughter and Grandmother's estate own after application of § 318?

2. All the 100 shares of Xerxes Corporation are owned by Partnership, in which A, B, C and D (all unrelated to each other) are equal partners. W, A's wife, owns all of the 100 shares of Yancy Corporation.

(a) How many shares, if any, of Xerxes Corporation are owned by A, W and M (W's mother)?

(b) How many shares, if any, of Xerxes are owned by Yancy? Would Yancy constructively own any shares of Xerxes if W owned only 10 percent of Yancy?

(c) How many shares, if any, of Yancy are owned by Partnership, B, C, D and Xerxes?

C. REDEMPTIONS TESTED AT THE SHAREHOLDER LEVEL

1. SUBSTANTIALLY DISPROPORTIONATE REDEMPTIONS

Code: § 302(b)(2).

Regulations: § 1.302–3.

The virtue of Section 302(b)(2) is its certainty. If a shareholder's reduction in voting stock as a result of a redemption satisfies three mechanical requirements, the redemption will be treated as an exchange. To qualify as "substantially disproportionate," a redemption must satisfy the following requirements:

1. Immediately after the redemption, the shareholder must own (actually and constructively) less than 50 percent of the total com-

---

15. I.R.C. § 318(a)(5)(E). This rule applies for purposes of attributing stock to and from the S corporation, but not for determining constructive ownership of stock in the S corporation. Id.

bined voting power of all classes of stock entitled to vote,[1]

2. The percentage of total outstanding voting stock owned by the shareholder immediately after the redemption must be less than 80 percent of the percentage of total voting stock owned by the shareholder immediately before the redemption,[2] and

3. The shareholder's percentage ownership of common stock (whether voting or nonvoting) after the redemption also must be less than 80 percent of the percentage of common stock owned before the redemption.[3] If there is more than one class of common stock, the 80 percent test is applied by reference to fair market value.[4]

The attribution rules of Section 318 are applicable in measuring stock ownership for purposes of all these percentage tests.

To illustrate, assume Redeemer owns 60 percent of the common stock of a corporation which has only one class of stock outstanding. A redemption which reduces Redeemer's stock interest to a percentage below 48 percent would satisfy Section 302(b)(2). Below that level, Redeemer would own less than 50 percent of the corporation's total combined voting power, and his percentage of voting stock after the redemption (below 48 percent) would be less than 80 percent of his percentage of voting stock before the redemption (60 percent).

The regulations elaborate on the operation of Section 302(b)(2). Stock with voting rights only upon the happening of a specific event (e.g., a default in a payment of dividends on preferred stock) is not considered voting stock until the event occurs.[5] A redemption of solely nonvoting stock will never satisfy Section 302(b)(2) because there will not be a sufficient reduction in the shareholder's interest in voting stock. But if a redemption qualifies as substantially disproportionate under Section 302(b)(2), a simultaneous redemption of nonvoting preferred stock (which is not Section 306

---

1. I.R.C. § 302(b)(2)(B).

2. I.R.C. § 302(b)(2)(C). This requirement may be expressed by the following formula:

$$\frac{\text{Voting shares owned after redemption}}{\text{Total voting shares outstanding after redemption}} \text{ must be less than: } .80 \times \frac{\text{Voting shares owned before redemption}}{\text{Total voting shares outstanding before redemption}}$$

3. I.R.C. § 302(b)(2)(C).

4. The common stock cutback test is applied on an aggregate rather than a class-by-class basis. Thus, if a shareholder's aggregate reduction in all classes of common stock (measured by value) meets the percentage tests in Section 302(b)(2)(C), the redemption will be treated as an exchange even if the shareholder continues to own 100 percent of one class of outstanding common stock. Rev. Rul. 87–88, 1987–2 C.B. 81.

5. Reg. § 1.302–3(a).

stock)[6] will be treated as an exchange.[7] The Service also has ruled that a redemption of voting preferred stock from a shareholder owning no common stock (either directly or by way of attribution) may qualify under Section 302(b)(2), even though the shareholder can not satisfy the 80 percent test relating to common stock.[8]

The substantially disproportionate redemption safe harbor does not apply to any redemption made pursuant to a plan which has the purpose or effect of a series of redemptions that, taken together, result in a distribution that is not substantially disproportionate with respect to the shareholder.[9] This statutory application of the step transaction doctrine is the subject of the ruling that follows.

Revenue Ruling 85–14

1985–1 Cum.Bull. 83.

ISSUE   .

Should qualification under section 302(b)(2) of the Internal Revenue Code of a redemption of one shareholder be measured immediately after that redemption, or after a second redemption of another shareholder that followed soon after the first redemption, under the following facts?

FACTS

X, a corporation founded by *A*, is engaged in an ongoing business. As of January 1, 1983, *X*'s sole class of stock, voting common stock, was held by *A, B, C,* and *D*, who are unrelated to each other. *A* owned 1,466 shares, *B* owned 210 shares, *C* owned 200 shares, and *D* owned 155 shares of *X* stock. *A* was president and *B* was vice-president of *X*.

X has a repurchase agreement with all *X* shareholders, except *A*. This agreement provides that if any such shareholder ceases to be actively connected with the business operations of *X*, such shareholder must promptly tender to *X* the then-held *X* shares for an amount equal to the book value of such stock. *X* has a reciprocal obligation to purchase such shares at book value within 6 months of such shareholder's ceasing to be actively connected with *X*'s business operations.

On January 1, 1983, *B* informed *A* of *B*'s intention to resign as of March 22, 1983. Based on this information, *A* caused *X* to adopt a plan of redemption and to redeem 902 shares of *A*'s *X* stock, on March 15, 1983, for which *A* received 700x dollars. Thus, *A* then held 564 shares of the 1129 shares (49.96 percent) of the *X* stock still outstanding, temporarily yielding majority control over the affairs of *X* until *B* ceased to be a shareholder. On March 22, 1983, *B* resigned from *X* and, in accordance with the *X* stock purchase agreement, *X* redeemed for cash all of *B*'s shares within the next

---

6. See Chapter 6C, infra.

7. Reg. § 1.302–3(a).

8. Rev.Rul. 81–41, 1981–1 C.B. 121.

9. I.R.C. § 302(b)(2)(D).

6 months, thus leaving 919 shares of X stock outstanding, restoring majority control to A.

LAW AND ANALYSIS

Section 302(a) of the Code provides that if a corporation redeems its stock and if one of the paragraphs of subsection (b) applies, then such redemption will be treated as a distribution in part or full payment in exchange for the stock.

Section 302(b)(2) of the Code provides that a redemption will be treated as an exchange pursuant to section 302(a) if the redemption is substantially disproportionate with respect to the shareholder, but that this paragraph will not apply unless immediately after the redemption the shareholder owns less than 50 percent of the total combined voting power of all classes of stock entitled to vote.

Under section 302(b)(2)(C) of the Code, one of the requirements for the distribution to be substantially disproportionate is that the ratio that the voting stock of the corporation owned by the shareholder immediately after the redemption bears to all the voting stock of the corporation at such time, is less than 80 percent of the ratio that the voting stock of the corporation owned by the shareholder immediately before the redemption bears to all the voting stock of the corporation at such time.

Section 302(b)(2)(D) of the Code, in dealing with a series of redemptions, provides that section 302(b)(2) is not applicable to any redemption made pursuant to a plan the purpose or effect of which is a series of redemptions resulting in a distribution which (in the aggregate) is not substantially disproportionate with respect to the shareholder.

The percentage provisions contained in sections 302(b)(2)(B) and 302(b)(2)(C) of the Code provide "safe harbor" exchange treatment. Examined separately, the transaction that occurred on March 15, 1983, would qualify as a substantially disproportionate redemption because (i) A's ownership of X's voting stock immediately after the redemption was less than 50 percent of the total combined voting power of all the X stock and (ii) A's ownership of X's voting stock was reduced from 72.18 percent to 49.96 percent, which meets the 80 percent requirement of section 302(b)(2)(C). However, if A's redemption is considered to be part of a section 302(b)(2)(D) series of redemptions which included X's redemption of B's shares, then A's redemption would not constitute a substantially disproportionate redemption because (i) A's ownership of X's voting stock after the redemptions exceeded 50 percent of the total combined voting power of X and (ii) A's ownership of X's voting stock after the redemptions was reduced from 72.18 percent to 61.37 percent, which does not meet the 80 percent requirement of section 302(b)(2)(C).

Section 1.302–3(a) of the Income Tax Regulations states that whether or not a plan described in section 302(b)(2)(D) of the Code exists will be determined from all the facts and circumstances.

In the present situation, although A and B had no joint plan, arrangement, or agreement for a series of redemptions, the redemption of A's shares was causally related to the redemption of B's shares in that A saw an apparent opportunity to secure exchange treatment under section 302(b)(2) of the Code by temporarily yielding majority control over the affairs of X.

Nothing in section 302(b)(2)(D) of the Code or in the legislative history of this section * * * indicates that the existence of a plan depends upon an agreement between two or more shareholders. Thus, a "plan" for purposes of section 302(b)(2)(D) need be nothing more than a design by a single redeemed shareholder to arrange a redemption as part of a sequence of events that ultimately restores to such shareholder the control that was apparently reduced in the redemption.

Under the facts and circumstances here, section 302(b)(2)(D) of the Code requires that the redemptions of A and B be considered in the aggregate. Accordingly, A's redemption meets neither the 50 percent limitation of section 302(b)(2)(B) nor the 80 percent test of section 302(b)(2)(C). Thus, the redemption of A's shares was not substantially disproportionate within the meaning of section 302(b)(2).

HOLDING

Under the facts of this ruling, qualification under section 302(b)(2) of the Code of A's redemption should not be measured immediately after that redemption, but, instead, should be measured after B's redemption that followed soon after A's redemption.

PROBLEMS

1. Y Corporation has 100 shares of common stock and 200 shares of nonvoting preferred stock outstanding. Alice owns 80 shares of Y common stock and 100 shares of its preferred stock. Cathy owns the remaining 20 shares of Y common and 100 shares of Y preferred stock. Alice and Cathy are not related. In each of the following alternative situations, determine whether the redemption satisfies the requirements of § 302(b)(2):

(a) On January 15, Y Corporation redeems 75 of Alice's preferred shares.

(b) Same as (a), above, except that Y also redeems 60 shares of Alice's common stock.

(c) Same as (a), above, except that Y also redeems 70 shares of Alice's common stock.

(d) What difference would it make in (c), above, if, on December 1 of the same year, Y redeems 10 shares of Cathy's common stock?

2. Z Corporation has 100 shares of voting common stock and 200 shares of nonvoting common stock outstanding. Every share of Z common stock has a fair market value of $100. Don owns 60 shares of Z voting common stock and 100 shares of Z nonvoting common stock. Jerry owns all of the remaining Z stock. Don and Jerry are not related to one another. If Z redeems 30 of Don's voting common shares, will the redemption qualify for exchange treatment under § 302(b)(2)?

2.   COMPLETE TERMINATION OF A SHAREHOLDER'S INTEREST

a.   WAIVER OF FAMILY ATTRIBUTION

Code: § 302(b)(3), (c).

Regulations: § 1.302–4.

The theory of the substantially disproportionate safe harbor is that exchange rather than dividend treatment is appropriate when a distribution in redemption causes a significant reduction in the shareholder's interest in the corporation's voting stock. This policy applies with even greater force in the case of a complete termination of a shareholder's interest, which qualifies for exchange treatment under Section 302(b)(3). For shareholders of a closely held family corporation, however, the attribution rules present a substantial roadblock to a complete termination. Even if all of the stock of a retiring shareholder is redeemed, she will continue to be treated as a 100 percent owner if her children or other related parties hold the remaining shares.

To provide relief where the redeemed shareholder is willing to cut the corporate cord, Section 302(c)(2) eases the path toward a complete termination by waiving the family attribution rules if certain conditions are met. This attribution amnesty is a useful planning tool for shareholders of family corporations, permitting a shareholder to achieve a complete termination even though the remaining shares are held by close relatives. The waiver applies, however, only to *family* attribution; the entity and option attribution rules remain fully applicable.

Waiver of the family attribution rules is available only if immediately after the distribution the redeemed shareholder retains no "interest" in the corporation (other than as a creditor). The ban extends to interests as an officer, director or employee. Section 302(c)(2)(A) also includes a "ten year look forward" rule, under which the shareholder may not retain or acquire (other than by bequest or inheritance) any of the forbidden interests in the corporation "other than an interest as a creditor."[1] To prevent anticipatory bailouts, Section 302(c)(2)(B) provides a "ten year look back" rule, under which the family attribution rules may not be waived if during the ten years preceding the redemption either: (1) the redeemed shareholder acquired any of the redeemed stock from a "Section 318" relative or (2) any such close relative acquired stock from the redeemed shareholder.

---

1. This rule is enforced by requiring the redeemed shareholder to file a form in which the shareholder agrees to notify the Service of any acquisition of a forbidden interest within ten years from the redemption and to retain such records as may be necessary to permit enforcement of this rule by the Service. The normal three year statute of limitations is extended to one year after the shareholder gives notice of acquisition of a forbidden interest in order to permit the Service to make a retroactive assessment of a deficiency. I.R.C. § 302(c)(2)(A).

Neither of these exceptions applies, however, if "tax avoidance" was not one of the principal purposes of the otherwise tainted transfer.[2]

The materials that follow illustrate how the Service and the courts have interpreted these intricate requirements.

Lynch v. Commissioner

United States Court of Appeals, Ninth Circuit, 1986.
801 F.2d 1176.

■ CYNTHIA HOLCOMB HALL, CIRCUIT JUDGE:

The Commissioner of the Internal Revenue Service (Commissioner) petitions for review of a Tax Court decision holding that a corporate redemption of a taxpayer's stock was a sale or exchange subject to capital gains treatment. The Commissioner argues that the taxpayer held a prohibited interest in the corporation after the redemption and therefore the transaction should be characterized as a dividend distribution taxable as ordinary income. We agree with the Commissioner and reverse the Tax Court.

I

Taxpayers, William and Mima Lynch, formed the W.M. Lynch Co. on April 1, 1960. The corporation issued all of its outstanding stock to William Lynch (taxpayer). The taxpayer specialized in leasing cast-in-place concrete pipe machines. He owned the machines individually but leased them to the corporation which in turn subleased the equipment to independent contractors.

On December 17, 1975 the taxpayer sold 50 shares of the corporation's stock to his son, Gilbert Lynch (Gilbert), for $17,170. Gilbert paid for the stock with a $16,000 check given to him by the taxpayer and $1,170 from his own savings. The taxpayer and his wife also resigned as directors and officers of the corporation on the same day.

On December 31, 1975 the corporation redeemed all 2300 shares of the taxpayer's stock. In exchange for his stock, the taxpayer received $17,900 of property and a promissory note for $771,920. Gilbert, as the sole remaining shareholder, pledged his 50 shares as a guarantee for the note. In the event that the corporation defaulted on any of the note payments, the taxpayer would have the right to vote or sell Gilbert's 50 shares.

In the years immediately preceding the redemption, Gilbert had assumed greater managerial responsibility in the corporation. He wished, however, to retain the taxpayer's technical expertise with cast-in-place concrete pipe machines. On the date of the redemption, the taxpayer also entered into a consulting agreement with the corporation. The consulting agreement provided the taxpayer with payments of $500 per month for five

2. See generally Kuntz, "Stock Redemptions Following Stock Transfers—An Expanding 'Safe Harbor,' Under Section 302(c)(2)(B)," 58 Taxes 29 (1980).

years, plus reimbursement for business related travel, entertainment, and automobile expenses.[2] In February 1977, the corporation and the taxpayer mutually agreed to reduce the monthly payments to $250. The corporation never withheld payroll taxes from payments made to the taxpayer.

After the redemption, the taxpayer shared his former office with Gilbert. The taxpayer came to the office daily for approximately one year; thereafter his appearances dwindled to about once or twice per week. When the corporation moved to a new building in 1979, the taxpayer received a private office.

In addition to the consulting agreement, the taxpayer had other ties to the corporation. He remained covered by the corporation's group medical insurance policy until 1980. When his coverage ended, the taxpayer had received the benefit of $4,487.54 in premiums paid by the corporation. He was also covered by a medical reimbursement plan, created the day of the redemption, which provided a maximum annual payment of $1,000 per member. Payments to the taxpayer under the plan totaled $96.05.

II

We must decide whether the redemption of the taxpayer's stock in this case is taxable as a dividend distribution under 26 U.S.C. § 301 or as long-term capital gain under 26 U.S.C. § 302(a). Section 302(a) provides that a corporate distribution of property in redemption of a shareholder's stock is treated as a sale or exchange of such stock if the redemption falls within one of four categories described in section 302(b). If the redemption falls outside of these categories, then it is treated as a dividend distribution under section 301 to the extent of the corporation's earnings and profits.[4]

Section 302(b)(3) provides that a shareholder is entitled to sale or exchange treatment if the corporation redeems all of the shareholder's stock. In order to determine whether there is a complete redemption for purposes of section 302(b)(3), the family attribution rules of section 318(a) must be applied unless the requirements of section 302(c)(2) are satisfied. Here, if the family attribution rules apply, the taxpayer will be deemed to own constructively the 50 shares held by Gilbert (100% of the corporation's stock) and the transaction would not qualify as a complete redemption within the meaning of section 302(b)(3).

Section 302(c)(2)(A) states in relevant part:

> In the case of a distribution described in subsection (b)(3), [the family attribution rules in] section 318(a)(1) shall not apply if—

---

2. The corporation leased or purchased a pickup truck for the taxpayer's use in 1977. If someone at the corporation needed the truck, the taxpayer would make it available to him.

4. On the date of the redemption, W.M. Lynch Co. had accumulated earnings and profits of $315,863, and had never paid a dividend.

> (i) immediately after the distribution the distributee has no interest in the corporation (including an interest as officer, director, or employee), other than an interest as a creditor * * *.

The Commissioner argues that in every case the performance of post-redemption services is a prohibited interest under section 302(c)(2)(A)(i), regardless of whether the taxpayer is an officer, director, employee, or independent contractor.

The Tax Court rejected the Commissioner's argument, finding that the services rendered by the taxpayer did not amount to a prohibited interest in the corporation. In reaching this conclusion, the Tax Court relied on a test derived from Lewis v. Commissioner, 47 T.C. 129, 136 (1966)(Simpson, J., concurring):

> Immediately after the enactment of the 1954 Code, it was recognized that section 302(c)(2)(A)(i) did not prohibit office holding per se, but was concerned with a retained financial stake in the corporation, such as a profit-sharing plan, or in the creation of an ostensible sale that really changed nothing so far as corporate management was concerned. Thus, in determining whether a prohibited interest has been retained under section 302(c)(2)(A)(i), we must look to whether the former stockholder has either retained a financial stake in the corporation or continued to control the corporation and benefit by its operations. In particular, where the interest retained is not that of an officer, director, or employee, we must examine the facts and circumstances to determine whether a prohibited interest has been retained under section 302(c)(2)(A)(i).

Lynch v. Commissioner, 83 T.C. 597, 605 (1984)(citations omitted).

After citing the "control or financial stake" standard, the Tax Court engaged in a two-step analysis. First, the court concluded that the taxpayer was an independent contractor rather than an employee because the corporation had no right under the consulting agreement to control his actions.[5] Id. at 606. Second, the court undertook a "facts and circumstances" analysis to determine whether the taxpayer had a financial stake in the corporation or managerial control after the redemption. Because the consulting agreement was not linked to the future profitability of the corporation, the court found that the taxpayer had no financial stake. *Id.* at 606–07. The court also found no evidence that the taxpayer exerted control over the corporation. Id. at 607. Thus, the Tax Court determined that the taxpayer held no interest prohibited by section 302(c)(2)(A)(i).

III

We review the decisions of the Tax Court on the same basis as decisions in civil bench trials in district courts, * * * The Tax Court's

---

5. Finding that the taxpayer was not an employee obviated the need to decide whether the parenthetical language in section 302(c)(2)(A)(i) prohibited employment relationships per se. See Seda v. Commissioner, 82 T.C. 484, 488 (1984)(court stated that "section 302(c)(2)(A)(i) may not prohibit the retention of all employment relationships").

interpretation of what constitutes a prohibited interest under section 302(c)(2)(A)(i) is a question of law reviewed de novo.

We reject the Tax Court's interpretation of section 302(c)(2)(A)(i). An individualized determination of whether a taxpayer has retained a financial stake or continued to control the corporation after the redemption is inconsistent with Congress' desire to bring a measure of certainty to the tax consequences of a corporate redemption. We hold that a taxpayer who provides post-redemption services, either as an employee or an independent contractor, holds a prohibited interest in the corporation because he is not a creditor.

The legislative history of section 302 states that Congress intended to provide "definite standards in order to provide certainty in specific instances." S.Rep. No. 1622, 83d Cong., 2d Sess. 233, reprinted in 1954 U.S.Code Cong. & Ad.News 4017, 4621, 4870. "In lieu of a factual inquiry in every case, [section 302] is intended to prescribe specific conditions from which the taxpayer may ascertain whether a given redemption" will qualify as a sale or be treated as a dividend distribution. H.R.Rep.No. 1337, 83d Cong.2d Sess. 35, reprinted in 1954 U.S.Cong. & Ad.News 4017, 4210. The facts and circumstances approach created by the Tax Court undermines the ability of taxpayers to execute a redemption and know the tax consequences with certainty.

The taxpayer's claim that the Senate rejected the mechanical operation of the House's version of section 302 is misleading. The Senate did reject the House bill because the "definitive conditions" were "unnecessarily restrictive." S.Rep.No.1622, 83d Cong., 2d Sess. 44, reprinted in 1954 U.S.Code Cong. & Ad.News 4621, 4675. However, the Senate's response was to add paragraph (b)(1) to section 302, which reestablished the flexible, but notoriously vague, "not essentially equivalent to a dividend" test. This test provided that all payments from a corporation that were not essentially equivalent to a dividend should be taxed as capital gains. The confusion that stemmed from a case-by-case inquiry into "dividend equivalence" prompted the Congress to enact definite standards for the safe harbors in section 302(b)(2) and (b)(3). The Tax Court's refusal to recognize that section 302(c)(2)(A)(i) prohibits *all* noncreditor interests in the corporation creates the same uncertainty as the "dividend equivalence" test.

The problem with the Tax Court's approach is apparent when this case is compared with Seda v. Commissioner, 82 T.C. 484 (1984). In *Seda*, a former shareholder, at his son's insistence, continued working for the corporation for two years after the redemption. He received a salary of $1,000 per month. The Tax Court refused to hold that section 302(c)(2)(A)(i) prohibits the retention of employment relations per se, despite the unequivocal language in the statute.[6] Id. at 488. Instead, the court applied the facts and circumstances approach to determine whether

---

6. Eight of the seventeen Tax Court judges who reviewed *Seda* concurred in the result but would have classified all officer, director, or employee relationships as prohibited interests under section 302(c)(2)(A)(i).

the former shareholder retained a financial stake or continued to control the corporation. The Tax Court found that the monthly payments of $1,000 constituted a financial stake in the corporation. Id. This result is at odds with the holding in *Lynch* that payments of $500 per month do *not* constitute a financial stake in the corporation. Compare Lynch, 83 T.C. at 606–07 with Seda, 82 T.C. at 488. The court also found in *Seda* no evidence that the former shareholder had ceased to manage the corporation. 82 T.C. at 488. Again, this finding is contrary to the holding in *Lynch* that the taxpayer exercised no control over the corporation after the redemption, even though he worked daily for a year and shared his old office with his son. Compare Lynch, 83 T.C. at 607 with Seda, 82 T.C. at 488. *Seda* and *Lynch* thus vividly demonstrate the perils of making an ad hoc determination of "control" or "financial stake."

A recent Tax Court opinion further illustrates the imprecision of the facts and circumstances approach. In Cerone v. Commissioner, 87 T.C. 1 (1986), a father and son owned all the shares of a corporation formed to operate their restaurant. The corporation agreed to redeem all of the father's shares in order to resolve certain disagreements between the father and son concerning the management of the business. However, the father remained an employee of the corporation for at least five years after the redemption, drawing a salary of $14,400 for the first three years and less thereafter. The father claimed that he was entitled to capital gains treatment on the redemption because he had terminated his interest in the corporation within the meaning of section 302(b)(3).

Even on the facts of *Cerone,* the Tax Court refused to find that the father held a prohibited employment interest per se. * * * Instead, the Tax Court engaged in a lengthy analysis, citing both *Seda* and *Lynch.* The court proclaimed that *Lynch* reaffirmed the rationale of *Seda,* even though *Lynch* involved an independent contractor rather than an employee. After comparing the facts of *Seda* and *Cerone,* the Tax Court eventually concluded that the father in *Cerone* held a financial stake in the corporation because he had drawn a salary that was $2,400 per year more than the taxpayer in *Seda* and had been employed by the corporation for a longer period after the redemption. *Cerone,* slip op. at 53. However, the Tax Court was still concerned that prohibited interest in *Seda* might have been based on the finding in that case that the taxpayer had both a financial stake *and* continued control of the corporation. The Tax Court, citing *Lynch,* held that the "test is whether he retained a financial stake *or* continued to control the corporation." * * * Thus, the Tax Court found that the father in *Cerone* held a prohibited interest because he had a financial stake as defined by *Seda.*

Although the Tax Court reached the correct result in *Cerone,* its approach undermines the definite contours of the safe harbor Congress intended to create with sections 302(b)(3) and 302(c)(2)(A)(i). Whether a taxpayer has a financial stake according to the Tax Court seems to depend on two factors, length of employment and the amount of salary. Length of employment after the redemption is irrelevant because Congress wanted taxpayers to know whether they were entitled to capital gains treatment on the date their shares were redeemed. * * * As for the amount of annual salary, the Tax Court's present benchmark appears to be the $12,000 figure in *Seda.* Salary at or above this level will be deemed to be a financial stake in the enterprise, though the $6,000 annual payments in this case were held not to be a financial stake. There is no support in the legislative history of section 302 for the idea that Congress meant only to prohibit service contracts of a certain worth, and taxpayers should not be left to speculate as to what income level will give rise to a financial stake.

In this case, the taxpayer points to the fact that the taxpayers in *Seda* and *Cerone* were employees, while he was an independent contractor. On appeal, the Commissioner concedes the taxpayer's independent contractor status. We fail to see, however, any meaningful way to distinguish *Seda* and *Cerone* from *Lynch* by differentiating between employees and independent contractors. All of the taxpayers performed services for their corporations following the redemption. To hold that only the employee taxpayers held a prohibited interest would elevate form over substance. The parenthetical language in section 302(c)(2)(A)(i) merely provides a subset of prohibited interests from the universe of such interests, and in no way limits us from finding that an independent contractor retains a prohibited interest. Furthermore, the Tax Court has in effect come to ignore the parenthetical language. If employment relationships are not prohibited interests per se, then the taxpayer's status as an employee or independent contractor is irrelevant. What really matters under the Tax Court's approach is how the taxpayer fares under a facts and circumstances review of whether he has a financial stake in the corporation or managerial control.[7] Tax planners are left to guess where along the continuum of monthly payments from $500 to $1000 capital gains treatment ends and ordinary income tax begins.

Our holding today that taxpayers who provide post-redemption services have a prohibited interest under section 302(c)(2)(A)(i) is inconsistent with the Tax Court's decision in Estate of Lennard v. Commissioner, 61 T.C. 554 (1974). That case held that a former shareholder who, as an independent contractor, provided post-redemption accounting services for a corporation did not have a prohibited interest. The Tax Court found that "Congress did not intend to include independent contractors possessing no financial stake

---

7. The Tax Court's focus on managerial control or a financial stake originated with Judge Simpson's concurrence in *Lewis,* 47 T.C. at 136–38. His interpretation of section 302(c)(2)(A) is supported by Bittker, Stock Redemptions and Partial Liquidations Under the Internal Revenue Code of 1954, 9 Stan. L.Rev. 13, 33 n. 72 (1956). Professor Bittker argues that Congress' goal was to ensure that taxpayers who transferred only ostensible control or maintained a financial stake in the corporation did not receive the benefit of capital gains treatment. He is no doubt correct. However, the means selected by Congress to achieve this goal do not allow for an individualized determination of control and financial stakes. Instead, section 302(c)(2)(A)(i) operates mechanically: the taxpayer must sever all but a creditor's interest to avoid the family attribution rules and thereby receive capital gains treatment. Nowhere in the legislative history of section 302(c) does Congress intimate that courts may use a flexible facts and circumstances test to determine the existence of managerial control or a financial stake.

in the corporation among those who are considered as retaining an interest in the corporation for purposes of the attribution waiver rules." Id. at 561. We disagree. In the context of *Lennard,* the Tax Court appears to be using financial stake in the sense of having an equity interest or some other claim linked to the future profit of the corporation. Yet, in cases such as *Seda* and *Cerone,* the Tax Court has found that fixed salaries of $12,000 and $14,400, respectively, constitute a financial stake. Fees for accounting services could easily exceed these amounts, and it would be irrational to argue that the definition of financial stake varies depending on whether the taxpayer is an employee or an independent contractor. In order to avoid these inconsistencies, we conclude that those who provide post-redemption services, whether as independent contractors or employees, hold an interest prohibited by section 302(c)(2)(A)(i) because they are more than merely creditors.

In addition, both the Tax Court and the Commissioner have agreed that taxpayers who enter into management consulting contracts after the redemption possess prohibited interests. Chertkof v. Commissioner, 72 T.C. 1113, 1124–25 (1979), *aff'd,* 649 F.2d 264 (4th Cir.1981); Rev.Ruling 70–104, 1970–1 C.B. 66 (1970). Taxpayers who provide such services are, of course, independent contractors. However, unlike the Commissioner's opinion in Rev. Ruling 70–104 that all management consulting agreements are prohibited interests, the Tax Court applies the financial stake or managerial control test. In *Chertkof,* the court found that because the services provided under the contract "went to the essence" of the corporation's existence, the taxpayer had not effectively ceded control. 72 T.C. at 1124. Here, the Tax Court distinguished *Chertkof* on the ground that the taxpayer did not retain control of the corporation, but instead provided only limited consulting services. *Lynch,* 83 T.C. at 608. We believe that any attempt to define prohibited interests based on the level of control leads to the same difficulties inherent in making a case-by-case determination of what constitutes a financial stake.[8]

IV

Our decision today comports with the plain language of section 302 and its legislative history. See Gardner & Randall, Distributions in Redemption of Stock: Changing Definitions for a Termination of Interest, 8 J. Corp. Tax'n 240, 247–48 (1981); Marusic, The Prohibited Interest of I.R.C. Section 302(c)(2)(A)(i) After Seda and Lynch, 65 Neb.L.Rev. 486, 502, 518–19 (1986); Rose, The Prohibited Interest of Section 302(c)(2)(A), 36 Tax L.Rev. 131, 145–49 (1981). Taxpayers who wish to receive capital gains treatment upon the redemption of their shares must completely sever all

---

8. Determining the existence of control is particularly difficult in the context of a family-held corporation. The exercise of control often will not be obvious because a parent may influence a child, and hence corporate decisionmaking, in myriad ways. Our rule that the provision of services is a prohib- ited interest eliminates the need to make a speculative inquiry into whether the parent still controls the corporation after the redemption. Of course, no rule could or should prohibit post-redemption parent-child communication concerning the management of the corporation.

noncreditor interests in the corporation.[9] We hold that the taxpayer, as an independent contractor, held such a noncreditor interest, and so cannot find shelter in the safe harbor of section 302(c)(2)(A)(i). Accordingly, the family attribution rules of section 318 apply and the taxpayer fails to qualify for a complete redemption under section 302(b)(3). The payments from the corporation in redemption of the taxpayer's shares must be characterized as a dividend distribution taxable as ordinary income under section 301.

Reversed.

Revenue Ruling 59–119

1959–1 Cum.Bull. 68.

A stock redemption agreement between the corporation and the instant shareholder provides that a total of $350x$ dollars will be paid to such shareholder for all his stock interest in the corporation, $100x$ dollars to be paid on the closing date and $250x$ dollars to be paid by the corporation within eight years, payable in quarter-annual installments. The corporation executed an installment judgment note to the shareholder and the judgment note and shares of stock of the corporation to be redeemed are retained by an escrow holder as security for installment payments due. In the event the installment and interest payments are in default, then pursuant to the agreement the escrow holder, upon notice from the taxpayer, may sell the stock of the corporation held by him at public or private sale to satisfy such obligations, however, in no event will the taxpayer become the purchaser of said stock at such sale.

The stock redemption agreement also states that so long as the corporation owes funds to such shareholder it will not, without first receiving the written consent of the shareholder, declare dividends; pay salaries in excess of a certain amount to officers; sell its assets except in the ordinary course of business; or engage in a reorganization, recapitalization, merger, consolidation or liquidation.

Because of the substantial sums due the shareholder, because he plans to reside permanently in another state and will be far removed from the base of operations of the corporation, and pursuant to the advice of persons

---

9. Our definition of a prohibited interest still leaves an open question as to the permissible scope of a creditor's interest under section 302(c)(2)(A)(i). See, e.g., Treas. Reg. § 1.302–4(d)(a creditor's claim must not be subordinate to the claims of general creditors or in any other sense proprietary, i.e., principal payments or interest rates must not be contingent on the earnings of the corporation).

The taxpayer argues that some creditor relationships might result in an "opportunity to influence" as great or greater than any officer, director, or employee relationship. He cites Rev.Ruling 77–467, 1977–2 C.B. 92 which concluded that a taxpayer who leased real property to a corporation, after the corporation redeemed his shares, held a creditor's interest under section 302(c)(2)(A)(i). While the taxpayer here may be correct in his assessment of a creditor's "opportunity to influence" a corporation, he overlooks the fact that Congress specifically allowed the right to retain such an interest.

skilled in creditor protection matters, he considers it advisable to have a member of the law firm representing him serve on the board of directors of the corporation. Therefore, the instant shareholder and the remaining shareholders, all related, entered into a second agreement whereby a nominee of his law firm will serve on the board of directors as long as the corporation is indebted to the shareholder. Such nominee will be paid x dollars by the corporation for each meeting he attends and such additional sums as determined in the sole discretion of the instant shareholder for other services which may be reasonably necessary to determine that his interests as a creditor are being protected in accordance with the agreements.

The sole purpose of this arrangement is to protect the shareholder as a creditor by determining that the aforementioned conditions are being met rather than running the risk of having to engage in extended litigation at some future date if it is then determined that the conditions of the stock redemption agreement were violated.

* * *

According to the agreement in question, the remaining shareholders and the instant shareholder will appoint, indirectly through the law firm representing such shareholder, a member of that law firm to serve on the board of directors of the corporation. Such a nominee director will be acting solely on the taxpayer's behalf and, therefore, will in effect be his agent. The fact that the nominee director will receive remuneration for his service from someone other than the taxpayer does not make him any less the taxpayer's agent, for the source of remuneration to an agent is only one factor to be considered in determining whether an agency exists between two parties. Such an appointment of an agent to the board of directors is contrary to the condition prescribed in section 302(c)(2) of the Code. For the purposes of section 302(c)(2), it is immaterial whether an interest in the corporation is asserted directly or through an agent.

The fact that the director is a "limited" director in that his only duty will be to determine whether the conditions set forth in the stock redemption agreement are being observed is not material, for section 302(c)(2) of the Code does not make any exception for such directors. Furthermore, that section of the Code does not make an exception for a director whose power is limited because he is a minority member of a board.

In view of the foregoing, it is held that the agreement between the instant shareholder and the remaining shareholders of the corporation, under which a nominee is appointed to serve on the board of directors of the corporation, violates the condition prescribed in section 302(c)(2)(A)(i) of the Code. Accordingly, in the event of such an agreement, the redemption of the taxpayer's stock of the corporation shall be treated as a distribution of property to which section 301 of the Code applies.

However, if the taxpayer-shareholder designates a representative of his law firm to attend the board of director's meetings of the corporation solely for the purposes of determining whether the provisions of the agreement described above have been complied with, and not in the capacity of a director, officer or employee, or advisor, such action will not adversely affect section 302(c)(2) of the Code.

Revenue Ruling 77–293

1977–2 Cum.Bull. 91.

Corporation X had 120 shares of common stock outstanding, all of which were owned by A, its president. A's son, B, had been employed by X for many years as its vice-president and general assistant to the president. Realizing that the future successful operation of X required a thorough knowledge of its operation, products lines, and customer needs, A had trained and supervised B in all phases of the business so that upon A's retirement B would be able to assume responsibility for managing the business.

As part of A's plan to retire from the business and to give ownership of the business to B, A gave 60 shares of X stock to B as a gift, and not as consideration for past, present, or future services. Shortly thereafter, A resigned and B assumed the position of chairman of the board and president of X. X redeemed the remaining 60 shares of stock owned by A in exchange for property. Immediately after the redemption, A was not an officer, director, or employee of X and no longer had any interest in X. A's gift of stock to B was for the purpose of giving B complete ownership and control of X. The earnings and profits of X exceeded the amount of the distribution in redemption of the X stock.

* * *

In the instant case, neither section 302(b)(1) of the Code nor section 302(b)(2) applies since A, through the constructive ownership rules of section 318(a), owned 100 percent of the stock of X both before and after the redemption. Therefore, there was no meaningful reduction under section 302(b)(1) or a substantially disproportionate reduction under section 302(b)(2) of A's stock ownership.

Section 302(c)(2)(A) of the Code provides that for purposes of section 302(b)(3), 318(a)(1) will not apply if (i) immediately after the distribution the distributee has no interest in the corporation (including an interest as an officer, director, or employee), other than an interest as a creditor, (ii) the distributee does not acquire any such interest (other than stock acquired by bequest or inheritance) within ten years from the date of such distribution, and (iii) the distributee files an agreement to notify the district director of any acquisition of any such interest in the corporation. However, pursuant to section 302(c)(2)(B)(ii), the provisions of section 302(c)(2)(A) are not applicable if any person owns (at the time of the distribution) stock the ownership of which is attributable to the distributee under section 318(a) and such person acquired any stock in the corporation, directly or indirectly, from the distributee within the ten-year period ending on the date of the distribution, unless such stock so acquired from the distributee is redeemed in the same transaction. However, section 302(c)(2)(B)(ii) will not apply if the disposition by the distributee did not have as one of its principal purposes the avoidance of Federal income tax.

The structure and legislative history of section 302 of the Code make it clear that the purpose of section 302(c)(2)(B) is not to prevent the reduction of capital gains through gifts of appreciated stock prior to the redemption of the remaining stock of the transferor, but to prevent the withdrawal of earnings at capital gains rates by a shareholder of a family controlled corporation who seeks continued control and/or economic interest in the corporation through the stock given to a related person or the stock he retains. Application of this provision thus prevents a taxpayer from bailing out earnings by transferring part of the taxpayer's stock to such a related person and then qualifying the redemption of either the taxpayer's stock or the transferee's stock as a complete termination of interest by virtue of the division of ownership thus created and the availability of the attribution waiver provisions.

Tax avoidance within the meaning of section 302(c)(2)(B) of the Code would occur, for example, if a taxpayer transfers stock of a corporation to a spouse in contemplation of the redemption of the remaining stock of the corporation and terminates all direct interest in the corporation in compliance with section 302(c)(2)(A), but with the intention of retaining effective control of the corporation indirectly through the stock held by the spouse. Another example, which would generally constitute tax avoidance within the meaning of this provision, is the transfer by a taxpayer of part of the stock of a corporation to a spouse in contemplation of the subsequent redemption of the transferred stock from the spouse. * * *

Whether one of the principal purposes of an acquisition or disposition of stock is tax avoidance within the meaning of section 302(c)(2)(B) of the Code can be determined only by an analysis of all of the facts and circumstances of a particular situation. Here, the gift of X stock by A was to B who is active and knowledgeable in the affairs of the business of X and who intends to control and manage the corporation in the future. The gift of stock was intended solely for the purpose of enabling A to retire while leaving the business to B. Therefore, the avoidance of Federal income tax will not be deemed to have been one of the principal purposes of the gift of stock from A to B, notwithstanding the reduction of the capital gains tax payable by A as a result of the gift of appreciated stock prior to the redemption.

Accordingly, if A files the agreement specified in section 302(c)(2)(A)(iii) of the Code, the redemption by X of its stock from A qualifies as a termination of interest under section 302(b)(3).

Rev.Rul. 57–387, 1957–2 C.B. 225, is modified to the extent that it contains implications to the contrary concerning the reduction of the capital gains tax.

NOTE

Ten-Year–Look–Forward Rule. The prohibition on retaining or acquiring any post-redemption "interest" (other than as a creditor or by bequest or inheritance) in the corporation is one of the major hurdles to utilizing Section 302(c)(2).[1] Until the Ninth Circuit's decision in *Lynch,* the courts generally rejected the Service's strict view that *any* performances of services, with or without compensation, constitutes a forbidden corporate interest.[2]

The results are mixed in the many other factual contexts arising under the ten-year look-forward rule. The Service has ruled that a prohibited interest is obtained if the redeemed shareholder becomes a custodian under the Uniform Gifts to Minors Act or a voting trustee of corporate stock during the restricted ten year period.[3] But if the shareholder becomes executor of a deceased shareholder's estate and can vote the stock held by the estate, the protection of Section 302(c)(2) is still available by virtue of the exception for stock acquired by bequest or inheritance.[4] In Revenue Ruling 72–380,[5] the Service ruled that since a redeemed shareholder may reacquire a direct stock interest by bequest or inheritance, it was reasonable to permit "acquisition under identical circumstances of the significantly lesser interest embodied in the * * * right of an executor to vote stock in an estate * * *."[6] In Revenue Ruling 79–334[7] the same reasoning was applied to an appointment by will of a previously redeemed shareholder as a trustee of a trust. The ruling concludes that a redeemed shareholder may waive family attribution even though, as trustee, he can vote stock of the corporation in which he once had an interest.

Deferred Payment Redemptions. In the area of deferred payment redemptions, the Service and the courts have disagreed over what constitutes a forbidden proprietary interest. The regulations provide that to be considered a creditor, the rights of the redeemed shareholder must not be greater than necessary to enforce the claim. An obligation may be treated as proprietary if it is subordinated to claims of general creditors, if payments of principal depend upon corporate earnings, or if the interest rate fluctuates with the corporation's success.[8] Acquisition of corporate property as a

---

1. See generally Rose, "The Prohibited Interest of Section 302(c)(2)(A)," 36 Tax L.Rev. 131 (1981).

2. Compare Rev.Rul. 56–556, 1956–2 C.B. 177 and Rev.Rul. 59–119, 1959–1 C.B. 68 with Estate of Lennard v. Commissioner, 61 T.C. 554 (1974), nonacq. 1978–2 C.B. 3, and Lewis v. Commissioner, 47 T.C. 129 (1966).

3. Rev.Rul. 81–233, 1981–2 C.B. 83; Rev.Rul. 71–426, 1971–2 C.B. 173.

4. I.R.C. § 302(c)(2)(A)(ii).

5. 1972–2 C.B. 201.

6. An executor who also becomes an officer of the corporation acquires a prohibited interest and loses Section 302(c)(2)'s protection. Rev.Rul. 75–2, 1975–1 C.B. 99.

7. 1979–2 C.B. 127.

8. Reg. § 1.302–4(d). A shareholder's ability to defer gain on a credit redemption under the installment method is a separate issue. Section 453(k)(2)(A) denies use of the installment method for sales of stock or securities which are traded on an established securities market. This provision thus limits the tax advantage of deferral on a credit redemption to redemptions of stock in closely held corporations.

result of enforcement of rights as a creditor does not run afoul of Section 302(c)(2) unless the redeemed shareholder acquires stock in the corporation, its parent corporation, or a subsidiary.[9]

The standards applied by the courts to credit redemptions are not as rigid. In Dunn v. Commissioner,[10] a redemption agreement provided for postponement of principal and interest payments on corporate notes given in payment for the shareholder's stock if such payments would violate financial requirements in the corporation's franchise agreement with General Motors. The court concluded that the postponement provision did not require the notes to be classified as equity or give the shareholder an interest in the corporation other than as a creditor. In Estate of Lennard v. Commissioner,[11] the court found that a subordinated demand note, which was paid approximately three months after issuance, did not represent a proprietary interest in the corporation.

The Service has specific guidelines for granting a favorable ruling on an installment redemption. It ordinarily will not rule on the tax consequences of a redemption of stock for notes when the note payment period extends beyond 15 years.[12] Nor will a ruling be issued under Section 302(b) if the shareholder's stock is held in escrow or as security for payments on corporate notes given as consideration for the redeemed stock because of the possibility that the stock may be returned to the shareholder as a result of a default by the corporation.[13]

Once again, however, the courts have been far more lenient. For example, in Lisle v. Commissioner[14] the Tax Court found a Section 302(b)(3) complete termination where the redeemed shareholders were to be paid for their stock over a 20 year period, the shareholders retained their voting rights pursuant to a security agreement, the stock was held in escrow and could be returned to the shareholders and the shareholders continued to serve as corporate directors and officers. The court concluded that the shareholders were directors and officers in name only and that, based upon the facts present in the case, the security provisions were not inconsistent with a finding that the transaction qualified as a complete redemption.

Other Post–Redemption Interests. Finally, the Service will permit a redeemed shareholder to lease property to the corporation on an arms length basis provided that the rental payments are not dependent on corporate earnings or subordinated to the claims of the corporation's general creditors.[15]

b.   WAIVER OF ATTRIBUTION BY ENTITIES

Section 302(c)(2) only permits waiver of the *family* attribution rules and requires the "distributee" to file an agreement promising to notify the

9. Reg. § 1.302–4(e).
10. 615 F.2d 578 (2d Cir.1980).
11. Note 2, supra.
12. Rev.Proc. 2005–3, § 4.01(21), 2005–1 C.B. 118, 123.
13. Id. at 682.
14. 35 T.C.M. 627 (1976).
15. Rev.Rul. 77–467, 1977–2 C.B. 92.

Service of the acquisition of a forbidden interest within the ten year period following the redemption. What if the redeemed shareholder is a trust, estate or other entity that completely terminates its *actual* interest in the corporation but continues to own shares attributed to a beneficiary from a related family member which then are reattributed from the beneficiary to the entity?[1] May the entity waive family attribution or is the waiver opportunity limited to individual shareholders?

At one time, the Service contended that only individuals could waive family attribution.[2] The Tax Court disagreed, however, holding that an estate or trust that completely terminated its actual interest in a redemption could waive family attribution from a family member to a beneficiary.[3] One appellate court, rejecting what it called a "crabbed reading" of the Code, even held that an entity could waive attribution from a beneficiary to the entity.[4] The problem with these decisions was that they did not prevent the beneficiary from acquiring an interest in the corporation during the ten years after the redemption or require an agreement from the beneficiary to notify the Service if such a forbidden interest were acquired.

Technical as it may seem, this issue was of considerable interest to shareholders of closely held corporations and their estate planners. The Service's rigid position often was an impediment to a redemption of the stock of an estate or trust where family members of the beneficiaries continued to own shares of the company. In the midst of continuing litigation, Congress enacted a special rule for waiver by entities, incorporating appropriate safeguards to preclude the beneficiaries from reacquiring an interest.[5] The Joint Committee on Taxation explained the rule as follows:[6]

> The Act permits an entity to waive the family attribution rules if those through whom ownership is attributed to the entity join in the waiver. Thus, a trust and its beneficiaries may waive family attribution to the beneficiaries if, after the redemption, neither the trust nor the beneficiaries hold an interest in the

---

1. For example, assume Mother's Estate, of which Father is the sole beneficiary, owns 50 of the 100 outstanding shares of X Corporation stock. The other 50 shares are owned by Child. If X redeems Estate's 50 shares, Estate continues to constructively own Child's 50 shares, which are attributed from Child to Father via family attribution and then reattributed from Father to Estate. May Estate break the family attribution chain in order to qualify the redemption as a complete termination?

2. Rev.Rul. 59–233, 1959–2 C.B. 106, Rev.Rul. 68–388, 1968–2 C.B. 122.

3. See Crawford v. Commissioner, 59 T.C. 830 (1973); Johnson Trust v. Commissioner, 71 T.C. 941 (1979); but see Metzger

Trust v. Commissioner, 76 T.C. 42 (1981), affirmed, 693 F.2d 459 (5th Cir.1982).

4. Rickey v. United States, 592 F.2d 1251 (5th Cir.1979). This remarkable example of "flexible" statutory construction was sharply criticized. See Andrews, "Comment: Estate Waiver of the Estate–Beneficiary Attribution Rules in Nonliquidating Redemptions Under Section 302 and Related Matters: The *Rickey* Case in the Fifth Circuit," 35 Tax L.Rev. 147 (1979).

5. I.R.C. § 302(c)(2)(C).

6. Staff of Joint Committee on Taxation, General Explanation of the Tax Equity and Fiscal Responsibility Act of 1982, 98th Cong.2d Sess. 146–47 (1982).

corporation, do not acquire such an interest within the 10–year period, and join in the agreement to notify the IRS of any acquisition. The entity and beneficiaries are jointly and severally liable in the event of an acquisition by any of them within the 10–year period and the statute of limitations remains open to assess any deficiency. The tax increase is a deficiency in the entity's tax but may be asserted as a deficiency against any beneficiary liable under the rules. Congress intended that the tax will be collected from a beneficiary only when it cannot be assessed against or collected from the entity, such as when the entity no longer exists or has insufficient funds. Further, it was intended that the tax will be assessed and collected from the beneficiary whose acquisition causes the deficiency before it is asserted against any other beneficiary.

Under the Act, only family attribution under Section 318(a)(1) may be waived by an entity and its beneficiaries. The waiver rules are not extended to waivers of attribution to and from entities and their beneficiaries (secs. 318(a)(2) and 318(a)(3)). The Act thus is intended to overrule Rickey v. United States, 592 F.2d 1251 (5th Cir.1979). Congress intended that the Act should not be construed to provide any inference as to whether the *Rickey* decision adopts a proper construction of prior law. Nor was any inference intended as to whether the other cases extending the waiver rules for family attribution to entities adopt a proper construction of prior law.

Certain anti-avoidance rules applicable where the redeemed stock was acquired by the distributee from a related party or a related party at the time of the redemption owns stock acquired from the distributee are extended to the entity and affected beneficiaries.

PROBLEMS

1. Randall Corporation is owned by John, John's daughter Alison and Alison's son Chuck. John owns 100 shares of Randall stock, Alison owns 50 shares and Chuck owns 25 shares. Consider whether the following redemptions (in year one) qualify as an exchange under 302(b)(3):

(a) Randall redeems Alison's entire 50 shares for cash.

(b) Same as (a), above, except that Alison fails to file the agreement required in § 302(c)(2)(A)(iii)? What is the purpose of this requirement?

(c) Same as (a), above, except the price paid for Alison's shares is contingent upon Randall's future profits?

(d) Randall redeems 20 of Alison's shares for cash on January 1 of year one and the remaining 30 shares for cash on January 1 of year two.

(e) Same as (a), above, except Alison remains as a director of Randall?

(f) Same as (a), above, except that, two years after the redemption, Randall forms a new subsidiary and Alison becomes an employee of the subsidiary?

(g) Same as (a), above, except that two years after the redemption Chuck dies and leaves his Randall shares to Alison?

2.   The B & B Windshield Wiper Corporation ("B & B") was organized ten years ago by Betty and Billy, who are wife and husband. Betty and Billy formed B & B by transferring cash and other property to the corporation in exchange for 150 shares of the corporation's common stock. Betty and Billy own B & B's manufacturing plant and lease the plant to the corporation for an annual rental fee. B & B has been very successful and has a large amount of accumulated earnings and profits.

Five years ago, Betty and Billy's youngest Son, Junior, began working for B & B as a clerk in the domestic subcompact wiper division. Junior's managerial talents were quickly recognized and he has risen rapidly in B & B's corporate structure. Today, Junior is B & B's Vice President in charge of operations and has overall responsibility for production at B & B's manufacturing plant.

Shortly after Junior came to B & B, his parents agreed that he would eventually take over control and management of the company. Betty and Billy have now decided that the time has come to retire. To implement this decision, their accountant has suggested the following plan:

(1) Betty and Billy will give 30 of their 150 B & B shares to Junior to provide him with an ownership interest in the corporation.

(2) B & B will redeem Betty and Billy's remaining 120 shares for $50,000 plus a $400,000 B & B note paying market rate interest. The note will be payable monthly over a 20–year term and will be secured by an interest in the corporation's assets. Additionally, B & B will agree to restrict dividend payments, limit new indebtedness, and refrain from taking certain extraordinary corporate action (e.g., merger or liquidation) during the term of the note.

(3) Betty and Billy will continue to lease the manufacturing plant to B & B under a lease which has a rent escalation clause dependent upon the consumer price index. They also will grant B & B a five year option to purchase the plant at its appraised fair market value.

(a) Will Betty and Billy's redemption be classified as an exchange under Section 302(a)?

(b) Suppose Betty establishes a management consulting firm after leaving B & B. What would be the tax impact on the redemption if B & B hired Betty's firm to perform an analysis of its proposed entry into the Australian windshield wiper market?

3.   Cinelab Corporation has 100 shares of common stock outstanding. John owns 50 shares and Mary, John's sister, owns 30 shares. The other 20 shares are owned by the Estate of Sam; Sam was John and Mary's father.

Their mother, Bella, is the sole beneficiary of the estate. Consider the tax consequences of the following redemptions of Cinelab stock:

(a) Cinelab redeems Estate's 20 shares.

(b) Same as (a), above, except that Bella is the residuary beneficiary of the estate and John and Mary each receive specific legacies.

(c) Same as (a), above, except that John and Mary are the residuary beneficiaries of the estate.

(d) Same as (a), above, except the 20 shares were owned and redeemed from a trust established under Sam's will providing income to Bella for her life and the remainder to Nancy, another child of Sam and Bella. The life estate and remainder have equal actuarial values.

(e) Any change in the result in (d), above, if Nancy acquires stock in Cinelab three years after the redemption by the trust?

3.   REDEMPTIONS NOT ESSENTIALLY EQUIVALENT TO A DIVIDEND

Code: § 302(b)(1).

Regulations: § 1.302–2.

United States v. Davis

Supreme Court of the United States, 1970.
397 U.S. 301, 90 S.Ct. 1041, rehearing denied, 397 U.S. 1071, 90 S.Ct. 1495 (1970).

■ MR. JUSTICE MARSHALL delivered the opinion of the Court.

In 1945, taxpayer and E.B. Bradley organized a corporation. In exchange for property transferred to the new company, Bradley received 500 shares of common stock, and taxpayer and his wife similarly each received 250 such shares. Shortly thereafter, taxpayer made an additional contribution to the corporation, purchasing 1,000 shares of preferred stock at a par value of $25 per share.

The purpose of this latter transaction was to increase the company's working capital and thereby to qualify for a loan previously negotiated through the Reconstruction Finance Corporation. It was understood that the corporation would redeem the preferred stock when the RFC loan had been repaid. Although in the interim taxpayer bought Bradley's 500 shares and divided them between his son and daughter, the total capitalization of the company remained the same until 1963. That year, after the loan was fully repaid and in accordance with the original understanding, the company redeemed taxpayer's preferred stock.

In his 1963 personal income tax return taxpayer did not report the $25,000 received by him upon the redemption of his preferred stock as income. Rather, taxpayer considered the redemption as a sale of his preferred stock to the company—a capital gains transaction under § 302 of the Internal Revenue Code of 1954 resulting in no tax since taxpayer's basis in the stock equaled the amount he received for it. The Commissioner of Internal Revenue, however, did not approve this tax treatment. According to the Commissioner, the redemption of taxpayer's stock was essentially equivalent to a dividend and was thus taxable as ordinary income under §§ 301 and 316 of the Code. Taxpayer paid the resulting deficiency and brought this suit for a refund. The District Court ruled in his favor, 274 F.Supp. 466 (D.C.M.D.Tenn.1967), and on appeal the Court of Appeals affirmed. 408 F.2d 1139 (C.A.6th Cir.1969).

The Court of Appeals held that the $25,000 received by taxpayer was "not essentially equivalent to a dividend" within the meaning of that phrase in § 302(b)(1) of the Code because the redemption was the final step in a course of action that had a legitimate business (as opposed to a tax avoidance) purpose. That holding represents only one of a variety of treatments accorded similar transactions under § 302(b)(1) in the circuit courts of appeals. We granted certiorari, 396 U.S. 815 (1969), in order to resolve this recurring tax question involving stock redemptions by closely held corporations. We reverse.

I

The Internal Revenue Code of 1954 provides generally in §§ 301 and 316 for the tax treatment of distributions by a corporation to its shareholders; under those provisions, a distribution is includable in a taxpayer's gross income as a dividend out of earnings and profits to the extent such earnings exist. There are exceptions to the application of these general provisions, however, and among them are those found in § 302 involving certain distributions for redeemed stock. The basic question in this case is whether the $25,000 distribution by the corporation to taxpayer falls under that section—more specifically, whether its legitimate business motivation qualifies the distribution under § 302(b)(1) of the Code. Preliminarily, however, we must consider the relationship between § 302(b)(1) and the rules regarding the attribution of stock ownership found in § 318(a) of the Code.

Under subsection (a) of § 302, a distribution is treated as "payment in exchange for the stock," thus qualifying for capital gains rather than ordinary income treatment, if the conditions contained in any one of the four paragraphs of subsection (b) are met. In addition to paragraph (1)'s "not essentially equivalent to a dividend" test, capital gains treatment is available where (2) the taxpayer's voting strength is substantially diminished, [or] (3) his interest in the company is completely terminated. * * * [T]axpayer admits that paragraphs (2) and (3) do not apply. Moreover, taxpayer agrees that for the purposes of §§ 302(b)(2) and (3) the attribution rules of § 318(a) apply and he is considered to own the 750 outstanding shares of common stock held by his wife and children in addition to the 250 shares in his own name.

Taxpayer, however, argues that the attribution rules do not apply in considering whether a distribution is essentially equivalent to a dividend under § 302(b)(1). According to taxpayer, he should thus be considered to own only 25 percent of the corporation's common stock, and the distribution would then qualify under § 302(b)(1) since it was not pro rata or proportionate to his stock interest, the fundamental test of dividend equivalency. See Treas.Reg. 1.302–2(b). However, the plain language of the statute compels rejection of the argument. In subsection (c) of § 302, the attribution rules are made specifically applicable "in determining the ownership of stock for purposes of this section." Applying this language, both courts below held that § 318(a) applies to all of § 302, including § 302(b)(1)—a view in accord with the decisions of the other courts of appeals, a longstanding treasury regulation,[6] and the opinion of the leading commentators.[7]

Against this weight of authority, taxpayer argues that the result under paragraph (1) should be different because there is no explicit reference to stock ownership as there is in paragraphs (2) and (3). Neither that fact, however, nor the purpose and history of § 302(b)(1) support taxpayer's argument. The attribution rules—designed to provide a clear answer to what would otherwise be a difficult tax question—formed part of the tax bill that was subsequently enacted as the 1954 Code. As is discussed further, infra, the bill as passed by the House of Representatives contained no provision comparable to § 302(b)(1). When that provision was added in the Senate, no purpose was evidenced to restrict the applicability of § 318(a). Rather, the attribution rules continued to be made specifically applicable to the entire section, and we believe that Congress intended that they be taken into account wherever ownership of stock was relevant.

Indeed, it was necessary that the attribution rules apply to § 302(b)(1) unless they were to be effectively eliminated from consideration with regard to §§ 302(b)(2) and (3) also. For if a transaction failed to qualify under one of those sections solely because of the attribution rules, it would according to taxpayer's argument nonetheless qualify under § 302(b)(1). We cannot agree that Congress intended so to nullify its explicit directive. We conclude, therefore, that the attribution rules of § 318(a) do apply; and, for the purposes of deciding whether a distribution is "not essentially equivalent to a dividend" under § 302(b)(1), taxpayer must be deemed the owner of all 1,000 shares of the company's common stock.

II

After application of the stock ownership attribution rules, this case viewed most simply involves a sole stockholder who causes part of his shares to be redeemed by the corporation. We conclude that such a redemption is always "essentially equivalent to a dividend" within the meaning of that phrase in § 302(b)(1)[8] and therefore do not reach the

---

6. See Treas.Reg. 1.302–2(b).

7. See B. Bittker & J. Eustice, Federal Income Taxation of Corporations and Shareholders 292 n. 32 (2d ed. 1966).

8. Of course, this just means that a distribution in redemption to a sole share-holder will be treated under the general provisions of § 301, and it will only be taxed as a dividend under § 316 to the extent that there are earnings and profits.

Government's alternative argument that in any event the distribution should not on the facts of this case qualify for capital gains treatment.[9]

The predecessor of § 302(b)(1) came into the tax law as § 201(d) of the Revenue Act of 1921, 42 Stat. 228:

"A stock dividend shall not be subject to tax but if after the distribution of any such dividend the corporation proceeds to cancel or redeem its stock at such time and in such manner as to make the distribution and cancellation or redemption essentially equivalent to the distribution of a taxable dividend, the amount received in redemption or cancellation of the stock shall be treated as a taxable dividend * * *."

Enacted in response to this Court's decision that pro rata stock dividends do not constitute taxable income, Eisner v. Macomber, 252 U.S. 189 (1920), the provision had the obvious purpose of preventing a corporation from avoiding dividend tax treatment by distributing earnings to its shareholders in two transactions—a pro rata stock dividend followed by a pro rata redemption—that would have the same economic consequences as a simple dividend. Congress, however, soon recognized that even without a prior stock dividend essentially the same result could be effected whereby any corporation, "especially one which has only a few stockholders, might be able to make a distribution to its stockholders which would have the same effect as a taxable dividend." H.R.Rep. No. 1, 69th Cong., 1st Sess., 5. In order to cover this situation, the law was amended to apply "(whether or not such stock was issued as a stock dividend)" whenever a distribution in redemption of stock was made "at such time and in such manner" that it was essentially equivalent to a taxable dividend. Revenue Act of 1926, § 201(g), 44 Stat. 11.

This provision of the 1926 Act was carried forward in each subsequent revenue act and finally became § 115(g)(1) of the Internal Revenue Code of 1939. Unfortunately, however, the policies encompassed within the general language of § 115(g)(1) and its predecessors were not clear, and there resulted much confusion in the tax law. At first, courts assumed that the provision was aimed at tax avoidance schemes and sought only to determine whether such a scheme existed. * * * Although later the emphasis changed and the focus was more on the effect of the distribution, many courts continued to find that distributions otherwise like a dividend were not "essentially equivalent" if, for example, they were motivated by a sufficiently strong nontax business purpose. See cases cited n. 2, supra. There was general disagreement, however, about what would qualify as such a purpose, and the result was a case-by-case determination with each case decided "on the basis of the particular facts of the transaction in question." Bains v. United States, 289 F.2d 644, 646, 153 Ct.Cl. 599, 603 (1961).

---

9. The Government argues that even if business purpose were relevant under § 302(b)(1), the business purpose present here related only to the original investment and not at all to the necessity for redemption. Under either view, taxpayer does not lose his basis in the preferred stock. Under Treas. Reg. 1.302–2(c) that basis is applied to taxpayer's common stock.

By the time of the general revision resulting in the Internal Revenue Code of 1954, the draftsmen were faced with what has aptly been described as "the morass created by the decisions." Ballenger v. United States, 301 F.2d 192, 196 (C.A.4th Cir.1962). In an effort to eliminate "the considerable confusion which exists in this area" and thereby to facilitate tax planning, H.R.Rep. No. 1337, 83d Cong., 2d Sess., 35, the authors of the new Code sought to provide objective tests to govern the tax consequences of stock redemptions. Thus, the tax bill passed by the House of Representatives contained no "essentially equivalent" language. Rather, it provided for "safe harbors" where capital gains treatment would be accorded to corporate redemptions that met the conditions now found in §§ 302(b)(2) and (3) of the Code.

It was in the Senate Finance Committee's consideration of the tax bill that § 302(b)(1) was added, and Congress thereby provided that capital gains treatment should be available "if the redemption is not essentially equivalent to a dividend." Taxpayer argues that the purpose was to continue "existing law," and there is support in the legislative history that § 302(b)(1) reverted "in part" or "in general" to the "essentially equivalent" provision of § 115(g)(1) of the 1939 Code. According to the Government, even under the old law it would have been improper for the Court of Appeals to rely on "a business purpose for the redemption" and "an absence of the proscribed tax avoidance purpose to bail out dividends at favorable tax rates." * * * However, we need not decide that question, for we find from the history of the 1954 revisions and the purpose of § 302(b)(1) that Congress intended more than merely to re-enact the prior law.

In explaining the reason for adding the "essentially equivalent" test, the Senate Committee stated that the House provisions "appeared unnecessarily restrictive, particularly, in the case of redemptions of preferred stock which might be called by the corporation without the shareholder having any control over when the redemption may take place." S.Rep. No. 1622, 83d Cong., 2d Sess., 44. This explanation gives no indication that the purpose behind the redemption should affect the result.[10] Rather, in its more detailed technical evaluation of § 302(b)(1), the Senate Committee reported as follows:

> "The test intended to be incorporated in the interpretation of paragraph (1) is in general that currently employed under section 115(g)(1) of the 1939 Code. Your committee further intends that in applying this test for the future * * * the inquiry will be devoted solely to the question of whether or not the transaction by its nature may properly be characterized as a sale of stock by the redeeming shareholder to the corporation. For this purpose the presence or absence of earnings and profits of the corporation is not material. Example: X, the sole shareholder of a corporation

---

10. See Bittker & Eustice, supra, n. 7, at 291: "It is not easy to give § 302(b)(1) an expansive construction in view of this indica-tion that its major function was the narrow one of immunizing redemptions of minority holdings of preferred stock."

having no earnings or profits causes the corporation to redeem half of its stock. Paragraph (1) does not apply to such redemption notwithstanding the absence of earnings and profits." S.Rep. No. 1622, supra, at 234.

The intended scope of § 302(b)(1) as revealed by this legislative history is certainly not free from doubt. However, we agree with the Government that by making the sole inquiry relevant for the future the narrow one whether the redemption could be characterized as a sale, Congress was apparently rejecting past court decisions that had also considered factors indicating the presence or absence of a tax-avoidance motive.[11] At least that is the implication of the example given. Congress clearly mandated that pro rata distributions be treated under the general rules laid down in §§ 301 and 316 rather than under § 302, and nothing suggests that there should be a different result if there were a "business purpose" for the redemption. Indeed, just the opposite inference must be drawn since there would not likely be a tax-avoidance purpose in a situation where there were no earnings or profits. We conclude that the Court of Appeals was therefore wrong in looking for a business purpose and considering it in deciding whether the redemption was equivalent to a dividend. Rather, we agree with the Court of Appeals for the Second Circuit that "the business purpose of a transaction is irrelevant in determining dividend equivalence" under § 302(b)(1). Hasbrook v. United States, 343 F.2d 811, 814 (1965).

Taxpayer strongly argues that to treat the redemption involved here as essentially equivalent to a dividend is to elevate form over substance. Thus, taxpayer argues, had he not bought Bradley's shares or had he made a subordinated loan to the company instead of buying preferred stock, he could have gotten back his $25,000 with favorable tax treatment. However, the difference between form and substance in the tax law is largely problematical, and taxpayer's complaints have little to do with whether a business purpose is relevant under § 302(b)(1). It was clearly proper for Congress to treat distributions generally as taxable dividends when made out of earnings and profits and then to prevent avoidance of that result without regard to motivation where the distribution is in exchange for redeemed stock.

We conclude that that is what Congress did when enacting § 302(b)(1). If a corporation distributes property as a simple dividend, the effect is to

---

11. This rejection is confirmed by the Committee's acceptance of the House treatment of distributions involving corporate contractions—a factor present in many of the earlier "business purpose" redemptions. In describing its action, the Committee stated as follows:

"Your committee, as did the House bill, separates into their significant elements the kind of transactions now incoherently aggregated in the definition of a partial liquidation. Those distributions which may have capital-gain characteristics *because they are not made pro rata* among the various shareholders would be subjected, at the shareholder level, to the separate tests described in [§§ 301 to 318]. On the other hand, those distributions characterized by what happens solely at the corporate level by reason of the assets distributed would be included as within the concept of a partial liquidation." S.Rep. No. 1622, supra, at 49. (Emphasis added.)

transfer the property from the company to its shareholders without a change in the relative economic interests or rights of the stockholders. Where a redemption has that same effect, it cannot be said to have satisfied the "not essentially equivalent to a dividend" requirement of § 302(b)(1). Rather, to qualify for preferred treatment under that section, a redemption must result in a meaningful reduction of the shareholder's proportionate interest in the corporation. Clearly, taxpayer here, who (after application of the attribution rules) was the sole shareholder of the corporation both before and after the redemption, did not qualify under this test. The decision of the Court of Appeals must therefore be reversed and the case remanded to the District Court for dismissal of the complaint.

It is so ordered.

■ MR. JUSTICE DOUGLAS, with whom THE CHIEF JUSTICE AND MR. JUSTICE BRENNAN concur, dissenting.

I agree with the District Court, 274 F.Supp. 466, and with the Court of Appeals, 408 F.2d 1139, that respondent's contribution of working capital in the amount of $25,000 in exchange for 1,000 shares of preferred stock with a par value of $25 was made in order for the corporation to obtain a loan from the RFC and that the preferred stock was to be redeemed when the loan was repaid. For the reasons stated by the two lower courts, this redemption was not "essentially equivalent to a dividend," for the bona fide business purpose of the redemption belies the payment of a dividend. As stated by the Court of Appeals:

> "Although closely-held corporations call for close scrutiny under the tax law, we will not, under the facts and circumstances of this case, allow mechanical attribution rules to transform a legitimate corporate transaction into a tax avoidance scheme." 408 F.2d, at 1143–1144.

When the Court holds it was a dividend, it effectively cancels § 302(b)(1) from the Code. This result is not a matter of conjecture, for the Court says that in the case of closely held or one-man corporations a redemption of stock is "always" equivalent to a dividend. I would leave such revision to the Congress.

Revenue Ruling 85–106

1985–2 Cum.Bull. 116.

ISSUE

Is a redemption of nonvoting preferred stock not essentially equivalent to a dividend within the meaning of section 302(b)(1) of the Internal Revenue Code when there is no reduction in the percentage of voting and nonvoting common stock owned by the redeemed shareholder, and when the redeemed shareholder continues to have an undiminished opportunity to act in concert with other shareholders as a control group, under the circumstances described below?

FACTS

Corporation *X* had outstanding three classes of stock consisting of 100 shares of voting common stock, 100 shares of nonvoting common stock, and 50 shares of nonvoting 9 percent cumulative preferred stock. The fair market value of each share of common stock was approximately half the fair market value of each share of preferred stock. The voting common stock was held as follows:

Shareholders	*Shares*
A	19
B	19
C	18
Minority shareholders	44
Total	100

None of the minority shareholders owned more than five shares. None of the holders of the voting common stock were related within the meaning of section 318(a) of the Code. The combined voting power of *A, B,* and *C* was sufficient to elect a majority of the board of directors of *X*.

The nonvoting common stock and the preferred stock were held (directly and indirectly) in approximately the same proportions as the common stock. *C* held no nonvoting common stock or preferred stock directly, but was the sole remaining beneficiary of a trust, *T*, which owned 18 percent of both the nonvoting common stock and the preferred stock.

The trustees of *T* decided that it would be in the best interests of that trust if most of the *X* preferred stock held by *T* could be converted into cash. After negotiation, *X* redeemed six shares of preferred stock for its fair market value of 6*x* dollars. Following this redemption, *T* continued to hold three shares of preferred stock, and 18 percent of the nonvoting common stock. Under section 318(a)(3)(B) of the Code, *T* is also considered to own the voting common stock owned by its sole beneficiary, *C*.

LAW AND ANALYSIS

Section 302(a) of the Code provides, in part, that if a corporation redeems its stock, and if section 302(b)(1), (2), (3), or (4) applies, such redemption will be treated as a distribution in part or full payment in exchange for the stock.

* * *

The lack of any reduction in *T*'s 18 percent vote prevented this redemption from qualifying under section 302(b)(2) of the Code, and the lack of complete termination of interest prevented it from qualifying under section 302(b)(3). The question remains whether the redemption should be considered not essentially equivalent to a dividend so as to qualify under section 302(b)(1). Under section 1.302–2(b) of the Income Tax Regulations, this determination depends upon the facts and circumstances of each case.

In United States v. Davis, 397 U.S. 301 (1970), 1970–1 C.B. 62, the Supreme Court of the United States held that in order to qualify under section 302(b)(1) of the Code, a redemption must result in a meaningful reduction of the shareholder's proportionate interest in the corporation, and that, for this purpose, the attribution rules of section 318 apply.

In determining whether a reduction in interest is "meaningful", the rights inherent in a shareholder's interest must be examined. The three elements of a shareholder's interest that are generally considered most significant are: (1) the right to vote and thereby exercise control; (2) the right to participate in current earnings and accumulated surplus; and (3) the right to share in net assets on liquidation. Rev.Rul. 81–289, 1981–2 C.B. 82.

In applying the above principles, it is significant that (as a result of section 318(a)(3)(B) of the Code) the redemption did not reduce T's percentage of the vote in X. It is true that T reduced its percentage interest in current earnings, accumulated surplus, and net assets upon liquidation, and reduced the fair market value of its ownership in X. However, when the redeemed shareholder has a voting interest (either directly or by attribution), a reduction in voting power is a key factor in determining the applicability of section 302(b)(1) of the Code.

It is also true that T was not the largest shareholder. A and B each held slightly larger voting interests, and larger interests measured by fair market value. T, however, was not in the position of a minority shareholder isolated from corporate management and control. Compare Rev.Rul. 75–512, where the majority of the redeeming corporation's voting stock was held by a shareholder unrelated (within the meaning of section 318(a)) to the redeemed trust. Also compare Rev.Rul. 76–385, 1976–2 C.B. 92, where the redeemed shareholder's total interest was *de minimis*.

In the present situation, a significant aspect of T's failure to reduce voting power is the fact that the redemption leaves unchanged T's potential (by attribution from C) for participating in a control group by acting in concert with A and B. Compare Rev.Rul. 76–364, 1976–2 C.B. 91, where a reduction in voting interest was found meaningful in itself when it caused the redeemed shareholder to give up a potential for control by acting in concert with one other shareholder. In addition, the Tax Court has indicated significance for this factor of potential group control (*Johnson Trust*, at 947). See also Bloch v. United States, 261 F.Supp. 597, 611–612 (S.D.Tex. 1966), aff'd per curiam, 386 F.2d 839 (5th Cir.1967), where, in finding that "the distributions in question were essentially equivalent to a dividend," the court noted that there was no change in the redeemed shareholder's potential for exercising control "by aligning himself with one or more of the other stockholders."

Although there was a reduction of T's economic interest in X, such reduction was not sufficiently large to result in a meaningful reduction of T's interest. The absence of any reduction of T's voting interest in X (through C) and T's potential (through C) for control group participation are compelling factors in this situation.

In Himmel v. Commissioner, 338 F.2d 815 (2d Cir.1964), dealing with a similar question, a decision was reached permitting the applicability of section 302(b)(1) of the Code. That case, however, was decided prior to the decision of the Supreme Court in *Davis*. Thus, *Himmel* fails to reflect the development in the law represented by the *Davis* limitation on section 302(b)(1) applicability where there is no meaningful reduction of the shareholder's proportionate interest in the corporation. Thus, pursuant to *Davis,* it is proper to view *Himmel* as incorrect to the extent it conflicts with the position contained in this revenue ruling.

HOLDING

The redemption of nonvoting preferred stock held by T does not qualify as a redemption under section 302(b)(1) of the Code, under the facts of this ruling when there is no reduction in the percentage of voting and nonvoting common stock owned by T, and when T continues to have an undiminished opportunity to act in concert with other shareholders as a control group. Since the redemption does not otherwise qualify under section 302(b), it is not a distribution in part or full payment for the stock under section 302(a). Consequently, under section 302(d), the redemption will be treated as a distribution of property to which section 301 applies.

NOTE

The Meaningful Reduction Standard. In interpreting the "meaningful reduction" standard of *Davis*, the Service's rulings have considered the effect of the redemption on the redeemed shareholder's voting power, rights to participate in current and future corporate earnings, and rights to share in net assets on liquidation.[1] As illustrated by Revenue Ruling 85–106, if the shareholder has a voting interest, the key factor in measuring dividend equivalence is the reduction in the shareholder's voting power as opposed to other important economic rights. Whether such a reduction is "meaningful" is essentially a question of fact, but some guidelines have emerged from published rulings. For example, in Revenue Ruling 75–502,[2] the Service ruled that a shareholder's reduction of voting common stock ownership from 57 percent to 50 percent was meaningful where the remaining stock was held by a single unrelated shareholder. The ruling also states that a lesser reduction would not have qualified under Section 302(b)(1) because the shareholder would have continued to have "dominant voting rights."[3]

Turning to minority shareholders, the Service held in Revenue Ruling 75–512[4] that a reduction of common stock ownership from 30 percent to 24.3 percent—a near-miss under the substantially disproportionate redemption safe harbor—was meaningful because the redeemed shareholder experienced a reduction in three significant rights: voting, earnings, and assets on liquidation. A reduction in common stock ownership from 27

---

1. See, e.g., Rev. Rul. 81–289, 1981–2 C.B. 82.

2. 1975–2 C.B. 111.

3. Id.

4. 1975–2 C.B. 112.

percent to 22 percent also was held to be meaningful where the remaining shares were owned by three unrelated shareholders because the redeemed shareholder lost the ability to control the corporation in concert with only one other shareholder.[5]

The Section 302 regulations also focus upon the effect of the redemption upon the shareholder's control of corporate affairs. Thus, pro rata redemptions of a corporation's single class of stock do not qualify for exchange treatment, and the redemption of all of one class of stock also fails if all outstanding classes of stock are held proportionately.[6] Any redemption of stock from a shareholder owning only nonvoting preferred stock, however, is not essentially equivalent a dividend since the shareholder does not have control over whether the redemption occurs.[7] The Service also has ruled that a redemption of publicly traded common stock that reduces a shareholder's interest from .0001118 percent to .0001081 percent qualifies for exchange treatment since such a shareholder cannot exercise control over corporate affairs.[8] The same reasoning should apply to redemptions by closely held companies of stock held by minority shareholders who reduce their percentage interests, even if the reduction is slight. But a pro rata redemption of stock in a publicly traded corporation will not satisfy the "meaningful reduction" standard even if the shareholder owns only small noncontrolling interest in the corporation.[9]

Suppose that under state law a simple majority of a corporation's outstanding shares can control day-to-day corporate activities through the board of directors but extraordinary corporate action, such as a merger or liquidation, requires approval by two-thirds of the shares. Should a redemption in which a shareholder loses control of extraordinary corporate action but retains control of routine matters (e.g. a reduction to 60% voting control) qualify for exchange treatment under Section 302(b)(1)? In Wright v. United States,[10] the Eighth Circuit determined that such a redemption is not essentially equivalent to a dividend because of the loss of two-thirds control of the corporation. In Revenue Ruling 78–401,[11] the Service takes a more restrictive view of the application of Section 302(b)(1) to these facts. The ruling concludes that if extraordinary corporate action is not "imminent," the retention of day-to-day control of corporate activities is a "predominant factor" and the redemption does not result in a meaningful reduction in the shareholder's interest. It is unclear what position the Service would take if a merger or similar corporate transaction were contemplated or what evidence would substantiate the likelihood of corporate action.

---

5. Rev. Rul. 76–364, 1976–2 C.B. 91.

6. Reg. § 1.302–2(b).

7. Reg. § 1.302–2(a). In Rev.Rul. 77–426, 1977–2 C.B. 87, a redemption of five percent of the outstanding preferred stock from a shareholder owning all of the preferred stock (and only preferred stock) qualified for exchange treatment under Section 302(b)(1).

8. Rev.Rul. 76–385, 1976–2 C.B. 92.

9. Rev.Rul. 81–289, 1981–2 C.B. 82.

10. 482 F.2d 600 (8th Cir.1973).

11. 1978–2 C.B. 127.

Family Discord. One of the more titillating issues to arise under Section 302(b)(1) involves whether the Section 318(a)(1) family attribution rules should be ignored when there is evidence of family discord between the redeemed shareholder and related continuing shareholders. A typical factual context in which this "family fight" question arises is well illustrated in the following introduction to a leading Tax Court decision:[12]

> Petitioner Michael N. Cerone * * * and his son Michael L. Cerone * * * owned and operated the Stockade Cafe * * * each owning 50 percent of the stock of the corporation. The father and son had a volatile relationship and frequently disagreed over management decisions. Over the years their disagreements became more serious, and finally they decided one of them should buy the other's interest in the business. Petitioner did not think he could run the business alone, so it was decided that the corporation would redeem all of his stock. After the redemption, petitioner worked at the Stockade Cafe for several years, but he did not exercise any control over the corporation. This case involves the tax treatment of the payments or distributions petitioner received for his stock.

If the family attribution rules applied to the above fact pattern, the redemption of the father's 50 percent stock interest would not qualify under Section 302(b)(1) because he continued to own 100 percent of the company through attribution from his son. If the attribution chain could be broken, however, the father's reduction of his interest from 50 percent to zero would be "meaningful" and the redemption would qualify for exchange treatment under Section 302(b)(1) even if he failed to meet the specific requirements for waiver of family attribution under Section 302(c).[13]

After its victory in United States v. Davis, the Service consistently rejected attempts by taxpayers to break the chain of family attribution by proving family hostility.[14] Most courts to consider the question agree that the attribution rules apply without regard to family squabbles. Although the First Circuit once held that family discord might "negate the presumption" of the attribution rules,[15] the Tax Court and the Fifth Circuit have

---

12. Cerone v. Commissioner, 87 T.C. 1 (1986). See also the colorful introduction to the Fifth Circuit's opinion in Metzger Trust v. Commissioner, 693 F.2d 459 (5th Cir. 1982)("We decide today a story driven by tensions as old as Genesis but told in the modern lexicon of the tax law. It is the story of David who built a business and left it in the charge of his eldest son Jacob to be shared with Jacob's two sisters Catherine and Cecilia, of their alienation and resulting quarrel with the tax collectors.")

13. See Section C2 of this chapter, supra. Mr. Cerone was unable to waive family attribution under Section 302(c) because he retained a prohibited employment relationship with the corporation after the redemption. 87 T.C. at 29–33.

14. See, e.g., Rev.Rul. 80–26, 1980–1 C.B. 66.

15. Haft Trust v. Commissioner, 510 F.2d 43 (1st Cir.1975), vacating and remanding 61 T.C. 398 (1973).

refused to allow family discord to nullify the attribution rules in applying Section 302(b)(1).[16]

More recently, the Tax Court has suggested that family discord may be relevant in testing for dividend equivalency under Section 302(b)(1) *after* the attribution rules have been applied. In Cerone v. Commissioner,[17] the court summarized its view of the proper role of family hostility:[18]

> Although we [have] rejected the * * * argument that family discord could preclude application of the attribution rules, we nonetheless noted that family discord does have a role, albeit a limited one, in testing for dividend equivalence under section 302(b)(1). We reasoned that under *United States v. Davis,* supra, the proper analysis is as follows: First, the attribution rules are plainly and straightforwardly applied. Second, a determination is made whether there has been a reduction in the stockholder's proportionate interest in the corporation. If not, the inquiry ends because, if there is no change in the stockholder's interest, dividend equivalency results. If there has been a reduction, then all the facts and circumstances must be examined to see if the reduction was meaningful under *United States v. Davis,* supra. It is at this point, *and only then,* that family hostility becomes an appropriate factor for consideration. * * *.

PROBLEMS

1. Z Corporation has 100 shares of common stock outstanding, owned by A (28 shares), B (25 shares), C (23 shares) and D (24 shares.) Unless otherwise indicated, assume the shareholders are not related. In each of the following alternative situations, determine whether the redemption is not essentially equivalent to a dividend under § 302(b)(1):

(a) Z redeems 7 shares from A.

(b) Z redeems 5 shares from A, and A and D are mother and daughter.

(c) Z redeems 5 shares from A, and A and B are mother and daughter.

(d) Same as (c), above, except that A has not spoken to B since B married "outside her faith."

2. Y Corporation has 100 shares of common stock and 100 shares of nonvoting preferred stock outstanding. The preferred stock is not convertible into Y common stock and is not Section 306 stock (i.e., not stock treated specially in § 306 because of its tax avoidance potential). The Y

---

16. Cerone v. Commissioner, supra note 12; Metzger Trust v. Commissioner, 76 T.C. 42 (1981), affirmed, 693 F.2d 459 (5th Cir.1982), cert. denied, 463 U.S. 1207, 103 S.Ct. 3537 (1983); Haft Trust v. Commissioner, 61 T.C. 398 (1973), vacated and remanded, 510 F.2d 43 (1st Cir.1975).

17. Supra note 12.

18. 87 T.C. at 22. See also Henry T. Patterson Trust v. United States, 729 F.2d 1089 (6th Cir.1984)(percentage reduction from 97 to 93 percent, after applying attribution rules, is meaningful under *Davis* in view of hostility.)

common and preferred stock are owned by the following unrelated shareholders:

Shareholder	Common Shares	Preferred Shares
A	40	0
B	20	55
C	25	10
D	15	15
E	0	20

Will the following alternative redemptions qualify for exchange treatment under § 302(b)?

(a) Y redeems 5 preferred shares from E.

(b) Y redeems all of its outstanding preferred stock.

3. Suppose an individual shareholder owns ten shares of common stock with a basis of $15,000. What happens to the shareholder's basis if five shares are redeemed in a transaction which is properly classified as a dividend? What if all ten shares are redeemed in a transaction which is properly classified as a dividend because a § 302(c)(2) waiver of family attribution is unavailable?

D.   REDEMPTIONS TESTED AT THE CORPORATE LEVEL: PARTIAL LIQUIDATIONS

Code: § 302(b)(4), (e).

Section 302(b)(4) provides exchange treatment for redemptions of stock held by noncorporate shareholders if the distribution qualifies as a "partial liquidation." Under Section 302(e)(1), a distribution is treated as in partial liquidation if it is pursuant to a plan, occurs within the taxable year in which the plan is adopted or the succeeding taxable year, and is "not essentially equivalent to a dividend." Although the "not essentially equivalent to a dividend" standard mirrors the language in Section 302(b)(1), the two provisions have a very different focus. For partial liquidation purposes, dividend equivalency is determined at the corporate rather than the shareholder level. Thus, while a pro rata redemption could never escape dividend classification under Section 302(b)(1), any redemption that results in a genuine contraction of the corporation's business may qualify for exchange treatment as a partial liquidation if the distribution is made to a shareholder other than a C corporation. The legislative history of the predecessor of Section 302(e) explains the corporate contraction standard:[1]

> The general language of the proposed draft would include within the definition of a partial liquidation the type of cases involving the contraction of the corporate business. Such as for

---

1. S.Rep. No. 1622, 83d Cong., 2d Sess. 49 (1954). See Imler v. Commissioner, 11 T.C. 836 (1948)(the "contraction-by-fire" case referred to in the Senate Report).

example, cases which hold that if the entire floor of a factory is destroyed by fire, the insurance proceeds received may be distributed pro rata to the shareholders without the imposition of a tax at the rates applicable to the distribution of a dividend, if the corporation no longer continues its operations to the same extent maintained by the destroyed facility. Voluntary bona fide contraction of the corporate business may of course also qualify to the same extent as under existing law. In addition to the general definition of what constitutes a partial liquidation, your committee's bill provides a rule to indicate one type of distribution that will in any event constitute a partial liquidation. Under this rule, if a corporation is engaged in two or more active businesses which has [sic] been carried on for at least 5 years, it may distribute the assets of either one of the businesses in kind, or the proceeds of their sale.

The amorphous corporate contraction doctrine is a perilous yardstick for the tax planner.[2] Recognizing the need for greater certainty, Congress has provided a safe harbor in Section 302(e)(2), which assures partial liquidation status if the distribution consists of the assets of a "qualified trade or business" or is attributable to the termination of such a trade or business, and immediately after the distribution the corporation continues to conduct another qualified trade or business. To be "qualified," a trade or business must have been actively conducted throughout the five-year period ending on the date of the distribution and must not have been acquired by the distributing corporation in a taxable transaction during that period.[3] The active trade or business that the corporation continues to conduct must have a similar five-year business history. The "active" business requirement is designed to patrol against the accumulation of earnings in the form of investment assets, such as real estate or securities, followed by prompt bailout distributions masquerading as corporate contractions.[4]

A distribution may qualify as a partial liquidation even if the shareholders do not actually surrender any stock.[5] If the other requirements of either the general corporate contraction doctrine or the statutory safe harbor are met, the transaction will be treated as a constructive redemption of stock.[6]

Distributions to corporate shareholders do not qualify for partial liquidation treatment even if all the other statutory requirements are met.[7]

2. For the Service's ruling policy on whether a distribution qualifies as a corporate contraction, see Rev.Proc. 2005–3, § 4.01(22), 2005–1 C.B. 118, 123 (ordinarily no ruling unless distribution results in a 20 percent or greater reduction in gross revenue, net fair market value of assets, and employees).

3. I.R.C. § 302(e)(3).

4. For the definition of an active trade or business, see Reg. § 1.355–3(b), (c), which

govern corporate divisions under Section 355. See Chapter 10B, infra.

5. Fowler Hosiery Co. v. Commissioner, 301 F.2d 394 (7th Cir.1962); Rev.Rul. 90–13, 1990–1 C.B. 65.

6. See Rev.Rul. 77–245, 1977–2 C.B. 105, for the method of computing the tax consequences of a partial liquidation.

7. I.R.C. § 302(b)(4).

For purposes of determining whether a shareholder is corporate or noncorporate, stock held by a partnership, estate, or trust (but not an S corporation) is treated as if held proportionately by the partners or beneficiaries.[8] S corporations are thus treated as corporate shareholders and do not qualify for exchange treatment on a partial liquidation under Section 302(b)(4).

At first glance, it might seem that C corporation shareholders would welcome their eviction from the partial liquidation safe harbor because distributions that otherwise would give rise to taxable capital gain would become dividends sheltered by the dividends received deduction. But Congress was not acting in a spirit of generosity. Rather, it was attempting to put an end to several widely publicized acquisition techniques that used the partial liquidation as a vehicle for obtaining the best of all tax worlds: a stepped-up basis for selected assets of the acquired corporation along with the preservation of favorable tax attributes (e.g., earnings and profits deficits, loss and credit carryovers, etc.)—all at little or no tax cost.[9]

Congress inflicted further punishment on corporate shareholders when it enacted restrictions to prevent abuse of the dividends received deduction.[10] Any amount treated as a dividend to a corporate shareholder under Section 301 is an "extraordinary dividend" under Section 1059 if it is a distribution in redemption of stock which is part of a partial liquidation of the redeeming corporation, regardless of the shareholder's holding period or the size of the distribution.[11] As a result, a corporate shareholder that receives a dividend in a transaction treated as a partial liquidation must reduce its basis in the stock of the redeeming corporation by the portion of the dividend that was not taxed because of the dividends received deduction.[12]

Revenue Ruling 79–184

1979–1 Cum.Bull. 143.

Advice has been requested whether the sale by a parent corporation of all the stock of a wholly owned subsidiary and the distribution of the sales proceeds by the parent to its shareholders qualifies as a distribution in partial liquidation within the meaning of section 346(a)(2) of the Internal Revenue Code of 1954 [now Section 302(e). Ed.].

Corporation *P* owned all of the single class of outstanding stock of Corporation *S* for many years, during which time each had been engaged in the active conduct of a trade or business.

8. I.R.C. § 302(e)(5).

9. See, e.g., Henderson, "Federal Tax Techniques for Asset Redeployment Transactions," 37 Tax L.Rev. 325 (1982); Ginsburg, "Taxing Corporate Acquisitions," 38 Tax L.Rev. 171 (1983).

10. See Chapter 12F, supra.

11. I.R.C. § 1059(e)(1).

12. I.R.C. § 1059(a), (b). If the non-taxed portion of the dividend exceeds the shareholder's basis in the redeemed stock, the excess is treated as gain from a sale or exchange of the stock. I.R.C. § 1059(a)(2).

Pursuant to a plan, *P* sold all of the stock of *S* to an unrelated party for cash and distributed the proceeds of the sale pro rata to its shareholders in redemption of part of their *P* stock.

Section [302(e)(1)] of the Code provides, in part, that a distribution will be treated as a partial liquidation of a corporation if it is not essentially equivalent to a dividend, is in redemption of a part of the stock of the corporation pursuant to a plan, and occurs within the taxable year in which the plan is adopted or within the succeeding taxable year. Section 1.346–1(a)(2) of the Income Tax Regulations provides that a distribution resulting from a genuine contraction of the corporate business is an example of a distribution that will qualify as a partial liquidation under section [302(e)(1)].

Generally, for purposes of section [302(e)] of the Code, the business that is terminated or contracted must be operated directly by the corporation making the distribution. See *H.L. Morgenstern,* 56 T.C. 44 (1971). However, Rev.Rul. 75–223, 1975–1 C.B. 109, provides that when a parent corporation liquidates a wholly owned subsidiary and distributes the subsidiary's assets, or the proceeds from the sale of those assets, to its shareholders, the fact that the distributions were attributable to assets used by the subsidiary rather than directly by the parent will not prevent the distribution from qualifying as a "genuine contraction of the corporate business" to the parent within the meaning of section 1.346–1(a)(2) of the regulations. The basis for this holding is that under section 381 a parent corporation that liquidates a subsidiary under section 332 (when section 334(b)(1) applies) inherits attributes (for example, earnings and profits) of the liquidated subsidiary so that after the liquidation of the subsidiary the parent is viewed as if it had always operated the business of the liquidated subsidiary.

However, when a parent corporation distributes the stock of its subsidiary, as in *Situation 3* of Rev.Rul. 75–223, section 381 of the Code does not apply to integrate the past business results of the subsidiary with those of the parent. Therefore, distribution by the parent of subsidiary's stock does not result in the parent corporation taking into account the past operations of the subsidiary. Thus, there is no analogy between a distribution of stock of the subsidiary and a distribution of the assets of a liquidated subsidiary or the proceeds of a sale of such assets. A distribution of the stock of the subsidiary under such circumstances is a corporate separation, governed by section 355, and not a corporate contraction.

Similarly, as in the present case, where *P* sells all of the stock of its wholly owned subsidiary, *S,* and distributes the proceeds to its shareholders, there is no basis for attributing the business activities of *S* to *P*. It is well established that a corporation is a legal entity separate and distinct from its shareholders. New Colonial Ice Co. v. Helvering, 292 U.S. 435 (1934), XIII–1 C.B. 194 (1934); Moline Properties, Inc. v. Commissioner, 319 U.S. 436 (1943), 1943 C.B. 1011. Although the assets of *P* are reduced by the subsequent distribution of the sale proceeds, the sale by *P* of the *S* stock is not in and of itself sufficient to effect a contraction of the business operations of P within the contemplation of section 346(a)(2) of the Code. Rather, the overall transaction has the economic significance of the sale of an investment and distribution of the proceeds.

Accordingly, the distribution by P to its shareholders of the proceeds of the sale of the S stock does not qualify as a distribution in partial liquidation within the meaning of section [302(e)(1)] of the Code, and the distribution will be treated as a distribution by P of property taxable to the P shareholders under section 301 by reason of section 302(d). See section 1.302–2(b) of the regulations, which provides that all distributions in pro rata redemption of a part of the stock of a corporation generally will be treated as distributions under section 301 if the corporation has only one class of stock outstanding.

PROBLEM

Alpha Corporation operates a book publishing business ("Books") and a bar exam review course ("Cram") as divisions (i.e., not as separately incorporated entities). Alpha's single class of common stock outstanding is owned in equal shares by Michael, Pamela (Michael's wife) and Iris Corporation. Neither Michael nor Pamela owns any stock in Iris. Alpha also owns all of the stock of Beta Corporation, a separately incorporated company which is engaged in the beta processing business, and it directly owns a diversified securities portfolio.

What are the shareholder level tax consequences of the following alternative transactions:

(a) Alpha has operated Books and Cram for more than five years and it distributes the assets of Books to its three equal shareholders in redemption of 50 shares from each shareholder. Any different result if the redemption is made without an actual surrender of shares?

(b) Is there a different result in (a), above, if Alpha had purchased Books three years ago for cash? If so, why should that matter? What if Alpha acquired Books three years ago in a tax-free reorganization?

(c) What if all the assets of Books were destroyed by fire and Alpha distributes one-half of the insurance proceeds equally to its three shareholders in redemption of an appropriate number of shares of stock and retains the remaining proceeds to carry on its book publishing business on a somewhat smaller scale?

(d) Same as (a), above, except that Alpha distributes the assets of Books to Michael in redemption of all of his stock.

(e) Same as (a), above except that Alpha distributes the assets of Books to Iris in redemption of all of its Alpha stock.

(f) Alpha distributes the securities portfolio to its three equal shareholders in redemption of 20 shares from each shareholder.

(g) Alpha sells all of its Beta stock and distributes the proceeds pro rata to the shareholders in redemption of 20 shares from each.

(h) Same as (g), above, except that Alpha liquidates Beta and then distributes the assets of Beta's business, which Beta has operated for more than five years.

E.   CONSEQUENCES TO THE DISTRIBUTING CORPORATION

1.   DISTRIBUTIONS OF APPRECIATED PROPERTY IN REDEMPTION

Code: § 311.

In the preceding chapter, the story of the decline of the *General Utilities* doctrine began to unfold.[1] The assault on *General Utilities* in the redemption setting gained momentum when Congress discovered that several insurance companies were redeeming large amounts of their own stock by distributing appreciated securities while avoiding recognition of gain at the corporate level.[2] Congress curtailed this perceived abuse by enacting a rule that required a corporation to recognize gain on a distribution of appreciated property in a redemption as if the property had been sold for its fair market value. Partial liquidation distributions, however, continued to qualify for nonrecognition at the corporate level, and numerous exceptions demonstrated that Congress was not yet ready to give *General Utilities* a proper burial.[3]

Corporate takeover specialists were quick to exploit these remaining vestiges of the *General Utilities* doctrine. Through carefully orchestrated transactions, they sought to convert a direct sale of property by a corporation, normally a taxable event to the seller, into a tax-free distribution.[4] After several of these schemes were publicized, Congress responded by further narrowing the opportunity for nonrecognition on nonliquidating distributions of appreciated property in redemption.[5] The final demise of *General Utilities* in the redemption context came with the Tax Reform Act of 1986. In adopting Section 311(b), which also applies to nonliquidating distributions, Congress repealed all the remaining exceptions that had provided for nonrecognition of gain to the distributing corporation. As a result, a corporation distributing property in redemption of stock (including a partial liquidation) always recognizes gain but may not recognize loss.

---

1. See Chapter 4D1, supra.

2. See S.Rep. No. 91–552, 91st Cong., 1st Sess. 279, reprinted in 1969–3 C.B. 423,-600.

3. See I.R.C. § 311(d)(2)(pre–1982).

4. See Henderson, "Federal Tax Techniques for Asset Redeployment Transactions," 37 Tax L.Rev. 325 (1982). The Service's attack or this strategy was rejected in

Esmark, Inc. v. Commissioner, 90 T.C. 171 (1988), aff'd, 886 F.2d 1318 (7th Cir.1989).

5. For a description of some of the abuses at which the 1982 changes were directed, see Staff of Joint Committee on Taxation, General Explanation of Tax Equity and Fiscal Responsibility Act of 1982, 97th Cong., 2d Sess. 125 (1982).

2.   EFFECT ON EARNINGS AND PROFITS

Code: § 312(n)(7).

The effect of a stock redemption on the distributing corporation's earnings and profits initially depends upon the tax consequences of the redemption at the shareholder level. If the redemption is treated as a distribution to which Section 301 applies, the distributing corporation adjusts its earnings and profits in the same manner as on other nonliquidating distributions—i.e., earnings and profits are decreased by the amount of cash and the principal amount of any obligations, and by the greater of the adjusted basis or the fair market value of any property distributed.[1] In addition, the corporation always recognizes gain and correspondingly increases its current earnings and profits on a distribution of appreciated property, and it reduces current earnings and profits by any taxes paid on that gain.[2]

If a redemption (including a partial liquidation) is treated as an exchange to the redeemed shareholder, the effect on earnings and profits is more complex. In that situation, Section 312(n)(7) provides that the part of the distribution in redemption that is properly chargeable to earnings and profits shall be an amount which does not exceed the ratable share of the corporation's accumulated earnings and profits attributable to the redeemed stock. Congress also expressed its intention that earnings and profits never would be reduced by more than the amount of the redemption.[3]

To illustrate the operation of this rule, assume that X Corporation has 1,000 shares of common stock outstanding, and that A and B each acquire 500 of these shares at issuance at a price of $20 per share. Assume further that X is a profitable business that holds $100,000 of net assets, consisting of $50,000 cash and $50,000 of appreciated real property, and X has $50,000 of accumulated earnings and profits. If X distributes $50,000 cash to A in redemption of A's 500 shares, Section 312(n)(7) reduces X's earnings and profits by $25,000—the ratable share of X's $50,000 earnings and profits attributable to A's 50 percent stock interest that was redeemed. The remaining $25,000 of the distribution is charged to X's capital account and, after the redemption, X would have $25,000 of remaining accumulated earnings and profits. The following excerpt from the legislative history of the Tax Reform Act of 1984 explains the operation of this rule in the case of a corporation with a more complex capital structure:[4]

> If a corporation has more than one class of stock outstanding, its earnings and profits generally should be allocated among the different classes in determining the amount by which a redemption of all or a part of one class of stock reduces earnings and

---

1. I.R.C. § 312(a), (b).

2. I.R.C. § 311(b); 312(b).

3. S.Rep. No. 98–169, 98th Cong., 2d Sess. 202 (1984).

4. Staff of Joint Committee on Taxation, General Explanation of the Tax Reform Act of 1984, 98th Cong., 2d Sess. 181 (1984).

profits. However, earnings and profits generally should not be allocated to preferred stock which is not convertible and which does not participate to any significant extent in corporate growth. Therefore, a redemption of such preferred stock should result in a reduction of the capital account only, unless the distribution includes dividend arrearages, which will reduce earnings and profits.

Similarly, priorities legally required as between different classes of stock should be taken into account in allocating earnings and profits between classes. For example, assume that corporation X has 1,000 shares of class A common stock and 1,000 shares of class B common stock. Both classes are $10 par value stock and were issued at the same time at a price of $20. The class A common has a preference as to dividends and liquidating distributions in a 2:1 ratio to the class B common, and only the class B common has voting rights. Assume further that Corporation X holds net assets worth $210,000 and has current and accumulated earnings and profits of $120,000. If X distributes $140,000 in cash in redemption of all of the class A common, earnings and profits should be reduced by $80,000 and capital account by $60,000.

PROBLEM

X Corporation has 200 shares of common stock outstanding. A and B each acquired 100 shares of X upon their issuance at a price of $1,000 per share, and they each thus have an adjusted basis of $100,000 in their X stock. At the beginning of the current year, X has $100,000 of accumulated earnings and profits and it has $50,000 of earnings and profits from operations during the year. What are the tax consequences to X of the following alternative redemptions of A's stock, assuming in each case that the redemption qualifies for exchange treatment under § 302(a)?

(a) In redemption of A's 100 shares, X distributes land ($250,000 fair market value; $200,000 adjusted basis) held as an investment.

(b) Same as (a), above, except X's adjusted basis in the land is $300,000.

3.   STOCK REACQUISITION EXPENSES

Code: § 162(k).

Amounts paid to acquire stock generally must be capitalized as part of the stock's basis.[1] The capitalization requirement applies to the original purchase price of the stock as well as to acquisition expenses, such as brokerage commissions and legal fees.[2] Some older authority held, however,

---

1. I.R.C. §§ 263(a), 1012.

2. Reg. § 1.263(a)–2(c), (e). See Woodward v. Commissioner, 397 U.S. 572, 90 S.Ct.

1302 (1970); United States v. Hilton Hotels Corp., 397 U.S. 580, 90 S.Ct. 1307 (1970).

that expenses incurred by a corporation to repurchase its stock, in limited circumstances, might be ordinary and necessary expenses deductible under Section 162.[3] In the midst of the frenzy of hostile corporate takeovers in the 1980's, Congress became concerned that corporate expenditures incurred to fend off unwanted corporate suitors by purchasing their shares—so-called "greenmail" payments—were being characterized as deductible business expenses.[4] Section 162(k)(1) was enacted to make it clear that all expenditures by a corporation incurred in purchasing its own stock, whether representing amounts paid for the stock, a premium paid in excess of the stock's value, or expenses connected with the purchase, are nondeductible, nonamortizable capital expenditures.[5] Section 162(k)(2) contains exceptions for interest payments deductible under Section 163, and several more specialized situations. In 1996, Congress broadened the scope of Section 162(k)(1) by extending its application to any "reacquisition" of stock regardless of whether the transaction is technically treated as a redemption under Subchapter C.

One difficult interpretive problem under the Section 162(k) disallowance rule revolves around the question of what amounts are paid to shareholders "in connection with" a redemption of stock. The legislative history states that while the phrase "in connection with" is to be construed broadly, it is not intended to deny a deduction for "otherwise deductible amounts paid in a transaction which has no nexus with the redemption other than being proximate in time or arising out of the same circumstances."[6] The Conference Report goes on to expand upon this standard:[7]

> For example, if a corporation redeems a departing employee's stock and makes a payment to the employee in discharge of the corporation's obligations under an employment contract, the payment in discharge of the contractual obligation is not subject to disallowance under this provision. Payments in discharge of other types of contractual obligations, in settlement of litigation, or pursuant to other actual or potential legal obligations or rights, may also be outside the intended scope of the provision to the extent it is clearly established that the payment does not represent consideration for the stock or expenses related to its acquisition, and is not a payment that is a fundamental part of a "standstill" or similar agreement.

> The conferees anticipate that, where a transaction is not directly related to a redemption but is proximate in time, the Internal Revenue Service will scrutinize the transaction to deter-

---

3. Five Star Manufacturing Co. v. Commissioner, 355 F.2d 724 (5th Cir.1966). See generally Note, "Deductibility of Stock Redemption Expenses and the Corporate Survival Doctrine," 58 So.Cal.L.Rev. 895 (1985).

4. S.Rep. No. 99–313, 99th Cong., 2d Sess. 223 (1986).

5. Id.

6. H.R.Rep. No. 841, 99th Cong., 2d Sess. II—168 (1986).

7. Id. at II—168–69.

mine whether the amount purportedly paid in the transaction is reasonable. Thus, even where the parties have countervailing tax interests, the parties' stated allocation of the total consideration between the redemption and the unrelated transaction will be respected only if it is supported by all the facts and circumstances.

However, the conferees intend that agreements to refrain from purchasing stock of a corporation or other similar types of "standstill" agreements in all events will be considered related to any redemption of the payee's stock. Accordingly, payments pursuant to such agreements are nondeductible under this provision provided there is an actual purchase of all or part of the payee's stock. The conferees intend no inference regarding the deductibility of payments under standstill or similar agreements that are unrelated to any redemption of stock owned by the payee.

The most controversial interpretive issue to arise since the enactment of Section 162(k) involves the deductibility of loan fees and related expenses incurred by corporations that have engaged in leveraged stock repurchase transactions. The courts have disagreed on the scope of the disallowance rule in this setting. The Ninth Circuit upheld the deductibility of various fees incurred to finance a stock redemption in a case where a public corporation sought to amortize $4 million in loan fees incurred in connection with a leveraged buyout designed to enable the company to go private.[8] The Service had disallowed the deductions, contending that the fees were stock redemption expenses subject to disallowance under Section 162(k). The court reasoned that Section 162(k) did not extend to financing costs because the borrowing was a transaction separate from the redemption. In so holding, the court rejected the Service's view that the disallowance rule extended to all costs (other than interest expenses, which is specifically excepted by statute) directly or indirectly related to a stock redemption, including financing fees. The Tax Court has taken a contrary view, holding that fees paid to an investment banking firm to obtain loans to finance a stock repurchase as part of a leveraged buyout were not deductible because they were incurred "in connection with redemption of stock."[9] The court agreed with the Service's broader view of Section 162(k), finding that the various steps taken to effect a leveraged buyout were integrated.

Congress eventually interceded, settling the controversy with a "technical correction" that amended Section 162(k) to make it clear that amounts properly allocable to indebtedness on which interest is deductible may be amortized over the term of the loan even if the debt is incurred by a corporation to repurchase its stock.[10]

8. In re Kroy (Europe) Ltd., 27 F.3d 367 (9th Cir.1994).

9. Fort Howard Corp. v. Commissioner, 103 T.C. 345 (1994).

10. I.R.C. § 162(k)(2)(ii).

F.   Redemption Planning Techniques

1.   Bootstrap Acquisitions

Revenue Ruling 75–447

1975–2 Cum.Bull. 113.

Advice has been requested as to the Federal income tax consequences, in the situations described below, of the redemption by a corporation of part of its stock.

Situation 1

Corporation X had outstanding 100 shares of voting common stock of which A and B each owned 50 shares. In order to bring C into the business with an equal stock interest, and pursuant to an integrated plan, A and B caused X to issue, at fair market value, 25 new shares of voting common stock to C. Immediately thereafter, as part of the same plan, A and B caused X to redeem 25 shares of X voting common stock from each of them. Neither A, B, nor C owned any stock of X indirectly under section 318 of the Internal Revenue Code of 1954.

Situation 2

Corporation X had outstanding 100 shares of voting common stock of which A and B each owned 50 shares. In order to bring C into the business with an equal stock interest, and pursuant to an integrated plan, A and B each sold 15 shares of X voting common stock to C at fair market value and then caused X to redeem five shares from both A and B. Neither A, B, nor C owned any stock of X indirectly under section 318 of the Code.

Section 302(b)(2) of the Code states that section 302(a), which provides for treating a redemption of stock as a distribution in part or full payment in exchange for the stock, will apply if the distribution is substantially disproportionate with respect to the shareholder. * * *

In Zenz v. Quinlivan, 213 F.2d 914 (6th Cir.1954), a sole shareholder of a corporation, desiring to dispose of her entire interest therein, sold part of her stock to a competitor and shortly thereafter sold the remainder of her stock to the corporation for an amount of cash and property approximately equal to its earned surplus. The Government contended that the redemption was a dividend on the grounds that the result was the same as if the steps had been reversed, that is, as if the stock had been redeemed first and the sale of stock to the competitor had followed. The United States Court of Appeals rejected the Government's contention and held that the purchase of the stock by the corporation (when coupled with the sale of stock to the competitor) was not a dividend to the selling shareholder and that the proceeds should be treated as payment for the stock surrendered under the provisions of the Internal Revenue Code of 1939.

Rev.Rul. 55–745, 1955–2 C.B. 223, states that in situations similar to that in *Zenz,* the amount received by the shareholder from the corporation will be treated as received in payment for the stock surrendered under section 302(a) of the Code since the transaction when viewed as a whole results in the shareholder terminating his interest in the corporation within the meaning of section 302(b)(3).

In determining whether the "substantially disproportionate" provisions of section 302(b)(2) of the Code have been satisfied in *Situation 1* and in *Situation 2,* it is proper to rely upon the holding in *Zenz* that the sequence in which the events (that is, the redemption and sale) occur is irrelevant as long as both events are clearly part of an overall plan. Therefore, in situations where the redemption is accompanied by an issuance of new stock (as in *Situation 1*), or a sale of stock (as in *Situation 2*), and both steps (the sale, or issuance, of stock, as the case may be, and the redemption) are clearly part of an integrated plan to reduce a shareholder's interest, effect will be given only to the overall result for purposes of section 302(b)(2) and the sequence in which the events occur will be disregarded.

Since the *Zenz* holding requires that effect be given only to the overall result and proscribes the fragmenting of the whole transaction into its component parts, the computation of the voting stock of the corporation owned by the shareholder *immediately before* the redemption for purposes of section 302(b)(2)(C)(ii) of the Code should be made before any part of the transaction occurs. Likewise, the computation of the voting stock of the corporation owned by the shareholder *immediately after* the redemption for purposes of section 302(b)(2)(C)(i) should be made after the whole transaction is consummated. Making the immediately before and the immediately after computations in this manner properly reflects the extent to which the shareholder involved in each situation actually reduces his stock holdings as a result of the whole transaction.

Therefore, for purposes of the computations required by section 302(b)(2)(C) of the Code, A and B, in *Situation 1,* will each be viewed as having owned 50 percent (50/100 shares) of X before the transaction and 33⅓ percent (25/75 shares) immediately thereafter. In *Situation 2,* A and B will each be viewed as having owned 50 percent (50/100 shares) of X before the transaction and 33⅓ percent (30/90 shares) immediately thereafter. Furthermore, in each situation, the result would be the same if the redemption had preceded the issuance, or sale, of stock.

Accordingly, in both *Situations 1* and *2,* the requirements of section 302(b)(2) of the Code are satisfied. Therefore, the amounts distributed to A and B in both situations are distributions in full payment in exchange for the stock redeemed pursuant to section 302(a).

NOTE

The classic bootstrap acquisition is a transaction where the buyer purchases all or part of the stock of the target corporation in conjunction with a redemption of some of the selling shareholder's stock. In Zenz v. Quinlivan,[1] which is discussed in Revenue Ruling 75–447, the sole shareholder of a corporation sold part of her stock for cash and, three weeks later, the corporation redeemed her remaining shares. The combined sale and redemption structure was used because the buyer wanted to minimize future dividend exposure by reducing the corporation's earnings and profits. The seller's agenda was to be taxed on both the sale and redemption at then favorable capital gains rates and avoid dividend treatment on the redemption.

The Service argued that the redemption would have been a dividend to the target's shareholder if the distribution had preceded the sale and should not be treated any differently where the parties orchestrated a different order of events. The Sixth Circuit disagreed. Finding that the taxpayer intended from the outset to terminate her entire interest in the corporation, it held that the redemption qualified as an exchange rather than a dividend. The Service subsequently acquiesced to the result in *Zenz* and extended its reasoning to substantially disproportionate redemptions in Revenue Ruling 75–447.

In the case of a noncorporate shareholder, *Zenz* and its progeny have far less significance as long as qualified dividends are taxed at preferential capital gains rates. In a combined sale and redemption transaction, a noncorporate seller ordinarily will suffer no tax disadvantage if the distribution in redemption is characterized as a dividend. The distinction still matters, however, to corporate shareholders. As discussed in Chapter 12,[2] corporate sellers who are seeking to extract liquid assets prior to a sale of stock normally prefer a pre-sale dividend for two reasons: (1) the availability of the dividends received deduction, and (2) corporate capital gains are not taxed at preferential rates.

PROBLEM

Strap is the sole shareholder of Target Corporation. Boot is a prospective buyer and is willing to purchase all of the Target stock, but Boot is unable to pay the $500,000 price demanded by Strap even though he believes it to be fair. Target has $100,000 cash on hand. Should Strap and Boot structure Boot's acquisition of Target along the lines of the *Zenz* case? Is there a better alternative? What additional facts would you like to know? (Compare to *TSN Liquidating* and the problem on page 206, supra.)

2. BUY–SELL AGREEMENTS

a. IN GENERAL

Code: §§ 101(a), 264(a)(1); skim § 2703.

Closely held corporations frequently use buy-sell stock purchase agreements to ensure continuity of the business, to satisfy economic and tax

---

1. 213 F.2d 914 (6th Cir. 1954).   **2.** See Chapter 4G, infra.

goals when a shareholder dies or retires, and to resolve shareholder disputes. There are two basic forms of buy-sell agreements. Under a "cross-purchase" agreement, the departing shareholder or the shareholder's estate sells stock to the continuing shareholders. Under the more commonly employed "entity-purchase" agreement, the corporation redeems the departing shareholder's stock, funding the redemption with available cash, borrowed funds, an installment note, or the proceeds of a corporate-owned life insurance policy. The obligation to buy (or sell) may be mandatory or optional, as the parties agree, and is triggered by certain events specified in the agreement. The most common trigger event is a shareholder's death. Other typical trigger events are retirement or disability.

Buy-sell provisions frequently are part of a more comprehensive shareholders' agreement that includes restrictions on the transfer of stock, rights of first refusal to the corporation in the event a shareholder wishes to sell, and provisions to determine the value of any stock purchased pursuant to the agreement. Some primitive agreements set the price based on "book value," an accounting concept that often bears little or no relationship to the economic value of the company. More sophisticated agreements will use a formula based on earnings or provide for an appraisal mechanism on the occurrence of a trigger event.

A goal of many buy-sell agreements for closely-held family businesses is to establish the federal estate tax valuation of the stock upon a shareholder's death. A decedent's gross estate generally includes all property held by the decedent, valued either at the date of death or six months thereafter (the alternate valuation date).[1] In the case of unlisted stock, which cannot be valued by market quotations, fair market value is determined by taking into account a variety of factors, including the corporation's net worth, its earnings history and dividend-paying capacity, and the value of stock of publicly traded companies in the same line of business.[2] If stock is subject to an option or contract to purchase, such as a buy-sell agreement, the regulations provide that the agreement will establish the value if it represents a bona fide business arrangement and is not a device to pass the stock to the natural objects of the decedent's bounty for less than adequate and full consideration.[3] But if the decedent was free to dispose of the stock during his lifetime without price restrictions, "little weight" is given to the price set at death by the option or contract.[4] The courts agree that maintaining control of a closely held business constitutes a bona fide

---

1. I.R.C. §§ 2031; 2032.

2. I.R.C. § 2031(b); Reg. § 20.2031–2(f)(2). See also Rev. Rul. 59–60, 1959–1 C.B. 237.

3. Reg. § 20.2031–2(h). For the buy-sell agreement price to be binding, the decedent's estate must be obligated to sell the dece-dent's stock; the buyer either must be obligated to buy the decedent's interest or have an option to do so; and the price specified must have been fair at the time the agreement was made. Id.

4. Id.

business purpose but they require a separate examination of whether a restriction or option constitutes a "testamentary device."[5]

For buy-sell agreements entered into or substantially modified after October 8, 1990, Congress has added some statutory restrictions on the valuation of property subject to an option or contract to purchase. Section 2703(a) provides that the value of any property for estate, gift and generation-skipping tax purposes shall be determined without regard to (1) any option, agreement or other right to acquire or use property at a price less than the fair market value of the property, disregarding the option agreement or right, or (2) any restriction on the right to sell or use such property. Under this general rule, the effect of a buy-sell agreement on valuation would be disregarded. Section 2703(b), however, provides an exception for any option, agreement, right or restriction which satisfies the standards of the regulations (bona fide business arrangement and not a testamentary device) and has terms "comparable to similar arrangements entered into by persons in an arm's length transaction." In adding this comparability standard, Congress intended the taxpayer to show that the agreement was one that could have been obtained in an arm's length bargain with an unrelated party, considering such factors as the term of the agreement, the present value of the affected property, and its expected value at the time of exercise.[6] In noting that this standard would not be met "by showing isolated comparables but requires a demonstration of the general practice of unrelated parties," the Senate Finance Committee stated that expert testimony—e.g., by an appraiser familiar with the industry—would be evidence of such general practice.[7]

Even with the enactment of Section 2703, drafters of buy-sell agreements still have some flexibility in their use of valuation methodologies. For example, the Conference Report accompanying the 1990 Act states that a buy-sell agreement should not be disregarded merely because its terms differ from those used by another similarly situated company.[8] Noting that general business practice may recognize more than one valuation methodology, even within the same industry, the conferees went on to state that "[i]n such situations, one of several generally accepted methodologies may satisfy the standard contained in the conference agreement."[9]

Section 2703 has not resulted in the demise of buy-sell agreements to fix estate tax valuation. It merely places a greater premium on an evidentiary showing that the arrangement is bona fide and not merely a tax-avoidance device to transfer a family business to the next generation for less than adequate and full consideration.

As developed in the next section of the text, buy-sell agreements also may raise constructive dividend issues if they are not properly structured

5. See, e.g., St. Louis County Bank v. United States, 674 F.2d 1207 (8th Cir.1982).

6. Senate Finance Committee Explanation of Revenue Provisions, 1991 Budget Reconciliation Bill (Oct. 13, 1990), 101st Cong., 2d Sess. 68 (1990).

7. Id. See also Reg. § 25.2703–1.

8. H.Rep. No. 101–964, 101st Cong., 2d Sess. 157 (1990).

9. Id. See also Reg. § 25.2703–1(b)(4).

and implemented. With most dividends now taxed at 15 percent, these issues may or may not be important depending on other variables, such as the shareholder's stock basis, the need for capital gains to absorb otherwise unavailable capital losses, and the shareholder's other tax characteristics.

b.   CONSTRUCTIVE DIVIDEND ISSUES

Revenue Ruling 69–608

1969–2 Cum.Bull. 42.

Advice has been requested as to the treatment for Federal income tax purposes of the redemption by a corporation of a retiring shareholder's stock where the remaining shareholder of the corporation has entered into a contract to purchase such stock.

Where the stock of a corporation is held by a small group of people, it is often considered necessary to the continuity of the corporation to have the individuals enter into agreements among themselves to provide for the disposition of the stock of the corporation in the event of the resignation, death, or incapacity of one of them. Such agreements are generally reciprocal among the shareholders and usually provide that on the resignation, death, or incapacity of one of the principal shareholders, the remaining shareholders will purchase his stock. Frequently such agreements are assigned to the corporation by the remaining shareholder and the corporation actually redeems its stock from the retiring shareholder.

Where a corporation redeems stock from a retiring shareholder, the fact that the corporation in purchasing the shares satisfies the continuing shareholder's executory contractual obligation to purchase the redeemed shares does not result in a distribution to the continuing shareholder provided that the continuing shareholder is not subject to an existing primary and unconditional obligation to perform the contract and that the corporation pays no more than fair market value for the stock redeemed.

On the other hand, if the continuing shareholder, at the time of the assignment to the corporation of his contract to purchase the retiring shareholder's stock, is subject to an unconditional obligation to purchase the retiring shareholder's stock, the satisfaction by the corporation of his obligation results in a constructive distribution to him. The constructive distribution is taxable as a distribution under section 301 of the Internal Revenue Code of 1954.

If the continuing shareholder assigns his stock purchase contract to the redeeming corporation prior to the time when he incurs a primary and unconditional obligation to pay for the shares of stock, no distribution to him will result. If, on the other hand, the assignment takes place after the time when the continuing shareholder is so obligated, a distribution to him will result. While a pre-existing obligation to perform in the future is a necessary element in establishing a distribution in this type of case, it is not until the obligor's duty to perform becomes unconditional that it can be said a primary and unconditional obligation arises.

The application of the above principles may be illustrated by the situations described below.

Situation 1

A and B are unrelated individuals who own all of the outstanding stock of corporation X. A and B enter into an agreement that provides in the event B leaves the employ of X, he will sell his X stock to A at a price fixed by the agreement. The agreement provides that within a specified number of days of B's offer to sell, A will purchase at the price fixed by the agreement all of the X stock owned by B. B terminates his employment and tenders the X stock to A. Instead of purchasing the stock himself in accordance with the terms of the agreement, A causes X to assume the contract and to redeem its stock held by B. In this case, A had a primary and unconditional obligation to perform his contract with B at the time the contract was assigned to X. Therefore, the redemption by X of its stock held by B will result in a constructive distribution to A. See William J. and Georgia K. Sullivan v. United States of America, 244 F.Supp. 605 (1965), affirmed, 363 F.2d 724 (1966), certiorari denied, 387 U.S. 905, 87 S.Ct. 1683 (1967), rehearing denied, 388 U.S. 924, 87 S.Ct. 2104 (1967).

Situation 2

A and B are unrelated individuals who own all of the outstanding stock of corporation X. An agreement between them provides unconditionally that within ninety days of the death of either A or B, the survivor will purchase the decedent's stock of X from his estate. Following the death of B, A causes X to assume the contract and redeem the stock from B 's estate.

The assignment of the contract to X followed by the redemption by X of the stock owned by B's estate will result in a constructive distribution to A because immediately on the death of B, A had a primary and unconditional obligation to perform the contract.

Situation 3

All of the stock of X corporation was owned by a trust that was to terminate in 1968. Individuals A and B were the beneficiaries of the trust. Since B was the trustee of the trust, he had exclusive management authority over X through his control of the board of directors. In 1966, A paid to B the sum of 25x dollars and promised to pay an additional 20x dollars to B in 1969 for B's interest in the corpus and accumulations of the trust plus B's agreement to resign immediately as supervisor of the trust and release his control over the management of the corporation. The actual transfer of the stock held in trust was to take place on termination of the trust in 1968. In 1969, X reimbursed A for the 25x dollars previously paid to B, paid 20x dollars to B, and received the X stock held by B.

For all practical purposes, A became the owner of B's shares in 1966. Although naked legal title to the shares could not be transferred until the trust terminated in 1968, B did transfer all of his beneficial and equitable ownership of the X stock to A in exchange for an immediate payment by A of $25x$ dollars and an unconditional promise to pay an additional $20x$ dollars upon termination of the trust. The payment by X of $20x$ dollars to B and $25x$ dollars to A in 1969 constituted a constructive distribution to A in the amount of $45x$ dollars. See Schalk Chemical Company v. Commissioner, 32 T.C. 879 (1959), affirmed 304 F.2d 48 (1962).

Situation 4

A and B owned all of the outstanding stock of X corporation. A and B entered into a contract under which, if B desired to sell his X stock, A agreed to purchase the stock or to cause such stock to be purchased. If B chose to sell his X stock to any person other than A, he could do so at any time. In accordance with the terms of the contract, A caused X to redeem all of B's stock in X.

At the time of the redemption, B was free to sell his stock to A or to any other person, and A had no unconditional obligation to purchase the stock and no fixed liability to pay for the stock. Accordingly, the redemption by X did not result in a constructive distribution to A. See S.K. Ames, Inc. v. Commissioner, 46 B.T.A. 1020 (1942), acquiescence, C.B. 1942–1, 1.

Situation 5

A and B owned all of the outstanding stock of X corporation. An agreement between A and B provided that upon the death of either, X will redeem all of the X stock owned by the decedent at the time of his death. In the event that X does not redeem the shares from the estate, the agreement provided that the surviving shareholder would purchase the unredeemed shares from the decedent's estate. B died and, in accordance with the agreement, X redeemed all of the shares owned by his estate.

In this case A was only secondarily liable under the agreement between A and B. Since A was not primarily obligated to purchase the X stock from the estate of B, he received no constructive distribution when X redeemed the stock.

Situation 6

B owned all of the outstanding stock of X corporation. A and B entered into an agreement under which A was to purchase all of the X stock from B. A did not contemplate purchasing the X stock in his own name. Therefore, the contract between A and B specifically provided that it could be assigned by A to a corporation and that, if the corporation agreed to be bound by the terms, A would be released from the contract.

A organized Y corporation and assigned the stock purchase contract to it. Y borrowed funds and purchased all of the X stock from B pursuant to the agreement. Subsequently Y was merged into X and X assumed the liabilities that Y incurred in connection with the purchase of the X stock and subsequently satisfied these liabilities.

The purchase by *Y* of the stock of *X* did not result in a constructive distribution to *A*. Since *A* did not contemplate purchasing the *X* stock in his own name, he provided in the contract that it could be assigned to a corporation prior to the closing date. *A* chose this latter alternative and assigned the contract to *Y*. *A* was not personally subject to an unconditional obligation to purchase the *X* stock from *B*. See Arthur J. Kobacker and Sara Jo Kobacker, et al. v. Commissioner, 37 T.C. 882 (1962), acquiescence, C.B. 1964 2, 6. Compare Ray Edenfield v. Commissioner, 19 T.C. 13 (1952), acquiescence, C.B. 1953–1, 4.

Situation 7

A and *B* owned all of the outstanding stock of *X* corporation. An agreement between the shareholders provided that upon the death of either, the survivor would purchase the decedent's shares from his estate at a price provided in the agreement. Subsequently, the agreement was rescinded and a new agreement entered into which provided that upon the death of either *A* or *B, X* would redeem all of the decedent's shares of *X* stock from his estate.

The cancellation of the original contract between the parties in favor of the new contract did not result in a constructive distribution to either *A* or *B*. At the time *X* agreed to purchase the stock pursuant to the terms of the new agreement, neither *A* nor *B* had an unconditional obligation to purchase shares of *X* stock. The subsequent redemption of the stock from the estate of either pursuant to the terms of the new agreement will not constitute a constructive distribution to the surviving shareholder.

PROBLEM

A, B and C, who are unrelated, each own one-third of Y Corporation's outstanding common stock. The shareholders have entered into a cross-purchase agreement under which they agree that the two surviving share-holders will purchase the Y stock owned by the estate of the first share-holder to die. Y purchased a life insurance policy on the life of each shareholder and has continued to pay the annual premiums. Y is the beneficiary under the policies. B died this year, and Y used the proceeds from the policy on B's life to completely redeem the stock held by B's estate. What will be the tax consequences of these events to A, C and Y?

c.   REDEMPTIONS INCIDENT TO DIVORCE

Regulations: § 1.1041–2(a), (b), (c), (d).

Arnes v. United States

United States Court of Appeals, Ninth Circuit, 1992.
981 F.2d 456.

■ Hug, Circuit Judge:

The issue in this case is whether a taxpayer must recognize for income tax purposes the gain that she realized when, pursuant to a divorce settlement, a corporation redeemed her half of the stock in the corporation, the remaining stock of which was owned by her former husband. The district court, ruling on cross-motions for summary judgment, held that Section 1041 of the Internal Revenue Code of 1986 (I.R.C.) relieved the taxpayer of having to recognize the gain, and awarded the taxpayer a refund of $53,053 for 1988. * * * We affirm.

I.

Joann Arnes, the Taxpayer–Appellee, married John Arnes in 1970. In 1980, they formed a corporation, "Moriah," to operate a McDonald's franchise in Ellensburg, Washington. That corporation issued 5,000 shares of stock in the joint names of John Arnes and Joann Arnes. In 1987, the couple agreed to divorce. McDonald's Corporation required 100% ownership of the equity and profits by the owner/operator, and informed John Arnes that there should be no joint ownership of the restaurant after the divorce.

Joann and John Arnes entered into an agreement to have their corporation redeem Joann Arnes' 50 percent interest in the outstanding stock for $450,000. The corporation would pay that money to Joann Arnes by forgiving a debt of approximately $110,000 that she owed the corporation, by making two payments of $25,000 to her during 1988, and by paying the remainder of approximately $290,000 to her in monthly installments over ten years beginning in February 1988. The agreement was incorporated into the decree of dissolution of the marriage, dated January 7, 1988. Joann Arnes surrendered her 2,500 shares to the corporation on December 31, 1987, and the corporation cancelled her stock certificate on May 4, 1988, then issuing another 2,500 shares to John Arnes.

On her federal income tax return for 1988, Joann Arnes reported that she sold her stock in Moriah on January 2, 1988, for a price of $450,000, and that her basis was $2,500, resulting in a profit of $447,500. She received $178,042 in 1988 as part of the sales price. Using an installment method, she treated $177,045 as long-term capital gain and the remainder as recovery of a portion of her basis.

On December 27, 1989, she filed a timely claim for refund of $53,053 for 1988 on the ground that she was not required to recognize any gain on the transfer of her stock because the transfer was made pursuant to a divorce instrument. The IRS did not allow the claim for refund, and Joann Arnes initiated this suit.

The district court found that the redemption of Joann Arnes' stock in Moriah was required by a divorce instrument, and that John Arnes had benefitted from the transaction because it was part of the marital property settlement, which limited future community property claims that Joann Arnes might have brought against him. The court, in applying the IRS regulations, found that, although Joann transferred her stock directly to Moriah, the transfer was made on behalf of John and should have been treated as having been made to John. Therefore, the transfer qualified for nonrecognition of gain pursuant to the I.R.C. exemption for transfers made to spouses or former spouses incident to a divorce settlement. See 26 U.S.C. § 1041 (1988). Summary judgment was granted in favor of Joann Arnes.

The Government appeals. Meanwhile, in order to insure that the capital gain will be taxed, the Government has asserted a protective income tax deficiency against John Arnes, who has contested the deficiency by filing a petition with the Tax Court. His case is pending but not before this court. The Government maintains that, although Joann Arnes is the appropriate party to be taxed for the gain, John Arnes should be taxed if the district court's ruling is upheld. If neither John nor Joann is taxed, the $450,000 used to redeem Joann's appreciated stock apparently will be taken out of the corporation tax-free.

* * *

III.

The Government contends that the gain resulting from Moriah's redemption of Joann Arnes' stock does not qualify for exemption under section 1041, which is limited to transfers made directly to one's spouse or former spouse, or transfers made into trust for that person. Joann Arnes' transfer to Moriah, the Government contends, is outside the scope of the exemption. Joann Arnes contends that her transfer of stock to Moriah should be considered a transfer to John, resulting in a benefit to John, and absolving her of the obligation to bear the burden of any resulting tax.

* * *

The purpose of [Section 1041] is to defer the tax consequences of transfers between spouses or former spouses. See H.R.Rep. No. 432, Pt. II, 98th Cong., 2d Sess. 1491 (1984), reprinted in 1984 U.S.Code Cong. & Admin.News 697, 1134 ("a husband and wife are a single economic unit"). Property received in such a transfer is excluded from the recipient's gross income. The recipient's basis is then equal to the transferor's basis. 26 U.S.C. § 1041(b)(2)(1988). Later, when the recipient transfers the property to a third party, the gain or loss must be recognized.

After section 1041 was enacted, the Treasury Department published a temporary regulation to implement the statute. Temp. Treas. Reg. § 1.1041–1T (1992). The regulation explains that in certain cases a transfer of property to a third party "on behalf of" a spouse or former spouse should be treated as a transfer to the spouse or former spouse. Id. at Q–9, A–9. One example supplied in the regulation is the case where the transfer to the third party is required by a divorce or separation instrument. Such a transfer of property will be treated as made directly to the nontransferring spouse (or former spouse) and the nontransferring spouse will be treated as immediately transferring the property to the third party. The deemed transfer from the nontransferring spouse (or former spouse) to the third party is not a transaction that qualifies for nonrecognition of gain under section 1041. Temp.Treas.Reg. § 1.1041–1T, A–9 (1992).

The example suggests that the tax consequences of any gain or loss arising from the transaction would fall upon the nontransferring spouse for whose benefit the transfer was made, rather than upon the transferring spouse. Consistent with the policy of the statute, which is to defer recognition until the property is conveyed to a party outside the marital unit, the regulation seems to provide for shifting the tax burden from one spouse to the other, where appropriate.

Thus, a transfer by a spouse to a third party can be treated as a transfer to the other spouse when it is "on behalf of" the other spouse. Whether the redemption of Joann's stock can be construed as a transfer to John, pursuant to the regulation example in A–9, depends upon the meaning of "on behalf of." The district court interpreted the regulation as meaning that a transfer was made "on behalf of" John Arnes if he received a benefit from the transfer. The court then concluded that John did receive a benefit, because the transfer was part of the marital property agreement which settled any future community property claims that Joann Arnes could have asserted against John.

Although no case is directly on point, many tax cases concern transfers made on behalf of other persons. Generally, a transfer is considered to have been made "on behalf of" someone if it satisfied an obligation or a liability of that person. If an employer pays an employee's income tax, that payment is income to the employee. See Old Colony Trust Co. v. Commissioner, 279 U.S. 716, 729–31, 49 S.Ct. 499, 504, 73 L.Ed. 918 (1929). If a corporation assumes a shareholder's bank note in exchange for stock, the shareholder receives a taxable constructive dividend. Schroeder v. Commissioner, 831 F.2d 856, 859 (9th Cir.1987).

In *Schroeder*, the taxpayer borrowed money from a bank to buy stock in the corporation. The corporation later redeemed part of that stock, assumed the taxpayer's bank note, and forgave a debt owed by the taxpayer to the corporation. At the time that the taxpayer borrowed the money from the bank, he owned no part of the corporation and had no authority to act on behalf of the corporation. See id. at 859–60 & n. 7. The taxpayer had the primary obligation to repay the loan, and the corporation's assumption of the loan relieved the taxpayer of that obligation. We held that the redemption of Schroeder's stock was a taxable constructive dividend. Id. at 859.

The Government argues that the Arnes stock transfer is more properly analogized to Holsey v. Commissioner, 258 F.2d 865 (3d Cir.1958), where the Third Circuit held that a shareholder who owned fifty percent of the stock in a corporation did not receive a taxable benefit when the corporation redeemed the other fifty percent of the stock. The court found that the redemption "did not discharge any obligation of [the taxpayer] and did not benefit him in any direct sense," although the result was that the shareholder gained control of the company. Id. at 868.

John Arnes had an obligation to Joann Arnes that was relieved by Moriah's payment to Joann. That obligation was based in their divorce property settlement, which called for the redemption of Joann's stock. Although John and Joann were the sole stockholders in Moriah, the obligation to purchase Joann's stock was John's, not Moriah's. Furthermore, John personally guaranteed Moriah's note to Joann. Under Washington law, Joann could sue John for payment without suing Moriah. See Wash.Rev.Code Ann. § 62A.3–416(1)(West 1979). Thus, John was liable, with Moriah, for the payments due Joann.

We hold that Joann's transfer to Moriah did relieve John of an obligation, and therefore constituted a benefit to John. Joann's transfer of stock should be treated as a constructive transfer to John, who then transferred the stock to Moriah. The $450,000 was paid to Joann by Moriah on behalf of John. The transfer of $450,000 from the corporate treasury need not escape taxation, if we hold, as we do, that Joann is not required to recognize any gain on the transfer of her stock, because it is subject to section 1041. The tax result for Joann is the same as if she had conveyed the property directly to John.

The Government argues that because Joann transferred her stock to the corporation, rather than to John, the exception in section 1041 should not apply. The corporation cancelled Joann's stock and agreed to pay Joann $450,000. As a result, no asset with a carryover basis exists. John received an additional 2,500 shares from the corporation after Joann's shares were cancelled, but he did not carry over Joann's basis, because the transfer was not made directly to him. Under this literal application of the statute, Joann's gain, from the appreciation of the stock, would not be recognized by John if he were to dispose of his stock. Although John became the sole owner of the corporation as a result of the transfer, the net worth of the corporation was depleted, because the corporation incurred the debt of $450,000 to Joann. As the Government puts it, before the stock redemption, John owned half of a corporation worth $900,000; after the redemption, he owned all of a corporation worth $450,000. John has realized no gain; the value of his stock is still in the corporation, and the redemption did not increase the value of John's stock. In contrast, Joann received cash (and debt forgiveness) for her transfer of stock.

We reject the Government's application of the statute. The regulations, particularly as explained by Question and Answer 9, in Temp. Treas. Reg. § 1.1041–1T, demonstrate that the statute is meant to apply to situations such as this one, where a transfer is made on behalf of one's former spouse.

Finally, the Government points to one other example in the Temporary Treasury Regulations interpreting section 1041. Question 2 describes a situation in which a corporation wholly owned by one spouse sells property to the other spouse. That sale is not subject to the exemption rule of section 1041. See Temp. Treas. Reg. § 1.1041–1T(a), Q–2, A–2, ex. 3 (1992). The example does not apply to the Arnes transaction because Moriah was owned one-half each by John and Joann.

The judgment of the district court is AFFIRMED.

NOTE

Tax Consequences to Nontransferor Spouse. The Ninth Circuit found that the disposition of Mrs. Arnes' stock was not a redemption but rather a sale to Mr. Arnes in a tax-free transaction under Section 1041. What then are the tax consequences to Mr. Arnes, who was not a party to the case? Assuming that Moriah was a C corporation with sufficient earnings and profits, Mr. Arnes would appear to have a $450,000 constructive dividend (taxable, under current law, at a maximum rate of 15 percent but with no recovery of basis) under the Ninth Circuit's characterization of the transaction. But appearances can be deceiving. Mr. Arnes took his controversy to the Tax Court, which held in a reviewed decision that he did not have a constructive dividend because he was not primarily and unconditionally obligated to acquire his wife's stock.[1] The court supported its decision with the following example from Revenue Ruling 69–608:[2]

> A and B owned all the outstanding stock of X corporation. An agreement between A and B provided that upon the death of either, X will redeem all the X stock owned by the decedent at the time of death. In the event that X does not redeem the shares from the estate, the agreement provided that the surviving shareholder would purchase the unredeemed shares from the decedent's estate. B died and, in accordance with the agreement, X redeemed all of the shares owned by his estate.
>
> In this case A was only secondarily liable under the agreement between A and B. Since A was not primarily obligated to purchase the X stock from the estate of B he received no constructive distribution when X redeemed the stock.

As a result, neither Mr. nor Mrs. Arnes was taxable on the transaction— the dreaded "whipsaw" result that the Service was trying to avoid.

Which result was more favorable overall for the taxpayers—the Ninth Circuit's or the Tax Court's? Remember that it is usually desirable in a marital dissolution setting for the parties to plan to reduce their overall tax liability. In a concurring opinion in *Arnes*, Tax Court Judge Beghe offered this observation:[3]

> Hewing to the bright line rules of Rev. Rul. 69–608 * * * in the marital dissolution context will reduce the tax costs of divorce for the owners of small businesses held and operated in corporate form. If the shareholder spouses can negotiate their separation agreement with the assurance that the redemption will be tax free to the remaining shareholder and a capital gain transaction to the terminating shareholder, the overall tax costs will ordinarily be less than if the terminating spouse qualifies for nonrecognition under Section 1041, but the remaining spouse suffers a dividend

---

1. Arnes v. Commissioner, 102 T.C. 522 (1994). See also Blatt v. Commissioner, 102 T.C. 77 (1994)(wife taxable on redemption; no Section 1041 transfer because redemption did not satisfy any legal obligation of husband and wife was not acting "on behalf of" husband at time of acquisition); Hayes v. Commissioner, 101 T.C. 593 (1993) (redemption of wife's stock was a constructive dividend to husband where husband had a primary and unconditional obligation to purchase that stock; no Section 1041 issue before the court).

2. See supra p. 263.

3. 102 T.C. at 541.

tax. This will leave a bigger pie to be divided in setting the consideration for the share to be redeemed.

Confusion in the Courts: Inconsistent Standards. The Ninth Circuit held that Mrs. Arnes was not taxable under Section 1041 because her transfer was "on behalf of" her husband within the meaning of the Section 1041 regulations. But the Tax Court held that Mr. Arnes did not have a constructive dividend because the corporation did not satisfy his "primary and unconditional" obligation to acquire his wife's stock. So neither spouse was taxed and the Service was whipsawed because different standards were applied to the transferor and nontransferor spouse to determine the tax consequences of the same transaction.

The Tax Court has revisited this issue, but its multiple and conflicting opinions in Read v. Commissioner[4] only added to the confusion. The fact pattern in *Read* was fairly typical. Prior to their marital dissolution, Mr. and Mrs. Read owned virtually all the stock of Mulberry Motor Parts, Inc. ("MMP"), a C corporation. Mrs. Read ("W") agreed to sell her MMP stock to Mr. Read ("H") for cash and a promissory note bearing market rate interest unless H elected to cause MMP or its separate employee stock ownership plan to buy the stock on the same terms. H elected to have MMP redeem W's stock. Although W reported the interest paid by MMP on the promissory note as income, neither W nor H reported any taxable gain on the redemption. Fearing a whipsaw, the Service issued deficiency notices to both parties. But it ultimately aligned itself with W by arguing in the Tax Court that H had received a constructive dividend from MMP in the full amount of the principal and interest payments received by W.

The Tax Court majority viewed the central issue to be whether W's transfer of MMP stock to MMP was made "on behalf of H" so that W was entitled to nonrecognition of gain under the Section 1041 regulations.[5] W argued that the regulations squarely applied to her situation, while H, seeking to avoid a constructive dividend, relied on established case law in arguing that he should not be taxed because he never had a "primary and unconditional obligation" to purchase W's stock.

The Tax Court majority sided with W, holding for the first time that application of the venerable "primary and unconditional" standard to the nontransferor spouse was inappropriate in divorce-related redemptions. Instead, the majority based its decision on the Section 1041 regulations in holding that W's transfer of MMP stock to MMP was a transfer made "on behalf of" H. The court found that H's election to have MMP redeem W's stock caused W to be acting as H's representative in connection with the redemption. In light of these holdings, the majority sustained the deficiencies asserted against H, noting that H had "indicated" that he would be taxable if the court found that W was entitled to nonrecognition under Section 1041. Because it found H's "indication" as tantamount to a concession, the Tax Court majority offered no analysis of the proper standard to be applied to the nonredeeming spouse. As discussed earlier in

4. 114 T.C. 14 (2000).   **5.** See Reg. § 1.1041–1T(c), Q & A–9.

this Note, however, the Tax Court previously had applied the "primary and unconditional" standard in holding that a nontransferor spouse does not invariably receive a constructive dividend in a divorce-related redemption.

Nine judges joined the majority opinion in *Read*; six of the nine wrote a concurring opinion with more extensive analysis of the unfavorable tax consequences to H. Seven judges dissented in four separate opinions. Despite differences in emphasis, the essence of the dissents was that the majority should not have discarded the "primary and unconditional" standard in the divorce setting. Armed with these forceful dissents and a trickle of commentary critical of the majority's opinion,[6] Mr. Read and MMP[7] appealed to the Eleventh Circuit, arguing that the Tax Court erred by recasting MMP's redemption of Mrs. Read's stock as a constructive dividend to Mr. Read.

Regulations to the Rescue. Reacting to the confusion in the courts, the Service amended the Section 1041 regulations to provide greater certainty in determining the tax consequences of divorce-related redemptions. Unlike the Tax Court majority in *Read*, the regulations seek to harmonize the well recognized "primary and unconditional obligation" standard for constructive dividends with the policy of Section 1041.

The threshold question posed by the regulations is whether a divorce-related redemption results in a constructive distribution to the nontransferor spouse under applicable tax law. For this purpose, "applicable tax law" means the primary and unconditional obligation standard.[8] If the redemption does result in a constructive distribution, the redeemed stock is deemed to have been transferred by the transferor spouse to the nontransferor spouse in a tax-free Section 1041 transaction (provided the requirements of Section 1041 are otherwise met), and then retransferred by the nontransferor spouse to the redeeming corporation.[9] The tax consequences of the deemed redemption are then determined under Section 302.[10] As a result, the transferor spouse has no gain or loss on the deemed transfer of stock to the nontransferor spouse, and the nontransferor spouse most likely has a constructive dividend.[11]

If the redemption does not result in a constructive distribution—e.g., because it does not satisfy a primary and unconditional obligation of the nontransferor spouse—the regulations respect the form of the transac-

---

6. See Kalinka, *"C.M. Read and the Tax Consequences of Divorce–Related Redemptions,"* 78 Taxes 21 (2000); Raby & Raby, "Confusion Surrounds Stock Redemptions Incident to Divorce," 86 Tax Notes 1121 (2000).

7. MMP was a party to the case because the Service disallowed corporate-level deductions for interest paid on MMP's to Mrs. Read on the ground that they were constructive dividends to Mr. Read. As this book went to press, no decision had yet been issued on the appeal.

8. Reg. § 1.1041–2(a), (d) Examples 1 & 3.

9. Reg. § 1.1041–2(a)(2), –2(b)(2).

10. Reg. § 1.1041–2(b)(2).

11. Whether or not the constructive distribution is a dividend depends on whether the corporation has earnings and profits and whether any of the tests for exchange treatment in Section 302 are met (unlikely in the typical fact pattern).

tion.[12] That means that the corporation is treated as having redeemed stock directly from the transferor spouse in a transaction in which the non-transferor spouse is not a party. As a result, Section 1041 does not apply, the transferor spouse's tax treatment is determined under Section 302 (likely a capital gain), and the nontransferor spouse is not taxed.[13]

The regulations provide a "special rule" permitting spouses to depart from "applicable tax law" and treat a divorce-related redemption as either taxable to the transferor spouse (even if it would have been a constructive dividend to the nontransferor spouse under applicable tax law) or as a constructive distribution to the nontransferor spouse and a tax-free Section 1041 transfer to the transferor spouse (even in the absence of a primary and unconditional obligation).[14] This rule is consistent with the general policy allowing the parties to a divorce to negotiate and ultimately determine the tax consequences of divorce-related transactions (e.g., spousal and child support payments, property transfers, dependency exemptions) as long as they treat the transactions consistently. To utilize the special rule, the parties must memorialize their intent in a written agreement prior to the date on which the nontransferor spouse files his or her first timely filed federal income tax return for the year that includes the date of the stock redemption but no later than the due date of the return (including extensions).[15]

If the regulations had applied to the redemption in the *Arnes* case and the parties had not elected to utilize the special rule, which spouse would have been taxed?

Planning. In light of these permissive regulations, how should the parties plan a divorce-related redemption? For example, how should a redemption be structured if the parties wish to minimize their overall joint tax liability and preserve more dollars for the family? What is the best advice to a transferor or nontransferor spouse who wishes to avoid tax on the redemption? In what circumstances would the parties wish to invoke the "special rule?" Is it still possible, either through separate or joint planning, to structure a redemption so that neither spouse is taxed? Do the regulations eliminate all legal controversies over the proper tax treatment of divorce-related redemptions?

3. CHARITABLE CONTRIBUTION AND REDEMPTION

Grove v. Commissioner

United States Court of Appeals, Second Circuit, 1973.
490 F.2d 241.

■ KAUFMAN, CHIEF JUDGE:

We are called upon, once again, to wrestle with the tangled web that is the Internal Revenue Code and decipher the often intricate and ingenious

12.	Reg. § 1.1041–2(a)(1).	**14.**	Reg. § 1.1041–2(c).
13.	Reg. § 1.1041–2(b)(1).	**15.**	Reg. § 1.1041–2(c)(3).

strategies devised by taxpayers to minimize their tax burdens. We undertake this effort mindful that taxpayer ingenuity, although channelled into an effort to reduce or eliminate the incidence of taxation, is ground for neither legal nor moral opprobrium. As Learned Hand so eloquently stated, "any one may so arrange his affairs that his taxes shall be as low as possible: he is not bound to choose that pattern which will best pay the Treasury: there is not even a patriotic duty to increase one's taxes * * *." Helvering v. Gregory, 69 F.2d 809, 810 (2d Cir.1934), aff'd 293 U.S. 465, 55 S.Ct. 266, 79 L.Ed. 596 (1935).

* * *

I.

A full recitation of the undisputed facts underlying this controversy will aid in placing the legal issues raised on appeal in their proper context.

Philip Grove received an engineering degree in 1924 from Rensselaer Polytechnic Institute, a private, tax-exempt educational institution. During the Depression, he founded what is now Grove Shepherd Wilson & Kruge, Inc. and at all times since has controlled a majority of its shares. The balance of the Corporation's shares, with the exception of those held by RPI, are owned by officers and employees of the Corporation or their relatives.

The Corporation's business is building airfields, highways, tunnels, canals, and other similar heavy construction projects in both the United States and foreign countries. These projects usually involve the investment of large sums of money over an extended period of time and involve a high degree of risk. Since, in this industry, contract payments normally are made only after specified levels of progress are achieved, a firm must always commit substantial amounts of its own funds, whether borrowed or internally generated, to a project. Moreover, a company can determine an acceptable contract price based only on its best estimate of the cost to complete the project. A bad "guess" or unforeseen contingency may require a firm to complete a project while incurring a loss. Not surprisingly, the mortality rate in this industry is high. To protect against such adverse developments, successful firms seek to maintain liquidity by holding ample cash or other assets easily converted to cash. One method of conserving cash, adopted by the Corporation, is to retain all earnings and refrain from paying dividends.

As we have noted, RPI, like all universities and colleges, pursued its alumni with a wide variety of contribution plans. One plan employed "life income funds," and its terms were simple. An alumnus would make a gift of securities to RPI and retain a life interest in the income from the donated securities. Whatever dividends and interest were paid during the donor's life would belong to the donor, while any capital appreciation would inure to RPI. Upon the death of the donor, RPI would obtain full title to the securities.

In 1954, Dr. Livingston Houston, RPI's president, suggested to Grove that he make a gift under the "life income funds" plan. Grove explained that his only significant holdings were shares of his own corporation, but expressed a willingness to donate some of these shares under the plan, with certain qualifications. The Corporation, he stated, could not agree to any obligation or understanding to redeem shares held by RPI. This condition, of course, stemmed from a fear that RPI might seek redemption at a time when the Corporation was hard pressed for cash, which, as we have noted, was an asset crucial to a company in the heavy construction business. Moreover, since Grove at that time was unsure of RPI's money-management qualifications, he further conditioned his gift on a requirement that if RPI disposed of the shares, any proceeds would be invested and managed by an established professional firm.

RPI found these terms acceptable and on December 30, 1954, Grove made an initial gift of 200 shares, valued at $25,560. A letter accompanying the donation set forth the conditions we have recited. Moreover, in addition to retaining an interest in the income from the gift for his life, Grove specified that in the event he should predecease his wife Harriet, she would receive the income until her death.

On the same day, the Corporation and RPI signed a minority shareholder agreement. RPI agreed not to "sell, transfer, give, pledge or hypothecate, or in any way dispose of the whole or any part of the common stock of the Corporation now or hereafter owned * * * until [RPI] shall have first offered the Corporation the opportunity to purchase said shares upon the terms and conditions hereinafter provided." The redemption price was established at book value of the shares as noted on the Corporation's most recent certified financial statement prior to the offer. Pursuant to the contract, the Corporation was "entitled (but not obligated) to purchase all or any part of the shares of stock so offered." If the Corporation did not exercise its option to purchase within sixty days, RPI could transfer the shares to any other party and the Corporation's right of first refusal would not subsequently attach to such transferred shares.[3]

The 1954 gift was the first in a series of annual contributions to RPI by Grove. From 1954 to 1968, Grove donated to RPI between 165 and 250 shares of the Corporation each year, reaching a cumulative total of 2,652 shares, subject to terms substantially similar to those noted earlier.

Generally, RPI offered donated shares to the Corporation for redemption, between one and two years after they were donated by Grove. The transactions followed a similar pattern. On each occasion, the Finance Committee of RPI's Board of Trustees first authorized the sale of specific shares of the Corporation. RPI's treasurer or controller would then write to Sidney Houck, the Corporation's treasurer, informing him of RPI's desire to dispose of the shares. Upon receipt of this letter, Houck would call a

---

3. Other minority shareholders of the Corporation signed similar agreements, which, in effect put in writing the Corporation's practice of redeeming, when financial conditions permitted, any minority-owner shares offered to it, for example, by a departing employee or a deceased employee's widow.

special meeting of the Corporation's board of directors to consider whether or not to exercise the Corporation's right of first refusal. The Board would adopt a resolution authorizing redemption and Houck would so inform RPI's financial officer, enclosing a company check for the amount due. By return mail, RPI would forward the appropriate stock certificate to the Corporation for cancellation.

At the time of the first redemption, in December, 1955, RPI opened an investment account at the Albany, New York, office of Merrill Lynch, Pierce, Fenner & Beane ("Merrill Lynch"). The account was captioned "Rensselaer Polytechnic Institute (Philip H. Grove Fund) Account." In accordance with Grove's wishes concerning the management of disposition proceeds, RPI authorized Merrill Lynch to act directly upon investment recommendations made by Scudder, Stevens, & Clark, Grove's personal investment adviser. RPI deposited the proceeds of each redemption transaction into this account which, pursuant to Scudder, Stevens & Clark's instructions, were generally invested in securities of large corporations whose shares traded on organized stock exchanges. Merrill Lynch paid the income from these investments to RPI on a monthly basis. RPI, in turn, made quarterly remittances to Grove, accompanied by an analysis of all account transactions.

On his personal income tax return for 1963, Grove reported as taxable income dividends of $4,939.28 and interest of $2,535.73 paid to him by RPI from the Merrill Lynch account. For 1964, Grove reported $6,096.05 in dividends and $3,540.81 in interest. The Commissioner, however, assessed deficiencies in Grove's taxable income for these years, asserting that Grove "realized additional dividends in the amounts of $29,000 and $25,800 in 1963 and 1964, respectively, as the result of the redemption of stock by Grove Shepherd Wilson & Kruge, Inc." Accordingly, the Commissioner increased Grove's taxable income by these amounts and demanded payment of additional taxes—in excess of $13,000 for each year. Grove refused to pay and petitioned the Tax Court for a redetermination of his tax liability. The Court, concluding that Grove had made a bona fide gift to RPI, ruled in favor of the taxpayer and the Commissioner appealed.

II.

The Commissioner's view of this case is relatively simple. In essence, we are urged to disregard the actual form of the Grove–RPI–Corporation donations and redemptions and to rewrite the actual events so that Grove's tax liability is seen in a wholly different light. Support for this position, it is argued, flows from the Supreme Court's decision in Commissioner of Internal Revenue v. Court Holding Co., 324 U.S. 331, 65 S.Ct. 707, 89 L.Ed. 981 (1945), which, in language familiar to law students, cautions that "[t]he incidence of taxation depends upon the substance of a transaction * * *. To permit the true nature of a transaction to be disguised by mere formalisms, which exist solely to alter tax liabilities, would seriously impair the effective administration of the tax policies of Congress." Id. at 334, 65 S.Ct. at 708. In an effort to bring the instant case within this language, the

Commissioner insists that whatever the appearance of the transactions here under consideration, their "true nature" is quite different. He maintains that Grove, with the cooperation of RPI, withdrew substantial funds from the Corporation and manipulated them in a manner designed to produce income for his benefit. In the Commissioner's view, the transaction is properly characterized as a redemption by the Corporation of Grove's, not RIP's shares, followed by a cash gift to RPI by Grove. This result, it is said, more accurately reflects "economic reality."

The Commissioner's motives for insisting upon this formulation are easily understood once its tax consequences are examined. Although Grove reported taxable dividends and interest received from the Merrill Lynch account on his 1963 and 1964 tax returns, amounts paid by the Corporation to redeem the donated shares from RPI were not taxed upon distribution. If, however, the transactions are viewed in the manner suggested by the Commissioner, the redemption proceeds would be taxable as income to Grove. Moreover, because the redemptions did not in substance alter Grove's relationship to the Corporation—he continued throughout to control a majority of the outstanding shares—the entire proceeds would be taxed as a dividend payment at high, progressive ordinary-income rates, rather than as a sale of shares, at the fixed, and relatively low, capital gains rate. See, 26 U.S.C. § 302; United States v. Davis, 397 U.S. 301, 90 S.Ct. 1041, 25 L.Ed.2d 323 (1970).

Clearly, then, the stakes involved are high. We do not quarrel with the maxim that substance must prevail over form, but this proposition marks the beginning, not the end, of our inquiry. The court in Sheppard v. United States, 361 F.2d 972, 176 Ct.Cl. 244 (1966) perceptively remarked that "all such 'maxims' should rather be called 'minims' since they convey a minimum of information with a maximum of pretense." Id. at 977 n. 9. Each case requires detailed consideration of its unique facts. Here, our aim is to determine whether Grove's gifts of the Corporation's shares to RPI prior to redemption should be given independent significance or whether they should be regarded as meaningless intervening steps in a single, integrated transaction designed to avoid tax liability by the use of mere formalisms.

The guideposts for our analysis are well marked by earlier judicial encounters with this problem. "The law with respect to gifts of appreciated property is well established. A gift of appreciated property does not result in income to the donor so long as he gives the property away absolutely and parts with title thereto before the property gives rise to income by way of sale." Carrington v. Commissioner of Internal Revenue, 476 F.2d 704, 708 (5th Cir.1973), quoting Humacid Co., 42 T.C. 894, 913 (1964). As noted below by the Tax Court, the Commissioner here "does not contend that the gifts of stock by [Grove] to RPI in 1961 and 1962 were sham transactions, or that they were not completed gifts when made." If Grove made a valid, binding, and irrevocable gift of the Corporation's shares to RPI, it would be the purest fiction to treat the redemption proceeds as having actually been received by Grove. The Tax Court concluded that the gift was complete and irrevocable when made. The Commissioner conceded as much and we so find.[9]

It is argued, however, that notwithstanding the conceded validity of the gifts, other circumstances establish that Grove employed RPI merely as a convenient conduit for withdrawing funds from the Corporation for his personal use without incurring tax liability. The Commissioner would have us infer from the systematic nature of the gift-redemption cycle that Grove and RPI reached a mutually beneficial understanding: RPI would permit Grove to use its tax-exempt status to drain funds from the Corporation in return for a donation of a future interest in such funds.

We are not persuaded by this argument and the totality of the facts and circumstances lead us to a contrary conclusion. Grove testified before the Tax Court concerning the circumstances of these gifts. The court, based on the evidence and the witnesses' credibility, specifically found that "[t]here was no informal agreement between [Grove] and RPI that RPI would offer the stock in question to the corporation for redemption or that, if offered, the corporation would redeem it." Findings of fact by the Tax Court, like those of the district court, are binding upon us unless they are clearly erroneous, 26 U.S.C. § 7482(a); Rule 52, F.R.Civ.P., and "the rule * * * applies also to factual inferences [drawn] from undisputed basic facts." Commissioner of Internal Revenue v. Duberstein, 363 U.S. 278, 291, 80 S.Ct. 1190, 1200, 4 L.Ed.2d 1218 (1960). It cannot seriously be contended that the Tax Court's findings here are "clearly erroneous" and no tax liability can be predicated upon a nonexistent agreement between Grove and RPI or by a fictional one created by the Commissioner.

Grove, of course, owned a substantial majority of the Corporation's shares. His vote alone was sufficient to insure redemption of any shares offered by RPI. But such considerations, without more, are insufficient to permit the Commissioner to ride roughshod over the actual understanding found by the Tax Court to exist between the donor and the donee. Behrend v. United States (4th Cir.1972), 73–1 USTC ¶ 9123, is particularly instructive. There, two brothers donated preferred shares of a corporation jointly controlled by them to a charitable foundation over which they also exercised control. The preferred shares were subsequently redeemed from the foundation by the corporation and the Commissioner sought to tax the redemption as a corporate dividend payment to the brothers. The court, in denying liability, concluded that although "it was understood that the corporation would at intervals take up the preferred according to its financial ability * * *, this factor did not convert into a constructive

---

9. The Commissioner might have argued that at least that portion of the redemption proceeds allocable to Grove's retained life income interest was taxable as a dividend. He chose not to do so and the Tax Court "express[ed] no opinion upon the question, if it were properly presented, whether petition- er derived taxable income upon the redemption of stock to the extent of the life estate which he retained * * *." Since the Commissioner has bypassed this aspect, it would be inappropriate in our discussions of the gifts to attach any special significance to the retained life interest feature.

dividend the proceeds of the redemption * * * [because] the gifts were absolutely perfected before the corporation redeemed the stock." Id.

Nothing in the December, 1954, minority shareholder agreement between the Corporation and RPI serves as a basis for disturbing the conclusion of the Tax Court. Although the Corporation desired a right of first refusal on minority shares—understandably so, in order to reduce the possibility of unrelated, outside ownership interests—it assumed no obligation to redeem any shares so offered. In the absence of such an obligation, the Commissioner's contention that Grove's initial donation was only the first step in a prearranged series of transactions is little more than wishful thinking grounded in a shaky foundation. * * *

We are not so naive as to believe that tax considerations played no role in Grove's planning. But foresight and planning do not transform a non-taxable event into one that is taxable. Were we to adopt the Commissioner's view, we would be required to recast two actual transactions—a gift by Grove to RPI and a redemption from RPI by the Corporation—into two completely fictional transactions—a redemption from Grove by the Corporation and a gift by Grove to RPI. Based upon the facts as found by the Tax Court, we can discover no basis for elevating the Commissioner's "form" over that employed by the taxpayer in good faith. "Useful as the step transaction doctrine may be in the interpretation of equivocal contracts and ambiguous events, it cannot generate events which never took place just so an additional tax liability might be asserted." Sheppard v. United States, supra, at 978. In the absence of any supporting facts in the record we are unable to adopt the Commissioner's view; to do so would be to engage in a process of decision that is arbitrary, capricious and ultimately destructive of traditional notions of judicial review. We decline to embark on such a course.

Accordingly, the judgment of the Tax Court is affirmed.

■ OAKES, CIRCUIT JUDGE (dissenting):

Review of the tax consequences of a business transaction requires consideration of the economic realities of the entire transaction. See Gregory v. Helvering, 293 U.S. 465, 55 S.Ct. 266, 79 L.Ed. 596 (1935); South Bay Corp. v. Commissioner of Internal Revenue, 345 F.2d 698, 703, 705 (2d Cir.1965). Whether a transaction should be viewed as two or more steps or as one integrated transaction may result in entirely different tax consequences. * * *

Here, as I see it, the form of the transaction was two-step: a gift of stock followed by a redemption of the stock by the donor controlled corporation. The substance of the transaction, however, was a payment out of corporate earnings and profits to a charity designated by the donor who retained a life interest in the gift.

The factors which distinguish the RPI–Grove transactions from other charitable donations of securities and which persuade me to treat this as an integrated transaction are two: first, the gifts made by the Groves were of stock in a closed corporation that was inevitably redeemed annually;

second, by virtue of retaining a life income from the reinvested proceeds and by retaining a measure of control over how those proceeds should be reinvested (by designating the investment adviser who was also the Groves' personal adviser), the Groves were able to achieve a bail-out from their non-dividend-paying closed corporation.

* * *

The majority opinion relies heavily on two cases which I believe are readily distinguishable from the situation here. One is Carrington v. Commissioner of Internal Revenue, 476 F.2d 704 (5th Cir.1973), relied on for the proposition that "[a] gift of appreciated property does not result in income to the donor so long as he gives the property away absolutely and parts with title before the property gives rise to income by way of sale." Here the Groves did not part with all interest in the construction company stock. The reservation of a life interest in the stock (or its reinvested proceeds), when coupled with taxpayer's right, however indirect, to direct the manner in which proceeds would be invested, gave the Groves a very great continuing interest and control, a fact of not inconsiderable tax significance. Cf. Corliss v. Bowers, 281 U.S. 376, 378, 50 S.Ct. 336, 74 L.Ed. 916 (1930) (Holmes, J.) ("taxation is not so much concerned with the refinements of title as it is with actual command over the property taxed. * * * "). More importantly, Carrington involved only one contribution of stock and one redemption; there was no pattern of redemption of stock as was clearly established here at least by the time of the tax years in question.

In Behrend v. United States, CCH 1973 Stand.Fed.Tax Rep. ¶ 9123 (4th Cir.1972), also relied upon by the majority, the proceeds of the redemption were used wholly for the benefit of the charitable foundation which was the recipient of the stock; there was no life estate reserved for the personal benefit of the donors. See 1973 Stand.Fed.Tax Rep. ¶ 9123 at 80,067 ("[P]redominant force" in Behrend decision is "indisputable fact" that the taxpayers therein "did not participate whatsoever in the beneficence of the foundation").

Thus, I believe that when, as here, the nature and conditions of the charitable gift and the pattern of donor-charity behavior are such as to make it for all practical purposes inevitable that the stock given will be offered for redemption and accepted by the closely held corporation, resulting in providing the equivalent of a safe pension fund for the donor stockholders, then the transaction must be treated as a distribution of dividends under §§ 301(a), 301(c) and 316(a) of the Internal Revenue Code of 1954. The majority opinion refers to an "absence of any supporting facts in the record" for the Commissioner's position, but omits to rely upon the one most important fact on which the case should turn: the pattern of redemption over years of giving. I accordingly dissent.

NOTE

The *Grove* case illustrates an effective charitable giving technique for the shareholders of a closely held corporation. After losing several similar cases, the Service stopped challenging "charitable bailouts," announcing in Revenue Ruling 78–197[1] that a charitable contribution of stock followed by a redemption would be treated as a dividend to the donor only if the donee is legally bound or can be compelled by the corporation to surrender the shares for redemption.[2] Although they may not be legally obligated to do so, most charities will be highly motivated to offer the shares for redemption in order to convert the stock into a more liquid and diversified investment.

One desirable aspect of the transaction in *Grove* was Mr. Grove's ability to retain a life income interest in a diversified portfolio managed by his personal investment advisor. This format is no longer available to the philanthropic shareholder unless certain additional requirements are met. In general, a donor who wishes to retain a life income interest in contributed property will not qualify for charitable income and gift tax deductions unless the gift is made to a qualified charitable remainder annuity trust or unitrust or a pooled income fund.[3]

PROBLEMS

Philanthropist ("P") owns 25,000 shares of Family Corporation. The fair market value of P's Family stock is $2,500,000 ($100 per share); P's basis is $25,000 ($1 per share). Family has 100,000 shares of common stock (its only class) outstanding; the remaining shares are owned by P's spouse and children. Family has ample accumulated earnings and profits. The Family bylaws require all shareholders to grant the corporation a right of first refusal to buy their stock at fair market value before the shares are offered for sale to an outsider, but the corporation is not required to redeem the stock.

On the occasion of his 25th college reunion, P wishes to make a $100,000 contribution to State University ("SU"). Consider the tax consequences of the following alternative plans:

(a) Family Corporation distributes $100,000 to P in redemption of 1,000 shares of stock. P then contributes $100,000 to SU.

(b) P contributes 1,000 shares of Family stock to SU. Two months later, pursuant to an oral understanding, Family distributes $100,000 to SU in redemption of its 1,000 shares. SU was not legally obligated to surrender the shares for redemption.

(c) Same as (b), above, except that P contributes 250 shares of Family stock to SU in each of the four years following his reunion.

---

1. 1978–1 C.B. 83.

2. See also Palmer v. Commissioner, 62 T.C. 684 (1974), affirmed on another issue, 523 F.2d 1308 (8th Cir.1975), where the gift was made to a private foundation controlled by the taxpayer. The Service, however, may continue to challenge transactions where the donated property is later reacquired by the donor, or where the charity uses the redemption proceeds to acquire other property from the donor, pursuant to an informal prearranged understanding. See Blake v. Commissioner, 697 F.2d 473 (2d Cir.1982).

3. See I.R.C. §§ 170(f)(2), (3); 664; 2522(c)(2).

(Assume that the value of the stock was $100 per share throughout this period.) Two months after each contribution, Family distributes $25,000 to SU in redemption of the 250 shares.

G.   REDEMPTIONS THROUGH RELATED CORPORATIONS

Code: § 304 (except § 304(b)(3)(C), (D), (b)(4)).

Regulations: § 1.304–2(a), (c) Examples (1) & (3), –3(a).

Section 304 is an intricate statutory watchdog designed to prevent an end run around Sections 301 and 302. Despite its complexity, the basic purpose of Section 304—to prevent controlling shareholders from claiming basis recovery and capital gain treatment on transactions that result in a "bailout" of corporate earnings without a significant reduction in control—can be illustrated by a simple example. Assume that Shareholder A owns all of the common stock (the only class outstanding) of X Corporation and Y Corporation, and both corporations have ample earnings and profits. Having read the *Davis* case, A knows that a redemption of either her X or Y stock will result in a dividend and no recovery of basis. But what if A sells some of her X shares to Y or vice versa? Because this is a "sale" rather than a redemption or a distribution, A hopes to extract cash while enjoying exchange treatment, but in substance A's "sale" is indistinguishable from a dividend. Section 304 ensures this result by requiring shareholder sales involving "brother-sister" and "parent-subsidiary" corporations to satisfy one of the tests in Section 302 in order to qualify for capital gain status and recovery of basis.

Section 304 is yet another area where the tax stakes are less significant as long as dividends and long-term capital gains are taxed at the same preferential rates. As with conventional redemptions and other transactions to be studied later in this text, the importance of dividend classification will depend on variables such as the basis of the stock and the type of shareholder (individual vs. corporate) involved.

Brother-Sister Acquisitions. Section 304(a)(1) applies when one or more persons who are in "control" of each of two corporations transfer stock of one corporation (the "issuing corporation") to the other (the "acquiring corporation") in exchange for cash or other property.[1] "Control" for this purpose is defined as at least 50 percent ownership of either the corporate voting power or of the total value of all classes of stock.[2]

---

1. For this purpose, "property" does not include stock of the acquiring corporation. I.R.C. § 317(a). See Bhada v. Commissioner, 892 F.2d 39 (6th Cir.1989).

2. I.R.C. § 304(c)(1). In determining control, the Section 318 attribution rules are applicable with certain modifications relating to shareholder-corporation attribution. I.R.C. § 304(c)(3). In the case of a corporation with more than one class of stock, the value prong of the "control" test is applied to the aggregate value of all classes of stock, not class-by-class. Rev.Rul. 89–57, 1989–1 C.B. 90. Thus, a shareholder who owns 50 percent or more of the value of all the corporation's stock has "control" even if that shareholder owns less than 50 percent of a particular class.

If Section 304(a)(1) applies, Congress devised an intricate method to test the "sale" for dividend equivalence. Returning to the example, when A sells X Corporation stock to Y Corporation for cash, she is treated as having received a distribution of cash in redemption of Y stock (Y being the "acquiring corporation").[3] This hypothetical distribution is then tested under Section 302(b) standards to determine whether A may treat the transaction as an exchange. Dividend equivalence is tested by reference to A's stock ownership of X (the "issuing corporation"—i.e., the company whose stock is sold) before and after the transaction.[4]

In the example, A owned 100 percent of the X stock before the sale to Y. After the sale, A continued to own 100 percent of the stock directly and constructively by virtue of her ownership of Y. Since the sale does not reduce A's interest in X, it fails to satisfy any of the Section 302(b) tests for exchange treatment and thus will be treated as a Section 301 distribution from Y to A. In determining the amount of the distribution that is a dividend, Section 304(b)(2) requires the transaction to be treated as a dividend to A by Y (the "acquiring corporation") to the extent of its earnings and profits and then by X (the "issuing corporation") to the extent of its earnings and profits. Thus, the earnings and profits of both corporations are available to characterize the distribution to A as a dividend.[5]

Parent-Subsidiary Acquisitions. Section 304(a)(2) applies similar principles when a controlled subsidiary acquires stock of its parent from a shareholder of the parent in return for property. The parent-subsidiary relationship is defined by the same 50 percent "control" test described above.[6] The "property" used to make the acquisition is treated as a distribution in redemption of the parent's stock for purposes of testing dividend equivalency under Section 302.[7] If the redemption fails to qualify as an exchange and thus is treated as a Section 301 distribution, the amount and source of any dividend is first determined by reference to the earnings and profits of the acquiring (subsidiary) corporation and then, if necessary, by the earnings and profits of the issuing (parent) corporation.[8] If the constructive redemption is treated as an exchange, the selling shareholders recognize gain or loss under normal tax principles.

---

3. To the extent that the distribution is treated as a distribution to which Section 301 applies, A is treated as having transferred the X stock to Y (the acquiring corporation) in exchange for Y stock in a tax-free Section 351(a) transaction, and then Y is treated as having redeemed the Y stock that it (hypothetically) issued in the deemed Section 351 transaction. I.R.C. § 304(a)(1); Prop. Reg. § 1.304–2(a)(3). If the distribution is treated as an exchange under Section 302(a), Y is treated as purchasing the stock of X. See S. Rep. No. 99–313, 99th Cong., 2d Sess. 1048 (1986); Prop. Reg. § 1.304–2(a)(4). These deemed transactions are relevant in determining the basis consequences to the parties. See infra notes 11–12 and accompanying text.

4. I.R.C. § 304(b)(1). Once again, modified Section 318 corporation-to-shareholder (and vice versa) attribution rules apply in measuring the effect of this hypothetical transaction on A's interest in X. Id.

5. I.R.C. § 304(b)(2).

6. I.R.C. § 304(c)(1).

7. I.R.C. § 304(b)(1).

8. I.R.C. § 304(b)(2).

If a transaction is both a brother-sister and a parent-subsidiary acquisition, the parent-subsidiary rules take precedence.[9] But because the attribution rules transform most actual brother and sister corporations into a constructive parent and subsidiary, the regulations provide that an actual brother-sister relationship takes precedence over a constructive parent-subsidiary affiliation, causing Section 304(a)(1) to govern acquisitions by related nonsubsidiary corporations.[10]

Collateral Tax Consequences. In the basic Section 304(a)(1) brother-sister acquisition where the amount paid is treated as a Section 301 distribution, A is deemed to have transferred the X stock to Y in exchange for Y stock in a Section 351(a) transaction. Y thus takes a transferred basis from A in the X stock under Section 362, and A's basis in the Y stock received in the deemed Section 351 exchange is equal to A's basis in the X stock that A actually transferred to X.[11] Under the current regulations, A's basis in the Y stock is decreased on the subsequent deemed distribution of Y stock only if part of the distribution is applied against the Y stock's basis under Section 301(c)(2). The proposed regulations discussed earlier in connection with actual redemptions would produce a different result. Those regulations generally treat the unutilized basis in the hypothetical Y stock treated as redeemed by Y as a deferred loss recognized by A at the time of the deemed redemption but not taken into account until a later time (the "final inclusion date"), such as a complete termination of A's interest in the issuing corporation or A's death, or when A sells part of the stock (of which corporation?) at a gain to the extent of that gain (the "accelerated loss inclusion date").[12] The reduction in earnings and profits resulting from any dividend logically should follow the ordering rules in Section 304(b)(2)—i.e., first reduce the acquiring corporation's earnings and profits insofar as they are the source of the dividend and then, if necessary, reduce the issuing corporation's earnings and profits.

If Section 304(a)(1) applies and A's sale of X Corporation stock to Y Corporation is treated as an exchange under Section 302(a), Y is treated as having acquired the X stock by purchase and it thus takes a cost basis under Section 1012, and A's original basis in his Y stock remains unchanged.[13] The theory, based on various fictional transactions (i.e., A is deemed to receive Y stock in exchange for X stock and then Y is deemed to redeem that Y stock from A for cash or other property) is that A "sold" Y stock (to Y) with a basis equal to the basis of the X stock actually transferred by A to Y. As in any actual sale or exchange, the basis of the (hypothetical) Y stock "sold" by A is fully recovered in determining gain or

---

9. I.R.C. § 304(a)(1).

10. Reg. § 1.304–2(c) Example (1).

11. I.R.C. § 304(a)(1). See Prop. Reg. § 1.304–2(a)(3). Reg. § 1.304–2(a) and (c) Example (1) reach the same result using a different approach based on the statute before it was amended in 1997.

12. Prop. Reg. §§ 1.304–2(a)(3), –2(c) Example 2; 1.302–5. Similar rules apply to parent-subsidiary redemptions. See Prop. Reg. § 1.304–3(a).

13. Prop. Reg. § 1.304–2(a)(4).

loss on the sale, and thus A's basis in her Y stock is the same as it was before the transaction.[14]

In the brother-sister scenario where the redemption is treated as an exchange, any reduction of earnings and profits is limited by Section 312(n)(7) to an amount not in excess of the redeemed stock's ratable share of earnings and profits.[15] The more difficult question is *which* corporation's earnings and profits? The Code and regulations are silent on this technical teaser. Possibilities include the acquiring corporation's (the transaction is treated as a constructive redemption of acquiring corporation stock and the distributed "property" comes from that entity), the issuing corporation's (the redemption is tested by reference to its stock), neither (the transaction is simply a purchase, not a reduction of either corporation's wealth), or both (pro rata?).[16] One defensible answer is that the required reduction should be made first to the acquiring corporation's earnings and profits and, if necessary, then to the issuing corporation's earnings and profits.

The collateral tax consequences of a parent-subsidiary acquisition are also not entirely settled. If the constructive redemption of the parent's stock is treated as a dividend, the selling shareholder's basis in the parent stock transferred to the subsidiary is added to the basis in the shareholder's remaining parent stock under the current regulations. Under the proposed regulations dealing with actual redemptions, the shareholder is treated as recognizing a deferred loss that may be taken into account at a later time.[17] The subsidiary takes a cost basis in the parent stock that it acquires.[18] Tracking Section 304(b)(2), it is logical to first reduce the acquiring subsidiary's earnings and profits to the extent they are the source of the dividend and then move on, if necessary, to reduce the parent's earnings and profits. If the redemption is treated as an exchange, the selling shareholder recovers his basis in the transferred parent stock and recognizes capital gain or loss under normal tax principles. The subsidiary takes a cost basis in the acquired parent stock. If the constructive redemption is treated as an exchange, Section 312(n)(7) again should apply, but it is unclear which corporation's earnings and profits are reduced, leaving taxpayers to apply any reasonable approach.

Coordination with Section 351. Enactment of an intricate statute such as Section 304 inevitably whets the appetite of tax lawyers. Consider the sole shareholder of a profitable company with a desire for cash and a distaste for dividends at a time when dividends were taxed at much higher rates than capital gains. Assume that the shareholder borrows against his

---

14. Id. See also Reg. § 1.304–2(c) Example 1.

15. See Section E2 of this Chapter, supra.

16. See Bittker & Eustice, Federal Income Taxation of Corporations and Shareholders ¶ 9.24[4] (7th ed. 2000).

17. Prop. Reg. § 1.304–3(a).

18. Cf. Rev.Rul. 80–189, 1980–2 C.B. 106; Broadview Lumber Co. v. United States, 561 F.2d 698 (7th Cir.1977).

stock for valid business reasons and then contributes the stock to a newly formed holding company in exchange for the holding company's stock plus its assumption of the shareholder's liability. Or assume that the shareholder transferred all the stock of the operating company to a wholly owned holding company in exchange for additional stock of the holding company plus cash. Are the tax consequences of these transactions determined under Section 351? Or should they be governed by Section 304? Initially, the courts disagreed on which provision should control in these overlap situations.[19]

In an effort to strengthen the anti-bailout objectives of Subchapter C, Congress settled the overlap issue by providing that Section 304 generally will take precedence.[20] The Joint Committee on Taxation explained the amendment as follows:[21]

> The Act extends the anti-bailout rules of sections 304 * * * to the use of corporations, including holding companies, formed or availed of to avoid such rules. Such rules are made applicable to a transaction that otherwise qualifies as a tax-free incorporation under section 351.

> Section 351 generally will not apply to transactions described in section 304. Thus, section 351, if otherwise applicable, will generally apply only to the extent such transaction consists of an exchange of stock for stock in the acquiring corporation. However, section 304 will not apply to debt incurred to acquire the stock of an operating company and assumed by a controlled corporation acquiring the stock since assumption of such debt is an alternative to a debt-financed direct acquisition by the acquiring company. This exception for acquisition indebtedness applies to an extension, renewal, or refinancing of such indebtedness. The provisions of section 357 (other than sec. 357(b)) and Section 358 apply to such acquisition indebtedness provided they would be applicable to such transaction without regard to section 304. In applying these rules, indebtedness includes debt to which the stock is subject as well as debt assumed by the acquiring company.

* * *

This rule, like several other anti-bailout measures in Subchapter C, is much less significant as long as dividends and long-term capital gains are taxed at the same low rate.

---

19. Compare Gunther v. Commissioner, 92 T.C. 39 (1989), affirmed, 909 F.2d 291 (7th Cir.1990); Commissioner v. Haserot, 355 F.2d 200 (6th Cir.1965) and Haserot v. Commissioner, 46 T.C. 864 (1966), affirmed sub nom. Commissioner v. Stickney, 399 F.2d 828 (6th Cir.1968) with Coates Trust v. Commissioner, 480 F.2d 468 (9th Cir.1973), cert. denied, 414 U.S. 1045, 94 S.Ct. 551 (1973).

20. I.R.C. § 304(b)(3).

21. Staff of Joint Committee on Taxation, General Explanation of Tax Equity and Fiscal Responsibility Act of 1982, 98th Cong., 2d Sess. 142–43 (1982).

Niedermeyer v. Commissioner

United States Tax Court, 1974.
62 T.C. 280, affirmed per curiam 535 F.2d 500 (9th Cir.1976), cert. denied 429 U.S. 1000, 97 S.Ct. 528 (1976).

■ Sterrett, Judge: * * *

[In 1966, the taxpayers, Bernard and Tessie Niedermeyer, owned 22.58% of the common stock of American Timber & Trading Co., Inc. ("AT & T"). They also owned 125 of the 2,136 outstanding shares of AT & T preferred stock. Two of the taxpayers' sons, Bernard, Jr. and Walter, owned 67.91% of the common stock of AT & T.

Lents Industries ("Lents") was another corporation controlled by the Niedermeyer family. In 1966, the taxpayers and their sons, Bernard, Jr. and Walter, did not own any stock of Lents, but three other sons (Ed, Linus and Thomas) each owned 22⅓% of the Lents common stock.

On September 8, 1966, the taxpayers sold their AT & T stock to Lents for $174,975.12, but they retained all their preferred stock until December 28, 1966, when they contributed the preferred to a family foundation. After this contribution, the taxpayers ceased to have any interest in AT & T. Since the time of their sale of AT & T common stock, neither of the taxpayers was an officer, director or employee of the company.

The Niedermeyer family had long been active in the business of manufacturing special wood products in Oregon. During 1963, a family dispute arose between Bernard, Jr. and his brothers, Ed, Linus and Thomas. The brothers had been partners in Niedermeyer–Martin Co., another wood product enterprise, but the dispute caused the partnership to incorporate. During the mid–1960's, Bernard, Jr., as controlling shareholder of AT & T, refused to allow AT & T to do any business with Niedermeyer–Martin Co., which became a competitor. The acquisition by Lents of the taxpayers' common stock in AT & T was part of an effort by Ed, Linus and Thomas Niedermeyer to gain control of AT & T.

On their joint federal income tax return for 1966, the taxpayers reported a long-term capital gain of $168,321.58 on the sale of their AT & T common stock to Lents. The Commissioner determined that the entire proceeds of the sale were taxable as ordinary income because the transaction was covered by Section 304(a) and was essentially equivalent to a dividend. Ed.]

OPINION

The ultimate question to be decided in this case is whether petitioners realized a capital gain or received a dividend on the sale of their AT & T common stock to Lents in 1966. The resolution of this question depends on whether the sale in question was a redemption through the use of a related corporation under the provisions of section 304(a)(1) and, if so, whether the distribution by Lents to petitioners is to be treated as in exchange for the redeemed stock under the provisions of section 302(a) or as of property to which section 301 applies.

Section 304(a)(1) provides, in pertinent part, that, if one or more persons are in "control" of each of two corporations and if one of those corporations acquires stock in the other corporation from the person or persons in control, then the transaction shall be treated as a distribution in redemption for purposes of section 302. Section 304(c)(1) defines the term "control" as "the ownership of stock possessing at least 50 percent of the total combined voting power of all classes of stock entitled to vote, or at least 50 percent of the total value of shares of all classes of stock." Section 304(c)[(3)] then states that the constructive ownership of stock rules contained in section 318(a) shall apply for the purpose of determining "control," except that the 50-percent limitations of sections 318(a)(2)(C) and 318(a)(3)(C) shall be disregarded for such purpose.

It is clear that by its terms section 304(a)(1) applies to the factual situation of this case. Prior to the transaction here in question, petitioners, husband and wife, together actually owned 1,083.117 shares out of the 4,803.083 outstanding shares of AT & T common stock, its only class of stock entitled to vote. Two of petitioners' sons owned 3,263.072 shares. Thus a total of 4,346.189 shares, or 90.49 percent, of the outstanding voting stock of AT & T was actually or constructively owned by petitioners. Three of petitioners' other sons owned 48 out of 72 shares, or 67 percent, of the outstanding stock of Lents, the ownership of such stock being constructively attributable to petitioners. Consequently, under section 304(c)(1), either petitioner, or both, are regarded as the person or persons in control of both AT & T and Lents prior to the transaction in question. Accordingly, under section 304(a)(1) the transaction in which Lents acquired petitioners' AT & T common stock must be treated as a redemption. The fact that neither petitioner actually owned stock in the acquiring corporation is of no concern here. * * *

Petitioners object to the applicability of section 304 on the ground that the attribution rules of section 318(a) should not be applied in this case. They base this position upon what they term the "bad blood" exception to the attribution rules as applied in Estate of Arthur H. Squier, 35 T.C. 950 (1961). In *Squier,* a case under section 302 involving the question of whether a distribution was essentially equivalent to a dividend, this Court decided that, based in part on a "sharp cleavage" between the executor of the taxpayer estate and members of the Squier family, and notwithstanding the attribution rules, the redemption in fact resulted in a crucial reduction of the estate's control over the corporation. The Court held that the distribution there was not essentially equivalent to a dividend and implicit in this conclusion was the belief that the attribution rules were not conclusive in all events in determining whether there had been a significant change of control which would allow the conclusion that the distribution was not essentially equivalent to a dividend. We note that in Robin Haft Trust, 61 T.C. 398 (1973), this Court decided that, in light of United States v. Davis, 397 U.S. 301 (1970), the rationale of *Squier* was no longer applicable to section 302(b)(1).

Besides here, as was not the case with *Squier,* no evidence was adduced to show that there were any disputes or cleavage between petitioners and any of their sons. The falling out was apparently between petitioners' sons. Apparently, petitioners would have us infer from the disagreements between Bernard E. Niedermeyer, Jr., majority shareholder of AT & T, and three other of their sons, who together were majority shareholders of Lents, that petitioners did not in fact control either corporation. We are unwilling to make this assumption and consequently petitioners' argument fails on its facts.

Moreover, we are of the opinion that the "control" test of sections 304(a)(1) and 304(c) requires that the attribution rules be applied in every case. Congress expressly indicated that the attribution rules of section 318 are to be applied in determining "control" for section 304 purposes. Section 304(c)(2) states that "Section 318(a)(relating to the constructive ownership of stock) *shall* apply for purposes of determining control under paragraph (1)." (Emphasis supplied.) Under section 304(c)(1) "control" is defined only as the ownership (either actually or constructively) of certain amounts of stock. Through the use of precise rules of attribution Congress intended to remove the uncertainties existing under prior law, which had no specific statutory guidance for constructive ownership of stock in the area of corporate distributions and adjustments, in the administration of the provisions where attribution was deemed appropriate. H.Rept. No. 1337, to accompany H.R. 8300 (Pub.L. No. 591), 83d Cong., 2d Sess., p. A96 (1954). See also *Coyle v. United States,* supra at 490. We think the attribution rules require, through their employment in section 304, that petitioners be treated as in actual control of both AT & T and Lents, notwithstanding any "bad blood" between petitioners' sons.

Petitioners assert that even though the sale is to be treated as a distribution in redemption of Lents' stock under section 304(a)(1), they are entitled to treat the distribution as in full payment in exchange for their stock under section 302(a) by meeting one of the tests contained in section 302(b). The determination under section 302(b) is to be made by reference to the issuing corporation's stock, here the AT & T stock, except that the 50–percent limitations of sections 318(a)(2)(C) and 318(a)(3)(C) are to be disregarded in applying the attribution rules of section 318(a). Sec. 304(b)(1).

Section 302(b) sets forth certain conditions under which a redemption of stock shall be treated as an exchange. If none of those conditions are met, section 302(d) provides that the distribution will then be treated as one to which section 301 applies. Petitioners do not contend that section 302(b)(2) or 302(b)(4) is applicable but they argue that the transaction in question meets the test of either section 302(b)(1) or 302(b)(3).

The test of section 302(b)(1) requires that the redemption be "not essentially equivalent to a dividend." To meet the test of nondividend equivalency the redemption must, after application of the attribution rules of section 318(a) to the stock ownership interests as they existed both before and after the redemption, result in "a meaningful reduction of the shareholder's proportionate interest in the corporation." *United States v. Davis,* supra at 313. In resolution of the question of dividend equivalency, the fact that the transaction in issue may have had a bona fide business purpose is no longer relevant. *United States v. Davis,* supra at 312. Furthermore, the applicability of the attribution rules in section 302(b)(1) is not affected by any "bad blood" between petitioners' sons. *Robin Haft Trust,* supra at 402–403.

As stated above, prior to the redemption petitioners owned, either actually or constructively, 90.49 percent of the outstanding common stock of AT & T. After the redemption, petitioners actually owned no AT & T common stock, although they did own 125 shares out of 2,136 outstanding shares of that corporation's preferred stock. However, petitioners constructively owned 82.96 percent of the outstanding common stock of AT & T comprised as follows: 3,055.221 shares actually owned by their son Bernard E. Niedermeyer, Jr., 207.851 shares actually owned by their son Walter E. Niedermeyer, and 67 percent of the 1,083.117 shares, or 725.688 shares, actually owned by Lents and constructively owned by their sons E. C., L. J., and T.J. Niedermeyer. Sec. 318(a)(5)(A). We do not think a reduction in ownership of the AT & T common stock from 90.49 percent to 82.96 percent constitutes a meaningful reduction of petitioners' proportionate interest in AT & T in the instant case. See Friend v. United States, 345 F.2d 761, 764 (C.A.1, 1965); Stanley F. Grabowski Trust, 58 T.C. 650, 659 (1972); *Fehrs Finance Co.,* supra at 185–186. With such a small change in a high percentage interest, petitioners' control and ownership of AT & T is essentially unaltered and cannot be considered to have undergone a meaningful reduction. An 82.96–percent interest clearly is sufficient to dominate and control the policies of the corporation.

Petitioners next assert, under several theories, that they terminated their interest in AT & T as contemplated in section 302(b)(3). The test provided therein allows the redemption to be treated as an exchange "if the redemption is in complete redemption of all of the stock of the corporation owned by the shareholder." Unless the conditions of section 302(c)(2) are satisfied to exempt petitioners from application of the family attribution rules of section 318(a)(1), these rules apply in their entirety in determining whether there has been a redemption of petitioners' complete stock interest in AT & T.

Petitioners sold all their AT & T common stock to Lents on September 8, 1966, and contributed all their AT & T preferred stock to the Niedermeyer Foundation on December 28, 1966. On September 24, 1968, petitioners filed an amended return for the calendar year 1966 to which was attached the agreement called for in section 302(c)(2)(A)(iii).

It is clear that, if they are to meet the requirements of the test of section 302(b)(3), petitioners must show that they completely terminated their stock interest in AT & T and in so doing they must be able to effect a waiver of the family attribution rules of section 318(a)(1) through use of section 302(c)(2).

While section 1.302–4(b), Income Tax Regs., states that the agreement specified in section 302(c)(2)(A)(iii) must be attached to a return timely filed for the year in which the distribution occurs, several cases have held that some delay in filing the agreement does not vitiate it, and we find those cases to be applicable here where petitioners filed the agreement upon discovering their inadvertent failure to do so earlier. United States v. G.W. Van Keppel, 321 F.2d 717 (C.A.10, 1963); Georgie S. Cary, 41 T.C. 214 (1963).

However, the fact that a proper agreement was filed alone does not effect a waiver of the family attribution rules unless the other requirements of section 302(c)(2) are satisfied. The only other requirement in question here is that petitioners must have had no interest in AT & T, other than an interest as a creditor, immediately after the distribution referred to in section 302(b)(3). In the instant case, however, petitioners retained their 125 shares of AT & T preferred stock, at least until December 28, 1966, after the redemption of all their AT & T common stock on September 8, 1966.

Petitioners contend that ownership of these 125 shares of AT & T preferred stock until December 28, 1966, does not prevent application of the exemption provided in section 302(c)(2) and consequently qualification under section 302(b)(3) as having completely terminated their stock interest in AT & T. Petitioners make the following arguments to show that the AT & T preferred stock retained until December 28, 1966, was not the retention of an interest other than that of a creditor and implicitly was not the retention of a stock interest in AT & T: (1) The preferred stock was actually debt; (2) a de minimis rule should be applied; (3) the relinquishment of their preferred stock interest in AT & T on December 28, 1966, was "immediately after" the sale of their AT & T common stock on September 8, 1966; and (4) at the time of the sale of their AT & T common stock they intended to donate their AT & T preferred stock to charity before the year's end.

While citing no cases in their support, petitioners first argue here that the characteristics of the AT & T preferred stock are those commonly associated with debt instruments. We do not agree. A number of factors have been considered in resolution of this question of fact, see O.H. Kruse Grain & Milling v. Commissioner, 279 F.2d 123, 125–126 (C.A.9, 1960), affirming a Memorandum Opinion of this Court; Wilbur Security Co., 31 T.C. 938, 948 (1959), affd. 279 F.2d 657 (C.A.9, 1960); however, we see no useful purpose in reciting all the factors but will confine discussion herein only to those we think relevant.

While it is true that the preferred stockholders had no right to participate in the management of the corporation, such fact is not so uncharacteristic of preferred stock rights as to be conclusive, standing alone, of the question at hand. John Kelley Co. v. Commissioner, 326 U.S. 521, 530 (1946). We think that the following facts are indicative of the equity flavor of the preferred stock: There was no unconditional obligation to pay a principal sum certain on or before a fixed maturity date; the timing of preferred "dividends" was discretionary with the corporate directors; upon liquidation the preferred stockholders would be paid "from the money and/or property available for distribution to shareholders," which indicates to us that the preferred stock was subordinated in priority to the general creditors; AT & T's articles of amendment to the articles of incorporation used the terms "dividends," "preferred stock," and "shareholders" with reference to the instruments in question; and the preferred stock was created during a reorganization by a transfer of earned surplus to AT & T's capital account.

We think petitioners' second argument attempting to interject a de minimis rule allowing the retention of some small stock interest while qualifying under section 302(b)(3) is wholly without merit. Section 302(b)(3) clearly requires no less than a complete termination of all petitioners' stock interest in the corporation.

Petitioners next assert that they had no interest in AT & T "immediately after the distribution," as the phrase is used in section 302(c)(2)(A)(i), because the December 28, 1966, contribution should be considered to have occurred immediately after the September 8, 1966, redemption. We assume petitioners believe that if they satisfy this requirement of having no interest "immediately after" the redemption, they will also satisfy the requirement in section 302(b)(3) of having completely terminated their stock interest in AT & T. While we express no opinion on petitioners' apparent belief, we think the words "immediately after" must be given their ordinary meaning and that consequently December 28 cannot be considered "immediately after" September 8. Cf. Commissioner v. Brown, 380 U.S. 563, 570–571 (1965).

Petitioners' final argument to satisfy the requirements of sections 302(b)(3) and 302(c)(2)(A)(i) is that, at the time of the transfer of their AT & T common stock to Lents, they intended to donate their remaining AT & T preferred stock to charity by the end of 1966. Petitioners did in fact contribute their 125 shares of AT & T preferred stock to the Niedermeyer Foundation on December 28, 1966.

While petitioners' contention in this regard is not entirely clear, their argument appears to be that the September 8, 1966, transfer was but one step in a plan to terminate completely their interest in AT & T, the final step in such plan being their December 28, 1966, contribution of their remaining preferred stock. The only case cited by petitioners, Arthur D. McDonald, 52 T.C. 82 (1969), involved the question of whether a plan, calling for the redemption of that taxpayer's E & M preferred stock which was followed by a reorganization in which the taxpayer exchanged his E & M common stock for Borden stock, resulted in a distribution with respect to the preferred stock, which was essentially equivalent to a dividend under section 302(b)(1). The Court concluded that, after completion of the plan, the taxpayer's direct interest in E & M was terminated and consequently the redemption was not essentially equivalent to a dividend. Petitioners have not urged, and we consider it wise since the attribution rules would frustrate them, that their intention to donate the AT & T preferred stock by year's end shows that the redemption comes within the provisions of section 302(b)(1). Rather, they apparently contend that their intentions to donate the AT & T preferred stock constituted a plan to terminate their interest in AT & T which, with use of section 302(c)(2)(A), satisfies the requirements of section 302(b)(3).

Where redemptions were executed pursuant to a plan to terminate one's interest in a corporation, it has been held that dividend equivalency may be avoided where the individual redemptions are component parts of a single sale or exchange of an entire stock interest. In Re Lukens' Estate, 246 F.2d 403 (C.A.3, 1957), reversing 26 T.C. 900 (1956); Jackson Howell, 26 T.C. 846 (1956), affd. 247 F.2d 156 (C.A.9, 1957); Carter Tiffany, 16 T.C. 1443 (1951).[4] Where there is a plan which is comprised of several steps, one involving the redemption of stock that results in a complete termination of the taxpayer's interest in a corporation, section 302(b)(3) may apply. Otis P. Leleux, 54 T.C. 408 (1970); Estate of Oscar L. Mathis, 47 T.C. 248 (1966). However, the redemption must occur as part of a plan which is firm and fixed and in which the steps are clearly integrated. *Otis P. Leleux,* supra at 418.

We regard the evidence presented on petitioners' behalf as too insubstantial to prove the existence of such a plan. Petitioner Bernard E. Niedermeyer's self-serving statement during the trial that at the time of transfer of the AT & T common stock on September 28, 1966, he intended to donate the AT & T preferred stock to charity by year's end, and petitioners' prior history of contributions do not establish to us a firm and fixed plan in which all the steps are clearly integrated.

The plan certainly was not in writing and there was no evidence of communication of petitioners' asserted donative intention to the charity or to anyone. One of petitioners' sons testified that Lents acquired petitioners' AT & T common stock in an attempt to gain control of AT & T. However, no mention at all was made by this son of any desire on petitioners' part to terminate their total interest in AT & T. Petitioners could easily have changed their minds with regard to any intent to donate the preferred stock. Clearly petitioners' decision to donate the preferred stock has not been shown to be in any way fixed or binding. * * * We note that *Arthur D. McDonald,* supra, cited by petitioners, involved a written plan which was fixed as to its terms and apparently binding. By the above discussion we do not mean to indicate that all such plans need to be in writing, absolutely binding, or communicated to others, but we do think that the above-mentioned factors, all of which are lacking here, tend to show a plan which is fixed and firm.

---

4. The cited cases were decided under the "essentially equivalent to the distribution of a taxable dividend" standard of sec. 115(g)(1), I.R.C. 1939. Sec. 29.115–9, Regs. 111, provided that "a cancellation or redemption by a corporation of all of the stock of a particular shareholder, so that the shareholder ceases to be interested in the affairs of the corporation, does not effect a distribution of a taxable dividend." Under present law, sec. 302(b)(1) would now appear applicable if completion of the plan results in a meaningful reduction in the taxpayer's proportionate interest in the corporation.

Since petitioners have not established that the redemption is to be treated as an exchange under section 302(a), the proceeds are to be treated as a distribution of property to which section 301 applies and as a dividend as determined by the respondent.

Decision will be entered for the respondent.

PROBLEMS

1. The *Niedermeyer* case is a good example of a tax planning blunder. It illustrates the need for sensitivity to provisions such as § 304. In reading the case, make sure you can answer the following questions:

(a) Why did § 304 apply to the sale by the taxpayers of their AT & T common stock to Lents?

(b) Given that § 304 applies, how do you test the "redemption" to determine if the taxpayers have a dividend?

(c) Why were the taxpayers unable to waive family attribution and qualify for "sale" treatment under § 302(b)(3)?

(d) How could they have avoided this unfortunate result?

2. Bail Corporation and Out Corporation each have 100 shares of common stock outstanding. Claude owns 80 shares of Bail stock (with a basis of $40,000, or $500 per share) and 60 shares of Out stock (with a basis of $9,000, or $150 per share.) The remaining Bail and Out shares are owned by one individual who is not related to Claude. Bail has no current or accumulated earnings and profits. Out has no current and $5,000 of accumulated earnings and profits. Determine the tax consequences to the various parties in each of the following alternative transactions:

(a) Claude sells 20 of his Out shares, in which he has a $3,000 adjusted basis, to Bail for $4,000.

(b) Claude sells all of his Out shares to Bail for $12,000.

(c) Same as (a), above, except that Claude receives $3,000 and one share of Bail stock (fair market value—$1,000) for his 20 Out shares.

(d) Same as (a), above, except that Claude receives one share of Bail stock (fair market value—$1,000) and Bail takes the 20 Out shares subject to a $3,000 liability that Claude incurred to buy the 20 shares of Out stock.

3. Is Section 304 still necessary?

H.   REDEMPTIONS TO PAY DEATH TAXES

Code: § 303(a), (b)(1)–(3), (c). Skim § 6166.

When a shareholder of a closely held corporation dies, it often is necessary to liquidate all or part of the decedent's stock to raise cash to pay death taxes and other expenses. Since the shares are not readily marketable and the family as a whole may be unwilling to risk loss of control, a redemption may be an important component of the decedent's estate plan. Since the basis of the stock normally will have been stepped-up to its fair market value at the decedent's death,[1] a redemption qualifying for exchange treatment can be accomplished virtually tax-free—a once-in-a-lifetime opportunity for a painless withdrawal of corporate earnings. Section 303, one of several income and estate tax provisions offering relief for owners of closely held businesses,[2] makes it possible to avoid dividend treatment and achieve full recovery of basis on a redemption even if the transaction does not come within one of the Section 302(b) tests.

The purpose of Section 303 is to remove any income tax impediments to a redemption when an estate faces a liquidity problem. If several detailed requirements are met, distributions in redemption are treated as a sale or exchange rather than a dividend up to the sum of federal and state death taxes and allowable funeral and administrative expenses.[3] Curiously, however, the estate is not required to use (or even need) the redemption proceeds to pay taxes and expenses.

To qualify under Section 303, the value of the redeemed stock must be included in determining the decedent's gross estate for federal estate tax purposes.[4] The other principal requirements relate to the relationship of the decedent's holdings in the corporation to his total gross estate and the timing of the distribution.

Relationship of Stock to Decedent's Estate. Congress concluded that income tax relief was justified only when a decedent's holdings in the corporation represented a substantial portion of his gross estate. Section 303(b)(2) requires that the value of all the stock of the distributing corporation included in the decedent's gross estate must exceed 35 percent of the total gross estate less certain expenses deductible for federal estate tax purposes. A special rule permits the stock of two or more corporations to be aggregated for purposes of this 35 percent test if 20 percent or more in value of each such corporation's total outstanding stock is included in the gross estate. For purposes of the 20 percent requirement, stock held by the decedent's surviving spouse as community property, or held with the decedent prior to death in joint tenancy, tenancy-by-the-entirety, or tenancy-in-common, is treated as if it were included in determining the value of the decedent's gross estate.[5] If a decedent's holdings are close to the 35

---

1. I.R.C. § 1014(a). This assumes that the estate tax remains in place, and the Section 1022 carryover basis regime enacted in 2001 never goes into effect.

2. E.g., I.R.C. §§ 302(c)(2)(waiver of family attribution when testing redemptions), 2032A (estate tax valuation of certain real property), 6166 (extension of time to pay

estate tax). Section 303 contains no "closely held" business requirement, but the vast majority of Section 303 redemptions involve close corporations.

3. I.R.C. § 303(a).

4. Id.

5. I.R.C. § 303(b)(2)(B).

percent mark, it may be desirable to engage in various lifetime and post-mortem maneuvers to ensure that Section 303 will be available.[6]

Timing of the Redemption. Section 303 applies only to amounts distributed within a reasonable time after the decedent's death. The redemption must occur within 90 days after the expiration of the three year assessment period for federal estate taxes.[7] If the estate becomes embroiled in a controversy with the Service and files a petition for redetermination of estate tax with the Tax Court, the period is extended to 60 days after the Tax Court's decision becomes final.[8] A further extension is provided if the estate is eligible and elects to pay estate taxes in installments over the extended period (up to 15 years) provided by Section 6166.[9] But if the redemption occurs more than four years after death, the amount that can qualify for Section 303 treatment is limited to the lesser of unpaid death taxes and administrative expenses immediately before the distribution or death taxes and expenses actually paid during the one year period beginning on the date of distribution.[10]

Eligible Shareholders. Although Section 303 is most commonly used by the decedent's estate, other shareholder-beneficiaries sometimes are eligible for its benefits if their interest "is reduced directly (or through a binding obligation to contribute) by any payment" of death taxes or administrative expenses.[11] In the normal case where the decedent's will provides that taxes and expenses are payable out of the residuary estate, specific legatees of stock (including a spouse receiving a bequest eligible for the unlimited marital deduction) are not eligible to use Section 303.

Distributions of Appreciated Property. The most likely asset for a Section 303 redemption is cash, but a corporation that distributes appreciated property to redeem its shares must recognize gain under the now familiar rule in Section 311(b).

PROBLEM

George died last year and his gross estate for federal estate tax purposes is $2,000,000. George's estate expects to incur a total of $100,000 of death taxes and allowable deductions for expenses and losses under §§ 2053 and 2054. George's gross estate includes stock in X Corporation (fair market value—$200,000) and Y Corporation (fair market value—$400,000). The fair market value of all of the outstanding X and Y stock is $1,400,000 and $1,600,000, respectively. George's wife, Adele, also owns $200,000 of X stock. (She and George held a total of $400,000 of X stock as tenants-in-common during his life.)

If Y Corporation redeems shares from George's estate, will the redemption qualify for exchange treatment under § 303?

---

6. See Kahn, "Closely Held Stocks—Deferral and Financing of Estate Tax Costs through Sections 303 and 6166," 35 Tax Lawyer 639, 676–681 (1982).

7. I.R.C. § 303(b)(1)(A). See I.R.C. § 6501(a).

8. I.R.C. § 303(b)(1)(B).

9. I.R.C. § 303(b)(1)(C).

10. I.R.C. § 303(b)(4).

11. I.R.C. § 303(b)(3).

CHAPTER 6

STOCK DIVIDENDS AND SECTION 306 STOCK

A. INTRODUCTION

Code: Skim §§ 305; 306; 317(a).

It should be evident by now that Subchapter C has been the backdrop for a continuing cops and robbers saga. The goals of the robbers are clear enough, even if their methods may be a bit obscure. When they ran out of ideas to avoid the double tax, the robbers historically shifted their focus to bailing out corporate earnings at the least tax cost. The cops were quick to respond, but they sometimes lacked direction and even were known to engage in isolated acts of police brutality. Nowhere does this drama have a richer history than in the area of stock dividends and Section 306 stock. But for many of these skirmishes, the operative word may now be "history," at least as long as dividends and long-term capital gains are taxed at the same preferential rate.

The evolving plot is best appreciated by first putting the underlying transactions into perspective. A stock dividend is simply a distribution of stock (or rights to acquire stock)[1] by a corporation to some or all of its shareholders. If the distributed stock is of the same class as the shareholder's underlying holdings, a stock dividend is similar to what is known as a "stock split." The only difference is that a stock dividend requires the corporation to transfer an appropriate amount from retained earnings to paid-in capital while a stock split merely increases the number of outstanding shares without any adjustment to the corporate capital account.[2] A stock dividend, however, need not be of the same class of stock as the shareholder's existing interest in the corporation. Preferred stock may be distributed with respect to common or vice versa, and more complex capital structures present the opportunity for countless variations.

---

1. I.R.C. § 305(d)(1) defines the term "stock" to include rights to acquire such stock.

2. Apart from the financial accounting distinctions, the line of demarcation between a stock dividend and a stock split usually is drawn by the relationship of the number of shares distributed to the previously outstanding shares. To better inform shareholders, the rules of the New York Stock Exchange provide that a distribution of less than 25 percent of the shares outstanding prior to the distribution will be a stock dividend. Larger distributions (e.g., distributions of one share for each share held) are labelled splits. New York Stock Exchange Company Manual, § 703.02.

298

Stock dividends accomplish a variety of business objectives. Some public companies periodically pay small "common on common" stock dividends instead of cash ostensibly to provide their shareholders with some tangible evidence of their interest in corporate earnings while allowing the corporation to retain cash for use in the business. Although these distributions may have an incidental impact on the price of the stock, they are more of a shareholder public relations gesture than an event of any financial consequence. Stock splits often are prompted by a desire to increase the number of outstanding shares and thus reduce the price per share in an attempt to increase the marketability (and market value) of the stock on a listed exchange.

The business objectives may be different in the case of a closely held corporation. In that setting, stock distributions frequently are a vehicle to shift corporate control.[3] To illustrate, assume that all the outstanding stock of Family Corporation is owned by Mrs. Older and has a fair market value of $1,000 per share. Mr. Younger, Older's son, has been employed by Family for several years and Older expects to gradually shift control of the business to Younger. Older's plan faces several obstacles. Gifts of Family common stock to Younger may not be feasible because Older is unwilling to part with that much wealth or the gift tax liability may be prohibitive. Younger also may not be able to afford a significant purchase of stock from his mother because the current price of Family common stock is too high.

As an alternative, Family might distribute a new class of preferred stock to Older. The preferred stock could be structured with dividend rights and a liquidation preference so that its value absorbs most of the net worth of the company, leaving the common stock with only nominal value. The distribution of preferred stock to Older will be tax-free[4] and, since the value of the common stock will be substantially reduced, Older more easily may shift control to Younger through gifts or even sales of common stock.[5]

The tax consequences of the stock distribution to Older in our example are governed by Section 305, which remains significant in the current tax rate environment. Section 305(a) generally provides that gross income does not include a distribution of stock by a corporation to its shareholders with respect to its stock. This exclusion, however, is subject to various exceptions, the most important of which are found in Section 305(b). Consequently, the applicability of the Section 305(b) exceptions is the critical inquiry in analyzing the tax consequences of a stock distribution. These exceptions are examined more closely in the next section of this chapter. It is sufficient for now to note that the preferred stock distribution to Older is

---

3. A recapitalization frequently is an alternative method for making adjustments to the corporation's capital structure. In certain situations, a recapitalization may provide more favorable income tax results. See Chapter 11, infra.

4. I.R.C. § 305(a). The preferred stock, however, would be Section 306 stock assuming Family has earnings and profits. See Section C of this chapter, infra.

5. But see I.R.C. § 2701 et seq., which limits the estate planning advantages of this strategy.

not a taxable stock dividend. What do you suppose is the rationale for that result?

Lest we forget the cops and robbers saga, there is one other aspect of the previous example to consider. Recall that Older owns 100 percent of the outstanding Family common stock, and Family makes a tax-free distribution of a new class of preferred stock to Older. Assume further that Family has ample earnings and profits. If Older retained her common stock rather than giving it to her son, the preferred stock distribution historically provided her with an opportunity for tax avoidance. She could sell the preferred stock to Facilitator for cash and, after a short period of time, the corporation could redeem the preferred stock, paying Facilitator an appropriate premium for the shares. When the dust settled, this series of transactions had virtually the same economic effect as a cash distribution by Family to Older: Older has cash in hand, Family's corporate treasury has been depleted, and Older still owned 100 percent of the company. But the tax consequences appeared to be dramatically different. Rather than being stuck with a taxable dividend, Older hoped to enjoy "sale" treatment on the disposition of the preferred stock to Facilitator. A sale enabled Older to recover her basis in the preferred stock and to recognize a long-term capital gain to the extent the amount realized on the sale exceeded her basis.[6] A closer examination reveals that this potential loophole (is it still?) was closed by Section 306, which was the legislative response to Older's tax avoidance plan—the so-called "preferred stock bailout." In our simple example, the preferred stock will bear the taint of "Section 306 Stock," and Section 306(a)(1) will characterize Older's amount realized on the sale to Facilitator as ordinary (dividend?) income.[7] The last section of this chapter explores the details of Section 306 and evaluates its continuing significance.

B.   TAXATION OF STOCK DIVIDENDS UNDER SECTION 305

Code: §§ 305(a), (b), (c), (d); 307; 312(d)(1)(B), (f)(2); 1223(5).

Regulations: §§ 1.305–1;–2;–3(a), (b), (c); (e) Examples (1), (2), (3), (4), (8), (10) and (11);–4;–5(a);–6;–7(a); 1.307–1.

The current scheme for taxing stock distributions is a distant cousin of statutes fashioned during the infancy of the income tax and is the product of a checkered legislative history. The Revenue Act of 1916 provided that a "stock dividend shall be considered income, to the amount of its cash value."[1] In 1920, the Supreme Court considered the constitutionality of this

---

6. This assumes that Older had a long-term holding period in the Family common stock, which could be tacked in determining the holding period of the preferred. I.R.C. § 1223(5).

7. I.R.C. § 306(a)(1)(A), (c)(1)(A). Prior to the enactment of Section 306 as part of the 1954 Code, the Service argued that in sub-

stance these transactions were equivalent to a cash distribution. The argument met with sporadic success. Compare Chamberlin v. Commissioner, at p. 309 infra, with Rosenberg v. Commissioner, 36 T.C. 716 (1961).

1. Revenue Act of 1916, § 2(a). In Towne v. Eisner, 245 U.S. 418, 38 S.Ct. 158 (1918), the Supreme Court concluded that a

provision in Eisner v. Macomber.[2] Mrs. Macomber, a common shareholder of a corporation with no other class of stock outstanding, received a proportionate distribution of additional common stock. The Supreme Court held that the distribution was not taxable because it did not constitute "income" within the meaning of the 16th Amendment to the Constitution. Although the Court's constitutional commentary has been discredited,[3] the result in *Macomber* is eminently logical and has been codified in Section 305(a). Whatever reshuffling may occur in the corporation's capital account, a common-on-common stock dividend does little more than crowd the shareholder's safe deposit box (or brokerage account) with additional stock certificates or book entry shares evidencing the same ownership interest held before the distribution.

An obedient Congress swiftly responded to the Supreme Court's interpretation of the 16th Amendment with a primitive declaration that stock dividends "shall not be subject to tax."[4] The stock dividend terrain remained calm until the Supreme Court generated a minor tremor in 1936 with its decision in Koshland v. Helvering.[5] Corinne Koshland, a shareholder who owned cumulative nonvoting preferred stock, received a distribution of voting common stock. She subsequently disposed of her preferred stock and asserted that she was entitled to use the stock's full cost basis in determining her gain. Since the prior common stock distribution was received tax-free, the Service contended that a proportionate amount of Mrs. Koshland's basis in her preferred shares should be allocated to the common, thereby increasing the gain on the disposition of her preferred stock. The Supreme Court agreed with the shareholder's contention and in the course of its opinion shed additional light on the meaning of Eisner v. Macomber:[6]

> Although *Eisner v. Macomber* affected only the taxation of dividends declared in the same stock as that presently held by the taxpayer, the Treasury gave the decision a broader interpretation which Congress followed in the Act of 1921. Soon after the passage of that Act, this court pointed out the distinction between a stock dividend which worked no change in the corporate entity, the same interest in the same corporation being represented after the distribution by more shares of precisely the same character, and such a dividend where there had either been changes of corporate identity or a change in the nature of the shares issued as dividends whereby the proportional interest of the stockholder after the distribution was essentially different from his former interest. Nevertheless the successive statutes and Treasury regulations

---

stock dividend was not "income" or "dividends" under the Revenue Act of 1913.

2. 252 U.S. 189, 40 S.Ct. 189 (1920).

3. See Bittker & Eustice, Federal Income Taxation of Corporations and Shareholders ¶ 8.40[1] (7th ed. 2000).

4. Revenue Act of 1921, § 201(d).

5. 298 U.S. 441, 56 S.Ct. 767 (1936).

6. 298 U.S. at 445–46, 56 S.Ct. at 769–70. In Helvering v. Gowran, 302 U.S. 238, 58 S.Ct. 154 (1937), the Court held that a shareholder took a zero basis in preferred shares received as a nontaxable distribution on common stock.

respecting taxation of stock dividends remained unaltered. We give great weight to an administrative interpretation long and consistently followed, particularly when the Congress, presumably with that construction in mind, has reenacted the statute without change. The question here, however, is not merely of our adopting the administrative construction but whether it should be adopted if in effect it converts an income tax into a capital levy.

We are dealing solely with an income tax act. Under our decisions the payment of a dividend of new common shares, conferring no different rights or interests than did the old—the new certificates, plus the old, representing the same proportionate interest in the net assets of the corporation as did the old—does not constitute the receipt of income by the stockholder. On the other hand, where a stock dividend gives the stockholder an interest different from that which his former stock holdings represented he receives income. The latter type of dividend is taxable as income under the Sixteenth Amendment. Whether Congress has taxed it as of the time of its receipt, is immaterial for present purposes.

Koshland at least educated Congress on the subtleties of taxing stock dividends, but the legislators were not yet up to the task of devising a precise statutory solution. Instead, they tossed the ball back into the judiciary's court by providing in the Revenue Act of 1936 that a distribution of stock or rights to acquire stock was not to be treated as a dividend to the extent it did "not constitute income to the shareholder within the meaning of the Sixteenth Amendment to the Constitution."[7] The Supreme Court declined the invitation to reconsider *Eisner v. Macomber,* preferring to develop a "proportionate interest test", under which a stock dividend was taxable if it increased a shareholder's proportionate interest in the corporation.[8]

It was back to the drawing board, however, with the enactment of the Internal Revenue Code of 1954. Seeking a simple approach, Congress enacted the predecessor of current Section 305, largely as an expression of dissatisfaction with the proportionate interest test. A far more elaborate system was adopted in the Tax Reform Act of 1969. The following excerpt of legislative history describes the 1954 Code provisions and explains the 1969 amendments.

7. Revenue Act of 1936, § 115(f)(1). This test was carried over to the 1939 Code.

8. See the legislative history in the text at pp. 303–304, infra. See also Helvering v. Sprouse, 318 U.S. 604, 63 S.Ct. 791 (1943), where the Supreme Court decided that a pro rata distribution of nonvoting common stock to a shareholder owning voting common stock was nontaxable because it did not change the proportionate interests of the shareholders, and Strassburger v. Commissioner, 318 U.S. 604, 63 S.Ct. 791 (1943), where the Court held that a distribution of cumulative nonvoting preferred stock to the corporation's sole shareholder was not taxable because "[b]oth before and after the event he owned exactly the same interest in the net value of the corporation as before." Id. at 607, 63 S.Ct. at 792.

Excerpt From Senate Finance Committee Report on Tax Reform Act of 1969

S.Rep. No. 91–552, 91st Cong., 1st Sess. 150–54 (1969).

Present law.—In its simplest form, a stock dividend is commonly thought of as a mere readjustment of the stockholder's interest, and not as income. For example, if a corporation with only common stock outstanding issues more common stock as a dividend, no basic change is made in the position of the corporation and its stockholders. No corporate assets are paid out, and the distribution merely gives each stockholder more pieces of paper to represent the same interest in the corporation.

On the other hand, stock dividends may also be used in a way that alters the interests of the stockholders. For example, if a corporation with only common stock outstanding declares a dividend payable at the election of each stockholder, either in additional common stock or in cash, the stockholder who receives a stock dividend is in the same position as if he received a taxable cash dividend and purchased additional stock with the proceeds. His interest in the corporation is increased relative to the interests of stockholders who took dividends in cash.

Present law (sec. 305(a)) provides that if a corporation pays a dividend to its shareholders in its own stock (or in rights to acquire its stock), the shareholders are not required to include the value of the dividend in income. There are two exceptions to this general rule. First, stock dividends paid in discharge of preference dividends for the current or immediately preceding taxable year are taxable. Second, a stock dividend is taxable if any shareholder may elect to receive his dividend in cash or other property instead of stock.

These provisions were enacted as part of the Internal Revenue Code of 1954. Before 1954 the taxability of stock dividends was determined under the "proportionate interest test," which developed out of a series of Supreme Court cases, beginning with Eisner v. Macomber, 252 U.S. 189 (1920) [T.D. 3010, C.B. 3, 25]. In these cases the Court held, in general, that a stock dividend was taxable if it increased any shareholder's proportionate interest in the corporation. The lower courts often had difficulty in applying the test as formulated in these cases, particularly where unusual corporate capital structures were involved.

Soon after the proportionate interest test was eliminated in the 1954 Code, corporations began to develop methods by which shareholders could, in effect, be given a choice between receiving cash dividends or increasing their proportionate interests in the corporation in much the same way as if they had received cash dividends and reinvested them in the corporation. The earliest of these methods involves dividing the common stock of the corporation into two classes, A and B. The two classes share equally in earnings and profits and in assets on liquidation. The only difference is that the class A stock pays only stock dividends and class B stock pays only cash dividends. The market value of the stock dividends paid on the class A stock is equated annually to the cash dividends paid on the class B stock.

Class A stock may be converted into class B stock at any time. The stockholders can choose, either when the classes are established, when they purchase new stock, or through the convertibility option whether to own class A stock or class B stock.

In 1956, the Treasury Department issued proposed regulations which treated such arrangements as taxable (under sec. 305(b)(2)) as distributions subject to an election by the stockholder to receive cash instead of stock. In recent years, however, increasingly complex and sophisticated variations of this basic arrangement have been created. In some of these arrangements, the proportionate interest of one class of shareholders is increased even though no actual distribution of stock is made. This effect may be achieved, for example, by paying cash dividends on common stock and increasing by a corresponding amount the ratio at which convertible preferred stock or convertible debentures may be converted into common stock. Another method of achieving this result is a systematic periodic redemption plan, under which a small percentage, such as 5 percent, of each shareholder's stock may be redeemed annually at his election. Shareholders who do not choose to have their stock redeemed automatically increase their proportionate interest in the corporation.

On January 10, 1969, the Internal Revenue Service issued final regulations under which a number of methods of achieving the effect of a cash dividend to some shareholders and a corresponding increase in the proportionate interest of other shareholders are brought under the exceptions in section 305(b), with the result that shareholders who receive increases in proportionate interest are treated as receiving taxable distributions.

General reasons for change.—The final regulations * * * do not cover all of the arrangements by which cash dividends can be paid to some shareholders and other shareholders can be given corresponding increases in proportionate interest. For example, the periodic redemption plan described above is not covered by the regulations, and the committee believes it is not covered by the present statutory language (of sec. 305(b)(2)).

Methods have also been devised to give preferred stockholders the equivalent of dividends on preferred stock which are not taxable as such under present law. For example, a corporation may issue preferred stock for $100 per share which pays no dividends, but which may be redeemed in 20 years for $200. The effect is the same as if the corporation distributed preferred stock equal to 5 percent of the original stock each year during the 20-year period in lieu of cash dividends. The committee believes that dividends paid on preferred stock should be taxed whether they are received in cash or in another form, such as stock, rights to receive stock, or rights to receive an increased amount on redemption. Moreover, the committee believes that dividends on preferred stock should be taxed to the recipients whether they are attributable to the current or immediately preceding taxable year or to earlier taxable years.

Explanation of provisions.—The bill continues (in sec. 305(b)(1)) the provision of present law that a stock dividend is taxable if it is payable at the election of any shareholder in property instead of stock.

The bill provides (in sec. 305(b)(2)) that if there is a distribution or series of distributions of stock which has the result of the receipt of cash or other property by some shareholders and an increase in the proportionate interests of other shareholders in the assets or earnings and profits of the corporation, the shareholders receiving stock are to be taxable (under sec. 301).

For example, if a corporation has two classes of common stock, one paying regular cash dividends and the other paying corresponding stock dividends (whether in common or preferred stock), the stock dividends are to be taxable.

On the other hand, if a corporation has a single class of common stock and a class of preferred stock which pays cash dividends and is not convertible, and it distributes a pro rata common stock dividend with respect to its common stock, the stock distribution is not taxable because the distribution does not have the result of increasing the proportionate interests of any of the stockholders.

In determining whether there is a disproportionate distribution, any security convertible into stock or any right to acquire stock is to be treated as outstanding stock. For example, if a corporation has common stock and convertible debentures outstanding, and it pays interest on the convertible debentures and stock dividends on the common stock, there is a disproportionate distribution, and the stock dividends are to be taxable (under section 301). In addition, in determining whether there is a disproportionate distribution with respect to a shareholder, each class of stock is to be considered separately.

The committee has added two provisions to the House bill (secs. 305(b)(3) and (4)) which carry out more explicitly the intention of the House with regard to distributions of common and preferred stock on common stock, and stock distributions on preferred stock. The first of these provides that if a distribution or series of distributions has the result of the receipt of preferred stock by some common shareholders and the receipt of common stock by other common shareholders, all of the shareholders are taxable (under sec. 301) on the receipt of the stock.

The second of the provisions added by the committee (sec. 305(b)(4)) provides that distributions of stock with respect to preferred stock are taxable (under sec. 301). This provision applies to all distributions on preferred stock except increases in the conversion ratio of convertible preferred stock made solely to take account of stock dividends or stock splits with respect to the stock into which the convertible stock is convertible.

The bill provides (in section 305(b)(5)) that a distribution of convertible preferred stock is taxable (under sec. 301) unless it is established to the satisfaction of the Secretary or his delegate that it will not have the result of a disproportionate distribution described above. For example, if a corporation makes a pro rata distribution on its common stock of preferred stock convertible into common stock at a price slightly higher than the market price of the common stock on the date of distribution, and the period during which the stock must be converted is 4 months, it is likely that a distribution would have the result of a disproportionate distribution. Those stockholders who wish to increase their interests in the corporation would convert their stock into common stock at the end of the 4–month period, and those stockholders who wish to receive cash would sell their stock or have it redeemed. On the other hand, if the stock were convertible for a period of 20 years from the date of issuance, there would be a likelihood that substantially all of the stock would be converted into common stock, and there would be no change in the proportionate interest of the common shareholders.

The bill provides (in sec. 305(c)) that under regulations prescribed by the Secretary or his delegate, a change in conversion ratio, a change in redemption price, a difference between redemption price and issue price, a redemption treated as a section 301 distribution, or any transaction (including a recapitalization) having a similar effect on the interest of any shareholder is to be treated as a distribution with respect to each shareholder whose proportionate interest is thereby increased. The purpose of this provision is to give the Secretary authority to deal with transactions that have the effect of distributions, but in which stock is not actually distributed.

The proportionate interest of a shareholder can be increased not only by the payment of a stock dividend not paid to other shareholders, but by such methods as increasing the ratio at which his stock, convertible securities, or rights to stock may be converted into other stock, by decreasing the ratio at which other stock, convertible securities, or rights to stock can be converted into stock of the class he owns, or by the periodic redemption of stock owned by other shareholders. It is not clear under present law to what extent increases of this kind would be considered distributions of stock or rights to stock. In order to eliminate uncertainty, the committee has authorized the Secretary or his delegate to prescribe regulations governing the extent to which such transactions shall be treated as taxable distributions.

For example, if a corporation has a single class of common stock which pays no dividends and a class of preferred stock which pays regular cash dividends, and which is convertible into the common stock at a conversion ratio that decreases each year to adjust for the payment of the cash dividends on the preferred stock, it is anticipated that the regulations will provide in appropriate circumstances that the holders of the common stock will be treated as receiving stock in a disproportionate distribution (under sec. 305(b)(2)).

It is anticipated that the regulations will establish rules for determining when and to what extent the automatic increase in proportionate interest accruing to stockholders as a result of redemptions under periodic redemption plan are to be treated as taxable distributions. A periodic redemption plan may exist, for example, where a corporation agrees to redeem a small percentage of each common shareholder's stock annually at the election of the shareholder. The shareholders whose stock is redeemed receive cash, and the shareholders whose stock is not redeemed receive an automatic increase in their proportionate interests. However, the committee does not intend that this regulatory authority is to be used to bring isolated redemptions of stock under the disproportionate distribution rule (of sec. 305(b)(2)). For example, a 30 percent stockholder would not be treated as receiving a constructive dividend because a 70 percent stockholder causes a corporation to redeem 15 percent of its stock from him.

NOTE

Collateral Tax Consequences. The collateral tax consequences of a stock distribution (e.g., basis, holding period, and effect on earnings and profits) depend upon whether or not the distribution is taxable to the shareholders. Taxable distributions are governed by the rules in Section 301. The amount of the distribution is the fair market value of the stock.[1] The shareholder takes a fair market value basis in the distributed stock, and his holding period runs from the date of the distribution.[2] The distributing corporation recognizes no gain or loss under Section 311(a)(1), and it may reduce its earnings and profits by the fair market value of the distributed stock.[3]

If a stock distribution is nontaxable under Section 305(a), the shareholder must allocate the basis in the stock held prior to the distribution between the old and new stock in proportion to the relative fair market values of each on the date of distribution,[4] and the holding period of the old shares may be tacked on in determining the holding period of the distributed stock.[5] The distributing corporation recognizes no gain or loss on the distribution of its stock[6], and it may not reduce its earnings and profits.[7]

Stock Rights Distributions. Section 305 also governs distributions of stock rights (sometimes called warrants). Public companies occasionally issue rights to acquire additional stock at a favorable price as a means of raising equity capital.[8] Like stock dividends generally, rights distributions are not taxable unless they come within one of the Section 305(b) exceptions.[9] In the case of a nontaxable rights distribution, Section 307(a) generally requires an allocation of basis between the underlying stock and the rights in proportion to their relative fair market values on the date of the distribution.[10] In most cases, however, such an allocation is unneces-

---

1. Reg. § 1.305–1(b)(1). This rule also applies to corporate shareholders. Reg. § 1.301–1(d)(1)(ii).

2. Reg. § 1.301–1(h).

3. Reg. § 1.312–1(d).

4. I.R.C. § 307(a); Reg. § 1.307–1.

5. I.R.C. § 1223(5).

6. I.R.C. § 311(a)(1).

7. I.R.C. § 312(d)(1)(B).

8. See, e.g., Rev.Rul. 72–71, 1972–1 C.B. 99, which is the Service's ruling on a complex rights offering by American Telephone and Telegraph Co.

9. See I.R.C. § 305(d)(1), which treats rights as "stock" for purposes of Section 305.

10. But the regulations permit this allocation only if the rights are exercised (in which event the basis allocated to the rights is added to the cost of the new stock acquired) or sold. If the rights simply lapse, the shareholder recognizes no loss but the basis returns to the underlying stock. Reg. § 1.307–1(a).

sary because of an administrative convenience exception in Section 307(b), which provides that the rights shall take a zero basis if their fair market value is less than 15 percent of the value of the stock with respect to which they were distributed. Taxpayers with time on their hands (or the incentive to make an allocation) may elect to use the allocation method prescribed in Section 307(a).[11] Taxable rights distributions are treated as Section 301 distributions; as such, their value (if any) is a dividend to the extent of the distributing corporation's earnings and profits.

PROBLEMS

1. Hill Corporation is organized with two classes of voting common stock: Class A and Class B. Shares in each class of stock have an equal right to Hill's assets and earnings and profits. Frank owns 100 shares of Class A stock, and Fay and Joyce each own 50 shares of Class B stock.

Assuming that Hill Corporation has ample earnings and profits, determine whether the following distributions are taxable under § 301 or excludable under § 305(a):

(a) A pro rata distribution of nonconvertible preferred stock to both classes of shareholders.

(b) A pro rata distribution of Class A stock on Class A and Class B on Class B. The Class B shareholders also are given the option to take cash in lieu of additional Class B shares. Joyce exercises this option.

(c) A pro rata distribution of Class A stock on Class A and a cash distribution on Class B.

(d) Assume that Class B is a class of nonconvertible preferred stock which pays regular cash dividends and Hill distributes Class B stock to the Class A shareholder.

(e) Same as (d), above, except that Hill distributes a class of nonconvertible preferred stock which has rights to assets and earnings and profits subordinate to those of the existing Class B stock (i.e., "junior" nonconvertible preferred stock) to the Class A shareholder.

(f) Assume that Hill has only one class of common stock outstanding and also has issued a series of 10 percent debentures convertible into common stock at the rate of one share of common stock for each $1,000 debenture. Hill makes an annual interest payment to the debenture holders and one month later distributes a "common on common" stock dividend to the common shareholders without adjusting the conversion ratio on the debentures.

(g) Same as (f), above, except that the debentures are convertible preferred stock. The corporation declares a one-for-one split on the common stock (i.e., each shareholder receives one new share of

---

11. I.R.C. § 307(b)(2).

common stock for each old share) and the conversion ratio of the preferred is doubled.

(h) Assume again that Class A and Class B are both classes of voting common stock. Hill makes a pro rata distribution of Class A on Class A and a distribution of newly issued shares of nonconvertible preferred stock on Class B.

(i) Same as (h), above, except that the preferred stock which is distributed is convertible into Class B stock over 20 years at Class B's market price on the day of the distribution.

2. Z Corporation has one class of common stock outstanding, held by unrelated individuals A (500 shares), B (300 shares) and C (200 shares). Will § 305(c) create any tax problems if Z agrees to redeem annually 50 shares of stock at the election of each shareholder, and A makes such an election for two consecutive years?

C.   SECTION 306 STOCK

1.   THE PREFERRED STOCK BAILOUT

Chamberlin v. Commissioner

United States Court of Appeals, Sixth Circuit, 1953.
207 F.2d 462, certiorari denied 347 U.S. 918, 74 S.Ct. 516 (1954).

■ MILLER, CIRCUIT JUDGE.

[This case involved the tax consequences of a device known as the preferred stock bailout. Metal Moulding Corporation was a prosperous company engaged in manufacturing automobile molding and trim. From the time of its formation in 1924, the corporation had only common stock outstanding and was substantially controlled by the Chamberlin family. In December, 1946, after a long period during which it paid substantial cash dividends, the corporation declared a stock dividend of 1⅛ newly authorized preferred shares for each share of common stock outstanding. Two days later, as a result of lengthy prior negotiations, virtually all the shareholders agreed to sell their preferred stock to two insurance companies. The investment committees of those companies actually had approved the purchase prior to the issuance of the preferred stock. The terms of the preferred had been discussed with and shaped by the demands of the insurance companies. At all times, it was contemplated that the shares would be redeemed at a negotiated price over a seven-year period. The entire plan was designed to enable the shareholders to withdraw corporate earnings at preferential capital gains rates. The insurance companies were willing to act as amiable facilitators because they would receive dividends on the preferred stock and a premium on the redemption.

The shareholders treated the preferred stock dividend as nontaxable and reported the proceeds of sale of the preferred as capital gain. On audit, the Service ruled that the distribution of the preferred stock was a taxable dividend. The Tax Court agreed with the Service, reasoning that the distribution was not made for any bona fide business purpose and was in substance the equivalent of a cash distribution out of earnings and profits.

After reviewing the Supreme Court decisions involving the taxability of stock dividends, the Court of Appeals addressed the tax consequences of Metal Moulding's ingenious bailout device. Ed.]

In our opinion, the declaration and distribution of the preferred stock dividend, considered by itself, falls clearly within the principles established in Towne v. Eisner, supra, and Eisner v. Macomber, supra, and is controlled by the ruling in the Strassburger case. Accordingly, as a preliminary matter, we do not agree with the Tax Court's statement that the stock dividend is taxable because as a result of the dividend and immediate sale thereafter it substantially altered the common stockholders' preexisting proportional interests in the Corporation's net assets. The sale to the insurance companies of course resulted in such a change, but the legal effect of the dividend with respect to rights in the corporate assets is determined at the time of its distribution, not by what the stockholders do with it after its receipt. * * * It seems clear to us that if taxability exists it is not because of the change in pre-existing proportional interests caused by a later sale, but by reason of the other ground relied upon by the Tax Court, namely, that viewed in all its aspects it was a distribution of cash rather than a distribution of stock. That this is the real basis of the ruling appears from the statement in the opinion that "disregarding the circumstances and terms of the issue, it might be said as a matter of form the stock dividend constituted one which fell within the Sprouse and Strassburger cases. * * * However, * * *, not form but the real substance of the transaction is controlling."

The general principle is well settled that a taxpayer has the legal right to decrease the amount of what otherwise would be his taxes, or altogether avoid them, by means which the law permits; * * * and that the taxpayer's motive to avoid taxation will not establish liability if the transaction does not do so without it. * * *

It is equally well settled that this principle does not prevent the Government from going behind the form which the transaction takes and ascertaining the reality and genuineness of the component parts of the transaction in order to determine whether the transaction is really what it purports to be or is merely a formality without substance which for tax purposes can and should be disregarded. * * *

The question accordingly presented is not whether the overall transaction, admittedly carried out for the purpose of avoiding taxes, actually avoided taxes which would have been incurred if the transaction had taken a different form, but whether the stock dividend was a stock dividend in substance as well as in form.

No question is raised about the legality of the declaration of the dividend. Respondent does not contend that proper corporate procedure was not used in creating the preferred stock and in distributing it to the stockholders in the form of a dividend. If the transaction had stopped there we think it is clear that the dividend would not have been taxable in the hands of the stockholders. Strassburger v. Commissioner, supra. Whether the declaration of the dividend was in furtherance of any corporate business purpose or was the result of correct judgment and proper business policy on the part of the management, we believe is immaterial on this phase of the case. The Supreme Court cases in no way suggest that the taxability of a stock dividend depends on the purpose of its issuance or the good or bad judgment of the directors in capitalizing earnings instead of distributing them. The decisions are based squarely upon the proportional interest doctrine. * * * The presence or absence of a corporate business purpose may play a part in determining whether a stock dividend is a bona fide one, one in substance as well as in form, but it does not by itself change an otherwise valid dividend into an invalid one. A stock dividend, legally created and distributed, which is a dividend in substance as well as in form, does not change from a non-taxable dividend into a taxable one because of the purpose of its issuance or on account of the good or bad judgment of the directors in declaring it.

Nor is there any question about the genuineness and unconditional character of the sale of the preferred stock by the stockholders who received it to the two insurance companies. The facts show conclusively that title passed irrevocably from the stockholders to the insurance companies, and that the sellers received in cash without restriction a full consideration, the adequacy of which respondent does not question. But respondent contends that the sale of the stock following immediately upon its receipt resulted in the stockholder acquiring cash instead of stock, thus making it a taxable dividend * * *. There are two answers to this contention.

A non-taxable stock dividend does not become a taxable cash dividend upon its sale by the recipient. On the contrary, it is a sale of a capital asset. * * * [I]ts character as a capital asset is in no way dependent upon how long it is held by the taxpayer before its sale. * * *

The other answer to the contention is that although the stockholder *acquired* money in the final analysis, he did not *receive* either money or property *from* the corporation. Sec. [301(a)], in dealing with taxable dividends, defines a dividend as "any distribution *made by a corporation* to its shareholders, whether in money or in other property * * * out of its earnings or profits * * *." (Emphasis added.) The money he received was received from the insurance companies. It was not a "distribution" by the corporation declaring the dividend, as required by the statute.

We come then to what in our opinion is the dominant and decisive issue in the case, namely, whether the stock dividend, which, by reason of its redemption feature, enabled the Corporation to ultimately distribute its earnings to its stockholders on a taxable basis materially lower than would have been the case by declaring and paying the usual cash dividend, was a bona fide one, one in substance as well as in form. * * *

In our opinion, the stock dividend in this case * * * was an issue of stock in substance as well as in form. According to its terms, and in the absence of a finding that it was immediately or shortly thereafter redeemed at a premium, we assume that a large portion of it has remained outstanding over a period of years with some of it still unredeemed after nearly seven years. It has been in the hands of the investing public, free of any control by the corporation over its owners, whose enforceable rights with respect to operations of the corporation would not be waived or neglected. Substantial sums have been paid in dividends. The insurance companies bought it in the regular course of their business and have held it as approved investments. For the Court to now tell them that they have been holding a sham issue of stock would be most startling and disturbing news.

It also seems clear that the insurance companies were not purchasers in form only without acquiring any real interest in the property conveyed. The character of the transaction as a bona fide investment on the part of the insurance companies is not challenged by the respondent. The element of a formal conduit without any business interest is entirely lacking.

If the transaction lacks the good faith necessary to avoid the assessment it must be because of the redemption feature of the stock, which, in the final analysis, is what ultimately permitted the distribution of the corporate earnings and is the key factor in the overall transaction. Redemption features are well known and often used in corporate financing. If the one in question was a reasonable one, not violative of the general principles of bona fide corporate financing, and acceptable to experienced bona fide investors familiar with investment fundamentals and the opportunities afforded by the investment market we fail to see how a court can properly classify the issue, by reason of the redemption feature, as lacking in good faith or as not being what it purports to be. The insurance companies, conservative, experienced investors, analyzed the stock issue very carefully, provisions were required to make it conform to sound investment requirements, and each of the two companies, acting independently of the other, purchased a very substantial amount in the regular course of their investment purchases. If the redemption feature was unreasonable or not in accord with generally accepted investment principles the stock would not have been approved as an investment and purchased by the two insurance companies. In our opinion, the redemption feature, qualified as it was with respect to premiums, amounts subject to redemption in each year, and the length of time the stock would be outstanding, together with the acceptance of the stock as an investment issue, did not destroy the bona fide quality of the issue. We cannot say that the preferred stock was not in fact what it purported to be, namely, an issue of stock in substance as well as in form. * * *

Each case necessarily depends upon its own facts. The facts in this case show tax avoidance, and it is so conceded by petitioner. But they also show a series of legal transactions, no one of which is fictitious or so lacking in substance as to be anything different from what it purports to be. Unless we are to adopt the broad policy of holding taxable any series of transactions, the purpose and result of which is the avoidance of taxes which would otherwise accrue if handled in a different way, regardless of the legality and realities of the component parts, the tax assessed by the Commissioner was successfully avoided in the present case. We do not construe the controlling decisions as having adopted that view. * * *

In deciding this case it must be kept in mind that it does not involve a ruling that the profit derived from the sale of the stock dividend is or is not taxable income. Such profit is conceded to be taxable. The issue is whether it is taxable as income from a cash dividend or as income resulting from a long-term capital gain. Accordingly, it is not the usual case of total tax avoidance. Congress has adopted the policy of taxing long-term capital gains differently from ordinary income. By Sec. 115(g), Internal Revenue Code, it has specifically excluded certain transactions with respect to stock dividends from the classification of a capital gain. The present transaction is not within the exclusion. If the profit from a transaction like the one here involved is to be taxed at the same rate as ordinary income, it should be done by appropriate legislation, not court decision.

The judgment is reversed and the case remanded to the Tax Court for proceedings consistent with the views expressed herein.

NOTE

The *Chamberlin* case was decided under the 1939 Code. Left unchecked, the court's endorsement of the preferred stock bailout would have encouraged other closely held corporations to engage in similar profitable end runs around the distribution rules. Although the result in *Chamberlin* possibly would have been overturned in subsequent litigation, the Treasury wisely sought a prompt legislative solution. The central issue facing the drafters of the 1954 Code was whether to attack the bailout by taxing all "preferred on common" stock dividends or to defer the punishment until the shareholder disposed of stock with bailout potential.

Common shareholders who receive a proportionate preferred stock dividend have not increased their interest in the corporation. They simply have a tax opportunity which they may choose to forego for nontax reasons. For example, there may be valid business reasons (e.g., a shift of control from older to younger generation shareholders) for a preferred stock dividend. Recognizing these and other nontax objectives served by preferred stock dividends, Congress concluded that the *receipt* of the dividend was not the appropriate occasion for punitive action.[12] Instead, it chose to label stock with bailout potential as "Section 306 stock" and to require a shareholder to report ordinary income rather than capital gain when Section 306 stock is sold or redeemed. In the case of a sale, the ordinary income amount is generally determined by the amount that would have been a dividend at the time of the stock distribution if cash rather than

12. S.Rep. No. 1622, 83rd Cong., 2d Sess. 46 (1954).

stock had been distributed.[13] In the case of a redemption, the ordinary income amount is determined at the time of the cash distribution.[14] Other operational and planning aspects of Section 306 are examined below.

Now that dividends and long-term capital gains are taxed at the same low rate, the advantages to be achieved from a bailout of corporate earnings at "capital gains rates" have diminished considerably. As with redemptions and a few other classic bailout transactions to be studied later, the only remaining tax advantages to noncorporate shareholders of a sale rather than a dividend are recovery of stock basis and, in special situations, the ability to offset capital gains (but not qualified dividends) with capital losses. Section 306 nonetheless remains in the Code, in semi-hibernation until the distinction between dividends and capital gains is restored to its former glory, or until Congress decides that it is no longer necessary.

2.   THE OPERATION OF SECTION 306

a.   SECTION 306 STOCK DEFINED

Code: § 306(c)–(e).

Regulations: §§ 1.306–3(a)–(c), (e).

The definition of Section 306 stock is consistent with the original anti-bailout objectives of the statute. The principal category is stock distributed to a shareholder as a tax-free stock dividend under Section 305(a)—other than "common on common."[1] Ordinarily, this is preferred stock distributed to common shareholders by a corporation with earnings and profits. As the *Chamberlin* case illustrates, preferred stock is the primary vehicle for a bailout because it can be sold without diminishing the shareholder's control or right to share in future corporate growth. "Common" stock is excepted because it lacks bailout potential; it may not be sold without diminishing the shareholder's control and interest in corporate growth.[2]

Although the Service has not defined "common stock" for Section 306 purposes, its published rulings focus on whether a sale of the stock would cause a reduction of the shareholder's equity position in the company. The fundamental inquiry is thus whether the stock has a realistic and unrestricted opportunity to participate in the growth of corporate equity.[3] If stock has either a limited right to dividends or to assets upon liquidation, it is not "common" stock for Section 306 purposes.[4] But voting common stock that is subject to the issuing corporation's first refusal right to purchase the stock at net book value whenever a shareholder wishes to make a transfer is common stock because, upon a transfer, the shareholder will

---

13.   I.R.C. § 306(a)(1).

14.   I.R.C. § 306(a)(2). See Section C2b of this chapter, infra.

1.   I.R.C. § 306(c)(1)(A).

2.   See Walter, " 'Preferred Stock' and 'Common Stock': The Meaning of the Terms

and the Importance of the Distinction for Tax Purposes," 5 J.Corp.Tax'n 211 (1978).

3.   See, e.g., Rev.Rul. 75–222, 1975–1 C.B. 105; Rev.Rul. 79–163, 1979–1 C.B. 131.

4.   Rev. Rul. 79–163, supra note 3.

part with some or all of his interest in the future growth of the corporation vis a vis other shareholders.[5]

Congress also concluded that a tax-free stock dividend issued by a corporation with no current or accumulated earnings and profits for the year of the distribution has limited bailout potential. If cash instead of stock had been distributed, the shareholder would not have realized ordinary income whenever the distributing corporation has no earnings and profits. Consequently, Section 306 stock does not include stock which would not have been treated as a dividend at the time of distribution if cash had been distributed in lieu of the stock.[6]

To prevent an easy purge of the taint, Section 306 stock includes stock with a transferred or substituted basis.[7] This category encompasses stock received as a gift which takes a Section 1015 transferred basis, or stock received in exchange for Section 306 stock in a tax-free Section 351 transaction.[8] But the exorcist prevails when stock passes from a decedent and thus qualifies for a date-of-death basis under Section 1014. In that event, the Section 306 taint is buried along with the decedent and her old basis.

An important but more specialized category is stock (which is not common stock) received in a tax-free corporate reorganization or division when the effect of the transaction is substantially the same as the receipt of a stock dividend or when the stock is received in exchange for Section 306 stock. For example, preferred stock received by the shareholders of the target (i.e., acquired) corporation in a tax-free merger may be a prime candidate for Section 306 classification. This aspect of Section 306 is considered in a later chapter.[9]

The final category of Section 306 stock was added by Congress to thwart the use of a holding company to bail out earnings. Assume, for example, that Schemer holds only common stock in Profitable Co. Finding that Section 306 presents a substantial roadblock to a bailout, Schemer organizes Holding Co., exchanging her Profitable common stock for newly issued Holding common and preferred stock in a tax-free Section 351 transaction. At one time, the Holding preferred stock would not have been Section 306 stock because Holding had no earnings and profits at the time of its incorporation. This offered shareholders the very bailout opportunity that Congress was trying to prevent! Schemer could sell the Holding preferred stock to an institutional investor, recovering her basis and realizing a capital gain, and the stock later could be redeemed by the corporation—all without losing any of her control or share in the growth of Profitable.

5. Rev. Rul. 76–386, 1976–2 C.B. 95; see also Rev. Rul. 81–91, 1981–1 C.B. 123.

6. I.R.C. § 306(c)(2).

7. I.R.C. § 306(c)(1)(C).

8. In this situation, the old Section 306 stock remains tainted in the hands of the corporation, and the newly issued stock, whatever its class, also is Section 306 stock by virtue of its substituted basis under Section 358. See Rev.Rul. 77–108, 1977–1 C.B. 86.

9. See Chapter 11, infra.

Section 306(c)(3) blocks this maneuver by characterizing the preferred stock of Holding Co. (i.e., preferred stock acquired in a Section 351 exchange) as Section 306 stock if the receipt of money instead of the stock would have been treated as a dividend to any extent. Of course, Holding Co. has no earnings and profits so that a distribution of cash would not have been a dividend. To make the statute achieve its objective, Section 306(c)(3)(A) borrows the rules of Section 304 (relating to redemptions through the use of affiliated corporations). In our example, the Holding Co. preferred would be Section 306 stock if Profitable Co. has any current or accumulated earnings and profits. This is because a cash payment by Holding Co. for the Profitable common stock would have resulted in a dividend to Schemer under Section 304(a)(1). In effect, this means that we look to the earnings and profits of the original corporation (Profitable Co.) in determining whether the receipt of cash would have been a dividend.[10]

b. DISPOSITIONS OF SECTION 306 STOCK

Code: § 306(a).

Regulations: § 1.306–1.

The tax consequences of a disposition of Section 306 stock vary depending on whether the stock is sold or redeemed. On a sale of Section 306 stock, the amount realized is treated as dividend income to the extent of the stock's "ratable share" of the amount that would have been a dividend if the corporation had distributed cash in an amount equal to the fair market value of the stock at the time of the distribution.[11] This rule requires the shareholder to look back to the time of distribution and determine to what extent a cash distribution would have emanated from the corporation's current or accumulated earnings and profits at that time.[12] The balance, if any, of the amount realized is treated as a reduction of the basis of the Section 306 stock, and any excess is treated as gain from the sale or exchange of the stock.[13] Although the ordinary income amount is treated as a dividend received from the corporation to allow noncorporate

---

10. In testing for the effect of a dividend, the Section 318 attribution rules apply without regard to the 50 percent limitation in Sections 318(a)(2)(C) and 318(a)(3)(C). I.R.C. § 306(c)(4).

11. I.R.C. §§ 306(a)(1)(A), (a)(1)(D).

12. I.R.C. § 306(a)(1)(A). This provision also applies to other nonredemption "dispositions" such as certain pledges of Section 306 stock where the pledgee can only look to the stock as security (an unlikely scenario), but it does not apply to charitable contributions of Section 306 stock. Reg. § 1.306–1(b)(1); Rev.Rul. 57–328, 1957–2 C.B. 229. For charitable deduction purposes, however, a taxpayer who contributes appreciated Section 306 stock to a qualified donee must reduce the fair market value of the

donated stock by the amount that would have not have been long-term capital gain if the stock had been sold rather than donated. See I.R.C. § 170(e)(1)(A); Pescosolido v. Commissioner, 91 T.C. 52 (1988). It appears that the treatment of Section 306(a)(1) ordinary income as a dividend and thus, if "qualified," part of "adjusted net capital gain" under Section 1(h)(11), does not permit a donor-shareholder from escaping the reduction rule in Section 170 because the gain technically is not "long-term capital gain." Perhaps the Treasury will specify otherwise if and when it issues regulations under the authority of Section 306(a)(1)(D).

13. I.R.C. § 306(a)(1)(B).

shareholder to qualify for the preferred rates under Section 1(h), it is not clear if corporate shareholders are eligible for the Section 243 dividends received deduction, or whether the corporation is entitled to reduce its earnings and profits when Section 306 stock is sold.[14] No loss may be recognized if the shareholder's adjusted basis in the stock exceeds the amount realized, and any unrecovered basis must be allocated back to the stock with respect to which the Section 306 stock was distributed.[15]

A shareholder who receives a nontaxable stock dividend of Section 306 stock that later is redeemed by the corporation has used two steps to achieve what could have been accomplished in a single transaction: the withdrawal of cash from the corporation. To reflect that reality and treat the transactions as a single event, Section 306(a)(2) provides that the amount realized on a redemption of Section 306 stock is treated as a Section 301 distribution, taxable as a dividend (likely a qualified dividend) to the extent of the current or accumulated earnings and profits in the year of redemption.[16] The balance of the distribution, if any, is treated as a reduction of basis and then capital gain under the rules generally applicable to nonliquidating distributions.[17]

c. DISPOSITIONS EXEMPT FROM SECTION 306

Code: § 306(b).

Regulations: § 1.306–2.

Section 306 is aimed only at bailouts, and not every disposition of Section 306 stock presents that opportunity. For example, a shareholder who sells her entire interest in a corporation (including her Section 306 stock) is not withdrawing corporate earnings while preserving control. She is engaging in a transaction that easily could have qualified for capital gain treatment irrespective of any prior stock dividend. Section 306(b)(1) thus provides that the punitive general rule of Section 306(a) shall not apply to nonredemption dispositions if the shareholder completely terminates her interest in the corporation and does not dispose of the stock to a related person within the Section 318 attribution rules.[18] A similar exception is provided for redemptions of Section 306 stock that result in a complete termination of the shareholder's interest under Section 302(b)(3) or qualify as a partial liquidation under Section 302(b)(4).[19]

---

14. Section 306(a)(1)(D) provides that any amount treated as ordinary income on a sale of Section 306 stock shall be treated as a dividend "[f]or purposes of section 1(h)(11) and such other provisions as the Secretary shall specify * * *." As of early 2005, the Treasury had not yet "specified" and, until it does, it appears that corporate shareholders may not claim the dividends received deduction, and no earnings and profit reduction is authorized on a sale of Section 306 stock.

15. I.R.C. § 306(a)(1)(C); Reg. § 1.306–1(b)(2) Example (3).

16. I.R.C. § 306(a)(2).

17. See I.R.C. § 301(c)(2), (3).

18. For purposes of determining whether there has been a complete termination, the Section 318 attribution rules apply. I.R.C. § 306(b)(1)(A)(iii).

19. I.R.C. § 306(b)(1)(B).

Other exempt dispositions include: (1) redemptions of Section 306 stock in a complete liquidation;[20] (2) dispositions that are treated as nonrecognition transactions, such as tax-free Section 351 transfers, contributions to capital and the like;[21] and (3) distributions coupled with subsequent dispositions or redemptions of Section 306 stock if the taxpayer satisfies the Service that either: (a) the distribution and subsequent disposition or redemption, or (b) in the case of a prior or simultaneous disposition of the underlying common stock, just the disposition or redemption, was not made pursuant to a plan having tax avoidance as one of its principal purposes.[22]

Although Section 306 is aimed primarily at closely held companies, the Service's hard line position is that holders of Section 306 stock issued by public companies are not automatically entitled to relief under the "no tax avoidance" exception in Section 306(b)(4).[23] The "no tax avoidance" exception is explored in the *Fireoved* case, which follows.

Fireoved v. United States

United States Court of Appeals, Third Circuit, 1972.
462 F.2d 1281.

■ ADAMS, CIRCUIT JUDGE.

This appeal calls into question the application of section 306 of the Internal Revenue Code of 1954 and the "first in-first out rule" to a redemption of preferred stock in a corporation by plaintiff, one of its principal shareholders. In particular we are asked to decide whether the transaction here had "as one of its principal purposes the avoidance of Federal income tax," whether a prior sale of a portion of the underlying common stock immunized a like proportion of the section 306 stock from treatment as a noncapital asset, and whether another block of the redeemed stock should be considered to represent stock not subject to section 306.

I. Factual Background

On November 24, 1948, Fireoved and Company, Inc. was incorporated for the purpose of printing and selling business forms. At their first meeting, the incorporators elected Eugene Fireoved, his wife, Marie, the plaintiffs, and a nephew, Robert L. Fireoved, as directors of the corporation. Subsequently, the directors elected Eugene Fireoved as President and Treasurer and Marie Fireoved as Secretary. The corporation had authorized capital stock of 500 shares of $100 par value non-voting, non-cumulative preferred stock and 100 shares of $1 par value voting common stock. On December 31, 1948, in consideration for $100 cash, the corporation issued Eugene Fireoved 100 shares of common stock; for $500 cash, it

20. I.R.C. § 306(b)(2).
21. I.R.C. § 306(b)(3).
22. I.R.C. § 306(b)(4).

23. Rev. Rul. 89–63, 1989–1 C.B. 90, revoking Rev. Rul. 56–116, 1956–1 C.B. 164.

issued him five shares of preferred stock; and in payment for automotive equipment and furniture and fixtures, valued at $6,000, it issued him an additional 60 shares of preferred stock.

In 1954, when Mr. Fireoved learned that his nephew, Robert, was planning to leave the business, he began discussions with Karl Edelmayer and Kenneth Craver concerning the possibility of combining his business with their partnership, Girard Business Forms, that had been printing and selling business forms for some time prior to 1954. Messrs. Fireoved, Edelmayer and Craver agreed that voting control of the new enterprise should be divided equally among the three of them. Because Mr. Fireoved's contribution to capital would be approximately $60,000 whereas the partnership could contribute only $30,000, it was decided that preferred stock should be issued to Mr. Fireoved to compensate for the disparity. In furtherance of this plan, the directors and shareholders of Fireoved and Company, in late 1954 and early 1955, held several meetings at which the following corporate changes were accomplished: The name of the company was changed to Girard Business Forms; the authorized common stock was increased from 100 to 300 shares and the authorized preferred stock was increased to 1000 shares; Mr. Fireoved exchanged his 100 shares of common and 65 shares of preferred stock for equal amounts of the new stock; an agreement of purchase was authorized by which the company would buy all the assets of the Edelmayer–Craver partnership in return for 200 shares of common and 298 shares of preferred stock; and Mr. Fireoved was issued 535 shares of the new preferred stock as a dividend[6] on his 100 shares of common stock, thereby bringing his total holding of preferred stock to 600 shares to indicate his $60,000 capital contribution compared to the $29,800 contributed by the former partnership.

As the business progressed, Mr. Edelmayer demanded more control of the company. In response, Mr. Fireoved and Mr. Craver each sold 24 shares of common stock in the corporation to him on February 28, 1958.

On April 30, 1959, the company redeemed 451 of Mr. Fireoved's 600 shares of preferred stock at $105 per share, resulting in net proceeds to him of $47,355.[7] The gain from this transaction was reported by Mr. and Mrs. Fireoved on their joint return for the year 1959 as a long term capital gain. Subsequently, the Commissioner of Internal Revenue (Commissioner) assessed a deficiency against the Fireoveds of $15,337.13 based on the Commissioner's view that the proceeds from the redemption of the 451 shares of preferred stock should have been reported as ordinary income and the tax paid at that rate based on section 306. Mr. and Mrs. Fireoved paid the assessment on March 14, 1963, but on March 10, 1965, filed a claim for a refund with the Commissioner.

After the Commissioner disallowed the refund claim on March 8, 1966, the Fireoveds instituted the present action against the United States on

---

6. At the time Mr. Fireoved received his stock dividend, the company had accumulated earnings and profits of $52,993.06.

7. In 1959, the company had accumulated earnings and profits of $48,235.

August 4, 1967 seeking a refund of the $15,337.13 plus interest on the ground that the transaction came within an exception to section 306, and that they were therefore entitled to report the income as a long term capital gain. The case was tried to the court without a jury on stipulated facts. It is from the district court's determination, 318 F.Supp. 133, on October 29, 1970, that $8,885.50 should be refunded to the taxpayers that both parties appeal.

II. *Background of Section 306*

Because we are the first court of appeals asked to decide questions of law pursuant to section 306, it is appropriate that we first examine the circumstances that led to the inclusion in 1954 of this section in the Code.

Generally, a taxpayer will benefit monetarily if he is able to report income as a long term capital gain rather than as ordinary income. Under normal circumstances a cash dividend from a corporation constitutes ordinary income to the shareholder receiving such money. Therefore, it would be to the advantage of a shareholder if a method could be devised by which the money could be distributed to him, that would otherwise be paid out as cash dividends, in a form that would permit the shareholder to report such income as a long term capital gain.

A temporarily successful plan for converting ordinary income to long term capital gain is described by the facts of Chamberlin v. C.I.R., 207 F.2d 462 (6th Cir.1953). * * *

The legislative reaction to the Chamberlin decision was almost immediate, resulting in the addition of section 306 to the 1954 Code, in order to prevent shareholders from obtaining the tax advantage of such bail-outs when such shareholders retain their ownership interests in the company.

* * *

Based on the history of section 306 and its plain meaning evidenced by the provisions, it is not disputed that the 535 shares of preferred stock issued to Mr. Fireoved as a stock dividend in 1954 were section 306 stock. Additionally, it is clear that in 1959, when the company redeemed 451 shares of Mr. Fireoved's preferred stock, the general provisions of section 306aside from the exceptions—would require that any amount realized by Mr. Fireoved be taxed at ordinary income rates rather than long term capital gain rates, because the company had earnings at that time of $48,235more than the $47,355 required to redeem the stock at $105 per share.

Thus, the questions to be decided on this appeal are (1) whether certain of the exceptions to section 306 apply to permit the Fireoveds' reporting their gain as a long term capital gain, and (2) whether 65 of the 451 shares redeemed are not section 306 stock because of the first in-first out rule of Treasury Regulation § 1.1012–1(c).

III.   Was the distribution of the stock dividend "in pursuance of a plan having as one of its principal purposes avoidance of Federal income tax?"

Mr. Fireoved asserts that the entire transaction should fall within the exception established by section 306(b)(4)(A), which provides: "If it is established to the satisfaction of the Secretary or his delegate * * * that the distribution, and the disposition or redemption * * * was not in pursuance of a plan having as one of its principal purposes the avoidance of Federal income tax," then the general rule of section 306(a) will not apply.

As a threshold point on this issue, the Government maintains that because Mr. Fireoved never attempted to obtain a ruling from the "Secretary or his delegate" the redemption should be covered by section 306(a), and the district court should not have reached the question whether the exception applied to Mr. Fireoved. Mr. Fireoved urges that the district court had the power to consider the matter de novo, even without a request by the taxpayer to the Secretary or his delegate. Because the ultimate result we reach would not be altered by whichever of these two courses we choose, we do not resolve this potentially complex procedural problem.[10]

The district court, based on the assumption that it had the power to decide the question, found that although one of the purposes involved in the issuance of the preferred stock dividend may have been business related, another principal purpose was the avoidance of Federal income tax.

Mr. Fireoved's analysis of the facts presented in the stipulations would reach the conclusion that the sole purpose of the stock dividend was business related. He relies heavily on that portion of the stipulation which describes why the decision was made to combine his business with the Edelmayer–Craver partnership: "The partnership could provide the additional manpower which the expected departure of Robert L. Fireoved from the Corporation would require. Additionally, the partnership needed additional working capital which the Corporation had and could provide." Based primarily on the latter sentence, Mr. Fireoved asserts that the district court had no choice but to find that the transaction was business related and that it therefore had no avoidance incentive.

In making this argument, however, Mr. Fireoved overlooks the plain import of the language of section 306(b)(4). Whether the section requires the decision to be made by the Secretary or the district court, it is clear that "one of [the] principal purposes" of the stock dividend was not for "the avoidance of Federal income tax." The stipulation demonstrates no more than that the reorganized company required more capital than could be supplied by the partnership alone. The stipulation is completely in harmony with the following fact situation: After the partnership was combined with the corporation, the business required the $30,000 contributed by the partnership and all of the $60,000 Mr. Fireoved had in the corporation. Mr. Fireoved decided to take the stock dividend rather than to distribute the cash to himself as a dividend, and then to make a loan to the

---

10. For the same reason, we do not decide this issue in Part II, infra.

corporation of the necessary money because if he took the cash, he would subject himself to taxation at ordinary income rates. Therefore "one of the principal purposes" of the stock dividend would be for "the avoidance of Federal income tax."

In a situation such as the one presented in this case, where the facts necessary to determine the motives for the issuance of a stock dividend are peculiarly within the control of the taxpayer, it is reasonable to require the taxpayer to come forward with the facts that would relieve him of his liability. Here the stipulation was equivocal in determining the purpose of the dividend and is quite compatible with the thought that "one of the principal purposes" was motivated by "tax avoidance." We hold then that the district court did not err in refusing to apply the exception created by section 306(b)(4)(A).[11]

IV. Did the prior sale by Mr. Fireoved of 24% of his underlying common stock immunize such portion of the section 306 stock he redeemed in 1959?

The district court construed section 306(b)(4)(B) to mean that any time a taxpayer in Mr. Fireoved's position sells any portion of his underlying common stock and later sells or redeems his section 306 stock, an equivalent proportion of the section 306 stock redeemed will not be subject to the provisions of section 306(a). The Government has appealed from this portion of the district court's order and urges that we reverse it, based on the history and purpose of section 306 and the particular facts here.

The stipulations indicate that, "On February 28, 1958, Fireoved and Craver each sold 24 shares of common stock in the corporation to Edelmayer," and that appropriate stock certificates were issued. From this fact, Mr. Fireoved reasons that his sale of 24 of his 100 shares of common stock was undertaken solely for the business purpose of satisfying Mr. Edelmayer's desire for more control of the corporation, and therefore he should be given the benefit of section 306(b)(4)(B). In addition, Mr. Fireoved contends that the disposition of his section 306 stock was related to a business purpose because he used part of the proceeds to pay off a $20,000 loan that the company had made to him.

Mr. Fireoved has the same burden here of showing a lack of a tax avoidance purpose that he had in section III supra. It is clear from the limited facts set forth in the stipulations that he has not established that

---

11. It is important to note that apparently both Mr. Fireoved, in prosecuting this action for a refund, and the Government, in its defense, assumed that if the distribution and redemption of the preferred stock were not controlled by § 306(a), the gain would be subject to taxation as a long term capital gain. This is not necessarily the case at all. Whether or not § 306 governs the transaction, it nonetheless involves a redemption of stock by a corporation to which § 302 could apply. Under the tests set out in § 302(b)—the relevant one of which appears to be § 302(b)(1)—Mr. Fireoved, who had the burden of proof, may well have been unable to show that the redemption was not "essentially equivalent to a dividend." United States v. Davis, 397 U.S. 301, 90 S.Ct. 1041, 25 L.Ed.2d 323 (1970). We hold, however, that it is now too late for the Government to raise this issue.

the disposition of 24% of the 535 shares of the section 306 preferred stock he owned "was not in pursuance of a plan having as one of its principal purposes the avoidance of federal income tax."[12] More important, however, is that an examination of the relevant legislative history indicates that Congress did not intend to give capital gains treatment to a portion of the preferred stock redeemed on the facts presented here.

It is apparent from the reaction evinced by Congress to the Chamberlin case, supra, that by enacting section 306 Congress was particularly concerned with the tax advantages available to persons who controlled corporations and who could, without sacrificing their control, convert ordinary income to long term capital gains by the device of the preferred stock bailout. The illustration given in the Senate Report which accompanied section 306(b)(4)(B) is helpful in determining the sort of transactions meant to be exempted by section 306(a):

> Thus if a shareholder received a distribution of 100 shares of section 306 stock on his holdings of 100 shares of voting common stock in a corporation and sells his voting common stock before he disposes of his section 306 stock, the subsequent disposition of his section 306 stock would not ordinarily be considered a tax avoidance disposition since he has previously parted with the stock which allows him to participate in the ownership of the business. However, variations of the above example may give rise to tax avoidance possibilities which are not within the exception of subparagraph (B). Thus if a corporation has only one class of common stock outstanding and it issues stock under circumstances that characterize it as section 306 stock, a subsequent issue of a different Class of common having greater voting rights than the original common will not permit a simultaneous disposition of the section 306 stock together with the original common to escape the rules of subsection (a) of section 306.

Thus, it is reasonable to assume that Congress realized the general lack of a tax avoidance purpose when a person sells all of his control in a corporation and then either simultaneously or subsequently disposes of his section 306 stock. However, when only a portion of the underlying common stock is sold, and the taxpayer retains essentially all the control he had previously, it would be unrealistic to conclude that Congress meant to give

---

12. Consistent with Mr. Fireoved's sale of 24 shares of common stock in 1958 could have been his knowledge that one year later he would be selling his section 306 stock and a desire on his part to avoid taxation at ordinary income rates. As noted later in the opinion, the sale of just 24 shares was enough so that he retained effective control—in the form of veto power—over the corporation. Moreover, the fact that Mr. Fireoved needed $20,000 of the proceeds to pay off a loan to the corporation would not meet his burden.

The proceeds of the redemption totaled $47,355. Thus, although $20,000 of the redemption may not have been to avoid taxes, we can ascribe no purpose other than tax avoidance to the receipt of the additional $27,355. Therefore, since one of the principal purposes of the redemption of 451 shares of preferred stock was "the avoidance of Federal income tax," Mr. Fireoved may not take advantage of § 306(b)(4)(B) for any part of the redemption.

that taxpayer the advantage of section 306(b)(4)(B) when he ultimately sells his section 306 stock. Cf. United States v. Davis, 397 U.S. 301, 90 S.Ct. 1041, 25 L.Ed.2d 323 (1970).

Shortly after Mr. Fireoved's corporation had been combined with the Edelmayer–Craver partnership, significant changes to the by-laws were made. The by-laws provided that corporate action could be taken only with the unanimous consent of all the directors. In addition, the by-laws provided that they could be amended either by a vote of 76% of the outstanding common shares or a unanimous vote of the directors. When the businesses were combined in late 1954, each of the directors held ⅓ of the voting stock, thereby necessitating a unanimous vote for amendment to the by-laws. After Messrs. Fireoved and Craver each sold 24 shares of common stock to Mr. Edelmayer, Mr. Fireoved held 25⅛% of the common (voting) stock, Mr. Craver 25⅛% and Mr. Edelmayer 49⅛%. It is crucial to note that the by-laws provided for a unanimous vote for corporate action, and after the common stock transfer, the by-laws were capable of amendment only by a unanimous vote because no two shareholders could vote more than 74⅝% of the common stock and 76% of the common stock was necessary for amendment. Thus, although Mr. Fireoved did sell a portion of his voting stock prior to his disposition of the section 306 stock, he retained as much control in the corporation following the sale of his common stock as he had prior to the sale. Under these circumstances it is not consonant with the history of the legislation to conclude that Congress intended such a sale of underlying common stock to exempt the proceeds of the disposition of section 306 stock from treatment as ordinary income. Accordingly, the district court erred when it held that any of the preferred shares Mr. Fireoved redeemed were not subject to section 306(a) by virtue of section 306(b)(4)(B).[14]

V. Does the rule of first in-first out mean that 65 of the 451 redeemed shares were those which Mr. Fireoved acquired when he incorporated his business in 1948 and thus should not be treated as section 306 stock?

The district court held that 65 of 451 shares of preferred stock that Mr. Fireoved redeemed in 1959 represented the original shares issued to him in 1948 and were not, therefore, section 306 stock, and that the proceeds from their sales should be treated as a long term capital gain. The court reached this conclusion by applying Treas.Reg. § 1.1012–1(c). This regulation provides that when an individual acquires shares of the same class of stock in the same corporation on different dates and for different prices, sells a portion of those shares, and cannot adequately identify which lots were sold, for the purpose of determining the basis and the holding period, the first shares acquired are deemed to be the first shares sold.

---

14. It is important to note that our decision relates only to the facts of this case. We express no view on the situation in which less than all the voting shares are sold but enough are disposed of to relinquish effective control prior to or simultaneous with the sale of section 306 stock.

Both the district court and Mr. Fireoved reason that the 65 preferred shares he received in 1948 were the first such shares owned by him. In 1954, when the corporation was recapitalized, Mr. Fireoved surrendered his certificate for 65 shares, received a 535 share stock dividend and was issued a certificate representing 600 shares of preferred stock. When he disposed of 451 shares in 1959, it was impossible to identify which shares of the 600 share certificate were being sold. By applying the convenient tool of section 1.1012–1(c), one might conclude that the 65 original shares were sold first because they were received first.

Superficially, this analysis appears to be correct. However, it overlooks the existence of Section 1223(5) of the Code and the regulations issued pursuant thereto. This section governs the transaction in question because section 307 required Mr. Fireoved to allocate his investment in the underlying common stock between the stock and the preferred stock issued as a dividend. Section 1223(5) is then clear in that it will apply to all situations in which an allocation of basis has occurred pursuant to section 307. These provisions broadly state that the holding period for stock received as a stock dividend is equal to the period for which the underlying stock was held. Applying this test we discover that the preferred stock dividend of 535 shares was issued with respect to the original 100 shares of common received by Mr. Fireoved. Therefore, the holding period for the 535 shares dividend relates back to the date on which the underlying common was issued. Coincidentally, the original 65 shares of preferred stock were issued on the same date as the common. Because the constructive date of issuance for all of the 600 shares of preferred stock owned by Mr. Fireoved is identical, neither the 65 shares nor the 535 shares are first in, but rather are in at the same time.

Since it is impossible adequately to identify which shares were sold when Mr. Fireoved redeemed 451 shares of preferred stock, we hold that a pro rata portion of the 65 shares were redeemed in 1959. In other words, the percentage of the 600 shares of preferred which were not section 306 stock may be represented by the fraction $^{65}/_{600}$. That percentage of the 451 shares redeemed in 1959, therefore, would not be section 306 stock.[15]

* * *

PROBLEMS

1. In year one, Argonaut Corporation distributed nonconvertible nonvoting preferred stock worth $1,000 to each of its two unrelated equal common shareholders, Jason and Vera. The Argonaut common stock owned by each of the shareholders had a basis of $2,000 prior to the distribution and a value of $3,000 immediately after the distribution. At the time of the

---

15. The number of shares may be determined as follows: $^{65}/_{600}$ x 451 = 48.86   shares of non-section 306 stock.

distribution, Argonaut had $2,000 of earnings and profits. In year three, Argonaut had $3,000 of earnings and profits.

(a) What are the tax consequences to Jason, Vera and Argonaut of the distribution of preferred stock in year one?

(b) What results to Vera and Argonaut if Vera sells her preferred stock to Carl, an unrelated party, for $1,000 in year three?

(c) Same as (b), above, except that Vera sells her preferred stock to Carl for $1,750?

(d) Same as (b), above, except that Argonaut had no earnings and profits at the time of the distribution of the preferred stock?

(e) What results if Jason gives his preferred stock to his grandson, Claude, and Claude later sells the stock for $1,000? What if Jason dies and bequeaths his preferred stock to Claude?

(f) What results to Jason and Argonaut if in year three the corporation redeems half of Jason's common stock for $5,000 and all of his preferred stock for $1,500?

(g) Same as (f), above, except the corporate bylaws require unanimous shareholder agreement for corporate action, and the bylaws may be amended only with the concurrence of more than 75 percent of the shareholders.

(h) Same as (f), above, except that Argonaut has no accumulated or current earnings and profits in year three.

2. Zapco Corporation has 100 shares of common stock outstanding all of which are owned by Sam Shifty. Zapco has an ample supply of current and accumulated earnings and profits.

(a) If Sam forms Holding Co. by transferring 50 Zapco shares in exchange for 100 shares of Holding common stock and 100 shares of Holding preferred stock, will any of the Holding shares be Section 306 stock?

(b) What result if Zapco were owned equally (50 shares each) by Sam Shifty and Selma Zap, who is unrelated to Sam, and the two shareholders form Holding Co. by transferring all their Zapco stock with Sam taking back 100 shares of Holding Co. common stock and Selma taking back 50 shares of Holding Co. preferred stock and 50 shares of Holding Co. common stock?

CHAPTER 7

COMPLETE LIQUIDATIONS

A. INTRODUCTION

We have been present at the creation of a corporation and nurtured the corporate entity as it engaged in distributions, redemptions, partial liquidations and maneuvers to mitigate the double tax. This chapter shifts the focus to the end of a C corporation's life cycle.

A few definitions are in order to set the stage. The Code does not define "complete liquidation," but the regulations provide that liquidation status exists for tax purposes "when the corporation ceases to be a going concern and its activities are merely for the purpose of winding up its affairs, paying its debts, and distributing any remaining balance to its shareholders."[1] Legal dissolution under state law is not required for the liquidation to be complete, and a transaction will be treated as a liquidation even if the corporation retains a nominal amount of assets to pay any remaining debts and preserve its legal existence.[2]

Liquidations often are preceded by a sale of substantially all of a corporation's assets and a distribution of the sales proceeds to the shareholders in exchange for their stock. Alternatively, the buyer of a corporate business may acquire all the stock of the target company and either keep the old corporation alive or cause it to be liquidated. But liquidations do not necessarily involve sales. The corporation simply may distribute its assets in kind to the shareholders, who either may sell the assets or continue to operate the business outside of corporate solution. Or a parent corporation may wish to rearrange its holdings by liquidating or selling the stock of a subsidiary.

All these transactions raise challenging tax issues at the shareholder and corporate levels. Historically, individual shareholders have hoped to emerge from a complete liquidation or the sale of a profitable corporate business by realizing a capital gain on their stock and, on an installment sale, by deferring recognition of the gain until cash payments are received. At the corporate level, the goals generally have been to avoid recognition of gain on a distribution or sale of assets while providing the shareholders (in a liquidation) or the purchaser (in an acquisition) with a fair market value basis in the distributed or acquired assets. At one time, most of these objectives could be met with careful planning, but liquidations became far

---

1. Reg. § 1.332–2(c). This regulation technically applies only to the liquidation of a subsidiary, but it has long been assumed to apply also to ordinary liquidations.

2. See, e.g., Rev.Rul. 54–518, 1954–2 C.B. 142.

more expensive after the Tax Reform Act of 1986. This chapter surveys the current landscape, considering first the general shareholder and corporate level tax consequences of complete liquidations and then turning to the special problems raised on the liquidation of a subsidiary. Later chapters will consider the closely related topic of taxable acquisitions of corporate assets or stock, tax-free acquisition techniques known as corporate reorganizations, and the carryover of tax attributes following an acquisition.[3]

B.   COMPLETE LIQUIDATIONS UNDER SECTION 331

1.   CONSEQUENCES TO THE SHAREHOLDERS

Code: §§ 331; 334(a); 346(a); 453(h)(1)(A)–(B).

Regulations: §§ 1.331–1(a), (b), (e); 1.453–11(a)(1), (2)(i), (3), –11(d).

The complete liquidation of a corporation presents an opportunity to revisit several policy issues that recur throughout the study of Subchapter C. Consider the appropriate tax consequences to Owner, a sole shareholder of X Corporation, who desires to liquidate X and continue to operate its business as a proprietorship. Assume that X has been profitable and has ample earnings and profits at the time of its liquidation. From Owner's standpoint, should the liquidation be treated as: (1) a nonrecognition transaction akin to an incorporation, (2) a dividend distribution, (3) an exchange of the stock for the distributed assets or (4) some combination of the above?

If Owner continues to operate the business as a sole proprietorship, the liquidation results in a mere change in the form of his investment. Since Congress granted nonrecognition treatment to Owner when he transferred the business into corporate solution, is it not also appropriate to treat the transfer of those assets back into Owner's hands as a tax-free event? This analogy has a superficial appeal but Congress has never seriously considered it except in very limited situations.[1] Nonrecognition is inconsistent with the double tax regime of Subchapter C because it would facilitate the tax-free bailout of earnings and profits. Moreover, many complete liquidations involve the sale of a business followed by a distribution of the cash proceeds to the shareholders. Cash distributions do not lend themselves to a nonrecognition regime because it is impossible to assign money the substituted basis that would be necessary to preserve the shareholder's gain for recognition at a later time. Similarly, any attempt to preserve the liquidated corporation's earnings and profits in the hands of its former shareholders would be cumbersome and inconsistent with the termination of the corporation.

A stronger case can be made for treating a liquidating distribution as a dividend to the extent of the corporation's remaining earnings and profits.

---

3.   See Chapters 8, 9, and 12, infra.

1.   See, e.g., I.R.C. § 332, discussed in Section C of this chapter, infra.

Because earnings and profits disappear on a complete liquidation, this is the last chance to tax a shareholder's withdrawal of corporate profits as ordinary income. By triggering the distribution rules of Sections 301 and 316, this approach would focus on the source of the liquidating distribution rather than the shareholder's relationship to his investment. Dividend treatment, however, is inconsistent with Section 302, which treats a distribution in redemption as an exchange if the shareholder completely terminates or substantially reduces his interest in the corporation. Why should a complete termination of the interests of all the shareholders be treated any less favorably? Moreover, if liquidating distributions were treated as dividends to the extent of the corporation's earnings and profits, a shareholder's stock basis might never be recovered.

The redemption analogy suggests a third approach, which would treat a complete liquidation as a sale of stock by the shareholder. This solution is imperfect, if only because it ignores the disappearance of the earnings and profits account, a clean sweep that does not occur on a sale of stock. But after a period of waffling,[2] Congress opted to treat liquidations as exchanges, an approach that permits shareholders to avoid the dividend sting and be taxed at capital gains rates. Congress concluded that the dividend threat was "preventing liquidation of many corporations" because of the high tax cost it imposed and therefore was generating only minimal revenue.[3] It regarded exchange treatment as "consistent with the entire theory of the [Code]" and as "the only method * * * which can be easily administered."[4]

The Congressional policy is codified in Section 331(a), which provides that amounts received by a shareholder in complete liquidation are treated as full payment in exchange for the shareholder's stock. The vast majority of shareholders who hold their stock as a capital asset will recognize capital gain or loss in an amount equal to the difference between (1) the money and the fair market value of the property received and (2) the shareholder's adjusted basis in the stock surrendered. Section 334(a) provides that the shareholder's basis in property distributed by a corporation in a complete liquidation that is taxable at the shareholder level shall be the fair market value of the property at the time of the distribution.

Computation of a shareholder's gain or loss on a complete liquidation is ordinarily a straightforward affair. The shareholder's amount realized is the money and the fair market value of all other property received from the liquidating corporation. If a shareholder assumes corporate liabilities or receives property subject to a liability in a liquidating distribution, the amount realized is limited to the value of the property received, net of

---

2. Liquidations were first treated as exchanges in the Revenue Act of 1924. Congress changed its mind briefly from 1934 to 1936 and then reinstated the present system.

3. H.R.Rep. No. 2475, 74th Cong., 2d Sess. (1936), reprinted in 1939–1 (Part 2) C.B. 667, 674.

4. S.Rep. No. 368, 68th Cong., 1st Sess. (1924), reprinted in 1939–1 (Part 2) C.B. 266, 274.

liabilities. In keeping with the principles of the *Crane* case, however, it is assumed that the distributee shareholder will pay the liabilities and he thus obtains a full fair market value basis in the property under Section 334(a).

Shareholders who hold several blocks of stock with different bases and acquisition dates must compute their gain or loss separately for each block rather than on an aggregate basis.[5] This method generally makes a difference, however, only when some shares are held long-term and others short-term; otherwise, the tax consequences will be identical whether the shareholder uses a share-by-share or an aggregate approach.[6]

The timing of a shareholder's gain or loss on a complete liquidation raises thornier questions. A liquidating corporation often is unable to distribute all of its property at one time or within the same taxable year. Recognizing these practical constraints, Section 346(a) defines a complete liquidation to include a series of distributions occurring over a period of time if they are all pursuant to a plan of complete liquidation. Shareholders normally prefer to treat these "creeping complete" liquidations as open transactions so they can defer reporting any gain until the amounts received exceed their stock basis.[7] This cost recovery approach has been sanctioned by the Service in the liquidation context[8] even though it would appear to be foreclosed by Section 453, which requires ratable basis recovery as payments are received even in cases where the selling price cannot be readily ascertained.[9] Since liquidating distributions are treated as payments in exchange for the shareholders' stock, Section 453 technically seems to apply and, if so, shareholders wishing to defer their gain should be required to use the installment method, allocating each distribution between recovery of basis and taxable gain.[10] But taxpayers who wish to use

---

5. Reg. § 1.331–1(e). For example, assume that Shareholder ("S") holds 60 shares of X, Inc. stock long-term with a $30,000 basis and 40 shares short-term with a $50,000 basis. If S receives $100,000 in complete liquidation of X, he must allocate the amount realized ratably between the two blocks as follows:

6. For the problems of valuation of the liquidating distribution and handling contingent claims, see Bittker & Eustice, Federal Income Taxation of Corporations & Shareholders ¶ 10.03[2] (7th ed. 2000).

Long-Term 60 shares		Short–Term 40 shares	
A.R.	$60,000	A.R.	$40,000
A.B.	30,000	A.B.	50,000
LTCG	$30,000	STCL	$10,000

7. See, e.g., Burnet v. Logan, 283 U.S. 404, 51 S.Ct. 550 (1931). Cf. I.R.C. § 453(d)(installment method applies unless taxpayer elects out of Section 453).

8. Rev.Rul. 68–348, 1968–2 C.B. 141, amplified by Rev.Rul. 85–48, 1985–1 C.B. 126.

9. See I.R.C. § 453(j)(2); Reg. § 15A.453–1(c). See also S.Rep. No. 96–1000, 96th Cong., 2d Sess. 24 (1980), reprinted in 1980–2 C.B. 494, 506–507. But see Rev.Rul. 85–48, supra note 8, where the Service continued to sanction open transaction reporting of gain on a liquidation notwithstanding the limits imposed by Section 453.

10. Cf. Reg. § 1.453–11(d), which appears to support the position taken in the text but only when the liquidating corporation distributes an installment obligation described in Section 453(h). See infra notes 11–13 and accompanying text. Installment sale reporting is not available if the stock of the liquidating corporation is publicly traded. See I.R.C. § 453(k)(2), requiring current inclusion of gain on deferred payment dispositions of stock or securities traded on an established securities market. If open transaction report-

the cost recovery approach are not likely to be challenged in light of the Service's longstanding position in published rulings.

A different issue is presented when a liquidating corporation sells certain assets for installment obligations and then distributes the obligations in complete liquidation. In that situation, shareholders who receive the installment obligations may be able to defer part of their Section 331(a) gain on the liquidation by using the installment method of reporting under Section 453. Installment sale reporting is accomplished by treating the shareholders' receipt of payments on the distributed installment obligations as if they were received in exchange for the shareholder's stock.[11] To qualify for this treatment, the obligations must have been acquired by the corporation in respect of a sale or exchange of property during the 12–month period beginning on the date a plan of complete liquidation is adopted and the liquidation must be completed within that 12–month period.[12] Installment obligations arising from the sale of inventory or other "dealer" property by the corporation are eligible for installment sale treatment in the hands of the distributee shareholders only if the obligation resulted from a bulk sale—i.e., the sale was to one person in one transaction and involves substantially all of the property attributable to a trade or business of the corporation.[13] Installment sale reporting is not available, however, if the stock of the liquidating corporation is publicly traded,[14] or if the shareholder elects out of Section 453.[15]

PROBLEM

A owns 100 shares of Humdrum Corporation which he purchased several years ago for $10,000. Humdrum has $12,000 of accumulated earnings and profits. What are the tax consequences to A on the liquidation of Humdrum Corporation in the following alternative situations:

(a) Humdrum distributes $20,000 to A in exchange for his stock?

ing is still generally available to liquidating distributions, this restriction should not apply when a shareholder of a public company receives a series of distributions straddling two or more taxable years. See also I.R.C. § 453(d), which permits a taxpayer to "elect out" of installment sale treatment. In the case of a liquidation, an election out would require the shareholder to report his entire gain in the year of the first distribution except, perhaps, where the value of future distributions is unascertainable. See Reg. § 15A.453–1(d).

11. I.R.C. § 453(h)(1)(A); Reg. § 1.453–11. A shareholder who receives liquidating distributions that include installment obligations in more than one taxable year must reasonably estimate the gain attributable to distributions received in each taxable year based on the best available information and allocate his stock basis pro rata over all payments to be received. When the exact amount of gain is subsequently determined, any adjustment is made in the taxable year in which that determination is made. Alternatively, the shareholder may file an amended return for the earlier year. I.R.C. § 453(h)(2); Reg. § 1.453–11(d).

12. Id. See Reg. § 1.453–11(c).

13. I.R.C. § 453(h)(1)(B); Reg. § 1.453–11(c)(4).

14. I.R.C. § 453(k)(2); Reg. § 1.453–11(a)(2)(i). But if a nonpublicly traded liquidating corporation distributes an installment obligation arising from a corporate-level sale of publicly traded stock, the obligation generally qualifies for installment sale reporting under Section 453(h). Reg. § 1.453–11(c)(2).

15. I.R.C. § 453(d).

(b) What result in (a), above, if A receives $10,000 in the current year (year one) and $10,000 in year two? Would there be any problem if Humdrum does not adopt a formal plan of complete liquidation in year one?

(c) Humdrum distributes $8,000 cash and an installment obligation with a face and fair market value of $12,000, payable $1,000 per year for 12 years with market rate interest. The installment obligation was received by Humdrum two months ago, after the adoption of the plan of liquidation, on the sale of a capital asset. Would the result be different if Humdrum's stock were publicly traded? See I.R.C. § 453(k).

(d) Same as (c), above, except the installment obligation was received two years ago and no payments have yet been made.

(e) What result in (a), above, if two years later, A is required to pay a $5,000 judgment against Humdrum in his capacity as transferee of the corporation? Compare this with the result if the judgment had been rendered and paid by the corporation prior to the liquidation. See Arrowsmith v. Commissioner, 344 U.S. 6, 73 S.Ct. 71 (1952).

2.   CONSEQUENCES TO THE LIQUIDATING CORPORATION

Code: § 336(a), (b), (c), (d). Skim § 267(a)(1), (b), (c).

It should come as no surprise at this juncture that Subchapter C requires property distributions by corporations to their shareholders to be analyzed at both the corporate and shareholder levels. Earlier chapters have chronicled the gradual erosion of the *General Utilities*[1] doctrine, under which a corporation generally did not recognize gain on nonliquidating distributions of appreciated property. We have seen that recognition of gain (but not loss) is now the statutory norm in the nonliquidation setting.[2] Should the same rules apply to liquidating distributions and sales of assets by a liquidating corporation? Once again, a brief historical interlude is appropriate before considering the current answers to this much debated question.

a.   BACKGROUND

Although the *General Utilities* case involved a distribution of appreciated property by an ongoing business, the doctrine also applied to liquidating distributions. Until the enactment of the 1986 Code, a corporation generally did not recognize gain or loss on the distribution of property in complete liquidation.[3] Prior to the 1954 Code, however, sales of assets by a liquidating corporation were fully taxable.

---

1. General Utilities & Operating Co. v. Helvering, 296 U.S. 200, 56 S.Ct. 185 (1935); see Chapters 12D1 and 13E1, supra.

2. I.R.C. § 311(a), (b).

3. I.R.C. § 336(a)(pre–1987). This general nonrecognition rule was subject to various exceptions, such as the statutory recapture of depreciation provisions and the judicially created tax benefit rule and as-

To illustrate the disparate tax treatment of liquidating distributions and sales under the pre–1954 regime, assume that A is the sole shareholder of Target Corporation ("T") and has a $100,000 basis in her T stock. T's only asset is a parcel of undeveloped land ("Gainacre") with a fair market value of $400,000 and a zero adjusted basis. Purchaser ("P") wishes to acquire Gainacre for $400,000 cash. If T distributed Gainacre to A in complete liquidation, it recognized no gain under the *General Utilities* doctrine, and A took Gainacre with a $400,000 fair market value basis. On a sale of Gainacre to P for $400,000 following the liquidation, A thus would recognize no gain. If, instead, T had sold Gainacre directly to P, it would have recognized $400,000 gain under the pre–1954 regime. In either case, A recognized gain on the liquidation of T, measured by the difference between the amount of the distribution and her $100,000 adjusted basis in the T stock.

The different tax results of these economically equivalent transactions prompted savvy taxpayers to "postpone" sales of corporate assets until after a liquidation in order to avoid a corporate-level tax. The ignorant did what came naturally—and often was a practical necessity for large corporations with many assets and shareholders—by selling assets at the corporate level prior to the liquidation. With such high tax stakes, the courts were called upon to determine who *in substance* made the sale—an inquiry that engendered some anomalous results, as evidenced by the two Supreme Court decisions that follow.

Commissioner v. Court Holding Co.

Supreme Court of the United States, 1945.
324 U.S. 331, 65 S.Ct. 707.

■ MR. JUSTICE BLACK delivered the opinion of the Court.

An apartment house, which was the sole asset of the respondent corporation, was transferred in the form of a liquidating dividend to the corporation's two shareholders. They in turn formally conveyed it to a purchaser who had originally negotiated for the purchase from the corporation. The question is whether the Circuit Court of Appeals properly reversed the Tax Court's conclusion that the corporation was taxable under § 22 of the Internal Revenue Code for the gain which accrued from the sale. The answer depends upon whether the findings of the Tax Court that the whole transaction showed a sale by the corporation rather than by the stockholders were final and binding upon the Circuit Court of Appeals.

It is unnecessary to set out in detail the evidence introduced before the Tax Court or its findings. Despite conflicting evidence, the following findings of the Tax Court are supported by the record:

signment of income doctrine. See, e.g., 460 U.S. 370, 103 S.Ct. 1134 (1983).
Hillsboro National Bank v. Commissioner,

The respondent corporation was organized in 1934 solely to buy and hold the apartment building which was the only property ever owned by it. All of its outstanding stock was owned by Minnie Miller and her husband. Between October 1, 1939 and February, 1940, while the corporation still had legal title to the property, negotiations for its sale took place. These negotiations were between the corporation and the lessees of the property, together with a sister and brother-in-law. An oral agreement was reached as to the terms and conditions of sale, and on February 22, 1940, the parties met to reduce the agreement to writing. The purchaser was then advised by the corporation's attorney that the sale could not be consummated because it would result in the imposition of a large income tax on the corporation. The next day, the corporation declared a "liquidating dividend," which involved complete liquidation of its assets, and surrender of all outstanding stock. Mrs. Miller and her husband surrendered their stock, and the building was deeded to them. A sale contract was then drawn, naming the Millers individually as vendors, and the lessees' sister as vendee, which embodied substantially the same terms and conditions previously agreed upon. One thousand dollars, which a month and a half earlier had been paid to the corporation by the lessees, was applied in part payment of the purchase price. Three days later, the property was conveyed to the lessees' sister.

The Tax Court concluded from these facts that, despite the declaration of a "liquidating dividend" followed by the transfers of legal title, the corporation had not abandoned the sales negotiations; that these were mere formalities designed "to make the transaction appear to be other than what it was" in order to avoid tax liability. The Circuit Court of Appeals drawing different inferences from the record, held that the corporation had "called off" the sale, and treated the stockholders' sale as unrelated to the prior negotiations.

There was evidence to support the findings of the Tax Court, and its findings must therefore be accepted by the courts. Dobson v. Commissioner, 320 U.S. 489; Commissioner v. Heininger, 320 U.S. 467; Commissioner v. Scottish American Investment Co., 323 U.S. 119. On the basis of these findings, the Tax Court was justified in attributing the gain from the sale to respondent corporation. The incidence of taxation depends upon the substance of a transaction. The tax consequences which arise from gains from a sale of property are not finally to be determined solely by the means employed to transfer legal title. Rather, the transaction must be viewed as a whole, and each step, from the commencement of negotiations to the consummation of the sale, is relevant. A sale by one person cannot be transformed for tax purposes into a sale by another by using the latter as a conduit through which to pass title. To permit the true nature of a transaction to be disguised by mere formalisms, which exist solely to alter tax liabilities, would seriously impair the effective administration of the tax policies of Congress.

It is urged that respondent corporation never executed a written agreement, and that an oral agreement to sell land cannot be enforced in

Florida because of the Statute of Frauds, Comp.Gen.Laws of Florida, 1927, vol. 3, § 5779. But the fact that respondent corporation itself never executed a written contract is unimportant, since the Tax Court found from the facts of the entire transaction that the executed sale was in substance the sale of the corporation. The decision of the Circuit Court of Appeals is reversed, and that of the Tax Court affirmed.

It is so ordered.

United States v. Cumberland Public Service Co.

Supreme Court of the United States, 1950.
338 U.S. 451, 70 S.Ct. 280.

MR. JUSTICE BLACK delivered the opinion of the Court.

A corporation selling its physical properties is taxed on capital gains resulting from the sale. There is no corporate tax, however, on distribution of assets in kind to shareholders as part of a genuine liquidation. The respondent corporation transferred property to its shareholders as a liquidating dividend in kind. The shareholders transferred it to a purchaser. The question is whether, despite contrary findings by the Court of Claims, this record requires a holding that the transaction was in fact a sale by the corporation subjecting the corporation to a capital gains tax.

Details of the transaction are as follows. The respondent, a closely held corporation, was long engaged in the business of generating and distributing electric power in three Kentucky counties. In 1936 a local cooperative began to distribute Tennessee Valley Authority power in the area served by respondent. It soon became obvious that respondent's Diesel-generated power could not compete with TVA power, which respondent had been unable to obtain. Respondent's shareholders, realizing that the corporation must get out of the power business unless it obtained TVA power, accordingly offered to sell all the corporate stock to the cooperative, which was receiving such power. The cooperative refused to buy the stock, but countered with an offer to buy from the corporation its transmission and distribution equipment. The corporation rejected the offer because it would have been compelled to pay a heavy capital gains tax. At the same time the shareholders, desiring to save payment of the corporate capital gains tax, offered to acquire the transmission and distribution equipment and then sell to the cooperative. The cooperative accepted. The corporation transferred the transmission and distribution systems to its shareholders in partial liquidation. The remaining assets were sold and the corporation dissolved. The shareholders then executed the previously contemplated sale to the cooperative.

Upon this sale by the shareholders, the Commissioner assessed and collected a $17,000 tax from the corporation on the theory that the shareholders had been used as a mere conduit for effectuating what was really a corporate sale. Respondent corporation brought this action to recover the amount of the tax. The Court of Claims found that the method by which the stockholders disposed of the properties was avowedly chosen in order to reduce taxes, but that the liquidation and dissolution genuinely ended the corporation's activities and existence. The court also found that at no time did the corporation plan to make the sale itself. Accordingly it found as a fact that the sale was made by the shareholders rather than the corporation, and entered judgment for respondent. One judge dissented, believing that our opinion in Commissioner v. Court Holding Co., 324 U.S. 331, required a finding that the sale had been made by the corporation. Certiorari was granted, 338 U.S. 846, to clear up doubts arising out of the *Court Holding Co.* case.

Our *Court Holding Co.* decision rested on findings of fact by the Tax Court that a sale had been made and gains realized by the taxpayer corporation. There the corporation had negotiated for sale of its assets and had reached an oral agreement of sale. When the tax consequences of the corporate sale were belatedly recognized, the corporation purported to "call off" the sale at the last minute and distributed the physical properties in kind to the stockholders. They promptly conveyed these properties to the same persons who had negotiated with the corporation. The terms of purchase were substantially those of the previous oral agreement. One thousand dollars already paid to the corporation was applied as part payment of the purchase price. The Tax Court found that the corporation never really abandoned its sales negotiations, that it never did dissolve, and that the sole purpose of the so-called liquidation was to disguise a corporate sale through use of mere formalisms in order to avoid tax liability. The Circuit Court of Appeals took a different view of the evidence. In this Court the Government contended that whether a liquidation distribution was genuine or merely a sham was traditionally a question of fact. We agreed with this contention, and reinstated the Tax Court's findings and judgment. Discussing the evidence which supported the findings of fact, we went on to say that "the incidence of taxation depends upon the substance of a transaction" regardless of "mere formalisms," and that taxes on a corporate sale cannot be avoided by using the shareholders as a "conduit through which to pass title."

This language does not mean that a corporation can be taxed even when the sale has been made by its stockholders following a genuine liquidation and dissolution.[3] While the distinction between sales by a corporation as compared with distribution in kind followed by shareholder sales may be particularly shadowy and artificial when the corporation is closely held, Congress has chosen to recognize such a distinction for tax purposes. The corporate tax is thus aimed primarily at the profits of a

---

3. What we said in the *Court Holding Co.* case was an approval of the action of the Tax Court in looking beyond the papers executed by the corporation and shareholders in order to determine whether the sale there had actually been made by the corporation. We were but emphasizing the established principle that in resolving such questions as who made a sale, fact-finding tribunals in tax cases can consider motives, intent, and conduct in addition to what appears in written instruments used by parties to control rights as among themselves. See, e.g., Helvering v. Clifford, 309 U.S. 331, 335–337; Commissioner of Internal Revenue v. Tower, 327 U.S. 280.

going concern. This is true despite the fact that gains realized from corporate sales are taxed, perhaps to prevent tax evasions, even where the cash proceeds are at once distributed in liquidation.[4] But Congress has imposed no tax on liquidating distributions in kind or on dissolution, whatever may be the motive for such liquidation. Consequently, a corporation may liquidate or dissolve without subjecting itself to the corporate gains tax, even though a primary motive is to avoid the burden of corporate taxation.

Here, on the basis of adequate subsidiary findings, the Court of Claims has found that the sale in question was made by the stockholders rather than the corporation. The Government's argument that the shareholders acted as a mere "conduit" for a sale by respondent corporation must fall before this finding. The subsidiary finding that a major motive of the shareholders was to reduce taxes does not bar this conclusion. Whatever the motive and however relevant it may be in determining whether the transaction was real or a sham, sales of physical properties by shareholders following a genuine liquidation distribution cannot be attributed to the corporation for tax purposes.

The oddities in tax consequences that emerge from the tax provisions here controlling appear to be inherent in the present tax pattern. For a corporation is taxed if it sells all its physical properties and distributes the cash proceeds as liquidating dividends, yet is not taxed if that property is distributed in kind and is then sold by the shareholders. In both instances the interest of the shareholders in the business has been transferred to the purchaser. Again, if these stockholders had succeeded in their original effort to sell all their stock, their interest would have been transferred to the purchasers just as effectively. Yet on such a transaction the corporation would have realized no taxable gain.

Congress having determined that different tax consequences shall flow from different methods by which the shareholders of a closely held corporation may dispose of corporate property, we accept its mandate. It is for the trial court, upon consideration of an entire transaction, to determine the factual category in which a particular transaction belongs. Here as in the *Court Holding Co.* case we accept the ultimate findings of fact of the trial tribunal. Accordingly the judgment of the Court of Claims is

Affirmed.

■ MR. JUSTICE DOUGLAS took no part in the consideration or decision of this case.

NOTE

The difficulties faced by the courts in reconciling the results in *Court Holding* and *Cumberland* influenced Congress to extend the *General Utili-*

---

4. It has also been held that where corporate liquidations are effected through trustees or agents, gains from sales are taxable to the corporation as though it were a going concern. See, e.g., First National Bank v. United States, 10 Cir., 86 F.2d 938, 941; Treas.Reg. 103, § 19.22(a)–21.

ties doctrine to liquidating sales. Under the 1954 Code version of Section 337, a corporation generally did not recognize gain or loss on a sale of property pursuant to a plan of complete liquidation except for recapture of depreciation and a few other items.[1] Aptly named the "anti-*Court Holding*" provision, old Section 337 usually ensured that the tax consequences of liquidating sales and distributions were the same regardless of the form of the transaction. In either case, the corporation generally did not recognize gain or loss, while the buyer (or distributee shareholder) took a fair market value basis in the acquired or distributed assets. As a result, the principal tax cost of a complete liquidation or taxable disposition of assets by a liquidating corporation was the capital gain recognized at the shareholder level.

Shortly after this extension of the *General Utilities* doctrine, reformers began calling for its repeal.[2] Imposing a tax at the shareholder level, they argued, did not justify exempting a liquidating corporation from tax on the disposition of its appreciated property. Until the 1980's, however, support for repeal was limited to the academic community and a handful of principled practitioners. "The General," it was said, had the loyal backing of the troops—battalions of legislators and their business constituents who looked askance at the double tax.[3] A principal justification for retaining the *General Utilities* doctrine was that it provided relief from the double taxation of corporate earnings by partially integrating the corporate and individual taxes.[4] More specialized pleaders focused on the adverse impact of the double tax on the "largely inflationary gains" on long-held assets of small "Mom and Pop" businesses.[5]

Despite these arguments, the movement for legislative reform gained momentum in the 1980's.[6] Eventually, the House of Representatives included *General Utilities* repeal, along with a permanent exception for certain closely held corporations, in its version of the 1986 tax reform legislation.[7]

1. I.R.C. § 337 (pre–1987).

2. See, e.g., Lewis, "A Proposed New Treatment for Corporate Distributions and Sales in Liquidations," 86th Cong., 1st Sess., House Committee on Ways and Means, 3 Tax Revision Compendium 1643 (1959).

3. We are indebted to the late Professor Walter Blum for the military analogy. See Blum, "Behind the *General Utilities* Doctrine, or Why Does the General Have So Much Support from the Troops," 62 Taxes 292 (1984).

4. See, e.g., Nolan, "Taxing Corporate Distributions of Appreciated Property: Repeal of the *General Utilities* Doctrine and Relief Measures," 22 San Diego L.Rev. 97 (1985). For an excellent survey and critique of the arguments for retaining *General Utilities,* see Yin, "General Utilities Repeal: Is Tax Reform Really Going to Pass it By?" 31 Tax Notes 1111 (June 11, 1986).

5. See, e.g., "Reform of Corporate Taxation," Hearing before the Committee on Finance, United States Senate, 98th Cong., 1st Sess. 148, 151, 153–157, 174–176, 185, 268–270 (Oct. 24, 1983).

6. See Staff of the Senate Finance Committee, The Subchapter C Revision Act of 1985: A Final Report Prepared by the Staff, 99th Cong., 1st Sess. 6–8, 42–44, 52–54, 59–68 (S.Prt. 99–47, 1985), recommending repeal of the *General Utilities* doctrine except for liquidating distributions or sales of certain long-held (over five years) assets by closely held corporations with under $2 million in assets.

7. H.R. 3838, 99th Cong., 1st Sess. (1985), §§ 331–335.

The House Ways and Means Committee report summarized the rationale for repeal in the liquidation setting:[8]

> The committee believes that the *General Utilities* rule, even in the more limited form in which it exists today, produces many incongruities and inequities in the tax system. First, the rule may create significant distortions in business behavior. Economically, a liquidating distribution is indistinguishable from a nonliquidating distribution; yet the Code provides a substantial preference for the former. A corporation acquiring the assets of a liquidating corporation is able to obtain a basis in assets equal to their fair market value, although the transferor recognizes no gain (other than possibly recapture amounts) on the sale. The tax benefits may make the assets more valuable in the hands of the transferee than in the hands of the present owner. The effect may be to induce corporations with substantial appreciated assets to liquidate and transfer their assets to other corporations for tax reasons, when economic considerations might indicate a different course of action. Accordingly, the *General Utilities* rule may be responsible, at least in part, for the dramatic increase in corporate mergers and acquisitions in recent years. The committee believes that the Code should not artificially encourage corporate liquidations and acquisitions, and believes that repeal of the *General Utilities* rule is a major step towards that goal.

> Second, the *General Utilities* rule tends to undermine the corporate income tax. Under normally applicable tax principles, nonrecognition of gain is available only if the transferee takes a carryover basis in the transferred property, thus assuring that a tax will eventually be collected on the appreciation. Where the *General Utilities* rule applies, assets generally are permitted to leave corporate solution and to take a stepped-up basis in the hands of the transferee without the imposition of a corporate-level tax. Thus, the effect of the rule is to grant a permanent exemption from the corporate income tax.

The Senate had originally included *General Utilities* repeal in its version of the 1986 bill, but that provision was later dropped, reportedly because of concerns over its adverse impact on corporate entrepreneurs.[9] In reconciling the two bills, the Conference Committee adopted the House's approach. To the surprise of even the tax reformers, the conferees went beyond the earlier proposals by eliminating any permanent exceptions for closely held corporations and providing only limited transitional relief. The General, so it seemed, had been deserted by the troops once the battle went behind closed doors. Against that background we turn to the current corporate-level tax treatment of liquidating distributions and sales.

---

8. H.R.Rep. No. 99–426, 99th Cong., 1st Sess. 281 (1985).

9. See Yin, supra note 4, at 1112–1113.

b.   LIQUIDATING DISTRIBUTIONS AND SALES

The current version of Section 336(a) is the reverse of its 1954 Code predecessor. The general rule requires a liquidating corporation to recognize gain or loss on the distribution of property in complete liquidation as if the property were sold to the distributee at its fair market value. If the distributed property is subject to a liability or the distributee shareholder assumes a liability in connection with the distribution, the fair market value of the property is treated as being not less than the amount of the liability.[1] In strengthening the double tax regime of Subchapter C, Congress greatly increased the tax cost of a complete liquidation. Whenever a corporation makes a liquidating distribution of appreciated property, gain generally will be recognized at the corporate level and the distribution also will be a taxable event to the shareholders.[2]

Once Congress required a liquidating corporation to recognize gain or loss on liquidating distributions, it took the next logical step by conforming the tax treatment of liquidating sales. With the repeal of former Section 337, a corporation generally must recognize gain or loss on any sale of its assets pursuant to a complete liquidation plan.[3]

c.   LIMITATIONS ON RECOGNITION OF LOSS

The general rule in Section 336(a) differs in one important respect from the rules in Section 311 governing nonliquidating distributions. It allows the distributing corporation to recognize loss as well as gain. Moreover, although Section 267 disallows losses on sales of property by a corporation to a "related" party (e.g., a controlling shareholder), it does not disallow them on liquidating distributions to related parties.[4] This license to recognize corporate-level losses quickly rattled the Congressional nervous system. To prevent taxpayers from recognizing losses "in inappropriate situations" or inflating the amount of loss actually sustained on a liquidation, the Tax Reform Act of 1986 added the two separate limitations in Section 336(d).[5]

Distributions to Related Persons. Section 336(d)(1) partially reinstates the policy of Section 267 by providing that no loss shall be recognized by a liquidating corporation on the distribution of property to a Section 267 related person if either: (1) the distribution is not pro rata among the

---

1. I.R.C. § 336(b). Cf. I.R.C. § 7701(g); Commissioner v. Tufts, 461 U.S. 300, 103 S.Ct. 1826 (1983), rehearing denied, 463 U.S. 1215, 103 S.Ct. 3555 (1983).

2. The general rule is subject to two exceptions. Nonrecognition of gain or loss is preserved for: (1) distributions in complete liquidation of a controlled—i.e., 80 percent—subsidiary (I.R.C. § 337, see Section C2 of this chapter, infra), and (2) distributions in certain tax-free reorganizations (I.R.C. § 336(c), see Chapter 9C2, infra).

3. A corporation that sells or distributes stock in an 80 percent or more subsidiary may elect under Section 336(e), however, to treat the sale as a disposition of the subsidiary's assets and ignore any gain or loss on the sale or distribution of the stock. See also I.R.C. § 338(h)(10) and Chapter 8C3, infra.

4. I.R.C. § 267(a)(1).

5. See H.R.Rep. No. 99–841, 99th Cong., 2d Sess. II–200 (1986).

shareholders, or (2) the distributed property was acquired by the liquidating corporation in a Section 351 transaction or as a contribution to capital within the five-year period ending on the date of the distribution. These restrictions thus initially focus on the recipient of the loss property. For this purpose, related persons usually will be shareholders who own directly, or through the Section 267 attribution rules, more than 50 percent in value of the stock of the distributing corporation.[6]

Neither the statute nor the legislative history explains when a distribution is "not pro rata" among the shareholders. Congress presumably intended to single out situations where a majority shareholder receives an interest in loss property that is disproportionate to his stock interest in the corporation.[7] The legislative history provides scant illumination of the rationale for this rule. The conferees merely expressed an intent to restrict the ability of taxpayers to recognize losses in "inappropriate situations."[8] Perhaps Congress believed that it was necessary to apply the loss disallowance policy of Section 267 to liquidating distributions where the parties exercised a measure of control by targeting distributions of loss property to majority shareholders—but at the same time concluded that pro rata liquidating distributions were less likely to be motivated by tax avoidance.[9]

The rationale for limiting losses on distributions of recently contributed property to a related party is easier to discern—or at least it was before Congress imposed limitations on the transfer of built-in losses in Section 351 transactions.[10] Before the enactment of Section 362(e)(2), taxpayers could duplicate a single economic loss for tax purposes by transferring property with a built-in loss to a corporation in a Section 351 transaction or as a contribution to capital. For example, assume Sole Shareholder ("Sole") transferred Lossacre (adjusted basis—$1,000; fair market value—$500) to her wholly owned X Corporation ("X") in exchange for $500 of X stock in a Section 351 nonrecognition transaction. Under prior law, Sole took a $1,000 exchanged basis in her new X stock,[11] and X took Lossacre with a $1,000 transferred basis.[12] Assume further that, three years later, when Lossacre had the same basis and value, X liquidated, distributing Lossacre and its other assets to Sole. Without an "outbound" limitation, both Sole Shareholder and the corporation would recognize a $500 loss on the liquidation—two losses for the price of none considering that, when the

---

6. I.R.C. § 267(b)(2), (c).

7. For example, assume X Corporation has a net worth of $1,000 and is owned 75% by A and 25% by five unrelated shareholders. X distributes Lossacre (value—$750; basis $1,000) to A and $250 cash to the other shareholders. Since Lossacre was not distributed to the shareholders in proportion to their respective stock interests, the distribution is not pro rata and X may not recognize its $250 loss.

8. H.R.Rep. No. 99–841, supra note 5, at II–200.

9. Even if the distribution is pro rata, however, losses may be disallowed if the asset distributed to a related person is "disqualified property" within the meaning of Section 336(d)(1)(B). See text accompanying notes 10–15, infra.

10. See I.R.C. § 362(e)(2) and Chapter 2A, infra.

11. I.R.C. § 358(a).

12. I.R.C. § 362(a).

smoke cleared, Sole still owned Lossacre.[13] The same technique was effective for controlling shareholders who owned less than 100 percent of the corporation if on liquidation they received their pro rata share of each corporate asset.[14]

Section 336(d)(1)(A)(ii) attacks this form of "stuffing" with a rule that extends Section 267 principles to pro rata liquidating distributions of "disqualified property" to a related person. "Disqualified property" is defined as any property acquired by the liquidating corporation during the five-year period preceding the distribution in a Section 351 transaction or as a contribution to capital.[15] Section 362(e)(2), however, now imposes an inbound limitation on duplication of losses. Applying that limitation to the above example, Sole would still take a $1,000 exchanged basis in her X stock, but X's basis in Lossacre would be limited to its $500 fair market value at the time it was transferred to X. As a result, on its liquidation three years later, X would have no recognized loss and Section 336(d) would not apply.

In its haste to adopt an inbound loss limitation rule, Congress may not have paused to ask whether the outbound limitations in Section 336(d)(1) should be modified. One answer that may explain the continuing existence of Section 336(d)(1) is that it does not exclusively target *duplication* of losses. It also applies to liquidating distributions of loss property to related persons that are not pro rata or are of "disqualified property," even if the loss was realized while the property was held by the corporation. Although the policy for such a limitation is difficult to defend in the context of a complete liquidation, the Code often limits losses when property is transferred between corporations and shareholders as well as in other related party transactions.[16]

Losses With Tax Avoidance Purpose. Section 336(d)(2) prevents the duplication of *precontribution* built-in losses even on certain distributions to minority shareholders. This limitation applies only if the distributing corporation acquired property in a Section 351 transaction or as a contribution to capital as part of a plan the principal purpose of which was to recognize loss by the corporation on a liquidating sale, exchange or distribution of the property. In that event, Section 336(d)(2) limits the corporation's deductible loss to the amount that accrued after the corporation

---

13. Of course, Sole will now hold Lossacre with a stepped-down fair market value basis of $500, but she will have benefitted from two losses without ever having disposed of the property.

14. As noted previously, corporate-level losses on non pro rata ("bullet") distributions to controlling shareholders are disallowed under Section 336(d)(1)(A)(i).

15. I.R.C. § 336(d)(1)(B). The term also includes any property the adjusted basis of which is determined in whole or in part by reference to the adjusted basis of property

acquired in a Section 351 transaction or as a contribution to capital—e.g., like-kind property received in a Section 1031 transaction in exchange for property acquired by the corporation in a Section 351 transaction. Id.

16. See, e.g., I.R.C. § 351(b)(2) (no loss on transfers to controlled corporations even if transferor receives boot); § 267(a)(1)(disallowance of losses in related party transactions); § 1015(1)(donee's basis for loss reduced for gifts of built-in loss property).

acquired the property. Precontribution losses are disallowed by a basis step-down rule which requires the corporation to reduce its basis (but not below zero) in the affected property by the amount of built-in loss in the property at the time it was acquired by the corporation.[17]

Section 336(d)(2) is reinforced by a provision that treats any contribution of property after the date that is two years before the adoption of the plan of liquidation as part of a forbidden plan to recognize loss, except as the Treasury may provide in regulations.[18] Congress provided extensive guidance on the operation of this two-year presumption and the escape hatches that it expects to be included in future regulations. For example, although a contribution made more than two years prior to the adoption of a liquidation plan might be made with a prohibited purpose, the Conference Report states that in those circumstances the basis step-down rule in Section 336(d)(2) would apply only "in the most rare and unusual cases."[19] The legislative history also directed the Treasury to issue regulations generally providing that even contributions of property within the period covered by the presumption should be disregarded "*unless* there is no clear and substantial relationship between the contributed property and the conduct of the corporation's current or future business enterprises."[20] A "clear and substantial relationship" generally would include a requirement of a corporate business purpose for placing the property in the particular corporation to which it was contributed as compared to retaining the property outside that corporation.[21] If the contributed property has a built-in loss at the time of contribution that is "significant" relative to the built-in corporate gain at that time, "special scrutiny of the business purpose would be appropriate."[22]

Since the inbound loss limitation rule of Section 362(e)(2) effectively disallows most precontribution losses by stepping down the basis of property when it is acquired, Section 336(d)(2)'s role will be greatly reduced in the future. Section 362(e)(2) applies to transfers after October 22, 2004, and so contributions of loss property before that date will be monitored exclusively by Section 336(d)(2). Even after the effective date of Section 362(e)(2), there still will be situations where the inbound rule will not step down the basis of built-in loss property—e.g., where the corporation holds some properties with built-in losses that are subject to Section 336(d)(2) but the inbound stepdown rule did not apply because the aggregate basis of all properties transferred in a Section 351 transaction did not exceed their aggregate fair market value. Query, however, whether an outbound loss

---

17. The built-in loss is the excess of the adjusted basis of the property immediately after its acquisition over its fair market value at that time. I.R.C. § 336(d)(2)(A).

18. I.R.C. § 336(d)(2)(B)(ii).

19. H.R.Rep. No. 99–841, supra note 5, at 200. See also Staff of the Joint Committee on Taxation, General Explanation of the Tax Reform Act of 1986 ("1986 Act General Ex-

planation"), 100th Cong., 1st Sess. 343 (1987).

20. H.R.Rep. No. 99–841, supra note 5, at II–201.

21. 1986 Act General Explanation, supra note 19, at 343.

22. Id.

limitation rule is still necessary in this situation? Perhaps the best explanation is traditional Congressional paranoia regarding abuse of tax losses.

In short, Section 336(d)(2) still may operate to prevent recognition of a loss but only in very limited circumstances. We must wait and see if Congress decides to revisit these questions in its next tax bill.

Overlap Situations. If both Section 336(d)(1) and Section 336(d)(2) apply to the same transaction, the harsher rule in Section 336(d)(1) (which disallows the entire loss rather than just the precontribution built-in loss) takes precedence.[23]

PROBLEM

All the outstanding stock of X Corporation is owned by Ivan (60 shares) and Flo (40 shares), who are unrelated. X has no liabilities and the following assets:

Asset	Adj. Basis	F.M.V.
Gainacre	$100,000	$400,000
Lossacre	800,000	400,000
Cash	200,000	200,000

Unless otherwise indicated, assume that Gainacre and Lossacre each asset have been held by X for more than five years.

On January 1 of the current year, X adopted a plan of complete liquidation. What are the tax consequences to X on the distribution of its assets pursuant to the liquidation plan in each of the following alternatives?

(a) X distributes each of its assets to Ivan and Flo as tenants-in-common in proportion to their stock interests (i.e., Ivan takes a 60% interest and Flo a 40% interest in each asset).

(b) Same as (a), above, except X distributes Lossacre and the cash to Ivan and Gainacre to Flo.

(c) Same as (b), above, except X distributes Gainacre and the cash to Ivan and Lossacre to Flo.

(d) Same as (a), above, except X acquired Lossacre as a contribution to capital four years ago, and X was not required to reduce its basis under § 362(e). Is the result different if Lossacre had a value of $1,000,000 and a basis of $800,000 at the time it was contributed to the corporation?

(e) What result on the distributions in (c), above (i.e., Gainacre and cash to Ivan, Lossacre to Flo) if Lossacre, which had no relationship to X's business operations, was transferred to X by Ivan and Flo in a § 351 transaction 18 months prior to the adoption of the liquidation plan, when Lossacre had a fair market value of

23. 1986 Act General Explanation, supra note 19, at 342, n. 86.

$700,000 and an adjusted basis of $800,000? Assume, alternatively, that § 362(e)(2) did and did not apply to the contribution of Lossacre to X.

(f) Now assume that Ivan and Flow own 80% and 20%, respectively, of X, which was formed with Ivan contributing Gainacre and Lossacre (same adjusted basis and fair market values as in introductory facts above) and Flo contributing $200,000 cash. Assume further that Lossacre is § 336(d)(1) "disqualified property," § 362(e)(2) applied to Ivan's contributions to X but § 336(d)(2) does not apply to the liquidating distribution of Lossacre because there was no "plan" for X to recognize loss on that property. Pursuant to a liquidation plan, X distributes each of the assets to the two the shareholders in proportion to their stock interests.

(g) Same as (f), above, except assume that § 362(e)(2) applied to Ivan's contributions to X and § 336(d)(2) applies to Lossacre because there was a "plan" by X to recognize loss in that property.

C.   LIQUIDATION OF A SUBSIDIARY

1.   CONSEQUENCES TO THE SHAREHOLDERS

Code: §§ 332; 334(b)(1); 1223(1).

Regulations: §§ 1.332–1, –2, –5.

Nonrecognition treatment is inappropriate on an ordinary complete liquidation because it would permit individual shareholders to achieve a tax-free bailout as they watch the corporation's earnings and profits account disappear from the scene. Different policy considerations come into play when a parent corporation liquidates a controlled subsidiary. Since the assets of the subsidiary remain in corporate solution, the liquidation is a mere change in form that should not be impeded by the imposition of a tax. The subsidiary's tax attributes, including its earnings and profits, can be inherited by the parent without administrative burdens. Moreover, the subsidiary could have paid tax-free dividends to the parent under Section 243 or the consolidated return rules. All these factors, together with a desire to encourage the simplification of corporate structures, influenced Congress to adopt a nonrecognition scheme by enacting the statutory predecessor of Section 332.

Section 332 provides that a parent corporation recognizes no gain or loss on the receipt of property in complete liquidation of an 80 percent or more subsidiary if certain conditions are met. In that event, the parent takes the distributed assets with a transferred basis under Section 334(b)(1)[1] and inherits the subsidiary's earnings and profits and other tax

---

1. If the liquidating subsidiary is a foreign corporation not subject to U.S. tax and the transferee parent is a domestic corporation, the parent must reduce the basis of built-in loss property it receives in the liquidation to its fair market value. I.R.C. § 334(b)(1)(B).

attributes under Section 381(a)(1).[2]

To qualify under Section 332, the subsidiary must distribute property to its parent in complete cancellation or redemption of its stock pursuant to a plan of liquidation, and the liquidation must meet two formal requirements, one relating to control and the other to timing.

Control. Under Section 332(b)(1), the parent must own at least 80 percent of the total voting power of the stock of the subsidiary and 80 percent of the total value of all outstanding stock of the subsidiary from the date of adoption of the plan of complete liquidation and at all times thereafter until the parent receives the final distribution.[3] This condition normally is not a problem if the subsidiary is wholly owned, but any significant minority ownership creates a risk that the transaction will run afoul of the control requirement. Indeed, a parent corporation sometimes is motivated to intentionally violate the 80 percent tests in order to avoid Section 332 and recognize a loss on its stock in the subsidiary.[4] Conversely, an aspiring parent that does not meet the 80 percent control test may seek to qualify a liquidation under Section 332 by acquiring more stock of the subsidiary or causing the subsidiary to redeem stock held by minority shareholders shortly before the liquidation. As illustrated by the *Riggs* case, below, this strategy may trigger a controversy with the Service over when the liquidation plan was adopted.

Timing. Section 332 includes two timing alternatives. "One-shot" liquidations qualify if the subsidiary distributes all of its assets within one taxable year[5] even if it is not the same year in which the liquidation plan is adopted.[6] Where the distributions span more than one taxable year, the plan must provide that the subsidiary will transfer all of its property within three years after the close of the taxable year in which the first distribution is made.[7] Failure to meet the deadline will cause the liquidation to be retroactively disqualified.[8]

---

2. The parent's basis in the stock of a subsidiary is not taken into account in determining the tax consequences of a Section 332 liquidation and disappears from the scene. This creates the possibility that the parent may be deprived of a loss on its investment in the subsidiary even though it must inherit a low carryover basis in its assets.

3. The stock ownership requirements are derived from Section 1504(a)(2), which sets forth rules for determining whether a corporation is a member of an "affiliated group." For purposes of the stock ownership requirement, most nonconvertible preferred stock is disregarded. I.R.C. § 1504(a)(4). Reg. § 1.332–2(a), which states that the test is whether the parent owns at least 80 percent of the subsidiary's total combined voting power and 80 percent of all other classes of stock (except nonvoting stock limited and

preferred as to dividends), does not reflect legislative changes to Section 332(b)(1).

4. See Commissioner v. Day & Zimmermann, Inc., 151 F.2d 517 (3d Cir.1945).

5. I.R.C. § 332(b)(2); Reg. § 1.332–3. In this situation, the adoption by the shareholders of the resolution authorizing the distributions in liquidation is considered an adoption of a "plan" of liquidation even though it may not specify the time for completing the transfers.

6. Rev.Rul. 71–326, 1971–2 C.B. 177.

7. I.R.C. § 332(b)(3); Reg. § 1.332–4.

8. Id. To allow the Service to assert deficiencies for the early distributions in the event of a retroactive disqualification, the parent is required to file a waiver of the normal three year statute of limitations and may be asked to post a bond in order to

Minority Shareholders. Nonrecognition under Section 332 is only granted to the controlling parent corporation. It is not available to minority shareholders, who must determine their gain or loss in the normal manner under Section 331(a) unless the liquidation also qualifies as a tax-free reorganization—a rare situation that will be explored in a later chapter.[9]

George L. Riggs, Inc. v. Commissioner

United States Tax Court, 1975.
64 T.C. 474.

■ DRENNEN, JUDGE: Respondent determined a deficiency in petitioner's income tax for the taxable year ended March 31, 1969, in the amount of $589,882.28.

The sole issue for determination is whether the plan of liquidation of Riggs–Young Corp., a subsidiary of the petitioner, was adopted subsequent to the time when petitioner owned at least 80 percent of the outstanding stock of Riggs–Young, thereby rendering section 332, I.R.C. 1954, applicable to the liquidation so that the gain to petitioner thereon is not to be recognized.

FINDINGS OF FACT

[George L. Riggs, Inc., referred to throughout the opinion as "petitioner," was a holding company which as of December, 1967, owned approximately 35.6 percent (2,432 out of 6,840 shares) of the nonvoting preferred stock and 72.13 percent (8,047 out of 11,156 shares) of the common stock of The Standard Electric Time Co. ("Standard"). Standard owned 90 percent of the outstanding stock of a Delaware subsidiary and 99.5 percent of a California subsidiary. The corporations were in the business of manufacturing and marketing electric clocks and signal devices. Standard was the manufacturing arm of the business, and the two subsidiaries handled marketing.

On December 13, 1967, Frances Riggs–Young, the president of Standard and controlling shareholder of petitioner, notified all of Standard's shareholders that the company and its subsidiaries would be seeking approval for a sale of substantially all of the operating assets of the companies. In connection with the sale, Standard changed its name to Riggs–Young Corporation. The sales were consummated on December 29, 1967. In February, 1968, Riggs–Young (formerly Standard) redeemed all of its preferred stock. On April 17, 1968, the directors of Riggs–Young approved the liquidation of the Delaware and California subsidiaries, and authorized Riggs–Young to offer to redeem common stock from all of its shareholders with the exception of petitioner and Frances Riggs–Young. The stated purpose of this tender offer was to eliminate the minority shareholders and provide them with the opportunity to receive cash for

protect the Commissioner's ability to collect past due taxes.

9. Reg. § 1.332–5. See Chapter 9B1, infra.

their stock. The Tax Court also found that counsel to petitioner and the related subsidiaries "recognized the desirability of petitioner's owning 80 percent of the common stock of Riggs–Young (1) to permit the filing of consolidated returns, and (2) to permit the possible further liquidation of Riggs–Young under section 332 of the Code to simplify the corporate structure." 64 T.C. at 480. The letter informing shareholders of the redemption offer stated that "If this offer is accepted by substantially all of the stockholders to whom it is directed, the Directors will consider liquidation and final dissolution of the Corporation." 64 T.C. at 479.

At the time of its redemption offer, petitioner owned 72.13 percent of Riggs–Young's common stock. The remaining shares were owned by members of the Riggs family, related trusts and a small group of unrelated minority shareholders.

The tender offer was made on April 26, 1968 and expired on May 28, 1968. During this period, owners of 2,738 shares of common stock tendered their shares for redemption. As a result of these redemptions, petitioner owned at least 80 percent of Riggs–Young's common stock on May 9, 1968, and its ownership increased to 95.6 percent by May 28. On June 20, 1968, the directors and shareholders of Riggs–Young approved a plan of complete liquidation and dissolution of the corporation. Between June and December, 1968, when the liquidation was completed, Riggs–Young made distributions to petitioner in excess of $2.2 million.

Petitioner realized a gain of $2,168,975 from the liquidation of Riggs–Young, representing the difference between the liquidating distributions and petitioner's $42,465 basis in its Riggs–Young stock. The gain was reported on petitioner's tax return but not recognized under the authority of Section 332. Ed.]

OPINION

The only question for decision is whether petitioner owned at least 80 percent of the outstanding stock of its subsidiary, Riggs–Young Corp., at the time Riggs–Young Corp. adopted a plan of liquidation within the meaning of section 332, I.R.C. 1954, so that the gain realized by petitioner on the liquidation of Riggs–Young is not to be recognized by virtue of that section. The vital question is when did Riggs–Young adopt a plan of liquidation within the meaning of section 332.

Respondent argues that the plan of liquidation was adopted on December 27, 1967, when about 90 percent of the stock of Riggs–Young (then Standard) was voted in favor of selling substantially all of the assets of Riggs–Young and its two subsidiaries, Delaware and California, to SET; or not later than about April 17, 1968, when the board of directors of Riggs–Young voted to liquidate Delaware and California and to make an offer to purchase all of the common stock of Riggs–Young then outstanding with the exception of the stock owned by petitioner and Frances Riggs–Young.[2]

---

2. Respondent specifically does not rely on the "end-result" or "step-transaction" theory in this case. * * *

On the other hand petitioner contends that the plan of liquidation of Riggs–Young was first adopted when it was formally adopted by vote of the stockholders on June 20, 1968, or at the earliest when counsel for petitioner recommended to petitioner in the early days of June 1968 that it liquidate Riggs–Young. Petitioner also contends that section 332 is an elective section and a taxpayer, by taking appropriate steps, can render that section applicable or inapplicable.

The parties are in agreement that by May 9, 1968, petitioner was the owner of at least 80 percent of the outstanding stock of Riggs–Young.

Section 332(a) of the Code provides as a general rule: "No gain or loss shall be recognized on the receipt by a corporation of property distributed in complete liquidation of another corporation." Subsection (b) of section 332 establishes certain requirements which must be satisfied before subsection (a) becomes applicable. The only requirement of subsection (b) which is in issue in this case is whether petitioner, which received property from Riggs–Young in liquidation, was, on the date of the adoption of the plan of liquidation, the owner of at least 80 percent of the stock of Riggs–Young, the liquidating corporation.

Nowhere in the pertinent statute is the phrase "the date of the adoption of the plan of liquidation" defined. However, in attempting to define this phrase for purposes of the provision of [1954 Code] section 337, the regulations of the Commissioner provide:

> Ordinarily the date of the adoption of a plan of complete liquidation by a corporation is the date of adoption by the shareholders of the resolution authorizing the distribution of all the assets of the corporation (other than those retained to meet claims) in redemption of all of its stock. * * * [Sec. 1.337–2(b), Income Tax Regs.; accord, Virginia Ice & Freezing Corp., 30 T.C. 1251 (1958).]

The date of this shareholder resolution should ordinarily be considered the date of the adoption of the plan of liquidation for purposes of section 332. See sec. 332(b)(2).

This Court has noted, in interpreting section 112(b)(6), I.R.C. 1939 (the predecessor of section 332, I.R.C. 1954), that although the adoption of the plan of liquidation "need not be evidenced by formal action of the corporation or the stockholders. * * * even an informal adoption of the plan to liquidate presupposes some kind of definitive determination to achieve dissolution." Distributors Finance Corp., 20 T.C. 768, 784 (1953). The mere general intention to liquidate is not the adoption of a plan of liquidation. City Bank of Washington, 38 T.C. 713 (1962).

Based on the evidence introduced in the case at bar, we must conclude that a plan for the liquidation of Riggs–Young had not been adopted prior to the critical date of May 9, 1968.

Respondent, in an effort to show that the plan of liquidation of Riggs–Young was informally adopted on December 27, 1967, or no later than April 1968, alludes to actions and statements made in connection therewith taken between December 1967 and June 1968. Petitioner offered the testimony of persons involved in those actions to explain what the parties had in mind in taking those actions and making the statements which cast a quite different light on the reasons therefor. This testimony was creditable and not shaken by cross-examination. In light of such evidence, we cannot agree with respondent's inference that these actions constituted an informal adoption of a plan of liquidation of Riggs–Young prior to May 9, 1968.

Respondent argues that the letter dated December 13, 1967, sent to the common shareholders of Standard (Riggs–Young) notifying them of the proposed sale of its assets and that the corporation was contemplating an offer to purchase the common shares held by all shareholders other than petitioner if the sale was approved, clearly indicates that the shareholders at the meeting on December 27, 1967, intended to approve not only the sale of the assets, but also the liquidation of Standard (Riggs–Young).

We believe this infers too much. As petitioner points out, the use of the word "contemplated" shows the acquisition of the common stock of the minority shareholders was merely a possibility about which a final decision had not been made. In any event, from the possibility of a tender offer to the minority shareholders, we cannot conclude, ipso facto, that a plan for the liquidation had been adopted. Petitioner explained that the possibility of this tender offer was made known to the shareholders in order to avoid any possible disclosure problem with the securities law and to apprise the shareholders, from a fairness standpoint, of eventual possibilities resulting from the sale. This explanation is reasonable.

Respondent next points to the fact that on February 23, 1968, all of the 6,840 shares of preferred stock of Riggs–Young were called for redemption as additional evidence that a definite decision to liquidate the corporation had been made. We believe petitioner adequately explained that this redemption was based on sound business reasons. The preferred stock had a par value of $25 per share and a cumulative dividend of 8 percent. This stock was subject to redemption at the option of Riggs–Young upon payment of the par value and any accumulated dividend. The testimony of Norman Vester, a director of Riggs–Young and president of Security National Bank which was cotrustee of Riggs Trust, and Roger Stokey, the attorney for petitioner, Riggs–Young, and Frances Riggs–Young, reveal that the redemption of the preferred stock was motivated by the desire to eliminate the excessive burden of a cumulative dividend of 8 percent and to reduce the number of shareholders with whom Riggs–Young and National Security Bank, as cotrustee of the majority shareholder, would have to deal. Both Vester and Stokey testified that as of January 19, 1968, the date the board of directors of Riggs–Young voted to redeem the preferred stock, no decision had been made to liquidate the corporation, and, therefore, no plan had been adopted.

Respondent next claims that a letter dated April 23, 1968, from Stokey to Scott C. Jordan categorically shows that a plan to liquidate Riggs–Young had been adopted prior to the date of the letter. Stokey's letter was in response to a letter from Jordan on behalf of Frances Riggs–Young inquiring whether she could participate in the tender offer that was about to be made to the minority shareholders of Riggs–Young. In his letter, Stokey said that Frances Riggs–Young might run some tax risks if she accepted a tender offer by Riggs–Young, apparently basing this statement on his belief that the amount she received from a tender offer might be taxed to her at ordinary income rates. As a result of this potential risk, Stokey stated in the letter: "Accordingly, we are arranging for her to receive her money in a liquidation."

Respondent perceives this statement by Stokey as a clear indication that a plan of liquidation of Riggs–Young had been adopted by a definite decision by April 23, 1963. We cannot so conclude. Stokey testified that "we," referred to as arranging the liquidation, meant Stokey and another member of his law firm, William Gorham. This letter merely shows that the attorneys involved in these transactions were contemplating the possibility of a liquidation of Riggs–Young. It in no way proves that the directors or shareholders of the corporation had made a definite decision or informally adopted a plan of liquidation.

Finally, respondent views the letter dated April 26, 1968, drafted by Frances Riggs–Young as president of Riggs–Young, which contained the tender offer to the common shareholders, other than petitioner and Frances Riggs–Young, as an additional indication of a prior adoption of a plan to liquidate. In this letter, Frances Riggs–Young did state that if substantially all of the shareholders accepted the offer, the directors of the corporation would consider liquidation and final dissolution of Riggs–Young.

Stokey testified that Gorham and he inserted, in this April 26 letter, the reference to the possible consideration of liquidating Riggs–Young. He also candidly admitted that he had undoubtedly discussed the possibility of liquidation of Riggs–Young at some prior point with Frances Riggs–Young, but hastened to add that he neither recommended liquidation at this time nor did she direct steps be taken to liquidate. Further, Stokey testified that he would never have recommended liquidation of Riggs–Young if petitioner had failed to achieve the 80–percent ownership.

Petitioner contends that the tender offer to the minority shareholders was made solely for business considerations and not with an eye toward the eventual liquidation of Riggs–Young. Vester and Stokey both testified that since the assets of Riggs–Young had been exchanged for cash, the primary purpose of the tender offer was to eliminate minority shareholders who might have different investment objectives for this cash than the majority shareholder. The bank, as trustee of Riggs, did not want to have to deal with a large group of minority shareholders. Furthermore, Stokey testified that Frances Riggs–Young desired to have the minority shareholders, many of whom were former employees of Standard, receive cash for their stock rather than have them remain locked in as minority shareholders of a personal holding company.

Stokey testified that another objective of the tender offer was to increase petitioner's ownership of Riggs–Young to 80 percent thereby enabling them to file a consolidated return. According to petitioner, the ultimate liquidation of Riggs–Young was not motivated by tax considerations and the sole advantage to be achieved from the liquidation was the simplification of petitioner's corporate structure. Petitioner alleges that Riggs–Young could have been kept in existence without any tax disadvantage. In fact the liquidation of Riggs–Young actually resulted in a tax disadvantage to Frances Riggs–Young personally since she had to pay capital gains tax on her share of the liquidation proceeds. She was a wealthy woman in her seventies and not in need of these funds and could have left this money in corporate solution until her death to enable it to receive a stepped-up basis for the beneficiaries of her estate.

We believe petitioner's explanations of why the actions were taken and the statements were made are true and that the considerations mentioned were taken into account in making the decisions that followed. While the motives enumerated by petitioner do not directly negate the notion that a liquidation may have been contemplated, discussed, or even intended prior to May 9, 1968, they do serve to sufficiently undermine the conclusions drawn by respondent from the actions and statements to offset any presumptions that respondent's inferences are correct. Without more concrete evidence than we have before us, we cannot agree with respondent that a plan of liquidation of Riggs–Young was adopted within the meaning of section 332 prior to May 9, 1968. Lacking such a finding, we believe the date on which the resolution to liquidate was actually adopted by the shareholders should be controlling.

The very most that can be gleaned from the evidence favorable to respondent's contention is that there may have been a general intent on the part of petitioner's advisers somewhere along the line prior to May 9, 1968, to liquidate Riggs–Young when and if petitioner achieved 80–percent ownership of Riggs–Young stock as a result of the tender offer. However, the formation of a conditional general intention to liquidate in the future is not the adoption of a plan of liquidation. *City Bank of Washington,* supra.

A mere intent by a taxpayer-corporation to liquidate a subsidiary prior to meeting the 80–percent requirement of section 332 should not be tantamount to the adoption of a plan of liquidation for the subsidiary at the point in time when that intent is formulated or manifested. Such a result would thwart the congressional intent of section 332 and prior judicial interpretations of this section and its predecessor.

The predecessor of section 332, I.R.C. 1954, was section 112(b)(6), first enacted in 1935. The purpose of section 112(b)(6) was to encourage the simplification of corporation structures and allow the tax-free liquidation of a subsidiary. * * *

* * *

Based on legislative history of [Section 112(b)(6) of the 1939 Code] and prior judicial decisions, we conclude that section 332 is elective in the sense that with advance planning and properly structured transactions, a corporation should be able to render section 332 applicable or inapplicable. The Commissioner in his regulations has conceded corporations this power in a seemingly analogous situation. See sec. 1.337–2(b), Income Tax Regs.

Such power of planning presupposes some right to forethought and the accompanying intent to achieve the desired goal. It would be a logical inconsistency equivalent to a "Catch–22" to say that a corporation has the power to control the application of this section, but that once the corporation formulates the intent to do so (assuming that at or subsequent to the time the intent was formed, it owned less than the required 80 percent but enough stock to cause the liquidation of the subsidiary), it has adopted a plan of liquidation and has precluded itself from the section.

A basic tenet of our tax laws is that a taxpayer has the legal right to decrease or altogether avoid his taxes by means which the law permits. Gregory v. Helvering, 293 U.S. 465 (1935); Daniel D. Palmer, 62 T.C. 684 (1974). At most, petitioner did no more than follow this prerogative.

The shareholders of Riggs–Young formally adopted the plan of liquidation of the corporation on June 20, 1968. Stokey testified that based on the records contained in his office diary, he did not discuss definite liquidation of the corporation with the corporate officers prior to June 4, 5, or 6, 1968. He concluded that he recommended liquidation on either the 4th or 5th of June 1968, and that a definite decision to liquidate was probably made on June 6, 1968. The testimony of Vester corroborates these statements of Stokey. We recognize that the adoption of a plan of liquidation need not be evidenced by formal action of the corporation or shareholders, *Distributors Finance Corp.,* supra. In this case, however, we find on the evidence that the plan of liquidation was adopted when the formal action was taken on June 20, 1968. Furthermore, even if it can be said that a plan of liquidation was adopted when Stokey first recommended it to the management, see *Distributors Finance Corp.,* supra, this occurred in June 1968 and would satisfy the requirements of section 332.

Respondent has cited and relied on Rev.Rul. 70–106, 1970–1 C.B. 70, as supportive of his position. This Court is not bound by a revenue ruling. Andrew A. Sandor, 62 T.C. 469 (1974). In addition, we find the facts of this case are greatly dissimilar to those contained in the ruling. The ruling assumes a prior agreement between the minority and majority shareholders concerning the redemption of the minority stockholders' stock. The ruling concludes that the liquidation plan was adopted when this agreement was reached. In the case at bar, there is no evidence of an agreement between the minority and majority shareholders prior to the tender offer. *Madison Square Garden Corp.,* supra at 624 n. 4. Since this revenue ruling is inapplicable, proper judicial restraint dictates that we do not comment on the validity or invalidity of the ruling as limited to the facts contained therein. Ronald C. Packard, 63 T.C. 621 (1975).

Decision will be entered for the petitioner. Reviewed by the Court.

2. CONSEQUENCES TO THE LIQUIDATING SUBSIDIARY

Code: §§ 336(d)(3); 337(a), (b)(1), (c), (d). Skim §§ 381(a)(1), (c)(2), (3); 453B(d); 1245(b)(3); 1250(d)(3).

Regulations: § 1.332–7.

Distributions of Property. A liquidating corporation generally recognizes gain or loss on distributions of property in a complete liquidation.[1] A

1. I.R.C. § 336(a).

major exception to this general rule is contained in Section 337,[2] which provides that a liquidating subsidiary does not recognize gain or loss on distributions of property to its parent[3] in a complete liquidation to which Section 332 applies. A nonrecognition rule makes sense in this context because the subsidiary's tax attributes, including the built-in gain or loss in its assets, can be preserved in the hands of the parent. Section 334(b)(1) implements this policy by providing that the parent takes a transferred basis in property received from a subsidiary in a Section 332 liquidation. In keeping with this carryover of tax attributes theme, the depreciation recapture provisions do not override Section 337,[4] and recapture potential continues to lurk in the distributed property through the definition of "recomputed basis" in Section 1245 and "additional depreciation" in Section 1250.[5] A liquidating subsidiary likewise does not recognize gain or loss on the distribution of installment obligations if Section 332 applies,[6] and the parent will take a transferred basis in the obligations under Section 334(b)(1).

Distributions to Minority Shareholders. The nonrecognition rule in Section 337(a) is limited to distributions of property by a liquidating subsidiary to "the 80–percent distributee"—i.e., the parent corporation. Distributions to minority shareholders are treated in the same manner as a distribution in a nonliquidating redemption. Accordingly, the distributing corporation will recognize gain but not loss. Recognition of gain is appropriate because minority shareholders do not inherit any built-in gain in the distributed property through a transferred basis but instead take a fair market value basis under Section 334(a). Distributions of loss property are another matter. In order to prevent a controlled subsidiary from recognizing losses (but not gains) by "bullet" distributions of loss property to minority shareholders, Section 336(d)(3) provides that no loss shall be recognized to a subsidiary on a distribution of property to minority shareholders in a Section 332 liquidation.

Transfer of Property to Satisfy Indebtedness of Subsidiary to Parent. Section 337 applies only to liquidating *distributions.* If a subsidiary is indebted to its parent, a transfer of property to satisfy the debt normally

---

2. This "new" Section 337 is not to be confused with its 1954 Code counterpart, "old" Section 337, which provided for nonrecognition of gain or loss on certain liquidating sales. Old timers wish Congress had avoided confusion by retiring old Section 337's number and placing it on a monument in Yankee Stadium.

3. Section 337(a) refers to the parent as "the 80–percent distributee," which is defined in Section 337(c) as a corporation that meets the 80 percent stock ownership requirements specified in Section 332(b).

4. I.R.C. §§ 1245(b)(3); 1250(d)(3).

5. I.R.C. §§ 1245(a)(2); 1250(b)(1), (3). Issues of depreciation recapture on real estate have waned because virtually all depreciable real property placed in service after 1986 must be depreciated under the straight line method. I.R.C. § 168(b)(3).

6. I.R.C. § 453B(d)(1).

would be a taxable event rather than a nontaxable distribution governed by Section 337(a), causing the subsidiary to recognize gain or loss and the parent to take a fair market value basis in the distributed property. The disparate treatment of distributions in complete liquidation and transfers of property to satisfy intercorporate indebtedness might tempt a subsidiary to distribute appreciated property as part of the liquidation while simultaneously using loss property to extinguish any indebtedness to the parent. Section 337(b)(1) prevents this ploy by providing that any transfer of property in satisfaction of a subsidiary's debt to its parent shall be treated as a distribution, subjecting the transfer to the general nonrecognition rule of Section 337(a). As a necessary corollary, Section 334(b)(1) provides that the parent takes a transferred basis in the distributed property.

Distributions to Tax–Exempt and Foreign Parents. Ever vigilant, Congress was concerned that taxpayers might turn the deferral provided by Section 337 into a permanent exemption from the corporate-level tax. Consider the following possibility. A and B, the sole shareholders of highly appreciated X Corporation, wish to sell the business and avoid at least one level of tax. They sell all their stock to tax-exempt Charity, Inc. and recognize gain on the sale or donate the stock to Charity and take a charitable deduction. Charity now owns 100 percent of the X stock but it does not wish to operate the business. Charity causes X to liquidate in a tax-free transaction at both the corporate and shareholder levels under Sections 332 and 337(a). Although Charity must take a transferred basis in the property distributed by X, no tax ever would be collected on the subsequent sale of those assets because Charity is exempt from tax.

This technique might have been vulnerable under the step transaction and other judicial doctrines, but Congress decided to attack it from within the Code. Section 337(b)(2) thus provides that the general corporate-level nonrecognition rule for liquidations of a subsidiary shall not apply where the parent is a tax-exempt organization. Nonrecognition is restored, however, if the distributed property is used by the tax-exempt parent in an "unrelated trade or business" immediately after the distribution.[7] In that event, there is no loophole to plug because the tax-exempt organization is subject to tax on its unrelated business income.[8] A similar rule requires recognition of corporate-level gain in the case of a liquidating distribution to a parent that is a foreign corporation, except as the Treasury may provide in regulations. The legislative history indicates that the regulations should permit nonrecognition if the appreciation on the distributed property is not being removed from the U.S.'s taxing jurisdiction prior to recognition.[9] In both situations where the subsidiary recognizes gain or

7. Exempt organizations may be taxable on income from an "unrelated business"—i.e., a regularly carried on trade or business activity that is not substantially related to the organization's exempt purposes. See I.R.C. § 511 et seq.

8. If the tax-exempt parent later disposes of the distributed property or ceases to use it in an unrelated trade or business, any gain not recognized on the earlier liquidation becomes taxable as unrelated business income. I.R.C. § 337(b)(2)(B)(ii).

9. H.R.Rep. No. 99–841, 99th Cong., 2d Sess. II–202 (1986).

loss, the parent takes a fair market value basis in the distributed assets.[10]

PROBLEMS

1.   P, Inc. ("P") owns 90 percent of the outstanding stock of S, Inc. ("S"). Individual ("I") owns the remaining 10 percent of S. P's basis in its S stock is $3,000. I's basis in his S stock is $200. S has accumulated earnings and profits of $2,000 and the following assets:

Asset	Adjusted Basis	Fair Market Value
Land	$3,000	$8,000
Equipment	2,500	1,000
Inventory	100	1,000

S wishes to liquidate and distribute all of its assets to its shareholders. What are the tax consequences to P, S and I in the following alternative situations?

(a) S distributes the inventory to I and the other assets to P.

(b) S distributes the equipment to I and the other assets to P. How might S improve this result?

(c) What result in (b), above, if P's basis in its S stock were $30,000 and S had a $30,000 basis in the land?

(d) Is (c), above, a situation where P might wish to avoid the application of § 332? Why? How might this be accomplished? Consider in this regard the § 332 qualification requirements and how a parent might assure that they are not met.

2.   Child Corporation has 100 shares of common stock outstanding. Mother Corporation owns 75 shares (basis—$1,000) and Uncle, an individual who recently inherited his stock, owns 25 shares (basis—$3,000). Child has no earnings and profits, a $10,000 net operating loss carryover and the following assets (all held long-term):

Asset	Adjusted Basis	Fair Market Value
Cash	$2,000	$2,000
Installment Note	1,000	4,000
Land	100	1,000
Equipment (all § 1245 gain)	100	1,000
Total	$3,200	$8,000

What are the tax consequences in the following alternative situations, disregarding the impact of any tax paid by Child as a result of its liquidating distributions?

(a) Child adopts a plan of complete liquidation and distributes $2,000 cash to Uncle and all its remaining assets to Mother.

(b) Child distributes $2,000 cash to Uncle in redemption of his 25 shares. One week later, it adopts a plan of complete liquidation and

---

10.   I.R.C. § 334(b)(1)(A).

distributes its remaining assets to Mother pursuant to the plan. What are Mother and Child trying to accomplish through this reunion?

3.   Parent Corporation ("P") owns all the stock of Subsidiary Corporation ("S"). P has a $1,000 basis in its S stock and also holds S bonds with a basis and face amount of $1,000. S has the following assets:

Asset	Adjusted Basis	Fair Market Value
Inventory	$10,000	$ 1,000
Land	200	10,000
	$10,200	$11,000

P intends to liquidate S, but before adopting a formal plan S distributes the inventory in satisfaction of its outstanding $1,000 debt to P. On the next day, S liquidates, distributing the land to P. Why did P and S structure the transactions in this manner? Will they achieve their tax objectives?

CHAPTER 8

TAXABLE CORPORATE ACQUISITIONS

A. INTRODUCTION

There are many ways to structure a corporate acquisition. In the preceding chapter, we previewed one method: a sale by the target corporation[1] of all its assets followed by a distribution of the proceeds of sale to the shareholders in complete liquidation of the target.[2] An alternative is a sale by the shareholders of their stock in the target corporation. In either case, the business can be acquired in exchange for cash, notes, stock or bonds of the acquiring corporation, other property, or any combination of consideration. In an asset acquisition, the acquiring corporation may purchase the assets directly, drop them down to a controlled subsidiary or cause a subsidiary to make the acquisition. In a stock acquisition, the target may stay alive as a subsidiary of the acquiring corporation or liquidate. Variations abound on these basic formats.

Although we quickly will turn our attention to the tax consequences of corporate acquisitions, it may be useful at the outset to consider a few nontax factors that may influence the form of a transaction. Stock acquisitions are usually simpler to execute than asset acquisitions. To sell its assets, the target must prepare conveyance documents for many different items of property, give notice to creditors in compliance with local bulk sales laws, and incur sales or other local transfer taxes. In a stock acquisition, however, it is unnecessary to transfer any of the target's assets; instead, the acquiring corporation simply buys the target's stock directly from the T shareholders. A stock purchase thus may be desirable (or even essential) if the target holds certain nonassignable assets, such as a favorable lease or employment contract, or has valuable rights under state law that might be jeopardized if the corporation were dissolved. On the

---

1. In discussing acquisitions in this and later chapters, the acquired corporation generally will be called the "target," or "T," and the corporate purchaser will be called the "acquiring corporation," or "P." By using the term "target," we do not necessarily mean to suggest that the acquisition is a hostile takeover.

2. A target corporation that sells all or most of its assets usually will liquidate and distribute the proceeds to its shareholders. Alternatively, T could stay alive as an investment company after the sale. If T is closely held, staying alive likely would cause it to be classified as a personal holding company. For the perils of personal holding company status, see Chapter 14C, infra. For the possibility of a sale of assets by a C corporation followed by a conversion to S corporation status, see Chapter 15F, infra.

other hand, a stock acquisition may expose the buyer to liabilities of the target that may be unknown or contingent at the time of the transaction. This threat normally can be obviated by warranties and indemnity provisions in the stock purchase agreement. But some buyers still prefer to avoid the risk altogether by buying the assets and not assuming any burdens that might be connected with the corporate entity. The presence of unwanted assets, the unwillingness of minority shareholders of the target to sell their stock, and the requirements of regulatory agencies and local corporate and securities law are additional nontax factors that may influence the choice of form.

The principal tax issues raised on a corporate acquisition are best introduced by revisiting the simple example from the preceding chapter. Recall that A is the sole shareholder of Target Corporation ("T") and has a $100,000 basis in her T stock. T's only asset is a parcel of undeveloped land ("Gainacre") with a fair market value of $400,000 and a zero adjusted basis. Purchaser, Inc. ("P") wishes to acquire the land for $400,000 cash. Consider three simple methods of structuring the acquisition:

(1) *Liquidation of T Followed by Shareholder Sale of Assets.* T distributes Gainacre to A in complete liquidation and then A sells Gainacre to P for $400,000.

(2) *Sale of T Assets Followed by Liquidation.* T sells Gainacre to P for $400,000 and then liquidates, distributing the after-tax proceeds of sale to A.

(3) *Sale of T Stock.* A sells her T stock to P for $400,000 and P either keeps T alive as a wholly owned subsidiary or causes T to liquidate and distribute Gainacre to P.

Under any of these methods, one would expect A to recognize gain equal to the difference between her amount realized on the liquidation or sale of stock and the $100,000 adjusted basis in her T stock. In addition, T has $400,000 of corporate-level gain inherent in Gainacre. Should that gain also be recognized and, if so, should P (directly or indirectly through its ownership of T stock) take Gainacre with a $400,000 fair market value basis? If T does recognize gain, who bears the economic burden of the corporate-level tax? Alternatively, can the transaction be structured so that T's gain is deferred through a zero transferred basis in the land? Or, perish the thought, might T's gain be permanently forgiven, with P (or T, if it is still alive), taking Gainacre with a $400,000 cost basis? To what extent do (or should) the answers to these questions depend on the form of the transaction? And how are they affected if the seller is not an individual but a corporation that owns 100 percent of the T stock?

The after-tax economic outcome of these transactions may differ radically depending on the structure selected by the parties. The remainder of this chapter fills in the details, first considering asset acquisitions and then stock acquisitions.

B.   ASSET ACQUISITIONS

1.   TAX CONSEQUENCES TO THE PARTIES

A taxable asset acquisition occurs when a purchaser ("P"), which may be an individual or a business entity such as a corporation or partnership, acquires the assets of a target corporation ("T") in exchange for cash, notes, other property, or a mix of such consideration, and the acquisition does not qualify as a tax-free reorganization under Section 368.[1] Following the sale of its assets, T normally liquidates and distributes the sales proceeds to its shareholders, but the shareholders may choose to keep T alive and cause it to reinvest the proceeds. Under the corporate laws of most states, an asset acquisition also may be accomplished more efficiently by a cash merger of T into P (or a subsidiary of P). On the merger, T's shareholders receive cash or notes (or a combination) from P, and T's assets and liabilities automatically transfer to P (or its subsidiary). The Service views such a "cash merger" as if T sold its assets to P and then completely liquidated.[2]

To illustrate the tax consequences of the most basic asset acquisition methods, return again to the example of A, the sole shareholder (stock basis—$100,000) of T, whose only asset is appreciated Gainacre (basis—zero; fair market value—$400,000). Assume that C corporations and individuals are taxed at a flat 35 percent rate, with a 15 percent preferential rate for capital gains recognized by individual taxpayers.[3]

Liquidation of T Followed by Shareholder Sale of T Assets. If T distributes Gainacre to A in complete liquidation, it recognizes $400,000 gain under Section 336(a) and incurs a tax liability of $140,000 (35% × $400,000). A bears the economic burden of the tax and is obligated to pay it because T has no assets after it liquidates. A recognizes $160,000 gain on the liquidation ($400,000 distribution less $140,000 corporate-level tax less $100,000 basis in T stock) and incurs a shareholder-level capital gains tax of $24,000 (15% × $160,000). A takes Gainacre with a $400,000 basis under Section 334(a) and recognizes no further gain on a sale of Gainacre to P for its fair market value. When the smoke clears, the total corporate and shareholder-level tax on the liquidation and sale is $164,000, leaving A with $236,000. P takes Gainacre with a $400,000 cost basis and, if P is a corporation, it does not succeed to the tax attributes (e.g., earnings and profits, net operating losses, etc.) of T.

Sale of T Assets Followed by Liquidation. The result is identical if T sells Gainacre to P and then liquidates. T recognizes $400,000 gain on the sale, pays a corporate-level tax of $140,000, distributes the $260,000 net proceeds to A in complete liquidation, and A again recognizes $160,000 gain

---

1.   See Chapter 9B, infra.

2.   Rev.Rul. 69–6, 1969–1 C.B. 104.

3.   These assumptions approximate the actual rates in effect as this edition went to press in early 2005.

under Section 331(a) and incurs a $24,000 capital gains tax. P takes Gainacre with a $400,000 cost basis and does not succeed to any of T's tax attributes.

Sale of T Assets Not Followed by Liquidation. If T does not liquidate after selling Gainacre to P, T once again recognizes $400,000 gain and incurs $140,000 in corporate-level tax, but A does not recognize gain if T retains and reinvests the $260,000 net proceeds. Keeping T alive defers and may permanently eliminate any tax at the shareholder level. For example, if A holds the T stock until her death, A's heirs will take a stepped-up basis in the stock under Section 1014 and then may liquidate the corporation without paying a shareholder-level tax. This "no liquidation" strategy may have some appeal if A is elderly and her estate is on the verge of obtaining a stepped-up basis in the T stock, but it is rarely desirable if the liquidation will be postponed for many years. First, the double tax on corporate earnings must be navigated if A wants access to T's earnings.[4] Moreover, if T no longer conducts an ongoing business, it likely will be classified as a "personal holding company."[5] As such, it will be required to distribute its net investment income annually to A or face a penalty tax equal to 15 percent of any undistributed income.[6] In many situations, keeping T alive may be more expensive than liquidating, although not as expensive as it was before the tax rate on dividends was reduced to 15 percent.

Conversion to S Corporation. If T chooses to stay alive, it could avoid some of the problems just described by becoming an S corporation. For example, T's income would pass through to its shareholders and be subject to only one level of tax, albeit at slightly higher marginal rates for some high-income individual shareholders. But as an S corporation, T would face other obstacles. To name just two, an S corporation that was once a C corporation may lose its S status or be subject to a special corporate-level tax if it has Subchapter C earnings and profits and significant investment income.[7]

2. ALLOCATION OF PURCHASE PRICE

Code: § 1060. Skim § 197.

Regulations: §§ 1.338–6(a), (b), (c)(1); 1.1060–1(a)(1).

Background. The parties to an asset acquisition typically negotiate and agree upon a purchase price based on the value of the target corporation as a going concern. For tax purposes, however, a sale of the assets of a going

---

4. Dividends received by T, however, would qualify for the 70 percent dividends received deduction under Section 243(a), and corporate-level *regular* tax could be avoided altogether by investing the sales proceeds in tax-exempt municipal bonds. But unless it qualifies for the small corporation exception, T still may be subject to the corporate alternative minimum tax even if it is able to shelter its investment income from the regular tax. See, e.g., I.R.C. § 56(g) and Chapter 1B2, supra.

5. See § 541 et seq. and Chapter 14B, infra.

6. I.R.C. § 541.

7. See I.R.C. §§ 1362(d)(3); 1375; Chapter 15B and 15F, infra.

business for a lump sum is treated as a sale of each individual asset rather than of a single capital asset.[1] This fragmentation approach requires the parties to allocate the purchase price among the various tangible and intangible assets that have been sold. The allocation is used to determine the amount and character of the seller's gain or loss, and the buyer's cost basis in each asset for purposes of computing depreciation and amortization deductions and gain or loss on a subsequent disposition.

The parties historically had adverse interests when it came to allocating the purchase price among the assets. Buyers wished to allocate as much as possible to inventory, depreciable property and amortizable intangibles with the shortest recovery periods, and they resisted allocations to land and nondepreciable goodwill. Sellers, by contrast, benefitted by allocating a larger portion of the purchase price to assets yielding a capital gain and less to ordinary income assets. If the seller is a C corporation, these conflicts have diminished with the elimination of a corporate capital gains rate preference. But buyers are still motivated to allocate basis to assets that provide depreciation or amortization deductions over the shortest possible recovery period, and corporate sellers with unused capital losses still prefer capital gains over ordinary income.

The parties may include a negotiated purchase price allocation in their written agreement. Because buyers and sellers historically had adverse interests, negotiated allocations usually were respected by the Service. Indeed, the Service and some courts generally did not permit a party to take a tax reporting position inconsistent with an agreed allocation unless the contract was unenforceable because of mistake, undue influence, fraud or duress.[2] More often than not, however, agreements of sale did not contain any purchase price allocation, allowing the parties to go their separate ways and possibly "whipsaw" the government in the process by taking inconsistent positions. A typical controversy involved the tension between a covenant not to compete and goodwill. Amounts paid by the buyer that are attributable to a covenant by the seller not to compete with the buyer for a stated period of time result in ordinary income to the seller and, before enactment of Section 197, the payments were amortizable by the buyer over the life of the covenant. Payments for goodwill, on the other hand, could not be depreciated or amortized by the buyer before Section 197 was added to the Code, and gain on the sale of goodwill was capital gain to the seller. Thus, sellers preferred allocations to goodwill, while buyers, craving deductions, preferred allocations to a covenant not to compete.

Even without a covenant not to compete, some of the most contentious allocation controversies have involved the amount properly attributable to goodwill and the going concern value of an acquired business. The alloca-

---

1. Williams v. McGowan, 152 F.2d 570 (2d Cir.1945).

2. Commissioner v. Danielson, 378 F.2d 771 (3d Cir.1967), cert. denied, 389 U.S. 858, 88 S.Ct. 94 (1967). Other courts, using a more lenient standard, permitted a party to override a contractual allocation by a showing of "strong proof" that the agreement should not be respected. See, e.g., Ullman v. Commissioner, 264 F.2d 305 (2d Cir.1959).

tion is critical to a buyer who pays a premium—i.e., an amount that exceeds the fair market value of the target's identifiable tangible and intangible assets. Prior to the Internal Revenue Code of 1986, the Service permitted the "proportionate" method of allocation, under which the value of each acquired asset (including intangibles such as goodwill) was determined, and then the aggregate purchase price was allocated in proportion to the relative fair market value of each asset. The proportionate method often had the effect of shifting any premium paid for the business toward depreciable and amortizable assets and away from nondepreciable goodwill. The future tax benefits that resulted from this buyer-friendly allocation method were a stimulus to the corporate takeover mania of the 1980's.

Under another valuation approach, known as the residual method, each tangible and intangible asset (excluding goodwill and going concern value) is valued first. If the overall price paid for the business exceeds the aggregate fair market value of these assets, the excess ("residue") is allocated to goodwill and going concern value. In the case of a "bargain purchase," where the price paid for the business is less than the fair market value of T's assets, nothing is allocated to goodwill and the amount allocated to the identifiable assets (other than cash, cash equivalents and marketable securities) is proportionately reduced.

Congress first moved to regulate purchase price allocations in connection with stock purchases that are treated as asset acquisitions under Section 338 by directing the Treasury to prescribe regulations governing allocation of basis among the target's assets.[3] Not unexpectedly, the regulations mandated use of the residual method. Eventually, Congress extended this approach to asset acquisitions by enacting Section 1060, which includes reporting requirements to protect the Service from being whipsawed. Congress took another step toward certainty with the enactment of Section 197, which requires the cost of most acquired intangible assets, including a covenant not to compete, to be amortized over 15 years. Because a buyer's ability to amortize intangible assets and the timing of that amortization affects the economic stakes of a purchase price allocation, an overview of Section 197 is useful before turning to the specific requirements of Section 1060.

Amortization of Intangibles: Section 197. Section 197 permits taxpayers to amortize many intangible assets ratably over a 15–year period, regardless of their actual "useful life" or recovery period under prior law. Amortizable "Section 197 intangibles" include information bases, customer and subscription lists, patient files, know-how, licenses, franchises, trade names and, notably, goodwill, going concern value and covenants not to compete.[4] Some of these assets, such as goodwill and going concern value, were not amortizable at all under prior law, while others were being written off over periods considerably shorter than 15 years. Amortization

---

3. I.R.C. § 338(b)(5). See Section C2 of this chapter, infra.

4. I.R.C. § 197(c)(1), (d).

under Section 197 is available, however, only for acquired intangibles; it is generally not permitted for assets that are created by the taxpayer.[5]

Section 197 puts to rest many of the most contested tax issues in the area of business acquisitions. Litigated disputes abounded under prior law, including one case in which the Supreme Court held that "customer-based" intangibles (primarily subscriber lists) acquired by a publisher on the purchase of a newspaper were amortizable if they had an ascertainable value and a determinable useful life.[6] Rejecting the Service's argument that such intangibles were "nondepreciable per se," the Court concluded that eligibility for amortization turned on whether the asset was capable of being valued and whether that value diminished over time.[7] The Court's approach, and the factual controversies that it necessarily engendered, are now largely moot with the enactment of Section 197.

Allocation of Purchase Price Under Section 1060. The ability of the parties to make strategical purchase price allocations has been reduced with the enactment of Section 197 and the Section 1060 basis allocation rules. Section 1060 applies to any "applicable asset acquisition," defined as any transfer (direct or indirect) of assets which constitute a "trade or business" in the hands of either the buyer or the seller, and the purchaser's basis in the purchased assets is determined wholly by reference to the consideration paid for the assets.[8] This broad definition goes well beyond the typical corporate asset acquisition, extending to sales of sole proprietorships and partnership interests.

Section 1060 requires the buyer and seller to allocate the total consideration received or paid for a business among the various transferred assets using the residual method previewed above.[9] For this purpose, "consideration received" is the seller's aggregate amount realized from the sale of its assets determined under general tax principles, and "consideration paid" is the buyer's aggregate cost of purchasing the assets that is properly taken into account in determining basis.[10] Thus, liabilities assumed by the buyer or to which the transferred property is subject generally are included in total consideration. Aggregate consideration is then allocated among the assets using a refined version of the residual method that places all "acquisition date assets" into one of seven classes and allocates the consideration among those classes in priority order.[11] In general, the amount allocated to an asset (except for the last "residual" category) may not exceed its fair market value.[12] Specifically, total consideration is first reduced by cash and cash equivalents (known as "Class I acquisition date

---

5. I.R.C. § 197(c)(2).

6. Newark Morning Ledger Co. v. United States, 507 U.S. 546, 113 S.Ct. 1670 (1993).

7. Id. at 565–570, 113 S.Ct. at 1680–83.

8. I.R.C. § 1060(c); Reg. § 1.1060–1(b)(1).

9. Reg. § 1.1060–1(a)(1).

10. Reg. § 1.1060–1(c)(1).

11. Reg. § 1.1060–1(c)(2). The Section 1060 regulations incorporate by reference the residual method used under Reg. § 1.338–6 for certain stock acquisitions that are treated as asset acquisitions under Section 338. Id.

12. Reg. § 1.338–6(c)(1).

assets") transferred by the seller.[13] The remaining consideration is then allocated first to highly liquid assets such as actively traded personal property (e.g., marketable securities), foreign currencies, and certificates of deposit (Class II assets) in proportion to their fair market values, then to accounts receivable, mortgages, and credit card receivables (Class III), then to inventory and other dealer-type property (Class IV), then to all assets other than those in the other classes (Class V—a broad category that includes most tangible assets, such as equipment and real estate), and finally to all Section 197 intangibles except goodwill and going concern value (Class VI). Any remaining consideration, such as in acquisitions where the purchase price includes a "premium" that exceeds the liquidation value of the tangible and intangible assets acquired, is allocated to Class VII, a category limited to goodwill and going concern value.[14]

Effect of Agreement Between the Parties. As first enacted, Section 1060 did not address the question of whether the parties to a transaction should be bound by any written agreement they reach regarding allocation of the purchase price. Concerned that taxpayers might continue to take reporting positions that were inconsistent with their agreements, Congress amended Section 1060 to provide that a written agreement governing the allocation of consideration in an applicable asset acquisition shall be binding on both parties unless the Treasury determines that the allocation (or fair market value) is not appropriate.[15] The regulations provide that a party may refute an agreed allocation or valuation only by proving that the agreement was unenforceable due to mistake, undue influence, fraud or duress.[16] This is the standard long advanced by the Service and applied by the Third Circuit in the *Danielson* case.[17] In holding the parties to their agreement, however, Congress made it clear that it did not intend to restrict the Service's ability to challenge the taxpayers' allocation to any asset by any appropriate appraisal method, particularly where there is a lack of adverse tax interests between the parties.[18] For example, an allocation that departs from the mandated residual method will not be respected even if it is part of a negotiated agreement and it would be reasonable for the Service to make an independent showing of the value of goodwill in order to challenge the taxpayer's valuation of other assets.[19]

Reporting Requirements. The parties to an applicable asset acquisition must attach a statement (Form 8594) to their tax returns, reporting information concerning the amount of the total sales price and how it was

---

13. Reg. § 1.338–6(b)(1). In the unusual case where the total consideration to be allocated is less than the amount of Class I assets, then the purchaser must immediately recognize ordinary income to that extent. Id.

14. Reg. § 1.338–6(b)(2).

15. I.R.C. § 1060(a), last sentence.

16. Reg. § 1.1060–1(c)(4).

17. Commissioner v. Danielson, 378 F.2d 771 (3d Cir.1967), cert. denied, 389 U.S. 858, 88 S.Ct. 94 (1967).

18. H.Rep. No. 101–964, 101st Cong., 2d Sess. 1096 (1990). See Reg. § 1.1060–1(c)(4).

19. See generally Staff of the Joint Committee on Taxation, General Explanation of the Tax Reform Act of 1986, 100th Cong., 1st Sess. 355–360 (1987).

allocated among the various asset classes.[20] The purchaser also must report any collateral agreements related to an acquisition, such as covenants not to compete, employment agreements, licenses, leases and the like.[21]

C. STOCK ACQUISITIONS

1. BACKGROUND

In a taxable stock acquisition, the purchaser ("P") buys the stock of a target corporation ("T") from T's shareholders for cash or a combination of cash, notes and other consideration. A stock acquisition may be structured as a reverse triangular merger, in which P forms a wholly owned transitory subsidiary ("S"), and S merges into T under state law, with T's shareholders receiving cash and debt obligations of P. When the dust settles, P holds T as a wholly owned subsidiary.

Acquisitions of public companies are almost always stock acquisitions. They are sometimes launched when P begins acquiring T stock in the open market.[1] The next step may be a cash tender offer to T's shareholders or a friendly merger negotiated with T's management. If P succeeds in acquiring control of T, the final step is usually a "back-end" merger where recalcitrant minority shareholders are squeezed out of the picture, sometimes for the same price originally offered to tendering shareholders or perhaps on less attractive terms.[2]

Whether the transaction is structured as a direct stock purchase or a reverse triangular cash merger,[3] T's shareholders recognize gain or loss on the sale of their stock, measured by the difference between their amount realized and stock basis, and P takes a cost basis in the T stock it acquires. T shareholders who receive notes generally may report their gain on the installment method if the T stock is not publicly traded.[4] The more difficult

---

20. I.R.C. § 1060(b). See Reg. § 1.1060–1(e).

21. Reg. § 1.1060–1(e). Section 1060(e) also provides that where a person owns at least 10 percent of the value of an entity immediately before a transaction and transfers both an interest in the entity and enters into an employment contract, covenant not to compete, royalty, lease or other agreement with the buyer, the parties must report information concerning the transaction as the Service may require. In determining whether a person is a 10 percent owner, the Section 318 attribution rules shall apply. I.R.C. § 1060(e)(2)(B).

1. P may purchase up to five percent of T's stock without any requirement for public disclosure under the federal securities laws. Securities Exchange Act of 1934, § 13(d), 15 U.S.C.A. § 78m(d)(1981).

2. Squeeze outs are facilitated by the modern corporate laws of Delaware and other states where many public companies are incorporated. See, e.g., Del.Corp.Law § 251. For a good basic description of the mechanics, dynamics and economics of corporate takeovers, see Hamilton, Business Basics for Law Students, ch. 13 (3d. 2002).

3. A reverse triangular cash merger is treated for tax purposes as if P purchased T stock directly from the shareholders. Transitory "S" is disregarded. See Rev.Rul. 73–427, 1973–2 C.B. 301; Rev.Rul. 79–273, 1979–2 C.B. 125.

4. I.R.C. § 453(k)(2). Installment sales of very large blocks of stock may be affected by Section 453A, which imposes what amounts to an annual interest charge on a seller's tax liability that has been deferred by

conceptual questions relate to the tax consequences to T and the impact of a stock acquisition on the basis of T's assets and T's other tax attributes. Should a stock acquisition be treated as if it were a taxable asset acquisition coupled with a liquidation of T, or should the form of the transaction control? Should the parties be permitted to select which treatment they would prefer?

Not surprisingly, Congress has exhibited considerable hyperactivity in answering these questions. The *Kimbell-Diamond* case, which follows, is the best place to begin describing the evolution of the current tax treatment of stock acquisitions.

Kimbell–Diamond Milling Co. v. Commissioner

Tax Court of the United States, 1950.
14 T.C. 74.

■ BLACK, JUDGE.

[In August, 1942, taxpayer's milling plant was destroyed by fire and two months later the taxpayer collected insurance as a reimbursement for its loss. It then purchased for approximately $210,000 cash all the stock of Whaley Mill & Elevator Co. in order to use Whaley's plant and equipment to replace its own destroyed facilities. The purchase price consisted of $120,000 of insurance proceeds and $90,000 of additional funds. The taxpayer's sole intention in purchasing Whaley's stock was to acquire the assets of the company through a prompt liquidation.

Taxpayer liquidated Whaley three days after acquiring the stock. In a prior proceeding, reported at 10 T.C. 7, the Tax Court held that the acquisition of Whaley came within the 1939 Code predecessor of § 1033 so that the taxpayer's gain on the involuntary conversion was not recognized. Since the taxpayer's acquisition of the Whaley stock qualified under § 1033, its basis was $110,000 (the sum of the $20,000 adjusted basis of the destroyed assets and the $90,000 of additional funds that were paid in addition to the insurance proceeds). The assets of Whaley acquired by the taxpayer in the liquidation had an adjusted basis to Whaley of more than $300,000; the depreciable assets represented about $140,000 of this total.

The central dispute in the case was over the taxpayer's basis for depreciation in the assets acquired in the Whaley liquidation. After addressing a procedural issue, the Court proceeded to discuss the merits. Note that this case arose under the 1939 Code, which did not contain former § 334(b)(2) or present § 338. Ed.]

     * * *

OPINION

Having decided the issue of *res judicata* against petitioner, we must now determine the question of petitioner's basis in Whaley's assets on the

the installment method. In general, this provision applies only if the face amount of the seller's installment receivables during the taxable year exceed $5 million.

merits. Petitioner argues that the acquisition of Whaley's assets and the subsequent liquidation of Whaley brings petitioner within the provisions of [the predecessor of § 332] and, therefore, by reason of [the predecessor of § 334(b)(1)], petitioner's basis in these assets is the same as the basis in Whaley's hands. In so contending, petitioner asks that we treat the acquisition of Whaley's stock and the subsequent liquidation of Whaley as separate transactions. It is well settled that the incidence of taxation depends upon the substance of a transaction. Commissioner v. Court Holding Co., 324 U.S. 331. It is inescapable from petitioner's minutes set out above and from the "Agreement and Program of Complete Liquidation" entered into between petitioner and Whaley, that the only intention petitioner ever had was to acquire Whaley's assets.

We think that this proceeding is governed by the principles of Commissioner v. Ashland Oil & Refining Co., 99 Fed. (2d) 588, certiorari denied, 306 U.S. 661. In that case the stock was retained for almost a year before liquidation. Ruling on the question of whether the stock or the assets of the corporation were purchased, the court stated:

The question remains, however, whether if the entire transaction, whatever its form, was essentially in intent, purpose and result, a purchase by Swiss of property, its several steps may be treated separately and each be given an effect for tax purposes as though each constituted a distinct transaction. * * * And without regard to whether the result is imposition or relief from taxation, the courts have recognized that where the essential nature of a transaction is the acquisition of property, it will be viewed as a whole, and closely related steps will not be separated either at the instance of the taxpayer or the taxing authority. Prairie Oil & Gas Co. v. Motter, 10 Cir., 66 F.2d 309; Tulsa Tribune Co. v. Commissioner, 10 Cir., 58 F.2d 937, 940; Ahles Realty Corp. v. Commissioner, 2 Cir., 71 F.2d 150; Helvering v. Security Savings Bank, 4 Cir., 72 F.2d 874. * * *

See also *Koppers Coal Co.,* 6 T.C. 1209 and cases there cited.

We hold that the purchase of Whaley's stock and its subsequent liquidation must be considered as one transaction, namely, the purchase of Whaley's assets which was petitioner's sole intention. This was not a reorganization within section 112(b)(6), and petitioner's basis in these assets, both depreciable and nondepreciable, is, therefore, its cost, or $110,721.74 ($18,921.90, the basis of petitioner's assets destroyed by fire, plus $91,799.84, the amount expended over the insurance proceeds). Since petitioner does not controvert respondent's allocation of cost to the individual assets acquired from Whaley, both depreciable and nondepreciable, respondent's allocation is sustained.

* * *

NOTE

If the stock purchase and subsequent liquidation of the target-subsidiary in *Kimbell-Diamond* had been treated as separate transactions, the buyer would have taken a (higher) transferred basis in the target's assets under Section 334(b)(1). The court looked to the buyer's intent, however, in holding that the stock purchase was merely a transitory step in a transaction that was properly characterized as a purchase of assets. Under this application of the step transaction doctrine, the liquidation was disregarded, and the buyer took a cost basis in the assets.

In the 1954 Code, Congress replaced the elusive intent standard of *Kimbell-Diamond* with a more objective test.[1] If a corporation purchased a controlling (80 percent or more) stock interest in the target corporation and then liquidated the target within a specific period of time, the acquiring corporation was treated as if it had purchased the target's assets. In general, the acquiring corporation took a cost basis in the assets equal to what it paid for the stock rather than the usual transferred basis that results from the liquidation of a controlled subsidiary. Although more "objective" than *Kimbell-Diamond,* the 1954 Code rules were laden with timetables, control and "purchase" requirements and a host of adjustments for cash distributions, liabilities assumed and transactions occurring after the acquisition but prior to the liquidation. Additional problems were created by the requirement that the buyer liquidate the newly acquired target in order to secure a *Kimbell-Diamond* cost basis in the target's assets.[2]

Congress responded to these deficiencies by enacting Section 338, which refines the *Kimbell-Diamond* concept by allowing the acquiring corporation to elect to treat certain stock purchases as asset purchases. Unlike *Kimbell-Diamond* and the prior statutory scheme, Section 338 does not require a corporate buyer of stock to liquidate the target in order to get a cost basis in its assets. This is convenient when the buyer wishes to keep the target alive as a subsidiary. Under current law, a corporation that acquires control (i.e., at least 80 percent) of a target corporation in a transaction that is taxable to the selling shareholders is thus presented with four basic choices. It may: (1) not make the Section 338 election and keep T alive, leaving T's bases in its assets and other tax attributes unaffected; (2) not elect under Section 338, liquidate T tax-free under Section 332 and inherit its asset bases and other tax attributes;[3] (3) make the Section 338 election and treat the transaction as an asset acquisition under which "new T" takes a cost basis in its assets and is purged of all of its prior tax attributes; or (4) make the election and then liquidate T.[4]

---

1. I.R.C. § 334(b)(2)(pre–1982).

2. For historians and masochists, see Bittker & Eustice, Federal Income Taxation of Corporations and Shareholders ¶ 11.45 (5th ed. 1987).

3. Note that the tax treatment of this method is contrary to *Kimbell-Diamond,* which would have treated a stock purchase followed by a prompt intended liquidation of the target as an asset acquisition, giving P a cost basis in T's assets rather than a transferred basis and, under current law, causing T to recognize gain or loss on the sale.

4. T or P's ability to utilize T's net operating losses in the first two situations may be limited. See I.R.C. §§ 269(b); 382; and Chapter 12, infra.

Before proceeding further, it is important to keep in mind that *Kimbell-Diamond* and Section 338 originated in the *General Utilities* era, when liquidating distributions and sales generally did not trigger a corporate-level tax. The principal question then confronting a corporate buyer of stock was whether to take a cost basis or a transferred basis in the target's assets. If those assets were appreciated, a well advised corporate buyer would make the Section 338 election in order to step up the basis of the target's assets at little or no corporate-level tax cost. The stakes are vastly different today, where liquidating sales and distributions generally are taxable events. If a stock purchase is treated as an asset acquisition, the target must recognize gain or loss, and one of the parties (buyer or seller, or both) must bear the economic burden of the corporate tax imposed on any gain. Accordingly, the Section 338 election is undesirable in virtually all cases where the target's assets are appreciated because it rarely makes economic sense to elect to pay tax currently in order to step up the basis of assets and avoid tax later. Section 338 nonetheless survives in the 1986 Code, along with reams of annoyingly intricate regulations, and it remains an attractive option in just a few situations that are discussed below.

2. OPERATION OF SECTION 338

Code: §§ 338(a), (b)(omit (b)(3)), (d), (e)(1), (2)(A) and (D), (g), (h)(1), (2), (3)(A), (4)(A), (5), (6)(A), (9), (11).

Regulations: §§ 1.338–4(a), (b)(1) & (2), (c), (d)(1), (e), –5(a), (b)(1) & (2), (c), (d)(1), (e)(1)–(3).

Overview of Section 338. Section 338 is a complex statutory mechanism that seeks to equate for tax purposes the purchase of an 80 percent or more interest in the stock of the target corporation with a purchase of the target's assets. In general, the goals are to: (1) ensure that the target and its shareholders bear the same tax burden on a sale of the target's stock that they would have incurred on a sale of its assets followed by a complete liquidation; (2) provide the buyer with a cost basis in the assets of the target; and (3) terminate the tax attributes of the target and start afresh, without regard to whether or not the target is actually liquidated.

To achieve these goals, Section 338 provides that if a purchasing corporation ("P") purchases 80 percent or more of the stock of a target corporation ("T") within 12 months or less, it may elect to treat T as having sold all of its assets for their fair market value in a single transaction.[1] T must recognize gain or loss on the hypothetical asset sale, after which it returns as a virgin corporation ("new T") with a cost basis in its assets and none of its former tax attributes.[2] If T is liquidated, this cost basis simply carries over to the parent under the rules governing liquidations of a subsidiary.[3]

---

1. I.R.C. § 338(a).
2. I.R.C. § 338(b).

3. I.R.C. §§ 332; 334(b)(1). See Chapter 7C2, supra.

The contours of Section 338 are easier to explain than its details. The section is littered with anti-avoidance provisions, many of which are aimed at maneuvers that are beyond the scope of this book. Understanding Section 338 is eased by focusing on its fundamentals.

Qualification for Section 338. The Section 338 election is available only to a "purchasing corporation," which is defined as "any corporation which makes a qualified purchase of stock of another corporation."[4] A "qualified stock purchase" is a transaction or series of transactions in which one corporation acquires by "purchase" an 80 percent controlling interest in another corporation during a 12–month "acquisition period."[5] Roughly translated, all of this means that P must buy at least 80 percent of the stock of T within a 12–month period in transactions that are taxable to the sellers.[6]

The Election. If a corporation makes a qualified stock purchase and desires to make the Section 338 election, it must do so no later than the fifteenth day of the ninth month beginning after the month in which the "acquisition date" occurs.[7] The acquisition date is the day within the 12–month acquisition period on which the 80 percent purchase requirement is satisfied.[8] Once made, a Section 338 election is irrevocable.[9] There is no turning back, even with the Commissioner's permission, if the results prove to be undesirable.

Effect of Election: Deemed Sale of Target Assets and Termination of Old Target's Existence. If P makes a qualified stock purchase and follows up with a timely Section 338 election, T is treated as having sold all of its assets at the close of the acquisition date for their "fair market value" in a single transaction and is treated as a new corporation which purchased all of its assets as of the beginning of the day after the acquisition date.[10] As a result, T recognizes gain or loss on this hypothetical sale, just as if it actually had sold its assets.[11] For purposes of this deemed sale, Section 338 provides that T is not treated as a member of an affiliated group if it otherwise might have been.[12] Although the income realized on the deemed

---

4. I.R.C. § 338(d)(1).

5. I.R.C. §§ 338(d)(3); 338(h)(1). The requisite stock interest is defined in Section 338(d)(3) by reference to Section 1504(a)(2), which defines "control" as possession of at least 80 percent of the total voting power and 80 percent of the total value of a corporation's stock.

6. "Purchase" is defined to exclude transactions that would not have resulted in the full recognition of gain or loss to the seller (i.e., reorganizations, gifts, bequests, Section 351 transfers) and acquisitions from certain "related persons" within the attribution rules of Section 318. I.R.C. § 318(h)(3).

7. I.R.C. § 338(g)(1).

8. I.R.C. § 338(h)(2).

9. I.R.C. § 338(g)(3).

10. I.R.C. § 338(a).

11. See Section B1 of this chapter, supra.

12. I.R.C. § 338(h)(9). This means that losses of P or any P affiliate or losses of a corporate parent or affiliate of T may not be used to shelter gains resulting from T's deemed asset sale, but T may deduct its own net operating losses against the gains from the deemed sale. See Reg. § 1.338–1(f)(3)(iv). A "consolidated deemed sale return" may be filed, however, by all target corporations acquired by a purchasing corporation on the same acquisition date if the targets were members of the same selling consolidated group. I.R.C. § 338(h)(15). Cf. I.R.C.

asset sale may not be combined with the income of P or its affiliates for tax purposes, the economic burden of the tax liability resulting from the deemed sale is indirectly borne by P, which will factor it into the price to be paid for the stock. On the day after the deemed sale, T is reincarnated. It returns as a new corporation with no earnings and profits or other tax attributes from its pre-deemed sale era and with a cost basis in the assets that it hypothetically purchased from its former self.[13] If all this talk about deemed transactions seems mysterious, keep in mind that it is simply the mechanism used by the Code to equate purchases of assets and stock when a Section 338 election is made.

Aggregate Deemed Sale Price. In the hypothetical asset sale triggered by a Section 338 election, T is treated as selling its assets for their "aggregate deemed sale price" ("ADSP").[14] In general, ADSP is the sum: of (1) the grossed-up amount realized on the sale to P of P's recently purchased T stock, and (2) the liabilities of old T, including tax liabilities from the deemed sale.[15] "Recently purchased stock" is T stock purchased by P during the 12–month acquisition period and held by P at the time of the qualified stock purchase.[16] Thus, if P purchased all of T's stock during the 12–month acquisition period, the ADSP is the total amount realized by the selling T shareholders plus old T's liabilities. If P purchased less than 100 percent of T's outstanding shares during the 12–month acquisition period, then the concept of "grossed-up" amount realized comes into play. The grossed-up amount realized is an amount equal to the amount realized on the sale to P of P's recently purchased T stock determined as if the selling T shareholders used old T's accounting methods and without regard to costs of sale, divided by the percentage of T stock (by value) attributable to that recently purchased stock, less any selling costs (such as brokerage commissions) incurred by the selling T shareholders in connection with their sale of recently purchased stock that reduce their amount realized.[17] The function of this complex formula in situations where P does not acquire 100 percent of T stock is to approximate the total amount that would have been realized on the sale of T stock if P had purchased all the shares at the same average price that P paid for the shares actually purchased during the acquisition period. To illustrate, if during the 12–month acquisition period P purchased 80 percent of T's outstanding stock for $800,000, the grossed-up amount realized on the sale to P of P's recently purchased T stock would be $800,000/.80, or $1,000,000.

Remember that the theory underlying Section 338 is to replicate the tax consequences of an asset acquisition. If P were to purchase all of T's assets, the purchase price would reflect any T liabilities assumed or property transferred subject to liabilities as part of the transaction. Under the principles of the *Crane* case, T's amount realized in such an asset sale would include the amount of those liabilities. In a stock purchase, the

§ 338(h)(10) and Section C3 of this chapter, infra.

13. I.R.C. § 338(a)(2).

14. Reg. § 1.338–4(a).

15. Reg. § 1.338–4(b)(1), (d).

16. I.R.C. § 338(b)(6)(A).

17. Reg. § 1.338–4(c)(1).

amount paid by P for T's stock similarly will take into account the debts and liabilities on T's balance sheet as of the "acquisition date." To properly determine the deemed sale price of T's assets under Section 338, the ADSP is increased by liabilities of old T, including tax liabilities, that properly would be taken into account as amount realized on a disposition by T of its assets to an unrelated purchaser who assumed the liabilities or took assets subject to a liabilities of old T.[18]

Determination of Asset Basis After Deemed Purchase. New T's basis in its assets has been described as a *Kimbell-Diamond* type cost basis, but the actual approach used to determine the aggregate basis and allocate it among T's assets is not quite that simple. The regulations label new T's basis as the "adjusted grossed-up basis" ("AGUB").[19] The AGUB generally is the sum of: (1) the grossed-up basis in P's recently purchased T stock, (2) P's basis in nonrecently purchased T stock (e.g., T stock owned by P before the 12-month acquisition period), and (3) liabilities of new T, including any tax liabilities triggered by the deemed sale.[20] AGUB is similar but not necessarily identical to ADSP. If P holds only recently purchased stock in T and T has no contingent liabilities, the two calculations usually produce the same result.

To illustrate, assume again that during the 12-month acquisition period P purchased 80 percent of T's outstanding stock for $800,000 and assume P does not own any other T stock. In computing ADSP and AGUB, the grossed-up amount realized and the adjusted grossed-up basis are both $1,000,000.[21] But if P owns nonrecently purchased T stock with a per-share basis different than P's basis in its recently purchased stock, the calculation of the ADSP for old T's assets and the AGUB for new T's assets will produce different results.[22] The difference is attributable to the fact that the ADSP formula treats P's nonrecently purchased stock the same as stock that is held by T shareholders other than P, while the AGUB formula uses P's actual basis in its nonrecently purchased T stock. P can make an election to recognize gain on its nonrecently purchased T stock.[23] If such an election is made, the sum of the grossed-up basis in P's recently purchased T stock and P's basis in any nonrecently purchased stock will equal the

---

18. Reg. § 1.338–4(d)(1). General tax principles control the time that liabilities are taken into account. See Reg. § 1.338–4(d)(2). Since determination of the ADSP may depend, in part, on the tax liability triggered by the deemed sale, and old T's tax liability depends on the ADSP, the calculation is potentially circular. The regulations recognize that the determination of ADSP may require trial and error computations. Reg. § 1.338–4(e). They also include examples of a formula to resolve this mathematical teaser. To revisit high school algebra, see Reg. § 1.338–4(g) Examples.

19. Reg. § 1.338–5(a).

20. Reg. § 1.338–5(b)(1).

21. For ADSP, see Reg. § 1.338–4(c); for AGUB, see Reg. § 1.338–5(b), (c).

22. Contingent liabilities that are taken into account in determining a seller's amount realized but are not yet properly included in a purchaser's basis also may be the source of an initial disparity that usually will be corrected by later adjustments. See, e.g., Reg. § 1.338–5(b)(2)(ii).

23. I.R.C. 338(h)(3). Losses on nonrecently purchased stock are not allowed. Reg. § 1.338–5(d)(3)(iii).

ADSP.[24] The election, however, requires P to currently recognize gain on its nonrecently purchased T stock, and so it usually is not desirable from a tax standpoint.

Allocation of Adjusted Grossed–Up Basis Among Target Assets. If P makes a Section 338 election, new T's aggregate AGUB is allocated among its assets under regulations promulgated under Section 338(b)(5). These regulations utilize the same seven-class system and reporting requirements previously discussed with respect to basis allocations in asset acquisitions.[25]

Consistency Rules. Section 338 allows a purchasing corporation to take a transferred basis in T's assets (by not making the election) or, at the cost of paying a tax on any gain (or deducting any loss) inherent in the target's assets, to take essentially a fair market value basis in those assets. When Section 338 was enacted, the consistency requirement was designed to ensure that P was put to a choice: it could select one or the other, but not both (or some of each) of these options. To achieve that objective, Section 338(e) was intended to prevent P from acquiring some assets from T or an affiliate of T with a cost basis and other assets with a transferred basis during a "consistency period" that begins one year before the start of the acquisition period and lasts to one year after the acquisition date.[26] Under Section 338(e), if P acquired such an asset it was deemed to make a Section 338 election with respect to T, unless T sold the asset in the ordinary course of its business (e.g., a routine sale of inventory) or P took a transferred basis in the asset.[27] Section 338(f) was designed to ensure that if P makes a qualified stock purchase with respect to T and one or more affiliates (e.g., a wholly owned subsidiary) of T during any consistency period, then all such qualified stock purchases must be treated consistently under Section 338; an election with respect to the first applies to all later qualified stock purchases and if no election is made for the first purchase, none may be made for later ones.

In the final Section 338 regulations, the Treasury significantly narrowed the reach of the consistency period rules because they were designed to patrol against exploitation of the long ago repealed *General Utilities* doctrine. Under the regulations, the asset consistency rules of Section 338(e) generally apply only if P acquires an asset directly from T during the consistency period and T is a subsidiary of another corporation ("S") in a consolidated group.[28] The stock consistency rules of Section 338(f) are now limited by the regulations to preventing avoidance of the asset consistency rules.[29]

Understanding the limited application of the asset consistency period rules requires a very basic knowledge of the consolidated return regulations, which generally permit a parent corporation in a consolidated group

---

24. See Reg. § 1.338–5(d)(3).

25. See Section C4 of this chapter, supra; Reg. § 1.338–6.

26. I.R.C. § 338(h)(4)(A).

27. I.R.C. § 338(e)(2)(A) and (B).

28. Reg. § 1.338–8(a)(2). The rules are also extended to a few other limited abuse cases that are well beyond the coverage of this text. See Reg. § 1.338–8(a)(3),(4).

29. Reg. § 1.338–8(a)(6).

to increase the basis for its stock in a subsidiary when the subsidiary recognizes a taxable gain on the sale of one of its assets.[30] The relationship of this rule to Section 338 is best illustrated by the following example provided by the Treasury where P is the purchasing corporation, T is the target and S is T's parent:[31]

The proposed regulations apply the consistency rules in the context of consolidated groups to prevent acquisitions from being structured to take advantage of the investment adjustment rules. If the consistency rules did not apply in such a case, P could acquire assets from T with a stepped-up basis in the assets, and then acquire the T stock at no additional cost to the S group.

Example. S and T file a consolidated return. S has a $100x basis in the T stock, which has a fair market value of $200x. On January 1, 1993, T sells an asset to P and recognizes $100x of gain. Under § 1.1502–32 [of the consolidated return regulations], S's basis in the T stock is increased from $100x to $200x. On March 1, 1993, S sells the T stock to P for $200x and recognizes no gain or loss.

The consistency rules of the proposed regulations apply to the transaction because T's gain on the asset sale is reflected under § 1.1502–32 in S's basis in the T stock. However, under the proposed regulations, the District Director no longer has the discretion to impose a deemed section 338 election for T. Instead, under proposed [regulation] § 1.338–4(d), P takes a carryover basis in any asset acquired from T. (This is referred to as the carryover basis rule).

Section 338 Election Coupled With Liquidation of T. If P purchases 80 percent or more of T stock, makes a Section 338 election, and then promptly liquidates T, the stock purchase and subsequent liquidation of T are accorded independent significance for tax purposes—i.e., they are not stepped together and treated as an integrated transaction. P is treated as having made a qualified stock purchase rather than a direct acquisition of assets under the *Kimbell-Diamond* doctrine.[32] On the liquidation, P recognizes no gain or loss under Section 332, and T recognizes no gain or loss on the distribution of its assets to P under Section 337. In any event, neither P nor T would have any significant realized gain or loss because at least 80 percent of the T stock would have been recently purchased, and any built-in gain on T's assets was recognized as a result of the Section 338 deemed asset sale. After the liquidation, P succeeds to T's fair market value basis in its assets.

Stock Acquisitions Without Section 338 Election. The tax consequences of an acquisition of 80 percent or more of T's stock with no Section 338

---

30. See Reg. § 1.1502–32 and Chapter 13, infra.

31. See Preamble, Prop. Reg. §§ 1.338–4, –5 (CO–111–90), issued Jan. 14, 1992 (1992–1 C.B. 1000).

32. Reg. § 1.338–3(c)(1)(i). See also Rev.Rul. 90–95, 1990–2 C.B. 67 (stating that

"Section 338 replaced the *Kimbell-Diamond* doctrine"). But see Rev. Rul. 2001–46, 2001–2 C.B. 321, infra p. 477, where two-step transactions were integrated for purposes of the tax-free reorganization rules.

election are somewhat less complicated. T's shareholders, as always, recognize gain or loss on the sale of their stock. T becomes a subsidiary of P and retains its tax attributes, including the historic basis in its assets, earnings and profits, and the like. If P subsequently liquidates T, or T merges into P or another P subsidiary, neither P nor T recognizes gain or loss, and T's asset bases and other tax attributes carry over to the transferee.[33] Significantly, the initial qualified stock purchase and subsequent liquidation of T (or merger of T into P or a P affiliate) are not treated as an integrated transaction (e.g., as a direct purchase of T's assets by P) even if all the steps were planned from the outset. If the transactions were integrated, T would recognize gain or loss on its assets, a result which is fundamentally inconsistent with P's decision not to make a Section 338 election. The extent to which T (if it stays alive) or P (if it liquidates T) may utilize T's net operating losses after the acquisition is likely to be limited by Section 382, which is examined in a later chapter.[34]

3.   ACQUISITION OF STOCK OF A SUBSIDIARY

Section 338(h)(10) Election. The previous discussion assumed that T was not a subsidiary of another corporation. Consider, however, the situation where T is a wholly owned subsidiary of Seller, Inc. ("S"), and P wishes to acquire T. Assume that the value of T's stock (and also its underlying assets) is $400,000; S has a $100,000 basis in its T stock; and T has a $100,000 aggregate basis in its assets. T could sell its assets directly to P for $400,000 in a taxable transaction and then distribute the sales proceeds to S in a tax-free liquidation under Section 332, with the net result being $300,000 of taxable gain to T on the asset sale. Alternatively, T could distribute the assets to S in a tax-free liquidation. S would take the assets with a $100,000 transferred basis under Section 334(b) and recognize $300,000 gain on a sale to P. In either case, S does not recognize gain or loss on its T stock, and P acquires the assets with a $400,000 cost basis. If the disappearance of S's $300,000 gain on its T stock seems inconsistent with the double tax regime, remember that no assets have yet been distributed out of corporate solution to the shareholders of S, the real people who own the enterprise. The policy is to avoid three levels of tax on what may be a single economic gain.

Now assume that for nontax reasons P must acquire T's stock. Under general tax principles, S would recognize gain or loss on the sale of its T stock and P would take the stock with a cost basis. If P makes a Section 338 election, T also is treated as having sold its assets in a taxable transaction. If P does not elect, the bases of T's assets are unchanged and any built-in gain or loss is preserved. Either way, the result is double *corporate*-level gain, with the potential of a third round of taxation when S distributes the sales proceeds to its shareholders.

33. Rev. Rul. 90–95, supra note 32. See also Reg. § 1.338–2(c)(3)(i), discussed in Chapter 9B1, infra.

34. See Chapter 12, infra, and I.R.C. § 269(b).

Section 338(h)(10) offers relief from this potential triple tax by permitting the parties to ignore S's sale of its T stock and treat the transaction as if it were a sale of T's assets.[1] If a Section 338(h)(10) election is made,[2] the transaction is treated as if old T sold its assets to an unrelated person (new T) while a member of the S consolidated group, and T then distributed its assets (i.e., the proceeds of sale) to S and ceased to exist. In most cases, the final step of the various hypothetical transactions is treated as a tax-free liquidation of T under Sections 332 and 337.[3] The tax consequences of the election are: (1) S recognizes no gain or loss on the sale of its T stock; (2) S inherits T's tax attributes (e.g., earnings and profits);[4] (3) T is treated as having sold its assets for their fair market value in a taxable transaction,[5] and any gain or loss is included on the consolidated return filed by S and its affiliates; and (4) "new T," a subsidiary of P, is treated as having acquired old T's assets for an amount equal to their adjusted grossed-up basis.[6] Two levels of corporate-level gain are thus avoided, and the tax burden of the sale remains with the seller.

Returning to the example, if the parties make a Section 338(h)(10) election, S's $300,000 gain on the sale of its T stock is ignored, and the $300,000 gain on the deemed sale of T's assets[7] is included on the consolidated tax return filed by S and its affiliates. P takes a $400,000 cost basis in the T stock and "new T" takes a $400,000 basis in its assets.

Although the Section 338(h)(10) election is generally desirable because it eliminates two levels of corporate-level gain, it has particular allure when S has a large "outside" gain on its T stock relative to minimal "inside" gain on T's assets. In that scenario, P may purchase T's stock at little or no tax cost to S if the parties make a Section 338(h)(10) election. Of course, the same result could have been achieved if S first liquidated T under Section 332 and sold the assets to P, but this method might not be feasible if P needs to keep T alive as a corporate entity for nontax reasons.

---

1. In general, before the transaction T must be a member of "the selling consolidated group." I.R.C. § 338(h)(10)(A). A "selling consolidated group" is any group of corporations which, for the taxable period which includes the transaction, includes T and files a consolidated tax return. I.R.C. § 338(h)(10)(B). A qualified seller also may be any "affiliated group" of corporations (within the meaning of Section 1504) which includes T, whether or not the group files a consolidated return. See generally Reg. § 1.338(h)(10)–1(b)(3).

2. The election must be made jointly by the S group and P. See Reg. § 1.338(h)(10)–1(c)(2).

3. See Reg. § 1.338(h)(10)–1(d).

4. These inherited tax attributes generally are reduced in proportion to the percentage of old T stock held by minority shareholders. Cf. Reg. §§ 1.381(c)(2)–1(c)(2).

5. The deemed sale price is determined under a formula prescribed by the regulations, which refers to the actual purchase price paid by P for the T stock and is adjusted for liabilities of T. See Reg. §§ 1.338(h)(10)–1(d)(3)(i); 1.338–4.

6. I.R.C. § 338(b). The adjusted grossed-up basis for new T's assets is determined under Reg. § 1.338–5 and is allocated among the assets under the approach discussed earlier in this chapter. Reg. § 1.338(h)(10)–1(d)(2).

7. We have assumed for convenience that the deemed sale price equals the $400,000 fair market value of T's assets.

The election also is attractive when S's consolidated group has losses that can be applied to offset any gain recognized by T on the deemed sale of its assets. If Section 338 were elected without an accompanying Section 338(h)(10) election, T must file a separate one day return reporting the income from the deemed sale and it could not offset its gain with any losses from S's other operations. If a Section 338(h)(10) election is made, however, the gain on the deemed sale is reported on S's consolidated return and may be offset by losses of S and its other affiliates.

The regulations extend the availability of the Section 338(h)(10) election to two additional situations. First, they permit the election when T and S are affiliated corporations even if T is not a member of the S consolidated group if S sells stock representing at least 80 percent of the voting power and value of T to P on the "acquisition date."[8] Second, a Section 338(h)(10) election is permitted if T is an S corporation immediately before the acquisition date.[9] If T is an S corporation, the gain on the deemed sale of T's assets is reported on old T's final S corporation return and passes through to T's shareholders, who may make appropriate adjustments to the basis of their T stock.[10] These adjustments will affect the gain or loss recognized by these shareholders on the deemed liquidation of old T, and no additional gain or loss is recognized on the actual stock sale. The taxation of S corporations and their shareholders is examined in Chapter 20.

Section 336(e). Section 336(e) is a close but obscure relative of Section 338(h)(10). In some cases, it is an identical twin. Section 336(e) provides that, upon the promulgation of (still awaited) regulations, a corporation that owns at least 80 percent of the voting power and value of the stock of another corporation may elect to treat a sale, exchange or distribution of that subsidiary's stock as if it were a disposition of the subsidiary's assets. If a Section 336(e) election is made, the parent does not recognize gain or loss on the disposition of the subsidiary's stock. The legislative history of Section 336(e) states that "principles similar to those of Section 338(h)(10)" will be used in determining the operation of the Section 336(e) election.[11]

The overlap between Sections 336(e) and 338(h)(10) is apparent when a parent *sells* the stock of a controlled subsidiary to a corporate purchaser. Section 336(e) is potentially broader, but its scope will remain unclear until regulations are promulgated. Presumably, Section 336(e) could apply even if the buyer were an individual or entity (such as a partnership) that is not qualified to make a Section 338 election. Moreover, Section 336(e) is not confined to sales. It potentially encompasses both liquidating and perhaps even nonliquidating distributions of the stock of a subsidiary.

8. Reg. §§ 1.338(h)(10)–1(c)(1), –1(b)(3), –1(d)(4).

9. Reg. §§ 1.338(h)(10)–1(c)(1), –1(b)(4), –1(d)(4).

10. Reg. § 1.338(h)(10)–1(d)(5)(i).

11. H.R.Rep. No. 841, 99th Cong., 2d Sess. II–204.

D. COMPARISON OF ACQUISITION METHODS

A typical student's reaction to this chapter (or indeed the entire course up to now) might be something like this: "After considerable effort, I understand the workings of most Code sections as they are studied, but the course is becoming a conglomeration of random detail." The lament might continue with these questions about taxable corporate acquisitions: "How does it all fit together? Does it matter whether P buys T's assets or stock? What rational buyer ever would make the Section 338 election? Does substance control over form—or form over substance? When does the step transaction doctrine apply?" In short, the understandable plea is—"Give me some perspective!" This section attempts to respond by comparing taxable acquisition methods in a tax planning context, and by providing a comprehensive acquisitions problem.

The repeal of the *General Utilities* doctrine greatly altered the tax economics of corporate acquisitions. Prior to that time, the tax consequences of an asset purchase followed by a complete liquidation, or a stock purchase coupled with a Section 338 election, were essentially the same. T's shareholders recognized a capital gain on their investment; T did not recognize gain or loss on the actual or deemed transfer of its assets except for recapture of depreciation and a few other items; and P (or "new T") obtained a fair market value basis in T's assets. In short, taxable acquisitions involved only a single, shareholder-level tax, which could be deferred if P used installment notes as partial consideration for the purchase.

After *General Utilities* repeal, an asset acquisition requires both T and its shareholders to recognize gain unless T does not liquidate. A stock purchase coupled with a Section 338 election is no better because the deemed asset sale results in full recognition of corporate-level gain. In either case, P obtains a fair market value basis in T's assets—but at the price of an immediate corporate-level tax. Corporate-level tax is avoided, however, if P purchases T's stock and does not elect under Section 338. It is perhaps ironic that, after years of effort to equate the tax treatment of different corporate acquisition methods, we are left with an asymmetrical system under which asset acquisitions require two levels of tax with no opportunity for T to defer tax through a transferred basis, while a stock acquisition without a Section 338 election requires only a shareholder-level tax, albeit with the trade-off of a transferred basis in T's assets.[1]

It follows that the preferred alternative for most taxable acquisitions is a stock purchase with no Section 338 election. It is rarely desirable to pay a front-end corporate tax on the gain inherent in T's assets in order to achieve tax savings later from the additional depreciation, amortization and

1. These lingering discontinuities are discussed in Zolt, "The *General Utilities* Doctrine: Examining the Scope of Repeal," 65 Taxes 819 (1987); Yin, "A Carryover Basis Regime? A Few Words of Caution," 37 Tax Notes 415 (1987); and Lewis, "A Proposal for a Corporate Level Tax on Major Stock Sales," 37 Tax Notes 1041 (1987).

other deductions that would flow from the stepped-up basis in T's assets. The two principal exceptions are: (1) where T has large net operating loss carryovers that would be available to offset the gain recognized on the deemed asset sale;[2] and (2) where T is a subsidiary of another corporation.[3]

The prospect of a two-tier tax also may tilt the method of choice in corporate acquisitions more towards tax-free reorganizations, where neither T nor its shareholders currently recognize gain or loss, but tax attributes at both the corporate and shareholder levels are preserved through transferred and exchanged bases. Acquisitive reorganizations are examined in Chapter 17.

PROBLEMS

1. Target Corporation ("T") is a "C" corporation. T's 1,000 shares of common stock (its only class) are owned by three unrelated individual shareholders as follows:

Shareholder	No. Shs.	Adj. Basis	F.M.V.
A	500	$ 50,000	$ 500,000
B	400	40,000	400,000
C	100	140,000	100,000
	1,000	$230,000	$1,000,000

A and B are in their late 70's and have held their T stock since the company was founded many years ago. C recently inherited her stock.

T has $400,000 of accumulated earnings and profits and the following assets (all held long-term) and liabilities:

Assets	Adj. Basis	F.M.V.
Cash	$200,000	$ 200,000
Inventory	50,000	100,000
Equipment ($100,000 § 1245 recapture)	100,000	200,000
Building (no recapture)	50,000	300,000
Securities	400,000	300,000
Goodwill	0	200,000
	$800,000	$1,300,000
Liabilities		
Bank loan		300,000
		$ 300,000

T and its shareholders are considering a sale of the business. Purchaser Corporation ("P") is interested in acquiring T. If specific computations are required by your instructor, assume (for computational convenience)

2. These losses are available without limitation to offset the gain on T's deemed asset sale. If P acquired T and did not elect under Section 338, T's NOLs would not be purged but they likely would be limited in the future under Section 382. See Chapter 12, infra.

3. See I.R.C. § 338(h)(10) and Section C3 of this chapter, supra.

that C corporations are taxed on all their income at a flat corporate rate of 35 percent and individuals are taxed at a flat 35 percent rate on ordinary income and a 15 percent rate on long-term capital gains.

What are the tax consequences of the following alternative acquisition methods to T, T's shareholders, and P?

(a) T adopts a plan of complete liquidation, sells all of its assets (except the cash but subject to the bank loan) to P for $800,000 cash, and distributes the after-tax proceeds to its shareholders in proportion to their stock holdings.

(b) T adopts a plan of complete liquidation, distributes all of its assets (subject to the liability) to its shareholders in proportion to their stock holdings, and the shareholders then sell the assets (less any cash but subject to the bank loan) to P for $800,000.

(c) In general, how would the result in (a), above, change if P paid T $200,000 in cash and $600,000 in notes, with market rate interest payable annually and the entire principal payable in five years?

(d) T sells all of its assets (except for the cash but subject to the bank loan) to P as in (a), above, except that T does not liquidate and instead invests the after-tax sales proceeds in a portfolio of publicly traded securities.

(e) P purchases all the stock of T for $800 per share and makes a § 338 election. (Why didn't P pay $1,000 per share for the T stock?)

(f) P purchases all the stock of T for cash but does not make the § 338 election. (Consider generally what P should pay for the T stock.)

(g) Assuming P and T are indifferent to the form of the transaction, would you recommend the acquisition method in (b)(purchase of assets), (e) (purchase of stock with § 338 election) or (f)(purchase of stock without § 338 election), above?

(h) Would your recommendation in (g), above, change if T had $600,000 in net operating loss carryovers?

(i) Assume that T is a wholly-owned subsidiary of S, Inc., and S has a $200,000 adjusted basis in its T stock. What result if T distributes all of its assets (subject to the liability) to S in complete liquidation, and S then sells the assets to P?

(j) Same as (i), above, except P insists that the transaction must be structured as an acquisition of T stock.

2.   Should Congress enact legislation that treats taxable asset and stock acquisitions consistently for tax purposes? If so, what are its options and which would you support?

E.   TAX TREATMENT OF ACQUISITION EXPENSES

The expenses incurred in connection with a corporate acquisition may be substantial. Both the purchaser ("P") and the target ("T") ordinarily must pay fees to lawyers, accountants and investment bankers. P may incur additional expenses to obtain debt and equity financing, and T may be obligated to secure an opinion stating that the proposed acquisition is "fair" to T and its shareholders. In virtually all cases, the central tax question becomes whether the expenses are currently deductible, amortizable, capitalized and added to the basis of a particular tangible or intangible asset, or treated as a permanent nondepreciable capital expenditure.

The tax treatment of P's expenses are relatively settled. Costs of obtaining debt financing (such as fees for negotiating the loan and drafting loan documents, up-front commitment fees and other fees paid to the lender) generally must be amortized over the term of the loan to which the expenses relate.[1] Likewise, expenses of obtaining equity financing (e.g., to register newly issued stock, prepare offering documents, etc.) are treated as permanent capital expenditures that are neither currently deductible nor amortizable.[2] Costs attributable to the acquisition of particular T assets or T stock (e.g., legal expenses for drafting an acquisition agreement, closing costs, finder's fees) also are capital expenditures and must be added to the basis of the acquired property.[3] If P forms a new subsidiary to carry out the acquisition, the organizational expenses are currently deductible (up to $5,000, but reduced as total expenses exceed $50,000), with any excess over the deductible amount amortizable over 15 years if P elects to apply Section 248. In addition, P may attempt to classify certain expenses related to an acquisition as normal business expenses. Examples would include expenses related to employment agreements, executive compensation and retirement planning, tax planning, and the annual retainer paid to an investment banker that may have helped arrange the acquisition.

The tax treatment of T's expenses has been more controversial. Assume for example that the target in a friendly corporate takeover incurs legal, investment banking and other fees, including the cost of obtaining an opinion that the terms of the acquisition are fair to T and its shareholders. Are these expenses currently deductible by T as ordinary and necessary businesses expenses under Section 162 or must they be capitalized? In INDOPCO, Inc. v. Commissioner,[4] the Supreme Court held that investment banking fees and other expenses incurred by a target corporation in a friendly takeover were nondeductible capital expenditures because they produced significant long-term benefits, such as the availability of the acquiring corporation's resources, the opportunity for synergy, and the benefits resulting from the target's transformation from a public company to a wholly owned subsidiary. In ruling for the government, the Court held that the creation or enhancement of a separate or distinct asset was not controlling in resolving capital expenditure classification questions. In so

---

1. Rev.Rul. 70–359, 1970–2 C.B. 103; Rev.Rul. 70–360, 1970–2 C.B. 103.

2. Rev.Rul. 69–330, 1969–1 C.B. 51.

3. If P acquires T's stock and makes a Section 338 election, these capital expenditures become part of new T's adjusted grossed-up basis and may be allocated among T's assets in accordance with the rules in Sections 338(b)(5) and 1060. See Reg. § 1.338(b)–1(g)(1).

4. 503 U.S. 79, 112 S.Ct. 1039 (1992).

doing, it rejected the taxpayer's reliance on a line of appellate decisions that had interpreted the Court's opinion in Commissioner v. Lincoln Savings & Loan Association[5] as adopting a test under which creation or enhancement of an asset is a prerequisite to capitalization. The Court clarified its earlier decision in *Lincoln Savings*, stating that the creation of a separate and distinct asset may be a sufficient reason for capitalizing an expense but not an essential prerequisite. It noted further that *Lincoln Savings* did not prohibit reliance on "future benefit" as a test for distinguishing an ordinary business expense from a capital expenditure. However, the Court conceded that an "incidental future benefit" may not require capitalization but that the taxpayer's realization of benefits beyond the year in which the expenditure was incurred is an important factor in distinguishing ordinary business expenses from capital expenditures.

Soon after it was decided, commentators began to focus on the potential ripple effect of the Supreme Court's *INDOPCO* decision—specifically whether the Court's reasoning would be imported to deny deductibility of various other expenses. The Service has calmed most of these nerves, first in a series of rulings confirming that the deductibility of many expenditures was not affected by Rev.Rul. 69–330, 1969–1 C.B. 51[6] and more recently in extensive regulations.[7]

INDOPCO involved a friendly takeover. Should expenses incurred to resist a hostile takeover be treated differently? The contexts in which this issue arises include both defending against a hostile takeover by a corporate raider and arranging for a taxable acquisition by a more friendly "White Knight" buyer. The cases so far indicate that the tax treatment of such expenditures may depend on the eventual outcome of the transaction. In United States v. Federated Department Stores, Inc.,[8] a corporate taxpayer, faced with a hostile offer, arranged a White Knight transaction and agreed to pay "break-up" fees to the White Knight if their merger fell through. Eventually, the hostile bidder was successful and the break-up fees were paid to the White Knight. The Court held that the fees were currently deductible under either Section 162 or Section 165 (as costs incurred in an abandoned transaction). Distinguishing *INDOPCO*, the court found that the fees were incurred to defend the business against attack and not to restructure the corporation in hopes of some future benefit.

In A.E. Staley Manufacturing Co. v. Commissioner,[9] the Tax Court considered a situation where a corporation incurred $23 million in invest-

---

5. 403 U.S. 345, 91 S.Ct. 1893 (1971).

6. See Rev. Rul. 95–32, 1995–16 I.R.B. 5 (expenditures by a public utility for the implementation and operation of energy conservation and load management programs are deductible under Section 162); Rev. Rul. 94–77, 1994–2 C.B. 19 (severance payments to employees are generally deductible under Section 162); Rev. Rul. 94–38, 1994–1 C.B. 35 (costs to clean up land and treat groundwater contaminated by taxpayer are deductible under Section 162); Rev. Rul. 94–12, 1994–1 C.B. 36 (incidental repair costs are deductible under Section 162); Rev. Rul. 92–80, 1992–2 C.B. 57 (advertising costs are generally deductible under Section 162).

7. See generally Reg. § 1.263(a)–4, –5.

8. 171 B.R. 603 (S.D.Ohio 1994).

9. 105 T.C. 166 (1995).

ment bankers' fees and printing costs to respond to a series of hostile tender offers for its stock. The company's board of directors declined two offers but eventually accepted a third bid. Rejecting the taxpayer's argument that *INDOPCO* was distinguishable because the takeover in *Staley* was hostile, the Tax Court held that the fees and costs were nondeductible because they were incurred in connection with a change in the ownership of the taxpayer that "portended strategic changes * * * with long-term consequences" and were capital in nature.[10] The Tax Court also distinguished *Federated Department Stores* because (1) there was no White Knight transaction that could be treated as abandoned and eligible for a loss deduction, and (2) the taxpayer received significant future benefits as a result of the acquisition.[11] Thus, according to the Tax Court the critical question is not whether the transaction is "friendly" or "hostile" but whether an identifiable loss has been sustained and the costs were incurred to realize future benefits.[12]

On appeal, however, the Seventh Circuit reversed and permitted the target corporation to deduct most of the expenses it incurred in resisting a hostile takeover.[13] The court reasoned that *INDOPCO* did not change the law with respect to costs incurred to defend a business because those expenses were to preserve the status quo, not to produce future benefits. It concluded that most of the expenses incurred by the taxpayer in *A.E. Staley* were related to the defense of its business and corporate policy and thus were currently deductible under Section 162(a). Costs properly allocable to unsuccessful efforts to engage in an alternate transaction to prevent the acquisition, such as a financial restructuring, recapitalization, or joint venture, were held to be deductible losses under Section 165. The court also held that fees paid to evaluate the taxpayer's stock and to facilitate the eventual merger were nondeductible capital expenditures.

If either P or T incurs costs in investigating or attempting to consummate an acquisition that ultimately fails, the transactional costs generally are currently deductible as losses under Section 165.[14]

In 2003, the Service issued lengthy regulations under Section 263 relating to the tax treatment of amounts incurred to acquire, create, or enhance various kinds of intangible assets.[15] The regulations are intended to provide guidance on when taxpayers must treat these costs as capital expenditures. They do so by specifying, in extraordinary detail, various categories of rights, privileges and future benefits for which capitalization

10. Id. at 200.

11. Id. at 199.

12. The Service also does not seem to base the tax consequences of the expenditure on whether the takeover was hostile. In Tech. Adv. Memo. 9144042 (July 1, 1991), a target corporation was required to capitalize expenses incurred to thwart a hostile tender offer. On the facts presented (the target incurred expenses in repurchasing its own stock from a corporate raider), the Service reasoned that the taxpayer failed to prove that the expenditure did not confer a long-term benefit.

13. A.E. Staley Manufacturing Co. v. Commissioner, 119 F.3d 482 (7th Cir.1997).

14. Rev.Rul. 73–580, 1973–2 C.B. 86.

15. Reg. § 1.263(a)–4, –5, T.D. 9107, 69 Fed. Reg. 436 (Jan. 5, 2004).

is required. Particular goals of this regulations project were to bring greater clarity to (some would say "erode" or "discard") the "significant future benefit" standard enunciated by the Supreme Court in Indopco, Inc. v. Commissioner, and to resurrect the more taxpayer-friendly "separate and distinct asset" approach of the Court's earlier *Lincoln Savings* decision. The effect of this new liberalized regime is to presume that outlays related to intangible assets are currently deductible unless these or subsequently issued regulations specifically require capitalization.

The regulations include specific rules on an acquisition of a trade or business, a change in the capital structure of a business entity, and certain other transactions such as Section 351 exchanges.[16] Costs that "facilitate" such transactions must be capitalized.[17] This standard is consistent with the previously discussed case law on the purchaser's acquisition expenses. Transaction costs incurred to defend against a hostile takeover are not viewed as facilitating the acquisition. As a result, they may be currently deducted rather than capitalized.[18] This rule follows the Seventh Circuit's decision in *A.E. Staley*. If an initially hostile acquisition becomes friendly, the taxpayer must bifurcate the costs between those incurred to defend against the hostile takeover and those incurred to facilitate the friendly acquisition, using a "facts and circumstances" standard to draw the line.[19] Costs incurred to thwart a hostile acquisition, such as by merging with a White Knight, must be capitalized even if the taxpayer's overall purpose was to defend against a hostile acquisition.[20] But legal fees paid to seek an injunction against a hostile takeover and investment banking fees to locate a potential White Knight acquirer may be currently deducted.[21] And there's much more, including simplifying conventions (e.g., compensation to employees are treated as amounts that do not facilitate a transaction and thus are currently deductible),[22] de minimis exceptions (transaction costs of $5,000 or less generally do not have to be capitalized),[23] and timing rules.[24]

F.   TAX POLICY ISSUES

1.   RETHINKING *GENERAL UTILITIES* REPEAL

Much of this text has been devoted to the history and current status of the *General Utilities* doctrine—the venerable principle that permitted a corporation to distribute appreciated property to its shareholders and avoid a corporate-level tax.[1] In studying the demise of *General Utilities*, an

---

16. See Reg. § 1.263(a)–5(a). For accounting rules for debt issuance costs that must be capitalized, see Reg. § 1.446–5.

17. Id. Costs that facilitate the acquisition of an intangible generally must be capitalized under Reg. §§ 1.263(a)–4(b)(1)(v), (e).

18. Reg. § 1.263(a)–5(*l*) Example 11.

19. Id. See also Reg. § 1.263(a)–5(*l*) Example 12.

20. Reg. § 1.263(a)–5(*l*) Example 11.

21. Id.

22. Reg. § 1.263(a)–5(d)(2).

23. Reg. § 1.263(a)–5(d)(3).

24. Reg. § 1.263(a)–5(e).

1. See Chapters 4D1, 5E1, and 7B2, supra.

inquisitive student may have wondered how the principle remained embedded in the Code for so long. Was there opposition to its repeal? What rationale might have supported its retention in the federal tax laws for over 50 years?

The *General Utilities* doctrine had its supporters, especially in the liquidation context. The two excerpts below address the question of relief from full recognition of corporate gain on a liquidation and the possible form of such relief. The first is from the testimony of an experienced tax practitioner at hearings before the Senate Finance Committee concerning that committee staff's 1983 preliminary report on Subchapter C reform. In reading the excerpt, keep in mind that the references to some statutory references (e.g., Sections 336 and 337) are to sections of the Code as they existed prior to the Tax Reform Act of 1986, when liquidating distributions and sales could be made without a corporate-level tax. At the time this testimony was presented, the maximum capital gains rate for individuals was 20 percent and the maximum capital gains rate for corporations was 28 percent, for a combined effective corporate and shareholder rate of 42.4 percent. The combined rate under current law is actually higher (48 percent) because of the absence of any rate preference for corporate capital gains. The second excerpt is from the Senate Finance Committee staff's final report on reform and simplification of Subchapter C"The Subchapter C Revision Act of 1985."[2] It surveys various potential relief provisions and could be a model for legislative proposals in the future if Congress should ever reconsider its approach to the *General Utilities* issue.

Excerpt From Hearings Before the Senate Finance Committee, Reform of Corporate Taxation*

S.Hrg. 98–556, 98th Cong., 1st Sess. 150–70 (1983).

Statement of John S. Nolan

Corporate Tax: Asset Appreciation on Complete Liquidation (*General Utilities*)

The result of the Staff proposal as to the *General Utilities* rule would be to impose a double tax on the appreciation in value of corporate assets sold or distributed in the course of a complete liquidation. This would effectively raise the maximum capital gain tax on this increase in asset value from the 20% rate, applicable to all other capital gains, to 42.4% [the combined then effective capital gains rates at the corporate and shareholder levels, Ed.]. * * *

2. Staff of the Senate Committee on Finance, The Subchapter C Revision Act of 1985: A Final Report Prepared by the Staff, 99th Cong., 1st Sess. (S.Prt. 99–47, 1985). Although titled an "Act," this entire proposal was not enacted into law, but many of its recommendations (but not relief from General Utilities repeal) were incorporated in the Tax Reform Act of 1986.

* Some footnotes omitted.

The additional gain that would be taxed by the proposed repeal of *General Utilities* would in many cases be largely inflationary gain, not real gain, together in some cases with the value of intangible assets of the business. A tax rate of 42.4% on these kinds of gain is not justified.

The impact will be almost entirely on closely-held family businesses; large publicly-held companies very seldom undergo complete liquidation. The short-term result will be to bias the decisions of these families in favor of merging their family companies into large publicly-held corporations in a tax-free exchange for stock of those companies, rather than allocating their capital to other uses that could be more efficient. The tax law would thus further interfere with market allocation of capital.

In the longer run, business will tend to avoid incorporation wherever possible. Our capital markets, the largest and most efficient in the world, are based on financial instruments of corporations, not unincorporated businesses. These markets will adjust, to be sure, but at a significant cost to the capital formation process. New instruments subject to new dimensions of risk will be required to replace corporate capital instruments.

As a lawyer experienced in this field, and as a former law teacher of the subject matter, after taking into account the circumstances of my clients and others similarly situated, I strongly oppose this particular element of the Staff's report. While I agree with many of the other major elements of the report, and while I see no strong objection to repeal of the General Utilities rule in the case of ordinary distributions in kind, I think that its repeal with respect to complete liquidations would be a grave error in tax policy.[1] I have studied the detailed reasons given for its repeal in the Staff report, and I do not find them convincing. They proceed from a fundamentally erroneous premise and are based far too much on unjustified speculation. The reasons given against repeal are understated and require much further development.

I note that in recent letters to Senator Dole, two prestigious bar associations with great experience in this field, the Association of the Bar of the City of New York and the Tax Section of the New York State Bar Association, have singled out this same matter to urge further careful

---

1. I recognize that repeal of *General Utilities* is a key element in the major treatment of acquisitions proposed in the report—that is, the election between cost basis and carryover basis treatment at the corporate level and the separate tax treatment at the shareholder level. If *General Utilities* is not repealed in the corporate liquidation context as I recommend, it will be necessary to retain the basic elements of §§ 337 and 338; it obviously is not desirable to return to the uncertainties of Commissioner v. Court Holding Co., 324 U.S. 331, 65 S.Ct. 707 (1945) versus United States v. Cumberland Public Service Co., 338 U.S. 451, 70 S.Ct. 280 (1950), and Kimbell–Diamond Milling Co. v. Commissioner, 187 F.2d 718 (5th Cir.1951). If the acquisitions proposals are adopted, but General Utilities is not repealed in the complete liquidation context, recapture should be required, but gain or loss should not otherwise be recognized, in transactions generally of the type described in § 337 and § 338 if the acquiring company elects cost basis treatment. The operation of those two provisions could be improved and restricted to their true purpose. It may be that recapture should be required in any such case, whether the acquiring corporation elects cost basis or carryover basis treatment. These are matters which require a great deal more study.

evaluation. I strongly urge this Committee to exercise great caution in making such a fundamental change in our corporate tax structure.

Impact of the Proposed Change—Family–Held Businesses

As previously stated, by far the greatest impact of the proposed change will be on family-held businesses. These family businesses typically hold a wide range of business assets, including real estate from which the business may be operated, or real estate collected in a family investment company. These assets are likely to have appreciated substantially in value over a long period of years, in large part as a result of inflation. The business will often have developed patents, trademarks, trade secrets, know-how, or other valuable intangible assets. Many family companies have been operated through several generations, thus greatly increasing the inflationary components of these gains. The proposal will tax all of this gain at the corporate level, in addition to the same gain being taxed again at the shareholder level, on complete liquidation of the family company.

Even though the family company may have been operated for many years, the family may have become so large, or the interests of different family members may have become so diverse, that it may make greater economic sense for the family to liquidate the corporation, possibly selling all or part of its assets, or to sell their stock, and undertake other business ventures. It may have become economically more efficient for third parties to acquire the business. There are a wide range of reasons why it may become appropriate for the family to terminate the activities of their corporation by complete liquidation. These families have operated on certain fundamental assumptions as to our taxing system as it has existed at least for the last fifty years, even prior to the time the General Utilities case was decided in 1935. These include a clear understanding under our tax system that upon a decision to terminate their business and completely liquidate, they could do so incurring only a single capital gains tax on such a terminal transaction on the appreciation in value of the underlying assets of the business. This has been the case whether they sell the assets of the business to third parties, divide the business among themselves while it remains in corporate solution, or take their respective shares of the assets in kind and operate as sole proprietorships or partnerships.

In any such case, they seek to put their capital to its most effective uses in our economy. A single capital gains tax on this terminal transaction, just as if the gain had arisen from any other investment asset held by them, is entirely appropriate. As previously stated, much of the gain is probably inflationary gain, not real gain, and thus deserves only a single capital gain tax. Even the balance of the gain, likely to be largely attributable to real estate or intangible assets, is by nature essentially an investment gain, not income attributable to regular business activity that typically is taxed at higher rates. The gain in question by its nature is capital gain. It should attract only a single capital gain tax.

A capital gain tax of 42.4% on this gain is not justified. The result will be that families wishing to terminate their family businesses will effectively have only one option—find a publicly-held corporation and take its stock for their company * * *

[T]he family could no longer sell the assets of the business to a third party, via [the former version § 337, which generally allowed corporations to make tax-free sales of assets in connection with a liquidation] or indirectly via § 338, and apply their capital to other uses, except by incurring a 42.4% tax burden.[2] Nor could they liquidate the corporation and operate the business as a partnership or sole proprietorship, dividing the assets in kind among themselves as they see fit. Much of the healthy flexibility of our existing tax system as it applies to family businesses would be lost. I see no justification for removing this flexibility, which has been an important inducement to the formation of new, privately-held companies with fresh ideas and inventiveness.

The problem could be compounded by the fact that the family company may have been organized originally to incorporate business assets held in a sole proprietorship or partnership. The assets may have appreciated substantially in value, from inflation or otherwise, and specific intangible asset values may have arisen, before any such incorporation. The proposal would tax the pre-incorporation gain on these assets even though it did not arise in corporate solution. The result would be that the family would clearly pay a much greater tax than would have been payable if no corporation had been formed. There can be no tax policy justification for this result.

Staff Report: Questionable Assumptions as to *General Utilities* Rule

The Staff report commendably recognizes that there are substantial questions whether the *General Utilities* rule should be repealed:

> In addition to the preceding recommendations, the Staff has identified a number of options that ought to be considered if the Committee concludes that the outright repeal of the *General Utilities* rule is too harsh. * * *

The American Law Institute, the recommendations of which were a major source of reference for the Staff's report, recognized the severity of a double tax on the long-term appreciation in value of business assets in a complete liquidation. The Institute recommended that the shareholder be allowed a credit for his share of the corporate capital gains tax against his individual capital gains tax to eliminate the double taxation. The credit is extremely complex. It also accomplishes little, to the extent the corporate and individual capital gain tax rates are essentially the same (as they should be with respect to the kind of gain in question here). The Staff rejects the ALI credit proposal on grounds of complexity and taxpayer compliance.

The Staff report gives nine arguments favoring repeal of *General Utilities* and three arguments against it. Before reaching them, it is critical

---

2. Technically, in a § 338 transaction, the selling shareholders would not directly incur all of the 42.4% tax but they would bear the burden of it partly through a reduced selling price in a cost basis acquisition.

to focus upon the basic assumptions of the Report in recommending repeal of General Utilities. These assumptions are that: (1) we have an unintegrated corporate tax system, it should be continued, and it should be rigorously applied; (2) the primary consideration should be that the rules should be "simplest and least susceptible to abuse and manipulation"; and (3) tax abuse abounds, despite many Code provisions specifically developed to prevent it, because of the General Utilities rule. I respectfully submit that none of these assumptions is valid.

In fact, we have never had a truly unintegrated corporate tax system in which a tax is paid on income at the corporate level and a second tax is paid on corporate income by the shareholders. Over the seventy or more years that our corporate income tax system has developed, we have had a compromise system in which double tax has been imposed on ordinary earnings from regular operations to the extent they are distributed to shareholders as dividends, but only a single tax has been imposed upon extraordinary events, such as a sale or distribution of assets pursuant to a complete liquidation.

In reality, we have to a large extent had only a single ordinary income tax on regular corporate earnings because of the ability to retain earnings. By reason of our provision for step-up in basis of assets at death, earnings taxed at ordinary rates at the corporate level have to a large extent been retained and have not been taxed again at the shareholder level. At most, they have been subjected to a capital gains tax on sale of stock at the shareholder level. A large percentage of corporations in the U.S., both publicly-held and privately-held, retain and reinvest in their business a large percentage of their annual earnings, partly as a result of the tax advantages to their shareholders that flow from this policy.

This is an entirely healthy system. The corporate tax rate and top individual rate are roughly the same. There should be limits on the tax burden on income from capital so that capital formation is not inhibited or misdirected away from business investment. Further, to the extent we provide incentives through tax allowances, such as the investment credit, ACRS, the research and development credit, or the intangible drilling cost deduction, there should be no preference for operating in or out of the corporate structure.

Virtually all major foreign industrialized countries, including the entire European Economic Community and Canada, have moved toward a single integrated tax structure in which only a single income tax is paid on business earnings. Economists tend strongly to favor such a system to avoid undue burdens on capital investment. We have obviously greatly moderated our tax burden on capital by the types of tax incentives previously described. As a practical matter, the effect of our present corporate tax structure is that by a variety of means we have achieved what is a single tax on the returns from capital, and this allows us to remain competitive in the world economy.

There is no important reason at this time to disturb this carefully-developed balance that has resulted from seventy or more years of experience in refining our corporate tax system to accommodate the needs of our economy and our society. It is particularly unwise to do so in a way that would impact harshly on privately-held, smaller companies. The primary consideration affecting our corporate tax structure should be economic efficiency, not simplicity or over-reactive concern with abuse and manipulation.[3]

The preoccupation in this Report with abuse and manipulation is disturbing. Admittedly, the extensive provisions we have developed to prevent abuse of the *General Utilities* rule, such as the recapture rules, the collapsible corporation provisions, new section 338, the recent repeal of the partial liquidation provisions, the ACRS anti-churning rules, and others, are complex. Complexity, however, in a corporate tax context is manageable, and we have in fact learned to live with it. Further, despite the impressions suggested by the report, these anti-abuse provisions are effective in practice. In my thirty-plus years as a corporate tax lawyer, I have not seen any widespread circumvention of the collapsible corporation rules or these other provisions. When some special forms of abuse have developed, as they did in recent years, the Congressional response was swift and effective, as in TEFRA. We have developed a new legislative capacity to deal with these problems as they arise.

We must not make a fundamental change in our corporate tax structure to meet these relatively narrow concerns if it could substantially affect efficient allocation of capital resources in the United States. The effect of such a change has not yet been studied sufficiently in the context of repeal of the *General Utilities* rule in corporate complete liquidations. In addition, the possible effects of discouraging the use of corporations to operate privately-held businesses, in favor of partnerships the interests in which are not publicly-traded, royalty trusts, or other arrangements have not been fully evaluated. There are critical economic, legal, and social issues to be considered.

Accordingly, I urge this Committee to defer action on this critical matter at least until these kinds of evaluations have been done. Much more analysis is required to make the judgments that are required in changing the tax structure to increase burdens on privately-held companies.

Staff Report: Reasons For and Against Repeal of *General Utilities*

The report * * * argues for taxing gain on corporate assets at the corporate level in complete liquidations first on the ground that taxpayers pay less tax because of the *General Utilities* rule than would be paid in the absence of a corporate tax. This is difficult to understand, since the main

---

3. Integration of the corporate and individual tax has also been accomplished in other ways in our tax system. The obvious example is Subchapter S, but administrative considerations have forced the imposition of severe limitations on its use. Royalty trusts exist to receive and distribute certain forms of passive income. As recognized in the Staff report, publicly-traded limited partnerships now exist to operate going businesses. The report would treat publicly-traded limited partnerships as corporations. Widely-held limited partnerships, the interests in which are not publicly-traded, also exist, however, and the report would not reach these arrangements.

thrust of repealing the *General Utilities* rule is to impose a double tax on the appreciation in value of corporate assets, thereby raising the effective rate on such gain from 20% under existing law to 42.4%. No explanation of this argument in the report is given. Contrary to the impression given in the report, taxpayers will generally pay more tax if *General Utilities* is repealed than they would have paid in the absence of a corporate tax.

* * *

In the complete liquidation context, involving privately-held companies, it is useful to recognize that the shareholder's gain on liquidation consists of two elements—retained earnings and appreciation in value of the company's underlying assets. There is no other source of shareholder gain. The shareholder may have bought his shares at a time when such elements existed to some degree; if so, his predecessor will have paid tax at the shareholder level on such elements. Retained earnings and appreciation in value of corporate assets ultimately always incur a tax at the shareholder level, except to the extent that stepped-up basis at death occurs or the shareholder is tax-exempt.

Further, the recapture rules insure that the ordinary income portion of asset appreciation ultimately is taxed, and as ordinary income. Retained earnings by definition have been taxed at the corporate level. What remains then is the capital gain portion of appreciation in value of corporate assets, which, as stated above, is ultimately taxed at the shareholder level, except where there has been an intervening death of the shareholder. Repeal of *General Utilities* in complete liquidations would tax this latter portion twice, once at the corporate level, and again immediately at the shareholder level except where there has been an intervening death of the shareholder. If the business had operated in non-corporate form, this double tax would not have been incurred.

The anti-churning rules effectively prevent undue benefit from ACRS. The collapsible corporation rules, despite their complexity, prevent undue benefit from complete liquidations. There is no substantial opportunity to gain greater benefits by operating in corporate form than in non-corporate form.

The other reasons given in the report for this double taxation may be grouped. The second reason relates to complexity and abuse, a matter already discussed. Repeal of the collapsible corporation rules is not necessarily a useful end in and of itself, regardless of what must be done to make it possible. There are important economic and social consequences to be resolved here; the world has lived with the collapsible corporation anti-tax avoidance rules for more than thirty years and can continue to do so. It is said that repeal will block certain tax-motivated acquisitions, but no specifications are given. TEFRA addressed such problems, and if further problems arise, they can be addressed equally promptly and equally specifically. It is said that repeal of General Utilities will limit churning under ACRS, but we already have in place an effective set of rules for that purpose. Finally, I submit that the seriousness of the liquidation-reincorporation problem is overstated; in my extensive corporate tax practice, I have seen very few instances of successful liquidation-reincorporations that produce substantial tax benefits. It is a wonderful conversation piece and tax teaching tool; it is not much of a real problem. In point of fact, the report can be read to endorse a form of liquidation-reincorporation not presently available. It would tax the corporation at capital gain rates, permit a step-up in basis of the assets (even though continuity of interest clearly exists), and permit depreciation deductions by reference to stepped-up basis to offset subsequent ordinary income from ongoing business operations.

Otherwise, the reasons for double taxation seem to boil down to a preference for greater purity in an unintegrated tax system

iv. General recognition of gain provides uniformity. * * *

v. Recognition broadens the corporate tax base. * * *

vii. The *General Utilities* doctrine allows tax on corporate gain to be avoided entirely. * * *

All of these propositions assume there should be a double tax on appreciation in value of corporate assets at the time of a complete liquidation. As previously stated, there is no basis for this assumption, and it would have enormous adverse effects on privately-held companies in the U.S.

* * *

We have a generally efficient, fair, and workable system that presently stimulates capital formation by avoiding interference with allocation of capital to its most efficient uses in the economy. Initiative and productivity are stimulated by the ability to build up capital returns in a privately-held company. For the most part, all income and gain is taxed at least once, except to the extent we provide tax incentives for good reasons, whether economic (for example, business investment or R & D activity) or social (tax-exempt charitable or similar institutions). When abuses develop, they may be quickly corrected, particularly with the recent Congressional ability to move more promptly. We should not disturb the efficient functioning of the present system unless there are reasons of overriding importance. These have not yet been demonstrated.

The reasons given in the Report as against repeal of *General Utilities* are understated. It is not a theoretical argument as to "realization". It is a practical consideration. The repeal as applied in the complete liquidation context would greatly damage privately-held business in the United States.

To answer the question posed in the Report, a corporate liquidation is an event which warrants a single capital gains tax because it represents a liquidation of an investment, just as any other investment. The gain realized is likely to be largely inflationary rather than real. To the extent the gain reflects retained earnings, it represents income already subject to tax at the corporate level. If it has not been fully taxed at the corporate level, it is because some economic or social policy has been regarded by Congress as sufficiently important to call for a tax incentive provision.

Such gain is quite different from the regular earnings of an ongoing business. The comparisons drawn in the report to a 73% tax rate on ordinary income overstate reality. I doubt that any significant amount of income earned through corporations in the U.S. ever bears an effective tax rate even close to 73%.

The argument that liquidation of a corporation is often a highly formal step without economic substance is not valid. Few complete liquidations involve distributions of assets to the shareholders in kind. Most involve sales of assets pursuant to [former] § 337 or sales of stock deemed to be sales of assets under § 338. The liquidation-reincorporation problem, as previously stated, is given far more emphasis in the Report than it deserves. Further, it simply is not the fact that complete liquidations are often tax-driven transactions; they generally result from a business conclusion that someone else can operate the business more efficiently and that the shareholders can direct their capital to more effective uses in the economy.

The Report correctly notes the argument against repeal that 42.4% is too high a tax rate to impose on investment gain at the time of a complete liquidation. The answer, however, is not to tinker with this rate. Instead, we should simply avoid increasing the extent of double taxation. Extraordinary gains arising on complete liquidation of a corporation should be taxed once, at regular capital gains rates, just as is all other investment gain.

* * *

Conclusion

The Committee should not repeal *General Utilities* in the context of complete liquidations and impose a double tax burden on asset appreciation. An effective tax rate of 42.4% on such gain will have severe adverse effects on privately-held companies. It will create a bias, causing owners of family businesses contemplating liquidation to merge their corporations into publicly-held companies in exchange for stock of such companies. Capital will not be directed to its most efficient uses in the United States economy.

Excerpt From the Subchapter C Revision Act of 1985: A Final Report Prepared by the Staff of the Senate Finance Committee*

S.Prt. 99–47, 99th Cong., 1st Sess. 62–68 (1985).

C. *Relief from repeal of General Utilities doctrine*

Many people who testified at the October, 1983 hearing advocated some form of relief from the repeal of *General Utilities*. The original proposal contained in the Staff Report suggested the possibility of transitional relief in the form of a phase-in of the corporate capital gains tax over

* Some footnotes omitted.

a 10–year period. Several people testified that such relief would be inadequate, and that some permanent relief was essential.

In deciding what type of permanent relief, if any, might be appropriate, two questions had to be resolved: (1) in what type of transactions should relief be provided; and (2) what form should the relief take?

1. Eligible transactions

Almost all who testified in favor of some form of permanent relief confined their remarks to the need for relief in a complete liquidation or liquidating sale. No one testified as to the need for relief in a non-liquidating setting. Indeed, even as to liquidating transactions, most individuals indicated that any permanent relief should be appropriately limited to the potential "double tax" on long-held capital assets.

However, one of the reasons described above in favor of the repeal of *General Utilities* was the concern that current law creates a bias in favor of certain types of transactions over others, providing much complexity and abuse potential. If any General Utilities relief were limited as suggested by those who testified, there was the possibility that the same problems as under current law would be revived.

Providing across-the-board relief in all transactions, liquidating and non-liquidating, seemed out of the question because of revenue considerations.[160] It seemed advisable, therefore, that any permanent relief should be targeted as closely as possible to the specific need for the relief.

In the large majority of cases, opposition to the repeal of *General Utilities*, and support for some form of relief, was based upon the concern that a "double tax" on long-held assets of small businesses was too harsh. The view was expressed that a small businessman whose incorporated business holds appreciating capital assets for an extended period of time should not be required to pay both a corporate level and a shareholder level tax upon the liquidation or acquisition of the business. According to this view, this was particularly true because the gains might be largely inflationary. However sympathetic the preceding case might be, the case of a speculator who owns stock of a large publicly-held corporation just prior to the liquidation or acquisition of such corporation appeared clearly less appealing as to the need for "double tax" relief. Thus, it seemed appropriate to consider limiting any relief to long-held gains of small businesses.

Moreover, there was testimony that the impact of the repeal of *General Utilities* (and the consequent need for some form of relief) would fall almost exclusively upon small, closely-held businesses, and that large, publicly-held corporations would rarely be affected. Finally, to the extent the form of the

---

160. *But see* discussion below regarding the possibility of implementing the Treasury Department's dividends paid deduction proposal. The Treasury proposal, which would provide only partial cross-the-board relief, is estimated to cost approximately $85 billion during the first four years that it would be implemented. See "Tax Reform for Fairness, Simplicity, and Economic Growth: The Treasury Department Report to the President" (November 1984) (hereinafter "Treasury Tax Reform Proposals") Vol. 1 at 248.

relief (described below) was criticized at the hearing as being too complex, many of those concerns would be eliminated if the relief were limited to a tightly circumscribed number of cases involving smaller corporations.

Accordingly, the bill provides permanent *General Utilities* relief in the case of a small business which incurs gains on long-held assets in a liquidation or liquidating sale. In those circumstances, the "double tax" is effectively eliminated.

Five years was chosen as the appropriate dividing line for "long-held" capital assets because, to the extent the proposal is an attempt to mitigate the effects of inflation, it was believed that some significant holding period should be required.[164] Other proposals have suggested three years as the appropriate test.[165]

The $1 million fair market value test for "small" businesses was chosen because of similar standards used in other sections of the Code.[166] In addition, to avoid a cliff effect, the bill proposes to provide relief, in decreasing amounts, for corporations up to $2 million in value.

2.   Form of the relief

The two principal forms of relief that were considered were a share-holder credit and corporate-level exemption.[167] Testimony was almost even-ly divided between the two types of relief. The American Law Institute had recommended a shareholder credit in its proposal.[169] The special ABA Task Force recommended a corporate-level exemption.[170]

The corporate-level exemption was rejected for the same reasons that a complete repeal of *General Utilities* was considered essential. A corporate-level exemption is no more than a partial repeal of General Utilities. Thus, a corporate-level exemption was viewed as presenting many of the same problems that an incomplete repeal of General Utilities would have pre-sented.

For example, assume that relief were provided in the form of a corporate-level exemption on capital assets with a holding period of 5 years or more. Assume that P corporation acquires all of the assets of T corporation in exchange for P stock. Further, assume that all of the T assets consist of capital assets with a holding period of 5 years or more.

---

164. In that regard, should a proposal such as the Treasury Department's recom-mendation to index the basis of capital assets for inflation, be enacted, it may be appropri-ate to rethink the need for the proposed relief. See Treasury Department Tax Reform Proposals, Vol. 11 at 178.

165. ABA Task Force Report, 37 Tax Lawyer 625, 631. The Minority Report did not agree with taxing any capital gains.

166. See, e.g., section 1244 ($1 million paid-in capital test); cf. P.L. 96–223, sec. 403(b), as amended (LIFO recapture amount reduced by $1 million); section 11(b) ($1 mil-lion taxable income threshold for graduated rates).

167. Other relief provided by the bill, including special relief on an in-kind liqui-dation, is discussed in the next section.

169. American Law Institute, Federal Income Tax Project: Subchapter C (1982) at 134.

170. ABA Task Force Report, 37 Tax Lawyer 625, 631. The Minority Report did not agree with this recommendation.

In this example, a cost basis election could be made, resulting in a cost basis to P in the assets acquired. Because of the exemption, no gain or loss would be recognized by T in the transaction. Finally, in the distribution by T of the P stock, the T shareholders would not recognize any gain or loss because of the receipt of qualifying consideration. In short, the acquisition would result in a cost basis being obtained by the acquiring party without any immediate tax being paid by either the target corporation or its shareholders. No one who testified appeared to advocate this result.

Obviously, in most cases, all of T's assets would not consist of capital assets with a holding period of 5 years or more. However, in any transaction, to the extent T's assets did consist of such assets, the potentially inappropriate combination of a cost basis to the acquiring corporation without any immediate tax liability would be available. For many of these reasons, the Treasury Department opposed a corporate-level exemption.

Some consideration was also given to using the S corporation rules as a means to provide the appropriate relief. One individual recommended exploring this option.

The S corporation option was ultimately rejected for two reasons. First, it was clear that many corporations not eligible for S corporation status should, nevertheless, be entitled to relief, so that the S corporation rules would have to be significantly liberalized. While certain of the restrictions under current law defining an S corporation might appropriately be waived or eliminated, at least in the case of a liquidation or liquidating sale, it was unclear that all of the restrictions could be removed. There was concern that to the extent any S corporation limitations remained, some sympathetic cases would be unfairly excluded from relief.

Second, the S corporation relief was also viewed as too generous in certain cases. The S corporation rules do not limit the size of the eligible corporation in economic terms. To the extent relief would be provided only to a limited number of corporations and their shareholders, it was determined that it would be fairer and closer to the targeted goal to draw a distinction based upon economic size rather than upon some other criterion, such as the number of shareholders of the corporation.

Thus, the bill provides for a shareholder credit type of relief from the repeal of *General Utilities*. Each shareholder of a small corporation is provided a basis adjustment in his stock in the liquidating or acquired corporation to reflect the corporate-level tax on long-held capital assets. The basis adjustment approach rather than a shareholder credit was selected to increase administrative simplicity, in order to harmonize the treatment of shareholders in different tax situations and to reconcile the difference between the corporate and shareholder capital gains rates. The basis adjustment would operate to eliminate the "double tax" on long-held capital assets. Only those shareholders holding the stock for six months or more would be entitled to relief.

D.   Other forms of relief

In addition to the basis adjustment relief described above, the bill also provides several other forms of relief, including special relief in an in-kind liquidation. As noted, several witnesses recommended some form of special relief in that situation.

Under the bill, any shareholder of a corporation which liquidates in kind is entitled to defer the shareholder level tax with respect to any property distributed to the shareholder in the liquidation, except for cash, stock, securities, and similar property, received. In that respect, the relief is similar to section 333 of current law, except that several of the limitations of that section have been eliminated.

The relief is available to a shareholder of any corporation that liquidates in kind, not just "small" corporations. Shareholders of small corporations would have the option of selecting either the basis adjustment relief described earlier or the deferral of shareholder tax proposal.

Some consideration was given to a deferral of the corporate level tax rather than the shareholder level tax. Ultimately, this was rejected because of the view that the corporate level tax should not be permitted to be deferred beyond the termination of the corporation. Many provisions under current law permit the deferral of corporate tax while assets remain within the corporation or in corporate solution. However, if those benefits represent true "deferrals" rather than an exemption, it seemed appropriate to require the deferral to end upon the liquidation of the corporation, when the assets leave corporate solution.

In addition, the deferral of the shareholder level tax is analogous to the deferral permitted under the bill when a shareholder receives qualifying consideration.

Some thought was also given to a relief proposal in an in-kind liquidation that would permit both the shareholder and corporate level taxes to be deferred or avoided. It was noted by several witnesses that a shareholder, who organizes a corporation tax-free under section 351 by mistake and then chooses to liquidate the corporation, should be permitted to defer or avoid both the corporate and shareholder level taxes. This was viewed as particularly appealing in the case where the appreciation in the corporate assets occurred prior to the formation of the corporation—i.e., while the assets were held by the individual shareholder. Under this view, the "disincorporation" transaction should be permitted to be tax-free in the same way that an incorporation transaction is tax-free under section 351.

The potential discontinuity with the treatment under section 351 was a matter of some concern. But ultimately, it was determined that to the extent a discontinuity between incorporation and liquidation transactions exists, it is a problem created by section 351 and not by the proposed rules for an in-kind liquidation.

Section 351 arguably serves the policy goal of facilitating the formation of corporations. More importantly, that policy goal is achievable under section 351 with little or no tax avoidance potential. An individual who forms a corporation with appreciated property is moving that property from a potential "one-tax" system to a potential "two-tax" system. Therefore, permitting that individual to defer tax on the gain that would otherwise be recognized in the incorporation transaction will almost assuredly be a true deferral and not an exemption; indeed, the pre-incorporation appreciation may be taxed twice, not once, as a result of the act of incorporation.

The same cannot be said for a liquidation in kind. Arguably, it might be appropriate from a policy standpoint to facilitate certain "disincorporation" transactions by providing tax-free or tax-deferred treatment similar to section 351. But any such relief would be fraught with tax avoidance possibilities. Here, in contrast to section 351, the assets are moving from a potential "two-tax" system to, at most, a potential "one-tax" system. Thus, any "deferrals" permitted at the time of the liquidation may well result in complete exemptions. Possibilities of that sort might well necessitate certain of the complex anti-tax avoidance provisions of current law that are proposed to be eliminated by the bill.

Finally, a proposal to defer or exempt both the shareholder and corporate level taxes raised a number of unresolved issues with no clear policy direction. For example, should any such relief be limited to a short-term "mistake" case described above, or should it be available only where the shareholders have held the stock for some extended period of time, as was suggested by one witness? Should the relief be limited to built-in gains at the time of the incorporation transaction, or should it be extended to all corporate-level gains, whether they arose before or after the formation of the corporation? Finally, should any such relief be conditioned upon the elimination of a death step-up under section 1014, as was suggested by the Treasury Department? These and other issues raised significant problems of added complexity and potential uncertainty.

Another form of relief provided under the bill is the special election for goodwill and other unamortizable intangibles. Thus, at the election of the taxpayer, the corporate level tax burden of a cost basis election would not include any tax on the appreciation of such intangibles. This relief would not be inconsistent with the repeal of General Utilities because the acquiring party would be required to obtain a carryover basis in the intangibles.

A third form of relief is available under Subchapter S. Under current law, a C corporation with appreciated assets may be able to elect S corporation status and thereby avoid the corporate level tax on the appreciation. The bill would limit that possibility by generally not permitting an increase to a shareholder's stock basis in the case of gain (other than gain on long-held capital assets) recognized by the corporation which is attributable to periods when the corporation was a C corporation.[177] (This would have the effect of maintaining a potential "double tax" on gain (other than

---

177. The actual proposal permits an increase in stock basis to reflect the taxable portion of the gain. Thus, a tax-free distribution could be made by the S corporation to its shareholders to enable the shareholders to pay the pass-through tax on the corporate-level gain. Distributions in excess of that, however, would be taxable to the shareholders.

gain on long-held capital assets) arising when the corporation was a C corporation.) However, the S corporation modifications do not apply to corporations with a fair market value of $1 million or less, and apply only with limited impact to corporations under $2 million in value. This proposal, in combination with the shareholder credit proposal, should permit maximum flexibility in providing shareholder relief to small corporations.

A final form of relief provided is transitional relief. Although it was believed the existence of permanent relief would eliminate much of the need for transitional relief, it seemed appropriate to provide a specific prospective period of time during which businesses and investors could adjust to the new rules. Accordingly, the bill will not be effective any earlier than January 1, 1986.

Two other forms of relief are not specifically included in the bill, but are recommended, contingent upon certain other factors. First, in its November, 1984 Report to the President, the Treasury Department recommended an across-the-board 50 percent dividends paid deduction for all corporations. If that proposal, as well as the additional Treasury proposal to eliminate the capital gains preference, is enacted, it is recommended that the same relief should be considered in the case of liquidating distributions. The basis adjustment proposal could then be repealed if this relief were provided.

Second, to the extent necessary to keep this bill revenue-neutral, it is recommended that consideration be given to an across-the-board reduction of the corporate capital gains tax rate.

2. CORPORATE ACQUISITIONS AND THE PROBLEMS OF EXCESSIVE DEBT

The tax bias in favor of debt financing and the difficulties in distinguishing between debt and equity were discussed in Chapter 3 principally in the context of the capital structure of a closely held C corporation. The wave of corporate restructurings of public companies in the 1980's raised the stakes on this historically vexing issue. From 1984 to 1987, transactions such as corporate takeovers, redemptions of stock, debt-for-equity swaps and extraordinary distributions resulted in a reduction of $313.3 billion in corporate equity while new net corporate borrowing increased by $613.3 billion. The ratio of debt to equity of nonfinancial corporations increased from 30.3 percent in 1981 to 46 percent in 1987.[1] Although these developments undoubtedly were motivated by many factors other than the interest deduction allowed to corporate borrowers, the preferred tax treatment of debt has become a powerful influence on corporate financing behavior. And however difficult it may be to measure precisely the lost revenue resulting from this surge in debt financing,[2] it safely can be assumed that the erosion of the corporate tax base has been substantial.

1. Joint Committee on Taxation, Federal Income Aspects of Corporate Financial Structures, 101st Cong., 1st Sess. 2 (JCS 1–89, 1989).

2. It would not be enough, for example, to measure the revenue loss merely by looking at the increased corporate-level interest deductions. Among the many variables that

In early 1989, the Congressional tax-writing committees held hearings to examine the federal income tax aspects of corporate financial structures and to consider the problem of debt-financed acquisitions. In the wake of the $25 billion leveraged buyout of RJR Nabisco, Inc.,[3] a few influential legislators proposed to disallow interest deductions on any debt used to finance a corporate acquisition.[4] The Treasury attempted to change the subject by noting that if the corporate and individual income taxes were integrated, the problems of excessive debt would disappear.[5]

Some illustrative transactions, the policy issues and possible options for lessening the distinction between the tax treatment of debt and equity are addressed in the excerpts below from a study prepared by the Joint Committee on Taxation in connection with the 1989 hearings. The note following the excerpt discusses the narrowly targeted Congressional response to these concerns. Keep in mind that this discussion occurred before the introduction in 2003 of a preferential rate on qualified dividends, which reduces but does not eliminate the tax bias favoring debt over equity.

Excerpt From Joint Committee on Taxation, Federal Income Tax Aspects of Corporate Financial Structures

101st Cong., 1st Sess. (JCS 1–89, Jan. 18, 1989).

III. EXAMPLES OF TRANSACTIONS THAT INCREASE DEBT OR REDUCE EQUITY, AND TAX CONSEQUENCES

There are various transactions which can increase the debt of a corporation or reduce its equity. The discussion below describes broad categories of these transactions and uses examples to illustrate their tax consequences. The examples assume that no restrictions on interest deductions or other tax benefits stemming from interest expenses apply. In many cases, however, such limitations are applicable. * * *

Although there are significant tax reasons which may lead a corporation to engage in these transactions, such transactions may also be motivated by reasons apart from Federal income tax considerations. For example, such transactions may be undertaken to increase the value of a corporation's stock, to enhance earnings per share calculations, to concentrate

one also must consider are: the tax status of the creditor (e.g., individual, domestic or foreign corporation, pension fund or other tax-exempt entity, etc.); the contrasting tax result if earnings were distributed as dividends; the impact of the dividends received deduction available to corporate investors; and the result if corporate earnings were accumulated and reinvested.

3. See generally Burrough and Helyar, Barbarians at the Gate (Harper & Row, 1989).

4. For a survey of the "Stamp Out LBOs movement," see Mentz, Carlisle & Nevas, "Leveraged Buyouts: A Washington Perspective of 1989 Legislation and Prospects for 1990," 46 Tax Notes 1047 (Feb. 26, 1990).

5. Id, at 1049, quoting testimony by Secretary of the Treasury Nicholas Brady before the Senate Finance Committee, Jan. 24, 1989. For an overview of the integration issue, see Chapter 1B5, supra.

common stock holdings, to create treasury stock, as a defensive maneuver to ward off a takeover, or for other reasons.

* * *

B. Stock Repurchases

Description

A stock repurchase refers to a corporation redeeming (or buying back) its own shares from stockholders. A corporation may make a tender offer for a certain percentage of its shares at an announced price or a corporation may simply purchase its shares on the market. A corporation may fund a stock repurchase out of cash the corporation has on hand or it may borrow the funds.[67]

Tax consequences

A stock repurchase, whether financed out of cash the corporation has on hand or by borrowing, is generally a taxable transaction with respect to the redeeming shareholders. Taxable shareholders having their stock redeemed recognize any gain (i.e., the excess of the amount received over basis) or loss on the redemption of their shares.[68] There are no immediate tax consequences of a stock repurchase to the redeeming corporation.

A stock repurchase has further tax consequences to the redeeming corporation and to investors in the redeeming corporation over time. If a stock repurchase is financed with cash, the primary tax consequence is that the corporate assets of the redeeming corporation have been reduced. Corporate assets paid out to redeem shareholders' stock no longer produce earnings which are subject to the corporate income tax.[69] If the stock repurchase is financed through borrowing, the effect of the transaction is to replace the equity of the corporation with debt. Earnings of the corporation once available to be paid to shareholders as non-deductible dividends are instead paid to debtholders as deductible interest.[70] Thus, a stock redemption using borrowed funds enables the redeeming corporation to reduce its taxable income, or perhaps eliminate it (or even generate current tax losses which it could carry back to obtain tax refunds).[71]

---

67. As an alternative to borrowing funds from an outside lender and using the proceeds to repurchase the stock of shareholders, a corporation may repurchase stock by issuing debt directly to redeeming shareholders. This is sometimes called a "debt-for-equity swap."

68. Of course, there will be no tax imposed on those shareholders that are not subject to U.S. income tax on this income, i.e., certain foreign investors and tax-exempt investors such as pension funds.

69. This is also the result when the earnings of the distributing corporation are distributed to noncorporate shareholders in circumstances other than in connection with a stock repurchase.

70. A leveraged stock repurchase has exactly the same tax consequences as a leveraged distribution made by a corporation with respect to its stock.

71. A reduction in the redeeming corporation's Federal income tax liability could also increase its cash flow significantly. That increased cash flow might be sufficient to enable the redeeming corporation to cover most of its debt service obligations with re-

As indicated by the following example, the resulting reduction in Federal income taxes pays for increased returns to investors. To the extent increased investor returns are paid to taxable shareholders or debtholders, there may be an increase in investor-level taxes paid.

Example III–B

Consider the same facts as in Example III–A above [The facts were: Corporation M has $1.5 million annual income, 99,000 shares of stock outstanding and no debt. M's federal income tax is $510,000 ($1.5 million times 34 percent), resulting in after-tax income of $990,000 and earnings per share of $10. M's stock trades at $80 per share, or 8 times earnings. Ed.] except that Company M announces it will repurchase up to $11 million of its shares at a redemption price of $120 per share, 50 percent more than the price at which the stock has been trading on the market. Taxable redeeming shareholders recognize gain or loss on the redemption of their shares.

At $120 per share, $11 million will purchase approximately 93 percent of Company M's outstanding shares. To finance the share repurchase, Company M issues bonds for $11 million paying 12 percent interest. Approximately 93 percent of Company M's outstanding shares are redeemed.

The distribution of the operating income of Company M before and after the stock repurchase is as follows:

	Before	**After**
Redeeming shareholders	$ 920,700	0
Bondholders	0	$1,320,000
Continuing shareholders	69,300	118,800
Corporate income taxes	510,000	61,200
Total operating income	1,500,000	1,500,000
Earnings per share	10	16.20

The leveraged stock redemption has redistributed the income stream of Company M in the same way that the leveraged distribution with respect to stock redistributed the income stream, except that the continuing shareholders of Company M, rather than all the shareholders of Company M, receive the profit of $118,800. The redeeming shareholders of Company M who used to get $920,700 a year in dividends before the redemption receive no part of the income stream after the redemption. New bondholders receive interest of 12 percent a year on $11 million, or $1.32 million. This is one-third more than the entire amount of Company M's after-tax income before the stock repurchases even though the operating income of Company M is unchanged. Continuing shareholders of Company M receive the profit of $118,800 (the remainder of Company M's income after taxes and interest expense).

spect to the borrowed funds and retire much of the debt over a period of years (although the redeeming company might also have to sell some of its assets to raise cash to assist it in paying off the loan).

The taxable income of Company M has been reduced from $1.5 million to $180,000 ($1.5 million minus $1.32 million) because most of the earnings of Company M are now paid out as deductible interest payments. The resulting reduction of corporate Federal income taxes from $510,000 to $61,200 exactly pays for the increased returns to the new bondholders and the continuing shareholders. Depending on whether the increased returns are paid to taxable bondholders and shareholders, there may be an increase in investor-level Federal income taxes paid.

Note also that the earnings per share of Company M have gone up from $10 per share ($990,000 divided by 99,000 shares outstanding) before the leveraged buyout to $16.20 per share ($118,800 divided by 7,333 shares outstanding) after the leveraged buyout. If the stock will still sell for 8 times its earnings on the market after the leveraged buyout, the stock price would rise from $80 to $129.60 ($16.20 times 8).

Taxpayers have also sought similar tax results in connection with so-called "unbundled stock units." On December 5, 1988, four publicly traded companies—American Express Co., Dow Chemical Co., Pfizer Inc. and Sara Lee Corp.announced offers to their shareholders to exchange a certain portion of their outstanding common stock for unbundled stock units comprised of three separate securities:

(1) a 30–year deep-discount bond which will pay quarterly interest in an amount equal to the current dividend of the common stock exchanged;

(2) a share of preferred stock which will yield dividends equal to any increase in the dividend yield of the company's common stock; and

(3) an "equity appreciation certificate" which entitles the holder to acquire one share of common stock for an amount equal to the redemption value of the 30–year bond plus a share of the preferred stock. The new bond in effect would convert what had been nondeductible ordinary dividends into deductible interest payments, in addition to providing corporate deductions for an element of original issue discount.[72]

Actual transactions

Stock repurchases have become common corporate transactions. A list of the largest stock repurchases during 1988 published by The Wall Street Journal indicated that the largest 21 stock buy-back announcements of 1988 were intended to retire almost 500 million shares of stock worth approximately $23.8 billion. Ten transactions were listed with a value in excess of $1 billion. The largest transactions listed were the following: (1) UAL Corporation buying back 35.5 million common shares with a value of

---

72. The four companies currently plan to replace between 6.5 and 20 percent of their outstanding common stock with unbundled stock units. It has been estimated that the four corporations issuing unbundled stock units could save, in the aggregate, up to $5.9 billion in Federal income taxes over the 20–year life of the bonds. Aggregate tax savings in the first year after the exchange may be as much as $85 million, with annual tax savings steadily rising through the 30–year bond term. New York Times, December 7, 1988, p. D1. The Internal Revenue Service has not ruled on the tax treatment of unbundled stock units.

$2.84 billion; (2) International Business Machines Corporation buying back 17.8 million common shares with a value of $2 billion; (3) CSX Corp. buying back 60 million shares with a value of $1.86 billion; and (4) Sears Roebuck buying back 40 million common shares with a value of $1.75 billion.

C. Acquisitions Including Leveraged Buyouts

The acquisition of one corporation by another corporation may be structured in many different ways. An acquiring corporation may acquire control of the "target" corporation or it may acquire a small interest in the stock of another corporation as an investment. The acquiring corporation may finance the acquisition with debt (either by a new borrowing of the necessary funds or by keeping an old borrowing outstanding), or with its own retained earnings, or with funds contributed as new equity capital by investors.

An acquisition of the control of a target company may be a hostile or friendly transaction. It may be structured as an acquisition of the stock of the target company or an acquisition of the assets of the target company. The target company may continue to operate as an independent company in the same manner as before it was acquired, or it may be absorbed into the acquiring company or other companies owned by the acquiring company, or it may cease operations entirely and its assets be divided and sold.

1. Stock acquisitions out of retained earnings

A corporation may finance the acquisition of the stock of another corporation with internally generated funds (i.e., its retained earnings). The purchase of the stock has no tax consequences to the shareholders of the purchasing corporation. Likewise, there are no tax consequences to the acquired corporation as a result of the acquisition. The taxable shareholders of the acquired corporation recognize any gain or loss on the sale of their shares.

There are generally no immediate tax consequences to the purchasing corporation as a result of the transaction. However, the total amount of funds in corporate solution, the earnings of which are subject to a corporate-level tax, may be reduced by the amount spent for the acquisition to the extent that shares are acquired by the acquiring corporation from noncorporate shareholders. Moreover, no compensating additional corporate tax may arise when earnings of the acquired corporation are distributed to the acquiring corporation. This is because earnings of the target company which are distributed to the acquiring corporation as dividends will either be nontaxable under the consolidated return rules, or, if the corporations do not file a consolidated return, will be eligible for the dividends received deduction.

2. Debt-financed stock acquisitions including leveraged buyouts

A corporation may finance the acquisition of another corporation's stock by borrowing. The acquiring corporation may borrow using its own assets as security for the loan or it may borrow using the assets of the target company as security for the loan. In either case, debt has been substituted for equity at the corporate level. When the debt is secured by the acquired corporation's assets, the transaction is more likely to be called a "leveraged buyout."

Description

A leveraged buyout refers to a particular type of debt-financed acquisition of a "target" corporation.[74] The purchasers borrow most of the purchase price of the target company, using the assets of the target company as security for the loan. After the acquisition, the target corporation may be able to service the debt obligation out of its cash flow from operations or the purchaser may sell the assets of the target company and use the proceeds to retire the debt.

A leveraged buyout may occur in many different contexts and may be used by many different types of purchasers. The leveraged buyout, also sometimes called a bootstrap acquisition, has long been used to acquire private (i.e., closely held) corporations. More recently, leveraged buyouts have been used to acquire large public companies. A public company may be "taken private" through a leveraged buyout if the purchasers of the target public corporation are a relatively small group of investors. If the purchasers of the target corporation in a leveraged buyout include the current management of the target company, the transaction is sometimes called a "management buyout." A division or a subsidiary of a company also may be purchased through a leveraged buyout.

A leveraged buyout of a target company is usually accomplished by a debt-financed tender offer by the existing corporation for its outstanding publicly held stock, or, alternatively, by a tender offer for the target corporation's stock by a largely debt-financed shell corporation established for this purpose. The target corporation will repurchase its stock from its shareholders or the shell corporation will buy all the stock of the target corporation.[76] If a shell corporation is used, the target corporation and the shell corporation will typically merge immediately after the acquisition.

As mentioned above, most of the funds for a leveraged buyout transaction are borrowed, with the purchasers contributing only a small amount of their own funds as equity. Lenders for these transactions have been banks, investment banks, insurance companies, pension funds, and pools of investors. Debt terms reflect the degree of leverage and the loan security involved. Some of the debt incurred frequently is below investment grade, i.e., so-called "junk" bonds.

---

74. In what is called a "reverse leveraged buyout," public companies which had been converted to private companies in a leveraged buyout become public companies again, with their shares being sold in a public offering to shareholders.

76. Shareholders of the target company typically receive a premium for their stock above the price at which the stock has been trading on the market.

Tax consequences

A leveraged buyout is generally a taxable transaction with respect to the shareholders of the target corporation.[77] Taxable shareholders selling their stock recognize gain or loss on the sale of their shares.[78] There are no immediate tax consequences of a leveraged buyout at the corporate level since generally neither the repurchase by the target corporation of its own shares nor the purchase of the target corporation's shares by a shell corporation followed by the merger of the target and shell corporation is a taxable transaction.

The primary tax consequences of a leveraged buyout to the target corporation arise from the fact that the equity of the corporation has been replaced by debt. Income of the target corporation once paid to investors as nondeductible dividends on stock is instead paid to creditors as tax-deductible interest on debt.[79] As a result of the interest deductions generated by the borrowing in a leveraged buyout, the target corporation may have little, if any, taxable income in the years following a leveraged buyout and may claim loss carrybacks producing a refund of taxes paid prior to the acquisition.[80] Because the target corporation pays little, if any, of its operating income as Federal income taxes, the portion of the target corporation's income that was once being paid to the Federal government as Federal income taxes may instead be redirected to increase investor returns. However, to the extent increased investor returns are paid to taxable shareholders or holders of debt, there may be an increase in investor-level Federal income taxes paid.

Example III–C

Consider the same facts as in Example III–A [See p. 403, supra. Ed.] Rather than the management of Company M announcing a distribution with respect to its stock, Company M is acquired in a leveraged buyout. The acquirors pay $120 per share of stock, or 50 percent more than the price at which the stock has been trading on the market, for a total price of $11.88 million. Taxable selling shareholders recognize gain or loss on the sale of their shares.

The acquirors put up $880,000 of their own funds and raise the remaining $11 million of the purchase price by issuing notes paying 12 percent interest to be secured by the assets of Company M. The annual income of Company M after the leveraged buyout is unchanged.

---

77. Of course, there will be no tax imposed on those shareholders that are not subject to U.S. income tax on their income, i.e., certain foreign investors and tax-exempt investors such as pension funds.

78. Taxable shareholders will generally recognize gain (i.e., the excess of the amount received over their basis in the stock) because acquirors typically pay a substantial premium for stock in a leveraged buyout transaction.

79. A leveraged buyout has exactly the same tax effect as a leveraged distribution made by a corporation with respect to its stock and a leveraged stock redemption.

80. Indeed, the target corporation may be able to service its debt obligations out of a cash flow and reduced * * * taxes.

The distribution of the operating income of Company M before and after the leveraged buyout is as follows:

	Before	After
Company M shareholders	$ 990,000	0
Bondholders	0	$1,320,000
Acquirors	0	118,800
Corporate income taxes	510,000	61,200
Total operating income	1,500,000	1,500,000

The leveraged buyout has redistributed the income stream of Company M in the same way that the leveraged distribution with respect to stock, and the leveraged stock redemption, redistributed the income stream of Company M. However, the acquirors of Company M, rather than all the shareholders (in the case of a distribution with respect to stock) or the continuing shareholders of Company M (in the case of a stock redemption) receive the profit of $118,800. Company M shareholders who before the transaction received $990,000 a year in dividends now receive no distributions. New bondholders receive interest of 12 percent on $11 million, or $1.32 million. This is one third more than the entire amount of Company M's after-tax income before the leveraged buyout, even though the operating income of Company M is the same before and after the leveraged buyout.

The taxable income of Company M has, however, been reduced from $1.5 million to $180,000 ($1.5 million minus $1.32 million) because most of the income of the company is paid out to investors as interest rather than dividends. Federal income taxes are thereby reduced from $510,000 to $61,200. Acquirors make an after-tax profit of $118,800 (pre-tax profit of $180,000 reduced by Federal income tax of $61,200), a 13.4 percent return on their $880,000 equity investment. The income tax reduction of $448,800 exactly pays for the increased returns to investors (bondholders and the acquirors) as a result of the leveraged buyout. Depending on whether the increased investor returns are paid to taxable shareholders or holders of debt, there may be an increase in investor-level Federal income taxes paid.

Actual transactions

Leveraged buyouts of public companies have greatly increased in recent years, and the amounts involved in such transactions have risen dramatically. * * * The largest leveraged buyout transaction to date is the proposed acquisition of RJR Nabisco by the investment firm of Kohlberg Kravis Roberts & Co. ("KKR") for nearly $25 billion. It is expected that this acquisition will be completed by February 1989. Other large leveraged buyout transactions include the acquisition of Beatrice Companies by KKR for $6.25 billion in April 1986, and the management buyout of R.H. Macy & Co., Inc. for $3.5 billion in July 1986.

Newspaper reports indicate that out of the approximately $25 billion needed for the RJR Nabisco acquisition, more than $22.5 billion will be borrowed. Secured bank debt will account for approximately $17.5 billion of the borrowing, with most of the remainder being provided by investment banking firms. A pool of investors organized by KKR will put up $1.5 billion as an equity investment. It has been reported that KKR will contribute approximately $15 million of its own funds as equity. RJR Nabisco shareholders will be paid $109 for each share of common stock. This is almost twice the price at which the stock was trading immediately prior to the announcement of the possible sale of the company. It has been reported that due to increased interest deductions, RJR Nabisco could save up to $682 million annually in Federal and state income taxes and be able to seek the refund of additional amounts of taxes paid in prior years due to the carryback of net operating losses. Other reports have projected the annual savings at $370 million.

In the Beatrice transaction, each common shareholder received $50 per share ($40 in cash). This price of $50 per share was 45 percent higher than the market value of the stock one month prior to the announcement date of the first offer. Financing for the Beatrice leveraged buyout included $6.5 billion in debt and $1.35 billion in equity capital. Four billion dollars of the debt was lent by banks and $2.5 billion came from a new issue of high yield bonds. The equity came from two sources. Six hundred million came from a buyout fund organized by KKR and subscribed to by institutional investors and $750 million came from converting existing common stock to a new issue of preferred stock.

In the Macy transaction, each common share of stock outstanding received $68 in cash. This price of $68 per share was 55 percent higher than the market value of the stock one month prior to the announcement date of the first offer. On completion of the Macy leveraged buyout, the management group held 20 percent of the new company stock and an additional 20 percent was held by General Electric Co.'s credit union. Financing for the Macy leveraged buyout totalled approximately $3.7 billion. Out of this amount, almost $3.2 billion was debt: $770 million was lent from banks, $1.625 billion came from new issues of high yield bonds, and $800 million came from notes secured by mortgages. The remaining $500 million of the financing consisted of $200 million of excess cash of Macy's and $300 million was equity capital contributed by the acquirors.

* * *

V. Possible Options and Related Policy Considerations

A. Eliminate or Reduce the Distinction Between Debt and Equity by Integrating the Corporate and Individual Income Tax Systems

[Integration of the corporate and individual income taxes is discussed in the excerpts at pages 33–43, supra. Ed.]

* * *

B. Eliminate or Reduce the Distinction Between Debt and Equity by Limiting Interest Deductions

Interest disallowance proposals should be evaluated with reference to various policy issues. These issues include: the potential erosion of the business tax base (including but not necessarily limited to the corporate tax base); the proper measurement of economic income; the non-tax economic impact of business leverage; and whether certain specified types of transactions should be discouraged for various other non-tax economic reasons. In addition, administrability and fairness issues may be raised.

Particular interest disallowance proposals may address one or more of these issues. The proposals may be more or less comprehensive in treatment of the issues they do address. Because the proposals differ widely in the nature of the issues they address, it is necessary to determine which policy issues are considered significant in order to evaluate the desirability of any particular proposal.

The following discussion first describes a number of interest disallowance proposals and discusses the principal issues they address. The discussion then describes certain additional issues common to many of the proposals.

1. Broad interest disallowance proposals not dependent on particular types of corporate transactions

All interest deductions above a specified amount could be disallowed. There are several variations of this approach, each of which computes the amount of the disallowance based on different factors. The factors selected indicate the policy objectives of the proposals.

a. *Disallow a flat percentage of all interest deductions*

Under this approach, the amount of nondeductible interest would be a percentage of total interest expense. This approach principally addresses concerns about erosion of the revenue base and about the role of debt in facilitating tax arbitrage. It does not address issues of the proper measurement of income (either by trying to distinguish debt from equity, or by trying to limit interest deductions where the debt supports activities that do not produce income taxable to the entity incurring the debt). It also is not limited to any particular types of transactions that might be considered undesirable for non-tax reasons.

While revenue concerns are the main basis for this particular approach, issues arise regarding its effectiveness. For example, if the deduction denial is related only to a percentage of total interest expense, it might be possible for taxpayers in some circumstances to increase the stated interest amount beyond the amount they might have stated absent this provision, thus continuing to reap the benefit of the deduction. Present law provides certain bright-line rules designed to prevent the interest component of an obligation from being understated; but it has no comparable rules designed to prevent the overstatement of interest. Issues related to the design of such rules are addressed below in connection with other proposals.

The impact of this proposal will vary dramatically from industry to industry. For example, financial intermediaries, such as banks, may see enormous increases in taxable income, even though their loans may bear low interest rates. Likewise, this proposal will disproportionately affect activities which support high degrees of leverage, such as real estate, even though the debt involved may not be particularly risky.

b. *Disallow interest deductions in excess of a specified rate of return to investors*

This approach would disallow interest deductions in excess of a specified rate of return to investors. Deductions not in excess of that rate still would be permitted. The rate could be determined by reference to a rate deemed to represent that of a relatively risk-free investment (for example, the rate on comparable-term Treasury obligations issued at the time of the borrowing, or a few points above that rate). The rate could fluctuate as the reference rate fluctuates.

As with the approach described above, this approach addresses concerns about erosion of the tax base, but to the extent the rate selected reflects a measurement of "risk," this approach also might be described as an attempt to properly measure economic income. If one accepts the premise that all interest on debt is properly deductible without regard to whether the debt supports an asset that produces taxable income, and the further premise that the most fundamental basis for distinguishing debt from equity is the degree of investor risk, this approach seeks to deny a deduction for the "risk" element of stated interest on the theory it more nearly resembles a dividend distribution, while continuing to permit the non-risk portion to be fully deductible.

A primary issue with respect to this type of approach is the selection of the permitted deductible interest rate. To the extent the rate is selected in an attempt to identify excessive risk, questions may be raised regarding the accuracy of a risk analysis based solely on interest rate. On the other hand, to the extent the proposal is viewed as one of administrative convenience designed to address revenue concerns and avoid the need to distinguish between debt and equity, the accuracy of any risk analysis may be considered less important.

Non-tax policy issues also may arise. For example, even though it is arguable that a high degree of risk suggests an equity investment, and that a high interest rate suggests a high degree of risk, the practical result of such an approach may be that certain start-up firms, or firms involved in inherently risky ventures, may be more restricted in their ability to deduct all of the interest demanded by investors than other more established or stable firms. Variations in the permitted rate might be adopted for such situations; however, arguments then may be raised that whichever taxpayers are permitted the higher deductions may obtain a competitive advantage over other ventures also involving risk, which may have implications for neutrality of the tax system in this respect.

c. Disallow interest deductions based on inflation: interest indexing

This approach would disallow a portion of interest deductions based on inflation. A corresponding portion of the recipient's interest income would be treated as nontaxable.

1984 Treasury proposal

The Treasury proposals in 1984 suggested a plan which generally would have rendered the same specified fraction of interest non-deductible and non-includable. Home mortgage interest and a de minimis amount of other individual interest were exempt from these provisions. The Treasury proposal assumed a specified real pre-tax interest rate and would have calculated a percentage each year based on this assumed real rate relative to the sum of inflation and the assumed real interest rate. The allowable interest deduction (and inclusion) each year would have been calculated by multiplying nominal interest payments (and receipts) by this percentage, which would be published periodically by the tax authorities.

As a method for indexing debt, the proposal was relatively simple. Even so, it still had numerous difficulties. Because it applied a single fraction to all interest it did a poor job of coping with debt of differing risk characteristics; in particular, it made too large a percentage of interest on risky debt nondeductible and non-includable. Also, if the fraction were applied to financial intermediaries (e.g., banks), their income could be very lightly taxed. As pointed out by Treasury at the time, even with its problems, the method was likely to provide a more appropriate measure of income than the current method of deducting and including all nominal interest.

Other proposals

Other methods of indexing may better measure real interest deductions but at the cost of increased complexity. One proposal would require the restatement of interest paid by subtracting out the inflationary component of the interest rate. For example, if one paid $100 of interest at a 10 percent nominal rate and the rate of inflation were 7 percent, then one would calculate the inflationary component of the interest paid at a 7 percent rate ($70) and subtract that amount from the interest actually paid. The difference ($30) would be the allowed amount of deductible interest. Similar calculations would be necessary for purposes of income inclusion. This proposal, while having fewer distortions than the Treasury proposal, is significantly more complex and administratively difficult. In general, proposals designed to measure the appropriate amount of interest make a trade-off between simplicity and accuracy.

Issues generally applicable to indexing

A number of issues arise with respect to interest indexing. A principal concern is determining the amount of correction to interest expense or income that accurately reflects inflation. It may be necessary to determine a "real" interest rate prior to risk considerations. Even assuming a correct adjustment is identified, it may be necessary for administrative convenience to apply that adjustment in a relatively rough manner that does not fully account for different real interest rates over different periods of a year. It may be difficult to provide an administrable adjustment that does not involve windfalls to some taxpayers.

Indexing only interest but not other long-term arrangements may put additional pressure on the determination as to whether an instrument is properly characterized as debt. For example, depending on the relative tax situations of the parties, indexing only interest may make it more desirable for a taxpayer with a relatively high effective tax rate to hold an instrument characterized as debt rather than equity. Similarly, it may be more desirable for an arrangement to be characterized as a lending arrangement rather than a lease. To the extent parties in different tax situations recharacterized their arrangements to take advantage of tax arbitrage potential in this additional new disparity between the treatment of debt and other arrangements, there could be a corresponding revenue concern. On the other hand, it can be argued that failure to index may perpetuate a far greater revenue loss if the holders of debt instruments tend to be entities with a low effective tax rate and borrowers tend to be taxpayers with a higher effective rate who are obtaining an excessive interest deduction.

Exempting certain classes of debt, such as home mortgages, from indexing proposals may cause large tax-induced distortions of asset portfolios. Thus, excluding home mortgages would increase further the tax incentives for owner-occupied housing.

Any proposal that reduces interest inclusions and deductions to the same degree will generally reduce nominal interest rates. Because of the fall in nominal interest, the value of tax exemption to pension funds and other tax-exempt institutions will be less than it would be under a system without indexing.

d.   Disallow interest deductions in excess of a specified percentage of taxable income (or earnings and profits) as computed before the deductions

This approach would limit the interest deduction by reference to taxable income (or alternatively, earnings and profits) determined prior to the deduction. For example, one version of this approach would limit the deduction to no more than 50 percent (or some other specified percentage) of the taxable income of the corporation computed without regard to the interest deduction. Such an approach was adopted in the 1986 Senate version of H.R. 3838 (the Tax Reform Act of 1986) but was limited to situations where the lender was related to the payor corporation by at least 50–percent ownership and was a tax-exempt or foreign entity that would not pay U.S. tax on interest received from the payor corporation (Senate amendment to H.R. 3838, sec. 984 (1986)). One variation would limit the deduction to no more than 50 percent (or some other specified percentage) of the earnings and profits of the corporation computed without regard to the deduction. Another variation would apply the limitation only for minimum tax purposes.

This approach is principally addressed to revenue concerns and attempts to provide a rough but practical alternative to complex rules for distinguishing equity from debt, which assures that interest alone does not shelter taxable income to an unacceptable degree.

The limitation to a specified percentage of taxable income (or earnings and profits) might arguably be viewed as reflecting concerns about proper measurement of income, on the theory that when interest deductions alone consume a significant proportion of otherwise taxable income, this may suggest excessive risk to the lender implying an equity interest. However, this particular approach is not a targeted method of identifying situations of risk. This is because the ability to pay back indebtedness depends largely on the capacity of the debtor to generate cash flow, either from current operations or from sales of appreciated assets. Neither taxable income nor earnings and profits is an adequate measure of such capacity. For example, an entity with significant cash flow potential may have low taxable income because of other tax deductions that do not reflect economic losses (for example, accelerated depreciation), or because assets are currently held for appreciation and not for current income. The use of earnings and profits as a limitation similarly does not take account of items such as unrealized appreciation, which may be sufficient to avoid undue risk to the debtholder.

This approach also raises an issue whether it is desirable to limit interest deductions, thus increasing the effective tax rate, in times of recession or when taxable income is otherwise small due to real economic losses.

[The report went on to discuss options under which corporate interest deductions would be disallowed in transactions that reduce the corporate equity base or in more specified acquisitions or stock purchase transactions—e.g., proposals introduced in Congress that would limit interest deductions in the case of certain corporate repurchase transactions involving identifiable "risk" or in certain debt-financed acquisitions where appreciation on corporate assets is untaxed, or in certain hostile takeover situations. Ed.]

* * *

C. Combination Interest Disallowance and Dividend Relief Options

1. Provide deductible rate of return for corporate-level equity and limit interest deductions to the same rate

This option would grant a limited corporate-level dividends paid deduction and conform the treatment of debt to that accorded equity by limiting allowable interest deductions to the same rate. The rate of return could be selected to approximate the rate an investor would demand for a relatively risk-free investment (e.g., the rate on comparable-term Treasury obligations, or a rate several points above that).

The major advantage of this proposal is that the treatment of debt and equity would be more closely aligned since the cost of all externally-raised capital generally would be deductible to the same extent. This could remove some of the importance of distinguishing debt from equity.

In addition, the proposal might alleviate pressure for the issuance of debt, and to this extent would address non-tax issues related to concern about the economic consequences of leverage. This proposal, standing alone, is not designed to address any issues related to the potential erosion of the tax base. Although the deduction with respect to debt would be limited, the new deduction for equity might offset that limit in many cases. Depending upon the rate selected and the transitional rules adopted, the total amount of available deductions might be reduced for some corporations, but might increase for others.

Moreover, the proposal does not address issues related to the reduction of the corporate tax base by debt-financed distributions or by other distributions. However, it could be combined with other proposals directed to such issues.

One issue with respect to this approach is the selection of the appropriate deductible rate. The selection of the effective date of the proposal involves additional issues. For example, granting a dividends paid deduction for capital contributed prior to the effective date of the proposal could arguably provide a windfall for such capital. Similarly, cutting back interest deductions for debt incurred prior to that date could be viewed as undermining existing expectations.

If the deduction for equity is granted only to "new" capital, rules would have to be provided to prevent the retirement of existing capital and its reissuance as "new" capital eligible for the deduction. The minimum distributions tax proposal described below at Part V.D.1. of this pamphlet, infra, might provide a method of enforcing such a limitation.

Providing a deduction only for "new" capital might also raise questions whether new equity (or new corporations) might obtain some advantage over old equity (and old corporations.) Such concerns might be addressed by allowing the deduction for all capital but phasing it in slowly, or by requiring the deduction for each infusion of new capital to be phased out over some period of time.

2. Allow an investor credit for interest and dividends and deny corporate interest deduction

This option would not permit a corporation to deduct any interest. Instead, shareholders and debtholders would be allowed a credit against taxes owed as a result of their receipt of dividends and interest. The credit would be based, in some fashion, on corporate taxes paid with respect to the dividends and interest distributed by a corporation.

One advantage of this option is that the tax treatment of debt and equity would be equalized. One issue raised by this option is the effect it would have on other business entities (e.g., partnerships), depending on whether the option applied only to corporations or to a broader class of business entities. The other issues raised by this option are similar to those discussed in connection with integration proposals generally * * *.

D. Other Options

1. Impose minimum tax on distributions

A minimum tax could be imposed on certain corporate distributions (for example, extraordinary dividends, stock redemption distributions, and amounts distributed in corporate acquisitions) to assure that the corporate revenue base is not reduced without payment of at least a minimum amount of tax.[172]

One approach would impose the tax at a rate equal to the rate on dividends received by individuals (e.g. 28 percent). The tax could be withheld from the dividend distribution by the distributing corporation and a credit provided to the shareholder against any shareholder tax on the distribution.

This approach directly addresses the issue of the erosion of the corporate base by focusing on the cause of the erosion, i.e., distributions out of corporate solution. The approach recognizes that the erosion can occur whether or not debt is incurred and whether or not an acquisition transaction such as a leveraged buyout is involved. Its application to all major corporate distribution transactions would ensure that a minimum tax would in fact be collected, regardless of the nature of the distributee and of the specific tax characterization of the distribution. At the shareholder level, any bias in the tax law in favor of non-dividend distributions (treated as sales) as opposed to dividend distributions would be eliminated.

One issue related to this approach is that certain arguably unfair results may occur from the distributee's standpoint because the same tax is withheld from a distribution regardless of a shareholder's basis in the shares. In addition, the proposal would collect tax with respect to certain distributions to tax-exempt investors that are not currently taxed. This effect would be mitigated to the extent that ordinary distributions (such as ordinary dividends) might be exempted from the proposal.

It is arguable that the proposal might subject corporate income to multiple taxation if the corporation is taxed on earnings, a taxable selling

---

172. A variation of this approach was suggested by Professor William D. Andrews in a Reporter's Study on Corporate Distributions, published as an Appendix to the American Law Institute's Federal Income Tax Project, Subchapter C, Proposals on Corporate Acquisitions and Dispositions (1982). The Reporter's Study made three specific proposals relating to the taxation of corporate income. The proposals would (1) provide a deduction for dividends paid on new corporate equity, (2) impose a compensatory tax on nondividend distributions, and (3) modify the tax treatment of intercorporate investment and distributions. The proposals contained in the Reporter's Study have not been adopted by the American Law Institute.

shareholder is taxed on gain that is attributable to retained earnings, and the purchasing shareholder is also taxed on the distribution in redemption of his recently-acquired shares. However, such multiple taxation would be mitigated to the extent tax is deferred or eliminated either at the corporate or the shareholder level. For example, the corporation might not pay current tax on corporate earnings or appreciation that may underlie a selling shareholder's gain (because of corporate-level tax deductions that do not reflect economic losses, or because appreciation has not been recognized at the corporate level). Similarly, a selling shareholder may obtain a deferral benefit by not recognizing gain until his stock is sold. Also, such multiple taxation would not occur to the extent that the purchasing shareholder anticipates the new minimum distributions tax (or anticipated a tax on distributions under present law), and accordingly reduced the price paid to the selling shareholder.

2. Require recognition of corporate-level gain to the extent corporate-level debt is incurred in excess of corporate-level underlying asset basis

A portion of corporate-level appreciation could be recognized whenever debt is incurred in excess of underlying corporate-level asset basis. This proposal could be limited to situations where the debt supports a distribution out of corporate solution.

Under this approach, the distributing corporation is viewed as having cashed out a portion of its asset appreciation, since it has removed that value from corporate solution rather than using the funds to pay down corporate-level debt supported in part by appreciation in corporate assets. * * * The approach addresses issues related to the erosion of the corporate revenue base and also issues related to the measurement of economic income.

It is arguable that since the corporation is still liable for its debt, it has not obtained any advantage from the borrowing and distribution and should not be required to accelerate recognition of corporate level gain. On the other hand, to the extent corporate asset appreciation supported the borrowing, the funds have been removed from corporate solution, and the remaining corporate assets are the only source of repayment, it is arguable that the benefits of the corporate appreciation have been realized at this point.

3. Impose excise tax on acquisition indebtedness

A nondeductible excise tax at a rate that would approximate denial of a corporate level interest deduction could be imposed in the case of certain distributions where debt is involved. This tax could be designed to parallel any of the interest disallowance proposals described above that address acquisitions or other types of corporate distributions.

To the extent the tax depends upon identification of an amount of indebtedness that supports a particular type of transaction, it will involve the debt allocation issues discussed above in connection with interest disallowance proposals.

To the extent the tax is imposed only on certain types of indebtedness (for example, where the interest rate or the debt-equity ratio exceeds a certain amount), it raises the further issue whether transactions could be structured to avoid the particular limitations while varying other aspects of the transaction to produce similar economic results.

Finally, to the extent the tax is imposed only on certain types of stock purchases (for example, purchases of 50 percent of the stock of a corporation within a specified time), it will be limited in the extent to which it addresses broader questions relating to erosion of the corporate tax base or the proper matching of corporate-level deductions with income.

The principal issue such an excise tax would attempt to address is the potential concern related to interest disallowance proposals that foreign acquirors able to borrow abroad might be advantaged over U.S. acquirors. However, to the extent the excise tax is dependent upon the identification of some amount of debt supporting the acquisition, it may involve administrative issues since it may be difficult to identify the amount of foreign incurred debt supporting a U.S. acquisition. A presumption might be established that all or a specified percentage of a foreign acquiror's purchase price was debt-financed. Possibly foreign acquirors could be given an opportunity to rebut the presumption. However, it might be difficult for the Internal Revenue Service to audit any such rebuttal statements, which could require obtaining information about the entity's foreign capital structure.

4. Develop objective standards for distinguishing between debt and equity

The possibility of issuing Treasury regulations under section 385 could be revisited. Such an approach could attempt to develop more objective standards for distinguishing between debt and equity. Prior attempts to develop such standards have been unsuccessful. * * *

* * *

NOTE

When Congress first held hearings on the problems of excessive debt, proposals were floated to limit the deductibility of interest used to finance certain "major" and "hostile" acquisitions. Some securities analysts believed that the breadth of these proposals contributed to the stock market crash of October, 1987. A cautious Congress, perhaps squeamish at the prospect of another chilly reception from Wall Street, failed to achieve a consensus on a comprehensive response when it revisited the excessive debt problem in 1989. Instead, the final product was typical of much recent tax legislation: a narrowly targeted set of limitations aimed at particular perceived abuses, accompanied by a delegation to the Treasury to elaborate through regulations. This legislation curbs some of the more egregious uses of "junk bonds," which are high-yield unsecured debt instruments used to finance corporate acquisitions. Other provisions were aimed at the excessive net operating losses generated by debt-financed corporate acquisitions and at corporations paying significant amounts of interest to related tax-exempt entities.

Applicable High–Yield Discount Obligations. The first victim of the 1989 legislation was a type of high-yield debt instrument that does not currently pay interest in cash to the lender. This type of junk bond is usually structured as a zero-coupon instrument with an issue price that is significantly lower than the stated redemption price at maturity.[1] The "spread" between the issue and redemption price is "original issue discount" ("OID"). In general, the issuer of an OID bond accrues and deducts the "spread" as interest over the life of the bond even though the interest is not actually paid until maturity, and the lender (even if a cash basis taxpayer) includes OID in income over the life of the bond.[2] A related device is the "payment-in-kind" ("PIK") bond, which purports to make interest payments in the form of other debt or stock of the corporate issuer rather than in cash. OID and PIK bonds were attractive financing paper for acquisitions because the issuer received a current interest deduction without a corresponding cash expenditure.

One proposal was to treat high-yield zero coupon and PIK bonds as preferred stock on the theory that their high level of risk and dependence on the profitability of the business causes them to more resemble equity than debt. The legislation ultimately enacted[3] did not go that far. Instead, Congress decided to defer (and in some cases disallow) the issuer's deduction until interest is actually paid in cash but continue to require the lender to recognize interest income as it accrues. This approach represents a new Congressional willingness to bifurcate certain hybrid securities into debt and equity components. The theory is that a portion of the return on certain junk bonds represents a distribution of corporate earnings with respect to an equity interest in the corporation and should be treated as such for tax purposes.

The restrictions in Section 163(e)(5) apply to an "applicable high-yield discount obligation," which is defined in Section 163(i) as an instrument with: (1) a more than five-year maturity, (2) a yield to maturity that is five percentage points or more than the applicable federal rate in effect for the month in which the obligation is issued, and (3) "significant original issue discount."[4] The OID amount on these bonds is divided between an interest element that is deductible but only when interest is actually paid,[5] and a

---

1. A zero coupon bond is a debt instrument that pays no interest and is sold at a significant discount from its face value.

2. See I.R.C. §§ 1272–1273.

3. See I.R.C. §§ 163(e)(5), (i).

4. A virtually incomprehensible definition of "significant original issue discount"

appears in Section 163(i)(2). Oversimplifying considerably, OID is "significant" if the OID income that accrues in periods ending more than five years after the bond is issued exceeds interest actually paid on the bond.

5. "Payments" for this purpose are limited to actual payments of cash or property

return of equity element ("the disqualified portion") for which no interest deduction is allowed but which may be eligible for the dividends received deduction in the case of a corporate lender.[6] This approach is a compromise between deferral and total disallowance of the issuer's interest deduction. An instrument generally will have a "disqualified portion" of OID and thus face disallowance of part of the interest deduction if it has significant OID and the yield on the instrument is more than six percentage points over the applicable federal rate.[7]

Limitation on Net Operating Losses Created by Debt–Financed Transactions. Congress also was concerned that corporations were financing leveraged buyouts and similar transactions in part through the tax refunds that were generated by net operating loss carrybacks resulting from the payment of interest expense on acquisition debt. In general, a corporation that has a net operating loss ("NOL") may carry the excess deductions back for three taxable years and forward for fifteen years.[8] If a corporation with NOLs had taxable income in the three prior taxable years, the carryback will result in a refund of federal income taxes paid in those years. The interest deductions resulting from debt-financed acquisitions and other corporate restructurings often were large enough to offset not only the corporation's current operating income but also to generate an NOL carryback. Reasoning that NOL carrybacks are intended as an averaging device to smooth out swings in taxable income caused by business cycle variations and unexpected financial losses, Congress concluded that the interest expense triggered by a takeover was not sufficiently related to business operations in prior taxable periods to justify a carryback of NOLs attributable to acquisition interest.[9]

Section 172(h) addresses this concern by limiting the ability of a corporation to carry back NOLs where the losses are created by interest deductions attributable to leveraged buyouts and other debt-financed transactions, such as corporate repurchases of stock (collectively referred to as "corporate equity reduction transactions" or "CERTs").[10] A CERT is either a "major stock acquisition" (a planned acquisition by one corporation of 50 percent or more of the voting power or value of the stock in another corporation[11]) or an "excess distribution" (generally, unusually large distributions relative to the corporation's prior distribution history or net worth[12]). Interest attributable to a CERT is generally defined as interest

---

other than the stock or debt of the issuer. I.R.C. § 163(i)(3)(B).

6. I.R.C. § 163(e)(5)(A), (B).

7. I.R.C. § 163(e)(5)(C).

8. See I.R.C. § 172 and Chapter 12, infra.

9. See H.R. Rep. No. 101–247, 101st Cong., 1st Sess. (1989).

10. It is important to note that Section 172(h) does not disallow the interest deduction or limit NOL carryforwards but merely

restricts a corporation from carrying back the losses generated by certain debt-financed transactions.

11. I.R.C. § 172(h)(3)(B). A major stock acquisition does not include a qualified stock purchase where the buyer makes a Section 338 election. I.R.C. § 172(h)(3)(B)(ii). A CERT may include the acquisition of a subsidiary of another corporation.

12. I.R.C. § 172(h)(3)(C).

allocable to debt that would not have been incurred but for the CERT.[13] A de minimis rule provides that the limitation applies only if the amount of interest expense at issue exceeds $1 million.[14]

Earnings Stripping. A third practice that was limited in 1989 is known as "earnings stripping"—i.e., the payment of deductible interest by a corporate borrower to an economically related lender that is effectively exempt from United States taxation. Deducting a payment to a tax-exempt entity whose economic interests coincide with the payor is a particularly attractive form of tax arbitrage. Earnings stripping payments, which are not necessarily related to acquisitions, are made primarily in the international setting (e.g., a payment from a U.S. subsidiary to a related foreign parent) or, domestically, where a taxable U.S. corporation is related to one or more tax-exempt charitable organizations.

The particulars of the Congressional response are well beyond the scope of this overview. It is sufficient to note that Section 163(j) defers the deduction for any interest paid or accrued by a corporation to certain related persons who are exempt from U.S. tax.[15] The limitation applies only if: (1) the payor corporation's debt-equity ratio exceeds 1.5 to 1,[16] and (2) the payor has "excess interest expense," which generally is any interest expense for the taxable year in excess of 50 percent of the corporation's taxable income without regard to net interest expense (i.e., interest expense less interest income) or net operating losses.[17] The corporation may carry forward any deduction deferred by Section 163(j) and treat it as interest paid to the related party in future years when it may be deductible if the corporation's debt-equity ratio has improved or if it does not have excess interest expense.[18]

---

13. I.R.C. § 172(h)(2).

14. I.R.C. § 172(h)(2)(D).

15. The definition of "related" for this purpose is borrowed from Sections 267 and 707(b). I.R.C. § 163(j)(4).

16. See I.R.C. § 163(j)(2)(A). Section 163(j)(2)(C) generally defines "ratio of debt to equity" as "the ratio which the total in-debtedness of the corporation bears to the sum of its money and all other assets less such total indebtedness." For this purpose, assets are taken into account at their adjusted basis for determining gain. Id.

17. I.R.C. § 163(j)(2)(B).

18. I.R.C. § 163(j)(1)(B).

CHAPTER 9

ACQUISITIVE REORGANIZATIONS

A. INTRODUCTION

1. HISTORICAL BACKGROUND

Some of the major litigation arising under the early federal income tax laws involved a variety of transactions loosely described as corporate reorganizations. Long before they became distracted by tax considerations, corporate lawyers and investment bankers were busy devising transactions ranging from complicated mergers, acquisitions and recapitalizations to routine changes in the state of incorporation. With the arrival of the income tax, the courts were required to determine whether and to what extent these fundamental changes in the structure of a corporate entity were taxable events.

Working with a pristine statute and an unsophisticated perspective, the Supreme Court became one of the first protectors of the comprehensive tax base. In a series of cases, the Court concluded that even minor changes in the form of a corporate business enterprise (e.g., changing the state of incorporation from New Jersey to Delaware) caused the shareholders to realize gain.[1] While these cases were pending, however, Congress quickly came to the rescue by enacting one of the earliest nonrecognition provisions. Preceding even the forerunner of Section 351, Section 202(b) of the Revenue Act of 1918 provided that no gain or loss would be recognized on the "reorganization, merger or consolidation of a corporation" where a person received "in place of stock or securities owned by him new stock or securities of no greater aggregate par face value."[2]

The rationale for the reorganization provisions reflects the broader policies of nonrecognition. Congress concluded that the tax collector should not impede these diverse transactions because they are mere readjustments of a continuing interest in property, albeit in modified corporate form,[3] and the new property received is "substantially a continuation of the old investment still unliquidated."[4] But to the extent that a shareholder

---

1. Marr v. United States, 268 U.S. 536, 45 S.Ct. 575 (1925). See also United States v. Phellis, 257 U.S. 156, 42 S.Ct. 63 (1921); Rockefeller v. United States, 257 U.S. 176, 42 S.Ct. 68 (1921).

2. Pub.L. No. 254, 40 Stat. 1057 (1919).

3. Reg. § 1.368–1(b). See also S.Rep. No. 275, 67th Cong., 1st Sess. (1921), reprinted in 1939–1 (Part 2) C.B. 181, 188–189,

where the Senate Finance Committee justified the principal forerunners of the modern nonrecognition provisions on the ground that they would permit businesses to proceed with necessary adjustments and remove "a source of grave uncertainty" in the law.

4. Reg. § 1.1002–1(c).

liquidates a corporate investment, recognition of gain or loss *is* appropriate. The 1921 predecessor of the present reorganization regime thus provided that shareholders must recognize their realized gain, if any, to the extent of the "boot" (money and other property) received.[5] Congress soon refined the statutory scheme by making clear what it had suggested in earlier versions: nonrecognition really means deferral rather than total forgiveness of gain or loss. The Revenue Act of 1928 introduced rules for carryover and substituted bases in order to preserve the unrecognized gain or loss for recognition at the time that the shareholder liquidated his investment.[6]

What began as a relatively simple concept has evolved into a vast and challenging body of law that governs some of the most financially significant transactions in the business world. It is important to recognize at the outset that the system you are about to study is not necessarily sensible. Functionally different transactions are lumped together and labelled "reorganizations." At the same time, economically equivalent acquisition methods are tested for reorganization status under sharply different criteria that often place a great premium on the form chosen by the parties. Moreover, determining the tax consequences of a corporate combination or readjustment requires an application of both precise statutory provisions and judicially created "common law" principles of uncertain scope. Analysis is further complicated by the possibility of an overlap between the reorganization provisions and other parts of Subchapter C.

In view of these defects in the reorganization scheme, it is not surprising that commentators have called for a complete overhaul of the current system.[7] Some modest reforms have come from the Service through recently issued regulations and rulings. Those pronouncements harmonize some of the requirements of Section 368 and in so doing increase flexibility in structuring tax-free acquisitions. But Congress has not yet fully embraced the simplification movement, and so we must turn to a more detailed examination of provisions that Professors Bittker and Eustice have described as "extraordinarily complex, even for the [Internal Revenue] Code."[8]

2. OVERVIEW OF REORGANIZATIONS

Code: Skim §§ 336(c); 354; 355; 356; 358; 361; 362(b); 368(a)(1), (b), (c); 381(a); 1032.

The term "reorganization" generally is associated with the rehabilitation of a bankrupt company. Under the Internal Revenue Code, however,

---

5. Revenue Act of 1921, § 202, Pub.L. No. 98, 42 Stat. 227.

6. Revenue Act of 1928, § 113(a)(6)–(9), Pub.L. No. 562, 45 Stat. 791.

7. See generally Federal Income Tax Project, Subchapter C, American Law Institute (1982); Staff of the Senate Finance Committee, The Subchapter C Revision Act of 1985: A Final Report Prepared by the Staff, 99th Cong., 1st Sess. 50–58 (S.Prt. 99–47, 1985). See Section E of this chapter, infra.

8. Bittker & Eustice, Federal Income Taxation of Corporations and Shareholders ¶ 12.01[4] (7th ed. 2000).

"reorganization" is a term of art[1] used to describe corporate combinations or readjustments that fall into the following three broad categories:

(1) *Acquisitive reorganizations,* which are considered in this chapter, are transactions in which one corporation (the "acquiring corporation") acquires the assets or stock of another corporation (the "acquired" or "target" corporation). Included in this category are statutory mergers or consolidations ("A" reorganizations); acquisitions of stock of the target for voting stock of the acquiring corporation ("B" reorganizations); acquisitions of assets of the target for voting stock of the acquiring corporation ("C" reorganizations, sometimes called "practical mergers" because of their similarity to statutory mergers); and several other more complex acquisition techniques involving the use of a subsidiary or multiple steps.

(2) *Divisive reorganizations,* which result in the division of a single corporation into two or more separate entities and which often are preceded by a "D" reorganization. Corporate divisions are considered in Chapter 10.

(3) *Nonacquisitive, nondivisive reorganizations,* which involve adjustments to the corporate structure of a single, continuing corporate enterprise. This residual category includes recapitalizations ("E" reorganizations); changes in identity, form or place of incorporation ("F" reorganizations); certain transfers of substantially all of the assets from one corporation to another, followed by a liquidation of the first corporation (nondivisive "D" reorganizations); and transfers of a corporation's assets to another corporation pursuant to a bankruptcy reorganization plan ("G" reorganizations). These transactions are considered in Chapter 11.

A common organizational thread weaves its way through these diverse categories. First, definitional provisions set forth requirements ranging from the general and very flexible test to qualify as a Type A reorganization to the complex criteria imposed by Section 355 for corporate divisions. To qualify as a reorganization, a transaction also must pass muster under "common law" doctrines developed by the courts to reinforce the rationale for nonrecognition. The principal judicial doctrines are continuity of shareholder proprietary interest, continuity of business enterprise and business purpose. In general, the continuity of interest doctrine requires that in substance a substantial part of the value of the proprietary (i.e., equity) interests in the target corporation must be preserved in the reorganization through an exchange of target stock or assets for stock in the acquiring corporation.[2] For some transactions, the continuity of interest doctrine has been incorporated into the statutory definition of "reorganization." For example, the only permissible consideration in a B reorganization is voting

---

1. See I.R.C. § 368(a)(1); Reg. § 1.368–1(c).

2. Reg. § 1.368–1(e)(1).

stock of the acquiring corporation.[3] The doctrine assumes far more importance if the statute is imprecise, as with Type A reorganizations, where the Code merely requires a "statutory merger or consolidation" without any elaboration on the permissible consideration.[4] We therefore examine continuity of interest questions in connection with Type A reorganizations—the context in which that doctrine most frequently arises.

The continuity of business enterprise doctrine, as its name implies, focuses on the continuing business operations of the target. This requirement has been incorporated in the regulations[5] and also is considered with "A" reorganizations. Because the business purpose doctrine was first applied and has the greatest importance in the context of a corporate division, it is discussed in Chapter 10. In general, all these requirements must be satisfied in order for a transaction to qualify as a reorganization.[6] To further complicate matters, the Service sometimes applies the step transaction doctrine to corporate reorganizations to convert what in form may be separate nontaxable steps into what in substance is a taxable transaction, or vice versa.[7]

If all these statutory and judicial requirements are met, they unlock the doors to the "operative provisions"—sections of the Code that provide for nonrecognition of gain or loss and that govern collateral matters such as the treatment of liabilities, basis, holding period and carryover of tax attributes.[8] For example, Sections 354 and 356 grant total or partial nonrecognition of gain to the shareholders of the target corporation in an acquisitive reorganization. Section 358, which we encountered earlier in connection with tax-free incorporations, provides a formula for determining the substituted basis of the stock or securities received by these shareholders in a reorganization. At the corporate level, Section 361(a) generally provides for nonrecognition when a corporation transfers its assets in a reorganization and distributes property in a liquidation pursuant to a reorganization plan,[9] and Section 357 generally ensures that the assumption of the target's liabilities is not treated as boot for this purpose. The acquiring corporation is accorded nonrecognition under Section 1032 with respect to stock used to make the acquisition and takes a transferred basis in the target's assets or stock under Section 362(b). In keeping with the continuity of investment principle, the tax attributes of the target corporation (e.g., earnings and profits and net operating losses) generally carry

---

3. I.R.C. § 368(a)(1)(B).

4. I.R.C. § 368(a)(1)(A).

5. Reg. § 1.368–1(d).

6. Reg. §§ 1.368–1(b); 1.368–2(g). However, since the "E" reorganization involves only a single corporation, there is neither a continuity of interest nor a continuity of business enterprise requirement. Microdot, Inc. v. United States, 728 F.2d 593 (2d Cir. 1984); Golden Nugget, Inc. v. Commissioner,

83 T.C. 28 (1984); Rev.Rul. 82–34, 1982–1 C.B. 59. In addition, the legislative history of the "G" reorganization indicates that both doctrines will be leniently applied in an insolvency situation. See Chapter 11D, infra.

7. See, e.g., Rev.Rul. 79–250, 1979–2 C.B. 156.

8. See Section C of this chapter, infra.

9. See also I.R.C. § 336(c).

over to the acquiring corporation under Section 381, subject to various limitations to patrol abuse.[10]

If a transaction does not qualify as a reorganization, these operative provisions do not apply and the tax consequences of the transaction must be determined under other parts of Subchapter C. For example, an asset acquisition that fails as a Type A or C reorganization ordinarily would be a taxable transaction to the shareholders under the rules considered in Chapters 7 and 8. But it is the rare reorganization that fails. Because of the high stakes involved, taxpayers historically were reluctant to proceed with reorganization transactions without first obtaining the Internal Revenue Service's blessing in the form of an advance ruling or, when time was of the essence, a reliable opinion letter from private counsel.[11] More recently, the Service has declined to grant "comfort rulings" on straightforward acquisitions,[12] but it will rule on transactions presenting a "significant issue."[13] As a result, the Service's administrative guidelines are often tantamount to the law in this area, and taxpayers who disagree with the government's viewpoint must proceed with a transaction at their substantial risk.

B.   TYPES OF ACQUISITIVE REORGANIZATIONS

1.   TYPE A: STATUTORY MERGERS AND CONSOLIDATIONS

Code: § 368(a)(1)(A). Skim §§ 354(a); 356(a); 357; 358(a); 361; 362(b); 368(a)(2)(C), (b); 381(a)(2); 1032.

Regulations: §§ 1.368–1(a), (b), (c), (d)(1)–(3) & (5) Examples 1–5, (e)(1) & (6) Example 1;–2(a), (b)(1), (g).

a.   THE MERGER OR CONSOLIDATION REQUIREMENT

In General. The Type A reorganization is defined in the Code as a statutory merger or consolidation. For this purpose, "statutory" refers to a merger or consolidation pursuant to local (usually corporate) law.[1] Under a typical state merger statute, the assets and liabilities of the target corporation are transferred to the acquiring corporation without the need for deeds or bills of sale, and the target dissolves by operation of law.[2] The consider-

---

10. See Section D of this chapter and Chapter 12, infra.

11. For the Service's administrative guidelines in evaluating reorganizations, see Rev.Proc. 77–37, 1977–2 C.B. 568. See also Rev. Proc. 86–42, 1986–2 C.B. 722 for the standard representations required in an acquisitive reorganization ruling request.

12. Rev. Proc. 90–56, 1990–2 C.B. 639.

13. See Rev. Proc. 2005–3, § 3.01(31), 2005–1 I.R.B. 118, 120. A "significant issue" is one that meets three tests: (1) it is not clearly and adequately addressed by a statute, regulation, judicial decision, tax treaty, or administrative authority; (2) its resolution is not essentially free from doubt; and (3) it is legally significant and germane to determining the major tax consequences of the transaction. Id. If there is a significant issue, the Service will rule on the entire transaction. Id.

1. Russell v. Commissioner, 40 T.C. 810 (1963), affirmed 345 F.2d 534 (5th Cir.1965).

2. See generally Oesterle, Mergers and Acquisitions in a Nutshell (2001).

ation received by the target's shareholders is specified in a formal agreement of merger between the two companies. The shareholders may receive stock or debt instruments of the acquiring corporation, cash or a combination of all three. A consolidation involves a similar transfer of the assets and liabilities of two corporations to a newly created entity followed by the dissolution of the transferor corporations, and the shareholders of the transferors become shareholders of the new entity by operation of law. Either transaction may require approval by a simple majority or two-thirds vote of the shareholders of both corporations,[3] and under state corporate law dissenting shareholders may be granted the right to sell their target stock at a price determined in an appraisal proceeding.[4]

"Divisive" Mergers. To qualify as a Type A reorganization, a merger must be an acquisitive rather than a divisive transaction. To be "acquisitive," the result of the transaction must be that one corporation acquires the assets of another (target) corporation by operation of law, and the target must cease to exist. By contrast, a "divisive" transaction is one in which a corporation's assets are divided among two or more corporations. In Revenue Ruling 2000–5,[5] the Service relied on this distinction in ruling that a transaction in which T "merged" under state law into P, transferring only some of its assets and liabilities, and T remained in existence, was not a Type A reorganization.[6] Similarly, a transaction where T transferred some of its assets and liabilities to each of two acquiring corporations and then T dissolved, with each T shareholder receiving stock in both acquiring corporations, was not a Type A reorganization even though it was a merger under state corporate law.[7] Although both transactions were called "mergers" under state law, they were divisive rather than acquisitive because T's assets were divided between two corporations, and T's shareholders wound up with stock in two separate companies.[8]

Revenue Ruling 2000–5 was the Service's response to a new form of corporate merger statute enacted by the Texas legislature in 1989 to permit divisive mergers.[9] The understandable concern was that permitting such

---

3. Id. As a general rule, most state corporate laws give voting rights to shareholders of the purchasing ("P") and target ("T") corporations. But where the amount of P stock used in the acquisition is less than 20 percent of its outstanding shares, P shareholders usually do not have the right to vote. In an acquisition initiated by a tender offer, there is no formal shareholder vote because T shareholders individually may decide whether or not to sell. Id. at 62. Some states, such as Delaware, also do not give P shareholders the right to vote on asset acquisitions not structured as a merger, triangular mergers where a P subsidiary makes the acquisition, stock acquisitions, or certain acquisitions for cash or cash equivalents. Id. at 63–64.

4. Under Delaware law, for example, dissenting target shareholders have appraisal rights in statutory mergers (even if they do not have voting rights) but not in asset acquisitions. 8 Del. Code §§ 262, 271. See Oesterle, supra note 2, at 65 et seq.

5. 2000–1 C.B. 436 (Situation 1).

6. Id. See also Reg. § 1.368–2T(b)(1)(iv) Example 1.

7. Rev. Rul. 2000–5, 2000–1 C.B. 436 (Situation 2).

8. Some divisive transactions also may be tax-free but they must satisfy the requirements of Section 355. See Chapter 10, infra.

9. For an analysis and critique of Revenue Ruling 2000–5, see Bank, "Taxing Divi-

mergers to qualify as Type A reorganizations would be inconsistent with the policy of Section 368 and undermine Section 355, which imposes strict and detailed requirements for corporate divisions to qualify for tax-free treatment.[10] The ruling serves as a reminder that simple compliance with a state corporate merger law does not ensure that a transaction will qualify as a Type A reorganization.

Mergers Involving Disregarded Entities. In a similar response to emerging acquisition techniques, the Service issued regulations addressing mergers between corporations and disregarded entities (such as a single-member limited liability company).[11] The regulations take a common sense approach to the two most typical transactional forms: (1) the merger of a single-member limited liability company ("LLC") with a corporate owner ("X") into an acquiring corporation ("P"), and (2) the merger of a target corporation ("T") into a single-member LLC in exchange for stock of LLC's corporate owner ("P"). In both situations, the LLC is a disregarded entity and thus is treated for tax purposes as a division of its corporate owner unless it elects to be taxed as a separate corporation. The first transaction does not qualify as a Type A reorganization because X's assets and liabilities are divided between X and P as a result of the merger.[12] But a merger of T into a single-member LLC in exchange for stock of the LLC's corporate owner ("P") may qualify as a Type A reorganization if the other requirements (e.g., the continuity of interest doctrine, discussed below) are met and the separate legal existence of T terminates.[13] This favorable result is consistent with the treatment of a disregarded entity as a division of its owner. It is as if T merged directly into P. Permitting statutory mergers into disregarded entities to qualify as Type A reorganizations offers more flexibility by eliminating the need for these transactions to pass muster under the stricter requirements applicable to Type C stock-for-assets acquisitions.[14]

Shareholder and Business Enterprise Continuity Requirements. The Code is strangely silent as to the permissible consideration in a Type A reorganization and the degree to which the target's historic business must be conducted by the acquiring corporation. To fill these gaps and preserve the integrity of the nonrecognition scheme, the courts developed the continuity of proprietary interest and continuity of business enterprise requirements.[15] Both doctrines are examined in the materials that follow.

---

sive and Disregarded Mergers," 34 Geo. L. Rev. 1523 (2000).

10. See Chapter 10, infra.

11. See Reg. § 301.7701–2(a) and Chapter 1D2, supra, for a discussion of disregarded entities—familiarly known as "tax nothings." Certain real estate investment trusts and S corporation subsidiaries also may be treated as disregarded entities for tax purposes.

12. Reg. § 1.368–2T(b)(1)(iv) Example 6.

13. Reg. § 1.368–2T(b)(1)(iv) Example 2.

14. For example, Type C reorganizations require the acquiring corporation to acquire substantially all of the target's properties and to use mostly voting stock and only a limited amount of boot in making the acquisition. See Section B3 of this chapter, infra.

15. The earliest continuity of interest cases involved Type C reorganizations but the doctrine now applies primarily to statutory mergers and consolidations.

b.   CONTINUITY OF PROPRIETARY INTEREST: QUANTITY AND QUALITY

Southwest Natural Gas Co. v. Commissioner

United States Court of Appeals, Fifth Circuit, 1951.
189 F.2d 332.

■ RUSSELL, CIRCUIT JUDGE.

The correctness of asserted deficiencies for corporate income tax for the year 1941 and of declared value excess profits tax and excess profits tax for 1942 due by Southwest Natural Gas Company depends upon whether a merger of Peoples Gas & Fuel Corporation with the taxpayer, effected in accordance with the laws of Delaware, was a sale, as asserted by the Commissioner, or a "reorganization" within the terms of Section 112(g) [the predecessor of Section 368] of the Internal Revenue Code, as contended by the taxpayer. The parties so stipulated the issue in the Tax Court. That Court upheld the Commissioner's determination. Southwest Natural Gas Company has petitioned this Court for review.

The facts found by the Tax Court (which, as facts, are not challenged) and the grounds for its judgment in law thereon are fully set forth in its published opinion. In substance that Court held that literal compliance with the provisions of a state law authorizing a merger would not in itself effect a "reorganization" within the terms applicable under Internal Revenue Statutes; that the test of continuity of interest was nevertheless applicable; and that the transaction in question did not meet this test. This ruling is assigned as error upon grounds which, while variously stated, require for their maintenance establishment of at least one of the propositions that: if the literal language of the statute is complied with, that is if there is a "statutory merger" duly effected in accordance with state law, the statute requires it be treated as a reorganization; or, at least where such merger has been effected the Tax Court must hold the transaction a reorganization in the absence of a finding that it was not in truth and in substance a merger; or, even if this be not correct, that the facts of this case disclose sufficient "continuity of interest." It is insisted in either view the Tax Court was required to hold under the facts found by it that the transaction in question was in truth a "statutory merger" and hence a "reorganization."

Consideration of the underlying purposes of the terms and provisions of Section 112 of the Internal Revenue Code in its entirety and of this Section (g)(1)(A) as involved here, in particular, as being enacted "to free from the imposition of an income tax purely 'paper profits or losses' wherein there is no realization of gain or loss in the business sense but merely the recasting of the same interests in a different form, the tax being postponed to a future date when a more tangible gain or loss is realized." Commissioner of Internal Revenue v. Gilmore's Estate, 3 Cir., 130 F.2d 791, 794, and thus applicable to transactions which effect only the "readjustment of continuing interest in property under modified corporate forms," clearly discloses, we think, that the accomplishment of a statutory merger does not *ipso facto* constitute a "reorganization" within the terms of the statute here involved. This has been expressly held by the Court of Appeals for the Third Circuit in a well considered opinion, supported by numerous authorities cited. Roebling v. Commissioner, 143 F.2d 810. There is no occasion for elaboration or reiteration of the reasoning and authorities set forth in that opinion. In Bazley v. Commissioner, 331 U.S. 737, 67 S.Ct. 1489, 1491, 91 L.Ed. 1782, the Supreme Court enforced a similar construction with reference to the "re-capitalization" provision of the section. The authorities are clearly to the effect that the terms expressed in the statute are not to be given merely a literal interpretation but are to be considered and applied in accordance with the purpose of Section 112. Thus the benefits of the reorganization provision have been withheld "in situations which might have satisfied provisions of the section treated as inert language, because they were not reorganizations of the kind with which § 112, in its purpose and particulars concerns itself. * * * "

It is thus clear that the test of "continuity of interest" announced and applied by these cited authorities, supra, must be met before a statutory merger may properly be held a reorganization within the terms of Section 112(g)(1)(A), supra. Each case must in its final analysis be controlled by its own peculiar facts. While no precise formula has been expressed for determining whether there has been retention of the requisite interest, it seems clear that the requirement of continuity of interest consistent with the statutory intent is not fulfilled in the absence of a showing: (1) that the transferor corporation or its shareholders retained a substantial proprietary stake in the enterprise represented by a material interest in the affairs of the transferee corporation, and, (2) that such retained interest represents a substantial part of the value of the property transferred.

Among other facts, the Tax Court found that under the merger all of Peoples' assets were acquired by the petitioner in exchange for specified amounts of stock, bonds, cash and the assumption of debts. There was a total of 18,875 shares common stock of Peoples' entitled to participate under the agreement of merger. The stockholders were offered Option A and Option B. The holders of 7,690 of such shares exercised Option B of that agreement and received $30.00 in cash for each share, or a total of $230,700.00. In respect to the stock now involved, the stockholders who exercised Option A, the holders of 59.2 percent of the common stock received in exchange 16.4 per cent of petitioner's outstanding common stock plus $340,350.00 principal amount of six per cent mortgage bonds (of the market value of 90 per cent of principal), which had been assumed by petitioner in a prior merger and $17,779.59 cash. The 16.4 per cent of the common stock referred to was represented by 111,850 shares having a market value of $5,592.50, or five cents per share, and represented the continuing proprietary interest of the participating stockholders in the enterprise. This was less than one per cent of the consideration paid by the taxpayers.

We think it clear that these and other facts found by the Tax Court find substantial support in the evidence, and the conclusion of the Tax Court that they failed to evidence sufficient continuity of interest to bring the transaction within the requirements of the applicable statute is correct.

The decision of the Tax Court is affirmed.

[The dissenting opinion of Chief Judge Hutcheson has been omitted. Ed.]

Revenue Ruling 66–224

1966–2 Cum.Bull. 114.

Corporation *X* was merged under state law into corporation *Y*. Corporation *X* had four stockholders (*A*, *B*, *C*, *D*), each of whom owned 25 percent of its stock. Corporation *Y* paid *A* and *B* each $50,000 in cash for their stock of corporation *X*, and *C* and *D* each received corporation *Y* stock with a value of $50,000 in exchange for their stock of corporation *X*. There are no other facts present that should be taken into account in determining whether the continuity of interest requirement of section 1.368–1(b) of the Income Tax Regulations has been satisfied, such as sales, redemptions or other dispositions of stock prior to or subsequent to the exchange which were part of the plan of reorganization.

Held, the continuity of interest requirement of section 1.368–1(b) of the regulations has been satisfied. It would also be satisfied if the facts were the same except corporation *Y* paid each stockholder $25,000 in cash and each stockholder received corporation *Y* stock with a value of $25,000.

NOTE

The continuity of interest doctrine historically required the shareholders of the target corporation to receive a sufficient proprietary interest in the acquiring corporation to justify treating the transaction as a wholly or partially tax-free reorganization rather than a taxable sale.[1] The early cases focused on both the quality of the consideration received by the target's shareholders and the percentage of equity consideration (relative to total consideration) received by those shareholders as a group. For example, in one of the first cases to apply the doctrine, the Supreme Court held that a transaction literally satisfying the definition of a reorganization nonetheless was a taxable sale because the T shareholders received only short-term notes of the acquiring corporation.[2] In a later case, the Court held that there was sufficient continuity of interest where the T shareholders re-

---

1. See Reg. §§ 1.368–1(b); 1.368–2(a), (e)(1)(i).

2. Pinellas Ice & Cold Storage Co. v. Commissioner, 287 U.S. 462, 53 S.Ct. 257

(1933). See also Helvering v. Minnesota Tea Co., 296 U.S. 378, 56 S.Ct. 269 (1935).

ceived 38 percent nonvoting preferred stock of the acquiring corporation and 62 percent cash.[3]

In evaluating continuity of interest, it is the overall continuity preserved in the transaction that controls, not the continuity of any individual shareholder.[4] All classes of stock, whether voting or nonvoting, provide the requisite continuity while any other consideration (cash, short-term notes, bonds, assumption of liabilities) will fail to meet the test.[5] The lines with respect to the percentage of stock that must be received are not so easily drawn if one refers to the case law,[6] but the Service has provided a practical benchmark by declaring that it will rule favorably on a Type A reorganization if P uses at least 50 percent equity consideration in making the acquisition.[7] Keep in mind that this "percentage" is the proportion of equity consideration relative to total consideration used by P to acquire T, not the percentage of P stock owned by former T shareholders after the P's acquisition of T. Moreover, overall qualification as a reorganization under this liberal standard does not mean that all T shareholders will be able to defer recognition of their gain. Those receiving nonequity consideration must recognize gain, if any, perhaps as ordinary income, to the extent they receive boot.[8] But if the entire transaction fails to qualify as a reorganization, all the parties (including T), not merely those receiving nonequity consideration, must recognize gain or loss.

These venerable principles have not been altered by the enactment in 1997 of Section 356(e), which treats certain debt-like preferred stock, defined in Section 351(g) as "nonqualified preferred stock," as other property (i.e. boot) for purposes of recognition of gain or loss by the T shareholders in a reorganization. In treating nonqualified preferred stock as boot for gain recognition purposes, Congress was responding to concerns about acquisitive transactions in which T shareholders received a relatively secure instrument labelled as "stock" but bearing many of the characteristics of debt in exchange for a riskier equity investment. In those circumstances, Congress believed it was appropriate to view the new debt-like preferred stock as taxable consideration because the T shareholder was obtaining a more secure form of investment. Congress indicated, however, that nonqualified preferred stock would continue to be treated as equity under other provisions of the Code, such as Sections 351 and 368, at least until prospective regulations provide otherwise.[9]

---

3. John A. Nelson Co. v. Helvering, 296 U.S. 374, 56 S.Ct. 273 (1935).

4. See Rev.Rul. 66–224 at p. 431, supra; Reg. § 1.368–2(e)(1)(i).

5. See, e.g., John A. Nelson Co. v. Helvering, supra note 3.

6. See, e.g., John A. Nelson Co. v. Helvering, supra note 3 (38% redeemable nonvoting preferred sufficient for continuity); Miller v. Commissioner, 84 F.2d 415 (6th Cir.1936) (25% stock sufficient).

7. Rev.Proc. 77–37, 1977–2 C.B. 568. See also Rev. Proc. 86–42, 1986–2 C.B. 722. Despite the Service's 50 percent rule of thumb, it is believed that 40 to 45 percent will suffice based on the case law. See, e.g, Ginsburg & Levin, Mergers, Acquisitions and Buyouts ¶ 610.2 (2004 ed.).

8. See Section C1 of this chapter, infra.

9. Staff of the Joint Committee on Taxation, General Explanation of Tax Legislation Enacted in 1997, 105th Cong., 1st Sess. 212–213 (1997).

Finally, although the continuity of interest test generally requires that the T stock or assets acquired in the reorganization be held directly by the corporation that issues its stock to T shareholders, the Code permits "drop-down" transfers to subsidiaries of the acquiring corporation.[10] The regulations go further by permitting multiple transfers of T stock or assets among various members of an affiliated group of corporations or to a partnership controlled by the acquiring corporation.[11]

c. CONTINUITY BY HISTORIC TARGET SHAREHOLDERS

J.E. Seagram Corp. v. Commissioner

United States Tax Court, 1995.
104 T.C. 75.

OPINION

■ NIMS, JUDGE:

[This case arose out of a 1981 takeover contest for Conoco, Inc. After an unsuccessful attempt to negotiate a friendly takeover, J.E. Seagram Corporation ("Seagram") commenced a cash tender offer for Conoco stock. Two weeks later, E.I DuPont de Nemours and Co. ("DuPont") and Conoco entered into an agreement for a two-step acquisition, under which a DuPont subsidiary ("DuPont Tenderor") commenced a competing tender offer to acquire all of Conoco's stock in exchange for a combination of cash and DuPont stock, to be followed by a merger of Conoco into a DuPont subsidiary. The agreement was subject to several conditions, including the requirement that at least 51 percent of Conoco's stock must be tendered.

When the smoke cleared after the various tender offers expired, Seagram had acquired 32 percent of Conoco stock for cash, and DuPont had acquired 46 percent of Conoco stock for cash. DuPont subsequently acquired the Conoco shares it did not own (including Seagram's holding) in exchange for DuPont stock as part of the tender offer and the merger of Conoco into DuPont Tenderor. When the smoke cleared, approximately 78 percent of the Conoco stock had changed hands for cash in the DuPont and Seagram tender offers, but 54 percent of the Conoco stock (including Seagram's stake) was exchanged for DuPont shares.

Seagram claimed a loss on its exchange of Conoco stock for DuPont stock. The Service disallowed the loss on the grounds that the transaction constituted a tax-free reorganization. Seagram argued that the exchange of its Conoco stock for DuPont stock was not carried out in pursuance of a reorganization plan, as required by Section 368.

In the first part of its lengthy opinion, the Tax Court held that because DuPont was contractually committed to undertake the merger once it completed its tender offer, the "carefully integrated transactions together constituted a plan of reorganization * * *."

---

10. I.R.C. § 368(a)(2)(C).   **11.** Reg. § 1.368–2(k).

Seagram's second argument was that DuPont's tender offer and merger did not constitute a reorganization because they failed the continuity of interest requirement. The Tax Court's resolution of that issue is set forth below. Ed.]

On the date of the Conoco/DuPont Agreement, July 6, 1981, there were approximately 85,991,896 Conoco shares outstanding. Petitioner is essentially arguing that because it acquired approximately 32 percent of these shares for cash pursuant to its own tender offer, and DuPont acquired approximately 46 percent of these shares for cash pursuant to its tender offer, the combined 78 percent of Conoco shares acquired for cash after the date of the Agreement destroyed the continuity of interest requisite for a valid reorganization. We think petitioner's argument, and the logic that supports it, miss the mark.

* * *

The parties stipulated that petitioner and DuPont, through their wholly owned subsidiaries, were acting independently of one another and pursuant to competing tender offers. Furthermore, there is of course nothing in the record to suggest any prearranged understanding between petitioner and DuPont that petitioner would tender the Conoco stock purchased for cash if petitioner by means of its own tender offer failed to achieve control of Conoco. Consequently, it cannot be argued that petitioner, although not a party to the reorganization, was somehow acting in concert with DuPont, which was a party to the reorganization. If such had been the case, the reorganization would fail because petitioner's cash purchases of Conoco stock could be attributed to DuPont, thereby destroying continuity.

* * *

Respondent points out, correctly we believe, that the concept of continuity of interest advocated by petitioner would go far toward eliminating the possibility of a tax-free reorganization of any corporation whose stock is actively traded. Because it would be impossible to track the large volume of third party transactions in the target's stock, all completed transactions would be suspect. Sales of target stock for cash after the date of the announcement of an acquisition can neither be predicted nor controlled by publicly held parties to a reorganization. A requirement that the identity of the acquired corporation's shareholders be tracked to assume a sufficient number of "historic" shareholders to satisfy some arbitrary minimal percentage receiving the acquiring corporation's stock would be completely unrealistic.

Such a mandate to look only to historic shareholder identity to determine continuity was rejected by the Supreme Court in Helvering v. Alabama Asphaltic Limestone Co., 315 U.S. 179 (1942). In *Alabama Asphaltic*, unsecured noteholders of an insolvent corporation commenced a bankruptcy proceeding against the corporation. The noteholders bought the corporate assets from the trustee and transferred them to a newly formed corporation in exchange for its stock. In discussing these facts, the Supreme Court stated:

> When the equity owners are excluded and the old creditors become the stockholders of the new corporation, it conforms to realities to date their equity ownership from the time when they invoked the processes of the law to enforce their rights of full priority. At that time they stepped into the shoes of the old stockholders. The sale "did nothing but recognize officially what had before been true in fact." * * *

* * *

> Some contention, however, is made that this transaction did not meet the statutory standard because the properties acquired by the new corporation belonged at that time to the committee and not to the old corporation. That is true. Yet, the separate steps were integrated parts of a single scheme. Transitory phases of an arrangement frequently are disregarded under these sections of the revenue acts where they add nothing of substance to the completed affair. Gregory v. Helvering, 293 U.S. 465; Helvering v. Bashford, 302 U.S. 454. Here they were no more than intermediate procedural devices utilized to enable the new corporation to acquire all the assets of the old one pursuant to a single reorganization plan. * * *

In reaching this conclusion, the Supreme Court upheld the finding of a valid "A" reorganization by this Court. * * *

In the "integrated" transaction before us petitioner, not DuPont, "stepped into the shoes" of 32 percent of the Conoco shareholders when petitioner acquired their stock for cash via the JES competing tender offer, held the 32 percent transitorily, and immediately tendered it in exchange for DuPont stock. For present purposes, there is no material distinction between petitioner's tender of the Conoco stock and a direct tender by the "old" Conoco shareholders themselves. Thus, the requirement of continuity of interest has been met.

* * *

For the reasons stated in this Opinion, we hold that a loss cannot be recognized by petitioner on its exchange of Conoco stock for DuPont stock, made pursuant to the DuPont–Conoco plan of reorganization. * * *

NOTE

The Historic Shareholder Concept After Seagram. The *Seagram* decision raises several questions about the role of the historic shareholder doctrine in applying the continuity of interest doctrine. In an earlier case,[1] the Tax Court concluded that continuity of interest "must be measured by

---

1. Kass v. Commissioner, 60 T.C. 218 (1973).

looking to all the pre-tender offer shareholders' and held that the sale for cash by more than 80 percent of those shareholders was sufficient to prevent the merger of T into P from meeting the quantitative test" of continuity of interest. Isn't that the very same argument that Seagram made to support recognition of its loss? Wasn't Seagram arguing that the DuPont–Conoco merger failed as a reorganization because 78 percent of the historic Conoco shareholders received cash for their stock?

Perhaps the cases can be reconciled by remembering that the attempts by Seagram and DuPont to acquire Conoco were independent of one another. Would it be reasonable to conclude that Seagram's purchase of Conoco stock was "old and cold" for purposes of the DuPont–Conoco merger, so that it was an "historic" shareholder for purposes of that transaction? Is that what the court meant when it said Seagram "stepped into the shoes" of the Conoco shareholders that it bought out?

Or was the Tax Court concerned with the practical effects of its decision in *Seagram* on the world of corporate acquisitions? It noted the difficulty of tracking third-party transactions and the absence of any control by publicly held corporations over their shareholders as practical considerations supporting its decision. The decision offers tax practitioners some interesting planning options. For example, assume Target Corporation ("T") is owned 60 percent by shareholder A and 40 percent by shareholder B, and Acquiring Corporation ("P") wishes to acquire T in a tax-free merger. Before *Seagram*, it was thought that P could not achieve its goal if A wished to cash out of T. Under *Seagram*, however, if A can find an independent third-party purchaser who is willing to buy A's T stock for cash and who eventually becomes a P shareholder after the merger, each of the party's business and tax objectives may be satisfied with careful planning.[2]

The Historic Shareholder Concept: In Memoriam? The Tax Court's decision in *Seagram* represented a significant erosion of the historic shareholder concept. Regulations issued in 1998 appear to go even further by eliminating the relevance of historic T shareholders except in limited situations. Following *Seagram*, the regulations provide that a "mere disposition" of T stock prior to a potential reorganization to buyers unrelated to T or P will be disregarded in applying the continuity of interest doctrine.[3] To illustrate, assume that A, an individual, owns 100 percent of the stock of T, Inc. (value-$100), and T plans to merge into P, Inc. Shortly before the merger is consummated, B, who is unrelated to T or P, purchases all of A's T stock for $100 cash, and then B exchanges her T stock for $50 of P stock and $50 cash furnished by P. Under the regulations, A's sale is disregarded and the continuity of interest requirement is met because B's T stock was exchanged for a sufficient amount of P stock (50 percent of total consider-

---

2. See Bloom, "Taxpayers Have More Planning Flexibility in Reorganizations After *Seagram* If It Survives," 82 J.Tax'n 334 (1995), for a discussion of this and other post-*Seagram* strategies. See also Willens, "Some Observations on the Tax Court's *Seagram* Decision," 66 Tax Notes 1465 (1995).

3. Reg. § 1.368–1(e)(1)(i).

ation) to preserve a substantial part of the value of the proprietary interest in T.[4]

Relationship of Continuity of Interest Doctrine to Taxable Stock Acquisitions. The tax-free reorganization rules often overlap with other provisions in Subchapter C. One potential jurisdictional conflict is between the treatment of a qualified stock purchase (e.g., P's purchase of 80 percent or more of T stock) as defined in Section 338 and an acquisitive reorganization. The Service has issued regulations addressing the tax consequences of the transfer of T's assets to P or an affiliate of P following a qualified stock purchase where P does not make a Section 338 election.[5] They provide that the T stock acquired by P in the qualified stock purchase will count for continuity of interest purposes if T later transfers its assets to a P subsidiary ("S"), enabling the second step of the transaction to qualify as a tax-free acquisitive reorganization.[6] As a result, T does not recognize gain on the transfer of its assets, which will take a transferred basis in S's hands.[7]

These regulations reverse the holding in Yoc Heating v. Commissioner,[8] a much discussed old Tax Court case where P bought 85 percent of T's stock for cash and notes and, as part of the same transaction, T subsequently transferred its assets to S, a newly formed P subsidiary and then dissolved. P received additional S stock in exchange for its T stock, and the T minority shareholders received cash in exchange for their T stock. The Tax Court viewed P's purchase of T stock and the subsequent T asset transfer to S as an integrated transaction in which P acquired all of T's assets for cash and notes. Consequently, it held that there was insufficient continuity of interest to qualify the asset transfer as a Section 368 reorganization because the historic shareholders of T did not receive any P stock. The upshot was that S received a cost basis in the T assets rather than the transferred basis it would have taken if the acquisition had qualified as a reorganization. Because the *General Utilities* doctrine was still alive at the time of this transaction, T did not recognize any corporate-level gain or loss as a result of the court's decision.

The Section 338 regulations take the position that the result in *Yoc Heating* is inconsistent with the policy of Section 338, which was intended to preempt the subjective *Kimbell-Diamond* doctrine.[9] The regulations also provide that the operative reorganization provisions applicable to share-

---

4. Reg. § 1.368–1(e)(6) Example 1(ii). Continuity may not be preserved, however, when the consideration received by A prior to or in connection with the reorganization is in a cash redemption of A's T stock (this usually is a problem only when P furnishes the cash) or if B cashes out the P stock received in the merger in a redemption. See Reg. § 1.368–1(e)(ii), –1(e)(6) Example (5) & (9).

5. Reg. § 1.338–3(d)(1). See Chapter 8C2, supra.

6. Reg. § 1.338–3(d)(2). Similarly, P is treated as a historic T shareholder for purposes of determining whether, immediately after the transfer of T assets, a T shareholder is in "control" of the corporation to which the assets are transferred for purposes of Section 368(a)(1)(D). Reg. § 1.338–3(d)(3). See Chapter 11B, infra.

7. Reg. § 1.338–3(d)(5) Example (iii).

8. 61 T.C. 168 (1973).

9. See Chapter 8C1, supra.

holders of the target corporation in an acquisitive reorganization do not apply to minority shareholders of T unless the transfer of T assets is pursuant to a reorganization under generally applicable tax rules without regard to the regulations.[10] To illustrate, assume P buys 85 percent of the stock of T for cash from shareholder A and does not make a Section 338 election. The remaining 15 percent of T is owned by Mrs. K. Shortly thereafter, as part of the same plan, T merges into S, a 100 percent subsidiary of P, and Mrs. K receives P (or S) stock in exchange for her T stock. Under the regulations, the continuity of interest requirement is not met in determining the tax consequences to Mrs. K, who thus recognizes gain or loss with respect to the exchange of her T stock.[11] Why? How can a transaction qualify as a reorganization for some purposes (T's transfer of its assets) but not for others (Mrs. K's exchange of her T stock)?

d. POST–ACQUISITION CONTINUITY

Another aspect of the continuity of interest doctrine relates to the length of time that the target shareholders must hold their stock in the acquiring corporation. For example, assume T merges into P in a tax-free reorganization in which the only consideration is P stock, but shareholders who hold 80 percent of the T stock are legally committed at the time of the merger to sell their P stock to a third party. Does the prearranged sale disqualify the merger as a Type A reorganization because the continuity of interest test is not met. The selling T shareholders will be taxed in either event, of course, although the timing of their gain may be affected if the merger and subsequent stock sale occur in different taxable years, but what about the 20 percent who retain their P stock? And what are the appropriate tax consequences to the target and acquiring corporations?

The Service has never required T's shareholders to maintain continuity of interest in P for any particular period of time after an acquisitive reorganization. But in determining if the continuity of interest requirement has been satisfied, the Service for many years considered sales and other dispositions of stock occurring subsequent to a merger which are part of the same overall "plan."[12] The courts disagreed over whether a pre-merger intent to sell (without any binding commitment) would defeat continuity of interest.[13]

Regulations issued in 1998 resolve the issue by providing that subsequent dispositions of P stock received in a potential reorganization by

10. Reg. § 1.338–3(d)(5) Example (v). See also Kass v. Commissioner, supra note 1.

11. Id. See also Reg. § 1.368–1(e)(6) Example 4(ii).

12. Rev. Proc. 77–37, 1977–2 C.B. 568.

13. See, e.g., McDonald's Restaurants of Illinois, Inc. v. Commissioner, 688 F.2d 520 (7th Cir.1982), rev'g 76 T.C. 972 (1981), where the Tax Court treated a post-merger sale of P stock by former T shareholders as a separate transaction because the shareholders were not contractually bound to sell, but the Seventh Circuit found that a pre-merger intent to sell was sufficient to invoke the step transaction doctrine and cause the merger to lack continuity of interest. See also Penrod v. Commissioner, 88 T.C. 1415 (1987) (no binding commitment or pre-merger intent to sell; continuity of interest test satisfied).

former T shareholders generally will be disregarded in determining whether the continuity of shareholder interest requirement is met, even if the dispositions were pursuant to a preexisting binding contract.[14] This is consistent with the Service's current position that the continuity of interest requirement is satisfied if a substantial part of the value of the proprietary interest in T is preserved through an exchange for a proprietary interest (i.e., stock) of P. But if the facts demonstrate that T shareholders have sold their P stock for cash to P or a related party (e.g., a P subsidiary) before or after the acquisition, the continuity of interest requirement may not be satisfied.[15] For example, if P reacquired stock that it issued in the reorganization from T shareholders in exchange for cash, the reacquisition would be considered in determining if the continuity of interest requirement was satisfied. But sales of P stock by former T shareholders to outsiders would be ignored, even if the sales were pursuant to a binding commitment entered into prior to the reorganization.[16]

Revenue Ruling 99–58, which follows, is another illustration of the Service's new tolerance toward post-acquisition continuity issues.

Revenue Ruling 99–58

1999–2 Cum. Bull. 701.

ISSUE

What is the effect on continuity of interest when a potential reorganization is followed by an open market reacquisition of P's stock?

FACTS

T merges into P, a corporation whose stock is widely held, and is publicly and actively traded. P has one class of common stock authorized and outstanding. In the merger, T shareholders receive 50 percent common stock of P and 50 percent cash. Viewed in isolation, the exchange would satisfy the continuity of interest requirement of § 1.368–1(e) of the Income Tax Regulations. However, in an effort to prevent dilution resulting from the issuance of P shares in the merger, P's preexisting stock repurchase program is modified to enable P to reacquire a number of its shares equal to the number issued in the acquisition of T. The number of shares repurchased will not exceed the total number of P shares issued and outstanding prior to the merger. The repurchases are made following the merger, on the open market, through a broker for the prevailing market price. P's intention to repurchase shares was announced prior to the T merger, but the repurchase program was not a matter negotiated with T or the T shareholders. There was not an understanding between the T shareholders and P that the T shareholders' ownership of P stock would be transitory. Because of the mechanics of an open market purchase, P does not know the identity of a seller of P stock, nor does a former T sharehold-

14. Reg. § 1.368–1(e)(1)(i), –1(e)(6) Example 1(i).

15. Reg. § 1.368–1(e)(1)(ii), –1(c)(2).

16. See Reg. § 1.368–1(e)(6) Example (4)(i).

er who receives P stock in the merger and subsequently sells it know whether P is the buyer. Without regard to the repurchase program, a market exists for the newly-issued P stock held by the former T shareholders. During the time P undertakes its repurchase program, there are sales of P stock on the open market, which may include sales of P shares by former T shareholders.

LAW AND ANALYSIS

Requisite to a reorganization under the Internal Revenue Code is a continuity of interest as described in § 1.368–1(e). Section 1.368–1(b). The general purpose of the continuity of interest requirement is "to prevent transactions that resemble sales from qualifying for nonrecognition of gain or loss available to corporate reorganizations." Section 1.368–1(e)(1)(i). To achieve this purpose, the regulation provides that a proprietary interest in the target corporation is not preserved to the extent that, "in connection with the potential reorganization, ... stock of the issuing corporation furnished in exchange for a proprietary interest in the target corporation in the potential reorganization is redeemed." Id. However, for purposes of the continuity requirement, "a mere disposition of stock of the issuing corporation received in the potential reorganization to persons not related ... to the issuing corporation is disregarded." Id. The regulation provides that all facts and circumstances will be considered in determining whether, in substance, a proprietary interest in the target corporation is preserved.

Under the facts set forth above, continuity of interest is satisfied. There was not an understanding between the T shareholders and P that the T shareholders' ownership of the P shares would be transitory. Further, because of the mechanics of an open market repurchase, the repurchase program does not favor participation by the former T shareholders. Therefore, even if it could be established that P has repurchased P shares from former T shareholders in the repurchase program, any such purchase would be coincidental. The merger and the stock repurchase together in substance would not resemble a sale of T stock to P by the former T shareholders and, thus, the repurchase would not be treated as "in connection with" the merger. Under the facts presented, a sale of P stock on the open market by a former T shareholder during the repurchase program will have the same effect on continuity of interest as a mere disposition to persons not related to P.

HOLDING

Under the facts presented, the open market repurchase of shares through a broker has no effect on continuity of interest in the potential reorganization.

e.   CONTINUITY OF BUSINESS ENTERPRISE

Bentsen v. Phinney

United States District Court, Southern District of Texas, 1961.
199 F.Supp. 363.

■ Garza, District Judge.

[Rio Development Company was a Texas corporation engaged in the land development business along with two other corporations. All three corporations were controlled by the Bentsen family. The three corporations transferred all their assets, subject to liabilities, to a newly formed life insurance company. The transferor corporations then liquidated, and their shareholders became shareholders of the new insurance company. The parties stipulated that there was a business purpose for the transaction.

After failing to obtain an advance ruling from the Service that their exchange of stock in the land development companies for stock in the insurance company was a tax-free transaction, the taxpayers reported a taxable gain and then took the necessary procedural steps to file a refund suit in federal district court. The taxpayers contended that the transaction qualified as a reorganization, while the Service argued that it failed to meet the requirements of Section 368 because of a lack of continuity of business enterprise. Ed.]

The question for the Court to decide is: Was such corporate transaction a corporate "reorganization", as the term "reorganization" is defined in Section 368(a)(1), Internal Revenue Code of 1954, 26 U.S.C.A. § 368(a)(1), even though Rio Development Company engaged in the land development business and thereafter the new Insurance Company engaged in the insurance business?

The plaintiff taxpayers contend there was a corporate reorganization. The Government, Defendant in this cause, maintains that there was not a corporate reorganization under Section 368(a)(1) of the Internal Revenue Code of 1954, because there was not a continuity of business enterprise before and after the reorganization; and that this is a prerequisite as set out in the Treasury Regulations.

This case is governed by the Internal Revenue Code of 1954, 26 U.S.C., the applicable sections of which provide:

"§ 368. Definitions relating to corporate reorganizations

"(a) Reorganization.—

"(1) In General.—For purposes of parts I and II and this part, the term 'reorganization' means—

* * *

"(C) the acquisition by one corporation, in exchange solely for all or a part of its voting stock (or in exchange solely for all or a part of the voting stock of a corporation which is in control of the acquiring corporation), of substantially all of the properties of another corporation, but in determining whether the exchange is solely for stock the assumption by the acquiring corporation of a liability of the other, or the fact that property acquired is subject to a liability, shall be disregarded;

"(D) a transfer by a corporation of all or a part of its assets to another corporation if immediately after the transfer the transferor, or one or more of its shareholders (including persons who were shareholders immediately before the transfer), or any combination thereof, is in control of the corporation to which the assets are transferred; but only if, in pursuance of the plan, stock or securities of the corporation to which the assets are transferred are distributed in a transaction which qualifies under section 354, 355, or 356;"

"Sec. 354. Exchanges of stock and securities in certain reorganizations

"(a) General rule.—

"(1) In General.—No gain or loss shall be recognized if stock or securities in a corporation a party to a reorganization are, in pursuance of the plan of reorganization, exchanged solely for stock or securities in such corporation or in another corporation a party to the reorganization."

It is conceded that the 1939 Internal Revenue Code was the same in this respect as the 1954 Code, and that the corresponding Treasury Regulations issued under the 1939 Code are similar to the corresponding Treasury Regulations issued under the 1954 Code.

The Treasury Regulation states: "Requisite to a reorganization under the Code, are a continuity of business enterprise under the modified corporate form."

The Government contends that since there was a lack of "continuity of the business enterprise", there was not a reorganization as contemplated under the statutes.

The question for this Court to decide is the meaning of "continuity of business enterprise", and whether or not it exists in this case.

The Government takes the position that "continuity of business enterprise" means that the new corporation must engage in the same identical or similar business. Stated in another manner, the Government maintains it is necessary that there must be an identity of type of business before and after the reorganization.

The plaintiff taxpayers have cited to the Court the case of Becher v. Commissioner, 221 F.2d 252 (2d Cir.1955) affirming 22 T.C. 932 (1954), which the Government has tried to distinguish. In this case the taxpayer owned all the stock in a corporation engaged in the sponge rubber and canvass-product manufacturing business. The new corporation engaged in the business of manufacturing upholstered furniture. In that case, the Government took the position that there had been a reorganization and that a cash distribution to the shareholders of the old corporation was taxable as "boot" and was ordinary income to the shareholders. The Government prevailed in that case, and the Court, at 221 F.2d 252, 253, said:

"* * * but the Tax Court here correctly held that a business purpose does not require an identity of business before and after the reorganization. * * *"

Other cases cited are Pebble Springs Distilling Co. v. Commissioner, 231 F.2d 288 (7th Cir.1956), cert. denied 352 U.S. 836, 77 S.Ct. 56, 1 L.Ed.2d 55 affirming 23 T.C. 196 (1954). There the old corporation had the power to carry on both a whiskey distilling business and a real estate business, but it engaged solely in the real estate business.

Another case cited to the Court is Morley Cypress Trust v. Commissioner, 3 T.C. 84 (1944). In that case the old corporation owned land held for timber and the land was conveyed to a new corporation engaged in the oil business.

The Government tries to distinguish these last two cases by saying that in the Pebble Springs Distilling Co. case the new corporation could engage in the whiskey distilling business if it had wanted to, and that in the Morley Cypress Trust case, after the problem of continuity of business enterprise had been presented, the required continuity could have been found because both the old and the new corporations were actively engaged in exploiting the natural resources of the same land.

The Government also contends that under Texas law an insurance company cannot engage in any business other than that of insurance.

The Morley Cypress Trust case cited above, this Court believes, is the case most like the case before the Court. In the Morley Cypress Trust case the land was held for timber. In this case it was held for development. In the Morley case land was conveyed to a new oil corporation for use in the oil business. In this case, land (plus proceeds from the sale of land) was conveyed to a new corporation to furnish the means to capitalize a new insurance business.

The Government contends that the corresponding Treasury Regulation issued under the 1939 Code was in existence when the 1954 Code was enacted and Congress did not see fit to make any changes; that Treasury Regulations have the force of law when the Code section which they interpret is reenacted after they have once been promulgated, and cites Roberts v. Commissioner, 9 Cir., 176 F.2d 221, 10 A.L.R.2d 186.

The Government has been unable to present the Court with any decision in which the meaning of "continuity of business enterprise" as used in the Treasury Regulations, has been interpreted. Since no Court had upheld the contention made by the Government as to the interpretation to be given said words in the Regulations, it is unfair to say that Congress had an opportunity to make a change in passing the 1954 Code. Congress was not apprised of the meaning that the Government wishes to give to said language in the Regulations, and therefore the rule expressed in Roberts v. Commissioner, supra, is not controlling here.

This Court finds that no court has passed on the question of whether "continuity of business enterprise", as used in the Regulations, means that the new corporation must engage in the identical type of business or a similar business; and it is, therefore, held that this Court is not bound by any Treasury Regulation since it is the province of the Court to decide whether the Treasury Regulation means what the Government contends it means; and whether or not if it means what the Government contends, said Regulation is one that could be promulgated under the appropriate sections of the Internal Revenue Code.

This Court finds that "continuity of business enterprise", as used in the Regulations, does not mean that the new corporation must engage in either the same type of business as the old or a similar business, for if this be the requirement, then said Regulation is without authority.

To qualify as a "reorganization" under the applicable statutes, the new corporation does not have to engage in an identical or similar type of business. All that is required is that there must be continuity of the business activity.

This Court therefore finds that there was a reorganization under the applicable sections of the Internal Revenue Code.

Under the facts stipulated in this case, it is found that there was a continuity of the business activity and all requisites having been complied with, the plaintiff taxpayers have a right to a refund of the income taxes paid on the exchange of stock. The amounts to be refunded by the Government are to be those as stated in the Stipulation.

The Clerk will notify Counsel for the plaintiffs to submit an appropriate order and judgment.

Revenue Ruling 81–25

1981–1 Cum.Bull. 132.

ISSUE

For a transaction to qualify as a reorganization under section 368(a)(1) of the Internal Revenue Code of 1954, does the continuity of business enterprise requirement apply to the business or business assets of the acquiring (transferee) corporation prior to the reorganization?

LAW AND ANALYSIS

Section 1.368–1(b) of the Income Tax Regulations states that in order for a reorganization to qualify under section 368(a)(1) of the Code there must be continuity of the business enterprise under the modified corporate form.

Rev.Rul. 63–29, 1963–1 C.B. 77, holds that the continuity of business enterprise requirement of section 1.368–1(b) of the regulations was satisfied where a transferee corporation sold its assets and discontinued its business, then acquired the assets of another corporation in exchange for its voting stock, and used the sales proceeds realized from the sale of its assets to expand the business formerly conducted by the acquired corporation. The holding of Rev.Rul. 63–29 is now reflected in the recent amendment to section 1.368–1 (1.368–1(d)) of the regulations, which looks only to the transferor's historic business or historic business assets for determining if the continuity of business enterprise requirement is satisfied.

HOLDING

In a section 368(a)(1) reorganization the continuity of business enterprise requirement does not apply to the business or business assets of the transferee corporation prior to the reorganization.

* * *

NOTE

The continuity of business enterprise doctrine requires P either to continue T's historic business or to use a significant portion of T's historic business assets in a business.[1] This determination is based on all the facts and circumstances, applying liberal final regulations issued by the Service in 1998. For example, the regulations treat the continuity of business enterprise doctrine as satisfied in the acquisitive reorganization setting even if P transfers the acquired T assets or stock to controlled P subsidiaries, or in certain cases even to a partnership that is controlled by the P corporate group.[2] Numerous examples in the regulations illustrate how the doctrine is applied to various transactional structures.[3]

PROBLEMS

1. Assume that Acquiring Corporation ("P") and Target Corporation ("T") are incorporated in a state with a merger and consolidation statute that provides in part:

> Any two or more domestic corporations may merge into one of such corporations pursuant to a plan of merger approved in the manner provided in this chapter, and any two or more domestic corporations may consolidate into a new corporation pursuant to a plan of consolidation approved in the manner provided in this chapter.

> A vote of the shareholders shall be taken on the proposed plan of merger or consolidation. The plan of merger or consolidation shall be approved upon receiving the affirmative vote of the holders of a majority of the shares entitled to vote thereon of each such corporation.

Consider whether the following alternative transactions involving P and T qualify as Type A reorganizations. Assume in all cases that any preferred stock is not "nonqualified preferred stock."

---

1. Reg. § 1.368–1(d)(1).

2. Reg. § 1.368–1(d)(4) & (5).

3. Reg. § 1.368–1(d)(5). For a rare case in which a transaction was found to fail the continuity of business enterprise require-ment, see Honbarrier v. Commissioner, 115 T.C. 300 (2000), where the acquiring corporation did not continue the target's historic business or use a significant portion of its historic business assets in a business.

(a) T merges into P in an "all cash" merger. T transfers all of its assets to P and dissolves. T shareholders receive cash in exchange for their stock.

(b) Same as (a), above, except that the merger agreement provides that all T shareholders shall receive a newly issued class of P nonvoting preferred stock in exchange for their T stock.

(c) Same as (b), above, except shareholders holding 75% of the old T stock make a binding commitment prior to the merger to sell their new P stock to a third party for cash one week after the merger.

(d) Same as (b), above, except shortly after the merger and as part of its original plan, P sells T's assets to an unrelated party at a nice profit and uses the sales proceeds to expand one of P's other businesses.

(e) Same as (b), above, except that the T shareholders, all of whom vote to approve the merger, receive nonvoting preferred stock of P worth $200,000 and P notes worth $100,000?

(f) Same as (b), above, except that the T shareholders receive nonvoting preferred stock of P worth $100,000 and P long-term bonds worth $200,000?

(g) Same as (f), above, except that the bonds are convertible at any time into P nonvoting preferred stock?

(h) Same as (b), above, except that 75% of the T shareholders (owning $33\frac{1}{3}\%$ of the T stock) receive the notes worth $100,000 and 25% of the T shareholders (owning $66\frac{2}{3}\%$ of the T stock) receive P stock worth $200,000?

(i) Assume that P acquired 70% of the T stock five years ago for cash. In the current year, T merges into P, and the minority shareholders of T receive P stock worth $18,000 and $72,000 cash (i.e., 20% stock and 80% cash).

(j) As part of a takeover plan, P acquired 80% of the T stock six months ago in a tender offer for $240,000 cash. T then merges into P, and the remaining T shareholders receive $60,000 of P stock in exchange for their T stock.

2. Reread Reg. § 1.368–1(d)(5) Example (5).

(a) Is the regulation consistent with the result in Bentsen v. Phinney?

(b) Would the continuity of business enterprise issue arise in the example if P were merged into T and T's farm machinery manufacturing business were sold but P's lumber mill business were continued?

2.   TYPE B: ACQUISITIONS OF STOCK SOLELY FOR VOTING STOCK

Code: §§ 368(a)(1)(B), (c). Skim §§ 354(a); 358; 362(b); 368(a)(2)(C), (b); 1032(a).

Regulations: § 1.368–2(c).

Chapman v. Commissioner

United States Court of Appeals, First Circuit, 1980.
618 F.2d 856.

■ LEVIN H. CAMPBELL, CIRCUIT JUDGE.

This appeal by the Internal Revenue Service from a decision of the Tax Court calls for the construction of certain corporate reorganization provisions of the Internal Revenue Code, 26 U.S.C. §§ 354(a)(1) and 368(a)(1). We must decide whether the requirement of Section 368(a)(1)(B) that the acquisition of stock in one corporation by another be solely in exchange for voting stock of the acquiring corporation is met where, in related transactions, the acquiring corporation first acquires 8 percent of the acquiree's stock for cash and then acquires more than 80 percent of the acquiree in an exchange of stock for voting stock. The Tax Court agreed with the taxpayers that the latter exchange constituted a valid tax-free reorganization. Reeves v. Commissioner, 71 T.C. 727 (1979).

The Facts

* * *

The events giving rise to this dispute began in 1968, when the management of ITT, a large multinational corporation, became interested in acquiring Hartford as part of a program of diversification. In October 1968, ITT executives approached Hartford about the possibility of merging the two corporations. This proposal was spurned by Hartford, which at the time was considering acquisitions of its own. In November 1968, ITT learned that approximately 1.3 million shares of Hartford, representing some 6 percent of Hartford's voting stock, were available for purchase from a mutual fund. After assuring Hartford's directors that ITT would not attempt to acquire Hartford against its will, ITT consummated the $63.7 million purchase from the mutual fund with Hartford's blessing. From November 13, 1968 to January 10, 1969, ITT also made a series of purchases on the open market totalling 458,000 shares which it acquired for approximately $24.4 million. A further purchase of 400 shares from an ITT subsidiary in March 1969 brought ITT's holdings to about 8 percent of Hartford's outstanding stock, all of which had been bought for cash.

In the midst of this flurry of stock-buying, ITT submitted a written proposal to the Hartford Board of Directors for the merger of Hartford into an ITT subsidiary, based on an exchange of Hartford stock for ITT's $2 cumulative convertible voting preferred stock. Received by Hartford in December of 1968, the proposal was rejected in February of 1969. A counterproposal by Hartford's directors led to further negotiations, and on April 9, 1969 a provisional plan and agreement of merger was executed by the two corporations. While not unlike the proposal Hartford had earlier rejected, this plan was somewhat more favorable to Hartford's stockholders.[4] The merger agreement was conditioned upon approval, as required under state law, by the shareholders of the two corporations and by the Connecticut Insurance Commissioner. In addition, Hartford had an unqualified right to terminate the agreement if it believed there was any likelihood that antitrust litigation would be initiated. Although such litigation in fact materialized, Hartford's board of directors pushed ahead with the merger, and in October 1969 a Justice Department motion to enjoin the merger was denied by the United States District Court for the District of Connecticut.

Meanwhile, on April 15, 1969, attorneys for the parties sought a ruling from the IRS that the proposed transaction would constitute a reorganization under Section 368(a)(1)(B) of the Internal Revenue Code of 1954, so that, among other things, gain realized on the exchange by Hartford shareholders would not be recognized, see 26 U.S.C. § 354(a)(1). By private letter ruling, the Service notified the parties on October 13, 1969 that the proposed merger would constitute a nontaxable reorganization, provided ITT unconditionally sold its 8 percent interest in Hartford to a third party before Hartford's shareholders voted to approve or disapprove the proposal. On October 21, the Service ruled that a proposed sale of the stock to Mediobanca, an Italian bank, would satisfy this condition, and such a sale was made on November 9.

On November 10, 1969, the shareholders of Hartford approved the merger, which had already won the support of ITT's shareholders in June. On December 13, 1969, however, the merger plan ground to a halt, as the Connecticut Insurance Commissioner refused to endorse the arrangement. ITT then proposed to proceed with a voluntary exchange offer to the shareholders of Hartford on essentially the same terms they would have obtained under the merger plan. After public hearings and the imposition of certain requirements on the post-acquisition operation of Hartford, the insurance commissioner approved the exchange offer on May 23, 1970, and three days later ITT submitted the exchange offer to all Hartford shareholders. More than 95 percent of Hartford's outstanding stock was exchanged for shares of ITT's $2.25 cumulative convertible voting preferred stock. The Italian bank to which ITT had conveyed its original 8 percent interest was among those tendering shares, as were the taxpayers in this case.

In March 1974, the Internal Revenue Service retroactively revoked its ruling approving the sale of Hartford stock to Mediobanca, on the ground that the request on which the ruling was based had misrepresented the nature of the proposed sale. Concluding that the entire transaction no longer constituted a nontaxable reorganization, the Service assessed tax deficiencies against a number of former Hartford shareholders who had accepted the exchange offer. Appellees, along with other taxpayers, contested this action in the Tax Court, where the case was decided on appellees'

---

4. In particular, the annual dividend on the preferred shares was to be $2.25 rather than $2.00, and the conversion ratio was set at a rate more favorable to Hartford shareholders.

motion for summary judgment. For purposes of this motion, the taxpayers conceded that questions of the merits of the revocation of the IRS rulings were not to be considered; the facts were to be viewed as though ITT had not sold the shares previously acquired for cash to Mediobanca. The taxpayers also conceded, solely for purposes of their motion for summary judgment, that the initial cash purchases of Hartford stock had been made for the purpose of furthering ITT's efforts to acquire Hartford.

The Issue

Taxpayers advanced two arguments in support of their motion for summary judgment. Their first argument related to the severability of the cash purchases from the 1970 exchange offer. Because 14 months had elapsed between the last of the cash purchases and the effective date of the exchange offer, and because the cash purchases were not part of the formal plan of reorganization entered into by ITT and Hartford, the taxpayers argued that the 1970 exchange offer should be examined in isolation to determine whether it satisfied the terms of Section 368(a)(1)(B) of the 1954 Code. The Service countered that the two sets of transactions—the cash purchases and the exchange offer—were linked by a common acquisitive purpose, and that they should be considered together for the purpose of determining whether the arrangement met the statutory requirement that the stock of the acquired corporation be exchanged "solely for * * * voting stock" of the acquiring corporation. The Tax Court did not reach this argument; in granting summary judgment it relied entirely on the taxpayers' second argument.

For purposes of the second argument, the taxpayers conceded arguendo that the 1968 and 1969 cash purchases should be considered "parts of the 1970 exchange offer reorganization." Even so, they insisted upon a right to judgment on the basis that the 1970 exchange of stock for stock satisfied the statutory requirements for a reorganization without regard to the presence of related cash purchases. The Tax Court agreed with the taxpayers, holding that the 1970 exchange in which ITT acquired more than 80 percent of Hartford's single class of stock for ITT voting stock satisfied the requirements of Section 368(a)(1)(B), so that no gain or loss need be recognized on the exchange under Section 354(a)(1). The sole issue on appeal is whether the Tax Court was correct in so holding.

I.

We turn first to the statutory scheme under which this case arose. The basic rule governing exchanges was imported from Section 1002 of the 1954 Code, 26 U.S.C. § 1002. Section 1002 stated that, except as otherwise provided, gain or loss on the exchange of property should be recognized and taken into account in computing a taxpayer's taxable income. One exception to that rule appears in Section 354(a)(1), which provides that gain or loss shall not be recognized if stock or securities in a corporation are, in pursuance of the plan of reorganization, exchanged solely for stock or securities in another corporation which is a party to the reorganization. This exception does not grant a complete tax exemption for reorganizations, but rather defers the recognition of gain or loss until some later event such as a sale of stock acquired in the exchange. Section 354(a)(1) does not apply to an exchange unless the exchange falls within one of the six categories of "reorganization" defined in Section 368(a)(1). The category relevant to the transactions involved in this case is defined in Section 368(a)(1)(B):

> "[T]he term 'reorganization' means
>
> (B) the acquisition by one corporation, in exchange solely for all or a part of its voting stock * * * of stock of another corporation if, immediately after the acquisition, the acquiring corporation has control of such other corporation (whether or not such acquiring corporation had control immediately before the acquisition)."

The concept of "control" is defined in Section 368(c) as "the ownership of stock possessing at least 80 percent of the total combined voting power of all classes of stock entitled to vote and at least 80 percent of the total number of shares of all other classes of stock of the corporation." Subsection (B) thus establishes two basic requirements for a valid, tax-free stock-for-stock reorganization. First, "the acquisition" of another's stock must be "solely for * * * voting stock." Second, the acquiring corporation must have control over the other corporation immediately after the acquisition.

The single issue raised on this appeal is whether "the acquisition" in this case complied with the requirement that it be "solely for * * * voting stock." It is well settled that the "solely" requirement is mandatory; if any part of "the acquisition" includes a form of consideration other than voting stock, the transaction will not qualify as a (B) reorganization. See Helvering v. Southwest Consolidated Corp., 315 U.S. 194, 198, 62 S.Ct. 546, 550, 86 L.Ed. 789 (1942) (" 'Solely' leaves no leeway. Voting stock plus some other consideration does not meet the statutory requirement"). The precise issue before us is thus how broadly to read the term "acquisition." The Internal Revenue Service argues that "the acquisition * * * of stock of another corporation" must be understood to encompass the 1968–69 cash purchases as well as the 1970 exchange offer. If the IRS is correct, "the acquisition" here fails as a (B) reorganization. The taxpayers, on the other hand, would limit "the acquisition" to the part of a sequential transaction of this nature which meets the requirements of subsection (B). They argue that the 1970 exchange of stock for stock was itself an "acquisition" by ITT of stock in Hartford solely in exchange for ITT's voting stock, such that after the exchange took place ITT controlled Hartford. Taxpayers contend that the earlier cash purchases of 8 percent, even if conceded to be part of the same acquisitive plan, are essentially irrelevant to the tax-free reorganization otherwise effected.

The Tax Court accepted the taxpayers' reading of the statute, effectively overruling its own prior decision in Howard v. Commissioner, 24 T.C. 792 (1955), rev'd on other grounds, 238 F.2d 943 (7th Cir.1956). The plurality opinion stated its "narrow" holding as follows:

"We hold that where, as is the case herein, 80 percent or more of the stock of a corporation is acquired in one transaction,[18] in exchange for which only voting stock is furnished as consideration, the 'solely for voting stock' requirement of section 368(a)(1)(B) is satisfied.

18.   "In determining what constitutes 'one transaction,' we include all the acquisitions from shareholders which were clearly part of the same transaction."

71 T.C. at 741. The plurality treated as "irrelevant" the 8 percent of Hartford's stock purchased for cash, although the opinion left somewhat ambiguous the question whether the 8 percent was irrelevant because of the 14–month time interval separating the transactions or because the statute was not concerned with transactions over and above those mathematically necessary to the acquiring corporation's attainment of control.[15]

II.

For reasons set forth extensively in section III of this opinion, we do not accept the position adopted by the Tax Court. Instead we side with the Commissioner on the narrow issue presented in this appeal, that is, the correctness of taxpayers' so-called "second" argument premised on an assumed relationship between the cash and stock transactions. As explained below, we find a strong implication in the language of the statute, in the legislative history, in the regulations, and in the decisions of other courts that cash purchases which are concededly "parts of" a stock-for-stock exchange must be considered constituent elements of the "acquisition" for purposes of applying the "solely for * * * voting stock" requirement of Section 368(a)(1)(B). We believe the presence of non-stock consideration in such an acquisition, regardless of whether such consideration is necessary to the gaining of control, is inconsistent with treatment of the acquisition as a non-taxable reorganization. It follows for purposes of taxpayers' second argument—which was premised on the assumption that the cash transactions were part of the 1970 exchange offer reorganization—that the stock transfers in question would not qualify for nonrecognition of gain or loss.

Our decision will not, unfortunately, end this case. The Tax Court has yet to rule on taxpayers' "first" argument. To be sure, appellees urge that in the event of our reversing the Tax Court on the single issue it chose to

---

15. If the holding rested on the former basis, it would be difficult to credit the Tax Court's repeated assertions that it was not reaching or deciding the severability issue. As the taxpayers conceded their cash purchases were "parts of the 1970 exchange offer reorganization," the Tax Court had no reason to consider the actual lapse of time which occurred as a factor in treating the cash purchases as legally irrelevant. We assume, therefore, that any indications in the Tax Court's opinion that the separation in time was necessary to its holding were inadvertent, and that the holding actually rests on the Tax Court's reading of the statute. If the Tax Court wishes explicitly to articulate a rule regarding the time period which will suffice to separate two transactions for purposes of Section 368(a)(1)(B), we think it will have an adequate opportunity to do so in considering on remand the issue of severability raised by taxpayers' first argument.

address, we should consider upholding its judgment on the alternative ground that the prior cash purchases in the instant case were, as a matter of law, unrelated to the exchange offer. The taxpayers are correct that an appellee may urge any contention appearing in the record in support of the decree, whether or not the issue was addressed by the lower court. * * * Taxpayers' so-called first argument deserves, however, a more focused and deliberate inquiry than we can give it in the present posture of the case. The Commissioner has briefed the issue in only a cursory fashion, and oral argument was devoted almost entirely to the treatment of cash and stock transactions which, while separate, were conceded to be a part of one another. The question of what factors should determine, for purposes of Section 368(a)(1)(B), whether a given cash purchase is truly "related" to a later exchange of stock requires further consideration by the Tax Court, as does the question of the application of those factors in the present case. We therefore will remand this case to the Tax Court for further proceedings on the question raised by the taxpayers' first argument in support of their motion for summary judgment.

We view the Tax Court's options on remand as threefold. It can hold that the cash and stock transactions here in question are related as a matter of law—the position urged by the Commissioner—in which case, under our present holding, there would not be a valid (B) reorganization. On the other hand, the Tax Court may find that the transactions are as a matter of law unrelated, so that the 1970 exchange offer was simply the final, nontaxable step in a permissible creeping acquisition. Finally, the court may decide that, under the legal standard it adopts, material factual issues remain to be decided, so that a grant of summary judgment would be inappropriate at this time.[17]

---

17. We do not intend to dictate to the Tax Court what legal standard it should apply in determining whether these transactions are related. We would suggest, however, that the possibilities should include at least the following; perhaps others may be developed by counsel or by the Tax Court itself.

One possibility—advanced by the taxpayers—is that the only transactions which should be considered related, and so parts of "the acquisition," are those which are included in the formal plan of reorganization adopted by the two corporations. The virtues of this approach—simplicity and clarity—may be outweighed by the considerable scope it would grant the parties to a reorganization to control the tax treatment of their formal plan of reorganization by arbitrarily including or excluding certain transactions. A second possibility—urged by the Commissioner—is that all transactions sharing a single acquisitive purpose should be considered related for purposes of Section 368(a)(1)(B). Relying on an example given in the legislative history, see S.Rep.No.1622, 83d Cong., 2d Sess. 273, reprinted in [1954] U.S.Code Cong. & Admin.News, pp. 4621, 4911 [hereinafter cited as 1954 Senate Report], the Commissioner would require a complete and thoroughgoing separation, both in time and purpose, between cash and stock acquisitions before the latter would qualify for reorganization treatment under subsection (B).

A third possible approach, lying somewhere between the other two, would be to focus on the mutual knowledge and intent of the corporate parties, so that one party could not suffer adverse tax consequences from unilateral activities of the other of which the former had no notice. Cf. Manning, "In Pursuance of the Plan of Reorganization": The Scope of the Reorganization Provisions of the Internal Revenue Code, 72 Harv.L.Rev. 881, 912–13 (1959). Such a rule would prevent, for example, the situation where the acquiree's shareholders expect to receive favorable tax treatment on an exchange offer, only to learn

III.

A.

Having summarized in advance our holding, and its intended scope, we shall now revert to the beginning of our analysis, and, in the remainder of this opinion, describe the thinking by which we reached the result just announced. We begin with the words of the statute itself. The reorganization definitions contained in Section 368(a)(1) are precise, technical, and comprehensive. They were intended to define the exclusive means by which nontaxable corporate reorganizations could be effected. See Treas.Reg. § 1.368–1 (1960); 3 J. Mertens, The Law of Federal Income Taxation § 20.86 at 364 (1972). In examining the language of the (B) provision, we discern two possible meanings. On the one hand, the statute could be read to say that a successful reorganization occurs whenever Corporation X exchanges its own voting stock for stock in Corporation Y, and, immediately after the transaction, Corporation X controls more than 80 percent of Y's stock. On this reading, purchases of shares for which any part of the consideration takes the form of "boot" should be ignored, since the definition is only concerned with transactions which meet the statutory requirements as to consideration and control. To take an example, if Corporation X bought 50 percent of the shares of Y, and then almost immediately exchanged part of its voting stock for the remaining 50 percent of Y's stock, the question would arise whether the second transaction was a (B) reorganization. Arguably, the statute can be read to support such a finding. In the second transaction, X exchanged only stock for stock (meeting the "solely" requirement), and after the transaction was completed X owned Y (meeting the "control" requirement).

The alternative reading of the statute—the one which we are persuaded to adopt—treats the (B) definition as prescriptive, rather than merely descriptive. We read the statute to mean that the entire transaction which constitutes "the acquisition" must not contain any nonstock consideration if the transaction is to qualify as a (B) reorganization. In the example given above, where X acquired 100 percent of Y's stock, half for cash and half for voting stock, we would interpret "the acquisition" as referring to the entire transaction, so that the "solely for * * * voting stock" requirement would not be met. We believe if Congress had intended the statute to be read as merely descriptive, this intent would have been more clearly spelled out in the statutory language.

We recognize that the Tax Court adopted neither of these two readings. For reasons to be discussed in connection with the legislative history which follows, the Tax Court purported to limit its holding to cases, such as

later that an apparently valid (B) reorganization has been nullified by anonymous cash purchases on the part of the acquiring corporation. See Bruce v. Helvering, 64 App.D.C. 192, 76 F.2d 442 (D.C.Cir.1935), rev'g, 30 B.T.A. 80 (1934).

Difficulties suggest themselves with each of these rules, and without benefit of thorough briefing and argument, as well as an informed decision by the lower court, we are reluctant to proceed further in exploring this issue. We leave to the Tax Court the task of breaking ground here.

this one, where more than 80 percent of the stock of Corporation Y passes to Corporation X in exchange solely for voting stock. The Tax Court presumably would assert that the $^{50}\!/_{50}$ hypothetical posited above can be distinguished from this case, and that its holding implies no view as to the hypothetical. The plurality opinion recognized that the position it adopted creates no small problem with respect to the proper reading of "the acquisition" in the statutory definition. In order to distinguish the 80 percent case from the 50 percent case, it is necessary to read "the acquisition" as referring to at least the amount of stock constituting "control" (80 percent) where related cash purchases are present. Yet the Tax Court recognized that "the acquisition" cannot always refer to the conveyance of an 80 percent bloc of stock in one transaction, since to do so would frustrate the intent of the 1954 amendments to permit so-called "creeping acquisitions."

The Tax Court's interpretation of the statute suffers from a more fundamental defect, as well. In order to justify the limitation of its holding to transactions involving 80 percent or more of the acquiree's stock, the Tax Court focused on the passage of control as the primary requirement of the (B) provision. This focus is misplaced. Under the present version of the statute, the passage of control is entirely irrelevant; the only material requirement is that the acquiring corporation have control immediately after the acquisition. As the statute explicitly states, it does not matter if the acquiring corporation already has control before the transaction begins, so long as such control exists at the completion of the reorganization. Whatever talismanic quality may have attached to the acquisition of control under previous versions of the Code, see Part III B infra, is altogether absent from the version we must apply to this case. In our view, the statute should be read to mean that the related transactions that constitute "the acquisition," whatever percentage of stock they may represent, must meet both the "solely for voting stock" and the "control immediately after" requirements of Section 368(a)(1)(B). Neither the reading given the statute by the Tax Court, nor that proposed as the first alternative above, adequately corresponds to the careful language Congress employed in this section of the Code.

B.

The 1924 Code defined reorganization, in part, as "a merger or consolidation (including the acquisition by one corporation of at least a majority of the voting stock and at least a majority of the total number of shares of all other classes of stock of another corporation, or substantially all the properties of another corporation)." Pub.L. No. 68–176, c. 234, § 203(h)(1), 43 Stat. 257. Although the statute did not specifically limit the consideration that could be given in exchange for stock or assets, courts eventually developed the so-called "continuity of interest" doctrine, which held that exchanges that did not include some quantum of stock as consideration were ineligible for reorganization treatment for lack of a continuing property interest on the part of the acquiree's shareholders.
* * *

Despite this judicial development, sentiment was widespread in Congress that the reorganization provisions lent themselves to abuse, particularly in the form of so-called "disguised sales." In 1934, the House Ways and Means Committee proposed abolition of the stock-acquisition and asset-acquisition reorganizations which had appeared in the parenthetical section of the 1924 Act quoted above. The Senate Finance Committee countered with a proposal to retain these provisions, but with "restrictions designed to prevent tax avoidance." S.Rep. No. 558, 73d Cong., 2d Sess. 15 (1939–1 Cum.Bull. (Part 2) 586, 598).[20] One of these restrictions was the requirement that the acquiring corporation obtain at least 80 percent, rather than a bare majority, of the stock of the acquiree. The second requirement was stated in the Senate Report as follows: "the acquisition, whether of stock or of substantially all the properties, must be in exchange solely for the voting stock of the acquiring corporation." Id. at 17. The Senate amendments were enacted as Section 112(g)(1) of the Revenue Act of 1934, 48 Stat. 680, which provided in pertinent part:

> "(1) The term 'reorganization' means (A) a statutory merger or consolidation, or (B) the acquisition by one corporation in exchange solely for all or a part of its voting stock: of at least 80 per centum of the voting stock and at least 80 per centum of the total number of shares of all other classes of stock of another corporation; or of substantially all the properties of another corporation * * *."

Congress revised this definition in 1939 in response to the Supreme Court's decision in United States v. Hendler, 303 U.S. 564, 58 S.Ct. 655, 82 L.Ed. 1018 (1938), which held that an acquiring corporation's assumption of the acquiree's liabilities in an asset-acquisition was equivalent to the receipt of "boot" by the acquiree. Since virtually all asset-acquisition reorganizations necessarily involve the assumption of the acquiree's liabilities, a literal application of the "solely for * * * voting stock" requirement would have effectively abolished this form of tax-free reorganization. In the Revenue Act of 1939, Congress separated the stock-acquisition and asset-acquisition provisions in order to exempt the assumption of liabilities in the latter category of cases from the "solely for * * * voting stock" requirement. Section 112(g)(1) of the revised statute then read, in pertinent part, as follows:

> "(1) the term 'reorganization' means (A) a statutory merger or consolidation, or (B) the acquisition by one corporation, in exchange solely for all or a part of its voting stock, of at least 80 per centum of the voting stock and at least 80 per centum of the total number of shares of all other classes of stock of another corporation, or (C) the acquisition by one corporation, in exchange solely for all or a part of its voting stock, of substantially all the

---

20. The Senate's purpose in retaining these provisions was apparently to make available an alternative to statutory merger or consolidation in those states where merger statutes were overly restrictive or nonexistent. See Howard v. Commissioner, 238 F.2d 943, 946 (7th Cir.1956).

properties of another corporation, but in determining whether the exchange is solely for voting stock the assumption by the acquiring corporation of a liability of the other, or the fact that property acquired is subject to liability, shall be disregarded * * *."

The next major change in this provision occurred in 1954. In that year, the House Bill, H.R. 8300, would have drastically altered the corporate reorganization sections of the Tax Code, permitting, for example, both stock and "boot" as consideration in a corporate acquisition, with gain recognized only to the extent of the "boot." The Senate Finance Committee, in order to preserve the familiar terminology and structure of the 1939 Code, proposed a new version of Section 112(g)(1), which would retain the "solely for * * * voting stock" requirement, but alter the existing control requirement to permit so-called "creeping acquisitions." Under the Senate Bill, it would no longer be necessary for the acquiring corporation to obtain 80 percent or more of the acquiree's stock in one "reorganization." The Senate's proposal permitted an acquisition to occur in stages; a bloc of shares representing less than 80 percent could be added to earlier acquisitions, regardless of the consideration given earlier, to meet the control requirement. The Report of the Senate Finance Committee gave this example of the operation of the creeping acquisition amendment:

> "[C]orporation A purchased 30 percent of the common stock of corporation W (the only class of stock outstanding) for cash in 1939. On March 1, 1955, corporation A offers to exchange its own voting stock, for all the stock of corporation W tendered within 6 months from the date of the offer. Within the 6 months period corporation A acquires an additional 60 percent of the stock of W for its own voting stock. As a result of the 1955 transactions, corporation A will own 90 percent of all of corporation W's stock. No gain or loss is recognized with respect to the exchanges of the A stock for the W stock."

1954 Senate Report, supra, at 273. See also Treas. Reg. § 1.368–2(c) (1960).

At the same time the Senate was revising the (B) provision, (while leaving intact the "solely for * * * voting stock" requirement), it was also rewriting the (C) provision to explicitly permit up to 20 percent of the consideration in an asset acquisition to take the form of money or other nonstock property. See 26 U.S.C. § 368(a)(2)(B). The Senate revisions of subsections (B) and (C) were ultimately passed, and have remained largely unchanged since 1954. * * * Proposals for altering the (B) provision to allow "boot" as consideration have been made, but none has been enacted.

As this history shows, Congress has had conflicting aims in this complex and difficult area. On the one hand, the 1934 Act evidences a strong intention to limit the reorganization provisions to prevent forms of tax avoidance that had proliferated under the earlier revenue acts. This intention arguably has been carried forward in the current versions through retention of the "solely for * * * voting stock" requirement in (B), even while the (C) provision was being loosened. On the other hand, both the 1939 and 1954 revisions represented attempts to make the reorganization procedures more accessible and practical in both the (B) and (C) areas. In light of the conflicting purposes, we can discern no clear Congressional mandate in the present structure of the (B) provision, either in terms of the abuses sought to be remedied or the beneficial transactions sought to be facilitated. At best, we think Congress has drawn somewhat arbitrary lines separating those transactions that resemble mere changes in form of ownership and those that contain elements of a sale or purchase arrangement. In such circumstances we believe it is more appropriate to examine the specific rules and requirements Congress enacted, rather than some questionably delineated "purpose" or "policy," to determine whether a particular transaction qualifies for favorable tax treatment.

To the extent there is any indication in the legislative history of Congress' intent with respect to the meaning of "acquisition" in the (B) provision, we believe the intent plainly was to apply the "solely" requirement to all related transactions. In those statutes where Congress intended to permit cash or other property to be used as consideration, it made explicit provision therefor. See, e.g., 26 U.S.C. § 368(a)(2)(B). It is argued that in a (B) reorganization the statute can be satisfied where only 80 percent of the acquiree's stock is obtained solely for voting stock, so that additional acquisitions are irrelevant and need not be considered. In light of Congress' repeated, and increasingly sophisticated, enactments in this area, we are unpersuaded that such an important question would have been left unaddressed had Congress intended to leave open such a possibility. We are not prepared to believe that Congress intended—either when it enacted the 1934, the 1939, or the 1954 statutes—to permit a corporation to exchange stock tax-free for 80 percent of the stock of another and in a related transaction to purchase the remaining 20 percent for cash. The only question we see clearly left open by the legislative history is the degree of separation required between the two transactions before they can qualify as a creeping acquisition under the 1954 amendments. This is precisely the issue the Tax Court chose not to address, and it is the issue we now remand to the Tax Court for consideration.

C.

Besides finding support for the IRS position both in the design of the statute and in the legislative history, we find support in the regulations adopted by the Treasury Department construing these statutory provisions. We of course give weight to the statutory construction contemporaneously developed by the agency entrusted by Congress with the task of applying these laws. * * * The views of the Treasury on tax matters, while by no means definitive, undoubtedly reflect a familiarity with the intricacies of the tax code that surpasses our own. * * *

D.

Finally, we turn to the body of case law that has developed concerning (B) reorganizations to determine how previous courts have dealt with this question. Of the seven prior cases in this area, all to a greater or lesser degree support the result we have reached, and none supports the result reached by the Tax Court. We recognize that the Tax Court purported to distinguish these precedents from the case before it, and that reasonable persons may differ on the extent to which some of these cases directly control the question raised here. Nevertheless, after carefully reviewing the precedents, we are satisfied that the decision of the Tax Court represents a sharp break with the previous judicial constructions of this statute, and a departure from the usual rule of stare decisis, which applies with special force in the tax field where uncertainty and variety are ordinarily to be avoided. * * *

IV.

We have stated our ruling, and the reasons that support it. In conclusion, we would like to respond briefly to the arguments raised by the Tax Court, the District Court of Delaware, and the taxpayers in this case against the rule we have reaffirmed today. The principal argument, repeated again and again, concerns the supposed lack of policy behind the rule forbidding cash in a (B) reorganization where the control requirement is met solely for voting stock. It is true that the Service has not pointed to tax loopholes that would be opened were the rule to be relaxed as appellees request. We also recognize, as the Tax Court and others have highlighted, that the rule may produce results which some would view as anomalous. For example, if Corporation X acquires 80 percent of Corporation Y's stock solely for voting stock, and is content to leave the remaining 20 percent outstanding, no one would question that a valid (B) reorganization has taken place. If Corporation X then decides to purchase stock from the remaining shareholders, the *Howard* rule might result in loss of nontaxable treatment for the stock acquisition if the two transactions were found to be related. The Tax Court asserted that there is no conceivable Congressional policy that would justify such a result. Further, it argued, Congress could not have felt that prior cash purchases would forever ban a later successful (B) reorganization since the 1954 amendments, as the legislative history makes clear, specifically provided that prior cash purchases would not prevent a creeping acquisition.

While not without force, this line of argument does not in the end persuade us. First of all, as already discussed, the language of the statute, and the longstanding interpretation given it by the courts, are persuasive reasons for our holding even in the absence of any clear policy behind Congress' expression of its will. Furthermore, we perceive statutory anomalies of another sort which the Tax Court's rule would only magnify. It is clear from the regulations, for example, that a corporation which already owned as much as 80 percent of another's stock, acquired solely for cash, could in some circumstances acquire all or a part of the remainder solely for voting stock as a valid (B) reorganization. Why, then, could not as little as 10 percent of an acquisition constitute a (B) reorganization, if made solely for voting stock, even though the remaining transactions—totaling more than 80 percent—were made for nonstock consideration? If it is true that Congress did not view related cash transactions as tainting a stock-acquisition reorganization, why would it enact a "solely for * * * voting stock" requirement at all, except to the extent necessary to prevent mixed consideration of the sort employed in the "disguised sales" of the twenties?

Possibly, Congress' insertion of the "solely for * * * voting stock" requirement into the 1934 Act was, as one commentator has suggested, an overreaction to a problem which could have been dealt with through more precise and discriminating measures. But we do not think it appropriate for a court to tell Congress how to do its job in an area such as this. If a more refined statutory scheme would be appropriate, such changes should be sought from the body empowered to make them. While we adhere to the general practice of construing statutes so as to further their demonstrated policies, we have no license to rework whole statutory schemes in pursuit of policy goals which Congress has nowhere articulated. Appellees have not shown us any reason to believe that reaffirmation of the settled rule in this area will frustrate the Congressional purpose of making the (B) reorganization provision generally available to those who comply with the statutory requirements.[40]

A second major argument, advanced primarily by the district court in *Pierson,* is that the previous cases construing this statute are suspect because they did not give proper weight to the changes wrought by the 1954 amendments. In particular, the court argued the liberalization of the "boot" allowance in (C) reorganizations and the allowance of creeping (B) acquisitions showed that Congress had no intent or desire to forbid "boot" of up to 20 percent in a (B) reorganization. As we have discussed earlier, we draw the opposite conclusion from the legislative history. Liberalization of the (C) provision shows only that Congress, when it wished to do so, could grant explicit leeway in the reorganization rules. Nor do the creeping acquisition rules mark such a departure from a strict reading of the "solely" requirement as to persuade us that Congress intended to weaken it with respect to related transactions. One has only to look at the illustration given in the legislative history, with its separation of 16 years between the cash and stock transactions, to see that Congress did not indicate positive approval of the type of acquisition covered by the district court's holding.[41]

A third argument asserts that reliance on the literal language of the 1954 Code, and in particular a focus on the interpretation of "acquisition," is unjustified because the 1954 Code was not intended to alter the status of

---

40. We do not see how the argument that cash purchases are necessary to buy out the interests of "dissenting shareholders" who decline to take part in the exchange advances taxpayers' cause. One of the purposes of stock-acquisition arrangements, as opposed to statutory mergers, is to provide the option to minority shareholders not to take part. In this case, had such protection not been afforded, the Connecticut Insurance Commissioner evidently would not have approved the acquisition.

41. We also see little merit in the argument that the IRS policy of granting minor deviations from the "solely for * * * voting stock" requirement for such practical purposes as allowing the acquiring corporation to pay transaction costs undermines the strict reading the IRS urges in this case. See Pierson, 472 F.Supp. at 972 n. 51. The same is true of revenue rulings permitting purchases of stock indirectly from the acquired corporation itself.

(B) reorganizations under the 1934 and 1939 Codes. According to this argument, the acquisition of at least 80 percent of the acquiree's stock solely for voting stock was allowed under the pre–1954 version, and must still be allowed even though the present statute refers only to "the acquisition * * * of stock" with no percentage specified. This argument assumes the answer to the question that is asked. As *Howard* and *Southwest Consolidated* illustrate, it has been the undeviating understanding of courts, until now, that the pre–1954 statutes did not allow cash or other "boot" in a (B) reorganization. It cannot be inferred that Congress left intact a rule which never existed by enacting language inconsistent with such a rule.

Finally, we see no merit at all in the suggestion that we should permit "boot" in a (B) reorganization simply because "boot" is permitted in some instances in (A) and (C) reorganizations. Congress has never indicated that these three distinct categories of transactions are to be interpreted in pari materia. In fact, striking differences in the treatment of the three subsections have been evident in the history of the reorganization statutes. We see no reason to believe a difference in the treatment of "boot" in these transactions is impermissible or irrational.

Accordingly, we vacate the judgment of the Tax Court insofar as it rests on a holding that taxpayers were entitled to summary judgment irrespective of whether the cash purchases in this case were related by purpose or timing to the stock exchange offer of 1970. The case will be remanded to the Tax Court for further proceedings consistent with this opinion.

Vacated and remanded.

[Editor's Note. If the ITT–Hartford litigation had continued, the Tax Court would have been required to resolve the factual question of whether the earlier cash purchases of Hartford stock were "old and cold"—i.e., unrelated to the subsequent stock-for-stock exchange—and, if not, whether the sale to Mediobanca was sufficient to cleanse the transaction. The Tax Court never had that opportunity, however, because the controversy was settled when ITT agreed to pay $18.5 million. The IRS, in turn, agreed not to pursue claims against Hartford shareholders, who were allowed to treat the transaction as a tax-free exchange if they did not claim a stepped-up basis when reporting their gain or loss on a subsequent sale of the ITT stock.

The settlement relieved ITT, which had agreed to reimburse Hartford shareholders for any tax liability resulting from the transaction, of an estimated liability of $100 million. Query, is ITT's $18.5 million payment on behalf of the former Hartford shareholders deductible by the company and taxable to the shareholders? These thorny questions were resolved as part of the settlement. ITT agreed not to claim any deduction and the IRS agreed that Hartford shareholders would not be deemed to receive additional income as a result of Hartford's payment. I.R. 81–53, (1981), reprinted in P–H Fed.Taxes ¶ 60,299.5 (May 14, 1981).]

Revenue Ruling 67–274

1967–2 Cum.Bull. 141.

Advice has been requested whether the transaction described below qualifies as a reorganization within the meaning of section 368(a)(1)(B) of the Internal Revenue Code of 1954.

Pursuant to a plan of reorganization, corporation Y acquired all of the outstanding stock of corporation X from the X shareholders in exchange solely for voting stock of Y. Thereafter X was completely liquidated as part of the same plan and all of its assets were transferred to Y which assumed all of the liabilities of X. Y continued to conduct the business previously conducted by X. The former shareholders of X continued to hold 16 percent of the fair market value of all the outstanding stock of Y.

Section 368(a)(1)(B) of the Code provides in part that a reorganization is the acquisition by one corporation, in exchange solely for all or a part of its voting stock, of stock of another corporation if, immediately after the acquisition, the acquiring corporation has control (as defined in section 368(c) of the Code) of such other corporation. Section 368(a)(1)(C) of the Code provides in part that a reorganization is the acquisition by one corporation, in exchange solely for all or a part of its voting stock, of substantially all of the properties of another corporation, but in determining whether the exchange is solely for stock the assumption by the acquiring corporation of a liability of the other, or the fact that property acquired is subject to a liability, is disregarded.

Under the circumstances of this case the acquisition of X stock by Y and the liquidation of X by Y are part of the overall plan of reorganization and the two steps may not be considered independently of each other for Federal income tax purposes. See Revenue Ruling 54–96, C.B. 1954–1, 111, as modified by Revenue Ruling 56–100, C.B. 1956–1, 624. The substance of the transaction is an acquisition of assets to which section 368(a)(1)(B) of the Code does not apply.

Accordingly, the acquisition by Y of the outstanding stock of X will not constitute a reorganization within the meaning of section 368(a)(1)(B) of the Code but will be considered an acquisition of the assets of X which in this case is a reorganization described in section 368(a)(1)(C) of the Code. * * *.

Revenue Ruling 55–440

1955–2 Cum.Bull. 226.

Advice has been requested with respect to the tax consequences of a reorganization under the following circumstances.

Pursuant to a plan of reorganization, the X corporation acquired not less than 80 percent of the outstanding common stock of the Y corporation in exchange solely for voting common stock of X. The offer of exchange by

X corporation was contingent upon its acceptance by the holders of at least 80 percent of the outstanding common stock of Y corporation.

Y corporation also has voting preferred stock outstanding. The certificate of incorporation provides, in part, that the preferred stock may be called at a specified price per share, plus accrued dividends, on any dividend date upon 30 days' notice to the stockholders of Y's intention to redeem the stock. Prior to the effective date of the exchange, the board of directors of Y resolved to call the preferred stock and the 30 days' notices of the call were mailed to the holders of the preferred stock. The redemption price of all the outstanding preferred stock was deposited with a bank as escrow agent.

After the exchange of common stock was consummated upon the tender of at least 80 percent of the common stock of Y corporation, all of the preferred stock of Y had been previously called, but there were certain shares of the preferred stock which had not been presented for redemption prior to the effective date of the exchange.

Section 368 of the Internal Revenue Code of 1954 provides, in part, as follows:

(a) REORGANIZATION.

(1) IN GENERAL. * * * the term "reorganization" means

* * *

(B) the acquisition by one corporation, in exchange solely for all or a part of its voting stock, of stock of another corporation if, immediately after the acquisition, the acquiring corporation has control of such other corporation (whether or not such acquiring corporation had control immediately before the acquisition);

* * *

(c) CONTROL. * * * the term "control" means the ownership of stock possessing at least 80 percent of the total combined voting power of all classes of stock entitled to vote and at least 80 percent of the total number of shares of all other classes of stock of the corporation.

The question at issue is whether preferred shares previously called for redemption but not yet surrendered at the effective date of the exchange would be considered to be "stock" within the meaning of section 368(c) of the Code for the purpose of determining whether the X corporation was in control of Y corporation after the exchange of common stock within the meaning of section 368(a)(1)(B) of the Code.

Under the terms of the preferred stock indenture pursuant to the certificate of incorporation, the Y corporation may call for redemption on any dividend date upon 30 days' notice to its stockholders to redeem such stock. Therefore, the rights as preferred stockholders terminated upon the call of the preferred shares. Thereafter, the holders of such shares had only the right to receive the call price upon the surrender of the shares for redemption, there being no issue regarding the rights of creditors. For the purpose of determining control under section 368(c), preferred shares which have been called but not yet presented for redemption will be disregarded.

In view of the foregoing, the acquisition by X corporation in exchange solely for shares of its voting common stock of at least 80 percent of the outstanding common stock of Y corporation constitutes a reorganization within the meaning of section 368(a)(1)(B) of the Code, regardless of the number of shares of preferred stock of Y corporation which, at the time of the consummation of the exchange, had not been presented for redemption. Accordingly, no gain or loss is recognizable to the common stockholders of Y as a result of the exchange of their common stock of Y for common stock of X. The basis in their hands of the common stock of X received upon the exchange is the same as the basis of the common stock of Y exchanged therefor.

NOTE

Solely for Voting Stock Requirement. Before the lower court opinions in the ITT litigation, the courts had uniformly held that "voting stock" was the only permissible consideration in a B reorganization. A divided Tax Court boldly broke with tradition when it held that ITT's acquisition of Hartford qualified as a B reorganization despite ITT's prior cash purchase of 8 percent of the Hartford stock in a "related" transaction. The appellate decisions in *Chapman* and Heverly v. Commissioner[1] restored the status quo: there could be "no boot in a B." But the nagging policy question remains: why should the requirements for a stock-for-stock acquisition be so strict when the acquiring corporation in other types of acquisitive reorganization has the leeway to use from 20 to 50 percent nonequity consideration?

The rigid requirements for a B reorganization have placed considerable pressure on the definition of "voting stock." Although the term is not specifically defined in the Code, "voting stock" has been interpreted to require an unconditional right to vote on regular corporate decisions (election of directors, shareholder proposals, etc.) and not merely extraordinary events such as mergers or liquidations.[2] The class of stock transferred is immaterial provided that it has voting rights. Although the Supreme Court has long held that hybrid equity securities, such as warrants to purchase additional voting stock, do not constitute voting stock, contractual rights to receive additional voting stock may qualify.[3]

The Service has allowed the parties to a B reorganization some flexibility despite the stringency of the voting stock requirement. For example, the "solely" requirement is not violated if the acquiring corpora-

---

1. 621 F.2d 1227 (3d Cir.1980).

2. Cf. Reg. § 1.302–3(a).

3. Helvering v. Southwest Consolidated Corp., 315 U.S. 194, 62 S.Ct. 546 (1942); Rev. Rul. 66–112, 1966–1 C.B. 68.

tion issues cash in lieu of fractional shares.[4] The acquiring corporation also may pay the target corporation's expenses (e.g., registration fees, legal and accounting fees and other administrative costs) related to the reorganization, but payment of legal, accounting or other expenses of the target's shareholders will constitute forbidden boot.[5] Certain preferred stock with debt-like characteristics, labelled by Section 351(g) as "nonqualified preferred stock,"[6] is treated as boot for gain recognition purposes but remains "stock" for all other purposes until the regulations are modified and provide to the contrary. Thus, the receipt by target shareholders of nonqualified preferred stock with voting rights (an unlikely occurrence) should not disqualify a transaction as a Type B reorganization, but T shareholders would recognize realized gain to the extent of the value of any nonqualified preferred stock received in exchange for their T stock.[7]

Buying Out Dissenting Shareholders. A particular challenge in planning a B reorganization involves shareholders of the target who insist on receiving cash. If the acquiring corporation pays cash directly to these dissenters, the transaction will violate the solely for voting stock requirement and all the target's shareholders must recognize gain. But the Service permits the target to redeem the shares of dissenters prior to a valid B reorganization provided that the cash does not emanate from the acquiring corporation and continuity of interest requirements are satisfied.[8] Another possible approach might be for the transaction to proceed as a stock-for-stock exchange, followed by a later redemption of the acquiring corporation stock held by the dissenters.[9] If they were truly dissenters, however, one would assume they would have sought some assurance, albeit informal, that the later redemption would occur. In that event, the redemption likely would be part of the original reorganization plan and, if so, the entire transaction would fail.

Creeping Acquisitions. The acquiring corporation is not required to *acquire* "control" of T in a Type B reorganization. It simply must emerge from the reorganization with control, as measured by the 80 percent benchmarks in Section 368(c). It thus is possible for a Type B reorganization to be the culmination of a series of acquisitions of T stock provided, of course, that only voting stock is used as consideration and any earlier acquisitions of T stock for cash, notes or other consideration were "old and cold"—i.e., unrelated to the final stock-for-stock exchange. Whether or not an earlier cash acquisition is unrelated is essentially a factual "step transaction" question. The regulations assume that acquisitions are related if they occur over a short time span (e.g., 12 months) but not if they are separated by very long interval (e.g., 16 years).[10] This leaves a vast middle ground of uncertainty.

4. Mills v. Commissioner, 39 T.C. 393 (1962), affirmed on other grounds, 331 F.2d 321 (5th Cir.1964); Rev.Rul. 66–365, 1966–2 C.B. 116.

5. Rev.Rul. 73–54, 1973–1 C.B. 187.

6. See Chapter 2B3, supra.

7. I.R.C. § 356(e).

8. Rev.Rul. 55–440, p. 449, infra. See also Rev.Rul. 68–285, 1968–1 C.B. 147.

9. See Rev.Rul. 56–345, 1956–2 C.B. 206; Rev.Rul. 57–114, 1957–1 C.B. 122.

10. Reg. § 1.368–2(c).

Contingent Payments and Escrowed Stock Arrangements. During the negotiations over an acquisitive reorganization, the parties may disagree over the price to be paid for the target corporation. The acquiring corporation may contend that the target's earnings are unpredictable or that the value of the business is clouded by contingent liabilities. The target may counter by producing optimistic earnings projections. A common method of breaking this type of stalemate is through a contingent consideration agreement. The acquiring corporation may issue a specified amount of stock or securities and agree to issue additional shares under specified contingencies. For example, additional shares may be issued to the former target shareholders if the earnings of the target attain certain levels during a specified time period after the acquisition.

There are a variety of methods to handle the payment of contingent consideration. The parties simply may agree that additional shares will be issued on the happening of specified events. The acquiring corporation may issue negotiable certificates of contingent interest. Or the parties may take the formal step of transferring the additional shares to an escrow agent with instructions to issue the shares if certain future events occur.

At one time, the Service contended that contingent rights to acquire additional stock violated the "solely for voting stock" requirement for a Type B (and Type C) reorganization. This position was not sustained by the courts, however, and the Service now concedes that contingent consideration will not disqualify an acquisitive reorganization if certain conditions are met.[11] The Service has issued guidelines for approval of contingent and escrowed stock arrangements. The more important requirements for contingent consideration agreements are:[12] (1) to ensure compliance with the continuity of interest doctrine, only additional stock can be received; (2) the acquiring corporation must issue the stock within five years after the reorganization; (3) the arrangement must be based on a valid business reason, such as a valuation dispute; (4) there is a maximum number of contingent shares that can be issued; (5) at least 50 percent of the maximum number of shares of each class of stock must be issued in the initial distribution; (6) the contingent rights may be neither assignable nor readily marketable; and (7) the events triggering the issuance of additional stock are not within the control of the shareholders. Similar requirements are imposed where the acquiring corporation goes beyond merely promising to issue more stock and actually places the shares in escrow with an independent agent. In addition, escrowed stock must be shown as issued and outstanding on the acquiring corporation's financial statements, and the target shareholders must be entitled to any dividends paid on the stock

---

11. See, e.g., Hamrick v. Commissioner, 43 T.C. 21 (1964), acq.; Carlberg v. United States, 281 F.2d 507 (8th Cir.1960). The Service now agrees that contingent consideration is not boot but only if the contingent rights to additional shares are not negotiable. See Rev.Rul. 66–112, 1966–1 C.B. 68.

12. See Rev.Proc. 77–37, 1977–2 C.B. 568, amplified by Rev.Proc. 84–42, 1984–1 C.B. 521.

and voting rights if, as is required in a Type B reorganization, the escrowed stock has voting rights.[13]

PROBLEMS

1. Acquiring Corporation ("P") wishes to acquire Target Corporation ("T"). Prior to the proposed acquisition, P has 1,000 shares of voting common stock outstanding with a value of $100 per share. Consider whether the following transactions qualify as Type B reorganizations:

    (a) In exchange for their T stock, T shareholders receive 100 shares of newly issued P voting preferred stock with a value of $1,000 per share. Each share of the preferred stock has the same voting rights per share as each share of P common stock.

    (b) Same as (a), above, except that P transfers 85 shares of newly issued P voting common stock worth $85,000 and warrants worth $15,000 to acquire P voting common stock.

    (c) T shareholders receive P voting common stock with the same terms as the existing shares outstanding except that shareholders entitled to fractional shares receive a cash payment in lieu of those shares.

    (d) Same as (c), above, except that P also pays T's legal, accounting and SEC registration expenses incurred in connection with the reorganization.

    (e) Same as (c), above, except that P also pays the attorneys' fees incurred by T's majority shareholders for legal and tax advice relating to the transaction.

2. Assume the same basic facts as in Problem 1, above, except that Dee Minimis, a 5% minority shareholder, does not wish to participate in the transaction and is unwilling to become a shareholder of P.

    (a) Can P just disregard Dee and simply deal with T's other shareholders?

    (b) What result if T redeemed Dee's stock prior to the transaction between P and the remaining T shareholders? Would it matter if the cash used by T to redeem Dee's stock was borrowed from P?

    (c) What result if Dee participates in the transaction and a month later, pursuant to an oral understanding, P redeems Dee's newly acquired P shares?

    (d) What result if the majority shareholders of T buy out Dee's interest and then proceed to engage in a stock-for-stock exchange with P?

3. In the same type of transaction described in the problems above, what are the consequences to the shareholders of Target Corporation in the following alternative situations:

13. Rev.Proc. 84–42, supra note 12.

(a) Acquiring Corporation ("P") acquired 30% of the stock of Target Corporation ("T") for cash five years ago. It acquires the remaining 70% from T's shareholders in a single transaction in return for newly issued voting common stock of P.

(b) P acquired 85% of the stock of T in a cash tender offer a year ago, and it acquires the remaining 15% from T shareholders in a single transaction in return for newly issued voting common stock of P.

(c) Same as (a), above (i.e., P already owned 30% of the T stock), except that P acquires the remaining 70% at two different times: 40% in year one and 30% in year two.

(d) Same as (c), above, except that the 40% is acquired for cash.

(e) P, with the hope of ultimately acquiring 100% of T, acquired 10% of the T stock from one shareholder for cash one year ago. Six months ago, P sold the 10% interest to Friendly National Bank, with whom it enjoyed friendly relations. It then acquired 100% of the T stock in a single transaction solely in exchange for newly issued P voting stock.

3.   TYPE C: ACQUISITIONS OF ASSETS FOR VOTING STOCK

Code: § 368(a)(1)(C), (a)(2)(B), (a)(2)(G); Skim §§ 336(c); 354(a); 356(a); 357; 358(a); 361; 362(b); 368(a)(2)(C), (b); 381(a)(2); 1032(a).

Regulations: § 1.368–2(d).

General Requirements. Type C reorganizations are known as "practical mergers" because their end result is generally the same as a merger. The only difference may be the form of the transaction under local corporate law. In a statutory merger, all the assets and liabilities of the target are absorbed by the acquiring corporation automatically, while an asset acquisition technically requires a "transfer" of assets and liabilities under a negotiated agreement and does not necessarily require the target to sell all of its assets or to liquidate.[1]

Despite their similarities in form, it is far more difficult to qualify as a Type C stock-for-assets exchange than as a Type A statutory merger because of the more stringent consideration requirements. Section 368(a)(1)(C) requires the target to transfer "substantially all" of its properties *solely* in exchange for voting stock of the acquiring corporation. Although "voting stock" has the same meaning for both B and C reorganizations, the term "solely" in Section 368(a)(1)(C) is subject to two important exceptions. First, the assumption of liabilities by the acquiring corporation (or the taking of property subject to liabilities) is not treated as disqualifying boot.[2] Second, a "boot relaxation rule" permits the acquiring corporation to use up to 20 percent boot, but for this purpose the trans-

---

1. See, e.g., Cal.Corp.Code § 1100; Del. Code Ann. title 8, § 251 (1979). A liquidation of the target is required in a Type C reorganization, however, unless the Commissioner waives the requirement. I.R.C. § 368(a)(2)(G)(ii).

2. I.R.C. § 368(a)(1)(C).

ferred liabilities are considered as cash consideration.[3] A transaction thus can qualify as a Type C reorganization when the consideration consists of a substantial amount of debt relief as long as no other boot is used and sufficient voting stock is transferred to maintain continuity of interest. But a combination of debt relief and other boot likely will spell doom for the transaction.

To illustrate the operation of these rules, assume that Target ("T") has gross assets of $120,000 and liabilities of $30,000. Acquiring Corporation ("A") proposes to acquire all of T's assets in exchange for the assumption of $30,000 of liabilities and $90,000 of A voting stock. The transaction qualifies as a C reorganization because the liabilities are not treated as boot. But if A assumes the $30,000 of liabilities and transfers $80,000 of voting stock and $10,000 of cash, the transaction does not qualify. The liabilities are treated as "money paid" for purposes of the boot relaxation rule, and thus A has acquired only 66⅔ percent of the $120,000 gross assets of T for voting stock. On these facts, A must use at least $96,000 of voting stock (80 percent of $120,000) in order for the transaction to qualify as a Type C reorganization under the boot relaxation rule. This example illustrates that in the normal situation where T's liabilities exceed 20 percent of the value of its gross assets, no boot may be used.

Substantially All of the Properties. The target also must transfer "substantially all" of its properties. The Service's longstanding administrative benchmark requires a transfer of "assets representing at least 90 percent of the fair market value of the net assets and at least 70 percent of the fair market value of the gross assets held by the target corporation immediately preceding the transfer."[4] These guidelines further provide that "all payments to dissenters and all redemptions and distributions (except for regular, normal distributions) made by the corporation immediately preceding the transfer and which are part of the plan of reorganization will be considered as assets held by the corporation immediately prior to the transfer."[5] Other authorities are not as stringent in defining "substantially all," and it is possible that a complete transfer of *operating* assets may qualify even if the Service's percentage tests are not met.[6] Moreover, the Service has ruled that the "substantially all" test is met when the target corporation sells 50 percent of its historic assets to unrelated parties for cash and then transfers all of its assets, including the sales proceeds, to the acquiring corporation.[7] The key to this favorable ruling is that the overall transaction is not "divisive" because the cash proceeds from the asset sale were not retained by the target or its shareholders.

Liquidation Requirement. Prior to 1984, the target corporation in a C reorganization was not required to distribute its assets (which ordinarily will consist primarily of voting stock of the acquiring corporation) in

3. I.R.C. § 368(a)(2)(B).

4. Rev.Proc. 77–37, § 3.01 1977–2 C.B. 568, 569.

5. Id.

6. See, e.g., Rev.Rul. 57–518, 1957–2 C.B. 253; Commissioner v. First National Bank of Altoona, 104 F.2d 865 (3d Cir.1939) (86% of net worth is "substantially all").

7. Rev. Rul. 88–48, 1988–1 C.B. 117.

complete liquidation. Some targets chose to stay alive as a holding company with a fresh set of tax attributes.[8] Others opted to distribute the voting stock acquired in the reorganization while retaining other assets that might trigger adverse tax consequences (e.g., a dividend) if distributed to the shareholders.[9] To prevent these and other perceived abuses, Congress added a new rule requiring the target to distribute all of its assets pursuant to the plan of reorganization unless the Service, pursuant to regulations that it has yet to issue, agrees to waive the distribution requirement.[10] In the event of a waiver, however, the legislative history states that the retained assets must be treated as if they had been distributed to the T shareholders and recontributed to the capital of a new corporation.[11]

Creeping Acquisitions. A final issue is the treatment of a transaction where the acquiring corporation has previously purchased some stock of the target and now seeks to assume complete control by acquiring all of T's assets through a liquidation of T. We have seen that a creeping acquisition will not necessarily poison the final stock-for-stock exchange in a B reorganization, at least if the stock previously acquired for cash is "old and cold"—i.e., acquired in an unrelated transaction. For many years, creeping C reorganizations were impeded by the Service's wooden interpretation of the "solely for voting stock" requirement.[12] This longstanding position has been reversed by regulations providing that P's prior ownership of a portion of T stock will not by itself prevent the "solely for voting stock" requirement from being met.[13] The Service finally came to its senses and concluded that a transaction in which P converts an indirect interest in T's assets to a direct interest in those assets does not necessarily resemble a taxable sale by T of those properties.

To enforce the statutory continuity of interest rules, the regulations provide that where the Section 368(a)(2)(B) boot relaxation rule applies to the final step of a creeping Type C reorganization, the sum of: (1) the money or other boot distributed to T shareholders other than P and to T's creditors, and (2) the liabilities of T assumed by P, may not exceed 20 percent of the value of all of T's properties.[14] But if P acquires T stock from a shareholder of T or T itself for cash or boot as part of the acquisition,

---

8. The tax attributes (e.g., earnings and profits) of the target automatically pass to the acquiring corporation on a Type C reorganization. I.R.C. § 381(a)(2).

9. See Rev.Rul. 73–552, 1973–2 C.B. 116.

10. I.R.C. § 368(a)(2)(G). See Rev.Proc. 89–50, 1989–2 C.B. 631, for representations which ordinarily must be included in a request for the Service to waive the liquidation requirement.

11. H.R.Rep. No. 98–861, 98th Cong., 2d Sess. 846 (1984).

12. Rev. Rul. 54–396, 1954–2 C.B. 147 (P, which owned 79 percent of S as result of prior unrelated cash purchase, acquired T's assets in exchange for P voting stock, after which T liquidated and distributed P stock to minority shareholders. The transaction was ruled not to qualify as a Type C reorganization because P acquired only 21 percent of T's assets for voting stock and the remaining 79 percent as a liquidating distribution in exchange for previously held T stock). The Service's position was sustained in Bausch & Lomb Optical Co. v. Commissioner, 267 F.2d 75 (2d Cir.1959).

13. Reg. § 1.368–2(d)(4)(i).

14. Id.

such consideration is counted as boot in applying the boot relaxation rule.[15] To illustrate, assume that in an unrelated transaction P acquired 60 percent of the stock of T for cash. T's assets have a value of $110, and it has $10 of liabilities. Assume T transfers all its assets to P and, in exchange, P assumes the liabilities and transfers to T $30 of P voting stock and $10 of cash, and then T distributes the P voting stock and cash to its shareholders (other than P) and liquidates. This transaction will qualify as a Type C reorganization because the sum of cash paid and liabilities assumed ($20) does not exceed 20 percent of the value of T's assets.[16] If, however, P's cash acquisition of 60 percent of T was not "old and cold"— i.e., was related to the subsequent asset acquisition—the transaction would not qualify as tax-free because only 30 percent of the consideration used by P was voting stock.[17]

PROBLEMS

1. Assuming the judicial requirements are met, determine whether the following transactions qualify as a Type C reorganization:

(a) Target Corporation ("T") has $70,000 of operating assets and $30,000 of cash and securities held as an investment. Acquiring Corporation ("P") issues its voting stock worth $70,000 in exchange for the operating assets and T liquidates, distributing the P stock and its cash and investment securities to its shareholders.

(b) Same as (a), above, except that P acquires $40,000 of operating assets and $30,000 of cash and investment securities in exchange for the P voting stock. T then liquidates, distributing $70,000 of P stock and $30,000 of operating assets to its shareholders.

(c) Same as (a), above, except that T has $100,000 of operating assets and $30,000 of liabilities. P issues $70,000 of its voting stock in exchange for T's assets and liabilities, and T liquidates, distributing the P stock to its shareholders.

(d) Same as (c), above, except that P issues $60,000 of its voting stock and $10,000 cash in exchange for all of T's assets and liabilities, and T liquidates, distributing the P stock and cash to its shareholders.

2. Determine whether the transactions below will qualify as tax-free reorganizations:

(a) Target Corporation ("T") owns $70,000 of operating assets and $30,000 cash and investment securities. T redeems 30% of its stock, distributing the cash and investment securities. Acquiring Corporation ("P") issues $70,000 worth of its voting stock to the remaining T shareholders in exchange for their T stock. P then liquidates T.

---

15. Id.

16. Reg. § 1.368–2(d)(4)(ii) Example 1.

17. Reg. § 1.368–2(d)(4)(ii) Example 2.

(b) Same as (a), above, except that T redeems the 30% shareholders by distributing operating assets rather than cash and investment securities.

(c) P has held 30% of T's stock for several years. P exchanges its voting stock for the remaining 70% of T stock. P then liquidates T.

4.   TRIANGULAR REORGANIZATIONS*

Code: § 368(a)(1)(B) (first parenthetical) and (C) (first parenthetical), (a)(2)(C), (D) and (E), (b).

Regulations: § 1.368–2(b)(2), (f), (j)(1), (3)–(6).

Background. The three basic types of reorganizations offer limited flexibility if the acquiring corporation desires to operate the target as a wholly owned subsidiary. Assume, for example, that P, Inc. wishes to acquire T, Inc. and keep T's business in a separate corporation for nontax reasons. Although this objective could be met by a Type B reorganization, the stringent "solely for voting stock" requirement might be an insurmountable obstacle if P desired to use nonvoting stock as consideration or if a large number of T shareholders were unwilling to accept any class of P stock. Even the flexible A reorganization may not be feasible from a nontax standpoint. P may not wish to incur the risk of T's unknown or contingent liabilities which would remain P's responsibility even if T's assets were dropped down to a subsidiary. P also may be reluctant to bear the expense and delay of seeking formal approval of its shareholders or unwilling to provide T shareholders with the appraisal rights to which they would be entitled under state law on a direct merger.

To maneuver around these problems, corporate lawyers developed other acquisition methods involving the use of a subsidiary. One approach is for P to acquire T's assets in a qualifying Type A or C reorganization and immediately drop down the acquired assets to a newly created subsidiary. This technique does not solve the hidden liability problem, however, and it may not obviate the need for shareholder approval and appraisal rights.[1] An alternative is for P to transfer its stock to a new subsidiary ("S"), and then cause T to merge directly into S, with the T shareholders receiving P stock and, perhaps, other consideration in exchange for their T stock. Or P could form S and have S acquire substantially all of the assets of T in exchange for P voting stock.

The tax consequences of these and other triangular acquisition techniques have been a major subplot within the reorganization drama. In two early cases, the Supreme Court constructed several large roadblocks by holding that transactions similar to those described above failed to satisfy

---

* See generally Ferguson & Ginsburg, "Triangular Reorganizations," 28 Tax L.Rev. 159 (1973).

1. "Drop downs" also are inconvenient because they usually require an inordinate amount of paperwork (e.g., deeds and other documents of transfer, with accompanying recording fees and transfer taxes) as the assets pass from the parent to the subsidiary.

the continuity of interest doctrine if: (1) T merges into S but T shareholders receive P stock in a triangular reorganization, or (2) P makes the acquisition using P stock but drops T or its assets down to a subsidiary.[2]

Over the years, Congress gradually came to recognize that there was no reason to deny tax-free status to "drop downs" or triangular reorganizations that were economically equivalent to the simpler acquisition methods authorized by Section 368. In the 1954 Code, it added Section 368(a)(2)(C), which provides that an otherwise qualifying Type A or C reorganization will not lose its tax-free status merely because the acquiring corporation drops down the acquired assets to a subsidiary and it later added a similar rule for Type B reorganizations. Congress also permitted the acquiring corporation in a B or C reorganization to use voting stock of its parent to make the acquisition. For both drop downs and triangular reorganizations, Section 368(b) now makes it clear that the controlling parent will be a "party" to the reorganization. But the Service persisted in ruling that a merger of the target into a controlled subsidiary of the acquiring corporation was not tax-free when the target shareholders received stock of the parent because the parent was not a "party" to the reorganization and the T shareholder lacked continuity of interest.[3] Once again, Congress responded by adding two new categories of tax-free reorganizations: the Section 368(a)(2)(D) forward triangular merger and the Section 368(a)(2)(E) reverse triangular merger.

Forward Triangular Mergers: Section 368(a)(2)(D). From the time it was authorized as a tax-free reorganization in 1969, the forward triangular merger has become one of the most widely used acquisition techniques. Section 368(a)(2)(D) permits S to acquire T in a statutory merger, using P stock as consideration, provided that: (1) S acquires "substantially all" of the properties of T; (2) no stock of S is used in the transaction; and (3) the transaction would have qualified as a Type A reorganization if T had merged directly into P. In typically perverse fashion, Congress—without expressly articulating its rationale—reached into its bag of requirements and borrowed one from the Type C model ("substantially all of the properties") and another from the Type A model (the tests for permissible consideration). Although the legislative history is obscure, it is now clear that the "could have merged with parent" test merely requires the transaction to pass muster under the continuity of interest doctrine.[4] As a result, T shareholders only must receive at least 50 percent P stock (voting or nonvoting) under the Service's continuity guidelines, allowing the parties the freedom to use up to 50 percent cash and other nonequity consideration. Of course, the T shareholders who receive boot must recognize their

---

2. Groman v. Commissioner, 302 U.S. 82, 58 S.Ct. 108 (1937); Helvering v. Bashford, 302 U.S. 454, 58 S.Ct. 307 (1938). These cases also suggested that in no event could the T shareholders receive stock in both S and P because the receipt of stock in two separate corporations violated continuity of interest requirements.

3. Rev.Rul. 67–448, 1967–2 C.B. 144.

4. Reg. § 1.368–2(b)(2).

realized gain to that extent, but those who receive solely stock will enjoy nonrecognition if the overall transaction qualifies under these liberal standards.

Reverse Triangular Mergers: Section 368(a)(2)(E). Before examining the tax consequences of a reverse triangular merger, the transaction itself must be explained. Suppose P desires to acquire the stock of T in a tax-free reorganization and keep T alive as a subsidiary, but P is unable (or unwilling) to structure the deal as a Type B reorganization because of the "solely for voting stock" requirement. Neither a merger nor an asset acquisition is feasible because T, as a corporate entity, has a number of intangible assets (e.g., grandfather rights under state law; franchises or leases; favorable loan agreements) that would be jeopardized if T were dissolved or it would simply take longer or involve cumbersome regulatory hoops to structure the deal as a merger. One ingenious solution to this dilemma is for P to create S, contributing to it P voting stock, and then for S to merge into T under an agreement providing that T shareholders will receive P stock (and, possibly, other consideration) in exchange for their T stock. A variation on the theme, albeit a rare one, would be to use an existing subsidiary with ongoing business activities. In that event, the reverse merger would result in T's business being augmented by S's, all conducted under the same corporate roof. In either case, when the smoke clears P will own all the stock of T and S will disappear as a result of the merger.

Section 368(a)(2)(E) provides that this type of reverse merger will qualify as a tax-free reorganization if: (1) the surviving corporation (T) holds substantially all of the properties formerly held by both corporations (T and S), and (2) the former T shareholders exchange stock constituting "control" (measured by the 80 percent tests in Section 368(c)(1)) for P voting stock.[5] Once again, Congress borrowed from its bag of requirements and combined tests from Type A (merger), Type B (control) and Type C (substantially all of the properties) reorganizations. The reverse merger is thus less flexible for tax purposes than the forward triangular merger, perhaps reflecting its Type B origins. But there *can* be boot in an "(a)(2)(E)" reorganization; only 80 percent of the T stock must be acquired for P voting stock, and the rest may be obtained for cash or other property—or simply not acquired at all if P is willing to put up with minority shareholders.

Although Congress deserves applause for abandoning the formalisms of the old case law, its piecemeal approach to triangular reorganizations is yet another example of the major flaw in the reorganization scheme. In enacting Sections 368(a)(2)(D) and (E), each with its own distinct requirements, Congress added further embroidery to what already had become a crazy quilt. As the Senate Finance Committee staff lamented in its prelimi-

5. I.R.C. § 368(a)(2)(E)(ii). See Reg. § 1.368–2(j)(3)(ii).

nary report on the reform and simplification of Subchapter C, many of the arcane distinctions in Section 368 "defy rationalization" and "[n]o discernible public policy would so sharply distinguish among the forms of an acquisition that are economically so similar."[6] Congress would be well advised to move toward a system that would impose consistent requirements on economically equivalent acquisition techniques.[7]

5. MULTI–STEP ACQUISITIONS

Regulations: § 1.338(h)(10)–1T(c)(2).

We have seen that choosing the optimal structure for a corporate acquisition involves a wide range of legal and strategic considerations. From the buyer's perspective, important factors include determining the price to be paid for the target corporation and the mix of consideration to be used. Apart from taxes, other factors driving deal structure are the accounting treatment, regulatory hurdles, stock exchange rules, treatment of employer stock options, and timing, to name just a few.

For all these reasons, it may be desirable for the parties to an acquisition to employ a multi-step structure. For example, acquisitions of public companies may proceed at a quicker pace if the first step does not require regulatory clearance, consents from lenders or others with a contractual relationship to P or T, or actions that could impede the momentum of the deal. A good example of a two-step acquisition is when P makes a tender offer for T's stock at an attractive price and acquires sufficient stock to achieve control (but not 100 percent ownership) of T, enabling P to orchestrate a merger of T into P (or more likely into a P subsidiary), squeezing out the minority shareholders. The details of this and other deal structures are complex and beyond the scope of this text. Our concern here is to what extent the federal tax laws have accommodated the multi-step acquisition phenomenon.

The two rulings below are a reflection of the Service's willingness to apply the step transaction doctrine to multi-step acquisitions.[1] This often results in qualifying the integrated transaction as a tax-free reorganization where the separate steps, if viewed in isolation, would not qualify.

Big picture →

6. See Staff of the Senate Finance Committee, Preliminary Report on the Reform and Simplification of the Income Taxation of Corporations, 98th Cong., 1st Sess., 26–27, 55–66 (Comm.Print S. 98–95, 1983).

7. See Staff of the Senate Finance Committee: The Subchapter C Revision Act of 1985, A Final Report Prepared by the Staff, 99th Cong., 1st Sess. (S.Prt. 99–47, 1985); Posin, "Taxing Corporate Reorganizations: Purging Penelope's Web," 133 U.Penn.L.Rev. 1335 (1985).

1. See also Rev. Rul. 2001–24, 2001–1 C.B. 1290 (following a forward triangular merger of T into S, a P subsidiary, P may drop down the S stock to another of its controlled subsidiaries); Rev. Rul. 2001–25, 2001–1 C.B. 1291 (following a reverse triangular merger of S, a transitory subsidiary of P, into T, T may sell 50 percent of its operating assets to an unrelated buyer without violating the "substantially all of its properties" requirement of Section 368(a)(2)(E) if it retains the sales proceeds).

Revenue Ruling 2001–26

2001–1 Cum Bull. 1297.

ISSUE

On the facts described below, is the control-for-voting-stock requirement of § 368(a)(2)(E) of the Internal Revenue Code satisfied, so that a series of integrated steps constitutes a tax-free reorganization under §§ 368(a)(1)(A) and 368(a)(2)(E) and § 354 or § 356 applies to each exchanging shareholder?

FACTS

Situation 1. Corporation P and Corporation T are widely held, manufacturing corporations organized under the laws of state A. T has only voting common stock outstanding, none of which is owned by P. P seeks to acquire all of the outstanding stock of T. For valid business reasons, the acquisition will be effected by a tender offer for at least 51 percent of the stock of T, to be acquired solely for P voting stock, followed by a merger of a subsidiary of P into T. P initiates a tender offer for T stock conditioned on the tender of at least 51 percent of the T shares. Pursuant to the tender offer, P acquires 51 percent of the T stock from T's shareholders for P voting stock. P forms S and S merges into T under the merger laws of state A. In the statutory merger, P's S stock is converted into T stock and each of the T shareholders holding the remaining 49 percent of the outstanding T stock exchanges its shares of T stock for a combination of consideration, two-thirds of which is P voting stock and one-third of which is cash. Assume that under general principles of tax law, including the step transaction doctrine, the tender offer and the statutory merger are treated as an integrated acquisition by P of all of the T stock. Also assume that all nonstatutory requirements for a reorganization under §§ 368(a)(1)(A) and 368(a)(2)(E) and all statutory requirements of § 368(a)(2)(E), other than the requirement under § 368(a)(2)(E)(ii) that P acquire control of T in exchange for its voting stock in the transaction, are satisfied.

Situation 2. The facts are the same as in Situation 1, except that S initiates the tender offer for T stock and, in the tender offer, acquires 51 percent of the T stock for P stock provided by P.

LAW AND ANALYSIS

Section 368(a)(1)(A) states that the term "reorganization" means a statutory merger or consolidation. Section 368(a)(2)(E) provides that a transaction otherwise qualifying under § 368(a)(1)(A) will not be disqualified by reason of the fact that stock of a corporation (the "controlling corporation") that before the merger was in control of the merged corporation is used in the transaction, if (1) after the transaction, the corporation surviving the merger holds substantially all of its properties and of the properties of the merged corporation (other than stock of the controlling corporation distributed in the transaction), and (2) in the transaction, former shareholders of the surviving corporation exchanged, for an amount of voting stock of the controlling corporation, an amount of stock in the surviving corporation that constitutes control of such corporation (the "control-for-voting-stock requirement"). For this purpose, control is defined in § 368(c).

court decision

In King Enterprises, Inc. v. United States, 418 F.2d 511 (Ct.Cl.1969), as part of an integrated plan, a corporation acquired all of the stock of a target corporation from the target corporation's shareholders for consideration, in excess of 50 percent of which was acquiring corporation stock, and subsequently merged the target corporation into the acquiring corporation. The court held that, because the merger was the intended result of the stock acquisition, the acquiring corporation's acquisition of the target corporation qualified as a reorganization under § 368(a)(1)(A).

Section 354(a)(1) provides that no gain or loss will be recognized if stock or securities in a corporation a party to a reorganization are, in pursuance of the plan of reorganization, exchanged solely for stock or securities in another corporation a party to the reorganization.

Section 356(a)(1) provides that, if § 354 would apply to the exchange except for the receipt of money or property other than stock or securities in a corporate party to the reorganization, the recipient shall recognize gain, but in an amount not in excess of the sum of the money and the fair market value of the other property.

Section 1.368–1(c) of the Income Tax Regulations provides that a plan of reorganization must contemplate the bona fide execution of one of the transactions specifically described as a reorganization in § 368(a) and the bona fide consummation of each of the requisite acts under which nonrecognition of gain is claimed. Section 1.368–2(g) provides that the term plan of reorganization is not to be construed as broadening the definition of reorganization as set forth in § 368(a), but is to be taken as limiting the nonrecognition of gain or loss to such exchanges or distributions as are directly a part of the transaction specifically described as a reorganization in § 368(a).

Answer

✳

As assumed in the facts, under general principles of tax law, including the step transaction doctrine, the tender offer and the statutory merger in both Situations 1 and 2 are treated as an integrated acquisition by P of all of the T stock. The principles of King Enterprises support the conclusion that, because the tender offer is integrated with the statutory merger in both Situations 1 and 2, the tender offer exchange is treated as part of the statutory merger (hereinafter the "Transaction") for purposes of the reorganization provisions. Cf. J.E. Seagram Corp. v. Commissioner, 104 T.C. 75 (1995) (treating a tender offer that was an integrated step in a plan that included a forward triangular merger as part of the merger transaction). Consequently, the integrated steps, which result in P acquiring all of the stock of T, must be examined together to determine whether the requirements of § 368(a)(2)(E) are satisfied. Cf. § 1.368–2(j)(3)(i); § 1.368–2(j)(6), Ex. 3 (suggesting that, absent a special exception, steps that are prior to the merger, but are part of the transaction intended to qualify as a reorganization under §§ 368(a)(1)(A) and 368(a)(2)(E), should be considered for purposes of determining whether the control-for-voting-stock requirement is satisfied).

In both situations, in the Transaction, the shareholders of T exchange, for P voting stock, an amount of T stock constituting in excess of 80 percent of the voting stock of T. Therefore, the control-for-voting-stock requirement is satisfied. Accordingly, in both Situations 1 and 2, the Transaction qualifies as a reorganization under §§ 368(a)(1)(A) and 368(a)(2)(E).

Under §§ 1.368–1(c) and 1.368–2(g), all of the T shareholders that exchange their T stock for P stock in the Transaction will be treated as exchanging their T stock for P stock in pursuance of a plan of reorganization. Therefore, T shareholders that exchange their T stock only for P stock in the Transaction will recognize no gain or loss under § 354. T shareholders that exchange their T stock for P stock and cash in the Transaction will recognize gain to the extent provided in § 356. In both Situations 1 and 2, none of P, S, or T will recognize any gain or loss in the Transaction, and P's basis in the T stock will be determined under § 1.358–6(c)(2) by treating P as acquiring all of the T stock in the Transaction and not acquiring any of the T stock before the Transaction.

HOLDING

On the facts set forth in Situations 1 and 2, the control-for-voting-stock requirement is satisfied in the Transaction, the Transaction constitutes a tax-free reorganization under §§ 368(a)(1)(A) and 368(a)(2)(E), and § 354 or § 356 applies to each exchanging shareholder.

Revenue Ruling 2001–46

2001–2 Cum.Bull. 321.

FACTS

Under the facts described below, what is the proper tax treatment if, pursuant to an integrated plan, a newly formed wholly owned subsidiary of an acquiring corporation merges into a target corporation, followed by the merger of the target corporation into the acquiring corporation?

Question

Situation (1). Corporation X owns all the stock of Corporation Y, a newly formed wholly owned subsidiary. Pursuant to an integrated plan, X acquires all of the stock of Corporation T, an unrelated corporation, in a statutory merger of Y into T (the "Acquisition Merger"), with T surviving. In the Acquisition Merger, the T shareholders exchange their T stock for consideration, 70 percent of which is X voting stock and 30 percent of which is cash. Following the Acquisition Merger and as part of the plan, T merges into X in a statutory merger (the "Upstream Merger"). Assume that, absent some prohibition against the application of the step transaction doctrine, the step transaction doctrine would apply to treat the Acquisition Merger and the Upstream Merger as a single integrated acquisition by X of all the assets of T. Also assume that the single integrated transaction would satisfy the nonstatutory requirements of a reorganization under section 368(a) of the Internal Revenue Code.

Situation (2). The facts are the same as in Situation (1) except that in the Acquisition Merger the T shareholders receive solely X voting stock in exchange for their T stock, so that the Acquisition Merger, if viewed independently of the Upstream Merger, would qualify as a reorganization under section 368(a)(1)(A) by reason of section 368(a)(2)(E).

Section 338(a) provides that if a corporation makes a qualified stock purchase and makes an election under that section, then the target corporation (i) shall be treated as having sold all of its assets at the close of the acquisition date at fair market value and (ii) shall be treated as a new corporation which purchased all of its assets as of the beginning of the day after the acquisition date. Section 338(d)(3) defines a qualified stock purchase as any transaction or series of transactions in which stock (meeting the requirements of section 1504(a)(2)) of one corporation is acquired by another corporation by purchase during a 12–month acquisition period. Section 338(h)(3) defines a purchase generally as any acquisition of stock, but excludes acquisitions of stock in exchanges to which section 351, section 354, section 355, or section 356 applies.

Rev. Rul. 90–95 (1990–2 C.B. 67) (Situation 2), holds that the merger of a newly formed wholly owned domestic subsidiary into a target corporation with the target corporation shareholders receiving solely cash in exchange for their stock, immediately followed by the merger of the target corporation into the domestic parent of the merged subsidiary, will be treated as a qualified stock purchase of the target corporation followed by a section 332 liquidation of the target corporation. As a result, the parent's basis in the target corporation's assets will be the same as the basis of the assets in the target corporation's hands. The ruling explains that even though "the step-transaction doctrine is properly applied to disregard the existence of the [merged subsidiary]," so that the first step is treated as a stock purchase, the acquisition of the target corporation's stock is accorded independent significance from the subsequent liquidation of the target corporation and, therefore, is treated as a qualified stock purchase regardless of whether a section 338 election is made.

Section 1.338–3(d) of the Income Tax Regulations incorporates the approach of Rev. Rul. 90–95 into the regulations by requiring the purchasing corporation (or a member of its affiliated group) to treat certain asset transfers following a qualified stock purchase (where no section 338 election is made) independently of the qualified stock purchase. In the example in section 1.338–3(d)(5), the purchase for cash of 85 percent of the stock of a target corporation, followed by the merger of the target corporation into a wholly owned subsidiary of the purchasing corporation, is treated (other than by certain minority shareholders) as a qualified stock purchase of the stock of the target corporation followed by a section 368 reorganization of the target corporation into the subsidiary. As a result, the subsidiary's basis in the target corporation's assets is the same as the basis of the assets in the target corporation's hands.

Section 368(a)(1)(A) defines the term "reorganization" as a statutory merger or consolidation. Section 368(a)(2)(E) provides that a transaction otherwise qualifying under section 368(a)(1)(A) shall not be disqualified by reason of the fact that stock of a corporation (controlling corporation), which before the merger was in control of the merged corporation, is used in the transaction if (i) after the transaction, the corporation surviving the merger holds substantially all of its properties and the properties of the merged corporation, and (ii) in the transaction, former shareholders of the surviving corporation exchange, for an amount of voting stock of the controlling corporation, an amount of stock in the surviving corporation which constitutes control of such corporation.

In Rev. Rul. 67–274 (1967–2 C.B. 141), Corporation Y acquires all of the stock of Corporation X in exchange for some of the voting stock of Y and, thereafter, X completely liquidates into Y. The ruling holds that because the two steps are parts of a plan of reorganization, they cannot be considered independently of each other. Thus, the steps do not qualify as a reorganization under section 368(a)(1)(B) followed by a liquidation under section 332, but instead qualify as an acquisition of X's assets in a reorganization under section 368(a)(1)(C).

Situation (1). Because of the amount of cash consideration paid to the T shareholders, the Acquisition Merger could not qualify as a reorganization under section 368(a)(1)(A) and section 368(a)(2)(E). If the Acquisition Merger and the Upstream Merger in Situation (1) were treated as separate from each other, as were the steps in Situation (2) of Rev. Rul. 90–95, the Acquisition Merger would be treated as a stock acquisition that is a qualified stock purchase, because the stock is not acquired in a section 354 or section 356 exchange. The Upstream Merger would qualify as a liquidation under section 332.Œ

However, if the approach reflected in Rev. Rul. 67–274 were applied to Situation (1), the transaction would be treated as an integrated acquisition of T's assets by X in a single statutory merger (without a preliminary stock acquisition). Accordingly, unless the policies underlying section 338 dictate otherwise, the integrated asset acquisition in Situation (1) is properly treated as a statutory merger of T into X that qualifies as a reorganization under section 368(a)(1)(A). See King Enterprises, Inc. v. United States, 418 F.2d 511 (Ct.Cl.1969) in a case that predated section 338, the court applied the step transaction doctrine to treat the acquisition of the stock of a target corporation followed by the merger of the target corporation into the acquiring corporation as a reorganization under section 368(a)(1)(A); J.E. Seagram Corp. v. Commissioner, 104 T.C. 75 (1995)(same). Therefore, it is necessary to determine whether the approach reflected in Rev. Rul. 90–95 applies where the step transaction doctrine would otherwise apply to treat the transaction as an asset acquisition that qualifies as a reorganization under section 368(a).

Rev. Rul. 90–95 and section 1.338–3(d) reject the approach reflected in Rev. Rul. 67–274 where the application of that approach would treat the purchase of a target corporation's stock without a section 338 election followed by the liquidation or merger of the target corporation as the purchase of the target corporation's assets resulting in a cost basis in the assets under section 1012. The rejection of step integration in Rev. Rul. 90–95 and section 1.338–3(d) is based on Congressional intent that section 338 "replace any nonstatutory treatment of a stock purchase as an asset purchase under the Kimbell–Diamond doctrine." H.R. Rep. No. 760, 97th Cong., 2d Sess. 536 (1982), 1982–2 C.B. 600, 632. (In Kimbell–Diamond Milling Co. v. Commissioner, * * *, the court held that the purchase of the stock of a target corporation for the purpose of obtaining its assets through a prompt liquidation should be treated by the purchaser as a purchase of the target corporation's assets with the purchaser receiving a cost basis in the assets.)

Rev. Rul. 90–95 and section 1.338–3(d) treat the acquisition of the stock of the target corporation as a qualified stock purchase followed by a separate carryover basis transaction in order to preclude any nonstatutory treatment of the steps as an integrated asset purchase. The policy underlying section 338 is not violated by treating Situation (1) as a single statutory merger of T into X because such treatment results in a transaction that qualifies as a reorganization under section 368(a)(1)(A) in which X acquires the assets of T with a carryover basis under section 362, and does not result in a cost basis for those assets under section 1012. Thus, in Situation (1), the step transaction doctrine applies to treat the Acquisition Merger and the Upstream Merger not as a stock acquisition that is a qualified stock purchase followed by a section 332 liquidation, but instead as an acquisition of T's assets through a single statutory merger of T into X that qualifies as a reorganization under section 368(a)(1)(A). Accordingly, a section 338 election may not be made in such a situation.

Situation (2). Situation (2) differs from Situation (1) only in that the Acquisition Merger, if viewed independently of the Upstream Merger, would qualify as a reorganization under section 368(a)(1)(A) by reason of section 368(a)(2)(E). This difference does not change the result from that in Situation (1). The transaction is treated as a single statutory merger of T into X that qualifies as a reorganization under section 368(a)(1)(A) without regard to section 368(a)(2)(E).

HOLDING

Under the facts presented, if, pursuant to an integrated plan, a newly formed wholly owned subsidiary of an acquiring corporation merges into a target corporation, followed by the merger of the target corporation into the acquiring corporation, the transaction is treated as a single statutory merger of the target corporation into the acquiring corporation that qualifies as a reorganization under section 368(a)(1)(A).

* * *

EFFECT ON OTHER DOCUMENTS

Rev. Rul. 67–274 is amplified and Rev. Rul. 90–95 is distinguished.

NOTE

Experienced tax professionals have come to understand that "the step-transaction doctrine generally applies ... except when it doesn't."[1] What factors in the two rulings above supported application of the doctrine? Was it because the first step was conditioned on the second occurring? Does Revenue Ruling 2001–26 offer any guiding principle for application of the doctrine, or does it simply assume for purposes of analysis that the tender offer and merger should be integrated?

A critical point made in Revenue Ruling 2001–46 is that application of the step transaction doctrine was permissible because it did not violate the policy of Section 338. What policy? Does that suggest that the step transaction doctrine should not be applied to the prototype *Kimbell-Diamond* transaction where P purchases 80 percent or more of T's stock and promptly liquidates T, winding up with direct ownership of its assets? If the step transaction doctrine did apply to this fact pattern, P would take a cost basis in T's assets even though no Section 338 election was made—a result clearly at variance with the policy of Section 338.

What if the first step is a qualified stock purchase under Section 338, and P and S (T's corporate parent) jointly make a Section 338(h)(10) election? In that situation, should the first step be viewed in isolation for tax purposes or should step transaction principles be applied, resulting in reorganization treatment and nullification of the Section 338 election? What if T is not a subsidiary and P unilaterally makes a Section 338 election?[2]

The Service has issued proposed regulations[3] answering some of these questions. They provide that the step transaction doctrine will not apply to a multi-step acquisition if the first step is a qualified stock purchase under Section 338 and the parties to the transaction make a joint Section 338(h)(10) election with respect to that step, whether or not the overall transaction would have qualified as a reorganization.[4] To illustrate, assume that P, Inc. owns all the stock of Y, Inc., a newly formed subsidiary, and S, Inc. owns all the stock of T, Inc. As the first step in P's acquisition of T's assets, Y, Inc. merges into T, with T surviving, and S (T's only shareholder) receives 50 percent P voting stock and 50 percent cash. This step, viewed independently, does not qualify as a reorganization and does constitute a qualified stock purchase. T then merges into P. If P and S do not make a Section 338(h)(10) election, the step transaction doctrine would be applied

1. See Stratton, "Step–Transaction Doctrine Tested Under Corporate Rulings," 93 Tax Notes 332 (Oct. 15, 2001), quoting an I.R.S. official who was quoting an unnamed law professor.

2. For some analysis of these and other ramifications of Revenue Ruling 2001–46, see Fowler, "Practical Transactional Aspects of Rev. Rul. 2001–46," 93 Tax Notes 963 (Nov. 12, 2001); Ginsburg & Levin, "Integrated Corporate Acquisitions: Comments on Rev. Rul. 2001–46," 93 Tax Notes 553 (Oct. 22, 2001).

3. The proposed regulations simultaneously were issued as temporary regulations, permitting them to become effective on a temporary basis while the Service continues to invite and consider comments. All citations are to the temporary regulations.

4. Reg. § 1.338(h)(10)–1T(c)(2).

under the principles of Revenue Ruling 2001–46, and the overall acquisition would be treated as a Section 368 reorganization. But if P and S jointly make a Section 338(h)(10) election, the regulations "turn off" the step transaction doctrine and treat P's acquisition of the T stock in the reverse merger as a qualified stock purchase, causing "old T" to recognize gain or loss on the deemed sale of its assets and "new T"—and then P, after the merger into P—to take a cost basis in its assets.[5] If, however, the first step does not constitute a qualified stock purchase under Section 338(d)(3)— such as in Situation 2 of Revenue Ruling 2001–46 where the first step, viewed independently, was a section 368 reorganization—then no Section 338(h)(10) election can be made and the overall acquisition will be treated as a reorganization.[6] The regulations do not address a situation where a unilateral Section 338 election is made by the acquiring corporation with respect to the first step.

PROBLEMS

1. Consider whether the transactions described below qualify as a tax-free reorganization. Assume in all cases that P is the acquiring corporation, T is the target corporation and S is a newly formed 100% subsidiary of P.

(a) T merges into P, with T shareholders receiving P stock, and then P transfers the T assets to S. (Why might this form of transaction be unattractive to the parties for nontax reasons?)

(b) P forms S by transferring P voting common stock to S in exchange for S stock. S then transfers the P stock to T in exchange for all of T's assets, and T liquidates.

(c) P forms S by transferring P voting common stock to S in exchange for S stock. T then merges into S, and T shareholders receive solely P voting stock in exchange for their T stock.

(d) Same as (c), above, except that the T shareholders receive voting stock of both P and S in exchange for their T stock.

(e) Same as (c), above, except that the T shareholders receive 50% P common voting stock and 50% S notes, some of which pass to dissenting shareholders of T.

(f) Same as (c), above, except that the T shareholders receive 30% P nonvoting preferred stock, 20% cash and 50% S notes.

(g) Same as (e), above, except that prior to the merger T redeems all the stock held by T's dissenting shareholders, who hold one-third of T's stock, in exchange for operating assets of T.

2. Consider whether the transactions described below qualify as a tax-free reorganization. Again assume in all cases that P is the acquiring corporation, T is the target and S is a wholly owned subsidiary of P.

5. Reg. § 1.338(h)(10)–1T(e) Examples 11 and 12.

6. Reg. § 1.338(h)(10)–1T(e) Example 14.

(a) P forms S by transferring P voting common stock to S in exchange for S stock. S then transfers the P stock to T's shareholders in exchange for all of their T stock.

(b) P forms S by transferring P voting common stock to S in exchange for S stock. S then merges into T, which has only one class of stock. In the merger, T shareholders holding 80% of the stock receive P stock in exchange for their T stock. Holders of the other 20% of T, who dissent from the merger, receive cash from P. After the transaction, T is a wholly owned subsidiary of P.

(c) Same as (b), above, except following the merger, T sells 50% of its operating assets to an unrelated buyer for cash.

(d) Same as (b), above, except P initiates the acquisition by a tender offer in which it acquires 60% of the T stock from T's shareholders for P voting stock. P then forms S and S merges into T. In the merger, T shareholders holding the remaining 40% of T stock receive a combination of consideration consisting of two-thirds P voting stock and one-third cash.

(e) Same as (b), above, except P acquires all the stock of T in a reverse statutory merger of S into T and, in the merger, T shareholders exchange their T stock for consideration consisting of 50% P voting stock and 50% cash. Following the merger and pursuant to P's original acquisition plan, T merges upstream into P.

(f) Same as (e), above, except P made a valid Section 338 election after it acquired T.

(g) Same as (e), above, except the final step is a merger of T into New S, a newly formed subsidiary of P.

(h) Same as (b), above, except that P transfers both P stock and P notes (worth 20% of the total consideration) to S; the stock and notes are then transferred to all of T's shareholders in exchange for their T stock. Shareholders holding 80% of the T stock receive P stock and the dissenting T shareholders receive notes.

(i) Same as (h), above, except that shareholders holding 80% of the T stock receive a combination of P stock and notes while the dissenting 20% T shareholders receive cash.

(j) Same as (b), above, except that P owned 30% of T's stock prior to the transaction and in the merger of S into T, T shareholders receive P voting stock in exchange for their T stock.

C. TREATMENT OF THE PARTIES TO AN ACQUISITIVE REORGANIZATION

Up to this point, we have been concentrating on the definition of a reorganization in Section 368. Compliance with those statutory requirements and the judicial doctrines unlocks the gate to the operative provisions, which govern the tax treatment of the target shareholders and corporations that are "a party to a reorganization" and provide for transferred and exchanged bases, tacked holding periods and the carryover of corporate tax attributes such as net operating losses. Section 368(b) broadly defines "a party to a reorganization" to include any corporation resulting from a qualifying reorganization (e.g., the surviving corporation in a consolidation), the acquiring and target corporations in a straight acquisitive reorganization and the parent corporation in a "drop down" or triangular reorganization.

This section summarizes the operative provisions, beginning with the tax consequences to the target's shareholders and security holders and then turning to the treatment of the target and acquiring corporations.

1.   CONSEQUENCES TO SHAREHOLDERS AND SECURITY HOLDERS

Code: §§ 354(a); 356(a), (c), (d), (e); 358(a), (b), (d), (f); 368(b). Skim §§ 351(g); 356(a).

Regulations: §§ 1.354–1(a), (b), (d) Example (3), (e); 1.356–1, –3, –4; 1.358–1, –2(a)(1)–(4), (b); 1.368–2(f), (g).

Recognition of Gain or Loss. One of the principal benefits of reorganization status is the nonrecognition granted to the shareholders and security holders of the target corporation under Section 354(a). Shareholders are entitled to complete nonrecognition only when they receive solely stock or securities of the acquiring corporation.[1] This invariably occurs in a Type B reorganization, but the target shareholders in a Type A, C or any form of triangular reorganization may receive some boot. In that event, the shareholder must recognize any realized gain to the extent of the money plus the fair market value of any other boot received.[2] For this purpose, boot includes any property other than stock or securities of a party to the reorganization. To prevent a bailout through the use of securities,[3] Section 356(d) provides that if the principal amount of securities received exceeds the principal amount of securities surrendered or if securities are received but none are surrendered, the fair market value of the excess is treated as boot.[4] Consequently, a shareholder holding no securities who receives bonds in connection with a reorganization is treated as having "cashed out" his investment to the extent of the bonds—an appropriate result under the continuity of interest principle. But security holders who change their investment to an equity interest or exchange securities for the same or lesser principal amount have not engaged in a bailout and therefore are entitled to nonrecognition treatment. As might be expected, however, a shareholder or security holder who receives boot may not recognize any realized loss.[5]

---

1. I.R.C. § 354(a)(1).

2. I.R.C. § 356(a)(1).

3. "Securities" are generally defined to encompass relatively long-term corporate debt instruments but not short-term notes, stock rights or warrants.

4. See I.R.C. § 354(a)(2)(A).

5. I.R.C. § 356(c).

Characterization of Gain. Section 356(a)(2) provides that any recognized gain is treated as a dividend to a target shareholder if the exchange "has the effect of the distribution of a dividend." In that event, each T shareholder must treat as a dividend the amount of his recognized gain that is not in excess of that shareholder's ratable share of the corporation's accumulated earnings and profits.[6] Any remaining gain is treated as gain from the sale or exchange of the target stock or securities transferred.

The "boot dividend" issue has been one of the most difficult questions arising under the operative provisions. The Service once contended that dividend treatment was automatic if boot were received,[7] but it later conceded that dividend equivalence should be determined by using the tests applicable to stock redemptions in Section 302(b),[8] treating the boot as if it were received as a distribution in redemption of the *target* corporation's stock immediately prior to the reorganization exchange.[9] Taxpayers argued, however, that dividend equivalence should be determined by examining the effect of the reorganization exchange as a whole, an approach that ultimately was adopted by the Supreme Court in Clark v. Commissioner.[10] Under the *Clark* test, each T shareholder is treated as initially receiving only P stock instead of the combination of P stock and boot actually received, and then P is treated as having distributed the boot in a redemption of the portion of P stock not actually received by the T shareholder. If this hypothetical redemption meets one of the tests for exchange treatment in Section 302(b), the receipt of boot does not have the effect of a dividend, and the shareholder recognizes capital gain or loss. Otherwise, as previewed above, the recognized gain is a dividend (likely a qualified dividend eligible for the 15 percent maximum rate) to the extent of the shareholder's ratable share of "the corporation's"[11] accumulated earnings and profits, and any remaining gain is capital gain.

Whenever there is a meaningful rate preference for long-term capital gains and dividends are taxed as ordinary income, individual taxpayers will benefit from the Supreme Court's holding in *Clark*.[12] Corporate shareholders, however, may prefer dividend classification in order to qualify for the dividends received deduction under Section 243.[13] Dividend treatment also

6. Note that the gain is not automatically characterized as ordinary income but, if it has the effect of a dividend, it is treated as a Section 301 distribution subject to the Section 243 dividends received deduction. See Rev.Rul. 72–327 at p. 493, infra. In addition, the earnings and profits of the target corporation are reduced under Section 312(a).

7. See Commissioner v. Bedford's Estate, 325 U.S. 283, 65 S.Ct. 1157 (1945).

8. In applying Section 302(b) principles, the Section 318 attribution rules are applicable. I.R.C. § 356(a)(2). Rev.Rul. 74–515, 1974–2 C.B. 118. See also Wright v. United States, 482 F.2d 600 (8th Cir.1973).

9. See, e.g., Shimberg v. United States, 577 F.2d 283 (5th Cir. 1978), cert. denied, 439 U.S. 1115, 99 S.Ct. 1019 (1979).

10. 489 U.S. 726, 109 S.Ct. 1455 (1989). See also Rev. Rul. 93–61, 1993–C.B. 118.

11. The statute is unclear, but the majority view appears to be that the dividend determination should be based on the target corporation's earnings and profits.

12. The Service, as it must, has announced that it will apply the *Clark* approach to an acquisitive reorganization. See Rev. Rul. 93–61, 1993–1 C.B. 118.

13. But see I.R.C. § 1059(e)(1)(B), which treats any amount treated as a divi-

may be preferable to the acquiring corporation because it reduces the earnings and profits that are inherited under Section 381 as a result of the reorganization. Finally, dividend classification may be undesirable where shareholders receiving notes from the acquiring corporation wish to report their gain on the installment method. Unless the target stock exchanged by the shareholder is publicly traded,[14] installment sale treatment generally would be available if the transaction is treated as a sale but not if the receipt of installment boot is treated as a dividend under Section 356(a)(2).[15]

The boot dividend issue rarely is important to individual shareholders, however, now that dividends and long-term capital gains are taxed at the same preferential rate. Since any amount characterized as a dividend under Section 356(a)(2) may not exceed the shareholder's recognized gain, the shareholder is always entitled to recovery of basis. If the dividend is "qualified," the rate is the same unless the capital gain is short-term (or the stock is not a capital asset), in which case dividend treatment is preferable. Corporate shareholders will continue to prefer dividend classification because of the dividends received deduction, and dividend treatment is preferable to the acquiring corporation because it reduces earnings and profits inherited from the target corporation on the reorganization.

Dividend Within Gain Approach: Policy Aspects. Section 356(a)(2) limits the amount of any boot dividend to the shareholder's recognized gain. This approach has been criticized as a "curious mixing of dividend and sale or exchange concepts" which "permits shareholders with a high basis in their stock * * * to withdraw corporate earnings in a reorganization without dividend consequences."[16] Allowing taxpayers to recover their basis even when a transaction is equivalent to a dividend is inconsistent with the rules applicable to stock redemptions in Section 302 and is difficult to justify.

Basis and Holding Period. Target shareholders determine the basis of nonrecognition property (i.e., the stock or nonboot securities received in the exchange) under Section 358 by reference to their basis in the stock that they relinquished, increased by any gain recognized and reduced by any boot received and liabilities assumed. Boot takes a fair market value basis under Section 358(a)(2). This is the same formula used many chapters ago in determining the basis of stock received in a Section 351 exchange. If different types of nonrecognition property are received (e.g., two classes of stock or stock and bonds), the aggregate exchanged basis is allocated among those properties in proportion to their relative fair market values under

---

dend on a non pro rata redemption of a corporate shareholder's stock as an "extraordinary dividend." See Chapter 12F3, supra.

14. See I.R.C. § 453(k)(2).

15. See I.R.C. § 453(f)(6); Prop.Reg. § 1.453–1(f)(2).

16. Staff of the Senate Committee on Finance, The Subchapter C Revision Act of 1985: A Final Report Prepared by the Staff, 99th Cong., 1st Sess. 45 (S.Prt. 99–47, 1985). See also Wolfman, "Subchapter C and the 100th Congress," 33 Tax Notes 669, 672 (Nov. 17, 1986).

rules provided in the regulations.[17] The nonrecognition property generally takes a tacked holding period under Section 1223(1) and the holding period of the boot commences on the date of its acquisition.

The transferred basis rule in Section 358 is simple enough to apply when a target shareholder acquired all of her T stock at the same time. But it is not uncommon for a shareholder to acquire stock in the same corporation at different times, for different prices. When these multiple "tax lots" of T stock are exchanged in a tax-free reorganization for stock of the acquiring corporation, can T shareholders use the average basis in their T shares to determine the basis for all their new P stock or must they use an approach under which the basis of the P stock received is traced to the basis of the different blocks of T stock surrendered? And does it matter how the shares are held—e.g., in certificates that can be physically identified, or a brokerage account where separate lots may be more difficult or impossible to track?[18]

From the standpoint of simplicity and administrative convenience, the average basis method has much to offer even when separate lots are easily identifiable. But to prevent potential tax avoidance and also allow taxpayers more flexibility, the Service has concluded that tracing is the preferable approach.[19] Under proposed regulations, the basis of the stock received in a reorganization transaction, to the greatest extent possible, must be an allocable portion of the basis of each block of stock surrendered.[20] Taxpayers who are unable to identify and match the particular shares of stock received and surrendered may designate which properties were exchanged for each other as long as the designation is consistent with the terms of the transaction.[21]

The proposed regulations illustrate the tracing approach with this example of a Type A statutory merger where Corporation N is the target and Corporation O is the acquiring corporation:[22]

---

17. I.R.C. § 358(a)(1); Reg. § 1.358–2.

18. Even without a reorganization, similar issues are raised when shares are sold by a taxpayer who acquired lots of that stock on different dates or at different prices. See, e.g., Reg. § 1.1012–1(c), providing that if the shares sold cannot be adequately identified, the earliest of the lots acquired is deemed to be sold first. In the reorganization setting, the cases are inconsistent. Compare, e.g., Arrott v. Commissioner, 136 F.2d 449 (3d Cir. 1943)(average basis) and Bloch v. Commissioner, 148 F.2d 452 (9th Cir. 1945)(tracing permissible).

19. Prop. Reg. § 1.358–2.

20. Prop. Reg. § 1.358–2(a)(2)(i). For simplicity, the discussion in the text is limited to exchanges of stock, but the proposed regulations use a similar approach for reorganization exchanges of debt securities. If more than one class of stock or security of the target corporation is exchanged for multiple classes of the acquiring corporation, an additional layer of allocation is required. See, e.g., Prop. Reg. § 1.358–2(c) Example 3.

21. The designation must be made on or before the date when it is first relevant (e.g., at the time of a sale of the P stock received by the selling shareholder). If no designation is made at the time of a sale or transfer, the taxpayer is treated as selling or transferring the P shares received in respect of the earliest T shares purchased or acquired. Prop. Reg. § 1.358–2(a)(2)(iii).

22. Prop. Reg. § 1.358–2(c) Example 1.

F, an individual, acquired 20 shares of Corporation N stock on Date 1 for $3 each and 10 shares of Corporation N stock on Date 2 for $6 each. On Date 3, Corporation O acquires the assets of Corporation N in a reorganization under Section 368(a)(1)(A). Pursuant to the terms of the plan of reorganization, F receives 2 shares of Corporation O stock for each share of Corporation N stock. Therefore, F receives 60 shares of Corporation O stock. Pursuant to Section 354, F recognizes no gain or loss on the exchange. F is not able to identify which shares of Corporation O stock are received for each share of Corporation N stock.

F has 40 shares of Corporation O each of which has a basis of $1.50 and is treated as having been acquired on Date 1 and 20 shares of Corporation O each of which has a basis of $3 and is treated as having been acquired on Date 2. On or before the date on which the basis of a share of Corporation O stock received becomes relevant, F may designate which of the shares of Corporation O stock have a basis of $1.50 and which have a basis of $3.

PROBLEM

Target Corporation ("T") has 10 equal shareholders, $100,000 of accumulated earnings and profits and a net worth of $500,000. Acquiring Corporation ("P") has 500,000 shares of voting common stock outstanding (value-$10 per share) and $500,000 of accumulated earnings and profits. Unless otherwise indicated, assume that each T shareholder owns 100 shares of voting common stock with a basis of $20,000 and a value of $50,000. T merges into P in a qualifying Type A reorganization. Discuss the tax consequences to the T shareholders under the following alternatives:

(a) Each T shareholder receives 4,000 shares of P voting common stock (value$40,000) and P nonvoting preferred stock (not "nonqualified preferred stock") worth $10,000.

(b) Same as (a), above, but instead of the preferred stock each shareholder receives 20–year market rate interest bearing P notes with a principal amount and fair market value of $10,000.

(c) Same as (b), above, except that each shareholder has a $45,000 basis in her T stock.

(d) Same as (b), above, except that two of the shareholders receive all the notes (with a principal amount and fair market value of $100,000), and the remaining shareholders receive voting common stock worth $400,000.

(e) Same as (b), above, except that T had $50,000 of accumulated earnings and profits.

2. CONSEQUENCES TO THE TARGET CORPORATION

Code: §§ 336(c); 357(a), (b), (c)(1); 358(a), (b)(1), (f); 361.

Regulations: § 1.357–1(a).

Treatment of the Reorganization Exchange. Without a nonrecognition provision, the target corporation in an acquisitive reorganization would recognize gain or loss on the transfer of its assets and the assumption of its liabilities by the acquiring corporation. If the acquisition qualifies as a reorganization, however, Section 361(a) comes to the rescue by providing that the target recognizes no gain or loss if it exchanges property, pursuant to the reorganization plan, solely for stock or securities in a corporation which also is a party to the reorganization. Section 357(a) offers similar protection by providing that the assumption of the target's liabilities in a reorganization exchange will not be treated as boot nor prevent the exchange from being tax-free under Section 361(a).[1] These rules apply primarily to Type A and C reorganizations and forward triangular mergers. In a Type B stock-for-stock exchange or a reverse triangular merger, no assets are transferred because the target corporation remains intact as a controlled subsidiary of the acquiring corporation.

The target in a Type C reorganization may receive a limited amount of boot without disqualifying the transaction under Section 368.[2] In that event, the target must recognize any realized gain (but may not recognize loss) on the reorganization exchange to the extent of the cash and the fair market value of the boot that the target does not distribute pursuant to the plan of reorganization.[3] Any transfer by the target of cash or other boot received in the exchange to creditors in connection with the reorganization is treated as a "distribution" pursuant to the reorganization plan.[4] Since the target in a Type C reorganization is generally required to distribute all of its properties pursuant to the plan,[5] gain or loss rarely will be recognized on the exchange.[6]

Section 361(a) only applies to the *receipt* of boot by the target pursuant to the reorganization plan. An acquiring corporation that transfers appreciated boot property to the target as partial consideration for the target's assets must recognize gain under Section 1001 because, to that extent, the transaction is considered to be a taxable exchange.[7] In that event, the target takes the boot property with a fair market value basis.[8]

---

1. As in the Section 351 incorporation area, the general nonrecognition rule in Section 357(a) is subject to an exception in Section 357(b) if the liability assumption is motivated by tax avoidance or lacks a bona fide business purpose. The Section 357(c) exception for liabilities assumed in excess of the basis of the transferred assets only applies to a Type D reorganization. See Chapters 11 and 12, infra.

2. I.R.C. § 368(a)(2)(B). Boot in a Type C reorganization would include any property other than stock or securities of the acquiring corporation (or its parent). See Section B3 of this Chapter, infra.

3. I.R.C. § 361(b)(1), (2).

4. I.R.C. § 361(b)(3). The Service may prescribe regulations as necessary to prevent tax avoidance through abuse of this rule. Id.

5. I.R.C. § 368(a)(2)(G).

6. A rare situation where gain might be recognized is where liabilities of the target are assumed in a transaction to which Section 357(b) or (c) applies.

7. Rev.Rul. 72–327 at p. 493, infra. Section 361(a) does not apply in this situation because it only provides nonrecognition to the *recipient* of distributed boot.

8. I.R.C. § 358(a)(2). See also I.R.C. § 358(f).

Treatment of Distributions. Section 361(c) generally provides that a corporation does not recognize gain or loss on the distribution of "qualified property" to its shareholders pursuant to a reorganization plan. "Qualified property" is: (1) stock (or rights to acquire stock) in, or obligations (e.g., bonds and notes) of the distributing corporation, or (2) stock (or rights to acquire stock) in, or obligations of, another party to the reorganization which were received by the distributing corporation in the exchange. Thus, any stock, securities or even short-term notes of the acquiring corporation received by the target in the exchange and then distributed to its shareholders would constitute "qualified property." Section 361(c)(3) makes it clear that a transfer of "qualified property" by a target to its creditors in satisfaction of corporate liabilities is treated as a "distribution" pursuant to the reorganization plan.

If the target distributes an asset other than qualified property, it must recognize gain (but may not recognize loss) in the same manner as if the property had been sold to the distributee at its fair market value.[9] For example, the target would recognize gain on the distribution of an appreciated retained asset (i.e., an asset not acquired in the reorganization) or boot (other than notes of the acquiring corporation) which appreciated between the time it was received and the distribution to shareholders.[10]

Sales Prior to Liquidation. Before liquidating, the target corporation in a Type C reorganization may sell some of the stock or securities received from the acquiring corporation in order to raise money to pay off creditors. Prior to the Tax Reform Act of 1986, the courts were divided over whether these sales were entitled to nonrecognition treatment.[11] The current version of Section 361 settles the debate by providing that only transfers of "qualified property" (i.e., stock or obligations of the acquiring corporation) or boot directly to creditors will qualify for nonrecognition because they are treated as "distributions" to the shareholders pursuant to the reorganization plan.[12] Sales of property to third parties are thus fully taxable events even if they were necessary to raise money to pay off creditors.

Basis and Holding Period. If the target corporation retains property received from the acquiring corporation, which only could occur in a Type C reorganization where the Commissioner waives the Section 368(a)(2)(G) distribution requirement, it is deemed to have distributed that property to its shareholders, who then are treated as having recontributed the property to a "new" corporation as a contribution to capital.[13] The basis and the holding period of the property in the hands of the "new" corporation depend upon the consequences to the shareholders. If the property is boot

---

9. I.R.C. § 361(c)(1), (2).

10. Since the target takes a fair market value basis in the boot under Section 358(a)(2) at the time of the exchange, it would recognize only post-acquisition appreciation on a later distribution of the boot.

11. Compare General Housewares Corp. v. United States, 615 F.2d 1056 (5th Cir.1980)(allowing nonrecognition under for-

mer Section 337) with FEC Liquidating Corp. v. United States, 548 F.2d 924 (Ct.Cl. 1977)(taxing such gains on the ground that former Section 337 and the reorganization provisions were conceptually incompatible).

12. I.R.C. § 361(b)(3), (c)(3).

13. See supra note 5.

to the shareholders, it receives a fair market value basis and no tacked holding period in the hands of either the shareholders or the "new" corporation to which it is constructively recontributed.[14] If the property is nonrecognition property (e.g., stock or securities of the acquiring corporation) to the shareholders, then their exchanged bases and tacked holding periods transfer to the "new" corporation.[15] These rules are irrelevant in the typical Type C reorganization where the target liquidates and distributes the stock, securities and boot received in the transaction, along with any retained assets, to its shareholders. In that event, basis and holding period are determined under the operative provisions governing shareholders and security holders.[16]

3. CONSEQUENCES TO THE ACQUIRING CORPORATION

Code: §§ 362(b); 368(b); 1032.

Regulations: § 1.1032–1.

Recognition of Gain or Loss. The acquiring corporation does not recognize gain or loss on the issuance of its stock or the stock of its parent in an acquisitive reorganization or, for that matter, in any other transaction.[1] To the extent that it may issue securities as consideration for the acquired property, the acquiring corporation recognizes no gain because the acquisition is a "purchase." If the acquiring corporation transfers other "boot" property to make the acquisition, however, it recognizes any realized gain or loss under general tax principles.[2]

Basis and Holding Period: In General. Under Section 362(b), the target assets acquired in a Type A, Type C or forward triangular reorganization take a transferred basis, increased by any gain recognized by the target on the transfer. Since Section 361(a) generally provides that the target does not recognize gain or loss on any exchange of property pursuant to the plan of reorganization, an upward basis adjustment for gain recognized by the target will occur only in the rare Type C reorganization where the target receives boot and does not distribute it to its shareholders or creditors. In the case of a Type B or reverse triangular reorganization, however, the property acquired is corporate stock whose transferred basis is determined by its basis in the hands of the target shareholders.[3] In either

---

14. I.R.C. §§ 358(a)(2); 362(a).

15. I.R.C. §§ 358(a)(1); 362(a); 1223(1) and (2).

16. See page 486, supra.

1. I.R.C. § 1032(a). It was once feared that Section 1032 would not apply where a controlled subsidiary acquired property in exchange for its *parent's* stock. The Service has ruled, however, that the subsidiary does not recognize gain or loss in this situation, presumably because such an acquisition is eco-

nomically indistinguishable from a direct acquisition by the parent followed by a drop down of the assets to the subsidiary. See Rev.Rul. 57–278, 1957–1 C.B. 124. Reg. § 1.1032–2(b).

2. See Rev.Rul. 72–327, at p. 493, infra.

3. See Rev.Proc. 81–70, 1981–2 C.B. 729, which provides an approach for determining this transferred basis when the large number of target shareholders makes precise determination of their bases impossible.

case, the property acquired is allowed a tacked holding period under Section 1223(2).

Limit on Importation of Built-in Losses. The effect of the Section 362(b) transferred basis rule is to preserve not only built-in gains but also built-in losses when P acquires T's assets in a tax-free reorganization. This rule made it possible for U.S. corporations to engage in what became known as "basis shift" transactions with U.S. tax-indifferent parties, such as foreign corporations. The primary goal was to shift unrealized economic losses to U.S. taxpayers, who could then realize the losses and shelter their taxable income.

Section 362(e)(1) attempts to block basis-shift shelters by providing that if a net built-in loss is "imported" in a tax-free reorganization, the basis of such loss property in the hands of the transferee corporation is limited to its fair market value immediately after the transaction.[4] A net built-in loss is imported into the United States if the aggregate adjusted basis of the properties received by a domestic transferee corporation from a person not subject to U.S. tax exceeds the fair market value of the transferred properties.[5]

Basis of Target Stock Received in Triangular Reorganizations. Determining the acquiring parent corporation's basis in the stock of a subsidiary acquired in a reverse triangular reorganization raises a tantalizing technical question. Under Section 368(a)(2)(E), the acquiring corporation either may form a "phantom" subsidiary or use a preexisting operating subsidiary to merge into the target corporation. It ordinarily will transfer voting stock and possibly some boot to the subsidiary which then transfers that property to the target shareholders as the consideration for the acquisition.

In a straight Type B reorganization, the parent determines its basis in the target stock under Section 362(b) by reference to the stock bases of the former target shareholders. In the case of a reverse subsidiary merger, however, Section 358 would appear to require the acquiring corporation to take an exchanged basis—i.e., its basis in the target stock acquired would be the same as its basis in the stock of the disappearing subsidiary. That basis likely would be zero if a phantom subsidiary were used to effect the merger. A similar issue arises in the case of forward triangular merger, where the target merges into a subsidiary formed by the acquiring corporation immediately prior to the reorganization. Since the parent normally forms the subsidiary by transferring its own stock, in which it presumably has a zero basis, it would appear that the parent would retain a zero basis in the stock of the subsidiary even after it absorbs the target.

The Treasury has issued regulations that address the zero basis problem. Those regulations seek to conform the tax consequences of a triangular reorganization with those of a "drop down" transaction in which

---

4. I.R.C. § 362(e)(1)(A). For a similar rule limiting the transfer of built-in losses in Section 351 transactions, see I.R.C. § 351(3)(2), discussed in Chapter 11A, infra.

5. I.R.C. § 362(e)(1)(B), (C).

P acquires T's assets or stock directly and then drops them down to a subsidiary ("S") in a tax-free transaction. To illustrate the operation of the regulations in a forward triangular merger in which T merges into S, a newly formed P subsidiary, the regulations permit P to increase its basis in its S stock by the net basis (assets less liabilities) of T's assets.[6] In a simple transaction where P had no prior basis in its S stock, the net effect is that P's basis in its S stock and S's basis in the acquired T assets will be the same.

In a simple reverse triangular merger where newly formed S merges into T, which survives as a P subsidiary, P's basis in its T stock is adjusted by assuming that T had merged into S in a forward triangular merger, applying the rules discussed above.[7] Thus, in a wholly tax-free reverse merger where 100 percent of the T stock is acquired, P's basis in its T stock would equal T's net basis in its assets plus any preexisting basis that P had in its S stock.

Revenue Ruling 72–327

1972–2 Cum.Bull. 197.

Advice has been requested as to the Federal income tax consequences of the transaction described below:

On July 1, 1969, corporation *X* merged into corporation *Y* in a reorganization qualifying under section 368(a)(1)(A) of the Internal Revenue Code of 1954. Pursuant to the reorganization, *M* corporation, a stockholder of *X*, received, in exchange for its *X* stock, *Y* stock having a fair market value of 100*x* dollars plus other property having a fair market value of 40*x* dollars but an adjusted basis in the hands of *Y* of 10*x* dollars. *M* had a basis of 90*x* dollars in its stock of *X*. *M*'s ratable share of the undistributed earnings and profits of *X* accumulated after February 28, 1913, was 30*x* dollars. *M* realized gain of 50*x* dollars (140*x* dollars less 90*x* dollars) on the exchange. Of the 50*x* dollar gain, 40*x* dollars was recognized to *M* pursuant to section 356(a)(1) of the Code. Pursuant to section 356(a)(2) of the Code, 30*x* dollars was treated as a dividend and 10*x* dollars was treated as gain from the exchange of property.

The Federal income tax consequences of the above described transaction are as follows:

(1) The 30*x* dollar gain, treated as a dividend to *M* under section 356(a)(2) of the Code, is eligible for the corporate dividends received deduction provided by section 243(a) of the Code. *M*'s basis in the stock of *Y* is 90*x* dollars. Section 358(a)(1) of the Code. *M*'s basis in the other property received is 40*x* dollars, the fair market value thereof. Section 358(a)(2) of the Code.

---

6.   Reg. § 1.358–6(c)(1).

7.   Reg. § 1.358–6(c)(2). Additional rules are provided for more specialized situations, such as where S was a preexisting subsidiary, the consideration is mixed, or less than all of T's stock is acquired in a reverse merger. See Reg. § 1.358–6(c)(2)(i)(C), –6(c)(4).

(2) Pursuant to section * * * 1001 of the Code, gain is recognized by Y in the amount of $30x$ dollars ($40x$ dollars minus $10x$ dollars). See, for example, United States v. Thomas Crawley Davis, 370 U.S. 65 (1962), Ct.D.1873, C.B. 1962–2, 15; E.F. Simms v. Commissioner, 28 B.T.A. 988, at 1029 (1933). Y's basis for the assets acquired from X is the basis of the assets in the hands of X. Section 362(b) of the Code.

(3) No gain or loss is recognized by X on the transaction. Section 361[(a) of the Code. Under Section 358(a)(2), X takes the other property with a basis of $40x$ dollars, and it recognizes no gain on distribution of the other property under Section 361(c). X does not recognize gain on the distribution of the Y stock. I.R.C. §§ 336(c); 361(c)(1). Ed.]

(4) Y's earnings and profits are increased by the $30x$ dollar gain that it recognized on the exchange of the other property. Section 312(f)(1) of the Code.

(5) Y succeeds to, and takes into account, X's earnings and profits, or deficit in earnings and profits, as of the close of the date of the transaction. Section 381(c)(2) of the Code. In computing the earnings and profits of X for purposes of section 381(c)(2) of the Code, account must be taken of the amount of X's earnings and profits properly applicable to the distribution to M. Section 1.381(c)(2)–1(c)(1) of the Income Tax Regulations. X's earnings and profits, for purposes of section 381(c)(2) of the Code, are computed as follows:

(a) X's earnings and profits are not increased by reason of the receipt [or distribution] of the other property. Sections 361[(a)] and 312(f)(1) of the Code.

(b) X's earnings and profits are reduced (but not below zero) by $40x$ dollars as a result of the distribution of the other property to M. Section 312(a)(3) of the Code. For purposes of determining earnings and profits, X [has] a basis of $40x$ dollars (fair market value) in the other property. Section [358(a)(2)] of the Code.

(6) M's earnings and profits are increased by $40x$ dollars, the amount of gain recognized on the transaction. Sections 356(a)(1) and (2) of the Code and section 312(f)(1) of the Code.

PROBLEMS

1. Acquiring Corporation ("P") has $100,000 of accumulated earnings and profits. Target Corporation ("T") has assets with a basis of $60,000 and a fair market value of $100,000 and $50,000 of accumulated earnings and profits. T's shareholders have a $20,000 aggregate basis in their stock. P acquires all the assets of T in a qualifying Type C reorganization. Discuss the tax consequences to P, T and T's shareholders under each of the following circumstances:

(a) P transfers its voting stock, worth $80,000, in exchange for all of T's assets which are subject to $20,000 of liabilities. T immediately distributes the stock to its shareholders in complete liquidation.

(b) Same as (a), above, except that P transfers $80,000 of voting stock and $20,000 cash to T, which uses the cash to pay off its liabilities and distributes the stock to its shareholders in complete liquidation. Which result in (a) or (b), above, would P prefer?

(c) Same as (a), above, except that P transfers voting stock worth $80,000 and investment securities with a basis of $10,000 and a value of $20,000 in return for all of T's assets which were not subject to any liabilities. T again immediately distributes the consideration it receives pro rata to its shareholders in complete liquidation.

(d) Same as (a), above, except that P transfers $80,000 of its voting stock, $10,000 of P bonds and $10,000 of cash to T in exchange for its assets. Because an immediate distribution would result in substantial hardship to T, T receives the Commissioner's permission not to liquidate and retains the cash, bonds and stock for eventual satisfaction of its liabilities and distribution of the remaining assets to its shareholders.

(e) For this part of the problem, assume T has no liabilities. P transfers $80,000 worth of its voting stock and $20,000 of nonvoting preferred stock to T in exchange for all of T's assets. T liquidates and distributes the voting and nonvoting preferred stock to its shareholders pro rata.

2. Target Corporation ("T") has operating assets with a basis of $18,000 and a value of $90,000, investment land with a basis of $2,000 and a value of $10,000 and liabilities of $40,000.

In a Type C reorganization, Acquiring Corporation ("P") acquires T's operating assets in exchange for P voting stock worth $80,000 and some stock in Bell, Inc. (an unrelated public company) with a basis of $2,000 and a value of $10,000. P does not assume T's liabilities.

Before liquidating, T sells $40,000 of P stock and uses the proceeds to pay off its liabilities. T then distributes the remaining $40,000 of P stock, its investment land and the Bell, Inc. stock (now worth $12,000) in complete liquidation to its shareholders, who have an aggregate basis of $10,000 in their T stock.

Prior to the reorganization, P had $20,000 of earnings and profits and T had $10,000 of earnings and profits.

(a) What are the tax consequences to T, P and T's shareholders?

(b) Would there be a different result in (a), above, if T transferred $40,000 of P stock to its creditors in connection with the liquidation?

3. Parent Corporation ("P") creates Subsidiary Corporation ("S") by transferring P stock as a preliminary step to acquiring the assets of Target Corporation ("T") in a separate subsidiary. T's shareholders own stock worth $200,000 with a basis of $50,000. T has assets worth $200,000 with a basis of $100,000.

(a) Assuming a valid § 368(a)(2)(D) forward triangular merger, what are the tax consequences to P, S, T and T's shareholders?

(b) Assuming a valid § 368(a)(2)(E) reverse triangular merger, what are the tax consequences to P, S, T and T's shareholders?

(c) What results in (a), above, if the transaction fails to qualify as a reorganization?

(d) What results in (b), above, if the transaction fails to qualify as a reorganization?

D.   CARRYOVER OF TAX ATTRIBUTES

1.   INTRODUCTION

Code: § 381(a). Skim § 381(c).

When one corporation acquires the assets of another corporation in a tax-free reorganization, the acquired properties retain both their bases and holding periods. But what happens to the remaining tax attributes of the target—its earnings and profits, depreciation and other accounting methods, unused net operating losses, capital loss carryforwards and the like?

Prior to 1954, the Code contained few rules regulating the carryover of corporate tax attributes. The Supreme Court merely followed the lead of lower courts[1] in holding that a corporation's earnings and profits could not be eliminated by means of a reorganization but that instead the acquiring corporation inherited the target's earnings and profits along with its assets.[2] Because any other approach would have allowed a profitable corporation to use a reorganization to sweep its earnings and profits account clean and diminish future dividends, the Court's decision was no more surprising than the reaction of the tax bar to the proposition that corporate attributes could survive a reorganization. They assumed, or at least hoped, that an acquiring corporation could inherit negative as well as positive tax attributes in a tax-free reorganization or liquidation. If that assumption proved true, profitable corporations could acquire the assets of their unprofitable brethren solely to succeed to the target's earnings and profits deficit and net operating losses (NOLs). The acquiring corporation thus could assure itself that future distributions would be sheltered by the newly acquired earnings and profits deficit and that future income would be effectively exempt from tax because of the newly acquired NOLs.

The Supreme Court responded by holding that earnings and profits deficits did *not* survive a reorganization[3] and that NOLs could be used only by the corporate entity that incurred them.[4] But tax advisors were not to be outdone. Shortly after these decisions, several reorganizations which followed a similar pattern appeared on the scene. Loss Corp., a corporation with NOLs but no current income to absorb them, would acquire the assets of Profit Corp., a successful company, in a tax-free reorganization. In the process, the Profit Corp. shareholders would receive more than enough Loss Corp. stock to control the continuing and expanded Loss Corp. Since Loss Corp. technically was the surviving entity, it retained its NOLs, which

---

1. See, e.g., Commissioner v. Sansome, 60 F.2d 931 (2d Cir.1932), cert. denied, 287 U.S. 667, 53 S.Ct. 291 (1932).

2. Commissioner v. Munter, 331 U.S. 210, 67 S.Ct. 1175 (1947).

3. Commissioner v. Phipps, 336 U.S. 410, 69 S.Ct. 616 (1949).

4. New Colonial Ice Co. v. Helvering, 292 U.S. 435, 54 S.Ct. 788 (1934). But see Helvering v. Metropolitan Edison, 306 U.S. 522, 59 S.Ct. 634 (1939), where the Court held that these attributes did follow the target's assets in certain mergers.

then were used to offset the gains generated by the new business. Once again, the Supreme Court was forced to respond to a device involving trafficking in tax attributes. In Libson Shops, Inc. v. Koehler,[5] the Court decided that even if a loss corporation survives a reorganization, NOLs incurred prior to the transaction only could be used to offset post-acquisition gains if they were generated by substantially the same *business* as well as the same entity which had incurred the losses.

With the arrival of the 1954 Internal Revenue Code, the case law regulating the carryover of tax attributes was replaced by a comprehensive statutory scheme.[6] The principal provisions are: (1) Section 381, which generally provides that a target corporation's tax attributes follow its assets in tax-free reorganizations (other than B and E reorganizations) and tax-free liquidations of a subsidiary; (2) Sections 382 and 383, which restrict the carryforward of net operating losses and certain other losses and credits following a substantial change of ownership; (3) Section 384, which limits the use of loss carryforwards to offset certain gains following a corporate acquisition; and (4) Section 269, which allows the Secretary to disallow deductions, credits or other allowances in certain situations where one corporation's stock or assets were acquired for the principal purpose of obtaining the specific deductions, credits or allowances in question. The limitations on carryforwards of net operating losses and Section 269 are considered in Chapter 13. The remainder of this chapter examines the general rules on carryover of tax attributes in corporate acquisitions.

5. 353 U.S. 382, 77 S.Ct. 990 (1957).

6. Some commentators and courts have suggested that the *Libson Shops* doctrine survived the 1954 Code, but Congress intended specifically not to incorporate the doctrine into the new statutory scheme governing limitations on net operating loss carryforwards. H.R.Rep. No. 99–841, 99th Cong., 2d Sess. II–194 (1986).

2.   SECTION 381 CARRYOVER RULES

Code: § 381(a), (b). Skim § 381(c).

General Carryover Rules. Section 381(a) provides that in a tax-free liquidation of a subsidiary or a reorganization (other than a Type B or E reorganization), the acquiring corporation shall "succeed to and take into account" some 26 specified attributes of the target,[1] including earnings and profits, NOLs, accounting and depreciation methods and capital loss, investment credit and charitable contribution carryovers.[2] In Type B stock-for-stock acquisition and Type E recapitalization, the acquired or recapitalized corporation remains intact after the transaction and thus no carryover mechanism is necessary. In a triangular reorganization where substantially all of the target's assets are transferred to a subsidiary of the issuing corporation, the subsidiary is the "acquiring corporation" and succeeds to the target's attributes.[3]

Earnings and Profits Deficits. Left unchecked, Section 381 would subject the revenue to some of the same abuses already discussed. As we have seen, one promising tax avoidance strategy is presented where Profit Corp. acquires Loss Corp.'s assets in a reorganization and inherits its earnings and profits deficit and NOL carryovers. To some extent, this abuse is limited by Section 381 itself. Section 381(c)(2) restricts Profit Corp.'s ability to rid itself of its own current or accumulated earnings and profits through a simple acquisition of Loss Corp. by providing that an earnings and profits deficit inherited from Loss Corp. may not be applied against any earnings and profits of Profit Corp. that existed prior to the acquisition. Loss Corp.'s deficit therefore only can be used to offset post-acquisition accumulated earnings and profits. If a distribution is made in a post-acquisition year in which there are current earnings and profits, any offsetting accumulated deficit acquired from Loss Corp. is irrelevant in any event, since the distribution will be deemed to come from the current earnings and profits of the taxable year and then from Profit Corp.'s own pre-acquisition accumulated earnings and profits.[4]

Net Operating Losses. Even though Profit Corp. receives little benefit from Loss Corp.'s earnings and profits deficit, Loss's NOL carryovers still might be used to eliminate Profit's own tax liability. Section 381(c)(1) provides complex rules governing the carryover of NOLs, but it does not prevent them from being misused by Profit Corp. Instead, Section 382, which is discussed later in this chapter, is the designated policing agent in this situation.

---

1.   I.R.C. § 381(c)(1)–(26).

2.   Cf. I.R.C. § 312(h)(2), which requires a "proper allocation" of earnings and profits between the acquiring corporation and the target if less than 100 percent of the assets are acquired in a Type C or Type D reorganization.

3.   Reg. § 1.381(a)–1(b)(2).

4.   I.R.C. § 381(c)(2)(B). See Chapter 4, supra. Thus, an acquired earnings and profits deficit will do no more than prevent undistributed current earnings and profits from becoming accumulated earnings and profits in a subsequent year.

Rather than Profit Corp. acquiring the assets and tax attributes of Loss Corp., Loss might acquire Profit's assets in a Type A or C reorganization, maintaining Loss's earnings and profits deficit and NOLs without assistance from Section 381, and then might use those negative tax attributes to offset Profit's past and future income. If Profit's shareholders receive sufficient Loss Corp. stock to control the combined company, the transaction in substance is identical to the acquisition of Loss Corp. by Profit. The benefits of this transaction also are limited by both Sections 381(b) and 382. The *Bercy Industries* case, which follows, explores the limits of Section 381(b)(3), which in part prevents Loss Corp. from carrying back any NOLs that it incurs subsequent to the acquisition to offset pre-acquisition income of Profit Corp.

Bercy Industries, Inc. v. Commissioner

United States Court of Appeals, Ninth Circuit, 1981.
640 F.2d 1058.

■ Trask, Circuit Judge:

Appellant Bercy Industries, Inc. (Bercy), appeals from a decision of the Tax Court affirming a deficiency assessment by the Commissioner of Internal Revenue (the Commissioner). This court has jurisdiction pursuant to I.R.C. [26 U.S.C.] § 7482. Bercy contends that the Commissioner improperly denied it a loss carryback under section 381 of the Internal Revenue Code (the Code). Subsection (b)(3) of that section limits post-reorganization loss carry-backs by the surviving corporation of certain tax-free reorganizations. Surviving corporations in other tax-free reorganizations, however, are permitted carryback of post reorganization losses without special limitation. Bercy argues that either Congress intended that corporations that reorganize as Bercy did be permitted to carryback their post-reorganization losses, or Bercy's reorganization qualifies as one of the types entitled to unrestricted carryback treatment. The Commissioner responds that the Code should be strictly construed and that Bercy does not qualify for unrestricted carryback treatment under the terms of section 381. We reverse.

I

Bercy Industries was incorporated in 1965. In 1968, a corporation named Beverly Enterprises established a subsidiary shell corporation, Beverly Manor. Beverly Manor remained a shell until April 23, 1970, the date of the reorganization here at issue. On that date, Bercy Industries (Old Bercy) was acquired by Beverly Manor by means of a triangular merger. Old Bercy was merged into Beverly Manor, which then changed its name to Bercy Industries (New Bercy). All shareholders of Old Bercy exchanged their stock for shares of stock in Beverly Enterprises, the parent. The Old Bercy stock was then cancelled.

Although it had been anticipated that New Bercy would be as profitable as Old Bercy had been, New Bercy suffered a loss for the post-reorganization period April 23 to December 31, 1970. Relying on the carryover provisions of section 172 of the Code, New Bercy attempted to carry back this loss to offset net operating income of Old Bercy in its two preceding tax years. It is this carryback that the Commissioner disallowed, and that is the subject of this appeal.

Appellant raises two issues: (1) whether Congress, in enacting section 381, intended to prevent the subsidiary corporation in a triangular merger from carrying back post-merger losses to offset pre-merger income of the transferor corporation, where the subsidiary was a mere shell before the merger, and (2) whether the reorganization here at issue should be classified as a type (B) reorganization for purposes of section 381. Both issues are of first impression in this circuit. We address only the first issue.

II

Under I.R.C. § 172, a corporation which incurs a net operating loss in any tax year may carry this loss back three tax years, or forward seven tax years, to offset net operating income earned during those years. Section 172 reflects congressional recognition that business income often fluctuates widely from year to year, and that, consequently, a carryover provision is necessary to mitigate the inequitable and excessive tax liabilities that would result from determination of income on a strictly annual basis. * * *

In 1954, Congress enacted section 381 as part of a substantial revision of the entire Code. The Commissioner argues that Congress intended this provision to preempt and replace prior caselaw with reliable and consistent rules for carrying over pre-and post-reorganization income and loss. Conceding this to be the general purpose of section 381, appellant nevertheless argues that it is an oversimplified characterization of congressional intent with respect to subsection (b)(3). We agree.

Prior to the 1954 revision of the Code, a significant tax avoidance problem for the Internal Revenue Service was the corporate practice of "trafficking in loss corporations."[3] The Commissioner had attempted to combat this practice by ruling that net operating losses could be carried over only to offset income of the particular legal entity that incurred the losses. See, e.g., Libson Shops, Inc. v. Koehler, supra, 353 U.S. at 385–86, 77 S.Ct. at 992 (decided under the 1939 Code). Thus, the acquiring corporation in a triangular merger was effectively prevented from carrying back any post-merger losses to offset pre-merger income of the transferor corporation.

Although approved by the Supreme Court in New Colonial Ice Co. v. Helvering, 292 U.S. 435, 440–41, 54 S.Ct. 788, 790, 78 L.Ed. 1348 (1934),

---

3. A profitable corporation would acquire an unprofitable corporation with losses eligible to be carried forward under section 172. After the acquisition, the transferor corporation's pre-reorganization losses were carried forward to offset current and expected income of the acquiring corporation, thereby reducing current tax liability. See generally D. Kahn & P. Gann, Corporate Taxation and the Taxation of Partnerships 848–49 (1979); Note, Section 368(a)(1)(F) and Loss Carrybacks in Corporate Reorganizations, 117 U.Pa.L.Rev. 764, 765 (1969).

the Commissioner's position was undercut by a succession of adverse court decisions, see, e.g., Helvering v. Metropolitan Edison Co., 306 U.S. 522, 529, 59 S.Ct. 634, 638, 83 L.Ed. 957 (1939); Stanton Brewery v. Commissioner, 176 F.2d 573, 575 (2d Cir.1949), which resulted in substantial confusion among corporations as to when post-reorganization loss carryovers were permitted, * * *. Section 381 and its companion, section 382, rejected the restrictive position taken by the Commissioner and clarified the availability of post-reorganization loss carryovers by prohibiting them only in limited circumstances specified in the two sections. * * *

With respect to the enactment of subsection (b)(3) of section 381, the legislative history shows that Congress was concerned with a complex accounting problem—deciding how a post-reorganization loss should be allocated between the acquiring corporation and the transferor corporations, and, therefore, how much of the loss should be carried back to offset each entity's income in the preceding three tax years. The Senate Finance Committee reported: "Some limitation upon carry-backs in reorganizations and mergers is justifiable on the ground that it is too complex in some cases to determine to which of several component corporations the loss of the surviving corporation is attributable." Senate Finance Committee, supra, at 404. This committee also stated, however, that

> [i]n two important areas * * * the problem of allocating the loss is not involved, and it is suggested that in such cases, at least, there should be no limit on carrybacks. One is the case of a reincorporation of the same corporation in a different state, or upon expiration of its charter. Another instance is that of the wholly owned subsidiary which is liquidated into its parent, which parent suffers a net operating loss in the following year.

Id. (emphasis added). This language strongly suggests that when a reorganization generates no complex problems of post-reorganization loss allocation, Congress intended that the surviving corporate taxpayer be able to carry back such losses without limitation.

Because Congress specifically identified two circumstances in which loss carrybacks should be permitted, the Commissioner argues that if Congress had also intended to permit carrybacks in a triangular merger involving a shell corporation, it would have specifically mentioned this circumstance as well. In 1954, however, the Code did not permit a corporation to use its parent's stock as consideration for the acquisition of another corporation's assets in a tax-free reorganization. This prevented the use of shells in effecting such reorganizations. Congress did not suggest that this type of tax-free reorganization be removed from the carryback restrictions of section 381(b)(3) because such a reorganization was not then tax-free. Such use of parent stock was sanctioned by amendments to the Code in 1968 and 1971. Act of Oct. 22, 1968, Pub.L. No. 90–621, § 1(a), 82 Stat. 1310–11 (triangular mergers); Act of Jan. 12, 1970, Pub.L. No. 91–693, § 1(a), 84 Stat. 2077 (reverse triangular mergers). We find nothing in the text or legislative history of these amendments that would suggest that they were intended to expand the scope of section 381(b)(3) beyond the problem to which it was originally directed, i.e., allocation of post-reorganization loss. * * *

The non-applicability of subsection (b)(3) to type (B), (E), and (F) reorganizations[4] supports our view of congressional intent with respect to this subsection. (B) reorganizations involve exchange of stock at the shareholder level only, (E) reorganizations are a recapitalization of a single corporation, and (F) reorganizations are a mere change in form or identity. A loss carryback after one of these reorganizations generally does not result in the offset of income earned by one corporation by losses incurred by another.[5] Thus, there are no post-reorganization allocation problems.

Both legislative history and statutory structure support the conclusion that Congress was preoccupied with post-reorganization allocation problems when it enacted the loss carryback restriction. We agree with the Second Circuit that the intent of Congress with respect to subsection (b)(3) of section 381 was to prohibit carryback of post-reorganization losses pursuant to section 172 only when such a carryback would entail complex problems of post-reorganization loss allocation. See Aetna Casualty & Surety Co. v. United States, supra, 568 F.2d at 819, 822, 824.

III

The Commissioner states that section 381(b)(3) reflects a policy of not permitting loss carrybacks when the legal and economic identity of the corporation has been substantially altered.[6] The Commissioner argues that Old Bercy was legally transformed by its merger into New Bercy and the subsequent cancellation of its stock. He further argues that the reorganization transformed Old Bercy economically by shifting control of that corporation from its own shareholders to those of Beverly Enterprises.

Even assuming that the Commissioner has correctly articulated the congressional policy underlying subsection (b)(3), we are not persuaded that a material change in identity resulted from the reorganization here at issue. The reorganization involved only one set of operating assets, one set of books, and one tax history. New Bercy is operating the same commercial business that Old Bercy operated. There is no problem of allocating a post-reorganization loss to different pre-reorganization businesses. Regardless of the formal technicalities of the transaction, the indisputable fact is that the

---

4. (F) reorganizations are explicitly exempted by the terms of the statute. See I.R.C. § 381(b). (B) and (E) reorganizations are exempted because they are not described in subsection (a)(2), to which subsection (b)(3) refers. See Treas.Reg. § 1.381(a)–1(b)(3)(i) (T.D.6500).

5. Such a result occurs in some (F) reorganizations. Such a reorganization, however, nearly always involves the consolidation of wholly owned subsidiaries into a parent corporation, so that the loss allocation problems are far less significant than would normally be the case. See e.g., Estate of Stauffer v. Commissioner, 403 F.2d 611 (9th Cir. 1968). See also B. Bittker & J. Eustice, supra, para. 16.12, at 16–22 to–23 & nn. 40–41.

6. In the Commissioner's view, subsection (b)(3) does not apply to type (B), (E), and (F) reorganizations only because such reorganizations leave the surviving corporation's pre-reorganization legal and economic identity essentially unchanged.

same business generated both the income and the loss.[7] The legislative history of section 381 shows that Congress intended that a loss carryback be available in circumstances such as these.

IV

It has long been judicial practice in reviewing tax cases to look through the form of a transaction to its substance when scrutiny of form alone would subvert the purposes of the Code. See, e.g., Gregory v. Helvering, 293 U.S. 465, 469–70, 55 S.Ct. 266, 267, 79 L.Ed. 596 (1935). We have discovered no tax policy, nor does the Commissioner articulate one, that would be promoted by denying a loss carryback in this instance.[8] On the contrary, section 172 manifests a congressional policy preference for loss carryovers which is not to be lightly set aside. Aetna Casualty & Surety Co. v. United States, supra, 568 F.2d at 822, 824. To deny a loss carryback on the facts of this case would exalt form over substance. Accordingly, we hold that subsection (b)(3) of section 381 does not prevent Bercy from using the loss carryback provisions of section 172. The judgment of the Tax Court is Reversed.

PROBLEMS

1. Acquiring Corporation ("P") acquires the assets of Target Corporation ("T") in a valid Type C reorganization. Both corporations are calendar year taxpayers and the transactions are completed on December 31, 2005.

   (a) If P has accumulated earnings and profits of $30,000 and T has an earnings and profits deficit of $50,000, what result to the P shareholders in 2005 if during that year P has $20,000 of current earnings and profits, T breaks even and P distributes $20,000 cash?

---

7. The Commissioner makes much of the fact that because of the reorganization, the benefit of the loss carryback will accrue to a different set of shareholders than the one that owned Bercy at the time it earned the income to be offset. We fail to see why this should prevent a carryback. Sections 381 and 382 are grounded on two competing theories: (1) A loss carryover ought to be available only when the shareholders who were the "beneficial sufferers" of such loss retain an interest in its use, as the Commissioner argues; and (2) a loss carryover ought to be available only for use against profits from business activities which gave rise to the loss. Kaufman, Application of a Loss Carryover of One Business Against Profits From Another Business; Libson Shops and Sections 381, 382, and 269, 24 N.Y.U.Inst.Fed.Tax. 1199, 1203 (1966). These two theories conflict in large degree, so that any particular subsection of 381 or 382 may favor one theory over the other. See id. As our discussion of con-

gressional intent indicates, see Part II supra, this was the case with section 381(b)(3); theory (2), rather than theory (1), clearly animates subsection (b)(3). Moreover, we note that the former shareholders of Old Bercy are now minority holders of Beverly Enterprises, and have a continuing, albeit diminished, interest in carryback of the post-reorganization loss. Finally, the Commissioner himself concedes that a loss carryback would have been permitted had Bercy reorganized pursuant to a reverse triangular merger, yet such a reorganization would have resulted in the same change in shareholder ownership which the Commissioner now argues should prevent the carryback.

8. We are unpersuaded by the Commissioner's argument that chaos and inconsistency will result from permitting loss carrybacks in circumstances such as those in this case.

(b) What result in (a), above, if P breaks even in 2005 and makes no distributions during that year but distributes $20,000 in 2006, a year when P also breaks even?

(c) What result in (b), above, if in 2005, P has a $10,000 current earnings and profits deficit?

(d) What result in (b), above, if in addition in 2007 P has a $10,000 current earnings and profits deficit and makes a $20,000 cash distribution?

(e) What result in (d), above, if in addition in 2008, P has $20,000 of current earnings and profits and makes a $20,000 cash distribution?

(f) What result in (e), above, if P makes no distribution in 2008, but distributes $40,000 in 2009, a year in which P breaks even.

2. T Corporation merges into P Corporation two-thirds of the way through P's year. What are the results in the following situations:

(a) P has $30,000 of deficit earnings and profits for the entire year of the acquisition and T has $30,000 of accumulated earnings and profits at the date of the acquisition. The combined corporation makes a distribution of $20,000 in the succeeding year when it breaks even.

(b) Same as (a), above, except that P Corporation has $30,000 of current earnings and profits for the year and T has a $30,000 earnings and profits deficit at the time of the acquisition. The combined corporation again makes a distribution of $20,000 in the succeeding year, when it breaks even.

(c) Same as (b), above, except that the combined corporation makes a distribution of $30,000 on the last day of the year of acquisition.

3. T Corporation merges into P Corporation in a tax-free Type A reorganization in which T shareholders receive 51 percent of the outstanding P stock. Both corporations are calendar year, accrual method taxpayers and the merger occurs on December 31, 2001. Both corporations have been in existence for two years, with T sustaining a $20,000 loss in each of those years and P earning a profit of $30,000 in each year.

(a) May the combined corporation carry back T's losses and apply them against P's profits for 2000 and 2001?

(b) Assuming that the loss and income patterns continue, determine the combined corporation's net income for the years 2002 through 2006.

(c) What results in (b), above, if T were a profitable corporation with net income of $20,000 in each of the prior and current years but P sustained a $100,000 loss in 2002 followed by a return to the regular gain pattern in 2003?

    (d) What result in (c), above, if T and P consolidated into C Corporation and C sustained the $100,000 loss in 2002 followed by $50,000 in gains in the succeeding years?

4. Consider the following questions concerning the carryover of net operating losses:

    (a) May a Type F reorganization be preferable to a Type A reorganization?

    (b) Is there ever an overlap between a Type F and a Type A reorganization?

    (c) How does the *Bercy Industries* case relate to these questions?

    (d) Does Bercy apply to all § 368(a)(2)(D) reorganizations?

E. POLICY: AN ELECTIVE CARRYOVER BASIS REGIME

Congress has been tinkering with Subchapter C since the enactment of the 1954 Code, but most revisions have been aimed at narrow technical problems. Prompted by recommendations from the organized tax bar and the American Law Institute, Congress cautiously began to reexamine a number of fundamental structural issues in 1982, when it enacted Section 338. Shortly thereafter, the Senate Finance Committee began a comprehensive study of Subchapter C. The staff reviewed recommendations of prominent bar and accounting groups and relied heavily on the Subchapter C project of the American Law Institute. In September, 1983, it issued its preliminary report—a controversial document that proposed revisions both large and small. Some of the staff's narrower recommendations were incorporated in the Tax Reform Act of 1984.

The Finance Committee staff followed up with its "final report"—the Subchapter C Revision Act of 1985. Some of its aspects, most notably further repeal of the General Utilities doctrine and a revised approach to limiting net operating loss carryforwards, were incorporated in the Tax Reform Act of 1986. But even the 1986 Act left for another day the centerpiece of both the ALI and the Senate Finance Committee projects— the adoption of an entirely new scheme governing corporate acquisitions, including the replacement of the tax-free reorganization provisions with an essentially elective system that would permit nonrecognition under consistent standards for any corporate acquisition at the price of a carryover basis in the assets of the target corporation. The following excerpt provides a summary of these acquisition proposals. Keep in mind that the excerpt assumes that *General Utilities* has not yet been fully repealed and makes references to the former versions of Section 336 and 337.

Excerpt From the Subchapter C Revision Act of 1985: A Final Report Prepared by the Staff of the Senate Finance Committee

S. Prt. 99–47, 99th Cong., 1st Sess. 50–53 (1985).

IV. SUMMARY OF PROPOSALS

The principal proposals contained in the bill are described below. A more detailed description of the proposals is set forth in the Technical Explanation accompanying the bill.

A. Definition of qualified acquisition (new section 364 of the Code)

In general, the bill consolidates, simplifies, and makes uniform the rules classifying corporate mergers and acquisitions, whether treated under current law as a "reorganization", a liquidating sale under section 337 of the Code, or a section 338 stock acquisition.

New section 364 defines "qualified acquisition" as meaning any "qualified stock acquisition" or any "qualified asset acquisition." A qualified stock acquisition is defined as any transaction or series of transactions during the 12–month acquisition period in which one corporation acquires stock representing control of another corporation. A qualified asset acquisition means (1) any statutory merger or consolidation, or (2) any other transaction in which one corporation acquires at least 70 percent of the gross fair market value and at least 90 percent of the net fair market value of the assets of another corporation held immediately before the acquisition, and the transferor corporation distributes, within 12 months of the acquisition date, all of its assets (other than assets retained to meet claims) to its shareholders or creditors.

For these purposes, the definition of "control" is conformed to that contained in section 1504(a)(2) of the Code.

Where an acquiring corporation makes a qualified stock acquisition of a target corporation and the target corporation owns stock in a subsidiary, a special rule would treat the acquiring corporation as having also acquired the stock of the subsidiary, for purposes of determining whether the acquiring corporation has made a qualified stock acquisition of the subsidiary.

A special rule is also provided where an acquisition might qualify as both a qualified asset acquisition and a qualified stock acquisition. For example, where an acquiring corporation acquires all of the assets of a target corporation, and certain of those assets consist of all of the stock of a subsidiary, the transaction is treated as a qualified stock acquisition of the subsidiary and a qualified asset acquisition of all of the other assets of the target corporation.

The common-law doctrines of continuity of interest, continuity of business enterprise, and business purpose would have no applicability in determining whether a transaction qualifies as a qualified acquisition.

The bill repeals section 368. Acquisitive reorganizations ("A", "B" and "C" reorganizations and subsidiary mergers) under current law would be replaced by the rules for qualified acquisitions. The "D" reorganization rules would be replaced by special rules (described below) relating to qualified acquisitions between related parties. Transactions qualifying under current law as an "E" reorganization (a recapitalization) and an "F" reorganization (a mere change in identity, form, or place of organization of one corporation) are conformed to the definition of qualified acquisitions. Finally, the "G" reorganization rules (bankruptcy reorganizations), developed largely in response to continuity of interest problems in those types of transactions, are no longer needed and therefore are repealed.

B. Elective tax treatment of qualified acquisitions (new section 365 of the Code)

The corporate level tax consequences of a qualified acquisition are explicitly made elective. Under new section 365, all qualified acquisitions are treated as "carryover basis acquisitions" unless an election to be treated as a "cost basis acquisition" is made.

In general, elections may be made on a corporation-by-corporation basis. Thus, for example, if an acquiring corporation makes a qualified stock acquisition of both a target corporation and a target subsidiary, a cost basis election may be made for the target corporation but, if desired, no such election need be made for the target subsidiary.

Within a single corporation, the same election must generally apply for all of the assets of the corporation. A consistency rule would provide that assets that are acquired which were held by a single corporation during the consistency period must be treated consistently, either as all cost basis or all carryover basis.

Notwithstanding the consistency rule, an inconsistent carryover basis election may be made with respect to goodwill and certain other unamortizable intangibles. For example, a separate carryover basis election may be made with respect to such property even though a cost basis election is made for all of the other assets of the target corporation.

In general, no cost basis election may be made with respect to any qualified acquisition between related parties. These generally refer to transactions where, after application of the attribution rules, there is 50 percent or greater common ownership between the target and acquiring corporations. In addition, no cost basis election may be made with respect to a transaction qualifying as an "E" or "F" reorganization under current law. Finally, a mandatory cost basis election generally applies to a qualified asset acquisition where the acquiring corporation is a non-taxable entity (such as a tax-exempt entity, a regulated investment company, or a foreign corporation).

An election must be made before the later of (1) the 15th day of the 9th month following the month in which the acquisition date occurs, or (2) the date prescribed in regulations. Once made, an election is irrevocable.

C. Corporate level tax consequences of qualified acquisitions (sections 361, 362 and 381 of the Code)

The corporate level tax consequences of a qualified acquisition result directly from the election made at the corporate level. For example, in the case of a carryover basis acquisition, no gain or loss is recognized by the target corporation and the acquiring corporation obtains a carryover basis in any assets acquired. Attributes carry over under section 381.

In the case of a cost basis acquisition, the target corporation recognizes gain or loss and the acquiring corporation obtains a basis in any assets acquired determined under section 1012. Attributes do not carry over. Where the cost basis acquisition is a qualified stock acquisition, the target corporation is deemed to have sold all of its assets for fair market value at the close of the acquisition date in a transaction in which gain or loss is recognized, and then is treated as a new corporation which purchased all of such assets as of the beginning of the day after the acquisition date.

A special rule is provided in the case where a target corporation is a member of an affiliated group and a cost basis election is made. In general, unless the parties elect otherwise, a target corporation in that situation shall not be treated as a member of such group with respect to the gain or loss recognized in the transaction.

The basis of any property received by a target corporation in a qualified asset acquisition is the fair market value of such property on the acquisition date. The basis of stock acquired by an acquiring corporation in a qualified stock acquisition is determined under new section 1020 of the Code (see description below for rules concerning basis of stock of controlled subsidiaries).

Under the bill, sections 337 and 338 of current law are repealed.

D. Shareholder level tax consequences of qualified acquisitions (sections 354, 356, and 358 of the Code)

In general, shareholder level tax consequences of a qualified acquisition are determined independent of the corporate level tax consequences and independent of the election made at the corporate level. Thus, even if a transaction is treated as a cost basis acquisition at the corporate level, it may be wholly or partly tax free at the shareholder level. In addition, shareholder level consequences are generally determined shareholder-by-shareholder, and the consequences to one shareholder do not affect the tax treatment of other shareholders or investors of the target corporation.

As a general rule, nonrecognition treatment is provided to shareholders or security holders of the target corporation upon receipt of "qualifying consideration," i.e., stock or securities of the acquiring corporation and, where the acquiring corporation is a member of an affiliated group, of the common parent of such group and any other member of such group specified in regulations. The nonrecognition rule applies to the receipt of securities only to the extent the issue price of any securities received does not exceed the adjusted basis of any securities surrendered.

A special rule is provided in the case of investment company stock. In general, stock or securities of an investment company does not qualify as qualifying consideration. An exception applies, however, and such stock or securities will qualify as qualifying consideration, if the target corporation is a diversified investment company. The term "investment company" and "diversified investment company" generally have the same meaning as under current law. In short, the existence of an investment company as the acquiring corporation may affect the tax treatment of the transaction at the shareholder level, but does not affect the corporate level tax consequences.

Receipt of "nonqualifying consideration" (i.e., any consideration other than qualifying consideration) generally results in recognition of gain to the shareholder or security holder. Such gain is treated as gain from the sale or exchange of property unless the receipt of nonqualifying consideration has the effect of a distribution of a dividend. The determination of dividend effect is made by treating the shareholder as having received only qualifying consideration in the exchange, and then as being redeemed of all or a portion of such qualifying consideration (to the extent of the nonqualifying consideration received). For these purposes, earnings and profits of both the target and acquiring corporations are generally taken into account.

Special rules are provided where there is a controlling corporate shareholder of the target corporation. In general, these rules are designed to avoid a second corporate level tax where the target corporation is acquired in a cost basis acquisition. In addition, where the target corporation is acquired in a carryover basis acquisition and all or part of the consideration is nonqualifying consideration, these rules are designed to insure that the controlling corporate shareholder or a distributee of such shareholder will recognize gain on the receipt of the nonqualifying consideration.

In general, shareholders or security holders obtain a substitute basis in any [qualifying] consideration received, and a fair market value basis in any nonqualifying consideration received. Controlling corporate shareholders of the target corporation generally obtain a basis in any qualifying consideration received equal to the lesser of substitute basis or fair market value basis.

CHAPTER 10

CORPORATE DIVISIONS

A. INTRODUCTION

1. TYPES OF CORPORATE DIVISIONS

Code: Skim §§ 355; 368(a)(1)(D), (c).

The preceding chapter examined acquisitive and nondivisive single-party reorganizations. We now turn to a variety of transactions in which a single corporate enterprise is divided into two or more separate corporations. Section 355 allows a corporation to make a tax-free distribution to its shareholders of stock and securities in one or more controlled subsidiaries. If an intricate set of statutory and judicial requirements are met, neither the distributing corporation nor its shareholders recognize gain or loss on the distribution. Section 355 also unlocks the gate to other provisions which govern the treatment and characterization of boot, and collateral matters such as basis, holding period and carryover of tax attributes.[1] The rationale for nonrecognition is that the division of a business conducted under one corporate shell into separate corporations is an inappropriate taxable event when no significant assets leave corporate solution and the historic shareholders continue to control all the resulting corporations.

The three types of corporate divisions are commonly known as spin-offs, split-offs and split-ups. To illustrate the elements of these transactions, assume that Alex and Bertha each own 50 percent of the stock of Diverse Corporation ("D"), which for many years has operated a winery and a chicken ranch as separate divisions. For reasons to be elaborated below, the shareholders wish to divide the business into two separate corporations on a tax-free basis. The division method they choose will be influenced by their nontax goals. The possibilities are:

1. *Spin-off.* Assume that to comply with a new state regulation, D is required to operate the chicken ranch and winery as separate corporations. To accomplish the division, D forms a new corporation, Poultry, Inc., contributing the assets of the chicken ranch. It then distributes the stock of Poultry pro rata to Alex and Bertha, who emerge as equal shareholders in each corporation. Because a spin-off involves a distribution of property to shareholders without the surrender of any stock, it resembles a dividend.

---

1. See, e.g., I.R.C. §§ 356; 357; 358; 361; 362; 381; 1223(1) and Section D of this chapter, infra.

2. *Split-off*. Alex and Bertha desire to part company, with Alex operating the winery and Bertha the chicken ranch. To help them go their separate ways, D again forms a new corporation, Poultry, Inc., contributing the assets of the chicken ranch. D then distributes the stock of Poultry to Bertha in complete redemption of her D stock. Alex becomes the sole shareholder of D, which now owns only the winery, and Bertha is the sole owner of the chicken ranch. If Alex and Bertha did not want to part company, D could have made a pro rata distribution of Poultry stock in redemption of an appropriate amount of D stock. In either situation, a split-off resembles a redemption because the shareholders have surrendered stock of D.

3. *Split-up*. To comply with a new state regulation, D is required to terminate its corporate existence and divide up its two businesses. The fission is accomplished by D forming Vineyard, Inc. and Poultry, Inc., contributing the winery assets to Vineyard and the chicken ranch assets to Poultry. D then distributes the stock of the two new corporations pro rata to Alex and Bertha in exchange for all their D stock. Because D has distributed all of its assets and dissolved, this transaction resembles a complete liquidation. If the objectives of the parties had been different (e.g., Alex and Bertha wanted to sever their relationship), the transaction could have been effected by distributing the Vineyard stock to Alex and the Poultry stock to Bertha.

As these examples demonstrate, spin-offs, split-offs and split-ups can be classified for tax purposes in two different ways: as a tax-free corporate division or as the taxable transaction that each method resembles. In order to qualify as tax free to the shareholders, the division must satisfy the requirements of Section 355 and its accompanying judicial doctrines. In general, Section 355 allows a corporation with one or more businesses that have been actively conducted for five years or more to make a tax-free distribution of the stock of a controlled subsidiary (or subsidiaries) provided that the transaction is being carried out for a legitimate business purpose and is not being used principally as a device to bail out earnings and profits. In the absence of Section 355, a spin-off likely would be treated as a dividend under Section 301; a split-off would be tested for dividend equivalency under the redemption rules in Section 302; and a split-up would be treated as a complete liquidation under Section 331.

There is one more piece to this introduction to the puzzle. In each of the examples above, Diverse Corporation was required to engage in a preliminary step in order to accomplish its division. Because its two businesses were operated as divisions under one corporate roof rather than as separately incorporated subsidiaries, D had to drop one or more of those businesses into a separate corporate shell before proceeding with the distribution to its shareholders. If that distribution satisfies the tests in Section 355, the initial transfer of assets by D to its new subsidiary (or subsidiaries) will constitute a divisive Type D reorganization.[2] As such, the transfer of assets will be tax free to D under Section 361(a), the assumption of liabilities will be governed by Section 357 and the basis of the transferred assets will carry over to the new subsidiary under Section 362(b).[3] Creation of a new subsidiary, however, is not a condition to qualifying for nonrecognition of gain under Section 355. If its requirements are met, Section 355 applies to distributions of stock of preexisting corporations as well as to new subsidiaries created solely to carry out the division.[4]

2. NON-TAX MOTIVES FOR CORPORATE DIVISIONS

Many different strategic and economic considerations can lead a company to the decision that its business should be divided. Some of the more routine motives include resolution of shareholder disputes, insulation of one business from the risks and creditors of another, and compliance with a regulatory decree.

In the world of publicly traded companies, one of the most common motives for a division is the desire to separate the distributing and controlled corporations so they each can devote their attention to a single line of business. In the parlance of Wall Street, focusing the old and new corporations on a single business allows investors to have a "pure play" on a particular industry. For example, a corporation engaged in the transportation, energy and real estate businesses might transfer the latter two businesses to newly formed corporations and then distribute all shares of the new entities to the distributing corporation's shareholders to create three companies, each with a single focus. The theory underlying this maneuver is that a more narrowly focused company will have greater success than a conglomerate by virtue of its ability to devote more energy and attention to the single enterprise. This renewed vigor, so the theory goes, will be derived in part from an increased incentive for corporate managers to perform. Because their performance (or at least the perception of their performance) will be reflected more directly in the stock value of a narrowly focused company than in the stock value of a conglomerate, the managers will be more accountable to shareholders. In addition, proponents of corporate divisions expect the resulting streamlined companies to benefit from the freedom of corporate managers to pursue growth opportunities that they otherwise would feel constrained to pursue.

Another common motive for a corporate division is the desire to increase market recognition of the value of a particular business. Executives of a corporation engaged in several lines of business often believe that stock market analysts fail to appreciate the collective value of the corporation's businesses. To overcome this problem, corporate managers often decide to place a particular business in an independent company in the

---

2. The initial transaction also would qualify for nonrecognition under Section 351, but Section 368(a)(1)(D) and its accompanying operative provisions take precedence if the transfer of assets is followed by a Section 355 distribution.

3. See Section D of this chapter, infra.

4. I.R.C. § 355(a)(2)(C).

hope that "the market" will recognize the value of that business (and perhaps also the value of the distributing corporation's remaining businesses) more clearly. Increased recognition of value, it is hoped, will attract more capital for both the old and new corporations and increase returns to shareholders. There is evidence to support the view that a corporate division will lead to increased recognition of shareholder value. Certain studies of corporate divisions have concluded that, following an initial period of investor uncertainty, the stocks of both distributing and controlled corporations that have engaged in a spin-off generally outperform the market.[1] This increase in stock value may be attributable in part to the fact that, following a spin-off, distributing and controlled corporations frequently are seen as attractive candidates for a corporate acquisition.

Yet another agenda driving some corporate divisions may be an acquiring corporation's need to pay down debt incurred in making an acquisition by selling off some of the target's businesses or, conversely, for a target to better position itself for an acquisition by shedding businesses that depress its value. Congress's desire to curb deferral of corporate-level tax in connection with these break-up acquisition strategies has contributed to much of the complexity of Section 355.

Alternatives exist to achieve many of the goals of a corporate division. For example, a corporation simply could sell the assets of an unwanted business. Similarly, if the business is conducted through a subsidiary, the parent could sell the subsidiary's stock. Because the selling corporation generally is taxed on the sale and its shareholders are taxed a second time when the sale proceeds are distributed, however, a sale often is more tax efficient. In contrast, the parties to a properly structured spin-off incur no current tax and the distributing corporation might even recoup its investment in a pre-existing subsidiary at far less of a tax cost than in a sale. Before the controlled corporation's shares are distributed, the controlled corporation can declare and pay a large dividend that likely will be eligible for the dividends received deduction provided by Section 243.[2]

Another alternative is for a corporation to issue tracking stock (sometimes referred to as alphabet or letter stock). The issuer pays dividends on tracking stock based on the performance of a particular division or subsidiary. The stock is listed and traded separately from the issuer's other shares, giving the illusion that there are shares outstanding in two distinct corporations. In theory, tracking stock allows for market recognition of the value of a business and provides incentives for corporate managers in the same way as a spin-off, but allows the issuing corporation to retain control of the business in question. Issuing tracking stock also does not involve the tax cost of a sale of the business. Tracking stock does not offer all the

---

1. See, e.g., P. Cusatis, J. Miles and R. Woolridge, Restructuring Through Spinoffs: The Stock Market Evidence, 33 J. Financial Economics 293 (1993).

2. See Chapter 4A, supra. The distributing corporation's dividends received deduction will be disallowed if the distributing corporation does not hold the controlled corporation's stock for a sufficient period of time. See I.R.C. § 246(c); Chapter 4F2, supra.

advantages of a spin-off, however, such as the ability to insulate one business from potential liabilities associated with another. It also may give rise to undesirable administrative and political issues, such as the necessity of satisfying two distinct groups of shareholders.

3.   HISTORICAL BACKGROUND OF SECTION 355

To better understand the technical requirements for a tax-free corporate division, it is helpful to look back at the historical background of Section 355. The early income tax provisions governing spin-offs were elegantly simple but dangerously naive. Interpreted literally, they permitted a corporation to transfer all or part of its assets to a newly formed subsidiary and then to make a tax-free distribution of the stock of that subsidiary to its shareholders as part of a plan of reorganization.[1] The tax avoidance potential of this blanket exemption from the dividend rules was enormous, and the judiciary swiftly responded by curtailing the use of a spin-off as a bailout device. In Gregory v. Helvering, which follows, the Supreme Court made one of its earliest contributions to the common law of taxation[2] and paved the way toward the enactment of a comprehensive statutory solution to the problem of corporate divisions.

Gregory v. Helvering

Supreme Court of the United States, 1935.
293 U.S. 465, 55 S.Ct. 266.

■ MR. JUSTICE SUTHERLAND delivered the opinion of the Court.

Petitioner in 1928 was the owner of all the stock of United Mortgage Corporation. That corporation held among its assets 1,000 shares of the Monitor Securities Corporation. For the sole purpose of procuring a transfer of these shares to herself in order to sell them for her individual profit, and, at the same time, diminish the amount of income tax which would result from a direct transfer by way of dividend, she sought to bring about a "reorganization" under § 112(g) of the Revenue Act of 1928, c. 852, 45 Stat. 791, 818, set forth later in this opinion. To that end, she caused the Averill Corporation to be organized under the laws of Delaware on September 18, 1928. Three days later, the United Mortgage Corporation transferred to the Averill Corporation the 1,000 shares of Monitor stock, for which all the shares of the Averill Corporation were issued to the petitioner. On September 24, the Averill Corporation was dissolved, and liquidated by distributing all its assets, namely, the Monitor shares, to the petitioner. No other business was ever transacted, or intended to be transacted, by that company. Petitioner immediately sold the Monitor shares for $133,333.33. She returned for taxation as capital net gain the sum of

1. See, e.g., Revenue Act of 1924, P.L. No. 176, § 203(c), 43 Stat. 253, 256.

2. See Blum, "Motive, Intent, and Purpose in Federal Income Taxation," 34 U.Chi. L.Rev. 485 (1967); Chirelstein, "Learned Hand's Contribution to the Law of Tax Avoidance," 77 Yale L.J. 440 (1968).

$76,007.88, based upon an apportioned cost of $57,325.45. Further details are unnecessary. It is not disputed that if the interposition of the so-called reorganization was ineffective, petitioner became liable for a much larger tax as a result of the transaction.

The Commissioner of Internal Revenue, being of opinion that the reorganization attempted was without substance and must be disregarded, held that petitioner was liable for a tax as though the United corporation had paid her a dividend consisting of the amount realized from the sale of the Monitor shares. In a proceeding before the Board of Tax Appeals, that body rejected the commissioner's view and upheld that of petitioner. 27 B.T.A. 223. Upon a review of the latter decision, the circuit court of appeals sustained the commissioner and reversed the board, holding that there had been no "reorganization" within the meaning of the statute. 69 F. (2d) 809. Petitioner applied to this court for a writ of certiorari, which the government, considering the question one of importance, did not oppose. We granted the writ.

Section 112 of the Revenue Act of 1928 deals with the subject of gain or loss resulting from the sale or exchange of property. Such gain or loss is to be recognized in computing the tax, except as provided in that section. The provisions of the section, so far as they are pertinent to the question here presented, follow:

"Sec. 112. (g) *Distribution of stock on reorganization.*—If there is distributed, in pursuance of a plan of reorganization, to a shareholder in a corporation a party to the reorganization, stock or securities in such corporation or in another corporation a party to the reorganization, without the surrender by such shareholder of stock or securities in such a corporation, no gain to the distributee from the receipt of such stock or securities shall be recognized * * *.

"(i) *Definition of reorganization.*—As used in this section * * *.

"(1) The term 'reorganization' means * * * (B) a transfer by a corporation of all or a part of its assets to another corporation if immediately after the transfer the transferor or its stockholders or both are in control of the corporation to which the assets are transferred, * * *."

It is earnestly contended on behalf of the taxpayer that since every element required by the foregoing subdivision (B) is to be found in what was done, a statutory reorganization was effected; and that the motive of the taxpayer thereby to escape payment of a tax will not alter the result or make unlawful what the statute allows. It is quite true that if a reorganization in reality was effected within the meaning of subdivision (B), the ulterior purpose mentioned will be disregarded. The legal right of a taxpayer to decrease the amount of what otherwise would be his taxes, or altogether avoid them, by means which the law permits, cannot be doubted. * * * But the question for determination is whether what was done, apart from the tax motive, was the thing which the statute intended. The reasoning of the court below in justification of a negative answer leaves little to be said.

When subdivision (B) speaks of a transfer of assets by one corporation to another, it means a transfer made "in pursuance of a plan of reorganization" [§ 112(g)] of corporate business; and not a transfer of assets by one corporation to another in pursuance of a plan having no relation to the business of either, as plainly is the case here. Putting aside, then, the question of motive in respect of taxation altogether, and fixing the character of the proceeding by what actually occurred, what do we find? Simply an operation having no business or corporate purpose—a mere device which put on the form of a corporate reorganization as a disguise for concealing its real character, and the sole object and accomplishment of which was the consummation of a preconceived plan, not to reorganize a business or any part of a business, but to transfer a parcel of corporate shares to the petitioner. No doubt, a new and valid corporation was created. But that corporation was nothing more than a contrivance to the end last described. It was brought into existence for no other purpose; it performed, as it was intended from the beginning it should perform, no other function. When that limited function had been exercised, it immediately was put to death.

In these circumstances, the facts speak for themselves and are susceptible of but one interpretation. The whole undertaking, though conducted according to the terms of subdivision (B), was in fact an elaborate and devious form of conveyance masquerading as a corporate reorganization, and nothing else. The rule which excludes from consideration the motive of tax avoidance is not pertinent to the situation, because the transaction upon its face lies outside the plain intent of the statute. To hold otherwise would be to exalt artifice above reality and to deprive the statutory provision in question of all serious purpose.

Judgment affirmed.

NOTE

The Board of Tax Appeals was more tolerant in its evaluation of Mrs. Gregory's maneuver. Adopting a strict constructionist approach, the Board reasoned that "[a] statute so meticulously drafted must be interpreted as a literal expression of the taxing policy, and leaves only the small interstices for judicial consideration."[1] On appeal to the Second Circuit, Judge Learned Hand—in one of his most famous pronouncements on tax avoidance—agreed that "[a]ny one may so arrange his affairs that his taxes shall be as low as possible; he is not bound to choose that pattern which will best pay the Treasury; there is not even a patriotic duty to increase one's taxes."[2] But he quickly eschewed literalism in favor of the big picture, reasoning that "the meaning of a sentence may be more than that of the separate words, as a melody is more than the notes, and no degree of particularity can ever obviate recourse to the setting in which all appear,

1. Gregory v. Commissioner, 27 B.T.A. 223, 225 (1932).

2. Helvering v. Gregory, 69 F.2d 809, 810 (2d Cir.1934).

and which all collectively create."[3] The Supreme Court's opinion was a less stylish but equally forceful reaffirmation that the language of the Code must be interpreted in light of its purpose.

Gregory v. Helvering has ramifications that go far beyond corporate divisions. It is one of the earliest articulations of the substance over form and step transaction doctrines. However amorphous they may be, those doctrines serve as a brooding omnipresence in the responsible tax advisor's conscience. When the system works properly (not always the reality), they also thwart the schemes of aggressive tax avoiders who rely on a literal interpretation of the Code to wreak havoc with its intended purpose. As we will see later in the chapter, the narrower business purpose doctrine emanating from *Gregory* also survives as one of the major requirements for qualification as a tax-free corporate division.[4]

While *Gregory* was pending, Congress saw the light and repealed the tax-free spin-off provision involved in that case. Curiously, split-ups (and, for a time, split-offs) continued to qualify for nonrecognition if they did not run afoul of the limitations in *Gregory*.[5] Congress ultimately realized, however, that not every spin-off is a bailout device, and in 1951 it enacted the statutory forerunner of Section 355 to remove any impediment to corporate divisions "undertaken for legitimate business purposes."[6] In general, the new statute granted nonrecognition to spin-offs that were pursuant to a plan of reorganization unless one of the corporate parties to the reorganization did not intend "to continue the active conduct of a trade or business" or "the corporation whose stock is distributed was used principally as a device for the distribution of earnings and profits * * *."[7] The contours of the present Section 355 thus were being shaped: to qualify as tax free, a spin-off had to be motivated by a genuine business purpose and consist of the separation of one or more active trades or businesses in a transaction that was not being used principally as a bailout device.

With the enactment of Section 355 in the 1954 Code, Congress finally provided a comprehensive statutory scheme governing all three types of corporate divisions.[8] At the same time, the business purpose and continuity of interest doctrines were preserved as independent nonstatutory requirements.

4. OVERVIEW OF SECTION 355

Code: §§ 355(a), (b), (c); 368(c).

Regulations: § 1.355–1(b).

Before becoming immersed in technical details, it is important to recall the purpose of Section 355. Congress intended to provide tax-free status to

---

3. Id.

4. See Section C1 of this chapter, infra.

5. For the history of corporate divisions before the 1954 Code, see Bittker & Eustice, Federal Income Taxation of Corporations and Shareholders ¶ 11.01 (7th ed. 2000).

6. S.Rep. No. 781, 82d Cong., 1st Sess. (1951), reprinted in 1951–2 C.B. 458, 499.

7. Revenue Act of 1951, ch. 521, § 317(a), 65 Stat. 493, amending Internal Revenue Code of 1939, § 112(b)(11).

8. The statute does not explicitly refer to spin-offs, split-offs and split-ups, but Section 355(a)(2) makes it clear that Section 355 applies to all three forms of corporate divisions. The different forms continue to be significant if the transaction fails the Section 355 tests.

corporate divisions serving legitimate business needs. At the same time, it included safeguards to patrol against the bailout of earnings and profits. Most of the statutory and judicial requirements are directed at these broad objectives. But their precise meaning and scope are often unclear, and the waters have been muddied further by piecemeal changes made over the years to address real and perceived abuses.

a. STATUTORY AND JUDICIAL REQUIREMENTS

A corporate division will qualify as tax free to the shareholders and the distributing corporation if it satisfies the requirements discussed below.

Control. One corporation (the "distributing corporation") must distribute to its shareholders (with respect to their stock) or to security holders (in exchange for their securities) the stock or securities of a "controlled corporation"—i.e., a corporation that the distributing corporation "controls" immediately before the distribution.[1] For this purpose, "control" is defined by Section 368(c), which requires ownership of 80 percent of the total combined voting power and 80 percent of the total number of shares of all other classes of stock, including nonvoting preferred stock.

Distribution of All Stock or Securities. The distributing corporation must distribute all the stock or securities of the controlled corporation that the distributing corporation holds or, alternatively, an amount of stock sufficient to constitute "control" within the meaning of Section 368(c).[2] If any stock or securities of the controlled corporation are retained, the distributing corporation also must establish to the satisfaction of the Service that the retention is not pursuant to a plan having tax avoidance as one of its principal purposes.[3]

Active Trade or Business Requirement. Both the distributing corporation and the controlled corporation—or in a split-up, both controlled corporations—must be engaged immediately after the distribution in an actively conducted trade or business which has been so conducted throughout the five-year period ending on the date of the distribution.[4] That business must not have been acquired within the five-year predistribution period in a taxable transaction (e.g., a sale of assets taxable to the seller).[5] Moreover, the distributing corporation must not have purchased a controlling stock interest in a corporation conducting the business in a taxable transaction during the five-year predistribution period.[6]

---

1. I.R.C. § 355(a)(1)(A).

2. I.R.C. § 355(a)(1)(D).

3. I.R.C. § 355(a)(1)(D)(ii); Rev. Proc. 96–30, 1996–1 C.B. 696. See also Rev.Rul. 75–469, 1975–2 C.B. 126; Rev.Rul. 75–321, 1975–2 C.B. 123.

4. I.R.C. § 355(a)(1)(C); (b).

5. I.R.C. § 355(b)(2)(C).

6. I.R.C. § 355(b)(2)(D). The active trade or business test also will be violated if the distributee shareholder is a corporation that acquired control of the distributing corporation within the five-year predistribution period. Id.

Not A "Device." The division must not be used "principally as a device for the distribution" of the earnings and profits of either the distributing or controlled corporations. The "mere fact" that stock or securities of either corporation are sold after the distribution is not to be considered as evidence of a device unless the sales were pursuant to a prearranged plan.[7]

Judicial Limitations: Business Purpose and Continuity of Interest. In addition to the statutory tests, the regulations incorporate two venerable judicially created limitations. Nonrecognition is available only if the distribution is carried out for an independent corporate business purpose[8] and the shareholders of the enterprise prior to the division maintain adequate continuity of interest in the distributing and controlled corporations after the distribution.[9]

All these requirements are applied without regard to the form the parties choose to accomplish the division. Thus, a distribution may qualify as tax-free under Section 355 irrespective of whether it is pro rata and whether or not the distributee shareholder surrenders stock in the distributing corporation or the distribution is preceded by the formation of a new controlled corporation in a Type D reorganization.[10]

b.   TAXATION OF THE PARTIES

Paralleling Section 354, which generally applies to nondivisive reorganizations, Section 355 provides total shareholder-level nonrecognition only where the distributing corporation distributes stock or securities of a controlled corporation.[11] Stock rights or warrants are not treated as "stock or securities" for this purpose and thus constitute taxable boot under Section 356.[12] In the case of a distribution of securities (e.g., long-term notes, bonds, debentures), if the principal amount of securities of the controlled corporation received by the distributee exceeds the principal amount of the distributing corporation's securities surrendered in connection with the distribution, the value of the excess is treated as boot.[13] If securities of the controlled corporation are received and no securities of the parent are surrendered, the entire value of the securities received is treated as boot.[14] In addition, any stock of a controlled corporation acquired in a taxable transaction within the five years preceding the distribution constitutes boot.[15] The distribution of boot does not necessarily disqualify a transaction under Section 355, but it will cause the distributee shareholder

---

7. I.R.C. § 355(a)(1)(B).

8. Reg. § 1.355–2(b).

9. Reg. § 1.355–2(c).

10. I.R.C. § 355(a)(2).

11. I.R.C. § 355(a)(1). For this purpose, "nonqualified preferred stock," as defined in section 351(g)(2), received in a distribution with respect to stock other than nonqualified preferred stock is not treated as "stock or securities"—i.e., it will be boot. I.R.C. § 355(a)(3)(D).

12. Reg. § 1.355–1(b).

13. I.R.C. §§ 355(a)(3)(A)(i); 356(d)(2)(C).

14. I.R.C. §§ 355(a)(3)(A)(ii); 356(d)(2)(C).

15. I.R.C. § 355(a)(3)(B). See Edna Louise Dunn Trust v. Commissioner, 86 T.C. 745 (1986).

to recognize any realized gain, normally as a qualified dividend taxable at preferential capital gains rates, to the extent of the boot received.[16] At the corporate level, the distributing corporation generally does not recognize gain on the distribution of stock or securities of its subsidiary but may recognize gain on the distribution of appreciated boot or in certain situations where a divisive transaction is used to facilitate the sale of a subsidiary.[17]

The principal hurdles to achieving nonrecognition under Section 355 are the active business test, the business purpose requirement and the "device" limitation. In interpreting these rules, the Treasury has waffled, first emphasizing the active business test and then shifting the emphasis to the "device" and business purpose limitations. The current government position is reflected in extensive regulations, which have largely supplanted the case law and are a principal focus of this chapter.

B.   THE ACTIVE TRADE OR BUSINESS REQUIREMENT

Code: § 355(a)(1)(C), (b).

Regulations: § 1.355–3.

Lockwood's Estate v. Commissioner

United States Court of Appeals, Eighth Circuit, 1965.
350 F.2d 712.

■ VOGEL, CIRCUIT JUDGE.

The single question involved in this review of an unreported decision of the Tax Court of the United States, entered August 26, 1964, is whether the "spin-off" of part of the business conducted by the Lockwood Grader Corporation of Gering, Nebraska, (hereinafter Lockwood) through the organization of a new corporation, Lockwood Graders of Maine, Inc. (hereinafter Maine, Inc.) was tax-free to petitioners, recipients of the stock of Maine, Inc., under 26 U.S.C.A. § 355 (Int.Rev.Code). The government contended that the spin-off was not tax-free since the requirements of § 355(b)(2)(B) relating to the conducting of an active business for five years prior to the date of distribution had not been met. The government apparently conceded and the Tax Court found that the petitioners had met all other requirements to qualify under § 355 for tax-free treatment. The Tax Court upheld the government's contention and petitioners appeal.

The now deceased Thorval J. Lockwood, whose interests herein are represented by his duly qualified executor, National Bank of Commerce Trust and Savings Association, and his wife Margaret were the sole

16.   I.R.C. §§ 355(a)(4)(A); 356. See Section C of this Chapter, infra, for a more detailed explanation of the treatment of boot and the other operative provisions that accompany Section 355.

17.   I.R.C. § 355(c), (d).

stockholders of Lockwood and had been so since its incorporation under Nebraska law in 1946. Lockwood's predecessor, Lockwood Graders, was a partnership formed in 1935 for the purpose of producing and selling a portable potato sorting machine invented by the decedent. Starting in the early spring of each year Thorval and Margaret drove to Alabama and worked their way north through Missouri to North Dakota for the purpose of selling Lockwood products. The equipment was sold in "all of the potato growing areas of the United States" but primarily in the biggest growing areas such as North Dakota, Idaho and Colorado.

From 1946 to 1951, inclusive, Lockwood operated its business of manufacturing and selling wash lines, potato machinery, parts and supplies to potato shippers in the potato growing areas. Though Lockwood continued to have its principal place of business at Gering, Nebraska, branches were opened, as the business expanded, in Grand Forks, North Dakota; Antigo, Wisconsin; Monte Vista, Colorado; and Rupert, Idaho. These branches performed both manufacturing and sales functions. In 1952, under a reorganization plan, these branches were separately incorporated to promote greater efficiency and to properly provide for expansion. Assets of Lockwood were exchanged for all of the stock of each new corporation and the stock so exchanged was passed without consideration to Thorval and Margaret as sole stockholders of Lockwood. The reorganization plan, among other things, was specifically designed to make use of the tax-free provisions of what is now § 355.

In the early 1950's Lockwood and the other controlled corporations changed the nature of their business somewhat by selling to individual farmers as well as to potato suppliers. Lockwood had previously dealt primarily in grading equipment but at this time it began to manufacture and sell field equipment such as harvesting pieces, bin holders and vine beaters as well.

Beginning as early as 1947 Lockwood began to make some sporadic and relatively inconsequential sales in the northeastern part of the United States. From 1949 to 1955 the primary sales of products and parts in that part of the country were made to Gould & Smith, Inc., a retailer of farming and industrial equipment, of Presque Isle, Maine (although there are no records of sales made to them in 1952). Such sales were found to be of a relatively small volume by the Tax Court. On November 15, 1954, Lockwood established a branch office in Presque Isle, Maine, from which to handle Lockwood products. On March 1, 1956, pursuant to the 1951 plan for reorganization set out in footnote 2, supra, the Maine branch office was incorporated under the laws of Maine with its principal place of business at Presque Isle, Maine. Maine, Inc., was a wholly owned subsidiary of Lockwood. On incorporating, Lockwood transferred to Maine, Inc., $23,500 in assets consisting of petty cash totalling $150.00, accounts receivable totalling $4,686.67, automobiles and trucks worth $1,100, shop equipment worth $295.00, office furniture and fixtures worth $81.60, and inventory worth $17,186.73. In return for these assets Maine, Inc., issued all of its stock, 235 shares at $100.00 par value, to Lockwood. On March 31, 1956,

Lockwood distributed 162 of these shares of Maine, Inc., to Thorval and 73 of them to Margaret. This distribution gave rise to the controversy here involved.

The Tax Court held this distribution to be outside of § 355. According to the Tax Court there was:

"* * * the absence of evidence that the *Maine business* was actively conducted during the months between March 31, 1951, and August 1953—a span of time totaling over 40 per cent of the requisite five-year period [required by § 355(b)(2)(B).]" (Emphasis supplied.)

The Tax Court found that the Maine business was not actively and continuously conducted until August 1953, at which time a Lockwood salesman traveled to Maine and personally solicited orders from farmers and businessmen other than Gould & Smith. We do not disagree with the factual finding of the Tax Court as to the active conduct of Lockwood's business in Maine prior to the incorporation of Maine, Inc. However, the Tax Court, for reasons set out below, erred in looking only at the business performed by Lockwood in Maine to determine if the five-year active business requirement had been met prior to the incorporation of Maine, Inc. Nothing in the language of § 355 suggests that prior business activity is only to be measured by looking at the business performed in a geographical area where the controlled corporation is eventually formed. In this case, when the entire Lockwood market is viewed, it can be seen that Lockwood was engaged in active business as required by § 355 for the five years prior to the incorporation of Maine, Inc. Since its incorporation Maine, Inc., has carried on the same kind of manufacturing and selling business previously and concurrently performed by Lockwood. Thus all § 355 prerequisites are met and the Tax Court erred in determining this was not a tax-free transfer.

At this point it would be helpful to look at the evolvement of what is now § 355. Prior to 1924 a distribution to stockholders pursuant to a spin-off was taxed as a dividend. From 1924 to 1932, however, the revenue acts changed position and provided spin-offs could be tax-free. From 1934 to 1950 tax-free spin-offs were again abolished since this device was being used as a method for distributing earnings and profits, which would otherwise be taxable dividends, through the issuance of stock in the controlled corporation. Such stock could be disposed of at the more favorable capital gain rates. Because of the usefulness of the spin-off device in the achievement of corporate growth and flexibility, Congress again accorded it tax-free status in 1951. At that time certain conditions were imposed to prevent any abuse from using this device. In 1954 the tax-free spin-off was continued as § 355 of the Code with additional tax avoidance safeguards which included the five-year active business requirement involved in this case.

As stated by the Second Circuit in Bonsall v. Commissioner, 2 Cir., 1963, 317 F.2d 61, at page 65:

" * * * Only long application may completely clarify the difficult terminology of section 355."

With this we agree. However, certain things have become clear since the enactment of § 355 in 1954. After much controversy it has been determined that tax-free treatment will not be denied to a transaction under § 355 merely because it represents an attempt to divide a single trade or business. See United States v. Marett, 5 Cir., 1963, 325 F.2d 28; Coady v. Commissioner, 33 T.C. 771, affirmed per curiam, 6 Cir., 1961, 289 F.2d 490. The Commissioner has acceded to the holdings of Marett and Coady in Rev.Rule 64–147, 1964–1, Cum.Bull. 136, even though the Commissioner had previously insisted, in § 1.355–1(a) of the Income Tax Regulations, that two or more existing businesses had to be actively operated the five years prior to distribution. The Tax Court in Coady, at pages 777–778 of 33 T.C., states:

"Respondent maintains that a reading of 355(b)(2)(B) [set out at footnote 1, supra] in conjunction with the requirement of 355(b)(1) [set out at footnote 4, infra] * * * indicates Congress intended the provisions of the statute to apply only where, immediately after the distribution, there exist two separate and distinct businesses, one operated by the distributing corporation and one operated by the controlled corporation, both of which were actively conducted for the 5–year period immediately preceding the distribution. In our judgment the statute does not support this construction.

"As noted, the only reference to plurality appears in section 355(b)(1), and deals with corporate entities, not businesses. Recognizing the divisive nature of the transaction, subsection (b)(1) contemplates that where there was only one corporate entity prior to the various transfers, immediately subsequent thereto, there will be two or more *corporations*. In order to insure that a tax-free separation will involve the separation only of those assets attributable to the carrying on of an active trade or business, and further to prevent the tax-free division of an active corporation into active and inactive entities, (b)(1) further provides that each of the surviving corporations must be engaged in the active conduct of *a* trade or business. [Emphasis by the court.]

"A careful reading of the definition of the active conduct of a trade or business contained in subsection (b)(2) indicates that its function is also to prevent the tax-free separation of *active* and *inactive* assets into *active* and *inactive* corporate entities. This is apparent from the use of the adjective 'such,' meaning beforementioned to modify 'trade or business' in subsection (b)(2)(B), thus providing that the trade or business, required by (b)(2)(B) to have had a 5–year active history prior to the distribution, is the same trade or business which (b)(2)(A) requires to be actively conducted immediately after the distribution. Nowhere in (b)(2) do we find, as respondent suggests we should, language denying the benefits of section 355 to the division of a single trade or business. [Emphasis by the court.]

"Nor can respondent derive support for his position by reading subsections (b)(1) and (b)(2) together, inasmuch as the plurality resulting therefrom is occasioned, not by any requirement that there be a multiplicity of businesses, but rather by the divisive nature of the transaction itself: i.e., one corporation becoming two or more corporations. *Moreover, from the fact that the statute requires, immediately after the distribution, that the surviving corporations each be engaged in the conduct of a trade or business with an active 5–year history, we do not think it inevitably follows that each such trade or business necessarily must have been conducted on an individual basis throughout that 5–year period. As long as the trade or business which has been divided has been actively conducted for 5 years preceding the distribution, and the resulting businesses (each of which in this case, happens to be half of the original whole) are actively conducted after the division, we are of the opinion that the active business requirements of the statute have been complied with.*" (Emphasis supplied.)

Respondent in the instant case, although claiming to accept the single business interpretation, points to the language of § 355(b)(1) and argues, as did the government in Coady, that the word "*and*" in that section means that, in determining whether or not the active business requirement was met, one has to look at both the business done by the distributing corporation (Lockwood) *and* the business done as such by the controlled corporation (Maine, Inc.) and its predecessors in Maine. Contrary to the government's position, once it has been ascertained that two or more trades or businesses are not required for § 355 to apply, the crucial question becomes whether or not the two corporations existing after distribution are doing the same type of work and using the same type of assets previously done and used by the prior *single* existing business. § 355(b)(1) has no relevance to respondent's point once it has been determined that only a single business is required.

Here the five years of prior activity we are concerned with involve the prior overall activity of Lockwood. Previous to 1956 Lockwood had carried on *in toto* what Maine, Inc., would later carry on in part in the northeast. We are not concerned with the prior activity of Lockwood in the northeast only, for Congress has never intimated that such a geographical test should be applied and we are not about to apply such a test now. A perusal of the House and Senate Reports indicates conclusively that at no time did the House or the Senate contemplate any kind of geographic test in applying the five-year active business requirement. The facts clearly show that Lockwood, in fact, was actively conducting the trade or business involved five years prior to the distribution period.

One case, Patricia W. Burke v. Commissioner, 1964, 42 T.C. 1021, did discuss the past business of a controlled corporation as performed in a limited geographical area in finding the prerequisites of § 355 had been met. That case did not, however, hold that there was in fact a geographical test. Further, at page 1028 that court set out what we believe to be the test:

> "* * * as long as the business which is divided has been actively conducted for 5 years before the distribution and the resulting businesses are actively conducted after the division, the active business requirements of the statute are met. Cf. also H. Grady Lester, 40 T.C. 947 (1963)."

Since there is no Congressional intent evidenced to the contrary, the test, restated, is not whether active business had been carried out in the geographic area later served by the controlled corporation but, simply, whether the distributing corporation, for five years prior to distribution, had been actively conducting the type of business now performed by the controlled corporation without reference to the geographic area. In the instant case the facts are abundantly clear that Lockwood had been actively engaged in the type of business later carried on by Maine, Inc., if one refers to a national rather than just the northeastern market.

It was mentioned earlier in this opinion that beginning in 1950 Lockwood began to sell field equipment as well as grading equipment. The respondent apparently does not contend, nor do we find, that Lockwood so changed its business as to be engaged in a new business that had been active for only two years prior to the incorporation of Maine, Inc. Lockwood meets the requirements of an existing five-year active business as set out by the Conference Committee in Conference Report No. 2543 at page 5298 of 3 U.S.C.Cong. & Adm.News, 1954:

> "It is the understanding of the managers on the part of the House, in agreeing to the active business requirements of section 355 and of section 346 (defining partial liquidations), that a trade or business which has been actively conducted throughout the 5-year period described in such sections will meet the requirements of such sections, even though such trade or business underwent change during such 5-year period, for example, *by the addition of new,* or the dropping of old, *products,* changes in production capacity, and the like, provided the changes are not of such a character as to constitute the acquisition of a new or different business." (Emphasis supplied.)

In § 1.355–4(b)(3) of the Income Tax Regulations the Commissioner specifically adopts the above-quoted portion of the Committee Report.

The respondent contends:

> "If the taxpayers' argument prevails, then any corporation with a five-year history could distribute any of its assets regardless of when they were acquired and regardless of what kind of business they are in after the division, as long as the distributing corporation is in an active business. In other words, taxpayer argues that the five-year history rule requires that only the business of the distributing corporation have a five-year history.

For instance, suppose a large manufacturing corporation with a ten-year life acquired some data processing machines in order to better control its inventory and work-in-process flow. If taxpayers' argument is correct, a year later this corporation could transfer all the data processing equipment to a new corporation in exchange for its stock, spin off the stock and claim a tax-free distribution under Section 355 since the manufacturing corporation had more than a five-year life and the data processing business, once an integral part of the original business, was being actively conducted after the spin-off. Moreover, the same logic would allow the spin-off of real estate owned by the manufacturing corporation and used in its business."

The fears of the government are unfounded. The example of the manufacturing company is more closely akin to the Bonsall case, supra, and is factually distinguishable from the instant case. Here Lockwood had not just recently acquired that part or segment of its business that was spun off. Rather, what was spun off was a part of the business Lockwood had always performed in the past and which it has continued to perform since the distribution. If Lockwood had, just before distribution, acquired or opened up a new or entirely different aspect of its business unrelated to prior activities and had spun this off to the controlled corporation, a different result might ensue. In Bonsall the distributing company, a dealer in floor covering materials, attempted to assert a tax-free spin-off occurred when a rental business of *de minimis* proportions was transferred to a subsidiary with the stock of the subsidiary being distributed to the distributor's shareholders. The Second Circuit held at page 64 of 317 F.2d:

"There is ample support for the factual determination that Albany Linoleum [the distributing company therein] was not actively conducting a real-estate rental business. * * * the portion of its income realized from real estate rentals was minute. * * * No activity appeared beyond a few casual conversations with prospective tenants. Moreover, most of the floor-space of the two buildings combined was occupied by the floor-covering business. Only a very small part was available for rental, and an even smaller part actually leased. The continuing rental to Armstrong Cork Co. which provided most of the rental income appeared to be an accommodation to a large supplier of the floor-covering business and thus an adjunct to it, rather than indicative of an independent business, for the Tax Court found that the premises were let at less than fair rental value over the five-year period. Finally, no separate records of rental income and expenses were kept. Absence of such records is at least probative of the fact that the managers of Albany Linoleum did not regard it as engaged in an independent rental business. The Tax Court was plainly justified in concluding that the small amount of rental activity was merely an incidental part of the sole business of the corporation—wholesale floor-coverings. * * * "

Thus it is clear that in respondent's example and in Bonsall the business sought to be spun off was not actively engaged in for five years prior to distribution, which is not the situation in the instant case. Here, what was spun off was merely an integral part of what had been Lockwood's primary and only business from its inception.

Further, it should be remembered that even if the five-year active business requirement is met, there is further protection in § 355 against spin-offs being used for mere tax avoidance, which would be contrary to Congressional intent. § 355(a)(1)(B) will only allow a tax-free spin-off transaction where " * * * the transaction was not used principally as a device for the distribution of the earnings and profits of the distributing corporation or the controlled corporation or both * * *." Under this section, the government and the courts have great latitude in preventing the abuses which the respondent fears will happen by finding for petitioners in this case. Cf. Gregory v. Helvering, 1935, 293 U.S. 465, 55 S.Ct. 266, 79 L.Ed. 596. Herein the respondent does not contend that the purpose of the spin off was designed primarily for tax avoidance. No earnings and profits were in fact distributed to Thorval and Margaret. The Tax Court stated that:

> " * * * we do not view the distribution as running afoul of the congressional purpose behind section 355, * * *."

This being so, and since petitioners otherwise complied with § 355, the decision of the Tax Court will be reversed. The transaction herein involved cannot be treated as a taxable distribution of dividends.

Revenue Ruling 2003–38

2003–1 Cum. Bull. 811.

ISSUE

Whether the creation by a corporation engaged in the retail shoe store business of an Internet web site on which the corporation will sell shoes at retail constitutes an expansion of the corporation's business rather than the acquisition of a new or different business under § 1.355–3(b)(3)(ii) of the Income Tax Regulations.

FACTS

Corporation D has operated a retail shoe store business, under the name "D," since Year 1 in a manner that meets the requirements of § 355(b) of the Internal Revenue Code. D's sales are made exclusively to customers who frequent its retail stores in shopping malls and other locations. D's business enjoys favorable name recognition, customer loyalty, and other elements of goodwill in the retail shoe market. In Year 8, D creates an Internet web site and begins selling shoes at retail on the web site. To a significant extent, the operation of the web site draws upon D's experience and know-how. The web site is named "D.com" to take advantage of the name recognition, customer loyalty, and other elements of goodwill associated with D and the D name and to enhance the web site's chances for success in its initial stages. In Year 10, D transfers all of the web site's assets and liabilities to corporation C, a newly formed, wholly owned subsidiary of D, and distributes the stock of C pro rata to D's shareholders. Apart from the issue of whether the web site is considered an expansion of D's business and therefore entitled to share the business's five-year history at the time of the distribution in Year 10, the distribution meets all the requirements of § 355.

LAW

Section 355(a) provides that a corporation may distribute stock and securities in a controlled corporation to its shareholders and security holders in a transaction that will not cause the distributees to recognize gain or loss, provided that, among other requirements, (i) each of the distributing corporation and controlled corporation is engaged, immediately after the distribution, in the active conduct of a trade or business, (ii) each trade or business has been actively conducted throughout the five-year period ending on the date of the distribution, and (iii) neither trade or business was acquired in a transaction in which gain or loss was recognized, in whole or in part, within the five-year period. Sections 355(b)(1)(A), 355(b)(2)(B), and 355(b)(2)(C).

In determining whether an active trade or business has been conducted by a corporation throughout the five-year period preceding the distribution, the fact that a trade or business underwent change during the five-year period (for example, by the addition of new or the dropping of old products, changes in production capacity, and the like) shall be disregarded, provided that the changes are not of such a character as to constitute the acquisition of a new or different business. Section 1.355–3(b)(3)(ii). In particular, if a corporation engaged in the active conduct of one trade or business during that five-year period purchased, created, or otherwise acquired another trade or business in the same line of business, then the acquisition of that other business is ordinarily treated as an expansion of the original business, all of which is treated as having been actively conducted during that five-year period, unless that purchase, creation, or other acquisition effects a change of such character as to constitute the acquisition of a new or different business. Id.

In Example (7) of § 1.355–3(c), corporation X had owned and operated a department store in the downtown area of the City of G for six years before acquiring a parcel of land in a suburban area of G and constructing a new department store. Three years after the construction, X transferred the suburban store and related business assets to new subsidiary Y and distributed the Y stock to X's shareholders. Citing § 1.355–3(b)(3)(i) and (ii), the example concludes that X and Y both satisfy the requirements of § 355(b).

In Example (8) of § 1.355–3(c), corporation X had owned and operated hardware stores in several states for four years before purchasing the assets of a hardware store in State M where X had not previously conducted business. Two years after the purchase, X transferred the State M store and related business assets to new subsidiary Y and distributed the Y stock to X's shareholders. Citing § 1.355–3(b)(3)(i) and (ii), the example concludes that X and Y both satisfy the requirements of § 355(b).

Rev. Rul. 2003–18, 2003–7 I.R.B. 467, concludes that the acquisition by a dealer engaged in the sale and service of brand X automobiles of a franchise (and the assets needed) to sell and service brand Y automobiles is an expansion of the brand X business and does not constitute the acquisition of a new or different business under § 1.355–3(b)(3)(ii) because (i) the product of the brand X automobile dealership is similar to the product of the brand Y automobile dealership, (ii) the business activities associated with the operation of the brand X automobile dealership (i.e., sales and service) are the same as the business activities associated with the operation of the brand Y automobile dealership, and (iii) the operation of the brand Y automobile dealership involves the use of the experience and know-how that the dealer developed in the operation of the brand X automobile dealership.

ANALYSIS

The product of the retail shoe store business and the product of the web site are the same (shoes), and the principal business activities of the retail shoe store business are the same as those of the web site (purchasing shoes at wholesale and reselling them at retail). Selling shoes on a web site requires some know-how not associated with operating a retail store, such as familiarity with different marketing approaches, distribution chains, and technical operations issues. Nevertheless, the web site's operation does draw to a significant extent on D's existing experience and know-how, and the web site's success will depend in large measure on the goodwill associated with D and the D name. Accordingly, the creation by D of the Internet web site does not constitute the acquisition of a new or different business under § 1.355–3(b)(3)(ii). Instead, it is an expansion of D's retail shoe store business. Therefore, each of D and C is engaged in the active conduct of a five-year active trade or business immediately after the distribution. See Rev. Rul. 2003–18 and § 1.355–3(c), Examples (7) and (8).

HOLDING

The creation by a corporation engaged in the retail shoe store business of an Internet web site that sells shoes at retail constitutes an expansion of the retail shoe store business rather than the acquisition of a new or different business under § 1.355–3(b)(3)(ii).

NOTE

Although the anti-bailout objective of the active business requirement is clear enough, this multifaceted test has engendered considerable litigation. The *Lockwood* case is typical of the Commissioner's unsuccessful early efforts to apply the test strictly. The Service retreated on a number of controversial issues and most of these concessions are reflected in the regulations. This Note surveys some settled and lingering questions.

Trade or Business. Both the distributing corporation and the controlled corporation (or the controlled corporations in the case of a split-up) must be engaged immediately after the distribution in a trade or business with a five-year history. The regulations treat a corporation as being engaged in a trade or business if:[1]

> * * * a specific group of activities are being carried on by the corporation for the purpose of earning income or profit, and the activities included in such group include every operation that forms a part of, or a step in, the process of earning income or profit. Such group of activities ordinarily must include the collection of income and the payment of expenses.

The regulations go on to create a dichotomy between active business and passive investment activities. Although the determination of whether a trade or business is "actively conducted" is a factual question turning on all the facts and circumstances, active business status generally requires the corporation to itself perform active and substantial management and operational functions.[2] For this purpose, the activities performed by persons outside the corporation, such as independent contractors, generally are not taken into account.[3] To preclude a tax-free separation of passive investment assets, "active conduct" does not include the holding of property for investment (e.g., raw land or portfolio securities) or the ownership and operation (including leasing) of real or personal property used in the owner's trade or business unless the owner performs significant management services with respect to the property.[4]

Vertical Divisions of a Single Integrated Business. Suppose a corporation wishes to divide a single trade or business that has been operated for more than five years? Does Section 355 require two separate predistribution trades or businesses, each with its own five-year history, or may one existing business be divided in two? After several defeats,[5] the Service came to acknowledge that Section 355 can apply to the separation of a single business. Thus, assuming the other statutory and judicial requirements are met, a corporation engaged in an integrated business at one location may transfer half of its assets to a new subsidiary and distribute the stock of the subsidiary to a 50 percent shareholder in a tax-free split-off.[6]

Functional Divisions. The treatment of functional divisions—i.e., separations of certain distinct functions of a single business enterprise—is more

---

1. Reg. § 1.355–3(b)(2)(ii).

2. Reg. § 1.355–3(b)(2)(iii). Some of the corporation's activities, however, can be performed by others. Id.

3. Id.

4. Reg. § 1.355–3(b)(2)(iv).

5. See Coady v. Commissioner, 33 T.C. 771 (1960), affirmed per curiam 289 F.2d 490 (6th Cir.1961)(single construction business divided into two businesses to resolve shareholder dispute); United States v. Marett, 325 F.2d 28 (5th Cir.1963)(food manufacturer operating at three factories spun off one factory opened eight months before the distribution).

6. See, e.g., Reg. § 1.355–3(c) Examples (4) & (5).

uncertain. To illustrate the issue, assume that a manufacturer of high technology equipment wishes to spin off its research and development function for valid business reasons. The Service once maintained that such support activities did not constitute a separate trade or business because they did not independently produce income.[7] The regulations now sanction some types of functional divisions, as illustrated in the following example:[8]

> For the past eight years, corporation X has engaged in the manufacture and sale of household products. Throughout this period, X has maintained a research department for use in connection with its manufacturing activities. The research department has 30 employees actively engaged in the development of new products. X transfers the research department to new subsidiary Y and distributes the stock of Y to X's shareholders. After the distribution, Y continues its research operations on a contractual basis with several corporations, including X. X and Y both satisfy the requirements of section 355(b). * * * The result in this example is the same if, after the distribution, Y continues its research operations but furnishes its services only to X. * * *

Similarly, if a steel manufacturer spins off a coal mine operated solely to supply its coal requirements, the manufacturing and captive coal mine activities will qualify as separate active businesses after the distribution.[9]

The regulations make it clear that the functional separation in the example above satisfies the active business test whether the research department subsequently provides services only to the business from which it was separated or also to other customers. The coal mine also was treated as an active business even though it did not derive income from outside third parties. These examples reflect the Service's abandonment of any requirement that an active business must ''independently'' produce income. But tax-free treatment for a functional division is still far from assured. The transaction also must have a corporate business purpose, and it must not run afoul of the ''device'' limitation. As we will discover shortly, the regulations provide that the same functional separations which pass muster under the active business test may present ''evidence'' of a prohibited bailout device.[10]

Geographical Divisions. The liberal approach of the *Lockwood* case has been incorporated into the regulations. Previously, the Service applied a strict geographic test under which, for example, a manufacturer with factories in two locations could not separate one from the other unless they both had a five-year business history. The current regulations dispense with geography and look to the character of the activity and commonality of functions in determining whether geographically dispersed operations constitute a single integrated business. Thus, a new activity in the same

---

7. Reg. § 1.355–1(c)(3)(pre–1989).

8. Reg. § 1.355–3(c) Example (9).

9. Reg. § 1.355–3(c) Example (11). See also Reg. § 1.355–3(c) Example (10), providing that the separation of the processing and sales functions of a meat products business satisfies the active business test.

10. See Reg. § 1.355–2(d)(2)(iv)(C).

line of business as an activity that has been actively conducted by the distributing corporation for more than five years ordinarily will not be considered a separate business. For example, the regulations would permit a nine year old department store to spin off a suburban branch constructed three years ago, where after the distribution each store has its own manager and is operated independently of the other store.[11]

Single or Multiple Businesses: The Section 355(b) Five–Year Rules. To satisfy the active business test, both the distributing and distributed (i.e., controlled) corporations—or both distributed corporations in a split-up— must operate businesses that were actively conducted for the five years prior to the distribution.[12] In addition, those businesses must not have been acquired within the five-year predistribution period in a transaction that was taxable to the seller, and must not have been conducted by a corporation the control (i.e., 80 percent) of which was acquired by the distributing or any distributee corporation in a taxable transaction during that five-year period.[13] A purpose of these requirements is to prevent a corporation from using Section 355 to avoid the dividend provisions of Subchapter C by temporarily investing its earnings in a business that it plans to spin off to its shareholders.

The five-year rules have spawned controversies over whether a particular activity is a separate business requiring its own five-year history or simply part of an integrated business which has been active for more than five years. We have seen, for example, that a recently opened suburban branch store may be treated as an integral part of an ongoing department store business with a more than five-year history.[14] On the other hand, businesses with clearly distinct products or services (e.g., a chicken ranch and a winery) are considered to be separate.[15] As *Lockwood* illustrates, similar problems arise in the case of a diversification or expansion of a business within the five-year predistribution period. The regulations offer some guidance on this question, suggesting that a newer activity in the same line of business will be treated as an expansion of the original business unless the "purchase, creation, or other acquisition effects a change of such a character as to constitute the acquisition of a new or different business."[16] If the earnings of one business are used to finance the

---

11. Reg. § 1.355–3(c) Example (7). See also Reg. § 1.355–3(c) Example (8), illustrating the same result where the new activity is purchased as a going concern.

12. I.R.C. § 355(b)(2)(B).

13. I.R.C. § 355(b)(2)(C)–(D); Reg. § 1.355–3(b)(1)–(5). For this purpose, a "taxable transaction" is one in which gain or loss was recognized in whole or in part by the seller. If a business is acquired in a tax-free reorganization, its previous history carries over (along with its tax attributes) for purposes of the five-year rule.

14. Reg. § 1.355–3(c) Example (7).

15. See, e.g., Rev.Rul. 56–655, 1956–2 C.B. 214 (retail appliance branch and retail furniture branch considered separate businesses); Rev.Rul. 56–451, 1956–2 C.B. 208 (metal industry magazine separate from magazine to serve electrical industry).

16. Reg. § 1.355–3(b)(3)(ii). See also Rev. Rul. 2002–49, 2002–2 C.B. 288, where a corporation that actively conducted a commercial real estate business in conjunction with another unrelated corporation through a limited liability company in which each corporation held a 20 percent interest continued to engage in the same trade or business (and did not acquire a new or different business)

growth of a separate enterprise, the Service has ruled that an attempted spin-off of one of the businesses may not qualify under Section 355, possibly because a new, insufficiently "aged" business has been created.[17]

Real Estate. The Service has consistently maintained that investment land and owner-occupied real estate ordinarily do not constitute actively conducted businesses.[18] The regulations provide that the separation of owner-occupied real estate will be subject to "careful scrutiny." Real estate qualifies as an active business only if the owner performs "significant services with respect to the operation and management of the property."[19] Thus, the Service will not approve the spin-off of vacant land or mineral rights on ranch land, even if development activities are imminent.[20] But it will sanction the separation of an office building substantially leased (10 of 11 floors) to outsiders and actively managed by the lessor.[21] More recently, reversing its longstanding position, the Service has ruled that a real estate investment trust's rental activities can constitute an active trade or business if, for example, the REIT provides significant services to its tenants.[22] Even if the active business hurdle is surmounted, however, separations of real estate may be vulnerable under the "device" and business purpose tests.[23]

Dispositions of Recently Acquired Businesses. A transaction will flunk the active business requirement if the distributing corporation acquired control (i.e., 80 percent of the stock) of a corporation conducting the trade or business in a taxable transaction within the five years preceding its distribution.[24] In addition, if a controlling stock interest in the corporation conducting the trade or business was acquired by a corporate distributee shareholder within the five-year period preceding the distribution, the active trade or business requirement will not be met.[25] This rule precludes a corporation ("P") from purchasing a controlling interest in another corporation ("T") which has a subsidiary ("S") and then causing T to distribute the S stock to P in a tax-free distribution to set the stage for a sale by P of the S stock without recognizing any of the gain inherent in S's assets. Under Section 355(b)(2)(D), the distribution of S stock would not qualify as tax-free because control of the distributing corporation (T) was acquired by a corporate distributee (P) within the five-year period preced-

after it acquired the remaining 80 percent of the LLC in a taxable transaction.

17. Rev. Rul. 59–400, 1959–2 C.B. 114.

18. Reg. § 1.355–3(b)(2)(iv).

19. Id. Real estate management services are "active" if a corporation provides them in its capacity as a corporate general partner of a general partnership or as a member-manager of a limited liability company. See Rev. Rul. 92–17, 1992–1 C.B. 142; Rev. Rul. 2002–49, supra note 16.

20. Reg. § 1.355–3(c) Examples (2) and (3).

21. Reg. § 1.355–3(c) Example (12). Compare Reg. § 1.355–3(c) Example (13), where the separation of a two-story office building did not qualify where the distributing corporation occupied the ground floor and half of the second floor in the conduct of its banking business and rented the remaining area as storage space.

22. Rev. Rul. 2001–29, 2001–1 C.B. 1348.

23. See, e.g., Reg. § 1.355–2(d)(2)(iv)(C).

24. I.R.C. § 355(b)(2)(D).

25. Id.

ing the distribution. This aspect of Section 355 and related obstacles to using a tax-free corporate division to facilitate an acquisition are discussed later in this chapter.[26]

PROBLEMS

1. Lemon Corporation has been engaged in the manufacture and sale of personal computer equipment for ten years at two plants, one in Boston, Massachusetts and the other in San Jose, California. During this same period, Lemon also has operated a separate research and development division at each location. Its common stock, the only class outstanding, is owned equally by Ms. Micro and Mr. Chips. In each of the following alternative transactions, consider whether the division of Lemon Corporation satisfies the active trade or business requirement:

   (a) As a result of a shareholder dispute, Ms. Micro wishes to say goodbye to Mr. Chips. To enable the shareholders to part company but continue in the computer business, Lemon contributes the assets and research division of the Boston facility to a new corporation, Peach, Inc., and distributes all the Peach, Inc. stock to Mr. Chips in redemption of his Lemon stock. Ms. Micro remains as the sole shareholder of Lemon.

   (b) Same as (a), above, except that the Boston facility was opened three years ago.

   (c) Same as (b), above, except the Boston facility was acquired three years ago in a taxable transaction.

   (d) To comply with a divestiture order, Lemon transfers the assets of the research divisions to a new corporation, Research, Inc. and distributes all the Research stock pro rata to the shareholders. After the distribution, Research, Inc. continues to perform services solely for Lemon.

   (e) In addition to the operations described above, assume that three years ago Lemon purchased all the stock of Floppy Disk, Inc., a computer software manufacturer, in a taxable transaction. To comply with a regulatory decree, Lemon distributes the stock of Floppy Disk pro rata to its shareholders.

   (f) Same as (e), above, except that Floppy Disk merged into Lemon three years ago in a Type A reorganization. The consideration for that acquisition consisted of Lemon nonvoting preferred stock (80%) and Lemon short-term notes (20%).

2. DC Enterprises ("DC") is a large manufacturing company which owns the 10 story building in which it conducts its business. For the past 15 years, it has used six floors for its own operations and rented the other four floors to unrelated tenants. Six years ago, DC formed a wholly owned subsidiary, Properties, Inc., which leases two other commercial buildings

---

26. See Section E1 of this chapter, infra.

previously owned by DC on a long-term net lease basis, under which the tenants are responsible for property taxes, insurance and maintenance. Consider whether the following alternative transactions satisfy the active trade or business requirement:

(a) On the advice of a management consultant, DC transfers its 10 story office building to a new corporation, Rental, Inc., and distributes the Rental stock pro rata to its shareholders. After the distribution, DC leases from Rental the six floors that it occupies; and Rental continues to rent the other four floors to unrelated tenants. Rental employees actively manage the building and perform repair and maintenance services.

(b) Same as (a), above, except that DC only occupies one floor and the remaining space is leased to unrelated tenants.

(c) Same as (b), above, except the nine floors are rented to outsiders under a long-term net lease.

(d) DC distributes all the stock of Properties, Inc. pro rata to the DC shareholders. After the distribution, Properties continues its rental activities.

C. JUDICIAL AND STATUTORY LIMITATIONS

1. BUSINESS PURPOSE

Regulations: § 1.355–2(b).

Background. The business purpose doctrine originated in Gregory v. Helvering[1] and rapidly assumed its role as one of the first "common law" principles of federal taxation. The doctrine has become an increasingly important limitation under Section 355 even though it is never mentioned in the Code. The business purpose and device limitations are conceptually linked, each focusing on the taxpayer's motivation for the transaction. It is appropriate to consider the business purpose requirement first because the strength or weakness of a corporate business purpose is evidence in determining whether a transaction was used principally as a device for distributing earnings and profits.[2] Moreover, the regulations have long provided that the "business purpose requirement is independent of the other requirements under section 355."[3] Thus, a corporate division lacking a business purpose can not be accomplished tax free even if it is not used principally as a device to bail out earnings and profits.[4]

Business Purpose Regulations. The regulations define a corporate business purpose as "a real and substantial non Federal tax purpose germane to the business of the distributing corporation, the controlled corporation or the affiliated group to which the distributing corporation

1. See p. 516, supra.

2. Reg. § 1.355–2(b)(4), (d)(3)(ii).

3. Reg. § 1.355–2(b)(1).

4. Reg. § 1.355–2(b)(1).

belongs.''[5] Valid business purposes include compliance with antitrust and other regulatory decrees, resolution of shareholder disputes, or even amicable partings to permit shareholders to pursue separate business interests.[6] Among other business purposes approved by the courts and the Service over the years are: facilitating a merger of the distributing or controlled corporation;[7] increasing access to credit or new equity investment (such as by enabling either the controlled or distributing corporations to raise capital on more favorable terms through a public offering);[8] resolving labor problems;[9] providing an equity interest to a newly-hired key employee;[10] and warding off a hostile takeover.[11]

A pure shareholder purpose, such as personal estate planning, does not suffice under the regulations,[12] but the transaction may pass muster if a shareholder purpose is "so nearly coextensive with a corporate business purpose as to preclude any distinction between them."[13] For example, in Revenue Ruling 2003–52,[14] the Service ruled that the division of a family farm business into two separate corporations, one to grow grain and the other to raise livestock, satisfied the business purpose requirement. The division was motivated by a desire to permit the two principal shareholders (a brother and sister who disagreed over the future direction of the family business) to go their separate ways and devote their undivided attention to the businesses in which they were most involved, and also to promote family harmony and further the estate planning goals of their parents, who also were shareholders. The Service concluded that since the principal motivation for the transaction was to benefit both businesses, the fact that it also facilitated personal estate planning of the shareholders and promoted family harmony was not fatal.

Similarly, the Service found nearly co-extensive corporate and shareholder purposes on a separation of two lines of business of a public company that was motivated by a desire to increase the aggregate trading price of the stock of both businesses after they became separate corpora-

---

5. Reg. § 1.355–2(b)(2). See also Rev. Proc. 96–30, App. A, 1996–1 C.B. 696, which provided detailed guidelines to be used for ruling purposes in evaluating whether a distribution satisfies the business purpose requirement. But in Rev. Proc. 2003–48, 2003–2 C.B. 86, the Service announced a "no ruling" policy on business purposes issues and deleted the guidelines, which still offer planning guidance. The "no ruling" policy is a pilot program and may be reevaluated by the Service in 2005.

6. Reg. § 1.355–2(b)(5) Examples (1) and (2).

7. Commissioner v. Morris Trust, 367 F.2d 794 (4th Cir.1966); Rev. Proc. 96–30, supra note 5, App. A, §§ 2.07–.08. But see I.R.C. § 355(e) and Section E2 of this chapter, infra.

8. See, e.g., Rev.Rul. 77–22, 1977–1 C.B. 91; Rev.Rul. 85–122, 1985–2 C.B. 119; Rev. Proc. 96–30, supra note 5, App. A, §§ 2.02–.03.

9. Olson v. Commissioner, 48 T.C. 855 (1967).

10. Rev. Rul. 88–34, 1988–1 C.B. 115.

11. See Ltr.Rul. 8819075 (Feb. 17, 1988).

12. Reg. § 1.355–2(b)(2). But see Estate of Parshelsky v. Commissioner, 303 F.2d 14 (2d Cir.1962), where the court held that a shareholder business purpose justified a spin-off even in the absence of a corporate business purpose.

13. Reg. § 1.355–2(b)(2).

14. 2003–1 C.B. 960.

tions.[15] In addition to the obvious shareholder benefit, the higher stock prices were found to benefit the distributing corporation in two alternative situations: (1) by enhancing an equity-based employee compensation plan without diluting the interests of existing shareholders by issuing more stock, and (2) by allowing the corporation to use its own (more valuable) stock as partial consideration for future acquisitions with significantly less dilution of existing shareholder interests.[16]

The Service has ruled that the reduction of state and local taxes can be a corporate business purpose.[17] But the regulations make it clear that the reduction of "non Federal" taxes is not an independent corporate business purpose if: (1) the transaction will result in a reduction in both Federal and non Federal taxes because of similarities in the respective laws, and (2) the reduction of Federal taxes is greater than or substantially coextensive with the reduction of non Federal taxes.[18] For example, a spin-off of a subsidiary to enable one or both of the resulting corporations to elect S corporation status is not a business purpose[19] even though the transaction may bear little resemblance to the original bailout evil of Gregory v. Helvering.

A business purpose for a distribution also does not exist if the same corporate objectives can be met through a nontaxable transaction that does not require a distribution of stock of a controlled corporation and which is neither impractical nor unduly expensive.[20] For example, assume that a corporation manufactures both toys and candy through divisions which are not separately incorporated, and the shareholders wish to insulate the candy business from the risks of the toy business. If that goal can be achieved by dropping down the assets of one of the businesses to a new subsidiary, a subsequent distribution of the subsidiary's stock to the parent's shareholders is not carried out for a corporate business purpose.[21]

The fact that Section 355 permits a distributing corporation to avoid corporate-level gain on the distribution of stock of a controlled corporation is not considered by the Service to present such a potential for avoidance of federal taxes that it overrides an otherwise valid corporate business purpose.[22] The Service also has ruled that as long as a distribution is motivated in whole or substantial part by a corporate business purpose at the time it is made, the corporation's later failure to succeed in meeting that purpose will not prevent the distribution from satisfying the business purpose requirement.[23] In addition, continuing relationships for a limited period of

15. Rev. Rul. 2004–23, 2004–1 C.B. 585.
16. Id.
17. Rev.Rul. 76–187, 1976–1 C.B. 97.
18. Reg. § 1.355–2(b)(2).
19. Reg. § 1.355–2(d)(5) Example (6); see Rev. Proc. 96–30, supra note 5, App. C.
20. Reg. § 1.355–2(b)(3).
21. Reg. §§ 1.355–2(b)(3), 1.355–2(b)(5) Example (3). See also Reg. § 1.355–2(b)(5) Examples (4) and (5).

22. Rev. Rul. 2003–110, 2003–2 C.B. 1083 (corporation used Section 355 to separate its baby food and pesticide businesses to improve a market perception problem arising from the baby food company's affiliation with a pesticide business).

23. Rev. Rul. 2003–55, 2003–1 C.B. 961, where the business purpose for a corporate separation was to facilitate the raising of capital through an initial public offering of the stock of what previously was a wholly

time between the distributing and spun-off companies do not necessarily jeopardize the distribution from qualifying under Section 355.[24]

A notable recent addition to the list of acceptable business purposes is known as "fit and focus." The Service has ruled[25] that a software company's spin-off of a paper products business satisfied the business purpose requirement because the distribution was motivated by a desire to allow senior management of the distributing corporation "to concentrate its efforts on the software business, which it believes presents better opportunities for growth and allow the management of the paper products business to secure for that business the management resources needed for its full development." The ruling also states that the existence of common directors of the distributing and spun-off companies does not necessarily preclude reliance on a "fit and focus" business purpose.

Advance Rulings. In Revenue Procedure 96–30,[26] the Service set forth in great detail the type of information taxpayers must submit in order to obtain an advance ruling in a Section 355 transaction and provided new insight on the Service's approach to the business purpose requirement. The revenue procedure also provided guidelines to be used by the Service in evaluating whether a distribution satisfies the corporate business purpose requirement and a nonexclusive list of valid business purposes. But in 2003, the Service announced a "pilot program" under which it would no longer issue advance rulings on the business purpose requirement and the device limitation.[27] In lieu of guidelines, the Service is releasing more published rulings (many are discussed in the text above) approving a business purpose in a variety of factual contexts.

2.   CONTINUITY OF INTEREST

Regulations: § 1.355–2(c).

The regulations require that those persons who historically owned an interest in the enterprise prior to a corporate division must own, in the aggregate, an amount of stock establishing a continuity of interest in each of the modified corporate forms in which the enterprise is conducted after the distribution.[1] This means that one or more of the shareholders of the distributing corporation must emerge from the transaction (in the aggregate) with at least a 50 percent equity interest in each of the corporations

---

owned subsidiary of the distributing corporation. Even though market conditions unexpectedly deteriorated and the public offering was postponed indefinitely, there was a valid business purpose at the time the distribution was made.

24.   See Rev. Rul. 2003–75, 2003–2 C.B. 79, where a distribution was made to resolve issues relating to the competition for capital between two businesses (pharmaceuticals and cosmetics) and, after the spin-off, the two companies entered into "transitional" agree-

ments (two years, after which the agreements were to be renegotiated at arm's length for a limited period) relating to information technology, benefits administration, and accounting and tax matters.

25.   Rev. Rul. 2003–74, 2003–2 C.B. 77.

26.   See supra note 5.

27.   Rev. Proc. 2003–48, 2003–2 C.B. 86.

1.   Reg. § 1.355–2(c)(1).

that conduct the enterprise after the division.[2] The continuity of interest test overlaps considerably with the device limitation, which patrols against prearranged postdistribution sales as part of its anti-bailout mission. The regulations nonetheless emphasize that continuity of interest is an independent test that must be met in addition to the other Section 355 requirements.[3]

A common divisive transaction involves the breakup of a corporate enterprise to allow feuding shareholders to part company, with each taking a share of the business in the form of stock in separate corporations. The regulations acknowledge that this type of transaction, whether structured as a split-off or split-up, satisfies the continuity of interest requirement because the prior owners of the integrated enterprise emerge in the aggregate with all the stock of two corporations that survive the separation. Assume, however, that A and B each own 50 percent of the stock of P, Inc., which is engaged in one business, and P owns all the stock of S, Inc., which is engaged in a different business. If new and unrelated shareholder C purchases all of A's stock in P and P then distributes all the stock of S to B in redemption of B's P stock, the transaction fails the continuity of interest test because the owners of P prior to the distribution (A and B) do not, in the aggregate, own an amount of stock establishing continuity of interest in both P and S after the distribution.[4] Only the historic shareholders of P (i.e., A and B) may be counted for continuity of interest purposes, and the smoking pistol is present if none of those shareholders owns any stock of P after the distribution. As for who qualifies as an historic shareholder, it appears that a shareholder who acquires P stock prior to the time that P decides to engage in a division should qualify even if the acquisition occurred shortly before the distribution.[5] Apparently, even a person who acquired P stock in contemplation of a distribution of S stock will be treated as an historic shareholder if the acquisition was more than two years prior to the distribution.[6]

The shareholders of the distributing corporation also must maintain continuity of interest after the distribution.[7] A post-distribution continuity

---

2. Without explicitly saying so, several examples in the regulations indicate that a 50 percent equity interest, the safe harbor benchmark for Type A reorganizations, is what is needed to "maintain" continuity of interest. See, e.g., Reg. § 1.355–2(c)(2) Example (2); Rev.Proc. 96–30, § 4.06, 1996–19 I.R.B. 8, 18. Although 50 percent continuity is required to obtain an advance ruling from the Service, the case law supports a lower percentage, and practitioners have been known to prepare opinion letters stating that 40 percent equity is sufficient to maintain continuity of interest. See Ginsburg & Levin, Mergers, Acquisitions & Buyouts, § 610.2 (2004).

3. Reg. § 1.355–2(c)(1). For a rare published ruling on the application of the continuity of interest doctrine to a spin-off, see Rev.Rul. 79–273, 1979–2 C.B. 125.

4. Reg. § 1.355–2(c)(2) Example (3).

5. See Kaden & Wolfe, "Spin-offs, Split-offs, and Split-ups: A Detailed Analysis of Section 355," 44 Tax Notes 565, 588–589 (July 31, 1989).

6. Id. at 589. Cf. Rev.Rul. 74–5, 1974–1 C.B. 82, declared obsolete on other grounds by Rev.Rul. 89–37, 1989–1 C.B. 107.

7. This is similar to the recently abandoned post-acquisition continuity requirement for acquisitive reorganizations. See Chapter 9B1, supra. It remains to be seen

issue might arise, for example, if shareholders sold more than 50 percent of the stock of either the distributing or controlled corporations shortly after the distribution. Shareholders who committed themselves to sell prior to the distribution or had a fixed intention to do so are not likely to have maintained continuity of interest, but an unanticipated sale should not be a problem.

3.   The "Device" Limitation

Code: § 355(a)(1)(B).

Regulations: § 1.355–2(d).

a.   IN GENERAL

Section 355(a)(1)(B) provides that a corporate division may not be "used principally as a device for the distribution of the earnings and profits" of the distributing corporation or the controlled subsidiary. The historic mission of this requirement has been to prevent the conversion of ordinary dividend income into preferentially taxed capital gain through a bailout masquerading as a corporate division.[1] This goal is reaffirmed in the regulations, which provide:[2]

> * * * a tax-free distribution of the stock of a controlled corporation presents a potential for tax avoidance by facilitating the avoidance of the dividend provisions of the Code through the subsequent sale or exchange of stock of one corporation and the retention of the stock of another corporation. A device can include a transaction that effects a recovery of basis.

Ever since the device limitation was added to the Code, its meaning and scope have been mired in obscurity. The regulations initially fail to burn off the fog, declaring that "generally, the determination of whether a transaction was used principally as a device will be made from all of the facts and circumstances."[3] They go on to offer some guidance by identifying certain "device" and "nondevice" factors which are "evidence" of the presence or absence of a device, but the strength of this "evidence" still depends on "the facts and circumstances."[4]

The role of the device limitation is diminished but not eliminated now that dividends and long-term capital gains of noncorporate taxpayers are taxed at the same preferential rate. A "device" still may include a transaction that effects a recovery of a shareholder's stock basis. In situations where shareholders have a nominal basis and are indifferent to dividend vs. capital gain treatment, the question remains whether the Service might

---

whether the Service will modify its post-distribution continuity rules in the corporate divisions context. For an extensive discussion of the Section 355 version of the continuity of interest doctrine, see Shores, "Reexamining Continuity of Shareholder Interest in Corporate Divisions," 18 Va. Tax Rev. 473 (1999).

1. See, e.g., Rev.Rul. 71–383, 1971–2 C.B. 180.

2. Reg. § 1.355–2(d)(1).

3. Reg. § 1.355–2(d)(1).

4. Reg. § 1.355–2(d)(2)(i), (3)(i).

invoke the device limitation to tax the distributing corporation, which would be required to recognize gain on the distribution if the transaction does not qualify under Section 355, or whether it is sufficient to rely on more targeted corporate-level statutory watchdogs, such as Sections 355(d) and 355(e), which are discussed later in this chapter.[5]

Transactions Ordinarily Not a Device. Notwithstanding the presence or absence of the "device factors" to be discussed below, three transactions "ordinarily" are not considered a tax avoidance device. Distributions are presumed innocent if:

(1) the distributing and controlled corporations have neither accumulated nor current earnings and profits as of the date of the distribution, taking into account the possibility that a distribution of appreciated property by the distributing corporation as part of a divisive transaction would create earnings and profits if Section 355 did not apply;[6]

(2) in the absence of Section 355, the distribution would qualify as a redemption to pay death taxes under Section 303;[7] and

(3) in the absence of Section 355, the distribution would qualify, with respect to each distributee shareholder, as an exchange redemption under Section 302(a).[8]

Section 303 and Section 302(a)-type redemptions lose the benefit of the presumption, however, if they involve the distribution of stock of more than one controlled corporation and facilitate the avoidance of the dividend provisions of the Code through the subsequent sale or exchange of stock of one corporation and the retention of the stock of another corporation.[9]

Device and Nondevice Factors: In General. The regulations specify three factors that are "evidence" of a device ("device factors") and three factors that are evidence of a nondevice ("nondevice factors"). The device factors are: (1) a pro rata distribution; (2) a subsequent sale or exchange of stock of either the distributing or controlled corporation; and (3) the nature and use of the assets of the distributing and controlled corporations immediately after the transaction.[10] The three nondevice factors are: (1) the corporate business purpose for the transaction; (2) the fact that the distributing corporation is publicly traded and widely held; and (3) the fact that the stock of the controlled corporation is distributed to one or more domestic corporations which would be entitled to a dividends received deduction under Section 243 if Section 355 does not apply to the transac-

---

5. See Section E of this chapter, infra.

6. Reg. § 1.355–2(d)(5)(ii).

7. Reg. § 1.355–2(d)(5)(iii). See Chapter 5H, supra.

8. Reg. § 1.355–2(d)(5)(iv). For this purpose, the waiver of family attribution rules apply without regard to the ten year

look forward rule and the requirement to file a waiver agreement in Sections 302(c)(2)(A)(ii) and (iii). See Chapter 5C, supra.

9. Reg. § 1.355–2(d)(5)(i). For an example, see Reg. § 1.355–2(d)(5)(v) Example (2).

10. Reg. § 1.355–2(d)(2).

tion.[11] The presence of one or more of these factors is not controlling, however, and the "strength" of the evidence depends on the facts and circumstances.[12]

b. DEVICE FACTORS

Pro Rata Distribution. A pro rata distribution—for example, a spin-off—is considered to present the greatest potential for avoidance of the dividend provisions of Subchapter C and thus is more likely to be used principally as a device. As a result, the regulations provide that a pro rata or substantially pro rata distribution is evidence of a device.[13]

Subsequent Sale or Exchange of Stock. A parenthetical clause in Section 355(a)(1)(B) cryptically provides that the "mere fact" that stock or securities of either the distributing or controlled corporations is sold by all or some of the shareholders is not to be construed to mean that the transaction was used principally as a device. But the Service has long contended that a sale of stock of the distributing or controlled corporation shortly after a corporate division is evidence that the transaction was used as a bailout device. The "strength" of the evidence depends upon the percentage of stock disposed of after the distribution, the length of time between the distribution and the subsequent sale and the extent to which the subsequent sale was prearranged.[14]

A subsequent sale or exchange negotiated or agreed upon before the distribution is "substantial evidence" of a device.[15] A sale is always prearranged if it was "pursuant to an arrangement negotiated or agreed upon before the distribution if enforceable rights to buy or sell existed before the distribution."[16] The regulations are more equivocal if a sale was merely discussed by the parties but was "reasonably to be anticipated." In that event, it "ordinarily" will be considered to be previously negotiated or agreed upon.[17] Seemingly ignoring the express language of Section 355(a)(1)(B), the regulations also provide that even in the absence of prior negotiations or agreement, a subsequent sale nonetheless is "evidence of a device."[18] Presumably, the evidence would be fairly weak if the decision to sell were not made until after the distribution.

The perceived bailout abuse of a subsequent sale normally is present only when the selling shareholders cash out their investment. The regulations logically provide that if the shareholders dispose of stock in a subsequent tax-free reorganization in which no more than an "insubstantial" amount of gain is recognized, the transaction will not be treated as a subsequent sale or exchange. Rather, because the shareholders maintain an interest in the continuing enterprise, the stock received in the exchange is

---

11. Reg. § 1.355–2(d)(3).

12. Reg. § 1.355–2(d)(2)(i);–2(d)(3)(i).

13. Reg. § 1.355–2(d)(2)(ii).

14. Reg. § 1.355–2(d)(2)(iii)(A).

15. Reg. § 1.355–2(d)(2)(iii)(B).

16. Reg. § 1.355–2(d)(2)(iii)(D).

17. Id.

18. Reg. § 1.355–2(d)(2)(iii)(C).

treated as equivalent to the stock surrendered.[19] But any sale of the new stock received will be subject to the "subsequent sale" rules and could be evidence of a device.[20]

The Service's reliance on subsequent stock sales (whether or not prearranged) as substantial evidence of a device has always been questionable. To return to the earlier introductory example, assume that Diverse Corporation has actively conducted profitable winery and chicken ranch businesses for more than five years. If Diverse wished to spin off the chicken ranch as Poultry, Inc., it would have no difficulty satisfying the active business test. But what if the spin-off were the prelude to a prearranged sale of the Poultry, Inc. stock by the controlling shareholders? If gain on that sale were taxable to the shareholders at capital gains rates, or even if it merely effected a recovery of part of the shareholders' basis in their Diverse Corp. stock, should the spin-off be viewed principally as a device to bail out Diverse's earnings and profits?

In considering these questions, keep in mind the alternatives available to Diverse. If the corporation simply had sold the chicken ranch assets and distributed the proceeds to its noncorporate shareholders, the distribution likely would have qualified as a partial liquidation, entitling noncorporate shareholders to exchange treatment.[21] The same result would have occurred if the chicken ranch assets were distributed pro rata to the shareholders and sold shortly thereafter. To be sure, a sale or distribution of the chicken ranch assets by the corporation would have triggered gain at the corporate and shareholder levels.[22] But, historically at least, the principal concern in Section 355 was not with the double taxation of corporate earnings but rather the tax treatment of a distribution to the shareholders. If an economically equivalent transaction (i.e., a partial liquidation) would have qualified for capital gain treatment, it seems anomalous to classify a spin-off followed by a prearranged sale of the same business as a device to convert ordinary dividend income to capital gain. In the last analysis, the correct answer may be to treat partial liquidation distributions as dividends to noncorporate shareholders. Moreover, even if it is not a device, a distribution followed by a taxable sale is unlikely to satisfy the business purpose test and, if the sale closely follows the distribution but somehow escapes the device limitation, the transaction also may fail the continuity of interest requirement. And, of course, much of this discussion is less important as long as dividends and capital gains of noncorporate taxpayers are taxed at the same preferential rate.

Nature and Use of the Assets. The regulations also enforce the device limitation by taking into account the "nature, kind, amount, and use of the assets of the distributing and the controlled corporations (and corporations

---

19. Reg. § 1.355–2(d)(2)(iii)(E).

20. Id.

21. See I.R.C. § 302(b)(4), (e). But see Rev.Rul. 75–223, 1975–1 C.B. 109, discussed at p. 251, supra, in which the Service ruled that a distribution of stock of a subsidiary may not qualify as a partial liquidation. See also Morgenstern v. Commissioner, 56 T.C. 44 (1971).

22. See Chapters 7 and 8, supra.

controlled by them) immediately after the transaction."[23] Thus, the existence of assets that are not used in an active trade or business, such as cash and other liquid assets that are not related to the reasonable needs of the active business, is evidence of a device.[24] To illustrate, assume that Corporation P spins off Corporation S in order to comply with certain regulatory requirements under state law. As part of the separation, P transfers excess cash (not related to the reasonable needs of P or S's business) to S and then distributes the S stock pro rata to P's shareholders. The result of this infusion of cash into S is that the percentage of liquid assets not related to the trade or business is substantially greater for S than for P. The regulations view this as suspect, providing in an example that the transfer of cash by P to S is "relatively strong evidence of device."[25] When coupled with the pro rata nature of the distribution, the transaction is considered to have been used principally as a device notwithstanding the "strong business purpose" because there was no business purpose for the infusion of cash into S.[26]

The regulations also consider the relationship between the distributing and controlled corporations and the effect of a sale of one of the businesses on the overall enterprise. Evidence of a device is presented if the distributing or controlled corporation is a business that principally serves the business of the other corporation (a "secondary business") and it can be sold without adversely affecting the business that it serves.[27] Thus, the spin-off of a captive coal mine from a steel manufacturer, a transaction which satisfied the active business test,[28] nonetheless presents evidence of a device if the principal function of the coal mine is to satisfy the requirements of the steel business and the coal mine could be sold without adversely affecting the steel business.[29] The apparent concern here is not so much with the potential for tax avoidance through non-arm's length intercorporate transactions between the separated corporations. That type of abuse is adequately policed by Section 482, which authorizes the Commissioner to allocate income or deductions between or among commonly controlled trades or businesses.[30] What appears to be bothering the Service is the likelihood for avoidance of the dividend provisions of the Code when the "related function" is not truly integral to the business from which it has been separated.

23. Reg. § 1.355–2(d)(2)(iv).

24. Reg. § 1.355–2(d)(2)(iv)(A), (B).

25. Reg. § 1.355–2(d)(4) Example (3).

26. Reg. § 1.355–2(d)(2)(iv)(B); 1.355–2(d)(4) Example (3). Compare Reg. § 1.355–2(d)(4) Example (2), where the transfer of cash and liquid securities from the distributing to the controlled corporation was "relatively weak evidence of device" because after the transfer the two corporations held liquid assets in amounts proportional to the values of their businesses.

27. Reg. § 1.355–2(d)(2)(iv)(C).

28. See Reg. § 1.355–3(c) Example (11).

29. Reg. § 1.355–2(d)(2)(iv)(C). Likewise, the separation of the sales and manufacturing functions will constitute evidence of a device if the principal function of the sales operation after the separation is to sell the output from the manufacturing operation and the sales operation could be sold without adversely affecting the manufacturing operation.

30. See Chapter 13A, infra.

c. NONDEVICE FACTORS

Acknowledging that the corporate business purposes for a transaction may be sufficiently compelling to outweigh any evidence of a device, the regulations provide that the corporate business purpose for a transaction is evidence of nondevice.[31] In keeping with the "sliding scale" approach that pervades the device regulations, the stronger the evidence of device, then the stronger is the business purpose required to prevent determination that the transaction was used principally as a device.[32] The strength of a corporate business purpose, of course, is based on all the facts and circumstances, including but not limited to the importance of achieving the purpose to the success of the business, the extent to which the transaction is prompted by a person not having a proprietary interest in either corporation or by other outside factors beyond the control of the distributing corporation, and the "immediacy of the conditions" prompting the transaction.[33]

The fact that the distributing corporation is publicly traded and widely held, having no shareholder who directly or indirectly owns more than five percent of any class of stock, also is evidence of nondevice.[34]

Finally, the fact that the stock of the controlled corporation is distributed to a domestic corporate distributee which, without Section 355, would be entitled to the Section 243 dividends received deduction, is evidence of a nondevice.[35]

PROBLEM

Assume that Lemon Corporation from Problem 1 at page 534, operates a computer manufacturing business at only one location where it also conducts research and development through a separate division. Lemon also owns all the stock of Floppy Disk, Inc., a computer software manufacturer that Lemon purchased six years ago in a taxable transaction. The net worths of the computer and software businesses are approximately the same, and both corporations have substantial accumulated earnings and profits. The common stock of Lemon is owned equally by Ms. Micro and Mr. Chips. In each of the following alternatives, assume that the active trade or business requirement is met and consider whether the transactions described satisfy the other requirements of Section 355.

(a) To resolve a shareholder dispute, Lemon distributes all the stock of Floppy Disk, Inc. to Mr. Chips in complete redemption of his stock in Lemon.

(b) Same as (a), above, except that Ms. Micro and Mr. Chips are mother and son.

---

31. Reg. § 1.355–2(d)(3)(ii).
32. Id.
33. Id.

34. Reg. § 1.355–2(d)(3)(iii).
35. Reg. § 1.355–2(d)(3)(iv).

(c) Same as (a), above, except that shortly before the distribution of Floppy Disk stock to Mr. Chips, Ms. Micro sold all of her Lemon stock to Mr. Modem, who wished to acquire the hardware business but not the software company.

(d) To enable the computer manufacturing business to maintain different retirement plans for its manufacturing and research employees, Lemon transfers the assets of the research division to a new corporation, Research, Inc., and distributes all the Research stock pro rata to Ms. Micro and Mr. Chips. After the distribution, Research, Inc. continues to perform services solely for Lemon.

(e) Same as (d), above, except that the purpose of the spin-off is to comply with a regulatory decree. (Compare your answer to Problem 1(d) at page 536).

(f) To comply with a state law providing that computer hardware and software businesses may not be conducted by parent and subsidiary corporations, Lemon must spin off or sell its Floppy Disk, Inc. subsidiary. In anticipation of the new law, Lemon's board of directors informally negotiated a sale of Floppy Disk to Suitor, Inc. Before the agreement is reduced to an enforceable writing, Lemon distributes the Floppy Disk stock to Ms. Micro and Mr. Chips. Two months later, the shareholders sell the Floppy Disk to Suitor on the same terms negotiated by the Lemon board of directors.

(g) Same as (f), above, except that the Lemon board rejects Suitor's offer and instead distributes the Floppy Disk stock pro rata to the shareholders. Four months later, the shareholders sell their Floppy Disk stock to White Knight, Inc.

(h) Same as (g), above, except the sale by the shareholders is made to Suitor, Inc. on essentially the same terms that had been rejected by the Lemon board of directors.

D. TAX TREATMENT OF THE PARTIES TO A CORPORATE DIVISION

Code: §§ 311(a), (b)(1) & (2); 312(a), (b), (h); 336(c); 355(a)(1)(A), (3), (c); 356; 358(a)–(c); 361; 362(b), (e)(1); 1032. Skim §§ 301; 302; 355(d); 381(a); 1223(1) & (2).

Regulations: §§ 1.312–10; 1.358–2.

1. INTRODUCTION

If the requirements of Section 355 and the accompanying judicial doctrines are satisfied, a set of provisions come into play to govern the specific tax consequences (e.g., total or partial nonrecognition of gain, basis, holding period, etc.) to the parties. In this section, we consider the tax consequences if a corporate division is preceded by the formation of one or more new corporations in a Type D reorganization, the consequences of the division itself, and the results if the division fails to satisfy the statutory and judicial requirements.

If one or more corporations are formed as a preparatory step to a qualifying corporate division, the formation of the new subsidiary is a Type D reorganization.[1] The parent corporation does not recognize gain or loss on the transfer of assets to the controlled corporation,[2] and it takes an exchanged basis[3] and may tack the holding period in the new stock or securities that it receives.[4] The newly formed controlled corporation does not recognize gain on the issuance of its stock[5] and it takes the assets with a transferred basis and a tacked holding period.[6] The earnings and profits of the parent corporation are apportioned between the parent and controlled corporations according to rules provided in the regulations.[7] Section 381, providing for carryover of corporate attributes in certain corporate acquisitions, does not apply to divisive reorganizations and thus the parent corporation retains its tax attributes other than the earnings and profits which are allocated to the controlled corporation.

2.   CONSEQUENCES TO SHAREHOLDERS AND SECURITY HOLDERS

No Boot Received. If the requirements of Section 355 are met, the shareholders or security holders of the distributing parent corporation will not recognize gain or loss on the distribution of stock or securities of the controlled corporation.[1] The aggregate basis of the stock or securities in the distributing corporation held by the shareholder is allocated among the stock and securities of both the distributing and controlled corporations in proportion to their relative fair market values,[2] and the shareholder's holding period in the stock or securities of the controlled corporation received in the distribution includes the holding period of the stock or securities of the distributing corporation.[3]

---

1. I.R.C. § 368(a)(1)(D). A "divisive" D reorganization involves a transfer by one corporation of part of its assets to another corporation if, immediately after the transfer, the transferor "controls" the transferee and, pursuant to the same plan, stock or securities of the controlled corporation are distributed to the shareholders of the transferor corporation in a transaction that qualifies under Section 355. Id. For this purpose, the fact that the shareholders of the distributing corporation dispose of part or all of their distributed stock, or that the distributing corporation issues additional stock, is not taken into account. I.R.C. § 368(a)(2)(H).

2. I.R.C. § 361(a).

3. I.R.C. § 358(a).

4. I.R.C. § 1223(1).

5. I.R.C. § 1032(a).

6. I.R.C. §§ 362(b); 1223(2).

7. I.R.C. § 312(h); Reg. § 1.312–10(a), (c). In the case of a newly created corporation, this allocation generally is made in proportion to the relative fair market values of the assets retained by the parent corporation and the assets transferred to the controlled corporation. Reg. § 1.312–10(a). In a "proper case," the regulations provide that this allocation should be made in proportion to the "net basis" (after reduction for liabilities) of the transferred and retained assets. Id.

1. I.R.C. § 355(a)(1).

2. I.R.C. § 358(b), (c).

3. I.R.C. § 1223(1).

Treatment of Boot. As with most other types of reorganizations, the receipt of boot in an otherwise qualifying corporate division does not necessarily spell doom for the transaction but results in the recognition of gain to the shareholder receiving the boot. For this purpose, boot includes cash, any property other than stock or securities of the controlled corporation (e.g., short-term debt obligations, stock rights or warrants), securities of the controlled corporation to the extent that their principal amount exceeds the principal amount of any securities surrendered, any stock of the controlled corporation that was acquired by the distributing corporation in a taxable transaction within the five-year period prior to the distribution, and nonqualified preferred stock received in a distribution with respect to stock other than nonqualified preferred stock.[4]

The treatment of boot depends on the form of the division. In the case of a spin-off, the boot is treated as a distribution to which Section 301 applies (without regard to the shareholder's realized gain) and is thus a dividend to the extent of the distributing corporation's current and accumulated earnings and profits and a return of capital to the extent of any balance.[5] In the case of a split-off or split-up, both of which involve an exchange rather than a distribution, Section 356(a)(1) requires the shareholder to recognize any realized gain to the extent of the boot received in the distribution. The characterization of that gain is more problematic. Section 356(a)(2) adopts the same rule used for acquisitive reorganizations by providing that if the exchange has "the effect of the distribution of a dividend," the gain recognized is treated as a dividend to the extent of the shareholder's ratable share of accumulated earnings and profits of the distributing corporation.[6] The balance of any recognized gain is treated as gain from the exchange of property.[7] Dividend equivalence is tested by applying the "before" and "after" ownership principles of Section 302 (i.e., meaningful reduction of the shareholder's proportionate interest) using an assumption that the shareholder had retained the distributing corporation stock that actually was exchanged for controlled corporation stock and then had received the boot in exchange for distributing corporation stock equal in value to the boot.[8] Whether or not this hypothetical redemption results in a dividend is tested by comparing the shareholder's percentage ownership in the distributing corporation before the transaction with the interest the shareholder would have retained in the distributing corporation if he surrendered only the stock exchanged for the boot. The test for dividend equivalence is illustrated by Revenue Ruling 93–62, which follows in the text.[9] Any loss realized by a shareholder in a Section 355 exchange may not

---

4. I.R.C. §§ 355(a)(3), (4); 356(a), (b), (d)(2)(C) & (D).

5. I.R.C. § 356(b).

6. In one of the many curiosities in the world of reorganizations, neither Section 356(a)(2) nor the applicable regulations refer to *current* earnings and profits.

7. See Reg. § 1.356–1(b)(2).

8. Rev.Rul. 93–62, 1993–2 C.B. 118. See also Commissioner v. Clark, 489 U.S. 726, 109 S.Ct. 1455 (1989), which uses a similar approach in testing for dividend equivalence in acquisitive reorganizations where T shareholders receive boot.

9. For discussion of the Service's approach, see Steinberg, "Selected Issues in the Taxation of Section 355 Transactions,"

be recognized.[10]

Section 358 again governs the basis of the boot and nonrecognition property received in the distribution. The boot takes a fair market value basis and its holding period commences as of the date of the distribution.[11] The aggregate basis of the nonrecognition property (i.e., stock and securities) is the same as the basis of the stock or securities of the distributing corporation plus any gain recognized and less any cash and the fair market value of any boot property received on the exchange.[12] That aggregate basis is then allocated among the old and new stock or securities (or the new stock or securities, in the case of a split-up) in proportion to their relative fair market values.[13] If the "old stock" was acquired at different times or for different prices, the distributee shareholders generally must trace their bases in the various blocks of old stock (rather than using an average basis) in determining the basis of the new stock under Section 358. If tracing is impossible, the taxpayer may designate how the Section 358 basis is to be allocated among the different lots.[14] The nonrecognition property ordinarily is eligible for a tacked holding period.[15]

Revenue Ruling 93–62

1993–2 Cum. Bull. 118.

ISSUE

Whether gain recognized on the receipt of cash in an exchange of stock that otherwise qualifies under section 355 of the Internal Revenue Code is treated as a dividend distribution under section 356(a)(2).

FACTS

Distributing is a corporation with 1,000 shares of a single class of stock outstanding. Each share has a fair market value of $lx. A, one of five unrelated individual shareholders, owns 400 shares of Distributing stock. Distributing owns all of the outstanding stock of a subsidiary corporation, Controlled. The Controlled stock has a fair market value of $200x.

---

52 Tax Lawyer 7, 11–16 (1997). The author suggests that Revenue Ruling 93–62, while purporting to follow the Supreme Court's approach to dividend equivalence in Commissioner v. Clark, discussed supra p. 485, actually is inconsistent with *Clark's* "post-reorganization" approach insofar as the ruling treats the boot as having been received in a hypothetical redemption occurring *prior* to the split-off.

10. I.R.C. § 356(c).

11. I.R.C. § 358(a)(2).

12. I.R.C. § 358(a)(1).

13. I.R.C. § 358(b)(2), (c); Reg. § 1.358–2. The Service has never provided any guidance as to the precise date to be used in valuing the corporations for purposes of this allocation. In the case of publicly held companies, the date selected ordinarily is the first day that the stock of the controlled corporation was traded on a listed exchange. For other possibilities, see Bittker & Eustice, Federal Income Taxation of Corporations and Shareholders ¶ 11.12[1] (7th ed. 2000).

14. See Prop. Reg. § 1.358–2(a)(2)(i), – 2(c) Example 7.

15. I.R.C. § 1223(1).

Distributing distributes all the stock of Controlled plus $200x cash to A in exchange for all of A's Distributing stock. The exchange satisfies the requirements of section 355 but for the receipt of the cash.

LAW AND ANALYSIS

Section 355(a)(1) of the code provides, in general, that the shareholders of a distributing corporation will not recognize gain or loss on the exchange of the distributing corporation's stock or securities solely for stock or securities of a controlled subsidiary if the requirements of section 355 are satisfied.

Section 356(a)(1) of the Code provides for recognition of gain on exchanges in which gain would otherwise not be recognized under section 354 (relating to tax-free acquisitive reorganizations) or section 355 if the property received in the exchange consists of property permitted to be received without gain recognition and other property or money ("boot"). The amount of gain recognized is limited to the sum of the money and the fair market value of the other property.

Under section 356(a)(2) of the Code, gain recognized in an exchange described in section 356(a)(1) that "has the effect of the distribution of a dividend" is treated as a dividend to the extent of the distributee's ratable share of the undistributed earnings and profits accumulated after February 28, 1913. Any remaining gain is treated as gain from the exchange of property.

Determinations of whether the receipt of boot has the effect of a dividend are made by applying the principles of section 302 of the Code. Commissioner v. Clark, 489 U.S. 726 (1989), 1989–2 C.B. 68. Section 302 contains rules for determining whether payments in redemption of stock are treated as payments in exchange for the stock or as distributions to which section 301 applies.

Under section 302(a) of the Code, a redemption will be treated as an exchange if it satisfies one of the tests of section 302(b). Section 302(b)(2) provides exchange treatment for substantially disproportionate redemptions of stock. A distribution is substantially disproportionate if (1) the shareholder's voting stock interest and common stock interest in the corporation immediately after the redemption are each less than 80 percent of those interests immediately before the redemption, and (2) the shareholder owns less than 50 percent of the voting power of all classes of stock immediately after the redemption.

In *Clark*, the Supreme Court determined whether gain recognized under section 356 of the Code on the receipt of boot in an acquisitive reorganization under section 368(a)(1)(A) and (a)(2)(D) should be treated as a dividend distribution. In that case, the sole shareholder of the target corporation exchanged his target stock for stock of the acquiring corporation and cash. In applying section 302 to determine whether the boot payment had the effect of a dividend distribution, the Court considered whether section 302 should be applied to the boot payment as if it were made (i) by the target corporation in a pre-reorganization hypothetical redemption of a portion of the shareholder's target stock, or (ii) by the acquiring corporation in a post-reorganization hypothetical redemption of the acquiring corporation stock that the shareholder would have received in the reorganization exchange if there had been no boot distribution.

The Supreme Court stated that the treatment of boot under section 356(a)(2) of the Code should be determined "by examining the effect of the exchange as a whole," and concluded that treating the boot as received in a redemption of target stock would improperly isolate the boot payment from the overall reorganization by disregarding the effect of the subsequent merger. Consequently, the Court tested whether the boot payment had the effect of a dividend distribution by comparing the interest the taxpayer actually received in the acquiring corporation with the interest the taxpayer would have had if solely stock in the acquiring corporation had been received in the reorganization exchange.

Prior to the decision in *Clark*, the Service considered the facts and issue presented in this revenue ruling in Rev. Rul. 74–516, 1974–2 C.B. 121. The determination of whether the exchange of Distributing stock for Controlled stock and boot under section 355 of the Code had the effect of a dividend distribution under section 356(a)(2) was made by comparing A's interest in Distributing prior to the exchange with the interest A would have retained if A had not received Controlled stock and had only surrendered the Distributing stock equal in value to the boot. The Court's decision in *Clark* does not change the conclusion in Rev. Rul. 74–516, because, like Clark, the ruling determined whether the exchange in question had the effect of a dividend distribution based on an analysis of the overall transaction.

The exchange of A's Distributing stock for stock of Controlled qualifies for non-recognition treatment under section 355 of the Code in part because the overall effect of the exchange is an adjustment of A's continuing interest in Distributing in a modified corporate form. See section 1.355–2(c) of the Income Tax Regulations. The Controlled stock received by A represents a continuing interest in a portion of Distributing's assets that were formerly held by A as an indirect equity interest. The boot payment has reduced A's proportionate interest in the overall corporate enterprise that includes both Distributing and Controlled. Thus, the boot is treated as received in redemption of A's Distributing stock, and A's interest in Distributing immediately before the exchange is compared to the interest A would have retained if A had surrendered only the Distributing shares equal in value to the boot.

Under the facts presented here, before the exchange, A owned 400 of the 1,000 shares, or 40 percent, of the outstanding Distributing stock. If A had surrendered only the 200 shares for which A received boot, A would still hold 200 of the 800 shares, or 25 percent, of the Distributing stock outstanding after the exchange. This 25 percent stock interest would represent 62.5 percent of A's pre-exchange stock interest in Distributing. Therefore, the deemed redemption would be treated as an exchange because it qualifies as substantially disproportionate under section 302(b)(2) of the Code.

HOLDING

In an exchange of stock that otherwise qualifies under section 355 of the Code, whether the payment of boot is treated as a dividend distribution under section 356(a)(2) is determined prior to the exchange. This determination is made by treating the recipient shareholder as if the shareholder had retained the distributing corporation stock actually exchanged for controlled corporation stock and received the boot in exchange for distributing corporation stock equal in value to the boot.

EFFECT ON OTHER RULINGS

Rev. Rul. 74–516 is superseded.

3. CONSEQUENCES TO THE DISTRIBUTING AND CONTROLLED CORPORATIONS

Nonrecognition of Gain or Loss: General Rules. The tax consequences to the distributing corporation in a Section 355 transaction initially are determined by Section 361(c) if the distribution is preceded by a Type D reorganization and by Section 355(c) if it is not. In either case, the results generally are the same. If a Section 355 transaction occurs in conjunction with certain changes in shareholder ownership, the distributing corporation also may be required to recognize gain under Section 355(d).[1]

If a Section 355 distribution is part of a reorganization plan—i.e., where the distributing corporation first contributes property to the controlled corporation—no gain or loss is recognized if the property is contributed solely in exchange for stock or securities of the controlled corporation.[2] The distributing corporation recognizes gain, however, if the liabilities assumed by the controlled corporation exceed the aggregate adjusted basis of the transferred property or if it otherwise receives boot that is not distributed to shareholders or creditors as part of the reorganization plan.[3]

The distributing corporation also does not recognize gain on the distribution to its shareholders of "qualified property"—i.e., stock or debt obligations of the controlled corporation.[4] Thus, in the typical spin-off or split-off, where the distributing corporation's basis in the stock of the controlled corporation is ordinarily less than its fair market value, no corporate-level gain is recognized on the distribution. Section 311(b), which otherwise might have required gain recognition, is not applicable because it only applies to distributions under Subpart A of Subchapter C (Sections

---

1. See Section E1 of this chapter, infra.

2. I.R.C. §§ 368(a)(1)(D); 361(a).

3. I.R.C. § 361(b). The amount of cash and property that a distributing corporation may distribute to creditors without gain rec-ognition is limited to the aggregate adjusted basis of the assets contributed to the controlled corporation in the Type D reorganization. I.R.C. § 361(b)(3).

4. I.R.C. § 361(c)(1), (2).

301–307), and Section 355 is not within that portion of the Code.[5] The same result occurs on a split-up. Section 336, which otherwise might have required the recognition of corporate-level gain on a liquidating distribution, does not apply to distributions that are part of a reorganization.[6] Gain is recognized, however, in the rare case where appreciated boot is distributed in a Section 355 transaction that is part of a reorganization.[7]

If the distribution is not preceded by a Type D reorganization—e.g., where the controlled corporation is not a newly formed subsidiary—Section 355(c) takes over for all forms of divisions,[8] providing generally that the distributing corporation recognizes no gain or loss on any distribution to which Section 355 applies.[9] Gain must be recognized, however, on a distribution of appreciated property other than "qualified property,"—i.e., other than stock or securities in the controlled corporation.[10] Thus, no gain will be recognized on a distribution of stock or securities of the controlled corporation in a qualifying corporate division even if the recipient shareholder is taxed,[11] but gain is recognized on a distribution of any other appreciated boot.[12]

In all cases, any stock of the controlled corporation that is acquired by the distributing corporation in a taxable transaction within the five-year period preceding the distribution will constitute boot.[13] For example, assume the distributing corporation had owned 90 percent of the stock of a controlled subsidiary for many years and acquired the remaining 10 percent shortly prior to an otherwise qualifying Section 355 distribution. Because the recently acquired stock is treated as boot, it is taxable to the shareholders and any gain accruing during the period between the acquisition and distribution of the stock will be taxable to the distributing corporation.

Recognition of Gain on Certain Disqualified Distributions. The general nonrecognition rule in Section 355(c) does not apply if the distributing corporation makes a "disqualified distribution" of "disqualified stock" within the meaning of Section 355(d). In general, a disqualified distribution is any distribution of stock or securities of a controlled subsidiary ("S") if, immediately after the distribution, any person holds a 50 percent or greater interest in either the distributing corporation or the controlled subsidiary and that interest consists of "disqualified stock," defined generally as any stock acquired by "purchase" within the five-year period preceding the

---

5. See also I.R.C. § 361(c)(4).

6. I.R.C. § 361(c)(4); see also § 336(c).

7. I.R.C. § 361(c)(2).

8. Section 355(c)(3) makes it clear that Sections 311 (relating to nonliquidating distributions) and 336 (relating to liquidating distributions) do not apply to a distribution governed by Section 355.

9. I.R.C. § 355(c)(1).

10. I.R.C. § 355(c)(2). The definition of "qualified property" in Section 355(c)(2)(B) is somewhat narrower than the one used to define the same term in Section 361(c)(2)(B), where "qualified property" includes both rights to acquire stock and nonsecurity debt obligations.

11. The recipient would be taxed, for example, if the principal amount of securities received exceeds the principal amount of any securities surrendered. I.R.C. § 355(a)(3)(A).

12. I.R.C. § 355(c)(2)(A).

13. I.R.C. § 355(a)(3)(B).

distribution.[14] This rule, which is designed to prevent the use of Section 355 to facilitate the tax-free sale of part of a business following a takeover (and in related transactions), is discussed later in the chapter,[15] as is Section 355(e), which taxes the distributing corporation on distributions of controlled corporation stock in certain situations where as part of a "plan" a 50–percent or greater interest in either the distributing or controlled corporations was acquired within two years before or after the distribution.[16]

Carryover of Tax Attributes. The method of allocating the earnings and profits of the various parties to a corporate division depends on the form of the transaction. If a division is preceded by a Type D reorganization, the earnings and profits of the distributing corporation are allocated between the distributing and controlled corporations in proportion to the relative fair market values of the assets retained by each corporation.[17] If the division is not preceded by a Type D reorganization—e.g., where the stock of a preexisting subsidiary or subsidiaries is distributed—the regulations provide methods for determining the decrease in the distributing corporation's earnings and profits.[18] In no event may any deficit of the distributing corporation be allocated to the controlled corporation.[19]

Earnings and profits are the only tax attributes affected by a corporate division. The carryover rules of Section 381 relating to other tax attributes are not applicable to divisive reorganizations, and thus the tax history of the distributing corporation will remain intact in a spin-off or a split-off. Since a split-up involves the liquidation of the distributing corporation, its tax attributes will disappear as a result of the transaction.[20]

4. Consequences of Failed Divisions

If a corporate division fails to qualify under Section 355, the tax consequences depend on the form of the transaction. If the defective division is preceded by the formation of a new corporation, that formation still qualifies for nonrecognition—but under Section 351 rather than Section 368(a)(1)(D).[1]

As for the division itself, the distribution of stock or securities in a nonqualifying spin-off is treated as an ordinary distribution to which Section 301 applies. That means it will be a dividend to the extent of

---

14. I.R.C. § 355(d)(2)–(5).

15. See Section E1 of this chapter, infra.

16. See Section E2 of this chapter, infra.

17. I.R.C. § 312(h); Reg. § 1.312–10(a). The regulations also state that in a "proper case" the allocation should be made in proportion to the net bases of the transferred and retained assets.

18. Reg. § 1.312–10(b).

19. Reg. § 1.312–10(c).

20. See Rev.Rul. 56–373, 1956–2 C.B. 217.

1. Although the formation of the new corporation still qualifies for nonrecognition, different operative provisions come into play to govern the transaction. See I.R.C. §§ 351; 358; 362(a); 1032. See Reg. § 1.312–11(a) for the allocation of earnings and profits in these circumstances.

current and accumulated earnings and profits and a return of capital to the extent of any balance. If the distribution takes the form of a split-off, it is tested under the stock redemption rules of Section 302. To avoid being subject to Section 301, the redemption thus must come within one of the Section 302(b) tests for exchange treatment.[2] If the failed division is a split-up, the transaction logically should be governed by the complete liquidation rules, allowing the shareholders to recognize capital gain or loss under Section 331(a).[3]

At the corporate level, the distributing corporation will be required to recognize gain on a distribution of appreciated property in a failed spin-off or split-off under Section 311(b). Section 311(a)(2), however, denies recognition of loss on a distribution of property that has declined in value. In a split-up, the distributing corporation will be required to recognize gain or loss under Section 336(a), subject to the limitations on recognition of loss in Section 336(b).

PROBLEM

Father is the sole shareholder of an incorporated department store which he has owned for 15 years. He has a basis of $200,000 in his Store Corporation stock, which is currently worth $2 million. Store has $400,000 of accumulated earnings and profits. Three years ago, Store acquired land in Suburb, where it constructed and then opened a new branch store. The branch has been quite successful and represents $500,000 of the $2 million net worth of Store Corporation. The assets of the branch have a $100,000 basis.

Father recently celebrated his 65th birthday and is exploring some estate planning alternatives. His attorney has suggested that he should have Store Corporation transfer the Suburb store to newly created Branch Corporation in exchange for Branch stock worth $400,000 and Branch securities worth $100,000. Store Corporation, which would be worth $1.5 million after this transaction, then would distribute the Branch stock and securities to Father who in turn would give the Branch stock to his children.

Discuss all the income tax consequences of the above transactions to Father, Store Corporation and Branch Corporation, assuming first that the corporate division totally or partially qualifies under Section 355 and then that it fails to qualify.

---

2. If the distribution is pro rata, dividend treatment is thus assured. The distribution of stock in a failed split-off would not qualify for partial liquidation treatment under Section 302(b)(4). See Morgenstern v. Commissioner, 56 T.C. 44 (1971); Rev.Rul. 75–223, 1975–1 C.B. 109.

3. It is possible, however, that certain split-ups may be treated as a reorganization coupled with a dividend. This might occur on a split-up involving a failed division of an operating business from liquid assets in preparation for a sale of the liquid assets. See Bittker & Eustice, Federal Income Taxation of Corporations and Shareholders ¶ 11.15[3] (7th ed. 2000). But it may not matter when dividends and long-term capital gains are taxed at the same rate.

E.   Use of Section 355 in Corporate Acquisitions

1.   Limitations on Use of Section 355 in Taxable Acquisitions

a.   INTRODUCTION

The repeal of the *General Utilities* doctrine required tax advisors to search for new techniques to avoid corporate-level gain on the sale of all or part of a business. In one common transactional pattern, a corporate buyer of a controlling stock interest in a target corporation may seek to dispose of unwanted pieces of the target, perhaps to help finance the acquisition or maximize overall shareholder value. The tax goal is to consummate those sales without recognizing gain. After Congress blocked several other promising techniques, taxpayers turned to Section 355 to facilitate tax-free sales of unwanted assets in corporate solution. Congress reacted by curtailing the benefits of nonrecognition for certain transactions that previously would have qualified as tax-free divisions. These new anti-avoidance limitations, which were previewed earlier in this chapter, are best explained in the context of the transactions at which they were directed.

b.   DISPOSITIONS OF RECENTLY ACQUIRED BUSINESSES

Code: § 355(a)(2)(D).

Congress's first line of attack was to amend the active trade or business requirement in Section 355(b)(2)(D) in order to prevent a purchasing corporation ("P") that had recently acquired a controlling stock interest in a target corporation ("T") from disposing of a target subsidiary ("S") without paying a corporate-level tax. To illustrate the prototype transaction at which this rule is aimed, assume that P purchases all the stock of T, which has engaged directly in the active conduct of a trade or business for more than five years. T owns the stock of S, which also has engaged in the active conduct of a trade or business for the requisite five-year period. Both T and S have highly appreciated assets. P does not make a Section 338 election when it purchases T's stock and, as a result, T and S retain their historic asset bases. P intends to dispose of S shortly after the takeover of T.

At one time, the parties could have used a two-step transaction to sell S without recognizing gain. T would first distribute the S stock to P in a tax-free distribution under Section 355.[1] The Service ruled that such a distribution qualified as tax-free and did not violate the active trade or business requirement unless P attempted a bailout by distributing the S

---

1. To avoid problems under the continuity of interest doctrine, P needed to hold the T stock for a respectable period of time (two years was considered safest) to become a "historic" shareholder of T. See Section C2 of this chapter, supra.

stock to its shareholders.[2] P would allocate the cost basis in its T stock under Section 358 between the T stock and the S stock it received in the distribution, obtaining essentially a fair market value basis in the stock of both corporations.[3] After a respectable interval, P then would sell the S stock without recognition of any corporate-level gain by S. Although the new buyer would take a cost basis in the S stock, S would retain its historic lower asset bases. This is noteworthy because the gain inherent in S's assets was not avoided by this technique; it merely was deferred. Moreover, that gain did not accrue while P owned T (and thus indirectly S), and any economic gain that did accrue during P's ownership would be taxed on P's sale of the S stock.[4]

Section 355(b)(2)(D) forecloses this strategy by providing that the active trade or business requirement is not met if control of the distributing corporation (T) was acquired by a corporate distributee (P) within the five-year period preceding the distribution of stock in the controlled corporation (S). The limitation does not apply, however, if P acquired T in a wholly tax-free transaction, such as an acquisitive reorganization.[5] Distributee corporations that are members of the same affiliated group (as defined in Section 1504(a)) are treated as a single corporate distributee for this purpose.[6]

The principal sanction from denying Section 355 treatment to the above fact pattern is that T must recognize gain on the distribution of its S stock to P. In addition, assuming that T has ample earnings and profits, P has a dividend on receipt of the S stock, but as a corporate parent of T, P likely would be entitled to a 100 percent dividends received deduction.[7] P would obtain a fair market value basis in the distributed S stock[8] and thus

---

2. Rev.Rul. 74–5, 1974–1 C.B. 82. The key to the ruling was that T (the distributing corporation) and S (the controlled corporation) both had been engaged in the active conduct of a trade or business for five years. It did not matter that P (the distributee shareholder of T) had acquired a controlling interest in T in a taxable transaction within the five-year period preceding the distribution.

3. P thus obtained a basis in the S stock that usually was significantly higher than T's basis in the S stock. T's basis would disappear if the spin-off qualified under Section 355. Cf. I.R.C. §§ 332; 336(e); 338(h)(10).

4. Of course, T could not have sold its S stock without recognizing at least one level of gain. Query whether P should be able to avoid gain on a sale of a piece of T's business when T could not have done so. On the other hand, no corporate-level gain was recognized when T's shareholders sold all their T stock to P and no Section 338 election was made.

Query why T or P should not be able to sell S without corporate-level gain provided that gain is preserved through transferred asset bases.

5. I.R.C. § 355(b)(2)(D)(ii); see also Rev. Rul. 89–37, 1989–1 C.B. 107.

6. Thus, if in the example P had two existing wholly owned subsidiaries (X and Y) and each acquired 50 percent of the T stock for cash, a distribution by T of its S stock within five years after the acquisition would not qualify under Section 355 because X and Y, as members of the same affiliated group, are treated as a single corporation that acquired a controlling stock interest in T within five years preceding the distribution.

7. I.R.C. § 243(a)(3), (b). If P, T and S were members of a consolidated group, the dividend would be deferred and P's basis in its T stock would be reduced by the amount of the distribution. Reg. §§ 1.1502–14(a)(1), 1.1502–32(b)(2).

8. I.R.C. § 301(d).

recognize no further gain on the subsequent sale. But in the likely event that the buyer of the S stock does not make a Section 338 election, the gain inherent in S's assets is preserved through their transferred bases, raising the specter of yet another corporate-level tax.[9]

PROBLEM

T Corporation ("T") and its wholly owned subsidiary, S Corporation ("S") each have actively conducted a trade or business for more than five years. P Corporation ("P") wishes to acquire T but is not interested in owning the business conducted by S. The assets of T (including its S stock) and S are highly appreciated, and the businesses operated by T and S are equal in value. Consider generally the tax consequences of the following alternative transactions:

(a) T sells its S stock to Buyer Corporation. T's shareholders then sell their T stock to P.

(b) In 2005, P purchases all of T's stock from T's shareholders for cash and does not make a Section 338 election. In 2007, for a valid business purpose, T distributes its S stock to P and nine months later P sells the S stock to Buyer Corporation.

(c) Same as (b), above, except that P is an individual.

(d) Same as (b), above, except that P acquired all the stock of T in a tax-free Type B reorganization.

(e) In 2005, P purchases 50% of the T stock from T's shareholders and Buyer Corporation ("B") purchases the remaining 50%. In 2007, T distributes all of its S stock to B in exchange for all the T stock held by B.

c. DIVISIVE TRANSACTIONS IN CONNECTION WITH CERTAIN CHANGES OF OWNERSHIP

Code: § 355(c), (d).

The active business requirement disqualifies a divisive transaction if P acquires a controlling stock interest in T within the five years preceding the distribution of S stock.[10] The requirement does not apply, however, in some other situations that offer promising avenues of escape from corporate-level tax in ostensibly divisive transactions that were really sales. For example, if P did not acquire a controlling stock interest in T, the active business limitation would not preclude essentially the same transaction described in the example above. This opportunity may be illustrated

9. This double *corporate*-level tax could be avoided if T sold its S stock directly to the new buyer, and the parties jointly made an election under Section 338(h)(10). In that event, T could ignore the gain on the sale of its S stock but S would recognize gain on a deemed sale of its assets, and "new S" would obtain a stepped-up basis in those assets. See Chapter 8C3, supra. Query why the result is worse in a comparable transaction caught by the Section 355(b)(2)(D) trap?

10. I.R.C. § 355(b)(2)(D).

through a simple fact pattern in which four unrelated corporations (A, B, C and D) each purchase a portion of the stock of T with the ultimate objective of winding up with different pieces of T's business that are conducted through separate T subsidiaries. After waiting two years to establish their status as historic shareholders for continuity of interest purposes, A, B and C could exchange their T stock for stock of the desired T subsidiary in a split-off that would qualify under Section 355.[11] All of this could be accomplished without waiting five years after the acquisition of T because no single corporate distributee acquired a controlling stock interest in T. The five-year holding period requirement also does not apply to acquisitions of a controlling interest in T through a partnership or by any other noncorporate purchaser. A variety of other avoidance techniques quickly revealed that Congress had not successfully curtailed the use of Section 355 to avoid corporate-level gain on essentially acquisitive transactions.

The Treasury might have attacked a Section 355 transaction that was inconsistent with *General Utilities* repeal by exercising its authority to issue regulations under Section 337(d).[12] Instead, it returned to Congress for a more comprehensive solution. The result is Section 355(d), which imposes a corporate-level tax on divisive transactions in connection with certain changes of ownership. The House Ways and Means Committee explained the reasons for the change:[13]

> Some corporate taxpayers may attempt, under present-law rules governing divisive transactions, to dispose of subsidiaries in transactions that resemble sales, or to obtain a fair market value stepped-up basis for any future dispositions, without incurring corporate-level tax. The avoidance of corporate-level tax is inconsistent with the repeal of the *General Utilities* doctrine as part of the Tax Reform Act of 1986.
>
> Under the present-law rules, individual purchasers, or corporate purchasers of less than 80 percent, of the stock of a parent corporation may attempt to utilize section 355 to acquire a subsidiary (or a division incorporated for this purpose) from the parent without the parent incurring any corporate-level tax. The purchaser may acquire stock of the parent equal in value to the value of the desired subsidiary or division, and later surrender that stock for stock of the subsidiary, in a transaction intended to qualify as a non-pro-rata tax-free divisive transaction. Alternatively, the transaction might be structured as a surrender of the parent stock by

11. For this purpose, it is assumed that all relevant business of T have a five-year history; the business purpose requirement can be satisfied; and the parties could structure the transaction to avoid the step transaction doctrine.

12. Section 337(d) grants the Service authority to promulgate regulations to prevent circumvention of the purposes of certain amendments made by The Tax Reform Act of 1986 (i.e., repeal of the *General Utilities* doctrine) through the use of any provision of the Code or regulations.

13. House Ways and Means Committee, Explanation of the Revenue Provisions to 1991 Budget Reconciliation Bill (Oct. 16, 1990), 101st Cong., 2d Sess. 90–92 (1990).

all shareholders other than the acquiror, in exchange for a distribution (intended to be tax-free) of all subsidiaries or activities other than those the acquiror desires.

In addition, a non-corporate purchaser, or a corporate purchaser of less than 80 percent of the stock of another corporation, may attempt to utilize section 355 to obtain a stepped up fair market value basis in a subsidiary of an acquired corporation, enabling a subsequent disposition of that subsidiary without a corporate-level tax.

The provisions for tax-free divisive transactions under section 355 were a limited exception to the repeal of the *General Utilities* doctrine, intended to permit historic shareholders to continue to carry on their historic corporate businesses in separate corporations. It is believed that the benefit of tax-free treatment should not apply where the divisive transaction, combined with a stock purchase resulting in a change of ownership, in effect results in the disposition of a significant part of the historic shareholders' interests in one or more of the divided corporations.

The present-law provisions granting tax-free treatment at the corporate level are particularly troublesome because they may offer taxpayers an opportunity to avoid the general rule that corporate-level gain is recognized when an asset (including the stock of a subsidiary) is disposed of. There is special concern about the possibility for the distributing corporation to avoid corporate-level tax on the transfer of a subsidiary. Therefore, although the provision does not affect shareholder treatment if section 355 is otherwise available, it does impose tax at the corporate level, in light of the potential avoidance of corporate tax on what is in effect a sale of a subsidiary.

The bill is not intended to limit in any way the continuing Treasury Department authority to issue regulations to prevent the avoidance of the repeal of the *General Utilities* doctrine through any provision of law or regulations, including Section 355.

Because Section 355(d) attempts to reach such a wide range of transactions, its operation is complex. Very generally, Section 355(d) requires recognition of gain by the distributing corporation (but not the distributee shareholders) on a "disqualified distribution" of stock or securities of a controlled corporation regardless of whether the distribution is part of a reorganization.[14] A "disqualified distribution" is any Section 355 distribution if, immediately after the distribution, any person holds "disqualified stock" in either the distributing corporation or any distributed controlled corporation constituting a 50 percent or greater interest (measured by total

---

14. This is technically accomplished by removing the stock or securities of the controlled corporation from the category of "qualified property" under Sections 361(c)(2) and 355(c)(2). I.R.C. § 355(d)(1). As a result, the distributing corporation must recognize gain as if the stock and securities were appreciated boot.

combined voting power or value) in such corporation.[15] "Disqualified stock" is any stock in either the distributing corporation or any controlled corporation acquired after October 9, 1990 by purchase during the five-year period before the distribution.[16]

In effect, Section 355(d) creates a five-year statutory predistribution continuity of interest test. If violated, the test requires the distributing corporation to recognize gain on the distribution of stock or securities of a subsidiary to a person who ends up with 50 percent or more of the stock of the subsidiary. Some typical examples of the application of Section 355(d) are illustrated by the following excerpt from the legislative history:[17]

> Example 1. Assume that after the effective date, individual A acquires by purchase a 20–percent interest in the stock of corporation P and a 10–percent interest in the stock of its subsidiary, S, and 40 percent or more of the stock of S is distributed to A within 5 years in exchange for his 20–percent interest in P. (The remainder of the S stock distributed in the section 355 distribution is distributed to other shareholders). Under the provision P must recognize gain with respect to the distributed stock of S because all 50 percent of the stock of S held by A is disqualified stock.

> Example 2. Assume that after the effective date individual A acquires by purchase a 20–percent interest in corporation P and P redeems stock of other shareholders so that A's interest in P increases to a 30 percent interest. Within 5 years of A's purchase, P distributes 50 percent of the stock of its subsidiary, S, to A in exchange for his 30 percent interest in P (the remainder of the stock of S distributed in the section 355 transaction is distributed to the other shareholders). P recognizes gain on the distribution of the stock of S because all 50 percent of the stock of S held by A is disqualified stock.

For purposes of the definition of disqualified stock, stock or securities generally are considered acquired by "purchase" if they do not have either a transferred basis or a Section 1014 date-of-death basis, and were not acquired in an exchange to which Section 351 or the corporate reorganization provisions apply.[18] An acquisition of property in a Section 351 exchange, however, is considered a purchase to the extent such property is acquired for cash or a cash item, marketable stock or securities, or any debt of the transferor.[19] In the case of carryover basis property which was

---

15. I.R.C. § 355(d)(2).

16. I.R.C. § 355(d)(3). See I.R.C. § 355(d)(5)(B) for the details on the "purchase" requirement.

17. H. Rep. No. 101–964, 101st Cong., 2d Sess. 85 (1990).

18. I.R.C. § 355(d)(5)(A). The legislative history states that there will be an exception for reorganization exchanges in which

gain is recognized on receipt of boot. H.Rep. No. 101–964, supra note 17, at 90.

19. I.R.C. § 355(d)(5)(B). The legislative history states that it is expected that regulations will provide an exception for Section 351 exchanges in which such items are transferred as part of an active trade or business (including debts incurred in the ordinary course of the trade or business) and do not exceed the reasonable needs of the busi-

purchased by the transferor, the acquirer of the property is treated as having purchased the property on the date it was purchased by the transferor.[20] This tacking rule may enable a distributing corporation to achieve purchase status and a five-year holding period, thus avoiding the gain triggered on a disqualified distribution.

To prevent easy avoidance of the 50 percent or more ownership test, an array of aggregation and attribution rules are applied to test shareholder ownership after a distribution. First, a shareholder and all persons related to the shareholder under Sections 267(b) or 707(b) are treated as one person.[21] If two or more otherwise unrelated persons act pursuant to a plan or arrangement with respect to acquisitions of distributing corporation or controlled corporation stock or securities, they are treated as a single person for purposes of Section 355(d).[22] Special rules also apply to attribution of stock from a corporation to its shareholders. The Section 318(a)(2) attribution rules apply to both stock and securities with the threshold for attribution from a corporation reduced to 10 percent.[23] In addition, if a person acquires by purchase an interest in an entity through which stock or securities are attributed, such stock or securities are deemed purchased on the later of the date of the purchase of the interest in the entity or the date the stock or securities are acquired by purchase by the entity.[24]

In yet another anti-avoidance provision, the running of the five-year predistribution period for holding stock or securities is suspended during any period in which the holder's risk of loss with respect to the stock or securities or any portion of the corporation's activities is substantially diminished. Such a reduction in risk can be accomplished by an option in favor of the holder, a short sale, a special class of stock or any other device or transaction.[25] The Service also is granted broad power to prescribe regulations which modify the definition of "purchase" and prevent avoidance of Section 355(d) through the use of related persons, intermediaries, pass-thru entities, options or other arrangements.

2.   DISPOSITIONS OF UNWANTED ASSETS IN CONJUNCTION WITH TAX-FREE REORGANIZATIONS

As discussed earlier in this chapter, a corporate division may be used as the vehicle for a tax-free spin-off of unwanted assets in preparation for an acquisition of the rest of the target corporation's business. Consider a typical scenario. An attractive takeover candidate ("T"), engaged in two different businesses, is approached by a motivated buyer ("P") whose interest is limited to only one of those businesses. To facilitate the transaction and maximize shareholder value, T spins off the unwanted business to its shareholders and then is acquired by P in a tax-free acquisitive reorga-

---

ness. H.Rep. No. 101–964, supra note 17, at 91.

20.   I.R.C. § 355(d)(5)(C).

21.   I.R.C. § 355(d)(7)(A).

22.   I.R.C. § 355(d)(7)(B).

23.   I.R.C. § 355(d)(8)(A).

24.   I.R.C. § 355(d)(8)(B).

25.   I.R.C. § 355(d)(6).

nization. Should the spin-off qualify under Section 355? What if T spins off the wanted business ("Newco") to its shareholders, who then exchange their Newco stock for P stock? Should the form of the transaction make any difference? These and other scenarios present a challenge to the target corporation's tax advisor and provide the student of Subchapter C with an opportunity to relate the requirements for a tax-free corporate division to the acquisitive reorganization concepts encountered in the previous chapter.

In Commissioner v. Morris Trust,[1] the Fourth Circuit held that a spin-off of an unwanted business followed by a prearranged merger of the parent "distributing" corporation with an unrelated acquiring corporation qualified as tax-free—specifically, a Type D reorganization coupled with a Section 355 corporate division, and a Section 368 Type A acquisitive reorganization. The Service ultimately blessed the *Morris Trust* form of transaction[2] and even acknowledged that a spin-off to prepare for an acquisition of a separate business was a valid Section 355 business purpose,[3] but it was less receptive to other transactional patterns despite their economic similarity. For example, a spin off of unwanted assets followed by a Type C reorganization or a forward triangular merger was likely to be treated as an integrated transaction, with the unfortunate result that the unwanted assets would be considered in determining whether P transferred substantially all of its properties in the subsequent reorganization. If the unwanted assets were a substantial part of P's overall business, the acquisition would not qualify as a reorganization, and the spin-off also was unlikely to qualify under Section 355.[4]

Other transactional forms also were vulnerable to challenge under the step transaction doctrine. For example, if P contributed the assets of a *wanted* business with a five-year history to newly created S, retained another (unwanted) business, distributed the S stock to its shareholders, and then S was acquired by an unrelated corporation ("X") in an attempt-

---

1. 367 F.2d 794 (4th Cir.1966).

2. Rev. Rul. 68–603, 1968–2 C.B. 148. See also Rev. Rul. 70–434, 1970–2 C.B. 83 (Type B reorganization followed spin-off of unwanted business).

3. Rev. Proc. 96–30, 1996–1 C.B. 36.

4. See, e.g., Helvering v. Elkhorn Coal Co., 95 F.2d 732 (4th Cir.1937), cert. denied, 305 U.S. 605, 59 S.Ct. 65 (1938). But see Rev. Rul. 2003–79, 2003–2 C.B. 80, where distributing corporation ("D") engaged in two businesses ("X" and "Y") of equal size. To facilitate an acquisition of business "X" by acquiring corporation ("P"), D contributed the wanted X assets to a new controlled corporation ("C"), distributed the C stock to its shareholders in a valid Section 355 spin-off, and then P acquired all of C's assets in exchange for P voting stock, and C liquidated. The Service ruled that the acquisition of C's assets qualified as a Type C reorganization even though, under *Elkhorn Coal*, P's acquisition of the same properties from D would have failed the "substantially all of the properties" requirement if D had retained the wanted business and spun-off the unwanted business to C before the attempted reorganization. In so ruling, the Service, citing Congressional intent, held that it was appropriate to consider the controlled corporation as independent of the distributing corporation in determining if the "substantially all" requirement of Section 368(a)(1)(C) is satisfied. The ruling is further evidence that the form of a transaction often matters in Subchapter C and that the Service is willing to turn off the step transaction doctrine when the overall policy of the Code dictates a more formalistic analysis.

ed tax-free reorganization, the Service took the position that neither the spin-off nor the reorganization qualified for tax-free treatment. If the steps were prearranged, S was disregarded and P was treated as having made a taxable sale of the wanted assets to X and having distributed the consideration received from X to P's shareholders as a dividend.[5] If P was publicly traded and S was an "old and cold" (i.e., not newly formed) subsidiary, however, the Service ruled that a spin-off of S stock followed by X's acquisition of S in a Type A or Type B reorganization did qualify as tax-free if no formal negotiations with respect to the subsequent acquisition took place prior to the spin-off.[6]

After repeal of the *General Utilities* doctrine, Congress became concerned (some might say paranoid) that Section 355 was being used to avoid corporate-level gain on the sale of a business. Section 355(d), discussed earlier in this chapter, was an early response. To further narrow the scope of Section 355, Congress followed up by enacting Section 355(e), which virtually eliminates the time-tested *Morris Trust* technique.[7] The legislative history explains that where new shareholders acquire ownership of a business in connection with a spin-off, the transaction more closely resembles a taxable corporate-level disposition of the portion of the business that is acquired rather than a tax-free division among existing shareholders.[8]

Section 355(e) is a typically complex anti-avoidance provision and this discussion is limited to an overview. It requires the distributing (parent) corporation to recognize gain as if it had sold the stock of the distributed controlled subsidiary for its fair market value on the date of the distribution if, as part of a "plan" or series of related transactions, one or more persons acquire[9] (directly or indirectly) a 50–percent or greater interest in either the distributing or controlled corporation within two years before or after the distribution.[10] Put differently (and, one hopes, more coherently), the distributing corporation (but not its shareholders) must recognize corporate-level gain on an otherwise tax-free spin-off if "pursuant to a plan" stock of either the distributing or controlled corporation is acquired and the historic shareholders of the distributing corporation do not retain more than 50 percent (by vote and value) of both corporations. Significantly

---

5. Rev. Rul. 70–225, 1970–1 C.B. 80.

6. Rev. Rul. 96–30, 1996–1 C.B. 36.

7. See also I.R.C. § 355(f), which disqualifies a transaction in its entirety under Section 355 when one member of an affiliated corporate group makes a distribution to another member if the distribution is part of a plan or series of related transactions to which Section 355(e) applies.

8. S.Rept. No. 105–33, 105th Cong., 1st Sess. 139–140 (1997).

9. Acquisitions, for this purpose, are not limited to cost basis purchase transactions but also can include tax-free acquisitions. Certain acquisitions that do not involve a shift in control are disregarded. I.R.C. § 355(e)(3)(A). If the assets rather than the stock of either corporation are acquired, the shareholders of the acquiring corporation are deemed to have acquired the target stock for purposes of determining whether the gain-triggering shift of control has occurred. I.R.C. § 355(e)(3)(B).

10. I.R.C. § 355(e)(1), (2). Technically, this result occurs because the stock or securities in the controlled corporation is not treated as "qualified property" for purposes of Section 355(c)(2) or Section 361(c)(2), and thus gain is recognized on the distribution under Section 311(b).

(and inexplicably), neither the distributing nor controlled corporations may adjust the basis of their assets or stock to reflect this recognition of Section 355(e) gain.

Section 355(e) applies only if the transaction is part of a "plan" (or a series of related transactions) to acquire the requisite 50 percent or greater interest in the target. For this purpose, if one or more persons directly or indirectly acquire a 50–percent or greater interest in the distributing corporation or any controlled corporation during the four-year period beginning two years before the distribution, the acquisition is presumed to be pursuant to a plan unless the taxpayer establishes that such a plan did not exist.[11] Whether or not a prohibited "plan" exists is based on all the facts and circumstances.[12]

The regulations have gone through several iterations, and the most recent version provides considerable flexibility in making this factual determination.[13] In the case of acquisitions (other than public offerings) of the distributing or controlled corporation after a distribution, the distribution and acquisition will be considered as part of a plan only if there was an agreement, understanding, arrangement, or substantial negotiations regarding the acquisition or a similar acquisition (collectively referred to below as "Talks") at some time during the two year period preceding the distribution.[14] Although not labelled as a safe harbor, this "two year lookback rule" operates as a security blanket in many situations, especially in light of the narrow definitions of several critical terms. An "agreement, understanding or arrangement," for example, is generally considered to exist only if the parties have reached a common understanding on most of the significant terms of the transaction.[15] "Substantial negotiations" exist only if the significant economic terms of the acquisition have been discussed at the highest levels (directors, officers, shareholders, or their representatives).[16] In short, for a plan to exist, the dealings must have reached a fairly advanced stage.

The regulations go on to provide that, even though the existence of Talks between the parties within the two years preceding the distribution "tend to show" that the distribution and acquisition are part of a plan, all the facts and circumstances still must be considered, and the existence of a corporate business purpose (apart from facilitating the acquisition) will help the taxpayer rebut the statutory presumption.[17] Further comfort is available from seven safe harbors.[18] A key factor under most of these safe harbors is whether there were bilateral Talks during a specified time period. For example, if the acquisition occurred more than six months after the distribution and there were no Talks during the period commencing on one year before and ending six months after the distribution, the transactions are not considered part of a plan if the distribution was motivated by

11. I.R.C. § 355(e)(2)(B).
12. Reg. § 1.355–7T(b)(1).
13. See generally Reg. § 1.355–7T.
14. Reg. § 1.355–7T(b)(2).
15. Reg. § 1.355–7T(h)(1)(i).
16. Reg. § 1.355–7T(h)(1)(ii).
17. Reg. § 1.355–7T(b)(2).
18. Reg. § 1.355–7T(d).

a substantial business purpose other than facilitating the acquisition.[19] If a transaction does not fit within any of the safe harbors, the regulations include a list of "plan" and "nonplan" factors to consider in determining whether a plan exists.[20]

In summary, Section 355(e) obliterates many typical "planned" *Morris Trust* transactions but leaves open the possibility that a spin-off followed by an acquisition will continue to qualify under Section 355 if there was a valid business purpose and Talks with potential acquirers did not occur prior to the distribution and within six months thereafter. On the other hand, the existence of an agreement, understanding or negotiations to sell either the distributing or controlled corporations at the time of the spin-off likely will doom the transaction. In an ironic twist, Section 355(e) would not have changed the tax-free treatment in the actual *Morris Trust* transaction, because the distributing corporation's shareholders received 54 percent of the equity of the acquiring corporation as part of the transaction and thus the "control shift" required to trigger Section 355(e) would not have occurred. As a practical matter, Section 355(e) does not apply when the equity value of the distributing corporation after the spin-off exceeds that of the acquiring corporation.

PROBLEM

Leisure, Inc. is a publicly held corporation that operates a chain of motels and manufactures leisure apparel. Each business has roughly the same net worth and has been operated by Leisure for over five years. Denim Corporation wishes to acquire the apparel business but is not interested in the motels. Leisure would like to dispose of the apparel business, preferably in a tax-free reorganization, and it will continue to operate the motel business for the indefinite future. Consider the tax consequences of the following alternative plans for carrying out the objectives of the parties:

   (a) Leisure will transfer the motel assets to a newly formed subsidiary, Motel, Inc., and distribute the Motel stock pro rata to the Leisure shareholders. Leisure then will transfer the assets and liabilities of the apparel business to Denim in exchange for Denim voting stock (representing less than 50 percent of the total outstanding voting stock of Denim after the acquisition), and then Leisure will liquidate, distributing the Denim stock pro rata to its shareholders.

   (b) Same as (a), above, except that after the spin-off, Leisure merges into Denim. Under the terms of the merger, Leisure shareholders receive Denim nonvoting preferred stock.

   (c) What result if Leisure transfers the apparel business to a new corporation, Cords, Inc., and then distributes the Cords stock pro rata to the Leisure shareholders. Leisure continues to operate the

19. Reg. § 1.355–7T(d)(1).   **20.** Reg. § 1.355–7T(b)(3) & (4).

motel business, but Cords, Inc. merges into Denim, Inc., and the Cords shareholders receive Denim voting stock.

(d) Same as (c), above, except that after the merger, the Denim voting stock received by Cords shareholders represents more than 50 percent of the total outstanding stock of Denim.

(e) Same as (b), above, except that the merger of Leisure into Denim occurred one year after the spin-off. What factors are relevant in determining whether the transaction was part of a "plan" to acquire Leisure?

(f) Same as (b), above, except that the business purpose for the spin-off was unrelated to any acquisition of the apparel business, and the merger of Leisure into Denim occurred three years after the spin-off.

(g) Is § 355(e) necessary? How did the typical *Morris Trust* transaction violate the policy of Subchapter C?

CHAPTER 11

NONACQUISITIVE, NONDIVISIVE REORGANIZATIONS

A. TYPE E: RECAPITALIZATIONS

1. INTRODUCTION

Code: §§ 368(a)(1)(E); 354; 356; 358; 1032; 1036; 1223(1). Skim §§ 305; 306.

Regulations: §§ 1.301–1(*l*); 1.305–7(c); 1.368–2(e).

A tax-free reorganization sometimes involves only a single corporation undergoing a readjustment to its capital structure. The most common form of nonacquisitive, nondivisive reorganization is the recapitalization, which qualifies as a Type E reorganization if certain requirements are met. Recapitalizations traditionally have been used for a variety of business and tax objectives. A corporation may reshuffle its capital structure by exchanging stock for bonds in order to improve its debt/equity ratio and calm the nerves of creditors or as a condition to borrowing additional funds. Alternatively, it may exchange debt instruments for stock in order to lessen the sting of the double tax by withdrawing earnings in the form of deductible interest rather than nondeductible dividends. For closely held corporations, recapitalizations may be used as a device to shift control among the shareholders.

This overview of recapitalizations begins with an examination of the applicable judicial requirements, many of which have been previously encountered in connection with acquisitive reorganizations. We then consider the most common type of recapitalization exchanges.

Revenue Ruling 82–34

1982–1 Cum.Bull. 59.

ISSUE

Advice has been requested regarding whether continuity of business enterprise is a requirement for a recapitalization to qualify as a reorganization under section 368(a)(1)(E) of the Internal Revenue Code.

LAW, ANALYSIS AND HOLDING

Section 368(a)(1)(E) of the Code provides that a "recapitalization" is a reorganization. A recapitalization has been defined as a "reshuffling of a capital structure within the framework of an existing corporation." Helvering v. Southwest Consolidated Corp., 315 U.S. 194 (1942), Ct.D. 1544, 1942–1 C.B. 218.

When a shareholder receives stock in a reorganization described in section 368(a)(1) and either before or after the transaction, the principal business assets of the transferor are sold or disposed of, a question arises whether the continuity of business enterprise requirement for a reorganization is satisfied. See sections 1.1002–1(c), 1.368–1(b) and 1.368–1(d) of the Income Tax Regulations.

The purpose of the reorganization provisions is to except from the general rule of recognizing gain or loss certain specifically described exchanges incident to corporate readjustments which effect only a readjustment of continuing interests in property under modified corporate forms. Section 1.368–1(b) of the regulations states that a continuity of the business enterprise under the modified corporate form is required in a reorganization.

Specifically, section 1.368–1(d) of the regulations provides, in general, that the transferee in a corporate reorganization must either (i) continue the transferor's historic business or (ii) use a significant portion of the transferor's historic business assets in a business.

The "continuity of business enterprise" requirement is closely related to the "continuity of shareholder interest" requirement in section 1.368–1(b) of the regulations in that both are concerned with determining whether a transaction involves an otherwise taxable transfer of stock or assets of one corporation to another corporation, as distinguished from a tax-free reorganization, which assumes only a readjustment of continuing interests under modified corporate form. The consideration of whether a transaction involves an otherwise taxable transfer of stock or assets of one corporation to another corporation is not present in a recapitalization because a recapitalization involves only a single corporation. Therefore, Rev.Rul. 77–415, 1977–2 C.B. 311, consistent with several court decisions, concludes that continuity of shareholder interest is not a requirement for a recapitalization to qualify as a reorganization under section 368(a)(1)(E) of the Code. Similarly, continuity of business enterprise is not a requirement for a recapitalization to qualify as a reorganization under section 368(a)(1)(E).

2.   TYPES OF RECAPITALIZATIONS

Although immune from the continuity of interest and the continuity of business enterprise requirements, a recapitalization still must serve some business purpose in order to qualify for nonrecognition.[1] The courts have been tolerant in this area, and most of the business objectives set forth in the introduction to this chapter are acceptable. Historically, the taxpayer must have demonstrated a *corporate* (as opposed to shareholder) business

---

1.   Reg. § 1.368–1(b).

purpose to obtain an advance ruling from the Service on the tax-free status of a recapitalization,[2] and presumably this requirement continues despite the Service's new aversion to issuing "comfort" rulings.[3] In analogous situations, the courts have recognized that it may be unrealistic and impractical to distinguish corporate from shareholder purposes in a closely held corporation.[4] Thus, shareholder objectives germane to the corporation's business have been sufficient to satisfy the business purpose requirement.[5]

Recapitalizations fall into four broad categories depending upon the consideration exchanged. These categories raise different issues and are best studied separately.

a. BONDS EXCHANGED FOR STOCK

If a corporation discharges outstanding bonds by issuing preferred or common stock to the bondholders, the transaction qualifies as a Type E reorganization.[6] Under Section 354(a), the bondholders generally will recognize no gain or loss on the exchange of their debt instruments solely for stock. Section 354(a)(2)(B) creates an exception to nonrecognition to the extent stock received is attributable to accrued and untaxed interest on the bonds. This interest component will be taxed as ordinary income under Section 61.[7] The basis of the stock received in a bonds-for-stock recapitalization will be determined under the familiar rules of Section 358, and the new shareholder will be entitled to a tacked holding period on the stock under Section 1223(1).

On the corporate side, matters are fairly routine. Since the corporation is issuing its stock, it initially will be excused from recognizing gain or loss by Section 1032. However, a debtor corporation that transfers its stock in satisfaction of its debt is treated as if it satisfied the debt with an amount of money equal to the fair market value of the transferred stock.[8] Only an insolvent or bankrupt corporation may exclude any resulting discharge of indebtedness income under Section 108 and must make a corresponding

---

2. Rev.Proc. 81–60, § 4.04, 1981–2 C.B. 680.

3. See, e.g., Rev. Proc. 2002–3, § 3.01(30), 2002–1 I.R.B. 117, 119, where the Service indicates that it no longer will issue advance rulings on the tax-free status of a recapitalization (and many other transactions) unless it determines that there is a "significant issue" to be resolved. See supra p. 409 for what it takes to be a "significant issue."

4. Lewis v. Commissioner, 176 F.2d 646 (1st Cir.1949); Estate of Parshelsky v. Commissioner, 303 F.2d 14 (2d Cir.1962). But see Reg. § 1.355–2(b)(2), requiring a corporate business purpose in a tax-free division under Section 355.

5. Cf. Rafferty v. Commissioner, 452 F.2d 767 (1st Cir.1971), cert. denied, 408 U.S. 922, 92 S.Ct. 2489 (1972).

6. Reg. § 1.368–2(e)(1). A recapitalization should be distinguished from conversion of a bond into stock pursuant to a conversion privilege in the bond. The Service has held that the latter situation does not constitute a taxable event as long as the bond is converted into stock of the same corporation. Rev.Rul. 72–265, 1972–1 C.B. 222; Rev.Rul. 79–155, 1979–1 C.B. 153.

7. I.R.C. § 354(a)(3)(B).

8. I.R.C. § 108(e)(8).

reduction in its tax attributes.[9] Thus, a bonds-for-stock recapitalization may result in gross income for the corporation.

b. BONDS FOR BONDS

After initially contesting the issue,[10] the Service now concedes that if a creditor exchanges outstanding bonds for newly issued bonds in the same corporation, the transaction qualifies as a Type E reorganization.[11] The bondholder in a bonds-for-bonds exchange generally does not recognize gain or loss unless the bonds received are attributable to accrued and untaxed interest[12] or the principal amount of the bonds received in the exchange exceeds the principal amount of the bonds surrendered.[13] Income attributable to interest will be ordinary in character while gain recognized as a result of receipt of excess bonds generally will be either short-or long-term capital gain.[14] The bondholder's basis in the new bonds will be determined under Section 358 and the new bonds will take a tacked holding period under Section 1223(1).

On the corporate side, the primary concern in a bonds-for-bonds recapitalization will be the discharge of indebtedness rules in Section 108.[15] In addition, a bonds-for-bonds recapitalization may subject the corporation and bondholders to the intricate original issue discount provisions.[16]

c. STOCK FOR STOCK

The regulations provide three examples of stock-for-stock exchanges which qualify as reorganizations. Two examples involve exchanges of outstanding preferred stock for common stock and the third involves an exchange of outstanding common for preferred.[17] Thus, virtually all equity-for-equity exchanges will qualify as Type E reorganizations.[18] In addition, exchanges of common stock in a corporation for common stock in the same corporation or preferred stock for preferred stock will qualify for nonrecog-

9. See I.R.C. § 108(a)(1)(A), (a)(1)(B), (b).

10. See I.T. 2035, III–1 C.B. 55 (1924); Commissioner v. Neustadt's Trust, 131 F.2d 528, 530 (2d Cir.1942), affirming 43 B.T.A. 848 (1941), nonacq. 1941–1 C.B. 17, nonacq. withdrawn, acq. 1951–1 C.B. 2.

11. See I.T. 4081, 1952–1 C.B. 65; Rev. Rul. 77–415, 1977–2 C.B. 311.

12. I.R.C. § 354(a)(2)(B). Cf. I.R.C. § 354(a)(3)(B).

13. I.R.C. §§ 354(a)(2)(A), 356(a)(1), (d).

14. I.R.C. §§ 354(a)(3)(A), 356(a)(1). See Rev.Rul. 71–427, 1971–2 C.B. 183.

15. See I.R.C. § 108(e)(10).

16. In particular, see I.R.C. §§ 163(e), 1272–1275. See Bittker & Eustice, Federal Income Taxation of Corporations and Shareholders ¶ 12.27[4][c] (7th ed. 2000).

17. Reg. § 1.368–2(e)(2)–(4).

18. It is unlikely that a conversion of preferred stock into common stock in the same corporation, or vice versa, pursuant to a conversion privilege in the stock would be a taxable event under the theory of Rev.Rul. 72–265, 1972–1 C.B. 222, which deals with convertible debt instruments. Rev.Rul. 77–238, 1977–2 C.B. 115, however, holds that conversion of stock in furtherance of a corporate business purpose pursuant to a privilege contained in the corporation's certificate of incorporation is a recapitalization under Section 368(a)(1)(E).

nition under Section 1036.[19]

Sections 354 and 356 govern the shareholder level tax consequences of a stock-for-stock recapitalization. The shareholders will recognize gain to the extent they receive boot in the exchange, and the gain will be characterized as gain from the exchange of the stock unless the transaction has "the effect of the distribution of a dividend."[20] The shareholders' basis in the stock received in the exchange will be determined under Section 358 and will take a tacked holding period under Section 1223(1). The corporation will be entitled to nonrecognition under Section 1032 on the exchange of its stock.

Sections 305 and 306 also may come into play in a stock-for-stock recapitalization. The regulations provide that a recapitalization will be deemed to result in a distribution to which Section 305(c) applies if it is (1) pursuant to a plan to periodically increase a shareholder's proportionate interest in the assets or earnings and profits of the corporation or (2) with respect to preferred stock with dividend arrearages and the preferred shareholder increases his proportionate interest in the corporation as a result of the exchange.[21] The second alternative essentially precludes recapitalizations designed to remedy preferred stock dividend arrearages by taxing them under Sections 305(c) and (b)(4).[22]

Stock received in a recapitalization constitutes "Section 306 stock" under Section 306(c)(1)(B) if: (1) it is not common stock, (2) it was received pursuant to a plan of reorganization, (3) on its receipt gain or loss was not recognized to any extent under Sections 354 and 356, and (4) the effect of the transaction was substantially the same as the receipt of a stock dividend or the stock was received in exchange for Section 306 stock. The regulations provide a cash substitute test for determining whether the transaction has the effect of a dividend.[23] If cash received in lieu of the stock obtained in the recapitalization would have been a dividend under Section 356(a)(2), the transaction has substantially the same effect as a dividend. Thus, if the shareholders exchange common stock for common stock and a proportionate amount of preferred stock, the preferred shares will be Section 306 stock.

---

19. Section 1036 also applies to exchanges between two individual stockholders. Reg. § 1.1036–1(a). For this purpose, boot generally includes "debt-like" nonqualified preferred stock within the meaning of Section 351(g) unless such preferred stock is exchanged for comparable preferred of the same or lesser value, or in certain recapitalizations of "family-owned" corporations. I.R.C. § 354(a)(1)(C).

20. I.R.C. § 356(a)(2). See Rev.Rul. 84–114, below.

21. Reg. § 1.305–7(c). A preferred shareholder's proportionate interest increases if the greater of the fair market value or

liquidation preference of the stock received in the exchange exceeds the issue price of the preferred stock surrendered. In such an exchange, the amount considered distributed to the preferred shareholder under Section 305(c) is the lesser of (1) the greater of fair market value or liquidation preference of the preferred stock received over the issue price of the preferred stock surrendered or (2) the amount of the dividend arrearages.

22. Reg. § 1.305–5(d) Example (1). See also Reg. § 1.305–3(e) Example (12); Reg. § 1.305–5(d) Examples (2), (3) and (6).

23. Reg. § 1.306–3(d).

Revenue Ruling 84–114

1984–2 Cum.Bull. 90.

ISSUE

When nonvoting preferred stock and cash are received in an integrated transaction by a shareholder in exchange for voting common stock in a recapitalization described in section 368(a)(1)(E) of the Internal Revenue Code, does the receipt of cash have the effect of the distribution of a dividend within the meaning of section 356(a)(2)?

FACTS

Corporation X had outstanding 420 shares of voting common stock of which A owned 120 shares and B, C and D each owned 100 shares. A, B, C and D were not related within the meaning of section 318(a) of the Code. X adopted a plan of recapitalization that permitted a shareholder to exchange each of 30 shares of voting common stock for either one share of nonvoting preferred stock or cash. Pursuant to the plan, A first exchanged 15 shares of voting common stock for cash and then exchanged 15 shares of voting common stock for 15 shares of nonvoting preferred stock. The facts and circumstances surrounding these exchanges were such that the exchanges constituted two steps in a single integrated transaction for purposes of sections 368(a)(1)(E) and 356(a)(2). The nonvoting preferred stock had no conversion features. In addition, the dividend and liquidation rights payable to A on 15 shares of nonvoting preferred stock were substantially less than the dividend and liquidation rights payable to A on 30 shares of voting common stock. B, C, and D did not participate in the exchange and will retain all their voting common stock in X. X had a substantial amount of post–1913 earnings and profits.

The exchange by A of voting common stock for nonvoting preferred stock and cash qualified as a recapitalization within the meaning of section 368(a)(1)(E) of the Code.

LAW AND ANALYSIS

Section 354(a)(1) of the Code provides that no gain or loss will be recognized if stock or securities in a corporation a party to a reorganization are, in pursuance of the plan of reorganization, exchanged solely for stock or securities in such corporation or in another corporation a party to the reorganization.

Section 356(a)(1) of the Code provides that if section 354 would apply to an exchange but for the fact that the property received in the exchange consists not only of property permitted by section 354 to be received without the recognition of gain but also of other property or money, then the gain, if any, will be recognized, but in an amount not in excess of the sum of the money and fair market value of the other property. Section 356(a)(2) provides that if such exchange has the effect of the distribution of a dividend (determined with the application of section 318(a)), then there will be treated as a dividend to each distributee such an amount of the gain recognized under section 356(a)(1) as is not in excess of each distributee's ratable share of the undistributed earnings and profits of the corporation accumulated after February 28, 1913.

Under section 302(b)(1) and section 302(a) of the Code a redemption will be treated as a distribution in part or full payment in exchange for stock if it is not essentially equivalent to a dividend to the shareholder.

Rev.Rul. 74–515, 1974–2 C.B. 118, and Rev.Rul. 74–516, 1974–2 C.B. 121, state that whether a reorganization distribution to which section 356 of the Code applies has the effect of a dividend must be determined by examining the facts and circumstances surrounding the distribution and looking to the principles for determining dividend equivalency developed under section 356(a)(2) and other provisions of the Code. See Ross v. United States, 173 F.Supp. 793 (Ct.Cl.1959), cert. denied, 361 U.S. 875 (1959). Rev.Rul. 74–516 indicates that in making a dividend equivalency determination under section 356(a)(2), it is proper to analogize to section 302 in appropriate cases. In Shimberg v. United States, 577 F.2d 283 (5th Cir.1978), cert. denied, 439 U.S. 1115 (1979), the courts indicated that in making a dividend equivalency determination under section 356(a)(2), an analogy to section 302 may be appropriate in cases involving single entity reorganizations.

In United States v. Davis, 397 U.S. 301 (1970), rehearing denied, 397 U.S. 1071 (1970), 1970–1 C.B. 62, the Supreme Court of the United States held that a redemption must result in a meaningful reduction of the shareholder's proportionate interest in the corporation in order not to be essentially equivalent to a dividend under section 302(b)(1) of the Code.

Rev.Rul. 75–502, 1975–2 C.B. 111, sets forth factors to be considered in determining whether a reduction in a shareholder's proportionate interest in a corporation is meaningful within the meaning of Davis. The factors considered are a shareholder's right to vote and exercise control, to participate in current earnings and accumulated surplus, and to share in net assets on liquidation. The reduction in the right to vote is of particular significance when a redemption causes a redeemed shareholder to lose the potential for controlling the redeeming corporation by acting in concert with only one other shareholder. See Rev.Rul. 76–364, 1976–2 C.B. 91.

The specific issue is whether, in determining dividend equivalency under section 356(a)(2) of the Code, it is proper to look solely at the change in A's proportionate interest in X that resulted from A's exchange of voting common stock for cash, or instead, whether consideration should be given to the total change in A's proportionate interest in X that resulted from the exchange of voting common stock for both cash and nonvoting preferred stock.

In Rev.Rul. 55–745, 1955–2 C.B. 223, the Internal Revenue Service announced that for purposes of section 302(b)(3) of the Code, it would follow the decision in Zenz v. Quinlivan, 213 F.2d 914 (6th Cir.1954), that a complete termination of shareholder interest may be achieved when a shareholder's entire stock interest in a corporation is disposed of partly through redemption and partly through sale. See also Rev.Rul. 75–447, 1975–2 C.B. 113, in which the Zenz rationale was applied to section 302(b)(2).

Since the exchange of voting common stock for cash and the exchange of voting common stock for nonvoting preferred stock constitute an integrated transaction, in this situation involving a single corporation, it is proper to apply the Zenz rationale so that both exchanges are taken into consideration in determining whether there has been a meaningful reduction of A's proportionate interest in X within the meaning of Davis. Compare Rev.Rul. 75–83, 1975–1 C.B. 112, which holds that a distribution in connection with a transaction qualifying under section 368(a)(1)(A) of the Code will be viewed as having been made by the acquired or transferor corporation and not by the acquiring or transferee corporation for purposes of making a dividend equivalency determination under section 356(a)(2).

If the exchange of voting common stock for preferred stock and cash in this situation had been tested under section 302 of the Code as a redemption, it would not have qualified under section 302(b)(2) or (3) because there was neither an adequate reduction in A's voting stock interest nor a complete termination of that interest. In determining whether this situation is analogous to a redemption meeting the requirements of section 302(b)(1), it is significant that A's interest in the voting common stock of X was reduced from 28.57 percent ($^{120}/_{420}$) to 23.08 percent ($^{90}/_{390}$) so that A went from a position of holding a number of shares of voting common stock that afforded A control of X if A acted in concert with only one other shareholder, to a position where such action was not possible. Moreover, it is significant that A no longer holds the largest voting stock interest in X. In addition, although A received dividend and liquidation rights from the 15 shares of nonvoting preferred stock, these were substantially less than the dividend and liquidation rights of the 30 shares of voting common stock A surrendered. Accordingly, the requirements of section 302(b)(1) would have been met if the transaction had been tested under section 302, and, therefore, the cash received by A did not have the effect of the distribution of a dividend within the meaning of section 356(a)(2).

HOLDING

When A received cash and nonvoting preferred stock of X in an integrated transaction in exchange for voting common stock of X in a recapitalization described in section 368(a)(1)(E) of the Code, the receipt of cash did not have the effect of the distribution of a dividend within the meaning of section 356(a)(2).

d.   STOCK EXCHANGED FOR BONDS

Bazley v. Commissioner

Supreme Court of the United States, 1947.
331 U.S. 737, 67 S.Ct. 1489.

■ MR. JUSTICE FRANKFURTER delivered the opinion of the Court.

* * *

In the *Bazley* case, No. 287, the Commissioner of Internal Revenue assessed an income tax deficiency against the taxpayer for the year 1939.

Its validity depends on the legal significance of the recapitalization in that year of a family corporation in which the taxpayer and his wife owned all but one of the Company's one thousand shares. These had a par value of $100. Under the plan of reorganization the taxpayer, his wife, and the holder of the additional share were to turn in their old shares and receive in exchange for each old share five new shares of no par value, but of a stated value of $60, and new debenture bonds, having a total face value of $400,000, payable in ten years but callable at any time. Accordingly, the taxpayer received 3,990 shares of the new stock for the 798 shares of his old holding and debentures in the amount of $319,200. At the time of these transactions the earned surplus of the corporation was $855,783.82.

The Commissioner charged to the taxpayer as income the full value of the debentures. The Tax Court affirmed the Commissioner's determination, against the taxpayer's contention that as a "recapitalization" the transaction was a tax-free "reorganization" and that the debentures were "securities in a corporation a party to a reorganization," "exchanged solely for stock or securities in such corporation" "in pursuance of the plan of reorganization," and as such no gain is recognized for income tax purposes. Internal Revenue Code, §§ 112(g)(1)(E) [the predecessor of § 368(a)(1)(E)] and 112(b)(3). The Tax Court found that the recapitalization had "no legitimate corporate business purpose" and was therefore not a "reorganization" within the statute. The distribution of debentures, it concluded, was a disguised dividend, taxable as earned income under §§ [61(a) and 301]. 4 T.C. 897. The Circuit Court of Appeals for the Third Circuit, sitting en banc, affirmed, two judges dissenting. 155 F.2d 237.

Unless a transaction is a reorganization contemplated by § [368], any exchange of "stock or securities" in connection with such transaction, cannot be "in pursuance of the plan of reorganization." While § [368(a)] informs us that "reorganization" means, among other things, "a recapitalization," it does not inform us what "recapitalization" means. "Recapitalization" in connection with the income tax has been part of the revenue laws since 1921. 42 Stat. 227, 230, § 202(c)(2). Congress has never defined it and the Treasury Regulations shed only limited light. Treas.Reg. 103, § 19.112(g). One thing is certain. Congress did not incorporate some technical concept, whether that of accountants or of other specialists, into § [368(a)], assuming that there is agreement among specialists as to the meaning of recapitalization. And so, recapitalization as used in § [368(a)] must draw its meaning from its function in that section. It is one of the forms of reorganization which obtains the privileges afforded by § [368(a)]. Therefore, "recapitalization" must be construed with reference to the presuppositions and purpose of § [368(a)]. It was not the purpose of the reorganization provision to exempt from payment of a tax what as a practical matter is realized gain. Normally, a distribution by a corporation, whatever form it takes, is a definite and rather unambiguous event. It furnishes the proper occasion for the determination and taxation of gain. But there are circumstances where a formal distribution, directly or through exchange of securities, represents merely a new form of the previous participation in an enterprise, involving no change of substance in the rights and relations of the interested parties one to another or to the corporate assets. As to these, Congress has said that they are not to be deemed significant occasions for determining taxable gain.

These considerations underlie § [368(a)] and they should dominate the scope to be given to the various sections, all of which converge toward a common purpose. Application of the language of such a revenue provision is not an exercise in framing abstract definitions. In a series of cases this Court has withheld the benefits of the reorganization provision in situations which might have satisfied provisions of the section treated as inert language, because they were not reorganizations of the kind with which § [368], in its purpose and particulars, concerns itself. See Pinellas Ice & Cold Storage Co. v. Commissioner, 287 U.S. 462; Gregory v. Helvering, 293 U.S. 465; LeTulle v. Scofield, 308 U.S. 415.

Congress has not attempted a definition of what is recapitalization and we shall follow its example. The search for relevant meaning is often satisfied not by a futile attempt at abstract definition but by pricking a line through concrete applications. Meaning frequently is built up by assured recognition of what does not come within a concept the content of which is in controversy. Since a recapitalization within the scope of § [368] is an aspect of reorganization, nothing can be a recapitalization for this purpose unless it partakes of those characteristics of a reorganization which underlie the purpose of Congress in postponing the tax liability.

No doubt there was a recapitalization of the Bazley corporation in the sense that the symbols that represented its capital were changed, so that the fiscal basis of its operations would appear very differently on its books. But the form of a transaction as reflected by correct corporate accounting opens questions as to the proper application of a taxing statute; it does not close them. Corporate accounting may represent that correspondence between change in the form of capital structure and essential identity in fact which is of the essence of a transaction relieved from taxation as a reorganization. What is controlling is that a new arrangement intrinsically partake of the elements of reorganization which underlie the Congressional exemption and not merely give the appearance of it to accomplish a distribution of earnings. In the case of a corporation which has undistributed earnings, the creation of new corporate obligations which are transferred to stockholders in relation to their former holdings, so as to produce, for all practical purposes, the same result as a distribution of cash earnings of equivalent value, cannot obtain tax immunity because cast in the form of a recapitalization-reorganization. The governing legal rule can hardly be stated more narrowly. To attempt to do so would only challenge astuteness in evading it. And so it is hard to escape the conclusion that whether in a particular case a paper recapitalization is no more than an admissible attempt to avoid the consequences of an outright distribution of earnings turns on details of corporate affairs, judgment on which must be left to the Tax Court. See Dobson v. Commissioner, 320 U.S. 489.

What have we here? No doubt, if the Bazley corporation had issued the debentures to Bazley and his wife without any recapitalization, it would have made a taxable distribution. Instead, these debentures were issued as part of a family arrangement, the only additional ingredient being an unrelated modification of the capital account. The debentures were found to be worth at least their principal amount, and they were virtually cash because they were callable at the will of the corporation which in this case was the will of the taxpayer. One does not have to pursue the motives behind actions, even in the more ascertainable forms of purpose, to find, as did the Tax Court, that the whole arrangement took this form instead of an outright distribution of cash or debentures, because the latter would undoubtedly have been taxable income whereas what was done could, with a show of reason, claim the shelter of the immunity of a recapitalization-reorganization.

The Commissioner, the Tax Court and the Circuit Court of Appeals agree that nothing was accomplished that would not have been accomplished by an outright debenture dividend. And since we find no misconception of law on the part of the Tax Court and the Circuit Court of Appeals, whatever may have been their choice of phrasing, their application of the law to the facts of this case must stand. A "reorganization" which is merely a vehicle, however elaborate or elegant, for conveying earnings from accumulations to the stockholders is not a reorganization under § [368]. This disposes of the case as a matter of law, since the facts as found by the Tax Court bring them within it. And even if this transaction were deemed a reorganization, the facts would equally sustain the imposition of the tax on the debentures under § [354 and 356]. Commissioner v. Estate of Bedford, 325 U.S. 283.

In the *Adams* case, the taxpayer owned all but a few of the 5914 shares of stock outstanding out of an authorized 6000, par value $100. By a plan of reorganization, the authorized capital was reduced by half, to $295,700, divided into 5914 shares of no par value but having a stated value of $50 per share. The 5914 old shares were cancelled and the corporation issued in exchange therefor 5914 shares of the new no-par common stock and 6 per cent 20 year debenture bonds in the principal amount of $295,700. The exchange was made on the basis of one new share of stock and one $50 bond for each old share. The old capital account was debited in the sum of $591,400, a new no-par capital account was credited with $295,700, and the balance of $295,700 was credited to a "Debenture Payable" account. The corporation at this time had accumulated earnings available for distribution in a sum not less than $164,514.82, and this account was left unchanged. At the time of the exchange, the debentures had a value not less than $164,208.82.

The Commissioner determined an income tax deficiency by treating the debenture bonds as a distribution of the corporation's accumulated earnings. The Tax Court sustained the Commissioner's determination, 5 T.C. 351, and the Circuit Court of Appeals affirmed. 155 F.2d 246. The case is governed by our treatment of the *Bazley* case. The finding by the Tax Court that the reorganization had no purpose other than to achieve the distribution of the earnings, is unaffected by the bookkeeping detail of leaving the surplus account unaffected. * * *

Other claims raised have been considered but their rejection does not call for discussion.

Judgments affirmed.

■ MR. JUSTICE DOUGLAS and MR. JUSTICE BURTON dissent in both cases for the reasons stated in the joint dissent of JUDGES MARIS and GOODRICH in the court below. Bazley v. Commissioner, 3 Cir., 155 F.2d 237, 244.

NOTE

The *Bazley* case involved a pro rata exchange of common stock for common stock and bonds. For noncorporate shareholders, its significance has diminished now that most dividends and long-term capital gains are taxed at the same preferential rate. Later cases have offered some hope for qualifying a stock-for-stock-and-bonds exchange under Section 368(a)(1)(E) if the exchange is not pro rata.[1] Several tax problems remain for an exchanging shareholder even if the transaction constitutes a Type E reorganization. The rules in Section 356(a)(2) and (d) will likely result in characterization of gain as a dividend to the extent of the fair market value of bonds received and the corporation's earnings and profits. Even if the shareholder does not realize a gain on the exchange, the regulations suggest that a stock-for-stock-and-bonds recapitalization may be separately analyzed with the receipt of bonds being treated simply as a Section 301 distribution.[2] Stock-for-bonds exchanges also may give rise to original issue discount.[3]

PROBLEMS

1. Recap Corporation has $100,000 of accumulated earnings and profits and makes a pro rata distribution to each of its ten shareholders of new common voting stock worth $20,000 and new callable preferred stock worth $10,000 in exchange for each shareholder's old common voting stock worth $30,000. Assume that the new Recap preferred stock is not nonqualified preferred stock.

    (a) What result to the shareholders on the exchange?

    (b) What result when Recap calls the preferred stock?

    (c) What result if a shareholder sells his preferred stock?

1. See Seide v. Commissioner, 18 T.C. 502 (1952).

2. Reg. § 1.301–1(*l*). Reg. § 1.354–1(d) Example (3) provides that if a shareholder surrenders all of his stock solely for bonds, the tax consequences of the exchange are determined under Section 302 whether or not the transaction is a recapitalization under Section 368(a)(1)(E).

3. See I.R.C. §§ 163(e), 1272–1275. See generally Bittker & Eustice, Federal Income Taxation of Corporations and Shareholders ¶ 12.27[5][d] (7th ed. 2000).

(d) What result if Recap had a deficit in its earnings and profits account at the time of the distribution but it foresaw future potential profits?

2. The ten equal shareholders of Shuffle Corporation each have a $10,000 basis in their Shuffle common voting stock which has a $50,000 fair market value. Shuffle has $250,000 of earnings and profits. What result if the ten shareholders each transfer all their common voting stock in return for common voting stock worth $25,000 and bonds worth $25,000.

3. Leverage Corporation has 8% interest bonds outstanding with a face amount of $1,000,000 and a fair market value of $800,000. It redeems these bonds and issues new 12% interest bonds with a fair market value and a face amount of $800,000.

(a) Will the transaction qualify as a reorganization?

(b) What result in (a), above, if 12% interest bearing bonds with a face amount of $800,000 are redeemed for 8% interest bonds with a face amount of $1,000,000 and both sets of bonds have the same fair market value of $800,000?

4. Does an exchange of bonds for stock qualify as an "E" reorganization? Why would a corporation engage in such an exchange?

B.   TYPE D: LIQUIDATION—REINCORPORATION

Code: §§ 368(a)(1)(D), (a)(2)(H); 354(b); 381(a)(2). Skim §§ 331; 336; 354(a); 356(a); 358; 361; 1032.

Smothers v. United States

United States Court of Appeals, Fifth Circuit, 1981.
642 F.2d 894.

■ WISDOM, CIRCUIT JUDGE:

J.E. and Doris Smothers filed this civil action to obtain a refund of federal income taxes they paid under protest. This dispute arises from the dissolution of one of their wholly-owned business corporations. The taxpayers contend that the assets distributed to them by that corporation should be taxed at the capital gain rate applicable to liquidating distributions. The Internal Revenue Service (IRS) counters by characterizing the dissolution as part of a reorganization, thereby rendering the taxpayers' receipt of the distributed assets taxable at ordinary income rates. The district court viewed the transaction as a reorganization and ruled for the IRS. We affirm.

I.

The facts were stipulated. J.E. and Doris Smothers are married and reside in Corpus Christi, Texas. In 1956, they and an unrelated third party organized Texas Industrial Laundries of San Antonio, Inc. (TIL). The

Smothers' owned all of its outstanding stock from 1956 through the tax year in issue, 1969. TIL engaged in the business of renting industrial uniforms and other industrial cleaning equipment, such as wiping cloths, dust control devices, and continuous toweling. It owned its own laundry equipment as well.

Shortly after the incorporation of TIL, the taxpayers organized another corporation, Industrial Uniform Services, Inc. (IUS), specifically to oppose a particular competitor in the San Antonio industrial laundry market. The taxpayers owned all of the stock of IUS from the time of its organization until its dissolution. Unlike TIL, IUS did not own laundry equipment; it had to contract with an unrelated company to launder the uniforms it rented to customers. J.E. Smothers personally managed IUS, as well as TIL, but chose not to pay himself a salary from IUS in any of the years of its existence.[1]

IUS evidently succeeded in drawing business away from competing firms, for TIL purchased its main competitor in 1965. IUS continued in business, however, until 1969. On the advice of their accountant, the taxpayers then decided to dissolve IUS and sell all of its non-liquid assets to TIL. On November 1, 1969, IUS adopted a plan of liquidation in compliance with I.R.C. § 337, and on November 30, it sold the following assets to TIL for cash at their fair market value (stipulated to be the same as their book value):

Assets	Amount
Noncompetitive covenant	$ 3,894.60
Fixed assets	491.25
Rental property	18,000.00
Prepaid insurance	240.21
Water deposit	7.50
Total	$22,637.56[3]

The noncompetitive covenant constituted part of the consideration received by IUS from its purchase of a small competitor. The fixed assets consisted of incidental equipment (baskets, shelves, and a sewing machine), two depreciated delivery vehicles, and IUS's part interest in an airplane. The rental property was an old apartment building in Corpus Christi on land with business potential. These assets collectively represented about 15% of IUS's net value. The parties stipulated that none of these assets were necessary to carry out IUS's business.

1. Although the record does not specifically so indicate, and although it is unnecessary to our resolution of this case, we think it instructive to note that IUS apparently did not pay any dividends during its existence, either. We deduce that from the following facts of record: (1) the Smothers' cost basis in their IUS stock was $1000.00; (2) IUS had "approximately $148,162.35" in accumulated earnings and profits at the time of its dissolution; (3) IUS's book value at the time of its dissolution was $149,162.35.

3. The parties stipulated that the purchase price was $22,637.56, and the district court found that as a fact. The items listed add to $22,633.56, however. We ignore the discrepancy and accept the stipulation.

After this sale, IUS promptly distributed its remaining assets to its shareholders, the taxpayers, and then dissolved under Texas law:

Assets	Amount
Cash (received from TIL)	$ 22,637.56
Cash (of IUS)	2,003.05
Notes receivable	138,000.00
Accrued interest receivable	35.42
Claim against the State of Texas	889.67
Liabilities assumed	(14,403.35)
Total	$149,162.35

TIL hired all three of IUS's employees immediately after the dissolution, and TIL continued to serve most of IUS's customers.

In computing their federal income tax liability for 1969, the taxpayers treated this distribution by IUS as a distribution in complete liquidation within § 331(a)(1). Accordingly, they reported the difference between the value of the assets they received in that distribution, $149,162.35, and the basis of their IUS stock, $1,000, as long-term capital gain. Upon audit, the IRS recharacterized the transaction between TIL and IUS as a reorganization within § 368(a)(1)(D), and therefore treated the distribution to the taxpayers as equivalent to a dividend under 356(a)(2). Because IUS had sufficient earnings and profits to cover that distribution, the entire distribution was therefore taxable to the Smothers' at ordinary income rates. The IRS timely assessed a $71,840.84 deficiency against the Smothers'. They paid that amount and filed this suit for a refund.

The district court held that the transaction constituted a reorganization and rendered judgment for the IRS. * * *

II.

Subchapter C of the Internal Revenue Code broadly contemplates that the retained earnings of a continuing business carried on in corporate form can be placed in the hands of its shareholders only after they pay a tax on those earnings at ordinary income rates. That general rule is, of course, primarily a consequence of § 301, which taxes dividend distributions as ordinary income. The Code provides for capital gain treatment of corporate distributions in a few limited circumstances, but only when there is either a significant change in relative ownership of the corporation, as in certain redemption transactions, or when the shareholders no longer conduct the business themselves in corporate form, as in true liquidation transactions. The history of Subchapter C in large part has been the story of how Congress, the courts, and the IRS have been called upon to foil attempts by taxpayers to abuse these exceptional provisions. Ingenious taxpayers have repeatedly devised transactions which formally come within these provisions, yet which have the effect of permitting shareholders to withdraw profits at capital gain rates while carrying on a continuing business enterprise in corporate form without substantial change in ownership. This is just such a case.

The transaction in issue here is of the genus known as liquidation-reincorporation, or reincorporation. The common denominator of such transactions is their use of the liquidation provisions of the Code, which permit liquidating distributions to be received at capital gain rates, as a device through which the dividend provisions may be circumvented.[7] Reincorporations come in two basic patterns. In one, the corporation is dissolved and its assets are distributed to its shareholders in liquidation. The shareholders then promptly reincorporate all the assets necessary to the operation of the business, while retaining accumulated cash or other surplus assets. The transaction in this case is of the alternate form. In it, the corporation transfers the assets necessary to its business to another corporation owned by the same shareholders in exchange for securities or, as here, for cash, and then liquidates. If the minimal technical requirements of § [former.] 337 are met, as they indisputably were here, the exchange at the corporate level will not result in the recognition of gain by the transferor corporation. If formal compliance with the liquidation provisions were the only necessity, both patterns would enable shareholders to withdraw profits from a continuing corporate business enterprise at capital gain rates by paper-shuffling. Unchecked, these reincorporation techniques would eviscerate the dividend provisions of the Code.

That result can be avoided by recharacterizing such transactions, in accordance with their true nature, as reorganizations. A reorganization is, in essence, a transaction between corporations that results merely in "a continuance of the proprietary interests in the continuing enterprise under modified corporate form"—a phrase that precisely describes the effect of a reincorporation. Lewis v. Commissioner, 1 Cir.1949, 176 F.2d 646, 648. Congress specifically recognized that the throw-off of surplus assets to shareholders in the course of a reorganization can be equivalent to a dividend, and if so, should be taxed as such. §§ 356(a)(1)–(2). The reincorporation transactions described above result in a dividend payment to the shareholders in every meaningful financial sense. The assets retained by the shareholders therefore should be taxed as dividends as long as the transaction can be fitted within the technical requirements of one of the six classes of reorganizations recognized by § 368(a)(1).

In general, reincorporation transactions are most easily assimilated into § 368(a)(1)(D)("D reorganization"), as the IRS attempted to do in this case.[9] A transaction qualifies as a D reorganization only if it meets six statutory requirements:

7. Other tax benefits may be reaped from reincorporation transactions in appropriate circumstances: e.g., elimination of the earnings and profits account of the old corporation in order to avoid the § 531 tax on unreasonable accumulation; and a step-up in the tax basis of depreciable corporate assets at capital gain rates to the extent permitted by § 1245 and § 1250. In light of IUS's rela-tively large earnings and profits account, the former benefit is not a trivial one here.

9. Reincorporations may also fit within § 368(a)(1)(F)("[a] mere change in identity, form or place of organization, however effected"). * * * The government did not press that theory on appeal. Doubtless that owes to its general reluctance to extend the scope of § 368(a)(1)(F) to acquisitive reorganizations, which derives from the fact that net operat-

(1) There must be a transfer by a corporation (§ 368(a)(1)(D));

(2) of substantially all of its assets (§ 354(b)(1)(A));

(3) to a corporation controlled by the shareholders of the transferor corporation, or by the transferor corporation itself (§ 368(a)(1)(D));

(4) in exchange for stock or securities of the transferee corporation (§ 354(a)(1));

(5) followed by a distribution of the stock or securities of the transferee corporation to the transferor's shareholders (§ 354(b)(1)(B));

(6) pursuant to a plan of reorganization (§ 368(a)(1)(D)).

On this appeal, the taxpayers concede that the transaction in issue meets every technical prerequisite for characterization as a D reorganization, except for one. They argue that since the assets sold by IUS to TIL amounted to only 15% of IUS's net worth, TIL did not acquire "substantially all of the assets" of IUS within the meaning of § 354(b)(1)(A).

We hold to the contrary. The words "substantially all assets" are not self-defining. What proportion of a corporation's assets is "substantially all" in this context, and less obviously, what "assets" are to be counted in making this determination, cannot be answered without reference to the structure of Subchapter C. To maintain the integrity of the dividend provisions of the Code, "substantially all assets" in this context must be interpreted as an inartistic way of expressing the concept of "transfer of a continuing business". As this Court implied in Reef Corp. v. Commissioner, 5 Cir.1966, 368 F.2d 125, 132, cert. denied, 1967, 386 U.S. 1018, 87 S.Ct. 1371, 18 L.Ed.2d 454, it is in a sense simply a limited codification of the general nonstatutory "continuity of business enterprise" requirement applicable to all reorganizations.

This interpretation finds support in the history of § 368(a)(1)(D) and § 354(b)(1)(A). The Internal Revenue Code of 1939 had no provision equivalent to the "substantially all assets" requirement, and courts almost uniformly approved attempts by the IRS to treat reincorporation transactions as reorganizations within the predecessor of § 368(a)(1)(D) in the 1939 Code. The "substantially all assets" requirement of § 354(b)(1)(A) and the amendment of § 368(a)(1)(D) incorporating that requirement were added during the 1954 recodification as part of a package of amendments aimed at plugging a different loophole—the bail-out of corporate earnings and profits at capital gains rates through divisive reorganizations. There is no indication that Congress wished to relax the application of the reorganization provisions to reincorporation transactions. Indeed, the committee reports indicate the contrary. The Senate report accompanying the bill that contained the "substantially all assets" requirement of § 354(b)(1)(A) and

ing losses may be carried back after an F reorganization. § 381(b)(3). See generally Cohen, The "New F" Reorganization, 36 N.Y.U.Inst.Fed.Tax. 833 (1978). The IRS has in the past occasionally advanced more exotic arguments against reincorporations—e.g., the theory that no real "liquidation" occurs in such transactions, and the theory that even if a liquidation does occur, the distribution of surplus assets is a dividend functionally unrelated to the liquidation—but it did not so argue here. * * *

the parallel amendment to § 368(a)(1)(D) stated that the purpose of those changes was only "to insure that the tax consequences of the distribution of stocks or securities to shareholders or security holders in connection with divisive reorganizations will be governed by the requirements of section 355". The report expressly noted that except with respect to divisive reorganizations, the reorganization provisions "are the same as under existing law and are stated in substantially the same form". Even more significantly, the original House version of the 1954 Code contained a provision specifically dealing with reincorporation transactions. That provision was dropped in conference because the conferees felt that such transactions "can appropriately be disposed of by judicial decision or by regulation within the framework of the other provisions of the bill". As the court said in Pridemark, Inc. v. Commissioner, 4 Cir.1965, 345 F.2d 35, 40, this response shows that "the committee was aware of the problem and thought the present statutory scheme adequate to deal with it". By implication, this passage approved the IRS's use of the predecessor of § 368(a)(1)(D) to meet the problem, and shows that the "substantially all assets" amendment was not thought to restrict its use.

Courts have almost unanimously so interpreted the "substantially all assets" language. Moreover, they have also interpreted the other technical conditions for a D reorganization in ways that accomplish the congressional intent to reach reincorporation transactions. For example, the literal language of § 368(a)(1)(D) and §§ 354(a), 354(b)(1)(B) requires that the transferee corporation "exchange" some of its "stock or securities" for the assets of the transferor, and that those items be "distributed" to the shareholders of the transferor, before a D reorganization can be found. Yet both of those requirements have uniformly been ignored as "meaningless gestures" in the reincorporation context, in which the same shareholders own all the stock of both corporations.[14] Smothers does not even challenge the applicability of that principle here.

Properly interpreted, therefore, the assets looked to when making the "substantially all assets" determination should be all the assets, and only the assets, necessary to operate the corporate business—whether or not those assets would appear on a corporate balance sheet constructed according to generally accepted accounting principles. Two errors in particular should be avoided. Inclusion of assets unnecessary to the operation of the business in the "substantially all assets" assessment would open the way

---

14. The "meaningless gesture" language is from James Armour, Inc., 1964, 43 T.C. 295, 307. See also, e.g., Atlas Tool Co. v. Commissioner, 3 Cir.1980, 614 F.2d 860, 865, cert. denied, 1980, 449 U.S. 836, 101 S.Ct. 110, 66 L.Ed.2d 43; Davant v. Commissioner, 5 Cir.1966, 366 F.2d 874, 886–87, cert. denied, 1967, 386 U.S. 1022, 87 S.Ct. 1370, 18 L.Ed.2d 460; Ralph C. Wilson, 1966, 46 T.C. 334, 344. Other technical requirements have been liberally construed in appropriate situations to foil reincorporations. For instance, § 354(b)(1)(B) technically requires that all properties received from the transferor corporation be distributed before a D reorganization can be found, but a "constructive distribution" was found in David T. Grubbs, 1962, 39 T.C. 42. Similarly, § 368(a)(1)(D) requires a "plan of reorganization", but a formal written plan is not necessary and the taxpayer's phraseology is not controlling if the transaction is in substance a reorganization. Atlas Tool Co. v. Commissioner, 614 F.2d at 866; Ralph C. Wilson, 46 T.C. at 345.

for the shareholders of any enterprise to turn dividends into capital gain at will. For example, if we assume that "substantially all" means greater than 90%, then a corporation need only cease declaring dividends and accumulate surplus liquid assets until their value exceeds 10% of the total value of all corporate assets. The shareholders could then transfer the assets actively used in the business to a second corporation owned by them and liquidate the old corporation. Such a liquidating distribution would be a dividend in any meaningful sense, but an interpretation of "substantially all assets" that took surplus assets into account would permit the shareholders to treat it as capital gain. Indeed, such an interpretation would perversely treat a merely nominal distribution of retained earnings as a dividend, but would permit substantial distributions to be made at capital gain rates. Courts therefore have invariably ignored all surplus assets and have focused on the operating assets of the business—the tangible assets actively used in the business—when making the "substantially all assets" assessment.[15]

Second, exclusion of assets not shown on a balance sheet constructed according to generally accepted accounting principles from the "substantially all assets" assessment would offer an unjustified windfall to the owners of service businesses conducted in corporate form. The most important assets of such a business may be its reputation and the availability of skilled management and trained employees, none of which show up on a standard balance sheet. Other courts have correctly recognized that in appropriate cases those intangible assets alone may constitute substantially all of the corporate assets. Otherwise, for example, a sole legal practitioner who owns nothing but a desk and chair could incorporate himself, accumulate earnings, and then set up a new corporation and liquidate the old at capital gain rates—as long as he is careful to buy a new desk and chair for the new corporation, rather than transferring the old.

When these principles are applied to this case, it is plain that "substantially all of the assets" of IUS were transferred to TIL, and that the transaction as a whole constituted a reorganization. TIL and IUS were both managed and wholly owned by Smothers. By the nature of its business, IUS was wholly a service enterprise; indeed, the parties stipulated that none of the tangible assets of IUS were necessary to the operation of its business. The extent to which those tangible assets were transferred to TIL is therefore entirely irrelevant. IUS's most important assets—its reputation, sales staff, and the managerial services of Smothers—were all transferred to TIL. TIL rehired all three of IUS's employees immediately after IUS's liquidation, and continued to serve IUS's old customers. The same business enterprise was conducted by the same people under the same ownership, and the only assets removed from corporate solution were accumulated liquid assets unnecessary to the operation of the business. To treat this transaction as other than a reorganization would deny economic reality; to

---

15. Note that liquid assets are "necessary" to the extent they represent working capital. See Swanson v. United States, 9 Cir. 1973, 479 F.2d 539, 545–46; Ross Michel Simon Trust v. United States, Ct.Cl. 1968, 402 F.2d 272, 280.

permit Smothers to extract the retained earnings of IUS at capital gain rates would make a mockery of the dividend provisions of the Internal Revenue Code.

We do not perceive ordinary income treatment here to be particularly harsh, or a "tax trap for the unwary". It places the Smothers' only in the position they would have been in if they had extracted the retained earnings of IUS as the Code contemplates they should have—by periodically declaring dividends.[18]

Affirmed.

■ GARZA, CIRCUIT JUDGE, dissenting:

After carefully reading the majority's opinion, I find that I must respectfully dissent. Unlike my Brothers, who apparently feel that it is their duty to "plug loopholes", I would remain content in applying the tax law as it reads leaving the United States Congress to deal with the consequences of the tax law as it has been drafted. The only issue before this Court on appeal is whether or not IUS transferred "substantially all of its assets" to TIL. Instead of dealing with this straightforward question, the majority has made a case of evil against liquidation-reincorporation abuses and, in an attempt to remedy every such perceived abuse, they have relieved the Congress of its burden to change the law heretofore requiring that "substantially all" of a corporation's assets be transferred to now read that "only those assets necessary to operate the corporate business" be transferred in order to meet the "D reorganization" requirements. Essentially, the majority has changed the definition of "substantially all assets" to mean only "necessary operating assets." I believe if Congress had meant "necessary operating assets" it would have said so instead of specifically requiring that "substantially all" of the assets be transferred. In my mind "substantially all" plainly means all of the assets except for an insubstantial amount. Under such a definition, the sale of 15% of IUS's assets to TIL could hardly be defined as "substantially all" of IUS's assets.

However, even after having redefined "substantially all" to mean "necessary operating assets", the IUS liquidation still falls short of the "D reorganization" requirements because the stipulated facts are that absolutely none of the assets sold from IUS to TIL were necessary operating assets for either corporation. Faced with an absence of a proper factual setting, the majority goes on to define necessary operating assets as including a corporation's intangible assets. Now while a sale of intangible assets might be an appropriate consideration in determining whether or

---

18. Of course, the progressive structure of the income tax in a sense penalizes the plaintiff, since dividend income that could have been spread over many years is concentrated in one year, but that result was avoidable at the taxpayer's discretion. Similarly, he could have taken out some of the earnings in the form of a salary. Note that in all probability, Smothers did not actually defer enjoyment of the retained earnings of IUS until the reincorporation transaction. IUS's major asset by far was $138,000 in "notes receivable". Although the record does not reveal who issued those notes, the inference could be drawn that Smothers took the earnings out of IUS as they were earned, tax-free, by simply borrowing them from the corporation.

not "substantially all" assets of a corporation have been transferred, such a consideration simply has no bearing in this case. All of the assets transferred to TIL were depreciated tangible objects sold at book value after which IUS completely ceased all business operations. There simply was no other transfer of IUS's intangible assets as a continuing business.

The majority has placed great emphasis on the fact that three of IUS's route salesmen were subsequently employed by TIL and that Mr. Smothers' managerial services were available to TIL. Regardless of whether or not these facts enhanced TIL's business, the fact remains that neither the route salesmen or Mr. Smothers' services were transferred as assets from one corporation to another. After IUS ceased business its route salesmen were free to seek any employment they desired. Likewise, Mr. Smothers was never obligated to perform services for TIL. From these facts I cannot agree that there was a transfer of a continuing business. The majority imputes adverse tax consequences to IUS's stockholders simply because TIL offered new employment to the route salesmen who were unemployed upon cessation of IUS's business operations. The majority places future stockholders, in Mr. Smothers' position, of choosing between unfavorable tax consequences and helping secure future employment to loyal and deserving employees whom otherwise would be unemployed.

Although the Internal Revenue Service has never questioned the bona fides of IUS's liquidation, the majority has gone beyond the stipulated facts by characterizing the liquidation as a tax avoidance scam. I simply cannot agree. After starting from scratch, Mr. Smothers worked for over a dozen years refraining from drawing salary in order that IUS could pay its taxes, employees and other operating expenses and in order for IUS to become a successful self-sustaining business enterprise. Mr. Smothers was successful but, now that he no longer could devote his service to IUS, his years of labor are now labeled by the majority as a mere "paper shuffle." I do not share the majority's attitude.

The reasons for my position can be more easily understood by a simple review of the bottom-line facts. After IUS began showing a profit and started accumulating a cash surplus, instead of immediately investing in a building or in other equipment for its operations, it continued its operations as before. Now, if IUS had purchased real property or depreciable personal property for its operations (instead of leasing as it had been) and had sold these properties pursuant to its plan of liquidation, certainly no argument would be made that the money initially invested in those properties should have been declared by IUS as dividends. However, instead of investing its accumulations, IUS simply put them in its bank account as the tax laws allow and presumably faced any tax consequences posed by such an accumulation.

After IUS ceased operations, was liquidated, and its assets distributed to its stockholders in exchange for their stock, the I.R.S. issued a deficiency, not because IUS was reorganized within the meaning of 26 U.S.C. § 368(a)(1)(D), but rather because the I.R.S. felt the accumulated earnings of IUS coupled with long-term capital gains rates applicable to the stock exchange provided an undesirable windfall to IUS's stockholders. In essence, the I.R.S. sought to expand the "D reorganization" provisions, lessen the availability of long-term capital gains treatment to corporate stockholders, and totally ignore the purpose of the tax upon improperly accumulated surplus as provided in 26 U.S.C. § 531. The majority seeks to do equity for the I.R.S. position by "treating" the IUS liquidation as a "D reorganization." I do not believe the taxpayers or the tax laws are served by upholding an I.R.S. deficiency for the sole purpose of "plugging loopholes." The lesson to be learned from the majority's opinion is clear—future corporations faced with similar circumstances need only invest their otherwise accumulated surplus in some method other than savings. In the process of liquidation they need sell whatever assets exist to third parties unrelated to their stockholders and their stockholders should make no effort to find future employment for the corporation's employees.

It seems to me that in its attempt to "plug" a perceived "loophole," the majority is giving this Court's imprimatur to a variation of the same so-called "mockery" of the tax laws sought to be prevented by its opinion.

For these reasons, I respectfully dissent.

NOTE

Type D reorganizations come in two basic forms. The "divisive D" involves a transfer by one corporation of some of its assets to a newly formed controlled subsidiary followed by a distribution of the stock of the subsidiary in a corporate division that qualifies under Section 355. This transaction has been examined in Chapter 10 along with the other aspects of corporate divisions. The second form of Type D reorganization is "nondivisive." It involves the transfer by one corporation of all or part of its assets to a corporation controlled immediately after the transfer by the transferor or its shareholders (or any combination) provided that the stock or securities of the controlled corporation are distributed in a transaction that qualifies under Section 354. Section 354(b) requires that the first corporation must transfer "substantially all" of its assets to the controlled corporation and the stock, securities and other properties that it receives must be distributed, along with its other properties, pursuant to a plan of reorganization.

The "nondivisive" D reorganization has always been an odd character in the reorganization alphabet. As the *Smothers* case illustrates, it historically has been invoked by the Service as a weapon to attack the liquidation-reincorporation transaction, a technique utilized by taxpayers in the days when the General Utilities doctrine and a capital gains preference worked in tandem to encourage bailouts of corporate earnings at capital gains rates without any corporate-level tax. To appreciate why, consider a gambit that might have been used in the "good old days" by Profit Corp., a family company with $800,000 of accumulated earnings and profits and a $2 million net worth, consisting of $1.5 million of operating assets and $500,000 of investment securities. Assume the shareholders wish to extract the securities from corporate solution without the sting of a dividend but to otherwise continue operating their business in a new corporation with fresh tax attributes (e.g., no earnings and profits) and no immediate exposure to the accumulated earnings tax.

One classic plan to accomplish these objectives was for the Profit Corp. shareholders to liquidate the corporation, retain the investment securities and, after an appropriate interval, reincorporate the operating assets under Section 351. Alternatively, Profit Corp. might transfer its operating assets to a new subsidiary in exchange for its stock and then liquidate, distributing the new stock and the investment securities to the shareholders. Whatever the format, the basic objective was to achieve what were then the tax benefits of a liquidation: capital gains at the shareholder level, nonrecognition at the corporate level, a step-up in basis of the assets in the reincorporated enterprise, and a fresh start for the earnings and profits account. The Service countered by arguing, with limited success, that the transaction was a reorganization coupled with the receipt of boot that should be taxed as a dividend.[1]

A liquidation-reincorporation rarely makes sense under current law if its form is respected for tax purposes. The liquidation will trigger corporate-level gain under Section 336 and significantly raise the tax cost of the strategy. Indeed, if the classic liquidation-reincorporation were carried out, it is now *taxpayers* who may prefer to characterize the transactions as a reorganization. Although they would recognize dividend income to the extent of the boot received, the good news is that noncorporate shareholders likely will qualify for the preferential qualified dividend rate, and the ongoing corporation would avoid recognizing gain on its assets because the asset bases would carry over to the transferee. The liquidation-reincorporation strategy may retain its vitality, however, in a few limited situations, such as when the corporation has losses to shelter the gains resulting from the distribution of appreciated assets, where the appreciation in the corporation's assets is negligible, or where the corporation has losses that it is trying to accelerate without removing the loss assets from corporate solution.

PROBLEM

Brother and Sister Corporation are owned by the same shareholders in the same proportionate amounts. The shareholders have a $200,000 basis in their Brother stock and Brother Corporation has operating assets with a value of $500,000 and basis of $200,000 as well as $200,000 of cash and $200,000 of earnings and profits. Sister Corporation, which has $300,000 of earnings and profits, purchases the operating assets for $500,000 cash and Brother Corporation immediately liquidates.

---

1. See, e.g., Davant v. Commissioner,   U.S. 1022, 87 S.Ct. 1370 (1967).
366 F.2d 874 (5th Cir.1966), cert. denied, 386

(a) What are the consequences of these transactions to the shareholders and to both corporations?

(b) Will the arguments of the taxpayers and the Service concerning the transactions differ from those advanced in the Smothers case?

(c) Is there any simpler way for the taxpayers to achieve their objectives?

C. TYPE F: MERE CHANGE IN IDENTITY, FORM, OR PLACE OF ORGANIZATION

Code: §§ 368(a)(1)(F); 381(b). Skim §§ 331; 351; 354(a); 356(a); 358; 361; 1032.

A Type F reorganization is defined by the Code as "a mere change in identity, form, or place of organization of one corporation, however effected." An example would be a merger of a closely held New York corporation into a newly formed Delaware corporation with the same shareholders in order to take advantage of Delaware corporate law in anticipation of a public offering of the company's stock.[1] Over fifty years ago a noted commentator stated that the Type F reorganization "is so little relied upon by taxpayers that this part of the statute has indeed perished through lack of use."[2] It has survived calls for repeal, however, and experienced a brief renaissance before resuming its historical role as a relatively dead letter in the tax-free reorganization alphabet.[3]

The resurgence of interest in the Type F reorganization was the result of attempts by taxpayers to carry back the post-acquisition losses of corporations which previously had been operated as an affiliated corporate group to pre-acquisition years of an acquired corporation. Since Section 381(b) only permits such a carryback of net operating losses in an F reorganization, the shareholders argued that the fusion of affiliated corporations qualified as an F reorganization. Although the language of the applicable statute implied that an F reorganization was limited to structural changes in a single corporation, the Commissioner, in his attempt to combat the liquidation-reincorporation bailout device, bolstered the argument that the F reorganization also applied to the merger of two or more active corporations. In the *Davant* case, the Commissioner asserted and the Court accepted the argument that an F reorganization could involve two operating corporations.[4] The Commissioner's argument, together with a

---

1. See, e.g., Rev. Rul. 96–29, 1996–1 C.B. 50.

2. Paul, Studies in Federal Taxation 82 (3d Ed. 1940). But see Pugh, "The F Reorganization: Reveille for a Sleeping Giant?" 24 Tax L.Rev. 437 (1969).

3. F reorganization issues occasionally resurface, usually in specialized situations.

See, e.g., Rev. Rul. 2003–19, 2003–1 C.B. 468. See also Prop. Reg. § 1.368–2(m), where the Service for the first time specifies the requirements to qualify as an F reorganization.

4. Davant v. Commissioner, 366 F.2d 874 (5th Cir.1966), cert. denied 386 U.S. 1022, 87 S.Ct. 1370 (1967). Actually the Commissioner made the argument at the trial

ruling in which the Service acknowledged that a reorganization meeting the definition of an F reorganization and some other type of reorganization would be treated as an F reorganization for purposes of Section 381(b),[5] opened the floodgates. The only remaining question was how far shareholders could push combinations of operating corporations into the F reorganization category.[6] In the 1970's, the Service conceded that a combination of active corporations under common control could qualify as an F reorganization if there was a complete continuity of shareholder and proprietary interests.[7] But Congress later slammed the door shut by limiting F reorganization status to a single operating corporation through the addition of the words "of one corporation" to Section 368(a)(1)(F). The Type F reorganization thus once again was relegated to its prior role as a minor provision governing reincorporations in another state and other merely formal changes. The following legislative history explains that amendment:[8]

Present law

A reorganization includes "a mere change in identity, form, or place of organization" (an F reorganization). Generally, present law requires a transferor corporation's taxable year to be closed on the date of a reorganization transfer and precludes a post-reorganization loss from being carried back to a taxable year of the transferor. However, F reorganizations are excluded from these limitations in recognition of the intended scope of such reorganizations as embracing only formal changes in a single operating corporation.

* * *

Conference agreement

The conference agreement limits the F reorganization definition to a change in identity, form, or place of organization of a single operating corporation.

This limitation does not preclude the use of more than one entity to consummate the transaction provided only one operating company is involved. The reincorporation of an operating company in a different State, for example, is an F reorganization that requires that more than one corporation be involved.

court level, 43 T.C. 540 (1965), and it was adopted by the appellate court in its opinion.

5. Rev.Rul. 57–276, 1957–1 C.B. 126.

6. Compare Movielab, Inc. v. United States, 204 Ct.Cl. 6, 494 F.2d 693 (1974), and Stauffer's Estate v. Commissioner, 403 F.2d 611 (9th Cir.1968), with Berger Machine Products, Inc. v. Commissioner, 68 T.C. 358 (1977), and Romy Hammes, Inc. v. Commissioner, 68 T.C. 900 (1977).

7. See Rev.Rul. 75–561, 1975–2 C.B. 129.

8. H.R.Rep. No. 97–760, 97th Cong., 2d Sess. 540–41 (1982), reprinted in 1982–2 C.B. 634–35.

Revenue Ruling 96–29

1996–1 Cum. Bull. 50.

ISSUE

Do the transactions described below qualify as reorganizations under § 368(a)(1)(F) of the Internal Revenue Code?

FACTS

Situation 1. Q is a manufacturing corporation all of the common stock of which is owned by twelve individuals. One class of nonvoting preferred stock, representing 40 percent of the aggregate value of Q, is held by a variety of corporate and noncorporate shareholders. Q is incorporated in state M. Pursuant to a plan to raise immediate additional capital and to enhance its ability to raise capital in the future by issuing additional stock, Q proposes to make a public offering of newly issued stock and to cause its stock to become publicly traded. Q entered into an underwriting agreement providing for the public offering and a change in its state of incorporation. The change in the state of incorporation was undertaken, in part, to enable the corporation to avail itself of the advantages that the corporate laws of state N afford to public companies and their officers and directors. In the absence of the public offering, Q would not have changed its state of incorporation. Pursuant to the underwriting agreement, Q changed its place of incorporation by merging with and into R, a newly organized corporation incorporated in state N. The shares of Q stock were converted into the right to receive an identical number of shares of R stock. Immediately thereafter, R sold additional shares of its stock to the public and redeemed all of the outstanding shares of nonvoting preferred stock. The number of new shares sold was equal to 60 percent of all the outstanding R stock following the sale and redemption.

Situation 2. W, a state M corporation, is a manufacturing corporation all of the stock of which is owned by two individuals. W conducted its business through several wholly owned subsidiaries. The management of W determined that it would be in the best interest of W to acquire the business of Z, an unrelated corporation, and combine it with the business of Y, one of its subsidiaries, and to change the state of incorporation of W. In order to accomplish these objectives, and pursuant to an overall plan, W entered into a plan and agreement of merger with Y and Z. In accordance with the agreement, Z merged with and into Y pursuant to the law of state M, with the former Z shareholders receiving shares of newly issued W preferred stock in exchange for their shares of Z stock. Immediately following the acquisition of Z, W changed its place of organization by merging with and into N, a newly organized corporation incorporated in state R. Upon W's change of place of organization, the holders of W common and preferred stock surrendered their W stock in exchange for identical N common and preferred stock, respectively.

LAW AND ANALYSIS

Section 368(a)(1)(F) provides that a reorganization includes a mere change in identity, form, or place of organization of one corporation, however effected. This provision was amended * * * in order to limit its application to one corporation. Certain limitations contained in § 381(b), including those precluding the corporation acquiring property in a reorganization from carrying back a net operating loss or a net capital loss for a taxable year ending after the date of transfer to a taxable year of the transferor, do not apply to reorganizations described in § 368(a)(1)(F) "in recognition of the intended scope of such reorganizations as embracing only formal changes in a single operating corporation." H.R.Rep. No. 760, 97th Cong., 2d Sess. 540, 541 (1982). Although a change in the place of organization usually must be effected through the merger of one corporation into another, such a transaction qualifies as a reorganization under § 368(a)(1)(F) because it involves only one operating corporation. The 1982 amendment of § 368(a)(1)(F) thus overruled several cases in which a merger of two or more operating corporations could be treated as a reorganization under § 368(a)(1)(F). See, e.g., Estate of Stauffer v. Commissioner, 403 F.2d 611 (9th Cir.1968); Associated Machine, Inc. v. Commissioner, 403 F.2d 622 (9th Cir.1968); and Davant v. Commissioner, 366 F.2d 874 (5th Cir.1966).

A transaction does not qualify as a reorganization under § 368(a)(1)(F) unless there is no change in existing shareholders or in the assets of the corporation. However, a transaction will not fail to qualify as a reorganization under § 368(a)(1)(F) if dissenters owning fewer than 1 percent of the outstanding shares of the corporation fail to participate in the transaction. Rev. Rul. 66–284, 1966–2 C.B. 115.

The rules applicable to corporate reorganizations as well as other provisions recognize the unique characteristics of reorganizations qualifying under § 368(a)(1)(F). In contrast to other types of reorganizations, which can involve two or more operating corporations, a reorganization of a corporation under § 368(a)(1)(F) is treated for most purposes of the Code as if there had been no change in the corporation and, thus, as if the reorganized corporation is the same entity as the corporation that was in existence prior to the reorganization. See § 381(b); § 1.381(b)–1(a)(2); see also Rev. Rul. 87–110, 1987–2 C.B. 159; Rev. Rul. 80–168, 1980–1 C.B. 178; Rev. Rul. 73–526, 1973–2 C.B. 404; Rev. Rul. 64–250, 1964–2 C.B. 333.

In Rev. Rul. 69–516, 1969–2 C.B. 56, the Internal Revenue Service treated as two separate transactions a reorganization under § 368(a)(1)(F) and a reorganization under § 368(a)(1)(C) undertaken as part of the same plan. Specifically, a corporation changed its place of organization by merging into a corporation formed under the laws of another state and immediately thereafter, it transferred substantially all of its assets in exchange for stock of an unrelated corporation. The ruling holds that the change in place of organization qualified as a reorganization under § 368(a)(1)(F).

Accordingly, in Situation 1, the reincorporation by Q in state N qualifies as a reorganization under § 368(a)(1)(F) even though it was a step in the transaction in which Q was issuing common stock in a public offering and redeeming stock having a value of 40 percent of the aggregate value of its outstanding stock prior to the offering.

In Situation 2, the reincorporation by W in state N qualifies as a reorganization under § 368(a)(1)(F) even though it was a step in the transaction in which W acquired the business of Z.

HOLDING

On the facts set forth in this ruling, in each of Situations 1 and 2, the reincorporation transaction qualifies as a reorganization under § 368(a)(1)(F), notwithstanding the other transactions effected pursuant to the same plan.

* * *

PROBLEM

Golden State Corporation is incorporated in California. It forms a new corporation in Arizona, Cactus Corporation, transferring all of its assets to Cactus Corporation in exchange for all of the Cactus stock. Golden State Corporation is then liquidated. What tax consequences to the Golden State shareholders?

D.   TYPE G: INSOLVENCY REORGANIZATIONS

Code: §§ 368(a)(1)(G); 354(b). Skim §§ 354; 355; 356.

Excerpt From Report of Senate Finance Committee on Bankruptcy Tax Bill of 1980*

S.Rep. No. 96–1035, 96th Cong., 2d Sess. 34–38, reprinted in 1980–2 Cum.Bull. 620, 637.

Present Law

Definition of reorganization

A transfer of all or part of a corporation's assets, pursuant to a court order in a proceeding under chapter X of the Bankruptcy Act (or in a receivership, foreclosure, or similar proceeding), to another corporation organized or utilized to effectuate a court-approved plan may qualify for tax-free reorganization treatment under special rules relating to "insolvency reorganizations" (secs. 371–374 of the Internal Revenue Code).

These special rules for insolvency reorganizations generally allow less flexibility in structuring tax-free transactions than the rules applicable to corporate reorganizations as defined in section 368 of the Code. Also, the special rules for insolvency reorganizations do not permit carryover of tax

---

* Some footnotes omitted.

attributes to the transferee corporation, and otherwise differ in important respects from the general reorganization rules.[1] While some reorganizations under chapter X of the Bankruptcy Act may be able to qualify for nonrecognition treatment under Code section 368, other chapter X reorganizations may be able to qualify only under the special rules of sections 371–374 and not under the general reorganization rules of section 368.

Triangular reorganizations

In the case of an insolvency reorganization which can qualify for nonrecognition treatment only under the special rules of Code sections 371–374, the stock or securities used to acquire the assets of the corporation in bankruptcy must be the acquiring corporation's own stock or securities. This limitation generally precludes corporations in bankruptcy from engaging in so-called triangular reorganizations, where the acquired corporation is acquired for stock of the parent of the acquiring corporation. By contrast, tax-free triangular reorganizations generally are permitted under the general rules of Code section 368.

Transfer to controlled subsidiary

In the case of an insolvency reorganization which can qualify for nonrecognition treatment only under the special rules of Code sections 371–374, it is not clear under present law whether and to what extent the acquiring corporation may transfer assets received into a controlled subsidiary. In the case of other corporate reorganizations, the statute expressly defines the situations where transfers to subsidiaries are permitted (Code sec. 368(a)(2)(C)).

Carryover of tax attributes

In the case of an insolvency reorganization which can qualify for nonrecognition treatment only under the special rules of Code sections 371–374, court cases have held that attributes (such as net operating losses) of the corporation in bankruptcy do not carry over to the new corporation. In the case of other corporate reorganizations, however, specific statutory rules permit carryover of tax attributes to the surviving corporation (Code sec. 381).

Reasons for change

The committee believes that the provisions of existing Federal income tax law which are generally applicable to tax-free corporate reorganizations

---

1. Under present law, it is not clear to what extent creditors of an insolvent corporation who receive stock in exchange for their claims may be considered to have "stepped into the shoes" of former shareholders for purposes of satisfying the nonstatutory "continuity of interest" rule, under which the owners of the acquired corporation must continue to have a proprietary interest in the acquiring corporation. Generally, the courts have found the "continuity of interest" test satisfied if the creditors' interests were transformed into proprietary interests prior to the reorganization (e.g., Helvering v. Alabama Asphaltic Limestone Co., 315 U.S. 179 (1942); Treas.Reg. § 1.371–1(a)(4)). It is unclear whether affirmative steps by the creditors are required or whether mere receipt of stock is sufficient.

should also apply to reorganizations of corporations in bankruptcy or similar proceedings, in order to facilitate the rehabilitation of financially troubled businesses.

Also, the committee believes that a creditor who exchanges securities in a corporate reorganization (including an insolvency reorganization) should be treated as receiving interest income on the exchange to the extent the creditor receives new securities, stock, or any other property for accrued but unpaid interest on the securities surrendered.

Explanation of provisions

Section 4 of the bill generally conforms the tax rules governing insolvency reorganizations with the existing rules applicable to other corporate reorganizations. These provisions are the same as section 4 of the House bill.

Definition of reorganization

In general

The bill adds a new category—"G" reorganizations—to the general Code definition of tax-free reorganizations (sec. 368(a)(1)). The new category includes certain transfers of assets pursuant to a court-approved reorganization plan in a bankruptcy case under new title 11 of the U.S. Code, or in a receivership, foreclosure, or similar proceeding in a Federal or State court.

* * *

In order to facilitate the rehabilitation of corporate debtors in bankruptcy, etc., these provisions are designed to eliminate many requirements which have effectively precluded financially troubled companies from utilizing the generally applicable tax-free reorganization provisions of present law. To achieve this purpose, the new "G" reorganization provision does not require compliance with State merger laws (as in category "A" reorganizations), does not require that the financially distressed corporation receive solely stock of the acquiring corporation in exchange for its assets (category "C"), and does not require that the former shareholders of the financially distressed corporation control the corporation which receives the assets (category "D").

The "G" reorganization provision added by the bill requires the transfer of assets by a corporation in a bankruptcy or similar case, and the distribution (in pursuance of the court-approved reorganization plan) of stock or securities of the acquiring corporation in a transaction which qualifies under sections 354, 355, or 356 of the Code. This distribution requirement is designed to assure that either substantially all of the assets of the financially troubled corporation, or assets which consist of an active business under the tests of section 355, are transferred to the acquiring corporation.

"Substantially all" test

The "substantially all" test in the "G" reorganization provision is to be interpreted in light of the underlying intent in adding the new "G" category, namely, to facilitate the reorganization of companies in bankruptcy or similar cases for rehabilitative purposes. Accordingly, it is intended that facts and circumstances relevant to this intent, such as the insolvent corporation's need to pay off creditors or to sell assets or divisions to raise cash, are to be taken into account in determining whether a transaction qualifies as a "G" reorganization. For example, a transaction is not precluded from satisfying the "substantially all" test for purposes of the new "G" category merely because, prior to a transfer to the acquiring corporation, payments to creditors and asset sales were made in order to leave the debtor with more manageable operating assets to continue in business.[5]

Relation to other provisions

A transaction which qualifies as a "G" reorganization is not to be treated as also qualifying as a liquidation under section 332, an incorporation under section 351, or a reorganization under another category of section 368(a)(1) of the Code.[6]

A transaction in a bankruptcy or similar case which does not satisfy the requirements of new category "G" is not thereby precluded from qualifying as a tax-free reorganization under one of the other categories of section 368(a)(1). For example, an acquisition of the stock of a company in bankruptcy, or a recapitalization of such a company, which transactions are not covered by the new "G" category, can qualify for nonrecognition treatment under sections 368(a)(1)(B) or (E), respectively.

Continuity of interest rules

The "continuity of interest" requirement which the courts and the Treasury have long imposed as a prerequisite for nonrecognition treatment for a corporate reorganization must be met in order to satisfy the requirements of new category "G". Only reorganizations—as distinguished from liquidations in bankruptcy and sales of property to either new or old

---

5. Because the stated intent for adding the new "G" category is not relevant to interpreting the "substantially all" test in the case of other reorganization categories, the comments in the text as to the appropriate interpretation of the "substantially all" test in the context of a "G" reorganization are not intended to apply to, or in any way to affect interpretations under present law of, the "substantially all" test for other reorganization categories.

6. However, if a transfer qualifying as a "G" reorganization also meets the requirements of section 351 or qualifies as a reorga-

nization under section 368(a)(1)(D) of the Code, the "excess liability" rule of section 357(c) applies if any former shareholder of the transferor corporation receives consideration for his stock, but does not apply if no former shareholder of the transferor corporation receives any consideration for his stock (i.e., if the corporation is insolvent). This rule parallels present law, under which insolvency reorganizations under sections 371 or 374 are excluded from the application of section 357(c).

interests supplying new capital and discharging the obligations of the debtor corporation—can qualify for tax-free treatment.

It is expected that the courts and the Treasury will apply to "G" reorganizations continuity-of-interest rules which take into account the modification by P.L. 95–598 of the "absolute priority" rule. As a result of that modification, shareholders or junior creditors, who might previously have been excluded, may now retain an interest in the reorganized corporation.

For example, if an insolvent corporation's assets are transferred to a second corporation in a bankruptcy case, the most senior class of creditor to receive stock, together with all equal and junior classes (including shareholders who receive any consideration for their stock), should generally be considered the proprietors of the insolvent corporation for "continuity" purposes. However, if the shareholders receive consideration other than stock of the acquiring corporation, the transaction should be examined to determine if it represents a purchase rather than a reorganization.

Thus, short-term creditors who receive stock for their claims may be counted toward satisfying the continuity of interest rule, although any gain or loss realized by such creditors will be recognized for income tax purposes.

Triangular reorganizations

The bill permits a corporation to acquire a debtor corporation in a "G" reorganization in exchange for stock of the parent of the acquiring corporation rather than for its own stock.

In addition, the bill permits an acquisition in the form of a "reverse merger" of an insolvent corporation (i.e., where no former shareholder of the surviving corporation receives any consideration for his stock) in a bankruptcy or similar case if the former creditors of the surviving corporation exchange their claims for voting stock of the controlling corporation which has a value equal to at least 80 percent of the value of the debt of the surviving corporation.

Transfer to controlled subsidiary

The bill permits a corporation which acquires substantially all the assets of a debtor corporation in a "G" reorganization to transfer the acquired assets to a controlled subsidiary without endangering the tax-free status of the reorganization. This provision places "G" reorganizations on a similar footing with other categories of reorganizations.

Carryover of tax attributes

Under the bill, the statutory rule generally governing carryover of tax attributes in corporate reorganizations (Code sec. 381) also applies in the case of a "G" reorganization. This eliminates the so-called "clean slate" doctrine.

"Principal amount" rule; "boot" test

Under the bill, "G" reorganizations are subject to the rules governing the tax treatment of exchanging shareholders and security holders which apply to other corporate reorganizations.

Accordingly, an exchanging shareholder or security holder of the debtor company who receives securities with a principal amount exceeding the principal amount of securities surrendered is taxable on the excess, and an exchanging shareholder or security holder who surrenders no securities is taxed on the principal amount of any securities received. Also, any "boot" received is subject to the general dividend-equivalence test of Code section 356.

Treatment of accrued interest

Under the bill, a creditor exchanging securities in any corporate reorganization described in section 368 of the Code (including a "G" reorganization) is treated as receiving interest income on the exchange to the extent the security holder receives new securities, stock, or any other property attributable to accrued but unpaid interest (including accrued original issue discount) on the securities surrendered. This provision, which reverses the so-called *Carman* rule, applies whether or not the exchanging security holder realizes gain on the exchange overall. Under this provision, a security holder which had previously accrued the interest (including original issue discount) as income recognizes a loss to the extent the interest is not paid in the exchange.

Example

The reorganization provisions of the bill are illustrated in part by the following example.

Assume that Corporation A is in a bankruptcy case commenced after December 31, 1980. Immediately prior to a transfer under a plan of reorganization, A's assets have an adjusted basis of $75,000 and a fair market value of $100,000. A has a net operating loss carryover of $200,000. A has outstanding bonds of $100,000 (on which there is no accrued but unpaid interest) and trade debts of $100,000.

Under the plan of reorganization, A is to transfer all its assets to Corporation B in exchange for $100,000 of B stock. Corporation A will distribute the stock, in exchange for their claims against A, one-half to the security holders and one-half to the trade creditors. A's shareholders will receive nothing.

The transaction qualifies as a reorganization under new section 368(a)(1)(G) of the Code, since all the creditors are here treated as proprietors for continuity of interest purposes. Thus, A recognizes no gain or loss on the transfer of its assets to B (Code sec. 361). B's basis in the assets is $75,000 (sec. 362), and B succeeds to A's net operating loss carryover (sec. 381).

Under the bill, the pro-rata distribution of B stock to A's creditors does not result in income from discharge of indebtedness [But see I.R.C. § 108(e)(8), which now makes stock-for-debt exchanges subject to Section 108. Ed.]

Assume the same facts as above except that B also transfers $10,000 in cash, which is distributed by A to its creditors. Although A would otherwise recognize gain on the receipt of boot in an exchange involving appreciated property, the distribution by A of the $10,000 cash to those creditors having a proprietary interest in the corporation's assets for continuity of interest purposes prevents A from recognizing any gain (Code sec. 361(b)(1)(A)).[10]

PROBLEM

Debtor Corporation is in bankruptcy. Debtor's assets have an adjusted basis of $75,000 and a value of $100,000, and the corporation has a net operating loss of $200,000, bonds outstanding (with no accrued unpaid interest) of $100,000 and trade debts of $100,000. Debtor transfers all of its assets to Relief Corporation in return for $100,000 of Relief stock which will pass half to the security holders and half to trade creditors. Debtor's shareholders will receive nothing. What are the tax consequences to the parties?

10. See Code sec. 371(a)(2)(A) and Treas.Reg. § 1.371–1(b) for a similar rule relating to distribution of boot to creditors in an insolvency reorganization under present law.

CHAPTER 12

LIMITATIONS ON CARRYOVERS OF CORPORATE ATTRIBUTES

A. INTRODUCTION

In traveling through Subchapter C, we have encountered a myriad of corporate acquisitions—some fully taxable, others partially taxable and still others tax-free. We have seen that tax considerations often influence the format of a particular acquisition but have yet to consider the possibility that not only the method but also the very fact of a corporate acquisition may be tax motivated. C corporations sometimes have been attractive takeover candidates not because of the inherent value of their assets or their future earning power but solely because of tax attributes. Indeed, the economics of an acquisition may be driven by the acquiring corporation's ability to utilize the target's net operating loss carryforwards as a shelter against profits from other business operations. If the stock of the target corporation is acquired, those carryforwards remain in the target and may benefit the acquiring corporation if the two companies are eligible to file consolidated tax returns.[1] If its assets are acquired in a reorganization (or in a tax-free Section 332 liquidation, if the target is already a controlled subsidiary), those loss carryforwards, along with the target's other tax attributes, are inherited by the acquiring corporation under Section 381.[2]

This chapter focuses primarily on the limitations imposed by the Code on the carryover of net operating losses after a corporate acquisition or other substantial change of ownership. The most significant limitations are in Section 382, which limits the use of net operating loss ("NOL") carryforwards and certain built-in losses following a change of corporate ownership. Section 383 limits the carryforward of certain other tax attributes, such as excess credits and capital losses. Other rules preclude a loss corporation from sheltering built-in gains of a previously unrelated gain corporation[3] and patrol against acquisitions motivated by a tax avoidance purpose.[4] In examining these intricate loss carryover limitations, this chapter makes a special effort to go beyond the sometimes overwhelming statutory mechanics by explaining the policies underlying these provisions.

Before proceeding to the limitations, the concept of a net operating loss should be reviewed. In general, a net operating loss, often identified by its "NOL" monogram, is the excess of business deductions allowed by the

---

1. See Section D3 of this chapter, infra.
2. See Chapter 9D, supra.
3. I.R.C. § 384.
4. I.R.C. § 269.

Code over the taxpayer's gross income in a single taxable period.[5] A net operating loss ordinarily may be carried back to the two taxable years preceding the loss year and may be carried forward to the 20 following years.[6] An NOL carryback reduces the taxpayer's taxable income in the earlier year and typically results in a refund. Carryforwards serve as deductions in the subsequent years to which they are carried and reduce the tax due for those periods. NOLs must first be carried to the earliest available year and, to the extent not used, are then carried forward to the next available taxable periods.[7] Net operating losses thus stand as an exception to the annual taxable year concept. The purpose of the carryover scheme is to serve as an averaging device that ameliorates the harsh consequences that would result for a business taxpayer with a fluctuating economic track record. As the Supreme Court has described NOL carryovers, "[t]hey were designed to permit a taxpayer to set off its lean years against its lush years, and to strike something like an average taxable income computed over a period longer than one year."[8] All of this works smoothly in the corporate setting if the owners of the entity are unchanged during the generally applicable 23–year carryback and carryforward period. This chapter addresses the problems that arise if the ownership of a loss corporation changes at a time that the company has unexpired net operating losses.

B.   LIMITATIONS ON NET OPERATING LOSS CARRYFORWARDS: SECTION 382

1.   INTRODUCTION

Code: Skim § 382(a), (b)(1), (g)(1), (i)(1)

A profitable company seeking tax savings may be tempted to acquire a corporation with NOL carryovers to use those deductions to shelter its taxable income. To illustrate, assume that Mr. Loser forms Loss Co. to engage in the manufacture and sale of passing fads. The company is initially capitalized with $1,000,000, all represented by Mr. Loser's equity investment. Despite Loser's high hopes, Loss Co. incurs $999,999 in deductible expenses in the first two years of its operation and never earns a cent. At the end of two years, the company has nothing left except $1 in its checking account and a $999,999 NOL deduction that is useless because Loss Co. has no income to offset. At that point, the company is worth $1 plus the value, if any, of its deductions. If Loss Co. is liquidated, the sad story ends. If Loser infuses new property or cash into the corporation to keep the business afloat, then Loss Co. may deduct its loss carryforwards against any future income as long as Loser continues to own a controlling interest in the company.

---

5. See generally I.R.C. § 172.

6. I.R.C. § 172(b)(1)(A).

7. I.R.C. § 172(b)(2).

8. United States v. Foster Lumber Co., 429 U.S. 32, 97 S.Ct. 204 (1976).

But what if Profit Co., shopping around for tax deductions, learns of Loss Co.'s difficulties? If Profit wishes to acquire Loss, it has many options. It could: (1) acquire all of Loss Co.'s assets (i.e., $1) in exchange for Profit Co. stock in an acquisitive Type A or C tax-free reorganization, as a result of which Profit Co. would inherit all of Loss Co.'s tax attributes (i.e., its $999,999 NOL deduction);[1] (2) acquire the stock of Loss Co. in either a taxable purchase, a tax-free Type B reorganization, or reverse triangular merger, and later liquidate Loss Co. under Section 332, thereby inheriting its NOL carryforwards;[2] (3) acquire Loss Co.'s stock and then transfer its own assets into Loss Co. in a Section 351 exchange; in that case Loss Co., now a wholly owned subsidiary of Profit Co., can operate the Profit business while retaining its own NOLs; or (4) Loss Co. can acquire the assets of Profit Co. in an acquisitive tax-free reorganization by exchanging enough Loss Co. stock to give the Profit Co. shareholders virtually 100 percent ownership of Loss Co. The Profit Co. shareholders then will own Loss Co., which will own all of old Profit Co.'s assets plus a $999,999 NOL carryforward.

Is something wrong here? If Loss Co. lost money, should its NOLs be available to offset Profit's future income or should the use of those NOLs be limited to offsetting later income earned by Loss? Should Profit be able to avoid tax on $999,999 of its future income by acquiring (or being acquired by) the corporate shell of an unsuccessful business?

After pondering these questions for many years, Congress enacted ineffective legislation in the 1954 Code aimed at limiting the use of NOL carryforwards in the corporate acquisitions setting. Amendments followed in 1976, but they were so unappealing that their effective date was delayed four times until 1986, when they were discarded completely in favor of a new Section 382.[3] The current statutory scheme is the outgrowth of decades of study, most notably the Subchapter C Project of the American Law Institute and the Senate Finance Committee staff's Subchapter C study.[4]

When applicable, Section 382 limits the use of a loss corporation's NOL carryforwards when there is a change of ownership of more than 50 percent of the stock of that company over a period of three years or less.[5] Stating this general rule in the language of the Code, the loss limitations are

---

1. I.R.C. § 381(a)(2).

2. I.R.C. § 381(a)(1). If the liquidation occurs immediately after a Type B reorganization, it would be treated as a Type C reorganization. See Rev.Rul. 67–274, 1967–2 C.B. 141; Chapter 9B3, supra. In addition, if Profit Co. acquires the Loss Co. stock and files a consolidated return, the availability of Loss Co.'s losses will be limited by the consolidated return regulations. See Section D3 of this chapter, infra.

3. See generally Jacobs, "Tax Treatment of Corporate Net Operating Losses and

Other Tax Attribute Carryovers," 5 Va. Tax Rev. 701 (1986).

4. See American Law Institute, Federal Income Tax Project, Subchapter C (1986); Staff of the Senate Finance Committee, The Subchapter C Revision Act of 1985: A Final Report Prepared by the Staff, 99th Cong., 1st Sess. 32–35, 55–56, 68–71 (S.Prt. 99–47, 1985); Eustice, "Alternatives for Limiting Loss Carryovers," 22 San Diego L.Rev. 149 (1985).

5. I.R.C. § 382(g)(1), (i).

triggered only after an "ownership change,"[6] which is either an "owner shift involving a 5–percent shareholder", or an "equity structure shift,"[7] coupled with a more than 50 percent increase in the stock ownership of "5–percent shareholders" which occurs during a three-year "testing period".[8] If Section 382 is triggered, it limits the use by a "new loss corporation" of any NOLs of an "old loss corporation" for any "post-change year" (i.e., any year after the ownership change).[9] In general, the taxable income of a new loss corporation that may be offset by preacquisition NOLs is limited to the value of the old loss corporation's stock on the date of the ownership change multiplied by a prescribed "long-term tax-exempt rate."[10] These and many other statutory terms will be explained in detail later in the chapter.

The rationale of Section 382 is to allow a loss company's NOLs to offset only the future income generated by that company's business. If the section is triggered by an ownership change, its limitations apply in two different ways. First, if the Loss Co. business is not continued (or substantially all of its assets are not used) for at least two years after the change of ownership, all of its NOLs are disallowed.[11] Second, if the Loss Co. business is continued or if its assets are used for at least two years, the losses are allowable only to the extent of the income generated from the old Loss Co.'s assets. Because the transactions that trigger Section 382 may involve the combining of a loss company with a profitable company, it may be impossible to determine exactly what part of the combined company's income is generated by the Loss Co.'s business or assets. Section 382 solves this problem by adopting a method to approximate Loss Co.'s income. It irrebuttably assumes that the return on Loss Co.'s equity will be the rate of return payable on long-term tax-exempt bonds. Thus, in any year, Loss Co.'s NOLs can be used by the combined company only to the extent of the value of old Loss Co. multiplied by an assumed return on equity known as the long-term tax-exempt rate.[12] These basic rules are augmented by attribution rules, technical adjustments and a swarm of anti-avoidance provisions that give new dimension to Congress's increasing paranoia.

Our study of Section 382 begins with an examination of the ownership change requirement and then turns to the effect of such a change on the ability to use Loss Co.'s NOL carryforwards.

2.   THE OWNERSHIP CHANGE REQUIREMENTS

Code: § 382(g), (i), (k), (*l*)(3) & (4). See § 318.

In General. Since the economic burden of corporate losses falls on the individuals who were shareholders when the corporation was losing money,

---

6. I.R.C. § 382(a), (g), (k)(3).

7. I.R.C. § 382(g), (k)(7).

8. I.R.C. § 382(g), (i), (k)(7).

9. I.R.C. § 382(a), (d)(2). The "new loss corporation" is the successor to Loss Co. in a merger or asset acquisition; it is Loss Co. itself in a stock acquisition. See I.R.C.

§ 382(k)(3). The "old loss corporation" is Loss Co. prior to the ownership change. I.R.C. § 382(k)(2).

10. I.R.C. § 382(b)(1).

11. I.R.C. § 382(c).

12. I.R.C. § 382(b)(1).

the Section 382 limitations do not intercede as long as those individuals continue as shareholders. After all, they suffered through the losses, so it is only fair to give them the benefit of the accompanying tax deductions. Consequently, Section 382 applies only if there is an "ownership change," which occurs if the percentage of Loss Co. stock owned by one or more "5-percent shareholders" increases by more than 50 percentage points[1] during the three-year "testing period."[2] Thus, if Profit Co. purchases 51 percent or more of Loss Co.'s stock within a three-year period, or if Loss Co. is acquired in a corporate reorganization and its ownership changes by more than 50 percent, the loss limitations will apply. Similarly, if ten unrelated individuals each purchase six percent of the Loss Co. stock, Section 382 applies.

These various types of ownership changes are divided by the statute into two categories: an "owner shift involving a 5-percent shareholder" and an "equity structure shift."[3] An "owner shift" generally occurs upon any change in the stock ownership (either an increase or a decrease) of any 5-percent or more shareholder (e.g., the taxable purchases illustrated above).[4] An "equity structure shift" includes tax-free reorganizations, certain public offerings and reorganization-type transactions such as cash mergers.[5]

Owner Shift Involving 5–Percent Shareholder. An owner shift involving a 5-percent shareholder is any change in stock ownership (increase or decrease) that affects the percentage of stock owned by any person who is a 5-percent shareholder before or after the change.[6] Most owner shifts are purchases. Thus, if Profit Co. purchases 10 percent of Loss Co. stock from one shareholder, an owner shift has occurred. Apart from purchases, owner shifts can occur as a result of Section 351 exchanges, redemptions, issuances of stock, or recapitalizations.[7] However, the statute specifically excludes owner shifts as a result of a gift, death or divorce transfer.[8] Changes in proportionate ownership attributable solely to fluctuations in the market value of different classes of stock also are disregarded, except to the extent provided in regulations.[9]

Keep in mind that a single "owner shift" is not enough to trigger Section 382; there also must be a more than 50 percent change in ownership of Loss Co.[10] And while a more than 50 percentage point change in ownership is an essential ingredient in the Section 382 recipe, it is not

1. I.R.C. § 382(g)(1).

2. Id. I.R.C. § 382(i)(1).

3. I.R.C. § 382(g)(2), (3).

4. I.R.C. § 382(g)(2).

5. I.R.C. § 382(g)(3). Regulations designating taxable reorganization-type transactions as equity structure shifts have not yet been issued. See Reg. § 1.382–2T(e)(2)(ii).

6. I.R.C. § 382(g)(2). A 5–percent shareholder is defined as any person holding 5 percent or more of the stock of the loss corporation at any time during the three year testing period. I.R.C. § 382(k)(7).

7. Reg. § 1.382–2T(e)(1).

8. I.R.C. § 382(*l*)(3)(B).

9. I.R.C. § 382(*l*)(3)(C).

10. I.R.C. § 382(g)(1).

the only one. Here is where the "5–percent shareholder" concept enters the scene. Consider, for example, the consequences of a simple 50 percent change in ownership rule to a publicly traded company that has loss carryforwards. Those NOLs might be limited as a result of random public trading if more than 50 percent of the company's shares happened to change hands during a three-year period. To preclude such a result, the type of "owner shift" required to trigger Section 382 occurs only if the percentage of stock of Loss Co. owned by one or more "5–percent shareholders" increases by the requisite 50 percent.[11]

A rule that only counted the increased ownership of 5–percent shareholders might be easily circumvented. For example, a shareholder who held Loss Co. stock while the losses were incurred might sell four percent interests to 25 equal purchasers rather than to a single individual. In so doing, the owner would avoid selling any of his stock to a 5–percent shareholder despite an obvious sale and purchase of tax benefits. To assure that the loss limitations apply in these circumstances, Section 382 generally treats all less than 5–percent shareholders as a single 5–percent shareholder.[12] Thus, the sales to 25 four percent shareholders in the example are treated as sales to a single 5–percent shareholder, and the Section 382 limits apply because that 5–percent shareholder's ownership shifts from zero percent to 100 percent. But in the earlier publicly traded example, the group of less than 5–percent shareholders always would have held 100 percent both before and after the transfers, and thus Section 382 would not apply. Unfortunately, not all "owner shifts" are the result of such simple purchases. The problems at the end of this section explore some of these additional complications.

Equity Structure Shifts. Recall that Section 382 first must be triggered by either an "owner shift involving a 5–percent shareholder" or an "equity structure shift,"[13] either of which must result in an "ownership change." An "equity structure shift" is defined to include tax-free reorganizations[14] and certain taxable "reorganization-type" transactions, public offerings and similar transactions.[15] Consequently, if there is a shift in the ownership of Loss Co. stock in a reorganization, which when combined with any other stock transfers within the three-year period results in a more than 50 percent change of ownership, such an equity structure shift will bring the Section 382 limitations into play.[16]

Special Rules for Determining Change in Ownership. In determining whether a change in ownership has occurred, reorganizations involve some

---

11. I.R.C. § 382(g)(1)(A).

12. I.R.C. § 382(g)(4)(A).

13. I.R.C. § 382(g)(1).

14. I.R.C. § 382(g)(3)(A). Some reorganizations are excluded from the definition of "equity structure shift." Section 382(g)(3)(A) excludes a Type D or G reorganization, unless the requirements of Section 354(b)(1) are met, and a Type F reorganization.

15. I.R.C. § 382(g)(3)(B). The regulations have not identified the reorganization-type transactions covered by this rule. See Reg. § 1.382–2T(e)(2)(ii).

16. The regulations acknowledge that any equity structure shift affecting a 5–percent shareholder is also an owner shift. Reg. § 1.382–2T(e)(2)(iii).

special complications. In a Type A or C reorganization, the acquiring company that inherits the loss is probably an entirely different company from Loss Co. In that event, what ownership is tested under Section 382? This question is answered indirectly by Section 382(k), which defines the "loss corporation" affected by Section 382 as the corporation entitled to use the loss after the ownership change. Thus, in a Type A statutory merger or a Type C stock-for-assets reorganization involving a loss corporation and another corporation, the limits apply to the survivor. In order to determine the extent of ownership change that has occurred, the ownership of the surviving corporation must be compared to the pre-reorganization ownership of the old Loss Co. In effect, the statute looks at the pre-and post-reorganization ownership of whatever company possesses the losses—whether this is the acquiring corporation or the target. For example, if Loss Co. is merged into Profit Co., Section 382 requires a comparison of the ownership of pre-merger Loss Co. and post-merger Profit Co. If the pre-merger Loss Co. shareholders own at least 50 percent of the post-merger Profit Co. (defined as "new loss corporation")[17] an ownership change within the meaning of Section 382(g) will not have occurred. On the other hand, if Loss Co. acquires the stock (in a Type B reorganization or reverse triangular merger) or assets (in a Type A or C reorganization, or a forward triangular merger) of Profit Co. in exchange for Loss Co. stock, Section 382 will apply unless at least 50 percent of the post-reorganization Loss Co. stock continues to be owned by the pre-reorganization Loss Co. shareholders.

In order to assure proper results in the context of the fusion of two corporations, one more special rule is required. All shareholders who own less than five percent of a company's stock generally are treated as a single 5–percent shareholder. In a reorganization, there may be at least two groups of less than 5–percent shareholders—in our examples, the shareholders of Loss Co. and those of Profit Co. If these two groups were treated as a single shareholder, virtually all reorganizations of publicly held companies would escape Section 382. For example, assume that Loss Co. and Profit Co. are both public companies, with no shareholder owning stock of both and no individual owning (directly or indirectly) five percent of either company. If Profit Co. acquires the Loss Co. assets in a merger pursuant to which the old Loss Co. shareholders receive enough Profit Co. stock to become, as a group, 15 percent shareholders of Profit Co., it would appear that Section 382 should apply because the Profit Co. shareholders went from zero to 85 percent ownership of the "new loss corporation." But if all less-than–5–percent shareholders of Loss Co. and Profit Co. are treated as a single shareholder, 100 percent ownership of Loss Co. has remained within the exclusive ownership of that "single" shareholder—i.e., the group of less than 5–percent shareholders owned all of Loss Co. and all of Profit Co. and still owns all of Profit Co. In order to assure that Section 382 will apply in this and similar situations, the statute segregates public shareholders by providing that the group of less than 5–percent shareholders of Profit Co.

17. I.R.C. § 382(k)(3).

and the group of less than 5–percent shareholders of Loss Co. are treated as separate shareholders.[18] In the example, ownership of Loss Co. by the Profit Co. shareholders will have increased from zero to 85 percent and Section 382 therefore will apply.

Attribution Rules. The rules outlined above are buttressed by a set of attribution rules that borrows from and expands upon the attribution rules in Section 318.[19] In general, under the attribution rules all stock is deemed owned by individuals, and only actual or constructive ownership by individuals is relevant in testing whether an ownership change has taken place under Section 382.

PROBLEMS

1. Loss Co. has 100 shares of common stock outstanding and is owned equally by Shareholders 1 through 25, who are not related to one another. Loss Co. has assets worth $1,000,000 and net operating loss carryovers of $8,000,000. Will the Section 382 loss limitations apply in the following situations?

    (a) All shareholders sell their stock to Ms. Julie ("J")?

    (b) Shareholders 1 through 13 sell their stock to J?

    (c) Shareholders 1 through 12 sell their stock to J?

    (d) What result in (c), above, if Loss Co. redeems the stock of Shareholders 13 and 14 two years later?

    (e) What result in (c), above, if Shareholder 13 sells his stock to New Shareholder 26?

    (f) What result in (e), above, if Shareholder 14 also sells her stock to New Shareholder 26?

    (g) What result if Shareholders 1 through 25 sell their stock to New Shareholders 26 through 50?

2. Loss Co. is owned 40 percent by Bill and 60 percent by the general public. Loss Co.'s stock is worth $10,000,000. Loss Co. acquires all the assets of Gain Co. (net worth—$10,500,000) in a Type C reorganization in exchange for $10,500,000 worth of Loss Co. voting stock. If no shareholders of Gain Co. owned any Loss Co. stock prior to the transaction, has there been an ownership change?

3. Whale Co. and Minnow Co. (which has loss carryovers) are both publicly held companies, neither of which has any 5–percent shareholder. Whale Co. purchases all the stock of Minnow Co. for cash. Does § 382 apply?

3. RESULTS OF AN OWNERSHIP CHANGE

Code: § 382(a)–(f), (h), (*l*)(1) & (4).

    In General. If an ownership change occurs, the Section 382 loss limitations then must be applied. Before considering any further details,

---

18. I.R.C. § 382(g)(4)(B)(i).   **19.** I.R.C. § 382(*l*)(3).

the function of the limitations must be examined. We have seen that Congress designed Section 382 to prevent taxpayers from selling and purchasing tax deductions. If that were the only relevant consideration, the rest would be easy—whenever there is an ownership change, simply eliminate all loss carryforwards. But our study of Subchapter C has revealed one other salient factor—a corporation is treated as a separate entity for tax purposes. Although the individual shareholder may bear the ultimate burden or reap the ultimate benefit of a corporation's losses or profits, it is the corporation itself that is the focus of the corporate income tax.

In Section 382, Congress has adopted a principle of "neutrality" toward a loss company. While the Section 382 limitations restrict trafficking in deductions, they permit the purchaser of a loss corporation to use that corporation's net operating losses to offset the old loss corporation's own subsequent income. What Section 382 seeks to prevent is the use of a corporation's losses to offset another taxpayer's income after an ownership change. It is from this policy that the two limitations in Section 382 directly flow.

Continuity of Business Enterprise Limit. The first limit is found in Section 382(c),[1] which incorporates the continuity of business enterprise doctrine[2] by disallowing all net operating loss carryovers if the old loss corporation business is not continued for at least two years after the ownership change.[3] As described in the reorganization regulations, continuity of business enterprise requires either that the historic business of the loss corporation be continued for at least two years or that a significant portion of its assets are used in some other business carried on by the new loss corporation.[4] As a result, a corporation that runs afoul of this first limit in the second year following an ownership change may be required to amend its tax return for the earlier year and remove any inherited NOL deductions that had been applied against taxable income.

The Section 382 Limitation. A second, more complex limitation is "the Section 382 limitation," under which losses can be used in any "post-change year" only to the extent of the value of the old loss corporation multiplied by the "long-term tax-exempt rate."[5] To illustrate, assume Loss Co. has a value of $200,000 and has losses of $800,000 at a time when the long-term tax-exempt rate is 6 percent. After an ownership change, New Loss Co. may use its loss carryforwards only to the extent of $200,000 multiplied by 6 percent, or $12,000 per year.

1. This limitation is inapplicable to the extent of any built-in gains or gains resulting from a Section 338 election as well as any Section 382(b)(2) carryovers related to such gains. See I.R.C. § 382(c)(2) and page 614, infra.

2. See Chapter 9B1d, supra.

3. I.R.C. § 382(c)(1).

4. Reg. § 1.368–1(d).

5. I.R.C. § 382(b)(1), (f). "Post-change year" is any taxable year ending after the "change date"—i.e., in the case of an owner shift, the date on which the shift occurs and, in the case of an equity structure shift, the date of the reorganization. I.R.C. § 382(d)(2), (j).

The theory of this limit is to allow the loss carryforwards to offset any income earned by the old loss business. But since many of the acquisitions that will trigger the limit involve combining a loss business with some other more profitable enterprise, it is impossible to determine exactly how much income will be generated by the old company. To solve this problem, Section 382 irrebuttably presumes that the old loss business will generate income on its assets at a predetermined rate—the long-term tax-exempt rate. Because the amount of available loss carryforwards depends on the value of the old loss company, the greater the value (and cost) of that company, the more loss carryforwards may be used each year. Although the object of this limit is to defer the use of loss carryforwards by limiting the amount that can be used in any one year, the deferral will turn into a complete disallowance if the losses cannot be used before their expiration under Section 172.

Carryforwards of Unused Limitation. The Section 382 limitation results in some further complexity if it exceeds a corporation's taxable income in a given post-change year. To illustrate, if Loss Co. in the example above, with a value of $200,000, had at least $12,000 of taxable income (disregarding its NOL carryover), the full $12,000 of NOLs that were available in each year after the change of ownership would be used. But if the combined taxable income of the new loss company were only $4,000, the full amount available under the Section 382(b)(1) limitation would not be utilized. In that situation, the $8,000 of available but unused NOLs may be carried forward and the limitation in the following year would be $20,000 (the sum of the regular $12,000 limitation plus the $8,000 carryover).[6]

Mid–Year Ownership Change. Another special rule applies if the "change date"[7] occurs on a date other than the last day of a year. In that event, the Section 382 limitation for the portion of the year after the change is a prorated amount derived by applying a ratio of the remaining days in the year to the total days in the year.[8] Thus, if the change occurs two-thirds of the way through the year, the limitation for that year is one-third of what otherwise would be available—i.e., $12,000 × ⅓, or $4,000 in the example above.[9]

The Long–Term Tax–Exempt Rate. Returning to the basic Section 382 limitation, recall that it is the value of the old loss corporation multiplied by the long-term tax-exempt rate. The use of this measure to predict the expected return on Loss Co.'s assets is the product of substantial Congressional debate.[10] Loss Co. presumably can generate earnings on its assets at

---

6. I.R.C. § 382(b)(2).

7. I.R.C. § 382(j).

8. I.R.C. § 382(b)(3)(B).

9. In addition, the limitation is inapplicable to the days of the year prior to the change date. I.R.C. § 382(b)(3)(A).

10. The long-term tax-exempt rate is defined by Section 382(f) as the highest federal long-term rate determined under Section 1274(d) in effect for the three-month period ending with the month of the ownership change, adjusted to reflect differences between returns on long-term taxable and tax-exempt obligations.

a rate at least equal to the higher federal long-term taxable rate. Indeed, if it could not do so some other way, Loss Co. simply could sell its assets and invest the proceeds in long-term federal obligations. Use of the lower tax-exempt rate to predict Loss Co.'s earnings is intended to offset the fact that the amount against which this rate is applied will exceed the real value of Loss Co.'s income-generating assets. How so? Because under Section 382(e)(1), the value of Loss Co. is the value of its stock immediately before the ownership change. Since Loss Co. has loss carryforwards to offset any income it earns in the near future, that income will be essentially tax-free. Loss Co.'s after-tax return will equal its before-tax profit, and the value of its stock will reflect not only the value of its income-generating assets but also the fact that the income which is generated will be tax free.

The Value of the Company. The second component of the Section 382 limitation is the value of the stock of the old loss corporation immediately preceding the ownership change.[11] Congress included several special rules to guard against predictable efforts to abuse this rule by inflating the value of the loss company.

One obvious technique to increase the available NOLs after an ownership change would be for the shareholders to increase the value of the loss company just prior to the change by contributing cash or other property to the corporation. Congress attacked this maneuver with an "anti-stuffing" rule, under which the value of any pre-change capital contribution received by the loss company as part of a plan to increase the Section 382 limitation is disregarded.[12] Any contribution received within two years before an ownership change is generally treated as part of such a plan.[13]

Even without "stuffing" in anticipation of a planned ownership change, shareholders of a loss company may be tempted to transfer cash or income-producing investments to the company. If there is a later ownership change, the allowable losses then would be greater; and if there is not a change, the investment income could be accumulated tax-free at the corporate level because it would be offset by the loss carryforwards. If the shareholders do not wish to transfer portfolio investments to the loss company, they at least might be tempted to prevent the company's profits (assuming it later becomes profitable) from being taken out of the company in order to reinvest these profits in portfolio investments which can accumulate tax-free at the corporate level and be available to increase the Section 382 limit in the event of a subsequent ownership change.

11. I.R.C. § 382(b)(1), (e)(1). For purposes of determining the value of the loss corporation, all stock is counted, even preferred stock that would be ignored in determining whether an ownership change has occurred. I.R.C. §§ 382(e)(1), (k)(6)(A); 1504(a)(4).

12. I.R.C. § 382(*l*)(1).

13. I.R.C. § 382(*l*)(1)(B). Exempted from this presumption are any contributions to be specified in regulations. The Conference Report instructs the Treasury that the regulations should generally exempt contributions only if they occurred prior to the accrual of the losses or if they were contributions of necessary operating capital. H.R.Rep. No. 99–841, 99th Cong., 2d Sess. II–182.

These possibilities did not go unnoticed by an ever suspicious Congress. If at least one-third of a loss corporation's assets consist of nonbusiness (i.e., investment) assets, the value of the corporation for purposes of Section 382 includes only the percentage of its actual net value that represents the percentage of its gross assets which are business assets.[14] To illustrate, if Loss Co. has $2,000,000 of investment assets, $3,000,000 of business assets and $1,000,000 of debt, it has a net value of $4,000,000, but only 60 percent of that value is taken into account for purposes of the Section 382 limitation because only 60 percent of its gross assets are business assets.[15]

If taxpayers are unable to increase useable NOLs by inflating the value of the loss corporation prior to an ownership change, they might be tempted to at least enable a profitable corporation to more easily avail itself of these losses by decreasing the value of the loss corporation after an ownership change. To illustrate, assume Loss Co. has a value of $1,000,000 and loss carryforwards of $1,000,000 and the tax-exempt rate is 6 percent. Profit Co. could acquire Loss Co. for $1,000,000 and use loss carryforwards at the rate of $60,000 per year, which probably would be enough only to offset Loss Co.'s own income. But what if Profit Co. pays $510,000 for 51 percent of Loss Co., and then Loss Co. redeems the remaining 49 percent of its outstanding shares? Loss Co.'s value has decreased by 49 percent (the amount paid to redeem its stock), and its revenues presumably will decrease by the same 49 percent. Profit Co. will have paid only $510,000, but the smaller New Loss Co. may deduct its loss carryovers to the extent of 6 percent times $1,000,000, or $60,000 per year. Once again, Congress cuts off a promising strategy at the pass. Section 382(e)(2) provides that if a redemption or other corporate contraction occurs in connection with an ownership change, the value of the loss corporation is determined only after taking the redemption or contraction into account.[16]

Limit on Built-in Losses. Finally, a corporation generally is subject to the Section 382 limitations only if it has loss carryforwards. A prospective buyer of deductions might be tempted to avoid the section by simply acquiring an asset that did not have the carryforwards themselves but rather the ability to produce them. Specifically, instead of acquiring a corporation that had loss carryforwards, a taxpayer could acquire a corporation that had substantial unrealized losses and other deductions built into its assets. Assuming a buyer is in the market for deductions, a company with assets having an aggregate basis of $1,000,000 and a value of $100,000 may be as attractive as a company with a $900,000 loss carryfor-

14. I.R.C. § 382(*l*)(4).

15. When it applies, Section 382(*l*)(4) specifically requires that the value of the loss corporation shall be reduced by the excess of the value of its nonbusiness assets over an amount of the corporation's debt which bears the same ratio to all the company's debt which the nonbusiness assets bear to all the company's assets. I.R.C. § 382(*l*)(4)(A). See

§ 382(*l*)(4)(D). The net result is as described in the text above.

16. The legislative history suggests that the "in connection with" standard should be broadly construed to include any redemption that is contemplated at the time of the ownership change. See H.R.Rep. No. 99–841, supra note 13, at II–187.

ward. Once the company is acquired, the profitable company could sell those assets and use the losses against its own profits.

In its eternal race to stay one step ahead of the taxpayer, Congress has extended the limitations in Section 382 to certain built-in unrealized losses and deductions that economically accrue prior to an ownership change but are not recognized until after the change.[17] If a corporation has assets whose aggregate bases exceed their total value—i.e., a "net unrealized built-in loss"[18]—then any built-in losses which are recognized within five years[19] of an ownership change are treated as loss carryforwards of the old loss corporation and are subject to the Section 382 deduction limits.[20] Depreciation, amortization or depletion deductions during the five-year recognition period are treated as recognized built-in losses for purposes of this rule unless the corporation establishes that such amounts are not attributable to the excess of the adjusted basis over the fair market value of the asset on the change date.[21] To the extent that the new loss corporation establishes that a loss recognized during the five-year period accrued after the ownership change, the loss may be deducted without limitation.[22] Even if the new loss company is unable to establish when any particular loss was accrued, the total amount of loss subject to this rule may not exceed the net unrealized loss built into the old loss corporation's assets.[23] A special de minimis rule provides that a corporation's net unrealized built-in loss is considered to be zero if it does not exceed the lesser of (1) 15 percent of the fair market value of the assets of the corporation, or (2) $10 million.[24]

Special Rules for Built-in Gains. On occasion, Congress is as eager to be fair as it is to be vigilant. In that spirit, the Section 382 limitation is increased to reflect built-in gains and other income items that accrued prior to the ownership change but are recognized within five years after the change. If on the change date the aggregate fair market value of a loss corporation's assets exceeds the aggregate adjusted basis of those assets—i.e., the corporation has a "net unrealized built-in gain"[25]—the Section 382 limitation is increased by any built-in gain (up to total net unrealized built-in gain) which is recognized during the five-year "recognition period" following an ownership change.[26] As a result, the new loss company can use its loss carryforwards (in addition to otherwise allowable post-change losses) to offset any built-in gains which it recognizes either on a disposition of an asset of the old loss corporation[27] or because of a Section 338

---

17. I.R.C. § 382(h)(1)(B).

18. I.R.C. § 382(h)(3)(A).

19. This is known as the "recognition period." I.R.C. § 382(h)(7).

20. I.R.C. § 382(h)(1)(B).

21. I.R.C. § 382(h)(2)(B). For example, depreciation deductions attributable to capital improvements made with respect to an asset after the change date would not be subject to the limitation.

22. I.R.C. § 382(h)(2)(B)(i).

23. I.R.C. § 382(h)(1)(B)(ii).

24. I.R.C. § 382(h)(3)(B)(i). For purposes of this test, cash, cash equivalents and marketable securities with a value not substantially different from their bases generally are disregarded. § 382(h)(3)(B)(ii).

25. I.R.C. § 382(h)(3)(A).

26. I.R.C. § 382(h)(1).

27. Id. The Service has announced that if a taxpayer sells a built-in gain asset prior to or during the recognition period in an

election made with respect to the loss corporation.[28] The corporation must be able to prove that the built-in gains accrued prior to the change date;[29] and the total increase in the Section 382 limitation may not exceed the net unrealized built-in gain as of the change date.[30] Once again, a de minimis rule provides that net unrealized built-in gains do not increase the Section 382 limitation if they do not exceed the lesser of (1) 15 percent of the fair market value of the corporation's assets, or (2) $10 million.[31]

PROBLEMS

1. Loss Co. has net operating loss carryforwards of $10,000,000. It has assets worth $10,000,000 and liabilities of $2,000,000. Profit Co. is a publicly held company worth $100,000,000.

   (a) On January 1, 2006, Profit Co. acquires all of the Loss Co. assets in a merger of Loss Co. into Profit Co. where Loss Co. shareholders receive Profit Co. stock worth $8,500,000. The long-term tax-exempt rate at that time is 5 percent. Assuming the Loss Co. business is continued, to what extent can Profit Co. deduct Loss Co.'s loss carryforwards in 2006?

   (b) What result in (a), above, if Profit Co. instead purchases all of the Loss Co. stock for $8,500,000?

   (c) What result in (a), above, if Profit Co.'s taxable income, disregarding any loss carryforward, is $300,000 in 2006?

   (d) What result in (a), above, if Profit Co. discontinues the Loss Co. business and disposes of its assets in 2006?

   (e) What result in (a), above, if the merger occurs on June 30, 2006? Assume the date is halfway through each corporation's taxable year.

2. Loss Co. has loss carryforwards of $10,000,000. It has the following assets, all of which have been held for more than two years unless otherwise indicated:

installment sale under Section 453, the provisions of Section 382(h) continue to apply to gain recognized from the sale (including a disposition of the installment obligations) after the recognition period. I.R.S. Notice 90–27, 1990–1 C.B. 336.

   28. I.R.C. § 382(h)(1)(C). If an ownership change and Section 338 qualified stock purchase occur simultaneously, the target is treated as selling its assets to itself ("new T") at the close of the acquisition date. I.R.C. § 338(a). In that situation, the Section 382 limit does not apply to the Section 338

deemed sale gain because the losses do not carry over to a "post-change year." I.R.C. § 382(a), (d)(2). When an ownership change takes place prior to a qualified stock purchase (i.e., a creeping qualified stock purchase), Section 382(h)(1)(C) provides special rules when the Section 382(h)(3)(B) de minimis threshold is not satisfied and the corporation's built-in gains are considered to be zero.

   29. I.R.C. § 382(h)(2)(A).

   30. I.R.C. § 382(h)(1)(A)(ii).

   31. I.R.C. § 382(h)(3)(B).

Asset	Adj. Basis	F.M.V.
Equipment	$2,000,000	$4,500,000
Land	6,000,000	3,000,000
IBM stock	2,000,000	2,000,000
Cash	500,000	500,000

Loss Co. has liabilities of $2,000,000. Profit Co. is a publicly held company worth $100,000,000. On January 1, 2006, Profit Co. acquires all of the Loss Co. assets in exchange for Profit Co. stock worth $8,500,000. The long-term tax-exempt rate is 5 percent.

(a) Assuming that the business conducted by Loss Co. is continued, to what extent can Profit Co. deduct Loss Co.'s loss carryforwards in 2006?

(b) What result in (a), above, if the stock and cash had been contributed to the capital of Loss Co. in November, 2005?

(c) What result in (a), above, if the IBM stock had a value and basis of $5,000,000?

(d) What result in (c), above, if IBM were a wholly owned subsidiary of Loss Co.?

(e) What result in (a), above, if Profit Co. acquires 70 percent of the Loss Co. stock for Profit Co. stock on January 1 and the IBM stock and the cash are distributed to Joe, a 30 percent shareholder of Loss Co., on March 1 in redemption of all of his stock?

(f) Will the result in (a), above, change if Profit Co. sells the equipment in February? Would the answer be different if the land had a basis of zero?

(g) Assume in (a), above, that the land had a basis of $8,000,000 and that Profit Co. sells the land for $3,000,000 two years later. Is the loss deductible? What if Profit Co. sells the land for $2,700,000?

C.   LIMITATIONS ON OTHER TAX ATTRIBUTES: SECTION 383

Code: § 383.

Section 383 is a brief section that is easily mastered if one understands the operation of Section 382. It essentially calls for the Treasury to issue regulations that will adopt the principles of Section 382 (i.e., the continuity of business enterprise requirement and ownership change rules coupled with limitations) to limit corporate attributes other than loss carryforwards. Section 383 applies to the Section 39 carryforward of the general business credit,[1] the Section 53 carryforward of the alternative minimum tax credit,[2] and the Section 904(c) carryforward of the foreign tax credit.[3]

---

1. I.R.C. § 383(a)(2)(A).   **3.** I.R.C. § 383(c).
2. I.R.C. § 383(a)(2)(B).

Section 383 also calls for regulations to employ Section 382 principles to limit capital loss carryforwards of a loss company.[4] In addition, the regulations must provide that any permitted use of a capital loss carryforward in any year will reduce the Section 382 limitation on loss carryforwards for that year.[5]

D.   OTHER LOSS LIMITATIONS

1.   ACQUISITIONS MADE TO EVADE TAX: SECTION 269

Code: § 269.

If a corporation surmounts the hurdles of Section 382, it still may find its losses limited by Section 269. The subjective approach of Section 269 is fundamentally different from the objective tests of Section 382. Section 269 applies to a transaction only if the principal purpose of the acquisition was "evasion or avoidance of Federal income tax by acquiring the benefit of a deduction, credit, or other allowance" which the taxpayer otherwise might not enjoy. Section 269(a) potentially applies to Type A and C reorganizations and forward triangular mergers and to Type B reorganizations or stock purchases where the acquiring corporation previously owned less than 50 percent of the target.[1] Section 269(b) applies to liquidations which occur within two years after a corporation makes a stock purchase which would have qualified for a Section 338 election but only if no such election was made.[2]

If Section 269 applies, the Commissioner has the power to deny any "deduction, credit or allowance." In theory, Section 269 thus has a potentially broader reach than Section 382. Although Congress has indicated that Section 269 should not be applied to a transaction where carryovers were limited by the prior versions of Section 382,[3] the proposed regulations make it clear that current Sections 382 and 383 do not limit the Service's ability to invoke Section 269.[4] Thus, if a tax avoidance device or scheme is detected, Section 269 can deny even those NOLs that otherwise slip by the limits of Section 382. It is expected, however, that Section 269 will be applied more sparingly now that the objective limits on loss carryovers have been strengthened.

---

4. I.R.C. § 383(b).

5. I.R.C. § 383(b). For regulations implementing Section 383, see Reg. § 1.383–1.

1. I.R.C. § 269(a)(2).

2. See Chapter 8C2, supra.

3. See, e.g., S.Rep. No. 94–938, 94th Cong., 2d Sess. 206 (1976), reprinted in 1976–3 C.B. (Part 1) 244; S.Rep. No. 1622, 83d Cong., 2d Sess. 284 (1954).

4. Reg. § 1.269–7 provides that Section 269 may be applied to disallow a deduction, credit or other allowance when the item is limited or reduced under Section 382 or 383. The fact that an item is limited under Section 382(a) or 383 is relevant to the determination of whether the principal purpose of the acquisition is evasion or avoidance of federal tax.

2.   LIMITATIONS ON USE OF PREACQUISITION LOSSES TO OFFSET BUILT-IN GAINS: SECTION 384

Code § 384.

Section 384 restricts an acquiring corporation from using its preacquisition losses to offset built-in gains of an acquired corporation. The policy and operation of Section 384 can best be illustrated by an example. Assume that Loss Corporation ("L") has $100,000 of net operating loss carryforwards. At the beginning of the current year, profitable Target Corporation ("T") merges into L in a tax-free Type A reorganization. L and T are owned by unrelated individual shareholders, and the merger does not result in a Section 382 ownership change to L. T's only asset, Gainacre, has a value of $200,000 and an adjusted basis of $125,000 which will transfer to L under Section 362(b). Assume that L sells Gainacre for $200,000 shortly after the merger, realizing a $75,000 gain.

Unless Section 269 or Section 382 applied, L could apply its preacquisition losses to shelter any gains recognized on the disposition of the assets acquired from T. Thus, L could use its net operating loss carryforwards to offset the $75,000 gain on the sale of Gainacre. Because it was not clear that Section 269 would effectively deter this strategy, Congress became concerned that loss corporations would become vehicles for "laundering" the built-in gains of profitable target companies. Section 384—yet another attack on the real and perceived abuses flowing from corporate acquisitions—is the legislative response. Its purpose is to preclude a corporation from using its preacquisition losses to shelter built-in gains of another (usually, a target) corporation which are recognized within five years of an acquisition of the gain corporation's assets or stock. In the example above, L would be prevented from using its preacquisition net operating loss as a deduction against the $75,000 "recognized built-in gain" on the disposition of Gainacre.

Section 384 is triggered in two situations: (1) stock acquisitions, where one corporation acquires "control" (defined by reference to the 80–percent-of-vote-and-value benchmark in Section 1504(a)(2)) of another corporation, and (2) asset acquisitions in an acquisitive Type A, C or D reorganization, if either corporation is a "gain corporation"—i.e., a corporation having built-in gains.[1] As originally enacted, Section 384 applied only when a loss corporation acquired the stock or assets of a gain corporation, but Congress later expanded the provision to apply regardless of which corporation acquired the other. If applicable, Section 384(a) provides that the corporation's income, to the extent attributable to "recognized built-in gains,"

---

1. I.R.C. § 384(a), (c)(4) and (5). Section 384 does not displace any of the other Code provisions limiting loss carryovers— e.g., Sections 269, 382, and certain provisions in the consolidated return regulations. Congress has indicated that the limitations of Section 384 apply independently of and in addition to the limitations of Section 382. Staff of the Joint Committee on Taxation, Description of the Technical Corrections Bill of 1988, 100th Cong., 2d Sess. 421 (1988). In contrast to Section 269, the application of Section 384 is not dependent on the subjective intent of the acquiring corporation.

shall not be offset by any "preacquisition loss" other than a preacquisition loss of the gain corporation. This punishment occurs during any "recognition period taxable year," which is any taxable year within the five-year period beginning on the "acquisition date."[2]

Understanding the operation of Section 384 requires a mastery of its glossary, much of which is borrowed from Section 382. The essential terms are as follows:

(1) The "acquisition date" is the date on which control is acquired, in the case of a stock acquisition, or the date of the transfer, in the case of an asset acquisition.[3]

(2) A "preacquisition loss" is any net operating loss carryforward to the taxable year in which the acquisition date occurs and the portion of any net operating loss for the taxable year of the acquisition to the extent the loss is allocable to the period before the acquisition date.[4]

(3) A "recognized built-in gain" is any gain recognized on the disposition of any asset during the five-year recognition period except to the extent that the gain corporation (in the case of an acquisition of control) or the acquiring corporation (in the case of an asset acquisition) establishes that the asset was not held by the gain corporation on the acquisition date, or that the gain accrued after the acquisition date.[5] Income items recognized after the acquisition date but attributable to prior periods are also treated as recognized built-in gain.[6] This definition should be familiar; it is similar to the definition of the same term in Section 382(h)(2)(A) except that the burden of proof is different. Under Section 382, the burden is on the taxpayer to establish that the asset was held by the old loss corporation before the change date and the recognized gain does not exceed the appreciation in the asset on that date. Under Section 384, it is presumed that a gain recognized during the recognition period is a built-in gain unless the corporation establishes that the asset was not held on the acquisition date or that the recognized gain exceeds the built-in gain at the time of the acquisition.

(4) The amount of recognized built-in gain for any taxable year is limited to the "net unrealized built-in gain" reduced by recognized built-in gains for prior years in the recognition period which, but for Section 384, would have been offset by preacquisition losses.[7] For this purpose, the definition of "net unrealized built-in gain" is

---

2. See I.R.C. §§ 384(c)(8); 382(h)(7). The Section 384 limitation also applies to any "successor" corporation to the same extent it applied to its predecessor. I.R.C. § 384(c)(7).

3. I.R.C. § 384(c)(2).

4. I.R.C. § 384(c)(3)(A). In the case of a corporation with a net unrealized built-in loss, as defined by Section 382(h)(1)(B), the term "preacquisition loss" also includes any built-in loss recognized during the five-year recognition period. I.R.C. § 384(c)(3)(B).

5. I.R.C. § 384(c)(1)(A).

6. I.R.C. § 384(c)(1)(B).

7. I.R.C. § 384(c)(1)(C).

borrowed from Section 382(h)(3), substituting the acquisition date for the ownership "change date."[8] Thus, it is the excess of the aggregate fair market value of the assets of the "gain corporation" over the aggregate adjusted bases of those assets, except that the net unrealized built-in gain will be deemed to be zero unless it is greater than the lesser of (1) 15 percent of the fair market value of the corporation's assets other than cash and certain marketable securities or (2) $10 million.[9]

The limitations in Section 384(a) do not apply to the preacquisition loss of any corporation that was a member of the same "controlled group" that included the gain corporation at all times during the five-year period ending on the acquisition date. For this purpose, the definition of controlled group is borrowed from Section 1563 (as modified to generally require more than 50 percent common ownership of both voting power and value).[10]

As if the foregoing rules were not enough, Section 384(f) authorizes the Treasury to promulgate regulations as may be necessary to carry out the anti-abuse mission of the section.[11]

PROBLEM

Gain Corp., which is wholly owned by individual A, has the following assets and no liabilities:

Asset	Adj. Basis	F.M.V.
Inventory	$150,000	$300,000
Machinery	300,000	200,000
Gainacre	100,000	350,000

Loss Corp., which is wholly owned by unrelated individual B, has $500,000 in net operating loss carryforwards.

Unless otherwise indicated below, assume that Loss Corp. acquired all the assets of Gain Corp. in a tax-free Type A reorganization on January 1, 2005. After the acquisition, B owned 80% and A owned 20% of the Loss Corp. stock. To what extent, if any, may Loss Corp. use its preacquisition net operating loss carryforwards against the gains recognized in the following alternative transactions?:

(a) Loss Corp. sells Gainacre for $500,000 in 2006.

(b) Same as (a), above, except that Loss Corp. acquired all of Gain Corp.'s stock from A for cash (not making a § 338 election) on January 1, 2005, after which it liquidated Gain Corp. under § 332.

(c) Same as (a), above, except Loss Corp. also sells the inventory for $400,000 in 2006.

---

8. I.R.C. § 384(c)(8).

9. I.R.C. §§ 384(c)(8); 382(h)(3)(B).

10. I.R.C. § 384(b). The common control testing period would be shortened if the gain corporation was not in existence for the full five-year preacquisition date period by substituting its period of existence. I.R.C. § 384(b)(3).

11. As of early 2005, no regulations had been issued.

(d) Instead of (a)–(c), above, Loss Corp. sells Gainacre for $900,000 in 2011.

(e) Same as (a), above, except that Loss Corp. has no net operating loss carryforwards at the time of the acquisition but its only asset is Lossacre, which had a fair market value of $300,000 and an adjusted basis of $500,000. In 2006, Loss Corp. sells Lossacre for $200,000 at the same time that it sells Gainacre for $500,000.

3. CONSOLIDATED RETURN RULES

C corporations generally determine their taxable income and tax liability without regard to the income and losses of other affiliated entities. The consolidated return rules are an exception to this separate entity principle. Section 1501 permits an "affiliated group of corporations" to elect to file a consolidated tax return in which their separate taxable income and losses are aggregated.[1] An "affiliated group" is defined as a chain of corporations linked by specific levels of stock ownership. The common parent of the group must own at least 80 percent of the total voting power and value of at least one corporation in the chain, and every corporation in the chain must be 80 percent owned (based on voting power and value) by other members of the group.[2]

When computing the consolidated taxable income or loss of an affiliated group of corporations, each member of the group first determines its separate taxable income or loss.[3] The separate taxable income or loss figures of the members of the group are then combined, and the Section 11 tax rates are applied to the aggregate figure to arrive at the group's tax liability.

Because the consolidated return rules permit aggregation of the separate taxable income and loss of the members, the potential exists for one member of the group to offset its taxable income with the losses of another member. For example, without a specific limitation, a profitable corporation could acquire the requisite ownership of a corporation with a large net operating loss, the two corporations could elect to file a consolidated return, and the joint tax liability of the corporate family would be reduced as the net operating losses of one member are deducted against the income of the other. A multi-layer of statutes and regulations limit the use of net operating losses by corporations filing a consolidated return. First, all of the statutory limitations on the use of NOLs studied earlier in this chapter (i.e., Sections 382, 383, 384 and 269) potentially apply to a consolidated group.[4] If any loss somehow should survive these statutory gatekeepers, the

---

1. See generally Chapter 1B3, supra, and Chapter 13, infra.

2. I.R.C. § 1504(a)(1), (2). In general, preferred stock is not counted for purposes of the ownership tests and certain corporations subject to special tax regimes, such as tax-exempt and foreign corporations, are not per-mitted to be part of an affiliated group. I.R.C. § 1504(a)(4), (b).

3. Reg. §§ 1.1502–2, 1.1502–11(a)(1), 1.1502–12.

4. See Reg. § 1.1502–90 through Reg. § 1.1502–99, which apply Section 382 to a consolidated group of corporations.

consolidated return regulations contain an additional rule to patrol abuse: the "separate return limitation year" ("SRLY") limitation.[5] The operation of these rules should be familiar because they reflect many of the same policies embodied in the generally applicable statutory limitations.

The SRLY limitation is designed to prevent the use by an affiliated group of net operating losses arising in a separate return limitation year of a member of the group. A separate return limitation year is a taxable year in which the member filed either its own separate tax return or filed as part of another affiliated group.[6] In general, the aggregate net operating losses of a member of an affiliated group arising in separate return years only may be carried over and used to offset the aggregate consolidated income attributable to that member.[7] Thus, if a profitable corporation ("P") acquires a target corporation ("T") with large net operating losses, and the two corporations file a consolidated tax return, preacquisition losses and built-in losses of T may not be used to reduce the post-acquisition tax liability on consolidated taxable income attributable to P.

The regulations include an important exception that restricts the application of the SRLY limitation. Generally, the SRLY limitation does not apply in any case where a corporation becomes a member of a consolidated group (where the limitation otherwise would apply) within six months of the change date of a Section 382(g) change of ownership.[8] As a result, in many acquisitions the SRLY limitation relinquishes jurisdiction over NOLs to Section 382.[9]

---

5. The regulations also include limitations on the use of built-in losses and capital loss carryovers and carrybacks. See Reg. §§ 1.1502–15; 1.1502–22(c), (d). These items are also subject to the SRLY limitation.

6. Reg. § 1.1502–1(e), (f).

7. Reg. § 1.1502–21(c).

8. Reg. § 1.1502–21(g)(1) & (2).

9. A similar rules applies in the case of recognized built-in losses. See Reg. § 1.1502–15(g).

CHAPTER 13

AFFILIATED CORPORATIONS

A. RESTRICTIONS ON AFFILIATED CORPORATIONS

1. INTRODUCTION

For a variety of reasons, business owners often conduct their activities through multiple corporations. For example, to protect a low-risk existing business from potential tort liability, the shareholders of a closely held corporation might form a separate corporation to conduct a new, high-risk activity. Similarly, a holding company with an operating subsidiary might determine that the regulatory requirements of a particular state or country are sufficiently stringent that a planned expansion into that jurisdiction should take place through a new subsidiary. Should these business decisions about the corporate structure affect the manner in which the enterprises are treated for tax purposes?

A corporation, like an individual, generally is treated as a separate taxable entity. If this rule were unqualified, however, business owners would have an incentive in many circumstances to create separate corporations solely to obtain tax benefits. Recognizing this incentive, the Code treats related corporations for many purposes as a single economic unit. There may also be an incentive for related corporations to reduce their tax liability through transactions where they deal with each other on terms which unrelated parties operating at arm's length would not agree. Congress again recognized this incentive and provided tax administrators with a powerful weapon to counteract it. This section of the chapter explores the Code's rules to address these and other concerns about the taxation of affiliated corporations.

2. LIMITATIONS ON MULTIPLE TAX BENEFITS

Code: § 1561(a). Skim §§ 11(b)(1); 535(c); 1551; 1563.

Section 1561. The basic purpose of Section 1561 is to prevent business owners from obtaining multiple tax benefits by subdividing their business among multiple corporations. In its current form, Section 1561 targets four specific benefits: (1) the progressive tax rate structure provided by Section 11(b), (2) the "accumulated earnings credit" provided by Section 535(c),[1] (3) the $40,000 exemption amount used by corporations in calculating their

---

1. The accumulated earnings credit reduces the tax liability of corporations subject to the special tax on accumulated earnings imposed by Section 531. See I.R.C. §§ 531, 532 and 535 and Chapter 14B, infra.

alternative minimum taxable income,[2] and (4) the $2 million exemption amount used by corporations in calculating their liability for the environmental tax imposed by Section 59A.

A simple example illustrates the abuse that Section 1561 is designed to prevent. Suppose that individual A is the sole shareholder of a corporation that both operates an automobile repair shop and sells automobile parts at retail. The parts are sold at a window in the back of the repair shop by employees who also serve as mechanics in the repair operations. Assume that the corporation has total taxable income of $100,000, of which $75,000 is from its repair operations and $25,000 is from its sales of parts. Under the tax rates imposed by § 11(b), the corporation's income tax liability would be:

Income	Tax Rate	Tax
$ 50,000	15%	$ 7,500
25,000	25%	6,250
25,000	34%	8,500
$100,000		$22,250

If A instead divides the corporation's business operations between two separate corporations, Parts, Inc. and Services, Inc., the total tax liability of the businesses would be reduced because more income would be taxed at the lowest 15 percent rate.

Parts			Services		
Income	Tax Rate	Tax	Income	Tax Rate	Tax
$25,000	15%	$3,750	$50,000	15%	$ 7,500
			25,000	25%	6,250
$25,000		$3,750	$75,000		$13,750

Combined Tax Liability

Parts:	$ 3,750
Services:	13,750
Total:	$17,500

Without a rule that takes into account the relationship between Parts and Services, A could obtain a corporate-level tax savings of $4,750 ($22,250—$17,500) simply by creating an additional corporation.

Section 1561 prevents this result (and similar results in the case of the other tax benefits listed above) by providing that the benefit received by certain related groups of corporations cannot exceed the benefit that the group would receive if it were a single corporation. With the exception of the accumulated earnings credit, the benefits targeted by Section 1561 must be divided equally among the group's members unless the members formally agree to a different allocation.[3] Thus, if Parts and Services do not

---

2. See I.R.C. §§ 55(b)(1)(B)(i), (d)(2).   **3.** I.R.C. § 1561(a).

enter into a formal allocation plan, the amounts of income in each taxable income bracket in Section 11(b) will be divided equally between them (to the extent that each corporation has taxable income), resulting in the same aggregate tax liability that they would have if they were a single corporation:

Income	Parts Tax Rate	Tax	Income	Services Tax Rate	Tax
$25,000	15%	$3,750	$25,000	15%	$ 3,750
			25,000	25%	6,250
			25,000	34%	8,500
$25,000		$3,750	$75,000		$18,500

Combined Tax Liability

Parts:	$ 3,750
Services:	18,500
Total:	$22,250

Component Members of a Controlled Group of Corporations. Section 1561 applies only to the "component members of a controlled group of corporations." The terms "component members" and "controlled group of corporations" are defined in Section 1563. Although simple in concept, these terms are defined in the Code and regulations with an extraordinary degree of complexity and specificity. Only a brief overview of those rules is provided here.

Section 1563 generally defines three principal types of controlled groups of corporations: a parent-subsidiary controlled group, a brother-sister controlled group, and a combined group.[4] A parent-subsidiary controlled group generally is defined as one or more chains of corporations connected through stock ownership to a common parent, if (1) stock possessing at least 80 percent of the total combined voting power or total value of all classes of stock of each corporation (other than the parent) is owned by one or more of the other corporations, and (2) the parent owns stock possessing at least 80 percent of the total combined voting power or total value of all classes of stock of at least one of the other corporations.[5] Thus, if corporation X owns 80 percent of the total combined voting power of corporations Y and Z, then X, Y and Z are members of a parent-subsidiary controlled group.[6] The definition of a brother-sister controlled group is two or more corporations where five or fewer shareholders who are individuals, estates, or trusts own stock possessing more than 50 percent of the total combined voting power or more than 50 percent of the total value of each corporation, taking into account the stock ownership of each person only to the extent such ownership is identical with respect to each such

4. I.R.C. § 1563(a).

5. I.R.C. § 1563(a)(1).

6. See Reg. § 1.1563–1(a)(2)(ii) Example 1.

corporation.[7] For example, assume shareholder A owns 25 percent of X Corporation's common stock and 35 percent of Y Corporation's common stock. Assume further that shareholder B owns 30 percent of X's common stock and 40 percent of Y's common stock. A's and B's identical ownership in X and Y is 25 percent and 30 percent, respectively. Since A's and B's identical ownership of common stock totals more than 50 percent of each corporation, X and Y are members of a brother-sister controlled group. A combined group is a group of three or more corporations, if (1) each corporation is a member of either a parent-subsidiary controlled group or a brother-sister controlled group, and (2) at least one of the corporations is the common parent of a parent-subsidiary controlled group and also is a member of a brother-sister controlled group.[8] For example, if an individual owns 80 percent of the total combined voting power of corporations X and Y, and Y owns 80 percent of the total combined voting power of corporation Z, then X, Y and Z are members of a combined group.[9] Several special rules apply in determining whether a controlled group of corporations exists, including limitations on what constitutes "stock" and an elaborate set of attribution rules similar to those under Section 318.[10]

A corporation generally qualifies as a "component member" of a controlled group of corporations for a taxable year if it is a member on the December 31 that falls within that taxable year.[11] If a corporation is not a member on December 31, it still can be treated as a member for its taxable year if it was a member at some point during the calendar year and was a member for at least one-half of the number of days during its taxable year that preceded December 31.[12] Certain corporations, referred to as "excluded corporations," cannot be component members. Among the excluded corporations are certain corporations that are exempt from tax under Section 501(a) and foreign corporations that are not engaged in a trade or business in the United States.[13] In some cases, a corporation may qualify as a component member of more than one controlled group. Section 1563(b)(4) makes clear that a corporation in this situation can be a member of only one controlled group, and the regulations provide rules for determining to which group it belongs.[14]

Broader Significance of a Controlled Group of Corporations. Section 1561 is one of many provisions in the Code that make use of Section 1563(a)'s definition of a "controlled group of corporations."[15] The definition thus has significance that extends beyond dividing up the four specific tax benefits targeted by Section 1561. Some of these provisions are similar to Section 1561 in that they limit the aggregate amount of a specific tax benefit available to a controlled group of corporations. For example, a

7.   I.R.C. § 1563(a)(2).

8.   I.R.C. § 1563(a)(3).

9.   Reg. § 1.1563–1(a)(2)(ii) Example 1.

10.   I.R.C. §§ 1563(c), (e).

11.   I.R.C. § 1563(b)(1)(A).

12.   I.R.C. § 1563(b)(1)(B), (b)(3).

13.   I.R.C. § 1563(b)(1)(A), (b)(2).

14.   Reg. § 1.1563–1(c).

15.   Section 1563 has a modified definition of a brother-sister controlled group that generally applies to other Code provisions. See I.R.C. § 1563(f)(5).

controlled group is limited to one $25,000 amount for purposes of computing the general business credit limitation under Section 38.[16] Similarly, the component members of a controlled group are treated as one taxpayer for purposes of deducting the cost of Section 179 property.[17] In other cases, provisions of the Code use Section 1563(a)'s definition for a slightly different purpose and with a different ownership threshold. For example, Section 267 provides that, in the case of property transferred from one member of a controlled group to another member, any loss realized on the transfer cannot be recognized until the property is transferred outside the controlled group.[18] For this purpose, Section 1563(a) is applied with a "more than 50 percent" rather than an "at least 80 percent" ownership threshold.[19]

3. SECTION 482

Code: § 482.

Regulations: §§ 1.482–1(a), (b), (c)(1).

a. INTRODUCTION

If a novice in the field of taxation were asked to peruse the Code and select several provisions that he or she thought were of most significance, Section 482 might seem an unlikely candidate. Weighing in at slightly more than 125 words, it could easily be perceived as innocuous. Nothing could be further from the truth. The sparse language of Section 482 is the statutory tip of a large and complex iceberg on which many a taxpayer has run aground.

Section 482 represents a broad Congressional grant of power to the Service to reallocate income, deductions and other tax items among certain commonly controlled taxpayers when the reallocation is necessary to prevent evasion of taxes or clearly to reflect income. Although originally designed to apply principally in the domestic context, Section 482 is of most significance today in international transactions, such as sales of goods by a foreign parent to its U.S. subsidiary. As one might expect of such a broad grant of authority, Section 482 has become one of the Service's principal weapons in its fight against devices used by taxpayers to reduce their tax liability and has spawned a large body of administrative guidance and judicial decisions.

b. STATUTORY ELEMENTS

Section 482 permits the Service to reallocate tax items when three basic elements are present: (1) there are two or more organizations, trades or businesses, (2) that are owned or controlled by the same interests, and

---

16. I.R.C. § 38(c)(4)(B).

17. I.R.C. § 179(d)(6), (7).

18. I.R.C. § 267(a)(1), (b)(3), (f).

19. I.R.C. § 267(f)(1)(A).

(3) the reallocation is necessary to prevent evasion of taxes or clearly to reflect the income of any of the organizations, trades or businesses.

Much of the power conferred by Section 482 derives from the broad meanings of the terms "organization" and "trade or business."[1] This first element is satisfied regardless of whether the taxpayers in question are incorporated, are domestic or foreign, or are affiliated.[2] Sole proprietorships, partnerships, trusts and estates (as well as corporations) all are subject to Section 482.[3] In several contexts, taxpayers have challenged Section 482 adjustments on the ground that the transaction in question did not involve two or more organizations, trades or businesses.[4] In the typical case, however, there is little dispute concerning this first element. When the Service proposes to reallocate income to a U.S. subsidiary from its foreign parent, for example, it generally is clear that two or more business entities are involved.

The second element similarly has received an expansive interpretation and typically is not the subject of most current disputes under Section 482 between taxpayers and the Service. According to the statute, ownership or control can be direct or indirect. The regulations elaborate on this by providing that "controlled" means any kind of control, whether or not legally enforceable, and that "[i]t is the reality of the control that is decisive, not its form or the mode of its exercise."[5] Control thus might exist as a result of a common interest between two otherwise unrelated taxpayers. For example in B. Forman Co. v. Commissioner,[6] two unrelated corporations operating competing department stores formed a new corporation to construct and operate an enclosed shopping mall and office complex, with each shareholder receiving 50 percent of the new corporation's stock and equal representation on its board. Finding that the common control requirement was satisfied, the court upheld the Service's authority to impose an arm's length interest rate on interest-free loans that the shareholders made to the new corporation.

The third element generally is "where the action is" in Section 482 disputes. Because Section 482 itself provides no standard regarding when it is necessary to make allocations to prevent tax evasion or clearly to reflect

---

1. Prior to 1934, the predecessor of Section 482 referred only to trades or businesses. In that year, Congress added the reference to organizations "to remove any doubt as to the application of this section to all kinds of business activity." H.R. Rep. No. 704, 73d Cong., 2d Sess. (1934), reprinted in 1939–1 (Part 2) C.B. 554, 572.

2. I.R.C. § 482.

3. Reg. § 1.482–1(i)(1).

4. See, e.g., Foglesong v. Commissioner, 691 F.2d 848 (7th Cir.1982) (individual and personal service corporation for which taxpayer performs services on an exclusive basis do not constitute two or more organizations, trades or businesses), nonacq., Rev. Rul. 88–38, 1988–1 C.B. 246; Asiatic Petroleum Co. v. Commissioner, 79 F.2d 234, 237 (2d Cir.) (holding company's sole activity of holding stock constitutes a business), cert. denied, 296 U.S. 645, 56 S.Ct. 248 (1935).

5. Reg. § 1.482–1(i)(4). If income or deductions are arbitrarily shifted between organizations or trades or businesses, a presumption of control arises. Id.

6. 453 F.2d 1144 (2d Cir.), cert. denied, 407 U.S. 934, 92 S.Ct. 2458 (1972).

income, the extensive interpretive regulations, administrative rulings, and judicial decisions are the main sources of guidance.

c. ALLOCATION STANDARD AND METHODS

The standard that the Service applies in examining transactions between commonly controlled taxpayers is that of uncontrolled taxpayers dealing with each other at arm's length.[7] That is, the Service compares the results of a transaction between commonly controlled taxpayers with those of a comparable transaction under comparable circumstances between uncontrolled taxpayers.[8] If the results of the two transactions are consistent, then the controlled transaction satisfies the arm's length standard.

For example, suppose that FP, a French manufacturer of perfume, distributes its finished products in the United States by selling them for resale to two U.S. corporations: Company A, a wholly owned subsidiary of FP, and Company B, a corporation not under common ownership or control with either FP or Company A. If the products that FP sells to Companies A and B are identical and the transactions between FP and Company A and FP and Company B are the same in all material respects (e.g., volume of sales and point of delivery), then the Service likely would determine whether the FP–Company A transactions satisfy the arm's length standard by comparing them with FP–Company B transactions. Thus, if FP sells the same product to Company A for $45 per bottle and to Company B for $20 per bottle, then, absent some factor that accounts for this difference, the Service likely would reallocate income from FP to Company A to ensure that the taxpayers do not use pricing to keep artificially low the income earned by the FP–Company A group that is subject to U.S. tax. The reallocation would be from FP to Company A because, by raising the price charged to Company A, FP effectively allocates a larger portion of income to its own taxing jurisdiction. That is, if Companies A and B both sell the same bottle of perfume in the U.S. for $50, Company B will realize a profit of $30 that is subject to U.S. tax. Absent a reallocation of income, Company A will realize a profit of only $5. In this simple example, the Service would reallocate $25 of income to Company A and thereby render that additional income subject to U.S. tax.

In determining whether an "uncontrolled" transaction is a comparable transaction under comparable circumstances, a variety of factors must be considered, such as the contractual terms of the controlled and uncontrolled transactions (e.g., volume of sales or purchases) and the degree of financial and other risks that the parties in each transaction assume.[9] Further, the regulations promulgated under Section 482 provide several methods for determining whether the results of a controlled transaction are at arm's length and, if they are not, for determining the appropriate arm's length result.[10] These methods often are referred to as "transfer pricing

---

7. Reg. § 1.482–1(b)(1).

8. Id.; Reg. § 1.482–1(d)(1).

9. Reg. § 1.482–1(d)(1).

6.

10. See Reg. §§ 1.482–2 through 1.482–

methodologies." The particular method that applies will depend in part on the type of transaction at issue. For example, the methods prescribed for a transfer of tangible property differ from those prescribed for a transfer of intangible property.[11] In choosing among the available methods, the "best method rule" dictates that the arm's length result of a controlled transaction be determined under the method that "provides the most reliable measure of an arm's length result."[12]

d. COLLATERAL ADJUSTMENTS

When the Service makes an adjustment under Section 482 with respect to one commonly controlled taxpayer, it also makes collateral adjustments to any other commonly controlled taxpayers involved.[13] The other taxpayer must reflect the collateral adjustment in the documents that it maintains for U.S. tax purposes.[14] A collateral adjustment might have an immediate effect, a deferred effect, or no effect at all (e.g., if the other taxpayer is not subject to U.S. tax and the collateral adjustment has no effect on intercorporate transfers). For example, if the Service uses Section 482 to impute interest income to a U.S. parent with respect to an interest-free loan that the parent makes to its foreign subsidiary, the foreign subsidiary must reflect imputed interest payments in the books that it maintains for U.S. tax purposes. The likely effect would be a decrease in the subsidiary's earnings and profits, which in turn would affect the tax treatment of dividends that the subsidiary pays to the U.S. parent.[15]

e. COMMON TRANSACTIONS

Although the Service has the authority to apply Section 482 to virtually any type of transaction between commonly controlled taxpayers, the regulations set forth five categories of transactions that are most likely to trigger adjustments. These are: (1) loans and advances,[16] (2) the performance of services,[17] (3) the use of tangible property (such as a lease of business premises),[18] (4) sales of tangible property,[19] and (5) the sale or use of intangible property.[20] In each case, the regulations provide guidelines—with varying degrees of specificity—for determining an arm's length result.

Transfers of intangible property such as copyrights, trademarks and patents historically have distinguished themselves as particularly difficult transactions to analyze under the arm's length standard, in part because of the common lack of comparable uncontrolled transactions. In 1986, Congress amended Section 482 by adding a second sentence, commonly referred

---

11. Compare Reg. § 1.482–3(a) with Reg. § 1.482–4.

12. Reg. § 1.482–1(c)(1); see also Reg. § 1.482–8.

13. Reg. § 1.482–1(g)(1) & (2).

14. Reg. § 1.482–1(g)(2)(ii).

15. Reg. § 1.482–1(g)(2)(iv) Example 3.

16. Reg. § 1.482–2(a). The application of Section 482 to loans with below-market interest rates has been superseded to a large extent by Section 7872.

17. Reg. § 1.482–2(b).

18. Reg. § 1.482–2(c).

19. Reg. § 1.482–3.

20. Reg. § 1.482–4.

to as the "super-royalty" provision, which requires that the income derived from a transfer of intangible property "be commensurate with the income attributable to the intangible." The provision was enacted in part as a result of concern that U.S. taxpayers were developing intangible property in the U.S.—often with the assistance of tax benefits designed to encourage such development—and then insulating the income generated by the intangible from U.S. tax by transferring the intangible to a foreign affiliate at a bargain price.[21] The super-royalty provision addresses this concern by directing that the adequacy of the consideration received by the transferor of an intangible (whether received in a lump sum or periodically) be determined by comparing the consideration with the income derived from the intangible by the transferee.[22] The "commensurate with income" standard generally must be satisfied not only in the year when the intangible is first transferred but also in all subsequent years that the arrangement between the controlled taxpayers is in effect.[23]

f. OTHER ISSUES

Advance Pricing Agreements. Disputes regarding the proper application of Section 482 to a transaction can be extraordinarily time consuming and expensive for everyone involved, particularly if the dispute leads to litigation.[24] In an effort to avoid such disputes, the Service has implemented a procedure under which taxpayers can secure an "advance pricing agreement" with the Service on how Section 482 will apply to one or more transactions between a taxpayer and other parties under common control.[25] The taxpayer initiates the process by proposing transfer pricing methodologies and data to show that the suggested methodologies are the best method for determining arm's length results between the taxpayer and specified affiliates.[26] The Service evaluates the taxpayer's request and if, after discussion, the proposal is acceptable, the parties execute an advance

---

21. H.R. Rep. No. 426, 99th Cong., 1st Sess. 423–425 (1986), reprinted in 1986–3 (vol. 2) C.B. 1, 423–425.

22. A 1988 study conducted by the Treasury Department, commonly known as the "White Paper," describes in detail the legislative, judicial and administrative history of Section 482, with particular emphasis on intangibles. U.S. Dep't of the Treasury, A Study of Intercompany Pricing Under Section 482 of the Code (1988), reprinted in Notice 88–123, 1988–2 C.B. 458. The White Paper reflects Treasury's preliminary analysis of the major problems encountered in administering Section 482 and the proper methods for determining arm's length prices with respect to transfers of intangibles. Many of the concepts set forth in the White Paper have been refined and incorporated in the current Section 482 regulations.

23. Reg. § 1.482–4(f)(2)(i). If the transferor receives consideration in a lump sum, the lump sum is treated as an advance payment of a stream of royalties payable over the shorter of the useful life of the intangible and the duration of the agreement between the parties. Reg. § 1.482–4(f)(5). That is, the lump sum must be converted into an equivalent stream of annual royalty payments taking into account certain specified factors, and each year the deemed royalty payment must satisfy the commensurate with income standard.

24. See, e.g., Ciba–Geigy Corp. v. Commissioner, 85 T.C. 172 (1985) (IRS challenge to royalties paid by U.S. subsidiary to Swiss parent in tax years 1965 through 1969 decided in 1985).

25. Rev. Proc. 96–53, 1996–2 C.B. 375.

26. Id. at § 2.

pricing agreement covering the proposed methodologies.[27] Although seeking an advance pricing agreement is by no means a small undertaking, the process can be significantly less burdensome than the alternative of an audit, administrative appeals and litigation.

Penalties and Reporting Requirements. In its 1988 study of intercompany transfer pricing, commonly known as the White Paper,[28] the Treasury Department identified the government's lack of access to taxpayer information and delay on the part of taxpayers in providing requested information as major problems in the government's efforts to administer Section 482. Since then, legislation strengthening the applicable penalty and reporting requirements has given the government some significant assistance in overcoming these obstacles.

In general, a taxpayer faces a 20 percent (and, in some cases, 40 percent) penalty if either (1) the taxpayer files a return that overstates or understates the price paid for property or services by more than a specified percentage of the amount determined to be correct under Section 482,[29] or (2) the Service makes Section 482 allocations that result in a net increase in the taxpayer's taxable income that exceeds a threshold amount.[30] Taxpayers can avoid the penalty in the second situation by reasonably using a method specified in the regulations for determining transfer prices (or, in some circumstances, another appropriate method), maintaining adequate contemporaneous documentation of the method used, and providing this documentation to the government within thirty days of the government's request.[31] A taxpayer desiring to minimize the risk of penalties resulting from a Section 482 adjustment thus may have to devote substantial time and resources at the time of a transaction to documenting the manner in which intercompany prices are determined. A taxpayer desirous of more certainty that penalties will not apply might consider seeking an advance pricing agreement.

As a result of the same concerns that prompted the penalty provisions discussed above, certain taxpayers are required to report to the government (and maintain adequate records with respect to) transactions with related parties. Generally, both U.S. corporations that are 25 percent foreign-owned and foreign corporations engaged in a trade or business in the U.S. are subject to this requirement.[32] Failure to comply can result in substantial penalties.[33]

---

27. Id.

28. Notice 88–123, 1988–2 C.B. 458. See supra note 22.

29. I.R.C. §§ 6662(e)(1)(B)(i); 6662(h).

30. I.R.C. §§ 6662(e)(1)(B)(ii); 6662(h). Taxpayers are subject to the 20 percent penalty if the net increase in taxable income resulting from a Section 482 adjustment exceeds the lesser of $5 million and 10 percent of the taxpayer's gross receipts.

31. I.R.C. § 6662(e)(3)(B).

32. I.R.C. §§ 6038A; 6038C.

33. I.R.C. §§ 6038A(d); 6038C(c). In comparison with Section 6038A, Section 6038C authorizes the Treasury Department to require corporations subject to the statute to maintain a broader range of records and to report a broader range of information. I.R.C. § 6038C(a)(2), (b)(2).

Proposed Changes to Section 482. Despite Section 482's broad grant of power to the Executive Branch, some tax policymakers have expressed the belief that certain taxpayers, particularly foreign-owned corporations, continue to use transactions with related parties to shift large amounts of income from the U.S. to foreign jurisdictions.[34] A 1992 proposal[35] would have amended Section 482 by requiring certain foreign corporations doing business in the U.S. and foreign-owned U.S. corporations to recognize a minimum amount of U.S. taxable income if they have more than a threshold level of transactions with foreign related parties. In general, the minimum U.S. taxable income for an affected corporation was a percentage of the corporation's gross receipts. The percentage was to be established by reference to data derived from domestic corporations in the same industry. Thus, the proposed legislation was designed to ensure that foreign and foreign-owned corporations report a level of income commensurate with that reported by a similarly-situated purely domestic corporation.

This proposal received harsh criticism on a number of grounds, including the soundness of its assumption that foreign-owned corporations with incomes below the industry average are shifting income and the possibility that the proposal violates provisions of tax treaties to which the U.S. is a party.[36] Although the proposal never became law, Congress's constant search for new revenue makes it quite possible that this or a similar provision could be resurrected.

B.   CONSOLIDATED RETURNS

Code §§ 1501; 1502; 1503(a); 1504(a) & (b); 1552. Skim § 243(a)(3), (b)(1) & (2)(A).

1.   INTRODUCTION

Earlier in this chapter, we saw that the Code limits certain tax benefits available to affiliated corporations by treating the corporations, for pur-

---

34. See, e.g., Hearings Before the Subcomm. on Oversight of the House Comm. on Ways and Means, 102d Cong., 2d Sess. (1992) (statement of the Honorable J.J. Pickle, Chairman of the Subcomm. on Oversight) ("The fact of the matter is that, in our society, a teacher or factory worker can pay more in Federal income tax than a major multinational corporation with billions in annual U.S. sales."); Hearings Before the Subcomm. on Oversight of the House Comm. on Ways and Means, 101st Cong., 2d Sess. (1990) (statement of Fred T. Goldberg, Jr., Commissioner of Internal Revenue) ("[T]he aggregate data, and our own examination activities, suggest that foreign controlled companies have adopted transfer pricing and other practices that may significantly understate their U.S. income tax liabilities.").

35. H.R. 5270 (1992), entitled the Foreign Income Tax Rationalization and Simplification Act of 1992, designating the current statutory language as Section 482(a) and adding a new Section 482(b).

36. The proposal was described as being "strongly opposed by the Treasury and, for that matter, by virtually everyone else." Bittker & Eustice, Federal Income Taxation of Corporations and Shareholders ¶ 13.20[4][i] (7th ed. 2000).

poses of determining their entitlement to the benefits, as a single taxpayer.[1] In this section, we explore a related concept: certain closely affiliated corporations are permitted to calculate and report their federal tax liability as if they were a single taxpaying unit.

As a general rule, every corporation subject to the federal income tax must report its tax liability on a separate return.[2] Section 1501 is an exception to this rule. Section 1501 permits an affiliated group of corporations to elect to report its tax liability on a single, consolidated return. The Code, however, provides little guidance on the manner in which an affiliated group must prepare a consolidated return. Congress has delegated that task to the Secretary of the Treasury, who is directed by Section 1502 to issue regulations. Rising to the occasion, the Treasury Department has issued extensive, detailed regulations that are the primary source of guidance on consolidated returns.

In reading the material that follows, consider the extent to which the consolidated return rules truly treat an affiliated group of corporations as a single entity. As you will discover, certain rules fully reflect a single entity model. Others continue to recognize the separate existence of each corporation in the group (a "separate entity" model). This conflict in the regulations is the source of much of their complexity.

2. ELIGIBILITY AND ELECTION TO FILE A CONSOLIDATED RETURN

a. ELIGIBILITY

Section 1501 grants the privilege of filing a consolidated return only to an "affiliated group of corporations." The term "affiliated group" is defined in Section 1504(a) as one or more chains of "includible corporations" connected through stock ownership to a common parent that is an includible corporation, if (1) the common parent owns directly stock possessing at least 80 percent of the total voting power and total value of the stock of at least one of the other includible corporations, and (2) stock possessing at least 80 percent of the total voting power and total value of the stock of each includible corporation (other than the common parent) is owned directly by one or more of the other includible corporations.[1] Thus, if corporation X owns stock possessing 80 percent of the total voting power and total value of corporations Y and Z, and if X, Y and Z all are includible corporations, then X, Y and Z are members of an affiliated group of corporations. The result would be the same if Z were an 80 percent-owned subsidiary of Y (i.e., if Z were a second-tier subsidiary of X).

The term "includible corporation" is defined in Section 1504(b) as any corporation, with seven specific exceptions. Among the corporations excluded from the definition are corporations exempt from tax under Section 501,

---

1. See Section A2 of this chapter, supra.

2. I.R.C. § 6012(a)(2); Reg. § 1.6012–2(a).

1. Several special rules modify the definition of "includible corporation." See I.R.C. § 1504(c)–(f).

insurance companies subject to tax under Section 801, and all foreign corporations.[2] Historically, S corporations by definition could not be a member of an affiliated group because they were not permitted to have subsidiaries. Under current law, however, S corporations may have both C and S corporation subsidiaries, but they are not allowed to join in the filing of a consolidated return with their C corporation affiliates.[3]

In determining whether an affiliated group of corporations exists, Section 1504(a)(4) provides that nonvoting, nonconvertible stock which is limited and preferred as to dividends and has redemption and liquidation rights which do not exceed the stock's issue price, except for a reasonable premium, is disregarded. The features described in Section 1504(a)(4) are those commonly associated with preferred stock. Merely because stock is labelled as preferred stock, however, does not mean that it is ignored in applying the stock ownership requirements of Section 1504(a); only stock that has each of the features listed in Section 1504(a)(4) is ignored. This provision generally is favorable to taxpayers in that it permits a corporation to raise capital by issuing stock described in Section 1504(a)(4) without making the corporation ineligible to join in the filing of a consolidated return.[4]

If a corporation is included (or required to be included) in a consolidated return filed by an affiliated group and subsequently ceases to be a member of the group, the corporation cannot be included in a consolidated return filed by the group (or certain related groups) during the succeeding five years.[5] This is an anti-abuse rule intended to foreclose the temporary elimination of a member from an affiliated group in order to improve the group's or the member's tax results. The Secretary of the Treasury has authority to waive this five-year waiting period under conditions that the Secretary prescribes.[6]

b.   ELECTION AND RELATED MATTERS

Even if two or more corporations constitute an affiliated group, the corporations must file separate returns unless they affirmatively elect to exercise their privilege of filing a consolidated return. An affiliated group exercises this privilege by filing a consolidated return not later than the last day prescribed by law (including extensions) for filing the common

---

2. Several special rules modify the definition of "includible corporation." See I.R.C. § 1504(c)–(f).

3. I.R.C. § 1504(b)(8). The C corporation affiliates still may file as a consolidated group, but without including their S corporation parent. See Chapter 15B, infra.

4. Sections 1504(a)(5)(A) and (B) similarly address what constitutes "stock" by directing the Secretary of the Treasury to issue regulations that treat (1) warrants, obligations convertible into stock and other similar interests as stock and stock as not stock,

and (2) options to acquire or sell stock as having been exercised. See Reg. § 1.1504–4.

5. I.R.C. § 1504(a)(3)(A). More precisely, the corporation cannot again be included in a consolidated return filed by the group before the sixty-first month beginning after the corporation's first taxable year in which it ceased to be a member of the group. Id.

6. I.R.C. § 1504(a)(3)(B). The general circumstances under which a waiver will be granted are set forth in Rev. Proc. 2003–32, 2002–1 C.B. 959.

parent's return.[7] As one might expect in such a regime, a consolidated return must be filed on the basis of the common parent's taxable year, and each subsidiary in the group must adopt the common parent's taxable year beginning with the first consolidated return year[8] for which the subsidiary's income is includible in the consolidated return.[9] In contrast, the method of accounting that each member of the group must use is determined without regard to the method used by the common parent.[10]

As a condition to the privilege of filing a consolidated return, Section 1501 requires that all corporations that were members of the affiliated group at any time during the taxable year consent to all of the regulations prescribed under Section 1502 that are in existence on the last day prescribed by law for filing the return. This requirement presumably is designed to minimize taxpayer challenges to the regulations.[11] In general, a corporation consents to the regulations by joining in the making of a consolidated return.[12]

The decision to file a consolidated return is a significant one, in part because an affiliated group that does so generally must continue to file on a consolidated basis for all succeeding tax years unless the group no longer remains in existence or the Secretary grants permission to discontinue filing for "good cause."[13] In general, an affiliated group no longer remains in existence if the common parent no longer remains as the common parent (e.g., if the parent sells the stock of all of its subsidiaries to one or more third parties).[14] The Service generally grants permission to discontinue filing for good cause only when there are certain changes in the Code or regulations that have a substantial adverse effect on the group's consolidated tax liability relative to the aggregate tax liability the members would incur if they filed separate returns, or when certain other factors demonstrate that there exists good cause for the discontinuance.[15] In short, the decision to file a consolidated return is one with which an affiliated group likely will have to live for an extended period of time.

3.   COMPUTATION OF CONSOLIDATED TAXABLE INCOME

a.   OVERVIEW

An affiliated group of corporations that files (or is required to file) a consolidated return is referred to in the regulations as a "consolidated group."[1] A consolidated group is subject to federal income tax on its

---

7.   Reg. § 1.1502–75(a)(1).

8.   A consolidated return year is a taxable year for which a consolidated return is filed or required to be filed. Reg. § 1.1502–1(d).

9.   Reg. § 1.1502–76(a)(1).

10.   Reg. § 1.1502–17(a).

11.   Not all taxpayers are so easily dissuaded. See American Standard, Inc. v. United States, 602 F.2d 256 (Ct.Cl.1979) (successful challenge to regulations).

12.   I.R.C. § 1501; Reg. § 1.1502–75(b)(1).

13.   Reg. § 1.1502–75(a)(2), (c)(1), (d)(1).

14.   Reg. § 1.1502–75(d)(1).

15.   Reg. § 1.1502–75(c)(1)(ii), (c)(1)(iii).

1.   Reg. § 1.1502–1(a), (h).

consolidated taxable income.[2]

The first step in determining a group's consolidated taxable income is to determine the separate taxable income (or loss) of each member.[3] Each member's separate taxable income must be determined by making several adjustments, the most significant of which are (1) the adjustments that take into account transactions between members of the group (so-called "intercompany transactions") and transactions that relate to the stock, bonds and other obligations of the members (such as intercompany distributions), and (2) the omission of certain items of income and deduction that must be determined on a consolidated basis.[4] After these adjustments, the separate taxable incomes of the members are combined. Next, the items of income and deduction that must be determined on a consolidated basis are calculated in accordance with the regulations and then added to or subtracted from the combined separate taxable incomes. The resulting amount is the group's consolidated taxable income, which is subject to tax at the rates specified in Section 11. Subject to certain restrictions, the consolidated group is allowed credits against this tax (and the other federal taxes to which it is subject), including the general business and foreign tax credits.[5] For purposes of determining each member's earnings and profits, the group's consolidated tax liability also must be allocated among the members.[6]

b.   COMPUTATION OF SEPARATE TAXABLE INCOME

Intercompany Transactions.[7] As the first step in determining a consolidated group's consolidated taxable income, each member's separate taxable income (or loss) must be determined as if the member were a separate corporation, with certain modifications.[8] One modification is that "intercompany transactions" must be taken into account in accordance with the detailed rules set forth in the regulations. An intercompany transaction is a transaction between corporations that are members of the same consolidated group immediately after the transaction.[9] Examples include sales or

---

2. Reg. § 1.1502–2(a). A consolidated group also is subject to other federal taxes, including the personal holding company tax, the accumulated earnings tax, and the alternative minimum tax. See Reg. § 1.1502–2; Prop. Reg. § 1.1502–2.

3. Reg. § 1.1502–11(a)(1).

4. See Reg. § 1.1502–12(a), –12(b) through (r).

5. Reg. §§ 1502–2; 1.1502–3; 1.1502–4.

6. I.R.C. § 1552.

7. In 1995, the Treasury Department substantially revised the regulations that govern intercompany transactions. These reg-

ulations generally apply to transactions that occur in years beginning on or after July 12, 1995. Reg. § 1.1502–13(*l*)(1). Unless otherwise noted, references in this chapter to the regulations governing intercompany transactions are to the 1995 regulations. Although there are significant differences in the terminology and analysis employed in the old and new regulations, the results for most common intercompany transactions are the same under each version. See Preamble to Final Intercompany Transaction Regulations, T.D. 8597, 1995–2 C.B. 6.

8. Reg. § 1.1502–11(a)(1), –12

9. Reg. § 1.1502–13(b)(1)(i).

rentals of property, the performance of services, the licensing of technology (such as a patent), and the lending of money.[10]

The essence of the rules governing intercompany transactions can best be understood by first considering the effect of a transaction between two divisions of a single corporation. For example, assume that corporation X has two divisions, S and B, and that division S transfers land with a fair market value of $100 and a basis of $70 to division B in exchange for $100 cash. No taxable event occurs as a result of the transfers because corporation X continues to hold both the land and the cash. Corporation X would retain a $70 basis in the land and the transaction would have no effect on X's taxable income. If, three years later, division B sells the land to an unrelated third party for $110, then corporation X would realize and recognize $40 of income at that time. The character and other tax attributes of this income generally would depend on the activities of divisions S and B with respect to the land.[11] Similarly, if division S leases office space to division B in exchange for an annual rental payment of $100, corporation X's taxable income would be unaffected because the arrangement would constitute a mere shifting of assets within one taxable entity.

The regulations governing intercompany transactions contain a "matching rule" and an "acceleration rule" that generally attempt to approximate the results of a transaction between divisions of a single corporation. Before illustrating this point, the rather complex terminology employed by the regulations deserves some mention. The regulations refer to the selling member in a transaction as "S" and to the buying member as "B." S's items of income, gain, deduction and loss from an intercompany transaction are referred to as its "intercompany items."[12] B's tax items arising from an intercompany transaction (or property acquired in an intercompany transaction) are referred to as "corresponding items."[13] A "recomputed corresponding item" is the corresponding item that B would take into account if S and B were divisions in a single corporation and the intercompany transaction were between those divisions.[14]

To return to the illustrations set forth above in the context of a consolidated return, assume that corporations S and B are at all relevant times members of a consolidated group and that, in year 1, S sells land with a fair market value of $100 and a basis of $70 to B for $100 cash. In year 3, B sells the land to an unrelated third party for $110. The sale from S to B is an intercompany transaction, and the $30 gain realized by S is S's intercompany item. Under the matching rule prescribed by the regulations, S takes its intercompany gain into account in computing its separate

---

10. Id.

11. For example, the character of the income as capital gain, Section 1231 gain, or ordinary income generally would depend on whether corporation X held the land for investment, for use in its trade or business, or for sale to customers in the ordinary course of its business. Determining the purpose for which X held the land would require an evaluation of the purposes for which divisions S and B held the land.

12. Reg. § 1.1502–13(b)(2)(i).

13. Reg. § 1.1502–13(b)(3)(i).

14. Reg. § 1.1502–13(b)(4).

taxable income only when B takes into account its corresponding item.[15] B has no corresponding item in year 1, and therefore S's $30 gain is deferred. In year 3, B realizes a gain of $10 ($110 amount realized less $100 basis in the land),[16] which is B's corresponding item. B must take this $10 into account in accordance with its method of accounting.[17] Assume that under B's method of accounting B takes the $10 gain into account in year 3 in computing its separate taxable income. Under the matching rule, S takes its $30 intercompany gain into account to reflect the difference between B's corresponding item ($10) and the recomputed corresponding item, i.e., the gain that B would have taken into account in year 3 if S and B were divisions of a single corporation. If S and B were divisions, B would have received the land from S with a $70 basis and therefore would have realized on the sale in year 3 a $40 gain, which is the recomputed corresponding item. Thus, S would take into account in year 3 the difference between this recomputed corresponding item ($40) and B's corresponding item ($10), or $30.

The result in this example is similar to the illustration above when S and B were divisions of a single corporation. There, as here, no gain with respect to the land was taken into account in determining taxable income until the land was transferred to a third party. In this respect, the regulations treat S and B as parts of a single taxpaying entity. The regulations similarly adopt a single entity approach with respect to the tax attributes of the $40 gain realized by the group, such as the gain's character: the character of S's $30 intercompany gain and B's $10 corresponding gain will depend upon the combined activities of S and B with respect to the land.[18] In other respects, the regulations adopt a separate entity approach. For example, the total $40 gain realized is allocated partly to S and partly to B, each of whom takes its portion of the gain into account in determining its separate taxable income. In general, no similar allocation would take place for tax purposes if S and B were divisions of a single corporation.

The matching rule also would apply to any other intercompany transactions between S and B, such as a lease of office space from S to B in exchange for an annual rental payment of $100. Assuming that B's payments of rent are currently deductible under B's method of accounting, S would take into account as current income the difference between B's $100 rental deduction and the recomputed rental deduction (zero), or $100.[19] Although S and B would take the income and deduction into account in computing their separate taxable incomes, the items effectively would offset

---

15. Reg. § 1.1502–13(c)(2)(ii).

16. B obtained a $100 cost basis in the land under Section 1012 when it purchased the land from S. Reg. § 1.1502–13(a)(2).

17. Reg. § 1.1502–13(c)(2)(i).

18. Reg. § 1.1502–13(c)(1)(i).

19. Reg. § 1.1502–13(c)(7)(ii) Example 8. The recomputed rental deduction is zero because B's payments to S would not generate tax deductions if S and B were divisions of a single corporation.

each other when the separate taxable incomes are combined, so that the transaction generally would have no net effect on the group's consolidated taxable income.

The second cornerstone of the intercompany transaction regulations, the acceleration rule, guards against situations in which S's intercompany items and B's corresponding items cannot be taken into account under the matching rule to produce the effect of treating S and B as divisions of a single corporation.[20] In that case, B continues to take its corresponding items into account in accordance with its method of accounting, but S's intercompany items are taken into account immediately before it first becomes impossible to achieve the effect of treating S and B as divisions, i.e., S's intercompany items are accelerated.[21] To illustrate, assume that immediately after S sells the land to B in year 1 in the example above, the common parent sells all the stock of B to an unrelated third party. Because B no longer is a member of the consolidated group that includes S, the effect of treating S and B as divisions cannot be achieved. The acceleration rule therefore requires S to take its $30 of intercompany gain into account in year 1.[22] B would take any gain or loss on a subsequent sale of the land to a third party into account in accordance with B's method of accounting, and this gain or loss would be reported either on B's separate return or, if B is a member of another consolidated group, on that group's consolidated return.

Even if an item is taken into account under the intercompany transaction rules described above, the item can be deferred or disallowed under another provision. For example, Sections 267(f) (deferral of certain losses), 269 (acquisitions to evade or avoid tax), and 482 (allocations among commonly controlled taxpayers) all potentially may apply.[23]

Intercompany Distributions. The regulations also require adjustments to the separate taxable incomes of group members for certain transactions with respect to a member's stock and other obligations. This discussion will be confined to an overview of the treatment of distributions to which Section 301 applies.[24]

An "intercompany distribution" is an intercompany transaction to which § 301 applies.[25] Thus, an ordinary cash distribution made by corporation S to its parent, corporation P, both of whom are members of the same affiliated group immediately after the distribution, is an intercompany distribution.

Intercompany distributions generally are excluded from the gross income of the distributee member.[26] This exclusion from income is available,

---

20. Reg. § 1.1502–13(d).

21. Reg. § 1.1502–13(d)(1)(i), (d)(2)(ii).

22. See Reg. § 1.1502–13(d)(3) Example 1(e).

23. Reg. § 1.1502–13(a)(4).

24. See Chapter 4, supra.

25. Reg. § 1.1502–13(f)(2)(i).

26. Reg. § 1.1502–13(f)(2)(ii).

however, only to the extent that there is a corresponding negative adjustment in the distributee member's basis in the stock of the distributing member.[27] This negative adjustment is made pursuant to the basis adjustment rules set forth in the regulations.[28] Under the basis adjustment rules, a distribution (and certain other tax items) effectively can reduce the distributee member's basis below zero.[29] This negative amount is referred to as the distributee member's "excess loss account."[30] Thus, provided that the distributee member reduces its basis in the distributing member's stock, the distributee does not recognize gain on an intercompany distribution, even if the distribution exceeds the distributee member's basis.[31] A subsequent disposition of the distributing member's stock, however, will cause the amount of the excess loss account to be included in the distributee member's gross income. In the case of distributions of property, the distributee member generally takes the property with a fair market value basis.[32]

A corporation that distributes appreciated property to its shareholders generally recognizes gain, but not loss.[33] These rules are modified in the context of a consolidated return. From the distributing member's perspective, intercompany distributions of property in effect are treated in the same manner as the intercompany sales of property examined earlier. Thus, if in year 1 distributing member S distributes appreciated property to its parent, member P, and P sells the property to an unrelated third party in year 3, S would not take its gain into account in computing its separate taxable income until year 3.[34] If instead S realizes a loss on the distribution, then the tax consequences to S depend on P's actions with respect to the property. If P sells the property in year 3 to an unrelated third party, and under P's method of accounting P takes into account in that year its gain or loss on the sale, then S would take its loss into account in year 3.[35] In contrast, if P distributes the property to its shareholders and realizes no further gain or loss, then S's loss is disallowed and never taken into account.[36] The general effect of these rules is to treat P and S as divisions of a single corporation: both gain and loss are taken into account if the property is sold outside the group but, in accordance with the general rules of Sections 311(a) and (b), only gain is taken into account if the property is transferred outside the group in a distribution to a shareholder.

27. Id.

28. See Reg. § 1.1502–32. The stock basis adjustment rules are discussed in more detail in Section B4 of this chapter, infra.

29. Reg. § 1.1502–32(a)(3)(ii).

30. Id.

31. This rule, of course, is contrary to the general rule of Section 301(c)(3)(A).

32. I.R.C. § 301(d); Reg. § 1.1502–13(f)(7) Example 1(a).

33. I.R.C. § 311(a), (b).

34. Reg. § 1.1502–13(f)(2)(iii), –13(f)(7) Example 1.

35. See Reg. § 1.1502–13(c)(6)(i), –13(f)(7) Example 1(d). If S distributed the property to a shareholder who is not a member of the affiliated group, however, then S would not recognize its loss under the general rule of Section 311(a). Reg. § 1.1502–13(f)(2)(iii).

36. See Reg. § 1.1502–13(c)(6)(i), –13(f)(7) Example 1(d).

c.   CONSOLIDATED ITEMS

In calculating consolidated taxable income, certain items of income and deduction are taken into account on a consolidated basis. That is, these items generally are omitted in calculating the separate taxable income of each consolidated group member and aggregated with like items from the other members. The net amount of each item is added to or subtracted from the sum of the members' separate taxable incomes (as determined by omitting the consolidated items).[37] The items that must be taken into account on a consolidated basis include capital gain or loss, gain or loss with respect to Section 1231 property, the charitable and dividends received deductions, and the deduction for net operating losses.[38] The regulations provide detailed rules on the manner in which the consolidated amounts of these items must be determined.[39]

Consolidated items may be affected by the intercompany transaction rules. For example, if one member of a consolidated group realizes a capital gain from the sale of property to another member, the selling member's gain may be deferred until a later year. If so, then the gain would not be taken into account in determining the group's consolidated capital gain or loss.[40]

d.   ALLOCATION OF TAX LIABILITY

Once the total tax liability of a consolidated group is determined, the liability must be allocated among the members for purposes of determining each member's earnings and profits.[41] A corporation's federal income tax liability during the year generally reduces its earnings and profits.[42] Among other effects, this reduction in earnings and profits may affect the characterization under Section 301 of distributions made by the members.

Section 1552 provides three methods pursuant to which an affiliated group can make this allocation and also permits the group to select any other allocation method with the approval of the Secretary of the Treasury.[43] Under the first method, the group's tax liability generally is allocated based on the ratio of each member's separate taxable income to the sum of the separate taxable incomes of all members.[44] For this purpose, a member's separate taxable income generally is calculated under the rules discussed earlier (e.g., by applying the intercompany transaction rules) and then adjusted for certain items specified in the regulations.[45] Under the second method, the group's tax liability similarly also is allocated using a

37.   Reg. § 1.1502–11(a).

38.   Id. See Chapter 12B3 for the limitations on the use of a member's net operating loss carryovers.

39.   See Reg. §§ 1.1502–21 (net operating losses); 1.1502–22 (capital gain or loss); 1.1502–23 (Section 1231 property); 1.1502–24 (charitable contributions); 1.1502–26 (dividends received deduction).

40.   See Section B3b of this chapter, infra.

41.   I.R.C. § 1552.

42.   See Chapter 4B, supra.

43.   I.R.C. § 1552(a).

44.   I.R.C. § 1552(a)(1); Reg. § 1.1552–1(a)(1).

45.   Reg. § 1.1552–1(a)(1)(ii).

ratio, but in this case each member's separately computed tax liability is compared to the sum of the members' separately computed tax liabilities.[46] Again, certain adjustments are required in computing the separate tax liability of each member.[47] The third method generally involves comparing each member's tax liability determined on both a consolidated basis (under the first method) and a separate basis (under the second method) and reallocating any increases in tax liability resulting from consolidation (i.e., any excess of the amount allocated to a member under the first method over the amount allocated under the second method) to those members who experience decreases in tax liability due to the consolidation.[48]

The regulations issued under Section 1502 that address adjustments to earnings and profits for members of a consolidated group provide certain additional allocation methods.[49]

4. STOCK BASIS ADJUSTMENTS

Consistent with the general purpose of the consolidated return rules to treat members of an affiliated group as a single taxpaying unit, a member's basis in the stock of another member is adjusted upward or downward to reflect the subsidiary member's distributions and its items of income, gain, deduction and loss.[1] This rolling basis mechanism prevents the shareholder-member ("P") from incurring a second round of corporate level tax, or enjoying a double deduction, with respect to its investment in S when S's income or loss already has been reflected in the group's consolidated return.

In general, P's stock basis is increased by S's taxable and tax-exempt income, and is decreased by S's taxable loss, any noncapital, nondeductible expenses of S, and any distributions that S makes with respect to its stock.[2] The regulations contain a host of special rules for computing each of these items. Contrary to the Code's conventional wisdom that a negative basis is impermissible, the consolidated return rules allow the effective equivalent of a negative basis. When the items that decrease basis reduce P's basis to zero, any further reductions create an "excess loss account."[3] In general, P must take into account as income or gain the amount of its excess loss account when it is treated as having disposed of the S stock.[4]

For example, assume that the S stock held by P has a fair market value of $100 and an adjusted basis of zero, and that during the taxable year S has $10 of tax-exempt income and also makes a $20 distribution to P. The $10 of tax-exempt income would increase P's basis by $10. The $20 distribution would reduce P's basis to zero and also would create a $10 excess loss account. If P then sells the S stock for $100, P will have a $110

---

46. I.R.C. § 1552(a)(2); Reg. § 1.1552–1(a)(2).

47. Reg. § 1.1552–1(a)(2)(ii).

48. I.R.C. § 1552(a)(3); Reg. § 1.1552–1(a)(3).

49. Reg. § 1.1502–33(d).

1. Reg. § 1.1502–32(a)(1).

2. Reg. § 1.1502–32(b)(2).

3. Reg. § 1.1502–32(a)(3)(ii); 1.1502–19(a)(2).

4. Reg. § 1.1502–19(b)(1), (c).

gain ($100 excess of amount realized over adjusted basis plus $10 excess loss account).

5. ADVANTAGES AND DISADVANTAGES OF FILING A CONSOLIDATED RETURN

Given the highly complex rules confronting filers of consolidated returns, one might well ask whether the ordeal is really a "privilege." The answer is that filing a consolidated return is not always advantageous. An affiliated group, with the aid of its accountants and tax counsel, must carefully assess the potential pros and cons. To a large extent, this assessment involves predicting the future direction that the group will take in its business and the likely performance and tax position of each member.

The advantages of filing a consolidated return include the ability to offset income of one member with the losses of another, the exclusion of dividends from the distributee member's gross income, and the ability to defer recognition of gain on intercompany transactions. Disadvantages include compliance with a complex set of regulations, and the permanent nature of the election to file a consolidated return (i.e., the group generally must continue to file a consolidated return even if doing so turns out to be disadvantageous relative to filing separate returns). Thus, an assessment of the desirability of filing a consolidated return involves considering issues such as the extent to which each member will have taxable income or loss, whether any limitations exist on the ability to use losses of one member against income of another, the extent to which the members will engage in intercompany transactions and the effect of the intercompany transaction rules on those transactions, and the likelihood of current members leaving or new members entering the group.

PROBLEMS

1. Corporation P owns 90% of Corporations A and B. Corporations A and B each own 40% of Corporation C. Corporation C owns 80% of Corporation D. Corporation D owns 100% of Corporation E, a tax-exempt organization. Corporation E owns 100% of Corporation F which owns 100% of Corporation G. All of the indicated percentages reflect total voting power and total value owned by the shareholder.

  (a) To what extent do the above corporations constitute an "affiliated group"?

  (b) What result in (a), above, if Corporation B sells 10% of its stock in Corporation C?

2. P, Inc. owns all of the only class of S, Inc. stock, and P and S are in a consolidated group. During year 1, P performs services for S in exchange for $10,000, and P incurs $8,000 of expenses in performing those services. Assume that S must capitalize its $10,000 cost for the services and takes into account $1,000 of cost recovery deductions in each of years 2 through 11. How will the P–S consolidated group be taxed on this transaction?

CHAPTER 14

ANTI–AVOIDANCE PROVISIONS

A. INTRODUCTION

The preceding chapters have demonstrated that C corporations and their shareholders historically have sought to lessen the impact of the double tax on corporate profits, avoid the higher marginal individual tax rates on ordinary income, and convert ordinary income to capital gain. Congress has responded with a host of anti-avoidance rules, many targeting discrete problems and others seeking a more global solution to errant taxpayer behavior.

This chapter examines two anti-avoidance provisions that have been major roadblocks to taxpayer exploitation of Subchapter C: the accumulated earnings tax and the personal holding company tax. These penalty taxes were designed to prevent taxpayers from escaping the higher individual tax rates by accumulating operating income of a business in a more lightly taxed C corporation or using the corporation as a vehicle to reduce the tax burden on personal service and investment income. The complex penalty regimes remain intact in the Code, but their importance has diminished now that the top corporate and individual rates are the same and long-term capital gains and dividends received by noncorporate shareholders are taxed at the same preferential rate.

For the benefit of corporate tax historians and others with a need to know, this chapter attempts to provide an overview of the two penalty taxes by exploring their contours without becoming distracted by too many details.

B. THE ACCUMULATED EARNINGS TAX

1. INTRODUCTION

For most of our income tax history, the graduated rates applicable to individuals greatly exceeded the relatively flat corporate rates. During the 1950's, the top corporate rate was roughly 50 percent while individuals were taxed at rates ranging up to 88 percent. This rate gap provided an incentive for taxpayers to accumulate business profits or investment income in a corporation. As Professors Bittker and Eustice once said, "use of a corporation as a temporary or permanent refuge from individual income tax rates has been one of the principal landmarks of our tax landscape."[1]

---

1. Bittker & Eustice, Federal Income Taxation of Corporations and Shareholders ¶ 1.02 (5th ed. 1987).

To illustrate a typical accumulation plan that would have invited the tax collector's scrutiny, consider the goals of Accumulator ("A"), a sole proprietor with a profitable business in the days of the 70 percent individual marginal rates. Tempted by the allure of the lower corporate tax rate, A incorporates his business with a healthy (but permissible) dose of debt and pays himself a hefty (but reasonable) salary. His personal consumption needs are fully satisfied by the salary, the interest payments on the debt, and as many nontaxable fringe benefits as the corporation can legally provide. Any additional profits from the business are left to accumulate in the corporation, where they work to increase the value of A's stock. If A needs more funds or later wishes to retire, he can "cash in" on his accumulated profits by selling some stock or liquidating the company, in either case reporting those profits as favored long-term capital gain. An even more attractive alternative would be to avoid entirely the individual income tax by holding the stock until death, when A's heirs would be entitled to a stepped-up basis under Section 1014. Or A might dispose of the business in a tax-free reorganization, emerging with publicly traded stock, albeit with a low substituted basis, which could be sold or held until A's death.[2]

The accumulated earnings tax was enacted to prevent the use of a C corporation to escape the individual income tax by an unreasonable accumulation of earnings. Although not part of its original design, it also serves the broader purpose of inducing corporations to pay dividends and subject their earnings to the double tax when those profits are not required for the reasonable needs of the business.[3]

For a brief time between 1987 and 1992, the corporate income tax rates exceeded the individual rates—an inversion from the historic norm that caused some commentators to propose repeal of the accumulated earnings tax on the ground that it was no longer necessary.[4] Under current law, the top individual and corporate rates are the same. This rate parity, along with the introduction of a preferential rate on dividends received by noncorporate shareholders, has reduced the incentive to organize a business as a C corporation. As a result, the accumulated earnings tax is less influential, but its lurking presence still may act as an enforcer of the double tax regime by encouraging profitable companies to distribute some of their earnings as dividends.

2.   THE PROSCRIBED TAX AVOIDANCE PURPOSE

Code: §§ 531; 532.

The accumulated earnings tax is a penalty imposed on a corporation "formed or availed of for the purpose of avoiding the income tax with

---

2. See I.R.C. §§ 354; 358; 368.

3. See Staff of Senate Finance Committee, Preliminary Report on the Reform and Simplification of the Income Taxation of Corporations, 98th Cong., 1st Sess. 23 (Comm. Print S. 98–95, 1983).

4. See, e.g., Wolfman, "Subchapter C and the 100th Congress," 33 Tax Notes 669, 674 (Nov. 17, 1986).

respect to its shareholders * * * by permitting earnings and profits to accumulate instead of being divided or distributed."[1] The tax is levied at 15 percent on a C corporation's "accumulated taxable income," which is generally defined as taxable income with certain adjustments (e.g., subtracting taxes and dividends paid and adding back the dividends received deduction) to reflect the true dividend paying capacity of the corporation.[2] Most corporations, regardless of motives, are given an accumulated earnings credit that in effect permits an accumulation of up to $250,000.[3] Although closely held corporations are the principal target of the tax, Section 532(c) provides that its application is to be determined "without regard to the number of shareholders," and the Tax Court has held that in theory the tax can apply to a publicly traded corporation even where ownership is not concentrated in a small group of shareholders.[4] As a practical matter, however, publicly traded companies are rarely threatened because of the difficulty of proving that they were formed for the proscribed tax avoidance purpose.[5] In addition, Section 532(b) provides specific exceptions from the tax for personal holding companies, foreign personal holding companies, tax-exempt organizations and passive foreign investment companies.

The central issue under the accumulated earnings tax is whether the corporation has been formed or availed of for the proscribed tax avoidance purpose. The statutory standard is met if tax avoidance is one of several factors motivating corporate accumulations.[6] Two statutory presumptions assist in determining the presence of a tax avoidance purpose. First, the fact that corporate earnings and profits are permitted to accumulate "beyond the reasonable needs of the business" is determinative of a tax avoidance purpose unless the corporation proves to the contrary by a "preponderance of the evidence."[7] In addition, the fact that the corporation is "a mere holding or investment company" is prima facie evidence of a tax avoidance purpose.[8]

The regulations generally provide that the presence of the proscribed tax avoidance purpose is determined by all the circumstances of the particular case, including:[9]

1. Dealings between the corporation and its shareholders, such as shareholder loans or corporate expenditures benefiting the shareholders personally;

1. I.R.C. § 532(a).

2. I.R.C. §§ 531; 535.

3. I.R.C. § 535(a), (c). A corporation is only permitted a $150,000 credit if its principal function is the performance of services in the field of health, law engineering, architecture, accounting, actuarial science, performing arts or consulting. I.R.C. § 535(c)(2)(B).

4. Technalysis Corp. v. Commissioner, 101 T.C. 397 (1993).

5. See, e.g., the legislative history of Section 532(c), which states that "it may be difficult to establish [a tax avoidance purpose] in the case of a widely-held operating company where no individual or small group of individuals has legal or effective control of the company." S.Rep. No. 98–169, 98th Cong., 2d Sess. 187 (1984); H.R.Rep. No. 98–861, 98th Cong., 2d Sess. 829 (1984).

6. United States v. Donruss, 393 U.S. 297, 89 S.Ct. 501 (1969).

7. I.R.C. § 533(a).

8. I.R.C. § 533(b).

9. Reg. § 1.533–1(a)(2).

2. The presence of corporate investments having no reasonable connection with the corporation's business; and

3. The extent to which the corporation has made dividend distributions.

These factors are not conclusive, but the presence of shareholder loans, unrelated corporate investments and a poor dividend history tend to poison the atmosphere on the question of the proscribed tax avoidance purpose.

Application of the accumulated earnings tax thus ultimately depends on the corporation's purpose. In United States v. Donruss,[10] a decision that significantly strengthened the tax, the Supreme Court held that the statutory standard was satisfied if tax avoidance is merely one of the purposes for the accumulation even if it is not the corporation's dominant or principal purpose. After reviewing the legislative history, the Court acknowledged the difficulties in applying such a subjective standard and expressed its preference for more objective criteria:[11]

> Two conclusions can be drawn from Congress' efforts. First, Congress recognized the tremendous difficulty of ascertaining the purpose of corporate accumulations. Second, it saw that accumulation was often necessary for legitimate and reasonable business purposes. It appears clear to us that the congressional response to these facts has been to emphasize unreasonable accumulation as the most significant factor in the incidence of the tax. The reasonableness of an accumulation, while subject to honest difference of opinion, is a much more objective inquiry, and is susceptible of more effective scrutiny, than are the vagaries of corporate motive.

> Respondent would have us adopt a test that requires that tax avoidance purpose need be dominant, impelling or controlling. It seems to us that such a test would exacerbate the problems that Congress was trying to avoid. Rarely is there one motive, or even one dominant motive, for corporate decisions. Numerous factors contribute to the action ultimately decided upon. Respondent's test would allow taxpayers to escape the tax when it is proved that at least one other motive was equal to tax avoidance. We doubt that such a determination can be made with any accuracy, and it is certainly one which will depend almost exclusively on the interested testimony of corporate management. Respondent's test would thus go a long way toward destroying the presumption that Congress created to meet this very problem. As Judge Learned Hand said of the much weaker presumption contained in the Revenue Act of 1921 * * *, "[a] statute which stands on the footing of the participants' state of mind may need the support of presumption, indeed be practically unenforceable without it * * *." * * * And, "[t]he utility of * * * [that] presumption * * * is well nigh destroyed if * * * [it] is saddled with requirement of

---

10. 393 U.S. 297, 89 S.Ct. 501 (1969).

11. 393 U.S. at 307–08, 89 S.Ct. at 506–07.

proof of the primary or dominant purpose of the accumulation.'' Barrow Manufacturing Co. v. Commissioner, 294 F.2d 79, 82 (C.A. 5th Cir.1961), cert. denied 369 U.S. 817, 82 S.Ct. 827 (1962).

After *Donruss*, it became clear that the critical inquiry is the reasonableness of the accumulation. As previewed above, Congress came to the aid of the fact finder by creating a statutory presumption under which an accumulation beyond the reasonable needs of the corporation's business is determinative of the proscribed tax avoidance purpose unless the corporation proves to the contrary by a preponderance of the evidence.[12] This procedural device eases the Government's burden of proof and immunizes a growing corporation that accumulates profits for purposes such as bona fide expansion, potential acquisitions, working capital needs and other valid business objectives.

The presumption is rebuttable, and in theory a corporation that accumulates earnings beyond its reasonable needs can avoid the tax by proving that the accumulation was not motivated by a tax avoidance purpose. As the Supreme Court stated in Donruss:[13]

> [W]e cannot subscribe to respondent's suggestion that our holding would make purpose totally irrelevant. It still serves to isolate those cases in which tax avoidance motives did not contribute to the decision to accumulate. Obviously in such a case imposition of the tax would be futile. In addition, ''purpose'' means more than mere knowledge, undoubtedly present in nearly every case. It is still open for the taxpayer to show that even though knowledge of the tax consequences was present, that knowledge did not contribute to the decision to accumulate earnings.

Few corporations, however, are able to make the requisite showing once it is determined that accumulations are unreasonable.[14] Conversely, even if an accumulation is found to be reasonable, the government theoretically might attempt to show the existence of the proscribed purpose.[15] In practice, however, the reasonable business needs standard is almost always the main event, and it therefore will be the focus of our coverage.

3. THE REASONABLE NEEDS OF THE BUSINESS

Code: §§ 533(a); 534(a)–(c); 537(a), (b)(1)

Regulations: §§ 1.537–1(a), (b), (c), –2, –3.

---

12. I.R.C. § 533(a).

13. 393 U.S. at 309.

14. For one isolated example, see T.C. Heyward & Co. v. United States, 66–2 U.S.T.C. ¶ 9667 (W.D.N.C.1966), where a federal district judge held that the corporation's accumulations were so large that it never could have intended to avoid the shareholder tax because no one would be so obvious. Such cases are aberrational. In the future, however, it is still conceivable that a publicly held corporation that is found to have made an unreasonable accumulation might contend that it lacked the proscribed purpose because it is not controlled by any single shareholder or insider group.

15. Such a showing ultimately would be futile, however, in light of Section 535(c)(1), which provides a credit against the accumulated earnings tax in an amount equal to those earnings which have been accumulated for the reasonable needs of the business.

Myron's Enterprises v. United States

United States Court of Appeals, Ninth Circuit, 1977.
548 F.2d 331.

■ Sneed, Circuit Judge:

Taxpayer-corporations sued in district court below for a refund of accumulated earnings taxes imposed by the Commissioner. The Commissioner had based the tax on his determination that for taxpayers' fiscal years 1966 through 1968 the reasonable needs of the business stemmed entirely from working capital needs and never exceeded $21,272. The taxpayers contended that their retained earnings for the years in question of $316,000, $374,316, and $415,766 respectively were needed to cover both working capital requirements of $100,000 and the planned purchase and remodeling of the ballroom operated by taxpayers, at an estimated cost of $375,000.

The district court, in Myron's Ballroom v. United States, 382 F.Supp. 582 (C.D.Cal.1974), held that taxpayers had accumulated earnings in excess of the reasonable needs of their business, but not to the extent claimed by the Commissioner. The court also found that the taxpayers had been availed of for the purpose of avoiding income taxes. Thus, the court upheld the surtax, but required a partial refund in light of the Commissioner's underestimation of taxpayers' reasonable business needs.

The taxpayers argue on appeal that they are entitled to a full refund (i) because all of the retained earnings in the years in question were required to meet the reasonable needs of their business, and (ii) because they proved by the preponderance of the evidence that they were not availed of to avoid taxes, despite the contrary finding by the district court. The Government argues, in response, that taxpayers were not even entitled to a partial refund—that the Commissioner's initial determination of the reasonable needs of the business was correct and that taxpayers failed to prove lack of tax-avoidance motivation. We conclude that the taxpayers are entitled to the full refund they seek. Therefore, we reverse and remand for such necessary proceedings as are consistent with this opinion.

I.

Taxpayer-corporations operate a ballroom and adjoining cocktail lounge. At all times since taxpayers were formed, they have leased their operating premises from Miss Pearl Rose, an elderly lady who has owned the property for approximately 30 years. The taxpayers began inquiring into the possibilities of purchasing the property in 1957, in part because they did not wish to make needed improvements unless they owned the building. Taxpayers made offers to Miss Rose of $100,000 and $150,000 for the property in the late 1950s—early 1960s, neither of which was accepted. However, at the time of the second offer, Miss Rose told taxpayers that they would have "first choice" if and when she decided to sell the ballroom.

In 1963, taxpayers learned that Russ Morgan, a former orchestra leader at the ballroom, had offered Miss Rose $300,000 cash for the property, in an attempt apparently to take over the ballroom operation. The price offered by Morgan probably reflected the goodwill that taxpayers had built up in their operations and therefore was considerably higher than the value of the ballroom property by itself. Morgan's actions convinced taxpayers that their business could be involuntarily "acquired" by someone purchasing the ballroom from Miss Rose;[3] taxpayers, therefore, promptly offered Miss Rose the identical sum of $300,000. This offer was renewed in 1964, 1965, 1966, 1967, 1968 and 1970. While Miss Rose never objected to the terms of the offers, she never sold and still owned the ballroom at the time of trial.

As the Government points out, Miss Rose was never particularly clear as to when and if she would sell her building. Nevertheless, the district court found (a) that taxpayers "expected at any time during the years 1966, 1967 and 1968 that [they] would be able to purchase the ballroom property from Pearl Rose for a price of $300,000 cash, no less than that amount, and maybe more," 382 F.Supp. at 587, and moreover (b) that the "expectation that the ballroom property would be acquired at any time during the years in issue was a reasonable expectation," id. at 588. Thus,

> "During the years in issue, the acquisition of the ballroom property and the planned improvements and repairs were reasonably anticipated business needs of [taxpayers], and said needs were directly connected with the businesses of the corporations." Id.

The district court further concluded that "[c]onsidering the reasonably anticipated business need of the corporations to purchase the ballroom property * * * the corporations combined required at least $375,000, in addition to their combined working capital needs of $100,000." Id. However, the court went on to hold that in light of taxpayers' sole-shareholder Mrs. Myrna Myron's willingness to loan up to $200,000 to her corporations for purchase of the ballroom "if the corporations did not have sufficient funds to consummate the transactions, * * * a reasonable accumulation [for the purchase] would be $250,000, with Mrs. Myron loaning the balance of funds required," id., thus leading to an excess accumulation in 1967 and 1968.

II.

Section 537 of the Internal Revenue Code provides that the reasonable needs of a business, for purposes of determining whether there has been an excess accumulation of earnings, include "the reasonably anticipated needs of the business." Treas.Reg. § 1.537–1(b)(1) provides that to justify an

---

3. While taxpayers had a lease and an option to renew on the ballroom property at the time Morgan made his $300,000 offer to Miss Rose, there was always the possibility that the lease could be broken or evaded. According to Mrs. Myron, Morgan had asked his attorney and Miss Rose's agent "to review [the lease] line by line to see if there was some way or some word—something that could break the lease." R.T. at 73. This possibility of a loophole in the lease left the door open for an involuntary "acquisition."

accumulation of earnings on grounds of reasonably anticipated business needs, a corporation must have "specific, definite, and feasible plans for the use of such accumulation" and must not postpone execution of the plan "indefinitely."[4]

The Government contends that the district court erred in concluding that the taxpayers had a "specific, definite, and feasible plan" to acquire and remodel the ballroom. The Government notes that Miss Rose never agreed to sell the ballroom and argues that taxpayers could not have reasonably expected Miss Rose to so agree within the taxable years in question after nearly a decade of unsuccessful negotiations.

We agree with other circuits that a determination by the trial court of the reasonably anticipated business needs of a corporation is a finding of fact which must be sustained unless clearly erroneous. * * * A court should be particularly wary of overturning a finding of a trial court supporting the taxpayer's determination of its anticipated business needs, since, in the first instance, the "reasonableness of the needs is necessarily for determination by those concerned with the management of the particular enterprise. This determination must prevail unless the facts show clearly the accumulations were for prohibited purposes." * * * We conclude that the district court was not clearly erroneous in finding that taxpayers' expected purchase and remodeling of the ballroom for $375,000 was a "reasonably anticipated need of the business."

The Government argues that if the instant plan to purchase the ballroom is held to be a reasonably anticipated business need,

> "any individual could organize a one-man corporation, lease a building and discuss with the lessor the purchase of the building at some future time, and then assert that in the meantime business needs required accumulation of corporate earnings." I.A. Dress Co. v. Commissioner of Internal Revenue, 273 F.2d 543, 544 (2d Cir.), cert. denied, 362 U.S. 976, 80 S.Ct. 1060, 4 L.Ed.2d 1011 (1960).

Such fears of artificially constructed needs were well-founded in the quoted case of I.A. Dress Co.; there, the owner of the building that the taxpayer sought to purchase "was willing to sell but at a price some $300,000 more than the taxpayer was willing to pay." Id. The offer of the taxpayer lacked substance and could easily have been a facade. In the instant case, however, the taxpayers were extremely diligent in their attempts to purchase the

---

4. "In order for a corporation to justify an accumulation of earnings and profits for reasonably anticipated future needs, there must be an indication that the future needs of the business require such accumulation, and the corporation must have specific, definite, and feasible plans for the use of such accumulation. Such an accumulation need not be used immediately, nor must the plans for its use be consummated within a short period after the close of the taxable year, provided that such accumulation will be used within a reasonable time depending upon all the facts and circumstances relating to the future needs of the business. Where the future needs of the business are uncertain or vague, where the plans for the future use of an accumulation are not specific, definite, and feasible, or where the execution of such a plan is postponed indefinitely, an accumulation cannot be justified on the grounds of reasonably anticipated needs of the business." Treas. Reg. § 1.537–1(b)(1).

ballroom; the taxpayers agreed to all of Miss Rose's stated terms—including payment in all cash; the price offered, far from being criticized by Miss Rose as too low, was apparently in excess of the property's fair market value.[5]

Neither do we have a situation where taxpayers' planned purchase of the ballroom was clearly infeasible. See Colonial Amusement Corp., 1948 Tax.Ct.Mem.Dec. (P–H) 48,149 (building restrictions and priorities prevented carrying out of expansion plans). Here, as in Universal Steel Co., 5 T.C. 627 (1945) (war priority restrictions temporarily blocked purchase of pickling plant), the taxpayers "had a right to hope, if not expect," id. at 638, that Miss Rose would sell to them in the near future. Miss Rose never foreclosed the possibility of sale on the terms offered by taxpayers; she merely wanted to "think it over some more." As expressed by Miss Rose's agent at one point during the negotiations, Miss Rose "was an elderly lady and had a very definite mind"; her answers, according to the agent, would differ depending on how she felt on getting up in the morning. Taxpayers were encouraged at several points in the negotiations; in 1965, Miss Rose's agent had told taxpayers, "Be prepared and ready to go." In light of the reasonable possibility that Miss Rose might have decided to accept the offer at any time during the taxable years in issue, calling for quick collection of $375,000 in cash, it would have been unreasonable to force taxpayers to pay out all of their earnings in dividends. Section 537 allows taxpayers to provide for "reasonably anticipated needs," not merely for certainties.

The district court's finding is supported by several tax court cases. In Magic Mart, Inc., 51 T.C. 775 (1969), acq., 1969–2 C.B. xxiv, the Tax Court held that the taxpayer's accumulation of earnings for 1959 through 1962 was reasonable in light of taxpayer's plan to acquire enlarged and expanded facilities, even though it had tried unsuccessfully to buy larger facilities since 1957 and was not able to close a deal until 1967, five years after the taxable years in question. In Breitfeller Sales, Inc., 28 T.C. 1164 (1957), acq., 1958–2 C.B. 4, the Tax Court held that a General Motors dealership's accumulation of earnings was justified, inter alia, by "the continuing possibility that it might [to avoid harmful competition] be required to finance a new dealership in [a neighboring community]." Id. at 1168 (emphasis added). See also Universal Steel Co., supra.

---

5. The Government argues that in addition to these steps the taxpayers also should have investigated purchasing other property in the general area, once Miss Rose did not prove totally disposing. Cf. Magic Mart, Inc., 51 T.C. 775 (1969), acq., 1969 2 C.B. xxiv. We agree that the failure of a taxpayer to look into the possibility of purchasing alternative properties generally will be a relevant factor in determining whether the taxpayer actually had a reasonably anticipated business need to purchase the sought-after property. However, other factors also must be considered, including the uniqueness of the sought property. Here, as was testified to at trial, a substantial amount of good will was tied up in the ballroom occupied by taxpayers; given that this value would have been lost if taxpayer had moved to another location, we do not believe that taxpayers' failure to pursue other possible properties (if other ballrooms even existed) calls for reversing the finding of the district court.

III.

The Government rests its entire case upon the argued lack of a specific, definite, and feasible plan. No attempt is made to support the trial court's use of Mrs. Myrna Myron's capacity to loan to the taxpayers to reduce the amount of the reasonable accumulation. The Government thus agrees with taxpayers that, assuming a feasible plan, the district court, in determining whether taxpayers unreasonably accumulated earnings, erred in subtracting from the cash needed to purchase the ballroom an amount that Mrs. Myron stated that she would be willing to loan to the taxpayers if necessary. We also agree. Having found that the reasonably anticipated business need of the taxpayers to purchase the ballroom property required at least $375,000 in cash, the district court erred in concluding that a reasonable accumulation was any less.[6]

Having determined that the reasonable business needs of taxpayers, within the meaning of section 535, equalled or exceeded the accumulated earnings of taxpayers for the taxable years in question, it is unnecessary for us to consider whether the district court was correct in holding that taxpayers had been availed of to avoid taxes within the meaning of section 531. Taxpayers are entitled to a full refund. The case is remanded to the district court for such necessary proceedings as are consistent with this opinion.

Reversed and remanded.

NOTE

The *Myron's Enterprises* case illustrates the essentially factual nature of the "reasonable business needs" issue. By the time a case reaches the courts, the corporation normally has compiled a laundry list of reasonable

---

6. That the reasonableness of accumulations should be judged without regard to the borrowing capabilities of the corporation-taxpayer is well established by the case law. See, e.g., General Smelting Co., 4 T.C. 313, 323 (1944), acq., 1945 C.B. 3; B. Bittker & J. Eustice, Federal Income Taxation of Corporations and Shareholders 8–20 to 8–21 & n. 42 (3rd ed. 1971). In computing "accumulated taxable income," which forms the base for the accumulated earnings tax, I.R.C. § 535 provides that a credit will be provided for the amount "retained for the reasonable needs of the business." There is no authority for reducing the credit to reflect the lending capacity of taxpayer's shareholders. If the reasonable business needs of taxpayer equal or outstrip the retained earnings, no surtax can be imposed, even though the needs could be financed by borrowing from outside—such financing decisions are for the taxpayer, not the courts to make.

The district court's logic could conceivably be extended to the point of totally nullifying Congress' expressed policy of allowing corporate taxpayers to accumulate earnings necessary for reasonable business needs. A sole shareholder can always loan back any cash distributed by his corporation in dividends if the corporation later needs the money (minus, of course, any income taxes paid). Therefore, to take into account the ability of a shareholder to loan money to the corporation could be construed as virtual authority "for denying all sole stockholder corporations the right ever to maintain accumulations even for reasonable needs. The test expressed by the statute would then be completely abandoned." Smoot Sand & Gravel Corp. v. Commissioner of Internal Revenue, 241 F.2d 197, 206 (4th Cir.), cert. denied, 354 U.S. 922, 77 S.Ct. 1383, 1 L.Ed.2d 1437 (1957).

business needs to justify the accumulation, and triers of fact typically are reluctant to second guess the business judgment of corporate management in the absence of a clear pattern of abuse. This note and the materials that follow it survey the principal factors taken into account by the Service and the courts in evaluating the reasonableness of a corporation's accumulation.

Reasonable and Unreasonable Needs: In General. After a general reminder that the reasonableness of a particular accumulation of earnings and profits is dependent "upon the particular circumstances of the case,"[1] the regulations provide guidance on what constitutes reasonable and unreasonable accumulations. If supported by the facts, the following grounds "may indicate" that accumulations are being made for the reasonable needs of the business:[2]

1. To provide for bona fide expansion of the business or replacement of plant;

2. To acquire a business enterprise through a stock or asset purchase;

3. To provide for retirement of bona fide indebtedness incurred in the trade or business;

4. To provide necessary working capital for the business; or

5. To provide for investments or loans to suppliers or customers in order to maintain the corporation's business.

The following nonexclusive list of purposes "may indicate" that the accumulations are beyond the reasonable needs of the business:[3]

1. Loans to shareholders or expenditures for the personal benefit of the shareholders;

2. Loans having no reasonable relation to the conduct of the business made to relatives or friends of shareholders or other persons;

3. Loans to another corporation in a different business if the two corporations are controlled, directly or indirectly, by the same shareholders;

4. Investments unrelated to the corporation's business; or

5. Retention of earnings and profits to provide against unrealistic hazards.

Anticipated Needs. Section 537(a) defines the "reasonable needs of the business" as including the reasonably anticipated needs. To justify an accumulation as being for a reasonably anticipated need, a corporation must have a business need for the accumulation and must have plans for the use of the funds which are "specific, definite and feasible."[4] The

1. Reg. § 1.537–2(a). The Supreme Court has held that in ascertaining the reasonable needs of a business, "readily marketable portfolio securities" are to be taken into account at their "net realizable value" rather than cost. Ivan Allen Co. v. United States, 422 U.S. 617, 95 S.Ct. 2501 (1975).

2. Reg. § 1.537–2(b).

3. Reg. § 1.537–2(c).

4. Reg. § 1.537–1(b)(1).

accumulation does not have to be used immediately or even within a short period of time as long as it is used within a "reasonable period," taking into account all the facts and circumstances.[5] The corporation's reasonably anticipated needs are determined based on facts present at the close of the taxable year; subsequent events may not be used to show that the accumulation was unreasonable. Subsequent events, however, can be considered to determine whether the corporation actually intended to consummate its plans for the accumulation.[6] Moreover, if the future plans are not completed, the presence of the accumulation is considered in determining the reasonableness of future accumulations.[7]

The "Business." The regulations expansively define the "business" of a corporation. The "business" includes not only the one in which the corporation has previously engaged but also "any line of business which it may undertake."[8] This definition should provide ample protection for accumulations intended for expansion into activities related to the corporation's existing businesses, and possibly may permit accumulations to finance any line of business permitted by the corporation's charter.[9] If a corporation owns and, in effect, operates a subsidiary, the subsidiary's business may be considered to be the business of the parent for purposes of evaluating the parent's reasonable business needs.[10] The regulations further provide that a subsidiary will be considered a "mere instrumentality" of its parent if the parent owns at least 80 percent of the subsidiary's voting stock.[11] Below the 80 percent figure, the question of attributing the subsidiary's business to the parent is determined by the particular circumstances of the case.[12]

Working Capital. The regulations recognize the need to accumulate earnings to provide "necessary working capital for the business." Working capital needs vary from industry to industry and among enterprises within the same industry, and the courts have struggled to develop standards to ascertain the working capital requirements of any particular business.[13] The judiciary's efforts have evolved into the so-called *Bardahl* formula, named for a 1965 Tax Court case which first employed the approach.[14] The formula, which is a mathematician's delight, attempts to identify a corporation's working capital needs by reference to its "operating cycle"—a concept that remains unsettled.[15] The *Bardahl* formula is viewed as a guidepost rather than a controlling legal principle,[16] and the following

---

5. Id.

6. Reg. § 1.537–1(b)(2).

7. Id.

8. Reg. § 1.537–3(a).

9. See Bittker & Eustice, Federal Income Taxation of Corporations and Shareholders ¶ 7.06 (7th ed. 2000).

10. Reg. § 1.537–3(b).

11. Id.

12. Id.

13. See Cunningham, "More Than You Ever Wanted to Know About the Accumulated Earnings Tax," 6 J. Corp. Tax'n 187, 209 (1979).

14. Bardahl Manufacturing Corp. v. Commissioner, 24 T.C.M. 1030 (1965).

15. See Cunningham, supra note 13, at 212.

16. See generally Thompson Engineering Co. v. Commissioner, 80 T.C. 672 (1983); Atlantic Commerce & Shipping Co. v. Com-

excerpt provides some insight into its nature and purpose:[17]

The formula represents a procedure for arriving at working capital needs by calculating the requirements of capital funds for one "operating cycle" of a business entity. One operating cycle is the length of time (usually expressed as a percentage of a year) it takes to purchase raw materials inventory, process those raw materials into finished goods, sell the finished product, and turn any accounts receivable into cash so that the process may be repeated. Hence, the ultimate percentage which represents this cycle must speak to the turnover time of raw materials, accounts receivable, and any credit cycle. The time it takes to turn over inventory can be computed by dividing either the highest or the average inventory for the year by the costs of the goods sold in that year. This results in a percentage of a year. In similar fashion, the time it takes to turn over a receivable account is computed by dividing the highest receivables for the year by the sales for that year. This likewise is expressed as a percentage of a year. Adding inventory cycle to receivables cycle, one arrives at a theoretical time period, again expressed as a percentage of a year, that is required for the total productive process.

The *Bardahl International* case took the additional step of recognizing that those who supply raw materials and labor are not paid immediately. An appropriate credit period, usually 15 or 30 days, is stated as a percentage of a year (divided by 365 days per year), and this is subtracted from the total of the inventory and receivables percentages. When this ultimate percentage rate is applied to the net operating expenses for the year, the result represents the expenses for one business operating cycle * * *. To this are added reasonably anticipated extraordinary expenses during the tax year in question * * *. The sum represents the total requirements of the firm for liquid assets * * *. This is contrasted against the sum of liquid assets such as cash and equivalents * * * and investments which can be converted into cash readily if necessary * * * in order to ascertain whether there is an excess or shortage of available capital * * *. Cognizance must also be taken of any loans unrelated to the business * * *.

The result of this whole process is a figure * * * indicating how much the subject firm has accumulated beyond its reasonable needs. This, in conjunction with its findings on the intent of the parties, should permit a factfinder to ascertain whether or not the corporate entity has been availed of for the purpose of avoiding income tax by one or more of the shareholders. * * *

Stock Redemptions. Corporations sometimes contend that an accumulation of earnings is necessary to create a fund for a later redemption of

missioner, 32 T.C.M. 473 (1973), affirmed, 500 F.2d 937 (2d Cir.1974).

17. Grob, Inc. v. United States, 565 F.Supp. 391, 395 (E.D.Wis.1983).

stock. In response to conflicting results in the courts, Congress has specifically provided that the term "reasonable needs of the business" encompasses accumulations in the year of a shareholder's death or in any subsequent year to the extent they are necessary to make a stock redemption to pay death taxes under Section 303.[18]

The cases are inconsistent as to other types of future redemptions. Some courts have found accumulations to redeem dissenting minority or 50 percent shareholders to be a reasonable need of the business.[19] But corporations have encountered more difficulty when they have attempted to justify an accumulation on the ground that reasonable business needs include accumulating earnings to redeem either a friendly minority shareholder[20] or a majority shareholder.[21] In each case, the question is whether the redemption satisfies a corporate (e.g., preventing continuous deadlocks in the boardroom) as opposed to a shareholder (e.g., funding a redemption of a retiring shareholder under a buy-sell agreement) purpose.[22] The *Gazette Publishing* case, which follows, illustrates how a redemption can be characterized as a valid response to a threat to the corporation's existence.

Gazette Publishing Co. v. Self

United States District Court, Eastern District of Arkansas, 1952.
103 F.Supp. 779.

■ TRIMBLE, CHIEF JUDGE.

This is an action by the plaintiff, Gazette Publishing Company, a corporation, against the acting collector of Internal Revenue for this district for the recovery of a Section 102, [Now Section 531. Ed.] 26 U.S.C.A. § 102, assessment made for the calendar years, 1946 and 1947.

Plaintiff was incorporated under the laws of Arkansas on June 5, 1889, for the purpose of publishing a newspaper, The Arkansas Gazette, and conducting related business enterprises, and has carried on such business since its incorporation. * * *

* * *

During the years, 1946 and 1947, Mr. J.N. Heiskell was president of the corporation, and Mr. Fred Allsopp was secretary-treasurer and general manager until his death in March, 1946. Upon his death, his son, W.C. Allsopp, who had been assistant business manager, succeeded to the posi-

---

18. I.R.C. § 537(a)(2); 537(b)(1). Similarly, reasonable needs are considered to include amounts necessary to redeem stock held by a private foundation that is required to shed its excess business holdings. I.R.C. §§ 537(a)(3); 537(b)(2). See I.R.C. § 4943.

19. See, e.g., Wilcox Manufacturing Co. v. Commissioner, 38 T.C.M. 378 (1979); Mountain State Steel Foundries, Inc. v. Commissioner, 284 F.2d 737 (4th Cir.1960).

20. See John B. Lambert & Associates v. United States, 212 Ct.Cl. 71 (1976).

21. See Lamark Shipping Agency, Inc. v. Commissioner, 42 T.C.M. 38 (1981); Pelton Steel Casting Co. v. Commissioner, 251 F.2d 278 (7th Cir.1958).

22. See generally Rudolph, "Stock Redemptions and the Accumulated Earnings Tax—an Update," 4 J.Corp. Tax'n 101 (1977).

tions held by his father. This situation had existed for many years. The business was run by informal conferences between these men, and no formal meetings of the Board of Directors or stockholders were held in which minutes were kept between March 24, 1944, and November, 1948. Formal meetings were only held when it was necessary to approve or ratify some action of the officers. * * *

* * *

The plaintiff corporation had a long history of paying generous dividends. For the twenty years ending with 1945, the year immediately preceding the questioned years, the corporation had net earnings after taxes of $2,288,000 and paid out $2,167,000 in dividends, retaining in the business for this period no more than $120,000 of the earnings. A study of the record discloses that the dividends paid in 1946 and 1947 were above the Corporation's average dividend in amount over the preceding ten year period. The 1947 dividend of $107,000 was the highest dividend paid since 1936. The record also discloses that more than half of the substantial increase in retained earnings during the period in question over prior years was due to the repeal of World War II excess profits tax. This gave to the officers of the Corporation an opportunity to begin to accumulate funds to meet the reasonable needs of the business, and without the necessity of reducing dividends.

The sale of the Allsopp stock, in 1948, was not the purpose for which the funds were accumulated during 1946 and 1947. The uncontroverted evidence in this case is that the proposed sale of the stock first came up in a flare of temper between Mr. Patterson and W.C. Allsopp in 1948, and that when the sale was proposed in 1948 it was a complete surprise to the president and the board of directors of the corporation. * * *

* * *

Defendant contends that the price of $1,000,000 paid for the Allsopp stock in 1948 was so far in excess of the true market value of that stock, that it is evident that there was in fact no reasonable need for the accumulation of the funds in 1946 and 1947.

It is in evidence that certain special interests have for many years sought to purchase or acquire stock in the corporation, and an interest in the publication of the Arkansas Gazette, the newspaper published by the corporation. The officers testified that the management has always watched the matter closely, fearing that if some group of special interests should acquire stock in the corporation, however minor it might be, such group of special interests would endeavor to break up the harmony existing in the management, and change the editorial and business policy of the corporation, which had conducted the business of the corporation so successfully so many years. When the Allsopp stock was offered for sale at $1,000,000, all the officers and directors of the plaintiff corporation knew this was in excess of its true market value. They were informed by the attorney for the Allsopp stockholders that the stock could be sold to an outsider for that amount of money. They recognized this as a business crisis. Knowing that their failure to acquire this stock for the corporation might in the future affect the interest of the corporation and its stockholders adversely, it was decided to make the acquisition and promote and keep intact the harmony of management and editorial policy of the corporation.

Defendant does not seem to recognize that this business is subject to changes in circumstances and conditions, and that good business judgment upon the part of management requires changes in plans to meet these changes of circumstances. This is true with this plaintiff as with all other business enterprises, and the courts have recognized that this is so. All business needs are relative. The most pressing needs today may not be the most pressing at a later date, because even more pressing needs may arise because of changed circumstances, and courts have frequently refused to sustain Section 102 Assessments where the funds accumulated for reasonable needs and owing to change in circumstances the funds were used only partially or not at all as originally planned.

In Dill Manufacturing Co., 39 B.T.A. 1023, it was the purchase of the minority stock which forced the postponement of plans for a new plant, and the Board of Tax Appeals, in reversing a Section 102 Assessment by the Commissioner, held the purchase of the minority stock was a reasonable business need of the company. The Board of Tax Appeals, said in that case: "The issue of preferred stock with the obligation to retire it within five years evidenced a debt, (cases cited). And this record, at most, does not establish that the liquidation of the syndicate stock by the partial use of that preferred stock, under the circumstances here, was not required as a reasonable business necessity. Cf. Sauk Investment Co., 34 B.T.A. 732; Mellbank Corporation, 38 B.T.A. 1108."

See also National Yarn Corporation, 9 TCM 603; General Smelting Co., 4 T.C. 313; The Wean Engineering Co., Inc., 2 TCM 510; Emeloid Co., Inc., v. Commissioner of Internal Revenue, 3 Cir., 189 F.2d 230. In the case of Fred F. Fisher, 6 TCM 520, the Tax Court held that the promotion of harmony in the conduct of the business is a proper business purpose. There, taxpayer's sister, a minority stockholder, had been constantly complaining about the conduct of the business. To put an end to the dissension, the company purchased the sister's stock at a price considerably in excess of its fair market value. The Commissioner, contending that the stock purchase was prompted by reasons personal to the stockholders and not in furtherance of any corporate purpose, assessed a deficiency on the other stockholders on the theory that the excessive portion of the purchase price constituted a constructive dividend. But the Tax Court held that the Company's purchase of the sister's stock was in furtherance of corporate purposes. The Tax Court pointed out that "there is no foundation for an assumption that a corporation would never, in its own interests, pay more than the fair market value of its stock in order to rid itself of a complaining minority stockholder," and that the excessive price paid for the stock "was not unreasonable for the purpose of promoting harmony in the conduct of the business and securing it from annoying interference and threats of legal proceedings." The Court said, "regardless of whether * * * complaints were justified, they had a nuisance value sufficient to warrant the action of the corporation in purchasing her stock."

The Arkansas Gazette, published by the plaintiff, is said to be the oldest daily paper west of the Mississippi River. It has enjoyed a long, honorable and successful career under able and eminent editors, among them the present President of the Corporation. It has a well established policy, standing firmly and stoutly for all the great moral issues arising from time to time, has had a great part in the development of the whole state, and has at all times supported worthy public causes and men in public life with telling effect. It has consistently over a long term of years refused to accept advertisements for alcoholic liquors of any kind. It also has had and still has strong editorial policies on many issues which special interests might and would oppose. For this Allsopp stock to have fallen into the hands of some special interest antagonistic to the present and the general policy of the paper, could and probably would have been most disruptive of the harmony of the corporation, even though it constituted a minority of all the stock. The purchase of this stock, even at the advanced price paid, was a reasonable need of the corporation, and was a change in circumstances which fully justified a change in the use of funds accumulated for other needs, and justified the borrowing of the $600,000 in addition to using the funds on hand.

* * *

The Court finds from all the evidence in the case, and giving such weight to the statutory presumptions as the law requires, that the earnings and profits were not accumulated in 1946 and 1947 beyond the reasonable needs of the corporation. Nor were such earnings accumulated for the purpose of preventing the imposition of a surtax upon the stockholders.

NOTE

Sections 533 and 534 work together to provide an unusual procedure for regulating the burden of proof if an accumulated earnings tax controversy is litigated in the Tax Court. As we have seen, an accumulation beyond the reasonable needs of the business is determinative of the forbidden purpose unless the corporation proves otherwise by a preponderance of the evidence.[1] The regulations provide that this presumption adds "still more weight" to the usual presumption of correctness that accompanies the Service's determinations of tax liability.[2] The Commissioner nonetheless will bear the burden of proof on the question of unreasonable accumulations unless it has informed the taxpayer, prior to sending a formal notice of deficiency, that the proposed notice includes an accumulated earnings tax deficiency.[3] Even in the likely case where the Commissioner provides notice, the taxpayer can shift the burden of proof back to the Commissioner by submitting a statement setting forth the grounds on which it relies to establish that all or part of its earnings and profits have

---

1. I.R.C. § 533(a).

2. Reg. § 1.533–1(b).

3. I.R.C. § 534(a), (b).

not been permitted to accumulate beyond the reasonable needs of the business.[4] The statement must be filed within 30 days of the Commissioner's notification under Section 534(b).[5] To shift the burden of proof, the taxpayer's statement may not consist merely of vague generalities. It must set forth with specificity and clarity the grounds on which it will rely to prove that its accumulations were reasonable.[6]

4. Calculation of Accumulated Taxable Income

Code: 535(a), (b), (c); 561; 562(a), (b), (c); 563(a), (d); 565(a)–(d), (f).

The base for the accumulated earnings tax is accumulated taxable income, which Section 535(a) defines as taxable income of the corporation, adjusted under Section 535(b), less the sum of the dividends paid deduction and the accumulated earnings credit.

Adjustments to Taxable Income. The base figure for computing accumulated taxable income is the current year's taxable income. The accumulated earnings tax, however, is directed at real retained economic profits because they are a more accurate measure of the corporation's capacity to pay dividends. As a result, taxable income is adjusted in a manner somewhat similar to that used to adjust taxable income to determine earnings and profits. For example, to arrive at accumulated taxable income, taxable income is reduced by certain nondeductible taxes[1] and charitable contributions in excess of the percentage limitations.[2] These items do not affect taxable income but nonetheless result in a decrease in the corporation's wealth. On the other hand, certain deductions allowed for income tax purposes that do not currently reduce the corporation's real wealth are disallowed in computing accumulated taxable income. These include the dividends received deduction[3] and the net operating loss deduction.[4]

Section 535(b) contains special rules governing the treatment of net capital gains and losses for purposes of determining accumulated taxable income.[5] Section 535(b)(6) permits a corporation to reduce taxable income by its net capital gain for the year less attributable taxes. But for purposes of determining net capital gain prior net capital losses are treated as short-term capital losses in succeeding taxable years.[6] Under Section 535(b)(5)(A) and (B), a corporation can deduct the amount of a net capital loss reduced by the lesser of its "nonrecaptured capital gains deductions" or its earnings and profits as of the close of the preceding year. "Nonrecaptured capital gains deductions" are generally defined by Section 535(b)(5)(C) as the excess of the aggregate amount allowable as a deduction in prior years for net capital gains over the aggregate reductions to capital losses for prior years.

---

4. I.R.C. § 534(c); Reg. § 1.534–2(a), (b).

5. I.R.C. § 534(c).

6. Reg. § 1.534–2(d).

1. I.R.C. § 535(b)(1).

2. I.R.C. § 535(b)(2).

3. I.R.C. § 535(b)(3).

4. I.R.C. § 535(b)(4).

5. A separate set of rules applies to a "mere holding or investment company." I.R.C. § 535(b)(8).

6. I.R.C. § 535(b)(6), (7).

Dividends Paid Deduction. Section 535(a) logically permits a corporation to reduce accumulated taxable income by dividends paid during the taxable year. Section 561(a) defines the "dividends paid" to include dividends[7] paid during the taxable year and certain "consent dividends." Generally, distributions must be pro rata in order to qualify for the dividends paid deduction.[8] Liquidating distributions and redemptions also may produce a deduction for dividends paid.[9] Because a corporation frequently may not have the facts available to determine its liability for the accumulated earnings tax, Section 563(a) provides that dividends paid on or before the 15th day of the third month following the close of a taxable year are considered paid in the earlier year.

Consent Dividends. Section 565 permits shareholders to file a consent with the corporation's tax return to include in income as dividends amounts which were not in fact distributed. Consent dividends are treated as if they were distributed in cash to the shareholders and then contributed back to the corporation on the last day of the corporation's taxable year.[10]

Accumulated Earnings Credit. To the extent that a corporation's earnings are retained for the reasonable needs of the business, they are not within the ambit of the accumulated earnings tax. To remove these earnings from the grasp of the tax, a corporation is permitted a deduction for the accumulated earnings credit in determining accumulated taxable income. The accumulated earnings credit is equal to the amount of current earnings and profits (less the dividends paid deduction) retained for the reasonable needs of the business minus the deduction permitted for net capital gains.[11] Section 535(c)(2) provides that the credit shall in no case be less than the amount by which $250,000 ($150,000 in the case of certain service corporations) exceeds accumulated earnings and profits at the close of the preceding taxable year.[12] This has the effect of enabling a corporation to accumulate a minimum of $250,000 regardless of its business needs.

PROBLEMS

1. Which of the following accumulations are likely to be for the reasonable needs of the business?

7. Section 562(a) generally employs the Section 316 definition of "dividend" for purposes of determining the dividends paid deduction. Reg. § 1.562–1(a) provides that if a dividend is paid in property (other than money) the amount of the dividends paid deduction is the corporation's adjusted basis in the property. The regulation was upheld in Fulman v. United States, 434 U.S. 528, 98 S.Ct. 841 (1978).

8. I.R.C. § 562(c). Differences in dividend rights among classes of stock not attributable to shareholder waivers are permitted.

9. I.R.C. § 562(b)(1).

10. I.R.C. § 565(c).

11. I.R.C. § 535(c)(1). Net capital gains are excluded from accumulated taxable income by Section 535(b)(6) but they are part of earnings and profits. If a net capital gain was not excluded from the accumulated earnings credit it would reduce accumulated taxable income twice: once under Section 535(b)(6) and again under Section 535(c).

12. Accumulated earnings and profits at the close of the preceding year are reduced by dividends treated as paid in such year under Section 563(a). I.R.C. § 535(c)(4).

(a) A corporation retains $200,000 of earnings and profits per year for five years to finance a $1,000,000 expansion of its manufacturing plant. Should it matter if the corporation could have borrowed 80% of the expansion costs?

(b) A corporation which manufactures computer chips accumulates $2,000,000 in order to acquire an office building which is rented to an insurance company under a net lease.

(c) Assume Parent Corporation owns all of the outstanding stock of Brother and Sister Corporations. Can Parent accumulate earnings and profits for Brother? Brother for Parent? Brother for Sister? See Reg. §§ 1.537–2(c)(3), –3(b).

(d) A corporation accumulates earnings and profits for potential § 531 tax liability.

(e) A corporation accumulates earnings and profits in order to redeem a class of limited and preferred stock.

2. T Corporation (a shoe manufacturer) is a calendar year, accrual method corporation which is not a personal holding company and which has accumulated earnings and profits at the end of year one of $200,000. T is a closely held corporation with three shareholders. In year two T has taxable income (all of which is ordinary income) of $60,000. T also has taxable income of $60,000 in both years three and four. There are no distributions to shareholders in any year.

(a) What tax results to T under §§ 11 and 531, assuming current § 11 rates on all income in years two, three, and four?

(b) What possible defenses may T have to the application of § 531?

(c) What effect will § 534 have on these facts?

C. THE PERSONAL HOLDING COMPANY TAX

1. INTRODUCTION

Code: §§ 541, 542(a).

The accumulated earnings tax was not an entirely effective vehicle to prevent the use of a corporation to avoid the individual tax rates (when they were higher than the corporate rates) because it is not imposed unless a corporation has accumulations that are motivated at least in part by tax avoidance. Moreover, the accumulated earnings credit may shelter substantial accumulations from the Section 531 tax. Partially in response to these shortcomings and in order to prevent certain other tax avoidance devices, Congress enacted the personal holding company tax.[1]

The original purpose of the personal holding company tax was to prevent taxpayers from avoiding the higher graduated individual tax rates

1. H.Rep. No. 704, 73rd Cong., 2d Sess. (1934), reprinted in 1939–1 C.B. 554, 562.

by using devices known as "incorporated pocketbooks," "incorporated talents" and "incorporated properties." These schemes were structured as follows:

1. *Incorporated Pocketbooks.* A high bracket individual would transfer passive investments (e.g., stocks, bonds, rental property) to a corporation in exchange for its stock. The corporation then could take advantage of the lower corporate rates and the dividends received deduction for any dividends that it received. The income could be realized at a later date at capital gain rates through a liquidation of the company or, ideally, the stock could be held until the taxpayer's death when his heirs would take a stepped-up basis.

2. *Incorporated Talents.* A highly compensated individual, such as a movie star, would form a wholly owned corporation and agree to work for the corporation at a small salary. The corporation then would contract out the services of its owner-employee for a substantial sum, and the great bulk of the income would be taxed at the lower corporate rates.[2]

3. *Incorporated Properties.* A taxpayer would transfer both investment property and property which did not generate income, such as a yacht or home, to a corporation. The shareholder then would lease back the property for a nominal amount, and the corporation would attempt to shelter both the rental income and its other income by claiming deductions for depreciation and maintenance on the property.[3]

To combat these plans, Section 541 imposes a penalty tax of 15 percent on the "undistributed personal holding company income" of every "personal holding company." The personal holding company tax is imposed in addition to a corporation's regular income tax. To avoid overlap, personal holding companies are not subject to the accumulated earnings tax.[4] The remaining sections of this chapter consider the details and operation of the personal holding company tax, first examining the definition of a personal holding company and then turning to the determination of the tax.

2.   DEFINITION OF A PERSONAL HOLDING COMPANY

Code: § 542(a). Skim § 542(c).

A personal holding company is a corporation which satisfies a stock ownership requirement and an adjusted ordinary gross income test. Unlike the accumulated earnings tax, the determination of whether a corporation is a personal holding company is an objective inquiry that does not depend on whether there is a tax avoidance motive.

---

2. See Commissioner v. Laughton, 113 F.2d 103 (9th Cir.1940).

3. Bittker & Eustice, Federal Income Taxation of Corporations and Shareholders ¶ 7.20 (7th ed. 2000).

4. I.R.C. § 532(b)(1).

a. STOCK OWNERSHIP REQUIREMENT

Code: §§ 542(a)(2); 544.

The first leg of the definition of a personal holding company looks to whether the corporation is closely held. The stock ownership requirement in Section 542(a)(2) is satisfied if at any time during the last half of the taxable year more than 50 percent in value of the corporation's outstanding stock is owned, directly or indirectly, by or for not more than five individuals. Not surprisingly, this test is accompanied by special attribution rules in Section 544(a), under which stock owned by a corporation, partnership, estate or trust is considered owned proportionately by its shareholders, partners or beneficiaries.[1] An individual is considered to own stock owned by his family (brothers, sisters, spouse, ancestors and lineal descendants) or partners,[2] as well as stock held under an option to purchase.[3] Section 544(b)(1) provides that securities convertible into stock are considered stock for purposes of Section 542(a)(2) if the effect of their inclusion is to make the corporation a personal holding company.

b. INCOME TEST

Code: §§ 542(a)(1); 543.

The income test seeks to identify corporations with a significant amount of passive investment income or income attributable to the personal services of a major shareholder. Under Section 542(a)(1), at least 60 percent of a corporation's "adjusted ordinary gross income" (AOGI) must be "personal holding company income" before the corporation will be classified as a personal holding company. To apply this test, one must master some special terminology.

Adjusted Ordinary Gross Income. The function of AOGI is to provide an accurate measuring rod against which to compare a corporation's passive investment and personal service income. Its computation begins with the corporation's gross income, which is then reduced by capital and Section 1231 gains to arrive at ordinary gross income (OGI).[4] These gains are excluded from gross income in order to prevent corporations from timing gains (and inflating their income) to avoid the income test.[5]

Next, a series of adjustments must be made to OGI to determine AOGI. These adjustments also are designed to prevent easy avoidance of the income test by manipulation of the corporation's gross income. For example, gross income includes the full amount of receipts from the rental of property or royalties from mineral exploration. Absent some adjustment mechanism, corporations could generate enough gross income from leveraged investments in these properties to inflate AOGI and escape the personal holding company tax. In order to prevent this technique, AOGI

---

1. I.R.C. § 544(a)(1).
2. I.R.C. § 544(a)(2).
3. I.R.C. § 544(a)(3).
4. I.R.C. § 543(b)(1)(A), (B).

5. S.Rep. No. 830, 88th Cong., 2d Sess. (1964), reprinted in 1964–1 (pt. 2) C.B. 505, 611.

includes not all gross ordinary income but only the corporation's adjusted income from rents and royalties.[6] This amount includes income from rents and mineral, oil and gas royalties only to the extent that the gross income from these activities exceeds the amount deductible for depreciation or depletion, property taxes, interest and rent.[7] Since copyright royalties, royalties from films produced by the corporation and royalties from computer software produced by the corporation generally require more active participation than mineral or oil and gas royalties, the gross amount of royalties from copyrights, produced films or qualifying computer software businesses is included in AOGI.[8] Interest earned by dealers on obligations of the United States and interest on condemnation awards, judgments and tax refunds also is excluded from AOGI.[9]

Personal Holding Company Income. Students of the Internal Revenue Code have come to expect a large degree of complexity when Congress seeks to prevent tax avoidance. Congress must anticipate new efforts to avoid its corrective legislation while not penalizing taxpayers engaged in legitimate business or investment activities. These dual and often competing goals contribute to a web of special rules and exceptions. And so it is that the definition of personal holding company income in Section 543(a) is one of the Code's most diabolical provisions. Before turning to the necessary details, a few generalizations are in order. Incorporated pocketbooks and incorporated talents were Congress's prime targets when it first enacted and expanded the personal holding company tax. Consistent with that purpose, passive investment income and certain income from personal service contracts are the principal components of personal holding company income. But it is possible for rents, royalties, and other forms of income that appear to be passive to result from a corporation's legitimate active business pursuits. Section 543 attempts to identify the purely passive income and the types of personal service income targeted by the personal holding company provisions through the use of various mechanical tests, some of which are examined in more detail below.

Passive Investment Income Items: In General. Passive investment income items are the principal target of the personal holding company tax. Personal holding company income thus includes dividends, interest, annuities, royalties and rents.[10] Capital gains and Section 1231 gains are excluded because they historically have enjoyed preferential rates at both the corporate and individual levels. Dividends are defined by reference to Section 316 and are not reduced by the dividends received deduction. Interest includes imputed interest under provisions such as Sections 483 and 7872, but the types of interest excluded from AOGI (e.g., interest on condemnation awards, judgments or tax refunds) do not constitute personal holding company income. The inclusion of most forms of interest income may create unexpected difficulties for an otherwise active corporation

---

6.   S.Rep. No. 830, 88th Cong., 2d Sess. (1964), reprinted in 1964–1 (pt. 2) C.B. 505, 610.

7.   I.R.C. § 543(b)(2)(A), (B).

8.   I.R.C. § 543(b)(1), (3).

9.   I.R.C. § 543(b)(2)(C).

10.   I.R.C. § 543(a)(1).

which has sold a substantial portion of its assets on credit in a year when other receipts are minimal.[11] Royalties include income from licenses to use various types of intangible property (e.g., patents, trademarks, technical know-how)[12]a broad definition that may threaten a high technology company, such as a computer software manufacturer, that chooses to license its technology rather than market it directly. Royalties from natural resources, films, copyrights and computer software are treated separately and are discussed below.

Rents. One of the major sources of complexity in Section 543 results from its attempt to draw objective lines between passive investment income and profits from an active operating business. Nowhere is this better illustrated than in the area of rents. The treatment of rents was overhauled as part of substantial revisions to the personal holding company tax enacted in 1964. The following excerpt from the legislative history describes the Congressional solution:[13]

> *(c)(v) Rental income.*Under present law rental income is classified as personal holding company income only if it represents less than 50 percent of total gross income. This is based on the concept that where rental income represents the major activity, the activity involved is more likely to be of an active rather than passive character. The House bill retains this 50–percent test (applying it, however, to adjusted income from rents and to adjusted ordinary gross income) but adds a second test providing that rental income may be characterized as passive, or personal holding company income even where it represents 50 percent or more of the adjusted ordinary gross income if, apart from the rental income, more than 10 percent of the ordinary gross income (gross income excluding capital gains) of the company is personal holding company income. For this purpose, income derived from the use of corporate property by shareholders is not viewed as personal holding company income, but income from copyright royalties and the adjusted income from mineral, oil, and gas royalties is included for this purpose as personal holding company income.

> Your committee has accepted the House changes in the 50–percent test with one modification. Your committee has made an amendment to this test with regard to rentals of tangible personal property retained by the lessee for three years or less. Under the amendment, in the case of such property, the income is not to be reduced by depreciation attributable to it for purposes of the 50–percent test and also for purposes of computing ordinary gross income. However, in the case of the provision in the House bill that the personal holding company income (apart from rent) may not exceed 10 percent of the ordinary gross income, your commit-

11. See, e.g., O'Sullivan Rubber Co. v. Commissioner, 120 F.2d 845 (2d Cir.1941).

12. Reg. § 1.543–1(b)(3).

13. S.Rep. No. 830, 88th Cong., 2d Sess. (1964), reprinted in 1964–1 (pt. 2) C.B. 505, 611–613.

tee's amendments provide that the personal holding company income for this purpose may be reduced by dividends paid during the year, by dividends paid in the next year which are treated as if paid in the year in question, and by consent dividends. Your committee believes that this prevents the 10–percent rule from working harshly where the personal holding company income other than rents may exceed 10 percent of ordinary gross income, perhaps by only a small amount but under the House bill, nevertheless, result in the entire amount of rental income being classified as personal holding company income. Your committee's amendment in effect permits taxpayers to meet the 10–percent test after dividend payments (or amounts treated as paid in dividends). At the same time it gives assurance that the personal holding company income (apart from rent) sheltered in the company may not exceed 10 percent of its ordinary gross income.

The fact that rental income, both in applying the 60–percent test and also in applying the 50–percent provision to the rental income itself, is determined on the basis of reducing rental income by depreciation, amortization, property taxes, interest, and rents paid has already been noted above. However, as previously indicated, tangible personal property rented for three years or less is not reduced by depreciation attributable to it for purposes of these tests, under your committee's amendments.

Mineral, Oil and Gas Royalties. Income from mineral, oil and gas royalties also are singled out for special treatment. The "adjusted income" from these royalties constitutes personal holding company income unless: (1) such adjusted income constitutes 50 percent or more of the corporation's AOGI, (2) certain other forms of the corporation's personal holding company income do not exceed 10 percent of its OGI, and (3) the corporation's trade or business deductions, other than salaries and deductions specifically allowed by sections other than Section 162 (e.g., depreciation, interest, state taxes) exceed 15 percent of AOGI.[14]

Copyright Royalties. Under rules similar to those applicable to mineral royalties, copyright royalties are personal holding company income unless: (1) they constitute 50 percent or more of the corporation's OGI, (2) other personal holding company income after certain adjustments, does not exceed 10 percent of the corporation's OGI, and (3) Section 162 business deductions allocable to the copyright royalties, other than salaries, deductions for royalties paid and deductions specifically allowed by sections other than Section 162, equal or exceed 25 percent of OGI reduced by royalties paid and depreciation deductions attributable to the copyrights.[15]

Produced Film Rents. "Produced film rents" are personal holding company income unless they constitute 50 percent or more of OGI. Active motion picture companies thus have nothing to fear from this provision.

14. I.R.C. § 543(a)(3).   **15.** I.R.C. § 543(a)(4).

The purpose and scope of Section 543(a)(5) are explained in the following excerpt from the 1964 legislative history:[16]

> *(c)(viii) Produced film rents.*Under present law payments received from the distribution and exhibition of motion picture films are treated as rentals. As a result, under present law, a corporation may be formed by an individual who owns a motion picture negative and have its earnings treated as rents for purposes of the personal holding company tax. Since in such a case more than 50 percent of its gross income would be considered to be from rents, there would be no personal holding company tax payable in this case.
>
> To meet this problem, the bill provides that payments received from the use of, or the right to use, films generally will be characterized as copyright royalty income. Thus, such income will be classified as personal holding company income unless 50 percent or more of the company's ordinary income is from this source, not more than 10 percent of the company's ordinary gross income is personal holding company income, and the deductions properly allocable to this film income represent 25 percent or more of the gross income from this source reduced by royalties paid and depreciation taken.
>
> The bill, however, retains what is essentially the treatment of present law for "produced film rents." Produced film rents are rents arising from an interest in a film acquired before the production of the film was substantially complete. It was thought that less severe tests should be applied in such cases because the participation in the production of the film in itself indicates an active business enterprise in this case. For produced film rent to escape characterization as personal holding company income, as under present law, these rents need constitute only 50 percent or more of the ordinary gross income of the company.

Computer Software Royalties. Prior to 1987, a closely held company that manufactured computer software was confronted with the personal holding company tax if it licensed its technology instead of marketing it directly.[17] Despite the fact that the company was an active operating business, the payments received under the licensing agreements likely constituted personal holding company income under Section 543, which includes both "royalties" and certain "copyright royalties" in the definition of personal holding company income.[18] Congress responded to this problem by providing that computer software royalties do not constitute personal holding company income if they are "active business computer software

---

16.   S.Rep. No. 830, 88th Cong., 2d Sess. (1964), reprinted in 1964–1 (pt. 2) C.B. 505, 612–13.

17.   See generally Morgan, "The Domestic Technology Base Company: The Di-

lemma of an Operating Company Which Might Be a Personal Holding Company," 33 Tax L.Rev. 233 (1978).

18.   I.R.C. § 543(a)(1), (4).

royalties.''[19] That term is defined in Section 543(d)(1) as royalties, received by a corporation in connection with the licensing of computer software, which satisfy four requirements that generally are designed to restrict the exception to corporations earning a substantial portion of their income and incurring significant expenses in the active conduct of the trade or business of developing, manufacturing, or producing computer software.[20]

Personal Service Income. The final major category of personal holding company income is aimed at the incorporated talent. Income from contracts to furnish personal services, including income from the sale or other disposition of such contracts, is tainted if: (1) the individual who is to perform the services is designated by name or description in the contract or can be designated by some person other than the corporation, and (2) the designated individual owns (directly or through attribution) 25 percent or more of the value of the corporation's stock at any time during the year.[21]

Other Items. Personal holding company income also includes rents for the use of tangible property received from a 25 percent shareholder under certain conditions[22] and income derived by the corporation in its capacity as a beneficiary of an estate or trust.[23]

Revenue Ruling 75–67

1975–1 Cum.Bull. 169.

Advice has been requested whether, under the circumstances described below, a corporation will be considered to have received personal holding company income within the meaning of section 543(a)(7) of the Internal Revenue Code of 1954.

B, a doctor specializing in a certain area of medical services, owns 80 percent of the outstanding stock of L, a domestic professional service corporation. B is the only officer of L who is active in the production of income for L, and he is the only medical doctor presently employed by L. B performs medical services under an employment contract with L. L furnishes office quarters and equipment, and employs a receptionist to assist B. P, a patient, solicited the services of and was treated by B.

Section 543(a)(7) of the Code provides, in part, that the term personal holding company income includes amounts received under a contract whereby a corporation is to furnish personal services if some person other than the corporation has the right to designate, by name or description, the individual who is to perform the services, or if the individual who is to perform the services is designated, by name or description, in the contract.

---

19. I.R.C.§ 543(a)(1)(C),   (a)(4)   (last sentence).

20. I.R.C. § 543(d)(2)–(5).

21. I.R.C. § 543(a)(7). For detailed examples of the operation of this provision, see Reg. § 1.543–1(b)(8).

22. I.R.C. § 543(a)(6).

23. I.R.C. § 543(a)(8).

In dealing with a professional service corporation providing medical services, an individual will customarily solicit and expect to receive the services of a particular physician, and he will usually be treated by the physician sought.

A physician-patient relationship arises from such a general agreement of treatment. Either party may terminate the relationship at will, although the physician must give the patient reasonable notice of his withdrawal and may not abandon the patient until a replacement, if necessary, can be obtained. C. Morris & A. Mortiz, Doctor and Patient and the Law 135 (5th ed. 1971). Moreover, if a physician who has entered into a general agreement of treatment is unable to treat the patient when his services are needed, he may provide a qualified and competent substitute physician to render the services. C. Morris & A. Moritz, supra, at 138, 374–75.

Thus, when an individual solicits, and expects, the services of a particular physician and that physician accepts the individual as a patient and treats him, the relationship of physician-patient established in this manner does not constitute a designation of the individual who is to perform the services under a contract for personal services within the meaning of section 543(a)(7) of the Code.

If, however, the physician or the professional service corporation contracts with the patient that the physician personally will perform particular services for the patient, and he has no right to substitute another physician to perform such services, there is a designation of that physician as the individual to perform services under a contract for personal services within the meaning of section 543(a)(7) of the Code.

The designation of a physician as an individual to perform services can be accomplished by either an oral or written contract. See Rev.Rul. 69–299, 1969–1 C.B. 165.

Moreover, if L agreed to perform the type of services that are so unique as to preclude substitution of another physician to perform such services, there is also a designation.

Accordingly, since in the instant case there is no indication that L has contracted that B will personally perform the services or that the services are so unique as to preclude substitution, it is held that income earned by L from providing medical service contracts will not be considered income from personal service contracts within the meaning of section 543(a)(7) of the Code.

Revenue Ruling 84–137

1984–2 Cum.Bull. 116.

ISSUE

Is rental income received by a corporate lessor from a corporate lessee, which [sic] both corporations are owned by the same individual shareholder, compensation for the use of or right to use corporate property by a shareholder under section 543(a)(6) of the Internal Revenue Code for purposes of the personal holding company tax provisions?

FACTS

A, an individual, owns all of the shares of two corporations, X and Y. X's primary business activity is the leasing of realty and tangible personal property to its sister corporation Y for a fair market rental value. A makes no personal use of X's leased assets, which are used solely in Y's manufacturing business. In 1983, X received 100x dollars of rental income from Y and 12x dollars of interest income from its various bank deposits. The 12x dollars of interest income is personal holding company income as defined in section 543(a)(1) of the Code.

LAW AND ANALYSIS

Section 543(a)(6)(A) of the Code provides that amounts received as compensation for the use of, or the right to use, tangible property of the corporation in any case where at any time during the taxable year, 25 percent or more in value of the outstanding stock of the corporation is owned, directly or indirectly, by or for an individual entitled to the use of the property (whether such right is obtained directly from the corporation or by means of a sublease or other arrangement) is personal holding company income.

Section 543(a)(6)(B) of the Code provides that section 543(a)(6)(A) of the Code will apply only to a corporation which has other personal holding company income (as determined under section 543(a)(6)(C)) in excess of 10 percent of its ordinary gross income.

Rev.Rul. 65–259, 1965–2 C.B. 174, states that where rental income is derived from a corporate lessee, any one of whose shareholders also directly or indirectly owns 25 percent or more in value of the outstanding stock of the lessor corporation, the shareholder of the lessee corporation indirectly has the right to use the leased property and such indirect right is obtained by means of an "other arrangement". See 320 East 47th Street Corporation v. Commissioner, 243 F.2d 894 (2d Cir.1957), rev'g in part, 26 T.C. 545 (1956). Thus, Rev.Rul. 65–259 holds that the rental income is personal holding company income under section 543(a)(6) of the Code.

The Tax Court in Allied Industrial Cartage Co. v. Commissioner, 72 T.C. 515 (1979), aff'd, 647 F.2d 713 (6th Cir.1981), and Silverman and Sons Realty Trust v. Commissioner, T.C.M. 1979–404, aff'd, 620 F.2d 314 (1st Cir.1980), disagreed with the holding in 320 East 47th Street Corp. These cases hold that, as between brother and sister corporations, unless a corporate lessee is shown to be a vehicle for facilitating the individual or personal use of leased property by its shareholders, its separate status should not be disregarded so as to impose the personal holding company tax upon the lessor corporation. See also New Colonial Ice v. Helvering, 292 U.S. 435 (1934) XIII–2 C.B. 194; Minnesota Mortuaries, Inc. v. Commissioner, 4 T.C. 280 (1944); acq., 1945 C.B. 5, nonacq., 1965–2 C.B. 7, acq. page 5, this Bulletin.

HOLDING

If rental income is received by a corporate lessor from a corporate lessee, when both corporations are wholly owned by the same individual shareholder and the rented property is used solely in the trade or business of the lessee corporation and not for the individual or personal benefit of the shareholder, then such rental income is not compensation for the use of or right to use corporate property by a shareholder under section 543(a)(6) of the Code for purpose of the personal holding company tax provisions.

* * *

3.   TAXATION OF PERSONAL HOLDING COMPANIES

Code: §§ 541; 545(a).

Personal holding companies are subject to a tax of 15 percent of their undistributed personal holding company income.[1] The key to understanding the computation of the personal holding company tax is the concept of undistributed personal holding company income (UPHCI). The definition of UPHCI bears no relationship to the definition of personal holding company income. As defined in Section 545(a), UPHCI is essentially the corporation's after-tax profits less a dividends paid deduction.

a.   ADJUSTMENTS TO TAXABLE INCOME

Code: § 545(b).

The personal holding company tax is imposed on the corporation's real after-tax profits rather than its taxable income. Accordingly, in determining the tax base, certain adjustments are made to the corporation's taxable income so that it more nearly resembles the corporation's true economic income. Deductions are allowed for payments, such as federal taxes[2] and certain excess charitable contributions, which reduce the corporation's real wealth but are not allowable in computing taxable income.[3] Conversely, certain deductions which are allowable in determining taxable income but which do not decrease the corporation's real earnings for the year are not allowed in determining UPHCI. An example is the Section 243 dividends received deduction.[4] Net operating losses also receive special treatment.[5] Finally, in order to exempt long-term capital gains from the personal holding company tax, corporations may eliminate net capital gains less attributable taxes in determining UPHCI.[6]

Another Section 545(b) adjustment relates to a specific tax avoidance scheme mentioned earlier. Individuals cannot depreciate their homes, yachts, vacation homes or other property held for personal use. In order to

---

1. I.R.C. § 541.

2. I.R.C. § 545(b)(1).

3. I.R.C. § 545(b)(2). A special mixture of individual and corporate rules apply to determine the amount of the adjustment.

4. I.R.C. § 545(b)(3).

5. I.R.C. § 545(b)(4).

6. I.R.C. § 545(b)(5).

obtain the benefits of depreciation, individuals would transfer these assets to a corporation with other income and then lease them back in an attempt to convert the assets to income-producing status in the hands of the corporation. We have already seen that the resulting rental income will likely be personal holding company income. Section 545(b)(6) attacks this same scheme from a different angle. For purposes of determining UPHCI, if the corporation leases its property, the allocable business and depreciation deductions are limited to the rental income from the property unless the corporation can establish that: (1) the rent received for the property was the highest obtainable, (2) the property was held by the corporation in the course of a business for profit, and (3) there either was a reasonable expectation of profit from the property or the property was necessary to the conduct of the business.

b. DIVIDENDS PAID DEDUCTION

Code: §§ 561, 316(b), 562(a), (b), (c), 563, 564, 565. Skim § 547.

The purpose of the personal holding company tax is to force personal holding companies to distribute earnings to their individual shareholders. It follows that to the extent a personal holding company distributes its earnings, the Section 541 tax should not apply. To qualify for the dividends paid deduction, distributions generally must be pro rata.[7] Under Section 561(a), the dividends paid deduction equals the sum of the dividends paid during the taxable year, consent dividends, and the dividend carryover under Section 564. The combination of these provisions make it highly unlikely that any well informed personal holding company ever will be subject to the penalty tax.

Dividends Paid During the Year. Dividends paid during the year are determined by reference to the definition of a dividend in Section 316. For purposes of the dividends paid deduction, the regulations provide that a dividend in kind of appreciated property may only be deducted to the extent of the corporation's basis in the distributed property.[8] This rule is at variance with the treatment of such dividends to shareholders, for whom the "amount" of the distribution is the full fair market value of the distributed property under Section 301(b)(1)(A). But the regulation was upheld by the Supreme Court on the general ground that Treasury Regulations should be sustained by the courts whenever they have a "reasonable basis."[9] Query whether the same approach should be used for distributions of property that has declined in value?

Distributions and redemptions treated as Section 301 distributions are, of course, taxable as dividends to the shareholders to the extent of the corporation's available earnings and profits. If a corporation is a personal holding company, however, distributions may be taxed as dividends even if there are no available earnings and profits. Under Section 316(b)(2), if a

---

7. I.R.C. § 562(c).

8. Reg. § 1.562–1(a).

9. Fulman v. United States, 434 U.S. 528, 98 S.Ct. 841 (1978).

personal holding company makes distributions in excess of the available earnings and profits, the distributions are nonetheless treated as dividends for all purposes to the extent of the corporation's UPHCI. This rule also applies if a corporation is considered to make a distribution under Section 563(b) (dividends paid after the year) or Section 547 (deficiency dividends) in a year in which it is a personal holding company.

Section 563(b) Election. If a corporation elects under Section 563(b), dividends paid or on before the 15th day of the third month following the close of a taxable year will be treated as having been paid during the prior year. The amount allowed as a dividend under Section 563(b) can not exceed either the corporation's UPHCI for the prior taxable year or 20 percent of the actual dividends paid during the prior year.[10]

Consent Dividends. If a corporation does not make actual distributions during the relevant period, it still can qualify for a dividends paid deduction to the extent that its shareholders consent to be taxed as if they had received pro rata distributions during the year and had immediately made capital contributions of the same amount.[11] Consent dividends are deductible only to the extent that all the shareholders consent to be taxed on a pro rata basis[12] and only to the extent that actual distributions would be dividends under Section 316(a) or 316(b).

Dividend Carryover. Even if a corporation pays no actual or consent dividends, it is entitled to a current dividend deduction if it has paid sufficient dividends in either or both of the two preceding years. Under Section 564 the amount of this deduction is the greater of the excess of the dividends paid deduction (without carryovers) over taxable income, as adjusted in Section 545, for the preceding year, or the excess of the combined dividends paid deduction (without carryovers) for the preceding two years over the total taxable income (again adjusted under Section 545) for the same two years. Roughly translated, this means that a corporation that over distributes in prior years may distribute less in the current year in determining its exposure to the tax.

Liquidating Distributions. If a corporation is liquidating, it still may be a personal holding company. Indeed, an operating company may become a personal holding company during the process of liquidating if it ceases its operations in a taxable year prior to its final liquidating distribution and has only passive investment income in that terminal year. In order to avoid penalizing liquidating corporations by denying them a dividends paid deduction for actual liquidating distributions, Section 562(b)(2) provides that if the corporation liquidates within 24 months of adopting a plan of liquidation, liquidating distributions to corporate shareholders are treated as dividends for purposes of the dividends paid deduction to the extent of the shareholder's proportionate share of UPHCI for the year of the distribution. At the corporation's election, liquidating distributions to noncorpo-

---

10. The timing of the shareholder's income is not affected by the Section 563(b) election.

11. I.R.C. § 565(c).

12. I.R.C. § 565(b)(1).

rate shareholders also may be treated as dividends under Section 316(b)(2)(B) to the extent of the shareholders' proportionate share of UPHCI. If they are so treated, the corporation is entitled to take the dividends paid deduction. Unlike corporate shareholders, however, noncorporate shareholders must treat such liquidating distributions as dividend income under Section 316(b) rather than capital gain under Section 331.

Deficiency Dividends. If a corporation is determined to be a personal holding company for a particular year, Section 547 permits the corporation to reduce its personal holding company tax base (but not interest or penalties) by the amount of its "deficiency dividends." Deficiency dividends are defined as amounts paid within 90 days of the determination of personal holding company tax liability which would have been eligible for the dividends paid deduction if distributed in the year in which Section 541 tax liability exists.[13] A deficiency dividend is allowed as of the date a claim for dividend is filed.[14]

PROBLEMS

1. X Corporation is wholly owned by A. Determine whether X is a personal holding company under each of the following alternatives:

(a) X manufactures umbrellas. In year one, X has $2,000,000 gross receipts from sales, and its cost of goods sold is $800,000. It has no other income or expenses and makes no distributions.

(b) X's business hits a dry spell in year two. Its gross receipts from sales are $900,000, and its cost of goods sold is $890,000. X also receives $30,000 interest on its $200,000 profit from year one, which it deposited in a savings account.

(c) What result in (b), above, if X also had $30,000 of § 1231 gains in year two? What about $10,000 of § 1231 gains and $20,000 of § 1245 gain?

2. Consider whether the following corporations are personal holding companies:

(a) Basketball Corporation is wholly owned by Dr. K, who plays professional basketball. Dr. K contracts to work for the corporation for $150,000 per year. Basketball Corporation then contracts with Team to provide Dr. K's services to Team for $300,000 per year.

(b) What result in (a), above, if Basketball purchases a movie theater by paying $20,000 down and taking the theater subject to a $180,000 mortgage. During the year, the theater has receipts of $300,000 and deductible expenses (depreciation interest, salaries and film rents) of $300,000?

13. I.R.C. § 547(d)(1).

14. I.R.C. § 547(b)(1). A claim must be filed within 120 days after the determination of personal holding company tax liability. I.R.C. § 547(e).

(c) Attorney forms Professional Corporation and incorporates his private practice. During the year the corporation earns fees of $300,000 and pays Attorney a salary of $150,000.

(d) Aside from the personal holding company tax, what other challenges might the Service assert in parts (a)–(c)?

3. Iris Securities Company is wholly owned by Investor. Determine whether Iris is a personal holding company, and if so, the amount of the § 541 tax, under the following circumstances:

(a) Iris earns a total of $30,000 of interest and dividends in year one. Iris also owns an apartment complex. During the past year, it collected rents of $100,000. Iris's only deductions were depreciation of $35,000, mortgage interest of $30,000, and property taxes of $5,000. Iris makes no distributions during the year.

(b) Assume that Investor comes to you for tax advice on December 15 of year one. If Iris uses the calendar year as its taxable year, can it avoid personal holding company status? What if Investor comes to you in January of year two?

4. Operating Company is owned equally by Ms. Active and by X Corporation. Operating Company has been engaged in the retail sales business. In June of year one, Operating Company adopts a plan to liquidate. In December of year one, it sells all its assets for $1,000,000, which it deposits in a short-term savings account. In June of year two, after having earned $50,000 interest during the year, Operating Company liquidates by distributing $525,000 to each shareholder.

(a) What are the tax consequences to Operating and its shareholders?

(b) What alternatives are available?

PART THREE

Taxation of S Corporations

CHAPTER 15

S CORPORATIONS*

A. INTRODUCTION

We have seen that a C corporation's net income is subject to tax at rates ranging from 15 to 35 percent,[1] and those earnings are taxed again when distributed as dividends to individual shareholders.[2] Although many techniques have been devised to avoid the double tax, it nonetheless remains the principal feature distinguishing the taxation of incorporated and unincorporated businesses. We also have seen that partnerships and limited liability companies are treated for tax purposes as conduits whose income and deductions pass through to the partners or members as they are realized, with the various items retaining their original character in the process.[3] Because income is taxed at the partner level, partnership distributions of cash and property generally do not produce any additional tax liability.[4]

Taxpayers have long sought to obtain the state law benefits of the corporate form (limited liability, centralized management, etc.) without the sting of the double tax. Congress attempted to accommodate this desire in 1958 when it enacted Subchapter S, which then permitted the shareholders of a "small business corporation" to elect to avoid a corporate level tax in most situations. The stated purpose of Subchapter S was to permit a business to select its legal form "without the necessity of taking into account major differences in tax consequence."[5]

As originally adopted, Subchapter S was a modified corporate scheme of taxation rather than a partnership-like pass-through regime. This early version was a strange hybrid of corporate and partnership concepts, laden with complexity. In these formative years, an electing small business necessarily depended on skilled lawyers and accountants to avoid Subchapter S's many technical traps. Calls for reform began with a 1969 Treasury Department study, which in general proposed a liberalization of the eligibility requirements and the adoption of a conduit approach more closely conforming to the tax treatment of partnerships.[6] Congress gradually

---

* See generally Eustice and Kuntz, Federal Income Taxation of Subchapter S Corporations (4th ed. 2001).

1. I.R.C. § 11.

2. I.R.C. §§ 61(a)(7), 301.

3. I.R.C. § 702(a), (b). Most limited liability companies are treated as partnerships for tax purposes. See Chapter 1C2a, supra, and Lind, Schwarz, Lathrope & Rosenberg,

Fundamentals of Partnership Taxation (7th ed. 2005).

4. I.R.C. § 731(a).

5. S.Rep. No. 1983, 85th Cong., 2d Sess. § 68 (1958), reprinted in 1958–3 C.B. 922.

6. See U.S. Treasury Department, Technical Explanation of Treasury Tax Reform Proposals: Hearings Before the House

relaxed the eligibility requirements through piecemeal legislation, most notably the Subchapter S Revision Act of 1982.[7] The 1982 Act greatly reduced the tax disparities between Subchapter S corporations and partnerships by replacing the modified corporate structure of Subchapter S with a statutory scheme which is similar but not identical to the tax treatment of partnerships and partners under Subchapter K. The Act also introduced the terminology now used in the Code. Electing small business corporations are called "S corporations" while other corporations are known as "C corporations."[8]

Subsequent legislation, culminating with the American Jobs Creation Act of 2004, further liberalized the Subchapter S eligibility requirements and eliminated technical traps for corporations seeking to elect and maintain S corporation status. As a result of these reforms, the tax differences between partnerships and S corporations have narrowed, making operation as an S corporation a viable, albeit less flexible, alternative for some closely held businesses. But significant differences in tax treatment remain between S corporations and unincorporated businesses. For example, Subchapter S status is available only for corporations that satisfy the statutory definition of "small business corporation" in Section 1361(b). This definition restricts eligibility to corporations with 100 or fewer shareholders; prohibits more than one class of stock; and limits the types of permissible shareholders. Moreover, partners' bases in their partnership interests are increased by their share of partnership liabilities,[9] while debts incurred by an S corporation have no effect on the bases of the corporation's shareholders in their stock. This difference may have an impact upon the ability of investors to utilize losses generated by the enterprise and the treatment of distributions.[10] Subchapter K also offers partners more flexibility in determining their individual tax results from partnership operations. Partnership allocations of specific items of income or deduction to a particular partner will be respected as long as the allocation has substantial economic effect, while shareholders of an S corporation are required to report a pro rata share of each corporate item.[11]

For a brief time, the inverted rate structure introduced by the Tax Reform Act of 1986 expanded the role of S corporations by reducing the top individual rate below the maximum rate for C corporations and broadening the corporate tax base. As a result, many closely held businesses requiring the corporate form and able to meet the eligibility requirements chose to operate as S corporations. The current maximum individual rate on ordinary income now equals the top corporate rate. More importantly, the emergence of the limited liability company, with its far greater flexibility, and the Service's willingness to allow any unincorporated business entity to

---

Comm. on Ways and Means, 91st Cong., 1st Sess. 5228–5275 (April 22, 1969).

7. Pub.L. No. 97–354 (1982), reprinted in 1982–2 C.B. 702.

8. I.R.C. § 1361(a).

9. I.R.C. § 752(a).

10. See also I.R.C. § 469, limiting the current deductibility of losses from certain passive activities.

11. Compare I.R.C. § 704(b)(2) with I.R.C. §§ 1366(a) & 1377(a).

elect partnership status for tax purposes, have profoundly influenced the choice of entity decision.[12] At least for newly formed businesses, many predicted that these developments would threaten to send S corporations to the sidelines, despite the more liberal eligibility requirements introduced by Congress. Many existing S corporations remain on the scene, however, and the S corporation tax regime and governance structure are relatively simple and familiar. In fact, S corporations became the most common corporate entity type in 1997 and, for taxable year 2001, 58.2 percent of all corporations filing tax returns were S corporations.[13] Thus, S corporations continue to be an important option for investors and a study of the fundamentals of Subchapter S is essential for a comprehensive understanding of business enterprise taxation. It also is instructive to compare the provisions of Subchapters S and K and to consider which of these pass-through taxation models is preferable from a policy standpoint.[14]

B.   ELIGIBILITY FOR S CORPORATION STATUS

Code: § 1361.

Eligibility to make a Subchapter S election is limited to a "small business corporation," defined in Section 1361(b) as a domestic corporation[1] which is not an "ineligible corporation" and which has: (1) no more than 100 shareholders, (2) only shareholders who are individuals, estates, and certain types of trusts and tax-exempt organizations, (3) no nonresident alien shareholders, and (4) not more than one class of stock. The 100–shareholder limit disqualifies publicly traded corporations from S status, and the one-class-of-stock rule shuts the door to corporations with complex capital structures. Significantly, however, a "small business corporation" need not be small when measured by income or value as a going concern, and some very large enterprises operate as S corporations.

Some remaining aspects of the S corporation eligibility requirements are summarized below.

Ineligible Corporations and Subsidiaries. An "ineligible corporation" may not qualify as a "small business corporation."[2] Certain types of corporations, such as banks and insurance companies, are "ineligible" because they are governed by other specialized tax regimes.[3] At one time, any corporation that was a member of an "affiliated group" also was ineligible to be an S corporation—a rule that effectively precluded S corporations from owning 80 percent or more of the stock of another C or S

---

12. See Chapter 1C2a, supra.

13. Bennett, "S Corporation Returns," 2001, 23 SOI Bulletin 47 (2004).

14. See Section H of this chapter, infra.

1. I.R.C. § 1361(b)(1). A domestic corporation is defined as a corporation created

or organized in the United States or under the laws of the United States or of any state or territory. Reg. §§ 1.1361–1(c); 301.7701–5.

2. I.R.C. § 1361(b)(1).

3. I.R.C. § 1361(b)(2).

corporation.[4] Under current law, S corporations may hold subsidiaries under certain conditions. C corporation subsidiaries generally are permitted,[5] and a parent-subsidiary relationship between two S corporations also is allowed if the parent elects to treat its offspring as a "qualified subchapter S subsidiary" ("QSSS"), which generally is defined as a 100 percent owned domestic corporation that is not an "ineligible corporation" and otherwise would qualify for S status if all of its stock were held by the shareholders of its parent.[6] If this QSSS election is made, the subsidiary is disregarded for tax purposes, and all of its assets, liabilities, income, deductions, and credits are treated as belonging to its S parent.[7] The regulations provide detailed procedures to govern revocation and other terminations of a QSSS election. In general, they treat a terminating event as a deemed incorporation of a new subsidiary that is governed by general tax principles.[8]

Number of Shareholders. Congress has made S corporations more widely available by gradually increasing the number of permissible shareholders. The current 100-shareholder limit[9] is nearly triple an earlier 35-shareholder cap. For purposes of this limit, a husband and wife (and their estates) are counted as one shareholder regardless of their form of ownership.[10] If stock is jointly owned (e.g., as tenants in common or joint tenants) by other than a husband and wife, each joint owner is considered a separate shareholder.[11] In the case of a nominee, guardian, custodian, or agent holding stock in a representative capacity, the beneficial owners of the stock are counted toward the 100-shareholder limit.[12]

In addition to the special rule for a husband and wife, all the members of a "family" may elect to be treated as a single shareholder for purposes of the 100-shareholder limit.[13] A family is defined as the lineal descendants (and their spouses and former spouses) of a common ancestor who is no more than six generations removed from the youngest generation shareholder at the time the election is made.[14] The election to be treated as one shareholder may be made by any member of the family and remains in

---

4. I.R.C. § 1361(b)(2)(A)(pre–1997).

5. I.R.C. § 1504(b)(8). The S parent, however, may not join in a consolidated return with the C corporation. See Chapter 13B for a discussion of consolidated returns.

6. I.R.C. § 1361(b)(3)(B). For election procedures, see Reg. § 1.1361–3(a).

7. I.R.C. § 1361(b)(3)(A). See Reg. § 1.1361–4(a)(1). If a subsidiary was in existence and had a prior tax history, the QSSS election triggers a deemed liquidation of the subsidiary under Sections 332 and 337 as of the day before the election is effective. Reg. § 1.1361–4(a).

8. See Reg. § 1.1361–5(b).

9. I.R.C. § 1361(b)(1)(A).

10. I.R.C. § 1361(c)(1)(A)(i); Reg. § 1.1361–1(e)(2).

11. I.R.C. § 1.1361–1(e)(2).

12. Reg. § 1.1361–1(e)(1).

13. I.R.C. § 1361(c)(1)(A)(ii). If a husband and wife are part of an electing family they are counted as part of that family. I.R.C. § 1361(c)(1)(A)(i).

14. I.R.C. § 1361(c)(1)(B). Adopted children and foster children are treated as children by blood. I.R.C. § 1361(c)(1)(C) (mistakenly citing I.R.C. § 152(b)(2).). A spouse is considered to be of the same generation as the individual to whom the spouse is married. I.R.C. § 1361(c)(1)(B)(ii).

effect until terminated as provided in regulations that will be issued by the Service.[15]

Eligible Shareholders. Congress also has gradually expanded the eligible S corporation shareholder pool. Once limited to individuals who were U.S. citizens or resident aliens, the permissible shareholder list now also includes decedent's and bankruptcy estates,[16] certain types of trusts discussed in more detail below,[17] qualified pension trusts, and charitable organizations that are exempt from tax under Section 501(c)(3).[18] A corporation still may not make an S election if any of its shareholders are C corporations, partnerships, ineligible trusts, or nonresident aliens.[19]

When Subchapter S was first enacted, trusts were not eligible shareholders, primarily because of Congress's desire for a relatively simple one-tier corporate tax regime where all beneficial owners were clearly identifiable. In response to the pleas of tax advisors to closely held businesses, Congress gradually relented by permitting various widely used types of trusts to be S corporation shareholders if certain conditions are met. Under current law, the trusts that are permissible shareholders include:

(1) Voting trusts, in which case each beneficial owner is treated as a separate shareholder;[20]

(2) Grantor trusts—i.e., domestic trusts treated for tax purposes as owned by their grantor—provided the grantor is an individual who is a U.S. citizen or resident.[21] An example would be the commonly used revocable living trust created to provide for continuity of asset management in the event of the grantor's disability and to avoid probate administration on death. For purposes of the 100–shareholder limit, the deemed owner of the trust is treated as the shareholder.[22]

(3) Former grantor trusts that continue as testamentary trusts, but only for the two-year period following the grantor's death.[23] The former deemed owner's estate is treated as the S corporation shareholder.[24]

(4) Testamentary trusts that receive S corporation stock under the terms of a will, but again only for the two-year period after the date of transfer of the stock to the trust.[25] The testator's estate

---

15. I.R.C. § 1361(c)(1)(1). Regulations may also change the rule that the election may be made by one family member.

16. I.R.C. §§ 1361(b)(1)(B), (c)(3).

17. See infra text accompanying notes 20–35.

18. I.R.C. §§ 1361(b)(1)(B), (c)(6). The trade-off for tax-exempt pension trusts and Section 501(c)(3) organizations is that their interest in the S corporation is treated as an interest in an "unrelated trade or business," and any net income is generally taxable at the trust or corporate rates. I.R.C. § 512(e)(1).

19. I.R.C. § 1361(b)(1)(B).

20. I.R.C. § 1361(c)(2)(A)(iv), (B)(iv).

21. I.R.C. § 1361(c)(2)(A)(i). Foreign grantor trusts are not eligible shareholders. I.R.C. § 1361(c)(2)(A), flush language.

22. I.R.C. § 1361(c)(2)(B)(i).

23. I.R.C. § 1361(c)(2)(A)(ii).

24. I.R.C. § 1361(c)(2)(B)(ii).

25. I.R.C. § 1361(c)(2)(A)(iii).

continues to be treated as the S corporation shareholder.[26]

(5) Qualified Subchapter S trusts ("QSSTs"), defined generally as trusts all of the income of which is actually distributed or must be distributed currently to one individual who is a U.S. citizen or resident.[27] A QSST may only have one current income beneficiary, who must elect QSST status and, as a result, is treated as the owner for tax purposes of the portion of the trust consisting of the S corporation stock with respect to which the election was made.[28] Among other things, the QSST definition permits a Qualified Terminable Interest Property ("QTIP") Trust,[29] the most widely used type of estate tax marital deduction trust created for the benefit of a surviving spouse, to hold S corporation stock.

(6) Electing small business trusts ("ESBTs"), a statutory creation that potentially expands the usefulness of S corporations in estate planning for a family business. All the beneficiaries of an ESBT must be individuals or estates who are eligible S corporation shareholders, or charitable organizations holding contingent remainder interests.[30] The beneficial interests in an ESBT must have been acquired by gift or bequest, not purchase,[31] and the trust must elect ESBT status to qualify as an S corporation shareholder.[32] Each potential current beneficiary of the trust is treated as a shareholder for purposes of the 100–shareholder limit,[33] but the trust's pro rata share of S corporation income is taxable to the trust at the highest individual marginal rates under rules specially designed for this purpose.[34] The significance of the ESBT category is that it permits inter vivos and testamentary trusts with more than one beneficiary—e.g., a "sprinkling" trust where the trustee has discretion to determine whether and how much income or corpus to distribute among several beneficiaries—to qualify as an S corporation shareholder.

The legislative history of the rule treating a family as one shareholder for the 100–shareholder limit explains that the rule applies to family members who own stock directly as well as those who are shareholders because they are beneficiaries of a QSST or ESBT.[35]

---

26. I.R.C. § 1361(c)(2)(B)(iii).

27. I.R.C. § 1361(d).

28. Id.

29. See I.R.C. § 2056(b)(7).

30. I.R.C. § 1361(e)(1)(A)(i). Charitable remainder trusts, however, may not be S corporation shareholders. I.R.C. § 1361(e)(1)(B)(iii). See also Rev. Rul. 92–48, 1992–1 C.B. 301.

31. I.R.C. § 1361(e)(1)(A)(ii).

32. I.R.C. § 1361(e)(1)(A)(iii). Trusts that already have made a QSST election or are wholly exempt from tax do not qualify as ESBTs. I.R.C. § 1361(e)(1)(B).

33. I.R.C. § 1361(c)(2)(B)(v). If there are no potential current income beneficiaries, then the trust is treated as the shareholder for that period. Id.

34. I.R.C. § 641(d).

35. H.Rep. No.108–755, 108th Cong., 2d Sess. 34 (2004).

One-Class-of-Stock Requirement. An S corporation may issue both stock and debt, but it may not have more than one class of stock.[36] The purpose of this rule is to simplify the allocation of income and deductions among an S corporation's shareholders and prevent "special allocations" and their potential for income shifting. The one-class-of-stock requirement has spawned many controversies over its history, but the issuance of final regulations has resolved the most contentious issues.

An S corporation generally is treated as having one class of stock if all of its outstanding shares confer identical rights to distributions and liquidation proceeds.[37] Significantly, differences in voting rights among classes of common stock are disregarded, permitting an S corporation to issue both voting and nonvoting common stock.[38] In determining whether outstanding stock confers identical rights to distribution and liquidation proceeds, the regulations look to the corporate charter, articles of incorporation, bylaws, applicable state law, and binding shareholders' agreements.[39]

Commercial contractual arrangements, such as leases, employment agreements, or loan agreements, are disregarded in determining whether a second class of stock is present unless a principal purpose of the agreement is to circumvent the one class of stock requirement.[40] For example, differences in salary or fringe benefits paid to employee-shareholders under compensation agreements will not result in a second class of stock if the agreements are not designed to circumvent the requirement.[41] Bona fide agreements to redeem or purchase stock at the time of death, divorce, disability or termination of employment also are disregarded in determining whether an S corporation has a second class of stock.[42] Other shareholder buy-sell, stock transfer and redemption agreements are disregarded in determining whether a corporation's outstanding shares confer identical distribution and liquidation rights unless: (1) a principal purpose of the agreement is to circumvent the one-class-of-stock requirement, and (2) the purchase price under the agreement is significantly in excess of or below the fair market value of the stock. Agreements that provide for a purchase or redemption of stock at book value or at a price between book value and fair market value satisfy the purchase price standard.[43]

36. I.R.C. § 1361(b)(1)(D).

37. Reg. § 1.1361–1(*l*)(1). "Outstanding stock" generally does not include stock that is subject to a substantial risk of forfeiture under Section 83 unless the holder has made the Section 83(b) election. Reg. § 1.1361–1(*l*)(3).

38. I.R.C. § 1361(c)(4); Reg. § 1.1361–1(*l*)(1).

39. Reg. § 1.1361–1(*l*)(2)(i).

40. Reg. § 1.1361–1(*l*)(2)(i).

41. Reg. § 1.1361–1(*l*)(2)(v) Examples (3) & (4). Any distributions (actual, constructive or deemed) that differ in timing or amount are given appropriate tax treatment.

For example, even though an employment agreement does not result in a second class of stock, excessive compensation paid under the agreement is not deductible. Reg. § 1.1361–1(*l*)(2)(i), (v) Example (3).

42. Reg. § 1.1361–1(*l*)(2)(iii)(B).

43. Reg. § 1.1361–1(*l*)(2)(iii)(A). A good faith determination of fair market value is respected unless it is substantially in error and was not determined with reasonable diligence. Id. A determination of book value is respected if it is determined in accordance with generally accepted accounting principles or used for any substantial nontax purpose. Reg. § 1.1361–1(*l*)(2)(iii)(C).

Unless the straight debt safe harbor applies,[44] any instrument, obligation or arrangement issued by a corporation (other than outstanding stock) is treated as a second class of stock if: (1) it constitutes equity under general tax principles, and (2) a principal purpose of issuing or entering into the instrument, obligation or arrangement is to circumvent the distribution and liquidation rights of outstanding shares or the limitation on eligible shareholders.[45] Safe harbors from reclassification are provided for short-term unwritten advances to the corporation that do not exceed $10,000 and obligations held proportionately among the shareholders.[46] The existence of various corporate instruments that give holders the right to acquire stock (e.g., call options or warrants) also may create a second class of stock depending upon whether the right is substantially certain to be exercised by the holder.[47]

Straight Debt Safe Harbor. The interaction of the one-class-of-stock limitation with the debt vs. equity classification issues encountered under Subchapter C[48] historically presented some knotty problems for S corporations with outstanding debt. In the formative years of Subchapter S, the Service adopted a practice of reclassifying nominal S corporation debt owed to shareholders as a second class of stock, causing the corporation to lose its S status.[49] This threat has diminished considerably by a safe harbor provision in Section 1361(c)(5) under which "straight debt" is not treated as a disqualifying second class of stock. "Straight debt" is defined as any written unconditional promise to pay on demand or on a specified date a sum certain in money if: (1) the interest rate and payment dates are not contingent on profits, the borrower's discretion or similar factors; (2) the instrument is not convertible (directly or indirectly) into stock; and (3) the creditor is an individual (other than a nonresident alien), an estate or trust that would be a qualifying shareholder in an S corporation, or a person that is actively and regularly engaged in the business of lending money.[50] The fact that an obligation is subordinated to other debt of the corporation does not prevent it from qualifying as straight debt.[51]

Obligations that qualify as straight debt are not classified as a second class of stock even if they would be considered equity under general tax principles and they generally are treated as debt for other purposes of the Code.[52] Thus, interest paid or accrued on straight debt is treated as such by the corporation and the recipient and does not constitute a distribution

---

44. See I.R.C. § 1361(c)(5) and notes 48–55, infra, and accompanying text.

45. Reg. § 1.1361–1(*l*)(4)(ii)(A).

46. Reg. § 1.1361–1(*l*)(4)(ii)(B).

47. Reg. § 1.1361–1(*l*)(4)(iii). Exceptions are provided for certain call options in connection with loans or to employees and independent contractors. If the strike price of a call option is at least 90 percent of its fair market value at its issuance, it is not substantially certain to be exercised. Reg. § 1.1361–1(*l*)(4)(iii)(B)–(C).

48. See generally I.R.C. § 385 and Chapter 3B, infra.

49. The courts, however, usually were not receptive to this argument. See, e.g., Portage Plastics Co. v. United States, 486 F.2d 632 (7th Cir.1973).

50. I.R.C. § 1361(c)(5)(B).

51. Reg. § 1.1361–1(*l*)(5)(ii).

52. I.R.C. § 1361(c)(5)(A); Reg. § 1.1361–1(*l*)(5)(iv).

governed by Section 1368.[53] But if a straight debt instrument bears an unreasonably high rate of interest, the regulations provide than an "appropriate" portion may be recharacterized and treated as a payment that is not interest.[54] If a C corporation has outstanding debt obligations that satisfy the straight debt definition but may be classified as equity under general tax principles, the safe harbor ensures that the obligation will not be treated as a second class of stock if the C corporation elects to convert to S status. The conversion and change of status also is not treated as an exchange of the debt instrument for stock.[55]

PROBLEM

Unless otherwise indicated, Z Corporation ("Z") is a domestic corporation which has 120 shares of voting common stock outstanding. In each of the following alternative situations, determine whether Z is eligible to elect S corporation status:

(a) Z has 99 unrelated individual shareholders, each of whom owns one share of Z stock. The remaining 21 shares are owned by A and his brother, B, as joint tenants with right of survivorship.

(b) Same as (a), above, except that A and B are married and own 11 of the 21 shares as community property. The remaining 10 shares are owned 5 by A as her separate property and 5 by B as his separate property.

(c) In (b), above, assume that the shareholders of Z elected S corporation status. What will be the effect on Z's election if one year later A dies and bequeaths her interest in Z stock to F, her long-time friend?

(d) Same as (a), above, except that the remaining 21 shares are held by a voting trust which has three beneficial owners.

(e) Same as (a), above, except that the remaining 21 shares are owned by a revocable living trust created by an individual, the income of which is taxed to the grantor under § 671.

(f) Same as (a), above, except that the remaining 21 shares are owned by a testamentary trust under which the surviving spouse has the right to income for her life, with the remainder passing to her children. The trust is a "qualified terminable interest trust" (see § 2056(b)(7)).

(g) Assume Z has 100 individual shareholders and forms a partnership with two other S corporations, each of which also have 100 individual shareholders, for the purposes of jointly operating a business. Z's one-third interest in this partnership is its only asset.

---

53. Id.

54. Id. Such a reclassification does not result in a second class of stock.

55. Reg. § 1.1361–1(*l*)(5)(v).

(h) Z has 100 shares of Class A voting common stock and 50 shares of Class B nonvoting common stock outstanding. Apart from the differences in voting rights, the two classes of common stock have equal rights with regard to dividends and liquidation distributions. Z also has an authorized but unissued class of nonvoting stock which would be limited and preferred as to dividends. The Class A common stock is owned by four individuals and the Class B common stock is owned by E and F (a married couple) as tenants-in-common.

(i) Same as (h), above, except that Z enters into a binding agreement with its shareholders to make larger annual distributions to shareholders who bear heavier state income tax burdens. The amount of the distributions is based on a formula that will give the shareholders equal after-tax distributions.

(j) Z has four individual shareholders each of whom own 100 shares of Z common stock for which each paid $10 per share. Each shareholder also owns $25,000 of 15–year Z bonds. The bonds bear interest at 3% above the prime lending rate established by the Chase Manhattan Bank, adjusted quarterly, and are subordinated to general creditors of Z.

C. ELECTION, REVOCATION AND TERMINATION

Code: §§ 1362 (omit (e)(5)–(6)); 1378. Skim §§ 444(a), (b), (c)(1), (e); 7519(a), (b), (d)(1), (e)(4).

Electing S Corporation Status. An otherwise eligible corporation may elect S corporation status under Section 1362 if all the shareholders consent.[1] Once made, an election remains effective until it is terminated under Section 1362(d).[2] An election is effective as of the beginning of a taxable year if it is made either during the preceding taxable year or on or before the fifteenth day of the third month of the current taxable year.[3] If the election is made during the first 2½ months of the year, the S corporation eligibility requirements must have been met for the portion of the taxable year prior to the election, and all shareholders at any time during the pre-election portion of the year must consent to the election.[4] If the eligibility requirements are not met during the pre-election period or if

---

1. I.R.C. § 1362(a). For rules and procedures on shareholders' consent to an S election, see Reg. § 1.1362–6.

2. I.R.C. § 1362(c). See generally Reg. § 1.1362–2.

3. I.R.C. § 1362(b)(1). Elections made not later than 2 months and 15 days after the first day of the taxable year are deemed made during the year even if the year is shorter than 2 months and 15 days. I.R.C.

§ 1362(b)(4). For rules on how to count months and days for this purpose, see Reg. § 1.1362–6(a)(2)(ii). For the Service's authority to treat a late election as timely if there was reasonable cause for the tardiness, see I.R.C. § 1362(b)(5). See Rev. Proc. 2004–48, 2004–2 C.B. 172, for the procedures to obtain relief for a late election.

4. I.R.C. § 1362(b)(2).

any shareholder who held stock during that period does not consent, the election does not become effective until the following taxable year.[5] In some cases, however, such as where an election is technically invalid because of the corporation's inadvertence or failure to obtain all the requisite shareholder consents on time, the Service may grant dispensation and waive the defect if there is reasonable cause.[6]

Revocation of Election. An S corporation election may be revoked if shareholders holding more than one-half of the corporation's shares (including nonvoting shares) consent to the revocation.[7] The revocation may specify a prospective effective date.[8] If a prospective effective date is not specified, a revocation made on or before the fifteenth day of the third month of the taxable year is effective on the first day of the taxable year and a revocation made after that date is effective on the first day of the following taxable year.[9]

Termination of Election. Apart from revocation, an S corporation election may be terminated if the corporation ceases to satisfy the definition of a small business corporation or, in certain circumstances, if the corporation earns an excessive amount of passive investment income.[10] The first ground for termination is easily illustrated. Terminating events include: (1) exceeding 100 shareholders; (2) issuance of a second class of stock; or (3) transfer of stock to an ineligible shareholder. In all those cases, the corporation will cease to be a small business corporation and its S corporation election will terminate on the day after the disqualifying event.[11] To prevent or cure transfers that may jeopardize a corporation's S corporation status, the shareholders will be well advised at the outset to enter into an agreement restricting stock transfers.

The limitation on passive investment income is more complex. Under Section 1362(d)(3), an election to be an S corporation will terminate if for three consecutive taxable years the corporation's "passive investment income" exceeds 25 percent of its gross receipts and the corporation has Subchapter C earnings and profits.[12] A termination triggered by excess passive investment income is effective beginning on the first day of the taxable year following the three year testing period.[13] It is important to note that the Subchapter C earnings and profits requirement has the effect

---

5. I.R.C. § 1362(b)(2)(B).

6. I.R.C. § 1362(f). An ineffective election to treat (1) a subsidiary as a qualified subchapter S subsidiary or (2) a family as one shareholder may also be salvaged under Section 1362(f).

7. I.R.C. § 1362(d)(1)(B). See Reg. § 1.1362–2(a).

8. I.R.C. § 1362(d)(1)(D).

9. I.R.C. § 1362(d)(1)(C). If the revocation is effective on a day other than the first day of a taxable year (e.g., because a prospective date is selected in the middle of the year), the taxable year will be an "S termi-

nation year," and the corporation will be taxed pursuant to rules in Section 1362(e). See Reg. § 1.1362–3 and infra text accompanying notes 19–21.

10. I.R.C. § 1362(d)(2), (3).

11. I.R.C. §§ 1361(b)(1)(A)–(D); 1362(d)(2)(B).

12. See Reg. § 1.1362–2(c). Prior years in which the corporation was not an S corporation are not considered for purposes of the passive investment income component of this test. I.R.C. § 1362(c)(3)(A)(iii)(II).

13. I.R.C. § 1362(c)(3)(A)(ii).

of rendering this limitation inapplicable to a corporation that has always been an S corporation or which has been purged of its earnings and profits.[14] Passive investment income generally is defined as gross receipts from royalties, rents, dividends, interest, annuities and gains from sales or exchanges of stock or securities,[15] but it does not include dividends received by an S corporation from a C corporation subsidiary to the extent they are attributable to earnings and profits of the subsidiary that are derived from the active conduct of a trade or business.[16] Gross receipts from sales or exchanges of stock or securities are considered only to the extent of gains.[17] For purposes of the overall gross receipts definition, gross receipts on the disposition of capital assets other than stock or securities are taken into account only to the extent of the excess of capital gains over capital losses from such dispositions.[18]

When an S corporation election terminates during the S corporation's taxable year, the corporation experiences an "S termination year," which is divided into two short years: an S short year and a C short year.[19] Income, gains, losses, deductions and credits for an S termination year generally may be allocated between the two short years on a pro rata basis or the corporation may elect to make the allocation under its normal accounting rules.[20] The corporation's tax liability for the short taxable year as a C corporation is then computed on an annualized basis.[21]

Inadvertent Terminations. If an S corporation election is terminated, the corporation generally is not eligible to make another election for five taxable years unless the Treasury consents to an earlier election.[22] Section 1362(f) provides relief if a termination is caused by the corporation ceasing to be a small business corporation or by excessive passive investment income. The corporation will be treated as continuing as an S corporation and the terminating event will be disregarded if: (1) the Service determines that the termination was inadvertent, (2) the corporation takes steps within a reasonable time to rectify the problem, and (3) the corporation and

---

14. An S corporation, however, may acquire earnings and profits under Section 381 in a corporate acquisition.

15. I.R.C. § 1362(d)(3)(C)(i). Losses from sales or exchanges of stock or securities do not offset gains for purposes of determining passive investment income. Id. The statute also contains rules for certain specialized items. See I.R.C. § 1362(d)(3)(C)(ii)–(iv).

16. I.R.C. § 1362(d)(3)(E).

17. I.R.C. § 1362(d)(3)(C)(i).

18. I.R.C. § 1362(d)(3)(B).

19. I.R.C. § 1362(e)(1). The C short year begins on the first day the termination is effective. I.R.C. § 1362(e)(1)(B).

20. See Reg. § 1.1362–3. To use normal accounting rules, an election must be filed by all persons who are shareholders during the S short year and all persons who are shareholders on the first day of the C short year. I.R.C. § 1362(e)(3). The pro rata allocation method may not be used in an S termination year if there is a sale or exchange of 50 percent or more of the stock in the corporation during the year. I.R.C. § 1362(e)(6)(D). For more rules on taxing an S termination year, see I.R.C. § 1362(e)(6).

21. I.R.C. § 1362(e)(5)(A).

22. I.R.C. § 1362(g). As a special act of amnesty, Section 1317(b) of the Small Business Job Protection Act of 1996 permits an automatic reelection after the date of enactment of the Act without regard to the five-year limit if the termination occurred in a taxable year beginning before January 1, 1997.

its shareholders agree to make whatever adjustments are required by the Service.[23] The corporation has the burden of establishing that under the relevant facts and circumstances the Commissioner should determine that the termination was inadvertent. Under the regulations, inadvertence may be established by showing that the terminating event was not reasonably within the control of the corporation and was not part of a plan to terminate the election, or that the event took place without the knowledge of the corporation notwithstanding its due diligence to prevent the termination.[24] For example, if a corporation in good faith determines that it has no Subchapter C earnings and profits but the Service later determines on audit that the corporation's S election terminated because it had excessive passive investment income for three consecutive years while it also had accumulated earnings and profits, it may be appropriate for the Service to find that the termination was inadvertent.

Taxable Year of an S Corporation. To preclude S corporations from using fiscal years to achieve a deferral of the shareholders' tax liability, S corporations must use a "permitted year," which is defined as either a calendar year or an accounting period for which the taxpayer establishes a business purpose.[25] The Service has ruled that the business purpose requirement may be satisfied if the desired tax accounting period coincides with a "natural business year"[26] and has quantified the concept with the same 25–percent test applicable to partnerships seeking to use a natural business fiscal year.[27] Under this test, a natural business year exists if 25 percent or more of the S corporation's gross receipts for the selected 12–month period are earned in the last two months. This 25–percent test must be met in each of the preceding three 12–month periods that correspond to the requested fiscal year.[28]

Section 1378 makes it clear that tax deferral for shareholders does not constitute a business purpose for a fiscal year. The legislative history also identifies several factors which generally do not support a claim of business purpose:[29]

> The conferees intend that (1) the use of a particular year for regulatory or financial accounting purposes; (2) the hiring patterns of a particular business, e.g., the fact that a firm typically hires staff during certain times of the year; (3) the use of a particular year for administrative purposes, such as the admission or retirement of partners or shareholders, promotion of staff, and compensation or retirement arrangements with staff, partners, or shareholders; and (4) the fact that a particular business involves the use

---

23. I.R.C. § 1362(f).

24. Reg. § 1.1362–4(b).

25. I.R.C. § 1378(b). See Reg. § 1.1378–1.

26. Rev.Proc. 74–33, 1974–2 C.B. 489.

27. Rev.Proc. 2002–38; §§ 2.02, 2.06, 5.05; 2002–1 C.B. 1037.

28. If the taxpayer does not have the required period of gross receipts, it cannot establish a natural business year under the revenue procedure. Rev. Proc. 2002–38, supra note 27.

29. H.R.Rep. No. 99–841, 99th Cong., 2d Sess. II–319 (1986).

of price lists, model year, or other items that change on an annual basis ordinarily will not be sufficient to establish that the business purpose requirement for a particular taxable year has been met.

Fiscal Year Election. Congress has modified these strict taxable year requirements by allowing S corporations to elect to adopt, retain or change to a fiscal year under certain conditions, including the payment of an entity-level tax designed to represent the value of any tax deferral to the shareholders that would result from the use of the fiscal year. The rules governing the fiscal year election and the required entity-level payment are found in Sections 444 and 7519.

Section 444 permits a newly formed S corporation to elect to use a taxable year other than the calendar year required by Section 1378 provided that the year elected results in no more than a three-month deferral of income to the shareholders.[30] An election and the Section 7519 payment is not required, however, for any S corporation that has established a business purpose for a fiscal year under Section 1378(b)(2).[31]

The trade-off for a Section 444 fiscal year election is that the corporation must make a "required payment" under Section 7519 for any taxable year for which the election is in effect. The mechanics of the required payment are annoyingly complex, but the concept is clear. An electing S corporation must pay and keep "on deposit" an amount roughly approximating the value of the tax deferral that the shareholders would have achieved from the use of a fiscal year. Thus, if an S corporation whose shareholders all used calendar years elected a fiscal year ending September 30, the corporation would be required to pay a tax that supposedly equalled the tax benefit from the three months deferral received by the shareholders.[32] Under a de minimis rule, no payment is required if the amount due is less than $500,[33] and a payment made in one year generates a balance "on deposit" that may be used in subsequent years.[34]

PROBLEM

Snowshoe, Inc. ("Snowshoe"), a ski resort located in Colorado, was organized by its four individual shareholders (A, B, C and D) and began operations on October 3 of the current year. A owns 300 shares of Snowshoe voting common stock and B, C and D each own 100 shares of Snowshoe nonvoting common stock. Each share of common stock has equal rights with respect to dividends and liquidation distributions. Consider the

---

30. I.R.C. § 444(a), (b)(1). S corporations formed or electing prior to 1987 also were permitted to retain a taxable year that was the same as the entity's last taxable year beginning in 1986. I.R.C. § 444(b)(3).

31. See I.R.S. Notice 88–10, 1988–1 C.B. 478.

32. We say "supposedly" because the Section 7519 "required payment" is determined mechanically, without regard to amounts actually deferred by the shareholders. See I.R.C. §§ 7519(b), (c) and (d) for the details.

33. I.R.C. § 7519(a)(2).

34. I.R.C. § 7519(b)(2), (e)(4).

following questions in connection with the election and termination of Snowshoe's S corporation status:

(a) If the shareholders wish to elect S corporation status for Snowshoe's first taxable year, who must consent to the election? What difference would it make if, prior to the election, B sold her stock to her brother, G? What difference would it make if B is a partnership which, prior to the election, sold its stock to H, an individual?

(b) What is the last day an effective Subchapter S election for Snowshoe's first taxable year is permitted?

(c) If the shareholders elect S corporation status, what taxable year will Snowshoe be allowed to select?

In the following parts of the problem, assume that Snowshoe elected S corporation status during its first taxable year.

(d) Can A revoke Snowshoe's Subchapter S election without the consent of B, C or D?

(e) If C sold all of his stock to Olga, a citizen of Sweden living in Stockholm, what effect would the sale have on Snowshoe's status as an S corporation?

(f) Same as (e), above, except that C only sold five shares to Olga and had no idea that the sale might adversely affect Snowshoe's S corporation status.

(g) Would it matter if Snowshoe's business is diversified and 45% of its gross receipts come from real estate rentals, dividends and interest?

D.   Treatment of the Shareholders

Code: §§ 1363(b), (c); 1366(a)–(e); 1367. Skim §§ 1366(f); 1371(b); 1377.

1.   Pass-Through of Income and Losses: Basic Rules

Entity Treatment. Although an S corporation is generally exempt from tax,[1] it nonetheless must determine its gross income,[2] deductions and other tax items in order to establish the amounts which pass through to the shareholders. Like a partnership, an S corporation computes its "taxable income" in the same manner as an individual except that certain deductions unique to individuals (e.g., personal exemptions, alimony, medical and moving expenses) are not allowed.[3] In addition, deductions normally available only to corporations, such as the dividends received deduction, are not

1. For the few limited exceptions, see Section F of this chapter, infra.

2. Section 1366(c) provides that a shareholder's pro rata share of the S corpora-

tion's gross income is used to determine the shareholder's gross income.

3. I.R.C. § 1363(b)(2).

allowed,[4] but an S corporation may elect to deduct and amortize its organizational expenses under Section 248.[5] Finally, a wide variety of items, ranging from charitable contributions and capital gains to depletion, must be separately computed in order to preserve their special tax character for purposes of the pass-through to the shareholders.[6] Thus, an S corporation is not entitled to any charitable deduction, but corporate charitable gifts may pass through to the shareholders without regard to the normal 10 percent limit on corporate contributions.

Although an S corporation is not a *taxable* entity, it is treated as an entity for various purposes. For example, tax elections affecting the computation of items derived from an S corporation (e.g., to defer recognition of gain on an involuntary conversion under Section 1033) generally are made at the corporate level.[7] Likewise, limitations on deductions (e.g., the dollar limitation under Section 179 on expensing the cost of certain recovery property) apply at the corporate level and often at the shareholder level as well.[8] And like a partnership, an S corporation is treated as an entity for filing tax returns and other procedural purposes.[9]

Pass-Through of Income and Deductions. Once the S corporation's tax items have been identified, the next step is to determine the manner in which they pass through to the shareholders. The pass-through scheme applicable to S corporations will have a familiar ring to a student who has endured the rigors of Subchapter K. First, income and deductions are characterized at the corporate level.[10] Section 1366(a)(1)(A) provides that items which may have potentially varying tax consequences to the individual shareholders must be separately reported. The most common separately stated items are capital and Section 1231 gains and losses, dividends taxed as net capital gain, interest and other types of "portfolio income" under the Section 469 passive loss limitations, tax-exempt interest, charitable contributions, investment interest, foreign taxes, intangible drilling expenses and depletion on oil and gas properties.[11] Thus, Section 1231 gains and losses do not fall into any corporate hotchpot; rather, they pass through and are aggregated with each shareholder's other Section 1231 gains and losses in order to determine their ultimate character. All the nonseparately stated items are aggregated and the resulting lump sum passes through as ordinary income or loss.

4. S.Rep. No. 97–640, 97th Cong., 2d Sess. 15 (1982), reprinted in 1982–2 C.B. 718, 724.

5. I.R.C. § 1363(b)(3).

6. I.R.C. §§ 1363(b)(1); 1366(a)(1)(A).

7. I.R.C. § 1363(c)(1).

8. See, e.g., I.R.C. § 179(d)(8).

9. I.R.C. § 6037. Cf. I.R.C. §§ 6221–6255.

10. I.R.C. § 1366(b). See Reg. § 1.1366–1(b). If shareholders are utilizing an S corporation for the principal purpose of converting ordinary income to capital gain or capital loss into ordinary loss on the sale or exchange of property, the regulations generally provide for the character of the gain or loss to be determined at the shareholder level. Reg. § 1.1366–1(b)(2), (3).

11. See generally Reg. § 1.1366–1(a)(2). See also Rev.Rul. 84–131, 1984–2 C.B. 37, where the Service ruled that a shareholder's share of an S corporation's investment interest is a separately stated item.

The timing of the shareholders' income and the allocation of pass-through items also is virtually a mirror image of the partnership rules. The shareholders of an S corporation take into account their respective pro rata shares of income, deductions and other separately stated items on a pro rata, per share daily basis.[12] These items are reported in the shareholder's taxable year in which the corporation's taxable year ends.[13] For example, if an S corporation with a natural business year uses a fiscal year ending January 31, 2006, the shareholders will report the respective pass-through items on their 2006 calendar year tax returns, thus achieving a healthy deferral of any gains or an unfortunate delay in recognizing any losses. A deceased shareholder's Subchapter S items are allocated on a daily basis between the shareholder's final income tax return and the initial return of the decedent's estate.[14]

Basis Adjustments. Section 1367 requires S corporation shareholders to increase the basis of their stock by their respective shares of income items (including tax-exempt income) and to reduce basis (but not below zero) by losses, deductions, and non-deductible expenses which do not constitute capital expenditures, and by tax-free distributions under Section 1368. Under the Code's ordering rules, basis is first increased by current income items, then decreased by distributions, and finally decreased (to the extent permitted) by any losses for the year.[15] Any additional losses in excess of a shareholder's stock basis must be applied to reduce the shareholder's basis (again, not below zero) in any corporate indebtedness to the shareholder.[16] If the basis of both stock and debt is reduced, any subsequent upward adjustments must first be applied to restore the basis in the indebtedness to the extent that it was previously reduced before increasing the basis of the stock.[17] These basis adjustments are generally made as of the close of the S corporation's taxable year unless a shareholder disposes of stock during the year, in which case the adjustments with respect to the transferred stock are made immediately prior to the disposition.[18]

2. LOSS LIMITATIONS

a. IN GENERAL

Section 1366(d) limits the amount of losses or deductions that may pass through to a shareholder to the sum of the shareholder's adjusted basis in the stock plus his adjusted basis in any indebtedness of the corporation to the shareholder. Losses disallowed because of an inadequate basis may be carried forward indefinitely and treated as a loss in any subsequent year in which the shareholder has a basis in either stock or

---

12. I.R.C. § 1366(a)(1). See § 1377(a)(1) for the method of determining each shareholder's "pro rata share."

13. I.R.C. § 1366(a)(1).

14. Id. See also Reg. § 1.1366–1(a)(1).

15. I.R.C. §§ 1366(d)(1)(A); 1368(d), last sentence. For other details on stock and

debt basis adjustments, see Reg. § 1.1367–1, –2.

16. I.R.C. § 1367(b)(2)(A).

17. I.R.C. § 1367(b)(2)(B).

18. Reg. § 1.1367–1(d)(1).

debt.[1] A special rule also provides that if a shareholder's stock is transferred under Section 1041 to a spouse or former spouse incident to a divorce, any suspended loss or deduction may be carried forward indefinitely by the transferee-spouse.[2] As illustrated by the *Harris* case, which follows this Note, one of the most litigated issues to arise under Subchapter S has involved the determination of a shareholder's basis in S corporation stock and debt for purposes of applying the general loss limitation rules in Section 1366(d).

Losses that pass through to a shareholder of an S corporation also may be restricted by the at-risk limitations in Section 465 and the passive activity loss limitations in Section 469.[3] The at-risk rules are applied on an activity-by-activity basis, except that activities constituting a trade or business generally are aggregated if the taxpayer actively participates in the management of the trade or business and at least 65 percent of the losses are allocable to persons actively engaged in the management of the trade or business.[4] The passive activity loss limitations cast a wider net and may delay an investor's ability to deduct legitimate start-up losses passing through from a new business operating as an S corporation unless the investor also materially participates in the activity.[5]

Harris v. United States

United States Court of Appeals, Fifth Circuit, 1990.
902 F.2d 439.

■ GARWOOD, CIRCUIT JUDGE:

Facts and Proceedings Below

In June 1982, Taxpayers contracted with Trans–Lux New Orleans Corporation to purchase for $665,585 cash a New Orleans pornographic theater that they intended to convert into a wedding hall. The Taxpayers' obligations under the contract were conditioned on their being able to secure from a third party a loan for not less than $600,000 repayable in fifteen to twenty years.[1] Shortly before this time, Taxpayers had contacted John Smith (Smith), a real estate loan officer with Hibernia National Bank (Hibernia), to discuss the possibility of obtaining financing for the impending acquisition. Smith orally committed to lend Taxpayers $700,000.[2]

---

1. I.R.C. §§ 1366(d)(2)(A), 1366(a)(1).

2. I.R.C. § 1366(d)(2)(B).

3. These limitations apply on a shareholder-by-shareholder basis rather than at the corporate level. I.R.C. §§ 465(a)(1)(A); 469(a)(2)(A).

4. I.R.C. § 465(c)(3)(B).

5. I.R.C. § 469(c)(1).

1. As part of the contract, Taxpayers deposited with the seller $32,500, all of which was to be applied to the purchase price. In the event Taxpayers were unable to procure the loan, the purchase contract called for their deposit to be refunded.

2. Smith asserted in his deposition that he did not know the purpose of the borrowed funds in excess of the purchase price, but he surmised that the money was intended for improvements to the theater. No written loan commitment was ever issued.

Subsequently, to shield themselves from the potential adverse publicity that could follow from the purchase of the pornographic theater, as well as to limit their personal liability and enhance their chances of qualifying for industrial revenue bonds to finance the theater's renovation, in July 1982 Taxpayers formed Harmar (Harmar), a Louisiana corporation, which elected to be taxed pursuant to Subchapter S of the Internal Revenue Code, to purchase and operate the subject property. Harris and Martin each initially contributed $1,000 to the corporation, receiving its stock in return, and each also loaned Harmar $47,500 to satisfy operating expenses. Harris and Martin were the sole shareholders of Harmar, each owning half of its stock.

The purchase of the theater closed on November 1, 1982, and the theater was conveyed to Harmar on that date. Hibernia furnished the $700,000 necessary to close the transaction. In borrowing the funds necessary to acquire the subject property, Harmar executed two promissory notes payable to Hibernia for $350,000 each, each dated November 1, 1982. One of these notes was secured by a $50,322.09 Hibernia certificate of deposit in Harris' name and another $304,972.49 certificate of deposit in the name of his wholly-owned corporation, Harris Mortgage Corporation. Harmar secured the other note, in accordance with its collateral pledge agreement, by its $3,000,000 note (which was unfunded apart from the $700,000) and its collateral mortgage on the theater, each executed by Harmar in favor of Hibernia and dated November 1, 1982. Under the terms of the collateral pledge agreement executed by Harmar in reference to the $3,000,000 note and mortgage, the mortgage secured "not only" Harmar's $350,000 note to Hibernia, "but also any and every other debts, liabilities and obligations" (other than consumer credit debt) of Harmar to Hibernia whether "due or to become due, or whether such debts, liabilities and obligations" of Harmar "are now existing or will arise in the future." Thus, the collateral mortgage secured the full $700,000 loan from Hibernia. Additionally, Taxpayers each executed personal continuing guarantees of Harmar indebtedness in the amount of $700,000 in favor of Hibernia. Smith testified in his deposition that the transaction was structured so that half the loan, as represented by one of the $350,000 notes, would be primarily secured by the certificates of deposit and the other half, represented by the other $350,000 note, primarily by the mortgage on the property purchased, with the entire amount also secured by Taxpayers' individual guarantees.

On its income tax return for the year ending December 31, 1982, Harmar reported a net operating loss of $104,013. Pursuant to [the predecessor of Section 1366], Taxpayers each claimed half of the loss as a deduction on their 1982 individual returns,[5] concluding that their bases in Harmar were in fact greater than Harmar's net operating loss for that year and that they therefore were entitled to deduct the entire loss on their personal returns. On audit, the Internal Revenue Service (IRS) found to

---

5. Harris and Martin claimed deductions for Harmar's loss of $52,006 and $52,007, respectively.

the contrary and determined that Harris and Martin each had a basis of $1,000 in his Harmar stock and an adjusted basis in Harmar's indebtedness to each of them as shareholders of $47,500. Pursuant to I.R.C. [§ 1366(d)], the IRS limited Taxpayers' deductions of the net operating loss to what it considered to be their bases in Harmar, $48,500 each. The IRS's disallowance of a portion of the deductions claimed by Taxpayers[6] resulted in additional tax liability, including interest, for Martin of $3,150.58 and for Harris of $1,280. Taxpayers paid the tax in dispute and now appeal the district court's summary judgment dismissing their suit for refund.

Discussion

Taxpayers contend on appeal that in determining the deduction allowable for Harmar's net operating loss, the IRS should have included in Taxpayers' bases in their Harmar stock the full value of the $700,000 Hibernia loan they guaranteed. I.R.C. [§ 1366] permits a Subchapter S shareholder to deduct from his personal return a proportionate share of his corporation's net operating loss to the extent that the loss does not exceed the sum of the adjusted basis of his Subchapter S corporation stock and any corporate indebtedness to him. See section [1366(d)(1)]. To arrive at their basis figure, Taxpayers seek to recast the transaction in question. They in essence urge that we disregard the form of the Hibernia loan—one from Hibernia to Harmar—in favor of what Taxpayers consider as the substance of the transaction—a $700,000 loan from Hibernia to them, the $700,000 proceeds of which they then equally contributed to Harmar's capital account. As evidence of their view of the substance of the transaction, Taxpayers point to the deposition testimony of Smith indicating that Hibernia looked primarily to Taxpayers, rather than to Harmar, for repayment of the loan, and they call attention to the $700,000 guarantees they each provided Hibernia as well as the $355,294.58 in certificates of deposit that Harris pledged to Hibernia as part of the November 1, 1982 loan transaction.

In its summary judgment memorandum, the district court declared that Brown v. Commissioner, 706 F.2d 755 (6th Cir.1983), was "on all fours" with the instant case and therefore resolved it. In *Brown,* the Sixth Circuit rejected shareholders' substance over form argument in ruling that the shareholders' guarantees of loans to their Subchapter S corporation could not increase their bases in their stock in the corporation unless the shareholders made an economic outlay by satisfying at least a portion of the guaranteed debt. Id. at 757. Without such an outlay, the *Brown* court concluded that " 'the substance matched the form' "of the transaction before it. Id. at 756. The reasoning of *Brown* was followed by the Fourth Circuit in Estate of Leavitt v. Commissioner, 875 F.2d 420 (4th Cir.1989), *aff'g,* 90 T.C. 206 (1988). There, the court, affirming the en banc Tax Court, held that shareholder guarantees of a loan to a Subchapter S corporation did not increase shareholders' stock basis because such guarantees had not "cost" shareholders anything and thus did not constitute an

---

6. The IRS disallowed $4,506 of Harris' deduction and $4,507 of Martin's.

economic outlay. *Leavitt,* 875 F.2d at 422 & n. 9.[7] In reaching this conclusion, the Fourth Circuit affirmed as not clearly erroneous a finding of the Tax Court that the loan, in form as well as in substance, was made to the corporation rather than to the shareholders.[8] Id. at 424. The court rejected appellants' suggestion that it employ the debt/equity principles espoused in Plantation Patterns, Inc. v. Commissioner, 462 F.2d 712 (5th Cir.1972), in determining whether the shareholders had actually made an economic outlay,[9] instead choosing to employ a debt/equity analysis only after making a finding that an economic outlay had occurred. *Leavitt,* 875 F.2d at 427. The *Leavitt* court reasoned that the legislative history of section [1366] limiting the basis of a Subchapter S shareholder to his corporate investment or outlay could not be circumvented through the use of debt/equity principles. Id. at 426 & n. 16. See generally Bogdanski, Shareholder Guarantees, Interest Deductions, and S Corporation Stock Basis: The Problems with Putnam, 13 J.Corp.Tax'n 264, 268–89 (1986).

Taxpayers press this Court to follow the contrary holding of Selfe v. United States, 778 F.2d 769 (11th Cir.1985). There, the Eleventh Circuit ruled that a shareholder's guaranty of a Subchapter S corporation loan could result in an increase in equity or debt basis even though the shareholder had not satisfied any portion of the obligation. *Selfe,* 778 F.2d at 775. The court remanded the case to the district court for it to employ debt/equity principles in determining if the loan in question was in substance one to the shareholder rather than to the corporation. Id.

The courts have uniformly ruled that a shareholder must make an economic outlay to increase his Subchapter S corporation stock basis. Taxpayers assert that if we look beyond the form of the transaction at what they contend is its substance—a loan from Hibernia to them, which in turn they contributed to Harmar as capital—we must find that a $700,000 outlay occurred and that their stock bases therefore correspondingly increased. They contend that use of debt/equity principles will lead us to such a conclusion.

---

7. In reasoning that the shareholders had not increased their stock bases as a result of their guarantees, the court turned to I.R.C. § 1012, which defines basis of property as its cost. Id. at 422 n. 9. Cost of property, in turn, is defined in the Treasury Regulations as the "amount paid for such property in cash or other property." 26 C.F.R. § 1.1012–1(a).

8. The court noted that the loan in question had been made by the bank directly to the corporation, the loan payments were made by the corporation directly to the bank, and neither the corporation nor the shareholders reported the payments as constructive dividends. Id.

Under *Leavitt,* the presumption is that the form will control and that presumption will not be surmounted absent the shareholder's satisfying the higher standard applicable to a taxpayer's seeking to disavow the form he selected and recast a transaction. See Bowers, Building Up an S Shareholder's Basis through Loans and Acquisitions, J. Tax'n S Corp., Fall 1989, at 22, 29.

9. In *Plantation Patterns,* this Court considered whether a Subchapter C corporation could deduct interest payments made on its debt and whether its shareholders had resulting dividend income. The Court, using a debt/equity analysis, affirmed a Tax Court finding that a corporation's interest payments on debentures were constructive dividends and could not be deducted as interest payments. Id. at 723–24. * * *

Ordinarily, taxpayers are bound by the form of the transaction they have chosen; taxpayers may not in hindsight recast the transaction as one that they might have made in order to obtain tax advantages. * * * The IRS, however, often may disregard form and recharacterize a transaction by looking to its substance. Higgins v. Smith, 308 U.S. 473, 60 S.Ct. 355, 357, 84 L.Ed. 406 (1940). The Tax Court has recognized an exception to the rule that a taxpayer may not question a transaction's form in cases such as this one in which the shareholder argues that guaranteed corporate debt should be recast as an equity investment on the shareholder's part. Blum v. Commissioner, 59 T.C. 436, 440 (1972).

In this case we find that the transaction as structured did not lack adequate substance or reality and that an economic outlay justifying the basis claimed by Taxpayers never occurred.

The summary judgment evidence reflects that the parties to this transaction intended that the Hibernia loan be one to the corporation. Each of the two $350,000 promissory notes was executed by and only in the name of Harmar. The notes have been renewed and remain in the same form, namely notes payable to Hibernia in which the sole maker is Harmar. Hibernia, an independent party, in substance earmarked the loan proceeds for use in purchasing the subject property to which Harmar took title, Harmar contemporaneously giving Hibernia a mortgage to secure Harmar's debt to Hibernia. The bank sent interest due notices to Harmar, and all note payments were made by checks to Hibernia drawn on Harmar's corporate account. Harmar's books and records for all years through the year ended December 31, 1985, prepared by its certified public accountant, reflect the $700,000 loan simply as an indebtedness of Harmar to Hibernia. They do not in any way account for or reflect any of the $700,000 as a capital contribution or loan by Taxpayers to Harmar, although they do reflect the $1,000 capital contribution each Taxpayer made and Harmar's indebtedness to Taxpayers for the various cash advances Taxpayers made to it. The Harmar financial statements for the year ended December 31, 1986, are the first to show any contributed capital attributable to the Hibernia loan. Further, Hibernia's records showed Harmar as the "borrower" in respect to the $700,000 loan and the renewals of it. Harmar's 1982 tax return, which covered August 15 through December 31, 1982, indicates that Harmar deducted $12,506 in interest expenses. Because only the Hibernia loan generated such expenses for that period, it is reasonably inferable that the deduction corresponded to that loan. The 1982 Harmar return showed no distribution to Taxpayers, as it should have if the $700,000 Hibernia loan on which Harmar paid interest was a loan to the Taxpayers. Further, the return shows the only capital contributed as $2,000 and the only loan from stockholders as $68,000, but shows other indebtedness of $675,000. In short, Harmar's 1982 income tax return is flatly inconsistent with Taxpayers' present position. Moreover, there is no indication that Taxpayers treated the loan as a personal one on their individual returns by reporting Harmar's interest payments to Hibernia as constructive dividend income. In sum, the parties' treatment of the transaction, from the time it was entered into and for years thereafter, has been wholly consistent with its unambiguous documentation and inconsistent with the way in which Taxpayers now seek to recast it. Hibernia was clearly an independent third party, and the real and bona fide, separate existence of Harmar is not challenged. The parties did what they intended to do, and the transaction as structured did not lack adequate reality or substance.

Moreover, if the transaction is to be "recast," it is by no means clear that it should be recast in the form sought by Taxpayers, namely as a cash loan to them from Hibernia followed by their payment of the cash to Harmar as a contribution to its capital, and Harmar's then using the cash to purchase the building. Such recasting does not account for Hibernia's mortgage on the building. In any event, if the transaction is to be recast, why should it not be recast as a loan by Hibernia to Taxpayers, with the Taxpayers using the funds to themselves purchase the building, giving Hibernia a mortgage on the building to secure their debt to it, and then transferring the building, subject to the mortgage, to Harmar as a contribution to capital? Presumably in that situation Taxpayers' bases in their Harmar stock would be reduced by the amount of the debt secured by the mortgage under I.R.C. § 358(d). See Wiebusch v. Commissioner, 59 T.C. 777, aff'd per curiam "on the basis of the opinion of the Tax Court," Wiebusch v. Commissioner, 487 F.2d 515 (8th Cir.1973).[15] While section 358(d) likely does not affect stockholder basis in the debt of the Subchapter S corporation to the stockholder, Taxpayers have not sought to recast the transaction as a loan by Hibernia to them followed by their loan of the proceeds to Harmar; indeed even after Harmar's books were rearranged starting with the year ending December 31, 1986, the books do not show any indebtedness in this respect of Harmar to Taxpayers and do continue to show Harmar as owing the money in question to Hibernia. There is simply no evidence of Harmar indebtedness to Taxpayers in respect to these funds.

Taxpayers' guarantees and Harris' pledge of certificates of deposit do not undermine the intent of the parties that Harmar be the borrower in this transaction. It certainly is not difficult to fathom that a careful lender to a new, small, closely held corporation such as Harmar would seek personal guarantees from all of its shareholders. See Bogdanski, supra, at 269. Moreover, the wholly unperformed guarantees do not satisfy the requirement that an economic outlay be made before a corresponding increase in basis can occur. See generally *Underwood,* 535 F.2d at 312. In

---

15. See also Megaard, No Stock Basis for Shareholder Guarantee of S Corporation Debt, 15 J.Corp.Tax'n 340 (1989). Megaard explains that "[u]nder Section 358(d), the assumption by a corporation of its shareholder's debt is treated as money received which reduces the shareholder's basis in the stock." Id. at 349. Cf. id. at 350 ("Having the corporation's assets encumbered by the shareholder's personal debt runs the risk of a basis reduction under Section 358 should the Service argue that the transaction was a purchase by the shareholder of the * * * assets followed by a contribution of the assets to the corporation subject to the debt.").

the same light, Harris' pledge to Hibernia of some $355,000 in certificates of deposit of his (and Harris Mortgage Corporation) does not provide such an outlay.[16]

We conclude that the transaction must be treated as it purports to be and as the parties treated it—namely as a loan by Hibernia to Harmar, all payments on which through the relevant time have been made by Harmar to Hibernia. For any funds or other assets Taxpayers have actually provided to Harmar as loans or contributions, Taxpayers are, of course, entitled to basis additions as of the time such contributions or loans were furnished by them to Harmar, but they are not entitled to a 1982 basis addition for Hibernia's 1982 $700,000 loan to Harmar, notwithstanding that it was also secured by Taxpayers' execution of guarantees and Harris' pledge to Hibernia of his and Harris Mortgage Corporation's certificates of deposit in the total face amount of some $355,000.

Conclusion

There was no genuine dispute as to any material fact necessary to sustain the Government's summary judgment motion. The district court's judgment is correct and it is therefore

Affirmed.

NOTE

In *Harris,* the Fifth Circuit joined several other circuits[1] and the Tax Court[2] in holding that the guarantee of an S corporation's loan by its shareholders may not be treated as an additional investment in the corporation which will increase the shareholders' bases for purposes of the loss limitation rule in Section 1366(d). In conflict with this line of authority is the Eleventh Circuit's decision in *Selfe v. United States.*[3] In *Selfe,* the court reasoned that debt-equity principles under Subchapter C were applicable in determining whether a shareholder-guaranteed debt should be characterized as a capital contribution. In remanding the case for a determination of whether the shareholder's guarantee amounted to either an equity investment or a shareholder loan to the corporation, the court directed the district court to apply the principles of *Plantation Patterns,* a Subchapter C case discussed in *Harris.*

16. Taxpayers would have us, in effect, convert this pledge to Hibernia into a $700,000 cash contribution made to Harmar by Taxpayers equally. But that did not happen. Taxpayers do not contend that the certificates of deposit were contributed to Harmar's capital.

1. Brown v. Commissioner, 706 F.2d 755 (6th Cir.1983); Estate of Leavitt v. Commissioner, 875 F.2d 420 (4th Cir.1989), cert. denied, 493 U.S. 958, 110 S.Ct. 376 (1989); Uri v. Commissioner, 949 F.2d 371 (10th Cir.1991); Sleiman v. Commissioner, 187 F.3d 1352 (11th Cir. 1999); Grojean v. Commissioner, 248 F.3d 572 (2001).

2. Estate of Leavitt v. Commissioner, 90 T.C. 206 (1988); Hitchins v. Commissioner, 103 T.C. 711 (1994).

3. 778 F.2d 769 (11th Cir.1985).

Despite the seeming conflict among the circuits, the Supreme Court has declined to add this fascinating tax issue to its docket.[4]

b.   SUBCHAPTER S LOSSES AND SECTION 362(e)(2)

Code: § 362(e)(2)

The rules for allocating and characterizing gains and losses that are inherent in property contributed to a partnership ("precontribution gains and losses") are one of the principal features of the Subchapter K partnership tax regime. Under Section 704(c)(1)(A), precontribution gains and losses generally must be taxed to the contributing partner, and Section 724 prevents partners from gaining a tax advantage by converting precontribution ordinary income into capital gain and precontribution capital loss into ordinary loss. Other provisions buttress these rules by preventing shifting of precontribution gains and losses through partnership distributions and dispositions of partnership interests.[1] In short, Subchapter K has an array of provisions designed to ensure that a partner who contributes property with a precontribution gain will be taxed on that gain and that precontribution losses may not be shifted to other partners.[2]

Subchapter S is relatively primitive compared to its Subchapter K cousin in the treatment of precontribution gains and losses. Under Section 1377, precontribution gains and losses are taxed like any other gain or loss under a per-share, per-day allocation method.[3] Precontribution gains and losses in an S corporation are thus routinely shifted to other shareholders.

As part of the American Jobs Creation Act of 2004,[4] Congress decided to attack various schemes by taxpayers to duplicate losses by way of transactions involving corporations. Section 362(e)(2) was one of the provisions enacted to curb those abuses. That section provides that if a shareholder transfers property with an aggregate built-in loss to a corporation in a Section 351 transaction, the corporation's basis in the property must be reduced to the fair market value of such property.[5] If more than one asset is contributed, the basis reduction is allocated among the property in proportion to their respective built-in losses immediately before the transaction.[6] As an alternative to reducing the property's basis, the shareholder and the corporation may elect to reduce the basis of the stock that was received for the property to the stock's fair market value immediately after the transfer.[7]

---

4. The Court denied the taxpayer's petition for certiorari in the *Estate of Leavitt* case, supra note 1.

1. I.R.C. §§ 704(c)(1)(B); 737; 751(a).

2. Section 704(c)(1)(C) prevents a shift of precontribution losses to other partners, even a transferee partner.

3. The regulations hold out the possibility of attacking plans to alter the character of precontribution gains and losses in an S corporation. See Reg. § 1366–1(b)(2) & (3).

4. Pub. L. No. 108–357, 108th Cong., 2d Sess. (2004).

5. I.R.C. § 362(e)(2)(A).

6. I.R.C. § 362(e)(2)(B).

7. I.R.C. § 362(e)(2)(C).

Section 362(e)(2) potentially will defer or limit precontribution losses in an S corporation, sometimes in a very unusual way. For example, assume that an individual decides to form an S corporation by contributing property with a $20,000 basis and $12,000 fair market value for all of the corporation's stock in a Section 351 exchange. Under Section 362(e)(2), the property's basis will be reduced to $12,000 and the precontribution loss in the property will disappear. If the corporation were to sell the property for $12,000, there would be no gain or loss recognized by the corporation. The shareholder's basis in the stock, however, would still be $20,000 so the loss would remain in the shares. The timing of the loss, however, would be deferred until the shareholder either liquidates the corporation or sells the stock. Alternatively, assume that the shareholder and the corporation elect to reduce the basis of the shareholder's stock to $12,000. In that case, the basis of the property in the corporation would remain at $20,000. If the corporation were to sell the property, it would recognize its $8,000 loss, which would pass through to the shareholder. The shareholder's stock basis would then be reduced by the loss down to $4,000, putting the shareholder in a position where a sale of the stock for its $12,000 fair market value would result in an $8,000 gain. Over time, the shareholder would report an $8,000 loss and an $8,000 gain, the net result being that the loss essentially disappeared. Finally, assume that the shareholder also contributed property with a $10,000 built-in gain to the S corporation at the same time as the transfer of the property with the built-in loss. In that case, no reduction in the basis of the loss property or the stock would be required under Section 362(e)(2) because the two properties that were transferred did not have an aggregate built-in loss.

It is hard to believe that Congress considered the effects on Subchapter S when it enacted Section 362(e)(2). That section now lurks as a trap for those who either receive poor advice or are not initiated in the ways of Subchapters C and S. Until Congress fixes this problem, taxpayers planning a new venture involving property with a built-in loss will be well advised to consider structuring the venture as a limited liability company or partnership governed by Subchapter K. Alternatively, another strategy for preserving a built-in loss in property would be to offer to make the property available to an S corporation through a leasing arrangement.

3. Sale of S Corporation Stock

Code: § 1(h).

The tax consequences of a sale of S corporation stock are determined by regulations promulgated under the "look-through" rules of Section 1(h). In general, S corporation stock is treated as a capital asset that gives rise to capital gain or loss on sale. Unlike the more complex approach taken by Subchapter K to the sale of a partnership interest, Subchapter S historically has not required selling shareholders to characterize a portion of their gain or loss on a stock sale by reference to the types of assets (e.g., ordinary income property) held by the corporation at the time of the sale. When

Congress enacted the Section 1(h) capital gains rate regime, however, it authorized the Service to prescribe appropriate regulations to apply the various maximum capital gains rates to the sale of interests in pass-through entities.[1]

The Section 1(h) regulations apply a partial capital gains "look-through" rule for sales and exchanges of interests in an S corporation.[2] Shareholders who sell S corporation stock held for more than one year may recognize collectibles gain (taxable at a maximum rate of 28 percent) and residual capital gain, which is generally taxable at a maximum rate of 15 percent.[3] The selling shareholder's share of collectibles gain is defined as the amount of the net collectibles gain (but not net collectibles loss) that would be allocated to that shareholder if the S corporation transferred all of its collectibles in a fully taxable transaction immediately before the transfer of the stock.[4] The selling shareholder's residual capital gain is the amount of long-term capital gain or loss that the shareholder would recognize on the sale of the stock ("pre-look-through capital gain or loss") minus the partner's share of collectibles gain.[5] The look-through rules do not extend to other corporate assets, such as inventory or depreciable real estate, that would generate ordinary income, or to real estate that would produce unrecaptured (i.e., 25–percent) Section 1250 gain on a corporate-level sale. What is the policy justification for this "pick and choose" look-through approach for S corporations?

The regulations illustrate these rules with the following example.[6] Assume that X, Inc., which always has been an S corporation and is owned equally by individuals A, B, and C, invests in antiques. After they were purchased, the antiques appreciated in value by $300. A owned one-third of the X stock and has held the stock for more than one year. A's adjusted basis in the X stock is $100. If A were to sell all of the X stock to T for $150, A would recognize $50 of pre-look-through long-term capital gain. If X were to sell all of the antiques in a fully taxable transaction immediately before the transfer to T, A would be allocated $100 of collectibles gain on account of the sale. Therefore, A will recognize $100 of collectibles gain on account of the collectibles held by X. The difference between A's pre-look-through capital gain or loss ($50) and the collectibles gain ($100) is A's residual long-term capital gain or loss on the sale of the X stock. Thus, A will recognize $100 of collectibles gain and $50 of residual long-term capital loss on the sale of A's X stock.

---

1. I.R.C. § 1(h)(11).

2. Reg. § 1.1(h)–1.

3. Reg. § 1.1(h)–1(a). In limited situations (e.g., where a transaction is governed by provisions of Subchapter C that treat gain on a sale or redemption of stock as ordinary income), shareholders also may recognize ordinary income on a sale of their S corporation stock. See, e.g., I.R.C. §§ 304, 306, 341.

4. Reg. § 1.1(h)–1(b)(2)(ii). A shareholder's share of collectibles gain is limited to the amount attributable to the portion of the stock transferred that was held for more than one year.

5. Reg. § 1.1(h)–1(c).

6. Reg. § 1.1(h)–1(f) Example 4.

PROBLEMS

1. S Corporation is a calendar year taxpayer which elected S corporation status in its first year of operation. S's common stock is owned by A (200 shares with a $12,000 basis) and B (100 shares with a $6,000 basis). During the current year, S will have the following income and expenses:

Business income	$ 92,000
Tax-exempt interest	1,000
Salary expense	44,000
Depreciation	8,000
Property taxes	7,000
Supplies	4,000
Interest expense paid on a margin account maintained with S Corp.'s stock broker	6,000
Gain from the sale of equipment:	
§ 1245 gain	7,000
§ 1231 gain	12,000
STCG from the sale of AT & T stock	7,500
LTCG from the sale of Chrysler stock held for two years	15,000
LTCL from the sale of investment real estate held for two years	9,000
Bribe of government official	6,000
Recovery of a bad debt previously deducted	4,500

(a) How will S Corporation, A and B report these events? Compare § 704(b)(2) and (c).

(b) What is A's basis in his S stock at the end of the current year?

(c) Whose accounting method will control the timing of income and deductions?

(d) If S realizes a gain upon an involuntary conversion, who makes the election under § 1033 to limit recognition of gain?

(e) Would it matter if the equipment would have been property described in § 1221(1) if held by A?

2. D, E and F each own one-third of the outstanding stock of R Corporation (an S corporation). During the current year, R will have $120,000 of net income from business operations. The net income is realized at a rate of $10,000 per month. Additionally, in January of this year R sold § 1231 property and recognized a $60,000 loss.

(a) Assume D's basis in her R stock at the beginning of the year is $10,000. If D sells one-half of her stock to G midway through the year for $25,000, what will be the tax results to D and G?

(b) What difference would it make in (a), above, if D sold all of her stock to G for $50,000?

3. The Ace Sporting Goods Store (an S corporation) is owned by Dick and Harry. Dick and Harry each own one-half of Ace's stock and have a $2,000 basis in their respective shares. At incorporation, Dick loaned $4,000 to Ace and received a five year, 12% note from the corporation.

   (a) If Ace has an $8,000 loss from business operations this year, what will be the results to Dick and Harry? Do you have any suggestions for Harry? Would it matter if on December 15 Ace borrowed $4,000 from its bank on a full recourse basis? What if Dick and Harry personally guaranteed the loan? Compare §§ 752(a) and 722.

   (b) If Ace has $6,000 of net income from business operations next year, what will be the results to Dick and Harry?

   (c) What difference would it make in (a), above, if the $8,000 loss was made up of $2,000 of losses from business operation and a $6,000 long-term capital loss? See Reg. § 1.704–1(d)(2).

   (d) What would be the effect in (a), above, if Ace's S corporation status was terminated at the end of the current year?

4. Allied Technologies, an S corporation, is owned by Betty (25%), Chuck (35%) and Diana (40%). Betty and Chuck also each own one-half of the stock of the Portland Exporting Corporation, also an S corporation.

   (a) If Allied sells investment real estate which it purchased two years ago for $40,000 to Portland for $20,000, what will be the result to Allied? See § 267.

   (b) What difference would it make in (a), above, if Portland were a C corporation?

   (c) Assume Allied is an accrual method taxpayer and owes $1,500 to Betty (a cash method taxpayer) for her December salary. If Allied pays the salary on January 15 of the following year, what will be the tax results to Allied and Betty (assuming both are calendar year taxpayers?) See § 267(e).

E.   DISTRIBUTIONS TO SHAREHOLDERS

Code: §§ 311(b); 1368; 1371(a)(1), (c), (e); Skim § 301(a), (b) and (d).

S Corporations Without Earnings and Profits. If an S corporation has no accumulated earnings and profits, distributions to shareholders are treated as a tax-free return of capital which is first applied to reduce the shareholder's stock basis.[1] Any distribution in excess of basis is treated as gain from the sale or exchange of property—capital gain if the stock is a capital asset.[2] Virtually all S corporations formed after 1982 do not generate earnings and profits[3] and are governed by this simple regime. This basic taxing pattern for distributions by S corporations also governs any distribu-

---

1. I.R.C. § 1368(b)(1).

2. I.R.C. § 1368(b)(2).

3. I.R.C. § 1371(c)(1). An S corporation formed after 1982 may generate earnings and profits for any year in which it is not an S corporation and may acquire earnings and profits under Section 381 in a corporate acquisition. See Chapter 9D, supra.

tion of property to which Section 301(c) would apply.[4] Thus, the tax consequences of transactions characterized as Section 301 distributions by other Code provisions, such as Sections 302 (redemptions) and 305 (stock dividends), are determined under Section 1368.

S Corporations With Earnings and Profits. S corporations with earnings and profits present more challenging problems because of the need to harmonize the Subchapter S rules with the corporation's prior C history. Distributions by a C corporation to its shareholders are taxable as dividends to the extent of the corporation's current and accumulated earnings and profits.[5] Some S corporations may have accumulated earnings and profits attributable to prior years when they were governed by Subchapter C. In addition, an S corporation may have inherited the earnings and profits of another company in a corporate acquisition subject to Section 381. In all these cases, the undistributed earnings have not been taxed at the shareholder level and represent an irresistible temptation for a tax-free bailout. There is no free lunch, however, and it thus becomes necessary to identify those distributions which should be taxed at the shareholder level because they are made out of accumulated earnings and profits.

The drafters of the 1982 Act devised a new tax concept—the "accumulated adjustments account" ("AAA")—to serve as the reference point for determining the source of distributions by an S corporation with accumulated earnings and profits. The AAA represents the post–1982 undistributed net income of the corporation. It begins at zero and is increased and decreased annually in a manner similar to the adjustment of the basis in a shareholder's stock.[6] Any distribution by an S corporation with accumulated earnings and profits is treated as a tax-free return of capital to the extent it does not exceed the AAA.[7] A distribution in excess of the AAA is treated as a dividend to the extent of accumulated earnings and profits,[8] and any portion of the distribution still remaining after both the AAA and accumulated earnings and profits are exhausted is treated first as a recovery of basis and then as gain from the sale of property.[9]

One might reasonably ask at this point: what is the purpose of this statutory scheme? The answer is more straightforward than it first appears. The function of the AAA is to identify the source of distributions by those few S corporations with accumulated earnings and profits. It permits the corporation to make a tax-free distribution of the net income recog-

---

4. I.R.C. § 1368(c). See Section G of this Chapter, infra.

5. I.R.C. §§ 301(c)(1), 316.

6. I.R.C. § 1368(e)(1)(A); Reg. § 1.1368–2. Unlike a shareholder's basis, however, the AAA is not increased by tax-exempt income items and is not decreased for expenses related to tax-exempt income. The adjustments also may result in a negative AAA. Reg. § 1.1368–2(a)(3)(ii). In addition, no adjustment is made for federal taxes at-

tributable to any taxable year in which the corporation was a C corporation. Id.

7. I.R.C. § 1368(c)(1). Except to the extent provided in regulations, the AAA is allocated proportionately among distributions if the distributions exceed the AAA. See Reg. § 1.1368–2(b), (c).

8. I.R.C. § 1368(c)(2).

9. I.R.C. § 1368(c)(2), (3). For lots of details about the AAA, see Reg. § 1.1368–2.

nized during its S corporation era which already was taxed at the share-holder level. Only after these previously taxed earnings are exhausted will a distribution be considered as emanating from accumulated earnings and profits.[10]

Distributions of Appreciated Property. At the shareholder level, the Section 1368 distribution rules make no distinction between distributions of cash and other property. At the corporate level, however, an S corporation that distributes appreciated property (other than its own obligations) recognizes gain in the same manner as if the property had been sold to the shareholder at its fair market value.[11] This familiar rule, borrowed from Subchapter C, applies to liquidating and nonliquidating distributions of property by an S corporation.[12] The gain is not taxed to the corporation but, like other corporate-level income, it passes through to the distributee shareholder, who takes a fair market value basis in the distributed proper-ty.[13] The shareholder's basis in his S corporation stock is reduced by the fair market value (not the adjusted basis) of the distributed property.[14] These rules are required to prevent the appreciation from escaping tax through a distribution which is tax-free at both the corporate and share-holder levels followed by a tax-free sale by the shareholder, who would take the property with a fair market value basis.

PROBLEMS

1. Ajax Corporation is a calendar year taxpayer which was organized two years ago and elected S corporation status for its first taxable year. Ajax's stock is owned one-third by Dewey and two-thirds by Milt. At the beginning of the current year, Dewey's basis in his Ajax shares was $3,000 and Milt's basis in his shares was $5,000. During the year, Ajax will earn $9,000 of net income from operations and have a $3,000 long-term capital gain on the sale of 100 shares of Exxon stock. What results to Dewey, Milt and Ajax in the following alternative situations?

(a) On October 15, Ajax distributes $5,000 to Dewey and $10,000 to Milt.

---

10. In lieu of these rules, an S corpo-ration may elect, with the consent of all shareholders who have received distributions during the year, to treat distributions as a dividend to the extent of accumulated earn-ings and profits. I.R.C. § 1368(e)(3); Reg. § 1.1368–1(f)(2). There normally is little in-centive to make this election. One possible motivation would be to enable the corpora-tion to sweep its Subchapter C earnings and profits account clean and thus avoid the cor-porate level tax and possible termination of S corporation status that would result from the co-existence of Subchapter C earnings and profits and excessive passive investment income. See I.R.C. § 1375. A similar election is provided during a post-termination transi-tion period. I.R.C. § 1371(e)(2).

11. I.R.C. § 311(b). An S corporation may not recognize loss, however, on a distri-bution of property that has declined in value. I.R.C. § 311(a).

12. See I.R.C. § 1371(a), which pro-vides that, except as otherwise provided in Subchapter S, the provisions of Subchapter C apply to S corporations and their sharehold-ers. For more on the coordination of Sub-chapters S and C, see Section G of this chap-ter, infra.

13. I.R.C. § 301(d)(1).

14. I.R.C. §§ 1367(a)(2)(A), 1368.

(b) On October 15, Ajax distributes $8,000 to Dewey and $16,000 to Milt.

(c) Ajax redeems all of Dewey's stock on the last day of the year for $20,000. What result to Dewey?

(d) On October 15, Ajax redeems one-fourth of Dewey's stock for $5,000 and one-fourth of Milt's stock for $10,000.

(e) Ajax distributes a parcel of land with a basis of $9,000 and a fair market value of $8,000 to Dewey and a different parcel with a basis of $13,000 and fair market value of $16,000 to Milt.

(f) On October 15, Ajax distributes its own notes to Dewey and Milt. Dewey receives an Ajax five year, 12% note with a face amount and fair market value of $8,000 and Milt receives an Ajax five year, 12% note with a face amount and fair market value of $16,000.

2. P Corporation was formed in 1981 by its two equal shareholders, Nancy and Opal, and elected S corporation status at the beginning of the current year. On January 1, Nancy had a $1,000 basis in her P stock and Opal had a $5,000 basis in her stock. P has $6,000 of accumulated earnings and profits from its prior C corporation operations and has the following results from operations this year:

Gross Income	$32,000
Long-term capital gain	4,000
Salary Expense	18,000
Depreciation	8,000

What are the tax consequences to Nancy, Opal and P Corporation in the following alternative situations.

(a) On November 1, P distributes $5,000 to Nancy and $5,000 to Opal.

(b) Same as (a), above, except that P distributes $10,000 to Nancy and $10,000 to Opal.

(c) What difference would it make in (a), above, if P also received $4,000 of tax-exempt interest during the year and distributed $2,000 of the interest to Nancy and $2,000 to Opal?

(d) During the current year P makes no distributions. On January 1 of next year Nancy sells her P stock to Rose for $6,000. If P breaks even on its operations next year, what will be the result to Rose if P distributes $6,000 to each of its shareholders next February 15?

(e) During the current year P makes no distributions. Nancy and Opal revoke P's Subchapter S election effective January 1 of next year. Assume P Co. has $5,000 of earnings and profits next year. What results to Nancy and Opal if P distributes $7,000 to each of them on August 1 of next year?

F.   TAXATION OF THE S CORPORATION

Code: §§ 1363; 1374; 1375.

The major benefit of a Subchapter S election is the elimination of tax at the corporate level. But this immunity from tax is not absolute. As part of its continuing mission to patrol abuse, Congress has provided that in certain limited situations an S corporation may be subject to tax under Section 1374 on certain built-in gains inherent in corporate property and under Section 1375 on a portion of its passive investment income.

Tax on Certain Built-in Gains: Section 1374. When Congress repealed the *General Utilities* doctrine, it recognized that the shareholders of a C corporation might elect S corporation status in order to avoid the corporate-level tax imposed under the new statutory scheme.[1] For example, assume Liquidating Co. is a C corporation, holds highly appreciated assets, and is owned by shareholders A and B, who also would realize large taxable gains if they sell their stock or liquidate the company. If A and B cause Liquidating Co. to sell its assets and liquidate, or to distribute its assets in complete liquidation, Liquidating Co. will be taxed on its gains and A and B also will be taxed on their stock gains.[2] If Liquidating Co. qualified as a "small business corporation," A and B could elect S corporation status in order to reduce the double-tax burden on the sale or liquidation. The company then could sell its assets and the gains would pass through to A and B, whose stock bases would be correspondingly increased. The effect of the S corporation/liquidation strategy would be to avoid the full impact of the double tax.

Section 1374 blocks this opportunity by taxing an S corporation that has a "net recognized built-in gain" at any time within ten years of the effective date of its S corporation election.[3] At the outset, two important limitations on this tax should be noted. First, Section 1374 applies only if the corporation's S election was made after December 31, 1986.[4] Second, it does not apply to a corporation that always has been subject to Subchapter S.[5]

In general, Section 1374 is designed to tax an S corporation on the net gain that accrued while it was subject to Subchapter C if that gain is subsequently recognized on sales, distributions and other dispositions of property within a ten-year "recognition period" beginning with the first taxable year in which the corporation was an S corporation. For this purpose, any gain recognized during the recognition period, including income from "ripe" items such as cash-basis accounts receivable or Section 453 installment obligations, is a "recognized built-in gain" unless the corporation establishes either that it did not hold the asset at the beginning of its first S taxable year or the recognized gain exceeds the gain inherent in the asset at that time.[6] Conversely, any loss recognized during the

---

1. See Chapters 4D, 5E and 7B2, supra.

2. See I.R.C. §§ 331; 336; 1001(a).

3. I.R.C. § 1374(a), (d)(7).

4. Tax Reform Act of 1986, P.L. No. 99–514, 99th Cong., 2d Sess. § 633(b) (1986).

5. I.R.C. § 1374(c)(1). This exemption may not apply, however, if the S corporation had a "predecessor" that was a C corporation. Id. This could occur, for example, where a C corporation was acquired by the S corporation in a tax-free reorganization.

6. I.R.C. § 1374(d)(3), (5)(A).

recognition period, including deductible items attributable to the corporation's pre-S life, is a "recognized built-in loss" to the extent that the S corporation establishes that it held the asset at the beginning of its first S year and the loss does not exceed the loss inherent in the asset at that time.[7] Since the taxpayer has the burden of proof under these definitions, a C corporation making an S election should obtain an independent appraisal of its assets to establish their value on the relevant date in order to avoid being taxed on gain arising under the S regime and to benefit from the losses that accrued during the corporation's C years.

The Section 1374 tax is computed by applying the highest rate applicable to C corporations (currently 35 percent) to the S corporation's "net recognized built-in gain," which is defined as the corporation's taxable income computed by taking into account only recognized built-in gains and losses but limited to the corporation's taxable income computed generally as if it were a C corporation.[8] The purpose of the taxable income limitation is to ensure that Section 1374 does not tax the corporation on more income than it actually realizes during the taxable year. To prevent taxpayers from avoiding the tax by manipulating the timing of post-conversion losses, Section 1374(d)(2)(B) provides that any net recognized built-in gains not taxed because of the taxable income limitation are carried forward and treated as recognized built-in gain in succeeding years in the recognition period.[9] Finally, the amount of net recognized built-in gain taken into account for any taxable year may not exceed the net unrealized built-in gain at the time the corporation became an S corporation reduced by any net recognized built-in gains which were subject to Section 1374 in prior taxable years.[10]

The Section 1374 tax easily could be avoided if it applied only to built-in gains recognized on the disposition of assets that were held by the S corporation at the beginning of its first S taxable year. For example, assume that a C corporation converting to S status holds an asset (Oldacre) with a built-in gain which it subsequently exchanges for property of like kind (Newacre) in a Section 1031 nonrecognition transaction. The gain inherent in Oldacre is preserved in Newacre's exchanged basis under Section 1031(d). If the corporation disposes of Newacre within ten years after switching to S status, the Section 1374 tax should apply to the built-in "C gain" even though Newacre was not held on the first day that the corporation was subject to Subchapter S. Section 1374(d)(6) ensures this result by providing that an asset taking an exchanged basis from another asset held by the corporation at the time it converted to S status shall be treated as having been held as of the beginning of the corporation's first S

---

7. I.R.C. § 1374(d)(4), (5)(B).

8. I.R.C. § 1374(b)(1), (d)(2). Taxable income, as defined in Section 63(a), is modified by disregarding certain deductions (e.g., the dividends received deduction) and net operating losses. I.R.C. §§ 1374(d)(2)(A)(ii); 1375(b)(1)(B). Net operating loss and capital loss carryforwards from prior years as a C

corporation are taken into account in computing the amount subject to tax under Section 1374. I.R.C. § 1374(b)(2).

9. The carryover rule applies only to corporations that elected S status on or after March 31, 1988. I.R.C. § 1374(d)(2)(B).

10. I.R.C. § 1374(c)(2), (d)(1).

year. In the above example, the built-in gain inherent in Oldacre on the conversion from C to S status is recognized under Section 1374 if the corporation disposes of Newacre at a gain during the recognition period.

Section 1374(d)(8) is another testament to Congress's protective attitude toward the double tax. It ensures that built-in gain in assets acquired by an S corporation from a C corporation in a tax-free reorganization does not escape a corporate level tax. For this purpose, the recognition period commences as of the date the asset is acquired rather than on the beginning of the first taxable year for which the corporation was an S corporation.[11]

Tax advisors began to plot strategies to reduce the impact of Section 1374 soon after it was enacted. For example, it was suggested that the tax might be avoided if an S corporation sold an asset with built-in gain during the 10–year recognition period on the installment method but delayed receipt of any payments (and thus any recognized gain) until after the recognition period had expired.[12] Not surprisingly, the Service has expressed its displeasure with this gambit. The regulations provide that the built-in gain rules will continue to apply to income recognized under the installment method during taxable years ending after the expiration of the recognition period. The gain, when recognized, will be subject to tax under Section 1374.[13]

Tax on Passive Investment Income. When it widened the gates to Subchapter S, Congress became concerned that a C corporation with earnings and profits might make an S election and redeploy substantial amounts in liquid assets yielding passive investment income such as dividends and interest. Left unchecked, this strategy would enable a profitable C corporation to move to the single-tax regime of Subchapter S and pass through the investment income to its shareholders, who might delay, perhaps forever, paying any shareholder-level tax on the Subchapter C earnings and profits. This plan had particular allure when a C corporation sold all of its operating assets and was seeking an alternative to the shareholder-level tax that would be imposed under Section 331 on a distribution of the proceeds in complete liquidation.[14]

The Code includes two weapons to foil the Subchapter S/passive income ploy. As discussed earlier, an S corporation with accumulated earnings and profits from its prior life as a C corporation will lose its S status if it has passive investment income that exceeds 25 percent of its gross receipts for three consecutive taxable years.[15] In addition, even before

11. I.R.C. § 1374(d)(8). See Section G of this chapter, infra, for an overview of the tax consequences when an S corporation is the acquiring or target corporation in a tax-free reorganization.

12. See, e.g., Taggart, "Emerging Tax Issues in Corporate Acquisitions," 44 Tax L.Rev. 459, 481 (1989).

13. Reg. § 1.1374–4(h)(1). For the relationship of this rule to other aspects of Section 1374, see Reg. § 1.1374–4(h)(2)–(5).

14. See Chapter 8B1, supra.

15. I.R.C. § 1362(d)(3). See Section C of this chapter, supra.

its S status is terminated, the corporation will be subject to a corporate-level tax under Section 1375. The tax, which equals 35 percent of the corporation's "excess net passive income," is imposed if an S corporation has earnings and profits from a taxable year prior to its S election and more than 25 percent of the corporation's gross receipts for the taxable year consist of "passive investment income."

For purposes of the Section 1375 tax, "passive investment income" is defined as gross receipts from royalties, rents, dividends, interest, and annuities, together with gains from sales or exchanges of stock or securities.[16] Interest earned on obligations acquired from the sale of inventory, the gross receipts of certain lending and finance institutions, and gains received as a result of the liquidation of a more than 50% controlled corporation are not passive investment income.[17] To prevent easy manipulation of the gross receipts test, only the excess of gains over losses from dispositions of capital assets (other than stock and securities) is included in gross receipts, and gross receipts from the sales or exchanges of stock or securities are taken into account only to the extent of gains.[18] The term "stock or securities" is interpreted expansively and includes stock rights, warrants, debentures, partnership interests, and "certificates of interest" in profit-sharing arrangements.[19]

The computation of the Section 1375 tax is a technician's dream (and a student's nightmare?). The base for the Section 1375 tax, "excess net passive income," is a percentage of the corporation's "net passive income," which is generally equal to passive investment income less deductions directly connected with the production of such income.[20] To arrive at excess net passive income, net passive income is multiplied by a ratio, which has a numerator equal to the excess of passive investment income over 25 percent of gross receipts for the year, and a denominator equal to passive investment income for the year.[21] There is one final caveat: excess net passive income cannot exceed the corporation's taxable income for the year computed with the special changes described in Section 1374(d)(4).[22]

An example may help control the pollution. Assume that X Corporation made a Subchapter S election last year and will have accumulated earnings and profits from prior C corporation operations at the end of its current taxable year, in which X has $50,000 of income from its regular business operations and $35,000 of business deductions. X also receives $15,000 of interest income and $10,000 of dividends and incurs $5,000 of expenses directly related to the production of the investment income.

Is X subject to the Section 1375 tax? The corporation will have Subchapter C earnings and profits at the close of its taxable year and more than 25 percent of its gross receipts are passive investment income ($25,-

---

16. I.R.C. §§ 1375(b)(3); 1362(d)(3)(D)(i).

17. I.R.C. § 1362(d)(3)(D)(ii)–(iv).

18. I.R.C. §§ 1375(b)(3); 1362(d)(3)(C); 1222(9).

19. See Reg. § 1.1362–3(d)(4)(ii)(B).

20. I.R.C. § 1375(b)(2).

21. I.R.C. § 1375(b)(1)(A).

22. I.R.C. § 1375(b)(1)(B).

000 out of $75,000 of gross receipts), so the tax is potentially applicable. X's net passive income is $20,000 ($25,000 of passive investment income less directly connected expenses), and it will have $5,000 of excess net passive income ($20,000 of net passive income multiplied by a ratio having $6,250 as the numerator ($25,000 of passive investment income reduced by 25 percent of gross receipts) and $25,000 as the denominator (passive investment income)). Since excess net passive income does not exceed X's taxable income as determined under Section 1374(d)(4), the corporation's tax liability will be $1,750 ($5,000 × 35 percent).

Section 1375(d) offers one avenue for relief from the Section 1375 tax. The tax may be waived if the S corporation establishes to the satisfaction of the Service that it determined, in good faith, that it had no earnings and profits at the close of a taxable year and, within a reasonable period after discovering earnings and profits, they were distributed. The addition of an "anti-blunder" provision to this complex area is a welcome sign and one hopes the Service will be merciful in its administration of Section 1375(d).

Because the definition of passive investment income includes gross receipts from sales or exchanges of stock or securities, the same gain might be taxed under both Sections 1374 and 1375. To prevent this possibility, Congress provided in Section 1375(b)(4) that the amount of passive investment income taken into account under Section 1375 is reduced by any recognized built-in gain or loss of the S corporation for any taxable year in the recognition period. Congress also considered the interaction of Sections 1374 and 1375 with the provisions taxing the shareholders of an S corporation. Any Section 1374 tax is treated as a loss (characterized according to the built-in gain subject to tax) sustained by the S corporation which will pass through to the shareholders, and each item of passive investment income is reduced by its proportionate share of the Section 1375 tax.[23]

It is important to keep the application of Sections 1374 and 1375 in perspective. A new corporation making a Subchapter S election generally does not have to be concerned with either provision. Section 1374(c)(1) will protect the corporation from the Section 1374 tax and, since the corporation's activities will not generate earnings and profits,[24] Section 1375 cannot apply to the corporation. Therefore, Sections 1374 and 1375 normally will not play a role in deciding whether to utilize a partnership or an S corporation for a new venture.

Additional considerations come into play if a C corporation is considering a move to a single tax regime. An operating C corporation must consider the impact of Sections 1374 and 1375 on a possible Subchapter S election. Weighed against these penalty provisions is the fact that a shift from C corporation status to partnership status requires a liquidation of the corporation, which may result in significant current corporate and shareholder tax liability.[25] The immediate tax cost of moving to a partnership format may be significant enough to tip the balance in favor of a

---

23. I.R.C. § 1366(f)(2), (3).

24. I.R.C. § 1371(c)(1).

25. See I.R.C. §§ 331, 336, 1001.

Subchapter S election and force an accommodation with Sections 1374 and 1375, if planning cannot successfully eliminate their impact.

PROBLEMS

1. Built-in Corporation ("B") was formed in 2000 as a C corporation. The shareholders of B elected S corporation status effective as of January 1, 2004, when it had no Subchapter C earnings and profits and the following assets:

Asset	Adj. Basis	F.M.V.
Land	$30,000	$20,000
Building	10,000	35,000
Machinery	15,000	30,000

For purposes of this problem, disregard any cost recovery deductions that may be available to B. Consider the shareholder and corporate level tax consequences of the following alternative transactions:

(a) B sells the building for $50,000 in 2005; its taxable income for 2005 if it were not an S corporation would be $75,000.

(b) Same as (a), above, except that B's taxable income for 2005 if it were not an S corporation would be $20,000.

(c) Same as (a), above, except that B also sells the machinery for $40,000 in 2006, when it would have substantial taxable income if it were not an S corporation.

(d) B trades the building for an apartment building in a tax-free § 1031 exchange and then sells the apartment building for $50,000 in 2005, when it would have substantial taxable income if it were not an S corporation.

(e) B sells the building for $90,000 in 2014.

2. S Corporation elected S corporation status beginning in 2001 and will have Subchapter C earnings and profits at the close of the current taxable year. This year, S expects that its business operations and investments will produce the following tax results:

Gross income from operations	$75,000
Business deductions	60,000
Tax-exempt interest	5,000
Dividends	12,000
Long-term capital gain from the sale of investment real property	35,000
Long-term capital gain from the sale of IBM stock	18,000
Long-term capital loss from the sale of General Motors stock	8,000

(a) Is S Corporation subject to the § 1375 tax on passive investment income? If so, compute the amount of tax.

(b) Same as (a), above, except that S receives an additional $5,000 of tax-exempt interest.

3.   The San Diego Bay Boat Storage and Marina Corporation ("Bay") was formed in 1999 as a C corporation and has substantial accumulated earnings and profits. Bay's business consists of three primary activities. About one-third of Bay's gross receipts are derived from marine service and repair work conducted by its two mechanics. Another one-third of Bay's total receipts come from the rental of berths to boat owners. Berthing fees vary depending upon the size of the particular boat. A boat owner renting a berth from Bay must pay a separate charge to have Bay's employees launch or haul out his boat. However, if given advance notice, Bay employees will fuel an owner's boat, charging only for the fuel. The remainder of bay's receipts come from dry storage of boats. Owners pay $200 per month for dry storage in Bay's warehouse where a Bay employee is on duty 24 hours a day. For this fee, Bay employees will launch, fuel (with a charge for fuel) and haul out the boat whenever requested by the owner. Bay's mechanics also will perform a free engine analysis every other year for owners of power boats in dry storage.

Bay is considering the possibility of making a Subchapter S election and has requested your advice concerning any problems which it may have. What difference would it make if Bay were a newly formed corporation?

G.   COORDINATION WITH SUBCHAPTER C

Code: §§ 1371; 1372.

It is important to remember that an S corporation is still a corporation for many tax purposes. It is organized in the same manner as other corporations, and it may engage in most of the transactions and experience the corporate adjustments encountered throughout this text. After incorporating or escaping from Subchapter C, S corporations may make nonliquidating distributions of property or stock, engage in redemptions, or acquire other businesses in either taxable or tax-free transactions. They may sell their assets and liquidate, be acquired by another corporation, or divide up into two or more separate corporations. The tax consequences of these and other events in an S corporation's life cycle are determined by a patchwork quilt of Code sections pieced together from Subchapters C and S. The resulting product provides a challenging opportunity to study the uneasy relationship between a double tax regime and a pass-through scheme.

Section 1371(a) begins the statutory snake dance with the deceptively simple general rule that the provisions of Subchapter C apply to an S corporation and its shareholders. This broad admonition is subject to two related exceptions. First, any provision in the Code specifically applicable to S corporations naturally will apply. Second, if the provisions of Subchapter C are "inconsistent with" Subchapter S, the S rules are controlling. Reliable authority is sparse on precisely how Congress intended to harmonize the rules, but the Service gradually has offered guidance. The details are best raised in the context of specific transactions.

Formation of a Corporation. All the basic rules studied in connection with the formation of a C corporation apply to newly formed S corporations.[1] Shareholders who comprise the founding 80 percent or more "control" group do not recognize gain or loss on the transfer of property to the corporation if the requirements of Section 351(a) are met, but realized gain is recognized to the extent the shareholder receives boot[2] or if the transferred liabilities exceed the shareholder's basis for the transferred property.[3] Shareholders determine their basis in stock, debt obligations and other boot received under Section 358. The corporation takes a transferred basis in any contributed assets under Section 362(a). Organizational expenditures may be deducted and amortized if the corporation elects to do so under Section 248, and the benefit of the deductions passes through to the shareholders.

Several other formation issues, most relating to the "small business corporation requirements," are unique to S corporations. To qualify for the S election, the corporation must be mindful of the 100–shareholder limit and the prohibition against certain types of shareholders (e.g., nonresident aliens, partnerships). As for capital structure, an S corporation is limited to one class of stock and thus may not issue preferred stock, but it is free to issue debt, preferably in a form that qualifies for the straight debt safe harbor.[4] Unlike a corporation facing the double tax, an S corporation has no particular incentive to issue pro rata debt to its shareholders.[5]

S Corporations as Shareholders. At one time, an S corporation in its capacity as a shareholder of another corporation was treated as an individual for purposes of Subchapter C. The purpose of this rule was to ensure that an S corporation would not qualify for the Section 243 dividends received deduction, which is designed to prevent double taxation at the corporate level and thus should not be available to a pass-through entity.[6] As drafted, however, the rule had a ripple effect on other transactions, leading Congress to repeal it in 1996 and clarify the tax consequences of many of the transactions discussed below. The legislative history includes a reminder that S corporations, like individuals, may not claim a dividends received deduction or treat any item of income or deduction in a manner inconsistent with the treatment accorded to individual taxpayers.[7]

Distributions and Liquidating Sales. As discussed earlier,[8] Subchapter S generally preempts Subchapter C in determining the tax consequences of nonliquidating distributions. Section 1368 specifically provides that it shall apply to any distribution to which Section 301(c) otherwise would apply. This means that Section 1368 is the reference point not only for routine

---

1. See generally Chapter 2, supra.

2. I.R.C. § 351(b).

3. I.R.C. § 357(c).

4. I.R.C. § 1361(c)(5).

5. For the advantages and disadvantages of issuing debt in the S corporation setting, see Eustice & Kuntz, Federal Income Taxation of S Corporations ¶ 6.03[1] (4th ed. 2001).

6. See, e.g., S.Rep. No. 640, 97th Cong., 2d Sess. 15, reprinted in 1982–2 C.B. 718, 724–725.

7. See H.R. Rep. 104–737, 104th Cong., 2d Sess. 56 (1996).

8. See Section E of this chapter, supra.

nonliquidating distributions but also other transactions, such as dividend-equivalent redemptions and taxable stock distributions, which are classified under Subchapter C as distributions to which Section 301 applies.[9] We have seen that an S corporation recognizes gain under Section 311(b) on a distribution of appreciated property but, unless Section 1374 applies, that gain is not taxed at the corporate level. Instead, the gain passes through to the shareholders, who may increase their stock basis by their respective shares of the gain.

In the case of liquidating distributions and sales, Subchapter C reassumes center stage. Liquidating distributions generally trigger recognition of gain or loss to an S corporation under Section 336 in the same manner as if the corporation were subject to Subchapter C. Sales of assets pursuant to a plan of complete liquidation also are taxable. In either case, however, these gains will pass through to the shareholders and be subject to a single shareholder-level tax unless Section 1374 intercedes. An S corporation also may make a liquidating sale on the installment method. Under certain conditions, these installment obligations may be distributed without triggering corporate-level gain (unless Section 1374 applies), and the shareholders may use the installment method to report the gain.[10] The *character* of the shareholder's gain in this situation is not determined by reference to their stock, which ordinarily would be a capital asset, but rather "in accordance with the principles of Section 1366(d)"[11]—i.e., as if the corporate-level gain on the sale of the asset had been passed through to the shareholders.[12]

Subchapter C also governs the shareholder-level consequences of a complete liquidation. An S corporation shareholder treats distributions in complete liquidation as in full payment in exchange for the stock under Section 331. Although liquidating distributions and sales result in only one level of tax to an S corporation and its shareholders,[13] variations between the shareholder's stock basis and the corporation's basis in its assets may have an impact on the character of the shareholder's gain or loss. For example, assume A owns all of the stock of S, Inc. (an S corporation with no prior C history) and has a $2,000 basis in her S stock. Assume S owns one ordinary income asset which has a $10,000 fair market value and a $1,000 adjusted basis. If S sells the asset, it will recognize $9,000 of ordinary income. The gain passes through to A, and her stock basis is increased by

---

9. See, e.g., I.R.C. §§ 302(d); 305(b). Section 306 is unlikely to apply in the S setting, however, because an S corporation may not issue preferred stock.

10. See I.R.C. § 453B(h). To qualify for corporate-level nonrecognition, the S corporation must distribute the obligation in complete liquidation. In addition, the obligations must result from sales of assets (other than nonbulk sales of inventory) during the 12–month period following the adoption of the liquidation plan. See I.R.C. § 453(h).

11. I.R.C. § 453B(h).

12. Thus, if the installment sale would have given rise to ordinary income, that character will pass through to the shareholders when they collect the installment obligations.

13. This is because the corporate-level gain on a liquidating distribution or sale results in upward basis adjustments to the shareholder's stock under Section 1367. A double tax would be imposed, however, if Section 1374 applies.

$9,000, to $11,000, under Section 1367. When S liquidates and distributes $10,000 cash to A, she recognizes a $1,000 long-term capital loss. Alternatively, if the ordinary income asset had a $2,000 basis, S would recognize $8,000 of ordinary income on its sale which would pass through to A, increasing her stock basis to $10,000. When S liquidates and distributes $10,000 cash to A, she would recognize no additional gain or loss.

Taxable Acquisitions of S Corporations. An acquisition of an S corporation may be structured as either a purchase of stock from the shareholders or a purchase of assets from the corporation. The method chosen affects not only the amount, character and timing of gain but also may have an impact on the tax status of the S corporation and perhaps even the acquiring party if it also is an S corporation.

An asset acquisition often is preferable because the purchaser will obtain a cost basis in the S corporation's assets at the cost of only a shareholder-level tax.[14] For example, assume P, Inc. wishes to acquire T, Inc. (an S corporation with no prior C history). If P purchases T's assets, any gain or loss recognized by T on the sale will pass through to its shareholders, and P will obtain a cost basis in the assets. T's shareholders will increase their stock basis by any gain recognized on the sale under Section 1367, thus avoiding a second tax on the same economic gain when T liquidates.

If P is a C corporation and purchases a controlling interest in the T stock, the T shareholders recognize gain or loss on the sale, and P takes a cost basis in the stock it acquires. T's S election will terminate, however, because an S corporation may not have any C corporation shareholders.[15] If P does not make a Section 338 election, T retains its historic bases in its assets, and as a new C corporation it will face the prospect of a corporate-level tax on any built-in gain. If P makes a Section 338 election to obtain a cost basis in T's assets, T—which loses its S status on the acquisition— must pay a corporate-level tax as a result of the deemed asset sale.[16] If P and T make a joint Section 338(h)(10) election, the regulations provide that old T (still considered an S corporation at this point) recognizes gain or loss on the deemed sale of its assets and then is deemed to have distributed those assets in complete liquidation. The gain or loss on the deemed asset sale passes through to T's shareholders, with resulting basis adjustments to their T stock. Those adjustments then may be taken into account in

---

14. Once again, this assumes that the corporation has no built-in gains that would be taxed under Section 1374. In contrast, an acquisition of assets from a C corporation generates tax at both the corporate and shareholder levels if the target liquidates. See Chapter 8B, supra.

15. I.R.C. §§ 1362(d)(2); 1361(b)(1)(B). After 1996, two or more S corporations may have a parent-subsidiary relationship in which case they are treated as one S corporation for tax purposes. I.R.C. § 1361(b)(3).

16. T's S election terminates when P acquires T's stock, and its short C year includes the day of the terminating event. Thus, the gain on the deemed asset sale must be reported on a one-day return for old T's "short C year." See I.R.C. §§ 1362(e)(1)(B); 338(a)(1). The economic burden of the corporate-level tax is borne by P unless it is reflected in the price paid for the stock.

determining the shareholders' gain or loss under Section 331 on the deemed complete liquidation of old T.[17]

Taxable Acquisitions by S Corporations. When the purchasing corporation ("P") is an S corporation, the primary concern usually is the preservation of P's S status. If P purchases the assets of T, the mix of consideration used in the transaction must be tailored to the S corporation eligibility requirements. P thus should avoid using its own stock or hybrid debt in order to avoid running afoul of the 100–shareholder limit or the prohibition against having more than one class of stock.[18]

When an S corporation acquires the stock of T, the acquisition will not necessarily result in a loss of the acquiring corporation's S status because S corporations may have controlled C corporation subsidiaries. In addition, an acquiring S corporation is eligible to make a Section 338 election, which will trigger immediate recognition of all T's gains and losses. Finally, if an S corporation acquires 80 percent or more of T's stock and liquidates T, the liquidation will be tax free to both corporations under Sections 332 and 337. Following that liquidation, however, any of T's built-in gains while it was a C corporation may later be subject to tax under Section 1374 upon a subsequent disposition.[19]

Tax-Free Reorganizations. An S corporation may be either the target or the acquiring corporation in a tax-free acquisitive reorganization. Looking first to situations where an S corporation is the target, it will lose its S status if it remains in existence as an 80 percent or more subsidiary following a tax-free acquisition of its stock by a C corporation in a Type B reorganization or reverse triangular merger. If an S corporation-target's assets are acquired in a merger or Type C reorganization, the transaction may proceed on a tax-free basis, and the target will terminate its existence as a result of the merger or the liquidation that necessary must follow a Type C reorganization.

If an S corporation is the acquiring corporation in a tax-free reorganization, it necessarily must issue new stock to the target shareholders. Whatever form of acquisition is used, care must be exercised to avoid termination of the election by exceeding the 100–shareholder limit or inheriting an ineligible shareholder. Now that S corporations may have subsidiaries, a Type B stock-for-stock acquisition, once impossible without losing S status, is now a feasible alternative. Similarly, acquisition of the assets of a C corporation in a Type A or C reorganization should not adversely affect the acquirer's S election, but the earnings and profits from the target's C years could jeopardize the acquiring corporation's S status or subject it to the Section 1375 tax if it has substantial passive investment income.[20] Moreover, an S corporation that is the acquiring corporation in a Type A or C reorganization or a forward triangular merger will inherit the target's tax attributes, including its earnings and profits, under Section

---

17.   See Reg. § 1.338(h)(10)–1.

18.   See generally I.R.C. § 1361(b).

19.   As to built-in gains, see I.R.C. § 1374(d)(8); Reg. § 1.1374–8.

20.   I.R.C. § 1362(b)(3); 1375.

381, and its accumulated adjustments account if the target is an S corporation with a prior C history.[21] Finally, any assets acquired from a C corporation in a tax-free reorganization trigger a new ten-year recognition period for purposes of the Section 1374 tax on built-in gains.[22]

Corporate Divisions. An S corporation may divide itself into separate corporations in a transaction that is tax-free at both the corporate and shareholder levels if all the requirements of Section 355 are met. Even when S corporations were not permitted to have subsidiaries, the Service was tolerant in this area, ignoring the transitory nature of a subsidiary formed in preparation for a division.[23] After the division, the new corporation (or corporations, in the case of a split-up) may immediately make an S election.[24]

PROBLEMS

1. Hi–Flying Co. is an aggressive growth company which was formed as a C corporation many years ago to develop new innovative technology. Hi–Flying has been successful and expects to receive inquiries concerning possible taxable and tax-free takeovers in the next few years. Can Hi–Flying's shareholders improve their tax situation in a future takeover by making an S election? In general, if Hi–Flying makes an S election, would you advise a potential corporate purchaser desiring a cost basis in Hi–Flying's assets to structure its acquisition as a purchase of stock or assets?

2. Target Corporation ("T") is a C corporation which has substantially appreciated assets and is a takeover candidate being pursued by several suitors. Purchasing Corporation ("P") has a Subchapter S election in effect and is considering making a bid for T. Consider the tax consequences of the following acquisition offers by P:

> (a) P will offer to purchase T's stock for cash or a combination of cash and P notes.

> (b) P will acquire T in a Type C reorganization.

H. COMPENSATION ISSUES

S corporation shareholders also commonly serve as officers, directors and employees of their corporation. Individuals with this multiple status may have a choice as to whether to withdraw cash as compensation or as a shareholder distribution. Payments of salary are deductible by the corporation as a business expense (with the benefit of the deduction passing through to the shareholders), and are includible in the employee's gross

---

21. For rules on AAA carryovers, see Reg. § 1.1368–2(d)(2).

22. I.R.C. § 1374(d)(8).

23. See, e.g., G.C.M. 39678 (1988).

24. For other issues, such as how to divide up the accumulated adjustments account, see Eustice & Kuntz, supra note 5, at ¶ 12.10.

income. Employee wages also are subject to various federal and state employment taxes imposed on both the employer and the employee (e.g., federal social security and medicare taxes).[1] Distributions, by contrast, generally may be received tax-free by shareholders to the extent of their stock basis, but they do not give rise to a deduction at the corporate level.

Because the payment of salaries to shareholders usually results in a tax "wash" in the case of a profitable corporation (the compensation deduction reduces the operating income that passes through to the shareholders), the *income* tax consequences of salaries and distributions may be identical.[2] The escalating employment tax base has influenced some S corporation shareholders to avoid this additional federal levy by foregoing salaries in lieu of larger shareholder distributions. The *Radtke* case, below, is one court's hostile reaction to this maneuver.

Joseph Radtke, S.C. v. United States

United States District Court, Eastern District of Wisconsin, 1989.
712 F.Supp. 143, affirmed 895 F.2d 1196 (7th Cir.1990).

ORDER

■ TERENCE T. EVANS, DISTRICT JUDGE.

* * *

FACTS

None of the facts are disputed.

Joseph Radtke received his law degree from Marquette University in 1978. The Radtke corporation was incorporated in 1979 to provide legal services in Milwaukee. Mr. Radtke is the firm's sole incorporator, director, and shareholder. In 1982, he also served as the unpaid president and treasurer of the corporation, while his wife Joyce was the unpaid and nominal vice-president and secretary. The corporation is an electing small business corporation, otherwise known as a subchapter S corporation. This means that it is not taxed at the corporate level. All corporate income is taxed to the shareholder, whether or not the income is distributed.

In 1982, Mr. Radtke was the only full-time employee of the corporation, though it employed a few other persons on a piece-meal and part-time basis. Under an employment contract executed between Mr. Radtke and his corporation in 1980, he received "an annual base salary, to be determined

---

1. In 2005, for example, both the employer and employee must pay social security ("FICA") taxes of 6.2% of the first $90,000 of an employee's taxable wages. I.R.C. §§ 3101; 3111; 3121. An additional medicare tax of 1.45%, again payable by both the employer and employee, is imposed on all of an employee's wages. I.R.C. § 3121(b). See generally Raby & Raby, "New Incentives for Avoiding SE and FICA Tax," 81 Tax Notes 1389 (Oct. 14, 1998).

2. The tax results are more complex, however, if the S corporation has losses for the taxable year. See Eustice & Kuntz, Federal Income Taxation of S Corporations ¶ 11.02[2] (4th ed. 2001).

by its board of directors, but in no event shall such annual salary be less than $0 per year * * *. Employee's original annual base salary shall be $0." This base salary of $0 continued through 1982, a year in which Mr. Radtke devoted all of his working time to representing the corporation's clients.

Mr. Radtke received $18,225 in dividends from the corporation in 1982. Whenever he needed money, and whenever the corporation was showing a profit—that is, when there was money in its bank account—he would do what was necessary under Wisconsin corporate law to have the board declare a dividend, and he would write a corporate check to himself.

Mr. Radtke paid personal income tax on the dividends in 1982. The Radtke corporation also declared the $18,225 on its form 1120S, the small business corporation income tax return. But the corporation did not file a federal employment tax form (Form 941) or a federal unemployment tax form (Form 940). In other words, it did not deduct a portion of the $18,225 for Social Security (FICA) and unemployment compensation (FUTA). The IRS subsequently assessed deficiencies as well as interest and penalties. The Radtke corporation paid the full amount that IRS demanded under FUTA—$366.44—and it also paid $593.75 toward the assessed FICA taxes, interest, and penalties. Then the corporation sued here after a fruitless claim for refunds.

DISCUSSION

* * *

The Radtke corporation acknowledges that wages are subject to FICA and FUTA taxes, but it argues that the Internal Revenue Code nowhere treats a shareholder-employee's dividends as wages for the purpose of employment taxes. The government, on the other hand, contends that "since Joseph Radtke performed substantial services for Joseph Radtke, S.C., and did not receive reasonable compensation for such services other than 'dividends', the 'dividends' constitute 'wages' subject to federal employment taxes." The government does not allege that the Radtke corporation is a fiction that somehow failed to comply with Wisconsin statutes governing corporations.

The Federal Insurance Contributions Act defines "wages" as "all remuneration for employment," with various exceptions that are not relevant to this dispute. 26 U.S.C. § 3121(a). Similarly, the Federal Unemployment Tax Act defines "wages" as "all remuneration for employment," with certain exceptions that are not relevant. 26 U.S.C. § 3306(b). (Dividends are not specifically excepted in either act, and "remuneration" is not defined.) Mr. Radtke was clearly an "employee" of the Radtke corporation, as the plaintiff concedes. *See* 26 U.S.C. §§ 3121(d) and 3306(i). Likewise, his work for the enterprise was obviously "employment." *See* 26 U.S.C. §§ 3121(b) and 3306(c).

According to the Radtke corporation, not all "income" can be characterized as "wages." I agree. See Royster Company v. United States, 479

F.2d 387, 390 (4th Cir.1973) (free lunches did not constitute "wages" subject to FICA and FUTA); Central Illinois Public Service Co. v. United States, 435 U.S. 21, 25, 98 S.Ct. 917, 919, 55 L.Ed.2d 82 (1978) (reimbursement for lunches not "wages" subject to withholding tax; Court says in dicta that dividends are not wages).

At the same time, however, I am not moved by the Radtke corporation's connected argument that "dividends" cannot be "wages." Courts reviewing tax questions are obligated to look at the substance, not the form, of the transactions at issue. Transactions between a closely held corporation and its principals, who may have multiple relationships with the corporation, are subject to particularly careful scrutiny. Whether dividends represent a distribution of profits or instead are compensation for employment is a matter to be determined in view of all the evidence.

In the circumstances of this case—where the corporation's only director had the corporation pay himself, the only significant employee, *no* salary for substantial services—I believe that Mr. Radtke's "dividends" were in fact "wages" subject to FICA and FUTA taxation. His "dividends" functioned as remuneration for employment.

It seems only logical that a corporation is required to pay employment taxes when it employs an employee. See Automated Typesetting, Inc. v. United States, 527 F.Supp. 515, 519 (E.D.Wis.1981) (corporation liable for employment taxes on payments to officers who performed more than nominal services for corporation); C.D. Ulrich, Ltd. v. United States, 692 F.Supp. 1053, 1055 (D.Minn.1988) (discussing case law defining who is an "employee"; court refuses to enjoin IRS from collecting employment taxes from S corporation that paid dividends but no salary to sole shareholder and director, a certified public accountant who worked for the firm). See also Rev.Rul. 73–361, 1973–2 C.B. 331 (stockholder-officer who performed substantial services for S corporation is "employee," and his salary is subject to FICA and FUTA tax); Rev.Rul. 71–86, 1971–1 C.B. 285 (president and sole stockholder of corporation is "employee" whose salary is subject to employment taxes, even though he alone fixes his salary and determines his duties).

An employer should not be permitted to evade FICA and FUTA by characterizing *all* of an employee's remuneration as something other than "wages." Cf. Greenlee v. United States, 87–1 U.S.T.C. Para. 9306 (corporation's interest-free loans to sole shareholder constituted "wages" for FICA and FUTA where loans were made at shareholder's discretion and he performed substantial services for corporation). This is simply the flip side of those instances in which corporations attempt to disguise profit distributions as salaries for whatever tax benefits that may produce. See, e.g., Miles–Conley Co. v. Commissioner, 173 F.2d 958, 960–61 (4th Cir.1949) (corporation could not deduct from its gross income excessive salary paid to president and sole stockholder).

Accordingly, the plaintiff's motion for summary judgment is DENIED, and the defendant's motion for summary judgment is GRANTED. The plaintiff is ORDERED to pay the remaining deficiency on its 1982 FICA taxes along with the assessed interest, penalties, and fees.

NOTE

Subsequent Developments. In accord with *Radtke* are Fred R. Esser, P.C. v. United States,[1] Dunn & Clark, P.A. v. Commissioner,[2] and Spicer Accounting Inc. v. United States.[3] A contrary result was reached in Davis v. United States,[4] where the court declined to recharacterize S corporation distributions as taxable wages. *Davis* is distinguishable, however, because the shareholders performed only minor services on behalf of the S corporation.

Fringe Benefits. Fringe benefits paid by an S corporation to its shareholder-employees also are subject to special treatment. Section 1372 provides that an S corporation shall be treated as a partnership for purposes of employee fringe benefits, and any shareholder owning either more than two percent of the corporation's outstanding stock or more than two percent of the total voting power of all stock will be treated as a partner. As a result, an S corporation seldom can provide benefits, such as a medical reimbursement plan or group-term life insurance, which are deductible by the corporation and excludable from gross income of its shareholder-employees.[5]

I. Tax Policy Issues: Subchapter K vs. Subchapter S*

The check-the-box elective classification regime discussed in Chapter 1 has made it easier for virtually any closely held business to obtain pass-through taxation treatment. This has resurrected the longstanding debate on the most desirable structure for a pass-through system. The excerpt below, from a study by the Joint Committee on Taxation, compares the tax treatment of partnerships and S corporations and surveys the competing views on the need to retain two different pass-through regimes.

Excerpt From Review of Selected Entity Classification and Partnership Tax Issues

Staff of Joint Committee on Taxation (JCS–6–97) 23–25 (April 8, 1997).

Need for multiple sets of rules for pass-through entities

[The issuance of final check-the-box classification regulations raises a set of issues regarding] whether there is a continuing need in the tax law

---

1. 750 F.Supp. 421 (D.Ariz.1990).
2. 57 F.3d 1076 (9th Cir.1995).
3. 918 F.2d 90 (9th Cir.1990).
4. 74 AFTR 2d 5618 (D.Colo.1994).
5. For special rules relating to health insurance, see I.R.C. § 162(*l*)(1), (5), and Rev. Rul. 91–26, 1991–1 C.B. 184.

* See generally Eustice, "Subchapter S Corporations and Partnerships: A Search for the Pass Through Paradigm (Some Preliminary Proposals)," 39 Tax L.Rev. 345 (1984).

for parallel pass-through systems for general business activities.[42] Although S corporations (and their shareholders) generally are treated similarly to partnerships (and their partners), significant differences exist, some of which favor S corporations while others favor partnerships.

For example, the items of income, gain, loss, deduction or credit of a partnership generally are taken into account by a partner pursuant to the partnership agreement (or in accordance with the partners' interest in the partnership if the agreement does not provide for an allocation) so long as such allocation has substantial economic effect.[43] Because of the one-class-of-stock rule for S corporations (sec. 1361(b)(1)(D)), the items of income, gain, loss, deduction or credit of an S corporation cannot be separately allocated to a particular shareholder, but are taken into account by all the shareholders on a per-share, per-day basis. Thus, partnerships generally are considered to be a more flexible vehicle for purposes of allocating particular entity-level items to investors.

Another important difference making partnerships more flexible than S corporations is the treatment of entity-level debt, for purposes of the owner's basis in his interest. A partner includes partnership-level debt in the basis of his interest (sec. 752), whereas an S corporation shareholder does not (sec. 1367). The amount of the partner's or S corporation shareholder's basis in his interest serves as a limit on the amount of losses that can be passed through (secs. 704(d), 1366(d)), which makes increases in basis for entity-level debt important.

The sale of stock in an S corporation generally results in capital gain or loss to the selling shareholder. The sale of an interest in a partnership also generally gives rise to capital gain or loss, but gives rise to ordinary income to the selling partner to the extent attributable to unrealized receivables and certain inventory items (sec. 751).

The distribution of appreciated property by an S corporation to a shareholder (as a dividend, in redemption of shares, or in liquidation) is treated as a taxable sale of such property. Any gain is allocated to all the shareholders on a per-share, per day basis and increases the shareholder's adjusted bases in their shares. The distributee shareholder then reduces his basis by the amount of the distribution (i.e., fair market value of the distributed property) and takes a fair market value basis in the property. By contrast, the distribution of appreciated property by a partnership to a partner generally is not treated as a taxable sale of the property (sec. 731).

An existing C corporation may elect to be treated as an S corporation on a tax-free basis, subject to certain special rules. Converting C corporations are subject to corporate-level tax on the recapture of LIFO benefits,[44]

---

42. Eliminating the two-tier corporate tax system, perhaps through some form of corporate integration, could also minimize the need for multiple sets of rules for pass-through entities, but is beyond the scope of this discussion.

43. Sections 704(a) and (b). The determination of whether an allocation has substantial economic effect is complex (Treas. Reg. sec. 1.704–1(b)(2)).

44. Sec. 1363(d).

on certain built-in gains recognized within a 10–year period after conversion,[45] and on certain passive investment income earned while the corporation retains its former C corporate earnings and profits.[46] The conversion of a C corporation to a partnership (or sole proprietorship) is treated as a liquidation of the entity, taxable to both the corporation and its shareholders.

The rules of subchapter C generally apply to an S corporation and its shareholders. Thus, for example, an S corporation may merge into a C corporation (or vice versa) on a tax-free basis. Similar rules do not apply to combinations of C corporations and partnerships.

Individual partners treated as general partners generally are subject to self-employment tax on their distributive shares of partnership income. Shareholders of an S corporation are not subject to self-employment tax on S corporation earnings, but are subject to payroll tax to the extent they receive salaries or wages from the corporation.

Partnerships, LLCs treated as partnerships, and S corporations may be treated differently for State income or franchise tax purposes.

Continuing utility of S corporations

If an LLC can provide limited liability to all owners and achieve pass-through status as a partnership under the check-the-box regulations (or under the Service's prior revenue rulings on LLCs), the need for S corporations could be questioned. Particularly in light of the growing use of LLCs, it could be argued that the great flexibility of the partnership tax rules outweigh the principal advantage of S corporations: relative simplicity. Thus, it is argued that the rules for S corporations could be repealed without detriment to taxpayers.[47]

Others say the continued existence of subchapter S is worthwhile. A corporate charter is a prerequisite imposed by regulators for some trades or businesses (e.g., for depository institutions or to hold certain licenses), and LLCs may not meet such regulatory requirements. Moreover, the corporate form is a familiar, time-tested format, while the LLC form is new and unfamiliar (particularly where a business undertakes interstate commerce).

---

45. Section 1374. For a discussion of how section 1374 allows the conversion of a C corporation to S corporation to be treated more favorably than the liquidation of a C corporation into a sole proprietorship or a partnership, despite the economic equivalence of the transactions, see, letter to Chairman Dan Rostenkowski from Ronald A. Pearlman, Chief of Staff of the Joint Committee on Taxation, recommending several simplification proposals, reprinted in Committee on Ways and Means, Written Proposals on Tax Simplification (WMCP 101–27), May 25, 1990, p. 24. In his 1995 and 1997 budget messages to the Congress, President Clinton recommended that section 1374 be repealed for C corporations above a certain size. [Later proposals made by the Clinton administration would have repealed Section 1374 for C-to-S conversions of corporations with a value of more than $5 million at the time of conversion and treated the transaction as a taxable liquidation of the C corporation followed by a contribution of the assets to an S corporation by the recipient shareholders. Ed.]

46. Section 1375.

47. W. Schwidetzky, "Is It Time to Give the S Corporation a Proper Burial?" 15 Virginia Tax Review 591 (1996).

Subchapter S supporters further point out that the rules of subchapter S are much simpler than the rules of subchapter K.[48] Others point to specific advantages of subchapter S over the partnership tax rules (primarily the ability to convert from C to S corporation status generally without current corporate tax on appreciation, and the availability of tax-free reorganization rules for business combinations and reorganizations). At least until LLC interests are as easily issued in capital markets as traditional corporate stock, the S corporation may continue to be an attractive vehicle in which to start a business, if it is anticipated that it will later go public. Finally, any repeal of subchapter S would require rules providing for the treatment of existing S corporations.[49]

Whether or not it is advisable to retain both the partnership rules and the S corporation rules, some argue that the complexity of either regime is excessive for small businesses, and a new, much simpler pass-through system should be provided for small businesses that would be consistent with the new simplicity for choice of entity under the check-the-box regulations.[50] A significant question, under such an approach, is the definition of a small business, which could depend on the number of owners, the value of the entity's assets, the amount of its gross or net income (if any), or some combination of these or other factors. Related questions involve the treatment of businesses that grow (or fluctuate in size), crossing the definitional line, and the treatment of tax attributes imported from a more complex tax regime. Weighing of simplicity against accuracy of income measurement and allocation would be a factor in designing a simpler regime.

Others would argue that there is nothing inherently complex in the application of the partnership tax rules to most small business transactions. Small businesses today can achieve the effect of a simplified partnership regime for most common business arrangements. Mandating the use of specific rules for small business would deny them the flexibility of present law partnership rules and, it could be argued, would represent a competitive disadvantage relative to larger businesses.

48. However, it must be pointed out that partners of a partnership may opt for a simple, subchapter-S like structure if they so desire. It could be said that the check-the-box regulations expand the appeal of subchapter S, because prior to those regulations, only entities structured as corporations for State law purposes could elect S corporation status, whereas now, a State-law partnership or LLC can be classified as a corporation for tax purposes and elect S status (provided applicable requirements are met).

49. See, for example, the letter of July 25, 1995, from Leslie B. Samuels, Assistant Treasury Secretary (Tax Policy) to Senator Orin Hatch, suggesting possible legislative proposals to allow S corporations to elect partnership status or to apply the check-the-box regulations to S corporations.

50. American Law Institute, Federal Income Tax Project—Taxation of Pass–Through Entities, Memorandum No. 2 96–105 (Sept. 2, 1996) (G. Yin and D. Shakow, reporters).

INDEX

References are to pages

†